JOHN

Baker Exegetical Commentary on the New Testament

ROBERT YARBROUGH AND ROBERT H. STEIN, EDITORS

Volumes now available:

Luke *Darrell L. Bock*
John *Andreas J. Köstenberger*
Romans *Thomas R. Schreiner*
1 Corinthians *David E. Garland*
Revelation *Grant R. Osborne*

Andreas J. Köstenberger (Ph.D., Trinity Evangelical Divinity School) is professor of New Testament and Greek and director of Ph.D./Th.M. studies at Southeastern Baptist Theological Seminary. He has written *The Missions of Jesus and the Disciples according to the Fourth Gospel* and an introduction to John's Gospel for the Encountering Biblical Studies series and has translated the two-volume New Testament theology written by Adolf Schlatter.

JOHN

ANDREAS J. KÖSTENBERGER

Baker Exegetical Commentary on the New Testament

B Baker Academic
Grand Rapids, Michigan

©2004 by Andreas J. Köstenberger

Published by Baker Academic
a division of Baker Publishing Group
P.O. Box 6287, Grand Rapids, MI 49516–6287
www.bakeracademic.com

Printed in the United States of America

Library of Congress Cataloging-in-Publication Data
Köstenberger, Andreas J., 1957–
    John / Andreas J. Köstenberger.
        p.   cm. — (Baker exegetical commentary on the New Testament)
    Includes bibliographical references and index.
    ISBN 0–8010–2644-X (hardcover)
    1. Bible. N.T. John—Commentaries. I. Title. II. Series.
BS2615.53.K67 2004
226.5′077—dc22   2004008418

For Timothy John,
my sweet son,
with my prayers
and affection
John 5:19–20

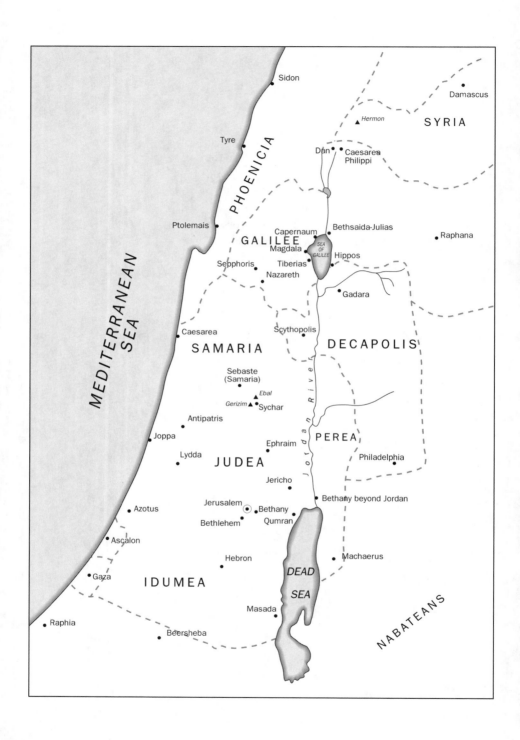

Sidon

Damascus

SYRIA

Hermon

Tyre

PHOENICIA

Dan • Caesarea
Philippi

Ptolemais

Capernaum • Bethsaida-Julias

Raphana

GALILEE

Magdala

SEA
OF
GALILEE

Hippos

Sepphoris

Tiberias

Nazareth

Gadara

MEDITERRANEAN
SEA

Caesarea

Scythopolis

DECAPOLIS

SAMARIA

Sebaste
(Samaria)

Ebal

Gerizim ▲ Sychar

Antipatris

Joppa

Ephraim

PEREA

Lydda

JUDEA

Philadelphia

Jericho

Jerusalem

Bethany

Bethany beyond Jordan

Bethlehem

Qumran

Azotus

Ascalon

Hebron

Machaerus

Gaza

IDUMEA

DEAD
SEA

Masada

Raphia

Beersheba

NABATEANS

Contents

Series Preface

The chief concern of the Baker Exegetical Commentary on the New Testament (BECNT) is to provide, within the framework of informed evangelical thought, commentaries that blend scholarly depth with readability, exegetical detail with sensitivity to the whole, and attention to critical problems with theological awareness. We hope thereby to attract the interest of a fairly wide audience, from the scholar who is looking for a thoughtful and independent examination of the text to the motivated lay Christian who craves a solid but accessible exposition.

Nevertheless, a major purpose is to address the needs of pastors and others involved in the preaching and exposition of the Scriptures as the uniquely inspired Word of God. This consideration affects directly the parameters of the series. For example, serious biblical expositors cannot afford to depend on a superficial treatment that avoids the difficult questions, but neither are they interested in encyclopedic commentaries that seek to cover every conceivable issue that may arise. Our aim, therefore, is to focus on those problems that have a direct bearing on the meaning of the text (although selected technical details are treated in the additional notes).

Similarly, a special effort is made to avoid treating exegetical questions for their own sake, that is, in relative isolation from the thrust of the argument as a whole. This effort may involve (at the discretion of the individual contributors) abandoning the verse-by-verse approach in favor of an exposition that focuses on the paragraph as the main unit of thought. In all cases, however, the commentaries will stress the development of the argument and explicitly relate each passage to what precedes and follows it so as to identify its function in context as clearly as possible.

We believe, moreover, that a responsible exegetical commentary must take fully into account the latest scholarly research regardless of its source. The attempt to do this in the context of a conservative theological tradition presents certain challenges, and in the past the results have not always been commendable. In some cases, evangelicals appear to make use of critical scholarship not for the purpose of genuine interaction but only to dismiss it. In other cases, the interaction glides over into assimilation, theological distinctives are ignored or suppressed, and the end product cannot be differentiated from works that arise from a fundamentally different starting point.

The contributors to this series attempt to avoid these pitfalls. On the one hand, they do not consider traditional opinions to be sacrosanct, and they are certainly committed to do justice to the biblical text whether or not it supports such opinions. On the other hand, they will not quickly abandon a long-standing view, if there is persuasive evidence in its favor, for the sake of fashionable theories. What is more important, the contributors share a belief in the trustworthiness and essential unity of Scripture. They also consider that the historic formulations of Christian doctrine, such as the ecumenical creeds and many of the documents originating in the sixteenth-century Reformation, arose from a legitimate reading of Scripture, thus providing a proper framework for its further interpretation. No doubt, the use of such a starting point sometimes results in the imposition of a foreign construct on the text, but we deny that it must necessarily do so or that the writers who claim to approach the text without prejudices are invulnerable to the same danger.

Accordingly, we do not consider theological assumptions—from which, in any case, no commentator is free—to be obstacles to biblical interpretation. On the contrary, an exegete who hopes to understand the apostle Paul in a theological vacuum might just as easily try to interpret Aristotle without regard for the philosophical framework of his whole work or without having recourse to those subsequent philosophical categories that make possible a meaningful contextualization of his thought. It must be emphasized, however, that the contributors to the present series come from a variety of theological traditions and that they do not all have identical views with regard to the proper implementation of these general principles. In the end, all that really matters is whether the series succeeds in representing the original text accurately, clearly, and meaningfully to the contemporary reader.

Shading has been used to assist the reader in locating the introductory comments for each section. Textual variants in the Greek text are signaled in the author's translation by means of half-brackets around the relevant word or phrase (e.g., ⌜Gerasenes⌝), thereby alerting the reader to turn to the additional notes at the end of each exegetical unit for a discussion of the textual problem. The documentation uses the author-date method, in which the basic reference consists of author's surname + year + page number(s) (e.g., Fitzmyer 1981: 297). The only exceptions to this system are well-known reference works (e.g., BDAG, LSJ, *TDNT*). Full publication data and a complete set of indexes can be found at the end of the volume.

Robert Yarbrough
Robert H. Stein

Author's Preface

This commentary represents the culmination of an intensive ten-year study of John's Gospel, issuing in a monograph on mission in John (Köstenberger 1998b), a basic historical, literary, and theological survey (1999a), and a historical-background commentary (2002c), in addition to several scholarly articles on selected themes (esp. 1995b; 1998a; 2001b: 49–63; 2002b; 2003; 2004). The present work represents an effort to provide a comprehensive (though not exhaustive),[1] balanced treatment of John's Gospel, both exegetically and theologically, based on the following convictions: (1) John's Gospel is historically reliable—it stands up well to historical research (Blomberg 2002; Köstenberger 2002c; Riesner 2002) and resists simplistic dichotomizations between history and theology; (2) the Gospel is a product of careful literary composition—though the book is not to be reduced to story, John employs devices of selection, characterization, and plot development (Culpepper 1983; but see the critiques by Carson 1991: 39–40, 63–68; Tovey 1997: 47–52), study of which has the potential of enhancing apprehension of John's theological message; and (3) John's ultimate concern is tied to theology—the presentation of Jesus as Messiah and Son of God is in order to lead others to place their faith in Jesus the way he himself had done when Jesus called him to discipleship.

In keeping with these basic convictions, the present commentary is, first, based on historical research pertaining both to the most likely life-setting of the Fourth Gospel and to various details provided by the Johannine narrative. It is hoped that the overall cumulative effect of incorporating this detailed historical research into a full-fledged commentary will be to further rehabilitate belief in the historical reliability of John's Gospel. A second distinctive of this work is the consistent drawing on the insights of literary studies on individual Johannine narratives. While in the past, the pendulum has at times swung too far in the historical direction—especially during the heyday of the historical-critical method—and at other times (more recently) toward an exclusive concern with literary aspects of the Gospel, the present

1. In light of the intended audience of this work, interaction is for the most part limited to commentaries, monographs, and periodical literature available in the English language. However, where judged essential, material in other languages is referenced as well.

commentary adopts a both-and approach, seeking to avoid both an unduly critical stance toward the Gospel's historical trustworthiness and a reductionism that moves almost entirely on a literary plane and neglects the historical dimension. As an inspired NT document and as the Word of God, John's Gospel demonstrably displays accurate historical detail as well as aesthetically pleasing literary sophistication, which jointly enhance the work's theological presentation and impact.

Hence, third, both historical and literary work are regarded as auxiliary to the theological appreciation of John's Gospel. Here (in the theological area) I have benefited most from the commentaries of my mentor, Don Carson, and the Dutch scholar Herman Ridderbos. While Carson's commentary excels both in its careful weighing of interpretive options and its theological grasp, Ridderbos is a master of theological synthesis, and I have found his treatment of "big-picture" issues particularly illumining. Leon Morris's commentary, too, is a very fine piece of work and consistently reflects mature judgment that has often pointed the way in my own research. Other major conversation partners in the present commentary are Rudolf Schnackenburg and Raymond Brown (occasional disagreements with them notwithstanding). Frequent reference is also made to the commentaries by Barrett, Beasley-Murray, Keener, and Moloney, not to mention Bultmann, who can be brilliant at one time and rather off course (in my view) at another. I have learned from Martin Hengel and his historical insights (though daring to differ at certain junctures), and I have benefited from the literary work of the likes of Mark Stibbe and R. Alan Culpepper (despite lodging criticisms at individual points of interpretation). Above all, I hope to have learned from Jesus as he speaks to us through the pages of the Gospel of John.

All these debts I gladly acknowledge, and the author and Scripture indexes at the back of this volume indicate further debts, here unacknowledged. The writing of this commentary was for the most part accomplished in a sixteen-month period, from September 2002 through December 2003. It would not have been possible without the wonderful, amazing support of my dear wife Margaret, who had recently given birth to our fourth child, Timothy John. In fact, Timothy's middle name has something to do with the present volume, which his father was in the process of birthing at the time he was born. Timothy, too, is the one to whom this commentary is lovingly dedicated. My other children, Lauren, Tahlia, and David, likewise were fully supportive and often prayed that God would help Daddy finish his commentary. Your prayers have been answered! I am also grateful for several who provided research assistance at various junctures in this project: Michael White, Alan Bandy, Mark Owens, David Croteau, Scott Kellum, and Corin Mihaila. Finally, I would be amiss if I did not acknowledge the contribution made to this work by my institution, Southeastern Baptist Theological Seminary, and its now former president, Dr. Paige Patterson, Dean Russ Bush, and the board of trustees. Thank you for allowing me enough space and time to pursue not only my teaching but also my writing ministry.

Soli Deo gloria.

Abbreviations

Bibliographic and General

ABD	*The Anchor Bible Dictionary,* edited by D. N. Freedman et al., 6 vols. (New York: Doubleday, 1992)
ASV	American Standard Version
BAGD	*A Greek-English Lexicon of the New Testament and Other Early Christian Literature,* by W. Bauer, W. F. Arndt, F. W. Gingrich, and F. W. Danker, 2d ed. (Chicago: University of Chicago Press, 1979)
BDAG	*A Greek-English Lexicon of the New Testament and Other Early Christian Literature,* by W. Bauer, F. W. Danker, W. F. Arndt, and F. W. Gingrich, 3d ed. (Chicago: University of Chicago Press, 2000)
BDF	*A Greek Grammar of the New Testament and Other Early Christian Literature,* by F. Blass, A. Debrunner, and R. W. Funk (Chicago: University of Chicago Press, 1961)
BEB	*Baker Encyclopedia of the Bible,* edited by W. A. Elwell, 2 vols. (Grand Rapids: Baker, 1988)
BGU	Aegyptische Urkunden aus den Königlichen (Staatlichen) Museen zu Berlin: Griechische Urkunden, 15 vols. (Berlin, 1895–1983)
Cant.	Canticles (= Song of Songs)
CEV	Contemporary English Version
DJG	*Dictionary of Jesus and the Gospels,* edited by J. B. Green, S. McKnight, and I. H. Marshall (Downers Grove, Ill.: InterVarsity, 1992)
DSS	Dead Sea Scrolls
EDNT	*Exegetical Dictionary of the New Testament,* edited by H. Balz and G. Schneider, 3 vols. (Grand Rapids: Eerdmans, 1990–93)
ESV	English Standard Version
HCSB	Holman Christian Standard Bible
ISBE	*The International Standard Bible Encyclopedia,* edited by G. W. Bromiley et al., 4 vols. (Grand Rapids: Eerdmans, 1979–88)
ISV	International Standard Version
JB	Jerusalem Bible
KJV	King James Version
LSJ	*A Greek-English Lexicon,* by H. G. Liddell, R. Scott, and H. S. Jones, 9th ed. (Oxford: Clarendon, 1968)
LXX	Septuagint
MM	*The Vocabulary of the Greek Testament: Illustrated from the Papyri and Other Non-literary Sources,* by J. H. Moulton and G. Milligan (1930; reprinted Grand Rapids: Eerdmans, 1976)
MS(S)	manuscript(s)
MT	Masoretic Text
NA[27]	*Novum Testamentum Graece,* edited by [E. and E. Nestle], B. Aland, K. Aland, J. Karavidopoulos, C. M. Martini, and B. M. Metzger, 27th rev. ed. (Stuttgart: Deutsche Bibelgesellschaft, 1993)

NAB	New American Bible
NASB	New American Standard Bible
NEAEHL	*The New Encyclopedia of Archaeological Excavations in the Holy Land*, edited by E. Stern, 4 vols. (Jerusalem: Israel Exploration Society & Carta/New York: Simon & Schuster, 1993)
NET	New English Translation
NewDocs	*New Documents Illustrating Early Christianity*, edited by G. H. R. Horsley and S. Llewelyn (North Ride, N.S.W.: Ancient History Documentary Research Centre, Macquarie University, 1981–)
NIDNTT	*The New International Dictionary of New Testament Theology*, edited by L. Coenen, E. Beyreuther, and H. Bietenhard; English translation edited by C. Brown, 4 vols. (Grand Rapids: Zondervan, 1975–86)
NIV	New International Version
NKJV	New King James Version
NLT	New Living Translation
NRSV	New Revised Standard Version
NT	New Testament
OT	Old Testament
par(s).	parallel(s)
P.Eger.	Egerton Papyrus
P.Oxy.	Oxyrhynchus Papyrus
Qoh.	Qoheleth (= Ecclesiastes)
RSV	Revised Standard Version
Str-B	*Kommentar zum Neuen Testament aus Talmud und Midrasch*, by H. L. Strack and P. Billerbeck, 6 vols. (Munich: Beck, 1922–61)
TDNT	*Theological Dictionary of the New Testament*, edited by G. Kittel and G. Friedrich; translated and edited by G. W. Bromiley, 10 vols. (Grand Rapids: Eerdmans, 1964–76)
TNIV	Today's New International Version
UBS[4]	*The Greek New Testament*, edited by B. Aland, K. Aland, J. Karavidopoulos, C. M. Martini, and B. M. Metzger, 4th rev. ed. (Stuttgart: Deutsche Bibelgesellschaft/United Bible Societies, 1993)
v.l.	*varia lectio* (variant reading)
ZPEB	*Zondervan Pictorial Encyclopedia of the Bible*, edited by M. C. Tenney, 5 vols. (Grand Rapids: Zondervan, 1975)

Hebrew Bible

Gen.	Genesis	2 Chron.	2 Chronicles	Dan.	Daniel
Exod.	Exodus	Ezra	Ezra	Hos.	Hosea
Lev.	Leviticus	Neh.	Nehemiah	Joel	Joel
Num.	Numbers	Esth.	Esther	Amos	Amos
Deut.	Deuteronomy	Job	Job	Obad.	Obadiah
Josh.	Joshua	Ps.	Psalms	Jon.	Jonah
Judg.	Judges	Prov.	Proverbs	Mic.	Micah
Ruth	Ruth	Eccles.	Ecclesiastes	Nah.	Nahum
1 Sam.	1 Samuel	Song	Song of Songs	Hab.	Habakkuk
2 Sam.	2 Samuel	Isa.	Isaiah	Zeph.	Zephaniah
1 Kings	1 Kings	Jer.	Jeremiah	Hag.	Haggai
2 Kings	2 Kings	Lam.	Lamentations	Zech.	Zechariah
1 Chron.	1 Chronicles	Ezek.	Ezekiel	Mal.	Malachi

Greek Testament

Matt.	Matthew	Eph.	Ephesians	Heb.	Hebrews
Mark	Mark	Phil.	Philippians	James	James
Luke	Luke	Col.	Colossians	1 Pet.	1 Peter
John	John	1 Thess.	1 Thessalonians	2 Pet.	2 Peter
Acts	Acts	2 Thess.	2 Thessalonians	1 John	1 John
Rom.	Romans	1 Tim.	1 Timothy	2 John	2 John
1 Cor.	1 Corinthians	2 Tim.	2 Timothy	3 John	3 John
2 Cor.	2 Corinthians	Titus	Titus	Jude	Jude
Gal.	Galatians	Philem.	Philemon	Rev.	Revelation

Other Jewish and Christian Writings

Acts Pet.	Acts of Peter
Apoc. Abr.	Apocalypse of Abraham
Apoc. Mos.	Apocalypse of Moses
Apol.	Tertullian, *Apologeticus* (*Apology*)
1 Apol.	Justin Martyr, *Apologia i* (*First Apology*)
As. Mos.	Assumption of Moses
Bar.	Baruch
2 Bar.	2 (Syriac Apocalypse of) Baruch
3 Bar.	3 (Greek Apocalypse of) Baruch
4 Bar.	4 Baruch
Barn.	Barnabas
Bel	Bel and the Dragon
Bib. Ant.	Pseudo-Philo, *Biblical Antiquities*
1–2 Clem.	1–2 Clement
Dial.	Justin Martyr, *Dialogus cum Tryphone* (*Dialogue with Trypho*)
Did.	Didache
1 Enoch	1 (Ethiopic) Enoch
2 Enoch	2 (Slavonic) Enoch
Epid.	Irenaeus, *Epideixis tou apostolikou kērygmatos* (*Demonstration of the Apostolic Preaching*)
1 Esdr.	1 Esdras
2 Esdr.	2 Esdras (= 4 Ezra)
Gos. Thom.	Gospel of Thomas
Gos. Truth	Gospel of Truth
Haer.	Irenaeus, *Adversus haereses* (*Against Heresies*)

Hist. eccl.	Eusebius, *Historia ecclesiastica* (*Ecclesiastical History*)
Jdt.	Judith
Jos. As.	Joseph and Aseneth
Jub.	Jubilees
Let. Arist.	Letter of Aristeas
Let. Jer.	Letter of Jeremiah
1–4 Macc.	1–4 Maccabees
Mart. Isa.	Martyrdom and Ascension of Isaiah
Mart. Pol.	Martyrdom of Polycarp
Odes Sol.	Odes of Solomon
Ps. Sol.	Psalms of Solomon
Sib. Or.	Sibylline Oracles
Sir.	Sirach (Ecclesiasticus)
T. Abr.	Testament of Abraham
T. Ash.	Testament of Asher
T. Ben.	Testament of Benjamin
T. Dan	Testament of Dan
T. Gad	Testament of Gad
T. Isaac	Testament of Isaac
T. Iss.	Testament of Issachar
T. Jacob	Testament of Jacob
T. Job	Testament of Job
T. Jos.	Testament of Joseph
T. Jud.	Testament of Judah
T. Levi	Testament of Levi
T. Naph.	Testament of Naphtali
T. Reub.	Testament of Reuben
T. Sim.	Testament of Simeon
T. Zeb.	Testament of Zebulun
Tob.	Tobit
Vir. ill.	Jerome, *De viris illustribus* (*On Illustrious Men*)
Wis.	Wisdom of Solomon

Josephus and Philo

Abr.	On Abraham	Husb.	On Husbandry
Ag. Ap.	Against Apion	J.W.	The Jewish War
Alleg. Interp.	Allegorical Interpretation	Life	The Life of Josephus
Ant.	Jewish Antiquities	Migr. Abr.	On the Migration of
Chang. Nam.	On the Change of Names		Abraham
Cher.	On the Cherubim	Mos.	On the Life of Moses
Conf. Tong.	On the Confusion of	Post. Cain	On the Posterity and
	Tongues		Exile of Cain
Creat.	On the Creation	Quest. Gen.	Questions and Answers
Decal.	On the Decalogue		on Genesis
Dreams	On Dreams	Sacr.	On the Sacrifices of Abel
Drunk.	On Drunkenness		and Cain
Flight	On Flight and Finding	Spec. Laws	On the Special Laws
Gaius	On the Embassy to Gaius	Unchang.	On the Unchangeableness
Heir	Who Is the Heir of Divine		of God
	Things?	Worse Att. Bet.	The Worse Attacks the
			Better

Rabbinic Tractates

The abbreviations below are used for the names of tractates in the Babylonian Talmud (indicated by a prefixed b.); Palestinian, or Jerusalem, Talmud (y.); Mishnah (m.); and Tosefta (t.).

ʿAbod. Zar.	ʿAbodah Zarah	Ḥul.	Ḥullin	Roš Haš.	Roš Haššanah
ʾAbot	ʾAbot	Kelim	Kelim	Šabb.	Šabbat
B. Bat.	Baba Batra	Ketub.	Ketubbot	Sanh.	Sanhedrin
B. Meṣiʿa	Baba Meṣiʿa	Mak.	Makkot	Šeb.	Šebiʿit
B. Qam.	Baba Qamma	Meg.	Megillah	Šeqal.	Šeqalim
Bek.	Bekorot	Menaḥ.	Menaḥot	Soṭah	Soṭah
Ber.	Berakot	Mid.	Middot	Sukkah	Sukkah
Beṣah	Beṣah	Moʿed Qaṭ.	Moʿed Qaṭan	Taʿan.	Taʿanit
Bik.	Bikkurim	Ned.	Nedarim	Tamid	Tamid
ʿEd.	ʿEduyyot	Nid.	Niddah	Ter.	Terumot
ʿErub.	ʿErubin	ʾOhal.	ʾOhalot	Yebam.	Yebamot
Giṭ.	Giṭṭin	Peʾah	Peʾah	Yoma	Yoma
Ḥag.	Ḥagigah	Pesaḥ.	Pesaḥim	Zebaḥ.	Zebaḥim
Hor.	Horayot	Qidd.	Qiddušin		

Targumim

Tg. Neof.	Targum Neofiti
Tg. Ps.-J.	Targum Pseudo-Jonathan

Other Rabbinic Works

Mek.	Mekilta	Midr. Rab.	Midrash Rabbah	Rab.	Rabbah
Midr.	Midrash	Pesiq. Rab.	Pesiqta Rabbati		

Qumran / Dead Sea Scrolls

1QH	Thanksgiving Hymns/Psalms (*Hôdāyôt*)
1QM	War Scroll (*Milḥāmâ*)
1QpHab	Commentary (*Pesher*) on Habakkuk
1QS	Manual of Discipline (*Serek Hayyaḥad*, Rule/Order of the Community)
1QSa	Rule of the Congregation (1Q28a, appendix A to 1QS)
3Q15	Copper Scroll
4Q159	Ordinances[a]
4Q246	Apocryphon of Daniel
4Q372	Apocryphon of Joseph[b]
4Q521	Messianic Apocalypse
4Q534	Elect of God (4QMess ar = 4QNoah[a] ar)
4QFlor	Florilegium (4Q174)
4QPBless	Commentary (*Pesher*) on Genesis[a] (4Q252)
4QpIsa[a]	Commentary (*Pesher*) on Isaiah[a] (4Q161)
4QpNahum	Commentary (*Pesher*) on Nahum (4Q169)
4QTest	Testimonia (4Q175)
11QMelch	Melchizedek (11Q13)
CD	Damascus Document

Greek Transliteration

α	a	ζ	z	λ	l	π	p	φ	ph
β	b	η	ē	μ	m	ρ	r	χ	ch
γ	g (n)	θ	th	ν	n	σ ς	s	ψ	ps
δ	d	ι	i	ξ	x	τ	t	ω	ō
ε	e	κ	k	ο	o	υ	y (u)	˙	h

Notes on the transliteration of Greek
1. Accents, lenis (smooth breathing), and *iota* subscript are not shown in transliteration.
2. The transliteration of asper (rough breathing) precedes a vowel or diphthong (e.g., ἁ = *ha;* ἁί = *hai*) and follows ρ (i.e., ῥ = *rh*).
3. *Gamma* is transliterated *n* only when it precedes γ, κ, ξ, or χ.
4. *Upsilon* is transliterated *u* only when it is part of a diphthong (i.e., αυ, ευ, ου, υι).

Hebrew Transliteration

א	ʾ		ת	t	
ב	b		בָ	ā	qāmeṣ
ג	g		בַ	a	pataḥ
ד	d		הַ	a	furtive pataḥ
ה	h		בֶ	e	sĕgôl
ו	w		בֵ	ē	ṣērê
ז	z		בִ	i	short ḥîreq
ח	ḥ		בִ	ī	long ḥîreq written defectively
ט	ṭ		בָ	o	qāmeṣ ḥāṭûp
י	y		בוֹ	ô	ḥôlem written fully
ך כ	k		בֹ	ō	ḥôlem written defectively
ל	l		בוּ	û	šûreq
ם מ	m		בֻ	u	short qibbûṣ
ן נ	n		בֻ	ū	long qibbûṣ written defectively
ס	s		בָה	â	final qāmeṣ hēʾ (בָה = āh)
ע	ʿ		בֶי	ê	sĕgôl yôd (בֶי = êy)
ף פ	p		בֵי	ê	ṣērê yôd (בֵי = êy)
ץ צ	ṣ		בִי	î	ḥîreq yôd (בִי = îy)
ק	q		בֲ	ă	ḥāṭēp pataḥ
ר	r		בֱ	ĕ	ḥāṭēp sĕgôl
שׂ	ś		בֳ	ŏ	ḥāṭēp qāmeṣ
שׁ	š		בְ	ĕ	vocal šĕwāʾ
			בְ	–	silent šĕwāʾ

Notes on the transliteration of Hebrew
1. Accents are not shown in transliteration.
2. Silent *šĕwāʾ* is not indicated in transliteration.
3. The unaspirated forms of ב ג ד כ פ ת are not specially indicated in transliteration.
4. *Dāgeš forte* is indicated by doubling the consonant. *Dāgeš* present for euphonious reasons is not indicated in transliteration.
5. *Maqqēp* is represented by a hyphen.

Introduction to the Gospel of John

Significance and Interpretation

John's Gospel, together with the Book of Romans, may well be considered the enduring "twin towers" of NT theology (Köstenberger 2000), soaring—to change metaphors—as an eagle over more pedestrian depictions of the life of Christ.[1] Very possibly written by John the apostle as the culmination of his long life and ministry (critical and postmodern objections to the Gospel's apostolic authorship notwithstanding),[2] the Gospel penetrates more deeply into the mystery of God's revelation in his Son than the other canonical Gospels and perhaps more deeply than any other biblical book. From the majestic prologue to the probing epilogue, the evangelist's words are as carefully chosen as they must be thoughtfully pondered by every reader of his magnificent work.

Over the course of history, the Fourth Gospel has exercised a remarkable influence commensurate with the profundity of its message. John's Christology, particularly affirmations of Jesus' deity and of his human and divine natures, decisively shaped the formulations adopted by the early church councils and creeds (J. N. Sanders 1943; Pollard 1970; Braun 1959; Grillmeier 1975: esp. 26–32). Many of the great minds of the Christian church, from the Fathers to modern times, have written

---

1. Taking their point of departure from the four beasts in Ezek. 1:10 and Rev. 4:6–8, the Fathers described John as an eagle. See, for example, Augustine, *De consensu evangelistarum* 6 (cited in Volfing 2001: 45 n. 67): "John flies like an eagle above the clouds of human weakness and gazes most keenly and steadily with the eye of his heart at the light of unchangeable truth." On John as fisherman, son of thunder, beloved disciple, elder and seer, apostle in second-century interpretation, saint depicted as an eagle, and hero and icon, see Culpepper 1994.

2. See the recent paper by O'Day (2002), who says that the abandonment of the apostolic authorship of the Fourth Gospel has "created space" for new readings of the Gospel. Others, however, view the results of the rejection of the apostolic authorship of John's Gospel in less positive terms. In any case, the summary way in which Johannine authorship is regularly dismissed in contemporary scholarship is without justification, for this theory of authorship has never been definitively refuted (Köstenberger 2001b: 17–47). Though only a theory, it continues to be a possible and, I would argue, eminently plausible hypothesis based on both external and internal evidence (see, e.g., Carson 1991: 68–81; Carson, Moo, and Morris 1992: 138–57; and the discussion below).

commentaries or monographs on John's Gospel.[3] Despite the massive assault on John's trustworthiness in the wake of the Enlightenment, especially by liberal German scholars, John's Gospel stands today widely rehabilitated as a reliable witness to the life, words, and deeds of our Lord Jesus Christ.[4]

Almost from its inception, the interpretation of John's Gospel was hotly contested. In the days of the early church, it was the gnostics who laid claim to this Gospel, asserting that it supported their message of salvation through knowledge (revelation) apart from redemption and forgiveness of sin (J. N. Sanders 1943: 47–87; Pollard 1970: 25). John's first epistle may be the first to bear witness to the way in which the Gospel was misunderstood, if not intentionally misrepresented (e.g., 1 John 1:1–3; 4:2–3). Subsequent to the Reformation, English deists as well as liberal German scholars initially preferred John's Gospel because of its lack of emphasis on demon exorcisms. In the wake of the Enlightenment, however, from Edward Evanson in England to Karl Bretschneider and David Strauss in Germany, attacks were mounted alleging contradictions between John's "spiritual Gospel" (Clement of Alexandria's term) and the Synoptics (Köstenberger 2001b: 17–47), pitting "history" against "theology," as if a Gospel that stresses the importance of eyewitness testimony and the careful evaluation of evidence must necessarily bend historical fact for the sake of theological expediency.[5] In the twentieth century, the towering figure of Rudolf Bultmann enlisted John in his program of demythologization (Carson 1991: 31–33).

3. On the Latin background, see Volfing 2001: 11–59. See also the works referenced in J. N. Sanders 1943; Pollard 1970; Braun 1959; and Grillmeier 1975.

4. The Fourth Gospel's integrity is not compromised by the inimitable Johannine style, enveloping narrative as well as discourse portions. For positive assessments of the historical reliability of John's Gospel, see Köstenberger 2002c; Blomberg 1993; 2001; 2002; contra M. Casey 1996. Nevertheless, there continues to be skepticism on the part of many; see the recent survey by Kysar (2002a), the largely positive assessment by Thompson (2002), and the very negative evaluation by Attridge (2002b).

5. The essays on history and theology in the Fourth Gospel and on the question of the Fourth Gospel's authorship by Morris (1969: 65–292) still repay careful study. For an interesting application of Clement's statement, see Thielman 1991: 183 in the context of his entire article. The reference to Clement's *Hypotyposeis* is found in Eusebius, *Hist. eccl.* 6.14. See also Thompson (2002: 2), who rightly notes, "Whatever Clement meant in calling John 'a spiritual Gospel,' it is doubtful that he meant to contrast 'facts' in the modern sense and 'interpretation.' . . . [A] 'spiritual' Gospel gives the inner meaning of an event or reality and, hence, its truth must be spiritually discerned." Thompson rightly maintains that "the modern view" that calls into question the historicity of any item in John that "stands in the service of his theological or interpretive agenda" constitutes "a very strange way to imagine that theology works, and perhaps could only have been thought of by people actually not doing theology." Thompson (2002: 3) proceeds to call for greater sophistication in biblical scholars' philosophy of history. Carson (1991: 29) similarly disavows attributing to Clement a dichotomy between "spiritual" and "historical"; he suggests that "spiritual" may mean "allegorical" or "symbol-laden."

Also, in recent years efforts have been made to transfer John's Gospel from the mainstream of apostolic Christianity to the margins of end-of-first-century sectarianism. The "Johannine community," "school," or "circle," rather than John the apostle, it is argued, was responsible for compiling the Gospel in light of its struggles against a parent synagogue that expelled some of its members because of their faith in Jesus as Messiah (Martyn 1977; 1979; R. Brown 1978; 1979; cf. Cullmann 1976). This reconstruction, it should be noted, is significantly based on the charge that the references to synagogue expulsion in John (esp. 9:22) are anachronistic. Yet the historical value of such reconstructions has itself come under serious scrutiny and has been increasingly questioned (Hengel 1993; Bauckham [ed.] 1998).[6] In a stunning "confession," Robert Kysar (2002b), at a recent session of the Johannine literature section convened under the auspices of the Society of Biblical Literature, has chronicled the rise and fall of the Martyn/Brown-style "Johannine community" hypothesis and expressed personal regret for ever having endorsed it. While Kysar himself opts for a postmodern paradigm that acknowledges the validity of a variety of "readings" of the Fourth Gospel, his critique has opened the way for a thorough reassessment of a paradigm that until recently was almost beyond question.[7]

Hermeneutical Presuppositions

No commentary is written without underlying hermeneutical presuppositions, whether conscious or unconscious, acknowledged or unacknowledged, explicit or implicit. Presuppositionless exegesis is impossible (Bultmann 1960), just as objective, neutral interpretation remains elusive. Every interpreter approaches the biblical text from a vantage point that reflects his or her ecclesiastical tradition, personal experience, and view of biblical authority, to name but a few of the most important factors in a person's preunderstanding (see, e.g., Klein, Blomberg, and Hubbard 1993: 81–116).

The present commentary is written in the conviction that although presuppositionless exegesis is an illusion, presuppositions do not necessarily preclude the kind of engagement with the biblical text by which the interpreter's understanding may be corrected by the scriptural message (Osborne 1991). What is more, an active, born-again faith in Jesus Christ as Lord is unashamedly acknowledged as the vantage point from which exegesis is undertaken (Schlatter, in Neuer 1996: 211–25). Rather than being a liability, this faith—together with the enabling work of

---

6. See, early on, Schlatter (1948: x), who comments that the term "Johannine school" appears to him to be "completely divorced from reality" (völlig phantastisch).

7. As late as 1990, D. M. Smith (1990: 293 n. 30) could write, "Martyn's thesis has become a paradigm. . . . It is a part of what students imbibe from standard works, such as commentaries and textbooks, as knowledge generally received and held to be valid."

the Holy Spirit in interpretation, if tempered with humility, exegetical work, and openness to the findings of others—can be a great strength (G. Maier 1994: 45–63). From the dialectic of the interpretive process, a reading of a given text (in the present instance, the Fourth Gospel) may be expected to emerge that can stake a legitimate claim at being more than merely one possible reading of this text (contra postmodern and reader-response approaches to John's Gospel).

Specifically, authorial intention, as conveyed in the context of a particular literary genre and as enshrined in the text itself, is here considered to be the yardstick by which the validity of a given interpretation is to be measured.[8] That is, the reading that conforms most closely to the authorially intended message to the original readers, in light of the historical-cultural background and in keeping with linguistic and literary conventions of the day, has the greatest claim to being the most accurate interpretation of a given passage.[9]

Although 100 percent certainty may be hard to come by, at least in the more difficult instances, we may hope to try to reconstruct beyond reasonable doubt a setting—historical, literary, and theological—that comports well with the internal evidence of the document of John's Gospel itself and coheres with what we know about early Christianity and its environment during the second half of the first century A.D. This remains not merely desirable, but a necessity, since the Gospel is part of the Christian canon, which ought to function authoritatively for the church in its preaching and teaching and application in life and practice (contra the "New Homiletic").

As a Gospel, the text under study here can reasonably be assumed to be focused on the life and (vicarious) death of Jesus, not the history of an alleged sectarian "Johannine community" (though clearly the evangelist's end-of-first-century vantage point can be expected to have informed his mode of presentation and selection). As to authorship,

8. The classic work is Hirsch 1967. Considerably more sophisticated is the recent work by Vanhoozer (1998), whose defense of authorially intended textual meaning is all the more to be taken seriously as Vanhoozer is keenly aware of, and sensitive to, the role of the reader in biblical interpretation, without, however, absolutizing it (cf. Vanhoozer 1995; see also the penetrating collection of essays in Vanhoozer 2002 and the following note).

9. An exceedingly clever defense of the author in general and of the author of John's Gospel in particular is provided by Vanhoozer's (1993 [= 2002: 257–74]) "hermeneutical exposition" of John 21:20–24. According to Vanhoozer, "The ethos of the Fourth Gospel largely depends on the identification of the author with the Beloved Disciple" (1993: 372). The "double Anselmian hermeneutics of 'I-witness testimony'" advocated by Vanhoozer urges that the beloved disciple's testimony be received on its own terms; unless it is believed, it is not understood. Over against the "death of the author" in much of recent scholarship and the prevailing "hermeneutic of suspicion," Vanhoozer asserts "authorial rights" and advocates a "hermeneutic of belief" that seems all the more justified because the beloved disciple is consistently identified in the Fourth Gospel as an eyewitness. In this context it may be significant that as late as the very last verse of the Gospel, the authorial "I" is still heard (see commentary at 21:20–25).

all options, including apostolic authorship, must remain on the table, without undue dogmatism on all sides (Köstenberger 2001b: 17–47). The literary artistry of the Gospel, which recently has received increased attention, ought to be appreciated, albeit without a lopsided emphasis on literary matters at the expense of historical ones.[10]

The deluge of literary explorations on various pericopes of the Fourth Gospel has yielded considerable insight regarding various details in the text, but any such literary light must be incorporated into a full-orbed understanding of the Gospel that is properly grounded historically and adequately informed theologically. Otherwise, such "readings" remain atomistic and isolated from the larger context of which they were originally a part and of which they must remain a part in order to function effectively in the life of the church collectively and of believers individually.

Below, I will postulate a tentative historical setting for the Fourth Gospel. This may serve as an overall framework for individual interpretations. Literary and narrative interpretive insights are incorporated throughout the commentary. There is no bias against insights from that quarter. To the contrary, traditional approaches have much to learn from more recent ones. Nevertheless, a more radical reader-response stance is eschewed, not least because of its postmodern consequence of eroding the authority of the biblical text beyond the narrow scope of a given interpretive community, but more importantly because this stance is at odds with the way the text of John's Gospel was likely to have been generated and to have functioned in the context of the interpersonal communication out of which it arose.

Underlying the present commentary is also an appreciation for previous efforts at interpreting the Fourth Gospel, be it in patristic or medieval times, during the Reformation period, or in the more recent history of interpretation. It is arrogant to assert the superiority of contemporary efforts at understanding a given biblical text merely because of our post-Enlightenment heritage (see Steinmetz 1980). At the same time, recent events such as the Holocaust and the development of gender-inclusive Bible translation have brought issues to the fore that have the potential for sharpening our understanding of certain passages in John's Gospel (see Köstenberger 2003), not to mention the discovery of biblical MSS that add to the available text-critical data on the basis of which interpretive decisions are made.[11]

---

10. See Köstenberger 1999a: 30–31. There has been a virtual avalanche of literary explorations of Johannine themes or specific Johannine portions of text pouring from the presses in the last two decades. Among those are Culpepper 1983; Duke 1985; Staley 1988; M. Davies 1992; Stibbe 1992; 1994; Lee 1994; Tovey 1997; Beck 1997; Conway 1999; and Harstine 2002, to list but a few.

11. For examples where recent MS finds made a difference in the assessment of the most likely original reading, see commentary at 1:18 and 1:34.

Finally, this commentary is written on the assumption (reasonable, I believe, though it is not possible to defend this assumption here) of a high view of Scripture, foremost its inerrancy and inspiration. This pertains particularly to the understanding of geographical and historical details in the Gospel (on which, see Köstenberger 2002c; Blomberg 2002). The commentary is written from a stance that expects any such details ultimately to be capable of a resolution that does not implicate the Johannine text in actual error or contradiction. A case in point is the dating of the crucifixion in this Gospel in relation to the Synoptics (see Köstenberger 2002a: 147–48).

Such an assumption flies in the face of the unfettered critical scholarship unleashed in full force with Bretschneider (though found in latent form at least as early as the 1790s).[12] Doubtless the present commentary will, in many quarters, be assailed as an exercise in mere confessionalism and traditional exegesis. This, however, is at least partially inaccurate. For even within an inerrant framework there remain exegetical options to be adjudicated and historical and literary questions to be solved, even though certain outcomes are regarded as unlikely at the outset (unless data were to surface that required a radical revision of one's presuppositions).

On this basis it is now possible to sketch out briefly, and in the spirit of the type of "critical realism" advocated by N. T. Wright (1992: 61–64), a plausible historical, literary, and theological setting for my interpretation of John's Gospel.[13] This, in turn, will serve as the general framework for the commentary itself.

Historical Setting

In reconstructing the historical setting of John's Gospel, one finds that a combination of internal and external evidence provides plausible grounds for concluding the following (Köstenberger 2000: 280). The author is (1) an apostle (1:14; cf. 2:11; 19:35); (2) one of the Twelve ("the disciple Jesus loved" [13:23]; cf. 19:26–27; 20:2–9; 21, esp. 21:24–25);[14]

12. Karl Gottlieb Bretschneider (1776–1848) pioneered an approach to John's Gospel that dated it to the late second century and rejected its veracity at most points (see Baird 1992: 312–14). In contrast, Bretschneider's contemporary Friedrich Schleiermacher (1768–1834) believed that "the Gospel of John bears such undeniable signs of authenticity, and so reveals on every page the eyewitness and personal participant, that one must be prejudiced and diverted from the natural course so as to doubt its authenticity" (cited in Baird 1992: 214).

13. See the magisterial "Part II: Tools for the Task" in Wright 1992: 29–144.

14. Note that the label "the disciple Jesus loved" occurs only in the second major portion of John's Gospel (first at 13:23). This is in keeping with the marked shift in perspective starting in 13:1, where the disciples' mission is viewed from the perspective of Jesus' exaltation (Köstenberger 1998b: 153). Hence, the casting of John in more elevated terms in chapters 13–21 is not unique in John's Gospel and may be seen as indicating that the

(3) John, the son of Zebedee. The disciple Jesus loved/John is consistently associated with Peter in the Fourth Gospel and elsewhere in the NT (13:23–24; 18:15–16; 20:2–9; 21; cf. Luke 22:8; Acts 1:13; 3–4; 8:14–25; Gal. 2:9).[15] Although the hypothesis of the apostolic authorship of the Fourth Gospel is regularly rejected in recent Johannine scholarship, the hypothesis has never been decisively refuted and continues to be at least as plausible as alternative explanations.[16] External evidence supports this identification (esp. Irenaeus, *Haer.* 3.1.2),[17] indicating that John lived to a ripe old age and that he was the last of the evangelists to write his Gospel.[18] It appears that John wrote his Gospel in Ephesus

apostle, as "the disciple Jesus loved," has an important part to play in the postexaltation mission of Jesus carried out through his commissioned followers.

15. The epithet "the disciple Jesus loved" is plausibly understood as an instance of authorial modesty (see Vanhoozer 1993: 374, who cites Augustine and Westcott, contra Barrett 1978: 117). On authorial modesty, see also Köstenberger 2004.

16. See Blomberg 2001: 72, referring to Westcott. Nevertheless, it should be acknowledged that apostolic authorship remains a hypothesis. In an essay surveying scholarship from the late eighteenth and early nineteenth centuries on the issue, I have shown that the apostolic paradigm was challenged on largely philosophical rather than evidential grounds and that there is therefore compelling reason to doubt that the Fourth Gospel's Johannine authorship has ever been refuted by actual argument (Köstenberger 2001b: 17–47). To assert the superiority of alternative hypotheses as virtually self-evident without adducing supporting evidence, as is commonly done today, hardly constitutes evenhanded scholarship. Cf. Keener 2003: 81–139, who at the outset of his thorough investigation of the authorship of John's Gospel (which concludes, tentatively, in favor of apostolic authorship) states that the Fourth Gospel's apostolic authorship has often been opposed out of dogmatism (p. 81) but that "traditional conservative scholars have made a better case for Johannine authorship of the Gospel . . . than other scholars have made against it" (p. 82).

17. One tricky piece of evidence concerns the second-century writer Papias (cited in Eusebius, *Hist. eccl.* 3.39.4–5), a contemporary of Polycarp, who, in turn, was a disciple of the apostle John (on the date of Papias, see Yarbrough 1983; Munck 1959). Papias (at least to Eusebius) seems to refer to two separate Johns, the apostle and a "John the elder." On this basis some have conjectured that the latter, rather than the former, wrote the Fourth Gospel. However, there is no need to drive a wedge between the two references to John in the passage in question. To the contrary, John may be designated "the elder" in the latter part of the quotation precisely because he is grouped with the elders mentioned earlier in the same passage. For a sound critique of the "John the elder" hypothesis, see Carson, Moo, and Morris 1992: 141–43. Keener (2003: 95–98) likewise challenges the reliability of Eusebius's interpretation of Papias, owing to the former's agenda of seeking to denigrate the Apocalypse. Keener (2003: 102–3) also includes an insightful discussion of the plausibility of John writing the Gospel at an advanced age. See also the works cited in Bauckham 1993: 27 n. 17 and the important essay by Hill (1998), who adduces from Eusebius's (*Hist. eccl.* 3.24.5–13, esp. 11) reference to Papias (without naming him) that Papias held John the apostle to be the author of the Fourth Gospel (contra Bauckham 1993; Hengel 1989a; note my review of Hengel's more extensive 1993 German monograph on the subject, Köstenberger 1996). For studies of the external evidence regarding the authorship of the Fourth Gospel, see Bauckham 1993: 24 n. 1.

18. Irenaeus, *Haer.* 2.22.5; 3.3.4 (quoted by Eusebius, *Hist. eccl.* 3.23.3–4), places John's death during the reign of Trajan (A.D. 98–117); Jerome (*Vir. ill.* 9) says that John died in the sixty-eighth year after Jesus' passion (i.e., A.D. 98 or 101). Regarding John being the

(so Irenaeus, *Haer.* 3.1.2; cf. Eusebius, *Hist. eccl.* 3.1.1) and that he ultimately envisioned—like the other canonical Gospels—a universal readership (Bauckham [ed.] 1998). John's original audience seems to have consisted primarily of Diaspora Jews and proselytes (Carson 1991: 91; see also Keener 2003: 175–80).

The purpose statement in 20:30–31 is perhaps most plausibly read as indicating that John wrote with an (indirect) evangelistic purpose, expecting to reach his unbelieving audience via Christian readers (Bauckham [ed.] 1998: 10). The Gospel originated within the matrix of the early Christian Gentile mission, the emergence of early gnostic thought, and, last but not least, the destruction of the Jerusalem temple in A.D. 70 (Motyer 1997; Kerr 2002; P. Walker 1996: 195; Draper 1997: 264, 285), a traumatic event that left Judaism in a national and religious void and caused Jews to look for ways to continue their ritual and worship.[19] Seizing the opportunity for (Jewish) evangelism, John presents Jesus as the temple's replacement (2:18–22; cf. 1:14; 4:21–24) and the fulfillment of the symbolism inherent in Jewish festivals (esp. chs. 5–12; see Hoskins 2002; Köstenberger forthcoming; Draper 1997: 264–65). If this reconstruction is correct, the Gospel most likely was written sometime after A.D. 70 but before A.D. 100.[20] If Thomas's confession of Jesus as "my Lord and my God" is intended to evoke associations of emperor worship under Domitian (A.D. 81–96), a date after A.D. 81 would appear most likely.[21]

last to write his Gospel, see Irenaeus, *Haer.* 3.1.1; Clement, cited by Eusebius, *Hist. eccl.* 6.14.7; and Eusebius himself, *Hist. eccl.* 3.24.7. See Carson 1991: 83.

19. See especially Alexander 1992 and Goodman 1992. For a fuller development and further bibliography, see Köstenberger forthcoming. For a critique of the Martyn/Brown-style "Johannine community" hypothesis, see Köstenberger 1998b: 200–210; Carson 1991: 35–36, 87–88, 369–72; and commentary at 9:22 below.

20. Very few would argue for a date prior to A.D. 70, as do J. A. T. Robinson 1976: 254–85 (but see the refutation in Kerr 2002: 19–25; see also Carson 1991: 82–86); Morris 1995: 25–30 (with reference to Cribbs 1970; Torrey 1936: x–xi); and Wallace 1990 (but see the present commentary at 5:2). However, the cumulative weight of the following internal evidence must be judged to favor a post–A.D. 70 date (cf. Croteau 2003): the references to the Sea of Tiberias in 6:1 and 21:1; Thomas's confession of Jesus as "my Lord and my God" in 20:28 (contra emperor worship in time of Domitian?); the reference to Peter's martyrdom (21:19); and the lack of reference to the Sadducees (Schlatter 1948: 44; though see the caution in Carson 1991: 84)—not to mention the comparative ease with which the Fourth Evangelist equates Jesus with God (e.g., 1:1, 14; 10:30; 20:28; see Carson 1991: 85, though note his caveats on p. 84) or external evidence such as Clement of Alexandria's statement, cited in Eusebius, *Hist. eccl.* 6.14.7, "Last of all, John, perceiving that the external facts had been made plain [in the Synoptics] . . . composed a spiritual gospel." This is true especially since the major pieces of evidence cited in support of a pre–A.D. 70 date—the lack of reference to the destruction of the temple and the use of a present-tense verb in 5:2 to refer to the Sheep Gate pool—are not determinative and are capable of alternative explanations (see, e.g., Schlatter 1948: 23–24).

21. See Carson (1991: 85), who tentatively suggests a date of A.D. 80–85, in part because he finds it "hard to believe that, if the Fourth Gospel were written after AD 70, the date was *immediately* after AD 70. . . . The reverberations around the Empire, for both Jews

Literary Features

John's overarching purpose is the demonstration that the Christ, the Son of God, is Jesus (20:30–31; see Carson 1987: 639–51) by weaving together several narrative strands. The prologue places the entire Gospel within the framework of the eternal, preexistent Word made flesh in Jesus (1:1–18). The first half of John's narrative sets forth evidence for Jesus' messiahship in the form of seven selected signs (1:19–12:50; cf. 20:30–31; see Köstenberger 1995b). John also includes Jesus' seven "I am" sayings (see "Theological Emphases" below) and calls numerous (seven?) witnesses in support of Jesus' claims, including Moses and the Scriptures, the Baptist, the Father, Jesus and his works, the Spirit, the disciples, and the evangelist himself (see commentary at 1:7). Representative questions concerning Jesus' messiahship serve to lead the Gospel's readers to the author's intended conclusion: the Christ is Jesus (e.g., 1:41; 4:25; 7:27, 31, 52; 10:24; 11:27; 12:34).

The second major section of John's Gospel shows how Jesus ensured the continuation of his mission by preparing his new messianic community for its mission. This portion opens with Jesus' farewell discourse (chs. 13–17): the new messianic community is cleansed (by the footwashing and Judas's departure; ch. 13), prepared (by instructions regarding the coming Paraclete and his ministry to the disciples; chs. 14–16), and prayed for (ch. 17). The disciples are made partners in the proclamation of salvation in Christ (15:15–16), their witness being aided by the Spirit (15:26–27), and taken into the life of the Godhead, which is characterized by perfect love and unity (17:20–26).

The Johannine passion narrative (chs. 18–19) presents Jesus' death both as an atonement for sin (cf. 1:29, 36; 6:48–58; 10:15, 17–18), though largely without the Synoptic emphasis on shame and humiliation, and as a stage in Jesus' return to the Father (e.g., 13:1; 16:28). The resurrection appearances and the disciples' commissioning by their risen Lord constitute the focal point of the penultimate chapter (ch. 20), where Jesus is cast as the paradigmatic Sent One (cf. 9:7), who now has become the sender of his new messianic community (20:21–23). The purpose statement of 20:30–31 reiterates the major motifs of the Gospel: the signs, believing, (eternal) life, and the identity of Jesus as Christ and Son of God. The epilogue portrays the relationship between Peter and the disciple Jesus loved in terms of differing yet equally legitimate roles of service within the believing community.

The structure of John's Gospel based on Jesus' seven signs may be delineated as follows:

---

and Christians, were doubtless still too powerful. A little time needed to elapse . . . before a document like the Fourth Gospel could be free *not* to make an *explicit* allusion to the destruction of the temple."

I. **Prologue: The Word made flesh (1:1–18)**
II. **The Book of Signs: The signs of the Messiah (1:19–12:50)**
   A. The forerunner, Jesus' inaugural signs, and representative conversations (1:19–4:54)
      1. The testimony of John the Baptist and the beginning of Jesus' ministry (1:19–51)
      2. The first sign: Turning water into wine at the wedding at Cana (2:1–12)
      3. One of Jesus' Jerusalem signs: The clearing of the temple (2:13–22)
      4. Further ministry in Jerusalem and Samaria (2:23–4:42)
         a. The "teacher of Israel," Nicodemus (2:23–3:21)
         b. Interlude: The testimony of John the Baptist (3:22–36)
         c. The Samaritan woman (4:1–42)
      5. The second sign at Cana: The healing of the royal official's son (4:43–54)
   B. Additional signs amid mounting unbelief (5:1–10:42)
      1. At an unnamed feast in Jerusalem: The healing of the lame man (5:1–47)
      2. Galilean Passover: Feeding the multitude and the bread of life discourse (6:1–71)
      3. Jesus at the Feast of Tabernacles (7:1–8:59)
         a. First teaching cycle (7:1–52)
         b. Second teaching cycle (8:12–59)
      4. The healing of the blind man and the good shepherd discourse (9:1–10:42)
         a. Jesus heals a blind man (9:1–41)
         b. Jesus the good shepherd (10:1–42)
   C. Final Passover: The climactic sign—the raising of Lazarus—and other events (11:1–12:19)
      1. The raising of Lazarus (11:1–57)
      2. The anointing at Bethany (12:1–11)
      3. The triumphal entry into Jerusalem (12:12–19)
   D. Conclusion (12:20–50)
      1. The dawning age of the Gentiles: Jesus predicts his death (12:20–36)
      2. The signs of the Messiah rejected by the old covenant community (12:37–50)
III. **The Book of Glory: Jesus' preparation of the new messianic community and his passion (13:1–20:31)**
   A. The cleansing and instruction of the new messianic community, including Jesus' final prayer (13:1–17:26)
      1. The cleansing of the community: The footwashing and Judas's departure (13:1–30)
         a. The footwashing (13:1–17)

    b. The betrayal (13:18–30)
  2. Jesus' final instructions: The farewell discourse (13:31–16:33)
    a. Jesus' departure and sending of the Spirit (13:31–14:31)
    b. Jesus the true vine (15:1–17)
    c. The Spirit and the disciples' witness to the world (15:18–16:33)
  3. Jesus' parting prayer (17:1–26)
  B. The passion narrative (18:1–19:42)
    1. The betrayal and arrest of Jesus (18:1–11)
    2. Jesus questioned by the high priest, denied by Peter (18:12–27)
    3. Jesus before Pilate (18:28–19:16a)
    4. Jesus' crucifixion and burial (19:16b–42)
  C. Jesus' resurrection and appearances and the commissioning of his disciples (20:1–29)
    1. The empty tomb (20:1–10)
    2. Jesus appears to Mary Magdalene (20:11–18)
    3. Jesus appears to his disciples (20:19–23)
    4. Jesus appears to Thomas (20:24–29)
  D. Conclusion: The signs of the Messiah witnessed by the new messianic community (20:30–31)
  IV. Epilogue: The complementary roles of Peter and the disciple Jesus loved (21:1–25)
  A. Jesus appears to seven disciples (21:1–14)
  B. Jesus and Peter (21:15–19)
  C. Jesus and the disciple Jesus loved (21:20–25)

The literary structure of John's Gospel, in turn, can be shown to follow a chronological time line.[22]

Chronology of Jesus' Ministry in John's Gospel

Time	Location/Event	John
Origin		*1:1–18*
eternity past	the Word was with God	1:1–18
Initial ministry, A.D. *29–30*		*1:19–2:12*
summer/fall 29	John the Baptist near the Jordan	1:19–34
subsequently	Jesus' calling of his first disciples	1:35–51

22. There are two main possibilities for the dating of Jesus' ministry, A.D. 26–30 or 29–33, with the latter set of dates to be preferred (see Hoehner 1977; Hoehner, *DJG* 118–22).

Time	Location/Event	John
winter 29/spring 30	the wedding at Cana of Galilee	2:1–12
First Passover and first full year of ministry, A.D. 30–31		*2:13–4:54*
April 7, 30	Jesus' first Passover (Jerusalem), temple clearing	2:13–3:21
spring/summer 30	John the Baptist near the Jordan	3:22–36
Dec./Jan./Feb. 30/31?	Jesus' ministry in Samaria	4:1–45
subsequently	the healing at Cana of Galilee	4:46–54
Second year of ministry, A.D. 31–32		*5:1–47*
March 27, 31	Passover not recorded in John	Matt. 12:1 pars.?
Oct. 21–28, 31?	the Sabbath controversy (Jerusalem)	5:1–47
Second Passover recorded in John and third year of ministry, A.D. 32–33		*6:1–11:54*
April 13 or 14, 32	Jesus' second Passover recorded in John (Galilee)	6:1–21
subsequently	Jesus' teaching in the synagogue of Capernaum	6:22–71
Sept. 10–17, 32	Jesus at the Feast of Tabernacles (Jerusalem)	7:1–52; 8:12–59
Oct./Nov. 32?	healing of blind man, good shepherd discourse	9:1–10:21
Dec. 18–25, 32	Jesus at the Feast of Dedication (Jerusalem)	10:22–39
Jan./Feb. 33?	Jesus' withdrawal to the area near the Jordan	10:40–42
March 33?	the raising of Lazarus (Bethany near Jerusalem)	11:1–53
March 33?	Jesus' withdrawal to Ephraim	11:54
Third Passover in John, passion week, resurrection appearances, A.D. 33		*11:55–21:25*
Friday, March 27, 33	Jesus arrives at Bethany	11:55–12:1
Saturday, March 28, 33	dinner with Lazarus and his sisters	12:2–11
Sunday, March 29, 33	"triumphal entry" into Jerusalem	12:12–50
Monday–Wednesday, March 30–April 1, 33	cursing of fig tree, temple clearing, temple controversy, Olivet discourse	Synoptics
Thursday, April 2, 33	Jesus' third Passover recorded in John (Jerusalem), betrayal, arrest	13:1–18:11

Time	Location/Event	John
Friday, April 3, 33	Jewish and Roman trials, crucifixion, burial	18:12–19:42
Sunday, April 5, 33	the empty tomb, first resurrection appearance	20:1–25
Sunday, April 12, 33	second resurrection appearance recorded in John	20:26–31
before May 14, 33	third resurrection appearance recorded in John	21:1–25[23]

Theological Emphases

The Messianic Mission of Jesus

In keeping with the Gospel genre, John's narrative focuses on Jesus and his messianic mission. At the very outset, John's account is based on OT theology. The Gospel's opening phrase, "In the beginning," recalls the first words of Genesis, which recount the creation of the world (1:1; cf. 1:3). According to John, the Word's coming into this world and being made flesh in Jesus constitutes an event of comparable magnitude (1:1, 14). Jesus is presented as the Word sent from heaven to accomplish a mission and, once the mission has been accomplished, to return to the place from which he came (cf. Isa. 55:11). John's use of the term λόγος (*logos*, word) with reference to Jesus also serves to contextualize the Christian message in the evangelist's culture.

Another OT concept taken up in John's prologue is that of light and darkness (1:4–5, 8–9; cf. 3:19–21; Gen. 1:3–4). In the Qumran literature, this contrast is set within the framework of an eschatological dualism. In John, however, Jesus is presented as the Word, active in creation, who has now brought final revelation from God. This revelation, in turn, is compared and contrasted with the revelation received by and mediated through Moses (1:17–18; cf. Exod. 33–34). Jesus brought "grace for grace" (1:16): though the law given through Moses also constituted a gracious gift from God, true grace—that is, final, eschatological grace—came only through Jesus (1:17). And no one, not even Moses, truly saw God (1:18; cf. Exod. 33:20, 23; 34:6–7); but now Jesus, with God at the beginning (1:1), and always, even during his earthly ministry, in closest relationship with the Father, has given a full account of him (1:18).

The Jewish milieu of John's Gospel and the firm grounding of its theology in OT antecedents are also borne out by the various component parts of the Gospel's christological teaching. John's favorite designation for Jesus is that of the Son sent by the Father (3:17, 34–36; 5:19–26; 6:40; 8:35–36; 14:13; 17:1). This metaphor is taken from Jewish life and the halakic concept of the *šālîaḥ*, according to which the sent one is like

23. For the dating of the four Passovers between A.D. 29 and 33 mentioned above, see Humphreys and Waddington 1992: 335.

the sender himself, faithfully pursuing his interests (cf. 13:16, 20). The image of the descending bread from heaven develops OT teaching on God's provision of manna in the wilderness (cf. Jesus as the antitype of the serpent in the wilderness [3:14]); the figure of the descending and ascending Son of Man (cf. the "lifted up" sayings in 3:14; 8:28; 12:34) probably derives from apocalyptic passages featuring one "like a son of man" (Dan. 7:13). Jesus is also shown to fulfill the symbolism of the Jewish Feast of Tabernacles (chs. 7–9) and the Passover (ch. 19), as well as that of Jewish institutions such as the Jerusalem temple (2:14–22; see "Historical Setting" above and discussion below).

Central to John's presentation of Jesus' work (esp. in chs. 1–12; see "Literary Features" above) is the concept of signs (Köstenberger 1995b). The trajectory of antecedent OT theology reaches back as far as the "signs and wonders" performed by Moses at the exodus; Jesus' signs point to a new exodus (cf. Luke 9:31). In John, however, the miraculous character of Jesus' works is blended with, and even superseded by, their prophetic symbolism (cf. Isa. 20:3). As with those of Moses and later prophets, the signs' function is primarily to authenticate the one who performs them as God's true representative. People are severely criticized for demanding spectacular evidence of Jesus' authority (4:48), yet signs are offered as an aid to faith (10:38). And though blessing is pronounced on those who "have not seen and yet have believed" (20:29), Jesus' signs clearly are designed to elicit faith among his audience, and when they fail to do so, people are held responsible.

Another crucial motif in John's theology is Jesus' fulfillment of the symbolism inherent in Jewish festivals and institutions. By pronouncing himself to be the "light of the world" (8:12; 9:5) and the source of "living water" (4:10–14; 7:37–38), Jesus claims to fulfill the torch-lighting and water-pouring ceremonies that formed part of the Feast of Tabernacles. By dying during Passover week, Jesus is revealed as the prototype of the Jewish Passover (19:14). By pointing to his own crucified and resurrected body as the true embodiment and functional substitute of the Jerusalem temple (2:14–22), Jesus indicates that Judaism is merely preparatory, anticipating the coming of God's Messiah. True worship must be rendered not in any particular physical location, but in spirit and truth (4:23–24).[24]

One final striking feature deserving comment is John's inclusion of seven "I am" sayings of Jesus. According to John, Jesus is (1) the bread of life, come down from heaven (6:35, 41); (2) the light of the world

---

24. On Jesus as the replacement and fulfillment of the temple in John's Gospel, see especially Coloe 2001; Johnson 2001; Hoskins 2002; and Kerr 2002. For a treatment that links this Johannine motif with the composition of the Fourth Gospel, see Motyer 1997 and Köstenberger forthcoming. On Jesus and Israel's traditions of judgment and restoration, see Bryan 2002.

(8:12 = 9:5); (3) both the gate for the sheep and (4) the good shepherd (10:7, 9, 11, 14); (5) the resurrection and the life (11:25); (6) the way, the truth, and the life (14:6); and (7) the true vine (15:1, 5). This terminology recalls God's self-identification to Moses at the outset of the exodus: "I am who I am" (Exod. 3:14). It is also reminiscent of Isaiah's consistent portrayal of the sovereign Lord God (e.g., Isa. 43:10–13, 25; 45:18; 48:12; 51:12; 52:6). In places, "I am" sayings and signs are linked (John 6:35; 11:25). Like the background to the Johannine signs, the background to Jesus' self-designation as the "I am" is therefore to be found in a trajectory ranging from Moses and the exodus to the OT prophets, particularly Isaiah (see John 12:38–41).

The Mission of the Messianic Community

Like his portrait of Jesus, John's presentation of the new messianic community follows a salvation-historical pattern (Pryor 1992a). In keeping with OT typology, believers are described as a "flock" (ch. 10) and as "branches" of the vine (ch. 15). John, however, does not teach that the church replaces Israel. Rather, he identifies *Jesus* as Israel's replacement: *he* is God's "vine" taking the place of God's OT "vineyard," Israel (Isa. 5). John acknowledges that "salvation comes from the Jews" (4:22), yet he portrays Israel as part of the unbelieving world that rejects Jesus. Jesus' "own" (the "Jews") did not receive him (1:11). In their place, the Twelve, who are now "his own," become the recipients of his love (13:1; cf. ch. 17). The Jewish leaders, on the other hand, are said not even to belong to Jesus' flock (10:26). This does not mean that the Jews are now shut out from God's salvation-historical program, but they, like everyone else, must come to Jesus *in faith* rather than presuming upon their Jewishness.[25]

Another instance of John's drawing on OT antecedents is Jesus' parting preparation of his followers in terms reminiscent of Moses' Deuteronomic farewell discourse ("love," "obey," "keep commandments," etc. [chs. 13–17]; cf. 1:17; see Köstenberger 1999a: 144). However, at this salvation-historical juncture it is not Israel but believers in Jesus who represent the core group through which he will pursue his redemptive purposes. The community is formally constituted in the commissioning narrative, where Jesus' breathing upon his gathered disciples marks a "new creation," recalling the creation of the first human being, Adam (20:22; cf. Gen. 2:7). Jesus' dependent and obedient relationship to his sender, the Father, is made the paradigm for the disciples' relationship with their sender, Jesus (Köstenberger 1998b: 190–98).

---

25. Keener (2003: 227–28) suggests that John's use of "the Jews" is ironic in that the evangelist grants the authorities the title they covet while ironically undermining their claim (citing Rev. 2:9; 3:9). Keener recommends putting "the Jews" in quotation marks in modern translations to indicate the irony.

In John's treatment of individual disciples, particular attention is given to two of Jesus' followers: Peter and the disciple Jesus loved. These two characters are regularly featured together (Quast 1989; see "Historical Setting" above): in the upper room (13:23–24); in the courtyard of the high priest (18:15–16); at the empty tomb (20:2–9); and at the Sea of Tiberias subsequent to Jesus' resurrection (ch. 21). Though Peter is considered to be the leader of the Twelve (cf. 6:67–79), he is presented as second to the disciple Jesus loved in terms of access to revelation (13:23) and faith (20:8). In the end, the ministry of the disciple Jesus loved is shown to be equally legitimate to that of Peter. Both of their ministries, in turn, are portrayed in terms that recall the ministry of Jesus: in Peter's case, the analogy is found in the death by which he would glorify God (21:19; cf. 12:33); in the case of the disciple Jesus loved, the parallel consists in his position "at Jesus' side," which qualified him supremely to "give a full account" of his Lord's person and work (13:23; cf. 1:18). Thus, the role of witness to Jesus may take forms as different as martyrdom and writing a Gospel, but witness must be borne, according to each person's calling (15:26–27).

Place in the Canon

Rather than constituting the product of a sectarian community at the end of the first century (as is held by certain proponents of the "Johannine community" hypothesis), John's Gospel is part of the fabric of canonical revelation, including the Synoptic Gospels, the other Johannine writings, the OT, and the rest of the NT.

Canonicity

Like the Synoptic Gospels, John was accepted as Christian Scripture by the end of the second century A.D. What is more, the second-century author Tatian, in his Gospel harmony, the *Diatessaron* (Greek: "through four"), used John's Gospel as the chronological framework for the other three Gospels (Bruce 1983: 8; 1988: 127; Carson 1991: 28). The first Christian writer to attribute the Fourth Gospel to John and to quote explicitly from the Gospel was Theophilus of Antioch (ca. A.D. 180) in his three-volume work *To Autolycus* (2.22; Pollard 1970: 40).[26] Soon thereafter, Clement of Alexandria famously wrote, "Last of all, John, perceiving that the external facts had been made plain in the Gospel, being urged by his friends, and inspired by the Spirit, composed a spiritual gospel" (cited in Eusebius, *Hist. eccl.* 6.14.7). Tertullian and Origen followed suit.

Except for the heretic Marcion and the fringe group the Alogoi, no one in the early church questioned the authenticity, authority, or can-

---

26. For a survey of second-century patristic references to John as the author of the Fourth Gospel, see Nixon 2003.

onicity of this Gospel. If John's Gospel took longer to gain universal recognition than the other Gospels, it likely was because it was almost instantaneously used by gnostic heretics to support their position.[27] In fact, John's first epistle may represent an attempt at responding to one such abuse. One of the earliest extant citations from the Gospel is by the gnostic Basilides (ca. A.D. 130); the earliest known commentary was penned by a gnostic, Heracleon, a student of Valentinus (ca. A.D. 180).[28] Irenaeus of Lyons, however, masterfully used the Fourth Gospel in refuting Gnosticism and thus dispelled any notion that the Gospel itself was tainted by gnostic thought (Pollard 1970: 42–48).

Relationship to the Synoptic Gospels

The relationship between John's Gospel and the Synoptics is a vast and complex topic that can in no way be treated here in depth. The relationship has been described in terms of mutual independence or varying degrees of literary interdependence (see the survey in D. M. Smith 1992). Despite efforts to demonstrate literary dependence, it seems hard to establish on purely literary grounds that John must have known or used one or more of the Synoptic Gospels. Historically, however, it seems difficult to believe that the Fourth Evangelist had not at least heard of the existence of the Synoptics and read some portions of them. But whether or not the author of the Fourth Gospel knew these other Gospels, clearly he did not make extensive use of them in composing his own narrative. Apart from the feeding of the five thousand, the anointing, and the passion narrative, John does not share any larger blocks of material with the Synoptic Gospels.[29]

27. See the introduction above. There is no good reason to believe that John's Gospel itself is based on a gnostic *Vorlage*, as Bultmann (1971: 25–31, and passim) held, or that it reflects Docetism and was erroneously included in the canon (the view of Käsemann 1968: 76–77 [cited in Sloyan 1996: 127, 129–30]).

28. See also the gnostic Gospel of Truth and P.Eger. 2 (cited in Pollard 1970: 25). Concerning Basilides, see Hippolytus, *Refutation of All Heresies* 7.22, 27; Heracleon's work is given extensive coverage in Origen's commentary on John's Gospel (see Bruce 1988: 128). Westcott (1896: i–ii, 184, 292) and Luthardt (1875: 96, 100–101), besides referring to Basilides, also discuss the possible acquaintance with John's Gospel reflected in Clement of Rome (2 Clem. 9:5 [ca. A.D. 150]: ἐγένετο σάρξ; cf. John 1:14), the Clementine Homilies (19.22; cf. John 9:1–3), and other patristic writings. Sloyan (1996: 130) cites an apparent reference to John 3:3, 5 in Justin Martyr, *1 Apol.* 61.4–5 (Carson 1991: 25; though see J. N. Sanders 1943: 27–28; Pollard 1970: 39; Osborn 1973: 137–38; Skarsaune 1987: 105–6; and Pryor 1992b). Carson (1991: 26) also mentions Tatian, Claudius Apollinaris, and Athenagoras (of Athens). Bauckham (1993) adds Polycrates, bishop of Ephesus (late second century). J. N. Sanders (1943: 86), on the other hand, maintains that "the Apostolic Fathers cannot be said to produce any certain traces of its [the Fourth Gospel's] use"; Pollard (1970: 24; cf. Bultmann 1971: 12) likewise acknowledges "the fact that in no extant 'orthodox' writing from before A.D. 170 is there any explicit quotation from the Gospel."

29. But note the "interlocking traditions" enumerated in Carson, Moo, and Morris 1992: 161–62. See also the internal evidence for John's awareness of Synoptic tradition, if not

Thus, unlike the Synoptics, John has no birth narrative, no Sermon on the Mount or Lord's Prayer, no accounts of Jesus' transfiguration or the Lord's Supper, no narrative parables, no demon exorcisms, and no eschatological discourse. Clearly, John has written his own book. This, however, does not make his a sectarian work apart from the mainstream of apostolic Christianity (Wenham 1997). Rather, John frequently transposes elements of the Gospel tradition into a different key (Köstenberger 2002a: 148–49). The Synoptic teaching on the kingdom of God corresponds to the Johannine theme of eternal life; narrative parables are replaced by extended discourses on the symbolism of Jesus' signs. Moreover, all four Gospels present Jesus as the Son of Man and as the Messiah fulfilling OT predictions and typology. Thus, the differences between the Synoptics and John should not be exaggerated.[30]

Relationship with the Other Johannine Writings

John's first epistle is quite apparently directed to defuse an early gnostic threat to the message of John's Gospel by showing that Jesus indeed has come in the flesh. John's Gospel portrays Jesus along similar lines, albeit without specific references to proto-Gnosticism. I have set forth some of the more striking similarities between John's Gospel and 1 John elsewhere (Köstenberger 1999a: 203–5; 2000: 283–84; see also Keener 2003: 123–26). The Book of Revelation is addressed to seven churches in Asia Minor (Rev. 2–3) and is intended to strengthen believers in the face of suffering at the end of the first century. Again, the reader is directed to my earlier presentation of common features of John's Gospel and the Apocalypse.[31]

---

one or more of the written Gospels, listed in Köstenberger 1999a: 36–37 (1:40: Andrew, "Simon Peter's brother"; 3:24: "This was before John [the Baptist] was put in prison"; 4:44: a prophet is without honor in his own country [cf. Mark 6:4 pars.]; 11:1–2: Bethany, "village of Mary and her sister Martha" [cf. Luke 10:38–42]; 6:67, 71: the Twelve; Judas, "one of the Twelve").

30. See the brief treatments in Köstenberger 1999a: 36–37, 198–200. Stuhlmacher (2002: 185–87) contends that John and the Synoptics do not merely represent different perspectives (what M. Hengel calls "aspective"), but that the Fourth Gospel "cultivates a[n] . . . idealized type of memory concerning Jesus." He urges, "The Johannine witness therefore needs to be consistently realigned with the Synoptics, the Pauline corpus and the OT, so that faith in Jesus Christ does not lose its historical roots" (p. 187). This, however, seems to be merely an oblique way of saying that John's Gospel is historically unreliable and that there are real contradictions between John and the Synoptics (cf. Stuhlmacher's more blunt statement in 1997: 287 [cited in Köstenberger 2002a: 144 n. 3]). I, of course, deny both accusations.

31. See Köstenberger 1999a: 205; 2000: 284; see also Keener 2003: 126–39, esp. 129. On the relationship between John's Gospel and the Pauline writings and the remainder of the NT, see Köstenberger 1999a: 205–7; 2000: 284–85.

I. Prologue: The Word Made Flesh (1:1–18)

The prologue is a kind of foyer to the Gospel (Carson 1991: 111).[1] In it John introduces the most important themes that he will develop in the rest of his work.[2] Unlike the Synoptics, John supplies neither a genealogy nor a birth narrative of Jesus. Rather, he reaches back all the way to eternity past, prior to creation (1:1; cf. Gen. 1:1). By linking Jesus' coming into the world to its creation, John signals that the incarnation of the Word (1:14) culminates a stream of salvation-historical events that command humanity's utmost attention. Thus the evangelist shows the progression from preexistence (1:1–2) to creation (1:3), the time subsequent to creation but prior to the incarnation (1:4–5), the Baptist (1:6–8), and the incarnation and its results and benefits (1:9–18) (van der Watt 1995: 321; Lindars 1972: 77).[3]

Though it is disputed whether the prologue is original with John or he adapted a preexisting hymn (inserting sections on the Baptist, 1:6–8, 15),[4] the prologue doubtless represents one of the most beautiful and

1. J. A. T. Robinson (1962–63) observes that "the themes of the gospel are played over beforehand, as in the overture to an opera" (cited in Viviano 1998: 183). Beasley-Murray (1992: 1867) calls it "an anticipatory description of the Mission of the Logos-Son to the World." The bibliography on the Johannine prologue is vast: see van der Watt 1995: 311 n. 1; Kurz 1997: 179 n. 1. For a chart showing themes anticipated in the prologue, see p. 586 below.

2. This is why the prologue has also been called the "proleptic quintessence" (Harnack 1892: 191), a "microcosm" (Valentine 1996), and an "adumbration" (Booser 1998: 13) of the entire Gospel (cited in MacLeod 2003: 48 n. 1).

3. For a comprehensive chart delineating narrative time in John's Gospel, see Culpepper 1983: 70. See also Burns 1971 and the chapter entitled "Structuring Time in the Fourth Gospel" in M. Davies 1992: 44–66.

4. Culpepper (1980–81: 1) quotes Barrett (1971: 27): "The Prologue is . . . one piece of solid theological writing. The evangelist wrote it all" (cf. Barrett 1975a: 20–35). Keener (2003: 333–34) maintains that the prologue is an original part of the Gospel, probably added by the author (the apostle John) after completing the first draft of the Gospel. According to Keener (2003: 333–34), ancient writers commonly introduced the main themes at the beginning of their work (see Keener 2003: 334 n. 10 for examples). Bultmann believed that the prologue originated as a pre-Christian gnostic hymn that stemmed from Baptist circles and was taken over and adapted by the Fourth Evangelist (Bultmann 1923: 4; summarized by Ashton 1986: 161). Valentine (1996), in contrast to many other Johannine scholars, argues that the prologue is an organic part of the book, a genuine preface intended to preview important theological themes, rather than a mere afterthought or postscript written after the body of the Gospel had been completed. E. Harris (1994: 26) contends that the prologue "was from the first the construction of the evangelist himself." See the survey in MacLeod 2003: 49–52.

carefully crafted poetic portions in the entire NT (R. Brown 1966: 22; Beasley-Murray 1999: 3).[5] In its opening lines (1:1–5), John uses a form of "staircase parallelism," introducing a concept at the end of one line and taking it up at the beginning of the next (Culpepper 1980–81: 9–10).[6] The pattern is broken in 1:6–9, which is written in more pedestrian prose, but is resumed in 1:10–11 and again in 1:17 (R. Edwards 1988: 8).[7] The literary artistry is most impressive in 1:1–2, which features both a staircase parallelism and a chiasm (Lund 1931: 42 [cited in Culpepper 1980–81: 9–10]; see also Staley 1986: 243; 1988: 50–51):[8]

A ἐν ἀρχῇ
  B ἦν
    C ὁ λόγος
      D καὶ ὁ λόγος
        E ἦν
          F πρὸς τὸν θεόν
          F′ καὶ θεός
        E′ ἦν
      D′ ὁ λόγος
    C′ οὗτος
  B′ ἦν
A′ ἐν ἀρχῇ πρὸς τὸν θεόν

The macrostructure of the opening section of John's Gospel most likely follows a chiastic pattern as well (though specific proposals

5. Morris (1995: 64) calls it "elevated prose." For a recent treatment of the Johannine prologue dealing with these and other questions, see MacLeod 2003: 48–64. For a discussion of the structure of the prologue, see Keener 2003: 334–37 (but Keener's [2003: 337] own tentative proposal—a three-stanza structure omitting the Baptist verses [1:6–8, 15]—is hardly convincing).

6. See the brilliant analysis of 1:1–2 by Cohee (1995: 471–72), who demonstrates that the passage features both "staircase parallelism" and chiasm (both between lines 1 and 2 and between lines 2 and 3) whereby the verb ἦν is placed in the center of each clause. He also notes how this enables θεός in line 3 to be in the emphatic position. See also Keener 2003: 364–65.

7. Cohee (1995: 474–75) rightly notes, "Although verses 6 through 9 seem to exhibit *some* patterns of verbal repetition or rhythmical system, or may in fact be a prose commentary inserted between verses of hymnic poetry, they do not yield to analysis . . . as easily as verses 1 through 5. The same seems to be true of verses 12 through 18. Verses 10 and 11, however, . . . do exhibit such a structure."

8. John's prologue has stimulated several highly creative structural proposals. Often the only limit seems to be the imagination of the interpreter. A case in point is the understanding of the prologue as a series of three successive "waves," each with three movements (La Potterie 1984; Moloney 1977: 35–39; 1993: 25–27; Viviano 1998). Coloe (1997: 44–46) sees 1:1–2 as introduction and 1:18 as conclusion, with 1:3–17 dividing into two sections of three strophes each (1:3–5, 6–8, 9–13 and 14, 15, 16–17), paralleling the six-day structure of Gen. 1:1–2:4. According to Coloe, the rest of the Gospel represents day seven.

differ: cf. Lund 1931: 44; Boismard 1957: 79–80; Lamarche 1964; Feuillet 1968: 160; Hooker 1969–70: 357; Borgen 1970; 1972; Culpepper 1980–81; Pryor 1990: 201–2; Booser 1998: 16; Kruse 2003: 59–60), with the Word's incarnation and the privilege of becoming God's children at the center, framed by references to the witness of John the Baptist:[9]

A The Word's activity in creation (1:1–5)
   B John's witness concerning the light (1:6–8)
      C The incarnation of the Word and the privilege
         of becoming God's children (1:9–14)
   B′ John's witness concerning the Word's preeminence (1:15)
A′ The final revelation brought by Jesus Christ (1:16–18)

By way of more detailed analysis, the correspondence between 1:1–2 and 1:18 can be seen in that (1) these are the only points at which the Word is "with God"; the Word's return to God's presence "conveys a sense of order, balance, and completion" (Culpepper 1980–81: 10); (2) θεός (*theos*, God) occurs three times in 1:1–2 and twice in 1:18 but only three times in the remainder of the prologue (note that two of these instances are at the center, 1:12–13); and (3) both 1:1–2 and 1:18 feature balancing references to eternal time (ἀρχῇ, *archē*, beginning; πώποτε, *pōpote*, ever).

Δι᾽ αὐτοῦ ἐγένετο (*di' autou egeneto*, through him were made) in 1:3 (affirming the Word's role in creation) is mirrored by διὰ Ἰησοῦ Χριστοῦ ἐγένετο (*dia Iēsou Christou egeneto*, came through Jesus Christ) in 1:17 (affirming the role of Jesus in revelation). The parallel between 1:4–5 and 1:16 is conceptual (dealing with divine blessings) rather than verbal, with "light and life" corresponding to "fullness of grace." The equivalence of 1:6–8 and 1:15 (references to John the Baptist) is self-evident. The incarnation is referred to in 1:9–11 and 1:14 (Culpepper 1980–81: 13–14).

In the center of the chiasm (the structure is clearer in Greek than in English translation), 1:11b and 1:13 correspond, as do 1:12a and 1:12c, which leaves 1:12b as the climax: "he gave the right to become children of God."[10] The term "children of God" occurs again in 11:52, where these are said to include also believing Gentiles (cf. 10:16), and in 8:41 at the nexus of this theme in John's Gospel (cf. 8:31–47), where true children of God are said to be those who not only have God's word (8:31–38) but also respond to it in faith (8:39–47).[11] In keeping with

9. Boismard (1957: 79–80)—and many writers after him—notes that while 1:1–11 deals with the Word's descent, 1:14–18 is characterized by a dynamic of ascent.

10. So Culpepper 1980–81: 15–17. This is supported by the observation of Pryor (1990: 202) that 1:14 is not to be considered as the prologue's "great incarnational turning point," but that "the ministry of the historical Jesus, which is unquestionably in focus in vv 12–13, ought to be projected back at least to v 9." Staley (1988: 53–55) suggests that the center is found in 1:12–13.

11. See Culpepper (1980–81: 26–31), who notes that in relation to John's first epistle, John 1:12 mirrors 1 John 3:1–2, while 1 John 3:10 (cf. 5:2) corresponds to John 8:31–47.

the above macrostructure, the prologue can be divided into strophes that mutually correspond by way of chiasm (see translation below): 1:1–2 with 1:18, 1:3 with 1:17, 1:4–5 with 1:16, 1:6–8 with 1:15, 1:9–10 with 1:14, and 1:11–13 at the center.[12]

The opening section of John's prologue (1:1–5) features the Word's participation in creation. Not only was the Word *with* God; it was itself God. The Word is presented as the giver of both light and life. By withholding the name of Jesus until 1:17, the evangelist creates suspense, allowing for certain christological anticipations to be seen in 1:1–5 without making them explicit until 1:9–14 and 1:16–18.[13] The present passage also sets the stage for the Word's rejection by the world at his "homecoming" (1:10) and the Word's incarnation as the one-of-a-kind Son from the Father (1:14, 18). John 1:5 sounds the note of the Word's victory over darkness, which foreshadows the Gospel's presentation of the ministry and passion of Jesus as a cosmic battle between God and Satan. Just as the entire prologue (1:1–18) is foundational for the remainder of the Gospel, 1:1–5 is foundational for the remainder of the prologue. Prior to the appearance of John the Baptist, who bore witness to Jesus, there already was the preexistent Word, who subsequently was made flesh in Jesus and revealed the Father to his followers (cf. 1:15).

In 1:6–8, the evangelist proceeds to anchor Jesus' ministry firmly in salvation history. Like the Synoptics, the present Gospel presents John the Baptist as "a man whose appearance and ministry belong integrally to the Christ-event" (Ridderbos 1997: 41). This reference to the Baptist, together with 1:15, anticipates the narrative commencing immediately after the prologue in 1:19. In light of the material's stylistic unity, it is not necessary to hold that the references to the Baptist were inserted into a non-Johannine, preexisting hymn.[14]

The climactic section of John's prologue (1:9–14) is framed by ref-

12. For a similar (but not identical) analysis, see Staley 1986: 245–46 (yet his suggested implications for the Gospel's narrative structure are rather idiosyncratic).

13. Stibbe (1993) sees elusiveness as Jesus' "major character trait in John's Gospel," contending that "Jesus is depicted throughout the story as the one who evades people both at the level of presence and at the level of language" (p. 25). Though this may be true at other places in the narrative, Stibbe's analysis of 1:18 hardly seems accurate: "What we have at the end of the Prologue is therefore the implication that the elusiveness of Jesus reflects the elusiveness of God" (p. 26). How does this square with the explicit statement in 1:18 that Jesus gives a full account of the Father? The Son must not be so elusive after all, since countless individuals down through the generations (including Jesus' own followers) have come to know the Father through the revelation of his Son (cf. 14:6).

14. Haenchen (1984: 1.117) holds that 1:6–8 represents a rather clumsy insertion into the original hymn. Bultmann (1971: 49) believes that the material is inserted to counter veneration of John the Baptist (cf. Schnackenburg 1990: 1.249–50). Ridderbos (1997: 42) ardently defends the prologue's unity. Moloney (1998: 37) notes that 1:6–8 is essential to the prologue in its current form.

erences to the coming of the true light into the world (1:9; a rather innocuous-sounding statement) and the Word becoming flesh (1:14; a truly startling claim). John 1:10–11 sounds a note of rejection by both the world (which was made through the Word [1:3]) and even his own people (i.e., Israel). John 1:12–13, with 1:12 as the major climax of the entire prologue (Culpepper 1980–81) and 1:13 as a clarifying addition, assigns to all those who believe "in his name" the right to become God's children. Both 1:11 and 1:13 make clear that the Jewish people must not presume upon their ethnic privilege. By centering his Gospel in the (sole) requirement of faith in Jesus, the evangelist strikes a universal note that achieves a further climax in 3:16. This universal scope transcends national (Jewish) boundaries and is in further development of the opening references to creation.

Pursuing his chiastic arrangement of presentation, the evangelist then returns to the witness of John the Baptist (1:15; cf. 1:6–8). The previous reference spoke of the bare fact of John's *identity*—now the evangelist elaborates regarding the *content* of John's testimony. The chiasm is completed in the final unit of the prologue (1:16–18), with 1:16 corresponding to 1:4–5, 1:17 to 1:3, and 1:18 to 1:1–2. Just as God's creation gifts through the Word were life and light (1:4–5), so God's gift through his one-of-a-kind Son is fullness of grace, indeed, "grace for grace" (1:16). Moreover, just as the world came into being through the Word, so grace and truth came through the Word-made-flesh, Jesus Christ (1:17; cf. 1:3). Finally, the evangelist closes the prologue the way he began it: with a reference to the Word (i.e., Jesus) as God (1:18; cf. 1:1). Jesus' ministry is thus cast as the creative Word's eschatological enfleshment and definitive revelation of God.

A. The Word's activity in creation (1:1–5)
B. John's witness concerning the light (1:6–8)
C. The incarnation of the Word and the privilege of becoming God's children (1:9–14)
D. John's witness concerning the Word's preeminence (1:15)
E. The final revelation brought by Jesus Christ (1:16–18)

Exegesis and Exposition[15]

[1]In the beginning was the Word,
and the Word was with God,

---

15. In the following translation, units are broken up to reflect the chiastic structure as discussed above, whereby 1:1–2 corresponds to 1:18, 1:3 to 1:17, 1:4–5 to 1:16, 1:6–8 to 1:15, and 1:9–10 to 1:14, with 1:11–13 forming the center of the chiasm.

and the Word was God.
[2]He was with God in the beginning.

[3]Through him all things were made,
and without him nothing was made
that has been made.

[4]In him was life,
and that life was the light of all people;
[5]and the light shines in the darkness,
but the darkness has not overcome it.

[6]There was a man sent from God, by the name of John.
[7]He came to give testimony concerning the light,
so that through him all might believe.
[8]That man was not the light; rather, he came to testify concerning the
light.

[9]The true light that enlightens every person was indeed coming into the
world.
[10]He was in the world,
and though the world was made through him,
yet the world did not recognize him.

[11]He came to that which was his own,
but his own did not receive him.
[12]Yet to all who did receive him,
to those who believed in his name,
to those he gave the right to become children of God—
[13]children born not of natural descent,
nor of human decision or a husband's will,
but born of God.

[14]And the Word was made flesh and pitched his tent among us,
and we have seen his glory,
glory as that of the one-of-a-kind Son from the Father,
full of grace and truth.

[15]John testifies concerning him
and cries out, saying, "This is the one of whom I said,
'The one who comes after me ranks ahead of me,
because he was before me.'"

[16]From his fullness we have all received grace for grace.

[17]For the law was given through Moses—
true, ultimate grace came through Jesus Christ.

[18]God no one has ever seen:
⌐the one-of-a-kind Son, God⌐ [in his own right],
who lives in closest relationship with the Father—
that one has given full account of him.

A. The Word's Activity in Creation (1:1–5)

The phrase "in the beginning" echoes the opening phrase of the Hebrew **1:1**
Bible (Gen. 1:1) and establishes a canonical link between the first words
of the OT Scriptures and the present Gospel. "Beginning" points to a time
prior to creation (R. Brown 1966: 4; Beasley-Murray 1999: 10; Schnackenburg 1990: 1.232).[16] Yet while John's first readers would have expected
the phrase "In the beginning *God*," the evangelist instead speaks of "the
Word" (Beasley-Murray 1999: 10). The focus of this verse is to show the
Word's preexistence (Ridderbos 1997: 25; Schnackenburg 1990: 1.232),
preparing for the later reference to a new "beginning," the incarnation
of the Word (cf. 1:14) (Morris 1995: 64; Carson 1991: 114).

The designation "Word"—used in a christological sense only in the
prologue (1:1, 14)—conveys the notion of divine self-expression or speech
(cf. Ps. 19:1–4).[17] The Genesis creation account establishes the effective-
ness of God's word: he speaks, and things come to pass (Gen. 1:3, 9;
cf. 1:11, 15, 24, 30). Psalmists and prophets alike portray God's word
in close-to-personal terms (Ps. 33:6; 107:20; 147:15, 18; Isa. 55:10–11).
Yet only John claims that this Word has appeared as an actual person,
Jesus Christ (cf. 1 John 1:1; Rev. 19:13). As a comprehensive christological designation, the expression "the Word" encompasses Jesus' entire
ministry, placing all of Jesus' works and words within the framework
of both his eternal being and existence[18] and God's self-revelation in
salvation history.[19]

16. Besides "beginning," the Greek term ἀρχή can also mean "first cause." It is possible
that John here seeks to convey both meanings, "in the beginning of history" and "at the
root of the universe" (Morris 1995: 65).

17. Calvin (1959: 7) remarks, "I think he calls the Son of God 'the Word' . . . simply
because, first, He is the eternal wisdom and will of God, and secondly, because He is the
express image of His purpose. For just as in men speech is called the expression of the
thoughts, so it is not inappropriate to apply this to God and say that He expresses Himself
to us by His Speech or Word."

18. Michaels (1989: 21) observes, "Elsewhere in John's Gospel, Jesus *speaks* the word,
but in the prologue he *is* the Word, the personal embodiment of all that he proclaims."

19. See the allusion to the tabernacle in 1:14 and the reference to God's giving the law
through Moses in 1:17 (see also 5:46). As Behr (2000: 94 [cf. M. Edwards 1995]) notes, for

The term "Word" appears to have been used by the evangelist at least partly in order to contextualize the gospel message among his Hellenistic audience. Keener (2003) provides thorough discussions of the gnostic Logos (pp. 339–41); the Logos of Hellenistic philosophy (pp. 341–43); Philo (pp. 343–47); wisdom, word, and Torah (pp. 350–60); and John's Logos and Torah (pp. 360–63). Three primary backgrounds have been proposed: (1) Greek philosophy (Stoicism, Philo); (2) the personification of wisdom; and (3) the OT.[20]

In Stoic thought, *logos* was Reason, the impersonal principle governing the universe. A spark of universal Reason was thought to reside within people (at least the best and wisest of them), who must live in keeping with it to attain dignity and meaning. Yet while John may well have been aware of the Stoic concept of the *logos*, it is doubtful that it constituted his primary conceptual framework (see the three reasons given in Köstenberger 1999a: 52).

Another candidate is the personification of wisdom in wisdom literature (see, e.g., Talbert 1992: 68–71). In Prov. 8 (esp. vv. 22–31), wisdom is called "the first of his [God's] works," "appointed from eternity, from the beginning, before the world began." Wisdom was "the craftsman at his side" when he marked out the earth's foundations, "rejoicing always in his presence." A whole corpus of apocryphal wisdom literature built on these notions (Sir. 1:1–10; Wisdom of Solomon). At first sight, the parallels between the characterization of wisdom in Prov. 8 and John's *logos* seem impressive. Wisdom, like John's *logos*, claims preexistence and participation in God's creative activity. Like the *logos*, wisdom is

---

the second-century church fathers, including Justin Martyr, "The revelation of God in the incarnate Logos is the last, even if the most important, in a series of discrete revelations." According to Irenaeus, "[t]he pre-existence of Christ, the Word of God, is inextricably connected with his seminal presence in Scripture, the word of God" (*inseminatus est ubique in Scripturis ejus Filius Dei*; Behr 2000: 98).

20. For a more thorough discussion, see E. Miller (1993: 448–49), who lists as many as nine different theories: (1) the OT *dbr*; (2) Wisdom (R. Harris 1917); (3) Greek philosophy (Stoicism); (4) Philo (Evans 1993: 100–145; Tobin 1990); (5) the Aramaic *mmrʾ* (Hayward 1978); (6) rabbinic speculation on the Torah; (7) gnostic sources, such as the Hermetic literature, especially Poimandres (Pagels 1999); (8) the Hellenistic-gnostic redeemer myth, Mandeans, and the Odes of Solomon (Bultmann 1923; 1973; 1971); and (9) the breaking of divine silence (Jeremias). Some, such as Epp (1975), combine two or more of the above (in Epp's case, Wisdom and Torah). Miller himself (1993: 452), building on his earlier work (1989), advances the thesis that the uses of λόγος in the Gospel proper, while not a christological title, are invested "with a certain christological transparency" (B. Reicke's term). Thus, startlingly, Miller, who believes that the prologue was written not only after the Gospel proper, but even after John's first epistle, finds the origin of the prologue's λόγος in the Fourth Gospel itself: "The one of whom it was said in John 7:46, 'Never has a man spoken like this!' eventually came to be called, appropriately, 'the Word.'" I find this thesis entirely unconvincing (Miller [1999] attempts to make the same case for ἀρχή). It is quite a tour de force to brush aside the massive OT substructure pervading the entire prologue. Not surprisingly, Miller's thesis has found few followers.

depicted as a vehicle of God's self-revelation, in creation as well as the law. Yet despite these surface similarities, John's *logos* differs from personified wisdom in several significant respects, and the term σοφία (*sophia*, wisdom) is absent from this Gospel (Schlatter 1948: 43; see the three differences noted in Köstenberger 1999a: 53).

Finally, the third proposed background is the depiction of the Word of God in the OT. There are several reasons why this option has the most to commend it: (1) the evangelist's deliberate effort to echo the opening words of the Hebrew Scriptures by the phrase "in the beginning"; (2) the reappearance of several significant terms from Gen. 1 in John 1 ("light," "darkness," "life"); (3) the prologue's OT allusions, be it to Israel's wilderness wanderings (1:14: "pitched his tent") or to the giving of the law (1:17–18); and (4) the evangelist's adaptation of Isa. 55:9–11 for his basic christological framework (Köstenberger 1999a: 54).[21]

Since the Word existed in the beginning, one might think that either the Word *was* God or the Word was *with* God. John affirms both. First, he states that the Word was "with God." The preposition πρός (*pros*, with) indicates place or accompaniment, but also disposition and orientation (Ridderbos 1997: 25 n. 23).[22] What is expressed is "not simple co-existence, but rather the idea of active relationship or intercourse 'with'" (Pollard 1977: 364–65).[23] In terms of relationship, not only does πρός establish a relationship between God and the Word, but also it distinguishes the two from each other (R. Brown 1966: 5).

The word ἦν (*ēn*, was) in 1:1 conveys the notions of existence, relationship, and predication (R. Brown 1966: 4; contrast ἐγένετο [*egeneto*, came, became] in 1:3, 6, 14). At the risk of overtranslation, the force may be, "the Word continually was" (Morris 1995: 65; though, of course, εἰμί has no past tense indicative forms other than the imperfect).[24] In context, the Word's existence is placed "outside the limits of time and place, neither of which existed *en archē*" (Moloney 1998: 35).

The term θεός (*theos*, God; used again in 1:2, 6, 12, 13, 18) is familiar to John's readers as a reference to the God revealed in the OT. The

21. Viviano (1998: 182) comments, "This passage of Isaiah [Isa. 55:10–11] almost certainly had *the* decisive effect on John 1:1–18."

22. Moloney (1998: 35) says that πρός connotes motion, not just "with," and translates it "turned toward." Yet any force of motion inherent in πρός is overridden by the stative verb (Wallace 1996: 358–59; Schnackenburg [1990: 1.234] also rejects the idea). Lindars (1972: 84) proposes "in company with," while Westcott (1908: 1.6) writes, "The personal being of the Word was realised in active intercourse with and in perfect communion with God." Bultmann (1971: 32–33) suggests that ἦν πρός is a Semitism equivalent to παρά plus the dative.

23. Seeking to combine the notions of "with" indicating accompaniment and "toward" signifying relationship, R. Brown (1966: 4–6) translates, "The Word was in God's presence"; A. T. Robertson (1934: 623 [cited in MacLeod 2003: 57]) glosses, "face to face with God."

24. Lindars (1972: 82) labels ἦν "past continuous" and thus "virtually timeless."

word occurs in Gen. 1:1 to refer to the Creator. The same expression is used for "god" in the Greco-Roman world, whose pantheon was made up of dozens of deities. The Jews, by contrast, believed in only one God (Deut. 6:4). John's favorite expression for God in his Gospel is "Father" of Jesus (cf. 1:14, 18).[25]

It is one thing for the Word to be *with* God (so were Isaiah's personified Word and Wisdom); it is quite another for the Word to *be* God.[26] Having distinguished the Word—Jesus, not mentioned by name until 1:17—from God, John now shows what they have in common: they are God (M. Harris 1992: 67; Luther 1957: 15). Clearly, calling Jesus "God" stretched the boundaries of first-century Jewish monotheism (though see Bauckham 1998a; Hurtado 1998b). From the patristic era (Arius) to the present (Jehovah's Witnesses), it has been argued that this verse merely identifies Jesus as *a* god rather than as God, because there is no definite article in front of θεός. Yet this is dubious for several reasons.[27]

First, John, as a monotheistic Jew, would hardly have referred to another person as "a god." Second, if John had placed a definite article before θεός, this would have so equated God and the Word that the distinction established between the two persons in the previous clause ("the Word was *with* God") would have been all but obliterated. Third, in Greek syntax it is common for a definite nominative predicate noun preceding a finite verb to be without the article (Colwell 1933: 12–31; McGaughy 1972; Wallace 1996: 256–70), so that it is illegitimate to infer indefiniteness from the lack of the article in the present passage.

In fact, if John had merely wanted to affirm that Jesus was divine, there was a perfectly proper Greek word for it: θεῖος (*theios*, divine) (R. Brown 1966: 5; Bultmann 1971: 33–34; Carson 1991: 117). Nevertheless, the force of the anarthrous θεός is probably not so much that of definiteness as that of quality: Jesus "shared the *essence* of the Father, though they differed in person" (Wallace 1996: 269). Everything that can

25. On "God" and "Father" in the Gospel of John, see especially the valuable and insightful monographs by Thompson (2000; 2001). On the characterization of God in the Fourth Gospel, see also Tolmie 1998; on God the Father, see Meyer 1996: 255–73 and Fisher 2003.

26. For a brief survey of the divinity and uniqueness of Jesus, particularly claims of Jesus' preexistence, see Köstenberger 1998b: 46–47 (see relevant bibliography in nn. 7–8).

27. See Hartley 1999 for an interaction with the arguments by Jehovah's Witnesses against Jesus' deity from 1:1c. Hartley first surveys the history of the debate, starting with Colwell (1933: 12–21), followed by contributions by Harner (1973: 75–87), P. Dixon (1975), and Hartley himself (1996). Hartley concludes that "the Word was *theos* (1:1c) in every *sense* the Father was *ton theon* (1:1b), rather than *a* god in a particular sense the Father was not" (1999: 1, summarizing 1996). See also MacLeod 2003: 59–60; and Keener 2003: 372–74, who points to the anarthrous instances of θεός designating God the Father later in the prologue (1:6, 12, 13, 18) and the articular use of θεός with reference to Jesus in 20:28 (p. 373).

be said about God also can be said about the Word (Morris 1995: 68; Wallace 1996: 735). By contrast, wisdom is never referred to as θεός.

The purpose of the verse is more than mere emphasis through repetition (the view of Borchert 1996: 106).[28] Now that the reader understands the contents of 1:1, the evangelist, by reiterating the second clause of 1:1, provides closure as well as preparing the reader for 1:3 (Carson 1991: 118). The pronoun οὗτος (houtos, he) points backward to the Word and forward to a human being (Moloney 1998: 35).

1:2

"Having declared that the Word is God and proclaimed His divine essence, he goes on to prove His divinity from His works" (Calvin 1959: 9). The affirmation that all things were made through *wisdom* or even through God's *word* would have been thoroughly in keeping with Jewish belief. John's contention, however, is that everything—that is, the κόσμος (kosmos, world) of 1:10 (Bultmann 1971: 36)—came into being through "him," that is, *Jesus*, God-made-flesh (the word διά [dia, through] conveys secondary agency on the part of the Son here and in 1:10, 17; 3:17; 14:6; 1 John 4:9; Pollard 1977: 366; Wallace 1996: 434).[29]

1:3

The phrase ὃ γέγονεν (ho gegonen, that has been made) can be construed with what precedes or with what follows.[30] The former is to be preferred, for the following reasons.[31] First, "without him nothing has been made that has been made" brings closure to the thought expressed in 1:3 by way of emphatic restatement of the converse. The alternative, "That which has been made in him was life," is hardly intelligible.[32]

28. See, rightly, MacLeod 2003: 62 (who in n. 66 cites further proponents of the view that 1:2 merely repeats 1:1), though it is far from certain that 1:2 should be read in sapiential terms as MacLeod avers.

29. Though note that Jesus is not explicitly mentioned until 1:17. "All things" (τὰ πάντα, ta panta) may echo Gen. 1:31 (cf. Gen. 9:3; Ashton 1986: 184 n. 37). Though startling, the substance of the present assertion is in no way unique to John; it pervades much of the NT (cf. 1 Cor. 8:6; Col. 1:16; Heb. 1:2). For extrabiblical parallels, see Köstenberger 2002c: 6. For a survey of possible backgrounds for 1:3, see Keener 2003: 375–81.

30. Cohee (1995: 476–77) adds a third alternative: he believes that ὃ γέγονεν was introduced into the text as a gloss on the οὐδὲ ἕν of verse 3b.

31. So the majority of commentators, including Morris 1995: 66; Carson 1991: 137; Haenchen 1984: 1.113–14; Schnackenburg 1970: 1.239–40; Barrett 1978: 156–57; and Schlatter 1948: 5–6. Among the translations that construe ὃ γέγονεν with what precedes are the NASB, NIV, NKJV, ISV, NLT, HCSB, ESV, and TNIV.

32. Note the comment on this alternative by Metzger (1994: 168): "whatever that may be supposed to mean." In Metzger's dissenting opinion (the majority of the UBS translation committee favors taking the phrase with what follows) he states, "Despite valiant attempts of commentators to bring sense out of taking ὃ γέγονεν with what follows, the passage remains intolerably clumsy and opaque" (similarly, Schnackenburg, cited by Ashton 1986: 172). Among the major translations, only the NRSV prefers this alternative. Commentators who advocate this option are R. Brown (1966: 6–7), Bultmann (1971: 39–40, esp. n. 4), Beasley-Murray (1999: 1–2, esp. n. a), and Whitacre (1999: 52). See also E. Miller (1989), who integrates his belief that the phrase is to be taken with what follows into his larger thesis that 1:1a–b and 1:3–5 constitute a christological hymn in four strophes extolling the

Second, John frequently begins a sentence or clause with ἐν (*en*, in) plus a demonstrative pronoun (cf. 13:35; 15:8; 16:26). Third, Johannine theology elsewhere favors taking the phrase with what precedes (5:26, 39; 6:53; cf. 1 John 5:11).[33]

The thrust of this verse is to point to creation, not incarnation (Ridderbos 1997: 37; Carson 1991: 118). The evangelist emphatically asserts that "everything owes its existence to the Word" (Morris 1995: 71). Restating a clause by way of negating the contrary is a common Johannine device (e.g., 1:12–13, 20; 3:16–17, 36) (Morris 1995: 71). The perfect γέγονεν (*gegonen*, has been made) underscores the permanent effect of ἐγένετο (*egeneto*, were made) earlier in the verse, denoting "the continuing existence of created things" (Morris 1995: 71; cf. Ridderbos 1997: 37 n. 62).

1:4–5   In 1:4–5, the evangelist continues to elaborate on the Word's involvement in creation, writing as one who looks at the present in light of its origin, with the imperfect verbs in 1:1–4 providing the general backdrop (Ridderbos 1997: 38, 40).[34] Both "life" and "light" are universal religious terms (D. H. Johnson, *DJG* 469–71; Schnackenburg 1990: 1.242–44), but John's teaching is deeply rooted in OT teaching.[35] At creation, calling forth "light" was God's first creative act (Gen. 1:3–5) (Morris 1995: 74–75). Later, God placed lights in the sky to separate between light and darkness (Gen. 1:14–18). Light, in turn, makes it possible for life to exist. Thus, on the fifth and sixth days of creation God made animate life to populate both the waters and dry land, culminating in his creation of humankind (Gen. 1:20–31; 2:7; 3:20). Now John asserts that life was "in him," Jesus. He is the source of life, both physical and spiritual ("eternal"). He also is the source of supernatural light, since only those who possess spiritual, eternal life have the capacity to "walk in the light," that is, to make moral decisions that are in accordance with God's revealed will.[36]

---

salvation-historical activity of the Word (he considers 1:1c and 1:2 to be interpolations). Brodie (1993: 138), because of the lack of punctuation, sees the text as inherently ambiguous and as being "part of a careful literary strategy" designed to focus on "the continuity between creation and the incarnation, between creation and redemption."

33. Cohee (1995: 473) also draws attention to parallels in Greek literature, such as the passage quoted by the apostle Paul in Acts 17:28 from Aratus, *Phaenomena* 5, and perhaps Cleanthes, *Hymn to Zeus* 4: Ἐν αὐτῷ γὰρ ζῶμεν . . . ("For in him we live . . .").

34. Schlatter (1948: 6) notes the characteristic Johannine asyndeton in 1:4 and that it does not detract from the flow of thought. Keener (2003: 382) identifies the chain life-life-light-light-darkness-darkness in 1:4–5 as a literary device called sorites (also adducing Wis. 6:17–20).

35. For an extensive discussion of the place of symbolism in the Fourth Gospel, see Culpepper 1983: 180–98. See also C. Koester 2003.

36. Hence, the present reference is to light that only believers possess; contra Calvin (1959: 11), who speaks of the "light" of common grace given to humans, that is, ethical rationality, which animals lack: "I think that this is a reference to that part of life in which men surpass the other animate creatures. It is as if he were saying that the life given to men was not life in general but life united with the light of reason."

"Light of [all] people" means "light *for* [all] people" (Bultmann 1971: 40), an objective genitive in Greek (Ridderbos 1997: 38 n. 64), pointing to the universal effects of the Word's appearance.

The statement "the light shines" anticipates "the light that came when Christ entered the world and that now shines" (Ridderbos 1997: 39). In the present Gospel, "darkness" is "the world estranged from God" (Schnackenburg 1990: 1.245), spiritually ignorant and blind, fallen and sinful (Witherington 1995: 55), dominated by Satan. The evangelist announces at the outset that the darkness has not "overcome" (κατέλαβεν, *katelaben*) the light (better translation than "understood"; cf. NIV footnote; Köstenberger 1999a: 55). This reading is suggested by, among other things, 12:35 (cf. 16:33), the closest parallel in John's Gospel (R. Brown 1966: 8).[37]

Once again, John contextualizes. While drawing on solidly OT concepts, he employs these universal terms to engage adherents of other religions and worldviews.[38] For some, light was wisdom (or wisdom was even superior to light; cf. Wis. 7:26–30). For others, light was given by the Mosaic law (2 Bar. 59:2) or Scripture (Ps. 19:8; 119:105, 130; Prov. 6:23). Still others looked for enlightenment in philosophy, morality, or a simple lifestyle. In this religiously pluralistic context, John proclaims Jesus as the supreme light, who is both eternal and universal and yet personal. Importantly, the coming of the light necessitated a choice to be made by those in the world who have seen it (Ridderbos 1997: 42).

37. "Overcome" or an equivalent is favored also by Morris 1995: 76; Moloney 1998: 36; Schnackenburg 1990: 1.245–46; Laney 1992: 39; Lindars 1972: 87; Schlatter 1948: 9 ("καταλαμβάνω never means 'understand' in John"); and Westcott 1908: 1.9–10. Carson (1991: 138) thinks that John might have both meanings ("overcome" and "comprehend") in mind (so also Whitacre 1999: 53) and likes the ambiguity in BAGD's translation, "master" (see BDAG 520). Keener (2003: 387) believes that John's use of κατέλαβεν in 1:5 is an instance of *traductio,* a play on the multiple meanings of a word (here "comprehend" and "overcome"). Keener notes that the word occurs in Wis. 7:30 but admits that there the term clearly means "overcome" and no wordplay is present. Burge (2000: 56) agrees that both are at work, but he sees "overcome" as being dominant. Calvin (1959: 12) translates "comprehend." The major translations divide more or less evenly between the two options, usually mentioning the one not chosen in a footnote: (1) NIV: "understood"; NASB, NKJV: "comprehend"; (2) NLT: "extinguish"; NET: "mastered"; ISV: "put out"; HCSB, ESV, NRSV: "overcome." Notably, the TNIV changed the NIV's "understood" to "overcome."

38. Some believe that John is alluding here to the Greek dualism between light and darkness. Rather than affirming belief in a personal God who is sovereign, all-powerful, and good, the Greeks viewed reality in terms of polar opposites, such as light and darkness or good and evil. John, however, refutes this kind of thinking in his first epistle, where he states emphatically, "God is light; in him there is no darkness at all" (1 John 1:5). Another kind of light/darkness dualism is found in the DSS, particularly the War Scroll (1QM) depicting the battle between the "sons of light" and the "sons of darkness." Yet, because of the sectarian nature of the Qumran community, light is never offered to those who live in darkness (cf. 1QS 3:21; 4:9–14) (Bauckham 1997). In John, on the other hand, Jesus urges his listeners, "Put your trust in the light while you have it, so that you may become sons of light" (12:36; cf. 8:12; 9:5).

Demonstrably, however, beneath this contrast between light and darkness lies a significant cluster of OT passages. Most interesting are several instances in Isaiah that depict the coming Messiah as a light entering the darkness. In Isa. 9:2, one reads, "The people walking in darkness have seen a great light; on those living in the land of the shadow of death a light has dawned." In Isa. 60:1–5, a time is envisioned when the nations will walk in God's light, and the glory of the Lord will shine brightly (cf. Isa. 42:6–7; 49:6; see also John 12:46; 1 John 1:5–7). In John, light and darkness are no equally matched duality, but in the battle between Jesus and Satan, Jesus, "the light," is the overwhelming victor.

B. John's Witness concerning the Light (1:6–8)

1:6 All four Gospels identify the Baptist as the forerunner of Jesus. Luke in particular provides a very thorough account of John's origins, including the unusual circumstances surrounding his birth (chs. 1–2). In the context of John's opening lines, the present description of John makes two things clear: (1) John was a man, not, as Jesus, God; and (2) John was sent by God to carry out a particular mission, in distinction from, but in relation to, Jesus. Ἐγένετο (*egeneto*, there was; contrast ἦν [*ēn*, was] in 1:1–4), together with ἄνθρωπος (*anthrōpos*, a man; contrast θεός [*theos*, God] in 1:1), sets the Baptist off from the Word or light: the Word existed from eternity. Yet although the Baptist was not the Word and certainly not God, he was indeed sent *from* God. The phrase "sent from God" is reminiscent of the OT description of a prophet whose role was to function as a spokesperson for God (e.g., 2 Chron. 24:19; 25:15; Jer. 7:25; 25:4; 28:9; 35:15; 44:4; Ezek. 2:3). The Jewish crowds thought of John as a prophet (Matt. 21:26 pars.), and that is how Jesus referred to him as well (Matt. 11:9 = Luke 7:26).

Luke records the unusual circumstances of how the Baptist got his name: initially he was to be named after his father, Zechariah, but his mother and his father concurred that his name should be John (Luke 1:59–63). The name "John," a common one in the Hellenistic world of that day, also occurred frequently among the members of the Jewish priesthood, which included John's father (Luke 1:5) (Carroll, *ABD* 3:886). "John" in the Fourth Gospel always refers to the Baptist.[39] The "other John" known from the Synoptics, that is, John the apostle, the son of Zebedee, is not referred to by name in this Gospel (though see 21:2). It is likely that he, as the author, conceals himself behind the phrase "the disciple Jesus loved" (first used in 13:23). Since the Fourth Evangelist is characteristically careful with names so as not to confuse his readers

---

39. Except, of course, for Simon's father (1:42; 21:15–17). For a list of named individual characters in the Fourth Gospel, see Beck 1997: 30. For a discussion of all the significant named characters in John (plus the mother of Jesus and the "beloved disciple"), see M. Davies 1992: 316–49.

(see 6:71; 12:4; 14:22: two Judases; 11:2; 12:3; 19:25: several Marys, plus Jesus' mother), this is evidence for apostolic authorship (Morris 1995: 79 n. 52; Carson 1991: 120).

Whereas the Synoptists portray John's ministry as more multifaceted, **1:7** John depicts him as the paradigmatic, though by no means only, witness to Jesus (Lincoln 2000: 58–73; the content of John's testimony is summarized in 1:15).[40] Like Luke (1:1–4), John stresses the accuracy of the facts set forth in his Gospel. In keeping with this concern, the Fourth Evangelist focuses on the Baptist's role as a witness to Jesus (cf. 1:7–8, 15, 19, 32–34; 3:26; 5:33–36). This makes the Baptist the first, though not the weightiest (5:36), among a whole series of witnesses to Jesus presented in this Gospel, which also include Jesus and his works (3:11, 32; 5:36; 8:14, 18; 10:25, 32, 37–38; 15:24; 18:37), Moses and the Scriptures (5:39, 46), the Father (5:32, 36–37; 8:18), the Spirit (chs. 14–16, esp. 15:26), the disciples (e.g., 15:27), and the Fourth Evangelist (19:35; 21:24).[41]

With regard to these witnesses, John's Gospel places particular emphasis on *eyewitnesses*, such as the Baptist (e.g., 1:32–34) and Jesus' first followers, including the evangelist (15:27; 19:35; 21:24). This role of eyewitness is both vital and humble. It is vital because eyewitnesses are required to establish the truthfulness of certain facts. Yet it is humble because the eyewitness is not the center of attention. Rather, eyewitnesses must testify truthfully to what they have seen and heard—no more and no less. The Baptist fulfilled this task with distinction. The last time he is mentioned in this Gospel, it is said of him that "all that John said about this man [Jesus] was true" (10:41).

"The light" has been cast as the life-giving, creative Word in 1:4, and as the illuminating, darkness-conquering force in 1:5. Now John (the Baptist) is said to give testimony to that light, with creation gradually receding into the background, and the focus increasingly shifting toward Jesus (cf. 1:9–14).

The desired, though not actual (Carson 1991: 121; Barrett 1978: 159), result of John's witness is that *all* might believe in Jesus (see commentary at 1:9) through him. Through the Word, "all things" were created; now it is God's purpose that "all people" might believe through John's

40. As Lincoln (2000: 21) notes, not only does the lawsuit motif (see Isa. 40–55, esp. 42:18–25; 43:22–28; 50:1–3) occur in each of the five main sections of John's narrative (prologue; 1:19–12:50; 13–17; 18–20; epilogue), but it does so in highly significant ways, forming the narrative framework of the Gospel (p. 141). According to Lincoln, just as there are seven signs and seven discourses in John's Gospel, there are seven witnesses: John the Baptist, Jesus himself, Jesus' works, God the Father, the Scriptures, the Samaritan woman, and the crowd. For a summary and appraisal of Lincoln's important monograph, see Köstenberger 2001a.

41. Keener (2003: 393) notes the literary purpose of opening and closing the Gospel with a witness (the Baptist and the evangelist respectively).

testimony (R. Brown 1966: 8–9). The word πιστεύω (*pisteuō*, believe) is found frequently in the Greek OT to describe the trust that God desires from his people.[42] In John's Gospel, πιστεύω, first used here in 1:7, occurs close to one hundred times, almost three times as often as in the Synoptics combined. John virtually never uses the noun πίστις (*pistis*, faith) in his writings (the only exceptions are 1 John 5:4; Rev. 2:13, 19; 13:10; and 14:12). Though he is not averse to understanding belief as the affirmation of certain religious truths, he is much more concerned about active, relational trust in Jesus Christ.

1:8   The disclaimer "That man was not the light; rather, he came to testify concerning the light" (cf. 1:15; 3:30; 5:36; 10:41) is taken by some as evidence that there were in John's day groups that elevated the Baptist above Jesus (R. Brown 1966: 28). There is some evidence for this in Ephesus in the 50s (Acts 18:25; 19:1–7). However, it is more likely that John's primary burden is to contrast (note the strong adversative ἀλλά [*alla*, but]) the respective ministries of John and Jesus (see 1:19–51; 3:22–24; 4:1–2), whereby the Baptist is cast in a positive light as a witness to Jesus (Ridderbos 1997: 42). John is not the light, but he is a lamp (5:35) (R. Brown 1966: 9; Morris 1995: 81; Keener 2003: 393). The phrase "testify concerning the light" does not occur in other literature and appears to be a Johannine coinage.[43] The phrase "he came" is not explicit in the text—an ellipsis—but follows from 1:7 (Morris 1995: 81 n. 61).[44]

C. The Incarnation of the Word and the Privilege of Becoming God's Children (1:9–14)

1:9   In 1:9–14, the categories of 1:1–5 are brought back, but this time they are explored in light of their "kerygmatic implications" (Ridderbos 1997: 43). The syntax of the sentence in 1:9 is complex. That what was "coming into the world" is the true light, not humankind, is clear enough (e.g., Pryor 1990: 203–4; Barrett 1978: 160–61; contra Haenchen 1984: 1.117). Since in Greek the periphrasis is separated ("was . . . coming," imperfect of εἶναι [*einai*, to be] plus the present participle), some translate the sentence as two somewhat independent clauses: "He was the true light . . . he was coming into the world" (see R. Brown 1966: 9–10).

"The true light is coming into the world" is a very subtle way of conveying the gospel to Hellenistic ears. It is hard to imagine a more discreet fashion of speaking of an event as momentous as the incarnation of

42. Abraham "believed the Lord" and thus became the father of all believers (Gen. 15:6; cf. Rom. 4:3, 20–24; Gal. 3:6; Heb. 11:8–12; James 2:23). Israel as a nation, however, is known in the OT primarily for unbelief (John 12:38; cf. Isa. 53:1).
43. On "the light" testifying, see 8:12–18.
44. Contra Wallace (1996: 477), who says that this may be an "imperatival ἵνα"—a conclusion called unlikely by Barrett (1978: 160).

the Word.[45] John uses the word κόσμος (*kosmos*, world) seventy-eight times in his Gospel (versus eight instances in Matthew and three each in Mark and Luke). The expression can mean "physical universe" (1:9, 10) or "a large number of people" (12:19). Most characteristically, however, the term refers to sinful humanity (e.g., 3:16). The phrase "come into the world," with its corollary "return to the Father," is used to depict Jesus as the one who enters the world from the outside and returns to his place of departure, that is, the presence of God the Father (cf. 13:1, 3; 14:12, 28; 16:28; 18:37). As in 3:19, the light was not received but rejected, resulting in judgment (cf. 9:39; 12:46–47) (Köstenberger 1998b: 121–23).

The coming of the Messiah frequently is depicted in the OT in terms of light.[46] By affirming that Jesus is the "true light"—just as he is the "true bread from heaven" (6:32) and the "true vine" (15:1)—John indicates that Jesus is the fulfillment of OT hopes and expectations. The term ἀληθινόν (*alēthinon*, true) here and elsewhere in John conveys the notion of genuineness in conjunction with typology: Moses gave the manna to OT Israel (though it was really God the Father who gave it; see 6:32); Jesus *is* the true bread from heaven—he gives life in an ultimate sense. Israel was God's vineyard; Jesus is God's vineyard—typified by fruitfulness—par excellence. Moreover, ἀληθινόν here also conveys a sense of ultimacy: in Jesus, God has revealed himself in an escalated, eschatological sense (Carson 1991: 122).

As the "true light," Jesus is here presented as the source of (spiritual) light.[47] That light enlightens every person.[48] The evangelist has already stated that "that life was the light of men" (1:4), that "the light shines in the darkness" (1:5), and that the Baptist bore witness "so that through him all might believe" (1:7). The present verse does not suggest universalism—the ultimate salvation of every person—for John does not speak of *internal* illumination in the sense of general revelation (contra Morris

45. Among those who take 1:9 as a preliminary reference to the incarnation are Ridderbos 1997: 43; Carson 1991: 122; Borchert 1996: 112–13; Schnackenburg 1990: 1.255; Laney 1992: 41. Moloney (1998: 37) sees a hint to the incarnation already in 1:3c–4. There also may be an implied contrast with Hellenistic religions that offered false "light."

46. On the general motif of "light," see commentary at 1:4–5. On the coming of the Messiah in terms of light, see especially Horbury (1998: 92–93, 99–100), who also discusses rabbinic interpretations. Important OT references include Num. 24:17 (cf. 4QTest 9–13); Isa. 9:2 (cf. 42:6–7; see commentary at John 1:5); and Mal. 4:2 (cf. Luke 1:78–79; see Köstenberger 2002c: 8).

47. Later in John's Gospel, Jesus calls himself "the light of the world" (8:12; 9:5). See also the depiction of Jesus in the Book of Revelation (1:14, 16; 2:18; 19:12; 21:23; 22:5, 16; cf. Matt. 17:2 pars.; Heb. 1:3; 2 Pet. 1:19). Köstenberger (2002c: 8) points out that the contrast conveyed by the expression "true light" is primarily between previous OT manifestations of God and God's final, definitive revelation through Jesus Christ.

48. This is the only instance of the term φωτίζω (*phōtizō*, enlighten) in the Fourth Gospel.

1995: 84), but of *external* illumination in the sense of objective revelation requiring a response (R. Brown 1966: 9). As the remainder of the Gospel illustrates, not all did in fact *receive* the light, though it was *available* to all through Jesus' presence and teaching (Borchert 1996: 113). John here stresses the universal scope of Jesus' coming and the potential spiritual enlightenment available to all who would believe, an enlightenment that is available not merely to Jews but to all people, including non-Jews (cf. 1:12–13; 3:16; 10:16; 12:32; contrast 1:10; 3:19–21).

1:10–11   He—the Word who was the light[49]—"was" (ἦν, *ēn*) in the world: not just paying a fleeting visit, but, as John goes on to elaborate in 1:14, "dwelling among us." Even though the world was created through the Word (an echo of 1:3), it did not recognize that Word, because it was estranged from him (Ridderbos 1997: 44). Yet the world should have recognized the one through whom it was made (Haenchen 1984: 1.117). The first half of John's Gospel documents how not only the pagan world, but even Israel—"his own" (R. Brown 1966: 10)—failed to recognize Jesus as Messiah and Savior of the world, rejecting the light, including all demonstrations of Jesus' deity and messiahship (his "signs"; cf. 12:37–43, citing Isa. 53:1) (Schlatter 1948: 17).[50]

Whether or not there is a progression in the evangelist's use of the term κόσμος,[51] the evangelist highlights the irony, even tragedy, of the world rejecting the one through whom it was made.[52] The senses "created universe," "universe inhabited by humankind," and "fallen, sinful humanity in darkness" all resonate in the background (note the connection between "the world" and the "darkness" mentioned in 1:5; Bultmann

49. Rather puzzlingly, R. Brown (1966: 10) claims that "he was" refers to the Word, not the light. But this surely is a false dichotomy, for the Word (1:1–2) is later in the prologue consistently referred to as the light.

50. Schnackenburg (1990: 1.256) claims that the reference is not to Jesus' earthly ministry but to Israel's history prior to the incarnation. Similarly, R. Brown (1966: 30) cites the parallel of Wisdom in 1 Enoch 42:2: "Wisdom came to make her dwelling place among the children of men and found no dwelling place." More likely, the reference is anticipatory of the Word's incarnation in 1:14 (Culpepper 1980–81: 13–14; Carson 1991: 122; Ridderbos 1997: 43; Moloney 1998: 37). On a literal level, see the reference in Luke 2:7 that there was "no guest room available" (TNIV) for Jesus and his parents at his birth, which may have spiritual overtones as well.

51. Barrett (1978: 162) sees only one sense of κόσμος in this verse. Morris (1995: 85) contends that the first two instances refer to everyone, while the third reference is to those who came in contact with Jesus. Beasley-Murray (1999: 12) sees a progression from "the world inhabited by humankind" in 1:10a to "the world including human beings" in 1:10b to "humanity, fallen and in darkness" in 1:10c. Carson (1991: 123) demonstrates that the word κόσμος never has a positive usage (contra Burge 2000: 57) and only a few neutral ones.

52. Stibbe (1993: 27) observes, "The fact that the world does not acknowledge Jesus shows that John has no time for what literary theorists call 'the pathetic fallacy'—the fallacious view that nature sympathizes with the poet and/or the hero. The world in John's story is actively hostile to the protagonist."

1971: 55). The thrice-repeated term κόσμος contributes to the solemnity and emphatic nature of the reference.[53]

"Did not recognize" translates the aorist of γινώσκω (*ginōskō*, know), referring to more than mere intellectual rejection and entailing a willful refusal to accept or believe (in) someone or something (Ridderbos 1997: 44; note the parallelism between πιστεύω [*pisteuō*, believe] and γινώσκω in 6:69). As R. Brown (1966: 10) points out, "The basic sin in John's Gospel is the failure to know and believe in Jesus." This refers first and foremost to a rejection of Jesus' claim of equality with God and his revelation of the Father through words and signs.

In 1:11, what is said first in general terms—"his own [lit., 'things']" (Greek neuter) refers to the Word's property (cf. the Greek of 16:32; 19:27; Acts 21:6; Kruse 2003: 66)—is then elaborated with specific reference to God's chosen people Israel: "his own [people]" (Greek masculine), a wordplay in the original (Pryor 1990).[54] Not only was Jesus not received by a world made through him, but also he was rejected by a people specially chosen by God as his very own (see Exod. 19:5).[55] The picture is that of the Word not being a welcomed guest among his own people, the very ones who should have received him with open arms.[56]

To substantiate this claim, John 1–12 narrates Jesus' performance of seven selected signs specifically for Israel, climaxing in a final statement regarding Israel's rejection of Jesus' signs in 12:37–43. In 13:1, then, the epithet "his own" is transferred from Israel to God's new messianic community, consisting of the inner circle of followers of Jesus the Messiah (Pryor 1992a: 55; Köstenberger 1998b: 162, 165–66). The entire Gospel is

53. On solemnity, see Thielman 1991: 177–78.

54. This is the view of, among others, Carson 1991: 125; Dodd 1953: 402; R. Brown 1966: 10; Morris 1995: 85; Borchert 1996: 114; Burge 2000: 59. For a demonstration that 1:11, properly interpreted and understood (particularly the world as God's property), refutes the notion, advanced by Bultmann, that John reflects gnostic thought, see Jervell 1956: 17–18. But see also the interaction with Jervell in Pryor 1990: 210–14.

55. Pryor (1990: 217) contends that "his own" here is "not a status term but a relational one," referring to the Jews as Jesus' "own kinsfolk," "his own people according to the flesh," "the people of his homeland," but that "nothing in the verse is implied of Israel as God's covenant people." For Pryor, 1:11 is thus equivalent to 4:44. But surely this dichotomy is unnecessary: consider the parallelism between 1:11 and 13:1 and the salvation-historical references pervading the prologue (e.g., tabernacle in 1:14, giving of the law through Moses in 1:17). On a different note, "did not recognize" in 1:10 and "did not receive" in 1:11 are equivalent in meaning (Bultmann 1971: 56), a Semitism (cf. "did receive" in 1:12; see Bultmann 1971: 57 n. 2).

56. According to Culpepper (1983: 169), the "foundational irony of the gospel is that the Jews rejected the Messiah they eagerly expected." A similar conclusion is reached by Duke (1985: 117), who suggests that 1:9–12 represents a summary of the dominant irony in the Fourth Gospel and notes how this primary irony (Jesus' rejection by the Jews) is played out in the narrative in John 9.

taken up with the narration of the ever-escalating confrontation between "the Jews" and Jesus, culminating in Jesus' crucifixion.[57]

1:12 John 1:12–13 is very possibly the climactic statement of the entire prologue, and by way of *inclusio* epitomizes the very purpose for which the Gospel was written: for people to "believe" and have life "in his name" (cf. 20:31) (Witherington 1995: 56).[58] The present statement sharply contrasts those who received him and believed with those who did not, marking out believers as those who "went against the current, who broke with the general pattern by which the world thinks, lives, and acts" (Ridderbos 1997: 45). John 1:12–13 also protects 1:5, 10, and 11 from being misunderstood.

The term ἔλαβον (*elabon*, did receive), a cognate of παρέλαβον (*parelabon*, received) in 1:11, is parallel to πιστεύω (*pisteuō*, believe; cf. 5:43–44) (Moloney 1998: 38; Schnackenburg 1990: 1.261). To "receive him" means to entrust oneself to Jesus, to acknowledge his claims, and to confess him (Carson 1991: 125–26). The grammatical construction uses a pendent nominative, with the following clause referring back to it with a personal pronoun (Wallace 1996: 52; Barrett 1978: 163). John 1:12–13 strikes the balance between human responsibility ("to receive," "to believe") and divine sovereignty ("born of God").

The expression "believe in the name" of Jesus is found only in the Johannine writings (cf. 2:23; 3:18; 1 John 3:23; 5:13) (Hawthorne, *ISBE* 3:480–83). In 1:7, "believing" has already been identified as the purpose of John's testimony to Jesus as "the light." Now, believing—the present participle may denote continual belief (Wallace 1996: 621)—is said to be "in his [Jesus'] name" (equated with "receiving" him). On one level, believing in "the name" of Jesus is nothing other than believing in Jesus (3:18) (R. Brown 1966: 11). Yet the phrase "believe *in the name* of Jesus" may place particular emphasis on the fact that in order to believe in Jesus, one must believe that he bears the divine name. For John, then, believing in Jesus entails accepting him "to the full extent of his self-revelation" (Schnackenburg 1990: 1.263). In the

57. Culpepper (1983: 125–32) has a helpful discussion of the evangelist's characterization of "the Jews." For a critique of Culpepper's methodology of characterization and an alternate proposal, see Stibbe 1992: 24–25.

58. For a helpful chart summarizing people's belief or lack thereof in the remainder of the Gospel, see Croteau 2002: 120 (on believing in John's Gospel, see also Gaffney 1965; Melick 1976; and H. Koester 1989). In the first half of the narrative, negative responses predominate; the few instances of believing in the second half are all positive. This seems to support the notion, defended in the present commentary, that Jesus' mission in John 1–12 is predominantly (though not exclusively) one of failure owing to people's lack of believing response, while John 13–21 is taken up with Jesus' focus on the nucleus of the new messianic community. Hence 1:12, as the pivot of the prologue, serves to encapsulate the entire scope of John's presentation of people's responses to the Messiah in terms of reception or rejection with the result of eternal life or judgment.

early church, the name of Jesus could simply be called "the Name" (Acts 5:40–41; 3 John 7).

Being a child of God is neither a quality possessed by all nor an exclusive prerogative for Israelites; it is an entitlement for those who believe in the Word (Ridderbos 1997: 46). The word translated "right" (ἐξουσία, exousia; cf. 5:27; 10:18; 17:2; 19:10) in the NIV/TNIV refers to the authorization or legitimate claim of becoming God's children,[59] a privilege (Ridderbos 1997: 46 n. 88) that now has been made available to all who believe in Jesus as Messiah. This assumes that, in one sense, sinful people are not God's children, even though they are created by God, unless and until they believe in Jesus Christ (cf. 1 John 3:1–2). John is careful to distinguish believers, who *become* children (τέκνα, tekna) of God, from Jesus, who *is* the unique Son (υἱός, huios) of God (Pollard 1977: esp. 364; Ridderbos 1997: 45; Oepke, *TDNT* 5:654; R. Brown 1966: 11; Beasley-Murray 1999: 13). In the OT, the Hebrews are called God's children (Deut. 14:1), even God's son and firstborn (Exod. 4:22). Yet OT saints did not call God "Father" or "Abba." The privilege of *being* God's children is extolled in 1 John 3:1–2; in John 1:12, the focus is on "becoming" God's children, indicating a change of status (Morris 1995: 87). The Word's ability to give this right is proof of his exclusive and unique relationship with God (Ridderbos 1997: 45).

The opposite of being born of God spiritually is natural procreation, mentioned by the evangelist in three different expressions (Ridderbos 1997: 47; Lindars 1972: 92). Spiritual birth is not the result of human initiative (Moloney 1998: 38) but of a supernatural origin (Schnackenburg 1990: 1.263).[60] **1:13**

"Natural descent" renders what is literally "bloods," that is, a blood relationship, on the basis of the belief that natural procreation entails the intermingling of bloods (cf. Ezek. 16:4–6; Wis. 7:1–2). Descent from the patriarchs was vital in the Jews' understanding of their divine sonship (see esp. John 8:31–41). John's point is that being a child of God is not a

---

59. Calvin (1959: 17) understands ἐξουσία in 1:12 as "honor"; Schlatter (1948: 19) glosses the word as "authorization" (Ermächtigung).

60. Some identify "children of God," not "those who believe," as the antecedent of the relative clause beginning 1:13 in order not to make faith follow regeneration (Bultmann 1971: 59 nn. 4–5). However, this is both syntactically awkward and implausible, as well as theologically unnecessary. In the Greek syntax, "those who believe" immediately precedes the relative clause and is thus most naturally taken as the antecedent, and the relationship between faith and rebirth is not easily reduced to a set sequential formula. The statement in 1 John 5:1, "Everyone who believes that Jesus is the Christ is born of God," allows one to deduce from a person's belief that person's regenerate state; regeneration (being "born of God") and saving faith thus go together and cannot be separated. Spiritual rebirth takes place at God's initiative; people are called to faith based on God's revelation in Christ. John nowhere elaborates on the precise temporal relationship of these two aspects. Here and elsewhere in his Gospel (6:44–45; 10:26; 12:37–40), he affirms both divine sovereignty and human responsibility, and interpreters should do no less (see Carson 1981).

result of blood relations, as if a Jew, for instance, could simply presume upon descent from Abraham or Moses (Morris 1995: 90). Rather, spiritual birth must be sought and received from God on the basis of faith (in Jesus as Messiah).[61]

The phrase "of human decision" renders the literal "will of flesh," whereby "flesh" does not denote what is sinful (as it does so often in Paul's writings), but merely relates to what is natural as opposed to what is supernatural. The reference to "a husband's will" implies the OT concept of male headship, in the present context perhaps with reference to the initiative usually taken by the husband in sexual intercourse resulting in procreation. Alternatively, the reference could more generally be to parental determination or will (Borchert 1996: 118). The expression "born of God" is reminiscent of OT passages in which God is said to have given birth to his people Israel (Deut. 32:18) (see further the commentary at John 3:3–5).

1:14 By way of *inclusio*, John now returns to the preexistent Word (cf. 1:1–2; see R. Brown 1966: 30; see also the oblique reference to the incarnation in 1:9).[62] The major burden of 1:14–18 is to identify the Word explicitly with Jesus.[63] Rather than using the words ἄνθρωπος (*anthrōpos*, man) or σῶμα (*sōma*, body), John here employs the almost crude term σάρξ (*sarx*, flesh; cf. Rom. 8:3). Σάρξ here denotes "all of the human person in creaturely existence as distinct from God" (Ridderbos 1997: 49; cf. Borchert 1996: 119 n. 72; Barrett 1978: 164). The powerful Word of God has been born into frail humanity (Mowvley 1984: 136). Ἐγένετο (*egeneto*, was made or born [more customarily, though somewhat misleadingly, rendered "became"]) does not mean "changed into" in the sense that Jesus, by becoming human, ceased to be God.[64] Nor does it mean "appeared" human (*pace* the docetists; see Morris 1995: 90–91) or even "took on" humanity (as is suggested by Witherington [1995: 55]). The main point is that God now has chosen to be with his people in a more personal way than ever before (Carson 1991: 127).

61. Cf. Borchert (1996: 118), who says that spiritual birth is not the result of bloodline relations. Witherington (1995: 56) paraphrases this as "ethnic origins," Carson (1991: 126) as "natural descent."

62. The second-century church father Irenaeus considered 1:14 to be a "summary" of 1:1–13 (cited in Behr 2000: 102).

63. Grappe (2000: 153–69) discusses 1:14–18 in light of Second Temple literature. He identifies the *shekinah* motif as the focal point of the passage, taking its point of departure from the revelation granted to Moses at Mount Sinai. For John, Jesus is the place where God's presence, glory, grace, and truth are revealed. "By virtue of his unique nature, he is the one who transcends the most prestigious figures and institutions of the past" (p. 153).

64. This point is made forcefully by O'Neill (1991: 127): "The Word did not turn into flesh, did not change its nature and become flesh, did not masquerade as flesh, and did not come on the scene as flesh. . . . 'The Word was born flesh' or 'the Word was made flesh.'"

The affirmation that "the Word was made flesh" takes the opening statement in 1:1 one step further: that same Word now has been born as a human being. Though John does not elaborate on the precise way in which Jesus was made flesh, his contention that deity assumed human nature in Jesus would have been anathema for Greeks who held to a spirit/matter dualism and could hardly have imagined immaterial Reason becoming a physical being. The idea of gods appearing in human form was not uncommon to the ancients. But John makes clear that the Word did not merely become manifest as an apparition—as was alleged by the docetists (from δοκέω, dokeō, seem)—but literally was made flesh (Talbert 1992: 74; cf. Pagels 1999; Grappe 2000).[65]

John's message is that the incarnation represents an event of equal importance with creation. Since the world—including God's chosen people (1:10–11)—is dark, fallen, and sinful, humanity's need is for spiritual rebirth (1:13; cf. 3:3, 5), available only through the preexistent, enfleshed Word (cf. 1:29, 36). This ran counter to gnostic thought, which denied not only Jesus' incarnation (on the grounds that it was inconceivable for God, who is spirit, to take on matter, which was considered evil), but also human sinfulness (cf. 1 John 1:8, 10) and hence the need for atonement (cf. 1 John 2:2; 4:10). The pronouncement that in Jesus, the Word, who was God, had been made flesh was therefore fundamentally at odds with the claims of *gnosis*, which did not acknowledge Jesus as "come in the flesh" (1 John 4:1–3; 2 John 7).

The Greek verb σκηνόω (skēnoō), commonly translated "dwelt," more literally means "to pitch one's tent." This rare term, used elsewhere in the NT only in the Book of Revelation (7:15; 12:12; 13:6; 21:3), suggests that in Jesus, God has come to take up residence among his people once again, in a way even more intimate than when he dwelt in the midst of wilderness Israel in the tabernacle (Exod. 40:34–35).[66] Moses met God and heard his word in the "tent of meeting" (Exod. 33:9); now, people may meet God and hear him in the flesh of Jesus (Mowvley 1984: 136). Jesus' "pitching his tent among us" is here related to the incarnation, that is, his being made human flesh; according to John, Jesus took the place of the temple (Schlatter 1948: 23; cf. Hoskins 2002: 170–74; Kerr 2002: 122–23). The aorist tense of σκηνόω could be viewed as ingressive ("began to dwell") or complexive ("dwelt" in its totality); perhaps both are in view: the Word took up residence, and then stayed (Ridderbos 1997: 51; Morris 1995: 91).[67]

65. On the background of "the Word" in John and on points of contact with John's contemporary culture, see commentary on 1:1.

66. While some see the tabernacle parallel (see Exod. 35–40), others look to the tent of meeting in Exod. 33 (Morris 1995: 92) or the exodus in general (Beasley-Murray 1999: 14).

67. Or, as Eugene Peterson's modern paraphrase (*The Message*) expresses it, "the Word moved into the neighborhood."

In Jesus, his followers saw the glory of God. "Us" and "we" probably refer not to all human beings or the church, but to those who lived with Jesus, particularly John and his fellow apostles, who "saw" (θεάομαι, *theaomai*)—a stronger word than mere "seeing," indicating "observing" or "perceiving" (Ridderbos 1997: 52; Schlatter 1948: 24)—him in faith (cf. 1:12) (Morris 1995: 93 n. 98; cf. Ridderbos 1997: 51; Carson 1991: 128).[68] Like Moses of old (2 Cor. 3:6–18; cf. Exod. 34:29–35; see Mowvley 1984: 136), the apostles were firsthand eyewitnesses of God's glory, which was in these last days displayed in Jesus, God's one-of-a-kind Son (Matt. 17:1–2 pars.; 2 Pet. 1:16; 1 John 1:1; cf. Heb. 1:3; 2:3–4).[69]

First mentioned here, δόξα (*doxa*, glory) is another important term introduced in the opening section of John's Gospel. In the OT, God's glory was said to dwell first in the tabernacle, and later in the temple.[70] The Second Temple period was marked by the relative paucity of God's revelation in light of Israel's apostasy. As John makes clear, now, in Jesus, God's glory has taken up residence in the midst of his people once again. To bring glory to God is said to be Jesus' overriding purpose in John's Gospel (9:3; 11:4, 40). As he brings glory to God, glory also comes to Jesus. This only continues what was already true of Jesus prior to his coming, for glory characterized both Jesus' eternal relationship with God (17:5) and his preincarnate state (12:41). While on earth, Jesus' glory is manifested to his first followers particularly through his "signs" (cf. 2:11; see Carson 1991: 128). As the obedient, dependent Son, Jesus brings glory to God the Father throughout his entire ministry, but he does so supremely by submitting to the cross, which for John is the place of God's—and Jesus'—ultimate glorification (cf. 12:23–33; 13:31–32; 14:13; 17:1, 4–5).

The believer cannot see the glory of the Father in the Son, but rather a glory "as of"; but what can possibly be seen, is seen (Moloney 1998: 39).[71] Jesus is God's "one-of-a-kind Son" (μονογενής, *monogenēs*).[72] The term is used in the OT and the Apocrypha to mean "only child" (Judg.

68. R. Brown (1966: 13) contends that "us" refers to humanity, and "we" to the apostolic witness (contra Barrett 1978: 166); Haenchen (1984: 1.119) takes "we" as a reference to the Christian community. Bultmann (1971: 69) unduly dichotomizes and dehistoricizes when he takes "seeing" as the unhistorical sight of faith.

69. Pryor (1990: 202 n. 6), in interaction with Schnackenburg, sees in 1:14–18 a polemic using the language of Exod. 33–34: whereas God's tent was pitched outside the camp of Israel and Moses was denied the vision of God's glory, Jesus' followers had the grace of the incarnate Word dwelling among them and have seen his glory.

70. For further discussion and relevant passages, see Köstenberger 1997: 230.

71. Ridderbos (1997: 53) renders ὡς as "in keeping with his nature as" (cf. Schnackenburg 1990: 1.270), R. Brown (1966: 13) as "in the quality of."

72. Winter (1953: 336) comments, "It is not *einzig*, but *einzigartig*" (cited in de Kruijf 1970: 112); cf. Schlatter (1948: 25): "not '*einzig geboren*,' but '*einzig der Art nach*.'" Commentators differ on the exact meaning of μονογενής. R. Brown (1966: 13–14) prefers "unique," pointing to the Latin *unicus*, and says that there is no reference to the Son's procession (similarly, Wallace 1996: 360, 363, charging S. Porter [1992: 142] with committing the

11:34; Tob. 3:15; 8:17). Being an only child, and thus irreplaceable, makes a child of special value to its parents (cf. Luke 7:12; 8:42; 9:38; see Pendrick 1995: 593–94).[73] Hence, the LXX often uses ἀγαπητός (*agapētos*, beloved) instead of μονογενής (Gen. 22:2, 12, 16; Amos 8:10; Jer. 6:26; Zech. 12:10; cf. Prov. 4:3; in Judg. [A] 11:34, both words are used).[74] The seminal event in OT history in this regard is Abraham's offering of Isaac, who in Gen. 22:2, 12, 16 is called Abraham's "one-of-a-kind son" (Hebrew, *yaḥîd*; note the probable allusion to this text in John 3:16), even though the patriarch earlier had fathered Ishmael (cf. Heb. 11:17; Josephus, *Ant.* 1.13.1 §222: μονογενής; see Fitzmyer, *EDNT* 2:440; Winter 1953: 337–40; Moody 1953: 213–19, esp. 217). Μονογενής therefore means not "only begotten," but "one-of-a-kind" son (in Isaac's case, son of promise; according to Heb. 11:17–19, Isaac is a prefigurement of Christ).[75]

In both OT and Second Temple literature, the Son of David and Israel are called God's "firstborn" or even "only" son (cf. Ps. 89:27; 2 Esdr. [4 Ezra] 6:58; Ps. Sol. 18:4; Jub. 18:2, 11, 15). In a decisive step further, John applies the designation μονογενής to God's "one-of-a-kind" Son par

---

"root fallacy"; Borchert 1996: 120). Morris (1995: 93) likewise favors "only" or "unique," disavowing any etymological relationship between μονογενής and γεννάω. Beasley-Murray (1999: 14 [cf. Haenchen 1984: 1.120]) concurs that the expression means "unique" and sees it as parallel to ἀγαπητός, "beloved" (cf. Carson 1991: 128). Ridderbos (1997: 53 [cf. Schnackenburg 1990: 1.270–71]) leans toward "only begotten" rather than simply "only," especially in light of the ensuing preposition "from." This is the view also of Dahms (1983), who points out that μονογενής often occurs in contexts where γεννάω is used as well (cf., e.g., 1:13; but see the refutation by Pendrick [1995]; see also Moody 1953). Laney (1992: 44) prefers "unique" or "one-of-a-kind," while Lindars (1972: 96) notes that "the phrase *of the Father* . . . is decisive." Keener (2003: 412–14) demonstrates that "only begotten" as a rendering of μονογενής fails the etymological test. He therefore glosses the meaning as "one of a kind," noting that Christians, like Israel, are called God's children (1:12–13), but Jesus is the special, one-of-a-kind Son (citing M. Harris 1992: 84–87). For a summary of the relevant passages and debate, see Cox 2001.

73. De Kruijf (1970: 114) notes that even though Luke 8:42 and 9:38 have parallels in the other Synoptics, only Luke uses the term μονογενής or even gives the information that the girl and the boy have no siblings. The presumable reason for this is Luke's desire to highlight the special value that the salvation of these children has for their parents.

74. But note that Aquila uses μονογενής to translate *yaḥîd* in Gen. 22:2, as does Symmachus in Gen. 22:12 (see Pendrick 1995: 593 n. 29).

75. For a very thorough and definitive demonstration that the notion of Jesus as the "only begotten" of the Father is foreign to Johannine thought and was read into the Gospel only later during the patristic period, see Pendrick 1995. Among other pieces of evidence, Pendrick cites ancient references where μονογενής is applied to an only child who was not the only begotten, "for the father might have begotten other children who died young and so the preservation of his name rests on the only surviving son" (p. 590). In light of the high infant mortality rate in the ancient world, Pendrick notes that "there must have been many only children who were not the only ones begotten by their parents" (p. 590 n. 23). See also Moody 1953: 213–19 and W. O. Walker 1994: 41 n. 37 (though when Walker contends that "the Greek of 1.14 does not include υἱός with μονογενής," he overlooks that "son" surely is implied in the term μονογενής, both semantically and by virtue of the juxtaposition with "from the Father").

excellence, Jesus (John 1:18; 3:16, 18; cf. 1 John 4:9). This is similar to the designation of Jesus as God's "beloved son," which surfaces in the Synoptics in the voice from heaven at Jesus' baptism and transfiguration and in the parable of the wicked tenants (see esp. Mark 1:11; 9:7; 12:6; cf. Luke 20:13) (Pendrick 1995: 595 n. 42). In keeping with the Isaac narrative and the parable of the wicked tenants, the term μονογενής in the present passage thus contains a significant soteriological dimension, culminating in John's assertion in 3:16, "God so loved the world that he sent his one-of-a-kind Son." This designation also provides the basis for Jesus' claim that no one can come to the Father except through him (14:6). It is also likely that "one of a kind" in John's context refers to Jesus' uniqueness in that "he is *both* the *human* Son of Joseph *and* the *divine* Son of God" (W. O. Walker 1994: 41 n. 37).

Jesus is the "one-of-a-kind Son" *from* (παρά, *para*), or alongside of, the Father, in the sense that he was "with" the Father (1:1), that he has come "from" the Father (16:27; 17:8), and that he will send the Paraclete "from" the Father (15:26). The Son also sees and hears (8:38, 40; 15:15) and receives from (10:18) the Father. Jesus *is* from the Father; the Baptist is *sent* from the Father (1:6) (Pollard 1977: 365).

While Jesus is God's "one-of-a-kind Son," God is Jesus' "Father." The word πατήρ (*patēr*, Father) is more personal than the term θεός (*theos*, God; see commentary at 1:1). It is Jesus' preferred way of referring to God in John. Although Jesus taught his disciples, who upon believing in Jesus had become God's "children" (1:12), to call God "Father" as well (Matt. 6:9 par.), Jesus' divine sonship remains unique. Thus, shortly after his resurrection, Jesus instructs Mary to tell his disciples, "I am returning to *my* Father and *your* Father, to *my* God and *your* God" (20:17). The relationship that Christians are able to enjoy with God their "Father" is unique among the world's religions, many of which portray God as remote, stern, impersonal, or mystical. The special fatherhood of God for believers is already implied in 1:12–13 in the reference to the "children of God" who are "born of God."[76]

According to John, Jesus is "full of grace and truth."[77] The introduction of the terms χάρις (*charis*, grace) and ἀλήθεια (*alētheia*, truth) marks another first in this Gospel. Χάρις occurs in John only in 1:14–17 in the phrases "grace and truth" and "grace for grace." Other than in Paul (where the word means "God's unmerited favor"; e.g., Eph. 2:8–9), χάρις in John's Gospel, in conjunction with ἀλήθεια, alludes to the OT phrase

---

76. On God the Father in the Gospel of John, see especially the work of Thompson (2000; 2001). See my largely appreciative review of her contribution (Köstenberger 2002d), yet note the concerns I raise regarding the overall thesis of her work.

77. The antecedent of πλήρης (*plērēs*, full) is subject to debate. If declinable, it refers to ὁ λόγος (R. Brown 1966: 14; Morris 1995: 94). If indeclinable, it should be taken with δόξαν (Carson 1991: 129) or αὐτοῦ, as is perhaps most likely (so BDAG 827; Ridderbos 1997: 54 n. 117). In any case, fullness of grace and truth is predicated of Jesus.

"loving-kindness [Hebrew, *ḥesed*] and truth [Hebrew, *emet*]" (Exod. 34:6; cf. 33:18–19; see Mowvley 1984: 137; Kuyper 1964: 3–13; cf. Ps. 25:10; 26:3; 40:10; Prov. 16:6; see also Ps. 83:12 LXX [= Ps. 84:11 Eng.]). In this expression, both "loving-kindness" and "truth" refer to God's covenant faithfulness to his people Israel.[78] According to John, this faithfulness found ultimate expression in God's sending of Jesus, his one-of-a-kind Son (Laney 1992: 44). John 1:14–18 displays numerous parallels to Exod. 33–34 (Köstenberger 2002c: 11; Swain 1998: 30; Mowvley 1984).

D. John's Witness concerning the Word's Preeminence (1:15)

The evangelist now returns to the witness of John the Baptist (cf. 1:8; 3:30; 5:36; 10:41). The Baptist serves as the prototypical OT prophetic witness to Jesus and his coming, which makes his testimony an integral part of the salvation history canvassed by the evangelist.[79] The dual phrase "testifies" and "cries out" (on which see further commentary at 7:28, 37, and at 12:44), a hendiadys (Ridderbos 1997: 55 n. 123) with μαρτυρεῖ (*martyrei*, he testifies) representing a "historic present" (R. Brown 1966: 15; Borchert 1996: 122) and κέκραγεν (*kekragen*, he cries out) a stative perfect, vividly envisions the Baptist's ministry as still continuing (Carson 1991: 130).

1:15

The Baptist was six months older than Jesus (Luke 1:24, 26) and began his ministry before Jesus did (Luke 3:1–20). The OT generally (though not without exception) supports the notion that rank and honor are tied to one's age (e.g., Gen. 49:3; Prov. 16:31). Thus, priority in time—such as being the firstborn—implied preeminence (cf. Deut. 21:17; Isa. 61:7).[80] Because of the Baptist's age and earlier ministry, both he and the evangelist are at pains to show that Jesus really was "before" John and therefore rightfully to be honored above him.

The Baptist, presumably unaware of Jesus' preexistence as the Word, may simply have intended to affirm that Jesus "surpassed him." If so, he spoke better than he knew (Kruse 2003: 72). For in the context of John's opening words (where Jesus is portrayed as having existed with God from eternity), the Baptist's confession also points to Jesus' eternal origin (1:14; cf. 8:58; 12:41) and thus preeminence. Interestingly, the Baptist's witness is anticipated here prior to its actual narration in 1:19–34 (Ridderbos 1997: 55). Studying the Baptist's quotation of himself (cf. 1:30) gives insight as to how ancients viewed quotations (paraphrasing the

78. On "truth," see the discerning study by Barr (1961: 161–205).

79. As in the case of 1:6–8, some see 1:15 as an addition to a preexisting hymn (R. Brown 1966: 15; contra Barrett 1978: 167); but again, this is unnecessary. Brodie (1993: 143) comments, "John appears to be . . . the embodiment of the OT. . . . John's crying, therefore, far from being an illogical interpolation, is altogether appropriate. It is as though, when the incarnation finally arrived, full of covenant love, the OT stood up and cheered."

80. See Harrison, *BEB* 1:791. For a different kind of argument from chronological priority, see 1 Tim. 2:13.

essential message but not necessarily repeating a statement verbatim; see Wallace 1996: 455).[81]

E. The Final Revelation Brought by Jesus Christ (1:16–18)

1:16 John 1:16 resumes the thought of 1:14.[82] The present statement, plus 1:17, coming as it does at one of the most climactic junctures of the prologue, is similar in function and import to Paul's letter to the Romans, where the apostle claims in 1:17 that in the gospel a righteousness from God is revealed "from faith[fulness] to faith." The term ὅτι (hoti, because) at the beginning of the clause conveys the notion that all believers can support the verdict that Jesus was greater than John (Morris 1995: 97). According to the evangelist—no longer the Baptist speaking (Borchert 1996: 122–23)—in the incarnate Word was found "fullness" (πλήρωμα, plērōma) (resuming the thought of 1:14 temporarily suspended by 1:15).[83] This expression occupied an important place in gnostic thought, the first major Christian heresy, which began to germinate in the second half of the first century (see 1 Tim. 6:20–21). It is to this type of teaching that the apostle Paul responds when he affirms that God's fullness dwelt in Jesus (Col. 1:19; 2:9; cf. Eph. 1:10, 23; 3:19; 4:13). For the Fourth Evangelist too, fullness can be found in one thing only: the grace of God displayed in Jesus, whose purpose was to bring "life . . . abundantly" (10:10). When the evangelist attributes "fullness of grace" to Jesus, he evokes parallels with similar descriptions of God in the OT (see Ps. 5:7; 51:1; 69:16; 106:45; Lam. 3:22–23; see also 1QS 4:4).

"We all" includes the "us" and "we" mentioned in 1:14—that is, the apostolic circle—but may, more comprehensively, refer to the entire believing community. Καί (kai; preceding "grace for grace" in the Greek) may be explicative ("that is"; Schnackenburg 1990: 1.275; Ridderbos 1997: 57 n. 131; contra Morris 1995: 98 n. 119) or resumptive ("even"; Beasley-Murray 1999: 15).

The major translations are inadequate in rendering the phrase χάριν ἀντὶ χάριτος (charin anti charitos) in 1:16 (NIV: "one blessing after another"; NASB: "grace upon grace").[84] M. Harris (NIDNTT 3:1179–80), while favoring the NIV rendering (the phrase "denotes a perpetual and rapid succession of blessings, as though there were no interval between the arrival of one blessing and the receipt of the next"),[85] points to a better way when he contends that "the idea of constant renewal may be less prominent than

81. Borchert (1996: 122) thinks that this verse constitutes evidence that the prologue was written after the Gospel proper.

82. For this reason R. Brown (1966: 15) and Ridderbos (1997: 56) believe that this verse was inserted later by the evangelist.

83. This is the only time that πλήρωμα is used in John's Gospel.

84. But note the TNIV: "grace in place of grace already given."

85. See also Bultmann 1971: 78; Lindars 1972: 97; Bruce 1983: 43; Beasley-Murray 1999: 15; Schnackenburg 1990: 1.275–76.

the notion of the replacement of 'old' grace by 'new' grace."[86] Importantly, the meaning "in return for" appears in the only two other occurrences in ancient literature (R. Edwards 1988: 4),[87] while there is no parallel to "grace upon grace" in all of ancient Greek literature. In fact, where "grace upon grace" is the intended meaning, the preposition used is ἐπί (*epi*, upon).[88] By portraying Jesus' coming in terms of the giving of "grace *[in exchange or return] for* [ἀντί, *anti*] grace,"[89] the evangelist affirms that the grace given through Moses was replaced by the grace bestowed through Christ (cf. Exod. 33:12, 13, 17) (Mowvley 1984: 137).[90]

True grace—that is, final, eschatological grace—came through Jesus **1:17** Christ.[91] Rather than offend the Gospel's Jewish audience, this verse is designed to draw it in: "If you want an even more gracious demonstration of God's covenant love and faithfulness," the evangelist tells his readers, "it is found in Jesus Christ." Jesus' ministry is superior to that of Moses, just as he is superior to Jacob (4:12) and Abraham (8:53). The absence of the word "but" between the two phrases suggests that John did not see a radical disjunction between God's giving of the law through Moses at Sinai (Hofius 1983: 278 n. 56, 279 n. 58) and the incarnation of Christ (R. Edwards 1988: 8; Lindars 1972: 98; Jeremias, *TDNT* 4:873).[92] Nevertheless, as in the following verse (1:18), the underlying dynamic is antithetical to some extent (Hofius 1989: 169 n. 44; contra Carson 1991:

86. See also Wallace 1996: 365–68, referring to Waltke 1958: 1.166–76; R. Brown 1966: 16; and especially the excellent, definitive discussion in Carson 1991: 131–34, referring also to R. Edwards 1988; La Potterie 1977: 1.145–50.

87. Euripides, *Helen* 1234: χάρις ἀντὶ χάριτος ἐλθέτω ("since favor is for favor due") and Dionysius of Antioch, *Epistle* 40: χάριν ἀντὶ χάριτος ἀπαιτήσαντες ("asking for one favor in exchange for another").

88. Cf. Sir. 26:15: χάρις ἐπὶ χάριτι γυνὴ αἰσχυντηρά ("a modest wife adds charm to charm"). Keener (2003: 421) contends that the phrase in John 1:16 conveys the sense of a "compensatory exchange," accumulation ("grace added to grace") rather than substitution, "an inexhaustible supply of blessing." Contra Keener, the use of ἐπί rather than ἀντί in Sir. 26:15 does put in question the relevance of Sir. 26:15 as a parallel for John 1:16.

89. So, earlier, Schlatter (1948: 32): "Gnade für Gnade" (grace for grace).

90. R. Edwards (1988: 7 nn. 17–21) cites the following leading fathers of the Greek church as holding that the phrase "grace for grace" referred to a replacement of the Mosaic law by the gospel: Chrysostom, Cyril of Alexandria, Origen, and Theophylact (also Jerome, the most learned of the Latin fathers). Somewhat curiously, Michaels (1989: 24) contends that "grace and truth" is "a circumlocution for the Holy Spirit" (with reference to passages in John and elsewhere that connect the Spirit with grace or truth; cf. John 4:23–24; 14:17; 15:26; 16:13; 1 John 5:6).

91. For the translation "true grace" I am indebted to R. Edwards (1988: 11, following R. Brown 1966: 16, with further reference to Montgomery 1939; Kuyper 1964), who notes that the Hebrew *Vorlage ḥesed wa-emet* constitutes a hendiadys meaning "faithful (or enduring) love." Edwards (ibid.) rightly cautions that John's appropriation of these OT expressions must be allowed to have a "fresh nuance": "The Old Testament symbols of God's gracious acts have been appropriated and Christianized."

92. Keener (2003: 422) states that the contrast in 1:17 is between something good and something better (citing *m. ᵓAbot* 2.7: "the more study of the Law the more life"). See also

132–34), though not in a strongly contrasting relationship such as might be indicated by the adversative conjunction ἀλλά (*alla*, but).

The connection with the preceding clause is one of cause (ὅτι, *hoti*, for; cf. Wallace 1996: 461): the law is seen as the gracious gift of God (Schlatter 1948: 32–33, 193 at 7:19; with ἐδόθη [*edothē*, it was given] as a "divine passive"; Hofius 1989: 170), albeit a gift that now has been superseded by God's gracious giving of his Son (Moloney 1998: 40, 46; see John 3:16; Rom. 8:32; Gal. 4:4; see also Heb. 1:1–2; 2:2–3; 3:1–6). Notably, what is referred to here is the event of the giving of the law at Sinai, not later abuses—such as legalism—by the Jews (cf. Paul, e.g., Rom. 3:19–21; 9:30–32; 10:3–4). The Pharisees (who call themselves "disciples of Moses" [John 9:28]) sharply contrast following Moses and Jesus—but not so the evangelist. In fact, later on in the Gospel, Jesus claims that Moses wrote of him (5:46–47).[93] This also, at long last, is the first mention of Jesus in the Gospel, culminating a string of references to the Word—both preexistent and incarnate—and the light. What is more, Jesus here is referred to by his fuller designation, "Jesus Christ," forming an *inclusio* with 17:3, the only other instance of this expression in John's Gospel.

1:18   At the conclusion of his prologue to the Gospel, the evangelist states emphatically, "God [first in the Greek word order] no one has ever seen." The present verse constitutes an *inclusio* with 1:1 (Keener 2003: 335 [with reference to Boismard 1957: 76–77], 338). There it was said that the Word was *with* God and the Word *was* God. Here in 1:18 it is similarly said that the "one-of-a-kind Son" was God and that he was with God in the closest way possible (Louw 1968: 38). This relationship, in turn, is presented as the all-important reason why Jesus, the enfleshed Word, was able to overcome the vast gulf that had existed between God and humankind up to that point—despite the law. For God no one had ever seen—not even Moses (1:17; cf. Num. 12:8) (Hofius 1989: 170). If there is a polemic here, it is not against the law itself (true also of Paul [e.g., Rom. 3:31]), but against the revelation contained in the law. As Jesus asserts later in the Gospel, anyone who has seen him has seen the Father (14:9; cf. 12:45), and no one can come to the Father except through him (14:6). Although the law is God's gracious revelation, it is not adequate as a vehicle of the "true, ultimate grace" (1:17) that came only through Jesus Christ.

The lack of a coordinating conjunction (asyndeton) indicates the causal relationship between 1:18 and 1:17 (Hofius 1989: 163 n. 4). Importantly, this theme is reiterated in the body of the Gospel during the course of Jesus' ministry in relation to the Jews (5:37; 6:46; cf. the close verbal parallel 1 John

---

Luther's (1957: 139–48) discussion of 1:17, summed up as follows: "It is as if he were to say: The Law, given through Moses, is indeed a Law of life, righteousness, and everything good. But far more was accomplished through Christ" (p. 144).

93. Other positive references to the law in John include 1:45; 7:19, 22–23, 51; 8:17; 10:34; 12:34 (cf. R. Edwards 1988: 8–9).

4:12). In the OT, God had stated clearly that no one could see his face and live (Exod. 33:20) (Mowvley 1984: 137). Moses received a glimpse of God's "back" (Exod. 33:23), as did Hagar (metaphorically; Gen. 16:13). The saints of the OT usually were terrified of seeing God (Exod. 3:6b; Judg. 13:21–22; Job 13:11; Isa. 6:5). The reason for humankind's inability to see God is two-fold: first, God is spirit (John 4:24); second, humankind fell into sin and was expelled from God's presence (Gen. 3; Isa. 59:2). Jesus surmounted both obstacles: he, himself God, became a human being, so that others could see God in him (John 1:14; 14:9–10; cf. 20:28); and, being sinless, he died for people, so that their sinfulness no longer keeps them from entering into fellowship with God (John 1:29; cf. Rom. 5:1–2, 6–11).

By way of *inclusio*, the phrase "the one-of-a-kind Son, God [in his own right]" provides a commentary on what is meant in 1:1c, where it is said that "the Word was God."[94] The Word was God, and so Jesus is "unique and divine, though flesh" (Mowvley 1984: 137). Rather than functioning attributively ("the one-of-a-kind God"), μονογενής probably is to be understood as a substantive in its own right as in 1:14 ("the one-of-a-kind Son"), with θεός in apposition ("God [in his own right]"; Hofius 1989: 164). The phrase "one-of-a-kind Son, God [in his own right]," which John here uses with reference to Jesus, is both striking and unusual (though note the equally clear ascriptions of deity to Jesus in 1:1 and 20:28). If this is what John actually wrote, it would identify Jesus even more closely as God than the phrase "one-of-a-kind Son." Judaism believed that there was only one God (Deut. 6:4). As John shows later in his Gospel, Jesus' claims of deity brought him into increasing conflict with the Jewish authorities. In the end, the primary charge leading to his crucifixion was blasphemy (19:7; cf. 10:33).[95]

The phrase "in closest relationship" (εἰς τὸν κόλπον, *eis ton kolpon*) refers to the unmatched intimacy of Jesus' relationship with the Father (Wallace 1996: 360), which enabled him to reveal the Father in an un-precedented way (cf. the contrast with Moses in 1:17; R. Brown 1966: 36). Literally, John here says that Jesus is "in the Father's lap," an idiom for greatest possible closeness (cf. Prov. 8:30) (Hofius 1989: 164–65, following Gese 1981). This is the way the term is used in the OT, where it portrays the devoted care of a parent or caregiver (Num. 11:12; Ruth 4:16; 2 Sam. 12:3; 1 Kings 3:20; 17:19; Lam. 2:12; cf. *b. Yebam.* 77a) (Hofius 1989: 166 nn. 19–21).[96] The most pertinent NT parallel is the reference to "Abraham's side" (TNIV) in Luke 16:22.

94. Regarding the important text-critical issue pertaining to 1:18, see additional note.
95. On the level of the original readers of John's Gospel, Keener (2003: 426) observes that "[t]o Jewish Christians needing to lay even their lives on the line because of their Christol-ogy, John reminds them that Christology is at the heart of their faith in Israel's God."
96. Greek parallels include Aristotle, *De mirabilibus auscultationibus* 846b.27; Demos-thenes, *Orations* 47.58.

These parallels show how deeply intimate John considered Jesus' relationship with the Father to be. The evangelist later uses a closely similar expression (ἐν τῷ κόλπῳ τοῦ Ἰησοῦ; lit., "in Jesus' bosom" [13:23]) with regard to himself, "the disciple Jesus loved," indicating that his closeness to Jesus during his earthly ministry made him the perfect person to write this Gospel. Access to divine revelation was also prized in the pagan mystery religions and Jewish apocalypticism and mysticism. Yet here John claims that Jesus' access to God far exceeds not only that claimed by other religions, but even that of Judaism. This is why Moses' system was inferior: under it, no one could see God (Morris 1995: 100).

John here does not use the more common term for "to make known," γνωρίζω (gnōrizō [15:15; 17:26]), but the rare expression ἐξηγέομαι (exēgeomai; found only here in this Gospel). In its Lukan occurrences (Luke 24:35; Acts 10:8; 15:12, 14; 21:19), the term regularly means "to give a full account" in the sense of "telling the whole story," the probable meaning here also (Louw 1968; Morris 1995: 101; contra Beasley-Murray [1999: 16], who likes the thought of the Logos "exegeting" the Father).[97] As he concludes his introduction, John therefore makes the important point that the entire Gospel to follow should be read as an account of Jesus "telling the whole story" of God the Father.

Additional Note

1:18. There is a question as to whether the original reading here is μονογενὴς υἱός (*monogenēs huios*, one-of-a-kind Son) or μονογενὴς θεός (*monogenēs theos*, one-of-a-kind [Son, himself] God). With the acquisition of 𝔓[66] and 𝔓[75], both of which read μονογενὴς θεός, the preponderance of the evidence now leans in the direction of the latter reading. M. Harris (1992: 78–80) expresses a "strong preference" for μονογενὴς θεός, for at least four reasons: (1) it has superior MS support; (2) it represents the more difficult reading; (3) it serves as a more proper climax to the entire prologue, attributing deity to the Son by way of *inclusio* with 1:1 and 1:14; (4) it seems to account best for the other variants. Most likely, then, μονογενὴς υἱός represents a scribal assimilation to 3:16 and 3:18.[98]

97. See also E. Harris (1994: 109, 115), who suggests the rendering "has communicated divine things," viewing the verb as a technical term describing the actions of religious figures in disclosing divine truth.

98. This also is the judgment of the majority of the UBS translation committee: see Metzger 1994: 169–70 for discussion and a more extended rationale. The type of evidence summarized above convinced the NIV, NASB, ISV, and ESV, though not the NKJV and HCSB; the NRSV ("God the only Son") and NLT ("his only Son, who is himself God") adopt a compromise solution. The TNIV, too, seeks to steer a middle course, though still affirms θεός as the original reading: "the one and only [Son], who is himself God." Among commentators, the reading μονογενὴς θεός is preferred by R. Brown 1966: 17; Lindars 1972: 98–99; Bruce 1983: 44–45; Carson 1991: 139; Morris 1995: 100–101; Borchert 1996: 124; Wallace 1996: 307; Beasley-Murray 1999: 2 n. e; Burge 2000: 61; Keener 2003: 425–26; see also E. Harris 1994: 102–5; contra Bultmann 1971: 81 n. 2; Schnackenburg 1990: 1.278–80 (tentatively); Ridderbos 1997: 59 n. 140; Moloney 1998: 46; and Schlatter 1948: 34–35. Note that Barrett (1978: 169) changed his position between the first edition (1955) and second edition of his commentary: "The added evidence of the two recently discovered papyri may seem to swing the verdict this way." Note also Wallace 1996: 360: "the unique One, God."

II. The Book of Signs: The Signs of the Messiah (1:19–12:50)

At the heart of Act I of John's Gospel drama is the demonstration of Jesus' messiahship by way of seven selected signs. Although Jesus is the "Savior of the world" (4:42; cf. 3:16), he is emphatic that "salvation is from the Jews" (4:22). Thus, Act I features a progressive display of signs of Jesus' messiahship directed to the Jews. Rather than lead the Jews to faith, however, the signs end up confirming their rejection of the Messiah (12:37–40).

John 1:19–2:11 narrates a week in Jesus' ministry. This bridge section overlaps with the narration of a ministry cycle from Cana to Cana in 2:1–4:54, with an intervening appearance by Jesus in the capital Jerusalem (2:13–3:21). Three signs are presented in this section: the turning of water into wine in 2:1–11 (the first sign in Cana [2:11]); the temple clearing in 2:13–22 (one of Jesus' Jerusalem signs; cf. 2:23; 3:2) (Köstenberger 1995b); and the healing of the official's son (second Cana sign [4:54]).

Chapters 5–10 form the second major subsection of Act I, narrating three additional signs. Characterized by mounting controversy between Jesus and his Jewish opponents, this section is built around Jesus' participation in several Jewish festivals, such as Tabernacles (chs. 5; 7–8), Passover (ch. 6), and Dedication (10:22–42).[1] The three signs featured in this subsection include the healing of a lame man (5:1–15), the feeding of the multitude (6:1–15), and the opening of a blind man's eyes (ch. 9).

Chapters 11–12, like 1:19–2:11, form a transitional section (note the signaling of Jesus' final week in 12:1, a possible *inclusio* with 1:19–2:11). On one level, the *inclusio* between 1:19–34 and 10:40–42 marks off 1:19–10:42 as a unit. It also sets off chapters 11–12 as special material, including accounts of the raising of Lazarus (ch. 11)—the seventh, climactic sign—and Jesus' anointing and triumphal entry (12:1–19). Further transitional material is found in 12:20–36 (the coming of the Greeks) and 12:37–50 (the grand tragic conclusion of Act I). Another element in the multilayered structure of this Gospel is the critical mass defection of the majority of Jesus' disciples followed by Peter's confession

1. The note of escalating conflict from 1:19–6:70 to 6:71–10:42 is recognized by Keener (2003: 427).

at the end of chapter 6, which comes halfway through Act I (possibly mirroring the structure of Mark and the Synoptics).[2]

The structure of the first major unit of John's Gospel can thus be diagrammed as follows:[3]

Act I: Jesus' Seven Signs and His Rejection by the Jews (1:19–12:50)

Transitional sections:	First week, sign (1:19–2:11)						Final sign, week (11:1–12:50)
Major literary units or cycles:	Start of public ministry (1:19–51)	Ministry cycle (chs. 2–4): various responses, elusive language		Festival cycle (chs. 5–10): Increased hostility, elusive movements		Conclusion of public ministry (chs. 11–12): Jesus withdraws (11:53–54)	
Inclusion markers (related to signs):	The Baptist (1:19–34)	Cana sign (2:1–11) Judean sign (2:13–22)	Cana sign (4:46–54)	Judean sign (5:1–15) Galilean and Judean signs (chs. 6; 9)	The Baptist (10:40–42)	Judean sign (11:1–44; 12:1–2, 9–11, 17–18)	Ending (12:37–50)
Midpoint crisis:				Moment of major crisis (6:60–71)			

2. Stibbe, in a fascinating article entitled "The Elusive Christ," has shown that John portrays Jesus as elusive both in his language (chs. 2–4) and in his movements (chs. 5–10). In chapters 11 and 12, "tension mounts as Jesus openly returns to the place of maximum danger and as the Sanhedrin formally plot to have Jesus killed" (Stibbe 1991: 36). Stibbe's literary analysis further confirms the divisions sketched above into an initial "Cana cycle" in chapters 2–4 and a "festival cycle" in chapters 5–10, with chapters 11–12 occupying a bridge function. Even the pivotal defection in chapter 6, followed by the narration of opposition in Jesus' family in chapter 7, seems to be borne out by Stibbe's study in that all but one of the references to the Jews seeking Jesus in order to kill (or arrest) him are found after this pivot (5:18; 7:1, 19, 20, 25, 30; 8:37, 40; 10:39; 11:8) (Stibbe 1991: 22).

3. Talbert (1970 [see esp. p. 343]) proposes unconvincingly that 1:19–5:47 displays the pattern of a macrochiasm. However, this comes at the expense of virtually ignoring the clear *inclusio* of 2:11 and 4:54, which marks this section off as a structural unit. Moreover, the very notion of a macrochiasm is far from established. An additional weakness is that at the heart of the chiasm Talbert groups 3:22–36 and 4:1–42 under the rubric "ritual and life," hardly a self-evident categorization. On the microlevel, however, Talbert's unit divisions are generally on target: 1:19–2:11; 2:13–22 (though there is no need to skip 2:12); 2:23–3:22; 3:23–36; 4:1–42; 4:43–54; 5:1–30; 5:31–47 (see the outline in the introduction above).

A. The Forerunner, Jesus' Inaugural Signs, and Representative Conversations (1:19–4:54)

John 1:19 marks the beginning of the actual Gospel narrative (Ridderbos 1997: 61; Carson 1991: 141). Most likely, the events from 1:19–2:11 describe one week in the ministry of Jesus (perhaps paralleling the first week recorded in the Book of Genesis, continuing to develop the motif of a "new creation"; see Hambly 1968: 69; Morris 1995: 114; Carson 1991: 148). John 1:19–51 may be divided into two parts: (1) John's witness (a) to the Jews (1:19–28) and (b) concerning Jesus Christ (1:29–34); and (2) the results of John's witness: (a) the coming of John's disciples to Jesus (1:35–40) and (b) the calling of Peter, Philip, and Nathanael (1:41–51) (Ridderbos 1997: 61).

In the wake of the prologue, the purpose of this section is at least twofold: (1) to show John's witness to Jesus at the inception of the latter's ministry; and (2) to clarify John's relationship to Jesus as one of witness rather than rivalry or antagonism. At this crucial salvation-historical juncture, John's testimony pointing his followers to the "Coming One" constitutes the impetus that triggers Jesus' messianic mission and the founding of his new messianic community (Ridderbos 1997: 61). On the first day, the Baptist is presented in contrast to the light; on the second day, he bears witness to the light; on the third day, he brings others to the light (R. Brown 1966: 45, following Dodd 1963: 248).

The present section also describes what it means to be a disciple of Jesus and to bear testimony to him (Burge 2000: 70; note diagram). The wine miracle at Cana in 2:1–11 occupies a bridge function as well, moving the narrative from the beginnings of Jesus' ministry to his first major public confrontation with his major protagonists in the Fourth Gospel, the Ἰουδαῖοι (*Ioudaioi*, Jews or Jewish leaders) (Moloney 1998: 51).[1] The overall intent of 1:19–4:54 seems to be to present the initiation of Jesus' self-disclosure and its reception among various types of groups and individuals (Schnackenburg 1990: 1.283–85).

---

1. On the term Ἰουδαῖοι, see commentary at 1:19. The new BDAG entry on Ἰουδαῖος, which systematically recasts all "Jews" as "Judeans" in order to avoid "anti-Judaism" by modern-day readers, constitutes an unduly extreme reaction and results in demonstrably inaccurate renderings that equate all Jews with inhabitants of Judea. However, Jews lived also in Galilee and adjacent provinces, not to mention the Diaspora. Note the appropriate criticism by Lowery (2003: 120–21).

The structure of 1:19–4:54 can be described as follows. John 1:19–51 serves a bridge function, narrating the Baptist's witness (1:19–34; cf. 1:6–8, 15) and Jesus' call of his first followers (1:35–51). Jesus' early ministry is narrated in chapters 2–4, commencing and concluding in Cana of Galilee (cf. 2:11; 4:54). In between are accounts of Jesus' ministry in Jerusalem and Samaria. The turning of water into wine is juxtaposed with the temple clearing (ch. 2), jointly presenting Jesus as Messiah and restorer of Israel. Jesus' encounter with Nicodemus stands opposite the one with the Samaritan woman, which in turn is followed by Jesus' healing of the royal official's son, showing the range of responses to Jesus' ministry on the part of different ethnic and religious groups (the familiar sequence: Judea, Samaria, and the Gentile world; cf. Acts 1:8). Chapter 3 alternates narrative scenes with the evangelist's commentary (3:16–21, 31–36). A section on the Baptist's witness in 3:22–30 provides continuity with the earlier treatment in 1:19–34.

1. The Testimony of John the Baptist and the Beginning of Jesus' Ministry (1:19–51)

After his magnificent, lofty introduction, the evangelist sets Jesus' ministry in historical perspective. Like the Synoptics, he links the beginning of Jesus' ministry with that of John the Baptist. In the prologue, mention was already made that John had been "sent from God" (1:6); that he had come as a witness to "the light" in order that all might believe through him (1:7); that he himself was not "the light" but merely witnessed to the light (1:8); and that John acknowledged the preeminence/preexistence of the Word-made-flesh and of the one-of-a-kind Son from the Father (1:15).

As in the prologue, John is cast in the ensuing narrative as a witness to Jesus. Rejecting any labels of greatness for himself, the Baptist, in response to the inquiry of a delegation from Jerusalem, denies being the Christ (1:20), Elijah (1:21), or the Prophet (1:21). Rather, he is the Isaianic figure of "a voice crying in the wilderness, 'Make straight the way of the Lord'" (1:23; cf. Isa. 40:3; Mark 1:3 pars.). John's baptism is designed to announce the Messiah's coming to Israel (1:26–28, 31); Jesus himself would baptize with the Holy Spirit (1:33; cf. Mark 1:8 pars.; Acts 1:5). He is "God's lamb who takes away the sin of the world" and "the Son of God" (1:29, 34). John 1:35–51 narrates Jesus' gathering of a group of disciples, with his initial followers transferring their allegiance from the Baptist.

There is a graceful transition from the prologue into the "Gospel proper" through the use of the conjunction "and" and a return to themes first sounded in the prologue (Ridderbos 1997: 61–62; Barrett 1978: 170).[1] The evangelist presents this account as if his readers were witnessing a trial scene where the evidence for and against Jesus is being set forth for them to evaluate (Burge 2000: 70–71; R. Brown 1966: 45; Borchert 1996: 126). He assumes that his readers are already aware of the Baptist and knowledgeable regarding his ministry.

The Baptist at this time was baptizing at the Jordan (1:28). Luke (3:1) informs us that it was the fifteenth year of the reign of Tiberius Caesar (A.D. 14–37), which would indicate A.D. 29.[2] Pontius Pilate was

---

1. This assessment contrasts with Keener (2003: 429), who characterizes the transition in 1:19 as abrupt (citing Homer's *Odyssey* as a parallel).
2. See Hoehner (1977: 31–37) and Messner (1998), with reference to the Roman historians Tacitus (*Annales* 4 §4) and Suetonius (*Tiberius* 73), both of whom date the beginning

governor of Judea (A.D. 26–36), Herod Antipas tetrarch of Galilee (4 B.C.–A.D. 39), and Herod Philip II tetrarch of Iturea and Trachonitis (4 B.C.–A.D. 34). In light of the information provided by Luke that Jesus was "about thirty years old" when he started his ministry (Luke 3:23; about thirty-three years, to be precise [see below]), the Baptist, six months Jesus' elder (Luke 1:26), was about thirty-three and a half years old at this time.

Starting in 1:29, John links his narrative sequence with the expression "the next day"; in 1:35, it is "the next day" again. Starting with John the Baptist's testimony in 1:19–28, it is possible to reconstruct an entire week of ministry (Carson 1991: 167–68; cf. Boismard 1956; Barrosse 1959):[3]

Day 1: John's testimony regarding Jesus (1:19–28)
Day 2: John's encounter with Jesus (1:29–34; "the next day")
Day 3: John's referral of two disciples to Jesus (1:35–39; "the next day")
Day 4: Andrew's introduction of his brother Peter to Jesus (1:40–42)
Day 5: Philip and Nathanael follow Jesus (1:43–51; "the next day")
[Day 6 not explicitly mentioned]
Day 7: Wedding at Cana (2:1–11; "on the third day")

Thus, John is found to open his Gospel with an account of Jesus' first week of ministry, culminating in his "first sign" at Cana.

Jesus' first week of ministry proceeds as follows. The Baptist's testimony is shown to trigger a chain reaction issuing in a string of followers attaching themselves to Jesus. John's initial witness causes Andrew and an unnamed disciple (John the son of Zebedee?) to follow Jesus (1:35, 40); Andrew's witness recruits his brother Peter (1:41–42); Jesus calls Philip, who is from the same town as Andrew and Peter, namely, Bethsaida (1:43–44); and Philip brings Nathanael (1:45–51), who probably is identical with the Bartholomew linked with Philip in the Synoptic apostolic lists (Mark 3:18 pars.). Nathanael's skepticism regarding Jesus, which is overcome by a demonstration of Jesus' true

---

of Tiberius's reign at A.D. 14 (the precise date is August 19, the day of Emperor Augustus's death); see also commentary at 2:20–21. It is unclear why Hengel (1999: 322) dates Tiberius's fifteenth year to ca. A.D. 27/28.

3. For an extensive summary of reconstructions, see Beasley-Murray 1999: 22; cf. Schnackenburg 1990: 1.285. Witherington (1995: 68) proposes that 1:35–2:11 describes three days, the first being narrated in 1:35–42, the second in 1:43–51, and the third in 2:1–12. Note also Moloney (1998: 50–51), who suggests that 1:19–2:11 represents an allusion to the giving of the law in Exod. 19.

identity, is later mirrored (an *inclusio*) by the "conversion" of "doubting Thomas" (20:24–29).

a. John's response to the Jerusalem delegation (1:19–28)
b. John's witness concerning Jesus (1:29–34)
c. John's referral of some of his disciples to Jesus and the subsequent chain reaction (1:35–51)

Exegesis and Exposition

¹⁹And this was John's testimony when the Jewish leaders in Jerusalem sent priests and Levites to him to ask him, "Who are you?" ²⁰He confessed and did not deny, but confessed, "I am not the Christ." ²¹So they asked him, "Then ⌜what are you⌝? Elijah?" He said, "I am not." "Are you the Prophet?" He answered, "No." ²²So they said to him, "Who are you? [Tell us] in order that we may give an answer to those who sent us. What do you say concerning yourself?" ²³He said, "I am a voice of one calling in the desert, 'Make the Lord's path straight,'" just as Isaiah the prophet said. ²⁴Now they had been sent from among the Pharisees. ²⁵And they asked and said to him, "Why then do you baptize, if you are neither the Christ nor Elijah nor the Prophet?" ²⁶John answered them and said, "I baptize with water; in your midst stands one whom you do not know, ²⁷who comes after me, the straps of whose sandals I am not worthy to untie." ²⁸These things took place in Bethany on the other side of the Jordan, where John was baptizing.

²⁹On the next day he saw Jesus coming toward him and said, "Look, God's lamb that takes away the sin of the world. ³⁰This is the one of whom I said, 'A man comes after me, who ranks ahead of me, because he was before me.' ³¹I had not known him, but it is in order that he might be revealed to Israel that I came baptizing with water." ³²And John testified, saying, "I have seen the Spirit descend from heaven like a dove, and it remained on him. ³³And I would not have known him, but the one who sent me to baptize with water told me, 'The one on whom you see the Spirit descend and remain—he is the one who baptizes with the Holy Spirit.' ³⁴And I have seen and have testified that he is ⌜the Chosen One of God⌝."

³⁵On the next day John stood there again, and so did two of his disciples; ³⁶and when he noticed Jesus walking around, he said, "Look, God's lamb." ³⁷When the two disciples heard him say [this], they in fact followed Jesus. ³⁸Yet when Jesus turned and noticed that they were following [him], he said to them, "What are you looking for?" And they said to him, "Rabbi" (which translated means "teacher"), "where are you staying?" ³⁹He said, "Come, and you will see." So they went and saw where he was staying, and they stayed with him that day: it was the tenth hour [about four in the afternoon].

⁴⁰Andrew, Simon Peter's brother, was one of the two who had heard these things from John and had followed him [Jesus]. ⁴¹He first went to get his own

brother Simon and said to him, "We have found the Messiah" (which translated means "Christ"). [42]He brought him to Jesus. When Jesus noticed him, he said, "You are Simon, ⌜the son of John⌝; you will be called Cephas" (which is translated as "Peter").

[43]On the next day he [Jesus] wanted to depart for Galilee and ran into Philip. And Jesus said to him, "Follow me." [44]Now Philip was from Bethsaida, the city of Andrew and Peter. [45]Philip went to get Nathanael and said to him, "We have found the one of whom Moses wrote in the law and of whom the prophets also wrote, Jesus the son of Joseph, the one from Nazareth." [46]And Nathanael said to him, "Can anything good be from Nazareth?" Philip said to him, "Come and see." [47]Jesus saw Nathanael come toward him and said to him, "Look, one who is truly an Israelite in whom there is no deceit." [48]Nathanael said to him, "From where do you know me?" Jesus answered and said to him, "Before Philip called you, when you were under the fig tree, I saw you." [49]Nathanael answered him, "Rabbi, you are the Son of God; you are the king of Israel." [50]Jesus answered and said to him, "Because I told you that I saw you under the fig tree, you believe? You will see greater things than these." [51]And he said to him, "Truly, truly, I say to all of you, you will see ⌜heaven open and God's angels ascend and descend⌝ on the Son of Man."

a. John's Response to the Jerusalem Delegation (1:19–28)[4]

1:19 What is at stake now is the Baptist's identity and the nature of his ministry; later the focus will shift to Jesus.[5] According to Luke, crowds came to John from all different walks of life (3:7–14). Matthew refers to both Pharisees and Sadducees (3:7). Here in the Fourth Gospel we are told of priests and Levites coming to John; later the evangelist mentions that Pharisees were coming to Jesus as well (1:24). Ministering mainly in and around the temple area in Jerusalem, priests and Levites were specialists in ritual purification and thus the ones most capable of dealing with issues arising from the Baptist's ministry (see 3:25) (Ridderbos 1997: 63; R. Brown 1966: 43; contra Barrett 1978: 172). The authorities

---

4. Stibbe (1993: 31) sees 1:19–28 as forming a chiasm, with 1:23 as its center.

5. Moloney (1998: 58) proposes that the question "Who are you?" could be taken as the *leitmotif* of John's Gospel. Barrett (1978: 172) considers the phrase an allusion to Jesus' "I am" statements in 6:35 and 8:24. Witherington (1995: 64) follows Painter in classifying the present pericope as a "quest story" that prepares the evangelist's audience to properly answer subsequent questions about Jesus' identity. He also contends—a rather dubious claim—that the evangelist presents Jesus as a Jewish sage à la Wisdom whom disciples were to seek and follow (adducing Sir. 51:23). The opening demonstrative "this" is classified by Wallace (1996: 334) as an instance of "inverse attraction," where the pronominal subject is linked with the gender of the preceding nominative (cf. Matt. 7:12; 13:38; Luke 2:12; 8:11; Rom. 11:27; Gal. 4:24). More questionable is Wallace's claim (1996: 532) that the present verb ἐστίν (*estin*, is) is a "*testimonium* present" (discussed under the rubric of "perfective present"). More likely, ἐστίν is a historical present (Wallace denies that εἰμί is ever used as a historical present in the NT).

also would have been keen on controlling any activity that might lead to subversive actions against Rome (Morris 1995: 115).

Although the present incident seems at first glance to be nothing but an innocent fact-finding mission, it reveals that the Jerusalem authorities[6] kept a watchful eye on John's activities. This casts an ominous shadow forward on Jesus' ministry, which is about to begin.[7] The Baptist seems to realize this; he responds to the interrogation rather guardedly and only gradually reveals his true identity. At the heart of the delegation's mission appears to be a challenge to the Baptist's legitimization for engaging in his ministry.[8] The very fact that emissaries from the Jerusalem authorities show up on John's doorstep serves as a show of power and as a signal that the authorities will not tolerate in the long run a ministry that runs counter to their own purposes.[9] In the end, John identifies himself, not as an OT messianic figure, but as Isaiah's "voice crying in the wilderness," a transitional figure calling for repentance and heralding God's salvation.

The present interrogation is reminiscent of a courtroom scene (Ridder-   **1:20**
bos 1997: 64; Schnackenburg 1990: 1.286).[10] The gravity of the Baptist's

6. Greek, Ἰουδαῖοι. Here and elsewhere in the Fourth Gospel, this Greek term ought to be rendered in keeping with the connotative meaning supplied by the respective context (see the TNIV). In a recent paper, S. Porter (2002), taking as his point of departure the recent compendium edited by Bieringer et al. (2001a; 2001b), contends that no single proposal explains all instances of the term in John's Gospel. He notes that only twenty-six out of seventy instances of Ἰουδαῖοι in John are negative (including 11:8, 54, but not 1:19; 5:10, 15; 8:22; 10:24; 18:12; 19:31). According to Porter, the singular referent of the term in John's Gospel is the Jewish people as a religious, ethnic group. However, a given context may limit the reference to a subgroup. A case in point is an articular, demonstrative use: "those Jews there." Anaphoric usage provides discourse continuity and cohesion. Partitive uses are found as well. Both literalistic views and "politically correct" views, according to Porter, are to be eschewed in favor of an understanding that is linguistically informed and contextually sensitive. When applied as part of a salvation-historical reading of the Johannine narrative and supplemented by other related terms, such as οἱ ἴδιοι in 1:11, the approach advocated by Porter is superior to woodenly literal or ideologically driven alternatives (see also Köstenberger 2003).

7. In his thorough discussion of 1:19–51, Culpepper (1983: 54–57) shows how the narrator uses analepses, prolepses, mixed analepses, and mixed prolepses, creating a distinction between the sequence of the narrative and the sequence of the story. Culpepper (1983: 89–98) also provides an extended discussion of the plot of the Fourth Gospel.

8. Whitacre (1999: 65) notes the disingenuous nature of the questioning, since the leaders sent others rather than going themselves, and the delegation asks only in order to provide a response to the Jewish authorities: "So even when they ask what seems to be an open question (v. 22), they do so with a closed attitude of indifference." Brodie (1993: 151) likewise notes that the delegation was concerned foremost with politics and bureaucracy: "to have some kind of manageable answer for some people back in Jerusalem."

9. As it turns out, Herod Antipas's act, recorded in the Synoptics, of imprisoning John and having him beheaded makes any further action on the part of the Jerusalem authorities to curb John's ministry unnecessary. Their attention consequently shifts to Jesus.

10. Brodie (1993: 148) uses "trial" terminology. Westcott (1908: 1.32) instead sees this as "in some sense, a Temptation of John corresponding to the (simultaneous) Temptation of Christ."

response is indicated by the pleonastic (and thus ungainly) syntax chosen by the evangelist: "He confessed and did not deny, but confessed" (Morris 1995: 117; Moloney 1998: 52; Schnackenburg 1990: 1.288).[11] John's statement is related first and foremost not to who he is, but who he emphatically is not: the Christ.[12] The confession—to be understood not in a religious sense but as a clear acknowledgment of his own identity (Ridderbos 1997: 64)—reiterates what the reader of John's Gospel already knows: the Baptist is not the expected deliverer or Messiah (1:15; see also 1:8: "not the light"; cf. 3:28).[13]

His insistent refusal to entertain messianic ambitions makes John an "ideal witness" (Ridderbos 1997: 64); his frank threefold confession stands in marked contrast to Peter's later threefold denial of Jesus (18:17, 25, 27; cf. 13:38). Rather than being the Messiah, the Baptist professes to be the voice of one calling in the desert, "Make straight the way for the Lord" (1:23, citing Isa. 40:3; cf. Matt. 3:1 pars.). Messianic hopes were widespread in early first-century Palestine (Horsley, *ABD* 4:791–97; Sacks, *BEB* 2:1446–49). Many Jews waited for the coming greater Son of David predicted in the OT (see 2 Sam. 7:11b–16; Hos. 3:5; cf. Matt. 1:1, 6, 17; Luke 3:31; Rom. 1:3). However, people were not necessarily united in their expectations, nor were these necessarily in keeping with scriptural predictions. The evangelist gathers several messianic expectations current in Jesus' day in chapter 7 of his Gospel.

1:21 "Then what are you? Elijah?" The question certainly was appropriate: John not only had the demeanor of a prophet, but also resembled Elijah in his rugged lifestyle (see Matt. 3:4; cf. 2 Kings 1:8) and powerful message of judgment (cf. Matt. 3:7–12; Luke 3:7–17) (Morris 1995: 119). Yet John also denied being Elijah (cf. John 5:35), the figure that many first-century Jews awaited in addition to the Messiah.[14] Elijah, who had never died (2 Kings 2:11), was to come "before that great and dreadful day of the Lord" (Mal. 4:5) (Morris 1995: 118). Some expected him to settle rabbinic disputes; others thought that he would perform great miracles

---

11. Ironically, in John's case it was virtuous to confess *not* to be someone. Humility prevented him from elevating himself as a messianic pretender (Ridderbos 1997: 65; cf. Barnett 1980–81).

12. The emphatic pronoun ἐγώ adds further firmness to the Baptist's denial (Barrett 1978: 172; Morris 1995: 117; Bultmann 1971: 88). Morris (1995: 117) renders the sense well: "It is not *I* who am the Christ."

13. The Greek word Χριστός, like its Hebrew counterpart, *mešiaḥ*, means "anointed one." Though the term was applied in the OT to a variety of men who were set apart and anointed to serve God and his people in a special capacity (such as priest or king), OT predictive prophecy gave rise to the expectation that there would be a future figure, *the* Anointed One, sent by God to deliver and rule his people. See especially Horbury 1998. For a convincing refutation of the claim that the present passage was written to counter a Baptist sect in the evangelist's day, see Ridderbos 1997: 64 (cf. R. Brown 1966: 48).

14. Matt. 16:14 pars.; 17:3–4, 10 pars.; 27:47, 49 par.; Sir. 48:10; *m. Šeqal.* 2.5; *m. Soṭah* 9.15; *m. B. Meṣiʿa* 1.8; *m. ʿEd.* 8.7; probably also 1QS 9:11.

or introduce the Messiah (e.g., 2 Esdr. [4 Ezra] 6:26–27; Justin, *1 Apol.* 35.1; see Beasley-Murray 1999: 24). In any case, he would "restore all things" (Matt. 17:11), turning the hearts of the fathers to their children and vice versa (Mal. 4:6; cf. Sir. 48:10; Luke 1:17).

John denied literally being the returning prophet Elijah. On the other hand, according to the Synoptics, Jesus clearly stated that the Baptist *was* "Elijah" (Matt. 11:14; 17:12; Mark 9:13), since his ministry constituted the typological fulfillment of the prophecy of Mal. 4:5 (cf. Luke 1:17) (Schnackenburg 1990: 1.289). Even before the Baptist's birth, an angel prophesied to his father, Zechariah, that John would "go on before the Lord *in the spirit and power of Elijah*" (Luke 1:17).[15] Did John perhaps not realize that he really *was* "Elijah"? Or do John and the Synoptics contradict each other? This is hardly the case. More likely, the Baptist denied being "Elijah" to counter the expectation (current in his day) that the same Elijah who escaped death in a fiery chariot would return in like spectacular manner.

"The Prophet" was yet a third end-time figure—not the Messiah— expected by the Jews (cf. 6:14; 7:40). There is thus a certain progression in the Jews' line of reasoning: if John was not the Messiah, was he one of the figures traditionally expected to prepare the way for the Messiah, be it Elijah or the Prophet? The coming of this Prophet was predicted by Moses (who was seen as the ideal Messiah because he brought both spiritual and political freedom for the Israelites; see Burge 2000: 71) in Deut. 18:15, 18.[16] Samaritans had a similar expectation (Macdonald 1964: 197–98, 362–71, 443; Carson 1991: 143). The Qumran community likewise was committed to waiting "until the prophet comes, and the Messiahs of Aaron and Israel" (1QS 9:11).[17] According to 2 Esdr. (4 Ezra) 2:18, God also would send his servants Isaiah and Jeremiah (cf. 2 Macc. 15:13–16; Matt. 16:14). Again, John denies being this expected end-time figure.[18]

Exasperated by the series of John's denials, the Jerusalem delegation demands a positive identification. The statement ἵνα ἀπόκρισιν δῶμεν (*hina apokrisin dōmen*, in order that we may give an answer [denoting the purpose of the question; see Morris 1995: 120 n. 23]) is elliptic: λέγε ἡμῖν (*lege hēmin*, tell us) or a similar phrase must be supplied to complete the thought (cf. 9:36; Barrett 1978: 173). Then, as now, one's

1:22

15. See also Mark's conflation of Mal. 3:1 ("I will send my messenger") and Isa. 40:3 (also found in John 1:23 and Synoptic parallels) in Mark 1:2–3. Carson (1991: 143) notes that false prophets sometimes dressed in a manner similar to Elijah (see Zech. 13:4).

16. Cf. Acts 3:22; 7:37; see also 1 Macc. 4:46; 14:41; T. Ben. 9:2.

17. See also the collection of messianic passages in 4QTest 5–8 citing Deut. 18:18–19.

18. Westcott (1908: 1.34) notes, "The replies grow shorter from time to time: 'I am not the Christ,' 'I am not,' 'No.'" Indeed, the Baptist must "decrease" (cf. John 3:30). Brodie (1993: 150) observes, "There is a faint evoking of a process of self-emptying."

origin goes a long way in ascertaining one's authority (cf. 2:18). These priests and Levites were not self-appointed, but rather had been sent officially by the Jewish authorities back in Jerusalem to find out about John (cf. Acts 9:1–2; 22:5; 26:10).[19] Remarkably, disciples of the Baptist are found decades after this event even outside Palestine (Acts 19:1–7). Jesus repeatedly attests to the Baptist's significant stature (e.g., Matt. 11:11 par.).

1:23 The Baptist's Jewish interrogators—as well as John's readers—already know who the Baptist is not; at long last, he is telling them who he is (Borchert 1996: 130).[20] Though Jesus is the Word, the Baptist is "a voice" directing his audience to Jesus (Morris 1995: 121). Rather than aligning himself with one of the expected end-time figures, John applies the words of Isa. 40:3 to himself, identifying himself as "the voice of one calling in the desert" (cf. Matt. 3:3 pars.). Thus, John presents himself as "the herald of a new exodus, announcing that God is about to redeem his people from captivity, as he had in the days of Moses" (Keener 1993: 266). The quotation also explains why the Baptist had chosen the Judean wilderness as the location for his ministry.[21] The desert had been the place of God's gathering and deliverance of his people from slavery in Egypt. Many leaders in the history of Israel, from Moses to Paul, were equipped for their divinely appointed task in the wilderness. The Baptist's statement makes clear that rather than being a messianic figure himself, his ministry was preparatory, yet in keeping with OT prophecy.

"Make the Lord's path straight" conveys the image of "preparing a roadway by clearing away the obstacles" (Morris 1995: 121).[22] The task of witnessing to Jesus today is similar: clearing away obstacles that may keep people from coming to Jesus, the most glaring being their

---

19. Note John's "sending" theme, especially 1:6, where the Baptist is said to have been "sent" from God; the Jewish delegation had been sent merely from Jerusalem. Note also the instance of stylistic variation of "sending" words: πέμπω in 1:22, ἀποστέλλω in 1:24 (Köstenberger 1999c). Wallace (1996: 621) cites the participle πέμψασιν in 1:22 as an example of an independent substantival participle.

20. Note the emphatic personal pronoun ἐγώ introducing the quotation; note also the implied contrast with Elijah in 1:21 (Wallace 1996: 322) and that a form of the verb "to be" needs to be supplied in the clause (Wallace 1996: 39).

21. Laney (1992: 48) remarks that John's voice crying out *in the wilderness* "is the first indication that things were not quite right in Jerusalem. The religious establishment of first-century Judaism was corrupt. The voice has abandoned Jerusalem and was calling out in the desert."

22. The quotation from Isa. 40:3 follows the LXX (Beasley-Murray 1999: 20 n. b) except that John uses εὐθύνατε instead of ἑτοιμάσατε (Barrett 1978: 173). This may be because (1) John was translating straight from the Hebrew; (2) he was influenced by the sound of εὐθεῖαν in the LXX shortly after the quotation; or (3) he took his cue from the use of εὐθύνειν with ὁδός in Sir. 2:6; 37:15; 49:9. Menken (1985: 202–3) suggests that the change was motivated by his desire "to make John the Baptist not so much the precursor of Jesus as a witness contemporaneous with Jesus."

sin and need of repentance. In its original Isaianic context, the statement refers figuratively to preparing the roads to allow for a return from the Babylonian exile to Jerusalem. Later on, Isaiah also speaks of the coming "Servant" (esp. Isa. 52:13–53:12), who will provide an even greater deliverance, which is consummated in the new heaven and new earth (Isa. 65–66). Thus, the Baptist remains faithful to this context by calling the people to repentance in preparation for the coming Servant (Carson 1991: 144).[23] Interestingly, the Qumran community applied the same passage in Isaiah to itself (1QS 8:12–14; see Burrows 1974: 246). Yet whereas these covenanters understood the passage as a call to dwell in the desert and to devote themselves to the study of God's word, the Baptist recognized it as a call to prepare the people of Israel for the coming Messiah (Morris 1995: 121).

The Pharisees, mentioned here almost incidentally, lead the charge **1:24–25** against Jesus in John's Gospel (see commentary at 3:1). Most likely, there was only one delegation of Jewish leaders, some of whom were Pharisees.[24] The Pharisees would have naturally been concerned, seeing that John's message and ministry attracted large crowds (Morris 1995: 122–23). Note that the Baptist does not fully answer the Pharisees' question until the next day (1:29) in 1:32, where he states that the purpose of his baptism is to prepare Israel for the Messiah. There is no clear indication in the Hebrew Scriptures that the coming of the Messiah to Israel would be preceded by a baptism of repentance for the Jews. Hence, the questioning of the Jewish delegation seems legitimate. However, the OT does use water as a symbol for cleansing and renewal (e.g., Ps. 51:2, 7; Ezek. 36:25; Zech. 13:1; cf. 1QS 4:20–21).

The Pharisees were particularly concerned about the connection proposed by the Baptist between baptism, repentance, and the final judgment (Ridderbos 1997: 66–67). Various forms of baptism and ritual purification were practiced in the first century, most notably proselyte baptism, which marked a Gentile's conversion to Judaism.[25] Gentiles were thought to be unclean and thus in need of the ceremonial cleans-

23. Alternatively, R. Brown (1966: 50) suggests that the Baptist is to prepare a road so that God might be able to come to his people.

24. So Ridderbos 1997: 66 n. 10; Morris 1995: 122; Carson 1991: 144; Beasley-Murray 1999: 20 n. c; Schnackenburg 1990: 1.292; contra R. Brown 1966: 44; Moloney 1998: 52. While thus the delegation included some Pharisees, this does not mean that the Pharisees were responsible for sending out the delegation, since the Sadducees had a majority on the Sanhedrin (Carson 1991: 144). This is true especially if an article is to be added (or implied) before ἀπεσταλμένοι (Beasley-Murray 1999: 20 n. c; Barrett 1978: 174; R. Brown 1966: 43–44; Schnackenburg 1990: 1.292). Ἀπεσταλμένοι ἦσαν (*apestalmenoi ēsan*, they had been sent) is a periphrastic pluperfect (Wallace [1996: 586] calls it "consummative").

25. For an extended treatment of the function of baptism in this Gospel, including discussions of proposed parallels with other ancient baptisms and John the Baptist and proselyte baptism, see Keener (2003: 440–48).

ing pictured in baptism. Yet John was baptizing not Gentiles, but fellow Jews. For John to propose that everyone, including Israelites, must be baptized was offensive to the Jewish mind, as it ignored their special standing as God's chosen people.[26] Also, though some Jewish communities practiced self-immersion, citing Ezek. 36:25 or Zech. 13:1 (Morris 1995: 123), John was baptizing other Jews, which was unknown (Carson 1991: 145). At times Jews might rebaptize themselves as they felt the need to be cleansed; John's baptism was once for all. The Pharisees' question "Why—and on whose authority—are you baptizing?" reflects their view that one who offered baptism as a means of escaping the final judgment must be an end-time figure of the stature of the Prophet, Christ, or Elijah (all of whom John the Baptist denied being).[27]

1:26–27   Overall, John's ministry may be compared to that of the OT prophets who beckoned a righteous remnant to come out of the people of Israel (Carson 1991: 146). "I baptize with water" (carrying a concessive connotation) implies a contrast that is not made explicit—unlike in the Synoptics—until 1:33, where John speaks of "one who baptizes with the Holy Spirit" (Ridderbos 1997: 67; Morris 1995: 123).[28]

Rather than dwell on his own ministry, John immediately shifts the focus to one whom his interrogators do not know, "one who comes after me" (i.e., his as-of-yet undeclared successor, an echo of 1:15; cf. 8:56–58).[29] Note that, by his own acknowledgment, not even John himself knew Jesus' true identity apart from divine revelation (1:31, 33) (Beasley-Murray 1999: 24).[30] John's self-confessed "ignorance" is a further instance

26. Cf. Mark 1:2–5; Matt. 3:1–10; Luke 3:3–14. So Morris 1995: 123; Beasley-Murray 1999: 24; Carson 1991: 145–46; Schnackenburg 1990: 1.293.

27. So Ridderbos 1997: 67; Burge 2000: 71; Barrett 1978: 174; R. Brown 1966: 51; Borchert 1996: 126.

28. In contrast to Mark 1:7, John uses ἄξιος not ἱκανός, does not use κύψας (Schlatter 1948: 45), and uses ἵνα plus subjunctive rather than an infinitive (Barrett 1978: 175). Staley (1988: 60) detects a progression from the Baptist's more active role in relation to Jesus in 1:26–34 to his taking a more passive role after 1:35 until the shift is completed in 3:22–36. See also the insightful comments on the nature of the Baptist's witness by Westcott 1908: 1.37.

29. Stibbe (1993: 33) again points to the theme of the "elusive Christ": "Even though Jesus is not visibly on stage, his elusive presence is felt in the Baptist's rather obscure remark. . . . The reference here is clearly to the mysterious and elusive presence of Jesus himself." Beyond this, the phrase "one whom you do not know" may also allude to the view held by some in that day that before commencing his public ministry, the Messiah would live a hidden life on earth (see commentary at 1:31; 7:27; see also Ridderbos 1997: 68; Beasley-Murray 1999: 20 n. d). The word "stand" (ἕστηκεν, hestēken), a perfect, has present force (cf. Mark 10:19; Acts 26:27; Heb. 6:9; see Wallace 1996: 579–80).

30. Borchert's argument (1996: 133) that John's "not knowing" is to be linked with the world's failure to recognize Jesus in 1:10, resulting in a "steady drumbeat of a dirgelike

of humility that throws into even starker relief the one who possesses original knowledge (1:18; 7:27–28) (Bultmann 1971: 92 n. 1).

In his own estimation, John is not even worthy to untie the straps of Jesus' sandals (cf. Mark 1:7 pars.; Acts 13:25).[31] Rabbi Joshua b. Levi (A.D. 250) taught, "All manner of service that a slave must render to his master, the pupil must render to his teacher—except that of taking off his shoe" (b. Ketub. 96a). The Baptist, however, acknowledged that he was unworthy to untie Jesus' shoelaces, a task judged too menial even for a disciple (Daube 1956: 266–67). This is a telling statement of how great the Baptist considered Jesus to be.

The reference to the physical setting of this event serves as a structural link indicating the end of the paragraph (cf. 6:59; 8:20; 11:54). It also helps transition to the climax of John's testimony in the ensuing verses (Ridderbos 1997: 68).[32] John takes care to distinguish this "Bethany beyond the Jordan" (cf. 10:40) from "Bethany near Jerusalem," the village where Lazarus was raised from the dead (11:1, 18).

1:28

The Bethany mentioned in the present passage, which was one of the places where John baptized (note the later reference to Aenon near Salim in 3:23), is probably not a village but the region of Batanea in the northeast (called Bashan in the OT; see Carson 1991: 147; followed by Keener 2003: 450; Witherington 1995: 66). This is suggested by the fact that Jesus is said to leave from Bethany for Galilee in 1:43 and apparently calls Philip to follow him still on the same day. Hence, Bethany must have been within a day's journey, and thus closer to Galilee than to Judea.[33]

If this reconstruction is correct, then "Bethany" would be a variant spelling of "Batanea" chosen by the evangelist to underscore that Jesus' ministry began and ended in "Bethany." At Bethany in the (Galilean) north, John the Baptist confesses Jesus as "God's lamb"; at Bethany in the (Judean) south, Jesus nears his crucifixion. The mention of all four major regions of the promised land—Judea, Samaria, Galilee, and the

---

march of rejection," is not only unduly melodramatic but also fails to acknowledge the all-important difference between the world's intransigence to divine revelation and the Baptist's receptivity to it.

31. Schlatter (1948: 45) notes the emphatic position of αὐτοῦ (autou, his), which, he argues, further accentuates the distance between the Coming One and the Baptist.

32. Moloney (1998: 53) notes, "Nowhere else in 1:19–51 is a day brought to such a formal close as this first day." Note also the periphrastic imperfect ἦν . . . βαπτίζων ("was baptizing"), indicating the continual nature of the Baptist's ministry (Barrett 1978: 175; Wallace 1996; 648).

33. This would seem to invalidate the recent claims made by Mohammed Waheeb (1999: 14–15), an archaeologist directing the Jordanian excavations in the Jordan area, to have discovered the "Bethany beyond the Jordan" at a site about five miles north of the Dead Sea. Cf. Riesner 1987: 47 (succinctly presented by idem, DJG 35–36); 2002. I am indebted to Riesner also for some of the following material.

Transjordan (of which Batanea was a part)—indicates that the sending of Jesus is for the whole of Israel.

b. John's Witness concerning Jesus (1:29–34)

1:29   This is now the second part of John's witness. After testifying to the Jewish delegation, John provides direct testimony concerning Jesus. The one glaring omission of the present narrative in comparison with the Synoptics is the account of Jesus' actual baptism by John. Apart from the fact that John appears to presuppose his readers' familiarity with the gospel story, Jesus' baptism by John could have been seen as indicative of submission on the part of Jesus, an inference that the evangelist would seek to avoid (Witherington 1995: 63). The section surely is historical, because if some of Jesus' early followers were previously disciples of the Baptist, something significant must have caused them to leave him at the climax of his ministry (Carson 1991: 148). Some question whether it is likely that the Baptist would have had foreknowledge of Jesus' death, but he may have spoken better than he knew (Ridderbos 1997: 69–72, esp. 71; contra Sandy 1991). The notion of sacrifice does not appear for the first time here in this Gospel; it is already hinted at in the prologue's portrayal of Jesus as God's "one-of-a-kind Son" à la Isaac (see commentary at 1:14).

Rather than focus on Jesus' baptism, the Fourth Evangelist concentrates on the christological interchange between Jesus and the Baptist.[34] John says that Jesus is "the," not just "a" lamb (ἀμνός, amnos) of God: he is the lamb par excellence. And he is *God's* lamb, that is, the lamb especially provided by God for the sins of the world.[35] As is common for characters in this Gospel (e.g., 11:49–52), the Baptist here speaks better than he knows. For he himself, it appears, merely thinks of the lamb led to the slaughter referred to in Isa. 53:7 (LXX: ἀμνός; elsewhere besides John in the NT only in Acts 8:32 [citing Isa. 53:7 LXX]; 1 Pet. 1:19 [cf. 2:21–25]), which contemporary Judaism interpreted, not in terms of a dying Messiah, but as substitutionary suffering for sin that fell short of actual death (cf. Matt. 11:2–3; Luke 7:18–20).[36]

34. The sense of ἐρχόμενον (*erchomenon*, coming) is that of John seeing Jesus coming toward him, though not for the first time. John 1:26 and 1:32–33 suggest that John had already recognized Jesus' true identity (Morris 1995: 126). Ἴδε (*ide*, look) indicates recognition; ὁ ἀμνός (*ho amnos*, the lamb) and its appositive represent a nominative of exclamation (Wallace 1996: 59–60), with the article preceding ἀμνός pointing to a one-of-a-kind substantive (a "monadic" article; Wallace 1996: 223–24).

35. A genitive of source. Alternatively, it may be a genitive of possession ("belonging to God"; see discussions in Morris 1995: 127; R. Brown 1966: 55). For a general survey of John's teaching on Jesus as the lamb of God, see Marshall, *DJG* 432–34. See also the survey of various interpretive options by Keener (2003: 452–54), who cites the apocalyptic lamb (judged unlikely), the language of the suffering servant (probable allusion to Isa. 53), and the sacrificial Passover lamb (considered primary).

36. Alternatively, the Baptist may have proclaimed Jesus as the apocalyptic warrior lamb who would bring judgment (e.g., 1 Enoch 90:9–12; T. Jos. 19:8; T. Ben. 3:8; Rev. 5:6, 12;

The evangelist, however, places the Baptist's declaration into the wider context of his passion narrative, where Jesus is shown to be the ultimate fulfillment of the yearly Passover lamb (see Exod. 12), whose bones must not be broken (John 19:36; cf. 19:14) (Burge 2000: 73–74; Barrett 1978: 176).[37] Another possible association is the lamb provided by God for Abraham when he was ready to offer up his son of promise, Isaac, in obedience to the divine command (Gen. 22:8, 13).[38] This is especially suggestive because John 3:16 probably alludes to this scene, highlighting one important difference: what Abraham was spared from doing at the last minute, God actually did—he gave his one and only Son (cf. Rom. 8:32).

This "God's lamb" will take away sin, presumably by means of a sacrificial, substitutionary death (Morris 1995: 130). The verb αἴρω (airō, take away) has the sense of "bearing off," "getting rid of," or "carrying away" (2:16; 5:8–12; 10:18; see Bultmann 1971: 96 n. 1), in association with the Hebrew kpr, which suggests the idea of sins being "wiped away" (Borchert 1996: 135–36).[39] "Takes away" is a present tense with future force (R. Brown 1966: 55–56), and "sin" is in the singular, "referring to the totality of the world's sin rather than to a number of individual acts" (Morris 1995: 130; cf. Schnackenburg 1990: 1.298). According to the pattern set by the OT sacrificial system, the shed blood of the substitute covered the sins of others and appeased the divine wrath by way of atonement (cf. 1 John 2:2; 4:10). As the Book of Hebrews makes clear, however, the entire OT sacrificial system was merely provisional until the coming of Christ.

Moreover, as God's lamb, Jesus takes upon himself the sin not merely of Israel, but of the entire world (cf. 1:10).[40] The idea that the Messiah would suffer for the sins of the world, rather than merely for Israel, was foreign to Jewish first-century ears; but John makes clear that Jesus

---

7:17); see R. Brown 1966: 59; Carson 1991: 150; and Beasley-Murray 1999: 24–25 (Schlatter [1948: 46–47] refers to both). For the Baptist's message of judgment, see esp. Matt. 3:7–12; Luke 3:7–17. Carson (1991: 149) notes also the doubts expressed by the Baptist in Matt. 11:2–3. Other options mentioned are the gentle lamb of Jer. 11:19 (with no overtones of bearing sin); the scapegoat of Lev. 16 that symbolically bore the sins of the people and was banished to the desert (albeit not a lamb); and the guilt offering of Lev. 14 and Num. 6 sacrificed to deal with sin (though it involved bulls and goats, not lambs).

37. The same point is made by the apostle Paul, who writes, "For Christ, our Passover lamb, has been sacrificed" (1 Cor. 5:7).

38. For a thorough discussion of several additional alternatives, see Morris 1995: 127–29; see also Barrett 1978: 176; Ridderbos 1997: 73–74.

39. Barrett (1978: 176–77) notes the LXX's tendency (except in Psalms) to translate the Hebrew verb nāśāʾ with a compound of αἱρεῖν. He also cites several OT parallels pertaining to the forgiveness of sin (Exod. 29:38; 34:7; Num. 14:18; 1 Sam. 15:25; Ps. 32:5; 85:3; Mic. 7:18).

40. See the classic exposition of 1:29 in its original Jewish context by Schlatter 1948: 48–49.

came to save the entire world (John 3:17; 1 John 2:2) and that he is the Savior of the world, not merely Israel (John 4:42; 1 John 4:14).[41] The NT's depiction of Jesus as "God's lamb" culminates in Revelation, where Jesus is the "lamb who was slain" who returns in universal triumph (see Rev. 5:6, 9, 12; 7:17; 12:11; 13:8; 17:14; 19:7, 9; 21:22–23; 22:1–3).

John's teaching on Jesus' substitutionary atonement builds on the evangelist's earlier reflection on Jesus' incarnation. For it is in the flesh that Christ suffered vicariously; his humanity was an indispensable prerequisite for his work on the cross on others' behalf. In fact, the atonement theme, far from being absent, is part of the warp and woof of John's Gospel: Jesus is the bread of life who will give his flesh for the life of the world (6:51); he is the good shepherd who lays down his life for his sheep (10:15); his sacrifice fulfills Passover symbolism (19:14, 31).

To argue that John, in good gnostic style, taught salvation through revelation rather than redemption (Bultmann 1955: 49–69; 1971; Forestell 1974; but see Köstenberger 1998b: 76–81; M. Turner 1990) is weak exegetically (in light of the passages just cited), defies logic (why would Christ die simply to demonstrate God's love rather than do so in some less painful way?), and suffers from reductionism (forcing an unnecessary either/or position; see Carson 1991: 152–53). It may be conceded, however, that John frequently assumes and presupposes the notions of substitutionary sacrifice and atonement rather than elaborating upon these elements as much as do the other evangelists (Köstenberger 1998b: 81).

1:30–31 "This is the one of whom[42] I said, 'A man comes after me, who ranks ahead of me, because he was before me.'" For the third time in short order the Gospel emphasizes Jesus' priority over the Baptist and his ministry (cf. 1:15, 27), continuing to develop themes first sounded in the prologue.[43] Once again, the statement affirms Jesus' preexistence and thus his preeminence (Carson 1991: 151), following up on the assertion made in 1:29 (Ridderbos 1997: 75).[44]

41. The expression "God's lamb" would have acquainted a Hellenistic audience with the Jewish roots of Christianity. Yet the added phrase "who takes upon himself the sin of the world" immediately points to the universal implications of the lamb's sacrifice.

42. The preposition used here is ὑπέρ, not the more common περί, but there is substantial overlap in meaning (cf. the use of περί in Matt. 26:28; John 17:9; Rom. 8:3; Eph. 6:18) (Wallace 1996: 363).

43. The reference to a previous statement is a recurring stylistic feature in this Gospel (Schlatter [1948: 50] cites 3:26, 28; 4:54; 5:33; 7:21; 8:24; 11:37; 13:33; 15:20; 18:9, 14, 32; 21:14). The statement is largely unchanged from 1:15 and 1:27, though the context is now Jesus' actual appearance (Ridderbos 1997: 75; Morris 1995: 132). The form of the verbs has been changed from participles to indicatives, enabling the author to stress the reality of the thought more forcefully (Morris 1995: 132). The inference that John includes this statement as a polemic against elements elevating the Baptist over Jesus in the evangelist's day (Beasley-Murray 1999: 25) is unnecessary.

44. Wallace (1996: 303) notes that πρῶτος (prōtos, before) in this verse is an instance of the superlative serving as a comparative.

John's testimony that he himself did not know Jesus (1:31; cf. Matt. 11:2–3; Luke 7:18–20) seems puzzling at first. It is hardly credible that John, a relative of Jesus (cf. Luke 1:36, and see commentary at 1:6), would literally not have known Jesus (cf. Matt. 3:14; see R. Brown 1966: 55). More likely, John here acknowledges that he did not know that Jesus was the Messiah until he saw the sign mentioned in 1:32–33 (Morris 1995: 132).[45] Again, this may play into the tendency among certain circles to perceive the Messiah as a clandestine figure prior to his public appearance (Justin, *Dial.* 8.49; cf. *m. Soṭah* 9.15; *m. ʿEd.* 8.7; see Barrett 1978: 177).

"It is in order that he might be revealed to Israel" seeks to reflect the emphatic construction of the purpose clause in the original, with ἵνα (*hina*, in order that) being placed first and διὰ τοῦτο (*dia touto*, therefore) following behind (Morris 1995: 132 n. 71; usually διὰ τοῦτο comes first; see Barrett 1978: 177). Despite the Baptist's self-deprecating comments, it was no mean task to introduce the Messiah to Israel (Morris 1995: 132). Note the quickly ensuing identification of Nathanael as one who is "truly an Israelite" (1:47) and contrast the use of Ἰουδαῖοι (*Ioudaioi*) in this Gospel (R. Brown 1966: 56; Schnackenburg 1990: 1.303). "The reason I came baptizing with water" (1:31) picks up on 1:25–26.

As we noted previously, the evangelist nowhere provides an actual account of Jesus' baptism by John, which, it may be inferred, took place some time prior to 1:32.[46] In the Synoptic Gospels, the descent of the Spirit as a dove (with the accompanying heavenly voice) was witnessed by Jesus (Matt. 3:16; Mark 1:10; Luke 3:22: "in bodily form"). In the Fourth Gospel, the function of this event is said to be the identification of Jesus as Messiah to the Baptist (1:33).[47] Although a dove was not a common figure for the Holy Spirit—though rabbinic tradition links a dove with the Spirit mentioned in Gen. 1:2 (Carson 1991: 153; R. Brown 1966: 57)—it was often associated with Israel, so that it is possible that Jesus is marked as the consummate Israelite at the point he receives the

1:32

45. See also the suggestion by D. M. Smith (1999: 70): "Possibly John denies knowledge of Jesus because in this Gospel knowledge of Jesus, that is, who he really is in relation to the Father, can only come by revelation."

46. "I have seen" (τεθέαμαι, *tetheamai*) is in the perfect, indicating the settledness of John's conviction (Carson 1991: 151). Less likely, the perfect points to the permanent effects of John's encounter with the Christ (Morris 1995: 132–33; R. Brown 1966: 56). Morris (1995: 133 n. 72) thinks that John's use of a different verb for seeing may be a mere instance of stylistic variation. More likely, θεάομαι in John conveys a more pronounced note of *perception* than other "seeing" verbs. This is borne out by all instances of θεάομαι in this Gospel: 1:14, 32, 38; 4:35; 6:5; 11:45.

47. The question of whether ἐξ οὐρανοῦ (*ex ouranou*, from heaven) should be related to καταβαῖνον (*katabainon*, descend) or περιστεράν (*peristeran*, dove) (discussed by Morris 1995: 133 n. 73) is ultimately an academic issue with little consequence. Wallace (1996: 223) considers the article with πνεῦμα (*pneuma*, Spirit) as an instance of a par excellence usage.

Spirit (Morris 1995: 133 n. 74).[48] In Jewish thought, the Messiah was the bearer of God's Spirit (1 Enoch 49:3; Ps. Sol. 17:37; T. Levi 18:2–14; T. Jud. 24:2–3; Kruse 2003: 72).

Importantly, the Baptist testifies that the Spirit did not merely descend on Jesus, but remained on him, a sign of Jesus' divine anointing.[49] For although in OT times the Holy Spirit came upon certain individuals for the purpose of temporary enablement for a particular task,[50] it was prophesied that the messianic age would involve the renewal of Israel through the power of God's Spirit (Isa. 32:15; Ezek. 36:26–27; 37:14; cf. Jub. 1:23), and that the Messiah would be full of the Spirit at all times (Isa. 11:2; 42:1; 61:1; cf. Luke 4:18; T. Jud. 24:1–3; see Köstenberger 1997: 229–30; Burge 1987: 58; 2000: 74; Borchert 1996: 138). Accordingly, the Baptist testifies later in John's Gospel that "God gives the Spirit without limit" (3:34). It is reasonable to assume that the Spirit remained with Jesus continually throughout his ministry (Morris 1995: 133; Burge 2000: 74; Barrett 1978: 178), just as Jesus remained in closest relationship with the Father (1:18).

1:33   The opening phrase "I would not have known him" mirrors perfectly the opening phrase of 1:31 (see commentary there). The expression "the one who sent me" in John's Gospel is a shorthand for God the Father (e.g., 4:34; 5:23, 24, 30, 37), who is identified as the sender of the Baptist in the prologue (1:6).[51] Βαπτίζειν (*baptizein*, to baptize) is an instance of an adverbial infinitive conveying the purpose for which the Baptist was sent (Wallace 1996: 591–92).

The divine revelation received by John the Baptist—reminiscent of an OT prophet occasionally receiving revelations from God (Witherington 1995: 67)—distinguishes him from Jesus' followers later in the chapter, since all other disciples needed human witnesses to become aware of Jesus' messiahship (cf. Matt. 11:11; see Morris 1995: 135). Later Jesus refers to John as the first of a chain of witnesses to his identity (5:33–35). The words "upon whom you see the Spirit descend and remain" echo 1:32.

Unlike John, who baptizes with water only, Jesus will baptize with the Holy Spirit (1:33; cf. Matt. 3:11 par.; Acts 1:5). He will be the "bearer" and the "dispenser" of the Spirit, effecting "the reality to which John

48. Calvin (1959: 34) here argues for an "unliteral and figurative" interpretation, with "dove" referring to the Spirit by metonymy.

49. Burge (1987: 50–52) notes that the Johannine account of Jesus' baptism focuses not on the baptism per se but on the Spirit's role in anointing Jesus and inaugurating his ministry. He suggests that this underscores the precrucifixion unity between Jesus and the Spirit.

50. See Num. 11:25; Judg. 3:10; 6:34; 11:29; 14:19; 1 Sam. 11:6; 16:13; 2 Chron. 15:1; 20:14.

51. Note also the emphatic pronoun ἐκεῖνος (*ekeinos*, that one) in the original (Morris 1995: 134 n. 77).

with his water baptism only pointed" (Ridderbos 1997: 76–77). The Messiah's "baptism with the Holy Spirit" was in keeping with the OT prediction that God would pour out his Spirit on all people in the last days (Isa. 32:15; 44:3; Ezek. 36:25–27; Joel 2:28–32; cf. Jub. 1:23; 2 Esdr. [4 Ezra] 6:26; T. Jud. 24:3; 1QS 4:20–21). In context, this also reveals a soteriological dimension of the Spirit's work in that Spirit baptism is related to the removal of sin (cf. 1QS 4:20–21; see Ridderbos 1997: 77; Morris 1995: 134 n. 79).

The consummative perfects ἑώρακα (heōraka, I have seen) and μεμαρτύ-   **1:34**
ρηκα (memartyrēka, I have testified) point to the abiding effect of John's words (Morris 1995: 134; Wallace 1996: 577; cf. μαρτυρεῖ [martyrei, he testifies] and κέκραγεν [kekragen, he cries out] in 1:15).[52] John 1:34 reads either "Son of God" (the designation for Jesus in 1:49) or "Chosen One of God" (see additional note). If "Chosen One of God" is what John wrote, this would closely parallel the wording of Isa. 42:1, where God promises to pour out his Spirit on his "chosen one" (Carson 1991: 152; Burge 2000: 74). While thus OT Israel was called God's "chosen people," and also Jesus' disciples are said to be "chosen" (e.g., 6:70; 13:18; 15:16, 19), Jesus is "the Chosen One" par excellence (Carson 1991: 152). The expression "chosen one of God" also occurs in the Qumran texts (4Q534), but its messianic nature is disputed (Abegg and Evans 1998: 202).[53]

c. John's Referral of Some of His Disciples to Jesus and the Subsequent Chain Reaction (1:35–51)

The present section shows that disciples attach themselves to Jesus as   **1:35–36**
followers for the first time.[54] They do so on the basis of remarkable christological confessions. Though frequent misunderstanding follows later in the Gospel, the spiritual development of these first followers of Jesus still shows the importance of taking steps of faith in response to one's present understanding of Jesus. Eventually, these disciples realized who he was—the Christ—and joined him in his suffering (Carson 1991: 148). Interestingly, Peter is assigned a very passive role in 1:37–42. In a sense, his actual "call narrative" is not found until the very end of the Gospel (21:15–23), an apparent inclusio (Franzmann and Klinger 1992).

Stepping out of the shadow of the Baptist, Jesus begins his own ministry by calling his first disciples.[55] According to Luke 3:23, Jesus was "about thirty years old" at this time. If Jesus was born in 5 or 4 B.C.

---

52. There seems to be little basis for the assertion by Barrett (1978: 178, citing G. Bornkamm) that "I have seen and I have testified" is a baptismal confession.

53. For a nonmessianic use of "son of God" at Qumran, see 4Q246 2:1.

54. For a detailed discussion of the characterization of Jesus' disciples in this Gospel, see Culpepper 1983: 119–25. See also chapter 4 in Köstenberger 1998b.

55. Contra Lindars (1972: 112–13), who contends that Jesus still remained a disciple of John according to the present Gospel in contrast to the Synoptics.

(as is commonly held to be the most likely date for his birth; see esp. P. Maier 1989: 113–30, who favors a date in late November of 5 B.C.), and if (as I argued in the introduction to 1:19–28) the Baptist's ministry started in A.D. 29, then Jesus would be about thirty-three years old at this point.[56] The events recorded in 1:35–4:42 all seem to belong to the period between Jesus' baptism and temptation and the beginning of his Galilean ministry narrated in Mark 1:14–15 pars.

A comparison with the call narratives in the Synoptic Gospels raises at least two important questions. How is it that in the Fourth Gospel disciples follow Jesus immediately while in the Synoptics they do so only at a later point in time (cf. Matt. 4:18–22; 9:9; Mark 1:16–20; 2:13–14; Luke 5:1–11, 27–28)? And why does John's initial chapter abound with high christological statements (1:29, 34, 36, 41, 45, 49) while the Synoptics (esp. Mark) seem to suggest that the disciples regularly failed to understand Jesus' true identity? By way of succinct reply: first, the Johannine narrative does not deny earlier encounters but focuses instead on Jesus' climactic call to discipleship; second, the confessions provide a credible motive why these men would make the dramatic decision to leave everything behind to follow Jesus.[57]

"The next day" is counted in relation to 1:29. Ridderbos (1995: 78) notes a certain progression during the course of the Baptist's three days of bearing witness to Jesus recorded in this chapter: on the first day, he testified to the Jews (1:19–28); on the second day, he bore direct witness regarding Jesus (1:29–34); and on the third day, he pointed his disciples to the Messiah (1:35–51). The verb form εἱστήκει (heistēkei, he stood) harks back to 1:26, where a similar form is applied to Jesus (ἕστηκεν, hestēken [though note textual variants]; see also 7:37) and gives the statement additional weight (Barrett 1978: 180). The preposition ἐκ (ek) in "two of his disciples" is partitive (Barrett 1978: 180). Intriguingly, the identity of these two disciples is not disclosed at this point (though Andrew is named later in 1:40; see Ridderbos 1997: 83).

Once again, a statement of the Baptist is reiterated, presumably to link it even more directly with the commencement of Jesus' ministry (Ridderbos 1997: 78). John's *private* testimony to two of his disciples concerning "God's lamb" in the present passage coheres closely with his earlier *public* declaration (1:29). The statement also effectively marks the end of the Baptist's significance in redemptive history. Similar to Moses, the Baptist "brought salvation history to a boundary that he himself was not allowed to cross (cf. Matt 11:11). All that was left for

56. See Hoehner 1977: 37–38; Hoehner, *DJG* 119; Humphreys and Waddington 1992: 351.
57. Moreover, it is far from certain whether those uttering these initial lofty confessions understood the full import of their words (cf. the Johannine "misunderstanding" theme). See further Köstenberger 1999a: 66–69; Carson 1991: 147–48, 153–54.

him to do was make room, to 'decrease,' to leave the scene (cf. 3:30)" (Ridderbos 1997: 78).

The present account represents an independent Johannine equivalent to the Synoptic call stories (Mark 1:16–20; Matt. 9:9). Interestingly, however, Jesus is shown to be rather passive; only once is he shown to "call" someone (Philip in 1:43). Generally, the future disciple either comes to Jesus on his own or is brought to him through the efforts of another disciple (Ridderbos 1997: 79; cf. Carson 1991: 153–54). As mentioned, the present account helps illumine the disciples' willingness (shown in the Synoptic call narratives) to abandon their trades and follow Jesus (Carson 1991: 154; Morris 1995: 136; contra Barrett 1978: 179).

This establishes the Baptist not only as a crucial witness to Jesus, but **1:37** also as the initial source from which Jesus drew his followers, further linking their ministries.[58] "To recommend disciples to a greater teacher was rare, required great humility and denoted confidence in the other teacher's superiority" (Keener 1993: 266). The present shift in allegiance from the Baptist to Jesus also illustrates John's humility and submission to the divine will: "It is the mark of a truly great man that he can gently, but firmly, detach them [his followers], so that they may go after a greater"—a refreshing example in a day when the human tendency is to build empires centered on certain individuals (Morris 1995: 137; cf. Borchert 1996: 141).

What is more, these early followers of Jesus show paradigmatically that with the appearance of Jesus the Messiah, those identified with old-style Judaism—even if part of a renewal movement such as the Baptist's—must leave their old religious system and associations behind for the sake of following the Messiah, Jesus. This is as relevant today as it was when the Gospel was first written and read (Burge 2000: 75). The term ἀκολουθέω (akoloutheō, follow), which occurs here for the first time in John, is used in all four Gospels (though not the rest of the NT) with reference to Jesus' disciples.[59] Disciples in that day literally "followed" or walked behind the one they had chosen as their teacher (e.g., y. Ḥag. 2.1).[60] In John's Gospel, however, the term gradually moves from this literal to a more figurative sense to denote a "following" of Jesus' teaching (8:12; 10:4–5, 27; 12:26; 21:19, 20, 22) (Köstenberger 1998b: 176–80, cf. 131–32).[61]

58. Note that there is no Johannine equivalent to the Synoptic accounts of Jesus choosing the twelve apostles (Morris 1995: 136).
59. Further references in the present Gospel are found in 1:38, 40, 43; 8:12; 10:4, 5, 27; 12:26; 13:36, 37; 21:19, 22. See Köstenberger 1998b: 145–47, 177–80.
60. For further rabbinic parallels, see Köstenberger 1998a: 119.
61. See the discussions in Morris 1995: 137; R. Brown 1966: 78; Carson 1991: 154; Barrett 1978: 180. See also comments on the term μένω (menō, stay) at 1:39.

1:38   As on other occasions, Jesus is asking nothing but a simple question: "What are you looking for?"[62] Beneath the surface, however, the question is both probing and challenging, and considering both the identity of the questioner and the Fourth Evangelist's penchant for double entendre, it is hard to believe that the question is not, on a secondary level, meant to challenge also the readers of John's Gospel to ask themselves what it is they are looking for (Carson 1991: 154–55; cf. Witherington 1995: 69; Bultmann 1971: 100).

Jesus is addressed as "rabbi" (which means "teacher").[63] The Semitic term *rabbi* (lit., "my great one") was a common honorific used by disciples to address their teacher. For the benefit of John's Greek-speaking readers, he translates the term into Greek (διδάσκαλος, *didaskalos*, teacher; cf. 20:16). By the end of the first century A.D., the expression had become a technical term for "ordained" teachers who had satisfied certain formal requirements of rabbinic training. At this point, however, the term was used more generally to refer to a respected Jewish religious teacher, such as Nicodemus (3:10), Jesus (1:38, 49; 3:2; 4:31; 6:25; 9:2; 11:8; 20:16), and even John the Baptist (3:26).

The designation is used by Jesus' first followers (1:38), Nathanael (1:49), Nicodemus (3:2), Jesus' disciples (4:31; 9:2; 11:8), and the multitudes (6:25). Interestingly, John translates the Hebrew (Aramaic) term *rabbi* in the first and last instances into Greek (1:38; 20:16) but otherwise leaves the original term *rabbi*. The Synoptic writers, on the other hand, especially Luke, prefer the Greek term διδάσκαλος. This indicates that contrary to common prejudice, John is very concerned to preserve reliable historical information regarding Jesus (Morris 1995: 137–38 n. 89; Carson 1991: 155). But even more important is that all four Gospel writers agree that Jesus was first and foremost perceived by his contemporares as a religious teacher, a rabbi (Köstenberger 1998a).

1:39   Apart from 1:32–33 (where the Spirit is said to "remain" on Jesus), 1:38–39 presents the first instances of the word μένω (*menō*, stay) in John's Gospel. Though here merely referring to Jesus' lodgings (cf. 2:12; 4:40; 10:40; 11:6, 54), the term gradually assumes a significant metaphorical dimension in John (8:31: "abide by my teaching"),

---

62. Note that these are the first words of Jesus in John's Gospel. Witherington (1995: 69) notes that in dramatic works the first words of the main character are often of special importance (more doubtful is Witherington's association of Jesus with Wisdom beckoning for an audience [pp. 69–70]). Whitacre (1999: 71) observes John's emphasis on Jesus' "almost mysterious silence" in comparison with the other Gospels, where "Jesus teaches, preaches and calls people to follow him, yet here Jesus has said almost nothing. . . . Compared with the Synoptics' picture, Jesus in John appears as one hidden and aloof." However, this comment surely must be balanced by the theme of Jesus' humanity in John's Gospel (see, e.g., Jesus' weariness from travel in John 4 or his bursting into tears in John 11).

63. See esp. Köstenberger 1998a: 97–128 (condensed in Köstenberger 1999a: 257–58).

especially in the farewell discourse (14:10, 17; 15:4–10: "remain in me/my love").[64] The invitation "Come, and you will see"—a conditional imperative conveying the sense "If you come—and I want you to—you will see" (Wallace 1996: 489–90)—is issued on Jesus' behalf by Philip to Nathanael in 1:46. Jesus' inviting these prospective disciples to his home may be compared to his statement in the Synoptics: "Foxes have holes and birds of the air have nests, but the Son of Man has nowhere to lay his head" (Luke 9:58; Matt. 8:20). Keener (2003: 470–71) proposes that hospitality required Jesus to offer the disciples a place for the night, since it was too far for them to travel back to their homes that night, whether the walk back to Bethsaida (1:44) was from Capernaum (2:12; a few hours' walk) or from Nazareth (1:45–46; a good day's walk).

The evangelist's reference to the "tenth hour" is the first reference to time in this Gospel (later instances are 4:6, 52; 19:14). Clearly, by mentioning the time, the evangelist gives evidence of eyewitness testimony (e.g., Morris 1995: 138–39). Though it is sometimes argued that Roman reckoning of time commenced at midnight—so that "tenth hour," for example, would mean "ten in the morning" (HCSB; NASB footnote)—the preponderance of evidence suggests that in the first century of Jesus' Palestine, time was counted from sunrise to sunset (i.e., from about 6 A.M. until about 6 P.M.; cf. John 11:9).[65] Moreover, the day was divided into three-hour intervals, with people approximating the estimated time to the next full three-hour segment.

Starting to count, then, as was customary, from sunrise at around 6 A.M., "tenth hour" would mean about 4 P.M. Because at that point daylight was going to run out before long, people refrained from engaging in major outdoor activities past that hour and began to make preparations for lodging, if necessary.[66] This was not confined to the Jewish world: "Caesar, for two reasons, would not fight that day; partly because he had no soldiers in the ships, and *partly because it was after the tenth hour of the day*" (Aulus Hirtius, *Alexandrian War* 10).[67] Since the main meal

---

64. Ridderbos (1997: 82–83) suggests a connection with 1:14: "Not only did they see *that* he lived among them and *where* he lived among them, but at his invitation they also stayed *with him* that day, and he spent time with them as a human among humans" (see also 4:40). A similar development from literal to figurative can be observed regarding the word ἀκολουθέω (see commentary at 1:37).

65. Carson (1991: 156–57) points out that the primary support for the Roman time-reckoning theory comes from Pliny the Elder, who notes that Roman authorities (like Egyptian ones) counted the official civil day from midnight to midnight—for example, in cases of leases and other documents that expired at day's end. But Pliny himself says that "common people everywhere" conceive of the day as running "from dawn to dark" (*Natural History* 2.188). See also the discussion in Morris 1995: 138 n. 91.

66. Contra Barrett (1978: 181), who comments that this is not a "natural point for the beginning of a day's stay."

67. As cited in J. Lightfoot 1859: 3.245.

was usually taken in the late afternoon, "tenth hour" may also indicate that Jesus extended table fellowship to these two disciples of John the Baptist (Jeremias 1966a: 45 n. 1).[68]

1:40   The reference to Andrew as "Simon Peter's brother" seems to presuppose the readers' knowledge of Synoptic tradition (written or oral), since Simon Peter is not mentioned until the following verse (for this phenomenon, see also 3:24; 4:44; 6:67 [reference to "the Twelve" without having mentioned them previously]; 11:1–2). It is also in recognition of the fact that Peter would have been more familiar to the readers (Ridderbos 1997: 84). Andrew is mentioned elsewhere in this Gospel only in 1:44; 6:8; 12:22. The name of the other disciple is not given. This unusual omission can best be explained if the disciple was John the evangelist, since he never refers to himself by name in this Gospel (Ridderbos 1997: 83; Morris 1995: 136; Burge 2000: 75; Witherington 1995: 70; see the present commentary at 1:6).[69]

1:41   John is the only NT author to use the term Μεσσίας (*Messias*, Messiah [here and in 4:25]; see Ridderbos 1997: 85). The expression is a transliteration of the Aramaic/Hebrew word meaning "the Anointed One."[70] In the OT, "anointed" variously refers to the king of Israel (1 Sam. 16:6; 2 Sam. 1:14), the high priest (Lev. 4:3), prophets (Ps. 105:15), or others who were set apart for a particular office.[71] Since John's Diaspora readership is not necessarily expected to know Aramaic, the predominant language of first-century Palestine (translations are also provided in 1:38, 42), John translates the Semitic term into the equivalent Greek expression (Χριστός, *Christos*, the Anointed One). The term "Messiah" is also found in Jewish writings preceding or roughly contemporary with

---

68. Bultmann's claim (1971: 100; accepted by Brodie 1993: 160) that "tenth hour" is the "hour of fulfillment" is very questionable. R. Brown (1966: 75) suggests that if the day was Friday, the disciples had to stay until Saturday evening in order to properly observe the Sabbath. Alternatively, the disciples stayed overnight because of the nature of the desired conversation. If so, this could refer to any day during the week (Morris 1995: 139; cf. Burge 2000: 76).

69. Ridderbos (1997: 84) thinks that this identification is all the more likely since Peter learns about Jesus from his brother Andrew and this unnamed disciple (1:41) and since Peter and John are closely associated in this and the other Gospels (so also Schlatter 1948: 55; more cautious assessments are found in Borchert 1996: 143; Schnackenburg 1990: 1.310; Carson 1991: 154). Note also the connection between Andrew and John in the Muratorian Canon (Bettenson 1967: 28). Michaels (1989: 37) thinks that the second disciple is Philip. Keener (2003: 468) likewise sees "no reason" to identify the other disciple with the beloved disciple, since he is not mentioned until 13:23. On a literary level, this is self-evident, but the absence of "beloved disciple" language prior to 13:23 does not seem to rule out the possibility that the apostle John appears in the Johannine narrative as a historical character that is left unnamed.

70. For a general survey of this title, see Hurtado, *DJG* 106–17.

71. On messianism in the OT, see chapter 1 of Horbury 1998.

the NT, such as the Qumran scrolls[72] and other literature.[73] Jesus' messiahship is developed further in 1:45 and 1:49.[74] Note also the *inclusio* provided by the Gospel's purpose statement (20:31).

Every time Andrew is mentioned in this Gospel, he is described as bringing or referring someone to Jesus (cf. 6:8; 12:22; see Morris 1995: 140).[75] The word for "noticed" (ἐμβλέψας, *emblepsas*) mirrors the earlier usage with reference to the Baptist in 1:36 (cf. βλέπει [*blepei*, sees] in 1:29) and may indicate perceptiveness (Barrett 1978: 182).[76] Last names as are used today were not in existence in biblical times. Instead, a person was known by who his or her father was (e.g., Simon, son of John) and/or by place of origin (e.g., Jesus of Nazareth; Simon of Cyrene). Also, in ancient cultures a name was thought to signify the personality of an individual. The underlying Greek in "son of John" transliterates the Aramaic and may abbreviate "son of Yohanan" (Aramaic for "John"; cf. Matt. 16:17; see Bruce 1983: 58). Peter is identified as "Simon, son of John" only here and in 21:15–17, which may be another instance of *inclusio*.[77]

1:42

"Cephas"—used only here in the Gospels but several times in Paul (1 Cor. 1:12; 3:22; 9:5; 15:5; Gal. 1:18; 2:9, 11, 14)—is an Aramaic word meaning "rock" (cf. Matt. 16:16–18). In OT times, God frequently changed people's names to indicate their special calling (e.g., Abraham, Jacob). Giving someone a new name demonstrated authority (2 Kings 23:34; 24:17). Rabbis in Jesus' day likewise occasionally gave characteristic names to their disciples. Jesus' "renaming" of Simon Peter is therefore in keeping with both biblical and rabbinic precedents. The evangelist adds that the translation of "Cephas" is "Peter" (1:42).

"Peter" does not appear to have been a proper name in ancient times. It may have been used by Jesus as a nickname[78] indicating Peter's strength of character (Ridderbos 1997: 86) and future role in the church.[79] Not

72. See CD 2:12; 12:23–13:1; 14:19; 19:10–11; 20:1; 1QSa 2:14, 20; 4Q521 line 1; 11QMelch line 18.

73. See Ps. Sol. 17:32; 1 Enoch 48:10; 52:4; 2 Esdr. (4 Ezra) 7:28–29; 12:32; 2 Bar. 29:3; 30:1; 40:1; 70:9; 72:2. See O'Neill 1995: 25–26; Abegg and Evans 1998: 191–94; Horbury 1998: chapter 2.

74. See also 3:28–29; 4:25–26, 29, 42; 5:45–46; 6:15; 7:26–27, 31, 40–43; 9:22; 10:24; 11:27; 12:34; 17:3; 20:31.

75. Wallace (1996: 559–60) classifies the aorist ἤγαγεν (*ēgagen*, brought) as a "consummative aorist" pointing to the completion of the act.

76. R. Brown (1966: 74) agrees that this is the case in 1:42 ("to look with penetration and insight"), but disputes that this is the connotation in 1:29.

77. Ridderbos (1997: 85–86) thinks that John is making use of a tradition that is distinct and earlier than that of the Synoptics, based on his use of the Aramaic Cephas and the fact that Simon's father is called John (rather than Jonah).

78. See Cullmann, *TDNT* 6:100–101; Borchert 1996: 143–44; Burge 2000: 76; Morris 1995: 140.

79. Cf. Matt. 16:16–19; see Schnackenburg 1990: 1.312–13; R. Brown 1966: 80; Beasley-Murray 1987: 27; Carson 1984: 368. It must be noted, however, that the evangelist himself

that Peter is worthy of such an epithet in himself; rather, the new name is proleptic of the new man whom God would someday create (Morris 1995: 141; cf. Carson 1991: 156). The focus instead is on Jesus as the one who intimately knows people and "so calls them that he makes them what he calls them to be" (Carson 1991: 156). This points to the "reliability of the apostolic witness . . . the historic foundations of which are laid bare here" (Ridderbos 1997: 86). In keeping with his supernatural knowledge displayed at other junctures (see commentary at 1:47–48), Jesus foresaw what the future held for Peter and their relationship (cf. 21:18–19; see Ridderbos 1997: 86).

1:43–44 "The next day" is now the fourth day in the week of Jesus' early ministry selected by the evangelist (cf. 1:29, 35).[80] The TNIV's "Jesus decided" is one possible way to construe the subject of the phrase (no subject is specified for the verb ἠθέλησεν [*ēthelēsen*, he decided]; see Morris 1995: 141; Barrett 1978: 183; R. Brown 1966: 81; Borchert 1996: 145; Moloney 1998: 55, 61).[81] Alternatively, though less likely, it may be Andrew, not Jesus, who decides to leave. Having just brought Peter to Jesus, it would be entirely natural for Andrew to bring (his friend) Philip as well. If this is correct, everyone who comes to Jesus in John 1 does so on the basis of someone else's witness (Carson 1991: 157–58). This would underscore the importance of testifying to others concerning Jesus.

Finding Philip, Jesus called him by saying, "Follow me."[82] Jesus' practice of calling his followers ran counter to the contemporary practice whereby disciples opted to attach themselves to a rabbi of their choice (cf. 15:16; see Köstenberger 1998a: 120). Even though Philip was not the kind of leader among the disciples that Peter turned out to be, Jesus still called him to follow him and included him in his apostolic circle (Morris [1995: 142] calls him a "limited man").[83] One factor may have been that Philip, like Andrew and Peter, was from the town of Bethsaida (1:44), so that Jesus could build on an already existing relationship among these men.[84]

---

does not comment explicitly, apparently leaving it up to the reader to draw the proper inference (see Barrett 1978: 183).

80. The suggestion by Borchert (1996: 145–46) that the three days mentioned in 1:29, 35, and 43 are meant to evoke in the reader's mind the fact that Jesus rose from the dead on the third day is improbable.

81. Schlatter (1948: 56) notes that the author implies that Jesus acted on his decision, citing 6:21. Schlatter also observes that nothing is said about Jesus' sojourn, but that a meeting place in Galilee is likely, since only a single day separates Jesus' encounter with Nathanael and the Cana wedding in 2:1 (p. 57).

82. On ἀκολουθέω, see commentary at 1:37. Philip is the only true example of a "call" in this Gospel (Morris 1995: 136); note also the Synoptic parallels. Morris (1995: 142) notes that the use here of the present tense of ἀκολουθέω points to a continuous action.

83. Though note that Philip plays a considerably larger role in the Fourth Gospel than in the Synoptics (cf. 6:5–7; 12:21–23; 14:8–9; see Ridderbos 1997: 87).

84. Note the plural "we have found" in 1:45 (Ridderbos 1997: 87). Westcott (1908: 1.45) suggests that "the very mixture of Hebrew (Simon, Nathanael) and Greek (Andrew,

Mark seems to indicate that Andrew and Peter were from Capernaum (1:29; cf. 1:21); here in John they are said to be from Bethsaida. Most likely, Andrew and Peter grew up in Bethsaida and subsequently moved to Capernaum (which is only a few miles directly west of Bethsaida; see Carson 1991: 158; R. Brown 1966: 82). This is similar to Jesus, who is regularly said to be from Nazareth (e.g., 1:45) although he had moved to Capernaum (Matt. 4:13). If they indeed were in the district of Batanea (see commentary at 1:28), then the city of Bethsaida, located in the district of Gaulanitis, would have been an appropriate destination.[85]

Bethsaida (meaning "place of the fishery") probably is to be identified with the mound called et-Tell, located east of the Jordan River about 1.5 miles before it enters the north shore of the Sea of Galilee. After Jerusalem and Capernaum, Bethsaida is the most frequently mentioned city in the Gospels (cf. Matt. 11:21 par.; Mark 6:45; 8:22; Luke 9:10; John 12:21),[86] and Jesus probably spent a significant amount of time there (Morris 1995: 142–43). Its significance was enhanced by its proximity to the Via Maris, an important thoroughfare (Burge 2000: 77). Mark records that a blind man was healed in this city, and the feeding of the four thousand took place in a deserted place nearby. Tragically, the city was condemned by Jesus, along with Chorazin and Capernaum, because of its unbelief.

"He went to get" (εὑρίσκει, *heuriskei*) indicates "a purposeful act of looking for and going to a person" (cf. 1:43; see Ridderbos 1997: 87).[87] The pattern is the same as that in 1:41: a declaration that someone has found the Messiah and the bringing of another to Jesus.[88] The plural "we have found" indicates that Philip had associated himself with the fledgling group of Jesus' followers (Morris 1995: 143).

1:45

Nathanael is mentioned also in 21:2 as one of the seven disciples to whom Jesus appears on the shore of the Sea of Galilee. There it is said that Nathanael came from Cana of Galilee—the site of two of Jesus' signs (cf. 2:1–11; 4:46–54). Since the name "Nathanael" is not mentioned in the Synoptics, it is likely that this was the personal name of Bartholomew (Bar-Tholomaios = son of Tholomaios), who is linked with Philip in all

---

Philip) names seems to indicate the representative character of this first group of disciples." Brodie (1993: 165) sees the call of Philip as "in some sense proleptic of . . . the call of the Greeks."

85. In Jesus' day, the term "Galilee" was used with reference to the territory east of the Jordan River (Carson 1991: 158; cf. Barrett 1978: 183; R. Brown 1966: 82; Morris 1995: 143 n. 100). After the beginning of the Jewish war in A.D. 66, apparently the entire region around the lake was called Galilee. If this is correct, John here follows contemporary usage (Beasley-Murray 1999: 21 n. k).

86. For general (including archaeological) information on Bethsaida, see Strickert 1998; Kuhn and Arav 1991; and Pixner 1985.

87. Though it is not explicitly stated exactly where Philip found Nathanael, it may have been Cana, Nathanael's hometown (21:2; see Ridderbos 1997: 88).

88. Carson (1991: 159) calls this the primary method of Christian growth.

three Synoptic apostolic lists (Matt. 10:3; Mark 3:18; Luke 6:14; though not in Acts 1:13) yet is not mentioned in John's Gospel (Leidig 1980).[89] Since "Bartholomew" was a patronymic, it is very plausible that this man was also known by another name (Morris 1995: 143; Hill 1997: 47; cf. Carson 1991: 159). Intriguingly, *b. Sanh.* 43a may provide independent attestation for the existence of a Nathanael among Jesus' disciples (Bauckham 1996: 34 [cited in Hill 1997: 46–47]).

"The law and the prophets" was a common Jewish designation for the Hebrew Scriptures in their entirety.[90] Philip had come to believe that Jesus was the Messiah foretold in the Scriptures, both in the law (cf. Deut. 18:15, 18; see commentary at 1:21) and in the prophets (e.g., Isa. 9:1–7; 11:1–5, 10–12; 52:13–53:12) (Carson 1991: 159).

Here, Jesus is said to be from Nazareth, and the son of Joseph.[91] Though born in Bethlehem, Jesus grew up in Nazareth, so that he could properly be said to be "from Nazareth." People knew him as "the son of Joseph" (John 6:42), even though he had been conceived in Mary's womb through the Holy Spirit (Matt. 1:18, 20; Luke 1:35) and existed with God from all eternity (John 1:1–2) (Morris 1995: 144). In any case, this would have been too early for Philip to know about the virgin birth.[92] Especially in

---

89. The identification of Nathanael with Bartholomew is favored by Ridderbos 1997: 87–88; Morris 1995: 143; Carson 1991: 159; Burge 2000: 77; contra Barrett 1978: 184; R. Brown 1966: 82; Schnackenburg 1990: 1.314. Barrett (1978: 179, 184) conjectures that the meaning of the name "Nathanael," "God has given," indicates that he represents an "ideal disciple" and that the passage should be interpreted allegorically. Somewhat along similar lines, Witherington (1995: 71) suggests that Nathanael's name implies that the disciples are the Father's gift to Jesus. It seems, however, that these kinds of conjectures leave the realm of well-founded exegesis and veer into the sphere of ultimately unverifiable speculation (see the critiques by Morris [1995: 143] and Carson [1991: 159], both of whom defend Nathanael's and the event's historicity). Hanhart (1970: 24–25) identifies Nathanael as Matthew; Hill (1997) somewhat cautiously advances the theory that Nathanael is identical with James of Alphaeus (cf. Epistle to the Apostles 2 [second century A.D.]).

90. Schlatter 1948: 57. Cf. Matt. 5:17; 7:12; 11:13; 22:40; Luke 16:16; 24:44; Acts 13:15; 24:14; 28:23; Rom. 3:21.

91. W. O. Walker (1994: 36) argues that "son of Joseph" is intended "to say something significant (and problematic) about Jesus' *origin* and thus about his *identity*: he is the son of a human father." He concludes, "If such is the case at 6.42, it may well also be the case at 1.45, particularly in light of the fact that 'from Nazareth' apparently has a similar import at 1.45." There is only one problem with this view: "son of Joseph, the one from Nazareth" is found on the lips of Philip, not Nathanael, in the wake of his claim "We have found the one of whom Moses wrote in the law and [of whom] the prophets [also wrote]." It is hard to conceive of Philip being derogatory about Jesus having a human father and coming from Nazareth (the latter is the case with Nathanael later!) while at the same time seeking to convince Nathanael that he and his fellow-seekers have found the one predicted in the Hebrew Scriptures. Moreover, as Kruse (2003: 86) notes, in the prologue the evangelist has already provided a clear presentation of Jesus' true origins, so he can refrain from commenting on Philip's rather incomplete description of Jesus here.

92. Calvin (1959: 40) trenchantly comments on Philip's witness to Jesus, "He foolishly calls Jesus the son of Joseph and ignorantly makes Him a Nazarene, but all the same, he leads Nathanael to none other than the Son of God who was born in Bethlehem."

light of the fact that the Pharisees use the same designation to discredit Jesus (6:42; see Carson 1991: 159), this is another instance of Johannine irony (Morris 1995: 144; Barrett 1978: 184; Witherington 1995: 71).

"Can anything good be from Nazareth?"[93] It is ironic that Nathanael, **1:46** himself from the small village of Cana in Galilee (21:2; cf. 2:1–11), here displays such prejudice against the relatively insignificant Galilean town of Nazareth (cf. 7:41, 52; note also that Jesus is called "the Nazarene" in 18:5, 7; 19:19).[94] There may be several reasons for his skepticism. First, there was Nazareth's insignificance. Mentioned neither in the OT nor in Josephus, Nazareth was a small town of no more than two thousand people, located about 3.5 miles southeast of the regional capital, Sepphoris.[95] Second, not only was Nazareth inconspicuous, but also people did not envision the Messiah as coming from Galilee (7:41, 52) (Ridderbos 1997: 88).[96] Third, some also think that there was a rivalry between the small cities of Nazareth and Cana (Morris 1995: 145; Burge 2000: 77). Finally, Nathanael, unlike some of Jesus' other early followers, probably had not benefited from the Baptist's testimony (Ridderbos 1997: 88). In any case, Nathanael features in this Gospel as "a type of the skeptical but honest [see the epithet "without deceit" applied to him by Jesus in 1:47] Jewish person who will require some evidence and convincing before believing in Jesus" (Witherington 1995: 71).

In regard to Philip's response to Nathanael's skepticism, he does not debate the skeptic, but instead he invites him to examine firsthand the veracity of his claim (Ridderbos 1997: 89; Borchert 1996: 147).[97] Though Philip may be unable to answer Nathanael's question, Jesus will provide the needed correction and instruction (1:50–51). What is more, the evangelist proceeds to answer Nathanael's question even more extensively in the remainder of his Gospel. Vicariously, the invitation to "come and see" is extended to every reader of John's Gospel, then as well as now (Carson 1991: 160). It underscores the importance of eyewitness testi-

93. Stibbe (1993: 42) observes that Nathanael's question "sounds very much like a local proverb." Westcott (1908: 1.55) notes that some of the church fathers took this expression positively: "Something good *can* come out of Nazareth."

94. Culpepper (1983: 176–77) suggests that the most common way of conveying irony in John's Gospel is through the use of unanswered questions (see 1:46; 4:12; 6:42, 52; 7:20, 26, 35, 42, 48; 8:22, 53; 9:40; 18:38). For a partial list of ironies, particularly unanswered questions, see also Duke 1985: 90–91.

95. The Nazarenes probably did have relations with their more cosmopolitan neighbors and more than likely also came into contact with the Greek-speaking Gentile traders who passed through Sepphoris in the north or the Esdraelon Valley in the south.

96. Though note the appearance of impostors in Galilee, such as Judas the Galilean (Acts 5:37), a man from Gamala in Gaulanitis who refused to pay tribute to Caesar in the days of the census in A.D. 6 (Josephus, *Ant.* 18.1.1 §4; 20.5.2 §102; *J.W.* 2.8.1 §118; see Burge 2000: 78; cf. R. Brown 1966: 83).

97. Morris (1995: 145) suggests that the reason for this approach was Philip's ineptitude.

mony and of a firsthand knowledge and personal relationship with Jesus. "Seeing"—together with "finding" and "knowing," part and parcel of the Johannine witness motif (Borchert 1996: 134)—relates to witnessing the revelation of God offered by Jesus (Ridderbos 1997: 89). The invitation to "come and see" (also used by other rabbis in Jesus' day) also implies an offer to go and find out together (Morris 1995: 145).[98]

1:47 This is the only instance of the term Ἰσραηλίτης (Israēlitēs, Israelite) in this Gospel.[99] The rendering "true Israelite" (NIV) probably is incorrect.[100] Rather, Jesus says, "truly," here is an Israelite in whom there is nothing false (lit., no "deceit," δόλος, dolos; see Ridderbos 1997: 90; Carson 1991: 160; Barrett 1978: 184–85; Schlatter 1948: 59).[101] In this, Nathanael differs from the original "Israel" (i.e., Jacob; see commentary at 1:50), who was deceitful (δόλος; cf. Gen. 27:35–36 LXX; see Carson 1991: 161; Morris 1995: 145; Burge 2000: 78).[102] Nathanael was free from such duplicity of heart (cf. Ps. 32:2) and thus prepared to consider whether the claims regarding Jesus were true or not. It is as if Jesus was saying, "Look, Israel without a trace of Jacob left in him!" (L. Trudinger 1982: 117). This attitude stood in sharp contrast not only with Jacob of old, but also with the hypocrisy of the Pharisees (Matt. 26:4; Mark 14:1: δόλος), and Nathanael becomes "a symbol of [true] Israel coming to God" (R. Brown 1966: 82; cf. Brodie 1993: 170). Nevertheless, this does not yet make him a "true Israelite" (he cannot be described as an actual convert at this point), but rather a "certain kind of Israelite, an Israelite in whom there is no guile" (Carson 1991: 160).[103]

1:48 John indicates throughout his Gospel that Jesus was endowed with supernatural knowledge.[104] In the Greco-Roman world, such knowledge was regularly attributed to magic or some other mysterious link to the gods.

98. Wallace (1996: 490–91) plausibly suggests that the trailing verb ἴδε (ide) is semantically equivalent to a future indicative (implying confidence on the part of the speaker: "Come, and you will see").

99. The expression occurs five times in Acts as an address for a Jewish audience and elsewhere in the NT only in Rom. 9:4; 11:1; 2 Cor. 11:22.

100. The TNIV properly changed this to "truly . . . an Israelite" (see discussion below).

101. Contra Bultmann 1971: 104; R. Brown 1966: 83, 499–501. Schnackenburg (1990: 1.316) describes Nathanael as "a genuine Israelite," then states in a footnote—wrongly—that this is an adverbial usage. Other instances of the adverb include 4:42; 6:14, 55 (v.l.); 7:26, 40; 8:31; 17:8.

102. Carson (1991: 161) notes, "Since Jesus is about to tell him of greater visions that will be his (1:50–51), there may also be an allusion to the popular etymology that related 'Israel' to ʾîš rōʾeh ʾēl, 'the man who sees God'" (cf. Philo, Alleg. Interp. 3.66 §186; similarly, Morris 1995: 148 n. 117). On Jacob traditions in nonbiblical Jewish sources, see Neyrey 1982; Rowland 1984.

103. Michaels (1989: 40) helpfully clarifies, "Jesus is not so much praising Nathanael's candor . . . as . . . looking at him and seeing not what he is but what he will become."

104. See, e.g., 1:42; 2:4, 19, 24–25; 4:17–18; 6:64, 70; 11:4, 11–14; 13:1, 10–11, 38; 21:18–19.

The Jews, on the other hand, considered access to divine revelation to be the mark of a true prophet. Jesus, however, was more than a prophet: he was the unique Son of God, whose place "at the Father's side" (1:18) provided him with an unlimited supply of divine insight. Nevertheless, Jesus did not display his supernatural knowledge to impress others, but rather to identify himself as the Messiah (1:49–51).

The fig tree sometimes is used in the OT as a figure for home or prosperity, at times in an end-time or even messianic context (1 Kings 4:25; Isa. 36:16; Mic. 4:4; Zech. 3:10) (Carson 1991: 161). In rabbinic literature, it is a place for meditation on the Scriptures and prayer (e.g., *Midr. Qoh.* 5.11 §2; see C. Koester 1990a: 31 nn. 2–3). Most notably, the wording of 1:48 echoes Zech. 3:10, which in turn alludes to 1 Kings 4:25 (C. Koester 1990a: 24). Thus, in keeping with other allusions in the context (cf. 1:45, 47, 51) and references to Zechariah elsewhere in this Gospel (cf. 12:13; 19:37), Jesus' statement about seeing Nathanael under the fig tree before Philip called him may signal that the time spoken of in Zech. 3:10, when everyone would "call his neighbor under the fig tree," was at hand.[105] It also may indicate the advent of the messianic "Branch," which was foretold in both the law (= "scepter" in Gen. 49:10 and Num. 24:17) and the prophets (Zech. 3:8; 6:12; Jer. 23:5; 33:15; cf. Isa. 11:1).[106] Alternatively, the phrase may simply indicate accurate knowledge of a person's whereabouts (cf. *m. Sanh.* 5.2; *b. Sanh.* 41a; see Moule 1954: 210–11).[107]

On the address "rabbi," see commentary at 1:38. "Son of God" and "king of Israel" are messianic titles that are equivalent in nature (Barrett 1978: 186; cf. Ridderbos 1997: 91).[108] Nevertheless, the climactic "king of Israel" may reflect a "strongly Hebraic [i.e., nationalistic] mentality" (Morris

1:49

---

105. C. Koester 1990a: 23–34; cf. Barrett 1978: 185; Nicklas (2000b: 201–2) is less than convinced. Other commentators consider the reference to be incidental, intended to show merely that Jesus "knew" Nathanael prior to their actual encounter (Ridderbos 1997: 90; cf. Burge 2000: 78; R. Brown 1966: 83; Moloney 1998: 56; contra Morris 1995: 146; Witherington 1995: 71; Borchert 1996: 148; Schnackenburg 1990: 1.317). Keener (2003: 486), too, rejects any deeper significance in the identification, suggesting that the fig tree may be mentioned simply because a specific landmark was necessary for some reason. Witherington's suggestion that Nathanael is being portrayed as an expert in the law who thus would know that the Messiah could not come from Nazareth seems far-fetched.

106. The DSS and other Jewish and early Christian texts indicate that the term "Branch" was a familiar designation for the Davidic messiah (4QFlor 10–12a; 4QPBless; 4QpIsa[a] 8–10; T. Jud. 24; Rev. 5:5). The DSS also show that the "Branch" was identified as God's "son" and king over Israel (C. Koester 1990a: 27–30).

107. Michaels (1966–67, reiterated in 1989: 41) proposes an allusion to Hos. 9:10.

108. Wallace (1996: 257, 263–64) notes the presence of the definite article in the original before "Son of God" but not "king of Israel" and points out that this was the actual passage that triggered Colwell's formulation of his famous rule. What Colwell concluded from the present passage is that the lack of the definite article need not indicate indefiniteness, given a certain syntax or word order. In other words, "king of Israel" (despite the lack of the article) is just as "definite" as "Son of God"; the reason why it has no article is that

1995: 147 n. 115; Jesus' response in 1:50–51 may provide a correction; cf. 6:15; 12:16; 18:36; see Painter 1977: 360–61).[109] Nathanael's judgment is vindicated, and his expectation apparently fulfilled, when Jesus is hailed as "king of Israel" at the "triumphal entry" in 12:13 (note that there, "king of Israel" is added by the evangelist to his quotation of Ps. 118:25–26). Nevertheless, there is no reason to believe that Nathanael's apparent glowing confession reveals greater insight than do previous confessions by disciples (Ridderbos 1997: 91; cf. Lindars 1972: 119). Still, since Nathanael is himself an Israelite, he is affirming Jesus as his own king as well as that of his nation.[110]

Specifically, by attaching to Jesus the label "Son of God," Nathanael identifies him as the Messiah predicted in the OT (2 Sam. 7:14; Ps. 2:7; cf. 1 Sam. 26:17, 21, 25; see commentary at 1:41; 20:31); the term "Son [of God]" was also a current messianic title in Jesus' day (cf. 1QSa 2:11–12; 2 Esdr. [4 Ezra] 7:28–29; but see 4Q246 2:1; and references below).[111] Likewise, "king of Israel" was a common designation for the Messiah (cf. 12:13, an *inclusio*; note also the phrase "king of the Jews" in John 18–19). Because of the expression's political overtones, however, Jesus was reluctant to identify himself in such terms (see 6:15), for his kingdom was "not of this world" (18:36) (Ridderbos 1997: 91). The terminologies converge in Jewish literature where the Davidic king is described as God's son.[112]

1:50–51 Jesus' response to Nathanael's confession is vintage Jesus, serving notice that this confession does not fully encompass all who Jesus is as the Messiah. Though the disciples have "seen" him, they have still more to experience and comprehend beyond Jesus' foreknowledge of events (Ridderbos 1997: 92; cf. Carson 1991: 162). The statement thus serves as a summation of the previous interaction (1:35–49), as well as dramatically anticipating what is to follow in the remainder of the narrative (Ridderbos 1997: 92; Beasley-Murray 1999: 22). Jesus is emphatic that his revelation to Nathanael was more than "the cheap trick of a clairvoyant" (Barrett 1978: 186): he is the apocalyptic Son of Man, who has come as a human being from transcendent origins in order to complete

---

both expressions are governed by the article preceding "Son of God." See also Morris 1995: 147 n. 114.

109. Though contrast "king of Israel" with "king of the Jews" (Schnackenburg 1990: 1.318). "King of Israel" is the designation used by Palestinian Jews (1:49; 12:13; cf. Mark 15:32; Matt. 27:42); "king of the Jews" is the term employed by Gentiles and Diaspora Jews (John 18:33, 39; 19:3, 19; cf. Luke 23:37–39).

110. Morris 1995: 147; cf. Witherington 1995: 72; R. Brown 1966: 87; Borchert 1996: 148.

111. For relevant literature, see Köstenberger 1998b: 48–49 n. 17.

112. See 4QFlor 1:6–7; 1QSa 2:11–12; 1 Enoch 105:2; 2 Esdr. (4 Ezra) 7:28–29; 13:52; 14:9; see Carson 1991: 162. Note also that "Messiah" and "king of Israel" are juxtaposed in Mark 15:32.

his mission and who will return to earth in the last days to serve as the end-time judge.

"I tell you the truth" represents the only instance of this expression addressed to Jesus' disciples in the first half of John's Gospel, which underscores the unusual nature and solemnity of the occasion. Note that the instances of "you" are now in the plural, referring to all the disciples present, not just Nathanael. "I tell you the truth" renders ἀμήν (amēn, it is firm), the Greek transliteration of the Hebrew term. While the Synoptics feature a single ἀμήν, John always uses the double expression ἀμὴν ἀμήν, perhaps in order to stress the authoritative nature of Jesus' pronouncements, both to the Jews and to the disciples (Morris 1995: 149). In the OT, the term confirms the truthfulness of someone else's statement. Jesus, on the other hand, uses the expression to assert the trustworthiness and importance of *his own* sayings (Carson 1991: 162).[113]

To see "heaven open" is to receive a vision of otherworldly realities (Acts 10:11; Rev. 4:1; 19:11).[114] An "open heaven" was every Jewish apocalyptic's dream. This spawned an entire genre of literature in the Second Temple period in which enigmatic figures such as Enoch (who, according to Gen. 5:24, was translated to heaven without dying) are depicted as traversing heaven and reporting what they see (1 Enoch is quoted in Jude 14–15). But, as Jesus maintains in John 3:13, "No one has ever gone into heaven except the one who came from heaven—the Son of Man." This Son of Man, in turn, is none other than the mysterious figure of Dan. 7:13, "one like a son of man, coming with the clouds of heaven." What Jesus claims is that he is that Son of Man prophesied in Daniel, the one who has seen God and given a full account of him (cf. John 1:18), the one who was "lifted up" at the cross (3:14; cf. 8:28; 12:32), and the one who will return in all his glory (Matt. 26:64).

The picture of "heaven open and God's angels ascending and descending" in the present context is drawn from Jacob's vision of the ladder "resting on the earth, with its top reaching to heaven, and the angels of God were ascending and descending on it [or 'him,' i.e., Jacob]" (Gen. 28:12).[115] As the angels ascended and descended on Jacob (who later was renamed "Israel")—a sign of God's revelation and reaffirmation of faithfulness to his promises made to Abraham (Ridderbos 1997: 93)—so the disciples are promised further divine confirmation of Jesus' messianic identity.[116] When Jacob awoke from his dream, he exclaimed, "How

113. See the surveys in Hawthorne, *DJG* 7–8; Moloney 1978: 1–22; Culpepper 1993: 57–101 (on 1:51, see pp. 61–63). See also Köstenberger 2002c: 22.

114. The perfect of ἀνοίγω (anoigō, open) suggests that heaven is in a state of openness (Morris 1995: 150).

115. See the discussion in Carson 1991: 163. On Jesus being "greater than Jacob," see 4:12. This is one of only three references to angels in this Gospel (cf. 12:29; 20:12).

116. The angels also serve as a resource for the "Son of Man" while he is absent from his heavenly abode (Matt. 26:53; Mark 1:13; Luke 22:43) (Ridderbos 1997: 94).

awesome is this place. This is none other than the house of God; this is the gate of heaven" (Gen. 28:17); and he called that place "Bethel," which means "house of God."

What Jesus tells Nathanael, then, is that he himself will be the place of much greater divine revelation than that given at previous occasions. He will mediate greater revelation than Abraham (8:58), Jacob (4:12–14), Moses (1:17–18; 5:45–47; 9:28–33), and Isaiah (12:37–41).[117] Jesus is the "new Bethel," the place where God is revealed, where heaven and earth, God and humankind, meet (Carson 1991: 163–64; Witherington 1995: 72; cf. Burge 2000: 79; Borchert 1996: 149; Schnackenburg 1990: 1.320; Keener 2003: 489–91). Importantly, though, Jesus is the very culmination of all of God's revelatory expressions (cf. 1:14–18), providing a fullness of divine self-disclosure about which even Jacob (Israel) could only dream; and these disciples, who as of yet know little of what awaits them, will soon be witnesses of revelation far exceeding that received by any Israelite in previous history (Ridderbos 1997: 93–94).

Moreover, the expression "heaven open and God's angels ascending and descending" also seems to convey an image of the "uninterrupted communion between Jesus and the Father" (cf. 8:16, 29; 10:30; 16:32), presenting the ensuing "signs" as manifestations of this communion (Bultmann 1971: 105–6). An "open heaven" is associated with apocalyptic imagery related to the "Son of Man" also in Matt. 26:64 pars. and Acts 7:56 (Ridderbos 1997: 93). With respect to the present passage, see especially Jesus' statement in response to large-scale defection later in this Gospel: "Does this offend you? What if you see the Son of Man ascend to where he was before?" (6:61b–62). In this related verse, the Son of Man's ascent clearly implies descent ("where he was before") in the context of preexistence (cf. 1:1–2; see Ham 1998: 79 n. 67; contra Pryor 1991a: 342).

The designation "Son of Man" for Jesus is common to all four Gospels (Marshall, *DJG* 775–81; Nickelsburg, *ABD* 6:137–50). Apart from functioning (as in the Synoptics) as Jesus' favorite self-reference (e.g., 6:27; 9:35; cf. Ezek. 2:1 et al.), the expression "Son of Man" is fused in Johannine theology to denote both Jesus' heavenly origin and destination (descent/ascent; 1:51; 3:13; 6:62; cf. Dan. 7:13) and his "lifting up" (substitutionary sacrifice) on the cross (3:14; 8:28; 12:34; cf. 6:53; 12:23; 13:31).[118] The Son of Man is also presented as the end-time judge (5:27).[119] Notably, the term is always found on Jesus' lips in John's Gospel (12:34 is no real

117. In this, John's argument is remarkably similar to that of the Book of Hebrews.

118. Note that although the Danielic "Son of Man" is a humanlike figure distinguishable from God, he is cast in entirely transcendent terms (Ridderbos 1997: 93).

119. This corresponds to the threefold division suggested by D. Guthrie (1981: 285–87): origin, authority, and exaltation (cited in Ham 1998: 78). For a bibliographic note, see Köstenberger 1998b: 50–51 n. 26. For a basic survey and relevant literature, see Ham 1998.

exception). Presumably, it is chosen by Jesus because it is less laden with political overtones than are designations such as the just-used "king of Israel" (Carson 1991: 164; Burge 2000: 79–80). In the context of the present chapter, "Son of Man" culminates the portrayal of Jesus as God's "one-of-a-kind Son," who, while nominally being the son of Joseph, is the Son of God (W. O. Walker 1994: 31–42).

The present reference is one of several in John's Gospel to "greater things" to come (Köstenberger 1995a). In 5:20, Jesus maintains that the Father "will show him even greater things than these," referring to his participation in the final judgment (cf. 5:27). In 14:12, Jesus predicts that believers after his death will do "even greater things than these, because I am going to the Father" (the Son's return). These pronouncements raise expectations for the reader of John's Gospel as he or she continues to follow John's narrative.[120] In the present case, the "greater things" that Jesus promises to Nathanael are bound up with greater revelation: "you will see heaven open, and the angels of God ascending and descending on the Son of Man."[121]

Specifically, "greater things" (i.e., revelations of God's glory in Christ) will be seen in the ever-escalating series of "signs" performed by Jesus (Ridderbos 1997: 95; Loader 1991: 255–74). Perhaps significantly, the pronouncement is made to Nathanael of Cana in Galilee (21:2), the site of Jesus' first and third "signs" framing John 2–4, the first major ministry portion of Jesus narrated in this Gospel (Burge 2000: 79). Yet according to the evangelist, an even greater revelation of the divine glory than Jesus' signs—spectacular as those may be—can be found at the cross (12:23–33; 13:31–32; 17:4–5; 19:30). As late as just prior to the crucifixion, however, Philip, one of Jesus' first followers and the very one who brought Nathanael to Jesus, can still ask Jesus to show him and his fellow disciples the Father—as if he had not consistently done so throughout his entire earthly ministry (14:8–12).

Additional Notes

1:21. There is some textual instability (presumably produced by the presence of the similar phrase τίς εἶ in 1:22) as to the emphatic pronoun σύ and the interrogative pronoun τί(ς) (Barrett 1978: 173). Τίς ("who?") is the reading in 𝔓⁶⁶, though virtually nowhere else. Σύ is found at the beginning (B), the middle (𝔓⁷⁵ C*), or the end of the clause (A). Yet little of interpretive significance rests on these minor differences.

---

120. See Culpepper (1983: 61–68) for a detailed discussion of prolepses in the Fourth Gospel (1:50 is listed in the same category as 2:4; 3:14, 17; 6:27, 64; 7:34, 38).

121. As Morris (1995: 148 n. 117) points out, this may be another reference to Nathanael as an "Israelite," in the sense that the name "Israel" (first applied to Jacob) was commonly derived from the Hebrew for "the man seeing God." Thus, Jacob was thought of as a prototypical man of vision, yet Nathanael would exceed his ancestor in the "greater things" that he would see as Jesus' follower.

1:34. While some early MSS read "the Son of God" (the reading adopted in the NIV, NASB, NRSV, NKJV, ISV, ESV, NLT, HCSB), others (such as ℵ* and 𝔓⁵ᵛⁱᵈ), including a recently published papyrus (𝔓¹⁰⁶), have "the Chosen One of God" (adopted by the TNIV).[122]

1:42. Some MSS read "the son of Jonah," which probably represents an assimilation to Matt. 16:17.

---

122. *The Oxyrhynchus Papyri,* vol. 65, was published in 1998 by the Egypt Exploration Society (see pp. 12–13). Among commentators, "Chosen One of God" is favored by Morris 1995: 134; Carson 1991: 152; Burge 1987: 59–61; 2000: 74; Barrett 1978: 178; R. Brown 1966: 57; Schnackenburg 1990: 1.305. "Son of God" is the reading advocated by Bultmann 1971: 92–93 n. 6; Borchert 1996: 139; Ridderbos 1997: 77; Beasley-Murray 1999: 21 n. g; Laney 1992: 53 (though all prior to the discovery of 𝔓¹⁰⁶). Rodgers (1999: 304) prefers both ("This is the only, the chosen Son of God"), while Michaels (1989: 36) proposes that the Baptist spoke "Chosen One of God" (hence the MS tradition), which the evangelist interpreted as "Son of God."

2. The First Sign: Turning Water into Wine at the Wedding at Cana (2:1–12)

In his concluding purpose statement, John writes that he recorded several of Jesus' "signs" in order to engender faith in his readers (20:30–31). The first one of these signs is Jesus' turning water into wine at the wedding of Cana (2:11). This is the first of the "greater things" promised in 1:51 (Ridderbos 1997: 113; Witherington 1995: 77; Schnackenburg 1990: 1.323; Williams 1997: 690). The events of 1:19–2:12 form a coherent unit in that they describe the first week of Jesus' ministry (including his first sign).[1]

The structure of the present narrative unfolds thus: 2:1–2 describes the setting; 2:3–5 reveals the need for intervention; 2:6–8 narrates the actual sign; 2:9–10 confirms the sign; and 2:11 provides the conclusion (cf. Beasley-Murray 1999: 33). John numbers another, later sign as "the second sign" that Jesus performed in Cana (4:54). This brings Jesus' first ministry circuit to a close, which spans John 2–4 (an *inclusio*). A complete list of Jesus' signs in John's Gospel can be constructed thus:

Jesus' Signs in John's Gospel

Event	John	Date
1. Changing water into wine	2:1–11	Winter/Spring, A.D. 30
2. Temple clearing[2]	2:13–22	Spring, A.D. 30
3. Healing of royal official's son	4:46–54	Spring, A.D. 31
4. Healing of lame man	5:1–15	Fall, A.D. 31
5. Feeding of multitude	6:1–15	Spring, A.D. 32
6. Healing of blind man	9:1–41	Fall, A.D. 32
7. Raising of Lazarus	11:1–44	Spring, A.D. 33

All of Jesus' signs occur in the first part of the Gospel, which deals with Jesus' public ministry to the Jews. In human terms, this min-

---

1. This is mirrored by the transitional section of John 11–12, which introduces Jesus' final week of public ministry, including his final sign.

2. For a defense of the temple clearing as a Johannine sign, see Köstenberger 1995b (cf. P. Trudinger 1997: 330), contra R. Brown (1966: 528), who claims that every use of σημεῖον (sēmeion, sign) refers to a "miraculous deed." By referring to the "temple cleansing" as "temple clearing," I take up a suggestion made by Mathews (1988–89: 101); cf. E. Sanders 1985: 61–76; Evans 1989: 237–70.

istry turns out to be a failure, as John makes clear in his summary statement in 12:37. While Jesus' disciples see in his signs a reflection of God's glory (2:11), the very same signs reveal the hardening of the Jewish leadership in its rejection of Israel's Messiah (see, e.g., 2:13–22; 9:1–41; 11:1–44). What the two events narrated in John 2 (a "diptych" [Beasley-Murray 1999: 31]) share in common is that they present Jesus as the restorer of Israel.[3] At the Cana wedding, Jesus is the bringer of messianic joy who fills up the depleted resources of Judaism. At the temple clearing, he removes from the center of Jewish worship any activity unworthy of the true worship of God (Witherington 1995: 86; Beasley-Murray 1999: 39).

It is fitting that the insignificant village of Cana in Galilee becomes the site of Jesus' first sign. For Jesus chose obscurity over fame (Matt. 4:5–7; Luke 4:9–12), and he came not to be served, but to serve (Mark 10:45). The fact that Cana is also Nathanael's hometown (21:2) ties 2:1–11 in with the end of John 1 (note that Nathanael is likely one of the disciples who accompanied Jesus to this wedding).[4] The entire event served as a foil for Jesus' revelation that "his time had not yet come" (2:4; cf. 7:30; 8:20; and the arrival of the "hour" in 12:23, 27; 13:1; 17:1). Nevertheless, Jesus finds a way to meet the need of the hour by performing a miracle "behind the scenes." Jesus not only turns water into wine; he creates wine of superior quality. This emphasis on the spectacular nature of Jesus' signs becomes a regular feature of John's narration.[5]

    a. The setting (2:1–2)
    b. Jesus turns water into wine (2:3–11)
    c. Return to Capernaum (2:12)

Exegesis and Exposition

[1]And on the third day there was a wedding at Cana in Galilee, and the mother of Jesus was there. [2]Now Jesus and his disciples also had been invited to the wedding. [3]And when the wine had run out, Jesus' mother said to him, "They do not have any more wine." [4]Jesus said to her, "What concern is that to me and to you, mother? My time has not yet come." [5]His mother said to the servants, "Do whatever he tells you to do." [6]Now there were six stone water jars standing there in keeping with the cleansing rituals of the Jews, each holding two or three

---

3. Cf. Keener (2003: 493), who prefers to read 2:1–11 in terms of Judaism's renewal rather than its obsolescence.

4. Witherington's (1995: 77) suggestions that the wedding may have involved Nathanael's family, and that Nathanael may have been the source of the story if the "disciple Jesus loved" was not present, are sheer conjecture, as is R. Brown's (1966: 98) suggestion that the bridegroom was actually John, the son of Zebedee (or Nathanael).

5. See commentary at 2:9–10.

measures [twenty to thirty gallons]. [7]Jesus said to them [the servants], "Fill the jars with water." And they filled them to the top. [8]And he told them, "Now draw some out and bring it to the master of the banquet." And they brought it to him. [9]Now when the master of the banquet tasted the water that had been turned into wine and did not know where it had come from—though the servants who had drawn the water knew—the master of the banquet called the bridegroom [10]and said to him, "Everyone serves the choice wine first, and when people have become drunk, the one of lesser quality. You have kept the choice wine until now." [11]This, the first of his signs, Jesus performed at Cana in Galilee, and he revealed his glory, and his disciples believed in him. [12]After this he went down to Capernaum, as did his mother and brothers and his disciples, and there they stayed for a short while.

a. The Setting (2:1–2)

After calling his first disciples, Jesus takes them along to a wedding in Cana of Galilee, not far from his hometown, Nazareth. There he performs the first of his startling signs, providing his followers with an initial glimpse of his messianic identity.[6] "The third day" is to be counted from the last event narrated: Jesus' encounter with Nathanael.[7] Including the first day in the calculation, this means two days later. In conjunction with John's initial testimony to Jesus in 1:19–28 and the three references to "the next day" in 1:29, 35, 43, this completes an entire week of activity (see chart at introduction to 1:19–12:50). If no information is given regarding the sixth day because it was a Sabbath, the Cana wedding—or at least the day on which Jesus and his friends joined the wedding party—would have fallen on a Sunday. This may not have been the first day of the wedding, since weddings lasted for a whole week (see Judg. 14:12), and it is unlikely that the wine ran out immediately.

2:1

The village of Cana is mentioned in the NT only in John (2:1, 11; 4:46; 21:2). Despite its insignificance (cf. the reference to Nazareth in 1:46; see Ridderbos 1997: 103–4), Cana becomes the site of Jesus' first and third signs recorded in this Gospel (cf. 4:46, 54: the second sign

---

6. Some in John's Ephesian audience may also have read the present account in light of the myth of Dionysus, the Greek god of wine and most popular deity in the Hellenistic world (Hengel 1995).

7. It is doubtful that the reference to "the third day" represents an allusion to the resurrection (so, rightly, Ridderbos 1997: 102; Carson 1991: 167; Burge 2000: 90; contra Borchert 1996: 153; Stibbe 1993: 46; Keener 2003: 497–98). The reference serves as a chronological connective with preceding events, perhaps indicating that the promise of 1:51 was quickly fulfilled (Beasley-Murray 1999: 34, citing Schnackenburg 1990: 1.325; cf. Talbert [1992: 86], who says that 2:1–11 serves as fulfillment of the prophecy in 1:51; and D. M. Smith [1999: 86], who speaks of the "first installment . . . of the revelation promised in 1:51"). The beginning of Jesus' final week is signaled in 12:1 (cf. Barrett 1978: 189–90).

in Cana). Several sites have been proposed for ancient Cana ("place of reeds"). Some older commentators suggest Kafr Kenn, some four miles northeast of Nazareth on the road to Tiberias, but this is rendered unlikely by the doubling of the letter *n* in "Kafr Kenn" (Mounce, *ISBE* 1:585). The probable location is Khirbet Qân in the Plain of Asochis, about eight miles northeast of Nazareth (cf. Josephus, *Life* 16 §86; 41 §207).[8] Fittingly, Khirbet Qân overlooks a marshy plain featuring plenty of reeds. To date, the site has not been excavated, but cisterns and the remains of buildings are visible, and nearby tombs are cut into the rocks. Some first-century coins also have been found on the site. The plain where Cana was located apparently was part of the royal domain of the Herodians and was cultivated by their tenants under the supervision of royal officials (cf. John 4:46; see Avi-Yonah 1964: 138). John's mention of "Cana in Galilee" seems to presuppose another Cana (not in Galilee), presumably the Cana in Lebanon referred to in Josh. 19:28 (cf. Josh. 16:8; 17:9).[9]

Jewish weddings were important and joyful occasions in the lives of the bride and the groom and their extended families, and the entire community joined in the celebration.[10] Cana was not far from Jesus' hometown of Nazareth (less than ten miles), and the fact that the guest list included Jesus and his disciples as well as his mother may indicate the wedding of a close family friend or relative.[11] This may also explain why Jesus' mother felt responsible to help when the hosts had run out of wine.

2:2 Note the order in which the evangelist lists those invited to the wedding: the mother of Jesus is mentioned first (though not by name), then Jesus and his disciples.[12] Mary may have been a friend of the family, helping behind the scenes.[13] Jesus may have been invited because of a childhood association, because he was one of the distinguished people

8. See Mackowski 1979; Dalman 1935: 101–6; Riesner, *DJG* 36–37; Deines 1993: 25 n. 38 (with further bibliography).

9. See Riesner 1987: 47, referring to Mackowski 1979: 278–79; cf. Dalman 1935: 101.

10. On Jewish weddings, see the sidebar in Köstenberger 2002c: 24. See also Safrai 1976; Derrett 1970: 227–38; Ferguson 1993: 68–69; Williams, *DJG* 86–88.

11. On Jesus' natural family, see the sidebar in Köstenberger 2002c: 25.

12. The use of a compound subject with a singular verb suggests that Jesus was invited to the wedding while his disciples simply accompanied him (Wallace 1996: 344). T. Martin (1998), surveying references to mothers in ancient writings, demonstrates that Mary is not mentioned by name because John assumed knowledge of her name among his readers (contra symbolic or polemical interpretations; see Beck 1993). For a list of unnamed characters in this Gospel, see Beck 1997: 31 (significant instances are the mother of Jesus, the Samaritan woman, the royal official, the lame man at the pool, the man born blind, and the beloved disciple). See also Beck's (1997: 54–62) treatment of the characterization of the mother of Jesus in John's Gospel.

13. See the helpful discussion of 2:1–11 in Derrett 1970: 229–44. For an examination of the evangelist's characterization of Mary, see Culpepper 1983: 133–34.

in the neighborhood, or both.[14] The group of Jesus' disciples presumably included the five mentioned in 1:35–51: Andrew, Simon Peter, Philip, Nathanael, and the unnamed disciple of 1:35 (possibly John the son of Zebedee).

b. Jesus Turns Water into Wine (2:3–11)

In Jewish thought, wine is a symbol of joy and celebration: "There **2:3** is no rejoicing save with wine" (*b. Pesaḥ.* 109a).[15] The running out of wine at the Cana wedding may be symbolic of the barrenness of Judaism. Prophetic expectation cast the messianic age as a time when wine would flow freely.[16] At a cultural level, running out of wine was considered to be a major social faux pas, since the host was responsible to provide the wedding guests with wine for seven days. There may even have been legal obligations. It is also possible that the hosts were of limited means (Morris 1995: 156, 158; cf. Carson 1991: 169; Burge 2000: 91; though note the presence of servants at the wedding). In the Greco-Roman world, and presumably in the Palestine of Jesus' day, three kinds of wine were in use: (1) fermented wines, which usually were mixed in the proportion of two or three parts of water to one of wine; (2) new wine, made of grape juice, and, similar to cider, not fermented; and (3) wines in which, by boiling the unfermented grape juice, the process of fermentation had been stopped and the formation of alcohol prevented.

The pattern "request–rebuke–assistance" occurs elsewhere in the NT (Matt. 15:21–28; cf. John 4:46–54; see Carson 1991: 173), though the specific form "suggestion–negative response–positive action" seems to be unique to John's Gospel, in each instance wedded to misunderstanding regarding the arrival of Jesus' "time," be it by Jesus' mother, brothers, or close friends (cf. 7:2–14; 11:1–44; see Giblin 1980).[17] Jesus' mother

---

14. Whitacre (1999: 78) conjectures that the way Jesus and his disciples are mentioned here may imply "that they got into town at the last minute and were invited to come along." Whitacre adds that it may have been their "unexpected presence at the wedding [that] may account for the wine shortage." Wine may have run out "because Jesus did not contribute, either because of his last minute arrival or because of his poverty." Whitacre here echoes suggestions already made by Westcott (1908: 1.81).

15. On wine in biblical times, see Watson, *DJG* 870–73; Keener 2003: 500–501.

16. See Jer. 31:12–14; Hos. 14:7; Amos 9:13–14; 2 Bar. 29:5; 1 Enoch 10:19; cf. Matt. 22:1–14 par.; 25:1–13.

17. Giblin's treatment is perceptive, but rather than including 4:46–54 with 2:1–11; 7:2–14; and 11:1–44, it is preferable to treat 4:46–54 in conjunction with the Synoptic "request–rebuke–assistance" pattern, since the pericope does not involve a misunderstanding regarding Jesus' "hour." Notably, each of the three instances of the "suggestion–negative response–positive action" pattern begin or conclude a subsection of John's Gospel, with 2:11 and 11:1–44 bracketing John's account of Jesus' seven signs as the first and last of these signs, and 7:2–14 beginning the second part of Jesus' public ministry after the watershed mass defection at the end of chapter 6.

is mentioned only here and in 19:25–27. It is possible that, apart from John's own eyewitness recollection, Mary was his major source for the present account. If women's quarters at ancient Jewish weddings were near the place where the wine was stored, Mary may have learned of the shortage of wine before word reached Jesus and the other men.[18] In what might have constituted a breach of etiquette, Mary informs Jesus of the problem, in the process disturbing the male guests.[19] Mary's request does not necessarily suggest that she expected her son to do a miracle (Williams 1997: 686; contra Laney 1992: 64). More likely, she is simply expressing her general reliance on the resourcefulness of Jesus (Carson 1991: 169–70).[20]

2:4   Jesus elsewhere makes clear that his relationship with his mother is constrained by kingdom concerns (cf. Matt. 12:46–50 pars.; Luke 2:48–51; 11:27–28). Jesus' address of his mother as "woman" (γύναι, *gynai*) sounds brusque (Ridderbos 1997: 105); at the very least, it establishes polite distance.[21] Yet the expression, while not particularly endearing, need not be harsh.[22] The unusual nature of Jesus' use of this address for his own mother is underscored by the fact that this practice is without parallel in ancient Jewish or Greco-Roman literature (R. Brown et al. 1978: 188). That this does not mark the absence of filial affection is indicated by the provision made by Jesus for his mother at the foot of the cross (19:25–27).

The underlying thrust of the phrase translated "Why do you involve me?" in the TNIV is "What do you and I have in common (as far as the matter at hand is concerned)?"[23] The implied answer: "Nothing." The expression occurs elsewhere in the Gospels exclusively on the lips of demons who strongly oppose Jesus (see Matt. 8:29 pars.; Mark 1:24 par.).

18. So Keener (1993: 268), perhaps following Derrett (1970: 235).

19. Williams (1997: 685–86) comments that there is "no indication that Mary enters the public space of the main dining room where the men are feasting, or that Jesus enters the private space of the women in the bridegroom's house. Some transitional space near a door or porch is the most likely physical location for this private and discreet interaction, as well as for storing the water jars."

20. Williams (1997: 686) makes the interesting suggestion that Jesus had been "off doing his own thing" in 1:29–51 and "that when he meets his family at Cana, his mother sees the opportunity to remind her wayward son of his duty as head of the family."

21. Compare 19:26; the NIV softens Jesus' address by translating the phrase as "dear woman," but there is no equivalent for "dear" in the original. Note the change in the TNIV to "mother" (the footnote says, "Or *Woman*; the Greek term does not denote any disrespect").

22. See 4:21; 20:13, 15; cf. Matt. 15:28; Luke 13:12; 22:57. Beasley-Murray (1999: 34) cites Josephus, *Ant.* 17.4.2 §74, as evidence that the address "woman" may be affectionate (but there it is ὦ γύναι).

23. See Wallace (1996: 150–51), who suggests that the statement makes use of the dative of possession, rendering it "What do we have in common?" Williams (1997: 688) paraphrases, "What concern is that (the shortage of wine) to me and to you? That is the groom's problem, why should you and I get involved?"

As OT parallels make clear, the phrase always distances two parties and frequently carries a reproachful connotation.[24] This suggests that Jesus here is issuing a fairly sharp rebuke to Mary (cf. Matt. 12:46–50), similar to his rebuke of Peter when he failed to understand the nature of Jesus' calling (cf. Matt. 16:23).[25] Alternatively, Jesus advises his mother that he had already decided to help and that he would do so in the manner and at the time of his own choosing rather than in response to her prompting (cf. 2 Kings 3:13; see Derrett 1970: 240–41; Beasley-Murray 1999: 35).[26]

The phrase "my time has not yet come" constitutes an internal prolepsis intended to alert the reader to anticipate the arrival of Jesus' time at a later point in the narrative (12:23, 27; 13:1; 17:1; see Carson 1991: 171; cf. Maccini 1996: 104–6).[27] In the framework of the entire Gospel, Jesus' ὥρα (hōra, time) refers to the moment at which God is fully glorified in him: the hour of his death, which for John constitutes also the moment of Jesus' exaltation (his "lifting up" [3:14; 8:28; 12:32]). In the present instance, Jesus does not want to be forced to a public manifestation of his identity on another's terms. Later, Jesus' brothers similarly urge Jesus to make himself known publicly, failing to perceive that the time (7:6, 8: καιρός, kairos) to do so had not yet come, and attempts to arrest Jesus fail for the same reason (7:30; 8:20).

Jesus' solution to the apparent quandary is to perform a miracle "behind the scenes." His timing is perfect, and the host is spared any embarrassment. By acting discreetly, Jesus avoids stealing the spotlight from the groom and his bride, to whom it rightfully belongs. Indeed, "the guest who was not likely to contribute any money, whose fellow-guests were likely to be expensive to entertain, gave the most valuable present of all: valuable for its quality, its quantity, its timeliness, and its non-reciprocating character" (Derrett 1970: 243).

Despite her son's cool response, Jesus' mother is not to be deterred.   **2:5**
Though she realizes that Jesus will do what he thinks best, she also expects that he will act on her behalf. Though she does not have authority over Jesus, she does express her faith (Ridderbos 1997: 106; cf. Carson 1991: 173; Moloney 1998: 68). The fact that Mary is able to give instructions to the servants may indicate that she was helping the bridegroom's mother with the preparation of dishes. The wording of

24. See Judg. 11:12; 2 Sam. 16:10; 1 Kings 17:18; 2 Kings 3:13; 2 Chron. 35:21. See Maccini (1996: 100–102), who concludes that Jesus is attempting to separate himself from his mother. Keener (2003: 505–6) likewise views 2:4 in terms of distancing.

25. Adducing the Petrine parallel, Maccini (1996: 102–4) calls Jesus' words to Mary here a "stern reprimand."

26. See also the lengthy note in Morris 1995: 159 n. 24.

27. For a list of the instances of "hour" in John's Gospel, see Keener 2003: 507.

Mary's instructions to the servants appears to constitute an allusion to Pharaoh's words to the Egyptians to go to Joseph and to "do what he tells you" (Gen. 41:55). Just as Joseph had provided famine relief, Jesus would be able to find a way out of the present dilemma. Jesus' mother takes what sounded like a sharp rebuke as an indication that Jesus is ready to help; her instructions to the servants express complete confidence.[28]

2:6 The mention of six stone water jars is one of several features of this account that appear to reflect eyewitness testimony; it is the kind of detail someone who witnessed the event might have remembered (Deines 1993: 274). The jars stood *there*: this means either in the dining room itself (Deines 1993: 274) or, perhaps more likely, in a passage near the courtyard where the well would be (Williams 1997: 685–86). There were *six* jars: in light of the significance that the number seven has for John, the number six may connote imperfection as falling one short of the perfect number seven (Moloney 1998: 72; note also that Jesus has the servants fill the jars *to the top*).[29] The jars were made of *stone*: this was because stone was not itself considered to contract uncleanness (Reich 1995; cf. Deines 1993: 29–34; Thomas 1991b: 162–65). For readers unfamiliar with Palestinian Jewish custom, the narrator further adds the explanatory aside that these jars were there "in keeping with the cleansing rituals of the Jews." This may have involved the washing of certain utensils used at the wedding and the washing of the guests' hands (cf. Mark 7:2–5; more broadly, John 3:25; see Deines 1993: 247–75, esp. 274).

Each jar held from twenty to thirty gallons. The original text has "two to three μετρηταί" (*metrētai*, measures), with one μετρητής equaling roughly ten gallons.[30] This adds up to a total of 120 to 180 gallons for all six jars combined. A large number of wedding guests must be accommodated for the course of an entire week of festivities. "The fact that there were servants, and more than one, indicates that the family was in at least comfortable if not opulent circumstances" (L. Abbott 1879:

---

28. In the context of John's theology, Mary's actions nonetheless seem to be characterized by a certain amount of ambiguity. On the one hand, she clearly expects Jesus to find a way to help (which does not necessarily mean that she expects him to do a miracle). If Joseph was dead by then, Mary, as a widow, would have relied on the labors and resourcefulness of Jesus, her firstborn (as the Synoptics indicate, Jesus had taken up Joseph's trade of a craftsman [Matt. 13:55; Mark 6:3]). On the other hand, Mary is shown to share in the "misunderstanding" motif that pervades the entire Gospel: she fails to see that Jesus' "time" has not yet come.

29. Though this is denied by most commentators (e.g., Morris 1995: 160–61; Barrett 1978: 191; Carson 1991: 174; R. Brown 1966: 100; Schnackenburg 1990: 1.332).

30. Cf. 1 Esdr. 8:20; Bel 3 (Theodotion); BDAG 643 further lists several inscriptions and papyri. See also Deines (1993: 28–29), who concludes that a μετρητής amounted to approximately thirty-nine liters. Schnelle (1996: 369, referring to Deines) adds up the total to about six hundred liters.

30; cf. Deines 1993: 25 n. 39). Beyond this, the evangelist probably seeks to indicate the abundance of Jesus' messianic provision.[31] The mention of Jewish purification (required by the law) may subtly reinforce the contrast drawn by the evangelist between the law given through Moses (1:17) and the new messianic provision by Jesus (Schlatter [1948: 69] cites 13:10).

Filling the jars with water (to the top) proves the impossibility of de- **2:7–8** ception or fraud (Morris 1995: 161). Apparently, the jars were at least partially empty, which may be significant in terms of John's subliminal message regarding contemporary Judaism (Deines 1993: 369). Jesus must have known that using the jars for a purpose other than ritual would temporarily defile them, but he puts meeting the need of the hour first (cf. 4:7–9). Somewhere between 2:7 and 2:8, Jesus must have turned the water into wine, because here the servants are told to draw some water (or so they thought) and to bring it to the "master of the banquet."[32]

The term ἀντλέω (*antleō*, draw out) frequently refers to drawing from a well (cf. John 4:7, 15 [the only other NT occurrences]). It therefore has been suggested that the servants did not take some of the water from the jars, but drew from a separate well. However, Dio Chrysostom, a first-century A.D. writer, uses the same term to refer to the "draining of wine casks" (*Orations* 45.11), which indicates that the verb used here does not necessarily refer to the drawing of water *from a well* (Morris 1995: 161; contra Carson 1991: 174, following Westcott 1908: 1.84). We

31. So, for example, Ridderbos 1997: 107; Morris 1995: 162; Carson 1991: 174; Beasley-Murray 1999: 35; R. Brown 1966: 105; Kruse 2003: 94–95. Ridderbos (1997: 108) cites OT allusions to the abundance of wine in the new age (Gen. 49:11; Isa. 25:6; Amos 9:13–14; Jer. 31:12–14; see also Joel 3:18). Keener (2003: 512) suggests a (proleptic) connection between the abundant "measure" of water turned into wine in 2:6 and the unlimited provision of the Spirit in 3:34.

32. The performance of the miracle is not actually narrated. For the Johannine pattern of implying movement without actually narrating it, see also 5:10, where the Jewish leaders challenging the healed lame man appear out of nowhere; 5:17 and 5:19, where Jesus is shown to respond to charges never made explicit; 6:10, where compliance with Jesus' command to have the people sit down is assumed but not stated; 6:59, where reference is made to Jesus' teaching in the synagogue in Capernaum though his arrival there has not previously been narrated; 9:7, where the movements of the man born blind are traced while Jesus fades from view; 11:16, where Thomas exhorts his fellow disciples to join him in going to Judea to die with Jesus, with the ensuing verse recording the group's arrival, but no reference being made to the actual departure or journey; 11:44, where the reader has to assume that some of the bystanders comply with Jesus' directive to take Lazarus's graveclothes off and let him go (note the shift signaled in both 11:16 and 11:44); 12:20, where the Greeks are shown to arrive, but their subsequent departure is not mentioned; Jesus' hearing before Pilate, where there are certain gaps in the narration of these two characters' movements (e.g., 19:5, 9); and 20:11, where Mary stands outside the tomb crying, without previous record of her approach. See Kellum 2005: 223–30, esp. 229, where he cites R. Brown 1966: 315.

therefore may assume that the servants were drawing water (or, as it turned out, wine) from the jars that had just been filled "to the top" (so, rightly, Keener 2003: 511).

The role of "master of the banquet" (ἀρχιτρίκλινος, *architriklinos*) was a position of honor, with one of the master's primary duties being the regulation of the distribution of wine. Sirach 32:1–2 (ca. 180 B.C.) gives instructions to those who are made "master of the feast" (ἡγούμενος, *hēgoumenos*). The position may represent an adaptation of the Greco-Roman "ruler of the feast" called a *symposiarch*, though differences may apply. Apparently, the "master of the banquet" did not join the wedding party at the table but rather, as a headwaiter in charge of catering, supervised the serving of food and drink, with several servants under him carrying out his orders. He may also have served as "master of ceremonies" (Aus 1998: 15–17).[33]

2:9–10 Now the focus shifts from the large quantity of the wine (six jars of two to three "measures" each, filled to the top [2:6–7]) to its superior quality (Morris 1995: 162–63; Ridderbos 1997: 107). Apparently, it was customary to serve the best wine first, when the wedding guests could still appreciate the taste of good wine before they had had too much to drink. The unsuspecting "master of the banquet" constitutes an independent witness to the occurrence of a miracle (Ridderbos 1997: 107–8; Schnackenburg 1990: 1.333; Barrett 1978: 193).[34] The touch of irony (underscored by the fact that the bridegroom never speaks; see Moloney 1998: 72–73) further highlights the wine's remarkable quality.

The emphasis on the excellent quality of the wine produced by Jesus coheres with John's customary emphasis on the extraordinary nature of Jesus' works. Thus, Jesus will raise the temple that was built forty-six years ago in only three days (2:20). He not only cures the royal official's son but does so long-distance, a highly unusual way of working miracles (4:50–53). He does not merely heal a lame man, but one who has been an invalid for thirty-eight years (5:5). He feeds the crowds from a supply of only five small barley loaves and two small fish, when it would have taken eight months' wages just for each person even to have one bite (6:7, 9). Jesus does not merely give sight to a man gone blind, but one who has been blind from birth (9:2). And he does not merely raise a dead man, but one who has been dead for four days (11:17), one day past the day when his spirit left him, according to contemporary Jewish belief, and his corpse exudes a stench (11:39).

33. Schlatter (1948: 70) takes the presence of a "master of the banquet" as indication of a well-to-do family (also citing 12:3).

34. Ridderbos (1997: 107–8) rightly notes that the master of the banquet's ignorance is not intended to portray him as a symbol for unbelieving Israel. R. Brown (1966: 107) makes the dubious suggestion that the man epitomizes blindness vis-à-vis wisdom.

In the end, Jesus has responded to the need of the hour (as communicated to him by his mother) in an amazing way (thus providing an early glimpse of his messianic identity), while still remaining in the background: his time had not yet come.[35] Only Jesus' mother, the master of the banquet, the servants, the bridegroom, and Jesus' disciples knew; there is no hint that the other wedding guests realized what Jesus had done. It may be surmised that the wedding festivities continued undisturbed. On this final day of his first week of ministry, Jesus the Messiah had provided his followers with his first sign.[36]

The present statement concludes John's account of Jesus' "first sign," selected by the evangelist to persuade his readers of Jesus' messianic identity (cf. 20:30–31). "First" (ἀρχή, archē) may also be translated "beginning" or "primary" (cf. 1:1; see Morris 1995: 163 n. 41; Carson 1991: 175; Barrett 1978: 193; Schlatter 1948: 72).[37] "Cana of Galilee" provides an *inclusio* with 2:1 (Carson 1991: 175) and serves to authenticate the just-narrated event (Morris 1995: 163).

2:11

"Revealed his glory" harks back to the prologue (1:14, 18). It surely is significant that this revelation of God's glory in Jesus consists not in a spectacular display of power, but in a quiet, behind-the-scenes work that remained largely unnoticed and impacted only a select few (cf. the temptation narratives in the Synoptics). It is in Jesus' humanity that God's glory is revealed. Moreover, this revelation culminates the history of God's dealings with his people in OT times, fulfilling prophetic symbolism and predictions and lending Jesus' work an end-time, definitive dimension that sets it apart from previous figures, servants, and spokespersons of God. The messianic age commonly was thought to be the period when God would reveal his glory.[38]

Jesus' first followers continue to show early signs of receptivity to Jesus' self-revelation (see 1:35–51), in contrast to the following responses of the Jewish leaders (2:18, 20) and the people of Jerusalem (2:23–25), including Nicodemus (see commentary at 3:1–15). Perhaps significantly, there is no mention of the impact that the sign had on the master of the banquet, the servants, and the bridegroom, or even Jesus' mother. Though benefiting from Jesus' physical provision, the wedding guests were untouched by Jesus' messianic self-revelation. The lack of reference to faith on the part of Jesus' mother may also be telling, especially since she is the focus of the earlier portion of

---

35. Moloney (1998: 69) notes that the next time a bridegroom is mentioned in this Gospel, it is Jesus who is identified as the bridegroom by John the Baptist.

36. Beyond this, Morris (1995: 162) suggests that Jesus provided a magnificent gift to a needy couple, saving them from incurring a significant liability that they would not have been able to afford.

37. Keener (2003: 515) gives the sense of ἀρχή as "paradigmatic."

38. Cf. Ps. 97:6; 102:16; Isa. 60:1–2; Ps. Sol. 17:30–32; 1 Enoch 49:2; see R. Brown 1966: 104.

the narrative, and should caution against any undue focus on Mary as an ideal disciple.[39]

c. Return to Capernaum (2:12)

2:12 "After this" (μετὰ τοῦτο, *meta touto*; the same phrase recurs in 11:7, 11; 19:28) indicates transition from one narrative to another, marking sequence but not tight chronology (Ridderbos 1997: 114; Bultmann 1971: 121; Barrett 1978: 194).[40] "A short while" (more lit., "not many days" [οὐ πολλὰς ἡμέρας, *ou pollas hēmeras*]) suggests that it was not very long before the group left for the Passover feast (Carson 1991: 176). This transitional verse may seek to show that Jesus' ministry was itself still in a transitional stage in which he remained closely tied to his physical family, though he was beginning to gather disciples. According to the Fourth Evangelist, the beginnings of Jesus' ministry find him gradually emerging from his associations with John the Baptist and his family ties (Witherington 1995: 80).

Jesus "went down" from Cana to Capernaum, since Cana was located in the hill country and Capernaum was situated directly at the Sea of Galilee at a lower elevation (the site has been excavated: Tel-Hûm; see Loffreda, *NEAEHL* 1:291–95). In the interim between the wine miracle and his journey to Jerusalem, Jesus returns to Capernaum, his base for ministry (the town is mentioned elsewhere in John only in 4:46; 6:17, 24, 59). Capernaum, located on the northwest corner of the Sea of Galilee, was not far from Cana (about sixteen miles to the northeast) and could be reached easily in a day's journey (about six to eight hours).[41] After the imprisonment of John the Baptist, and after encountering strong opposition in his hometown of Nazareth, Jesus permanently moved to Capernaum (see Matt. 4:12–13; cf. Luke 4:28–31). Matthew even ties Jesus' taking up residence in Capernaum to the fulfillment of OT prophecy, calling it "his own town" (Matt. 9:1; cf. Mark 2:1), owing to the length and variety of his activities there (cf. Matt. 4:12–17).[42]

---

39. Carson (1991: 169) rightly notes that there is little contextual support for the notion that Mary is here presented as a mediatrix between humanity and Jesus (contra those who see Mary here as representative of the people [e.g., Brodie 1993: 174]). Witherington (1995: 79, 378, referring to Ashton) may read too much into John's presentation when he sees Mary here depicted as a fledgling disciple who later becomes an "archetypal female disciple." Ridderbos (1997: 108) likewise seems to overreach when he suggests that Mary is symbolic of believing Israel, which has eagerly awaited the coming of the Savior. Another dubious suggestion is made by Stibbe (1993: 44), who proposes that Jesus' use of γύναι may constitute an allusion to Gen. 3:15, "in which case she is to be seen as the New Eve in the New Creation of Jesus' ministry."

40. A similar expression (μετὰ ταῦτα) is found in 3:22; 5:1, 14; 6:1; 19:38; 21:1.

41. For general information, see Laughlin (1993) and Schlatter (1997: 111–12).

42. Cf. Matt. 8:5 par.; 11:23 par.; 17:24; Mark 1:21 par.; 9:33; Luke 4:23.

Jesus' mother is not mentioned again until 19:25–27, and his brothers are referred to only here and at 7:3–9. More properly, they are half-brothers, children of Mary and Joseph (Carson 1991: 176; Morris 1995: 165; Burge 2000: 93; against the traditional Roman Catholic interpretation that denies that Mary had other children besides Jesus).[43] "His disciples" (as in 2:2) probably refers to those mentioned in 1:35–51 (Carson 1991: 176; Morris 1995: 165). Jesus' disciples are featured elsewhere in 2:17, 22, but otherwise not until 3:22. Nevertheless, they are presupposed as witnesses throughout (Bultmann 1971: 123 n. 3).

43. Implied also in the statement in Luke 2:7 that Jesus was Mary's "firstborn."

3. One of Jesus' Jerusalem Signs: The Clearing of the Temple (2:13–22)

The Jerusalem temple was a symbol of Jewish national and religious identity.[1] The original Solomonic temple was destroyed by the Babylonians and later rebuilt by Zerubbabel. It was renovated by Herod just prior to Jesus' coming. Both OT and Second Temple literature express the expectation of the establishment of a new temple for the messianic age.[2] It is against this backdrop that Jesus' rather striking action of clearing the temple must be understood.[3] What may at first appear to be an impetuous outburst of uncontrolled anger is cast by John as an outflow of genuine spiritual zeal. Thus, Jesus is shown to typify the pronouncement of Ps. 69:9: "Zeal for your house will consume me" (quoted in John 2:17).

In part, Jesus' actions are directed against the subversion of religious worship into commerce (Mark 11:17 pars.; cf. Jer. 7:9–11). This constitutes an offense to God, who is personally associated with the temple.[4] His holiness and purity cannot tolerate the consistent defilement of "his house"—judgment is inevitable. In prophetic style, the temple clearing therefore represents a symbolic act conveying the inner meaning of Jesus' crucifixion and bodily resurrection,[5] by which he becomes the temple's replacement in the life and worship of his people (2:19–21).[6] Tragically, the very place where God's glory is to be revealed—the temple—becomes the site where his glory in Jesus is rejected by his people, the Jews (cf. 1:11, 14; 2:11; see Lieu 1999).

1. See the sidebar in Köstenberger 2002c: 30.
2. For example, Ezek. 40–44; 1 Enoch 90:28–36; Ps. Sol. 17:30; 4QFlor 1:1–13; see Schnelle 1996: 368.
3. Interpreters differ as to whether Jesus' clearing of the temple was designed to "cleanse" temple worship (cf. E. Sanders 1985: 61–71; Neusner 1989; Evans 1989). In any case, the major point of the temple clearing in John is that Jesus serves as the temple's replacement in the life of the messianic community.
4. Note the repeated phrase "this house, which bears my name" (Jer. 7:10, 11, 14).
5. C. Brown (1984) notes that the Jews' demand for a sign to justify Jesus' clearing of the temple corresponds to their challenge of Jesus' authority in the Synoptics, and Brown sees the miracles of Jesus as standing in the tradition of prophetic signs that embody Jesus' message and personal identity.
6. For a detailed discussion of the prophetic symbolism entailed by Jesus' clearing of the temple and the argument that this event should be considered the second sign recorded in John's Gospel, see Köstenberger 1995b.

Furthermore, in Jesus' day the temple had become a Jewish "nationalistic stronghold," a place where Gentile worship was obstructed.[7] This ran counter to the original Solomonic vision (cf. 1 Kings 8:41–43; see Evans 1997: esp. 437–40). According to the prophet Isaiah, God wanted his "house" to "be called a house of prayer *for all the nations*" (Isa. 56:7), not only Israel. By selling sacrificial animals and setting up their currency exchange in the court of the Gentiles, the outer court of the temple, the merchants in effect torpedoed Gentile worship in the only place where it was possible. And that is what flew in the face of God's, and Jesus', desire for the temple to be a place of worship not just for Israel, but for people from all the nations.[8]

   a. The setting (2:13)
   b. Jesus clears the temple (2:14–22)

Exegesis and Exposition

[13]And the Jewish Passover was near, and Jesus went up to Jerusalem. [14]And in the temple area he noticed some who were selling cattle and sheep and doves, and others sitting at moneychangers' tables, [15]and after having made a whip out of cords, he drove all out from the temple area, both sheep and cattle, and he scattered the coins of the moneychangers and overturned their tables. [16]And to those who sold doves he said, "Take these things away! Stop turning my Father's house into a market!" [17]His disciples remembered that it was written, "Zeal for your house will consume me." [18]So the Jewish leaders answered and said to him, "What sign will you show us to prove your authority to do these things?" [19]Jesus answered and said to them, "Destroy this temple, and I will raise it up again in three days." [20]Then the Jewish leaders said, "This temple was built forty-six years ago, and you will raise it up again in three days?" [21]But he had spoken about the temple of his body. [22]So when he had been raised from the dead, his disciples remembered that he had been saying this, and they believed the Scripture and the word Jesus had spoken.

a. The Setting (2:13)

John 2:13 introduces not only 2:14–22 (see additional note on 2:13–22) but also the entire account of Jesus' initial Jerusalem ministry up until 3:21 (Ådna 2000: 179). John mentions at least three Passovers: the first in

2:13

---

7. The term is used by Barrett (1975).

8. Evans (1989: 265–67, citing Eppstein 1964) concludes that Caiaphas may have been the first high priest to authorize the sale of sacrificial animals in the temple precincts (perhaps because of a quarrel with the Sanhedrin), which may have provoked Jesus' response. Eppstein places this quarrel at A.D. 30, which would be precisely the time at which, according to my reconstruction, Jesus cleared the temple (the spring of A.D. 30; but see the cautionary comments in Evans 1989: 266–67).

2:13, 23, the second in 6:4, and the third in 11:55; 12:1 (see chart below). The Passover was the most important Jewish feast, commemorating God's dramatic deliverance of the Jews from Egypt on the night of the exodus, when the death angel "passed over" the firstborn in homes whose doorposts had been marked with blood (see Exod. 12, esp. 12:14–16).[9] It was celebrated on the fourteenth day of the lunar month Nisan (full moon at the end of March or the beginning of April), which marked the beginning of the festive calendar.

The Passover was one of the three annual pilgrim feasts that all Jewish men were to celebrate in Jerusalem (Deut. 16:16).[10] Large numbers of worshipers from the outlying provinces of Palestine (Luke 2:41–42) and the Diaspora (Acts 2:5) filled the capital city (cf. Josephus, *J.W.* 2.1.3 §10). The present Passover, the first during Jesus' public ministry, probably took place on April 7, A.D. 30 (Hoehner 1977: 60).[11] John mentions two Passovers later in his Gospel (6:4; 11:55 = 12:1).[12] "Was near" (ἐγγύς, *engys*) is John's customary way of referring to the approaching of a festival (cf. 6:4; 7:2; 11:55). People went "up" to Jerusalem because it was situated at a higher elevation than Galilee and because it was the capital city (Carson 1991: 176; Barrett 1978: 197).

Jewish Festivals in John's Gospel[13]

Name of Festival	Reference in John	Time Celebrated
Passover	2:13, 23	April 7, A.D. 30
"A feast of the Jews"	5:1	October 21–28, A.D. 31?
Passover	6:4	April 13/14, A.D. 32
Tabernacles (Booths)	7:2	September 10–17, A.D. 32
Dedication (Hanukkah)	10:22	December 18–25, A.D. 32
Passover	11:55; 12:1	April 3, A.D. 33

9. The phrase "Jewish Passover" has caused some controversy. Barrett (1978: 197) conjectures that the phrase may presuppose the existence of a Christian Passover at the time of writing (so, earlier, Westcott 1908: 1.89; cf. Borchert 1996: 162). Schnackenburg (1991: 1.345) and Beasley-Murray (1999: 39) suggest that the evangelist or the church had stopped participating in the Jewish Passover. Witherington (1995: 86–87) notes that the phrase indicates a certain distance between the author and Judaism and at least a partial Gentile audience (similarly, Morris 1995: 169). Carson (1991: 176) thinks that "Jewish" refers to the Jews of Judea in contrast to Galileans and Diaspora Jews.

10. Although this was not always possible for those living at a distance from Jerusalem, Galileans were not so remote as to be prevented from attending regularly (Ferguson 1993: 521).

11. Contra Carson (1991: 176), who cites a probable date of around A.D. 28.

12. The unspecified festival in 5:1 is probably not a Passover.

13. For a general survey, see Wise, *DJG* 234–41.

b. Jesus Clears the Temple (2:14–22)

"Temple area" (ἱερόν, *hieron*), in distinction from the temple building $\quad$ **2:14**
proper (ναός, *naos*; see commentary at 2:20), generally denotes the area
surrounding the temple, that is, "the whole of the Temple precincts, including the various courts as well as the holy place" (Morris 1995: 169).[14]
In the present instance, this probably refers to the outermost court, the
court of the Gentiles (Morris 1995: 170; Schnackenburg 1990: 1.346;
Beasley-Murray 1999: 37 n. b). Gentiles were barred from the inner
court of the temple.[15] The Jerusalem temple was a symbol of Jewish
national and religious identity.[16]

Two groups of people are portrayed as the target of Jesus' anger:
the sellers of cattle, sheep, and doves, and the moneychangers seated
at their tables. Those selling cattle and sheep are driven out by Jesus,
including their animals; those selling doves are told to leave; and the
moneychangers' tables are overturned and their coins scattered. The
message is one of judgment; Jesus' fury is unleashed against those who
defile the pure worship of God (compare the way in which the account
of Jesus' clearing of the temple is placed between Jesus' cursing of the
fig tree and its withering—a sign of judgment—in Mark 11:12–25 [cf.
Matt. 21:12–22]; note also Jesus' prediction of the destruction of the
temple in Matt. 24:2 pars.).

The sale of sacrificial animals rendered a valuable service to those
who traveled to the Passover from afar, enabling them to buy the animals on site rather than having to lead or carry them for long distances.
Cattle and sheep were needed for various kinds of offerings (e.g., Exod.
20:24; 22:30; 24:5; Lev. 1:3–9; 4:2–21; 5:7; 8:2; 22:21; Num. 7:6–9). Doves
were required for the purification of women (Lev. 12:6; Luke 2:22–24),
especially if they were poor (Lev. 12:8; cf. 5:7), the cleansing of those
with certain kinds of skin diseases (Lev. 14:22), and other purposes
(Lev. 15:14, 29).

The moneychangers likewise rendered a service: visitors to Jerusalem needed their money exchanged into the local currency because
the temple tax, paid by every conscientious Jewish male of twenty years
or more, had to be paid in that currency. The coinage of choice was Tyrian, owing to its high silver content (*m. Bek.* 8.7; see Carson 1991: 178;
Schnackenburg 1990: 1.346 n. 13).[17] The annual half-shekel equaled half
a Tyrian stater or tetradrachm, so that two Jews often joined together to

---

14. Cf. 5:14; 7:14, 28; 8:20, 59; 10:23; 11:56; 18:20.

15. See the Greek inscription (discovered in 1870) cited in Köstenberger 2002c: 29; cf.
Geva, *NEAEHL* 2:744; Millard 1997: 243. See also *m. Kelim* 1.8; Josephus, *Ant.* 15.11.4
§417; *J.W.* 5.5.1 §193; 6.2.4 §125.

16. See the sidebar in Köstenberger 2002c: 30.

17. On the temple tax, see Exod. 30:13–14; 2 Chron. 24:5, 9; Neh. 10:32; Matt. 17:24–27;
cf. Josephus, *Ant.* 3.8.1 §§193–96.

pay the tax in one coin (cf. Matt. 17:27). The temple tax was collected in Jerusalem from 25 Adar on, the lunar month preceding Nisan.[18] There may have been resistance to paying the annual temple tax, owing to the use of Tyrian currency and the annual requirement.[19]

2:15–16 In 2:14–15, the evangelist records Jesus' actions; not until 2:16 does Jesus speak (Moloney 1998: 77). The merchants,[20] sheep, and cattle, Jesus drove away with a whip (Morris 1995: 171).[21] The doves (which, being in cages, could not be driven out directly), Jesus ordered to be taken away (Moloney 1998: 77). The primary issue was not simply the existence of merchants and moneychangers or even the fact that they charged inflated prices for their services (though that was bad enough—note Jesus' charge at the clearing of the temple recorded in the Synoptics that the merchants and moneychangers had made the temple "a den of robbers" [Matt. 21:13 pars.]). Rather, Jesus faulted the merchants for disrupting Gentile worship in the only place that was open to them—the so-called court of the Gentiles—which was insensitive at best and evidence of religious arrogance at worst.[22] The temple establishment had amassed excessive wealth in Jesus' day, which made the merchants and moneychangers part of a system that exploited the poor for the purported goal of beautifying and administering the affairs of the temple.[23] The sale of sacrificial animals and money exchange should have been facilitated near the temple rather than within its walls. This is exactly

18. Cf. *m. Šeqal.* 1.3: "On the 25th thereof [the month of Adar] they [the tables of the moneychangers] were set up in the Temple." On Tyrian shekels, see Richardson 1992: 514–18. On the half-shekel offering, see Liver 1963.

19. Several commentators also mention that Tyrian coinage would have been preferred because it did not bear effigies (Moloney 1998: 76; Beasley-Murray 1999: 38 n. c; R. Brown 1966: 115; Borchert 1996: 163). However, this is disputed by Murphy-O'Connor (2000: 47, referring to Ben-David 1969), who cites evidence that Tyrian shekels "carried the head of the god Melkart (or Herakles) on the obverse and a Tyrian (Ptolemaic) eagle on the reverse with the inscription 'Tyre the holy and inviolable.'" Murphy-O'Connor also notes the minting of Jewish shekels carrying the legend "shekel of Israel/Jerusalem [is/the] holy" at the onset of the Jewish war in A.D. 66 (pp. 47–48, citing Schürer 1973–79: 1.605), and he points to the Qumran interpretation of a one-time requirement in 4Q159 frag. 1, col. 2, lines 6–7 (p. 49).

20. So Ridderbos 1997: 116; Moloney 1998: 81; Barrett 1978: 197; Witherington 1995: 87; contra TNIV.

21. Witherington (1995: 87) contends that in light of the large area—the outer court measured 300 by 450 meters—it is probable that some, but not all, were driven out. Many commentators (e.g., Borchert 1996: 164; Schlatter 1948: 75) mention that weapons (such as clubs) were not allowed in the temple courts.

22. See commentary at 2:14. See also Barrett 1975b; Evans 1997. On Gentile worship at the Jerusalem temple, see the appendix on Gentile participation in worship at Jerusalem in Schürer 1973–79: 2.309–13. Neusner (1989) adds another possible reason: the understanding that the daily whole offering, which was financed by the temple tax, provided atonement and expiation of sin.

23. Moreover, the use of Tyrian shekels likely involved religious compromise, if indeed these coins bore the image of the Tyrian god Melkart (P. Casey 1997: esp. 313–15).

what had been the case earlier in Israel's history when the animal merchants had set up shop across the Kidron Valley on the slopes of the Mount of Olives.

Jesus' temple action conjures up Zechariah's prophecy that "on that [final] day there will no longer be merchants in the house of the Lord Almighty" (14:21). It also calls to mind the words of Malachi that on the coming day of judgment, "suddenly the Lord . . . will come to his temple," so that people may once again offer acceptable sacrifices to the Lord (3:1, 3) (Carson 1991: 179; Hiers 1971: 86–89). "Stop turning" implies that the action is currently happening and must cease (Wallace 1996: 724; cf. Morris 1995: 171 n. 72). The first order issued by Jesus ("Take these things away!") is directed toward the sellers of doves; the second is addressed to all present (Moloney 1998: 81).

Jesus' clearing of the temple stirs in his disciples the memory of the righteous sufferer of Ps. 69:9 (compare John 2:16, "my Father's *house*," with Ps. 69:9, "zeal for your *house*").[24] Although God's people were warned against "zeal without knowledge" (Prov. 19:2; cf. Rom. 10:2), religious zeal was an important part of Jewish piety. In the OT, Phinehas is promised a covenant of a lasting priesthood "because he was zealous for the honor of his God" (Num. 25:13). In fact, God himself is shown to be zealous for his holy name (Isa. 59:17; Ezek. 39:25).

2:17

In the second century B.C., the Maccabees revived Jewish nationalistic fervor, while the Qumran community as well as the Pharisees were concerned for the religious state of Judaism. First-century Palestine was rife with religious as well as nationalistic zeal (Heard, *DJG* 688–98; Hengel 1989b). The Pharisees were concerned for the religious state of Judaism, while the Zealots played an important part in the rebellion against Rome in A.D. 66–70. Particularly notorious were the Sicarii (from Latin *sica*, dagger), religious terrorists who murdered people in broad daylight in an effort to destabilize the political situation in Roman-occupied Palestine.[25]

One of Jesus' disciples is nicknamed Simon "the Zealot" (Luke 6:15; Acts 1:13) for his religious zeal. Paul encourages believers to "never be lacking in zeal" (Rom. 12:11). Jesus' zeal, righteous rather than blindly nationalistic, was so great that it would "consume" him. This refers to his death, which would bring life to the world (cf. John 6:51; see Ridderbos 1997: 117; Schnackenburg 1990: 1.347).

---

24. The LXX reads "has consumed me" (Moloney 1998: 77). Unlike in 2:22 and 12:16, the present reference does not refer to the postresurrection period, but to the actual situation (so Ridderbos 1997: 116; Carson 1991: 180; R. Brown 1966: 115; Schnackenburg 1990: 1.347; Barrett 1978: 198; contra Witherington 1995: 88; Bultmann 1971: 122).

25. See the appendix on the Sicarii and the Zealots in Schürer 1973–79: 2.598–606.

2:18–19 Whereas the disciples accepted Jesus' actions (Moloney 1998: 78), the Ἰουδαῖοι (*Ioudaioi*, Jewish leaders) demanded evidence of Jesus' right to clear the temple (Ridderbos 1997: 117; Carson 1991: 180). Ἰουδαῖοι refers to the Jewish leaders, not the merchants (Barrett 1978: 199; Ridderbos 1997: 117; R. Brown 1966: 115; Bultmann 1971: 124), specifically, the temple authorities or members of the Sanhedrin (Carson 1991: 180). It was common for people to ask for proof of a prophet's divine legitimation (note, e.g., Matt. 12:38; 16:1); this seems to be the sense in which the Jews are using the term "sign" (Barrett 1978: 199; Moloney 1998: 81). Beyond this, the Messiah, too, was expected to perform "signs" (cf. John 7:31; see Morris 1995: 173–74).

Though Jesus was asked by the Jews several times to give them a sign (Matt. 12:38–39 pars.; 16:1 pars.; Luke 23:8), he never acceded to their demand (Ridderbos 1997: 117; Moloney 1998: 81). In the present case, Jesus proceeds instead to elaborate on the significance of the act that he had just performed (similarly, John 6:30; cf. Matt. 21:23–27 pars.)—the clearing of the temple (Köstenberger 1995b). True to the Jews' spiritual blindness, they had missed the sign performed right before their very eyes (Carson 1991: 181). The Jews demanded a sign (in the sense of divine legitimation); Jesus had just given it, thus asserting his messianic authority (Dodd 1953: 209). Moreover, for the evangelist, the symbolism underlying Jesus' act (including his accompanying pronouncement) anticipates Jesus' death and resurrection and the replacement of Jewish temple worship with faith in Jesus as Messiah.

Jesus' response recorded here, "Destroy this temple, and I will raise it up again in three days," provides the background for the testimony given at Jesus' trial as recorded in the Synoptics (Mark 14:58; Matt. 26:61; cf. Acts 6:13–14; see Carson 1991: 181; Morris 1995: 174; Ridderbos 1997: 118).[26] The phrase "in three days" (i.e., "a point three days hence") harks back to OT symbolic language (e.g., Exod. 19:11; Hos. 6:2) (Jeremias 1971: 227 and n. 18). If spoken several years prior to the trial, it is more readily understandable how the witnesses could not agree on the precise wording of Jesus' statement (Morris 1995: 168). Jesus' word for "temple" here is ναός (*naos*), referring to the temple building proper, rather than ἱερόν (*hieron*; cf. 2:14–15), denoting the temple area (see commentary at 2:14 and at 2:20–21). The Jews (in 2:20) and the evangelist (in 2:21) use the same word literally to refer to the temple building and figuratively

---

26. The terminology in 2:19 is similar to, but not identical with, Mark 14:58: John 2:19 uses λύω, ἐν + dative, and ἐγείρω; Mark 14:58 has καταλύω, διά + genitive, and οἰκοδομέω; τὸν ναὸν τοῦτον is shared. But note the use of ἐν + dative in Mark 15:29 (and Matt. 27:40), which leads Schlosser (1990: 400–402) to conclude that John depends on Mark in his account of the clearing of the temple. However, see the thorough analysis by Ådna (2000: 179–89), who comes to the opposite conclusion, that neither Mark nor Matthew/Luke served as literary sources for John's account of the clearing of the temple. Jeremias (1971: 221) notes that both ἐν + dative and διά + genitive are based on the Semitic ל.

to Jesus' body respectively. "Destroy" probably combines a (mild) conditional force with that of an imperative (Wallace 1996: 490).

The Synoptics mention Jesus' reference to "the sign of Jonah," who was **2:20–21** in the belly of the fish for three days and three nights (Matt. 12:40 pars.; cf. Jon. 1:17).[27] Jesus repeatedly predicted his death and subsequent resurrection "after three days" (e.g., Matt. 16:21 pars.). As elsewhere in the Gospel, misunderstanding results from a mistakenly literal construal of Jesus' words (which have a spiritually appraised, symbol-laden theological meaning; see Ridderbos 1997: 117; Schnackenburg 1990: 1.350). The pronoun "you" (σύ, *sy*) is added insolently (Moloney 1998: 79) and is emphatic (Morris 1995: 176), denoting an attitude of challenge and disrespect.

The TNIV rendering, "It has taken forty-six years to build this temple," suggests, almost certainly incorrectly, that the temple building was still under reconstruction at the time of the temple clearing by Jesus. This was true of the temple grounds at large, but not of the temple building itself. As historical records indicate, Herod the Great (reigned 37–4 B.C.) began the project of restoring the temple building proper (ναός, *naos*, the term used here) in the eighteenth year of his reign, 20/19 B.C. (Josephus, *Ant.* 15.11.1 §380),[28] with completion eighteen months later in 18/17 B.C. (*Ant.* 15.11.6 §421). Forty-six years later is A.D. 29/30 (there was no year 0), which places Jesus' first Passover in the spring of A.D. 30 (Wallace 1996: 560).[29] The restoration of the entire temple area (ἱερόν, *hieron*; see commentary at 2:14) was not completed until A.D. 63/64 under Herod Agrippa II and governor Albinus (*Ant.* 20.9.7 §219), shortly before its destruction by the Roman army in the Jewish war of A.D. 66–70 (cf. Schürer 1973–79: 1.308–9). The phrase "forty-six years" is in the dative (locative), not the accusative (durative), which also speaks against the rendering adopted by the TNIV. Likewise, it is unlikely that the aorist passive "was built" refers to an action still in progress (Wallace 1996: 560–61).[30]

27. C. Brown (1984: 321) says that Jesus' response in 2:19–22 corresponds to the sign of Jonah in Matthew and Luke.

28. In *J.W.* 1.21.1 §401, Josephus dates the beginning of the restoration of the temple in the fifteenth year of Herod's reign (i.e., three years earlier, in 23/22 B.C.), which may constitute an erroneous reference or indicate an earlier point in time when materials first started to be gathered.

29. Assuming a three-year ministry, we see that this puts the crucifixion at A.D. 33. This reading of John 2:20, and a date of A.D. 30 for Jesus' first Passover and the temple clearing, were advocated by Badcock (1935: 40–41). See also P. Maier (1968: 4–5); Hoehner (1977: 38–43; followed by Laney 1992: 72; cf. Hoehner, *DJG* 119); Humphreys and Waddington (1992: 351). MacAdam (1999: 31–33) concurs, but believes that this was Jesus' final Passover and that the Fourth Evangelist has transposed the temple clearing to the beginning of Jesus' ministry. Zahn (1921: 126–27 n. 23) comes close, arriving at the year A.D. 28 or 29.

30. The translation adopted here was adopted long ago by Badcock (1935: 40–41): "'Forty and six years was this temple in building' (A.V. and R.V.). . . . This is an impossible

The logic underlying Jesus' statement may become clearer when his opponents' question is understood as containing an ellipsis: "This temple was built forty-six years ago—and has stood all that time ever since then—and you want us to destroy it just so you can raise it up again in three days?" To be sure, they had demanded a sign, but to ask them to tear down the temple just so Jesus could provide the requested sign by rebuilding it within three days—an obvious impossibility—was clearly beyond the pale of what they were willing to do (Carson 1991: 181). Yet, as the evangelist duly notes, Jesus actually spoke of the "temple" of his body (a genitive of apposition [Wallace 1996: 98]), a veiled reference to his crucifixion and subsequent resurrection.[31]

In fact, the only other use of σῶμα (sōma, body) in John's Gospel is for the dead body of Jesus (19:38, 49 [including the other two who were crucified]; 20:12) (Schnackenburg 1990: 1.357; Barrett 1978: 201). As Barrett (1978: 201) notes, "The human body of Jesus was the place where a unique manifestation of God took place and consequently became the only true Temple, the only centre of true worship" (cf. 1:14, 18, 51). As to the Gentiles later on (12:20–36), Jesus' answer to the Jews is, in essence, "Not yet." Their unbelief currently kept them from discerning the true significance of Jesus' signs. As in Jesus' parables recorded in the Synoptics, the "mysteries of the kingdom" were not understood by those outside the circle of Jesus' close followers. This is true even subsequent to the resurrection: Jesus will show himself only to his own, not to the unbelieving world (14:22).

2:22 "So when" (ὅτε οὖν, hote oun) is a phrase unique to the NT and absent from the LXX, occurring a total of nine times in John's Gospel.[32] As elsewhere in the NT, the Father is the implied agent in Jesus' resurrection (cf. Acts 2:24, 32; 17:30–31; Gal 1:1). The disciples believed the Scripture and the words that Jesus had spoken. The Scripture passage in view may be Ps. 69:9, as in John 2:17; "Jesus' word" probably refers to the saying in 2:19. Though this is not made explicit here, the disciples' later understanding is aided by the Holy Spirit (cf. 7:39; 20:22; see Carson 1991: 183; Barrett 1978: 201; Morris 1995: 180).

---

translation on two counts; the substantive is in the dative of a point, and not duration, of time; and the verb is in the aorist and not in the imperfect, so the only possible translation is: 'This temple (or sanctuary) was built (before you were born) forty and six years ago.'" Badcock also, rightly in my opinion, dates the current Passover to A.D. 30 and the crucifixion to A.D. 33.

31. For a list of misunderstandings in John's Gospel, see Culpepper 1983: 161–62 (his list includes 2:19–21; 3:3–5; 4:10–15, 31–34; 6:32–35, 51–53; 7:33–36; 8:21–22, 31–35, 51–53, 56–58; 11:11–15, 23–25; 12:32–34; 13:36–38; 14:4–6, 7–9; 16:16–19). Culpepper (1983: 35) also identifies explanatory comments on the statements of Jesus by the evangelist (2:21; 6:6, 71; 7:39; 8:27; 12:33; 13:11; 18:32; 21:19, 23).

32. John 2:22; 4:45; 6:24; 13:12, 31; 19:6, 8, 30; 21:15.

Additional Note

2:13–22. John narrates a temple clearing at the beginning of Jesus' ministry; the Synoptics place a similar account at the inception of Jesus' final week in Jerusalem, just prior to his crucifixion (Mark 11:15–19 pars.).[33] The majority of commentators consider this to be an instance where John rearranges Synoptic material, following a topical rather than chronological arrangement.[34] Alternatively, this may represent a "doublet," a certain type of event occurring more than once during Jesus' ministry.[35] On balance, the latter explanation appears more likely.[36] If so, Jesus cleared the temple twice, with John recording only the first instance, and the Synoptists only the second.[37]

33. P. Trudinger (1997: 329, citing Daube 1966b: 1–6) suggests that Jesus' clearing of the temple at the beginning of his ministry resembles Hezekiah's similar action (see 2 Chron. 29:3–5, 17; 30:1).

34. Cf. Ridderbos 1997: 115; Schnackenburg 1990: 1.344; Barrett 1978: 195; R. Brown 1966: 117; Witherington 1995: 85–86; Borchert 1996: 160; Bultmann 1971: 122; Beasley-Murray 1999: 38–39; Dodd 1963: 162; Lindars 1972: 135–37; Keener 2003: 518–19. Keener contends that it is historically implausible that Jesus would challenge the temple system by overturning tables and yet continue in public ministry for two or three years afterward, sometimes even visiting Jerusalem (though he notes that Jesus faces considerable hostility there when he does). On the contrary, an early temple cleansing accounts well for Jewish hostility toward Jesus early on (5:18), and Jesus' continuing in ministry for two or three more years is eminently plausible historically in light of Jesus' pattern of withdrawal (3:22; 6:15; 7:9–10; 8:59; 10:40) and his caution from the very inception of his ministry because his "time" has not yet come (2:4; 7:6). Borchert (1996: 160) contends that two temple clearings are "a historiographic monstrosity that has no basis in the texts of the Gospels." Kreitzer (1998: 100–101) claims that the evangelist followed the motto "When the details of history no longer serve the functions of the story—discard them." R. Brown (1966: 118) concludes that Jesus uttered some prophetic saying concerning the destruction of the temple on his first visit but actually cleansed the temple at the end of his ministry. Wallace (1996: 561 n. 20) notes that this would require a crucifixion date of A.D. 33.

35. Cf., e.g., Mark's inclusion of two feedings of the multitudes (6:30–44; 8:1–13).

36. Cf. Carson 1991: 177; 1984: 441; Morris 1995: 167; Laney 1992: 70; Westcott 1908: 1.96–97; Calvin 1959: 51; Köstenberger 1999a: 76–78. Carson (1991: 177, referring to Morris) notes that virtually all of John 1–5 (except for the sections on John the Baptist) is non-Synoptic material. Morris (1995: 167 n. 55) states that "there are practically no resemblances between the two narratives, apart from the central act"; only five words are shared. Other commentators holding this view are Luther, W. Hendriksen, and R. V. G. Tasker (Kreitzer 1998: 94).

37. A third possibility (held by only a few) is that there was only one clearing, at the beginning of Jesus' ministry, and John got it right (J. A. T. Robinson 1985: 127–31; Campbell 1982: 117). Finally, fourth, Buchanan (1991: 284) says, "Jesus never cleansed the temple at all but instead this event had been attributed to him from the necessity of the doctrines and messianic expectations" (cited in Ådna 2000: 21 n. 67).

4. Further Ministry in Jerusalem and Samaria (2:23–4:42)

John 1:19–2:11 presents Jesus' first week of public ministry, taking its point of departure from the ministry of John the Baptist and culminating in Jesus' "first sign" in Cana of Galilee. Jesus' first followers indicate why they chose to attach themselves to Jesus: they believe Jesus to be the Christ, the Son of God. Jesus is also identified as "God's lamb" (1:29, 36), who would provide substitutionary atonement for "the sin of the world," and as the place of superior revelation (1:50–51). Jesus' clearing of the temple constitutes another sign (2:18), this time in Jerusalem (cf. 2:23; 3:2), which portrays Jesus as the restorer of true worship to Israel and the replacement of the temple in the life of God's people. With this, the stage is set for Jesus' encounters with Nicodemus and the Samaritan woman.

As the following chart illustrates, the contrast between these two characters could hardly be more pronounced:[1]

	Nicodemus	**Samaritan woman**
Place	Jerusalem	Samaria
Time	night	noon
Occasion	planned visit	providential encounter
Sex	male	female
Ethnic group	Jew	Samaritan
Social status	high; ruler/teacher	low; immoral woman
Attitude	respectful but incredulous	from antagonistic to witness
Discourse	from dialogue to monologue	dialogue throughout
Jesus' message	must be born again	worship God in spirit and truth

---

1. This chart comparing and contrasting Jesus' encounters with Nicodemus and the Samaritan woman in John 3–4 is adapted from Dockery 1988: 128–29.

a. The "Teacher of Israel," Nicodemus (2:23–3:21)

The present section (see Ridderbos 1997: 122) narrates Jesus' Jerusalem ministry subsequent to his clearing of the temple at the occasion of the Jewish Passover. Though 2:23–25 is transitional, it serves as the introduction to the Nicodemus narrative (Beasley-Murray 1999: 47; Blomberg 1995: 5). Only in 3:22 are Jesus and his disciples shown to move to the Judean countryside, where they engage in baptismal ministry for some time before returning to Galilee via Samaria (4:3). In a broader sense, therefore, 2:23–3:36 may be regarded as a literary unit (Julian 2000).[1]

The Nicodemus narrative alternates three questions asked by the "teacher of Israel" (3:2, 4, 9 [the first being an implicit question]) and Jesus' answers (all of which begin, "Truly, truly, I say to you" [3:3, 5, 11]; see R. Brown 1966: 136). Jesus is still in Jerusalem (cf. 2:13, 23; see Moloney 1998: 90). Cotterell (1985; followed by Conway 1999: 96) notes how Jesus' change of topic (in what Cotterell calls his "complex repartee") challenges the fundamental premise of Nicodemus's own priority. Although Nicodemus accepted Jesus' alternative range of topics, he did so somewhat reluctantly and was only marginally cooperative in the ensuing conversation. The contributions made by Nicodemus to the dialogue steadily decrease in length (from twenty-four words in 3:2, to eighteen words in 3:4, to four words in 3:9, to zero words in 3:10); Jesus' contribution steadily increases. Nicodemus is gradually relegated to the background, moving from senior rabbi to obdurate student of more-than-rabbi Jesus (note the hint of impatience in Jesus' words "Do not be surprised," and of irony, if not reproach, in his reference to Nicodemus as "teacher of Israel").[2]

Regarding the final subunit in the present section, opinions differ as to where Jesus' reply to Nicodemus ends—3:13–15 must be by Jesus, who alone uses the term "Son of Man" in this Gospel (12:34 is no real exception)—and the evangelist's commentary begins.[3] Most

---

1. For a helpful defense of the literary unity of John 3, see Lee 1994: 37–38.

2. Conway (1999: 85) describes Nicodemus as an "opaque rather than transparent character" whose inner motives are not disclosed by the narrator. Cotterell (1985: 241) draws attention to the portrayal of Nicodemus in his humanity as a Pharisee who was "inclined to patronize" and was "human enough to sulk" when "pierced in the presence of his own students." Meeks (1972: 53) calls Nicodemus a "rather stupid disciple."

3. Moloney (1998: 90) and R. Brown (1966: 149) believe that Jesus' words continue through 3:21; Witherington (1995: 99) thinks that the evangelist takes over in 3:12, or at

likely, for three reasons, the transition takes place in 3:16 (note there the introductory phrase οὕτως γάρ [*houtōs gar*, for this]; so Carson 1991: 185, 203; Morris 1995: 202; Burge 2000: 113, 117–18; apparently, Borchert 1996: 180): (1) the cross is spoken of as past (contra R. Brown 1966: 149); (2) μονογενής (*monogenēs*, one-of-a-kind Son) is used in this Gospel only by the evangelist (but not Jesus; see Tovey 1997: 155–56), as are πιστεύω εἰς ὄνομα (*pisteuō eis onoma*, believe in the name [3:18]) and ποιέω τὴν ἀλήθειαν (*poieō tēn alētheian*, practice the truth [3:21]) (Morris 1995: 202 n. 73; Steele 1988: 51–58); (3) 3:19–21 most likely represents the evangelist's expansion of the "light-darkness" motif first sounded in the prologue (1:4–5, 8–9). In light of the overlapping terminology of 3:15 and 3:16–18, it appears that the latter verses constitute the evangelist's expansion on Jesus' words in 3:13–15 (cf. ὁ πιστεύων [*ho pisteuōn*, the one who believes] and ἔχῃ ζωὴν αἰώνιον [*echē zōēn aiōnion*, may have eternal life] in 3:15 and 3:16). A similar transition can be observed between 3:27–30 and 3:31–36.

i. Dubious belief in Jerusalem (2:23–25)
ii. Jesus' conversation with Nicodemus (3:1–15)
iii. The evangelist's exposition (3:16–21)

Exegesis and Exposition

[2:23]Now while he was in Jerusalem at the Passover festival, many believed in his name when they saw the signs he performed. [24]But Jesus, for his part, would not entrust himself to them because he knew them all [25]and did not need anyone's testimony concerning the human being. For he knew what was in a person.

[3:1]Now there was a man of the Pharisees by the name of Nicodemus, a member of the Jewish ruling council. [2]He came to him [Jesus] by night and said to him, "Rabbi, we know that you are a teacher who has come from God. For no one could perform the signs you are performing unless God were with him." [3]Jesus answered and said to him, "Truly, truly, I say to you, unless someone has been born from above, he cannot see the kingdom of God." [4]Nicodemus said to him, "How can anyone be born when he is old? He cannot enter his mother's womb a second time and be born, can he?" [5]Jesus answered, "Truly, truly, I say to you, unless someone has been born of water and spirit, he cannot enter the kingdom of God. [6]What is born of flesh is flesh, and what is born of spirit is spirit. [7]Do not be surprised that I said to you, 'You all must be born from above.' [8]The wind [lit., 'the spirit'] blows where it pleases, and you hear its sound but cannot

least by 3:16. Schnackenburg (1990: 1.360, citing others as well) places the start of the evangelist's reflections at 3:13.

tell where it comes from or where it is going. That is the way it is with everyone born of spirit." [9]Nicodemus answered and said to him, "How can these things happen?" [10]Jesus answered and said to him, "You are Israel's teacher, and do not know these things? [11]Truly, truly, I say to you, we speak of what we know, and we testify to what we have seen, yet you people do not accept our testimony. [12]I told you earthly things and you don't believe—how will you believe if I tell you heavenly things? [13]Indeed, no one has ever ascended into heaven except for the one who descended from heaven, ⌜the Son of Man⌝. [14]And just as Moses lifted up the serpent in the wilderness, so the Son of Man must be 'lifted up,' [15]so that everyone who believes may ⌜in him⌝ have eternal life."

[16]For this is how much God loved the world: he gave his one-of-a-kind Son, so that everyone who believes in him may not perish but have eternal life. [17]For God did not send his Son into the world to condemn the world, but in order that the world might be saved through him. [18]Whoever believes in him is not condemned; but whoever does not believe stands condemned already, because he has not believed in the name of the one-of-a-kind Son of God. [19]This is the verdict: light has come into the world, but people preferred darkness to light; for their deeds were evil. [20]For everyone who perpetrates evil hates the light and does not come to the light, so that his deeds may not be exposed. [21]But whoever practices truth comes to the light, so that his deeds may be revealed as having been accomplished through God.

i. Dubious Belief in Jerusalem (2:23–25)

The reference to the Passover ties the transitional section of 2:23–25 in with its mention at the beginning of the previous section (2:13). John 2:23–25 summarizes the response to Jesus' ministry in Jerusalem by the general populace (in contrast to the hostility of the Jewish leadership [2:18, 20]; note in the Greek text the repeated use of the imperfect tense, indicating continuing action), sandwiched between Jesus' clearing of the temple and his encounter with Nicodemus. Perhaps more than concluding 2:13–22, these verses commence the Nicodemus narrative. This may be suggested by the overlapping terminology (ἄνθρωπος [anthrōpos, man or human being] in 2:25 and 3:1; σημεῖα [sēmeia, signs] in 2:23 and 3:2; the use of ἦν δέ [ēn de, now he/there was] in 2:23 and 3:1).[4]

2:23–25

If so, then the comments regarding Jesus' realistic attitude toward humans and his knowledge of the sinful human heart are designed to introduce the account of Nicodemus's coming to Jesus (Moloney 1998: 87; cf. Wallace 1996: 597; R. Brown 1966: 129). Nicodemus is one such person who "believed" on the basis of Jesus' "signs" but whose belief

---

4. See also the connection between Nicodemus's statement regarding τὰ σημεῖα . . . ἃ σὺ ποιεῖς (3:2) and the evangelist's comment regarding τὰ σημεῖα ἃ ἐποίει (2:23) (noted by Lee 1994: 39), which suggests that Nicodemus is one of those, described in 2:23–24, to whom Jesus did not entrust himself.

was not trusted by Jesus (Ridderbos 1997: 122–23; Beasley-Murray 1999: 47; contra Bultmann 1971: 133). In fact, not only Nicodemus, but also the Samaritan woman, the Gentile official, and the man at the pool of Bethesda, among others, illustrate Jesus' knowledge of all (kinds of) people (Carson 1991: 185).

The present scene takes place "in Jerusalem," or perhaps more precisely, "the precincts of Jerusalem" (Morris 1995: 180 n. 100, citing Bernard). The phrase "believed in his name" echoes the identical phrase at the pivot of the prologue (1:12) to the effect that those who believe in Jesus' name are given the privilege to become children of God (Ridderbos 1997: 122). Are these Jerusalem believers, then, God's children? This may be the natural conclusion, but the readers of the Gospel are quickly cautioned that such an inference is not necessarily warranted (Schnackenburg 1990: 1.358; R. Brown 1966: 126). As the evangelist indicates by way of a wordplay (a rhetorical technique similar to what some call *diaphora*; see Keener [2003: 531], who also cites δύναμαι and οἴδαμεν in 3:2–11), though these people "believed" (ἐπίστευσαν, *episteusan*; simple aorist, contra Moloney [1998: 87], who says that this "marks a definite, completed act") in *him*, Jesus, for his part (note the emphasizing pronoun αὐτός [*autos*, himself] and the mild adversative δέ [*de*, but]), did not "entrust" (ἐπίστευεν, *episteuen*; the imperfect indicates continuing action) himself to *them* (Borchert 1996: 168).[5] This prepares for the references later in the Gospel to massive unbelief even among Jesus' disciples, his own family, and the Jewish people (6:60–71; 7:1–9; 12:37–43).

Interestingly, the untrustworthy nature of people's belief is tied to its basis: Jesus' repeated performance (imperfect of ποιέω [*poieō*, do]) of signs (Carson 1991: 184; note the plural "signs"—this relativizes the reference to Jesus' "second sign" in 4:54 and restricts it to his performance of signs in Cana). Notably, this reference to Jesus' signs, too, is picked up in the Nicodemus narrative (3:2). Although it is through his signs that Jesus reveals his glory (2:11; cf. 1:14), and though they are the occasion for his disciples' faith (2:11), the seeing of signs does not necessarily lead to faith (Moloney 1998: 84).[6] This has already been

---

5. Carson (1991: 184) notes that the converse is also true: Jesus promises to entrust himself to those who truly trust in him. Wallace (1996: 349) comments that the emphasizing pronoun in "its very repetition contrasts Jesus with the rest of humanity, setting him apart in his sinlessness." Similar reflexive uses of πιστεύω in the NT include Luke 16:11; Rom. 3:2; 1 Cor. 9:17; Gal. 2:7; 1 Thess. 2:4; 1 Tim. 1:11; Titus 1:3 (Barrett 1978: 202).

6. As Michaels (1989: 53) notes, the problem is not signs-based faith, but cowardice and failure to acknowledge one's faith openly. Whitacre (1999: 86) similarly notes that signs-based faith is not the problem (citing 10:38; 12:37; 14:12; 20:30–31; cf. R. Brown 1966: 525–29), but that by its very nature, all faith prior to Jesus' glorification and the coming of the Spirit is immature. Borchert (1996: 167–69) wrongly includes even the disciples of 2:11 among the group whose faith is illegitimately signs-based in 2:23.

illustrated by the Jewish leadership's response to the temple clearing (2:18). Similarly, the Jews' "believing" at a later juncture occasions Jesus' cautious response (8:31), and in due course these people are exposed to be children not of God, but of Satan (8:39–59). The present passage thus inaugurates a thread of references to Jewish unbelief that builds to a crescendo in the dark conclusion of 12:37–50 (cf. 7:31; 8:30; 10:42; 11:45; 12:42; see Ridderbos 1997: 122).

Jesus knew what was in people's hearts. He had no need for any witnesses in this regard (Morris 1995: 182; contrast references to the Baptist in, e.g., 1:7–8, 15) (ἵνα [hina, that] in 2:25 is epexegetical; see Wallace 1996: 476). According to Jewish belief, God knows people's hearts and judges their motivations.[7] Perhaps the closest OT parallel is Solomon's statement at the occasion of the dedication of the temple that God alone knows the hearts of all people (1 Kings 8:39; see Morris 1995: 183). The present statement implies that Jesus is God or at least possesses a divine attribute. Jesus' knowledge of people's hearts is displayed in his encounters with Nicodemus and the Samaritan woman.[8] In both instances, Jesus immediately cuts to the heart of the problem: in Nicodemus's case, his lack of regeneration; in the Samaritan woman's case, a life of immorality and religious ignorance.

ii. Jesus' Conversation with Nicodemus (3:1–15)

The word ἄνθρωπος (anthrōpos, man) perhaps seems redundant in the En- 3:1
glish translation of 3:1 but may indicate that Nicodemus is to be included among the "all people" whose hearts are known by Jesus in 2:24–25 (Conway 1999: 87). Nicodemus is identified as one of the Pharisees, the preeminent Jewish sect mentioned almost incidentally in 1:24 (see Westerholm, *DJG* 609–14; Köstenberger 2002c: 34). Apparently, Nicodemus represents a more open element among this group, which shows that not all Pharisees were hostile toward Jesus (cf. 12:42; Acts 5:34–39). Although John focuses exclusively on the conversation between Jesus and Nicodemus, disciples of both teachers may have been present as well (cf. 3:11–12, where the Greek, with one exception, indicates Jesus addressing more than one person). Nicodemus is mentioned only in this Gospel (cf. 7:50–52; 19:39–42).[9] The

---

7. See 1 Sam. 16:7; 1 Chron. 28:9; Ps. 139:1–18, 23–24; Jer. 17:10; Rom. 8:27; Heb. 4:12–13; Wis. 1:6; Ps. Sol. 14:8; 17:25. Barrett (1978: 202) further cites *Mek. Exod.* 16.32: "There is no man who knows what is in his neighbor's heart."

8. See also 1:48; 2:4, 19; 3:14 (Jesus' knowledge extends to anticipating his crucifixion); 4:17–18; 6:51, 70; 7:6; 8:28; 9:3; 10:15–18; 11:4, 14; 12:24, 32; 13:10–11, 38; 15:13; 21:18–19.

9. Keener (2003: 536) states that Nicodemus (unlike the Samaritan woman) is probably named for literary reasons, since "it would be difficult for any but the most diligent reader to recognize his recurrence in 7:50 and 19:39 if he remained anonymous." This argument is unpersuasive, however, for it fails to account for the fact that the Fourth Evangelist manages to refrain from naming the "disciple Jesus loved" and yet avoids confusion.

name was common in first-century Palestine (Barrett 1978: 204). The fact that a wealthy philanthropic Jew by the same name was living in Jerusalem around A.D. 70 adds historical plausibility to John's account (*b. Giṭ.* 56a; *b. Ketub.* 66b; see Bauckham 1996; cf. Schlatter 1948: 84).

"Member of the Jewish ruling council" (lit., "ruler of the Jews" [ἄρχων τῶν Ἰουδαίων, *archōn tōn Ioudaiōn*]; cf. 7:26, 48; 12:42) almost certainly refers to the Sanhedrin (from συνέδριον [*synedrion*, gathering, assembly]), the highest national body in charge of Jewish affairs (Saldarini, *ABD* 5:975–80; Twelftree, *DJG* 728–32). Headquartered in Jerusalem, it was composed of Pharisees and Sadducees. When Judea became a Roman province in A.D. 6, the Sanhedrin became even more autonomous in handling internal Jewish matters. As John's Gospel progresses, the Sanhedrin turns out to be the driving force in the plot against Jesus. As a Pharisee, Nicodemus may have been less perturbed by Jesus' clearing of the temple than if he had been a Sadducee; the attribution "man of the Pharisees . . . member of the Jewish ruling council" identifies Nicodemus as part of the old Jewish religion (Morris 1995: 186).[10]

Commentators differ as to whether Nicodemus progressed in his understanding over time in this Gospel. Carson concludes that Nicodemus eventually came "to side with Jesus" (1991: 186; cf. 202; similarly, Cotterell 1985: 241). Morris likewise believes that Nicodemus, though a "timid soul," in the end "came right out for Jesus" (1995: 186). Moloney, too, thinks that he can detect a "journey of faith [on Nicodemus's part] within the unfolding narrative" (1998: 97). According to R. Brown (1966: 129), Nicodemus represents a group of Jewish leaders "who hesitantly came to believe in Jesus." Although Keener (2003: 533) says that Nicodemus here has "not yet crossed the threshold into discipleship" and is "at most a representative of some open-minded dialogue partners in the synagogues," he contends that Nicodemus later comes to "true, complete discipleship" (citing 19:39–42).[11] A closer analysis reveals, however, that not only is the term "believe" never attributed to Nicodemus (except for, indirectly, the inadequate signs-based faith of 2:23–25)—in fact, his lack of spiritual rebirth, in the context of 1:12–13, marks him off as an unbeliever—but also there is little actual progression in the way he is characterized in the Gospel.[12] Although he advocates fairness in dealing

10. In a puzzling statement, Conway (1999: 91) seems to drive a wedge between Pharisees and "rulers" in the Fourth Gospel ("given 12:42, the Pharisees seem to have greater authority and control than do the rulers"), and questions whether ἄρχων here refers to the Sanhedrin. But clearly, Nicodemus is presented here as both a Pharisee and an ἄρχων, so that he may accurately be described as a Pharisaic "ruler," which very likely means "Sanhedrin member."

11. Keener (2003: 536) proceeds to call Nicodemus a "secret believer" in 3:2 on account of his coming to Jesus by night. Yet this characterization is doubtful, since Jesus does not seem to treat Nicodemus as a "believer" here, secret or otherwise.

12. Arguably, repeated reference does not necessarily imply progression. For a mediating position, see Beck (1997: 63–70, esp. 69), who concludes that Nicodemus's "ambigu-

with Jesus (7:50–52; like Gamaliel in Acts 5:34–36, who usually is not credited with having become a believer) and ensures giving him a proper burial (19:39–42), none of this warrants the conclusion that Nicodemus actually came to believe.[13] Rather, he is a moral Jew, a decent man, who nonetheless falls short of regeneration.[14] For John, Nicodemus, though perhaps in transition, remains an outsider; he "moves through the narrative with one foot in each world, and in this Gospel that is just not good enough" (Bassler 1989: 646). Moreover, historically, by featuring Nicodemus, the evangelist shows that the Sanhedrin was not monolithic

---

ous characterization" is intended to challenge the reader to deeper faith. Beck (1997: 63) believes that Nicodemus's placement between two anonymous female characters suggests that his failure to respond positively serves as a foil for the positive responses of those two characters.

13. See Blomberg (1995: 5–7), who lists seven factors in favor of seeing John's portrait of Nicodemus as "substantially more negative" than the dominant view alleges: (1) the introduction of 2:23–25; (2) the labels "Pharisee" and "ruler of the Jews"; (3) Nicodemus's coming by night; (4) the identification of Jesus as a mere "teacher"; (5) Nicodemus's dependence on signs; (6) his astonishing ignorance; and (7) the evidence adduced by Cotterell regarding the increasingly negative portrayal of Nicodemus. According to Blomberg (cf. Bassler 1989), Nicodemus remains an ambivalent character, in contrast with the more positive progression found in the Samaritan woman in John 4. This overall conclusion is against Cotterell (1985: 241), who in his otherwise excellent discourse analysis exceeds the evidence when he credits Nicodemus with a "gradual dawning of true faith [culminating] in the presence of Nicodemus at the cross and in his ultimate identification with Jesus in his death." Rather than "take his place at Calvary," Nicodemus simply ensured giving Jesus a decent burial. (As Meeks [1972: 55] contends, Nicodemus's "ludicrous 'one hundred pounds' of embalming spices indicate clearly enough that he has not understood the 'lifting up' of the Son of Man.") Cotterell is on surer footing when he concludes that in the present narrative, "Nicodemus chose not to understand Jesus," characterizing the outcome of the present conversation as "inconclusive." Likewise mistaken, I believe, is Saayman (1995: 45), who detects in Nicodemus "a growing loyalty to Jesus."

14. Cf. Paulien (*ABD* 4:1106), who also refers to de Jonge 1971: 342; Sylva 1988: 148–49; Michel (1981: 231), who calls Nicodemus a "borderline character" ("personnage-frontière"); and Pamment (1985: 71, 73), who writes, "Nicodemus is the only individual character who fails to make a decision, remaining the good but uncommitted observer who tries to prevent injustice" (p. 73). Similarly, Conway (1999: 85–103) says that Nicodemus is a "pathetic character" who from beginning to end "is genuinely interested in Jesus, but is never able to gather the courage and conviction to confess his belief openly" (p. 103). Note also Pazdan (1987), who sees Nicodemus's portrayal as part of John's reversal of the traditional geographical polemic regarding Judeans, Samaritans, and Galileans; and Burge (2000: 124), who contends that Nicodemus never became a model disciple, because "disciples confess Jesus' identity, remain with him, and tell others." If my assessment of Nicodemus is correct, it runs counter to the notion, popular in current scholarship, that John's Gospel is "anti-Semitic," for here we have a Jewish person who, though not a believer in Jesus the Messiah, represents a fair-minded, moral, kind Jewish leader, providing a counterpoint to the more hostile element on the Sanhedrin. It is also possible that John includes the Nicodemus account at least in part because he had access to individuals among the Jewish leadership (cf. 18:15b: "that disciple [the 'other disciple' of 18:15a, presumably the evangelist; cf. 20:2; 21:24] was known to the high priest").

in its rejection of Jesus, but rather included moderate elements that were more cautious and conciliatory in their approach.

3:2 In keeping with Jewish culture, Nicodemus starts with a word of praise before stating his case (Louw 1986: 11; somewhat similarly, note the indirect statements in 2:3; 11:3).[15] Several of John's uses of νύξ (*nyx*, night) reveal a spiritual and moral darkness (cf. 9:4; 11:10; 13:30; but see 21:3). In the present instance, Nicodemus's coming to Jesus at night may be somewhat less negatively construed (contra Conway 1999: 92–93; contrast especially Judas in 13:30). He may have sought to avoid the crowds (Ridderbos 1997: 124; Morris 1995: 187; Paulien, *ABD* 4:1105).[16] Nevertheless, coming by night probably does indicate covertness of operation and perhaps also fear of publicity (cf. 12:42; 19:38–39).[17] Incidentally, the repeated reference to Nicodemus's coming "by night" in 19:39 may indicate the flatness of this character in John's Gospel.

It is remarkable that this highly respected Jewish teacher would honor the youngish (about thirty years old) Jesus as a fellow rabbi, especially since Jesus was known to lack formal rabbinic training (7:15). Nicodemus's comment "We know that you are a teacher who has come from God" (cf. Matt. 22:16; see Schlatter 1948: 86), though doubtless intended as a compliment (contrast the categorical denial of Jesus' divine commission by other Pharisees in 7:15), still falls far short of understanding Jesus' true nature; for he is the heaven-sent Son of Man (3:13). Nevertheless, Nicodemus is more open than are other Pharisees later in John's Gospel who declare categorically, "This man is not from God" (9:16).

15. Though note Goulder (1991: 154), who contends that "the tone [in the present passage] sounds greasy," and who adduces the parallel in Matt. 22:16, "a similarly insincere compliment, and one which led to a trap" (the second-century A.D. P.Eger. 2 links the present encounter with the question regarding paying tribute to Caesar in the Synoptics; see Bassler 1989: 636). Goulder, too, thinks that Nicodemus's portrayal in John's Gospel is "solidly negative" (p. 153), noting that "all Nicodemus can manage is two crass questions (3.4, 9) which show that he is totally without spiritual insight; and Jesus says so (3.10)"; that "at 7.50f Nicodemus speaks up weakly to his fellow Pharisees . . . but he is firmly snubbed, and does not stick to his point. . . . He is no real Christian: he is 'one of them' (7.50)"; and finally, that at the burial Nicodemus brings a large amount of spices, but Jesus has already been anointed for burial (12:7), and the ointments will be laid aside at the resurrection (pp. 155–56).

16. Cotterell (1985: 238–39) notes that νυκτός is not marked, not brought into emphatic position by fronting (he notes the general mobility of this element by reference to Acts 9:24–25; Matt. 28:13; Luke 21:37). He concludes that John's failure to front the expression tends to support the view that νυκτός is no more than a chronological discourse marker.

17. Contra several commentators (Barrett 1978: 205; Moloney 1998: 91; R. Brown 1966: 130; Witherington 1995: 94; Burge 2000: 114; Carson 1995: 187 n. 8; Blomberg 1995: 6), "by night" is likely not symbolic in the sense that Nicodemus came from darkness to light, while Judas went from light to darkness (cf. 6:70–71; 12:4–8; 13:2, 26–30; 18:2–5)—a view held by R. Brown (1966: 130) and Auwers (1990). Wallace (1996: 123–24) overreaches when he finds in the genitive of time an indication of "the *kind* of time in which Nicodemus came to see the Lord." Morris (1995: 187) suggests that John may have had more than one meaning in mind.

Nicodemus's use of the plural οἴδαμεν (*oidamen*, we know) may indicate that he was speaking for a group among the Sanhedrin (Pharisees) that was impressed by Jesus' signs (Carson 1991: 187; contra Barrett 1978: 202, 205; R. Brown 1966: 137). Perhaps more likely, Nicodemus is referring more generally to a group of people, be it his own disciples, other rabbis, or a variety of others (Cotterell 1985: 239).[18] The emphatic placement of ἀπὸ θεοῦ (*apo theou*, from God) accentuates Nicodemus's expressed belief of Jesus' divine calling (Barrett 1978: 205; Witherington 1995: 94). In light of Nicodemus's reference to Jesus as "come from God" and "God being with him," it is remarkable that he is nonetheless subsumed under the rubric of those to whom Jesus did not entrust himself, especially since Jesus says these things about himself later on in the Gospel (Ridderbos 1997: 124). Yet Nicodemus's lack of true understanding will be exposed shortly. Jesus is much more than a fellow rabbi (Morris 1995: 187; Köstenberger 1998a).

Nicodemus particularly singles out the signs that Jesus was performing (cf. 2:23).[19] It was commonly held in Judaism that miracles attest to God's presence. References to "signs" in the OT cluster around two major periods: (1) the "signs and wonders" performed by Moses at the exodus (e.g., Exod. 4:1–9); and (2) signs—with attendant symbolism, but not necessarily miraculous—acted out by various OT prophets (e.g., Isa. 20:3; see Köstenberger 1995b: 87–103). Though Jesus discourages dependence on "signs and wonders" (4:48), he does perform various signs, both miraculous (e.g., 2:1–11) and nonmiraculous (2:14–22). These signs show him to be not only a divine prophet (6:14; 7:40), but also the God-sent Messiah (7:31; 20:30–31). The present statement probably refers primarily to Jesus' Jerusalem signs (cf. 2:23) rather than to his first sign in Cana of Galilee (2:11; for a similar acknowledgment, see 11:47).

"If God were not with him" is a common Jewish locution, expressing a concept used by Jesus himself (8:29; 16:32) and frequently found in the OT (e.g., Gen. 21:20; 26:24; 28:15; 31:3; Deut. 31:23; Josh. 1:5; Jer. 1:19). Through his polite yet cautious introductory statement, Nicodemus tacitly inquires as to what new doctrine Jesus is propagating or, perhaps more precisely, who Jesus claims to be: the Prophet? the Messiah? (Carson 1991: 187).

As Westcott (1908: 1.105) aptly remarks, in what follows, "The Lord   3:3–5
answered not his words, but his thoughts. The Lord's answers to questions will be found generally to reveal the true thought of the questioner, and to be fitted to guide him to the truth which he is seeking." Specifically, Nicodemus's self-confident assertion, "We know," is met by

---

18. Schlatter (1948: 85) says that the "we" in 3:2 are "the many who believed in Jesus' name" in 2:23.

19. The iterative use of the present tense ποιεῖς points to Jesus' continuing practice of performing "signs" (in Jerusalem; see Morris 1995: 188 n. 14; Wallace 1996: 521).

Jesus' authoritative riposte, "Truly, truly, I say to you." The expression serves to draw a contrast between Nicodemus's opening statement and Jesus' response. Human understanding ("we know") is confronted with authoritative spiritual pronouncements (Ridderbos 1997: 124). Jesus' reply, which may involve a play on the word δύναται (*dynatai*, can[not]; Borchert 1996: 171), seems harsh; in essence, it amounts to a rejection of the process by which Nicodemus sought to discover who Jesus was. Not human observation, reasoning, and "believing" are required, but rather, a spiritual rebirth (Carson 1991: 187–88; cf. Morris 1995: 189). "Anyone" includes both Jews and Gentiles, that is, all of humanity.

The expression "see[20] the kingdom of God" (elsewhere in the NT also in Mark 9:1 = Luke 9:27) means "to participate in the kingdom at the end of the age, to experience eternal, resurrection life" (Carson 1991: 188; cf. Beasley-Murray 1999: 48).[21] The phrase has no exact counterpart in the OT, yet Nicodemus has no difficulty understanding its meaning. According to Jesus, Nicodemus and his fellow Jews cannot "see" God's kingdom apart from a supernatural birth. Unless their eyes are opened, they remain spiritually blind (cf. 9:39–41). The Hebrew Scriptures make clear that "the Lord is king" and that his sovereign reign extends to every creature (e.g., Exod. 15:18; Ps. 93:1; 103:19). The Jews expected a future kingdom ruled by the Son of David (Isa. 9:1–7; 11:1–5, 10–11; Ezek. 34:23–24; Zech. 9:9–10), the Lord's Servant (Isa. 42:1–7; 49:1–7), indeed, the Lord himself (Ezek. 34:11–16; 36:22–32; Zech. 14:9). Although not everyone was to be included in this kingdom, Jews in Jesus' day generally believed that all Israelites would have a share in the world to come, with the exception of those guilty of apostasy or some other blatant sin (*m. Sanh.* 10.1).

Jesus' reference to the kingdom of God is limited to the present instance (here and in 3:5) in John, which further underscores the authenticity of the present passage (D. M. Smith 1999: 94). At the only other occasion where the term "kingdom" occurs in this Gospel, Jesus affirms before Pilate that his kingdom is not of this world (18:36; cf. 6:15). This contrasts with the very frequent use of the term "kingdom" in the Synoptics, where Jewish expectations are shown to focus on a future "Son of David."[22] The expression is transposed into the more universal key of

---

20. "See" and "enter" are roughly synonymous (Barrett 1978: 207; R. Brown 1966: 130; Morris 1995: 189)—an instance of the Johannine penchant for stylistic variation (Barrett 1978: 208).

21. The phrase "enter the kingdom of God [or 'heaven']" is found in the NT also in Matt. 5:20; 7:21; 18:3; 19:23–24 par.; Mark 9:47; Acts 14:22. Pryor (1991b: 71–95 [cf., earlier, Lindars 1981: 287–88]) seeks to make a case for John's dependence on the tradition behind Matt. 18:3, but his argument is both unpersuasive and unnecessary (cf. Osburn 1989: 132: "unconvincing").

22. The virtual absence of the term "kingdom of God" in John's Gospel can further be seen as linked to the absence of narrative parables, whose subject in the Synoptics is predominantly that same kingdom.

4. Further Ministry in Jerusalem and Samaria
a. The "Teacher of Israel," Nicodemus
John 2:23–3:21

"eternal life" (cf. 3:16; see Morris 1995: 190; Ridderbos 1997: 128; Barrett 1978: 215; Bultmann 1971: 152 n. 2). That the expressions "kingdom of God" and "eternal life" are essentially equivalent is suggested by their parallel use in Matt. 19:16, 24 pars.

The reference to being "born again/from above" is startling and unexpected. Nevertheless, the notion of a new beginning and a decisive inner transformation of a person's life is also found in certain OT prophetic passages (e.g., Jer. 31:33–34; Ezek. 11:19–20; 36:25–27; see commentary at 3:5). This concept of a new spiritual birth is not dissimilar to that of a "new creation" (cf. 2 Cor. 5:17; Gal. 6:15). The term ἄνωθεν (anōthen, translated "again" in the TNIV here and in 3:7) can mean either "from above," be it figuratively (John 3:7, 31; 19:11; James 1:17; 3:15, 17) or literally ("from top to bottom": Matt. 27:51 par.; John 19:23), or "from the beginning" (Luke 1:3; Acts 26:5: "for a long time"; Gal. 4:9: "all over again" [with πάλιν, palin, again]). This potential ambiguity opens up the possibility of misunderstanding (R. Brown 1966: 130; Ridderbos 1997: 127; Barrett 1978: 208; Carson 1991: 190; Morris 1995: 190).[23] Nicodemus thought that the phrase meant literally "again," yet as John indicates, he misunderstood Jesus' true message, which pointed to the rabbi's need to be born "from above," that is, born spiritually (Beasley-Murray 1999: 45 n. b).[24]

"Born again/from above" in 3:3 is further explained as "born of water and spirit" in 3:5 (Louw 1986: 9–10).[25] Rather than referring to water and spirit baptism,[26] two kinds of birth,[27] or a variety of other things,[28]

23. Cotterell's (1985: 240) comment that there was no double meaning in Aramaic is unduly dismissive because it disregards the fact that John's Gospel has come to us in Greek, where misunderstanding is not only possible, but almost certainly intended by the evangelist. Thielman (1991: 179 n. 1) points to the frequency of double meanings in the present pericope (see 3:3, 7, 8), "which give the reader pause and serve to 'emphasize' the point at hand."

24. Morris (1995: 190) proposes that rather than being obtuse, Nicodemus may have been wistful, choosing not to understand because he was unwilling to accept the implications of Jesus' pronouncement.

25. Carson (1991: 195) rightly contends that the NIV's "water and the Spirit" is misleading (retained in the TNIV); "water and spirit" is preferable (see commentary at 3:6–8). Also incorrect, I believe, is the proposal by Talbert (1992: 99), who renders the phrase "of water which is Spirit."

26. Note in 3:5 the single Greek preposition governing both "water" and "spirit" (Ridderbos 1997: 127). Some have suggested that "born of water" refers to water baptism, be it John the Baptist's or Christian baptism, or both (Schnackenburg 1990: 1.369; Barrett 1978: 203, 208–9; R. Brown 1966: 141–42; Ridderbos 1997: 127–28; Beasley-Murray 1999: 49; Michaels 1989: 57). But it would hardly have been meaningful for Jesus to inform Nicodemus that he must be baptized in order to go to heaven. Nothing in the context indicates that this is the case, and it is unlikely that Jesus would have expected Nicodemus already to have known this. Moreover, the emphasis here is on the Spirit's activity, not on human ritual observance (Morris 1995: 193).

27. Contra those who say that "born of water" refers to physical birth, and "born of the Spirit" to spiritual birth (e.g., Witherington 1995: 97, referring to 1 John 5:6–8; Laney 1992: 78; but see Carson 1991: 191).

28. For a listing of options and discussion, see Carson 1991: 191–95.

the phrase probably denotes one spiritual birth (Carson 1991: 194). This is suggested by the fact that "born of water and spirit" in 3:5 further develops "born again/from above" in 3:3, by the use of one preposition (ἐξ, *ex*) to govern both phrases in 3:5, and by antecedent OT (prophetic) theology. The closest OT parallel is Ezek. 36:25–27, which presages God's cleansing of human hearts with water and their inner transformation by his Spirit (see also Isa. 44:3–5; Jub. 1:23–25).[29] The terminology may also be reminiscent of first-century proselyte baptism, in which the Gentile convert to Judaism was compared to a newborn child.[30]

3:6–8 Jesus here seeks to move Nicodemus from a woodenly literal to a spiritual understanding of what it means to be "born again/from above." In response to Nicodemus's question (3:4), Jesus maintains that even if it were possible for a person to be literally born a second time, this "second birth" would accomplish nothing, for it would still be a *physical* birth. However, what is needed is a *spiritual* birth (cf. 1:12–13; see also Gal. 4:29). "Born of flesh" refers to natural birth (cf. 1:13), "flesh" to "a person in his or her natural existence as begotten by a father and given birth to by a mother" (Ridderbos 1997: 128; cf. Morris 1995: 194; the Pauline connotation of sinfulness is absent here [contra Calvin 1959: 66]). "Spirit" represents "the principle of divine power and life operating in the human sphere" (R. Brown 1966: 131). Although the OT does not literally refer to God's Spirit "giving birth" to spirit (cf. John 6:63), it does hold out the vision that God, who is spirit (4:24), will "put a new spirit" in his people (Ezek. 36:26; cf. 37:5, 14).

Jesus here tells his rabbinic counterpart to "stop being surprised" (the force of the phrase in the Greek). Indeed, Jesus' teaching on the necessity of a spiritual birth was not a new doctrine. Rather, it reiterated a vision clearly laid out in OT prophetic literature. In the phrase "you must be born from above," "you" is in the plural, which shows that this requirement does not extend solely to Nicodemus but to the entire group he represents (cf. "someone" in 3:3, 5; "we" in 3:2, 11). This includes the Pharisees and the Sanhedrin—and thus the Jewish religious leadership—but ultimately the entire nation. Indeed, part of Nicodemus's dismay may stem not from actual ignorance of the OT, but from the fact that it is he and his Pharisaic colleagues who are said to be in need of spiritual regeneration (see commentary at 3:17).

Jesus illustrates his saying with an analogy between the wind and the person born of spirit. "Wind," a common image for the Spirit (Ridderbos 1997: 129), and "spirit" translate the same Greek and Hebrew words (Greek: πνεῦμα, *pneuma*; Hebrew: רוּחַ, *rûaḥ*). Both the OT and other

---

29. See, earlier, Schlatter 1948: 89. For helpful discussions, see Carson 1991: 191–96, esp. 194–95; McCabe 1999. See also Cotterell 1985: 241; Kynes, *DJG* 574–76, esp. 575.

30. Thus, Rabbi Yose ben Ḥalafta (ca. A.D. 130–160) said, "One who has become a proselyte is like a child newly born" (*b. Yebam.* 48b; cf. 22a; 62a; 97b; *b. Bek.* 47a).

Jewish literature contain numerous references to the mystery of the wind's origin (cf. Eccles. 8:8; 11:5; 1 Enoch 41:3; 60:12; 2 Bar. 48:3–4). In the present instance, the point of Jesus' analogy is that both wind and spiritual birth are mysterious in origin and movement—wind goes sovereignly where it pleases—yet though the wind's origin is invisible, its effects can be observed; it is the same with the Spirit (Ridderbos 1997: 129; Carson 1991: 197). Despite its inscrutability, spiritual birth is real, as real as the mysterious movements of the wind.[31] Moreover, just as the wind blows "where it pleases," so the Spirit's operation is not subject to human control, eluding all efforts at manipulation (Moloney 1998: 93).[32]

3:9–12 Nicodemus's second question (cf. 3:4) evidences his growing exasperation and lack of understanding. In this rabbinic dialogue, Jesus clearly is the teacher, and Nicodemus the student. In fact, from here on Nicodemus vanishes from sight, and the narrative drifts into a monologue, first by Jesus, and then, almost imperceptibly, by the evangelist himself (see commentary at 3:16). Nicodemus's question is frequently rendered "How can these things/this be?" (NIV, NASB, NRSV, NKJV, NLT, ESV, TNIV, et al.). However, the translation "How can these things happen?" is preferable (Barrett 1978: 211; Carson 1991: 198). By calling Nicodemus "Israel's teacher," Jesus may be returning Nicodemus's compliment in 3:2, where that rabbi had called Jesus "a teacher come from God" (cf. 3:11). The definite article before "teacher" in the original may suggest that Nicodemus was an established, recognized teacher (Bishop 1956; Ridderbos 1997: 132; Barrett 1978: 211; Morris 1995: 195); he was "the" teacher par excellence (Wallace 1996: 222–23; Bultmann 1971: 144 n. 2). The reason for Jesus' astonishment is that he had been speaking about things of which Nicodemus, as "Israel's teacher," should have been aware.[33]

With this, Nicodemus disappears from the scene (R. Brown 1966: 131). In his third, final, and most extensive pronouncement in the present narrative, introduced once again by the authoritative "truly, truly, I say to you," Jesus first confirms the reliability of the witness that Nicodemus has heard before proceeding to contrast earthly and heavenly things. Perhaps mirroring Nicodemus's opening gambit (Carson 1991: 198–99: "sardonically aping"; cf. R. Brown 1966: 132), Jesus' statement is phrased in plurals: "We speak of what we know, and we testify

31. Lindars (1972: 153–54) adduces Paul's statement in 1 Cor. 15:50 that "flesh and blood cannot inherit the kingdom of God."

32. Keener (2003: 556 n. 221) notes the verbal parallel between the wind blowing "where it wills" (3:7–8) and Jesus raising "whom he wills" (5:21). Keener (2003: 557–58) also recognizes another wordplay, involving the word for "voice" or "sound" (φωνή), applied to the wind in 2:8 and occurring later in the Gospel in 3:29; 5:25, 28, 37; 10:3–5, 16, 27; 11:43; 12:28, 30; 18:37.

33. Cf. Ezek. 11:19–20; 36:26–27; Isa. 44:3; 59:21; Jer. 31:31–34; Ps. 51:10; cf. Wis. 9:16–18; 1QS 3:13–4:26; see Ridderbos 1997: 132; Barrett 1978: 203; Moloney 1998: 94.

to what we have seen, yet you [plural] do not accept our testimony" (compare Nicodemus's comment in 3:2: "Rabbi, we know that you are a teacher come from God").[34] Nicodemus had approached Jesus as the representative of a group; Jesus responds that he and his group[35] also know a thing or two (cf. the "battle of knowledge" in 9:13–34, containing the formerly blind man's "we know" in 9:31).[36] What is more, their knowledge is firsthand rather than speculative or based on hearsay. In the early chapters of this Gospel, the words "testify" and "testimony" occur frequently to describe the Baptist's role as a "witness" to Jesus (1:7, 15, 19, 32, 34; 3:26; cf. 3:28); this is the first time the term is used by Jesus himself (cf. 3:32; 4:44; 5:31; 7:7; 8:14, 18; 13:21; 18:37; see Coenen, *NIDNTT* 3:1044–46). In the end, it is not that Nicodemus and his fellow rulers have not heard Jesus' witness, or even that they failed to understand it; at the root, their failure was not intellectual, but rather consisted in their unwillingness to "accept our testimony" (Carson 1991: 199).

Jesus' ensuing argument is *a minori ad maius*, from the lesser to the greater: "I told you earthly things and you don't believe—how will you believe if I tell you heavenly things?" (cf. 5:47; see Ridderbos 1997: 134). The implied answer: "There is no way; it is impossible." "Earthly things" (cf. 7:24; 8:15; see also Matt. 16:2–3 par.) may refer to the elementary teaching on the necessity of a spiritual birth ("the matters that have been discussed in the preceding dialogue" [Ridderbos 1997: 134]).[37] If "Israel's teacher" stumbles over such a foundational truth, how can Jesus enlighten him on "heavenly things" such as the more advanced teachings of the kingdom (Morris 1995: 197; Carson 1991: 199; Schnackenburg 1990: 1.377, referring to Heb. 6:1 and 1 Cor. 3:2)?[38]

34. It may be too early in Jesus' ministry for his disciples to be included (Carson 1991: 198–99; contra Ridderbos 1997: 134; Morris 1995: 196). Schnackenburg's (1990: 1.376) solution, that Jesus' statement is proleptic, looking "forward to the time when his disciples make his 'testimony' their own, as part of their preaching" (with reference to 3:22 and 9:4), likewise fails to convince. There is also no need to postulate that the "we" aligns Jesus with the OT prophets, reflects the Johannine community (Witherington 1995: 98; cf. Moloney 1998: 94), or denotes the church versus the synagogue (Barrett 1978: 211; Brodie 1993: 198).

35. Schlatter (1948: 91–92) refers to the Baptist (1:7, 34), but also to Abraham (8:56) and Isaiah (12:41).

36. Stibbe (1993: 55) observes, "Who is really the possessor of knowledge is the main subject of the dialogue."

37. Cf. Morris 1995: 196; Carson 1991: 199; R. Brown 1966: 132; Beasley-Murray 1999: 50; Witherington 1995: 98; Moloney 1998: 94; Schnackenburg 1990: 1.377; contra Barrett 1978: 212.

38. A similar sentiment is expressed in Wis. 9:16 (first century B.C.): "We can hardly guess at what is on the earth . . . but who has traced out what is in the heavens?" (cf. Jdt. 8:14). See also the anecdote involving Rabban Gamaliel (ca. A.D. 90) recounted in Köstenberger 2002c: 36.

Jesus here answers Nicodemus's question in 3:9: "these things" (i.e.,   **3:13–15**
spiritual rebirth) can happen only as a result of Jesus' crucifixion, resurrection, and ascension (Moloney 1998: 95).[39] Explaining how he has
knowledge of "heavenly things" (Ridderbos 1997: 135; Carson 1991:
199; Moloney 1998: 95), Jesus maintains that no one has ever gone
into heaven except for the one who descended *from* heaven—the Son
of Man (see commentary at 1:51; additional note to 3:13). The statement, as Carson (1991: 200) explains, is probably elliptical: "No-one
[else] has ascended into heaven and remained there [so as to be able to
speak authoritatively about heavenly things] but only the one who has
come down from heaven [is equipped to do so]." This characterization
is reminiscent of the prologue's portrayal of Jesus as the incarnate Word
and the one-of-a-kind Son from the Father, who has given a full account
of him (1:14, 18). The present passage combines elements of Num. 21:9
(the serpent in the wilderness), Isa. 52:13 ("lifted up"), and Dan 7:13–14
("Son of Man") (Borgen 1977: 252–53).[40]

The OT identifies heaven as the place where God dwells.[41] John's
Gospel refers several times to a descent *from* heaven, be it of the Spirit
(1:32–33), angels (1:51), the Son of Man (3:13), or the divine bread (6:33,
38, 41, 42, 50, 51, 58). However, this is one of only three instances where
it speaks of an ascent *into* heaven (angels [1:51]; the Son of Man [3:13];
the risen Lord [20:17]). Jesus here contrasts himself, the "Son of Man"
(cf. Dan. 7:13), with other human figures who allegedly entered heaven,
such as Enoch (Gen. 5:24; cf. Heb. 11:5), Elijah (2 Kings 2:1–12; cf.
2 Chron. 21:12–15), Moses (Exod. 24:9–11; 34:29–30), Isaiah (Isa. 6:1–3),
or Ezekiel (Ezek. 1; 10). A whole cottage industry of Second Temple
literature revolved around such figures and their heavenly exploits (e.g.,
1 Enoch; see Tabor, *ABD* 3:91–94; Borgen 1977). Although believers can
expect to join Christ in heaven one day (cf. John 14:1–3; 17:24), only
Jesus both descended from heaven and ascended back up to heaven (cf.
Luke 24:51; Acts 1:9; though note the similar ascent-descent pattern by
angels in John 1:51).

39. He does so despite his doubt that Nicodemus can follow his explanation (3:12),
but by this time the primary audience in John's Gospel has shifted from Nicodemus to
the readers (see the survey in Saayman 1995: 30–31). Grese (1988) maintains that 3:13–18
serves to explicate the references to "being born from above" in 3:3, 5, but this is doubtful,
for by 3:13–18 the monologue has moved on to a christological plane, while 3:3, 5 stipulate
the human requirement for entering God's kingdom.

40. Additionally, Hollis (1989: 475–78) draws attention to the use of "lift up" (נִשָּׂא) in
Gen. 40:13, 19, with reference to "lifting up" the butler's head and restoring him to office
and to "lifting up" the baker's head and hanging him on a tree (cf. Gen. 40:20–22). Thus,
this short narrative uses "lift up" both to refer to elevation in status and to indicate death
by hanging on a tree.

41. See, e.g., Ps. 14:2; 33:14; 103:19. See Schoonhoven, *ISBE* 2:654–55; Reddish, *ABD*
3:90–91.

The allusion to Moses lifting up the serpent in the wilderness is plainly to Num. 21:8–9, where God is shown to send poisonous snakes to judge rebellious Israel. When Moses intercedes for his people, God provides a way of salvation in the form of a raised bronze serpent, so that "when anyone was bitten by a snake and looked at the bronze snake, he lived." But the primary analogy established in the present passage is not that of the raised bronze serpent and the lifted-up Son of Man; rather, Jesus likens the restoration of people's physical lives as a result of looking at the bronze serpent to people's reception of eternal life as a result of "looking" in faith at the Son of Man (cf. 3:15–18; see Barrett 1978: 214; cf. Carson 1991: 202). Yet as in the case of wilderness Israel, the source of salvation ultimately is not a person's faith, but the God in whom the faith is placed (cf. Wis. 16:6–7). "Lifted up" (ὑψωθῆναι, hypsōthēnai) has a double meaning here (cf. 8:28; 12:32, 34), linking Jesus' exaltation with his elevation on a cross (Ridderbos 1997: 136–37). The expression draws on Isa. 52:13 LXX (ὑψωθήσεται, hypsōthēsetai; see Dodd 1953: 247).

The phrase "everyone who believes" strikes a markedly universal note. Although looking at the bronze serpent in the wilderness restored life to believing Israelites, there are no such ethnic restrictions on believing in Jesus. *Everyone* who believes will, "in him" (Jesus; see additional note), receive eternal life (cf. 3:16–18; see commentary at 1:4, 9, 12).[42] God sent Jesus to save not just Israel, but the entire world (3:17). Its insistence on the universality of the Christian message marks John's Gospel off from sects such as the Qumran community or the large number of mystery religions, all of which saw salvation limited to a select few. At the same time, however, John's Gospel does not teach universalism, that is, the notion that all will eventually be saved; rather, salvation is made contingent on believing "in him" (3:16), that is, Jesus the Messiah (cf. 20:30–31).

This, then, is the answer to Nicodemus's query in 3:9: these things (regeneration, entering the kingdom) can happen only through the "lifting up" of the Son of Man (Carson 1991: 202). The signs-based faith of 2:23 and 3:2 was founded on seeing Jesus in the flesh; the faith of 3:15 "is faith in the power of him who is powerless in the flesh and in the eyes of the flesh" (Ridderbos 1997: 137).

iii. The Evangelist's Exposition (3:16–21)

3:16 What is the reason (γάρ [gar, for]) that God made eternal life available (Wallace 1996: 668)? It is his love for the world.[43] This much-loved verse

42. This is the first reference to "eternal life" in John. The term occurs also in the Synoptics (e.g., Matt. 19:16, 29 pars.; 25:46; Luke 10:25), Acts (13:46, 48), the Pauline writings (e.g., Rom. 2:7; 5:21; 6:22, 23; Gal. 6:8; 1 Tim. 1:16; 6:12; Titus 1:2; 3:7), 1 John (1:2; 2:25; 3:15; 5:11, 13, 20), and Jude (21).

43. Gundry and Howell (1999: 24–39) argue that the Greek construction οὕτως . . . ὥστε should not be taken to mean "this is how much . . . so that," denoting high degree

is the only place in John where God the Father is said to love the world (cf. 1 John 4:9–10). The OT makes abundantly clear that God loves all that he has made, especially his people (e.g., Exod. 34:6–7; Deut. 7:7–8; Hos. 11:1–4, 8–11). In these last days, God has demonstrated his love for the world through the gift of his one-of-a-kind Son. Significantly, God's love extends not merely to Israel, but to "the world" (Morris 1995: 203; cf. Muller, *ISBE* 4:1115; Guhrt, *NIDNTT* 1:525–26), that is, sinful humanity (Carson 1991: 205). Just as God's love encompasses the entire world, so Jesus made atonement for the sins of the whole world (1 John 2:2).

In a major escalation from the giving of the law (cf. John 1:17; see Ridderbos 1997: 137), God gave his "one-of-a-kind Son" (see 1:14, 18; cf. Rom. 8:32; Gal. 4:4). While the Greek introductory construction οὕτως γάρ (*houtōs gar*, for thus) stresses the intensity of God's love (contra Kruse 2003: 113–14), the result clause, speaking of the giving of God's μονογενὴς υἱός (*monogenēs huios*, one-of-a-kind Son), stresses the greatness of that gift (Carson 1991: 204). The next verse says that God "sent" his Son (3:17); here, the term used is "gave" (Ridderbos 1997: 138 n. 108). This draws attention to the sacrifice involved for God the Father in sending his Son to save the world (Witherington 1995: 101).[44] Surely, to see his son die in such a cruel fashion would break any father's heart—much more so that of our heavenly Father. In a similar OT passage, Abraham was asked to give up his "one-of-a-kind son," Isaac (Gen. 22; see R. Brown 1966: 147; Dahl 1969: 28). Unlike Jesus, however, Isaac was not offered up, but spared when God provided a substitute.[45]

The stark alternatives in the following purpose clause (introduced by ἵνα [*hina*, in order that]) are either to perish or to obtain eternal life (Barrett 1978: 216; Morris 1995: 204). The term ἀπόλλυμι (*apollymi*, perish) occurs several times in this Gospel.[46] In the present context, "perish" is the antithesis of "have eternal life." Already in the OT, blessings for obedience correspond to curses for disobedience (Deut. 28–30). In John, likewise, there is no middle ground: believing in the Son (resulting in eternal life) or refusing to believe (resulting in destruction) are the

---

and result, but rather "in this way . . . and so," construing οὕτως with what precedes and taking ὥστε independently. This reading is novel, but it is hard to see how ὥστε could introduce a main clause and be rendered "and so." Also, these authors maintain that 3:16 is parallel to 3:14 (καθώς . . . οὕτως, "just as . . . so"), but the traditional rendering provides a much better parallelism ("so much . . . so") than the newly proposed one ("in this way . . . and so").

44. Contra Schnackenburg (1990: 1.399), who places heavy emphasis on the incarnation rather than the crucifixion. Morris (1995: 203) and others believe that both the incarnation and the crucifixion are in view.

45. Note also the parallel wording in the messianic prophecy of Isa. 9:6: "to us a son is given."

46. Later significant uses of this term in John (some of which reveal Jesus' commitment to keep his own from perishing) include 6:39; 10:28; 12:25; 17:12; 18:9 (cf. 3:36; 8:21, 24). See Hahn, *NIDNTT* 1:462–65; Morris 1965b: 146–49.

only options. Since "perish" is contrasted with *"eternal* life," it stands to reason that perishing is eternal as well. However, "perishing" does not mean annihilation in the sense of total destruction, but rather spending eternity apart from God and from Jesus Christ, in whom alone is life (1:4).[47] In John's Gospel it is particularly Judas, the "son of perdition" (17:12) and betrayer of Jesus Christ, who represents an example of those who are perishing.

3:17–18   Here, it is "God" who is said to have sent his Son (perhaps echoing terminology reflected also in Gal. 4:4); elsewhere in John it is "the Father." The construction of 3:17 is typical of the Fourth Evangelist, who has a penchant for explaining what he means by restating an idea in the negative (Bultmann 1971: 154 n. 1; Carson 1991: 206). The present verse stands in apparent contradiction with 5:27 and 9:39. However, the provision of "salvation for all who believe implies judgment for those who do not believe"; while "the purpose of Christ's coming was redemptive, . . . when His saving work is rejected, judgment results. Even though judgment results from unbelief, condemnatory judgment was not the purpose of the incarnation" (Laney 1992: 82). Hence, the sense of κρίνω (*krinō*, judge) in the context of the present passage is strongly negative ("condemn"), whereas in 5:27 and 9:39 it is neutral (Carson 1991: 207).

Not believing in the God-sent Son is tantamount to self-condemnation; God is not to blame, but rather the unbeliever. Humans remain responsible agents; no one is compelled to believe. Unbelievers face "the necessity of escaping an already existing condemnation" (Borchert 1996: 185). Whereas the emphasis in 3:1–8 was on the necessity of spiritual rebirth, the focus in 3:12–18 is on believing; thus, the themes of divine sovereignty and human responsibility are balanced (Ridderbos 1997: 140). The two verbs in the perfect tense in 3:18, κέκριται (*kekritai*, stands condemned) and μὴ πεπίστευκεν (*mē pepisteuken*, has not believed), underscore the settled state of unbelievers' condemnation and unbelief.[48]

The OT makes clear that God would rather save than condemn (e.g., Ezek. 18:23). The Jews, however, believed that the coming Messiah would save Israel but judge the Gentiles.[49] The Qumran sect even maintained that only its own members would be saved while the rest of the world would perish (1QM 1:5). The adherents of mystery religions likewise believed that only they were the initiated. Contrary to these expectations, John affirms that the coming of the Messiah manifested God's saving will for all, not just the Jews or a select few. John 3:18 contains echoes to terminology found in the prologue: the phrase "believe in the

---

47. For further study on hell, see L. Dixon 1992; Fernando 1994; and Peterson 1995.
48. The use of μή with an indicative is extremely rare (cf. Luke 11:35; Gal. 4:11; Col. 2:8; contrast οὐ πεπίστευκεν in 1 John 5:10; see Barrett 1978: 217).
49. See the references cited in Köstenberger 2002c: 38.

name" harks back to 1:12 (cf. 2:23); "one-of-a-kind Son of God" echoes 1:14 and 1:18 (cf. 3:16).

Here we encounter some of John's "courtroom" terminology, which includes terms such as μαρτυρέω (*martyreō*, testify), μαρτυρία (*martyria*, testimony), κρίσις (*krisis*, judgment), and κρίμα (*krima*, verdict) (see Lincoln 2000). Whereas in the Synoptics it is Jesus who is on trial, in John it is the world (including "the Jews"). The charge is that the world in its moral darkness sinfully rejected Jesus, God's Messiah. A significant number of witnesses are marshaled to establish John's case: Moses and the Scriptures, John the Baptist, Jesus and his works, the Father, and the Fourth Evangelist himself (see commentary at 1:7). In the end, John exposes the miscarriage of justice at the Jewish and Roman trials of Jesus and presents Jesus' resurrection as his ultimate triumph over the unbelieving world, including Satan (12:31; 16:11).

3:19–21

The contrast between light and darkness was introduced in the prologue (see commentary at 1:4–5).[50] In the present passage, "light" and "darkness" have clear moral connotations, grounding the world's rejection of Jesus in human depravity, which is the result of the fall (Gen. 3; Rom. 1:18–32). In the ultimate analysis, sin (including people's failure to recognize God's Messiah) is irrational and self-destructive. Notably, and contrary to Jewish self-perception, the Jews are not exempt from this pattern: they are shown to be in bondage to sin and spiritual blindness, refusing to face their guilt and preferring to suppress the truth instead (John 8:31–59; 9:39–41; cf. Matt. 21:33–46 pars.; Acts 7).[51]

A person in darkness does not come to the light for fear that his or her deeds will be exposed (John 3:20). The verb ἐλεγχθῇ (*elenchthē*, may be exposed) points further to the conviction and shame that come through such exposure (in 16:8, a function of the παράκλητος [*paraklētos*, Paraclete]). It is the opposite case with a person who "works truth."[52] "Works truth" contrasts with "perpetrates evil" in the preceding verse and represents a typical Jewish expression meaning "to act faithfully."[53] The rather unique phrase ἐν θεῷ εἰργασμένα (*en theō eirgasmena*, accomplished through God; cf. Mark 14:6) makes clear that these works are done through God rather than by one's own strength. This excludes

50. The translation "preferred" captures the Semitism underlying the more literal translation "loved more than" (R. Brown 1966: 134).
51. See the discussion of Plato's "Allegory of the Cave" (*Republic* 7.1–11 [ca. 390 B.C.]) in relation to John 3:19–21 by Köstenberger (2002c: 38–39), who notes that in Plato's allegory, the person who has seen the light is the philosopher who is cognizant of the world of ideas and thus is able better to explain reality, while in Jesus' teaching, the light is himself (cf. 1:4–5; 8:12; 9:5), and people's main problem is not ignorance but sin (cf. Ferguson 1993: 313–14).
52. The wording is similar at 5:29: "those who have done [what is] good."
53. It is found in the Greek OT (Neh. 9:33; Isa. 26:10), the apocryphal literature (Tob. 4:6; 13:6), and the Qumran scrolls (1QS 1:5; 5:3).

human pride.[54] For not just salvation, but also subsequent works are, properly understood, works "accomplished through God."

Additional Notes

3:13. Barrett (1978: 213 [followed by Laney 1992: 80]), against the vast majority of commentators (e.g., Morris 1995: 198; Carson 1991: 203; Schnackenburg 1990: 1.393–94; Moloney 1998: 101), accepts the variant "who is in heaven" after "Son of Man" because it is the more difficult reading (so also Black 1984). Carson (1991: 203) speaks for many when he states, "If no sensible copyist would have put it in, one wonders why we should think John would put it in."

3:15. The textual variant εἰς αὐτόν probably represents an assimilation to 3:16, so that ἐν αὐτῷ likely is original (Ridderbos 1997: 137 n. 107; R. Brown 1966: 133; Bultmann 1971: 152 n. 2). If so, the phrase seems to modify "have eternal life" rather than "believe" (Barrett 1978: 214; Morris 1995: 200 n. 68; Carson 1991: 202; Schnackenburg 1990: 1.397; contra Wallace 1996: 359). This is suggested by the fact that nowhere else in this Gospel is πιστεύω followed by ἐν. See discussion at 1:4.

---

54. On the exclusion of human "boasting," see especially Jer. 9:23–24, to which Paul harks back particularly in his dealings with the Corinthians: 1 Cor. 1:26–31; 2 Cor. 10:17; cf. Gal. 6:13–14; Eph. 2:8–9.

b. Interlude: The Testimony of John the Baptist (3:22–36)

By way of interlude between Jesus' conversation with Nicodemus and his encounter with the Samaritan woman, the evangelist returns to John the Baptist, whom he had already mentioned in the prologue (1:6–8, 15) and later in the opening chapter (1:19–37).[1] The present passage indicates that the Baptist had continued his practice of baptism up to this point (information consistent with that of the other Gospels), which raises the issue of the relationship between his ministry and that of Jesus.[2] In a poignant metaphor, John describes his role as that of "best man," as "friend of the bridegroom" (3:29), who rejoices with the groom (Jesus) without any sense of rivalry or competitiveness. As the evangelist will make clear at the very end of his Gospel, this is a lesson that all of Jesus' disciples need to learn (including the apostle Peter and John himself [21:15–23]).

As is the case in 3:16, 3:31 probably marks the transition from the speech of a character in the narrative to the evangelist's own exposition (Dodd 1953: 308–9; Morris 1995: 214–15; Carson 1991: 212; Borchert 1996: 192–93; Beasley-Murray 1999: 46, 53; Burge 1987: 81–82; 2000: 122; Witherington 1995: 110; Schnackenburg 1990: 1.381; contra Ridderbos 1997: 148; Barrett 1978: 224; and the NIV [though cf. the TNIV], NASB, and NKJV). Thus, 3:31–36 represents a "recapitulating epilogue," not merely of 3:22–30, but of the entire chapter (cf., e.g., 3:6 and 3:31; see Ridderbos 1997: 148–49).[3]

    i. Background (3:22–26)
    ii. John's testimony (3:27–30)
    iii. The evangelist's exposition (3:31–36)

---

1. On the connections between 3:22–36 and 3:11–21, see Klaiber 1990. Stegemann (1990: 514), in a very sound structural proposal, views 1:19–34 and 3:22–36 as *inclusios* encompassing 1:19–3:36, which in turn is a composite of 1:19–2:11 (John the Baptist; first week of Jesus' ministry; first sign) and 2:13–3:36 (Jesus' ministry in Jerusalem, including sign; John the Baptist [2:12 is transitional]).

2. There is no need to believe that the present verses were dislodged from their context (Morris 1995: 208–9; contra R. Brown 1966: 154–55) or to suppose that the placement of this section after 3:1–21 indicates that the prior section pertains to the rite of baptism (so, rightly, Carson 1991: 209).

3. Contra R. Brown (1966: 160), who suggests that these are actually the words of Jesus removed from their original context. Bultmann (1971: 160 n. 2) contends, without warrant, that these verses originally were located after 3:21.

Exegesis and Exposition

²²After these things Jesus and his disciples went into the Judean countryside. And there he spent some time with them and baptized. ²³But John also was baptizing at Aenon near Salim, because there was an ample supply of water, and people were coming and being baptized. ²⁴(For John had not yet been thrown into prison.) ²⁵Now there arose a dispute on the part of some of John's disciples with ⌜a certain Jew⌝ concerning purification. ²⁶And so they came to John and said to him, "Rabbi, the one who was with you on the other side of the Jordan—the one to whom you have borne witness—well, he is baptizing, and all are coming to him."

²⁷John answered and said, "A person can receive only what has been given him from heaven. ²⁸You yourselves bear witness that I said, 'I am not the Christ,' but 'I have been sent ahead of him.' ²⁹The one who has the bride is the bridegroom; the friend of the bridegroom is the one who stands and upon hearing him rejoices greatly on account of the bridegroom's voice. So, then, this my joy is now complete. ³⁰He must increase [in stature], but I must decrease."

³¹The one who comes from above is above all; the one who is from the earth is from the earth and speaks as one from the earth. The one who comes from heaven ⌜is above all⌝. ³²To what he has seen and heard he bears witness, yet no one accepts his testimony. ³³The one who receives his testimony confirms that God is truthful. ³⁴For the one whom God has sent speaks the words of God, for he [God] gives the Spirit without measure. ³⁵The Father loves the Son and has given everything into his hands. ³⁶Whoever believes in the Son has eternal life; but whoever does not believe in the Son will not see life, but God's wrath remains on him.

i. Background (3:22–26)

3:22
The brief reference to Jesus' baptizing ministry is meant to prepare the reader for the statement in 3:26. After his baptism by John, Jesus apparently continued to proclaim the coming of God's kingdom and the need for a baptism of repentance in accordance with the Baptist's message (see Matt. 4:17; cf. 3:2; see Ridderbos 1997: 143–44; cf. Moloney 1998: 109; Witherington 1995: 108; Burge 2000: 120; Beasley-Murray 1999: 52; contra Borchert 1996: 189; Schnackenburg 1990: 1.411–12). If so, the baptism described here is not Christian baptism (Morris 1995: 209; R. Brown 1966: 151; Witherington 1995: 108; D. M. Smith 1999: 103, contrasting the present reference with the Spirit baptism mentioned in 1:33).[4]

---

4. Some scholars (e.g., Witherington 1995: 108; Schnackenburg 1990: 1.411–12) suggest that it is those disciples of Jesus who had been followers of the Baptist who continued John's baptism, but this unduly shifts the focus regarding the nature of Jesus' ministry from Jesus to his disciples.

"After these things" (cf. 2:12) likely is meant to suggest that these events occurred at an unspecified time interval after Jesus' Jerusalem ministry (Ridderbos 1997: 143; Carson 1991: 209; cf. R. Brown 1966: 150).[5] The reference to the γῆς (gēs) of Judea seems puzzling at first.[6] The word γῆς usually means "land" or "region." However, this rendering seems to be excluded here, since Jesus has been in *the land of* Judea all along since attending the Passover from 2:23 to 3:21. More likely, the term here means "countryside" (TNIV; cf. Mark 1:5: χώρα [chōra]; so, earlier, Schlatter 1948: 103; also Carson 1991: 209). If so, Jesus is shown to leave the vicinity of Jerusalem and to head north. The next verse places him with John the Baptist at Aenon near Salim (see commentary at 3:23), while 4:3 indicates that Jesus leaves Judea altogether, returning to Galilee (cf. 2:12) via Samaria.

The expression διατρίβω (diatribō, spend some time) is deliberately vague. As in 11:54, the idea is an indefinite period of time that Jesus spent with his disciples. In the Book of Acts, the only other place in the NT where the term occurs, the stay may be longer but need not extend for more than "seven days" (20:6) or "eight or ten days" (25:6).[7] In John 3:22, both διέτριβεν (dietriben, spent some time) and ἐβάπτιζεν (ebaptizen, baptized) are in the imperfect, indicating continuing action (Morris 1995: 210; R. Brown 1966: 151; Moloney 1998: 105; Wallace 1996: 411–12, 547). Here it is said that "he" (Jesus) baptized; as the evangelist will soon clarify, Jesus, in fact, did not baptize at all, but rather his disciples did (4:2).

The periphrastic "was . . . baptizing" corresponds to the imperfect ἐβάπτι- **3:23–24** ζεν in the previous verse (Morris 1995: 210 n. 98; note also the imperfect verbs παρεγίνοντο [pareginonto, they were coming] and ἐβαπτίζοντο [ebaptizonto, they were baptized]). Perhaps John continued his ministry of baptism so as to have further opportunity to bear witness to Jesus as the Christ (Bultmann 1971: 170–71; cf. Ridderbos 1997: 145; Morris 1995: 210–11).

The site chosen for baptism was Aenon near Salim, because there was an ample supply of water. "Aenon" is a Semitic term meaning "springs"; hence John's mention of "plenty of water" (lit., "many waters," i.e., springs), which would have made this an ideal site for John's (and Jesus') baptismal preaching (Morris 1995: 210). "Salim" comes from the Hebrew word for "peace." The location of this place is disputed. The two primary sites that have been suggested both lie in Samaria (fore-

---

5. There is little evidence to support the various rearrangement theories that have been associated with these verses (Carson 1991: 209; Barrett 1978: 219).

6. On this and other purported examples of an *aporia*, or literary "seam," see the excursus in Köstenberger 1999a: 259–60. See also chapter 4 in Kellum 2005 (with special emphasis on 14:31).

7. Morris (1995: 209) refers to "an unhurried period."

shadowing things to come [see 4:1–42]): one is the Salim eight miles southeast of Beth Shean (Scythopolis); another is the Salim four miles southeast of Shechem, farther south.[8] The presence of a town (known from early times) called Sâlim in the latter location and of modern 'Ainûn, eight miles northeast of Sâlim, appears to favor the second site. Also, the latter location, being farther south, seems to cohere better with the geographical markers of 3:22 and 4:3. In either case, assuming the reconstruction of "Bethany on the other side of the Jordan" in 1:28 to be correct, John would have moved south by this time.

Despite increasing "competition" from Jesus, the Baptist's appeal shows no signs of abating; many keep coming and are being baptized. Nevertheless, John's disciples are concerned that Jesus is beginning to draw people away from him (see commentary at 3:25–30).

The parenthetical note "For John had not yet been thrown into prison" constitutes yet another instance where the readers of this Gospel are assumed to know an aspect of the Synoptic tradition (see commentary at 1:40; Bauckham 1998: 147–71, esp. 152–55). It may also be intended to assure them that the evangelist himself is aware of Synoptic chronology (Borchert 1996: 190). On one level, the evangelist seems to state the obvious: how could John have baptized after having been imprisoned? But the evangelist is concerned that those familiar with, say, the Gospel of Mark will see a contradiction between Mark's account (which does not record any Galilean ministry on the part of Jesus prior to John's imprisonment) and his own narrative (which does). In fact, a reading of the Synoptics seems to suggest that Jesus began his Galilean ministry *after* John's arrest (Mark 1:14; Matt. 4:12); only from the present Gospel do we learn that there was an interim period during which the Baptist's and Jesus' ministries overlapped. Rather than representing a discrepancy with the Synoptics, the Fourth Evangelist seeks to clarify the chronology, indicating that everything that happened up to this point in his Gospel took place prior to John's imprisonment by Herod Antipas, which is recorded in Mark 1:14 (cf. 6:17–29; see Carson 1991: 209–10; Burge 2000: 121; Ridderbos 1997: 145).

3:25–26   Nothing else is known about the "certain Jew" mentioned here (see additional note). The reference to "purification" is probably incidental. The issue of ritual purification, while of significant interest to first-century Jews (see the DSS; Morris 1995: 211), clearly is peripheral to the ministries of Jesus and John the Baptist. Hence, no further explanation is provided (cf. 2:6; 11:55; 18:28; 19:31). It is possible that the dispute centered around the issue of whose baptism was more efficacious, the

---

8. The first is mentioned as early as Eusebius's *Onomasticon* (fourth century A.D.). The second is defended by the eminent archaeologist Albright (1924), followed by Bacon (1929); see also Finegan (1992: 70). Yet another site is suggested in Riesner, *DJG* 35: Ain Farah, eight miles northwest of Shechem.

Baptist's or Jesus' (Ridderbos 1997: 146; cf. Beasley-Murray 1999: 52; Bultmann 1971; 171; Moloney 1998: 105). More likely, questions arose regarding the connection between John's baptism and more traditional ceremonies practiced in contemporary Judaism (Carson 1991: 210; Burge 2000: 121; Witherington 1995: 108; Moloney 1998: 109).

The manner in which John's disciples refer to Jesus betrays a degree of jealousy on their part (note the impersonal way of referring to Jesus and the hyperbolic statement "all are coming to him"; cf. 11:48; see Ridderbos 1997: 146). Not everyone among John's followers had responded to Jesus the way Jesus' first disciples had.[9] Intriguingly, this appears to have been a time when both the Baptist and Jesus had attractive, vibrant ministries (compare the imperfect verbs in 3:23 and the reference in 3:24; note also the disclaimer in 4:2). The perfect verb μεμαρτύρηκας (*memartyrēkas*, you have witnessed [with a dative of person, as in 3:28]) points to the abiding influence of John's witness (Morris 1995: 211 n. 105). The pronoun σύ (*sy*, you) is emphatic, contrasting the Baptist with Jesus (Morris 1995: 211).

This is the only place in John's Gospel where the Baptist is called "rabbi" (cf. 1:38). Though the Baptist, who engaged predominantly in a prophetic-style ministry, does not fit the stereotype of a Jewish rabbi, the term at that time was still sufficiently broad to characterize the Baptist. Later, the term came to be used only for those who underwent formal rabbinic training. The phrase "on the other side of the Jordan" suggests that Salim must be located on the west side of the Jordan (Schlatter 1948: 106; cf. 1:28: "Bethany on the other side of the Jordan," i.e., east of the Jordan).

ii. John's Testimony (3:27–30)

In keeping with contemporary practice, John uses the term "heaven" as a circumlocution for the name of God (similarly, Jesus in 19:11: "from above"). John here tells his disciples that he must neither exceed the calling he received from God nor compare himself with others (cf. 21:20–22; see Moloney 1998: 106).[10] The reference to Jesus' superior calling comports entirely with John's witness throughout (1:7–9, 15, 26–27, 30). Reminding his disciples of his consistent testimony—Jesus is greater than he is—the Baptist tells his devotees that they should not be surprised that Jesus has attracted a larger following (Ridderbos 1997: 147; cf. Morris 1995: 212; Carson 1991: 211; Borchert 1996: 191).[11]

3:27–30

---

9. It is not necessary to postulate that here the evangelist is addressing those who had remained followers of John the Baptist in his day (Carson 1991: 210; cf. Ridderbos 1997: 146; Morris 1995: 211; contra R. Brown 1966: 156; Barrett 1978: 219; Witherington 1995: 107; Schnackenburg 1990: 1.410).

10. The perfect participle δεδομένον (*dedomenon,* given) points to the permanence of the assignment (Morris 1995: 212).

11. Note the emphatic expression "you yourselves" (Morris 1995: 212). Schlatter (1948: 107) notes how closely οὐκ (*ouk,* not) is linked to εἰμί (*eimi,* I am) in 3:28.

The phrase "sent ahead" (an intensive perfect [Wallace 1996: 574–75]) is used in the OT for messengers sent ahead of a given person (e.g., Gen. 24:7; 32:3; 45:5; 46:28; cf. Ps. 105:17). John the Baptist now provides an illustration of what he said in plain language in 1:20–23 and 3:28. With Jesus on the ascendancy (3:26) and John at the height of his popularity (3:23), the issue of John's relationship to Jesus needed clarification. John likens himself to the best man (*šôšbîn*) at a wedding, who stands ready to do the bridegroom's bidding (e.g., *m. Sanh.* 3.5; *m. B. Bat.* 9.4).[12] In light of the OT background where Israel is depicted as "the bride of Yahweh" (Morris 1995: 213–14), the Baptist is suggesting that Jesus is Israel's awaited king and messiah (Carson 1991: 211; R. Brown 1966: 156; Barrett 1978: 223). In keeping with ancient law, the Baptist as the "best man" would be barred from ever marrying the bride (Carson 1991: 212; R. Brown 1966: 152).

The Baptist also makes clear that the purpose of his ministry was to elevate Jesus, so that there was no rivalry between the two men. Moreover, since Jesus is on the ascendancy, John perceives that his ministry is about to come to a close. This is not merely a personal issue; the transition from the Baptist to Jesus represents a crucial salvation-historical watershed from the OT prophetic era to that of the Messiah (Borchert 1996: 192; cf. Ridderbos 1997: 147). John's language here, "He must increase [in stature], but I must decrease," is reminiscent of the increase and decrease of light from the heavenly bodies. The more radiantly the rising sun begins to shine, the more John's star will grow dim.[13] The presence of the term καθαρισμός (*katharismos*, purification) in 3:25 (cf. 2:6) and the wedding metaphor in the present verse make it possible that the evangelist is alluding to Jesus' first "sign" at the wedding of Cana (Barrett 1978: 223).

iii. The Evangelist's Exposition (3:31–36)

3:31–34 The evangelist[14] here contrasts "the one who comes from above/heaven" (Jesus; cf. 3:13) with "the one who is from the earth" (the Baptist, representing humanity at large). The latter bears witness to what he has seen

---

12. Jesus calls himself "the bridegroom" in Matt. 9:15 pars. For the role of the bridegroom's friend, see Gower 1987: 64–66; Zimmermann and Zimmermann 1999. Joy was the overriding theme at Jewish weddings; the verb πληρόω (*plēroō*, fulfill, complete) is associated with joy throughout this Gospel (Carson 1991: 211–12; Barrett 1978: 223). The Baptist's words χαρᾷ χαίρει (*chara chairei*, lit., rejoices with joy), a Hebraism (χαρᾷ is a cognate dative [Wallace 1996: 168–69]), serve to intensify the verb (Ridderbos 1997: 147 n. 132; Morris 1995: 213 n. 112).

13. Note the reference to John by Jesus as a "lamp" in 5:35. See Ridderbos 1997: 147–48; cf. R. Brown 1966: 153; Moloney 1998: 110.

14. So, rightly, the TNIV (contra the NLT). The transition here is similar to that from 3:15 (Jesus) to 3:16 (the evangelist). Alternatively, the Baptist's words continue until the end of the chapter. See the introduction to this section.

and heard (though his witness is largely rejected);[15] the former speaks the words of God. Being "from the earth" here does not connote sinfulness, only finitude and limitation (Carson 1991: 212; Lee 1994: 43).

The discussion is strongly reminiscent of the similar contrast drawn in the prologue (cf. 1:6–10) and in the discussion between Nicodemus and Jesus earlier in the chapter. The clause "The one who is from the earth is from the earth"—in which the first part refers to origin and the second part to kind (Carson 1991: 212; Barrett 1978: 225; Schnackenburg 1990: 1.382)—echoes Jesus' words in 3:6 (cf. 1:13).

Rejecting John's testimony is tantamount to rejecting the truthfulness of God. The verb σφραγίζω (sphragizō, confirm) literally means "to seal," in the sense of certifying or authenticating something to be true (cf. Schippers, NIDNTT 3:497–501). The term is derived from the practice of signing important documents by pressing one's distinctive mark, which was engraved on one's signet ring, onto hot wax. Here the expression is used to indicate that everyone who accepts Christ's testimony about himself agrees ("seals") that God is truthful. In 6:27, it is said that God has put his "seal of approval" upon the Son of Man.

"The one whom God has sent" without further qualifier in this Gospel refers to Jesus (see esp. 9:7, where "Siloam" [sent] refers symbolically to Jesus, the Sent One par excellence; see Carson 1991: 364–65; and commentary at 9:7). The term lying behind "words" is ῥῆμα (rhēma). Jesus' words are "spirit and life" (6:63); he alone has "words of eternal life" (6:68). At times, Jesus' "words" simply refers to his teachings (8:20; 10:21). Ultimately, Jesus' words are the words of God (12:47–48; 14:10); they must remain in his followers (15:7) and were given to them by Jesus (17:8). The Jews, on the other hand, believe in neither Moses' (5:47) nor God's words (8:47).

"For he [God] gives the Spirit without measure."[16] Later Jewish rabbis were convinced that God gave his Spirit to the prophets in measured amounts (Lev. Rab. 15.2 on Lev. 13:2; attributed to Rabbi Aḥa [ca. A.D. 320]). Jesus, on the other hand, was the one on whom the Spirit had come to rest in all his fullness, as the Baptist had previously testified (cf. 1:32–33). Hence, Jesus is more than a mere prophet: he is "the distributor of the Spirit" (Burge 1987: 55). In keeping with this notion, the Book of Revelation portrays Jesus as the one who holds the seven spirits of God (3:1; cf. 5:6).

In 3:27, it was the Baptist's testimony that "a person can receive only   3:35–36
what has been given him from heaven." Here it is said what the Son
has been given by the Father: "all things." The ground of this bountiful

---

15. "No one" in 3:32 is hyperbolic; cf. 3:33 and see the similar progression in 1:11–12 (Morris 1995: 216–17; Borchert 1996: 193; Ridderbos 1997: 150).

16. So, e.g., Lee 1994: 41–42. It is possible that "he" refers to Jesus rather than God (Burge 1987: 83–84; cf. Hofius 1999: 131–34).

equipment is the Father's love for the Son, through whom believers also become objects of God's love (Calvin 1959: 85). Hence, also people must believe in the Son, resulting in eternal life, or else God's wrath remains on them (cf. 1 John 5:11–12).

The present tense "has" in the phrase "has eternal life" indicates that eternal life is not merely a future expectation but already a present experience. This exceeds OT hopes and claims made by other world religions. Similar to "see/enter the kingdom" and "practice the truth," "see life" is a typical Jewish expression meaning "experience or enjoy life." The corresponding expression "see death" is found in 8:51.[17]

The final verse of the chapter clearly attests to the fact that the wrath of God rests on unbelievers, which makes believing in the Son not optional but essential. The term ὀργή (orgē, wrath) is used only here in John's Gospel and the Johannine Epistles. In Revelation, both ὀργή and θύμος (thymos, the other Johannine word for "wrath") are used repeatedly to refer to God's holy outrage against rebellious humanity.[18]

Additional Notes

3:25. "A Jew" ($\mathfrak{P}^{75}$ A B) is the harder reading and more likely than the (anarthrous) reading "Jews" ($\mathfrak{P}^{66}$ ℵ*), which is contrary to Johannine style (Morris 1995: 211; Carson 1991: 210; R. Brown 1966: 152; Moloney 1998: 109; Barrett 1978: 221; Beasley-Murray 1999: 45; Pryor 1997: 15–16). The conjecture that the verse originally read "Jesus" instead of "Jew" (R. Brown 1966: 152; cf. Lindars 1972: 165) lacks MS support. Pryor (1997: 16–26) advances the unlikely proposal that the evangelist's source referred to Jesus, but he chose to change Ἰησοῦ τοῦ Ἰουδαίου to avoid any notion of dispute between Jesus and the Baptist.

3:31. The second occurrence of "is above all" in 3:31 constitutes a textual problem, but the phrase may well be original; the sense is the same in either case (Morris 1995: 216 n. 123; Ridderbos 1997: 149–50 n. 141; Barrett 1978: 225; contra Carson 1991: 213).

17. For OT parallels of "see life," see the LXX of Isa. 26:14; Job 10:22; Eccles. 9:9 (cf. Ps. 33:13 LXX, cited in 1 Pet. 3:10).
18. Ὀργή: Rev. 6:16–17; 11:18; 14:10; 16:19; 19:15; θυμός: Rev. 14:10, 19; 15:1, 7; 16:1, 19; 19:15.

c. The Samaritan Woman (4:1–42)

Jesus' return trip from the Jerusalem Passover back to Galilee led him, by divine necessity (4:4), through Samaria. Samaritans occupied a middle position between Jews and Gentiles, considering themselves Jews but being viewed by Jews as Gentiles.[1] This middle position required that the early church be a witness not just in Jerusalem and in all Judea, and then to the ends of the earth, but also in Samaria (Acts 1:8; cf. Acts 8). This sequence may also be reflected in the fact that in John, Jesus first witnesses to the Jew Nicodemus (ch. 3), then to the Samaritan woman (ch. 4), and then hears of approaching Gentiles (12:20–22; see also 4:45–53).

The relationship between Jews and Samaritans in Jesus' day was characterized by considerable acrimony. Indeed, John tells his readers that "Jews have no dealings with Samaritans" (4:9). This is why the Samaritan woman is surprised when Jesus asks her for a drink, for he must have known that using a drinking vessel handled by a Samaritan would defile him, since Samaritans were considered "unclean" by Jews. But contemporary Jewish scruples of that sort were of no concern to Jesus (cf. Mark 7:19). In fact, Jesus made a Samaritan the hero of one of his parables (Luke 10:25–37).

The setting for Jesus' encounter with the Samaritan woman is historic: Jacob's well. But their conversation has to bridge several major gulfs.[2] Ethnically, the history of Samaritan-Jewish relations was strained. The Samaritans had built a temple on Mount Gerizim (cf. Deut. 27:4–6) about 400 B.C., which was destroyed about 128 B.C. by the Jews, who claimed that proper worship must be conducted in Jerusalem. Religiously, the Samaritans' Scripture consisted only of the Pentateuch (the five books of Moses); the Jewish canon also included the Writings and the Prophets. Morally, Jesus, the Christ, the Son of God, stands opposite the Samaritan woman, who had had intimate relations with five men and was not married to her current partner (4:17–18).

In all of this, John highlights the divine condescension that caused the preexistent Word to become flesh and dwell among humans. In the fullness of his humanity, Jesus is tired (4:6) and thirsty (4:7) and asks

---

1. See the sidebar on Samaritans in Köstenberger 2002c: 45, including the listing of additional bibliography in footnote A-15 on p. 215.

2. On the moral, gender, and ethnic barriers separating Jesus from the Samaritan woman, see Keener 2003: 593–601.

a Samaritan woman for a drink. Yet it is precisely this condescension that opens up opportunities for revelation regarding Jesus' ability to grant eternal life ("living water" [4:10]), his supernatural knowledge (4:17–18; cf. 1:48), the proper way of worship (in spirit and truth [4:23–24]), and his true identity (he is the Christ [4:25–26]). In the end, the Samaritan woman invites her townspeople to come and see Jesus for themselves, and many believe (4:39). Hence, mission emerges as the primary topic of this narrative (see esp. 4:27–38).[3]

In structuring his narrative, the evangelist first sets the background (4:1–3), then narrates the dialogue between Jesus and the Samaritan woman (4:4–26), and finally describes the woman's return to her village, Jesus' interchange with his disciples, and the coming of more Samaritans (4:27–42) (Ridderbos 1997: 152).[4] Unlike Nicodemus (whose comments decrease in length and reveal ignorance), the Samaritan woman progresses in her understanding (Maccini 1996: 119–21), from calling Jesus a prophet (4:19; cf. 4:29, 39) to serving, albeit somewhat ambivalently, as a witness (4:27–30; see Blomberg 1995: 11).[5]

In addition, the conversation between Jesus and the Samaritan woman is fairly evenly balanced (Blomberg 1995: 9; though calling them "equal dialogue partners throughout the story" somewhat overstates the case). Unlike in Nicodemus's case, Jesus actually accepts the woman's "gambit" (4:21–24) and then responds to her implied question in 4:25, meeting her "immortal longings" (Cantwell 1983: 85). She will not call her husband, but soon she will call her entire village (Nortjé 1986: 25).

3. Beasley-Murray (1999: 58–59), after noting several lines of connection between chapters 2 and 4—the water/wine contrast in chapter 2, the well water/living water contrast in chapter 4, the Jerusalem temple versus Jesus' body in chapter 2, worship at Jerusalem/Mount Gerizim versus worship in spirit and truth in chapter 4—concludes that the form of chapter 4 is "controlled by the preceding signs," but the narrative is "set in a new dimension of mission to non-Israel."

4. See the various structural proposals in Beasley-Murray 1999: 59; R. Brown 1966: 176–78; Moloney 1998: 115. See also Carson 1991: 214.

5. Blomberg (1995: 8), with reference to Dockery (1988), lists five approaches to the present narrative: (1) allegorical (cf. 2 Kings 17:30–31); (2) existential (Bultmann 1971: 175–202); (3) pastoral (Milne 1993: 85–86); (4) salvation-historical (W. Davies 1974; Carson 1993); and (5) intertextual (focusing on OT parallels such as Gen. 24:10–61; 29:1–20; Exod. 2:15b–21) (Neyrey 1979). Acknowledging that all of these approaches capture elements of truth, Blomberg nevertheless finds them wanting and proposes a seven-pronged approach of his own. Stibbe (1993: 68–69) advocates a symbolic reading: "If the woman has had five husbands and is living *de facto* with a sixth, then Jesus is the seventh man in her life. Since seven is the perfect number in Judaism, the implicit commentary must be that Jesus is the man which she has been waiting for, the man in whose presence she will find wholeness." In the same vein, Brodie (1993: 217–18) sees this as a betrothal-type scene. See also Dockery (1988: 127–40), who distinguishes between author-, text-, and reader-oriented approaches, and Marshall 1974. R. Lightfoot (1956: 122) detects certain parallels between John 4 and 19.

Nevertheless, the woman's response is not as unequivocally positive as is usually maintained (Danna 1999: 219–23). First, as 4:29a makes clear, the woman, ignoring Jesus' open claim in 4:26, considers Jesus to be nothing more than a prophet (though, to her credit, she still goes to tell her townspeople).[6] Second, the interrogative particle μήτι (*mēti*) indicates that the woman, if not expecting a negative answer, at the very least appears somewhat hesitant:[7] "He couldn't be the Christ, could he?"[8]

Nor is there any explicit attribution of "believing" action to the woman. The woman's faith is at best tentative and uncertain.[9] Although there is a noticeable movement from her regarding Jesus as "a despised Jew to . . . someone who can make her life easier . . . to a prophet" (Danna 1999: 222), it is only the townspeople who complete the progression when they come to believe that Jesus is "Savior of the world" (4:42). Thus, the woman's response does not go far enough. Nevertheless, she acts like a disciple, and in some ways she is a better disciple than Jesus' actual followers.

The returning disciples (cf. 4:8) interrupt the conversation at its climax (Ridderbos 1997: 166). Jesus' dialogue with his disciples in 4:31–38 is set between the accounts of the Samaritan woman's witness to her people in 4:27–30 and their coming to believe in 4:39–42 (Beasley-Murray 1999: 59). This arrangement resembles a two-stage drama: on one stage, Jesus is conversing with his followers; on the other, the woman speaks to her fellow villagers and induces them to come and see Jesus. The scene ends with the final chorus of the townspeople who express faith in Jesus.[10]

6. In this she is only gradually better than Nicodemus, who perceives Jesus to be a "teacher come from God" (3:2).

7. O'Day (1986: 76) says that the question "is not a denial, but neither is it a full affirmative." BDAG 649 identifies 4:29b as a hesitant question, citing Matt. 12:23 as closest parallel; BDF §221: "perhaps this is the Messiah." See also the discussion in Beck 1997: 75–76.

8. Cf. LSJ 1130, *s.v.* μήτις; NRSV; Lindars 1972: 193. Westcott (1908: 1.163) comments, "The form of the sentence grammatically suggests a negative answer (v. 33), but hope bursts through it." The two other uses of μήτι in this Gospel (8:22; 18:35) unequivocally expect a negative response.

9. Moloney (1998: 196–99) considers the woman to be an example of "partial faith," and her fellow villagers to be one of "complete faith."

10. Dodd 1953: 315; Dockery 1988: 129–30, 133; Culpepper 1983: 136–37; Duke 1985: 100–103.

Exegesis and Exposition

[1]So when ⌐Jesus⌐ learned that the Pharisees had heard that Jesus was making and baptizing more disciples than John—[2]although in fact it was not Jesus himself who was baptizing, but his disciples—[3]he left Judea and departed again for Galilee.

[4]Yet it was necessary for him to pass through Samaria. [5]So he came to a Samaritan town called Sychar, in the vicinity of the plot of land that Jacob had given to his son Joseph. [6]And Jacob's well was there. So Jesus, worn out from the journey, sat down thus by the well. It was about the sixth hour [around noon].

[7]A woman from Samaria came to draw water. Jesus said to her, "Give me something to drink." [8](For his disciples had gone to the town to buy supplies.) [9]So the Samaritan woman said to him, "How is it that you, a Jew, ask me, a Samaritan woman, to give you something to drink?" (For Jews have no dealings with Samaritans.) [10]Jesus answered and said to her, "If you knew the gift of God and who it is that is telling you, 'Give me something to drink,' you would have asked him and he would have given you living water." [11]The woman said to him, "Sir, you have nothing to draw with, and the well is deep; so where do you get living water? [12]You are not greater than our father Jacob, are you, who gave us the well and himself drank from it, as also did his sons and his animals?" [13]Jesus answered and said to her, "Everyone who drinks from this water will thirst again. [14]But whoever drinks from the water that I will give him will never thirst again, but the water that I will give him will become in him a water supply welling up to eternal life." [15]The woman said to him, "Sir, give me this water, so that I won't get thirsty or have to keep coming here to draw water."

[16]He said to her, "Go, call your husband, and come back here." [17]The woman answered and said to him, "I don't have a husband." Jesus said to her, "Well you have said, 'I don't have a husband.' [18]For you have had five men, and the one you have now is not your husband. This you have said truthfully." [19]The woman said to him, "Sir, I see that you are a prophet. [20]Our ancestors worshiped on this mountain, yet you Jews say that the place where one ought to worship is in Jerusalem." [21]Jesus said to her, "Believe me, woman, a time is coming when you [Samaritans] will worship the Father neither on this mountain nor in Jerusalem. [22]You Samaritans worship what you do not know; we worship what we know, because salvation is from the Jews. [23]But the time is coming and in fact has arrived when true worshipers will worship the Father in spirit and truth. For, in fact, the Father is looking for those who worship him in such a way. [24]God is spirit, and those who worship him must worship in spirit and truth." [25]The woman said to him, "I know that the Messiah is coming—the one called Christ. When he comes, he will explain everything to us." [26]Jesus said to her, "I am the one—the one who is talking to you."

[27]Just then his disciples came and were surprised to find him talking with a woman. Yet no one said, "What are you seeking to accomplish?" or, "Why are

you talking with her?" ²⁸Then the woman left her water jar and headed back to the town and told the people, ²⁹"Come, see a man who told me everything I ever did; he couldn't be the Christ, could he?" ³⁰They set out from the town and were coming toward him.

³¹In the meantime his disciples were urging him, saying, "Rabbi, eat something!" ³²But he said to them, "I have food to eat that you do not know." ³³Then the disciples were saying to one another, "No one brought him food to eat, did he?" ³⁴Jesus said to them, "My food is to do the will of the one who sent me and to accomplish his work. ³⁵Don't you say, 'Four more months and then comes the harvest'? Look, I tell you, lift up your eyes and see the fields—they are ripe for harvest. Already ³⁶the reaper receives wages and gathers a crop for eternal life, so that the sower and the reaper may rejoice together. ³⁷For in this the saying is true, 'There is one who sows and another who reaps.' ³⁸I am sending you to reap that for which you have not labored; others have labored, and you have reaped the benefits of their labor."

³⁹Many of the Samaritans from that town believed in him on account of the woman testifying, "He told me everything I ever did." ⁴⁰So when the Samaritans came to him, they urged him to stay with them, and he stayed there for two days. ⁴¹And many more believed on account of his word, ⁴²and they were saying to the woman, "No longer do we believe on account of your testimony alone; for we have heard for ourselves, and we know that this one truly is the Savior of the world."

i. Background (4:1–3)

John's is the only Gospel that tells us of the baptizing ministries of Jesus and his disciples. "So" (οὖν, *oun*) loosely connects this passage to the previous section (Morris 1995: 222 n. 1). The reference to Jesus' knowledge is a recurring Johannine theme.[11] The Pharisees heard that Jesus was making and baptizing more disciples than John. They had investigated John's credentials (1:19–27); now they are looking into those of Jesus. There were others baptizing in Judea during this period, but Jesus and John were distinctive in that they used baptism as an initiatory rite for Jews.[12]

Ἐβάπτιζεν (*ebaptizen*, he was baptizing) in 4:2, an imperfect, indicates progressive or continual action (Morris 1995: 223 n. 7); the present tense verbs ποιεῖ (*poiei*, he is making) and βαπτίζει (*baptizei*, he is baptizing) in 4:1 have imperfect force as well (Wallace 1996: 456–58). "Departed again for Galilee" alludes to Jesus' attendance of the Cana wedding and his brief stay at Capernaum in John 2.[13] Jesus' departure, in continua-

4:1–3

---

11. See Culpepper 1983: 22 for a list of editorial comments presenting the internal thoughts of Jesus (4:1; 5:6; 6:6, 15, 61, 64; 11:5, 33, 38; 13:1, 11, 21; 16:19; 18:4; 19:28).

12. On the disclaimer of 4:2 and regarding Jesus' leaving of Judea, see commentary at 3:22 (cf. 1 Cor. 1:14–17).

13. Cf., in the Synoptics, Matt. 12:15; Mark 3:7; Luke 5:16 (see Borchert 1996: 198).

tion of 3:22, is part of a pattern, consistently chronicled in the present Gospel, of withdrawal by one whom one writer has termed "the elusive Christ" (Stibbe 1991: 19–38).[14]

ii. Setting (4:4–6)

4:4–6   The words "it was necessary" (ἔδει, *edei*) may indicate divine necessity: Jesus' going through Samaria was according to the plan and will of God (cf. 9:4; 10:16; 12:34; 20:9).[15] In any case, passing through (διέρχεσθαι, *dierchesthai* [the grammatical subject; Wallace 1996: 600–601]) Samaria also was strongly suggested geographically (cf. Luke 9:51–55). Hence "through Samaria" was the usual trek taken by travelers from Judea to Galilee (see Josephus, *Ant.* 20.6.1 §118; cf. *J.W.* 2.12.1 §232; *Life* 52 §269). Strict Jews, however, sought to bypass Samaria by opting for a longer, less direct route, which would have involved crossing the Jordan and traveling on the east side. Samaria (which here refers to the entire region, not just the city) had no separate political existence in Jesus' day. Together with Judea, it was under the jurisdiction of the Roman procurator.

The small town of Sychar probably was located at the site of modern ʿAskar, about two miles east of Nablus, centrally situated just east of Mount Gerizim and Mount Ebal.[16] ʿAskar may also be the ʿên Soker mentioned in the Mishnah (*m. Menaḥ.* 10.2; see Avi-Yonah 1964: 140). An identification of Sychar with biblical Shechem (about a mile from ʿAskar) is unlikely, since Shechem probably was destroyed in 128 B.C. (or at least prior to 107 B.C.) by the Hasmonean high priest John Hyrcanus I (Josephus, *J.W.* 1.2.6 §63; *Ant.* 13.9.1 §§255–56). Subsequent to the conquest of Jerusalem by the Roman general Pompey (63 B.C.), Sychar apparently replaced Shechem as the most important Samaritan city.[17] John is the first ancient author to mention Sychar/ʿAskar.[18]

"Near the plot of land that Jacob had given to his son Joseph" reflects the customary inference from Gen. 48:21–22 and Josh. 24:32 that Jacob gave his son Joseph the land at Shechem that he had bought from the sons of Hamor (Gen. 33:18–19) and that later served as Joseph's burial

---

14. Talbert (1992: 111) maintains, "Jesus has withdrawn from Judea because of sensed competition between his ministry and that of the Baptist (vv. 1–3)."

15. This represents the wide consensus of interpreters: see Ridderbos 1997: 153; Carson 1991: 215–16; Borchert 1996: 198–99; Beasley-Murray 1999: 59; Witherington 1995: 115; R. Brown 1966: 169; Morris 1995: 226; Barrett 1978: 230; Moloney 1998: 116, 120; Conway 1999: 105.

16. See Potter 1959: 331; Kippenberg 1971: 94; Riesner, *DJG* 40. A few late sources (such as Jerome) substitute "Shechem" for "Sychar," but this is clearly secondary (contra R. Brown 1966: 169; Burge 2000: 141).

17. See Hengel 1999: 299–300; contra Albright 1956: 160.

18. "A city in Samaria" in Acts 8:5 may refer to Sychar as well (see Hengel 1999: 301).

place (Exod. 13:19; Josh. 24:32; see Neyrey 1979; Dalman 1935: 212–16). The reference to Jacob's well and the later mention of Mount Gerizim (John 4:20) place Jesus' encounter with the Samaritan woman in the framework of "holy geography," which Jesus is shown to transcend. Apparently, Jacob's well was a convenient stop for pilgrims traveling between Galilee and Jerusalem.[19]

The site of Jacob's well is reasonably certain, although the OT nowhere mentions Joseph digging a well here (or anywhere). The current well is about one hundred feet deep. The existence of such a deep well is curious in an area where there are many springs. ʿAskar is nearly a mile to the north and has its own well, but perhaps it did not two thousand years ago. Shechem, on the other hand, is only about a hundred yards from Jacob's well, which suggests to some that Shechem and not ʿAskar is the true Sychar.

Jesus was worn out from the journey (ἐκ τῆς ὁδοιπορίας, ek tēs hodoiporias [denoting impersonal agency; Wallace 1996: 434–35]). Since it was about noon when Jesus sat down at the well, he and his disciples had been traveling for about six hours up to that point if they had started their journey at daybreak.[20] The evangelist's presentation of Jesus forestalls any docetic-style interpretation.[21] Jesus "sat down" by the well. Wells usually were carved out from solid limestone rock, with a small curb remaining to guard against accident (cf. Exod. 21:33). This is probably where Jesus sat down to rest (L. Abbott 1879: 52). Οὕτως (houtōs, thus) modifies ἐκαθέζετο (ekathezeto, sat down [R. Brown 1966: 169]).[22]

"About the sixth hour" means around noon if reckoning from the start of the day at sunrise (see commentary at 1:39).[23] There is a possible contrast between the time of day at which Jesus met the Samaritan woman and the time of Nicodemus's visit (noon versus night; so Burge 2000: 139; Conway 1999: 106). In an intriguing parallel, Josephus speaks of Moses, who, upon reaching a given town, "sat down on the brink of a well and there rested after his toil and hardships, at midday, not far from the town" (Ant. 2.11.1 §257).

19. Hengel 1999: 302, referring to Dalman.

20. Kruse (2003: 127) writes, "If Jesus had been baptizing in the same area as John (3:22, 26) and had left from there heading north-west to Sychar, he had covered a significant distance. As the crow flies, Sychar is about 30 miles from Aenon; but following the Roman roads it was about 40 miles. The journey would take a day and a half, so Jesus and his disciples would arrive in Sychar on the second day at about the sixth hour, i.e. about noon."

21. See Ridderbos 1997: 153; cf. Carson 1991: 217; Borchert 1996: 201; Morris 1995: 228; Burge 2000: 142.

22. Barrett (1978: 231) suggests the translation "at once" or "without more ado"; Bultmann (1971: 177 n. 4) proposes the simple rendering "so."

23. So N. Walker 1960 and the vast majority of commentators, including Beasley-Murray 1999: 58 n. e; Witherington 1995: 120; Barrett 1978: 231; Moloney 1998: 116, 121; Bultmann 1971: 178; contra Borchert 1996: 201.

iii. Jesus' Conversation with the Samaritan Woman (4:7–26)

4:7–9 Jesus' conversation with the Samaritan woman has two major topics: the "living water" that Jesus offers (4:7–18) and the worship sought by the Father (4:19–26) (Dockery 1988: 129). The evangelist's description of the woman is terse: "a woman from Samaria" (Ridderbos 1997: 154). Apparently, the woman was from the district, not the town, of Samaria (the town is located several miles north of Sychar). If Sychar is ʿAskar, it is surprising that the woman did not go to the well there (Ain ʿAskar). Perhaps that well did not always flow, or the woman lived closer to the well of Jacob. Women were more likely to come in groups to fetch water (Gen. 24:11; Exod. 2:16; 1 Sam. 9:11) and to do so either early in the morning or later in the day when the heat of the sun was not so fierce (Gen. 24:11: "toward evening"; cf. Gen. 29:7–8).[24] By contrast, this Samaritan woman came alone, and she came in the heat of the midday sun. Both observations suggest that this woman was looked down upon in her community on account of her low reputation (Neyrey 1994: 82; see 4:16–18).[25]

By asking for a drink from a woman who had come to the well alone (δός, *dos*, give [indicates a request; Wallace 1996: 478–88]), Jesus, himself being alone (4:8), broke all rules of Jewish piety (see below). His taking the initative invited the accusation of acting in a flirtatious manner. Jewish men usually did not speak to women in public (Borchert 1996: 202). The fact that Isaac's and Jacob's prospective wives were met at wells (Gen. 24:17; 29:10) created the sort of precedent that would further have cautioned devout Jews. The precedents were taken to suggest that, unless one is looking for a mate, one should avoid speaking to women in public, especially at wells, which were known to be places where men could "pick up" women.

The evangelist parenthetically informs readers that Jesus' disciples had gone into the town (i.e., Sychar; see Schlatter 1948: 118) to buy food. Apparently, Jesus and his disciples carried little or nothing to eat on their journeys (see Matt. 12:1 pars.; 16:5–7 par.; cf. 10:9–10 pars.). Rather, they brought with them money to buy what they needed on the way (cf. John 12:6; 13:29). Purchasing food, together with the preparation and cooking of food and waiting on tables, were common tasks of disciples.[26] That

---

24. But note that it may have been winter when Jesus met the Samaritan woman (see commentary at 4:35); if so, the midday sun would not have been as hot. Contra Keener (2003: 592–93), who repeatedly stresses that the noon hour would be hot and speaks of the "intensity of heat," without entertaining the possibility that noon would not be so hot in December (the likely time of year for this event, in my view).

25. See Carson 1991: 217; Witherington 1995: 120; Morris 1995: 228; Burge 2000: 142; Schnackenburg 1990: 1.424. As part of a series of putative "wisdom" parallels, Witherington (1995: 119) proposes that the Samaritan woman is depicted as the maidservant of Wisdom. I find this background reconstruction unconvincing.

26. See *y. Šeb.* 9.9; *Lam. Rab.* 3.17; *y. Ber.* 8.5; *t. Ber.* 6.4–5. See also Köstenberger 1998a: 122.

Jesus and his disciples were willing to purchase food from Samaritans indicates a certain freedom from the self-imposed regulations of the stricter sort of Jews who would have been unwilling to eat food that had been handled by Samaritans.[27] Moreover, with certain dry foods there was no conveyance of defilement.

The Samaritan woman (the article before γυνή, *gynē*, in 4:9 is anaphoric [Wallace 1996: 218]) was well aware of the ethnic gulf that separated Jews and Samaritans in that day, and she expressed puzzlement that Jesus, a Jew, would ask her, a Samaritan woman, for a drink.[28] For readers unfamiliar with this situation, the evangelist adds a note that Jews have no dealings with Samaritans.[29] Generally, Jews avoided contact with Samaritans, especially Samaritan women, although there would have been a certain spectrum depending on locale, class, education, and other factors.[30]

Some Jews were willing to eat with Samaritans (*m. Ber.* 7.1; 8.8), but many were not, owing to ritual defilement. Kruse (2003: 128) notes that ancient Jews distinguished between accepting food given to them by those considered unclean and buying it from them—the latter being viewed as inappropriate (citing 1QS 5:14–20). Samaritans were thought to convey uncleanness by what they lay, sat, or rode on, as well as by their saliva or urine. Samaritan women, like Gentiles, were considered to be in a continual state of ritual uncleanness (*m. Nid.* 4.1).[31] Apart from these ethnic sensibilities, men generally would not want to discuss theological issues with women. Hence the woman's surprise: did Jesus not know that even her water jar was considered unclean by his fellow Jews?

The verb δίδωμι (*didōmi*, give) dominates this section, occurring seven times between 4:7 and 4:15. Jesus' two-part response regarding God's gift (an objective genitive, as in "gift *from* God" [Moloney 1998: 117]) and his identity provides the structure for the remainder of the con-

4:10–15

---

27. As Rabbi Eliezer (ca. A.D. 90–130) used to say, "He that eats the bread of the Samaritans is like to one that eats the flesh of swine" (*m. Šeb.* 8.10 [cited by many, including Schlatter 1948: 118]).

28. As Barrett (1978: 232) notes, Samaritans in John's Gospel call Jesus "a Jew," while the Jews call him "a Samaritan" (8:48). By way of Johannine irony, this attests to Jesus' otherworldly nature.

29. Some interpreters, including Calvin (1959: 90), think that the words of 4:9b (missing from some MSS) are spoken by the Samaritan woman.

30. See Maccini 1996: 131–44. Daube (1956: 375–82) argues that "do not associate with" specifically refers to Jews not sharing vessels with Samaritans (cf. NIV text and note at 4:9). However, no common utensils (such as the woman's water jar) are specifically mentioned in 4:9. The explanatory aside, "For Jews have no dealings with [συγχρῶνται] Samaritans," probably is broader than the mere refusal to share drinking vessels (Ridderbos 1997: 154; Beasley-Murray 1999: 58 n. f; contra Carson 1991: 218; Borchert 1996: 203; Witherington 1995: 120; R. Brown 1966: 170; Morris 1995: 229; Barrett 1978: 232; Moloney 1998: 117, 121; Schnackenburg 1990: 1.425 n. 19).

31. See Danby 1933: 803; Daube 1950; 1956: 373–82; Derrett 1988.

versation (4:10–15 discusses the gift, 4:16–30 his identity; see Moloney 1998: 126–27). As with Nicodemus, Jesus immediately takes charge of the conversation, transposing the discourse from a literal, physical plane to a metaphorical, spiritual one (the woman's question in 4:9 is entirely ignored: Jewish/Samaritan distinctions are irrelevant in another world and reality; see Ridderbos 1997: 154–55).

Jesus' statement in 4:10 forms, in Greek syntax, a second-class condition (past contrary-to-fact [Wallace 1996: 694–95]): the woman knows neither God's gift nor Jesus' true identity. On a literal level, "living water" refers to highly coveted fresh springwater, as opposed to stagnant water (cf. Gen. 26:19; Lev. 14:6; Jer. 2:13).[32] Ultimately, it was God who was known to be the source and giver of life. In Num. 20:8–11, an incident to which Jesus perhaps alludes in the present passage, water gushes out of the rock, supplying the Israelites with badly needed refreshment. In Jer. 2:13, God laments that his people have forsaken him, "the spring of living water." In Isa. 12:3, the prophet envisions the joy with which people "will draw water from the wells of salvation" in the last days.[33]

In John, Jesus is identified explicitly with the Creator and life-giver (5:26), and he dispenses the gift of "living water," later unveiled as the Holy Spirit (7:37–39). This end-time blessing, bestowed after Jesus' exaltation, transcends John's water baptism (1:26, 33), Jewish ceremonial purification (2:6; 3:25), proselyte baptism (cf. 3:5), and the torch-lighting and water-pouring symbolism of the Feast of Tabernacles (chs. 7–8). It also supersedes nurturing or healing waters such as those from Jacob's well (ch. 4) or the pools of Bethesda and Siloam (chs. 5, 9). In fulfillment of the OT prophetic vision (Zech. 14:8; Ezek. 47:9), Jesus inaugurated the age of God's abundance.[34]

The term underlying "sir" is κύριος (kyrios), which can also mean "Lord." Here, however, it is simply a respectful address of Jesus without christological implications (cf. 4:15, 19, 49; 5:7; 6:34; 9:36; 12:21). The well today is still over one hundred feet deep and probably was deeper back then. In fact, Jacob's well may have been the deepest well in all

---

32. As Keener (2003: 605, citing ancient references) observes, water drawn from wells was not always living water (unless it was fed by an underground stream) and was therefore often thought to be less healthy than "living water," that is, water drawn from a spring or from rainwater.

33. For the ancient Jews, the greatest "gift of God" was the Torah (the law). Other "gifts of God," apart from the lights in the sky and rain, were considered to include peace, salvation, the land of Israel, and divine mercy (Gen. Rab. 6.5; attributed to Yoḥanan ben Zakkai [ca. A.D. 70] and other rabbis). Rabbinic thought associated the provision of water with the coming of the Messiah (Eccles. Rab. 1.9; see commentary at 6:31).

34. Borchert (1996: 203) sees the "gift of God" as the realization of God's promises; Morris (1995: 230) and Carson (1991: 218) identify it as eternal life, the latter with reference to the Torah (cf. R. Brown 1966: 176, 178–79); Schnackenburg (1990: 1.431) suggests that the gift is either the Holy Spirit or eternal life, or both; Burge (2000: 144) thinks that the reference is to the Spirit.

of Palestine (Potter 1959: 331). John's use of a different term for "well" in the present passage (φρέαρ, *phrear*; cf. 4:6: πηγή, *pēgē*) may indicate that the cistern (φρέαρ) is fed by an underground spring (πηγή) (Carson 1991: 217; Morris 1995: 228; Burge 2000: 142). Any band of travelers would have had a skin bucket (ἄντλημα, *antlēma*) for drawing water, which they lowered into the well with a rope. In the present instance, Jesus' disciples probably carried it with them, but they had left to buy supplies (4:8), presumably taking it along, and in any case Jesus could not get "living" water out of the well (see commentary at 4:10).

The woman's question "You are not greater than our father Jacob, are you?" reveals incredulity (Carson 1991: 219).[35] The particle μή (*mē*) indicates expectation of a negative answer (Schnackenburg 1990: 1.429): how could Jesus draw water out of such a deep well without a bucket? Or did he perhaps know of another source of ("living") water (Ridderbos 1997: 155)? Yet by way of Johannine irony (as well as misunderstanding [R. Brown 1966: 170; Morris 1995: 232; Barrett 1978: 228, 234; Carson 1991: 219]), Jesus' significance indeed surpasses that of all the luminaries in the history of God's people, be it Abraham (8:53), Moses (1:17), or Jonah or Solomon (Matt. 12:41–42). According to Josephus, the Samaritans claimed descent from Joseph through Ephraim and Manasseh (*Ant.* 11.8.6 §341). The Jews sharply disagreed (see Köstenberger 2002c: 45). Jesus himself seems to side with his fellow Jews when he refers to a Samaritan leper as a "foreigner" (ἀλλογενής, *allogenēs*, of another race [Luke 17:18]). Yet in the present passage, Jesus refuses to get sidetracked by this (for him) peripheral point (cf. 4:19–20).

Incidentally, the woman's claim that Jacob "gave us the well and drank from it himself" is purely traditional. The Book of Genesis does not record Jacob digging a well, much less his drinking from it or giving it to any of his sons. Mention is merely made of Jacob's buying and giving Shechem to Joseph (Gen. 33:19; 48:22), in the vicinity of which Jacob's well is located (see commentary at 4:5–6; cf. Neyrey 1979: 421–22).[36]

The repeated reference to thirst ("will thirst again . . . will never thirst again . . . so that I won't get thirsty") indicates that Jesus ministers to a keenly felt need. Even on a literal level, thirst is among the most intense and imperative human cravings. Hence, in Scripture thirst is used as a metaphor for spiritual desire (cf. Ps. 42:2; 63:1; 143:6; Isa. 55:1; Matt. 5:6). Jesus himself, in a function of his full humanity, is thirsty here and at the cross (John 19:28–30). However, he does not allow his actions to be controlled by his need for food and drink, instead looking beyond

35. Keener (2003: 601, 605) goes one step further, suggesting that the woman's statements in 4:12, 15 may have a mocking connotation.
36. On Jacob traditions in relation to a variety of subjects addressed in the present pericope, see Neyrey 1979.

his natural circumstances to deeper spiritual needs (4:30–34; cf. Matt. 4:1–4 par.).

"Will in him become a supply of water welling up to eternal life" is reminiscent of Isaiah's vision of people joyfully "drawing of water from the wells of salvation" in the last days (12:3; cf. 44:3; 49:10; 55:1; see also 6:53; 7:38; Sir. 24:21; 1 Enoch 48:1).[37] In a dry, hot climate such as that of Palestine, people are keenly aware of their need for water and of the blessing it represents. Crucially, in the present passage, Jesus is presented as the one who has been sent by God to satisfy the thirst of God's people (Ridderbos 1997: 157–58).

The phrase οὐ μὴ διψήσει εἰς τὸν αἰῶνα (*ou mē dipsēsei eis ton aiōna*, will never thirst again) is an instance of emphatic negation (Wallace 1996: 468, 568). Once again, however, the Samaritan woman transforms Jesus' promise of a gift to come into a request that Jesus provide her with immediate physical satisfaction (Moloney 1998: 118). Yet despite her ongoing confusion, the woman continues to engage in her quest for understanding (Ridderbos 1997: 158; cf. Moloney 1998: 123). She clearly is interested in the water that Jesus has to offer, but is still at a loss as to the water's origin (Carson 1991: 220).[38]

4:16–20   The woman's response, "I have no husband," seems designed to cut off further conversation along these lines (Carson 1991: 221). Cantwell (1983: 80) aptly sees her "clinging rather pathetically to her privacy and some semblance of respectability," using "a not very clever equivocation which Christ dramatically exposes, to reveal a life which is not so much immoral [though it is that!] as a mess, a broken series of false beginnings and shattered hopes." In fact, though technically truthful, the woman's statement is potentially misleading (Keener 2003: 605; hence Jesus' gentle yet firm response, in which he places ἄνδρα [*andra*, husband] in an emphatic grammatical position [Wallace 1996: 455]). On the face of it, it could be taken to imply that she was unattached and thus available (see commentary at 4:7; cf. Keener 1993: 273). Jesus, with fine irony, quickly removes all doubt: "You have had five men, and the one you have now is not your husband."

If the TNIV rendering, "five husbands," is correct, then the woman found herself in conflict with Jewish law (contra Westcott 1908: 1.154), since rabbis generally disapproved of more than three legal marriages in a lifetime, even in case of the death of previous husbands (*b. Yebam.* 64b; cf. *b. Nid.* 64a). However, it is perhaps more likely that this is another instance of a wordplay (a possibility not considered by Keener

---

37. See also Tg. Neof. of Gen. 28:10 (referring to the well at Haran; see Díaz 1963: 76–77), and the Samaritan liturgy for the Day of Atonement cited in Carson 1991: 220 (cf. Schnackenburg 1990: 1.430–32).

38. Conway (1999: 115–16) maintains that the woman's response in 4:15 does not indicate a development in her understanding of Jesus' identity.

2003: 605–8),[39] here involving the word ἀνήρ (*anēr*), which can mean either "man" or "husband." If so, Jesus may be telling the woman that she has had five "men" (with whom she lived in fornication) and that the one she is now living with is not her "man," that is, husband (though he may be that of another woman: note the emphatic position of "your" in the Greek). In other words, the woman is a serial fornicator (see Giblin 1999).[40]

The effect of Jesus' words seems to be that the woman "is hurt and sobered by his knowledge of her secret, but is liberated from the need to go on concealing it" (Cantwell 1983: 82). By calling Jesus "a prophet" (an indefinite qualitative noun [Wallace 1996: 265–66]; not "the Prophet" of Deut. 18), the woman acknowledges that Jesus knows her life circumstances without apparently having been told by anyone—hence, he must be "a prophet" (similarly, the formerly blind man in 9:17; cf. Luke 7:39). The Samaritans awaited the prophet like Moses (Deut. 18:15–18; cf. 34:10–12), who was, however, not identified with the Messiah (cf. John 4:25–26; see Kippenberg 1971: 325).

In another diversionary measure, the woman switches to a religious (hence "safer") topic: "Our ancestors worshiped on this mountain."[41] Though she meant to evade the subject, however, Jesus transforms the topic into one of extreme religious as well as personal relevance.[42] For, indeed, the woman's problems transcended her personal life and extended, significantly, also to her people's illegitimate way of worship (Cantwell 1983: 83). Just as Judaism was branded as lacking in experiential knowledge of true spiritual regeneration in John 3 (with Nicodemus serving as the paradigmatic representative), so here Samaritanism is cast as devoid of knowledge of what constitutes the true worship that God requires. All this follows on the heels of the temple clearing in 2:13–22.

"Our ancestors" refers back to Abraham (Gen. 12:7) and Jacob (Gen. 33:20), who built altars in this region. Mount Gerizim was the site where the Israelites were blessed by Moses (Deut. 11:29; 27:12). The Samaritans held that many other significant events during the patriarchal period

39. Note the three instances of wordplay on "again/from above," "wind/spirit," and "lift up/exalt" in 3:3–8, 14.
40. Some interpreters (such as Lindars [1972: 186]) argue that "five men/husbands" alludes to a tradition cited in Josephus, according to which the Samaritans had five gods (*Ant.* 9.14.3 §288; cf. 2 Kings 17:24, 30–31), just as "five colonnades" in 5:2 is taken to refer to the Jewish Pentateuch (Hengel 1999: 307, 315). As Blomberg (1995: 8 [cf. Schlatter 1948: 122]) points out, however, in reality the text lists seven gods of five nations (but see Prest 1992: 368; see also the discussion in C. Koester 1990b: 675–77).
41. But see Conway (1999: 119), who suggests that the woman in fact desires to return to the subject of Jewish/Samaritan relations, which she first introduced in 4:9.
42. Conway (1999: 118, citing Boers 1988: 171, 182) points out that whereas Jesus does not launch his revelatory monologue in John 3 until Nicodemus has faded from view, he does so here in the Samaritan woman's presence.

were associated with Mount Gerizim.[43] It is unclear precisely when the Samaritans built a temple at that location. Samaritan tradition places construction in the fifth century B.C., though Josephus claims that the temple was built in 332 B.C.[44] Since the names mentioned by Josephus coincide strikingly with those of Neh. 13:28, Samaritan tradition may be closer to the truth than is Josephus (Schnackenburg 1990: 1.434 n. 44). In Hellenistic times, Antiochus Epiphanes IV converted the Samaritan sanctuary into the temple of Zeus Horkios ("the Guardian of Oaths"), while the Samaritans continued their worship at an altar erected on another peak of the mountain (Avi-Yonah 1964: 141). In 129 B.C., it was razed by John Hyrcanus and the Jews (*Ant*. 13.9.1 §§254–56).

The dispute between Jews and Samaritans regarding the proper place of worship had thus been raging for centuries when the Samaritan woman broached the subject with Jesus. Josephus tells of an argument between Egyptian Jews and Samaritans before Ptolemy Philometor in around 150 B.C. as to whether the sanctuary was to be on Mount Gerizim or Mount Zion (*Ant*. 13.3.4 §74; cf. 12.1.1 §10). That Samaritan beliefs regarding the sanctity of Mount Gerizim continued unabated is illustrated by an incident in A.D. 36 (recounted in *Ant*. 18.4.1 §§85–87) involving a Samaritan troublemaker that was put down by Pilate. During Jesus' conversation with the Samaritan woman, Mount Gerizim would have been in full view. From Jacob's well, they may even have been able to see the temple's ruins, perhaps turning to look at them when the woman mentioned the place.

"Yet you Jews say that the place where one ought to worship is in Jerusalem." "You" (in the plural: ὑμεῖς, *hymeis*) is emphatic and refers to the Jewish people (whom the woman perceives Jesus to represent; see Burge 2000: 146; Moloney 1998: 128). Jesus responds in like manner, using plurals (4:21–22), treating the woman as a representative of the Samaritan people (Ridderbos 1997: 162; Carson 1991: 223). Jewish tradition widely affirmed the religious supremacy of Jerusalem (e.g., *Midr. Ps*. 91.7 on Gen. 28:17). The Pentateuch, however, does not specifically identify Jerusalem as the proper place of worship—though other portions of Scripture do (see 2 Chron. 6:6; 7:12; Ps. 78:68–69)—which led the Samaritans to establish their own sanctuary on Mount Gerizim.[45]

43. For Samaritan views about Mount Gerizim, see Macdonald 1964: 327–33.

44. See *Ant*. 11.8.4 §§321–24; cf. 13.9.1 §256. Josephus further attests to the temple's existence in 323 B.C., the year of Alexander the Great's death (*Ant*. 11.8.7 §346; cf. 11.8.2 §310). See Jeremias 1969: 352 n. 2. On archaeological excavations related to Mount Gerizim, see Crown 1989: 165–74.

45. C. Koester (1990b: 673–74) notes that while Samaritans claimed that Moses had hidden the vessels of the tabernacle on Mount Gerizim (see Josephus, *Ant*. 18.4.1 §85), the Jews traced the roots of Samaritan idolatry to when Jacob's wife Rachel stole and hid her father's household gods in that place (Gen. 31:19, 34; cf. 35:4; see *Gen. Rab*. 81.3 [ca. A.D. 180]; Pseudo-Philo, *Bib. Ant*. 25.10).

In response, Jesus points out that geographic locale soon will be a matter   **4:21–26**
of indifference as far as worship is concerned.[46] Jesus' response indicates,
first, that the woman would no longer be faced with a choice between
two places of worship; second, that the Samaritan worship at Mount
Gerizim was based on ignorance regarding Israel's role in God's plan of
salvation; and third, that such worship is not true worship (Ridderbos
1997: 162). "Believe me" (πίστευέ μοι, *pisteue moi*) is a simple assertive,
not as overt as "Truly, truly, I say to you" (Carson 1991: 223; contra Barrett [1978: 236], who thinks that the phrases are equivalent). "Woman"
(γύναι, *gynai*) is an unadorned address, neither particularly endearing
nor derogatory (cf. 2:4; 19:26; 20:13, 15).

"A time" (ὥρα, *hōra*) constitutes an eschatological marker. While often
in this Gospel the term is centered on Jesus' glorification (focused on
the cross), be it by way of disavowal that the time had come (2:4; 7:30;
8:20) or of affirmation that it had now arrived (12:23, 27; 13:1; 17:1),
the present reference seems more in line with a variety of general predictions pertaining to the end times inaugurated or realized by Jesus'
coming (cf. 4:23; 5:25, 28–29; 16:2, 4, 21, 25, 32; see Ridderbos 1997:
163; Beasley-Murray 1999: 61; R. Brown 1966: 172; Moloney 1998: 128;
contra Carson 1991: 223; Borchert 1996: 207).

The woman has just acknowledged Jesus as a prophet (4:19); now he
uses prophetic language: "a time is coming" (cf. 1 Sam. 2:31; 2 Kings
20:17; Jer. 31:31). Jesus' prophecy was literally fulfilled through the events
of A.D. 66–70 when the Romans, under Titus, razed Jerusalem, including the temple (cf. Luke 21:20, 24). Spiritually speaking, the crucified
and resurrected Christ would serve as a substitute for the Jerusalem
temple as the new center of worship for God's people (John 2:19–22).
The woman had spoken of the worship of "the fathers" (οἱ πατέρες, *hoi
pateres* [i.e., ancestors]); Jesus responds by speaking of worship of "the
Father" (Moloney 1998: 128; Conway 1999: 120; used in a universalistic
sense [Morris 1995: 238]). "The Father" is a direct object, a dative of
personal interest, suggesting personal relationship (Wallace 1996: 172),
that is, the new relationship created in the life of the genuine worshiper
(Schnackenburg 1990: 1.436–37).

Though seeking to engage the Samaritan woman in open interchange,
Jesus does not deny his Jewish heritage. First, he maintains that "you
Samaritans worship what you do not know." The Samaritans had greatly
truncated their knowledge of God by restricting their canon to the Pentateuch.[47] Proper worship in any age is critically predicated upon adequate

46. Schlatter (1948: 124) observes, "The new sacrifice (1:29) and the new temple (2:19)
constitute the grounds for a new worship."

47. Jesus refers to "what" (neuter) rather than "whom" (masculine) they do not know,
perhaps pointing to the less-than-personal character of Samaritan worship (Schlatter
1948: 125).

and accurate knowledge of the God worshiped (Borchert 1996: 208; cf. Morris 1995: 238). No matter how ceremonially elaborate, emotionally rousing, or sermonically eloquent, worship that is not offered from a proper understanding of who God is falls short. Evangelistically, too, the nature of proper worship must take precedence over discussions of secondary paraphernalia or liturgical trappings of worship.

Second, Jesus asserts that "salvation is from the Jews."[48] Jesus here affirms that the Jewish people are the instrument by which God's redemption is mediated to others. This contrasts with Samaritan religious ignorance (which here becomes a foil for Jesus' teaching on proper worship). Nevertheless, though Jesus freely acknowledges Jewish salvation-historical preeminence, he does not allow it to become a barrier keeping others from benefiting from divine salvation blessings.[49] It was precisely the fact that the Jews wanted to keep God's gifts to themselves that drew God's judgment. What is more, not only is Samaritan worship dismissed as being based on ignorance: Jewish worship in Jerusalem, too, is called obsolete (cf. 2:19–22). Coming from Jesus, a Jew, even one who affirmed that "salvation is from the Jews," this is truly revolutionary.

Because God is spirit, proper worship must be performed "in spirit and truth." Though not forming a hendiadys (contra Ridderbos 1997: 163–64),[50] "spirit" and "truth" are governed by the same preposition and thus encompass the same overall idea (Carson 1991: 225; cf. R. Brown 1966: 172, 180; Burge 2000: 147; Schnackenburg 1990: 1.437), perhaps sustaining an epexegetical relationship ("in spirit, that is, truth"; cf. the phrase "true worshipers" in 4:23).[51] "God is spirit" does not refer to the Holy Spirit (contra TNIV; though see discussion below)—much less to the human spirit (contra Morris 1995: 239; Collins 1995: 120–21)—but identifies God as a spiritual rather than material being.[52] The spiritual nature of God is taught clearly in the OT (cf. Isa. 31:3; Ezek. 11:19–20; 36:26–27).[53] Because God is spirit, the Israelites were not to make idols "in the form of anything" as did the surrounding nations (Exod. 20:4).

---

48. This is the only reference to σωτηρία (*sōtēria*, salvation) in this Gospel (cf. σωτήρ [*sōtēr*, savior] in 4:42).

49. Contra Keener (1993: 273), who reads the present passage in terms of "racial reconciliation." But this does not square with the emphasis of the present passage on the Jews being the source of salvation.

50. The two terms are separate (but epexegetically related) in the closest Johannine parallel, 1 John 3:18: "in deed and truth" (ἐν ἔργῳ καὶ ἀληθείᾳ), that is, "in deed, that is, in reality" (Collins 1995: 119, with reference to Schlatter).

51. Collins (1995: 120 n. 12) lists the following passages, featuring a similar construction with the second element serving an epexegetic function: 2 Pet. 3:7, 11; Jdt. 7:25; 1 Macc. 3:51; Sir. 45:4.

52. The reference is qualitative, "stressing the nature or essence of God" (Wallace 1996: 270); see the similar phrase in 3:6.

53. For a helpful discussion contrasting biblical with Hellenistic concepts of God, see Schnackenburg 1990: 1.440.

Jesus' point here is that since God is spirit, proper worship of him is also a matter of spirit rather than physical location (Jerusalem versus Mount Gerizim).[54]

The terms "spirit" and "truth" are joined later in the expression "Spirit of truth," referring to the Holy Spirit (see 14:17; 15:26; 16:13; cf. 1 John 4:6; 5:6; see also 2 Thess. 2:13). Though this may have been too advanced for the Samaritan woman, the present reference therefore seems to point John's readers ultimately to worship in the Holy Spirit. Thus, true worship is not a matter of geographical location (worship in a church building), physical posture (kneeling or standing), or following a particular liturgy or external rituals (cf. Matt. 6:5–13); it is a matter of the heart and of the Spirit (Talbert 1992: 115).[55] As Stibbe (1993: 64) puts it, "True worship is paternal in focus (the Father), personal in origin (the Son), and pneumatic in character (the Spirit)."

In a final attempt to end her embarrassment (Borchert 1996: 209), the woman affirms her belief that "Messiah (called Christ) is coming" (see commentary at 1:41). The woman's affirmation of her belief in the coming of the Messiah in the presence of just this Messiah constitutes an instance of supreme Johannine irony. The phrase "I know" is reminiscent of Nicodemus's "we know" in 3:2; in the more immediate context, Jesus contrasts the Jews' knowledge with Samaritan ignorance (4:22). The fact that the woman speaks of the coming Messiah in those terms indicates that she still has not recognized Jesus' true identity (Ridderbos 1997: 164; cf. Carson 1991: 226; contra Moloney 1998: 129).

Although the woman here refers to a coming "Messiah," the Samaritans did not regularly use this expression until the sixteenth century (Kippenberg 1971: 303 n. 216), preferring terms such as "Taheb" or "the Restorer." The figure of the Taheb, in turn, apparently originated independently of Deut. 18:15–18 and was only later identified with the "prophet like Moses."[56] The woman's affirmation, "He will explain ev-

---

54. Contra Keener (2003: 617), who suggests that the reference in 4:23–24 is to "worship empowered by the Spirit," the more probable reference in this context is to the distinction between the realm of spirit ("God is spirit") and that of physical location. Keener (2003: 618–19, esp. p. 619) also says "since God is spiritual but not physical, those who relate to him must do so through the gift of his Spirit," but a more logical way to complete his sentence would be "those who relate to him must do so on a spiritual rather than physical plane." Spirit, as in God's Spirit or the Holy Spirit, is only the derivative sense (see the discussion below).

55. The OT occasionally establishes a relationship between "word" and "spirit" (Neh. 9:20, 30; Ps. 33:6; 147:18; Isa. 59:21). In John's Gospel, Jesus is the Word (1:14), has received the fullness of the Spirit (3:34), and is himself the truth (14:6); in his final prayer, he affirms that God's Word is truth that sanctifies (17:17). Hence "spirit" and "truth" are part of a conceptual cluster that also includes "word" and "worship." On this connection, see Nelson 2001. See also Carson 1991: 226; Barrett 1978: 238–39; R. Brown 1966: 180.

56. See Bammel 1957: 381–85; Boring, Berger, and Colpe 1995: 264–65; Kippenberg 1971: 276–327.

erything to us," is consistent with the fact that rather than looking for a royal Messiah from the house of David (as did the Jews), Samaritans apparently expected a "teaching" Messiah (Bowman 1958: 298–308).

In a momentous self-disclosure that is unique to any Gospel narrative prior to Jesus' trials, Jesus now acknowledges frankly that he is the Messiah. The phrase ἐγώ εἰμι (egō eimi, I am) here initially serves as a vehicle of self-identification (cf. 6:20; note the similar assertions in 6:35 and esp. in 9:37; see Ridderbos 1997: 165; Bultmann 1971: 192, 226 n. 3), though on a secondary level it may also serve as a revelatory formula (Conway 1999: 121, citing O'Day 1986: 72) in allusion to Isa. 52:6 (Ball 1996: 178–81; Keener 2003: 620). This is the climactic pronouncement of the dialogue up to this point. It also is congruent with the Gospel's purpose statement (20:31). The woman knew about the coming of the Messiah, and she had encountered Jesus. Now she was faced with the claim that these two figures were one: Jesus is the Messiah, and the Messiah is Jesus (Ridderbos 1997: 165).

Jesus' conversation with the Samaritan woman constitutes a paradigm for sharing the gospel of Jesus Christ with those ignorant of Jesus' true identity and claims (Witherington 1995: 123–25; Burge 2000: 160–61).[57] It also shows how Jesus is ready to reveal himself to those who are open to his revelation, including non-Jews (though ministering to Samaritans is proleptic of the post-Pentecost mission [see Acts 1:8; 8:4–25]). Nevertheless, in the present context it is Jesus the Jew who bears witness to a Samaritan in a salvation-historical, eschatological setting. Remarkably, though Jesus generally is reluctant to identify himself openly as Messiah to the Jews (perhaps owing to the nationalistic overtones often associated with the term "messiah" in Jewish life), he apparently has no such hesitation in the case of the Samaritan woman (R. Brown 1966: 173; cf. Morris 1995: 241).

iv. The Disciples Rejoin Jesus (4:27–38)

4:27–30 Upon their return, Jesus' disciples were surprised to find him talking with a woman (Seim 1987: 59).[58] As Neyrey (1994: 82) remarks, "It is bad enough that a female is conversing with an unrelated male in a public place at an unusual hour. Worse, the reader is told that she considered the most significant item in this conversation Jesus' remarks on her shameless sexual behavior" (cf. Pazdan 1987: 148).

---

57. Blomberg (1995: 9), observing the woman's reputation of sexual immorality, contends that the pericope focuses "not nearly so much on the *how* of evangelism but on the *who*." If this presupposes that the Samaritan woman is the focus here, it must be said in response that Jesus is more properly in the center of the present passage, and if so, then the *how* of evangelism is certainly in view just the same.

58. Keener (2003: 621) suggests that the narrative technique at work in 4:27 is that of interruption (citing Acts 2:37; 10:44) immediately after the climax of a narrative (in the present instance, Jesus' self-revelation in 4:26).

Some rabbis (such as Yose ben Yoḥanan; see Goldin 1980: 41–61) held that to talk too much to a woman, even one's own wife, was a waste of time, diverting one's attention from the study of the Torah. Potentially, this habit could grow to be a great evil, even leading to hell (m. ʾAbot 1.5). Consequently, some rabbis taught that it was as inappropriate to provide one's daughter with a knowledge of the Torah as it was to sell her into prostitution (m. Soṭah 3.4; attributed to Rabbi Eliezer [ca. A.D. 90–130]).[59] As in other encounters with women, Jesus broke with his fellow rabbis' prejudice (see 7:53–8:11; 11:17–40; Luke 7:36–50; 8:2–3; 10:38–42).

The disciples' amazement at Jesus' engaging in prolonged conversation with a woman (imperfect, ἐλάλει [elalei, he was talking]) amounts to more than momentary surprise (imperfect, ἐθαύμαζον [ethaumazon, they were surprised]; see R. Brown 1966: 173).[60] But none of them asked "What are you seeking to accomplish?" or "Why are you talking with her?" At other occasions, the disciples were not so bashful (e.g., Matt. 19:13 pars.).[61] Perhaps the reason why they refrain from questioning Jesus here is that the woman is still there, so that an open challenge would have created an awkward situation (Carson 1991: 227). Also, the disciples' restraint may have been motivated by respect for Jesus (though not necessarily agreement with his judgment or practice). Generally, it was considered acceptable in first-century Judaism for disciples to question their rabbi's actions, as long as this was done respectfully and appropriately.[62]

The woman left her water jar, probably a large earthenware pitcher carried either on the shoulder or the hip (Gower 1987: 44). The woman here abandons her original purpose for coming to the well (to draw water) in order to tell her townspeople about Jesus. "Leaving her water jar" may therefore have symbolic overtones (R. Brown 1966: 173; Stibbe 1993: 67). Leaving behind one's natural occupation for the sake of witnessing to Jesus is also the mark of a disciple. This, too, stands in contrast to Nicodemus, who in 7:50–51 speaks out for fairness but does not positively witness to Jesus in front of his fellow Sanhedrin members.

The woman's witness is this: "Come, see a man who told me everything I ever did; he couldn't be the Christ, could he?"[63] The Greek interrogative

59. See Morris 1995: 242–43 n. 67 for other primary quotes.
60. Wallace (1996: 461, 553) interprets ὅτι (hoti, that, because) causally: "because he was speaking with a woman."
61. The spirit of open interchange between Jesus and his disciples, or even those of John the Baptist, is illustrated by passages such as John 9:2; 11:8, 12, 16; 13:6–10, 36–38; 14:5, 8, 22; 21:21; Matt. 9:14; 11:3; 13:10, 36; 15:12, 15; 17:10, 19; 18:21; 24:3 (and the parallels in Mark and Luke).
62. See the discussion and references in Köstenberger 1998a: 120–22. Contra Keener (1993: 274), who refers to "the general principle that one ought not to challenge one's teacher."
63. On the Samaritan Taheb as prophet-revealer, see commentary at 4:25. On the woman's witness in a Jewish-Samaritan context, see Maccini 1994.

particle μήτι (*mēti*) suggests, if not a negative answer, at least a hesitant question (Barrett 1978: 240; Beasley-Murray 1999: 58 n. h; cf. Morris 1995: 243–44; R. Brown 1966: 173).[64] This indicates that the woman, though clearly showing progress, has not arrived at an assured confidence regarding Jesus' identity (cf. 4:25); in fact, her testimony identifies him essentially as a prophet (4:29; cf. 4:19).[65] "Come and see" (δεῦτε ἴδετε, *deute idete*) resembles Jesus' invitation to his first followers in 1:39 (cf. 1:46). "A man" renders the Greek term ἄνθρωπος (*anthrōpos*), which is less gender-specific than ἀνήρ (*anēr*).[66]

"Who told me everything I ever did" is an obvious exaggeration, understandable in light of the woman's excitement. Perhaps the comment also highlights the woman's perception of the wretchedness of her past (Carson 1991: 228). Obviously, Jesus' knowledge of her private life had made a deep impression on her (Morris 1995: 243). Rabbinic literature is somewhat ambivalent on the validity of a Samaritan's testimony (cf. *m. Giṭ.* 1.5). The witness of Samaritan *women*, especially those of low repute, may have been subject to further limitations.[67] Yet the present instance represents not a formal courtroom scene, but an informal situation in which the Samaritan goes back to her town and tells her fellow villagers about a remarkable encounter she has had. Perhaps precisely *because* of the woman's reputation for immorality, her compatriots are curious to see for themselves what effected such a remarkable change in the woman's disposition.[68]

The reference to the Samaritans beginning to make their way toward Jesus in 4:30, together with 4:39–42, forms a "literary frame that encloses Jesus' discourse with the disciples" (Lee 1994: 70). This is another instance of the Fourth Evangelist's considerable narrative skill.

4:31–38 The disciples' urging their "rabbi" to eat something (see commentary at 1:38) is in keeping with disciples' customary care for the physical

---

64. See the discussion at the introduction to John 4 above. See also Schlatter (1948: 129), who says that, as in Matt. 12:23, the magnitude of the Christ concept allows only the question, not yet faith. Conway (1999: 123) may somewhat understate the significance of the particle when she says that it "may simply be an expression of the woman's excitement and the overall drama of the scene."

65. Borchert (1996: 211) is correct in pointing out that a person does not need to be fully convinced to function as a witness.

66. Morris (1995: 243 n. 70) suggests that by the use of this term, the evangelist may wish to affirm the humanity of Jesus (cf. 5:12; 8:40; 9:11, 24; 10:33; 11:47, 50; 18:14, 17, 29; 19:5).

67. Regarding women witnesses in general, Josephus writes, "From women let no evidence be accepted, because of the levity [lightness, triviality] and temerity [over-boldness, rashness] of their sex" (*Ant.* 4.8.15 §219). Maccini (1996: 139) too facilely subsumes the witness of Samaritan women under the witness of Samaritans in general.

68. The absence of a connective in 4:30 is worthy of note. It may accentuate the immediacy of the people's decision to see for themselves whether the woman's testimony concerning Jesus was true. Wallace (1996: 545) notes that ἤρχοντο (*ērchonto*, they were coming) is an instance of an ingressive imperfect.

well-being of their master, a concern that extended from buying food to tending to him when he was sick and burying him after he died (Köstenberger 1998a: 122–23). In response, Jesus asserts that fulfilling his mission is more important to him than physical food (cf. Matt. 6:25; Mark 3:20–21; see Schnackenburg 1990: 1.445).[69] The disciples, for their part, misunderstand, just as the Samaritan woman (and Nicodemus) did earlier (Carson 1991: 228; Ridderbos 1997: 167).[70] Yet the Samaritan woman failed to recognize what Jesus could offer her; the disciples do not understand what Jesus himself lived by: the satisfaction of doing his Father's will and of carrying out his mission (cf. 5:19–47; see Beasley-Murray 1999: 63; Carson 1991: 229).

It is startling for Jesus to claim that he must finish (τελειόω, teleioō; also in 5:36; 17:4; cf. 19:28, 30) God's work.[71] Was God's work, then, incomplete? In one sense, God was considered to have finished his work (Gen. 2:2). Yet, in another sense, it was recognized that God continues to sustain his creation (cf. John 5:17). In the present passage, Jesus affirms his commitment to complete the task that God has given him to do, that is, his redemptive work at the cross (12:23–24; 17:4; 19:30). The unity between Father and Son here relates primarily not to unity in essence and being, but to unity in purpose (Schnackenburg 1990: 1.448). The mention of food—first literal, then figurative—in 4:31–34 enables Jesus to develop the metaphor in 4:35 with reference to the fruit of his mission in the form of the approaching Samaritans (R. Brown 1966: 181).

The saying "Four more months and then comes the harvest" appears to have been a common proverb (cf. Matt. 16:2–3; see also Matt. 9:37–38 par.; see R. Brown 1966: 182),[72] though there is no independent evidence for its existence.[73] Jesus' statement could be taken to imply that four months remained until the harvest when the statement was made. In that case, the present event would have occurred during December

---

69. The present statement may echo Deut. 8:3; cf. Matt. 4:4; Luke 4:4; see Carson 1991: 228; Borchert 1996: 213; see also Jer. 15:16. Here the term used for "food" is βρῶσις (brōsis); in 4:34 it is βρῶμα (brōma). Apart from stylistic variation, the use of the latter term in 4:34 may be due to a desire to create assonance with θέλημα (thelēma, will) (R. Brown 1966: 173).

70. Another misunderstanding of the disciples involving food is Matt. 16:5–12. For other uses of the "the one who sent me" motif, see John 5:23–24, 30, 36–37; 6:38–39; 7:16, 18, 28, 33; 8:16, 18, 26, 29; 9:4; 12:44–45, 49; 13:20; 14:24; 16:5.

71. The present instance of the singular ἔργον (ergon, work) forms an inclusio with 17:4.

72. Argyle (1971: 247–48) argues for a Greek background, but most believe that the proverb is Semitic.

73. Somewhat similar, though in a context of judgment, is Jer. 51:33 (Schnackenburg 1990: 1.149 n. 86). Ensor (2000: 16) notes that the word θερισμός (therismos, harvest) occurs on Jesus' lips—but not those of the evangelists—in both John and the Synoptics, which supports the authenticity of John 4:35 as a saying uttered by Jesus (note also the instances that Ensor cites on p. 16 n. 17).

or January, since the time of harvest extended from March until May (barley was harvested in March, wheat from mid-April until the end of May).[74] Alternatively, the proverb as commonly used may simply indicate the need for patience, similar to the saying "Rome was not built in a day" (Ridderbos 1997: 168 n. 194).[75] In any case, Jesus' point may be that although sowing and reaping were separated by (a minimum of) four months, his coming ushered in the end-time harvest, so that sowing and harvest paradoxically coincide (cf. Amos 9:13; see Ensor 2000: 18 n. 23). If so, Jesus may be alerting his disciples to the fact that the events unfolding before their eyes do not correspond to the normal pattern of life, urging them to realign their priorities (Ridderbos 1997: 168; cf. Morris 1995: 247).

"Look at the fields! They are ripe [lit., 'white'] for harvest." "Harvest" terminology does not occur in this Gospel outside 4:35–38 (though it does on Jesus' lips in the Synoptics, confirming authenticity; see Ensor 2000: 16). If the proverb quoted in the previous verse is to be taken literally, the fields were not actually ripe for harvest. Rather, Jesus' statement may be metaphorical rather than literal, pointing his disciples to the approaching mass of white-clothed Samaritans (Beasley-Murray 1999: 63; Schnackenburg 1990: 1.449; Burge 2000: 149). Then again, Jesus' statement may be figurative, the emphasis being on the fact that in the case of his own ministry of "harvesting of souls," the customary waiting period was moot, and harvesting could begin immediately.

"Even now the reaper draws his wages." Payment usually was made only for work completed. Thus, the disciples must not delay getting to work when others are already receiving wages (Morris 1995: 247).[76] So sower (fronted syntactically for emphasis [Wallace 1996: 402]) and reaper may rejoice together (cf. Matt. 9:37 = Luke 10:2). The joy of reaping a harvest is universally known. The OT refers to it both literally (Deut. 16:13–14) and metaphorically (Ps. 126:5–6; Isa. 9:3). Sowing, on the other hand, was often laborious (Ps. 126:5). In the present instance, however, it is not just the reaper who is able to rejoice, but also the sower. Jesus here conjures up images of a glorious, restored Edenic prosperity (cf. Joel 3:18; Amos 9:13; see Carson 1991: 230), a time when streams of blessing will flow from God's presence (cf. Ps. 36:8; 46:4; 87:7; Ezek. 47:1–12).

74. See the table "Chronology of Jesus' Ministry in John's Gospel" in the introduction. Contra Kruse (2003: 139 n. 1), who thinks the event took place shortly after the Passover in March/April.

75. It is also possible that the saying was a general proverb *and* was uttered by Jesus about four months prior to harvesttime.

76. Rabbi Tarfon (ca. A.D. 130) used to say, "The day is short and the task is great and the laborers are idle and the wage is abundant and the master of the house is urgent" (*m.* ʾAbot 2.15).

"In this" at the start of 4:37 prepares for what follows (Carson 1991: 230; Barrett 1978: 242). Usually, the saying "One sows and another reaps" points to the sad inequality of life: one sows without enjoying the benefits of the resulting crop, while another, who has not sown, reaps the fruit of that person's labor at a later time (Lev. 26:16; Deut. 28:30; Job 31:8; see Borchert 1996: 214). In the case of the end-time spiritual harvest referred to by Jesus, however, the intervening time is collapsed, so that sower and reaper rejoice together (4:36). Nevertheless, as Jesus points out in the present verse, this does not mean that the distinction between sower and reaper is obliterated.[77]

Jesus explains to his followers that others have done the hard work; his followers are the beneficiaries of the labors of others (cf. 14:12; Matt. 13:16–17; see Ridderbos 1997: 171). These "others" are Jesus and his predecessors, most immediately John the Baptist, who was the final prophet associated with the OT era (Köstenberger 1998b: 180–84; cf. Carson 1991: 231; Morris 1995: 249).[78] The general principle stated by Jesus here is that a fruitful harvest often is contingent on the labors of others.

"I send you" (ἀπέστειλα ὑμᾶς, apesteila hymas) refers to the disciples, in anticipation of their later commissioning by Jesus (cf. 17:18; 20:21).[79] The threefold use of terms denoting "labor" (κεκοπιάκατε, κεκοπιάκα-σιν, κόπον, kekopiakate, kekopiakasin, kopon) appears to anticipate (reflect?) the usage of this expression in the early church with reference to Christian proclamation (Rom. 16:6; 1 Cor. 15:10; 16:16; Gal. 4:11; Phil. 2:16; Col. 1:29; 1 Thess. 5:12; 1 Tim. 4:10; 5:17; see Barrett 1978: 243; Schnackenburg 1990: 1.453); the twice-repeated perfect (κεκοπιάκατε, κεκοπιάκασιν) conveys the settled state of others' labors and the disciples' "nonlabor" up to that point.

v. More Samaritan Conversions (4:39–42)

There was at that time a significant influx of Samaritan believers. Apart from this instance, there is no precrucifixion evidence for a large contingent of Samaritan disciples (cf. Matt. 10:5); Acts 8:4–25 treats the evangelization of the Samaritans as a fresh venture. Historically, Jesus'

4:39–42

---

77. Barrett (1978: 242) points to Greek parallels such as Aristophanes, *Equites* 392. Partial parallels include Josh. 24:13; Eccles. 2:18–21; Matt. 25:24; see also 1 Cor. 3:6.

78. J. A. T. Robinson (1959) limits the "others" to John the Baptist and his followers (contra Cullmann [1956], who thinks that the "others" are the Hellenists of Acts 8:4ff.; see also the critique of this view by Carson 1991: 231). On entering into someone else's labor, see 1 Cor. 3:5–15 (contrast Rom. 15:20) and the parable of the workers in the vineyard in Matt. 20:1–16.

79. Though translations usually render ἀπέστειλα in the past tense ("sent"), it can be argued that "send" is a better rendering; if so, Jesus is talking here not about a sending in the past, but about the disciples' mission in general (on 4:34–38, see Köstenberger 1998b: 180–84).

Samaritan mission may have been preparatory for the early church's effort at evangelizing this group. Theologically, John may seek to show that the Samaritan mission of the early church was based on precedent in Jesus' own ministry (cf. Acts 1:8; 8:4–25). Jesus' pattern of ministry in John coincides with that of the mission of the early church (Acts 1:8): first Judea (ch. 3 [Nicodemus]), then Samaria (ch. 4), then the Gentiles (4:46–54? [it is not certain that the royal official was a Gentile]; 10:16; 11:52; 12:20–32).

The woman's fellow townspeople appear to progress beyond the woman's understanding of Jesus. The woman's testimony provided the initial impetus for them to come to Jesus, but now they have heard for themselves and have drawn their own conclusion (cf. 4:42; see Barrett 1978: 243–44). In fact, secondhand testimony is no substitute for a direct personal encounter with Christ (Morris 1995: 250–51). Moreover, faith overcomes any scandal that may be given by the external circumstances of the revealer's origin (contrast 6:42; 7:27, 41–42, 52; see Schnackenburg 1990: 455). This gap may represent yet another instance of Johannine irony (Morris 1995: 250).

The absence of the article before μαρτυρούσης (martyrousēs, testifying) in 4:39 suggests an adverbial (temporal) usage of the participle (Wallace 1996: 241). The town referred to as "that town" is Sychar (cf. 4:5; Acts 8:5?). When they urged him (note the imperfect ἠρώτων, ērōtōn; see Morris 1995: 250) to stay with them, he stayed there for two days (cf. 11:6; ἔμεινεν [emeinen] probably has no spiritual overtones in 4:40 [contra Barrett 1978: 243]). The Jews' scruples regarding ritual purity, which caused them to refrain from association with Samaritans, clearly was not a major concern for Jesus (cf. 4:9). Yet after two days, Jesus must move on, being directed, as always, by the Father.

Many had believed in Jesus on account of the Samaritan woman's testimony (4:39). Many more believed on account of Jesus' word (4:41; note the parallelism: διὰ τὸν λόγον, dia ton logon). "In him" is not repeated in 4:41, but is implied from 4:39. Λαλία (lalia, lit., "speech") in 4:42 probably represents mere stylistic variation in relation to λόγος (logos, word) in 4:41. The insistent nature of the townspeople's words to the woman is highlighted by the use of the imperfect "they were saying" (ἔλεγον, elegon); the settled state of their own conviction is expressed by two perfects, ἀκηκόαμεν (akēkoamen, we have heard) and οἴδαμεν (oidamen, we know).

After this foray beyond the Jewish nation, Jesus is called "Savior of the world" (elsewhere in the NT only in 1 John 4:14). Interestingly, the OT never calls the Messiah "savior," and the expression was not a messianic title in first-century Judaism. The Samaritans likewise did not view the Taheb as a redeemer. In the first century, the title "savior" was also applied to many Greek gods and Roman emperors, including Augustus (31 B.C.–A.D. 14), Tiberius (A.D. 14–37), and Nero (A.D.

54–68).[80] According to Josephus, the emperor Vespasian (A.D. 69–79) was hailed upon his arrival in a given city as savior and benefactor (*J. W.* 3.9.8 §459; 7.4.1 §§70–71), and his son Titus (A.D. 79–81) received a similar welcome (*J. W.* 4.2.5 §§112–13; 7.5.2 §§100–103; 7.5.3 §119; C. Koester 1990b: 666).

The LXX uses σωτήρ (*sōtēr*, savior) both for God (e.g., Isa. 45:15, 21; cf. 43:3, 11; 63:8–9) and for human deliverers such as Othniel and Ehud (Judg. 3:9, 15).[81] By recognizing Jesus as "Savior of the world," the Samaritans accept that salvation may be from the Jews, but it is ultimately for all people (C. Koester 1990b: 668). This universal note fits well with the evangelist's own consistent emphasis on the universality of salvation offered through Jesus.[82] Moreover, identifying Jesus, rather than the Roman emperor, as "Savior of the world" challenges the surrounding culture (cf. Rev. 13:18 [the "beast" may well be a Roman emperor]; see commentary at 20:28).[83] Jesus' harvest among the Samaritans therefore signals the return of a part of the unbelieving world to God as a first sign of the universal scope of Jesus' saving mission.

Additional Note

4:1. The reading ὁ κύριος ("the Lord"; adopted by the NIV, but not the TNIV, in 4:3 from a textual variant of 4:1), which would reflect hindsight (cf. 6:23; 11:2; Luke 7:13), probably is secondary and should be rejected (so Beasley-Murray 1999: 58 n. a; Moloney 1998: 119; Schnackenburg 1990: 1.422 n. 4; contra Morris 1995: 222); though it should be acknowledged that κύριος (which has not yet been used in this Gospel to refer to Jesus) is the harder reading and could constitute John's anticipation of the κύριος used by the Samaritan woman in 4:11, 15, 19.

---

80. C. Koester 1990b: 665–80, esp. 667; cf. Deissmann 1927: 364–65; Boring, Berger, and Colpe 1995: 268.

81. Philo occasionally calls God "savior of the world" (*Spec. Laws* 2.32 §198) or "savior of all" (*Unchang.* 34 §156; *Flight* 29 §162).

82. Though "savior" and "salvation" are not used outside the present pericope in John, the world, in its estrangement from God, is consistently portrayed as the object of God's saving purposes in Christ (3:16–21; 12:46–47).

83. An implied contrast with the Roman emperor is favored in Morris 1995: 251 n. 98; Beasley-Murray 1999: 65; contra Schnackenburg 1990: 1.458. C. Koester (1990b: 678) contends that the Samaritans' designation of Jesus as "Savior of the world" is part of the Johannine kingship theme, in contrast to the Jews' disavowal of Jesus as their king in 19:15 ("We have no king but Caesar"). Koester also points to the Roman presence in Samaria as evidence for the countercultural nature of the Samaritans' confession of Jesus (rather than the Roman emperor) as "Savior of the world" (pp. 678–79).

5. The Second Sign at Cana: The Healing of the Royal Official's Son (4:43–54)

Jesus' first major ministry circuit has almost come to a close. The healing of the royal official's son, labeled Jesus' "second sign" in Cana of Galilee by the evangelist, ties 4:43–54 in with 2:1–11, thus constituting 2:1–4:54 as the first major unit in John's narrative about Jesus (Moloney 1998: 113–14; Schnackenburg 1990: 1.419).[1] When Jesus returns to Galilee, he is "welcomed" there (4:45). Yet the welcome turns out to be shallow and conditional: people are interested only in miracles (4:44–45; cf. 4:48). Tellingly, the only recorded sign performed by Jesus at this occasion involves "a certain royal official" (βασιλικός, *basilikos* [4:46]), probably a (Gentile?) officer in Herod Antipas's service.[2] The story resembles that of the Gentile centurion in Matt. 8:5–13 and Luke 7:2–10, but this is not the same incident (Carson 1991: 233–34).[3] The literary structure of 4:47–54 resembles that of 4:39–42 (Moloney 1998: 151).

As in the case of the first sign in Cana, Jesus condescends to meet the need of the hour—in the present instance, the well-being of the royal official's son. But rather than "come down" to Capernaum, where the child lay sick, Jesus heals the boy long-distance—another instance of John's emphasis on "hard" miracles of Jesus. Indeed, when the official learns from his servants that his son got better at the seventh hour (i.e., about 1:00 P.M., counting from sunrise at 6:00 A.M.), he and his entire household believe (4:51–53). For this was the precise time at which Jesus had made the pronouncement that the official's son would live (4:53).

1. The inclusion with John 2 is created in more ways than one: note the mention of Cana ("where Jesus had turned the water into wine"), the reference to Capernaum, and the numbering of signs in Cana (Carson 1991: 237). Keener (2003: 630) also notes the geographical *inclusio* (i.e., references to Galilee in 4:43 and 4:54 serving to bracket the entire unit.

2. Herod was tetrarch (not king) of Galilee from 4 B.C. to A.D. 39, but he was commonly regarded as king (see, e.g., Mark 6:14); a similar designation is used for Blastus, "a trusted personal servant of the king" (Herod Agrippa I, Herod the Great's grandson) in Acts 12:20.

3. Lindars (1992a) proposes the rather daring hypothesis that John's source for the present account was Q, which he developed along different lines than did Matthew and Luke. However, the degree of difference between the respective accounts renders source-critical solutions less than convincing.

Also as in the case of the first Cana sign, no discourse accompanies the account of the healing of the royal official's son. The evangelist refrains from drawing out any specific christological symbolism that may be reflected in Jesus' performance of this particular sign. It is apparent that Jesus' performance of signs in Galilee (similar to Jerusalem [2:23–25; 3:2]) is unable to overcome the profound rejection he suffers from his own people (4:44). This rejection theme, already sounded in the prologue (1:11), will reach an intermediate culmination point at the end of John 6 and will climax in the pronouncement of 12:37.

    a. Jesus returns to Galilee (4:43–45)
    b. Jesus heals the royal official's son (4:46–54)

Exegesis and Exposition

⁴³But after the two days he left from there for Galilee. ⁴⁴(For Jesus himself had testified that a prophet has no honor in his own country.) ⁴⁵So when he came to Galilee, the Galileans received him, because they had seen all the things he had done in Jerusalem at the [Passover] festival; for they also had gone to the festival.

⁴⁶So he came again to Cana in Galilee, where he had turned the water into wine. And there was a certain royal official whose son lay sick in Capernaum. ⁴⁷When this man heard that Jesus had come from Judea to Galilee, he left and came to him and urged him to come down and heal his son; for he was about to die. ⁴⁸Then Jesus said to him, "Unless you people see signs and wonders, you will never believe." ⁴⁹The royal official said to him, "Sir, come down before my child dies." ⁵⁰Jesus said to him, "Go, your son is alive." The man believed the word Jesus had spoken to him and went away. ⁵¹And while he was still going down to Capernaum, his servants met him with the news that his ⌜child⌝ was alive. ⁵²So he inquired from them as to the time at which he [his son] had gotten better. They told him, "Yesterday, at the seventh hour [about 1:00 P.M.] the fever left him." ⁵³Then the father realized that it was at that hour that Jesus had told him, "Your son is alive"; and he believed, and his entire household. ⁵⁴Again, this was the second sign Jesus performed after he had come from Judea into Galilee.

a. Jesus Returns to Galilee (4:43–45)

Regarding the phrase "after the two days," compare 4:40 (note the anaphoric article in 4:43 [Wallace 1996: 219]). Jesus left for Galilee, yet there is no indication how long it took him to travel there. Also, we are not told exactly where in Galilee he went prior to his return visit to Cana (4:46). But from Sychar to Cana was about forty miles—a trip that could have been accomplished in two or three days.

4:43–45

The conjunction γάρ (*gar*, for) probably is anticipatory (cf. the continued rejection theme in Galilee in 6:41–42, 66) and has the sense "namely" or "now" (van Belle 1998: 39). John 4:44 (cf. 4:19), where τιμή (*timē*, honor) replaces the customary δόξα (*doxa*, glory) (Morris 1995: 254 n. 106), illustrates the opening reference to Jesus' rejection even by "his own" (1:11; see Pryor 1987; 1990: 216–17). The Galileans'[4] "welcome" (δέχομαι, *dechomai*, receive, welcome [only here in this Gospel]), in another instance of Johannine irony (Morris 1995: 254; Carson 1991: 236), was in fact a rejection (4:44), because Jesus' compatriots were interested only in his miracles (4:45: cf. 4:48; see also 6:14–15, 26, 30; see Stimpfle 1992: 86–96).[5] "Receiving" Jesus is not necessarily the same as accepting him (Schnackenburg 1990: 1.464), in keeping with the Johannine pattern of initial "faith" that is subsequently exposed as inadequate.

Regarding the statement in 4:45b, see 2:13–25, especially 2:23.[6] It was incumbent upon faithful Jews to go to Jerusalem for the three great pilgrim festivals, Passover, Pentecost, and Tabernacles. Large numbers of worshipers from the outlying provinces of Palestine (Luke 2:41–42) and the Diaspora (Acts 2:5) filled the capital city (cf. Josephus, *J.W.* 2.1.3 §10). Nevertheless, the biblical commands of Exod. 23:17 and Deut. 16:16 were not interpreted as requiring every person to travel to Jerusalem three times each year. Those living at a distance ought to go as they had the opportunity, and at least once in a lifetime (Ferguson 1993: 521).

b. Jesus Heals the Royal Official's Son (4:46–54)

4:46 Regarding the phrase "he came again to Cana," see 2:1–11 and 4:54. Although the ensuing account resembles Matt. 8:5–13 par. in certain

---

4. One school of interpretation identifies πατρίς (*patris*, homeland, hometown) in 4:44 with Jerusalem (so Barrett 1978: 246; Dodd 1953: 352; 1963: 238–41; Meeks 1966; 1967: 39–40; see, much earlier, Origen, *Commentarii in evangelium Joannis* 13.54–56, cited in van Belle 1998: 30). However, see the critiques by W. Davies (1974: 321–31) and Stimpfle (1992: 89) as summarized by van Belle (1998: 30–32). The Galilee/Nazareth explanation is found already in Augustine (cited by van Belle 1998: 33) and is defended by Stimpfle (1992: 86–96 [followed by van Belle 1998: 27–44]) and others (see van Belle 1998: 32–33; see also Ridderbos 1997: 174; Beasley-Murray 1999: 73; Schnackenburg 1990: 1.463). Still others think that both Galilee and Judea are in view (Carson 1991: 235–36; Burge 2000: 151–52; Witherington 1995: 126; W. Davies 1974: 321–31).

5. John may assume here his readers' familiarity with Synoptic tradition, according to which Jesus was rejected in his native Galilee, including Nazareth (Matt. 13:53–58 par.; Luke 4:16–30; cf. Matt. 11:19 par.). Other instances in which John appears to expect his readers' familiarity with Synoptic tradition include 1:40; 3:24; 6:67; 11:1–2. The present saying is found also in Gos. Thom. 31 and P.Oxy. 1.6 (van Belle 1998: 27–44). Michaels (1989: 78–79) links the present "welcome" to the Didache guideline that itinerant teachers not stay in a locale more than two days (cf. John 4:40). However, this seems to be both anachronistic and contextually far-fetched.

6. Wallace (1996: 631–32) notes that ἑωρακότες (*heōrakotes*, having seen) is an adverbial participle of cause.

respects, there are several significant differences. The Synoptic story occurs in Capernaum, John's in Cana. In the Synoptic account, Jesus heals the servant of a Roman Gentile. In John, the official's ethnic and national identity is unspecified (though he probably is a Genitle as well; see further below). In the Synoptics, the centurion declares himself unworthy to have Jesus come to his house. In John, the official pleads with Jesus to do so. For these reasons John 4:46–54 and Matt. 8:5–13 par. should be taken to refer to two separate occasions in Jesus' ministry.[7] Lack of reference to the disciples focuses attention on Jesus and his amazing feat (Witherington 1995: 127).

Jesus was approached by "a certain royal official."[8] If this man was a Gentile,[9] then this marks a progression from Jew (John 3) to Samaritan to Gentile (John 4) in Jesus' ministry, in keeping with the pattern followed also in the Book of Acts (cf. Acts 1:8; see Moloney 1998: 153). The term βασιλικός (basilikos, royal official) usually refers to someone in the service of a king.[10] In the present instance, the "king" probably was Herod Antipas (cf. Mark 6:14),[11] though Antipas technically did not hold that title, but rather was tetrarch of Galilee (4 B.C.–A.D. 39) (Hoehner 1972). This was the ruler whom Jesus later called "that fox" after hearing that he was out to kill him (Luke 13:31–32). Still later, when summoned before Herod at the occasion of his Jerusalem trial, Jesus refused to answer any of his questions (Luke 23:8–12). Presumably, one of the reasons for this frosty relationship was Herod's beheading of John the Baptist.[12] But the present event takes place at an earlier stage of Jesus' ministry, and Jesus in any case would not have held the royal official's employment with Herod Antipas against him personally.

Apparently, the official had heard (ἀκούσας, akousas [an aorist temporal participle denoting preceding action; Wallace 1996: 627]) reports from Galileans who had witnessed Jesus' signs in Jerusalem (4:47; cf. 4:45; see Moloney 1998: 153). His primary (only?) concern is not with Jesus'   **4:47**

---

7. So Carson 1991: 234; Ridderbos 1997: 174–75; Morris 1995: 255; Borchert 1996: 219–20; Burge 2000: 152–53; Witherington 1995: 127; contra R. Brown 1966: 193; Barrett 1978: 245; Beasley-Murray 1999: 71; Schnackenburg 1990: 1.471–75; Bultmann 1971: 205.

8. On the characterization of this official in John's Gospel, see the discussion in Beck 1997: 78–82.

9. So Mead 1985: 71; Barrett 1978: 245; Witherington 1995: 128; Moloney 1998: 153; Bultmann 1971: 206; but see the cautious assessment by Carson 1991: 234. Morris (1995: 255), somewhat idiosyncratically, suggests that the man was a Jew.

10. Keener (1993: 275) conjectures that perhaps he was "a wealthy aristocrat, probably much influenced by Greco-Roman culture and not very religious by general Palestinian Jewish standards." In his later commentary, Keener (2003: 630) similarly calls the man a "Galilean aristocrat." Some scholars speculate that the royal official is to be identified with Chuza, the manager of Herod's household mentioned in Luke 8:3.

11. So Carson 1991: 238; Morris 1995: 256; Borchert 1996: 219; R. Brown 1966: 190; Schnackenburg 1990: 1.465.

12. Matt. 14:1–12 par.; cf. Luke 9:7–9; for Jesus' reaction, see Matt. 14:12b–13.

identity but with his son's well-being (Carson 1991: 238; cf. Ridderbos 1997: 176). The sickness of the official's son involved some kind of fever (4:52) and apparently was terminal (4:47, 49). Capernaum is also the site of the healings of the centurion's servant (Matt. 8:5–13 par.), Peter's mother-in-law (Matt. 8:14–17 pars.), and a paralytic (Matt. 9:2–8 pars.), as well as (probably) the raising of Jairus's daughter (Matt. 9:18–26 pars.).[13]

Travel from Capernaum to Cana involved a day's journey of about fourteen miles. The trip was mostly uphill, since Cana lay in the Galilean hill country and Capernaum was located several hundred feet below sea level. If the royal official left Capernaum at sunrise, he could have reached Cana at noon, and at the seventh hour, 1:00 P.M., heard Jesus' comforting words that his son would live (4:50). On the way back, however, he would have been able to complete only half of his journey on the same day, so that his servants would have met him at the plain of Gennesaret on the following day (4:51–52) (Dalman 1935: 105).[14]

4:48   Jesus' comment reveals that people's earlier "welcome" (4:45) was rather shallow and based primarily on Jesus' miracle-working ability (see commentary at 4:45; cf. 2:23–25). "You people" (plural) refers not just to the royal official, but to the Galileans in general. The official is treated by Jesus as representative of the Galileans' signs-based response to him. Jesus' words—somewhat unexpected in light of the man's dire need (Moloney 1998: 153)—are designed to challenge this desperate, concerned father to go beyond self-interest and to recognize Jesus as more than a thaumaturge, thus summoning his Galilean audience to acknowledge his true identity (Ridderbos 1997: 176; note similar challenges in 2:4; 11:23–24; see Schnackenburg 1990: 1.468). The expression "signs and wonders" (a possible hendiadys; Laney 1992: 102) probably harks back to the "signs and wonders" performed by Moses at the exodus (Köstenberger 1998b: 58–59, esp. n. 43).[15]

4:49–50   The official's request is for Jesus to come to Capernaum *before* his "child"[16] would die. Once again, however, Jesus meets a request on his own terms:

13. On Capernaum, see commentary at 2:12.

14. The imperfect ἠρώτα (*ērōta*, urged) points to the official's determination (Ridderbos 1997: 175 n. 215; Morris 1995: 256). The urgency of the situation is further highlighted by the word ἤμελλεν (*ēmellen*, about to [Morris 1995: 256 n. 11]). "To come down" is a literal rendering of the Greek, for Capernaum was lower in elevation than Cana (see above and commentary at 4:51). Regarding the phrase "about to die," see the references to the royal official's son being "sick" (ἠσθένει, *ēsthenei*) in 4:46 and "having a fever" (ὁ πυρετός, *ho pyretos*) in 4:52.

15. Tellingly, the expression occurs elsewhere in the Gospels only in Jesus' eschatological discourse (Matt. 24:24 par.; cf. 2 Thess. 2:9), where Jesus warns that false messiahs and prophets will perform "signs and wonders" in order to deceive the elect. The semantic profile of this expression in Acts, Paul, and Hebrews is more positive.

16. The expression "child" indicates the close bond between father and son—a more emotional term than "son" in 4:47 (Morris 1995: 257; Moloney 1998: 153; Burge 2000: 158).

the present healing is a rare instance of a long-distance miracle.[17] The phrase "your son will live" may be an allusion to Elijah and the woman of Zarephath in 1 Kings 17:23 (Schnackenburg 1990: 1.467).[18] If so, Jesus' messianic activity is placed here within the compass of the miraculous healing ministry of Elijah in the OT (cf. Luke 4:23–27; though unlike Elijah, Jesus was able to heal the boy simply by his spoken word; see Schnackenburg 1990: 1.467).

The man—unlike other Galileans—takes Jesus at his word and departs, evidencing a remarkable progression from one who seeks out Jesus on the basis of his reputation as a thaumaturge (4:47, 49), to one who trusts in Jesus' word without (as of yet) seeing a miracle or validating sign that his son would be restored (4:50; cf. 4:41–42; see Witherington 1995: 128), to believing with his entire household (4:53; see Moloney 1998: 162). Previously, the official had merely believed in Jesus' ability to heal his son; now, he takes Jesus at his word (promise) that he has actually done so (Ridderbos 1997: 177).[19]

"While he was still on the way" reads, literally, "on the way down" (see commentary at 4:47). The distance from Cana to Capernaum could be covered in one day if the journey was begun in the morning. However, the royal official commenced his return trip in the afternoon and therefore had to stay overnight and complete his journey home on the following day (see commentary at 4:47). The phrase "his child was alive" (see additional note) repeats, with slight stylistic variation (Freed 1965a: 449), the earlier recorded utterance by Jesus, "your son [υἱός, huios (4:50)] is alive."   **4:51–52**

The word πυνθάνομαι (pynthanomai, inquire), used elsewhere in this Gospel only in 13:24, often connotes an element of curiosity or intrigue, coupled with a strong desire to know some piece of information of which the questioner is ignorant.[20] As in 2:5–10, the servants

---

17. On the unusual nature of Jesus' signs selected by John, see commentary at 2:10. A similar remarkable incident (that of the healing of the centurion's servant in Capernaum) is narrated in Matt. 8:5–13 par. Vermes (1972–73) seeks to adduce parallels with the first-century Jewish miracle worker and faith healer Ḥanina ben Dosa (cf. b. Ber. 34b; much more cautious is Bokser 1985). However, as Meier (1994: 581–88, citing Freyne 1980) points out, not only is Ḥanina ben Dosa not mentioned in Josephus, but also none of the three mishnaic references attribute miracle-working power to him; this takes place only in the talmudic tradition. Hence, all that can be said confidently about the "historical" Ḥanina is that he probably was a first-century Palestinian Jew who was noted for his efficacious prayers over the sick; there is not even early historical evidence linking him to Galilee.

18. Note the threefold repetition of the fact that the son is "alive" (John 4:50, 51, 43), emphasizing that Jesus is able to give/restore life (Morris 1995: 259; cf. Beasley-Murray 1999: 73).

19. Note also the progression from official to personal in the evangelist's description of the man: from "a certain official" (τις βασιλικός, tis basilikos [4:46, cf. 49]), to "the man" (ὁ ἄνθρωπος, ho anthrōpos [4:50]), to "the father" (ὁ πατήρ, ho patēr [4:53]) (Moloney 1998: 161).

20. Other NT instances of this word include Matt. 2:4; Luke 15:26; 18:36; Acts 4:7; 10:18, 29; 21:33; 23:19, 20, 34.

function as impartial witnesses, since they were unaware of what had transpired (Ridderbos 1997: 176; Schnackenburg 1990: 1.468; Bultmann 1971: 208).

"Seventh hour" indicates that the healing took place around 1:00 P.M. (see commentary at 1:39), the very time at which the official spoke to Jesus (Carson 1991: 239; Beasley-Murray 1999: 69; Moloney 1998: 162; Burge 2000: 152). "He had gotten better" (κομψότερον ἔσχεν, *kompsoteron eschen* [an ingressive aorist; Wallace 1996: 559]) is a Hellenistic expression (Barrett 1978: 248). "The fever left him" resembles the constructions in Matt. 8:15 pars. (the healing of Peter's mother-in-law).

4:53–54   The centurion and his entire household believed. Conversions of entire households are featured also in the Book of Acts in the cases of Cornelius (ch. 10; cf. 11:14), Lydia (16:15), the Philippian jailer (16:31), and Crispus (18:8) (Carson 1991: 239). The reference to a "second sign" here is to the second sign Jesus performed *after he had come from Judea to Galilee* (Ridderbos 1997: 179; cf. Morris 1995: 259). This invests Galilee with a certain strategic significance as the base for the manifestations of Jesus' messianic glory, contrary to all expectations and prejudices (cf. 1:46; 7:41, 52).[21] In the interim, other signs had been performed in Jerusalem and vicinity (2:23; 3:2; cf. 4:45). Thus John closes the cycle of Jesus' first ministry circuit, starting and ending in Cana of Galilee.[22]

Additional Note

4:51. The chosen rendering, "his child was alive," presupposes παῖς as the highly probable original reading (so Freed 1965a; contra Kilpatrick 1963). The reading υἱός appears to have arisen as a scribal assimilation to the context (cf. 4:46, 47, 50, 53; see Metzger 1994: 178).

---

21. Brodie (1993: 233) sees "a coherent picture": "Jesus' withdrawal from a superficial and hostile Judaism (2:23, 4:1–3), . . . followed . . . by allusions to his orientation toward the Gentiles—the coming, bridelike, of 'all' (3:26), the coming, in a betrothal scene, of the Samaritan woman and her people, and finally, from a border town, the coming of the royal official and his whole household." For Brodie, all of this adds up to "a journey to the Gentiles."

22. The numbering of the two Cana signs has suggested to some the existence of a "signs source" (Bultmann 1971: 206; Fortna 1970; 1989; Whitacre 1999: 116). However, this inference is not a necessary one (Ridderbos 1997: 178; Carson 1991: 178; Beasley-Murray 1999: 71; contra Barrett 1978: 246; Schnackenburg 1990: 1.469–71).

B. Additional Signs amid Mounting Unbelief (5:1–10:42)

After narrating Jesus' first ministry circuit, from Cana of Galilee to Jerusalem and via Samaria back to Cana in chapters 2–4, the evangelist embarks on a presentation of the remainder of Jesus' public ministry prior to his crucifixion. This presentation, in the form of a "festival cycle" built around Jesus' attendance of a variety of Jewish festivals (Borchert 1996: 235), takes up chapters 5–10.[1] As is clear also from the Synoptic Gospels, this phase of Jesus' ministry is characterized by escalating conflict. Once again, however, John is less concerned with comprehensiveness than are the Synoptists, selecting instead typical events and discourses that illustrate the responses that Jesus (the Christ) received.

As in the Cana cycle (chs. 2–4), John selects three signs to demonstrate further that Jesus is the Messiah and Son of God (cf. 12:37; 20:30–31) and features two major discourses. (1) The healing of the lame man (ch. 5) takes place at an unnamed feast (probably the Feast of Tabernacles) and issues in the most heated controversy up to this point and the first major attempt on Jesus' life recorded in the Gospel (5:18). (2) The feeding of the multitude (ch. 6) occurs at Jesus' only Galilean Passover recorded in the Gospel and presents Jesus as the Bread of Life, a teaching even many of Jesus' own disciples considered too difficult (6:60–71). (3) The next narrative unit, recounting Jesus' attendance at the Feast of Tabernacles (chs. 7–8, sans the pericope of the adulterous woman) perhaps the year following the healing of the lame man in chapter 5, is broken up into two major teaching cycles (7:1–52; 8:12–59), with the second teaching cycle culminating in the paternity dispute between Jesus and the Jewish leaders, who again seek to stone him on the charge of blasphemy (8:59). (4) The healing of the blind man and the ensuing Good Shepherd discourse (chs. 9–10) parabolically expose the spiritual blindness and irresponsible spiritual leadership of the Jewish authorities, who again attempt to arrest Jesus (10:39). Final closure is provided by the *inclusio* contrasting John the Baptist's lack of signs with Jesus' miraculous activities (10:40–42; cf. 1:19–51).

---

1. In light of the apparently abrupt reference to Jesus "crossing to the far shore of the Sea of Galilee" in 6:1 (ch. 5 has him in Jerusalem), it has been speculated that chapters 5 and 6 should be reversed (see Bultmann 1971: 209, 237; Schnackenburg 1990: 2.92); but see Carson 1991: 240; Morris 1995: 264; cf. Barrett 1978: 23–24; Borchert 1996: 250; and especially Ridderbos 1997: 183.

1. At an Unnamed Feast in Jerusalem: The Healing of the Lame Man (5:1–47)

After an extended stay in Galilee, Jesus returns to Jerusalem in order to attend an unspecified Jewish festival.[1] As in the cases of Nicodemus, the Samaritan woman, and the royal official, John shows Jesus' concern for a particular individual, in the present instance a man who has been an invalid for thirty-eight years.[2] If this were the Synoptic Gospels, the miracle itself would be sufficient to demonstrate Jesus' authority over sickness (cf. Mark 2:1–12) or his fulfillment of the messianic mission envisioned by Isaiah (cf. Matt. 8:17; 12:17–21; Luke 4:18–21). In John, however, the miracle is transmuted into a "sign" (cf. 7:21–24), an act with inherent christological symbolism. In the present scenario, the clue to understanding this symbolism is provided by the fact that Jesus performs this healing *on a Sabbath*.[3]

Notably, it is not the actual healing that is the Jews' primary concern. Rather, offense is taken at Jesus' telling the man to pick up his mat and walk; for oral tradition (though not the OT) forbade the carrying of a mat on the Sabbath. When confronted regarding this infraction, the man shifts the blame to the one who had healed him.[4] In the Johannine context, the healing and the ensuing controversy provide the occasion for Jesus to assert his oneness with God the Father. After defending himself against the charges of Sabbath-breaking and blasphemy, Jesus calls upon three major witnesses who can testify to the truthfulness of his claims: John the Baptist; Jesus' own works, including his miracles; and the Father, speaking primarily through the OT Scriptures.

1. For a survey of patristic literature on John 5:1–18, see Mees 1986. A close narrative reading of 5:1–18 is found in Culpepper 1993. A reading of 5:1–47 is provided by Lee 1994: 98–125.

2. Note that 6:2 mentions multiple "signs he [Jesus] had performed on the sick."

3. Note especially John 5:9–10, 16; cf. chapter 9, especially 9:14, 16. For Sabbath healings in the Synoptics, see Matt. 12:1–14 pars.; Mark 1:21–28 par.; Luke 13:10–17; 14:1–6.

4. For an unfavorable comparison between this character and the man born blind in John 9, see the discussion there. Keener (2003: 639, following Culpepper 1983: 139) contends that 5:1–15 serves as a (negative) foil for the (positive) characterization in chapter 9 of the man born blind, calling the contrasting of characters a common rhetorical device. See also Asiedu-Peprah 2001; Staley 1991. For a discussion of the similarities and differences between John 5 and 9, see Lee 1994: 105–7.

a. The setting (5:1–3)
b. The healing (5:5–9a)
c. The aftermath (5:9b–15)
d. The Sabbath controversy (5:16–47)
   i. Jesus' response to the charges of Sabbath-breaking and blasphemy (5:16–30)
   ii. Testimony regarding Jesus (5:31–47)

Exegesis and Exposition

[1]After these things there was ⌜a Jewish festival⌝, and Jesus went up to Jerusalem. [2]There was in Jerusalem by the Sheep Gate a pool (called ⌜"Bethesda"⌝ in Aramaic) that is surrounded by five colonnades. [3]Under those a large number of disabled—blind, lame, paralyzed—used to lie.[5]

[5]Now there was a certain man there who had been in his disabled state for thirty-eight years. [6]When Jesus saw him lying there and realized that he already had been in this condition for a long time, he said to him, "Would you like to get well?" [7]The invalid answered him, "Sir, I have no one to take me into the pool when the water is stirred. While I am going, someone else goes down ahead of me." [8]Jesus said to him, "Get up, take your mat, and go." [9]And at once the man got well and took his mat and went.

Now it was Sabbath on that day. [10]So the Jewish leaders were saying to the man who had been healed, "It is the Sabbath, and it is not lawful for you to carry your mat." [11]But he answered them, "The one who made me well, he told me, 'Take your mat and go.'" [12]They asked him, "Who is the man who told you, 'Take and go'?" [13]But the one who had been cured did not know who it was, for Jesus had slipped away, since there was a crowd in that place. [14]After these things Jesus ran into him in the temple area and said to him, "Look, you have become well; sin no longer, so that nothing worse may happen to you." [15]The man went and reported to the Jewish leaders that it was Jesus who had made him well.

[16]And for this reason the Jewish leaders were beginning to persecute Jesus, because he was doing these things on the Sabbath. [17]But ⌜Jesus⌝ answered them, "My Father is working until now, and I too am working." [18]So for this reason the Jewish leaders were all the more seeking to kill him, because not only was he breaking the Sabbath, but he was even calling God his own Father, making himself equal to God.

[19]So Jesus answered and kept saying to them, "Truly, truly, I say to you, the Son cannot do anything by himself unless he sees the Father do it. For whatever that one does, the Son does as well. [20]For the Father loves the Son and shows him all he does, and he will show him greater works than these, so that you will be amazed. [21]For just as the Father raises the dead and gives them life, so also the Son gives life to whomever he is pleased to give it. [22]For the Father judges

5. On 5:3b–4, see additional note.

no one, but has given all judgment to the Son, [23]so that all may honor the Son just as they honor the Father. Whoever does not honor the Son does not honor the Father who sent him.

[24]"Truly, truly, I say to you that whoever hears my word and believes the one who sent me has eternal life and does not come into judgment, but has passed from death to life. [25]Truly, truly, I say to you that a time is coming and in fact is now here when the dead will hear the voice of the Son of God, and those who have heard it will live. [26]For just as the Father has life in himself, so also he has given to the Son to have life in himself. [27]And he has given him authority to judge because he is the Son of Man.

[28]"Do not be surprised at this, because a time is coming when all who are in their graves will hear his voice [29]and come out, those who have done what is good to the resurrection of life, but those who have perpetrated wicked things to the resurrection of judgment. [30]I can do nothing by myself: just as I hear, I judge; and my judgment is just, because I do not seek my own will but the will of the one who sent me.

[31]"If I testify concerning myself, my testimony is not valid. [32]There is another who bears witness concerning me, and I know that his testimony that he renders concerning me is valid. [33]You have sent to John, and he has testified to the truth. [34]Not that I receive testimony from a human source, but I say these things in order that you may be saved. [35]He was the lamp that burned and shone, and you chose to enjoy his light for a season. [36]But I have testimony weightier than that of John. For the works that my Father has given me to accomplish—the very works that I am doing—they themselves bear witness concerning me that the Father has sent me. [37]And the Father who sent me—he has borne witness concerning me. You have never heard his voice or seen his form, [38]and you do not have his word residing in you, because the one whom the Father sent—in this one you do not believe. [39]You search the Scriptures because you think that in them you have eternal life. Yet it is they that testify concerning me; [40]and you do not want to come to me to have life.

[41]"I do not accept honor from mere humans, [42]but I know you: I know that you do not have love for God within yourselves. [43]I have come in my Father's name, and you do not accept me; if another comes in his own name, that one you will accept. [44]How can you believe, since you accept honor from one another but do not seek the honor that comes from the only God? [45]Do not think that I will accuse you before the Father; your accuser is Moses, on whom you have set your hopes. [46]For if you believed Moses, you would believe me; for he wrote concerning me. [47]Yet if you do not believe his writings, how will you believe my words?"

a. The Setting (5:1–3)

5:1   A little while after completing his first "ministry circuit," Jesus travels to Jerusalem to attend an unspecified festival (see additional note).[6] This

---

6. Brodie (1993: 236) finds the setting "thoroughly semitic. . . . The text evokes an image of the Jews as a suffering flock."

is the second of three trips by Jesus to the Jewish capital recorded in this Gospel (the time may be October, the year A.D. 31). Like the temple clearing, the present healing—the fourth sign in John's Gospel—takes place in Jerusalem. This is the only event selected by the evangelist from Jesus' second year of ministry.

The expression "after these things" marks the passing of an indefinite period of time (cf. 2:12; see Ridderbos 1997: 184; Keener 2003: 635).[7] Up to a year and a half may have passed since the last recorded festival, the Passover, at which Jesus had cleared the temple and met with Nicodemus. Now, after joining up with the Baptist in the Judean countryside, evangelizing in Samaria, and ministering for a while in Galilee, Jesus returns to the Jewish capital to celebrate an unnamed festival.[8]

The festival in question, the only one unnamed in this Gospel, may have been one of the several festivals taking place in Jerusalem in September/October, perhaps Tabernacles (which, if the year was A.D. 31, fell on October 21–28; see Hengel 1999: 308, 321). If so, Jesus' ministry lasted about three and a half years.[9] Tabernacles may be suggested by the fact that some MSS have "the" festival of the Jews, the conventional name for Tabernacles.[10]

The mention of the presence in Jerusalem (the definite article in the Greek may indicate the precincts of Jerusalem; cf. 2:23; see Morris 1995: 265 n. 7) of a pool near the Sheep Gate is controversial for at least two reasons.[11] First, the present tense form ἐστίν (estin, is) in 5:2 suggests to some a pre–A.D. 70 date for the composition of the Gospel, since the

5:2

---

7. On a literary level, Keener (2003: 634) observes that the shift from the end of chapter 4 to the beginning of chapter 5 is part of the Johannine pattern of leaving major chronological and geographical gaps (e.g., 7:2; 10:22; 11:55).

8. See Payne, *ZPEB* 3:460. "Jewish" festival, rather than pointing to a Gentile audience (Morris 1995: 265), indicates the "temporal and material distance that had developed at the time of the Gospel between the Christian church and the situation to which the story takes us" (Ridderbos 1997: 184). It was customary for Jews at any place and any elevation in Palestine to use the expression going "up" to Jerusalem.

9. See Carson 1991: 240. Bultmann (1971: 240) claims that the festival is Passover, based on his switching the order of John 5 and 6, but this is unlikely, since the evangelist clearly identifies Passover everywhere else in his Gospel. Also unlikely is Michaels's (1989: 85) theory that the present pericope was transposed from Jesus' first Passover in Jerusalem (cf. 2:23; 3:2). Many commentators choose to remain agnostic on which feast is in view (Keener 2003: 635), regarding its identity as either unknown (Ridderbos 1997: 184; Morris 1995: 265 n. 6) or of secondary interest (R. Brown 1966: 206), or both (Carson 1991: 241). Calvin (1959: 116) thinks that the feast probably is Pentecost.

10. See 1 Kings 8:2, 65; 12:32; 2 Chron. 5:3; 7:8; Neh. 8:14, 18; Ps. 81:3; Ezek. 45:25. See also additional note.

11. Helpful treatments include Avi-Yonah 1974: 142; Jeremias 1966b; Mackowski 1980: 79–83; Vardaman 1963; and Wieand 1965–66. Riesner (*DJG* 41) prefers the translation "There is in Jerusalem by the Sheep Pool the [site] with five porticoes called in Hebrew [i.e., Aramaic] Bethesda."

gate likely was destroyed during the events of A.D. 66–70.[12] Yet this may extract more from the present tense form than is warranted (Blomberg 2002: 43; Carson 1991: 241; Bultmann 1971: 240 n. 4; contra Wallace 1990: 197–205).

Questions also extend to the precise nature and location of the "Sheep Gate" (cf. Neh. 3:1, 32; 12:39), in part due to the elliptical reference involving the adjective προβατική (*probatikē*, pertaining to sheep) without accompanying substantive.[13] In Jesus' day, this apparently was a small opening in the north wall of the temple. The sheep were washed in the pool before being taken to the sanctuary. This was also the place where invalids lay in hopes of being healed. The upper class and those wishing to be ritually pure would have avoided this area, but not Jesus.

The five colonnades may have been erected by Herod the Great (Hengel 1999: 310–12). Four covered colonnades enclosed two separate pools (viewed as a unity)[14] in a rough trapezoid, with a fifth one separating them.[15] There, invalids could lie and be partially protected from the weather.[16] "Bethesda" in Aramaic may mean "house of (divine) mercy" (which would be a fitting term, given the desperate state of the people lying there in hope of miraculous healing), "house of the two springs," or be derived from the root "pour out" or "slope."[17]

12. See especially Wallace (1990: esp. 204; 1996: 531, with reference to McKay 1994: 40), who claims, "Since εἰμί is nowhere else clearly used as a historical present, the present tense should be taken as indicating present time from the viewpoint of the speaker." For evidence that εἰμί can function as a historical present, see 10:8: πάντες ὅσοι ἦλθον πρὸ ἐμοῦ κλέπται εἰσὶν καὶ λῃσταί, "all who have come before me *were* thieves and robbers" (note that "were" is the rendering chosen in the NIV, TNIV, NLT, and NET); cf. 19:40: καθὼς ἔθος ἐστὶν τοῖς Ἰουδαίοις ἐνταφιάζειν, "this *was* in accordance with Jewish burial customs" (NIV = TNIV; CEV: "which was how the Jewish people buried their dead"). See also Schlatter (1948: 141), who takes the present tense verb in 5:2 at face value but conjectures that the "sheep gate" must have been reconstructed subsequent to its destruction by Titus in A.D. 70.

13. A few commentators (Morris 1995: 265–66; Barrett 1978: 251; Moloney 1998: 171; R. Brown 1966: 206) think that προβατική modifies κολυμβήθρα (*kolymbēthra*, pool); others think that the implied noun is "gate" (Carson 1991: 241; so also the TNIV).

14. The existence of these pools, if not the name "Bethesda," may be attested by the Copper Scroll from Qumran (3Q15), which dates from between A.D. 35 and 65. See Hengel 1999: 309–10; Küchler 1999: 382, with further references.

15. The northern, smaller pool may go back to monarchial times; the southern pool may be that established in the second century B.C. by Simon the high priest (Sir. 50:3). For ancient sources, see Hengel 1999: 310. The site favored by most scholars is located under the monastery of St. Anne in the northeast quarter of the Old City. See Jeremias 1966b; Vardaman 1963: 28. Regarding the archaeological identification of Bethesda, see Wieand 1965–66: 396–400. The existence of the five porticoes is disputed by Broer (2001).

16. Some argue that "five" colonnades is also symbolic of the five books of Moses, the Pentateuch (see commentary at 4:18; cf. Hengel 1999: 315). Küchler (1999: 381–82) denies the historical existence of the five colonnades altogether and interprets the reference as exclusively allegorical.

17. See Barrett 1978: 252–53; Hengel 1999: 313, with further references in n. 74. On John's translation of Aramaic or Hebrew terms, see commentary at 1:38. "Aramaic" for

A large number of disabled persons used to lie (κατέκειτο, *katekeito*) at   5:3
that place.[18] Official Judaism almost certainly did not approve of the
superstition associated with the alleged healing powers of the pool of
Bethesda. After all, healing shrines were characteristic of pagan cults.
Apparently, however, the authorities looked the other way, tolerating
this expression of popular religion (see commentary at 5:7; additional
note on 5:3b–4). Among the disabled were the blind, the lame, and the
paralyzed.

b. The Healing (5:5–9a)

Passing by the pool of Bethesda, Jesus takes pity on a lame man and   5:5
heals him. Healers were much sought after in the ancient world, both
in Judaism and in Greco-Roman society. Rabbinic literature speaks of
one Ḥanina ben Dosa, who was recognized for his efficacious prayers on
behalf of the sick.[19] In the Hellenistic world, shrines were dedicated to
Asclepius and other gods of healing.[20] The man in the present instance
is identified as "an invalid."[21] Though his illness is not detailed, 5:7 suggests that he was paralyzed, lame, or extremely weak.[22]

The man had been an invalid for thirty-eight years—longer than many
people in antiquity lived (the average life expectancy for men barely
exceeded forty years), and roughly as long as Israel's wanderings in
the wilderness (Deut. 2:14; see Hengel 1999: 316; cf. Borchert 1996:
232). For all that time, nothing had cured him (cf. Mark 5:25–26; Luke
8:43). The length of the man's plight underscores the hopelessness of
his situation (Ridderbos 1997: 185; R. Brown 1966: 207) and is in keeping with John's selection of "difficult" miracles performed by Jesus (see
commentary at 2:9–10).

Jesus saw him and learned that he had been in this condition for a   5:6
long time. The Synoptics also introduce accounts of Jesus' miracles by
referring to Jesus "seeing" a person (Luke 7:13; 13:12). The Greek term

---

the Greek Ἑβραϊστί is favored by Carson 1991: 242; Ridderbos 1997: 185; Barrett 1978:
253; Witherington 1995: 137; Burge 2000: 173. R. Brown (1966: 206) says that the term
"is used loosely, often for names that are Aramaic." See also additional note.

18. The imperfect tense indicates that this was customary (Carson 1991: 242).

19. Though calling him a miracle worker and faith healer goes beyond the evidence;
see note on Ḥanina ben Dosa under commentary at 4:49–50.

20. Mackowski (1980: 81–83) even believes that behind 5:2–9 is the story of a pagan
sanctuary that he believes to have been an Asclepieum; but this is categorically ruled
out by Hengel (1999: 313), who nonetheless points to the significance of the Asclepius
cult for John's Asia Minor audience (p. 315, referring also to a work by K. H. Rengstorf
in n. 84). See also the ancient and bibliographic references cited in Boring, Berger, and
Colpe 1995: 266–67.

21. A similar healing is recorded in Matt. 9:1–8 pars. (Ridderbos 1997: 186).

22. Carson 1991: 242; the term used (ἀσθένεια, *astheneia*) represents the general expression for "disabled."

rendered "realized" (γνούς, *gnous*; TNIV: "learned") could just as well refer to supernatural knowledge as to knowledge gained through diligent inquiry.[23] Jesus' conversation with the invalid possibly was occasioned by the man's request for alms (cf. Acts 3:1–5). In contrast to the paralytic in Mark 2:1–12, whose four friends carried him to Jesus by lowering his mat through a roof, this man had no one to help him.

Jesus' offer, "Would you like to get well?" seems entirely redundant in light of the man's obvious need. Most likely, it is designed to elicit the man's perspective on the obstacle to his cure: the lack of those who would take him to the pool when the water was stirred. The stirring of the waters could have been created by intermittent springs or spring water. Superstition attributed the movement of the water to an angel of the Lord who would come down from time to time and stir up the waters (cf. the gloss in 5:3b–4 found in some later MSS; see Metzger 1994: 179).

5:7–9a The man's response makes clear that he could not see past the water as his healing agent (Ridderbos 1997: 185; Morris 1995: 269; Witherington 1995: 137). Jesus' response is striking for circumventing any human intermediate instrumentality: no healing springs, no human assistance was needed—Jesus' mere word sufficed.[24] At once[25] the man is cured, and he takes his mat and goes.[26]

A mat (κράβαττος, *krabattos*) was the bedding of the impoverished.[27] Normally made of straw, it was light and could be rolled up and carried about by any healthy person. Jesus' command underscores the reality and permanence of the cure: the man is able to pick up his mat and to walk away, in an amazing break with his thirty-eight years of living as an invalid.[28] Nevertheless, there is no mention of faith on the part of the healed man.[29]

23. Cf. 1:47–48; 4:17–18. So Barrett 1978: 254; Witherington 1995: 137; contra Morris 1995: 268 n. 18.

24. Brodie (1993: 237) notes that Jesus here acts "with a Creator-like knowledge and authority." The verb tenses focus on Jesus' command for the man to get up and go, with the action of taking up his mat preceding his departure, and the three actions prescribed in sequential order.

25. Εὐθέως (*eutheōs*, immediately), rare in John, stresses immediacy (Morris 1995: 269 n. 23; cf. R. Brown 1966: 208).

26. Again, the man's taking up his mat is presented as a mere preceding action to his progressive walking away.

27. The term occurs in John only in 5:8–11 (cf. Mark 2:4, 9, 11, 12; 6:55; Acts 5:15; 9:33). In Acts 5:15, it is used in distinction from κλινάριον (*klinarion*, cot).

28. Carson 1991: 244; Barrett 1978: 254. Though Ridderbos (1997: 186) perhaps gets carried away slightly when he sees the act as a sign of victory, exulting, "No longer does the bed carry a powerless man but, with vitality to spare, he (triumphantly) carries the bed."

29. Morris 1995: 269; Witherington 1995: 137. Puzzlingly, Moloney (1998: 172) concludes that the man's "obedience to the word of Jesus" "suggests that the man achieves a faith response."

c. The Aftermath (5:9b–15)

Only now, after the healing has taken place, does the evangelist introduce crucial new information:[30] the healing had been performed on a Sabbath (cf. 9:14; see Ridderbos 1997: 186).[31] What ensues is a controversy between Jesus and the Jewish leaders centering on proper Sabbath observance. In the context of the Johannine narrative, this ultimately leads to Jesus' discourse regarding his unique relationship with God the Father.[32]

5:9b–10

In a probable instance of Johannine irony (Carson 1991: 245), the Jewish leaders' primary objection is not against the healing itself but that the law allegedly forbade the man to carry his mat on the Sabbath (Bultmann 1971: 243; R. Brown 1966: 208).[33] Although the Jewish leaders may have thought of passages such as Exod. 31:12–17, Jer. 17:21–27, and Neh. 13:15–19, the man did not actually break any biblical Sabbath regulations. According to Jewish tradition, however, the man was violating a code that prohibited the carrying of an object "from one domain into another" (*m. Šabb.* 7.2; in the present instance, his mat). Apparently, it was permissible to carry a bed with a person lying on it, but not one that was empty (*m. Šabb.* 10.5). At this point, Jesus is accused not of violating the law himself, but of enticing someone else to sin by issuing a command that would have caused that person to break the law.

This man responds quite differently from the man healed in John 9 (Ridderbos 1997: 188). Essentially, he blames Jesus, the one who had "made him well."[34] "Later" (μετὰ ταῦτα, *meta tauta*; cf. 5:1) here may simply mean "later the same day." The pool of Bethesda was located just north

5:11–14

---

30. Lee (1994: 102, citing Robert Alter in n. 4) notes that the delayed reference to the Sabbath in 5:9b is in keeping with typical Hebrew narrative style.

31. The noun is qualitative, indicating the *kind* of day, not *which* day it was (so, rightly, Wallace 1996: 264). Thatcher (1999) calls this "the Sabbath trick," "a form of 'unstable irony' in which the narrator of the Fourth Gospel withholds critical information about an episode until the end of the story, forcing the reader to re-evaluate radically the nature of Jesus' activity." However, alternate explanations of the flow of the narrative are possible (if not more probable), and Thatcher's attempt at a poststructural reading of John 5 and 9 ultimately fails to convince. Highly improbable is the proposal by Laney (1992: 108–9) that the absence of the definite article suggests that this was not a Sabbath at all but a feast day when Sabbath regulations applied (citing Lev. 23:34–36).

32. Compare and contrast this healing especially with that of the blind man in John 9, which also takes place on a Sabbath (see the chart in Malina and Rohrbaugh 1998: 109). The Synoptics include at least five incidents that involve healing on the Sabbath and incur the wrath of the Jewish leaders: (1) Mark 1:21–28 par.; (2) Matt. 8:14–15 pars.; (3) Matt. 12:9–14 pars.; (4) Luke 13:10–17; (5) Luke 14:1–6 (Matthew features two, Mark three, and Luke all five incidents).

33. On Sabbath and Sunday observance, see the sidebar in Köstenberger 2002c: 59. On the Johannine characterization of "the Jews," see commentary at 1:19.

34. Ridderbos 1997: 188; Carson 1991: 245; Morris 1995: 271; Culpepper 1983: 138; 1993: 204–5; contra Staley 1991: 63–64. The term ὑγιής (*hygiēs*, well, healthy) occurs five times in this chapter, six times total in John, and only five other times in the rest of the NT (Morris 1995: 271–72 n. 30).

---

of the temple area. Jesus met the man again just a short distance from where the original healing had taken place. "Met" (εὑρίσκει, *heuriskei*) seems to indicate a chance encounter (rather than Jesus deliberately looking for the man [see Bultmann 1971: 243 n. 5]), though of course God's sovereign providence extends even over such events (Schnackenburg 1990: 2.98). "At the temple" does not necessarily imply that the man had gone to the temple *building* to offer thanks to God (the view of Morris 1995: 272; Laney 1992: 110).[35] More likely, he merely lingered in the temple precincts at large (Carson 1991: 245; R. Brown 1966: 208).

The perfect verb tense in "you have become well" (ὑγιὴς γέγονας, *hygiēs gegonas*) indicates the man's continual state of well-being, perhaps in contrast to other healings at that site that proved less than permanent (Morris 1995: 272). Jesus' comment, "Sin no longer, so that nothing worse may happen to you," seems to imply that at least sometimes (including in the case of the invalid?) sickness may be a result of sin (e.g., 1 Kings 13:4; 2 Kings 1:4; 2 Chron. 16:12).[36] The syntax of Jesus' command stresses urgency and possibly implies that the man must, in the future, desist from a pattern of sin.[37]

Jesus' Jewish contemporaries generally held that suffering was a direct result of sin (cf. John 9:2). Given expression already by the "miserable counselors" in the Book of Job, rabbinic literature states the principle succinctly: "There is no death without sin, and there is no suffering without iniquity" (*b. Šabb.* 55a, with reference to Ezek. 18:20).[38] However, the OT features several instances in which suffering is transparently not a result of sin (e.g., 2 Sam. 4:4; 1 Kings 14:4; 2 Kings 13:14). Jesus himself, likewise, rejected simple cause-and-effect explanations (cf. John 9:3; Luke 13:1–5). Nevertheless, though he did not attribute every instance of suffering to sin, Jesus acknowledged that sin may well lead to suffering. In the present instance, moreover, the "something worse" that Jesus threatened probably refers not to a worse physical condition at all but rather to eternal judgment for sin (cf. John 5:22–30).[39]

---

35. Also contra Brodie (1993: 238), who takes the man's presence "in the place of worship, the temple," as indication of "some receptivity toward God."

36. Some (such as Bultmann [1971: 243]) view 5:14 as being in contradiction with 9:2–3 (see discussion in Ridderbos 1997: 188). Though the ailment in the present passage may be the result of specific personal sin, and that in John 9 may not, however, this merely illustrates that caution must be exercised in individual cases and that sweeping theories must be avoided (cf. Carson 1991: 246; Morris 1995: 272).

37. See Ridderbos 1997: 189 n. 14; Morris 1995: 272. Carson (1991: 246 n. 1) rightly cautions against a simplistic generalization of negated present imperative = command to stop doing something (though he acknowledges that this may be the force here). More accurately, the present imperative regularly stresses urgency (with reference to S. Porter 1989: 335ff.).

38. The saying is attributed to Rabbi Ammi (ca. A.D. 300).

39. God's judgment: Ridderbos 1997: 189; Barrett 1978: 255; Gehenna or Hades: Beasley-Murray 1999: 74; Schnackenburg 1990: 2.98; eternal consequences: Morris 1995: 272; Witherington 1995: 139.

Rather laconically, the reader is told that the man's only response to Jesus' **5:15** exhortation was to report him to the Jewish authorities in compliance with their earlier request (5:12).[40] In the entire pericope there is no expression of gratitude or appreciation toward Jesus from the healed man (similar to the nine lepers in Luke 17:11–19). He was happy enough to have the use of his legs restored, but appears to be indifferent toward Jesus personally and content to let the authorities deal with him. This stands in marked contrast with the healed blind man in John 9, who defends Jesus and pays the price by being expelled from the synagogue (Ridderbos 1997: 190). Although the man clearly "represents a particular response to the gospel" (Ridderbos 1997: 190), "all interest in him ceases after v. 15" (Bultmann 1971: 243 n. 10). Indeed, he is a representative of unbelief and "is going nowhere in faith."[41]

d. The Sabbath Controversy (5:16–47)

In the present section Jesus elaborates on his statement in 5:17, defending himself against the charges that he is (1) a Sabbath-breaker and (2) a blasphemer who claims to be equal to God. In response, Jesus contends that everything he, the Son, does he is able to do because he has seen the Father do it first. This "apprenticeship analogy" may be rooted in Jesus' learning the trade of a craftsman from his adoptive father, Joseph (cf. Mark 6:3; Matt. 13:55; John 6:42).

Jesus thus identifies his "work" with that of his divine Father, whose work did not cease at creation. This Father continues to be active, and

40. Stibbe (1993: 75) observes, "By the end of the story he [the healed lame man] appears to be informing on the one who healed him."

41. Moloney 1998: 173; cf. Metzner 1999; Lee 1994: 110; Witkamp 1985: 24; Leidig 1979: 211; contra Thomas 1995: 18. Moloney (1998: 173) rightly notes, contra Beck (1993 [cf. 1997: 86–90]), who argues that anonymous characters in the Fourth Gospel draw the reader into an identification with the character, "The reader of the Fourth Gospel, however, hardly identifies with a man who is in league with 'the Jews' (vs. 15)." Keener (2003: 87), similarly, contends that a list of Johannine models of faith is not entirely coextensive with anonymous characters (citing esp. 5:14–15) and registers this as his only serious disagreement with Beck (p. 87 n. 49). Beck, in a review (2001), indirectly responds to my earlier criticism (Köstenberger 1999b, reviewing Beck 1997) that the man in John 5 disproves his theory by alleging, in effect, that I have no place for literary analysis in my hermeneutical method. Nothing could be further from the truth. My concern, rather, lies with an unqualified wholesale adoption of reader-response criticism by evangelicals who fail to realize that this methodology is part and parcel of a postmodern hermeneutic that is left with nothing but subjective readings devoid of any claim to authority or universal applicability. Moreover, I was concerned to point out that Beck's central thesis (i.e., that anonymity necessarily equals ideal function and positive characterization) is invalid. Note further this puzzling conclusion by Brodie (1993: 238): "The final picture . . . is . . . open to a positive interpretation: the man has finally come to mature (repentant) recognition of Jesus, and he is announcing the good news to the Jews." Precisely where Brodie finds the man "announcing the good news to the Jews" is unclear to me, nor can I see textual evidence for the man coming to "mature (repentant) recognition of Jesus."

Jesus colabors with him (5:17; cf. 4:34). As to healing on the Sabbath, the one who created the Sabbath has authority over it, determining its purpose, use, and limitations. In fact, even the Jews made exceptions to the rule of refraining from work on the Sabbath, most notably in the case of circumcision (7:23; cf. *m. Šabb.* 18.3; 19.2–3).

In fact, Jesus will do even "greater things": give eternal life and render judgment.[42] Jesus is the life-giver because, like the Father, he has life in himself. He "was with God in the beginning" (1:2), and "in him was life" (1:4). As God breathed life into the original creation, so Jesus gives life to those who believe in him (cf. 1:12–13; 3:3, 5, 7–8). Without such life people will remain in death (5:24), "darkness" (3:19), and under God's wrath (3:36).

For John, then, this fourth sign by Jesus points beyond itself to who Jesus is: the eternal life-giver. Tragically, Jesus' opponents, in their concern for legal obedience, miss the coming of the one who is life itself; in their concern for the study of the Scriptures, they miss the coming of the one of whom the Scriptures spoke (5:39–40, 45–47); and their discipleship of Moses keeps them from following their Messiah (9:28).

i. Jesus' Response to the Charges of Sabbath-Breaking and Blasphemy (5:16–30)

5:16 The following scene represents an informal interrogation; describing this as a "court scene" (Moloney 1998: 171) seems overblown.[43] John 5:16 marks the beginning of more overt, active hostility against Jesus (R. Brown 1966: 213).[44] John 5:18 says that the Jews were seeking to kill Jesus, though the exact form of persecution is not mentioned (Morris 1995: 273; Schnackenburg 1990: 2.100).[45] The Jews' initial indignation toward the healed man (5:10) now has been transferred to Jesus (Borchert 1996: 235).

5:17 Jesus' answer in 5:17 becomes the foundation for 5:19–47.[46] The introductory "truly, truly, I say to you" signals a significant pronouncement.

---

42. The giving of life is central to Jesus' mission in this Gospel (see 3:16–17; 6:33, 40, 44, 47, 50–58; 10:7–10; 17:2–3; cf. Köstenberger 1998b: 75–76).

43. Better is this characterization by Stibbe (1993: 77): "The passage is composed of five carefully related and sequential blocks of material. All of them are unified by the legal symbolism of the Gospel."

44. The imperfect Greek verbs in 5:16 and 5:18 (ἐδίωκον, ἐποίει, ἐζήτουν, ἔλυεν, ἔλεγεν) indicate the permanent pattern of hostility (Morris 1995: 275). Schlatter (1948: 146) views Jesus' opponents' urgency as an indication that they feared he might seek to escape.

45. Ridderbos (1997: 190) speaks of "the continuing position of 'the Jews' vis-à-vis Jesus." Bultmann (1971: 243–44) says that it shows "that the narrator is less interested in the details of the story than in portraying the Jews' habitual bearing towards the normal (or repeated) activity of Jesus."

46. "Jesus said to them" (5:17; see additional note): the Greek has "answered," not merely "said" (TNIV). The grammatical form of "answered" may suggest legal overtones (cf. 5:19; see Carson 1991: 247; Borchert 1996: 237).

Jesus' address of God as his "Father" is striking. It would have been highly unusual for a Jew of that day to address God simply as "my Father" without some qualifying phrase such as "in heaven" in order to avoid undue familiarity (Morris 1974: 31–35; Jeremias 1971: 61–67). The Jews' response in the next verse confirms the perceived inappropriateness of Jesus' terminology (see commentary at 5:18).

According to Jesus, God his "Father" has "always been at his work to this very day" (Bacchiocchi 1981: 3–19). According to Gen. 2:2–3, God rested on the seventh day of creation. But if God observes the Sabbath, who sustains the universe? The consensus among Jewish rabbis was that God does indeed work constantly, but that this does not amount to him breaking the Sabbath. Since the entire universe is his domain, he cannot be charged with transporting an object from one domain to another; and God lifts nothing to a height greater than himself.[47]

Jesus now adds that he, too, is working. He could have objected to the (inaccurate) Jewish interpretation of the OT Sabbath command that prohibited work normally done on the other six days of the week. These regulations (which referred to regular work) hardly applied to the man's picking up his mat after a miracle cure. But rather than taking this approach, Jesus places his own activity on the Sabbath plainly on the same level as that of God the Creator. If God is above Sabbath regulations, so is Jesus.[48]

John 5:18 contains the first reference in this Gospel to the plot to kill   **5:18**
Jesus.[49] This signals the escalation of controversy characteristic of the second major subsection of part one of John's Gospel (John 5–10, esp. the latter parts of chs. 5, 8, and 10). By now the issue of Sabbath observance (dealt with further in 7:19–24) has been dwarfed by the question of Jesus' relationship with God (Ridderbos 1997: 196). Just as Jesus is uniquely God's "own" Son (Rom. 8:32), God is uniquely "his own" Father (note the emphatic position of πατέρα ἴδιον, *patera idion*; cf. John 10:29–30). The designation "my Father" for God was extremely rare in the OT (but see Jer. 3:4, 19; cf. Ps. 89:26). The Jews were committed monotheists, believing in only one God.[50] This became an important distinguishing characteristic of Jewish religion in a polytheistic environment.[51] Jesus'

47. See *Gen. Rab.* 11.10; *Exod. Rab.* 30.9, citing Isa. 6:3; Jer. 23:24. The Letter of Aristeas (second century B.C.) says that God "is continually at work in everything" (210). See also Eusebius, *Praeparatio evangelica* 13.12.11, frg. 5 (cited in Boring, Berger, and Colpe 1995: 267).

48. Cf. Matt. 12:1–14 pars. (R. Brown 1966: 217; Barrett 1978: 256; Carson 1991: 247–48).

49. Cf. 7:1, 19–20, 25; 8:37, 40; 11:8, 16, 53.

50. See Num. 15:37–41; Deut. 6:4; 11:13–21. On the Jewish confession of God as "one God," called the Shema (from Hebrew, "to hear"), see Schürer 1973–79: 2.454–55. See also Hurtado 1998a.

51. Thus, the Roman historian Tacitus writes, "the Jews conceive of one God only" (*Historiae* 5 §5). See Cohon (1955), who also cites affirmations of God's uniqueness in

claim of a unique relationship with God seemed to compromise this belief by elevating Jesus to the same level as the Creator as a second God (Borchert 1996: 236).[52] The same charge later will lead to the crucifixion (Borchert 1996: 235).

5:19–20   Jesus' response in 5:19—note the shift from dialogue to monologue (cf. 3:10)—deals with both of the Jews' concerns: that of breaking the Sabbath and that of claiming equality with God (Ridderbos 1997: 191). Breaking the Sabbath was a serious offense, but making oneself equal to God "was challenging the fundamental distinction between the holy, infinite God and finite, fallen human beings" (Carson 1991: 249). In response, Jesus avers that he, while equal to God, is functionally subordinate to him as a son is to his father (Morris 1995: 277; Borchert 1996: 236; Carson 1991: 250; cf. Wright 1986). Their relationship preserves distinctness of role (Carson 1991: 251). Thus, Jesus does not assert independence from God, but dependence on him;[53] he is at once coeternal with and subordinate to the Father (Keener 1999).

The illustration in 5:19–20 (Keener 2003: 648 calls it an analogy) may reflect Jesus' own experience with his adoptive father, Joseph, from whom he learned the craftsman's trade (cf. Matt. 13:55; Mark 6:3).[54] Jesus' claim that "the Son can do nothing by himself" echoes Moses' affirmation that "the LORD has sent me to do all these things and that it was not my idea" (Num. 16:28) (R. Brown 1966: 214). "To do nothing on one's own authority" is a common Johannine idiom, underscoring Jesus' dependence on and obedience to God the Father, "who sent" him.[55] Jesus' logic implies that it is the Father who led him to the invalid and told him to heal him (Schnackenburg 1990: 2.103).

The latter part of 5:19 features the first of four consecutive γάρ-clauses (*gar*, for), asserting that "it is impossible for the Son to take independent,

---

Sib. Or. (3:11–12, 545–61); Let. Arist. (132–38); Wis. (13–15); Philo (*Mos.* 1.14 §75; *Decal.* 12–16 §§52–81); Josephus (*Ant.* 2.12.4 §§275–76).

52. Barrett (1978: 256) notes that those who had made themselves equal to God in past history included Hiram, Nebuchadnezzar, Pharaoh, and Joash. Ποιῶν (*poiōn*, making) is a participle of result (Wallace 1996: 638, 664).

53. See Beasley-Murray 1999: 75; Borchert 1996: 236; Moloney 1998: 174; Bultmann 1971: 245; Morris 1995: 274–75 n. 48 (referring to Odeberg 1968: 203), 277; Barrett 1978: 259; Keener 1999: 42–43. The use of ἐκεῖνος (*ekeinos*, that one) for God "lays stress upon the separate divine Person" in contrast with υἱός (*huios*, son). Also stressed is the Son's inability to do anything apart from the Father (again in 5:30; see Moloney 1998: 178; Barrett 1978: 264).

54. Though calling this a "parable" (Dodd 1968a; Burge 2000: 177; cf. R. Brown 1966: 218) may be an overstatement (Carson 1991: 250; Ridderbos 1997: 192; Beasley-Murray 1999: 75; Barrett 1978: 259–60).

55. Cf. 7:18; 11:51; 15:4; 16:13; 18:34; see Barrett 1978: 259; Bultmann 1971: 249; Carson 1991: 251; Borchert 1996: 237. Just as the Son depends on the Father, so believers can do nothing of eternal significance without Christ (15:5), but they can do all things through him who strengthens them (Phil. 4:13; see commentary at 5:23).

self-determined action that would set him over against the Father as another God" (Carson 1991: 251). The second γάρ-clause states the basis for the Son's dependence: the Father loves the Son (5:20) (Borchert 1996: 237). Clauses three and four speak of the Son's delegated authority to raise the dead and to exercise judgment (5:21, 22). In 5:20, "the Father loves the Son" features the verb φιλέω (*phileō*); in 3:35, in an otherwise identical phrase, the verb is ἀγαπάω (*agapaō*). This suggests that the two verbs are used as virtual synonyms in this Gospel.[56]

The Father's love for the Son expresses itself in his free self-disclosure, and the Son's love for the Father does so in his obedient submission to the Father's will, including death on the cross (Carson 1991: 251).[57] The "greater works," in context, refer to raising the dead and exercising judgment (5:21–23; see Morris 1995: 278; Moloney 1998: 178, 182; Schnackenburg 1990: 2.105). The raising of Lazarus, the climactic "sign" performed by Jesus in this Gospel, thus presents itself as proleptic of this kind of activity. The matching statement in John 13–21 may be the reference to believers' "greater works" in 14:12.[58]

According to Jesus, the Son gives life to whom he is pleased to give   **5:21** it, just as the Father raises the dead and gives them life.[59] The OT and Second Temple literature concur that raising the dead and giving life are the sole prerogatives of God.[60] Jesus' contemporaries therefore did not believe that the Messiah would be given authority to raise the dead.[61] This renders Jesus' claim of being able to raise the dead and to give them life at will all the more startling. Though Elijah sometimes was considered to be an exception because he was used by God to raise the dead, Jesus' claim is much bolder in that he claimed not merely to be God's instrument in raising other people, but to give life himself *to whom he is pleased to give it*.

The Father judges no one, but has entrusted all judgment to the Son.[62]   **5:22** This is a remarkable assertion, since according to the Hebrew Scriptures,

---

56. See Carson 1991: 251; Borchert 1996: 238; Barrett 1978: 259; contra Schnackenburg 1990: 2.104; Westcott 1908: 1.190.

57. The present tense forms φιλεῖ, δείκνυσιν, and ποιεῖ point to the habitual nature of the Father's love for the Son (Morris 1995: 278).

58. The ὑμεῖς in the final phrase in 5:20 is emphatic (Morris 1995: 278 n. 65; R. Brown 1966: 214) and "perhaps derogatory" (R. Brown 1966: 214).

59. The term ζῳοποιέω (*zōopoieō*, give life) is used elsewhere in this Gospel only in 6:63, there with reference to Jesus' words. The fact that ὥσπερ (*hōsper*, just as) is used only here and in 5:26 constitutes the latter passage, which talks about the Son as well as the Father having life in himself, as a close parallel (R. Brown 1966: 214).

60. See Deut. 32:39; 1 Sam. 2:6; 2 Kings 5:7; Tob. 13:2; Wis. 16:13.

61. Cf. *b. Taʿan.* 2a (attributed to Rabbi Yoḥanan, ca. A.D. 70 [cited in Köstenberger 2002c: 58]) and the *Shemoneh ʾEsreh* (ca. A.D. 70–100 [cited in Schürer 1973–79: 2.455–63]).

62. The present verse stands in apparent tension with 3:17, which is resolved by the semantic range of κρίνω (*krinō*, judge), which in 3:17 refers to "outright condemnation,"

judgment is the exclusive prerogative of God (e.g., Gen. 18:25; cf. Judg. 11:27; though see Ps. 2:2). In Second Temple literature, too, the Messiah remains very much in the background as far as judgment is concerned, apart from carrying out God's judgment on his enemies, in keeping with Jewish nationalistic expectations (e.g., Ps. Sol. 17:21–27).[63] Rabbinic writings likewise ascribe judging the world to God alone.

5:23   The purpose of the Father's delegation of life-giving and judgment-related authority to the Son is that people might honor the Son just as they honor the Father.[64] Conversely, anyone who does not honor the Son also fails to honor the Father who sent him. In the OT, Moses and the prophets were considered to be God's agents and mouthpieces who acted and spoke on God's behalf. The Jewish fundamental affirmation regarding a messenger (*šālîaḥ*) is that "a man's agent is like the man himself" (e.g., *m. Ber.* 5.5).[65] This is true of any messenger, particularly a trusted servant, and even more so of a man's son, especially his firstborn (Köstenberger 1998b: 115–21). Thus, anyone who fails to acknowledge the authority of Jesus (the sent Son) in fact rejects his sender, the Father.

Jesus' role as the sent Son highlights both Jesus' equality with the Father in purpose (and even nature) and his subordination to the Father in carrying out his mission: "it is a legal presumption that an agent will carry out his mission" (*b. ʿErub.* 31b–32a; cf. *b. Ketub.* 99b). According to John, this is precisely what Jesus did: he came to earth, accomplished the mission entrusted to him by the Father, and returned to the one who sent him (4:34; 17:4; cf. 19:30; see also 1:1, 14; cf. Isa. 55:11–12). Authorized representatives were not unique to Judaism. The Roman *legatus*, for instance, fulfilled a similar role. To this day, the failure to honor an ambassador is a failure to honor the government that he or she represents.

5:24–25   Both utterances in 5:24 and 5:25 are introduced by the solemn "truly, truly, I say to you." Jesus' statement that believers "have" eternal life in the here and now, having "crossed over from death to life" already in the past (5:24; cf. 1 John 3:14), ran counter to contemporary Judaism, which considered the attainment of eternal life to be a future event. The pronouncement represents one of the strongest affirmations of realized (inaugurated) eschatology in John's Gospel.[66] For John, hearing,

while in this passage it talks about the judicial "principle of discrimination" (Carson 1991: 254; cf. Borchert 1996: 239). Also, 3:17 has as its subject the purpose for the Son's coming into the world, whereas 5:22 addresses the issue of the distinctiveness of the Father's and Son's respective roles (Carson 1991: 254).

63. The single exception is the Son of Man (or "Chosen One") in the Similitudes of Enoch (1 Enoch 37–71; esp. 49:4; 61:9; 62:2–6; 63:11).

64. In effect, this establishes Jesus' right to be worshiped (Carson 1991: 255) and amounts to a claim to deity (Morris 1995: 279).

65. See Rengstorf, *TDNT* 1:414–20.

66. So Carson 1991: 256; Moloney 1998: 183; Ridderbos 1997: 197; Morris 1995: 280; Beasley-Murray 1999: 76.

like seeing, ought to be coupled with a believing response, in the present case with reference not to Jesus (as is customary in John) (Morris 1995: 280) but to the one who sent him (Carson 1991: 256).[67] "Word" is a collective term for Jesus' message (Morris 1995: 280). The statement "The dead will hear the voice of the Son of God, and those who have heard it will live" is reminiscent of Ezekiel's vision of the valley of dry bones (Ezek. 37).[68]

Jesus goes on to assert that just as the Father has life in himself, so he has given the Son to have life in himself (see commentary at 5:21).[69] The OT states repeatedly that God grants life to others.[70] But here Jesus claims that God granted him life *in himself*, a divine attribute.[71] The phrase rendered "he is the Son of Man" reads more literally "he is Son of Man"—the only instance of this christological title without articles before both "Son" and "Man" in the entire NT. This is accounted for in part by Colwell's rule (see commentary on "The Word was God" at 1:1; cf. Carson 1991: 259); it may also indicate an allusion to Dan. 7:13 LXX, where the expression "son of man" likewise does not feature the article (cf. Rev. 1:13; 14:14; see Carson 1991: 257–59; Ridderbos 1997: 200; Borchert 1996: 241 n. 37; R. Brown 1966: 215; Moloney 1998: 183). The title is designed "to express the transcendent character of Jesus' messiahship and the all-embracing, present-and-future-encompassing mission of Jesus as the Son of God" (Ridderbos 1997: 200).

5:26–27

The antecedent of "this" is what was taught in the preceding verses (Carson 1991: 258; Barrett 1978: 263); perhaps what follows is in view as well (R. Brown 1966: 215). Surprise would be due to people's unbelief (Ridderbos 1997: 201). Turning to the future ("and is now here" from 5:25 has been omitted here; see Moloney 1998: 180; cf. Barrett 1978: 263), Jesus states that all who are in their graves (the physically dead [Barrett 1978: 263]) will hear his voice and come out: those who have done what is good will rise to live, and those who have done evil will rise to be condemned.[72] Notably, the division will take place on the basis of what people have "done."

5:28–29

---

67. "Whoever hears and believes" is one unit, with one definite article governing both participles in the Greek (Barrett 1978: 261).

68. There are no similar texts in Second Temple literature. Paul refers to "the God who gives life to the dead and calls things that are not as though they were" (Rom. 4:17; cf. Eph. 2:1–5). On φωνή (*phōnē*, voice), see Betz, *TDNT* 9:285–86; McCann, *ISBE* 4:997; see also Rev. 1:10, 15.

69. The verse contains the only instance in the Greek NT of an anarthrous infinitive functioning as a direct object (Wallace 1996: 602).

70. For example, Gen. 2:7; Job 10:12; 33:4; Ps. 36:9.

71. The verse relates to the "eternal generation of the Son" (Carson 1991: 257).

72. The two genitives ζωῆς (*zōēs*, of life) and κρίσεως (*kriseōs*, of judgment) convey both purpose and result (Wallace 1996: 101).

Because believing often proves superficial (e.g., 2:23–25), a person is to be judged by what he or she does, not merely says (Borchert 1996: 241; contra Hodges 1979a). This does not amount to salvation by works; rather, the life that one lives forms "the test of the faith they profess" (Morris 1995: 285). In the first century there was no consensus as to whether all would be raised or only the righteous (but see Dan. 12:2). Sheol was thought of as containing chambers where the dead are kept until the great day of judgment.[73] A glimpse of the future resurrection was given moments after Jesus died on the cross (Matt. 27:52–53).[74]

5:30 The present verse marks a shift from Jesus referring to himself in the third person (5:25–29) to speaking about himself in the first person (nine references in Greek), which sets the stage for the remainder of the chapter (Borchert 1966: 242). Jesus emphatically states that by himself he can do nothing; he seeks not to please himself, but the one who sent him (see commentary at 5:19 and at 5:23).[75]

ii. Testimony regarding Jesus (5:31–47)

5:31 "If I testify about myself, my testimony is not valid."[76] Jesus here does not indicate that he actually will testify about himself; he is simply stating a supposition in order to comment on it (Wallace 1996: 471). If all that Jesus has is his own claims, this is insufficient (Carson 1991: 259; Morris 1995: 287 n. 95).[77] He ought not to "pose as an independent, self-authenticating authority" (Barrett 1978: 264), for that would be open to the charge of being motivated by self-interest (Bultmann 1971: 263). Even so, Jesus shortly will note that self-witness is valid if confirmed by other witnesses (Ridderbos 1997: 202). Moreover, since everything that Jesus says and does is in obedience to the Father, his witness is, in reality, that of God the Father (Carson 1991: 260; Beasley-Murray 1999: 78).[78]

The interrogation of witnesses was central to Jewish legal procedure.[79] This is clearly borne out by Jesus' trial before the Sanhedrin, where, to

---

73. See 1 Enoch 22:13; 51; 2 Esdr. (4 Ezra) 7:32; 2 Bar. 30:1–2; 42:7–8; 50:2.

74. See also John 3:19, 21; 6:40, 54; Acts 17:31; Rom. 2:5–11; 2 Cor. 5:10; 2 Tim. 4:1; 1 Pet. 4:5; see also commentary at 5:25.

75. On the double-negative construction underlying the phrase "by myself I can do nothing," see commentary at 14:30 and the close parallel 15:5. Cf. m. ʾAbot 2.4 (cited in Köstenberger 2002c: 60).

76. The rendering "not valid" (rather than "not true," indicating a courtroom setting) is suggested by Carson (1991: 259) and Morris (1995: 287) (contra Ridderbos 1997: 202).

77. Note the preponderance of emphatic first-person Greek pronouns in this section (5:30, 31, 34, 36, 43, 45; see Morris 1995: 286).

78. As Lee (1994: 104) notes, following Schnackenburg, instead of summoning three witnesses in 5:32–47, Jesus ultimately is only calling upon the witness of God, "whose testimony is effected through" John the Baptist, Jesus' own works, and the Scriptures.

79. On the trial motif in John's Gospel, see especially Lincoln 2000.

the dismay of the Jews accusing Jesus, witnesses did not agree (Mark 14:55–64; cf. Matt. 26:59–66). The need for multiple witnesses, already taught in the Hebrew Scriptures (Deut. 17:6; 19:15; cf. Num. 35:30), is reiterated by Jewish tradition (*m. Ketub.* 2.9; *m. Roš Haš.* 3.1; cf. Josephus, *Ant.* 4.8.15 §219).[80]

Anticipating his audience's need for additional witnesses, Jesus proceeds to refer to "another." The Jews initially may take this as a reference to the Baptist (cf. 5:33–35; so Chrysostom, cited in Morris 1995: 288 n. 96), but Jesus is referring to God the Father (5:37), in common Jewish fashion avoiding the name of God.[81] Jesus did not need the Baptist's witness (5:34); it was for the people (Carson 1991: 260; Bultmann 1971: 264–65). "You have sent to John" probably refers to the delegation sent by the Jews from Jerusalem to inquire about the nature of the Baptist's ministry (1:19–28).[82] "He has testified to the truth" reiterates the claim made already in the prologue (1:7; see Carson 1991: 260).[83]

5:32–34

Jesus calls John "a lamp" (λύχνος, *lychnos*) that burned and shone (see 1:7–9, which already made clear that John himself was not "the light" [φῶς, *phōs*], i.e., the Messiah). The verb ἦν (*ēn*, was) may indicate that John is now dead or at least in prison (cf. 3:24; see Morris 1995: 289; cf. Schlatter 1948: 156). "A lamp" is more accurately rendered "the lamp" (note the Greek article), pointing to a known person or phenomenon. Most likely, Ps. 132:17 is in view (so Carson 1991: 261; Morris 1995: 289 n. 100; Barrett 1978: 265), where it is said that God will "set up a lamp" (λύχνος) for his "anointed one." Though the Baptist earlier denied being Elijah (John 1:21), Jesus here identifies him as that "lamp" set up by God to cast its light on the coming Messiah.[84] Inherent in the designation of the Baptist as a "lamp" is the recognition that his witness was small (yet important) and of a temporary nature. He was a lamp that exuded light, but he was not the light itself (Carson 1991: 261).[85]

5:35–36

80. Relevant NT parallels include John 8:13–18; 2 Cor. 13:1 (citing Deut. 19:15); 1 John 5:7; Rev. 11:3.
81. That "another" refers to God the Father represents a broad consensus among commentators: so Ridderbos 1997: 202; Morris 1995: 288; Moloney 1998: 190; Beasley-Murray 1999: 78; Schnackenburg 1990: 2.121; Barrett 1978: 264; R. Brown 1966: 224.
82. "Have sent" and "have testified" are in the Greek perfect tense, indicating the settled condition resulting from the Baptist's witness to Jesus (cf. Barrett 1978: 264; Carson 1991: 260; Beasley-Murray 1999: 78; Morris 1995: 288; R. Brown 1966: 224; Wallace [1996: 577] calls this an "extensive perfect").
83. The idea of bearing witness to the truth occurs in the NT only in this Gospel (similarly, 18:37; cf. 3 John 3, 12); cf. 1QS 8:5–6.
84. Sir. 48:1 portrays Elijah as having arisen "like fire [πύρ, *pyr*], and his word burned like a torch [λάμπας, *lampas*]."
85. There may also be a hint at "burning up" in the sense that his witness was borne at a high personal cost (Morris 1995: 289), similar to Jesus being "consumed" by zeal for God (2:17).

"You chose to enjoy his light" indicates people's respect for John yet also indicts them for their superficiality and insincerity.[86] "For a season" points to the temporary nature of people's openness to John's message; the depth of people's commitment to John did not exceed the level of their allegiance to Jesus in 2:23–25 (Carson 1991: 261; Ridderbos 1997: 203). One witness weightier than the Baptist's is Jesus' "works" (ἔργα, *erga*).[87] What the evangelist may label "signs" is simply subsumed under his "works" by Jesus. Thus, his works include the signs but are not limited to them. Everything Jesus does, or even says (Ridderbos 1997: 203), that is, his entire ministry (Carson 1991: 261), constitutes his "works." Jesus does not ask people to believe in him by some blind leap of faith; he offers his works as evidence for his messianic claims. People ought to be able to see God's hand in Jesus' works, and God's voice in Jesus' words (Ridderbos 1997: 203).

5:37   By stating that "the Father . . . he has borne witness concerning me," Jesus may be referring to the voice at his baptism (Matt. 3:17 pars.), an event not explicitly mentioned in John, though the primary reference probably is to God's witness in Scripture (Beasley-Murray 1999: 78; Bultmann 1971: 266).[88] At another place John writes, "We accept man's testimony, but God's testimony is greater because it is the testimony of God, which he has given about his Son" (1 John 5:9).[89] The perfect μεμαρτύρηκεν (*memartyrēken*, he has borne witness) points to the confirmed state and continuing significance of the Father's witness.

"You have never heard his voice or seen his form." Old Testament figures who heard the voice of God include Noah (Gen. 7:1–4), Abraham (Gen. 12:1–3), Moses (Exod. 3:4–4:17; 19:3–6, 9–13; 33:11), Samuel (1 Sam. 3:4, 6, 8, 11–14), and Elijah (1 Kings 19:13, 15–18). Abraham (Gen. 18:1–2), Jacob (Gen. 32:24–30), Moses (Exod. 33:11), and Isaiah (Isa. 6:1–5) all "saw" the Lord in one sense or another (see Carson 1991: 262; Morris 1995: 291). Though not seeing God directly, Israel received the law at Mount Sinai and accepted it from God's servant Moses. Now, however, the Jews are rejecting greater revelation from an even greater messenger.[90]

86. The aorist ἠθελήσατε (*ethelēsate*, you chose) may be intended as a contrast to the perfect tense forms in 5:33, which indicate the settled condition of the Baptist's witness (Barrett 1978: 265). The word here for "enjoy" (ἀγαλλιάω, *agalliaō* [found elsewhere in John only in 8:56]) also occurs in the Greek text of Ps. 132:16. Josephus (*Ant.* 18.5.2 §118) writes that people "were aroused to the highest degree [variant: 'overjoyed']" by the Baptist's message.

87. See Köstenberger 1998b: 72–73. The term is repeated in 5:36 for emphasis (Morris 1995: 290).

88. See 5:45–47; Luke 24:27, 44; Acts 13:27; 1 John 5:9. Carson (1991: 262) sees here a "general reference to all of the Father's revealing work" (citing R. Lightfoot 1956: 146–47).

89. Cf. *m. ʾAbot* 4.22; *Exod. Rab.* 1.20; Wis. 1:6 (cited in Köstenberger 2002c: 61, 201 n. 164).

90. Cf. John 1:17–18; 8:56–58; 12:41; Heb. 1:1–3; 2:1–3; 3:1–6.

The defense turns into an indictment (Borchert 1996: 245): "and you do **5:38** not have his word residing in you."[91] If God's word had dwelt in Jesus' opponents, they would have accepted rather than rejected him (Ridderbos 1997: 204). Jesus' language harks back to the OT depiction of a God-fearing individual as someone who has the Word of God dwelling in his or her heart. Joshua (Josh. 1:8–9) and the psalmist (Ps. 119:11) are both characterized in this way. New Testament saints correspondingly are exhorted to let the word of Christ dwell in them richly (Col. 3:16). By contrast, Jesus' Jewish opponents do not have God's word dwelling in them, because they "do not believe the one he [God] sent" (5:38b).

Jewish diligence in studying the Torah was legendary.[92] But although **5:39–40** the Jews' zeal in studying Scripture was undeniable, Jesus maintained that such zeal was misguided, for alone it was insufficient for attaining eternal life.[93] What is required, rather, is an understanding of Scripture's true (christological) orientation and purpose. Not merely are individual sayings of Scripture fulfilled in Jesus;[94] Scripture in its entirety is oriented toward him.[95] Yet Jesus' Jewish opponents "did not want" to come to him (i.e., to accept his claims and believe in him): their refusal is deliberate (R. Brown 1966: 225).

Anticipating the charge that he is acting out of self-interest, Jesus asserts **5:41–43** that he is not seeking human acclaim, in contrast to his interrogators (5:41; cf. 5:44; see Carson 1991: 264), who are devoid of love for God (not "love of God"; see Bultmann 1971: 269 n. 2; Moloney 1998: 192) and whose self-love caused them to reject the God-sent Messiah (Carson 1991: 264). Jesus has come in his Father's name and was rejected;[96] false prophets, who come in their own name, the Jews will accept. This is nothing new: the false prophet Shemaiah is charged by the true prophet Jeremiah with speaking in his own name.[97] Jesus himself predicted the proliferation of false Christs as a sign of the end times (Matt. 24:5 pars.), and Josephus reports a string of charismatic figures in the years prior to A.D. 70 who at least temporarily accumulated a following (*Ant.*

91. Keener (2003: 658) lays out 5:38–44 as a "probable chiastic structure," with 5:42–43a as the center of the chiasm.
92. See Kenyon 1939: 38 (cited in Morris 1995: 292 n. 118). See also *b. Meg.* 18b (cf. Köstenberger 2002c: 61–62).
93. The famous first-century Jewish rabbi Hillel used to say, "The more study of the Law the more life. . . . If a man . . . has gained for himself words of the Law he has gained for himself life in the world to come" (*m. 'Abot* 2.7; cf. Bar. 4:1; *Gen. Rab.* 1.14). Paul argues against this view in Rom. 7:10 and Gal. 3:21.
94. See John 12:38; 13:18; 15:25; 17:12; 19:24, 36–37.
95. See John 1:45; 2:22; 3:10; 5:45–47; 12:41; 20:9; cf. Luke 24:27, 44–45; and Matthew's "fulfillment quotations." See Bruce 1978: 35–53.
96. On "name," see commentary at 1:12. On the Jewish concept of agency, see commentary at 5:23.
97. Jer. 29:25, 31; cf. Deut. 18:19–20; Jer. 14:14–15; 23:25; 29:9.

20.5.1 §§97–99; 20.8.6 §§171–72; *J.W.* 2.13.4–6 §§258–65).[98] The delegation sent to investigate the Baptist (1:19–22) may well have been aware of such stirrings.

5:44–45 Why were the Jewish leaders prepared to accept false prophets while rejecting their Messiah? Because they "accepted honor from one another," being so self-absorbed in the fulfillment of their religious duties that they had no room for God's revelation. Having turned blind spiritually, they had lost the ability to perceive God's work in their midst. In the rabbinical schools, Scripture study had become a means of self-advancement whereby authorities engaged in inconsequential verbal disputes (Morris 1995: 294 n. 125, with reference to Strachan 1955). "The only God" once again affirms Jewish monotheism, which is firmly embedded in the Torah and Second Temple literature (cf. 5:18; 17:3).

The Jews' hopes were set on Moses (see 9:28–29);[99] yet, ironically, it was precisely he who served as their accuser. In OT history, Moses frequently served as Israel's intercessor.[100] Yet both the "Song of Moses" and the Book of the Law function as witnesses against Israel (Deut. 31:19, 21, 26; cf. Rom. 3:19). In Jesus' day, many Jews, in keeping with the portrayal of Moses in OT and Second Temple literature, saw Moses' role as that of continuing mediator and advocate.[101] The Samaritans, too, regarded Moses as their heavenly intercessor.[102] Even many pagans knew him as Israel's lawgiver.[103] This widespread confidence in the efficacy of Moses' intercession shows how shocking Jesus' statement would have been for his Jewish audience.[104]

98. See Barnett 1980–81; Schlatter 1948: 160; Piper, *ISBE* 3:332–33; van der Woude, *TDNT* 9:509–27. However, calling these figures "messianic pretenders" goes beyond the evidence. Thus, Meier (1994: 611–12 n. 75) and R. Brown (1997: 820 n. 6) emphatically deny that any Jew (other than Jesus) claimed or was said to be the Messiah prior to, contemporaneous with, or even in the decades immediately following Jesus' ministry.

99. This is the only instance of the term "hope" (be it verb or noun) in John's Gospel (but the expression is also virtually absent from the Synoptics). The intensive perfect tense (ἠλπίκατε, *ēlpikate*) underscores the settled state of the Jews' hope set on Moses.

100. See Exod. 32:11–14, 30–32; Num. 12:13; 14:19–20; 21:7; Deut. 9:18–20, 25–29. See also As. Mos. 11:17 (cf. 12:6; Jub. 1:19–21; cited in Köstenberger 2002c: 62; cf. Beasley-Murray 1999: 79; Ridderbos 1997: 207; Carson 1991: 266).

101. See *Exod. Rab.* 18.3 on Exod. 12:29, where Moses is called "a good intercessor."

102. Schnackenburg 1990: 1.470 n. 139, with reference to Meeks 1967: 254–55.

103. E.g., Diodorus Siculus, *Bibliotheca historica* 1.94.2.8; 34/35.1.3.9 (first century B.C.).

104. For a treatment of Moses as a character in the Fourth Gospel, see Harstine (2002: 40–75), who treats 1:17, 45; 3:14; 5:45–46; 6:32; 7:19, 22, 23; 9:28–29. According to Harstine, Moses' dominant function throughout the narrative is as a witness to Jesus (p. 72), whereby Moses serves as a historical/legendary figure similar to Jacob (4:5, 12), David (7:42), and Abraham (8:33–58). On Moses in the Fourth Gospel, see also Glasson 1963; Meeks 1967; and Boismard 1993. Keener (2003: 662) observes how, on a literary level, the closing appeal to Moses in 5:45–47 prepares the way for chapter 6, where Jesus is presented as the new Moses providing God's people with the new "bread from heaven."

The present verses reveal the familiar Johannine pattern of a statement   5:46–47
in the affirmative followed by the converse. Belief in Moses and Jesus is
developed in terms of believing in Moses' writings and Jesus' words.[105]
"For if you believed Moses, you would believe me"[106] most likely refers to
the Jews' misdirected reading of the law. The reason why Moses would
accuse them was that he, as the lawgiver, knew the law's true purpose.
Rather than being an end in itself, it served to point to Christ (Carson 1991:
266). "Moses . . . wrote concerning me" (cf. 5:39) may refer to the first five
books of the OT (attributed to Moses) or to the prediction of a "prophet
like Moses" in Deut. 18:15, or both. "But if you do not believe his writings,
how will you believe my words?" refers to the Jews' failure to grasp the
true essence of the Scriptures, including their prophetic orientation toward
Jesus (cf. Matt. 5:17). The argument is from the lesser to the greater, a
customary rabbinic device.[107] "His writings" and "my words" are here set
in parallelism (cf. John 1:17), underscoring the correspondence between
the Hebrew Scriptures and Jesus' teaching (Moloney 1998: 192–93).

Additional Notes

5:1. The conclusion that the Feast of Tabernacles is the most likely referent stands, even though the anarthrous reading almost certainly is original.[108] The term ἑορτή has the article in all its twenty-five NT instances except here, in Matt. 27:15 = Mark 15:6 (there with κατά), and in Col. 2:16.

5:2. Some MSS read "Bethzatha" (preferred by NA²⁷; Bultmann 1971: 240 n. 7) or "Bethsaida" (cf. 1:44; 12:21), but "Bethesda" is attested much more widely and clearly is the superior reading.[109]

5:3b–4. These verses, which describe the periodic stirring of the water by a descended angel and the resulting healing of the first to enter the pool, clearly are inauthentic.[110] This is indicated by poor external attestation and the presence of as many as seven non-Johannine words in this one sentence (R. Brown 1966: 207).

5:17. Whether the word "Jesus" was added later or is original is uncertain (Beasley-Murray 1999: 70 n. k). The name is found in $\mathfrak{P}^{66}$ and A, but not in $\mathfrak{P}^{75}$, $\aleph$, and B.

---

105. The word πιστεύω (*pisteuō*, believe) is central, occurring four times in these two verses (see Morris 1995: 296–98).
106. On the grammatical construction, see Wallace 1996: 693, 695.
107. Jesus: Luke 16:31; John 3:12; 6:27; 7:23; 10:34–36; Paul: Rom. 5:15, 17; 2 Cor. 3:9, 11: other NT writers: Heb. 9:14; 12:9, 25. See Carson 1991: 266.
108. So the majority of commentators, including Barrett 1978: 250–51; Carson 1991: 240; Morris 1995: 265 n. 6; R. Brown (1966: 206), who says that the evidence is "overwhelming"; Beasley-Murray 1999: 69 n. e; Schnackenburg 1990: 2.93.
109. Hengel (1999: 309) comments, "One should by all means read 'Bethesda'"; so also Carson 1991: 241; Morris 1995: 267; Witherington 1995: 137; Borchert 1996: 231; Moloney 1998: 171; Schnackenburg 1990: 2.94; Schlatter 1948: 142; undecided are Ridderbos 1997: 185; R. Brown 1966: 206–7.
110. So Fee 1982 and the vast majority of commentators, including Ridderbos 1997: 185; Carson 1991: 242; Morris 1995: 267; Barrett 1978: 253; R. Brown 1966: 207; Beasley-Murray 1999: 70 n. h; Bultmann 1971: 241 n. 4; Borchert 1996: 232; Schnackenburg 1990: 2.94–95.

2. Galilean Passover: Feeding the Multitude and the Bread of Life Discourse (6:1–71)

Like the first and third signs (both in Cana of Galilee), Jesus' fifth sign recorded in John is again in Galilee (the second and fourth signs take place in Jerusalem; see also additional note on 6:1). The pattern of narration of chapter 6 is similar to chapter 5: Jesus' sign is followed by an extended discourse elaborating on the significance of the event (Ridderbos 1997: 208) (with the walking on the water incident serving as an interlude). The scene is the eastern shore of the Sea of Galilee; the time is spring, shortly before the Jewish Passover. While Jesus had spent an earlier Passover in Jerusalem (cf. 2:13), he now reveals his true nature in his native Galilee (cf. 4:44).[1]

The evangelist sets Jesus' ministry firmly in the context of salvation history, linking Jesus' signs with the two previous major periods of miraculous activity in the history of God's people: the ministries of Moses and of Elijah/Elisha. Once again, however, John does not content himself with narrating a mere miracle: what Jesus *does* is shown to reveal who he *is*—in the present case, the giver of eternal life. In keeping with Jewish expectation, Jesus is presented as the antitype to Moses: he is not merely used by God to provide bread for his people, but is himself sent by God as the life-giving "bread" who gives his life for the world.

In Jesus, the salvation-historical era predicted by the prophets has arrived, when "they will all be taught by God" (6:45; cf. Isa. 54:13). Yet on hearing Jesus' "bread of life discourse," many even of his disciples turn back and no longer follow him. Structurally, the present event thus marks a crucial watershed in Jesus' ministry. The halfway point of the first major portion of this Gospel reveals the failure, not of Jesus' ministry, but of a considerable portion of Jesus' followers (cf.

---

1. A comparison between John's account of the feeding of the five thousand and that of the Synoptics makes clear that John provides his own independent account (see esp. Schnackenburg 1990: 2.23–24; and the table in Anderson 1996: 187–88). John mentions several details that are not found in any of the other Gospels, such as the crossing of the sea (6:1); the approaching Passover (6:4); the involvement of Philip and Andrew (6:7–8); the fact that the five loaves contributed by the boy were made of barley (6:9); and Jesus' command to his disciples to gather all the fragments so that nothing would be lost (6:12).

12:37). Yet there is a silver lining: the enduring commitment of the Twelve (except for Judas) whom Jesus had chosen.

a. Jesus feeds the multitude (6:1–15)
b. Jesus walks on water (6:16–21)
c. The bread of life discourse (6:22–59)
d. Watershed: The Twelve remain, many others leave (6:60–71)

Exegesis and Exposition

[1]After these things Jesus left for the area on the other side of the Sea of Galilee (that is, of Tiberias). [2]And a large crowd was following him because they had been observing the signs he had been performing on the sick. [3]Then Jesus went up on the mountainside and there sat down with his disciples. [4]Now the Jewish festival of Passover was near. [5]So when Jesus lifted up his eyes and saw that a large crowd was coming toward him, he said to Philip, "Where shall we buy bread so that these may eat?" [6](He was saying this to test him; for he knew what he was about to do.) [7]Philip answered him, "Bread for two hundred denarii [eight months' wages] would not be sufficient for each one to receive a little." [8]Another one of his disciples, Andrew the brother of Simon Peter, said to him, [9]"Here is a boy who has five small barley loaves and two small fish; but what are these for so many?" [10]Jesus said, "Have the people sit down" (there was much grass in this place). So the men (numbering about five thousand) sat down. [11]Then Jesus took the loaves and, after giving thanks, distributed them to those who were seated, and did the same also with the fish—as much as they wanted. [12]And when all had had their fill, he said to his disciples, "Gather the leftover pieces, so that nothing may perish." [13]So they gathered them and filled twelve baskets with the pieces of the five barley loaves left over by those who had eaten. [14]So when the people saw ⌜the sign⌝ he had performed, they were saying, "This is truly the prophet who is to come into the world." [15]For this reason Jesus, who knew that they were about to come and seize him to make him king, withdrew again to the mountain by himself.

[16]Now when evening came, his disciples went down to the lake. [17]They boarded a boat and set off across the lake for Capernaum. Darkness had already settled, yet Jesus had not yet joined them, [18]and the lake was stirred because a strong wind was blowing. [19]So when they had rowed about twenty-five or thirty stadia [three or three and a half miles], they saw Jesus walking on the lake and coming near the boat, and they were terrified. [20]But he said to them, "It's me! Don't be afraid!" [21]Then they were willing to take him into the boat, and at once the boat was at the shore where they were heading.

[22]On the next day the crowd that had stayed on the other side of the lake realized that only ⌜one boat⌝ had been there and that Jesus had not entered the boat with his disciples but his disciples had left alone. [23]Yet boats from Tiberias

landed near the place where they had eaten the bread after the Lord had given thanks. ²⁴So when the crowd realized that neither Jesus nor his disciples were there, they got into their boats and went to Capernaum, looking for Jesus. ²⁵And when they found him on the other side of the lake, they said to him, "Rabbi, when did you get here?" ²⁶Jesus answered them and said, "Truly, truly, I say to you, you are looking for me not because you saw signs, but because you ate the loaves and had your fill. ²⁷Work not for food that perishes, but for food that lasts for eternal life, which the Son of Man will give you. For on him God the Father has put his seal of approval." ²⁸Then they said to him, "What must we do to perform the works of God?" ²⁹Jesus answered and said to them, "The work of God is this: to believe in the one he has sent." ³⁰So they said to him, "Then what sign will *you* perform that we may see it and believe you? What are you going to perform? ³¹Our ancestors ate the manna in the wilderness, as it is written, 'He gave them bread from heaven to eat.'" ³²Then Jesus said to them, "Truly, truly, I say to you, it is not Moses who has given you the bread from heaven, but it is my Father who gives you the true bread from heaven. ³³For the bread of God is that which comes down from heaven and gives life to the world."

³⁴Then they said to him, "Sir, from now on give us this bread all the time." ³⁵Jesus said to them, "*I am* the bread of life. Whoever comes to me will never go hungry, and whoever believes in me will never, ever thirst. ³⁶But as I told you, you have seen me and still do not believe. ³⁷Everyone the Father has given me will come to me, and whoever comes to me I will never cast out, ³⁸because I have come down from heaven not to do my own will, but the will of the one who sent me. ³⁹And this is the will of the one who sent me: that I lose none of those he has given me, but raise them up on the last day. ⁴⁰For my Father's will is this: that everyone who looks at the Son and believes in him have eternal life, and I will raise him up on the last day."

⁴¹Then the Jews there began to grumble concerning him because he said, "I am the bread that came down from heaven," ⁴²and they were saying, "Is this not Jesus the son of Joseph, whose father and mother we know? How can he now say, 'I came down from heaven'?" ⁴³Jesus answered and said to them, "Stop grumbling among yourselves. ⁴⁴No one can come to me unless the Father who sent me draws him, and I will raise him up on the last day. ⁴⁵It is written in the prophets, 'And they all will be taught by God.' Everyone who has heard from the Father and has learned comes to me. ⁴⁶Not that anyone has seen the Father except the one from God—only he has seen the Father. ⁴⁷Truly, truly, I say to you, whoever believes^r ˺has eternal life. ⁴⁸I am the bread of life. ⁴⁹Your ancestors ate the manna in the wilderness, yet they died; ⁵⁰this is the bread that comes down from heaven, that anyone may eat from it and not die. ⁵¹I am the living bread that came down from heaven. If anyone eats from this bread, he will live forever; in fact, the bread that I will give for the life of the world is my flesh."

⁵²Then the Jews began to argue sharply with one another, saying, "How can he give us his flesh to eat?" ⁵³So Jesus said to them, "Truly, truly, I say to you,

unless you eat the flesh of the Son of Man and drink his blood, you have no life in you. [54]Whoever eats my flesh and drinks my blood has eternal life, and I will raise him up on the last day. [55]For my flesh is real food, and my blood is real drink. [56]Whoever eats my flesh and drinks my blood resides in me, and I in him. [57]Just as the living Father sent me, and I live on account of the Father, so the one who eats me will live on account of me. [58]This is the bread that came down from heaven: not as your ancestors ate and died; whoever eats this bread will live forever." [59]These things he said while teaching in the synagogue at Capernaum.

[60]Therefore many of his disciples who had heard this said, "This message is hard. Who can accept it?" [61]Because he knew within himself that his disciples were grumbling about this, Jesus said to them, "Does this offend you? [62]Then what if you see the Son of Man ascend to where he was before? [63]The Spirit is the one who gives life; the flesh profits nothing. The words I have spoken to you are spirit and are life. [64]Yet there are some of you who do not believe." (For Jesus had known from the beginning which of them did not believe and who it was who would betray him.) [65]And he went on to say, "This is why I told you that no one can come to me unless it is given to him by the Father."

[66]From that time many of his disciples returned home and no longer walked with him. [67]So Jesus said to the Twelve, "You do not want to leave as well, do you?" [68]Simon Peter answered him, "Lord, to whom shall we go? You have words of eternal life. [69]And we have come to believe and know that you are ⌐the Holy One of God⌐." [70]Jesus answered them, "Have I not chosen you, the Twelve? Yet one of you is a devil." [71](He was talking about Judas, the son of Simon Iscariot; for he was about to betray him—one of the Twelve.)

a. Jesus Feeds the Multitude (6:1–15)

"After these things" is customarily vague (cf. 2:12; 5:1; see Carson 1991: 267). As much as half a year may have passed since the previous event recorded in John. The "other side" of the lake normally was considered to be the east side, since most Jewish activity occurred on the west side. In OT times, the Sea of Galilee was referred to as Kinnereth, because it was shaped like a lyre (Hebrew, *kinnôr*).[2] Around A.D. 17–18, Herod Antipas founded a city called Tiberias (cf. 6:23) on the west side in honor of his patron, Tiberius (A.D. 14–37; see Josephus, *Ant.* 18.2.3 §36). Gradually, the name of the city was transferred to the name of the lake. On a popular level, this transfer probably took place only around the time John wrote his Gospel, hence his choice to provide both names (cf. 21:1).[3]

6:1–2

---

2. Another explanation for the name is the proximity of the nearby town Tell el-'Oreimeth, which was lyrelike in shape. See Buehler, *ISBE* 2:391–92. For general information, see Riesner, *DJG* 37.

3. The name "Sea of Tiberias" is attested in first-century literature (Sib. Or. 12:104). It is also preserved in Jewish tradition (*Yamma shel Tiberya* [*t. Sukkah* 3.9]) and by the Arabs, who call the lake *Bahr Tabariyeh* (Avi-Yonah 1964: 143).

The verbs for "follow," "observe," and "perform" in 6:2 (ἠκολούθει, ἐθεώρουν, ἐποίει; *ēkolouthei, etheōroun, epoiei*) are all in the imperfect tense: people *kept* following Jesus and *continually* observed the signs that he *habitually* performed (Morris 1995: 302). Crowds were at hand when Jesus healed the lame man on the Sabbath (5:13). They were also present at various festivals in Jerusalem (7:12, 20, 31, 32, 40, 43, 49; 12:12, 17, 18, 29, 34) and at the raising of Lazarus (11:42; 12:9). Generally, John portrays the crowds as following Jesus only externally, as being drawn to Jesus primarily on account of his miracles, and as mired in confusion and ignorance (Köstenberger 1998b: 145–46).[4]

6:3–4 The word "mountainside" need not designate a specific mountain or hill but may refer simply to "the hill country" or "high ground" east of the lake known today as the Golan Heights (Morris 1995: 303; cf. Carson 1991: 268).[5] Like other rabbis, Jesus usually sat down to teach (Matt. 5:1; Mark 4:1; 9:35; Luke 4:20), although here teaching is not mentioned explicitly. The disciples have not been heard from since John 4:33.

Passover was near. This is the second of three Passovers mentioned by John, and the only one that Jesus spent in Galilee (in A.D. 32, Passover fell on April 13/14). In the life of the Jewish nation this festival marked a time of intense nationalistic zeal.[6] The nearness of the Jewish Passover provides the framework for the ensuing feeding of the multitude and Jesus' claim of being the "bread of life" (Schlatter 1948: 164).[7]

6:5–7 Jesus looks up and sees a large crowd coming toward him.[8] People apparently had walked the several miles around the (shorter) north side of the lake and caught up with Jesus and the disciples. Jesus involves Philip, who, like Andrew (cf. 6:8) and Peter, being a native of nearby Bethsaida (1:44), was the natural choice (Morris 1995: 303; Carson 1991: 269). Jesus' question serves to test Philip to gauge his response as a follower of Jesus the Messiah (6:6) (Ridderbos 1997: 210).[9]

4. For people's dependence on miracles, see 2:24 and 4:48.

5. Keener (2003: 664) observes that the references to mountains in 6:3 and 6:15 constitute a literary *inclusio*.

6. Kruse (2003: 161) notes that Passover was a time when the Jews expected the Prophet to provide manna from heaven the way Moses had done (citing 2 Bar. 29:3–30:1 [c. A.D. 100], see esp. 29:8, though there is in this text no specific mention of Passover).

7. Though some of the acts and words in John 6 have eucharistic significance, the feeding of the multitudes does not in itself constitute a eucharistic meal (so, rightly, Brodie 1993: 263; cf. Barrett [1978: 274], who adds that, to the contrary, "the eucharist, like the last supper. . . , must be understood in the context of the Jewish Passover"). See also R. Brown (1966: 246–49), who speaks of "eucharistic elements" in all four Gospel versions and considers "the eucharistic coloring of the Johannine account of the multiplication" as beyond doubt.

8. The phrase ἐπάρας οὖν τοὺς ὀφθαλμούς is reminiscent of 4:35 (Ridderbos 1997: 210; Keener 2003: 665).

9. Jesus' question is the first of several indications that he uses the present event to prepare and instruct his disciples (6:5–9, 12–13, 16–21; cf. 4:27–38). Anderson (1996: 173)

In the wilderness, Moses asked God a similar question: "Where can I get meat for all these people?"[10] "He knew what he was about to do" shows that Jesus fully intended to perform a miracle from the start.[11] "Eight months' wages" renders the phrase "two hundred denarii" (a genitive of price; see Barrett 1978: 274; Wallace 1996: 122). One denarius was approximately one day's pay (Matt. 20:2; cf. John 12:5). Philip quickly estimates that it would take over half a year's income to feed the entire crowd (no pay on Sabbaths or other holy days).

The παιδάριον (paidarion, boy) could have been a teenager or even in his early twenties, though he could have been younger as well.[12] The boy's lunch is rather modest: John emphasizes that both the five barley loaves and the two fish are small. In a similar account, Elisha fed one hundred men with twenty barley loaves and some ears of grain (2 Kings 4:42–44; see Ridderbos 1997: 211–12; Barrett 1978: 275 et al.).[13]

6:8–9

The common word for bread, ἄρτος (artos; used seventy-nine times in a literal sense in the NT), usually designates wheat bread; here (6:9, 13) it refers to bread made of barley (cf. in the LXX: Num. 5:15; Judg. 7:13; 2 Kings 4:42; Ezek. 4:12). Barley was common food for the poor, its "lower gluten content, low extraction rate, less desirable taste, and indigestibility" rendering it "the staple of the poor in Roman times" (Malina and Rohrbaugh 1998: 127; cf. Schlatter 1948: 165–66).[14]

notes that it is only in John that the source of the food is mentioned; see also Laney 1992: 121. The verb πειράζω (peirazō, test) occurs only here in John (cf. 8:6 in the non-Johannine pericope 7:53–8:11). It has negative connotations elsewhere in the Gospels but is used here in a neutral sense.

10. See Num. 11:13 (cf. R. Brown 1966: 233; Moloney 1998: 197; Burge 2000: 193). There are several other parallels between John 6 and Num. 11: the grumbling of the people (Num. 11:1; John 6:41, 43); the description of the manna (Num. 11:7–9; John 6:31); the reference to the eating of meat/[Jesus'] flesh (Num. 11:13; John 6:51); and the striking disproportion between the existing need and the available resources (Num. 11:22; John 6:7–9).

11. See Carson 1991: 269; also R. Brown 1966: 233; Schnackenburg 1990: 2.15. Note the personal pronoun setting Jesus apart from Philip and the verbs ᾔδει (ēdei, he knew; indicating prior knowledge) and ἔμελλεν (emellen, he was about; conveying certainty not associated with simple future) (Morris 1995: 304 n. 16). Compare also the reference to Jesus' supernatural insight in 2:24.

12. In the LXX, the term refers to young Joseph in Gen. 37:30, Daniel and his friends in Dan. 1, and Tobit's son, who is at a marriageable age, in Tob. 6.

13. The use of the word παιδάριον in John 6:9 (its only NT occurrence) and several times in the LXX of the 2 Kings passage (there referring to Elisha's servant) is one major verbal connection between these two narratives. Other links include the mention of barley and the overall mode of narration, including a question of disbelief, the command to distribute the loaves, and the fact that all ate with food left to spare.

14. Philo writes that barley products are "suited for irrational animals and people in unhappy circumstances" (Spec. Laws 3.10 §57). The more well-to-do preferred wheat bread (Spec. Laws 2.29 §175; see Schnackenburg 1990: 2.442 n. 25), which was traded at twice or even three times the value of barley (2 Kings 7:1, 16, 18; Rev. 6:6; m. Ketub. 5.8).

The fish probably were dried or preserved, perhaps pickled. The word used for "fish" here is the rare term ὀψάριον (*opsarion*; elsewhere in the NT only in John 6:11; 21:9, 10, 13), a diminutive form of ὄψον (*opson*), which originally meant cooked food and then came to refer to any relish taken with food. Much more common in the NT (nineteen occurrences) is ἰχθύς (*ichthys*; cf. ἰχθύδιον, *ichthydion*, in Matt. 15:34 = Mark 8:7).[15]

6:10–11   The reference to the large number of those present underscores the greatness of Jesus' miracle (Ridderbos 1997: 212). The men (presumably heads of households, reflecting "the patriarchy of the times" [Moloney 1998: 200]) sat down, about five thousand of them.[16] In addition, there were women and children (cf. Matt. 14:21; recall the presence of a boy with his lunch in John 6:9). The total may have been as many as twenty thousand people. This shows that Jesus could have had a substantial following had he been willing to be made king (cf. 6:14; see Carson 1991: 271–72).

There was much grass in that place (an allusion to the messianic age? cf. 10:9–10; Ps. 23:2; see Schnackenburg 1990: 2.16). Mark 6:39–40 mentions that the grass was green, which points to spring (near the Passover), before the summer heat would burn it brown. Jesus gave thanks.[17] If Jesus used the common Jewish form of thanksgiving, he would have uttered a prayer such as the following: "Blessed are you, O Lord our God, King of the universe, who brings forth bread from the earth" (cf. Carson 1991: 270). The bountiful meal evokes OT messianic prophecy.[18]

6:12–13   "Gather the leftover pieces, so that nothing may perish."[19] It was customary at Jewish meals to collect what was left over. Pieces of bread were not to be thrown around (*b. Ber.* 50b), and food the size of an olive or larger must be picked up (*b. Ber.* 52b).[20] Jesus applies the same care to preserving all that the Father has given him (10:28–29; 17:11–12, 15).

---

15. In light of the fact that the term ἰχθύς came to have eucharistic significance, it may be significant that John uses a different word (E. Johnston 1962: 153).

16. The words τὸν ἀριθμόν (*ton arithmon*, the number) form an accusative of respect or (general) reference (Wallace 1996: 203–4); Barrett (1978: 275) calls it an accusative of specification.

17. The word used here is εὐχαριστέω (*eucharisteō*, thank), used elsewhere in John only in 6:23; 11:41; the Synoptic parallels use εὐλογέω (*eulogeō*, bless), but cf., in the feeding of the four thousand, Matt. 15:36; Mark 8:6.

18. Cf. Isa. 25:6–8; 49:9–11; see also Matt. 22:1–14; Luke 22:15–30 (Ridderbos 1997: 213).

19. Similarly, it is said of Ruth, "She ate all she wanted and had some left over" (Ruth 2:14; see Daube 1956: 46–51). The concern that nothing "perish" (ἀπόληται, *apolētai*) may establish a link with the fate of Judas, who is described as "son of destruction" (ἀπωλείας, *apōleias*) in John 17:12. There may also be a link with the apostasy of most of Jesus' "disciples" in 6:66 (Anderson 1996: 174).

20. This reflects the views of Rabbis Hillel and Yoḥanan (cf. *b. Ḥul.* 105b, attributed to Abaye [ca. A.D. 280–339]). The expression "so that nothing may perish" is also documented

The baskets used to gather the leftovers probably were made of stiff material, perhaps wicker (Westcott 1908: 215). "Twelve" baskets may allude to Jesus' restoration of Israel (the twelve tribes) by calling twelve disciples to form the core of his new messianic community (Carson 1991: 271; see also Borchert 1996: 254).[21] Like Matthew and Luke, John mentions only the loaves (and not the fish) as having been gathered (but cf. Mark 6:43).[22]

When people saw the "sign" that Jesus had performed,[23] they asked whether Jesus was "the prophet who is to come into the world" (cf. 1:21; 7:40). This refers to Deut. 18:15–18, which also featured significantly in the messianic expectations at Qumran (cf. 4QTest 5–8; 1QS 9:11).[24] Jesus' multiplication of barley loaves is reminiscent of the miracle performed by Elijah's follower Elisha (2 Kings 4:42–44). In 1 Kings 19, a parallel is drawn between Elijah and Moses (cf. Exod. 24:18; 34:28). The popular expectation expressed in 6:14 may represent an amalgamation of the two figures (R. Brown 1966: 234–35). In Jesus' day, the notion of the "prophet" apparently was merged with that of "king" (6:15).[25] The figure also featured prominently in early Christian preaching (Acts 3:23; 7:37).

6:14–15

People were about to come and seize (ἁρπάζω, *harpazō*) him to make him king.[26] The present incident is reminiscent of the Zealots, a militant movement that had found in Galilee a fertile soil for its nationalistic brand of Judaism (perhaps reflected in Luke 13:1–3?). Jesus' true kingship becomes an issue later in John's Gospel (esp. 18:33–37). "But as the kingdom is God's gift and men cannot violently possess themselves of it, so Jesus, whom God gives (3:16) and who gives himself to men, cannot be violently constrained" (Barrett 1978: 278). Jesus, in his role as the "elusive Christ," withdraws to a mountain by himself (earlier he had withdrawn to this mountainous area with his disciples [6:1–3]),

---

in rabbinic literature with reference to food (*y. Sanh.* 6.6; *y. Ḥag.* 2.2; see Köstenberger 2002c: 65). Regarding Jewish care with respect to food, see E. Johnston 1962: 153–54; Daube 1956: 42.

21. Whitacre (1999: 144) notes, "The availability of twelve baskets for collecting the leftovers (v. 13) suggests this child was not the only one who had brought food."

22. The perfect participle βεβρωκόσιν (*bebrōkosin*, those who had eaten) may denote the sense of satisfaction provided by the meal (Morris 1995: 306 n. 27).

23. On the TNIV rendering "miraculous sign," see commentary at 2:11 (see also additional note on 6:14).

24. For an extensive discussion of the "prophet like Moses" theme, see Anderson 1996: 174–77.

25. Beasley-Murray (1999: 88) comments, "The step from a prophet like Moses (v 14), the first Redeemer and worker of miracles, to a messianic deliverer was a short one for enthusiasts in contemporary Israel to make" (cf. Horsley 1984).

26. The other instances of ἁρπάζω in the Gospels, all in John and Matthew, suggest that the term refers to robbery or the unlawful snatching away of something or someone (cf. John 10:12, 28, 29; Matt. 11:12; 12:29; 13:19).

going farther up what is known today as the Golan Heights (cf. Matt. 14:23; Mark 6:46).

b. Jesus Walks on Water (6:16–21)

6:16–19 From the mountaintop of participating in the feeding of the multitudes, the disciples descend to the valley of experiencing a violent storm as they try to cross the Sea of Galilee. Many of them were fishermen and well acquainted with the lake. When they see Jesus approaching, walking on the water, they are gripped by fear, at first failing to recognize him. This is all the more remarkable since a similar incident, Jesus' calming of the storm, had taken place earlier (Matt. 8:23–27 pars.). The account of Jesus' walking on the water is also found in two of the Synoptic Gospels (Matt. 14:22–33; Mark 6:45–52);[27] it does not constitute a Johannine sign (see commentary at 6:21).

It may be late afternoon, as only in 6:17 has darkness set in. The disciples are on the east side of the lake and will now attempt to row the six or seven miles back to Capernaum on the northwest side.[28] The focus of the narrative is not on the disciples' quandary but on Jesus' ability to get to them (Ridderbos 1997: 217).

The reference to darkness having settled is probably not a symbolic reference.[29] That Jesus had "not yet" joined them may imply that the disciples had expected Jesus to arrive sooner than he actually did.[30] The lake was stirred because a strong wind was blowing: "The Sea of Galilee lies about six hundred feet below sea level. Cool air from the south-eastern tablelands can rush in to displace the warm moist air over the lake, churning up the water in a violent squall" (Carson 1991: 275). Even today, powerboats are to remain docked as the winds buffet the water. How much more could violent storms have wreaked havoc on the wooden boats used in Jesus' time.

---

27. Mark and Matthew note that the disciples thought that Jesus was a ghost (Mark 6:49; Matt. 14:26). Mark also points out that the disciples had not understood about the loaves, for their hearts were hardened (Mark 6:52), while Matthew adds the episode with Peter and the response of worship when Jesus got into the boat (Matt. 14:28–33). John's account is terser, emphasizing primarily the calming effect of Jesus' presence on the disciples.

28. The imperfect ἤρχοντο (*ērchonto*) indicates that the disciples "were on their way" or that they were "trying to go" (Barrett 1978: 280; cf. Morris 1995: 308 n. 36; Moloney 1998: 203). Morris (1995: 309 n. 41), followed by Keener (2003: 673), suggests that the disciples were probably crossing not at the widest part of the lake but from the northeast to the northwest shores, the distance stated in 6:19 indicating that they were most of the way across the lake.

29. Cf. 3:2 and especially 21:3 (though note 13:30). So Moloney 1998: 203; contra Borchert 1996: 258; Carson 1991: 274. Ἐγεγόνει (*egegonei*, had come) is an intensive pluperfect (Wallace 1996: 585).

30. So, in essence, Westcott (1908: 218), who infers that Jesus had led the disciples "to expect that He would be with them, and that they clung in some way to the expectation even in their disappointment."

After rowing about three or three and a half miles,[31] the disciples were driven off course and found themselves halfway toward Magdala, where the lake was the widest (Schnackenburg 1990: 2.446 n. 65). The disciples' beholding (θεωροῦσιν, *theōrousin*) Jesus is reminiscent of 1:14.[32] The expression περιπατοῦντα (*peripatounta*, walking) describes the "effortlessness of Jesus going over the sea" (Ridderbos 1997: 217).[33] The fear of the disciples is concomitant with the sight they beheld. It is a fear appropriate for seeing the divine or supernatural (cf. Matt. 14:26; Luke 1:12; 2:9; see Ridderbos 1997: 217).

"The austere, nondramatic way in which everything is told climaxes in the simple saying of Jesus: 'It is I; do not be afraid'" (Ridderbos 1997: 217). On one level, ἐγώ εἰμι (*egō eimi*, it is I) is Jesus' self-identification to his disciples (Morris 1995: 310; Carson 1991: 275–76; Barrett 1978: 281; Ball 1996: 181). Beyond this, there may be overtones of epiphany ("I am" is God's name in the OT; see Exod. 3:14), especially in light of Jesus' walking on water. The statement may allude to Ps. 77:16, 19, describing God's manifestation to Israel during the exodus.[34]

6:20–21

The boat's arrival at the shore "at once" (εὐθέως, *eutheōs*) may indicate a second miracle,[35] in which case the "walking on water" would be followed by a "miraculous landing."[36] This contrasts with the crowd's expectations (6:14, 25; see Ridderbos 1997: 218; R. Brown 1966: 255). The walking on water constitutes a private manifestation of Jesus' messianic glory to his inner circle (similar to the transfiguration) and therefore does not qualify as a Johannine sign; nor is it identified as such by the Fourth Evangelist (Köstenberger 1995b; Carson 1991: 274).[37]

---

31. "Three or three and a half miles" translates "twenty-five or thirty stadia." A stadion was equivalent to 606.75 feet. The lake was about sixty-one stadia at its greatest width. If the multiplication of the loaves took place at the eastern shore of the Sea of Galilee, then the shortest distance to Capernaum would be five to six miles.

32. The use of the present tense adds a sense of vividness to the account (Morris 1995: 309).

33. Keener (2003: 673) suggests that there may be an allusion to Job 9:8 LXX, where God is said to walk on the waters (noting also the parallel wording in Mark 6:48 ["passing by"] and Job 9:11).

34. So Beasley-Murray 1999: 89–90; Witherington 1995: 153; Burge 2000: 193, 195. See further the discussion of ἐγώ εἰμι sayings in ancient culture and the OT in Beasley-Murray 1999: 89–90.

35. Keener (2003: 674) cites immediacy as a frequent mark of the miraculous.

36. For example, Michaels (1989: 107) observes, "The disciples wanted to take Jesus into the boat, but before they had a chance, they found themselves suddenly at their destination." Ridderbos (1997: 218) rejects the idea; many commentators do not arrive at a definitive conclusion (e.g., Morris 1995: 310). The phrase "and at once" is found elsewhere in John in 5:9 and 18:27 (the closely related term εὐθύς [*euthys*] is found in 13:30, 32; 19:34).

37. Schlatter (1948: 169) notes the contrasting ways in which Jesus deals with the crowd and his disciples. Whereas the former's desire to elevate Jesus as their king is frustrated, the latter's faith is mightily encouraged.

---

c. The Bread of Life Discourse (6:22–59)

6:22–25 The sequence of the ensuing events can be constructed, albeit with some difficulty (Morris 1995: 315–16; R. Brown 1966: 258–59; Borchert 1996: 260). Apparently, the crowd, which had been fed on "the other side" (6:1), had remained there during the events of 6:16–24. Next, "some boats from Tiberias" ended up where the crowd was (presumably east across the lake from Tiberias). Finally, the multitude and the people in the boats decided to head back to Capernaum across the northern quarter of the lake. Boats then arrived from Tiberias, the chief city on the west side of the lake (see commentary at 6:1). Whereas Capernaum was located on the northwest edge of the lake, Tiberias was several miles to the south, just about at the midpoint of the western shore.

The phrase "where they had eaten the bread" in 6:23 resumes the feeding narrative of 6:1–14 (see esp. 6:1, 3).[38] The expression "after *the Lord* had given thanks" (cf. 6:11 ["give thanks"] and 6:68 ["Lord"]) reveals hindsight from a post-Easter perspective (see, later, 11:2), though not necessarily later insertion of material (Moloney 1998: 206; Beasley-Murray 1999: 85 n. k; Barrett 1978: 285; contra Morris 1995: 316 n. 67; Anderson 1996: 182–83: "cultic gloss"), and may reflect eucharistic overtones (cf. 1 Cor. 11:23–24; see R. Brown 1966: 259; Moloney 1998: 206; contra Borchert 1996: 260 n. 84). This is the first time Jesus is called "Lord" (κύριος, *kyrios*) in this Gospel.[39]

"On the other side of the lake" refers to the area in or around Capernaum (see 6:24, 59). The phrase may allude to the supernatural manner in which Jesus crossed the lake (Carson 1991: 283). The two terms for "boat," πλοῖον (*ploion* [6:17, 19, 21, 22]) and its diminutive πλοιάριον (*ploiarion* [6:22, 23, 24]), seem to be used with no distinction in meaning (Barrett 1978: 285; R. Brown 1966: 257). While addressing him as "rabbi" (6:25; see commentary at 1:38), people engage in a discussion over Jesus' teaching, which once again reveals their lack of understanding of his true identity. "When did you get here?"[40] highlights the crowd's ignorance and confusion (Ridderbos 1997: 223).

6:26–27 As on previous occasions, Jesus discerns people's true motives (cf. 2:23–25; 3:3; 4:16–18): they were not really interested in the deeper significance of the signs (last mentioned in 6:2), but merely in having their stomachs filled (Ridderbos 1997: 224; Calvin 1959: 153).[41] Earlier,

---

38. The evangelist frequently refers to previous events in his Gospel: see 4:46 (cf. 2:1–11); 7:50 (cf. 3:1–2); 9:13, 18, 24 (cf. 9:1–7); 10:40 (cf. 1:28); 12:1–2, 9, 17 (cf. 11:1–44); 18:14 (cf. 11:49–51); 18:26 (cf. 18:10); 19:39 (cf. 3:1–2); 20:8 (cf. 20:4); 21:20 (cf. 13:23–25).

39. On the address κύριε as meaning "sir," see commentary at 4:11. See Witherington, *DJG* 484–92, esp. 490–91.

40. Thus, in effect, "How long have you been here?" (Morris 1995: 316 n. 68; Barrett 1978: 286; R. Brown 1966: 261; Carson 1991: 283).

41. Contra Beasley-Murray (1999: 91), who takes εἴδετε (*eidete*, you saw) literally, concluding that Jesus' present audience was not physically present when Jesus performed the

they had attempted to make Jesus king on account of the miraculous feeding (6:14–15). Rather than answer their question, therefore, Jesus exhorts them by taking things into a spiritual direction, telling people to work not for perishable food, but for food that lasts for eternal life, which the "Son of Man" will give them.[42] In their original context, Jesus' words refer not to the Eucharist (contra Schnackenburg 1990: 2.37) but to Jesus' identity as God's messenger (6:29) and the blessing of eternal life available through him (Ridderbos 1997: 225).

Since Jesus is the "food that lasts" spoken of here, and since he remains forever—in contrast to material bread and even the "bread from heaven" given during the exodus—the life he provides is eternal as well (Carson 1991: 284). On a literary level, there may be a connection between Jesus' earlier concern for gathering leftover food so that it might not perish and his reference to "food that lasts for eternal life" here. "Work for" shortly will be explained in terms of simple belief in Jesus. "On him" (τοῦτον, *touton*) is emphatic (Moloney 1998: 211) and points to Jesus' exclusive appointment and authorization by God as the bringer of salvation (Ridderbos 1997: 225; cf. Carson 1991: 284). More specifically, the reference may be to Jesus' reception of the Spirit at his baptism (cf. 1:33).[43]

The ensuing conversation apparently took place in the synagogue at Capernaum (cf. 6:59).[44] Similar questions are asked by the rich young ruler (Matt. 19:16 pars.) and by the crowd in Jerusalem at Pentecost (Acts 2:37). The crowd's response suggests a basic understanding that Jesus is urging them to look beyond their physical needs (Ridderbos 1997: 225). Nevertheless, there arises a misunderstanding concerning the words "work for" in the previous verse. What Jesus had intended as a reference to people's proper pursuit, the crowd took as an invitation to literally "work the works of God."[45] The phrase "works of God,"   **6:28–29**

---

sign. In the Synoptics, even the disciples are shown to misunderstand the implications of the miracle (Mark 6:52; cf. 8:14–21; see Carson 1991: 283). Barrett (1978: 286) views the use of ἐχορτάσθητε (*echortasthēte*, you had your fill) as evidence that John was familiar with Mark (cf. Mark 6:42; 8:8).

42. According to Schlatter (1948: 170), the present reference shows awareness of Galilean farmers' poverty, in part owing to heavy taxation. Regarding "I tell you the truth," see commentary at 1:51; on the "Son of Man," at 1:51; 3:13; concerning Jesus' "signs," at 2:11; 6:14. The relative pronoun ἥν (*hēn*, that) in 6:27 could refer either to "food" or to "eternal life" but probably has the entire phrase "food that lasts for eternal life" as its antecedent.

43. So Barrett 1978: 287; cf. Witherington 1995: 155; Schnackenburg 1990: 2.38; Burge 1987: 84–85. Less likely, the reference may be to his consecration (R. Brown 1966: 261) or to the incarnation (Moloney 1998: 211). On the phrase "seal of approval," see commentary at 3:33.

44. Carson (1991: 283) places the transition at 6:27. Morris (1995: 315) says the shift may have occurred as early as 6:25, but more likely "the discourse took place in stages, with only the concluding section in the synagogue."

45. See Carson 1991: 284–85. "To work works" is a common Semitic expression: see Matt. 26:10 par.; John 9:4; Acts 13:41, quoting Hab. 1:5; 1 Cor. 16:10. The verb ἐργάζομαι (*ergazomai*, work) occurs earlier in John in 3:21 and 5:17, and again in 9:4.

which may reflect Zealot parlance (Schlatter 1948: 171), refers in Jewish literature normally to works done by God, not those required by him (cf. 3:21; 9:3–4).[46] In light of the Jewish emphasis on "works of the law,"[47] Jesus' answer is nothing less than stunning: God's requirement is summed up as believing in "the one he has sent," that is, the Messiah. This contrasts with people's apparent confidence that they are able to meet the demands of God (Carson 1991: 285; Morris 1995: 319; Barrett 1978: 287).

6:30 Upon Jesus' stipulation that they believe in him, the Jews, in customary fashion, ask for a sign authenticating his authority (cf. 2:18; Matt. 12:38 par. Luke 11:16, 29; Matt. 16:1 par Mark 8:11).[48] People had just witnessed the feeding of the five thousand; it is hard to see why (though not uncharacteristic that [cf. 1 Cor. 1:22]) they demanded yet another sign. In Judaism, a "sign from heaven" was considered to be the highest form of legitimation.[49] Jesus' present audience indicates that if he were to perform the sign that they demanded, they would believe. This assertion constitutes yet another instance of Johannine irony, for Jesus had already performed several signs (including the feeding of the multitude), yet people persisted in their unbelief.

The present misunderstanding hinges on two different senses of the word "sign." The Jews demand further evidence for Jesus' claims; the evangelist presents as "signs" works of Jesus that are christologically significant (Ridderbos 1997: 226). In people's thinking, if Jesus was the prophet like Moses (6:14), he could be expected to perform further signs.[50] The crowd's emphasis on "seeing" as the basis for "believing" represents inferior faith at best in the context of the Johannine narrative (cf. esp. 20:29; see Morris 1995: 321). The question "What are you going to perform?" is a common OT expression of incredulity (Job 9:12; Eccles. 8:4; Isa. 45:9; see Derrett 1993: 142–44).

---

46. Similar terminology is found in the Qumran Scrolls (CD 2:14; cf. 1QS 4:4; 1QH 13:36; CD 1:1–2; 13:7–8). "Work of God" is also found (in a different context) in Rom. 14:20.

47. See Carson 1991: 285. See Rom. 3:20, 27–28; Gal. 2:16; 3:2, 5, 10; cf. Phil. 3:6, 9.

48. The parallelism between 6:30 and 2:18 is noted by Keener (2003: 678). Dodd (1953: 301, cf. 90) perceptively notes that Jesus, in response to the Jews' demand for a sign, "does not promise any significant event yet to happen," but rather "offers an interpretation of what has already happened," inviting them "to see in the actual occurrence of the Feeding of the Multitude the σημεῖον which they desire." People had seen the feeding, but they had not seen the sign; that is, they had not understood its symbolic, messianic significance as pointing to Jesus as the life-giving bread (pp. 334–35). Contra Whitacre (1999: 156), who claims that the crowd "is not asking for another sign to be given, but rather they want an interpretation of the feeding that has just occurred."

49. Cf. *Exod. Rab.* 9.1; *b. B. Meṣiʿa* 59b. Some of the rabbis, however, remained critical toward such signs (Schnackenburg 1990: 2.39–40).

50. Carson 1991: 285; cf. Beasley-Murray 1999: 91; Barrett 1978: 288; R. Brown 1966: 265; Moloney 1998: 212. The personal pronoun σύ (*sy*, you) is emphatic, possibly suggesting that people doubt Jesus' ability to furnish such a sign (Morris 1995: 321).

Three factors link the present chapter with the exodus account: (1) the **6:31**
Passover motif; (2) Jesus as the prophet like Moses; and (3) the expectation that God would again provide manna in the messianic age (Ridderbos 1997: 226; Morris 1995: 321; Beasley-Murray 1999: 91). The implicit
contrast is between Moses and Jesus (Ridderbos 1997: 226–27).

The topic of conversation may have spun off the Scripture reading
in the synagogue for that day (Burge 2000: 197; cf. Carson 1991: 285).
The crowd uses the exodus tradition in an attempt to question Jesus'
claims: "Our ancestors ate the manna in the wilderness" (cf. Ps. 78:23–
25). Indeed, it was expected that in the messianic age there would be a
recurrence of God's provision of manna (2 Bar. 29:8 [ca. A.D. 100]; cf.
Sib. Or. frg. 3:49 [second century B.C.?]; Rev. 2:17).[51]

The reference "He gave them bread from heaven to eat" seems to be
derived from several passages (see esp. Exod. 16:4, 15; Ps. 78:23–25; see
Carson 1991: 286; Schlatter [1948: 172–73] cites Neh. 9:15). The divine
provision of manna for wilderness Israel is celebrated in both OT and
Second Temple literature (Menken 1988).[52] Jesus' subsequent discourse
reflects a widespread homiletical pattern (Borgen 1965; Schnackenburg
1990: 2.40–41).

People's misunderstanding consists in their failure to see that it is not   **6:32–33**
Moses who is the giver of the true heavenly bread but Jesus' Father. The
use of the double ἀμήν (*amēn*, truly) heightens the force of Jesus' words
(cf. 6:26; see Ridderbos 1997: 227). The passages cited at 6:31 (see commentary at 6:31) convey the OT teaching that it is in fact God who is
the giver of the manna, with Moses as his mediator. In Jewish thought,
"bread (of God)" was taken to refer to the Torah or the showbread (*Gen.
Rab.* 70.5), in keeping with OT usage.[53] The last part of 6:32 indicates that
what is central in the present statement is the true bread from heaven
(τὸν ἀληθινόν [*ton alēthinon*, the true] is emphatic; see Barrett 1978:
290; Moloney 1998: 213; cf. Jesus as the "true vine" in 15:1).

As in 3:14, an event during Israel's wilderness wanderings at the
exodus is shown to anticipate typologically God's provision of salvation in and through Jesus (Barrett 1978: 290).[54] Moreover, whereas the

51. The expectation is also found in later rabbinic tradition (see quotations in Köstenberger 2002c: 68–69).

52. See Ps. 78:24; 105:40; Neh. 9:15; Wis. 16:20. See also Philo, *Alleg. Interp.* 3.59–61
§§169–76; *Worse Att. Bet.* 31 §118; *Heir* 15 §79; 39 §191; *Chang. Nam.* 44 §§259–60.

53. NIV: "food of God"; see Lev. 21:6, 8, 17, 21, 22; 22:25. Being essential for human
existence, bread and water are universal symbols of life. In Judaism, the Torah was commonly called "bread" (*Gen. Rab.* 54.1; 70.5; *Cant.* [Song] *Rab.* 1.2 §3); "bread" and "water"
symbolism was applied to salvation, the law, the Scriptures, and wisdom.

54. Since contemporary Judaism conceived of the Torah as "bread" from God (cf. Prov.
9:5), some suggest that Jesus may here claim to be superior to the Torah (Carson 1991:
286–87; cf. Barrett 1978: 290; R. Brown 1966: 262). However, in the Johannine context
such a claim seems unduly dichotomous and probably unlikely.

manna in the wilderness had Israel as its recipient, God's gift of Jesus is universal in scope (Carson 1991: 287). "Not Moses . . . but my Father" exhorts the Jews to see, behind Moses, God as the true provider of the heavenly bread. The present tense δίδωσιν (*didōsin*, he gives) could suggest that God was giving the true bread in the form of Christ in the present (Carson 1991: 286; Morris 1995: 322).

"Bread from heaven" points to Jesus' heavenly origin (cf. 3:13, 31; see Ridderbos 1997: 228). While the crowd interprets the words impersonally, the personal sense gradually builds up to 6:35 (R. Brown 1966: 263). The phrase "that which comes down from heaven" (6:33) occurs seven times in the present discourse.[55] Regarding the phrase "gives life to the world," note that in rabbinic teaching, the giving of the law at Mount Sinai was described in similar terms: "the earth trembled when he gave life to the world" (*Exod. Rab.* 29.9). In the present passage, the same function is said to be fulfilled by Jesus (cf. 5:39).

6:34–35   The words of the Jews here are reminiscent of those of the Samaritan woman at 4:15 (Ridderbos 1997: 228; Carson 1991: 287). Throughout the dialogue the Jews see Jesus in light of their preconceived notions and are entirely motivated by physical concerns (Ridderbos 1997: 229). "I am the bread of life" (6:35, reiterated in 6:48, 51) is the first of seven Johannine "I am" sayings.[56] Jesus' words are designed to correct the Jews' misunderstanding in the previous verse. In contrast to the need for a steady supply of bread as in the case of the manna in the wilderness, Jesus makes clear that people do not need to receive his bread repeatedly (cf. 13:9–10).[57]

By claiming, "Whoever comes to me will never go hungry, and whoever believes in me will never, ever thirst," Jesus plainly claims to fulfill OT messianic expectations (see esp. Isa. 55:1; cf. Isa. 49:10, cited in Rev. 7:16).[58] The present words help interpret the crasser statements in 6:54, clarifying what Jesus means by "eat my flesh" and "drink my blood" (defined as "coming" and "believing" respectively; cf. 6:64–65). They also foreshadow 6:53–56, underscoring the unity of the present discourse (Carson 1991: 288). Both instances of οὐ μή (*ou mē* [double

---

55. On John's portrayal of Jesus as the one who comes into the world and returns to the Father (descent/ascent), see Köstenberger 1998b: 121–30.

56. Subsequent sayings include 8:12 = 9:5; 10:7 = 10:9; 10:11 = 10:14; 11:25; 14:6; 15:1 (see the excursus in Witherington 1995: 156–58). The personal pronoun ἐγώ (*egō*, I) is emphatic (Ridderbos 1997: 229 n. 118); what is more, the "I am" saying of 6:35 forms the "narrative and theological centre of the scene," as it is based on what precedes it and is explained by what follows (Lee 1994: 135–36). "Of life" constitutes a verbal genitive (Carson 1991: 288 n. 1).

57. This does not remove the need of remaining in Christ (see John 15).

58. There is no need to resort to a sapiential interpretation here, understanding Christ as the true Wisdom (Carson 1991: 289; contra R. Brown 1966: 274–75; Witherington 1995: 149–50).

negative]), the second one also having πώποτε (*pōpote*, ever), are strongly emphatic.[59]

The present verses constitute a break in Jesus' discussion of the living "bread." Before returning to this topic, he addresses the Jews' persistent unbelief (Ridderbos 1997: 229). The Jews have not seen an additional sign of Jesus' authority (6:30; though they have seen his original sign), but they have seen *him*, and still they do not believe.[60] The precise referent of "I told you" in 6:36 is unclear; it is possible that the original occasion is not recorded in this Gospel (Morris 1995: 325). The thought of the Father giving individuals to Jesus is a repeated theme in the Gospel (cf. 6:39; 10:29; 17:2, 6; 18:9). Thus, Jesus takes no credit for attracting people to himself by his own oratory or miraculous power. As the Father's sent Son, he receives those who come to him because of the Father's prevenient work (Ridderbos 1997: 230). The present verse is significantly elaborated upon in 6:44, where Jesus states that no one can come to him "unless the Father who sent me draws him." Despite the rejection mentioned in 6:36, Jesus is confident that certain ones will come to him (Ridderbos 1997: 230; Carson 1991: 290). This seems to indicate the notion of divine predestination (cf. 6:39; see Carson 1991: 290; contra Witherington 1995: 158), which culminates in John 12.

6:36–40

John 6:37 encapsulates the Gospel's "universalism" (better: "universal scope"), "individualism," and "predestinarianism" (Barrett 1978: 294). On the basis of the Father's prevenient work, Jesus will receive the ones who come to him. What he *will not* do is fail to recognize these individuals as his own and eject them from his fellowship (Ridderbos 1997: 231 n. 123);[61] what he *will* do is keep and preserve them (Carson 1991: 290; Burge 2000: 200).[62] This motif culminates in the good shepherd discourse (esp. 10:28–29) (Schnackenburg 1990: 2.47) and continues through Jesus' final prayer (esp. 17:6, 9, 11–12; cf. 18:9) and his concluding commissioning of Peter and the "disciple Jesus loved" (ch. 21).[63]

59. The significance of the shift from the aorist subjunctive πεινάσῃ (*peinasē*, hunger) to the future indicative διψήσει (*dipsēsei*, thirst) is unclear (noted by Morris 1995: 324 n. 100; Barrett [1978: 292–93] thinks that John's use of the indicative is incorrect).

60. See discussion at 6:30. The second καί (*kai*, and) in 6:36 probably is adversative (so Barrett 1978: 293). The majority of commentators consider the word με (*me*, me) in 6:36 to be original (so Ridderbos 1997: 230 n. 120; Carson 1991: 289–90; Morris 1995: 325 n. 104; R. Brown 1966: 270; contra Barrett 1978: 293; Moloney 1998: 216; see also the discussions in Beasley-Murray 1999: 85; Schnackenburg 1990: 2.46).

61. "Everything" (πᾶν, *pan*) in 6:37 and 6:39 is neuter, used in a qualitative, collective sense (R. Brown 1966: 270; Barrett 1978: 294; Borchert 1966: 265), though ultimately people (not things) are in mind (BDF §138.1, with specific reference to John 6:37; cf. Morris 1995: 325; Moloney 1998: 216).

62. As Carson (1991: 290) notes, the present figure of speech is a litotes, a stylistic device declaring a certain truth by nullifying its corollary.

63. The idea of accepting someone called by God into the community and not rejecting that person is also found in the Qumran literature (e.g., 1QS 6:16, 19, 22; 9:15–16; 11:13–14).

Jesus' welcoming attitude is contrasted with the Pharisees' casting the formerly blind man out of the synagogue (9:34–35). Though the focus in the present verse seems to be on the Father's work of "giving" people to Jesus and on his receptive attitude, it is nonetheless true that persons must "come" to him. This underscores the need for a positive human response to the divine initiative (Borchert 1996: 265). Still, there is no indication here or elsewhere in this Gospel that God's predestinating purposes ever fail (contra Witherington 1995: 158).

Jesus' descent from heaven is cast in the perfect tense, καταβέβηκα (*katabebēka*, I have come down), as a settled condition, here with the preposition ἀπό (*apo*, from) rather than the customary ἐκ (*ek*, out of). This may place greater emphasis on Jesus' presence on earth (Schnackenburg 1990: 2.47). Jesus' purpose of doing the will of the one who sent him is stated in terms similar to 4:34, there as here in a mission context. The reason why (causal ὅτι, *hoti*, because [Carson 1991: 290]) Jesus certainly will receive those whom the Father brings to him is that he is committed to his Father's will rather than his own. Thus, the security of the believer rests on the faithfulness of the Son (Carson 1991: 291). The Father's will is further elaborated on in 6:39 and 6:40: that those given to Jesus should not perish but have eternal life and be raised on the last day.[64] The repetition of the words "on the last day" (6:39, 40, 44, 54) accentuates the heavenly, transcendent character of Jesus' mission, conveyed also by the title "Son of Man" (cf. 6:27, 53; cf. 3:13; 5:27–29; see Ridderbos 1997: 231). "The last day" is an expression found in the NT only in John (see also 5:28, 29; 11:24; 12:48).

"Eternal life" (6:40) as well as "raise up" (6:39, 40) continue the theme of life sounded in 6:33 and 6:35, underscoring the permanence of life made available in and through Jesus, in contrast to the temporary nature of God's provision of manna to wilderness Israel (Ridderbos 1997: 231). The possession of eternal life can be cast as in the present (6:40 and elsewhere in this Gospel), but this is balanced by repeated references to raising up on the last day. Thus, futuristic eschatology is not swallowed up by John's "realized" eschatology. Precisely because believers' future raising up by Jesus is a certainty, it can be said that they have eternal life already in the here and now.[65] The verb for "see" (θεωρέω, *theōreō*) may or may not signify the notion of perceptiveness (Carson 1991: 292). The relationship between "seeing" and "believing" in 6:40 is both positive (in contrast to 6:36) and close (Bultmann [1971: 233] goes so far as to

---

64. Both expressions in the aorist subjunctive in 6:39, μὴ ἀπολέσω (*mē apolesō*, I may not lose) and ἀναστήσω (*anastēsō*, I may raise), are part of the purpose clause indicating the Father's will (Barrett 1978: 295). The same dynamic seems to be at work in 6:40 (though note R. Brown 1966: 270).

65. Another important element in this regard is the giving of the Spirit, for "it is the Spirit who gives life," just as Jesus' words are "spirit and life" (6:63; cf. 1:33; 3:3–8, 34; 4:10–11; 7:38–39).

identify it as a hendiadys); the thought is similar to 3:13–14, where it is implied that the Hebrews "looked to" and "believed in" the lifted-up snake provided by God for "salvation." John 6:40 brings closure to the unit started with 6:35 by summarizing 6:35–39 (Borchert 1996: 266).

"The Jews" (Ἰουδαῖοι, *Ioudaioi*) who began to grumble (ἐγόγγυζον,   **6:41–42** *egongyzon* [iterative imperfect]) about Jesus probably are Galileans (Schlatter 1948: 175–76, citing 2:6, though that reference may be more general), which suggests that Ἰουδαῖοι in John does not necessarily refer to Judeans (Ridderbos 1997: 231). There are obvious parallels between Jesus' Jewish opponents and wilderness Israel (cf. Exod. 16:2, 8–9; Num. 11:4–23). Just as the Israelites grumbled about the first giver of bread, Moses, so now they grumbled about the second, Jesus (1 Cor. 10:10); and just as in the wilderness, the Jews' grumbling ultimately is directed against God himself (Moloney 1998: 217).

People raise another objection: how can Jesus claim heavenly origin when his human roots are all too plain?[66] Even the Jews in Jesus' part of Palestine are ignorant of his virgin conception. This is another instance of Johannine irony.[67] The Jews here object not to the notion that a man (like Jesus) could receive a divine calling, or even that someone like Elijah might appear on earth and dwell among human beings, but to Jesus' claim of descent from heaven in face of his obvious (or so it seemed) human origin (Odeberg 1968: 264–65 n. 3; also see commentary at 8:31–59 below, esp. 8:41).

Jesus proceeds to underscore the human inability to gain salvation apart   **6:43–44** from divine enablement. People can come to him only if the Father who sent Jesus draws them. Ultimately, therefore, salvation depends not on human believing, but on the "drawing" action of the Father (presumably by the Holy Spirit) by which God moves a person to faith in Christ (cf. 12:32; see also Jer. 31:3; Hos. 11:4; see Ridderbos 1997: 232). Rabbinic sources use the expression "to bring near to the Torah" with reference to conversion (e.g., Hillel [first century A.D.] in *m. ʾAbot* 1.12; see Moloney 1998: 220).[68] The reference to the Father "drawing" is balanced by people "coming" to Jesus.

---

66. The personal pronoun ἡμεῖς (*hēmeis*, we) may be emphatic, underscoring the certainty of people's conviction (Morris 1995: 328). R. Brown (1966: 270) detects a degree of animosity in the pronoun οὗτος (*houtos*, this one) and translates it "this fellow." Similarly, Westcott (1908: 233), who finds "perhaps a tinge of contemptuous surprise in the pronoun."

67. Carson 1991: 292 says, "John's record of their question is steeped in irony" (citing Duke 1985: 64–65). See also earlier, 4:44, where the evangelist refers to Jesus' saying that a prophet is not without honor except in his own country.

68. There is a certain affinity between John's teaching on predestination and the Qumran doctrine of the "two spirits" (1QS 3:14–4:6). The rabbinic view is summed up by a saying

In the present instance, Jesus' point is not merely general, but specific and salvation-historical. Because the Jews are refusing to come to God in his prescribed manner—through faith in the Messiah—they cannot receive eternal life. Jewish obduracy constitutes the focus of the "paternity dispute" in chapter 8; the healing of the blind man in chapter 9; the good shepherd discourse in chapter 10; and the events surrounding the raising of Lazarus in chapters 11–12. The Pharisee-led plot against Jesus that surfaces intermittently in the narrative (esp. during the "festival cycle" in chs. 5–10) is due to the Jews' unwillingness to come to God on his terms.

6:45–46 It is written in the prophets, "They will all be taught by God" (a paraphrase of Isa. 54:13; cf. Jer. 31:34). Jesus claims that this prophecy is realized in his ministry.[69] The expression "the prophets" could refer to the general tenor of prophetic OT teaching or to the prophetic writings as a division of the OT. In Judaism, it was held that to learn the Torah was to be taught by God himself.[70] Though the Jews prided themselves on being students of Scripture, Jesus here alleges that the reason why they refuse to "come to him" (i.e., believe in him as Messiah) is that they are unwilling to learn from God. It is unusual for Jesus to use a prophecy concerning the salvation of the Jews to point to their inability to be saved (Ridderbos 1997: 233). The focus here is on the fact that "all" will be taught by God and that "everyone" truly receptive to divine revelation will come to Jesus—not merely Jews (cf. 11:51–52; 12:32).

John 6:44 is the negative corollary to 6:37a (Carson 1991: 293); 6:46 clarifies 6:45 by noting that God's revelation is mediated exclusively through the Son, Jesus (Carson 1991: 294; Barrett 1978: 296; Schnackenburg 1990: 2.52). Also, a distinction is made between "hearing from the Father" (6:45) and "seeing the Father" (6:46). The former can occur only through Jesus, who alone has seen the Father. Per the prologue, this is something that not even Moses did; hence, God's revelation through Jesus is greater than that in the law (1:17–18; cf. 3:13; 5:37; 14:7–11; see Moloney 1998: 218). John 6:44–46 points to the cooperative effort between the Father and the Son in bringing a person to salvation. While salvation is the result of the Father's drawing work, it is brought about by an individual's believing reception of God's revelation in Jesus (Ridderbos 1997: 234; cf. Barrett 1978: 296).

---

attributed to Rabbi Akiba (ca. A.D. 135): "All is foreseen, but freedom of choice is given" (m. ʾAbot 3.16). Cf. Josephus, Ant. 18.1.3 §13; 18.1.4 §16; 18.1.5 §18; J.W. 2.8.14 §§162–65; see also the excursus in Schnackenburg 1990: 2.265–70.

69. Though shortly it will become apparent that his teaching is "too hard" for many of his followers (6:60). On Jesus as a rabbi in John's Gospel, see Köstenberger 1998a.

70. The expression "disciples of God" (i.e., the ones taught by God) is also found in the Qumran writings (CD 20:4; 1QH 10:39; 15:10, 14). See also the messianic parallel in Ps. Sol. 17:32 (prior to A.D. 70).

Jesus now returns to the subject of the "bread from heaven," introduced by another ἀμὴν ἀμήν statement: "Whoever believes has eternal life" (see additional note on 6:47). There are structural similarities between 6:32–35 and 6:48–51 (Schnackenburg 1990: 2.452 n. 146), though the latter section further clarifies the concept of "eating" (6:31, 35). In the present context, Jesus draws a distinction between the recipients of the manna in the wilderness—they still died—and those who eat from the "bread from heaven" and do not die but live forever (6:49–51; cf. 6:30–33). By referring to "your" ancestors, Jesus distances himself from his Jewish opponents.[71]

6:47–51

Jesus then elaborates on the significance of his statements regarding the "bread of life": (1) this "bread" is Jesus' flesh; and (2) he will give it for the life of the world. The fact that the term used for Jesus' body is "flesh," σάρξ (*sarx*), rather than σῶμα (*sōma* [more commonly used in relation to the Lord's Supper]) seems to caution against a sacramental or eucharistic understanding of these verses.[72] The term likely harks back to 1:14 (Carson 1991: 295; D. M. Smith 1999: 158). "Give for the life of the world" has a sacrificial connotation.[73] In the larger narrative context this refers to Jesus' body given on the cross for the sins of humanity (Ridderbos 1997: 238; Morris 1995: 331). The concept of "eating Jesus' flesh" is the subject of a follow-up question and Jesus' further explanation in 6:52–58.[74]

The Jews' fighting among themselves resembles their striving with Moses and God during the exodus (Exod. 17:2; Num. 20:3; see Beasley-Murray 1999: 94; Borchert 1996: 271; Schnackenburg 1990: 2.60).[75] As in 6:42, the pronoun οὗτος (*houtos*, this one) may be derogatory: "this fellow" (Morris 1995: 334 n. 130; Barrett 1978: 298; R. Brown 1966: 282). The question in 6:52 likely is intended to highlight the apparent meaninglessness of Jesus' words (cf. 3:4; 4:11; 8:52, 57; see Schnackenburg 1990: 2.60). Jesus, rather than responding directly (Ridderbos 1997: 239), clarifies further how he fulfills the gift of manna during

6:52–58

---

71. Similarly, 8:17: "your own law"; 8:56: "your father Abraham"; 15:25: "their law."

72. So Ridderbos 1997: 235–37; cf. Carson 1991: 295; Morris 1995: 331–32; contra Moloney 1998: 223; Schnackenburg 1990: 2.55; Lindars 1972: 267; Talbert 1992: 140. As Keener (2003: 690) observes, "John's words [in 6:27–63] invite his audience to look to Christ's death itself, not merely those symbols which point to his death." At best, any such overtones are derivative (Borchert 1996: 270–71; cf. Brodie 1993: 286; Calvin 1959: 170).

73. Carson (1991: 295) notes that the preposition ὑπέρ (*hyper*, for, in behalf of) is often found in the context of sacrificial language (10:11, 15; 11:51–52; 13:37–38; 15:13; 17:19; 18:14).

74. There is no reason to assume, as Bultmann (1971: 218–19) does, that these verses (starting with 6:51c) are the work of an "ecclesiastical redactor." See also the discussion in Schnackenburg 1990: 2.56–59.

75. The term μάχομαι (*machomai*, quarrel, fight) has a negative connotation in all of its three other NT uses (Acts 7:26; 2 Tim. 2:24; James 4:2).

the exodus (Moloney 1998: 222). This serves to intensify, rather than remove or diminish, people's hardening toward Jesus and his message (Ridderbos 1997: 239; cf. Carson 1991: 296; R. Brown 1966: 291–92; Schnackenburg 1990: 2.61).

Employing another solemn, authoritative ἀμὴν ἀμήν introduction, Jesus reiterates his earlier claims: stated negatively, "Unless you eat the flesh of the Son of Man and drink his blood, you have no life in you";[76] stated positively, "Whoever eats my flesh and drinks my blood has eternal life, and I will raise him up on the last day."[77] Jesus' use of the title "Son of Man" (see commentary at 1:51; in this discourse also in 6:27, 62) rules out a sacramental understanding. Jesus here speaks of the surrender of his "flesh and blood"—a Hebrew idiom referring to the whole person (cf. Matt. 16:17; 1 Cor. 15:50; Gal. 1:16; Eph. 6:12; Heb. 2:14)—unto death and of believers "eating and drinking" of it as the bread that came down from heaven and by which alone a human being can live. John 6:55, harking back to 6:27 and 6:32, emphatically states that Jesus' flesh and blood are real—that is, spiritual—food and drink. In Johannine parlance, "real" also carries the connotations of eschatological, typological fulfillment in relation to OT precursors.

John 6:56 adds the result of a believer's partaking of Jesus' flesh and blood: mutual indwelling.[78] This anticipates the fuller treatment of this phenomenon in John 15.[79] John 6:57 makes clear that the basis for believers' union with Jesus is Jesus' union with the Father. The ground of Jesus' own being is the "living Father" (cf. 5:26); likewise, Jesus is the ground of believers' spiritual existence (Carson 1991: 299; Moloney 1998: 222).[80] The personal pronoun με (me, me) instead of "my flesh/blood"

76. For the most part, 6:53 is a negative restatement of 6:51. However, 6:53 adds the reference to drinking Jesus' blood (a development of 6:35; see Beasley-Murray 1999: 94; Barrett 1978: 298).

77. John's use of τρώγω (trōgō, chew, eat) in 6:54 may be intended to heighten the vividness of Jesus' words (Ridderbos 1997: 242 n. 163; cf. Moloney 1998: 221; Bultmann 1971: 236), though it may merely be the evangelist's preferred verb for "eating" in the present tense (Carson 1991: 296; cf. Beasley-Murray 1999: 95; Barrett 1978: 299).

78. Lindars (1972: 269) observes, "This is the climax of the discourse. All the metaphors are dropped, and the whole thing is put into terms of personal relationship." Schlatter (1948: 179) notes aptly that the only "mysticism" that arises from this mutual indwelling is that of being "children of God."

79. There is no reason to conclude, on the basis of the present tense participles in this verse, that this partaking is an act to be repeated (contra Ridderbos 1997: 243; Morris 1995: 336). The logic of this section rather seems to demand that partaking of Jesus' flesh and blood is to be understood as an action that takes place once for all. Mutual indwelling ought not to be understood in egalitarian terms, as if Jesus and the believer were fulfilling equal roles. Jesus' sacrifice is foundational, and the believer's responsibility is the appropriation of this gift (Carson 1991: 298). Moreover, contrary to what might be expected, such mutual indwelling does not imply surrender of personality (Schnackenburg 1990: 2.63–64).

80. The construction κἀγὼ ζῶ . . . κἀκεῖνος ζήσει harks back to previous statements in 5:21, 24–30. Once again, however, the analogy breaks down in that believers do not

further seems to suggest that sacramental overtones are at best secondary (Carson 1991: 299). John 6:58, by way of *inclusio* (Ridderbos 1997: 244), returns to the events of the exodus account. However, now Jesus' audience and John's readers know the true identity of the bread—Jesus—and the necessity of partaking of it for salvation.[81] The summary nature of the present verse is highlighted by verbal allusions to 6:49 ("ancestors" [though here in Greek it says "the," not "your"]) and 6:51b ("live forever") (Schnackenburg 1990: 2.65; note also possible allusions to 6:33, 50).

Although later rabbinic teaching in fact speaks (figuratively) of "eating the Messiah" (*b. Sanh.* 99a; see Talbert 1992: 138),[82] a literal understanding of Jesus' words here militates against people's scruples against the drinking of blood and the eating of meat containing blood, both of which were proscribed by the Hebrew Scriptures, in particular the Mosaic law.[83] Against a sacramental understanding are further that (1) the Jews would not have understood Jesus' words in a sacramental sense; (2) the term "flesh" is never used in the NT to refer to the Lord's Supper; and (3) to do so would attribute inappropriate significance to such a practice (Ridderbos 1997: 240–41).[84] On a secondary level, however, John may expect his readers to read Jesus' words in light of the church's observance of the Lord's Supper, though not necessarily in a sacramental sense (Carson 1991: 296–97; Beasley-Murray 1999: 95).

John closes by saying that Jesus said these things while teaching in the synagogue in Capernaum (cf. 6:17, 24; see commentary at 2:12).[85] There is evidence that some synagogue services allowed the kind of exchange found in the present passage (Abrahams 1917: 1.1–17, esp. 4). When questioned about his disciples and his teaching by the high priest, Jesus referred to his habit of speaking openly in synagogues or at the temple (18:19–20; cf. Matt. 13:54; Mark 1:21; 6:2; Luke 4:15; 6:6). The anarthrous "in synagogue" may seek to accentuate the generic nature rather than specific identity of the location.[86]

6:59

---

have life in themselves (as does Jesus), even though they partake of Jesus' flesh and blood (Carson 1991: 299; cf. Beasley-Murray 1999: 95).

81. The consistent use of singular forms in contrast to the plural "the ancestors" may further accentuate the need for *individuals* to enter into right relationship with God through Jesus (Morris 1995: 337).

82. A later midrash on Eccles. 2:24 reads, "All the references to eating and drinking in this book signify Torah and good deeds" (see also on Eccles. 8:15).

83. See Gen. 9:4; Lev. 17:10–14; Deut. 12:16. See C. Koester 2003: 102–4.

84. Contra Schnackenburg (1990: 2.61), who suggests that John makes the sacrament an essential ceremony to gain eternal life because he was writing against a gnostic or docetic group within the Johannine community. Schnackenburg also (erroneously, in my opinion) suggests that eternal life, while gained through birth of water and the Spirit, must be maintained through participation in the sacrament.

85. It is possible that the second-century synagogue excavated at Capernaum was located on the site of the synagogue mentioned here. See the sidebar in Köstenberger 2002c: 70.

86. Schlatter (1948: 179–80, adducing Rev. 2:9; 3:9) contends that the anarthrous συναγωγή refers not to a building but to the congregation.

d. Watershed: The Twelve Remain, Many Others Leave (6:60–71)

6:60–62 Jesus' teaching on the "bread of life" is impossible to tolerate even for many of his disciples.[87] The ensuing large-scale defection marks a watershed in John's Gospel. As later will chapter 12, chapter 6 ends on a note of failure. As a result, the scope of Jesus' followers is narrowed, so that only a believing remnant remains, which constitutes the core of the new messianic community that is gathered to be instructed by the Messiah (chs. 13–16).

Those departing are not merely followers from a distance; they are "his disciples" (6:60–61, 66).[88] Many of them fall away, but not the Twelve (cf. 6:66, 67). "Hard" or "difficult" (σκληρός, *skleros* [elsewhere in the NT only in Matt. 25:24; Acts 26:14; James 3:4; Jude 15; cf. Gen. 21:11; 42:7]) does not mean "hard to understand," but "offensive"; note the parallel expression "Does this offend [σκανδαλίζει, *skandalizei*] you?" in the following verse.

Ἀκούειν (*akouein*, hear) means "accept," that is, listen with a view toward obeying (cf. 5:25); αὐτοῦ (*autou*, it [neuter], him [masculine]) probably relates to Jesus' message rather than Jesus himself, though ultimately the distinction is moot. Apparently, this group found it difficult to believe in one or all of the following: (1) Jesus' heavenly origin; (2) the notion that believers' appropriation of eternal life was contingent on Jesus' death; (3) the terminology of "eating and drinking [Jesus'] flesh and blood." Moreover, many had wrong motives, be it worldly materialism or political interests, or were unwilling to yield control of their lives to follow Christ (Carson 1991: 300).

The phrase "he knew within himself" probably suggests supernatural knowledge beyond what could be learned by natural means (R. Brown 1966: 296). "Grumble" (γογγύζω, *gongyzō*) harks back to 6:41 and ultimately to Israel's wilderness generation during the exodus. Many of Jesus' disciples now display the same spirit as that earlier of the Jews. "This" (τούτου, τοῦτο; *toutou, touto*) has as its global reference point the necessity for Jesus to die for the sins of the world.

Jesus' followers are "offended" by his teaching.[89] Indeed, the notion of a crucified Messiah proved offensive to many in the first and subse-

---

87. Calvin (1959: 177) comments, "It is dreadful and monstrous that so kind and friendly an invitation of Christ should have alienated the minds of many, especially those who had earlier been on His side and were even His close disciples. But this example is put before us as a mirror to see how great is the world's depravity and ingratitude, which heaps up material to stumble over even on the smooth way of life, that it may not come to Christ."

88. The use of the term μαθητής (*mathētēs*, disciple) is striking in conjunction with these followers' desertion of Jesus. Just as there are different kinds of faith (e.g., 2:23–25), there are different kinds of disciples (Carson 1991: 300).

89. The verb σκανδαλίζω (*skandalizō*, offend) occurs in John only here and in 16:1. In the other Gospels, Jesus' Jewish opponents are frequently shown to take offense at Jesus

quent centuries (cf. 12:34). The reference to Jesus' ascent in 6:62 (cf. 20:17), including an affirmation of his preexistence (cf. 17:5), by way of aposiopesis (the omission of the apodosis) (Ridderbos 1997: 245) suggests that crucifixion is not the end of the story and that his ascension would be every bit as striking as his forceful death (an argument from the lesser to the greater).[90]

"The Spirit is the one who gives life; the flesh profits nothing" (cf. Isa.   **6:63**
40:6–8).[91] Jesus' words here resemble his earlier comments to Nicodemus (3:6; see also 5:21; cf. 1 Cor. 15:45).[92] In the present instance, Jesus' point seems to be that human reason unaided by the Spirit is unable to discern what is spiritual (Ridderbos 1997: 246; Morris 1995: 340; cf. 1 Cor. 2:6–16).[93] The reference to Jesus' ascension in John 6:62 further suggests that here he states the necessity of the Spirit's work (cf. 7:37–39; see Carson 1991: 302; Beasley-Murray 1999: 96).

According to the Hebrew Scriptures, life was created by God's Spirit (Gen. 1:2; cf. 2:7) through his word ("And/Then God said"; Gen. 1:3, 6, 9, 11, 14, 20, 24, 26). Later, Moses instructed his fellow Israelites that "man does not live on bread alone but on every word that comes from the mouth of the LORD" (Deut. 8:3). Ezekiel memorably depicts the Spirit as life-giving (e.g., 37:1–14, esp. v. 5), and Jeremiah exemplifies receptivity to God's word (Jer. 15:16; cf. Ezek. 2:8–3:3) (Carson 1991: 302; Barrett 1978: 305). Both OT and NT view God's word as fully efficacious (Isa. 55:11; Jer. 23:29; Heb. 4:12). Here it is stated that it is *Jesus'* words (ῥήματα, *rhēmata*) that are spirit and life (cf. 5:24, 40, 46–47; 6:68),[94] which is in keeping with God's nature as spirit (4:24; see Schlatter [1948:

---

and his teaching (cf. Matt. 13:57 par.; 15:12), even though he seeks to avoid giving offense when possible (e.g., Matt. 17:27). At times the term is used as a synonym for religious apostasy (Matt. 11:6 par.; 24:10). Both Paul (Rom. 9:33 [cf. Isa. 8:14; 28:16]; 1 Cor. 1:23; Gal. 5:11) and Peter (1 Pet. 2:4–8 [cf. Ps. 118:22]) draw on seminal OT passages that refer to a "stumbling stone" rejected by people but made a "cornerstone" by God.

90. The conjunction οὖν (*oun*, then) is inferential; the argument is akin to 1:51. The question is rhetorical, with the answer being left open. The "ascent" of the "Son of Man" complements references to the "descent" (though not ascent) of the "bread of life" in the preceding discourse (cf. 6:33, 38, 41, 42, 50, 51, 58).

91. On the grammatical construction of this phrase, see commentary at 14:30.

92. At Qumran, the dualism is between two spirits; here and in 3:6, it is between flesh and spirit. Paul's strikingly similar pronouncement in 2 Cor. 3:6 indicates either dependence on Jesus or common drawing on conventional Jewish wisdom.

93. Note that "flesh" here takes on a different meaning than in the preceding discourse, where it referred to Jesus' body (so, rightly, Ridderbos 1997: 247; contra Schnackenburg 1990: 2.72).

94. The absence of the article before πνεῦμα (*pneuma*, spirit) and ζωή (*zōē*, life) indicates the quality or essential nature of Jesus' words (cf. 4:24). Ἐγώ (*egō*, I) may be emphatic (Barrett 1978: 305); the perfect λελάληκα (*lelalēka*, I have spoken), together with the plural ῥήματα (*rhēmata*, words), refers to the body of Jesus' teaching in its totality. The repetition of the stative verb (ἐστίν, *estin*) establishes "spirit" and "life" as distinct concepts (Morris 1995: 341 n. 152).

182], who also cites 1:1) and contrasts with the Jewish belief that life is found in the words of the law (5:39; cf. *Mek. Exod.* 15.26, citing Prov. 4:22; *m. ʾAbot* 6.7).

6:64–65 Jesus' focus now turns from the wider circle of his followers to the Twelve. In particular, he notes that one of them (identified specifically in 6:71 as Judas) would betray him. He now explains that this is the actual point of reference of his statement in 6:44 (reiterated in 6:65): in the final analysis, even faith (or lack thereof!) is sovereignly assigned by God.[95] "From the beginning" (ἐξ ἀρχῆς, *ex archēs*) probably refers to the point at which the Twelve attached themselves to Jesus (cf. 15:27: ἀπ' ἀρχῆς, *ap' archēs*). The emphasis thus is on Jesus' foreknowledge of this future event (Morris 1995: 341–42; see also in 6:64 the rare future participle, used to predict the betrayal, παραδώσων, *paradōsōn*). This, in turn, is "in keeping with John's picture of Jesus as going on his serene way well aware of all that concerned him, and of the crucifixion as divinely predestined" (Morris 1995: 342).

6:66–67 John 6:66 marks a watershed in this Gospel. The opening phase ἐκ τούτου (*ek toutou*) may mean "from that time" or "for this reason."[96] The magnitude of the event is apparent by the fact that not few, but many, of Jesus' followers are deserting him, and that these are called "disciples" (see commentary at 6:60–61). These former followers, literally, "went away to the things they had left behind" (ἀπῆλθον εἰς τὰ ὀπίσω, *apēlthon eis ta opisō*; cf. Luke 9:57–62) and no longer "kept moving about" (περιεπάτουν, *periepatoun* [customary imperfect]) with Jesus. In other words, they renounced their discipleship and fell away. Jesus was not the Messiah they expected.[97] The incident illustrates the truth embodied in Jesus' parable of the sower and the soils (Matt. 13:1–23 pars.).

This raises the question of whether Jesus' inner circle will desert him as well. Hence, Jesus asks, "You do not want to leave as well, do you?" However, the interrogative participle μή (*mē*) indicates that Jesus expects a negative answer (Carson 1991: 303; R. Brown 1966: 297).[98] The phrase καὶ ὑμεῖς (*kai hymeis*, you also) draws a distinction between the Twelve and other followers of Jesus (Barrett 1978: 306; cf. καὶ ἡμεῖς [*kai hēmeis*, we also] in 6:69). Remarkably, this is the first reference to "the Twelve"

95. Ridderbos 1997: 248; Carson 1991: 302; Morris 1995: 342; Barrett 1978: 305. Elsewhere in this Gospel, Jesus is shown to reiterate his earlier teaching: 8:24 (cf. 8:21); 15:20 (cf. 13:16); 16:15 (cf. 16:14).

96. So Moloney 1998: 231; Schnackenburg 1990: 2.75; Wallace (1996: 658) translates it "as a result of this"; Barrett (1978: 306) opts for both.

97. Morris 1995: 342. For further reasons, see commentary at 6:60. On people's expectations of the Messiah, see John 7 and commentary there.

98. Contra Barrett (1978: 306), who suggests that Jesus is venturing a hesitant question. This is grammatically possible but unlikely in light of the predestinarian language pervading this passage.

in this Gospel (cf. 6:70, 71; 20:24). There is no Johannine equivalent to the Synoptic account of the appointing of the twelve apostles (Matt. 10:1–4 pars.). Quite apparently, and as at other points, John assumes his readers' familiarity with the Synoptic tradition.

Although Peter's Synoptic and Johannine confessions apparently are separate events (Morris 1995: 343–44 n. 161; Witherington 1995: 160), the present passage seems to represent the Johannine equivalent to Peter's great confession at Caesarea Philippi in the Synoptics (Matt. 16:16 pars.). Since the term κύριος (*kyrios*) here (6:68; see commentary at 4:11; 6:23; 13:13) introduces a confession of Jesus as the "Holy One of God" (6:69), it does not merely (as in previous passages) address Jesus as "sir," but rather acknowledges him as Lord, which at least means "Master" and may allude to the name used for God in the LXX (Morris 1995: 344).[99] "To whom shall we go?" may refer to the possibility of transferring allegiance to a better rabbi (cf. 1:35–37). Peter's reference to "words of eternal life" in 6:68 harks back to Jesus' words in 6:63.[100]

6:68–69

The phrase "we have believed and come to know" constitutes a hendiadys (Ridderbos 1997: 249 n. 177; Schnackenburg 1990: 2.76) expressing the firmness of conviction arrived at by the Twelve as a result of a thoroughgoing process.[101] Σὺ εἶ (*sy ei*, you are) in 6:69 is emphatic (as are ὑμεῖς [*hymeis*, you] and ἡμεῖς [*hēmeis*, we] in 6:67 and 6:69). Peter's confession of Jesus as "the Holy One of God" (see additional note) anticipates later references to Jesus being set apart for God in 10:36 and 17:19. Though there is no evidence that the expression functioned as a messianic title in Judaism,[102] it clearly does so here. In the Synoptic equivalent, Peter confesses Jesus as "the Christ, the Son of the living God" (Matt. 16:16; Mark 8:29: "the Christ"; Luke 9:20: "the Christ of God"). This rare expression occurs elsewhere in the NT only in Mark 1:24 (= Luke 4:34), there uttered by a demon.[103]

Since Peter's words are representative of the Twelve, Jesus addresses them collectively.[104] Jesus' words serve to remind Peter and his associates of the origin of their calling in light of the slightly arrogant nature of Peter's statement (Carson 1991: 304). In the OT, the Israelites were

6:70–71

99. Elsewhere, Peter addresses Jesus as "Lord" in 13:6, 9, 36, 37. Later confessions of Jesus as Lord include 9:38 (the blind man) and 20:28 (Thomas).

100. The absence of the article before "words" in 6:68 points generically to the nature of Jesus' words (Morris 1995: 344–45 n. 164).

101. The words "believe" and "come to know" are roughly equivalent in John's Gospel (cf. 17:8; see Carson 1991: 303; R. Brown 1966: 298).

102. But cf. Ps. 16:10, applied to Jesus in Acts 2:27; 13:35.

103. Though see Luke 1:35; Acts 3:14 [cf. Ps. 16:10]; 4:27; 1 John 2:20; Rev. 3:7. The term is also seldom used in the OT, occasionally occurring with regard to men consecrated to God (Judg. 13:7; 16:17; Ps. 106:16).

104. Jesus' choice of *twelve* disciples likely was intended to correspond to the number of tribes of Israel (Ridderbos 1997: 250).

God's "chosen people" (Deut. 10:15; 1 Sam. 12:22). In the NT, this designation is transferred to the community of believers in Jesus (e.g., Eph. 1:4, 11; 1 Pet. 1:1–2; 2:9). Several times in John's Gospel, Jesus refers to the choosing of his disciples (cf. 13:18; 15:16, 19). Peter's confession here is taken as a confirmation of the efficacy of Jesus' choice of the Twelve (with the exception of Judas). This doubtless was intended to affirm Jesus' inner circle in their belief in light of the mass defection by other followers.

Jesus' statement regarding his choice of the Twelve is sharply contrasted with the designation of Judas (the betrayer [6:71]) as "a devil."[105] Later in the Gospel, the connection between Satan and Judas is made even more explicit (13:2, 27). As Schlatter (1948: 185) notes, Judas's apostasy does not truly frustrate God's election, for this election (in a broader sense) allows for the possibility of human failure. Yet John refrained from formulating a comprehensive theory or making this the subject of etiological or teleological conjecture. What was required was the total surrender of one's human religious ideas in sheer faith.

As to the phrase "Judas, the son of Simon Iscariot," at least six interpretations of "Iscariot" have been advanced, the most likely being "man of Kerioth" (Carson 1984: 239–40; Morris 1995: 345 n. 167; Beasley-Murray 1999: 85 n. u; Borchert 1996: 276). It was common in that day for father and son to have the same last name—especially here if "Kerioth" refers to their hometown. "Kerioth" may refer to the Kerioth Hezron in Judea (i.e., Hazor) mentioned in Josh. 15:25 or to the Kerioth in Moab referred to in Jer. 48:24. This would mean that Judas was the only non-Galilean among the Twelve.

The final explanatory phrase makes explicit why Judas is called "a devil" in the preceding verse: he later was to betray Jesus. The verb ἔμελλεν (emellen, he was about) before παραδιδόναι (paradidonai, to betray) gives a sense of certainty to Judas's betrayal (Morris 1995: 346). The concluding phrase, "one of the Twelve," sounds an ominous note, underscoring the gravity of one of Jesus' inner circle betraying his master.

Additional Notes

6:1. Bultmann (1971: 209–10) famously suggested switching the order of John 5 and 6, based on the seemingly abrupt reference to Galilee in 6:1. However, the traditional order should be maintained, especially in light of the complete absence of MSS evidence to the contrary.[106] Rather

105. Though the phrase could be rendered "one of you is *the* devil" (see Carson 1991: 304; Wallace 1996: 249, 265), this is not necessary, and contextually is less likely than the rendering "a devil." See also Matt. 16:23 (= Mark 8:33), where Peter is rebuked as "Satan" by Jesus. In John 8:44, Jesus calls the Pharisees children of the devil.

106. So Carson 1991: 267; cf. Ridderbos 1997: 208–9; Barrett 1978: 272; Witherington 1995: 385; contra R. Brown 1966: 235–36; Schnackenburg 1990: 2.5–9.

than geography, the references to the festivals should be considered determinative in reconstructing the sequence of events in these chapters (Moloney 1998: 193–94).[107]

6:14. There is some question as to whether the plural reading σημεῖα (𝔓⁷⁵ B) or the singular reading σημεῖον (the vast majority of MSS and commentators) is original. Among the few who prefer the plural is Anderson (1996: 174); though see the opinion of the UBS committee (Metzger 1994: 181) that the plural likely arose from scribal assimilation to 2:23 and 6:2.

6:22. The additional words after ἕν in 6:22 are scribal additions intended to illumine the text, specifically about the boat in question (Beasley-Murray 1999: 84 n. h; Barrett 1978: 285).

6:47. The reading "in me," which follows "believes" in some MSS, probably is not original. See Schnackenburg 1990: 2.53; Beasley-Murray 1999: 85 n. p.

6:69. The reading "the Holy One of God" clearly is original (𝔓⁷⁵ ℵ B C*); the variants "the Christ, the Holy One of God" (𝔓⁶⁶) and "the Christ the Son of [the living] God" (Byzantine MSS and some Fathers) represent rather transparent attempts at aligning the present passage with Matt. 16:16 (Beasley-Murray 1999: 85 n. t). See also additional note on 1:34.

---

107. See also Thielman (1991: 180), who suggests that the seemingly abrupt transition from 5:47 to 6:1 may be an instance of "a purposeful attempt at obscurity" (on which, see ibid., pp. 175–77). According to Thielman, the Fourth Evangelist may have "obscured the organizational pattern of his Gospel by design—to keep out those whose eyes were blind and whose hearts hard (12.40)" (p. 181). See also the work of Kellum (2005), especially pp. 225–26.

3. Jesus at the Feast of Tabernacles (7:1–8:59)

The Feast of Tabernacles was celebrated in the fall (September/October), while the next festival mentioned in John's Gospel, the Feast of Dedication, fell in the winter (10:22), later followed by Jesus' final Passover (13:1).[1] We thus enter the last half year of Jesus' public ministry. Chapters 7 and 8 (excluding the story of the adulterous woman) form a narrative unit (Moloney 2002),[2] followed by the account of the man born blind (ch. 9)—the sixth sign—and Jesus' good shepherd discourse (ch. 10). With this, Jesus' public ministry nears its conclusion. He returns to the place where John first baptized, hence where he started his own ministry (10:40), thus completing the cycle.[3] The controversy with the Jews culminates in Jesus' climactic sign (ch. 11) and his preparation for burial (ch. 12), followed by the final instruction of his inner circle (chs. 13–17).

In chapter 7, conflict continues to escalate. Several months have passed since the events surrounding Jesus' Galilean Passover. By all appearances, Jesus' ministry is in a state of crisis. Jesus stays away from Judea, ministering in Galilee instead, because the Jews in Judea were waiting to take his life.[4] The dynamic of rejection builds steadily: Jesus is rejected not only in his native Galilee (4:44) and in Judea (7:1)—and

1. For a thorough discussion of the historical background for the Feast of Tabernacles, see Moloney 1998: 232–36; 2002. See also Carson 1991: 304–5.

2. Keener (2003: 703) notes that chapters 7 and 8 are framed by ἐν κρυπτῷ and ἐκρύβη in 7:4 and 8:59 respectively to form a messianic secret motif.

3. Ridderbos (1997: 253) considers chapters 7–10 to constitute a unit, marked by Jesus' "encounters, conversations, and confrontations" with the Jews. More in depth is the analysis by Schenke (1989: esp. 186), who likewise defends the unity of chapters 7–10 dramatically developing the escalating conflict regarding Jesus. Schenke discerns three major scenes (7:10–8:59; 9:1–10:21; 10:22–39) plus a prologue (7:1–9) and an epilogue (10:40–42). In chapters 7–8 (scene I, taking place in the Jerusalem temple), Schenke finds seven smaller scenes (7:10–13, 14–31, 32–36, 37–44, 45–52; 8:12–20, 21–59) moving from diversity of opinion regarding Jesus to a united front against him. Scene II is staged in Jerusalem and can also be divided into seven smaller scenes (9:1–7, 8–12, 13–17, 18–23, 24–34, 35–39; 9:40–10:21). The location of scene III is once again the temple. A very similar division of chapter 7 is found in Neyrey 1996 (followed in the discussion below). On the thematic unity of the present unit, see also Dodd 1953: 345–54. On the thematic unity and development of 7:1–36, see Attridge 1980.

4. Stibbe (1993: 92) notes, "Throughout chapter 7, Jesus is elusive in relation to his past origins, his present language and movements, and to his future destiny in glory."

thus by the Jewry as a whole (cf. 1:11)—but even by the members of his own family. The evangelist has already revealed that one of the Twelve will betray Jesus (6:71). Thus, when the curtain opens to the second act of the first half of the Johannine drama, it does so on a note of profound uncertainty. An entire year may have passed since Jesus' last major clash with the Jerusalem authorities. In what may be the following year's Feast of Tabernacles (A.D. 32), Jesus braces himself once again for intense opposition.[5]

5. It may not be coincidental that chapters 7 and 8 contain not a single reference to Jesus' disciples (see commentary at 9:2).

a. First Teaching Cycle (7:1–52)

This is now the third (and, as it turns out, final) trip of Jesus to the Jewish capital (cf. 2:13; 5:1), which finds Jesus spending two months in Jerusalem from the Feast of Tabernacles to the Feast of Dedication (10:22). At this stage of Jesus' ministry, he is increasingly viewed within the matrix of messianic expectations. Was the Coming One to emerge from secret, mysterious beginnings (7:4, 10, 27) or was he a known figure of Davidic descent (7:41–42)? Did Jesus' miracles identify him as Messiah (7:21, 31)? Two important purposes guide the evangelist's presentation: Jesus' fulfillment of Tabernacles symbolism, and representative questions regarding Jesus' identity (Köstenberger 1998b: 94–96).[1]

The following pattern of three recurring cycles can be discerned: (1) Jesus travels to Jerusalem and teaches there (7:10–24, 37–39); (2) Jesus' teaching elicits debate and speculation (7:25–31, 40–44); (3) the Jewish authorities attempt to arrest Jesus (7:32–36, 45–52) (Carson 1991: 310–11; Barrett 1978: 316). The narrative builds toward the climax of 7:37b–38, where Jesus issues the invitation to all who are thirsty to come to him and drink, so that believers would, once the Spirit had been given, become sources of "streams of living water." Thus, in keeping with the theme underlying Tabernacles, "With joy you will draw water from the wells of salvation" (Isa. 12:3), the prophetic vision of Isa. 58:11 would be fulfilled.

   i. The unbelief of Jesus' brothers (7:1–9)
   ii. Jesus goes to the feast (7:10–13)
  iii. Jesus teaches at the feast (7:14–24)
  iv. Is Jesus the Christ? (7:25–44)
   v. The unbelief of the Jewish leaders (7:45–52)

Exegesis and Exposition

[1]And after these things Jesus was moving about in Galilee. For he did not want to move about in Judea, because the Jews there were seeking to kill him.

---

1. The story of the adulterous woman in 7:53–8:11 is not found in the earliest MSS of John's Gospel and was almost certainly not part of the Gospel the way John wrote it. Once this account is removed from the Gospel, it becomes evident that 8:12 picks up where 7:52 left off, restoring the unity of 7:1–52 and 8:12–59, which will be dealt with here as one coherent section. See further the excursus on 7:53–8:11 below.

²Yet the Jewish Feast of Tabernacles was near. ³So his brothers said to him, "Leave from here and go to Judea, so that your disciples there may also see the works that you are performing. ⁴For no one does anything in secret yet himself seeks to be a public figure. Since you are doing these things, show yourself to the world." ⁵(For not even his brothers were believing in him.) ⁶So Jesus said to them, "My time has not yet come—but your time is always right. ⁷The world cannot hate you, but it hates me, because I bear witness concerning it—that its works are evil. ⁸You go up to the feast; I am ⌜not⌝ going up to this feast, because my time has not yet been completed." ⁹And having said these things, he stayed in Galilee.

¹⁰But when his brothers had gone up to the feast, then he also went up, not publicly, ⌜but in secret⌝. ¹¹Now the Jewish leaders were looking for him at the feast and were saying, "Where is that fellow?" ¹²And there was much grumbling about him among the crowds. Some were saying, "He is a good man." But others were saying, "No, he is deceiving the people." ¹³Yet no one was speaking about him in public for fear of the Jews.

¹⁴Yet when it was already halfway through the feast, Jesus went up to the temple area and started teaching. ¹⁵So the Jews were amazed, saying, "How can he be so educated without having been formally taught?" ¹⁶So Jesus answered them and said, "My teaching is not my own, but is from the one who sent me. ¹⁷If anyone wants to do his will, he will know whether my teaching is from God or whether I speak of my own accord. ¹⁸The one who speaks on his own accord seeks his own honor. The one who seeks the honor of the one who sent him is true, and there is no unrighteousness in him. ¹⁹Has not Moses given you the law? And yet not one of you does what is written in the law. Why are you trying to kill me?" ²⁰The crowd answered, "You have a demon! Who is trying to kill you?" ²¹Jesus answered and said to them, "I did one work, and all of you are amazed. ²²This is why Moses gave you circumcision—yet it was not Moses but the patriarchs—and you circumcise a boy on the Sabbath. ²³If a boy can receive circumcision on the Sabbath, so that the law of Moses may not be broken, why are you angry with me because I made an entire man well on the Sabbath? ²⁴Stop judging by mere appearances, but exercise righteous judgment."

²⁵Then some from Jerusalem were saying, "Isn't this the one they are trying to kill? ²⁶But look, he's speaking openly, and no one is saying a thing to him! The rulers have not concluded that he is the Christ, have they? ²⁷But we know where this one is from; yet when the Christ comes, no one will know where he is from." ²⁸Then Jesus, still teaching in the temple area, cried out, saying, "You know me, and you know where I am from. I have not come on my own accord, but the one who sent me is true—the one whom you do not know. ²⁹Yet I know him, because I am from him, and he sent me." ³⁰At this they were trying to arrest him, yet no one laid a hand on him, because his time had not yet come. ³¹And many in the crowd believed in him and were saying, "The Christ, when he comes, will not perform more signs than he has done, will he?"

³²The Pharisees heard the crowd whispering these things about him, and the chief priests and Pharisees sent temple guards to arrest him. ³³So Jesus said, "I am with you a little longer, and then I go to the one who sent me. ³⁴You will look for me, but you will not find me, and where I am, you cannot come." ³⁵Then the Jews said to one another, "Where is he about to go that we will not be able to find him? Surely, he isn't planning to go into the Greek diaspora and teach the Greeks! ³⁶What is this statement that he made, 'You will look for me, but you will not find me, and where I am, you cannot come'?"

³⁷On the last, greatest day of the feast, Jesus stood up and cried out, saying, "If anyone thirsts, let him come to me and drink. ³⁸Whoever believes in me, as Scripture has said, rivers of living water will flow from within him." ³⁹(This he said concerning the Spirit, whom those who believed in him were about to receive. For the Spirit had not yet been given, because Jesus had not yet been glorified.)

⁴⁰So some from the crowd who had heard these words were saying, "He truly is the Prophet." ⁴¹Others were saying, "He is the Christ." Yet others were saying, "The Christ doesn't come from Galilee, does he? ⁴²Doesn't Scripture say that the Christ will come from the seed of David and from Bethlehem, the village where David was?" ⁴³So there arose division in the crowd on account of him. ⁴⁴And some of them wanted to arrest him, but no one laid hands on him.

⁴⁵Then the temple guards went to the chief priests and Pharisees, and they said to them, "Why didn't you bring him?" ⁴⁶The guards answered, "No one ever spoke like this man." ⁴⁷So the Pharisees answered them, "You have not been deceived as well, have you? ⁴⁸Has anyone of the rulers believed in him, or any of the Pharisees? ⁴⁹But this crowd that does not know the law—they are accursed." ⁵⁰Nicodemus (the one who had come to him [Jesus] earlier, being one of them) said to them, ⁵¹"Our law does not condemn a man unless you first hear from him and know what he is doing, does it?" ⁵²They answered and said to him, "You are not from Galilee as well, are you? Look, and you will see that no ⌜prophet⌝ arises from Galilee."

i. The Unbelief of Jesus' Brothers (7:1–9)

7:1–2 The scene is set in the opening two verses. "After this" does not establish tight connections but provides only a sequence of events;[2] it loosely connects what follows with events surrounding the miraculous feeding (Westcott 1908: 261). Jesus, as the Johannine "elusive Christ," "moved about" (περιεπάτει, *periepatei*) in Galilee[3] rather than Judea, because "the Jews there were seeking to kill him." This continues the escalating

---

2. Carson 1991: 305; Borchert 1996: 279; Barrett 1978: 309; see commentary at 2:12 and at 7:2.
3. The verb tense (a progressive imperfect [Wallace 1996: 543–44]) conveys the notion of Jesus continually moving about through the region of Galilee. Carson (1991: 305) proposes the rendering "continued around Galilee."

pattern of hostility (cf. 5:10, 18; 7:19–20).[4] Because Galilee and Judea were under different jurisdictions (Herod Antipas and the Roman prefect, respectively), it would have afforded a certain amount of protection for Jesus to stay away from Judea, where the Jews were looking for a way to take his life (but see Luke 13:31).

Tabernacles was celebrated from 15 to 21 Tishri, which fell in September or October (Lev. 23:34; in A.D. 32, it was celebrated September 10–17), after the grape harvest and two months prior to Dedication.[5] It followed shortly after the Day of Atonement and marked the conclusion of the annual cycle of religious festivals that began with Passover and Unleavened Bread six months earlier. Originally a harvest festival, Tabernacles (also called the "Feast of Booths") recalled God's provision for his people during the wilderness wanderings (Lev. 23:42–43; cf. Matt. 17:4 pars.). Festivities lasted seven days, culminating in an eighth day of special celebration and festive assembly. Owing to the daily solemn outpouring of water during the festival (cf. Num. 28:7; Isa. 12:3), Tabernacles came to be associated with eschatological hopes (cf. Zech. 14:16–19). Immensely popular, it was simply called "the Feast" by the Jews.[6]

The most natural understanding of the expression "Jesus' brothers" is that "brothers" refers to other naturally born sons of Mary, younger, of course, than Jesus (see commentary at 2:12). His brothers' urging for Jesus to display his credentials publicly in Judea "so that your disciples there may also see the works you are performing"[7] could have stung: though the Twelve continued with Jesus (6:67–69), many—most—of his other followers had fallen away (6:60, 66). At the upcoming Jerusalem festival, Jesus (so his brothers tell him) has an opportunity to reverse his fortunes.[8]

7:3–9

---

4. Beasley-Murray (1999: 106 [cf. Schnackenburg 1990: 2.143]) plausibly suggests that the references to the Jews in 7:1 and 7:13 form an *inclusio*, rendering the passage an introduction to the following narrative.

5. For helpful information on the particulars of the feast, see Avi-Yonah 1964: 144. See also the mishnaic tractate *Sukkah* (esp. *m. Sukkah* 5.2–4). Old Testament references include Lev. 23:33–43; Num. 29:12–39; Neh. 8:13–18; Hos. 12:9; Zech. 14:16–19.

6. For example, 1 Kings 8:2, 65; 12:32; 2 Chron. 5:3; 7:8; Neh. 8:14, 18; Ps. 81:3; Ezek. 45:25; Str-B 2:774. Josephus (*Ant.* 8.4.1 §100) called it "the greatest and holiest feast of the Jews."

7. The conjunction ἵνα (*hina*, so that) used with the future indicative represents a Johannine style characteristic (Wallace 1996: 699).

8. See Laney 1992: 138–39. The background for this may be the brothers' memory of Jesus' feat at the wedding of Cana (2:1–12) and his subsequent apparent popularity in Jerusalem (2:23–25; Ridderbos 1997: 257–58; Barrett 1978: 311). Kruse (2003: 182) proposes that the recent defection of many disciples may have been to the detriment of the family honor, which Jesus' brothers wanted restored. Ποιεῖ καὶ ζητεῖ in 7:4 represents Hebraic parataxis (Schnackenburg 1990: 2.139).

In principle, the advice of Jesus' brothers is correct, although their statement betrays ignorance regarding the Jewish authorities' plot against Jesus. What is more, for Jesus' brothers to think that the Messiah and Son of God is in need of their advice and coaching constitutes the height of presumption. The brothers' words also betray misunderstanding, for it is not Jesus' failure to "show himself to the world" that impedes the reception of his message but the world's sinful rejection of its Creator (Carson 1991: 305–6). Worse still, their attitude resembles Satan's at Jesus' temptation, who misconstrued Jesus' messianic calling in self-seeking terms (Matt. 4:5–7 par.; see R. Brown 1966: 306–8; Borchert 1996: 280–81). This reveals not so much doubt in Jesus' miracle-working abilities as it does a fundamental misunderstanding of who he is (Carson 1991: 307).

To be sure, Jesus ultimately must be revealed as Messiah. But in the face of persecution, he chooses a more gradual, judicious approach (though this is not a matter of secrecy or deception: see 18:20; cf. 7:14).[9] Jesus' brothers, by contrast, persist in their unbelief (ἐπίστευον [episteuon, they were (not) believing] is an imperfect; see Morris 1995: 349, 351), so the world cannot hate them (7:7).[10] For this reason, Jesus tells his brothers, "My time has not yet come; but your time is always right."[11] Jesus' situation is different from that of his unbelieving relatives: what they do is inconsequential; Jesus is a marked man who must plan his steps carefully (Schnackenburg 1990: 2.140). It was well-established Jewish belief that every man had his time;[12] Jesus' statement that his brothers had no particular "time" but that their "time" was always present was therefore striking, even novel.

Jesus asserts that the world cannot hate his brothers (presumably because they were part of it—quite an indictment [so Carson 1991: 308]), but the world "hates me, because I bear witness concerning it—that its works are evil" (7:7).[13] Jesus' comment "I am not [yet] going up to

9. Note the *inclusio* of 7:4 and 8:59 (Keener 2003: 703). Cf. Matt. 10:26 and the "messianic secret" motif in the Synoptics (Barrett 1978: 311; Carson 1991: 310, referring to Lindars 1972: 283).

10. Keener (2003: 705) observes that the statement in 7:5 ("not even his brothers were believing in him") follows on the heels of the apostasy of many of Jesus' disciples (6:66), adding to a wave of unbelief mounting against Jesus. Keener (2003: 706, citing D. M. Smith 1999: 168) also adduces the incident recounted in Mark 3:21, 31–35.

11. Paraphrased, this may mean "You can go anywhere you please, any time you want; I cannot" (cf. Ridderbos 1997: 258–59). Only in the present context is the term καιρός (*kairos*, time) used to denote Jesus' (God-appointed) "time"; elsewhere the expression is ὥρα, *hōra* (e.g., 2:4; see R. Brown 1966: 306; Carson 1991: 307–8; Morris 1995: 351–53).

12. See Eccles. 3:1 (cf. *Eccles. Rab.* 3.1) and the rabbinic and Qumran material cited in Köstenberger 2002c: 73.

13. The personal pronoun ἐμέ (*eme*, me) is emphatic (Morris 1995: 353 n. 20). The statement harks back to the evangelist's comments in 3:19–20 (Ridderbos 1997: 258–59; see, later, 7:19; 8:31–59; 9:39–41; 16:8–11).

this feast" (7:8 [see additional note]) may merely imply that he is not going up *now* (Morris 1995: 354–55) until the Father directs him to do so (Carson 1991: 308–9). As at 2:4, Jesus is not going to be pressured to act before his time.[14] The statement in 7:10 that Jesus went up "not publicly, but in secret" may also be designed to alleviate the apparent contradiction (Ridderbos 1997: 259–60).[15] "This feast" may be emphatic (so Moloney 1998: 238): Jesus may attend later festivals, but not necessarily this one. Note that apparently Jesus had already chosen to celebrate the Passover in Galilee (6:1–4), perhaps to stay out of harm's way for the time being.

ii. Jesus Goes to the Feast (7:10–13)

7:10–13

After setting the stage, the evangelist now commences his narration of the dramatically escalating conflict surrounding Jesus. The reader is told that despite what might have seemed to be the implication from 7:1–9, Jesus later follows, "not publicly, but in secret" (cf. 7:4; see additional note). Rather than making the journey to Jerusalem with the pilgrim caravan, Jesus goes later by himself. This he judges necessary in order not to hasten the time of his execution in light of mounting opposition. Moreover, the fact that he does not travel with his extended family (which was customary) points to Jesus' increasing isolation even among his flesh-and-blood relations.[16]

Now the Jewish leaders were looking for him at the feast (cf. 7:1).[17] In the following narratives John frequently resorts to the device of "contradictory voices" (7:12, 40–42; 9:16; 10:19–21). Later, the Ἰουδαῖοι (*Ioudaioi*) are identified as Pharisees (7:32, 47–48) and members of the Sanhedrin ("authorities," "rulers," "chief priests" [7:26, 32b, 45, 48]), which would have included Sadducees as well. "Where is that fellow?" echoes similar statements at other occasions (cf. 5:12; 9:12).[18] This being the time of a Jewish festival in Jerusalem, the crowds are composed of Judeans, Galileans, and Diaspora Jews.[19] The crowds play an important role particularly in chapters 7–12.

---

14. Schnackenburg 1990: 2.142. Barrett (1978: 313) notes the similar dynamic at a different time in Jesus' ministry (Mark 9:30; 10:1).

15. To "go up" (ἀναβαίνω, *anabainō*) to Jerusalem is a common expression no matter what one's geographical origination (cf. 5:1). Because the term is used later with reference to Jesus' ascension to the Father, some see an allusion to Jesus' glorification (Carson 1991: 309: "just possible"). This is unlikely (Michaels 1989: 127; Lindars 1972: 285) and in any case is not the primary referent (contra R. Brown 1966: 308).

16. How large the company of travelers might be can be seen from the incident recounted in Luke 2:44, in which Joseph and Mary looked for the boy Jesus for the better part of an entire day.

17. The use of ζητέω (*zēteō*, look for) in 7:11 reinforces the hostile intent from its use in 7:1 (Schnackenburg 1990: 2.143).

18. Westcott (1908: 264–65) detects in the question a mixture of ill will and curiosity.

19. The plural "crowds" (see commentary at 6:2) is used only here in John.

"Some" translates οἱ (*hoi*); a mild contrast is implied (Wallace 1996: 212–13). "No, he is deceiving the people" resembles a similar charge recorded by Matthew (27:63; cf. Luke 23:2; see R. Brown 1966: 307). Josephus names several first-century deceivers.[20] Jesus himself is called a deceiver in later Jewish literature (*b. Sanh.* 43a; cf. *b. Soṭah* 47a). According to Jewish law, the punishment for leading people astray was stoning, further distinguishing between those who mislead an individual and those who lead an entire town astray (*m. Sanh.* 7.4, 10). Deuteronomy 13:1–11 stipulates that a false prophet must die "because he . . . has tried to turn you from the way the Lord your God commanded you to follow." "The Jews" who are feared are the Jerusalem authorities, represented by the Sanhedrin (cf. John 9:22; 12:42; 19:12, 38; 20:19).

iii. Jesus Teaches at the Feast (7:14–24)

7:14–15   The present section constitutes the second smaller scene in the unfolding drama.[21] "Halfway" through the feast is a vague expression that may refer to the exact middle of the feast (i.e., the fourth day) or merely to a time other than the first or the last day (cf. 7:37). "Jesus went up to the temple courts and began to teach" is one of the few references to Jesus teaching in John.[22] The main temple building (ναός, *naos* [cf. 2:19–21]) was surrounded by several courts (ἱερόν, *hieron*, temple area), including the court of women, the court of (Israelite) men, and the court of the Gentiles (cf. 2:14–15; 5:14; 8:59; 10:23; 11:56). Jesus probably is teaching here in one of the outer porticoes (cf. 7:28; 8:20; 18:20; see commentary at 7:4). "The Jews" here probably refers to the Judean crowds as well as to the Jewish authorities (Ridderbos 1997: 262 n. 28).

"How can he be so educated without having been formally taught?"[23] It was common for Jewish males in Jesus' day to be able both to read and write and to have a basic understanding of the Scriptures. What was unusual, however, was Jesus' ability to carry on a sustained discourse in the manner of the rabbis, including frequent references to Scripture. Moreover, whereas the rabbis of Jesus' day would teach by frequent

20. See the list in Köstenberger 2002c: 74. For a general survey, see Heard, *DJG* 688–98.

21. Motyer (1997: 152–53) plausibly suggests that 7:14–24 is designed to enable the reader to make an appropriate judgment concerning the death of Jesus. If the Jews are correct, Jesus is a sinner, demon-possessed, and the like. If Jesus' claims are valid, it is the Jews who are misleading the people, not Jesus. Keener (2003: 721) discerns a common structure in 7:14–36 and 7:37–52: (1) Jesus teaches in the temple (7:14–24; 7:37–39), (2) people speculate about his identity (7:25–29, 31; 7:40–43), and (3) an attempt to arrest him fails (7:30, 32–36; 7:44–52, citing Talbert 1992: 145, following Lindars).

22. See 6:59; 8:20; cf. Mark 11:27; see Ridderbos 1997: 261–62. As in 5:1 and 7:8, there is the idea of "going up," to Jerusalem and then to the temple itself.

23. Note that many in Jerusalem were pilgrims from places where Jesus had never been, so this was their first acquaintance with his teachings (Morris 1995: 359). A similar question is raised regarding Jesus' followers in Acts 4:13.

appeal to other authorities, Jesus regularly prefaced his teachings by asserting unique authority: "You have heard that it was said, but I tell you"; "I tell you the truth"; "Truly, truly, I say to you" (Riesner 1981: 97–245). Increasingly, however, it was not enough for a Jew to master the written Scriptures or even the oral law; formal rabbinic training became the norm.[24]

"My teaching is not my own."[25] The age in which Jesus lived did not prize   **7:16–17**
originality. If Jesus had acknowledged that he was self-taught or had originated his own message, he would have been immediately discredited for arrogance. In the Judaism of his day, there was only one way to teach and learn the word and will of God: through Scripture (Torah) and its interpretation. In appealing to someone other than himself as the authority for his teaching, Jesus is not unlike other rabbis of his day. The rabbis referred back to the earlier rabbis; Jesus appeals to the Father, claiming direct knowledge from God (8:28) (Carson 1991: 312; Morris 1995: 359–60).

Anyone who is prepared to do God's will is promised that he or she will know whether Jesus' teaching is of human or divine origin. Discipleship is not merely embracing certain ideas; it also involves acting on them ("do God's will"; cf. 6:29).[26] Jesus knew this from personal experience (5:19–20). The same truth was commonly recognized by contemporary rabbis and their followers. Jesus' disciples frequently were called to act on the basis of their convictions. They left their natural relations and walk of life and helped their master in his ministry in a variety of ways (Köstenberger 1998b: 122–24).

"The one who speaks . . . there is no unrighteousness in him" recalls   **7:18–20**
5:41–47 and may respond to the earlier remark by Jesus' brothers (see 7:3–4) (R. Brown 1966: 312). This verse is composed of maxims. The central contrast seems to be between a false prophet, who deserves to be executed (Deut. 18:9–22), and Jesus, the Son of God, who must be followed.

"Has not Moses given you the law?" It was cause for great pride among the Jews that they were the recipients of the law (Rom. 2:17; 9:4). The Pharisees saw themselves as disciples of Moses (John 9:28). Jesus returns to Moses here in order to develop more thoroughly what God's will is and to point out that people fail to recognize Jesus' teaching because

---

24. In the post-Jamnia period (after ca. A.D. 90), the term "rabbi" came to refer exclusively to those who had undergone formal rabbinic training. See *b. Soṭah* 22a (cited in Köstenberger 2002c: 74–75; cf. Str-B 2:486; Beasley-Murray 1999: 108). See also commentary at 7:49.

25. Apart from 7:16–17, διδαχή (*didachē*, teaching) occurs in John's Gospel only in 18:19.

26. So Carson 1991: 312–13; R. Brown 1966: 316; Morris 1995: 360; Barrett 1978: 318; Kruse 2003: 185.

they have chosen not to do God's will, to obey the law (Carson 1991: 313–14). "Keeps the law" (lit., "does the law") is a rabbinic expression meaning to act in such a way that the law is done. Thus, it is said of Abraham that he "kept [lit., 'did'] the entire Torah even before it had come" (*t. Qidd.* 5.21).[27]

The accusation "you have a demon" has parallels in this and in the other canonical Gospels (cf. 8:48; 10:20; Matt. 12:24 pars.).[28] The same charge was leveled against the Baptist (Matt. 11:18). Interestingly, John features no accounts of demon exorcisms. People's ignorance of their leaders' scheming, and their attribution to Jesus of paranoia and delusions of grandeur, represent yet another instance of Johannine irony (Carson 1991: 314; Moloney 1998: 245; Lindars 1972: 295–96).

7:21–24 "I did one work." Here Jesus probably is referring to the healing of the invalid in John 5. "This is why Moses gave you circumcision—yet it was not Moses but the patriarchs." As Jesus (John?) parenthetically points out, circumcision actually was instituted before Moses with Abraham (Gen. 17:9–14) in the time of the patriarchs. "And you circumcise a boy on the Sabbath. If a boy can receive circumcision on the Sabbath, so that the law of Moses may not be broken, why are you angry with me because I made an entire man well on the Sabbath?" Jesus here uses the common rabbinic argument "from the lesser to the greater" (Ridderbos 1997: 265–66; see commentary at 5:47). The difficulty that Jesus raised was that two commandments of God apparently conflicted with one another. The Jews were to circumcise their males on the eighth day after birth (Lev. 12:3); yet, no regular work was to be performed on the Sabbath. What should be done when the eighth day fell on a Sabbath? The Jews had always concluded that it was permissible to go ahead and circumcise on the eighth day regardless of whether it fell on a Sabbath or not.[29]

This settled the "lesser" issue. But what about the "greater" one of "making an entire man well on the Sabbath"? Again, later rabbinic teaching generally concurred that, granted the lesser premise that circumcision (which "perfects" but one member of the human body) supersedes the Sabbath commandment, the saving of the entire body transcends it all the more.[30] Jesus concludes his argument with a stinging rebuke: "Stop judging by mere appearances, but exercise righteous judgment." This

---

27. See also Rom. 2:13; Gal. 3:10 (quoting Deut. 27:26), 12 (citing Lev. 18:5).

28. See also Josephus, *J.W.* 6.5.3 §§300–309 (cited in Köstenberger 2002c: 75). Keener (2003: 715) observes that Jesus will reverse this charge and in 8:41, 44 identify the devil as the "father" of "the Jews."

29. Thus Rabbi Yose b. Ḥalafta (ca. A.D. 140–65) said, "Great is circumcision which overrides even the rigor of the Sabbath" (*m. Ned.* 3.11; cf. *m. Šabb.* 18.3; 19.1–3; the midrash *Tanḥuma* 19b).

30. See the material cited in Köstenberger 2002c: 76 and Keener 2003: 717.

challenge has many formal OT parallels.[31] While in the first instance it is a general warning and exhortation to Jesus' original audience, the verse on a secondary level also addresses the readers of John's Gospel (Ridderbos 1997: 266). Had the Jews judged righteously, they would have realized that Jesus fulfilled the law in a manner indicated by the law (cf. 1:17; see Ridderbos 1997: 266; Carson 1991: 316). The repeated appeals to the law (7:19, 23) and the legal terminology (7:24) strike a forensic note that serves to continue the trial set in motion in John 5: "The fact that a death sentence hangs precariously over Jesus' head shows that the outcome of the argument here is a matter of life and death" (Stibbe 1993: 91).

iv. Is Jesus the Christ? (7:25–44)

The next three smaller scenes (7:25–31, 32–36, 37–44) center on the critical question "Is Jesus the Christ?" The people referred to by the term Ἰεροσολυμῖται (*Ierosolymitai*, people of Jerusalem [elsewhere in the NT only in Mark 1:5]) may represent a third group, along with "the Jews" (7:1, 11) and "the crowd" (7:20, 31). These Jerusalem residents would have been more familiar with the conflict between Jesus and the Jewish leaders than would the crowd of pilgrims (Barrett 1978: 321; Ridderbos 1997: 267; Carson 1991: 317). Thus, they ask tentatively, "The rulers have not concluded that he is the Christ, have they?"[32] Perhaps, they argue, "the rulers"—that is, the Sanhedrin (cf. 7:48; 12:42; see Schürer 1973–79: 2.199–226)—have uncovered new evidence to suggest that Jesus is indeed the Christ (Carson 1991: 317; Morris 1995: 365; Barrett 1978: 321).

7:25–27

"But" (ἀλλά, *alla*)—a strong adversative (Morris 1995: 365 n. 52)—the crowd quickly discards the possibility that Jesus might be the Christ. For they know where "this one" (the expression seems at least mildly disdainful [Ridderbos 1997: 268]) is from (Galilee; cf. 6:42); the Christ's origins, on the other hand, will be unknown—an instance of Johannine irony (cf. 9:29).[33] According to rabbinic teaching, some believed that

31. E.g., Deut. 16:18–19; Isa. 11:3–4; Zech. 7:9. See also John 5:22–30 (esp. 5:30). Grammatically, Μὴ κρίνετε (*mē krinete*, stop judging) enjoins people to cease an action rather than merely prohibiting it (Carson 1991: 316). Κρίσιν κρίνετε (*krisin krinete*, lit., "judge judgment") represents a cognate accusative construction (Ridderbos 1997: 266 n. 40; Wallace 1996: 190).

32. Παρρησίᾳ (*parrēsia*, openly) is a dative of manner or adverbial dative (Wallace 1996: 162). "They are not saying a word to him" is a rabbinic expression reflecting tacit approval (R. Brown 1966: 313). "Said R. Judah, 'Helene's *sukkah* [tabernacle] was twenty cubits tall, and sages went in and out, when visiting her, and not one of them said a thing'" (*t. Sukkah* 1.1). The interrogative particle μήποτε (*mēpote*) signals a tentative question (Carson 1991: 317; Barrett 1978: 321), the gist being "Do the rulers perhaps actually [μήποτε ἀληθῶς] know that he is the Christ?"

33. For OT information regarding the origins of the Messiah, see Mic. 5:2; Dan. 7:13. For apocalyptic references, see 1 Enoch 48:6; 2 Esdr. (4 Ezra) 13:51–52 (these may be post-Christian). See also Justin, *Dial.* 8.4 (cited in Kruse 2003: 188).

the Messiah would be born of flesh and blood yet be wholly unknown until he set out to procure Israel's redemption (Carson 1991: 317–18). Others in Judaism, such as the priests and scribes summoned by Herod in Matt. 2:1–6, were quite sure about the geographic origin of the Messiah (cf. John 7:42).[34] Apparently, however, those authorities could tell Herod little else about the Messiah's family, circumstances, or other information.

7:28–31   The cumulative christological thought of 7:28–29 is closely related to Matt. 11:27 and Luke 10:22 (Carson 1991: 318). Then Jesus, still teaching in the temple courts (see commentary at 7:14), "cried out."[35] He proceeds to affirm the people's statement, but he points out that, ironically, they do not know all there is to know (Ridderbos 1997: 269; Carson 1991: 318; Morris 1995: 366):[36] "As they celebrate their loyalty to the one true God at the feast, they are rejecting Jesus, the Sent One of the one true God" (Moloney 1998: 247).

"The one whom you do not know": this flat denial would have been a tremendous insult to the faithful Jews gathered at this greatest of feasts (cf. 4:22; Rom. 2:17–21). Jesus will elaborate on this charge in the context of the ensuing "paternity dispute" (see 8:19, 27, 55). Just as Jesus denied devising his own teaching (7:16), so also he denies that his mission is self-initiated (Morris 1995: 366–67). By implication (cf. 7:27), the question regarding Jesus' origin is not primarily geographical in nature (Judea versus Galilee), but spiritual: is his authority merely of human derivation, or has he been divinely commissioned? Jesus claims the latter (cf. 2:18–22; 3:1–15; 4:19–24). Again, an attempt at arresting (πιάζω, *piazō*, seize) Jesus is made.[37] Yet his time still has not come (cf. 2:4; 8:20, 59; 10:39; 12:36; cf. Ps. 31:15 [cited in Kruse 2003: 189]).

"The Christ, when he comes, will not perform more signs than he has done, will he?" In 6:15, after the feeding of the multitude, people are

---

34. In a civilization without family names, the place of origin is equivalent to an identifying name, such as Joseph "of Arimathea" or Jesus "of Nazareth" (cf. Gen. 29:4; Judg. 13:6).

35. Ἔκραξεν (*ekraxen*, he cried out) denotes a loud shout (Morris 1995: 366), indicating a public, solemn pronouncement (Carson 1991: 318; Barrett 1978: 322) (cf. 1:15; 7:37; 12:44).

36. The καί (*kai*, but) preceding ἀπ' ἐμαυτοῦ (*ap' emautou*, on my own accord) is adversative (Ridderbos 1997: 268 n. 45; Barrett 1978: 323; Schnackenburg 1990: 2.147). The ἐγώ (*egō*, I) at the beginning of 7:29 is emphatic, set against the ὑμεῖς (*hymeis*, you) in 7:28 (Schnackenburg 1990: 2.147). The alternating use of two words meaning "send," πέμπω (*pempō*) and ἀποστέλλω (*apostellō*), in 7:28–29 represents stylistic variation (Morris 1995: 367 n. 58; Barrett 1978: 323; R. Brown 1966: 313).

37. This is the first time that this word occurs in John. It is used eight times in John's Gospel (compared to only four times elsewhere in the NT), of which six refer to attempts to arrest Jesus (7:30, 32, 44; 8:20; 10:39; 11:57). In the present chapter, 7:30 may refer to an informal attempt, and 7:32 and 7:44 to formal attempts (Barrett 1978: 323), though the distinction should not be exaggerated.

ready to crown Jesus as king. Signs-based faith, while not ideal (e.g., 2:11, 23; 4:48), is better than no faith at all (10:38) (Carson 1991: 319; Morris 1995: 368). There is little direct evidence in the OT that miracles were expected of the Messiah, though this may be implied from the fact that Jews expected a prophet like Moses (Deut. 18:15, 18), who performed miraculous signs at the exodus (Exod. 7–11).[38] The application of certain messianic passages to Jesus' healing ministry in Matthew and Luke likewise may point in this direction.[39] In any case, it would have been natural for people to wonder, upon witnessing Jesus' miracles, whether he might not be the Messiah (see Mark 13:22; cf. Deut. 13:1–3; see Meeks 1967: 162–64).[40]

Then the chief priests (Sadducees) and the Pharisees sent temple guards   **7:32–36** to arrest him (cf. 5:18; 7:30). Though technically there was only one *"chief* priest" at a given time (cf. 11:49, 51; 18:13), there were others who had formerly held this office and who apparently retained the title. The designation may also have extended to other members of the high-priestly families. Annas in particular, the patriarch of his family, skillfully controlled matters through his relations. Alternately, "chief priests" may not refer to present and past high priests but to principal priests, that is, higher temple officials including, besides the high priest himself, the captain of the temple, the temple overseer, and the treasurers (Schürer 1973–79: 2.275–308; Jeremias 1969: 160–81).

The Pharisees belonged to the Sanhedrin, not as a party, but as members of a group of men who knew the Scriptures. Josephus points to the Pharisees' influence among the people (*Ant.* 13.10.5 §288; 18.1.4 §17). Almost all of the chief priests would have been Sadducees (see Acts 5:17; Josephus, *Ant.* 20.9.1 §199). The Sadducees and Pharisees made strange bedfellows (Carson 1991: 319). Faced with a common threat in the person of Jesus, they banded together (John 7:32, 45; 11:47, 57; 18:3).[41] Technically, only the chief priests, and not the Pharisees, had authority to arrest Jesus. The implication here is that the chief priests sought to arrest Jesus with Pharisaic support, perhaps even at Pharisaic urging. From the beginning, the Pharisees are prominent in the plot to arrest Jesus (cf. 5:18; see Ridderbos 1997: 270).

The primary responsibility of the temple guards, who were drawn from the Levites, was to maintain order in the temple precincts as a

38. Schlatter (1948: 197, citing *Mek. Exod.* 15.11), refers to the "Jewish view," "the more miracles, the more grounds for faith."

39. See esp. Matt. 11:2–6 par.; see also Matt. 8:17 (cf. Isa. 53:4); Luke 4:18–19 (cf. Isa. 61:1–2).

40. Barrett (1978: 323) infers from the emphatic position of ἐκ τοῦ ὄχλου (*ek tou ochlou,* of the crowd) that the evangelist sets the crowd off from the Jerusalemites.

41. There is no need to charge the evangelist here with "ignorance" or lack of "concern for accuracy," as do Barrett (1978: 324) and, less strongly, Schnackenburg (1990: 2.149).

kind of temple police force. Moreover, since the Romans granted the Jews a significant degree of autonomy in managing their own affairs, the Sanhedrin was able to deploy the temple guards also in matters quite removed from the actual sanctuary. In fact, if Jesus was still teaching in the vicinity of the temple, they would not have had to go far. The guards were commanded by "the captain of the temple," who also was drawn from one of the priestly families and whose authority in practical matters was second only to that of the high priest (Carson 1991: 319–20).

"I am with you a little longer." This is September/October (A.D. 32). Half a year later (March/April of A.D. 33), Jesus would be crucified. When people later will look for Jesus (presumably in order to escape judgment; cf. 3:36; 8:21; see Lindars 1972: 295–96), he will be inaccessible to them, and it will be too late (Ridderbos 1997: 271; Barrett 1978: 325). The implicit threat is that some will die in their sins (cf. 8:21, 24; Carson 1991: 320). Note that even Jesus' close followers will not be able to follow him immediately subsequent to his physical departure. Jesus' return to his sender ("I go to the one who sent me") is part of the Johannine mission theme (Köstenberger 1998b).[42]

The "Jews" (which may refer to the authorities or the crowd in general) said to one another, "Where is he about to go that we will not be able to find him?"[43] "Surely, he isn't planning to go into the Greek diaspora and teach the Greeks!" As in 6:41–42, 52, the Jews, who understand Jesus' words only on the surface, are perplexed and uneasy (cf. 7:36; see Morris 1995: 371), and so they entertain possibilities that seem ridiculous even to them (Ridderbos 1997: 271).[44] The present statement may, by way of Johannine irony, constitute a prophetic reference to the later Christian mission.[45] The world of Jesus and of the Father is beyond the Jews' ability to comprehend or enter (Moloney 1998: 249).

The expression "Greek diaspora" is a technical term referring to the large number of Jews living outside Palestine in various parts of the em-

---

42. This is the first occurrence of the frequent Johannine phrase indicating that Jesus will return to "him who sent me" (Ridderbos 1997: 271). The term ὑπάγω (hypagō, go) is favored by John (32 times, compared to 19 times in Matthew, 15 in Mark, and 5 in Luke; see Morris 1995: 369 n. 67; Moloney 1998: 250; Schnackenburg 1990: 2.476 n. 47). It is used seventeen times to refer to Jesus' departure to the Father.

43. Old Testament parallels to "Where does this man intend to go that we cannot find him?" may include Hos. 5:6; Amos 8:12; Isa. 55:6.

44. The interrogative particle μή (mē) indicates a hesitant suggestion (Barrett 1978: 325).

45. Cf. 11:50–52. So Beasley-Murray 1999: 112; Schnackenburg 1990: 2.150; Bultmann 1971: 309. Ridderbos (1997: 271–72) thinks that it merely indicates a presumed place of refuge for Jesus. Schlatter (1948: 150) sees in 7:35 not only an objection that Jesus' departure from Jerusalem would compromise the Jews' privilege as God's chosen people but also an acknowledgment of the oppressive superiority of Greek learning, the profundity of the Greeks' antipathy toward the Jews, and the firmness of religious traditions in Greek-speaking areas.

pire and beyond.[46] A rabbinic source (*b. Sanh.* 11b) has Rabban Gamaliel II (ca. A.D. 90) address a letter "to our brethren the Exiles in Babylon and to those in Media, and to all the other exiled [sons] of Israel." Jews had been living outside Palestine ever since the Babylonian exile. When they were allowed to return from exile, some went back, but many did not. In later years, many cities boasted a considerable Jewish population, including Antioch, Alexandria, and Rome.

The "Greeks" mentioned here (cf. 12:20) probably are Gentiles and perhaps proselytes.[47] The term is regularly used in the NT in contrast with "Jews,"[48] which suggests that reference is made to non-Jews, be it Greeks or Gentile proselytes. The phrase seems to have functioned as an umbrella term for Gentiles, owing to the dominance of Greek culture and language in the Greco-Roman world at large.[49] Interestingly, Jesus' Jewish interrogators think that Jesus will go into the Diaspora not to teach Jews, but Gentiles, presumably because it was assumed that only the latter needed instruction in the Scriptures.[50] The question arises as to how the Jews will be able to interpret Scripture if they have such difficulty understanding Jesus' words.

It is now the last and greatest day of the festival. Every day during Tabernacles, priests marched in solemn procession from the pool of Siloam to the temple and poured out water at the base of the altar. The seventh day of the festival, the last day proper (Lev. 23:34, 41–42), was marked by a special water-pouring rite and lights ceremony (*m. Sukkah* 4.1, 9–10). This was to be followed by a sacred assembly on the eighth day, which was set apart for sacrifices, the joyful dismantling of the booths, and repeated singing of the Hallel (Ps. 113–18).[51] Hence, by the

7:37–39

46. For uses of διασπορά (*diaspora*, dispersion) in the LXX, see Deut. 28:25; 30:4; Neh. 1:9; Ps. 146:2 (147:2 Eng.); Isa. 49:6; Jer. 15:7; 41:17; Dan. 12:2; Jdt. 5:19; 2 Macc. 1:27; cf. Ps. Sol. 8:28; 9:2.

47. See R. Brown 1966: 314; Schnackenburg 1990: 2.150; Schlatter 1948: 198. Contra Ridderbos (1997: 271), who opts for Greek-speaking Diaspora Jews. Carson (1991: 320 [cf. Barrett 1978: 325; Witherington 1995: 173]) thinks that Gentile proselytes probably are in view.

48. See Acts 14:1; 16:1; 18:4; 19:10, 17; 20:21; Rom. 1:16; 2:9, 10; 3:9; 10:12; 1 Cor. 1:22, 24; 10:32; 12:13; Gal. 3:28; Col. 3:11.

49. Note that there is a separate term for "Greek-speaking (or Grecian) Jews," Ἑλληνιστής, which occurs in Acts 6:1; 9:29; 11:20.

50. Does this imply that Jesus' contemporaries thought him capable of instructing Gentiles in the Diaspora by using Greek? If so, the present passage would provide indirect evidence that Jesus was known to at least speak (if not write) Greek. On the question of the language of Jesus, see the surveys by C. Rabin and G. Mussies in Safrai and Stern 1976: 1007–64 (plus the bibliography cited there); see also Silva 1991 (plus the bibliography cited there on p. 222 n. 3).

51. See Lev. 23:36; Num. 29:35; Neh. 8:18. The eighth day of this feast was also the last festival day in the Jewish year. Philo (*Spec. Laws* 2.33 §213) speaks of it as "a sort of complement [πλήρωμα] and conclusion of all the feasts in the year."

first century, many Jews had come to think of the Feast of Tabernacles as an eight-day event.[52]

Whether Jesus' words in 7:37–38 and 8:12 were uttered on the climactic seventh day, with its water-pouring and torch-lighting ceremonies, or on the eighth day of joyful assembly and celebration, they would have had a tremendous impact on the pilgrims.[53] Just when the events of the feast, and their attendant symbolism, were beginning to sink into people's memories, Jesus' words promised a continuous supply of water and light, perhaps also alluding to the supply of water from the rock in the wilderness.

Jesus cried out (see commentary at 7:28), "If anyone thirsts, let him come to me and drink."[54] Tabernacles was associated with adequate rainfall (Zech. 14:16–17), and this passage was read on the first day of the feast according to the liturgy in *b. Meg.* 31a. Another OT passage associated with this feast was Isa. 12:3: "With joy you will draw water from the wells of salvation." This water rite, though not prescribed in the OT, was firmly in place well before the first century A.D.[55] The festival seems to speak of the joyful restoration of Israel and the ingathering of the nations. Here Jesus presents himself as God's agent to make these end-time events a reality.

"As Scripture has said, rivers of living water will flow from within him." Calvin (1959: 198–99) suggests that reference is made here not to any particular passage of Scripture but to common prophetic teaching. Possible scriptural allusions include those promising spiritual blessings,[56] including the blessing of the Spirit,[57] in line with the feast itself.[58] "From within him" probably refers to the one who believes in Jesus the Messiah, with the first clause of 7:38 functioning as a pendent subject.[59]

---

52. See Josephus, *Ant.* 11.5.5 §157; *b. Sukkah* 48b; *m. Sukkah* 5.6; 2 Macc. 10:6.

53. Most commentators favor a time immediately following cessation of ceremonies on the eighth day (Carson 1991: 321; Morris 1995: 373, esp. n. 79; Barrett 1978: 326; Moloney 1998: 256; Schlatter 1948: 199). Some believe that Jesus' words fit better with the ceremonies of the seventh day (R. Brown 1966: 320; Bultmann 1971: 302 n. 5; Schnackenburg 1990: 2.152; Ridderbos 1997: 272; Burge 2000: 227). On the water-drawing ceremony, see Keener 2003: 722–24.

54. Cf. Isa. 55:1; also Ps. 42–43; Matt. 5:6; John 4:10–14; 6:35; Rev. 22:1–2, 17; Sir. 24:19–21; 51:23–24. Beasley-Murray (1999: 113 [cf. Burge 2000: 227]) sees a close parallel in form and content between 6:35 and 7:37–38.

55. See, perhaps, 1 Sam. 7:6. Some rabbinic sources, which may or may not reach back to the first century, are *Pesiq. Rab.* 52.3–6; *t. Sukkah* 3.3–12. See Grigsby 1986.

56. Isa. 58:11; cf. Prov. 4:23; 5:15; Zech. 14:8. Menken (1996) favors Ps. 77:16, 20 LXX, with the epithet "living" coming from Zech. 14:8.

57. Isa. 12:3; 44:3; 49:10; Ezek. 36:25–27; 47:1; Joel 3:18; Amos 9:11–15; Zech. 13:1. Ezekiel 47:1–11 is favored by Hodges (1979b) and Knapp (1997: 116–17).

58. See Neh. 9:15, 19–20; other relevant passages include Exod. 17:6; Ps. 105:41; Prov. 18:4; Isa. 43:19–20; 55:1; Jer. 2:13; 17:13; see also 1QH 16:4–40. See Menken 1996.

59. Ridderbos 1997: 273; Carson 1991: 323–25; Barrett 1978: 326–27; Lindars 1972: 300–301; Calvin 1959: 198; cf. Wallace 1996: 51–52, 654. Carson (1991: 324–25) notes Fee's

Jewish parallels abound.[60] According to certain traditions,[61] Jerusalem was situated in the navel of the earth, so John may be using "belly" (κοιλία, *koilia*) in 7:38 as a synonym for Jerusalem (Abrahams 1917: 1.11, referring to Zech. 14:8).[62]

"This he said concerning the Spirit."[63] Occasionally in the OT, water is used as a symbol for the Holy Spirit (cf. Isa. 44:3; Ezek. 36:25–27; Joel 2:28). Manna/water and the gift of the Spirit are linked in Neh. 9:20 (cf. 9:13, 15; see Carson 1991: 326–28; Shidemantle 2001). In John, this motif dovetails with 5:46 and the portrayal of Jesus as the true bread of heaven in John 6 (cf. 6:35).[64] Yet the giving of the Spirit, evoked by Jewish Tabernacles traditions, was contingent on Jesus being "glorified" (Ridderbos 1997: 275), a Johannine euphemism for the cluster of events centering in the crucifixion. The present statement thus anticipates the farewell discourse and the commissioning scene in 20:22.

Regarding the sequence "some from the crowd . . . others . . . yet others," see commentary at 7:11. "The prophet" refers to "the prophet like Moses" (Deut. 18:15–18; see commentary at 6:14; so Carson 1991: 329; contra Ridderbos 1997: 276–77). In first-century thinking, the Prophet and the Christ were often viewed as two separate personages (cf. John 1:21).[65] The Qumran community looked forward to the coming of the Prophet and the Anointed Ones of Aaron and Israel (1QS 9:11), whereby the Prophet was held to be different from the priestly and royal Messiahs. Concerning the eschatological successor to Moses, *Eccles. Rab.* 1.9 states, "As the former redeemer made a well to rise [Num. 21:17–18], so will the latter Redeemer bring up water [Joel 4:18]" (see commentary at 4:10 and at 6:31).

7:40–44

"He is the Christ" (see commentary at 1:41). "The Christ doesn't come from Galilee, does he? Doesn't Scripture say that the Christ will come from the seed of David and from Bethlehem, the village where David was?" This is the third public conjecture highlighted in this section (cf.

---

observation (1978) that the phrase τοῦτο δὲ εἶπεν (*touto de eipen*, and he said this) customarily refers to the words of Jesus in John. If this is the case here, then 7:38b is from Jesus and not the evangelist, and thus "from within him" refers to "whoever believes in me." Other instances of the pendent nominative in John are 1:12; 6:39; 15:2; 17:2 (Hodges 1979b: 241, citing Cortés 1967: 79). Less likely, Jesus here is presented as the source of "rivers of living water" (R. Brown 1966: 320; Beasley-Murray 1999: 115; Schnackenburg 1990: 2.154; Menken 1996: 165–66; Burge 1987: 88–93; 2000: 228; Keener 2003: 728–30).

60. See the material cited in Köstenberger 2002c: 78–79. See also Grigsby 1986.

61. See *b. Sanh.* 37a; Ezek. 5:5; 38:12; Jub. 8:19.

62. See the material cited in Köstenberger 2002c: 79. See also Marcus 1998; and Schnackenburg (1990: 2.156), who connects κοιλία with the water flowing from Jesus' side at 19:34.

63. For other explanatory phrases, see 2:11, 21–22; 12:16, 33; 21:19, 23.

64. For rabbinic and Qumran parallels, see Köstenberger 2002c: 79.

65. Though see Meeks 1967 and Martyn 1979: 113–14 for the view that the roles of the Prophet and the Messiah were interwined in the minds of many.

7:27, 31). There was ample scriptural support for people's contention that the Messiah would come from David's family and from Bethlehem, a village (κώμη, kōmē [elsewhere in John only applied to Bethany: 11:1, 30]) located south of Jerusalem in the heart of Judea.[66] Matthew 2:5–6 confirms that at least by the beginning of the first century A.D., Jewish scholars generally expected the Messiah to be born in Bethlehem (cf. Luke 2:1–20). No comparable evidence existed for a Galilean origin (cf. John 7:52).

Again, one cannot help but note the irony (Carson 1991: 330; Morris 1995: 380; contra Ridderbos 1997: 278). For whereas people (erroneously) thought that Jesus hailed from Galilee, John's readers clearly are expected to know that Jesus had in fact been born in Bethlehem, thus fulfilling messianic prophecy (cf. Matt. 2:5–6; Luke 2:4, 15). Jesus' interrogators are unmasked as ignorant (cf. John 7:52, where Jesus' Pharisaic opposition is shown to be in error). The apparent difficulty of Jesus' supposed Galilean origin was one that Christian apologists (including John) had to deal with already in the first century.[67] The division (σχίσμα, schisma) that arose among the crowd indicates, historically, that there was a diversity of opinions regarding Jesus' legitimacy during his earthly ministry.[68]

v. The Unbelief of the Jewish Leaders (7:45–52)

7:45–49 In this seventh and final short section of John 7, the Jewish leaders—absent in 7:33–44 (Wallace 1996: 327)—reenter the scene.[69] The guards answered, "No one ever spoke like this man."[70] These guards were chosen from the Levites. They were religiously trained and therefore not merely "brutal thugs." In the fulfillment of their duties they would have heard many teachers in the temple courts. Even as biblical nonexperts, they recognize that Jesus' teaching is unique. The guards' response to the Sanhedrin is all the more amazing in that they did not try to blame their failure to arrest Jesus on the shifting crowd; they merely spoke of Jesus' mesmerizing effect (Morris 1995: 382). Again, John intends, and

66. See 2 Sam. 7:12–16; Ps. 89:3–4; Isa. 9:7; 11:1; 55:3; see esp. Mic. 5:2.

67. The sharp disjunction drawn by several commentators between Jesus' earthly and heavenly origins in John is overdrawn (cf. Ridderbos 1997: 278; Barrett 1978: 331; Schnackenburg 1980: 2.158). On the verb πιάζω (piazō, seize) in 7:44, see commentary at 7:30.

68. Beasley-Murray (1999: 119) notes that those who are exposed to God's revelation cannot remain neutral and connects the division here to the division that will occur before the judgment seat. On "schisma" as a unifying formal element in John 7–10, see Schenke 1989: 177–78.

69. On temple guards, chief priests, and Pharisees, see commentary at 7:32.

70. For other times where Jesus' speech elicits similar responses, see Matt. 7:29; Mark 1:22; 12:17, 32–34, 37 pars.; John 4:42; cf. 18:6. The adverb οὕτως (houtōs, like this) focuses on the way Jesus spoke rather than on the substance of his teaching (Morris 1995: 382 n. 103).

the reader notes, irony and double meaning. After all, Jesus is no mere man (Carson 1991: 331; Morris 1995: 382; Barrett 1978: 331).[71]

The Sanhedrin's response is one of anger and contempt (Ridderbos 1997: 279).[72] The officers are said to have lowered themselves to the level of the ignorant crowds: "This crowd that does not know the law—they are accursed" (7:49; cf. Deut. 27:26; 28:15; Ps. 119:21; see R. Brown 1966: 325).[73] The disparaging remark regarding the crowd that is ignorant of the law constitutes an instance of heaping scorn and abuse on others in order to ridicule their viewpoint (see commentary at 9:28–29).[74] How ironic that only the masses who are said to be scripturally illiterate have a clue regarding Jesus' actual identity, while those who boast of their scriptural expertise are ignorant of who Jesus truly is (Burge 2000: 230; cf. Carson 1991: 331).

Enter Nicodemus, "the one who had come to him [Jesus] earlier, being one of them" (see 3:1–15, esp. 3:1; also 19:39). He who, unlike his colleagues, previously had engaged in dialogue with Jesus—yet remained one of them—comes to Jesus' aid, not as a "confessor" or "defender of Jesus' teaching," but on the common ground that he shared with his fellow Sanhedrin members: the law.[75] Michaels (1989: 142) puts it well: "His [Nicodemus's] remark (v. 51) is no ringing confession, but merely a plea for fairness. He appears in the narrative scene more to demonstrate the Pharisees' intransigence than to mark a stage in his own spiritual development." 7:50–52

71. Regarding "You have not been deceived as well, have you?" see commentary at 7:12. Note the perfect tense of πεπλάνησθε (*peplanēsthe*, you have been deceived) (Morris 1995: 382) as well as the passive voice, avoiding explicit reference to agency so as not to detract from the subject (i.e., the officers who are led astray) (Wallace 1996: 436). Carson (1991: 331) also sees irony in 7:48, for whatever one makes of Nicodemus, he is about to speak out on Jesus' behalf.

72. The particle μή (*mē*) at the beginning of the sentence is indicative of the Sanhedrin's "enraged frustration" (Ridderbos 1997: 279 n. 74). Stibbe (1993: 94) detects narrative echoes of the Nicodemus story in 3:1–21.

73. See Ridderbos 1997: 279–80; Carson 1991: 331–32. Morris (1995: 383) adds that it is not that the people are (entirely) unfamiliar with the law, but that they do not "know" (observe) it the way the Pharisees do: keeping the 613 commandments and so forth.

74. Care must be taken not to identify the crowd in the present instance with the "people of the land" (Hebrew: ʿammê hāʾāreṣ) in later rabbinic literature. As Meier (2001: 28–29) notes, first, the reference here is not necessarily to common people in general but specifically to the crowd of pilgrims who are in Jerusalem for the Feast of Tabernacles; second, the dispute here concerns not rules of purity and tithing in the Mosaic law (the context in which later rabbinic literature refers to ordinary Jews as "people of the land" with a pejorative connotation) but the proper identification of Jesus; and third, the crowd acts here (as throughout much of John 7) as the evangelist's sounding board for the christological revelation of Jesus (see further ibid., pp. 38–39 n. 36).

75. Ridderbos 1997: 280 (contra Moloney [1998: 255], who says that Nicodemus "now advocates a new way of understanding God's design for the people . . . in the words and deeds of Jesus"; see also Ridderbos's excursus on Nicodemus at the end of ch. 7).

Most likely, Nicodemus here is pressing for an official hearing (Motyer 1997: 154–55; contra Pancaro 1975). The fact that such does not yet occur continues the suspense of the narrative and allows the readers to keep pursuing their own examination of Jesus' claims (Motyer 1997: 155). The supreme irony in the present instance is that the guardians of the law themselves do not keep the law (Morris 1995: 384).[76] Old Testament law charges judges to investigate accusations against a person fairly (Deut. 1:16) and thoroughly (Deut. 17:4; 19:18). In light of the fact that Nicodemus's fellow Sanhedrin members have just expressed contempt toward the masses who are ignorant of the law, the evangelist surely sees irony in Nicodemus's calling them to task on a point of simple Jewish—indeed, universal—legal procedure (cf. *m. Sanh.* 5.4).[77]

The Fourth Evangelist proceeds to recount another dubious claim made by Nicodemus's colleagues: "You are not from Galilee as well, are you? Look, and you will see that no prophet arises from Galilee."[78] Yet, contrary to these confident assertions, prophets had indeed come out of Galilee in the past, including Jonah (2 Kings 14:25) and possibly Elijah (1 Kings 17:1) and Nahum (Nah. 1:1).[79]

Additional Notes

7:8. Textual tradition is split between "not" (ℵ D) and "not yet" ($\mathfrak{P}^{66, 75}$ B). It is possible that later scribes changed "not" to "not yet" in order to "protect" John's Gospel from a seeming untruth. In light of the papyrus readings, however, if so, this change would have had to occur fairly early.[80]

7:10. The ὡς in some MSS should probably be read (so $\mathfrak{P}^{66, 75}$ B; and Morris 1995: 356 n. 27; against ℵ D; Barrett 1978: 313: "perhaps"; Moloney 1998: 240). Note the NRSV: "not publicly but *as it were* in secret" (italics added).

7:52. The text may say either "a prophet" (more likely; so Morris 1995: 385 n. 115) or "the prophet" ($\mathfrak{P}^{66}$*; so Smothers 1958).[81]

---

76. In Acts 5:34–39, Gamaliel, another rabbi, perhaps only two years later, acts very much like Nicodemus does here.

77. Cf. Acts 25:16; Josephus, *Ant.* 14.9.3 §167; *J.W.* 1.10.6 §209; see Pancaro 1972. Later rabbinic rulings concur (*Exod. Rab.* 21.3 [cited in Köstenberger 2002c: 81]).

78. Ridderbos (1997: 281 n. 81) again notes the introductory particle μή, which here indicates ridicule. Ἐραύνησον (*eraunēson*, search) is a conditional imperative, with the verb in the apodosis, ἴδε (*ide*, see), being another imperative (Wallace 1996: 489). The present tense of ἐγείρεται (*egeiretai*, he arises) states a (supposedly) timeless truth (so, rightly, Ridderbos 1997: 281) rather than emphasizing presentness (Morris 1995: 385 n. 114). See also additional note. As to the brashness of the comment, cf. 11:49.

79. See the rabbinic literature cited in Köstenberger 2002c: 81. For another doubtful assertion by Jesus' antagonists, see 8:33.

80. For an argument supporting "not yet" as the original reading, see Caragounis 1998.

81. For further discussion of this issue, including bibliographic references, see Morris 1995: 385 n. 115. Motyer (1997: 154) suggests that the reference is to "the prophet" of Deut. 18:15.

Excursus: The Pericope of the Adulterous Woman (7:53–8:11)

As is widely recognized, the status of the pericope of the adulterous woman in 7:53–8:11 as an original part of John's Gospel is highly in doubt. Virtually all translations (for good reasons, as will be seen) place the passage in square brackets, indicating probable noninclusion in the original Gospel.[1] What follows here is a brief presentation of the internal and external evidence, whereby external considerations should be given primary weight.

Internal Evidence

As is helpfully summarized by Morgenthaler (1958: 60–62), fourteen out of eighty-two words used in this pericope (or 17 percent) are unique to John. The following words are not found elsewhere in this Gospel:

8:1   ἐλαία
8:2   ὄρθρος
8:3   μοιχεία
8:4   αὐτόφωρος, μοιχεύω
8:6   κύπτω, καταγράφω
8:7   ἐπιμένω, ἀνακύπτω, ἀναμάρτητος
8:8   κατακύπτω
8:9   πρεσβύτερος, καταλείπω
8:10 ἀνακύπτω (2x), κατακρίνω
8:11 κατακρίνω (2x)

The pattern is consistent: virtually every verse from 8:1–11 (the sole exception being 8:5) contains words found nowhere else in the Gospel (and, except for πρεσβύτερος, rarely or not at all in the other Johannine writings). Moreover, several other words occur only once or twice elsewhere in the Gospel. To this should be added the conspicuous nonoccurrence of standard Johannine vocabulary: ἀλλά, ἐάν, ἐκ, ἡμεῖς, ἵνα μή, μαθητής, οἶδα, ὅς, ὅτι, οὐ, ὑμᾶς, ὑμεῖς (detailed in Morgenthaler 1958: 61). On a syntactical level, one notes that δέ only here typically connects the clauses in the narrative (the particle is found in 8:1, 2, 3, 5,

---

1. The sole exception being the KJV and NKJV. Note the progression from the NIV (disclaimer, separating line, same size font) to the TNIV (disclaimer, separating line, considerably smaller size font).

6 [*bis*], 7, 9, 10, 11 [*bis*]; see Morgenthaler 1958: 61–62; Wallace 1993: 291; Burge 1984: 144).

Still, a closer look at the fourteen words used only here in John's Gospel yields less than conclusive results. First, the subject of adultery is not addressed elsewhere in this Gospel, which explains that the verb and noun for "adultery" are limited to the present context. Second, three closely related verbs describing Jesus' bending down and straightening up account for three additional Johannine *hapax legomena*: κύπτω, ἀνακύπτω, and κατακύπτω. "Without sin," too, may be explained as unique to the present context (though see 8:46). Thus, only a few words remain whose presence may be truly significant in suggesting non-Johannine authorship. One such word may be πρεσβύτερος (*presbyteros*, elder), which, one surmises, John would have had occasion to use elsewhere in his Gospel as well.[2]

Also, one notes a penchant for verbal κατα-prefixes among the non-Johannine vocabulary in the present pericope (καταγράφω, κατακύπτω, καταλείπω, κατακρίνω), which seems a bit unusual. There even appears to be counterevidence suggesting possible Johannine authorship of the pericope. A case in point is the almost identical wording of 6:6 and 8:6:

6:6: τοῦτο δὲ ἔλεγεν πειράζων αὐτόν
8:6: τοῦτο δὲ ἔλεγον πειράζοντες αὐτόν

This similarity could, of course, be explained as an attempted assimilation to Johannine style by another author. It is still interesting to note, however, that although the Synoptic material recounts occasions where Jesus' opponents approached him in order to test him, the wording is different (e.g., Matt. 16:1; 19:3; 22:35 pars.).[3] For this reason, word statistics should not be accorded definitive status in the present argument.[4] More significant, however, are Johannine style characteristics. Strikingly, Ruckstuhl and Dschulnigg (1991: 185–86) identify only two such characteristics in the entire pericope (7:53–8:11), a ratio of 21:1.[5] This represents overwhelming evidence that the section is non-Johannine.

2. O'Day (1992: 639) further notes that "scribes and Pharisees" (as well as "Mount of Olives") occurs nowhere else in John.

3. Though note that in *content* the Synoptic accounts provide much closer parallels to 8:6 than to 6:6, since in the latter it is Jesus testing one of his followers rather than Jesus' opponents testing him.

4. In my judgment, not even Wallace's (1993: 291–93) attempted refutation of Heil (1991) succeeds in completely enlisting the internal lexical and syntactical evidence in favor of non-Johannine authorship, though many of his individual points are well taken (Metzger [1994: 188 n. 3] calls Wallace's refutation of Heil a "convincing rebuttal").

5. The two characteristics are (1) ταῦτα without complement and with an antecedent referent, and (2) the verb ἐρωτάω.

External Evidence

The external evidence is most exhaustively treated by Petersen (1997: 191–221).[6] He notes that "the entire twelve verses of the *pericope adulterae* are completely absent from *all* of the oldest manuscripts of the Gospel of John," the pericope first appearing in the fifth-century Codex Bezae (D). Even after this, the spread into the MS tradition is very slow. Thus, scholarship has, almost universally, regarded the pericope as a later insertion for, in Petersen's words, "reasons [that] are massive, convincing, and obvious":[7]

1. Its utter absence from all pre-fifth-century A.D. MSS, including $\mathfrak{P}^{66}$, $\mathfrak{P}^{75}$, $\aleph$, B, and probably A and C (Metzger 1994: 187–88);
2. Its appearance in no fewer than five different places in the MS tradition (after John 7:36, 44, or 52; at the end of John's Gospel; or after Luke 21:38), bearing all the marks of a "bouncing around . . . 'floating' logion" (Petersen 1997: 193); one should also note the large number of variants pertaining to the entire pericope, which also suggests an unstable MS tradition (Burge 1984: 144; O'Day 1992: 639 n. 22; contra J. A. Sanders 1990: 337);
3. Non-Johannine literary features (see above);
4. The interruption of the narrative flow from 7:52 to 8:12, breaking up the literary unit 7:1–8:59; on a historical level, the setting of 7:53–8:1 suggests most plausibly Jesus' pattern during the week before his passion (cf. Mark 11:11, 19; 13:3; and esp. Luke 21:37; see Carson 1991: 334; Burge 1984: 144);
5. The lack of citation in early patristic writings up to the fourth century (the earliest Greek patristic reference of a variation of this narrative occurring in a commentary by Didymus the Blind [d. 398]; see Ehrman 1988; Beck 1997: 102–3; but cf. McDonald 1995);
6. The suggested scenario that the pericope passed from its original place in the Gospel according to the Hebrews to John's Gospel (Eusebius, *Hist. eccl.* 3.39.17, citing Papias).[8]

---

6. A briefer and more dated (but still helpful) survey is found in Burge 1984: 142–43. Further bibliographic references to materials dealing with both external and internal evidence can be found in Wallace 1993: 290 n. 2; J. A. Sanders 1990: 346 n. 1; Burge 1984: 141 n. 5. Also regularly cited is the monograph by Becker (1963).

7. See also Metzger (1994: 187–89), who calls the evidence for the non-Johannine origin of the pericope "overwhelming" and "conclusive." Keener (2003: 735–36), too, strongly contends that 7:53–8:11 is an interpolation, based on its suspect textual history and its large non-Johannine vocabulary. One of the few scholars favoring originality (on the grounds of Byzantine priority) is M. Robinson (1998: 1–17).

8. The attribution, recorded by Eusebius and reported by Papias (*Hist. eccl.* 3.39.17), of a similar pericope to a contemporary source probably refers to the sinful woman in Luke 7:36–50 rather than to the adulterous woman considered here (Petersen 1997: 196–97; contra Burge 1984: 143).

True, Augustine (and Ambrose) liked the pericope and suggested that it may have been removed by "enemies of the true faith" who feared "that their wives be given impunity in sinning" (cited in Petersen 1997: 199; a theory recently revived by O'Day 1992: 631–40; cf. Riesenfeld 1970); true, Jerome included the pericope in his Latin Vulgate; true, portions of the story are quoted in the *Didascalia apostolorum*, which usually is dated to the first half of the third century—but none of this overturns the weighty external considerations against regarding the pericope as Johannine and original.

Petersen himself (1997: 204–21) makes a strong case that the earliest extant reference to the pericope (specifically, the phrase οὐδὲ ἐγὼ [κατα]κρίνω (*oude egō [kata]krinō*, neither do I condemn [8:11]) is actually found in the Protevangelium of James (second half of the second century A.D.?), an apocryphal Christian romance. But rather than regarding John as this document's source, Petersen opts for joint dependence on an earlier source, presumably the aforementioned Gospel according to the Hebrews, which meets all the criteria: antedating A.D. 150; composed in Greek; preserving narrative portions as well as *logia Jesu*; and circulation in Egypt at an early date (Petersen 1997: 215–16).[9] This theory would explain the non-Johannine style, awkward position, and absence of the pericope from all the oldest MSS of John (Petersen 1997: 217).

Thus, though Burge (1984: 148) may be right when he classifies the pericope as "an edifying *agraphon* of Jesus," the fact remains that the account almost certainly was not part of the original Gospel and therefore should not be regarded as part of the Christian canon. Nor does inspiration extend to it. In principle, the pericope is no different from other possibly authentic sayings of Jesus that may be found in NT apocryphal literature. Thus, though it may be possible to derive a certain degree of edification from the study of this pericope, proper conservatism and caution suggest that the passage be omitted from preaching in the churches (not to mention inclusion in the main body of translations, even within square brackets [Köstenberger 2003]).[10] The present com-

9. This was first suggested by J. Drusius (1595), followed by Hugo Grotius (1641) and J. A. Fabricius (1703–19) (see Petersen 1997: 217). M. Robinson (1998: 5) wrongly attributes to Petersen the view that the pericope of the adulterous woman "was circulating *as part of John's gospel* in the mid-second century" (italics added). Apart from the fact that Petersen speaks of "the second half of the second century," his actual conclusion is that "three constitutive elements of the *pericope adulterae, as it is now know* [sic] *to us from the Gospel of John*, were known in the second half of the second century" (1997: 207 [italics added]). Nowhere does he suggest that John's Gospel was the source of the Protevangelium of James or that John's Gospel already contained the pericope in the mid–second century (and even if it did, this still would not prove that the pericope is original).

10. The unfortunate precedent of including the pericope may have been set by Erasmus, who, though doubting the originality of the passage, nonetheless included it in his 1516 edition of the Greek NT in deference to its popularity by readers of the Latin Vulgate. From there, the pericope found its way into the seventeenth-century Textus Receptus

mentary therefore will follow the precedent of Origen (d. 253), who moved directly from 7:52 to 8:12 (Heine 1993: 192; Burge 1984: 142), and refrain from further comment on 7:53–8:11.[11]

(Burge 1984: 148 n. 29). See also Beck (1997: 101–7, esp. 103–4), who concludes that the pericope is inauthentic but nonetheless incorporates it in his study by analyzing its effect on the reader. This judgment, however, is of doubtful merit in that it fails to consider the original and the earliest readers of the Gospel (who would not have read the Gospel with this pericope), and in that it unduly neglects issues such as canonicity, inspiration, and biblical authority.

11. A survey of major commentaries shows that about half provide a regular commentary (Carson, Laney, Lindars, Whitacre, Calvin, Westcott), while the other half refrain from comment (Michaels, Talbert, Stibbe, Brodie, D. M. Smith), in some cases choosing not to address the issue at all (e.g., Schlatter [1948: 205], who in his scholarly commentary moves directly from 7:52 to 8:12 without comment, though his popular commentary [1962: 139–41] does treat the *pericope adulterae* in deference to "ecclesiastical tradition"; see also Zahn [1921: 404], who, like Schlatter, moves immediately from 7:52 to 8:12 and deals with the pericope in a lengthy excursus on pp. 723–30).

b. Second Teaching Cycle (8:12–59)

The present passage covers the aftermath of Jesus' controversy with the Jewish leaders (ch. 7, with 7:45–52 serving as a transition). The roots are found even further back, in Jesus' healing of a lame man on the Sabbath (5:1–15; cf. 7:21). This is part of the dynamic of escalating conflict in the first half of this Gospel (esp. chs. 5–12). In a reversal of the Synoptic portrayal of Jesus as on trial before the Romans and the Jews, John shows how it is not Jesus, but ultimately the world (including the Jews), that is on trial.[1] To this end, the evangelist marshals a series of witnesses in defense of the truthfulness of Jesus' claims (see commentary at 1:7). In the present section the Jews dispute the validity of Jesus' witness and challenge Jesus' identification with God the Father.

The motif of light and darkness (sounded in 8:12) ties in several thematic strands in the Gospel:[2] (1) the Word's participation in creation (1:3); (2) the moral contrast between spiritual life and spiritual death (12:35–36); (3) Jesus' fulfillment of Feast of Tabernacles symbolism (ch. 7; 8:12); and (4) Jesus' healing of the man born blind (9:4–5), which becomes a parable of the Pharisees' spiritual blindness in contrast to the man's newfound vision. Whereas that man knew himself to be blind and in need of sight, the Pharisees, spiritually blind, claimed to be able to see, thus cutting themselves off from God's mercy (cf. Matt. 23:16–24). The evangelist returns to the "light" motif at the raising of Lazarus (John 11:9–10) and at Jesus' final indictment of Jewish unbelief (12:37–50).

---

1. See Charles 1989; Lincoln 2000. Stibbe (1993: 99) contends that the present pericope constitutes a "trial scene," whereby "the implicit commentary . . . supports the narrator's defence of the divinity of Jesus and the concomitant satire of the diabolism of the Jews." According to Stibbe, much of the irony in this chapter comes from Jesus taking on the role of Yahweh, and the Jews that of the false, pagan gods.

2. The term φῶς (phōs, light) spans the entire first half of John's Gospel, from the prologue (1:4, 5, 7, 8, 9) to the concluding section (12:35, 36, 46), in each of which it occurs six times. The term is absent from the second half of John's Gospel, which suggests that it is part of John's presentation of Jesus' entrance into the world and ministry to the Jews in chapters 1–12. The occurrences of φῶς are clustered in 1:4–9; 3:19–21; 5:35; 8:12; 9:5; 11:9–10; 12:35–46. Φῶς is linked with ζωή (zōē, life) in 1:4 and 8:12; ζωή is used more frequently than φῶς, especially in the phrase ζωὴ αἰώνιος (zōē aiōnios, eternal life). At times, φῶς serves as a metaphor for eternal life in its spiritual, moral, and present-day implications.

The present section elaborates further on the brewing "paternity dispute" between the Pharisees and Jesus. Claiming Abraham as their father, the Jews in effect deny their own sinfulness and need for salvation.[3] Jesus, in turn, charges that his opponents, owing to their persistent unbelief, in truth have the devil as their spiritual father. In the end, the face-off remains unresolved. When Jesus unequivocally calls God his Father and asserts that "before Abraham was born, I am," the Jews get ready to stone him on account of blasphemy. Yet for now, Jesus eludes their grasp and leaves the temple area.

   i. Jesus the light of the world (8:12–30)
  ii. The paternity dispute: The Jews' and Jesus' relationship to Abraham (8:31–59)

Exegesis and Exposition

[12]So Jesus spoke to them again, saying, "I am the light of the world. Whoever follows me will not walk in darkness but will have the light of life." [13]Then the Pharisees said to him, "You testify concerning yourself; your testimony is not valid." [14]Jesus answered and said to them, "Even if I bear witness concerning myself, my testimony is valid, because I know where I have come from and where I am going. But you do not know where I came from or where I am going. [15]You judge in a fleshly manner; I do not judge anyone. [16]And yet, if I judge, my judgment is valid, because I am not alone, but it is I and the ⌜Father⌝ who sent me. [17]And in your law it is written that the testimony of two persons is valid. [18]I am one who bears witness concerning myself, and the Father who sent me bears witness concerning me." [19]So they were saying to him, "Where is your father?" Jesus answered, "You know neither me nor my Father. If you knew me, you would also know my Father." [20]He spoke these words in the temple treasury while teaching in the temple area. Yet no one arrested him, because his time had not yet come.

[21]Then again he said to them, "I am going away, and you will look for me, and you will die in your sin. Where I go, you cannot come." [22]So the Jews were saying, "Will he kill himself, because he is saying, 'Where I go, you cannot come'?" [23]And he was saying to them, "You are from below, I am from above; you are from this world, I am not from this world. [24]I told you that you would die in your sins. For if you don't believe that I am [the one I claim to be], you will die in your sins." [25]So they were saying to him, "Who are you?" Jesus said to them, "Have I not told you from the beginning? [26]I have many things to say, and to judge, concerning you, but the one who sent me is true, and I—what I have heard from him, these things I speak to the world." [27](They did not understand

---

3. Besides 8:33–58, Abraham is not referred to anywhere in John's Gospel. Other significant NT references to Abraham include Matt. 3:9 par.; Rom. 4; Gal. 3; Heb. 11.

that he was speaking to them about the Father.) [28]So Jesus said to them, "When you have lifted up the Son of Man, then you will know that I am [the one I claim to be], and that I do nothing on my own accord, but speak just what the Father has taught me. [29]And the one who sent me is with me. He has not left me alone, because I always do the things that please him." [30]As he was speaking these things, many believed in him.

[31]Then Jesus was saying to the Jews who had believed in him, "If you abide by my teaching, you will truly be my disciples. [32]And you will know the truth, and the truth will set you free." [33]They answered him, "We are the seed of Abraham and have never been enslaved to anyone. How can you say, 'You will be set free'?" [34]Jesus answered them, "Truly, truly, I say to you, everyone who perpetrates sin is a slave ⌜to sin⌝. [35]And a slave does not remain in the house forever; the son remains forever. [36]So if the Son sets you free, you will be free indeed. [37]I know that you are the seed of Abraham. Yet you are trying to kill me, because my message has no place in you. [38]I speak what I have seen with the Father; so then, ⌜you too do what you've heard from your father⌝."

[39]They answered and said to him, "Abraham is our father." Jesus said to them, "⌜If you were⌝ children of Abraham, ⌜you would do⌝ the works of Abraham. [40]But now you are trying to kill me, a man who has told you the truth that I heard from God. This, Abraham did not do. [41]You are doing the works of your father." They said to him, "We are not children born out of wedlock! We have one father—God." [42]Jesus said to them, "If God were your father, you would love me, for I came from God and am now here; for I did not come on my own accord, but he sent me. [43]Why do you not understand my message? Because you cannot listen to my word. [44]You are from your father the devil, and you want to carry out your father's desires! He was a murderer from the beginning and does not ⌜stand⌝ in the truth, because there is no truth in him. When he tells a lie, he does what comes naturally, because he is a liar and the father of lies. [45]But I—because I speak the truth, you do not believe me. [46]Who among you can convict me of sin? If I am telling the truth, why don't you believe me? [47]Whoever is from God hears the words of God. This is why you do not hear: because you are not from God."

[48]The Jews answered and said to him, "Did we not rightly say that you are a Samaritan and have a demon?" [49]Jesus answered, "I don't have a demon, but I honor my Father, and you dishonor me. [50]I am not seeking my own honor; there is one who seeks it, and who judges. [51]Truly, truly, I say to you, whoever keeps my teaching will never, ever see death." [52]The Jews said to him, "Now we know that you have a demon! Abraham died, as did the prophets, yet you say, 'Whoever keeps my teaching will never, ever taste death.' [53]You are not greater than our father Abraham, are you? He died; and the prophets died. Who do you make yourself out to be?" [54]Jesus answered, "If I honor myself, my honor amounts to nothing. It is my Father who honors me, the one whom you claim to be ⌜your⌝ God, [55]and yet you do not know him; but I know him. And if I said

that I did not know him, I would be a liar like you; but I do know him and keep his word. ⁵⁶Abraham your father looked forward to the time when he would see my day, and he saw it and was glad." ⁵⁷Then the Jews said to him, "You are not yet fifty years old, and ⌜you have seen Abraham⌝?" ⁵⁸Jesus said to them, "Truly, truly, I say to you, before Abraham came to be, I am." ⁵⁹So they took up stones in order to cast them on him. But Jesus was hidden and left the temple area.

i. Jesus the Light of the World (8:12–30)

Again (cf. 7:37–38; see Barrett 1978: 335; Schnackenburg 1990: 2.189), Jesus launches a major discourse, commencing with the startling claim "I am the light of the world."[4] This is the second "I am" saying in John (see commentary at 6:35). Earlier in the Gospel, the Word is called "the light of all people" (1:4), and Jesus' confrontation with his opponents is cast as a battle between light and darkness (1:5; 3:19–21; cf. 9:4–5; 12:35–36, 46). Together with the manna (ch. 6) and the rivers of living water (ch. 7), the reference to Jesus as "light" in chapter 8 may be part of a "wilderness theme," alluding to God's presence with the Israelites as a pillar of fire.[5] In the OT, God himself (Ps. 27:1; 36:9) as well as his word (or "law"; Ps. 119:105; Prov. 6:23) are called a "light." "Light" imagery is also applied to the end-time Servant of the Lord (Isa. 49:6; cf. 42:6) and to the Lord's own presence in the midst of his people in the last days.[6] Here, "light" terminology is applied to Tabernacles symbolism (cf. *m. Sukkah* 5.2–4).[7]

8:12

Importantly, for Jesus to be the "light of the world" does not imply a universal bestowal of light upon all of humanity (Morris 1995: 389).[8] Rather, light from Jesus that results in personal salvation always assumes

4. The conjunction οὖν (*oun*, so, then) in 8:12 and 8:13, as elsewhere in this Gospel (cf. 8:21, 22, 25), is transitional in nature (Wallace 1996: 674). Motyer (1997: 155–56) plausibly suggests that this conjunction in 8:12 connects with 7:37–38, noting the continuation of themes from the Feast of Tabernacles. He also suggests that the same conjunction in 8:12 also corresponds to 7:52 because John is going to show that the Messiah can indeed come from Galilee. This is based on the prophecy of Isa. 9:1–2.

5. So Morris 1995: 388; R. Brown 1966: 344; Burge 2000: 255; Moloney 1998: 268; Borchert 1996: 295.

6. See Isa. 60:19–22; Zech. 14:5b–8; cf. Rev. 21:23–24. Contemporary Judaism applied the phrase "light of the world" not only to God but also to Israel, Jerusalem, the patriarchs, the Messiah, famous rabbis (e.g., Yoḥanan ben Zakkai), the Torah, the temple, and even Adam (Keener 1993: 285; see also Beasley-Murray 1999: 128; R. Brown 1966: 344; Schnackenburg 1990: 2.190; Moloney 1998: 266). The universality of "light" symbolism in religious language issues in numerous non-Jewish parallels (see Barrett 1978: 335–37; Bultmann 1971: 40–44, 342–43; Dodd 1953: 201–8; Odeberg 1968: 286–92).

7. For a detailed description of Tabernacles festivities and their relevance for the portrayal of Jesus in John 7–8, see Köstenberger 2002c: 82.

8. Commentators also debate the ontological nature and implications of Jesus' claim here. Talbert (1992: 152) maintains that the statement is "not primarily ontological . . . but soteriological," yet Brodie (1993: 324) rightly notes that Jesus' words are uttered "in the context of showing himself to be in union with the Father. The light, therefore, is not an

a faith commitment to Jesus in John's Gospel. The entire earthly sphere (controlled by the "ruler of this world," Satan) is in darkness (Morris 1995: 389); but Jesus has come as "the light of the world."[9] Those who follow him will therefore never "walk in darkness."[10] This entails more than mere ethical behavior; it involves one's "conduct of life in a more comprehensive sense" (cf. 12:35; Matt. 6:22–23; see Ridderbos 1997: 293). For John, "believing" and "following" are virtual synonyms (Bultmann 1971: 344). The "following" motif is also found in the exodus narrative, with the Israelites following the pillar of fire.[11] The phrase "light of life" is found in the OT as well as in other Jewish literature.[12] In the present context, "light of life" could have several specific nuances.[13]

8:13–14 The Pharisees' primary point is not so much that Jesus is wrong, but that he is not adhering to standard legal procedure (Morris 1995: 390): "You testify concerning yourself; your testimony is not valid."[14] Earlier, Jesus himself had acknowledged as much: "If I testify concerning myself, my testimony is not valid" (5:31). Old Testament law required multiple witnesses in capital cases and other crimes (Num. 35:30; Deut. 17:6; 19:15). Later Jewish legislation adopted the principle and applied it to other legal situations (*m. Ketub.* 2.9; cf. *m. Roš Haš.* 3.1).

Jesus' response to the Pharisees differs from that of 5:31–47, where he enumerates several corroborating witnesses (R. Brown 1966: 340; Bultmann 1971: 279). In the present instance Jesus opts to demonstrate the acceptability of his testimony, though later he shows that he is in agreement with their law (cf. 8:17; see Ridderbos 1997: 294; cf. Morris 1995: 390–91; Pancaro 1975: 264–65). Jesus bases the acceptability of his

isolated Jesus but a Jesus in relationship. The same is implied in the prologue: the light comes from the Word who is in relationship with God."

9. On the contrast between light and darkness in John, see commentary at 1:5.

10. See esp. 12:35; cf. 9:4–5; 11:9–10; and further 1:4–5, 9; 3:19–21; 12:46; Matt. 4:16, citing Isa. 9:1; 1 John 1:5–6; 2:8–9, 11.

11. See Beasley-Murray 1999: 128–29. Moloney (1998: 268, citing Talbert) notes that there was an expectation that the pillar of fire would return "at the end of time." For Qumran and Second Temple parallels, see Köstenberger 2002c: 82.

12. Cf. Ps. 36:9; 56:13; Ps. Sol. 3:12 (cf. 4 Bar. 9:3); 1QS 3:7; 1 Enoch 58:3 (cf. 58:4–6; 92:4).

13. Morris (1995: 389 n. 10 [similarly, Laney 1992: 159]) suggests the following possibilities: "gives life," "is life," "springs from life," or "illuminates life." Schnackenburg (1990: 2.191) adds that this may be an instance of an epexegetical genitive in the sense of "the life which frees a person from the sphere of death."

14. Commentators vary as to whether to regard as synonyms the two words used in the present context for "true" or "valid," ἀληθής (*alēthēs*; 8:13, 14, 17) and ἀληθινός (*alēthinos*; 8:16). Beasley-Murray (1999: 125 n. a [contra R. Brown 1966: 341; Lindars 1972: 317; Barrett 1978: 339]) opts to distinguish between the former meaning "true" or "valid" and the latter meaning "just" or "authentic" (similarly, Schnackenburg 1990: 2.194). Ridderbos (1997: 294) suggests the meaning "just" for ἀληθινός; Barrett (1978: 339) opts for "authentic"; and Carson (1991: 340) prefers "right."

testimony on his origin and destination.[15] Since ultimately he is derived from the Father, he is able to verify the legitimacy of his words.[16]

In Jesus' case, he witnesses not as an ordinary human being, but as the Son of God (R. Brown 1966: 341). As Schnackenburg (1990: 2.192–93) notes, "Words which in a human being would inevitably look like exaggerated arrogance, can take no other form in the mouth of the eschatological revealer." Jesus is not limited by mere creatureliness, so that in awareness of his true identity and divine origin, he is able to give a trustworthy testimony (Barrett 1978: 338). The Jews' failure to appreciate this produces the remainder of the discourse.

Jesus does not deny his right to judge, nor does he describe the man- **8:15–16**
ner in which he judges. Rather, he claims that his words and actions are legitimate because they are in conformity with the mission given to him by the Father (Ridderbos 1997: 294–95). Turning the tables,[17] Jesus charges his Pharisaic opponents with judging in a merely human manner.[18] People rejected Jesus as Messiah at least in part because he did not come with regal fanfare or bring political liberation to Israel as they expected (cf. 6:15; 18:36). Yet, appearances can be deceiving.[19]

In fact, Jesus is not alone in his rendering of judgment.[20] In this regard, too, there is complete unity between him and the Father (Barrett 1978: 339; cf. Morris 1995: 392). Jesus' mode of judgment is entirely distinct from that of the Pharisees (Morris 1995: 391). His judgment of individuals is the natural result of their unwillingness to believe his evidence.[21] The words "It is I and the Father who sent me" constitute a Semitism.[22] Jesus' words "I and the Father who sent me" may cor-

15. The words "where I have come from and where I am going" are an allusion to Jesus' words in John 7 (7:28, 33–34) (Schnackenburg 1990: 2.193).

16. See Ridderbos 1997: 294; Carson 1991: 339; Beasley-Murray 1999: 129; Schnackenburg 1990: 2.192.

17. Stibbe (1993: 101) comments, "The irony of the chapter is the fact that Jesus himself becomes the prosecutor. Having begun a process of questioning and prosecuting Jesus, the three Jewish groups find themselves almost imperceptibly taking on the role of defendants. The old irony of the judged becoming the judge is played out here."

18. Cf. 7:24. "By human standards" more literally reads "according to the flesh" (only here in John). This is another implicit instance of the dualism between flesh and spirit (cf. 3:6; 6:63).

19. Cf. 2 Cor. 5:16; Isa. 53:2–3; 1 Sam. 16:7; see Barrett 1978: 338; Moloney 1998: 266–67.

20. Cf. 16:32. See also *m. ʾAbot* 4.8. The conjunction δέ (*de*, but) serves to "reverse" the negative statement in 8:15b (Barrett 1978: 339). Morris (1995: 392) suggests that δέ (given its relationship with καί [*kai*, even]) means "even if."

21. Schnackenburg 1990: 2.194; cf. Moloney 1998: 267; R. Brown 1966: 345. Carson (1991: 339 [cf. Burge 2000: 257]) denies the suggestion that κρίνω (*krinō*, judge) has the meaning "to pass judicial sentence" and the conclusion on that basis that Jesus came not to convict but to save.

22. According to later Jewish tradition, when the priests marched in procession around the altar at the Feast of Tabernacles, singing the *hosanna* of Ps. 118:25, they did not sing "O Lord,"

respondingly indicate that Christ had now taken the place of Israel in relation to God (cf. 15:1) (contra Ridderbos 1997: 295).

8:17–19 With δέ (*de*, but) delayed in 8:17, the expression preceding it ("in your law") is emphatic (Barrett 1978: 339). The expression "your law"[23] indicates that Jesus distanced himself from his Jewish opponents.[24] The Pharisees' "law" was, of course, the Hebrew Scriptures (including messianic predictions and typological prefigurations), yet the Pharisees had added numerous pieces of oral tradition that in many cases effectively subverted the law's original message. Nevertheless, even by their own standards, the Jews were in the wrong, for the law bore witness to Jesus (cf. 5:39, 46–47; see Morris 1995: 392; R. Brown 1966: 341). Thus, rather than being law-observant, the Pharisees are in fact hostile to the law's true and ultimate point of reference.

On the two-witness requirement, see commentary at 8:13. Apparently, "the Jews took this so seriously that they interpreted Scripture to mean 'two witnesses' wherever a witness is mentioned unless it is specifically laid down that only one is required" (Morris 1995: 393 n. 24, citing Str-B 1:790). The pronouncement "I am one who bears witness concerning myself, and the Father who sent me bears witness" is presented in the form of a chiasm (Ridderbos 1997: 295). Jesus here states plainly that he and his Father are the two witnesses that attest to his truthfulness (Pancaro 1975: 275–78; Neyrey 1987: 512–15; Cory 1997: 104–5).[25]

There may be a hint of deity in Jesus' "I am" statement, recalling passages such as Isa. 43:10 (Morris 1995: 393 n. 25; Ball 1996: 186). In Jewish tradition, the combined witness of father and son was not acceptable, at least for certain purposes (*m. Roš Haš.* 1.7). In the present instance the Jews, of course, expect witnesses whose statements can be heard and compared with each other, so that it can be determined whether they agree. In 5:31–39, Jesus had listed a whole series of witnesses, including the Father, John the Baptist, Jesus' own works, and the Scriptures (see commentary at 1:7). Here, Jesus focuses exclusively on the Father as corroborating his own testimony (Morris 1995: 393).

---

but rather "I and he" in order to avoid using the name of God (*m. Sukkah* 4.5; cf. *m. Yoma* 6.2), whereby "I and he" lent expression to the fellowship between Israel and Yahweh.

23. Apparently, this is also how Gentiles referred to the law when in dialogue with Jews (Dodd 1953: 82).

24. Cf. 10:34; see also 6:49: "your ancestors"; 8:56: "your father Abraham"; 15:25: "their law" (see Augenstein 1997). Barrett (1978: 339) seems to deny the historicity of the words "in your law," suggesting that they are a creation of the evangelist intended to show the separation that occurred between Christianity and official Judaism. However, in light of the consistent pattern throughout John's Gospel, and the undeniable acrimony between Jesus and his Jewish opponents historically, this expedient is unnecessary. In favor of historicity are Morris (1995: 392 n. 19) and Carson (1991: 340).

25. Witherington (1995: 175) notes that for someone to call upon God as witness is akin to making a serious oath. Also, not believing a statement made under oath was as precarious as lying under oath.

"Where is your father?" By asking such a question, the Pharisees (by way of Johannine irony/misunderstanding) admit that they really do not know who Jesus is, despite the earlier claims of some inhabitants of Jerusalem (7:27). This attests to the Pharisees' estrangement from God (Ridderbos 1997: 297). The immediate point of the question may be that if Jesus' father is going to be his witness, he should present him (Ridderbos 1997: 297). Yet according to Jesus, anyone who has seen him has seen the Father (14:9; cf. Matt. 11:27), who is spiritually present with him throughout his ministry (John 1:18) and has testified to him in Scripture (cf. 5:37–38).[26] The Pharisees, who were proud of their knowledge of God (cf. Rom. 2:17; Kruse 2003: 204), would have been predictably offended by Jesus' statement.

These things took place in the temple area,[27] near the place where the offerings were made.[28] The treasury stood in the women's court (Mark 12:41–44 par.), not far from the hall where the Sanhedrin met.[29] The court of women also was the place where the celebration of lights took place during the Feast of Tabernacles (see commentary at 8:12). Each of the thirteen trumpet-shaped receptacles had inscriptions indicating the intended use of the various offerings: "gold for the mercy seat," "frankincense," "bird offerings," "wood," "freewill offerings," and so on (*m. Šeqal.* 6.5).[30]

8:20–22

"Yet" (concessive καί, *kai* [Ridderbos 1997: 299]) no one arrested him (see commentary at 7:30). Remarkably, even though Jesus was in a highly public location, he eluded arrest. This the evangelist attributes to divine sovereign providence and protection: "because his time had not yet come" (cf. 7:28–30). Only at the appointed hour would Judas (the instrument of Satan) and the Sanhedrin be permitted to arrest Jesus and hand him over to be crucified. "Not yet" (οὔπω, *oupō*) continues the narrative tension (Moloney 1998: 268).

Jesus, the light shining in the world's darkness, now issues a warning, indicating that time is running out for the Jews to accept his testimony. He is about to "go," and even though the Jews will look for him, they

---

26. "Like father, like son"—like the equivalent "Like mother, like daughter" (Ezek. 16:44)—was a truism in the ancient Near East. This family resemblance pertains both to external physical features and to character traits.

27. Ἱερόν (*hieron*, temple area) refers to the "general structure" of the temple (Wallace 1996: 561; see commentary at 2:14).

28. The preposition ἐν (*en*) is to be rendered "at," "near," or "by," since not just anyone would have been allowed inside (Ridderbos 1997: 298 n. 137). There may be irony in the location where the Jews manifest their ignorance of Jesus' true identity (Moloney 1998: 298). There may also be an element of judgment (Bultmann 1971: 283).

29. So Morris 1995: 394; Carson 1991: 341; Beasley-Murray 1999: 125 n. b; Burge 2000: 257. Barrett (1978: 340) alone seems to express some reservation.

30. There may actually have been several treasuries (cf. Josephus, *J.W.* 5.5.2 §200), the treasury, so-called, being the place where the alms boxes were set up. Several chambers were also used to store valuable items, both temple and private property (cf. *J.W.* 6.5.2 §282; *Ant.* 19.6.1 §294).

will not find him, and they will die in their sin.[31] For where he goes, they cannot come. Dying with one's sins unrepented of and unatoned for renders a person subject to the wrath and judgment of a holy God (3:36).[32] How much better to repent, confess one's sins, believe, and live (Deut. 24:16; cf. Ezek. 3:16–21; 18).

"Will he kill himself?" In 7:35, the Jews thought that perhaps Jesus was going away to the Diaspora to teach the Gentiles. Here, in another instance of misunderstanding, they interpret Jesus' statement "Where I go, you cannot come" as implying that he may commit suicide. This reveals the contempt (or low moral esteem) in which the Jews held Jesus (Schnackenburg 1990: 2.198) or at least evidences their heightened degree of exasperation.[33] Exceptional cases—such as Samson (Judg. 16:30) or the holdouts against the Romans committing mass suicide at Masada (A.D. 73)—were viewed favorably, but generally Jewish people shuddered at the thought of taking one's own life (e.g., Judas: Matt. 27:3–10; Acts 1:18–19). The corpse of such a person was left unburied until sunset (Josephus, J.W. 3.8.5 §377), and there was no public mourning. Moreover, it was believed that suicide excluded one from the future age.[34]

8:23–27 "You are from below, I am from above; you are from this world, I am not from this world" (cf. 3:12, 31). The contrast between an "upper" heavenly realm and a "lower" earthly one was recognized in Judaism, yet these two spheres were considered to be related through the concept of creation. The realm of the dead was imagined as being under the earth, and in Jubilees (ca. 150 B.C.) this underworld, the "darkness of the depths" (Jub. 7:29; cf. 5:14), was also regarded as the place of judgment (Jub. 22:22).

Whereas in Judaism a certain mystery attached to the division between what is above and what is below (m. Ḥag. 2.1), and gnostic thought assigned both knowledge (Gos. Truth 22:3–4) and salvation to the realm "above" (25:35–26:1; 35:1–2), the present passage distinguishes between "above" as the realm of God and "below" as that of humanity. The

---

31. Carson (1991: 341) takes the reference to the Jews' "looking for" Jesus to refer to their continued search for the Messiah after Jesus' death. Morris (1995: 396) thinks that the reference is to the Jews coming to realize who Jesus truly is when it is too late, or to their continued opposition after Jesus leaves their presence.

32. "Sin" in 8:21 is in the singular, which may refer to the "cardinal sin of rejecting Jesus" (Barrett 1978: 340; Carson 1991: 341; R. Brown 1966: 350; Schnackenburg 1990: 2.197). Alternatively, "sin" may be used generically to refer to a person's sinful state apart from Christ. The preposition ἐν (en, in) probably is locative ("in a state of sin"), though it also could be instrumental ("by reason of sin") (Barrett 1978: 341; cf. Morris 1995: 395).

33. D. M. Smith (1999: 184) says that "the Jews" here "at once manifest their ignorance and feign their innocence." Whitacre (1999: 215) notes that, ironically, it is really "the Jews" whose unbelief amounts to spiritual suicide.

34. According to the rabbis, the person who committed suicide could not pay with his life for the shedding of his blood (cf. Gen. 9:5), so that he must spend the afterlife in a state of damnation (see also Josephus, J.W. 3.8.5 §375; cf. 7.8.6–7.9.1 §§320–401). In contrast, pagan philosophers often considered suicide to be an "honorable death" (Droge and Tabor 1991).

repeated personal pronouns ὑμεῖς (*hymeis*, you) and ἐγώ (*egō*, I) and the repeated reference to "this" world combine to accentuate the gulf between the Jews' earthly orientation and Jesus' heavenly provenance (Moloney 1998: 273; Morris 1995: 396).[35]

John 8:24 provides the reason for Jesus' words in 8:21 (Ridderbos 1997: 300).[36] The OT background of the statement "If you don't believe that I am [the one I claim to be]" (cf. 8:28, 58) appears to be Exod. 3:13–14 as further developed in Isa. 40–55.[37] The purpose stated in Isa. 43:10 is "that you may know and believe me and understand that I am he.'" In context, "I am he" here means "I am (forever) the same," and perhaps even "I am Yahweh" (alluding to Exod. 3:14; see Ridderbos 1997: 301–2). Anyone other than God who appropriated this designation was guilty of blasphemy and subject to God's wrath (Isa. 47:8–9; Zeph. 2:15).[38]

The question "Who are you?" (another instance of Johannine misunderstanding [Barrett 1978: 342]) may be in response to Jesus' use of the predicateless ἐγώ εἰμι (*egō eimi*, I am) in 8:24 (Beasley-Murray 1999: 131; R. Brown 1966: 350). The emphatic "you" (noted by Morris 1995: 398, citing A. Plummer) implies direct challenge: "Who do you think you are?" (cf. 8:53).[39] Jesus' response may be rendered as a statement, "Just as I've told you from the beginning,"[40] or as a question, "Have I not told you from the beginning?"[41] John 8:26 implies that Jesus has every right to judge the "Jews," yet his messiahship depends not on their response to him, but on the Father.[42] The Father's "all-determining significance" is underscored by the statement in 8:27 (Moloney 1998: 271).[43]

---

35. The imperfect ἔλεγεν (*elegen*, he was saying) accentuates the progressive nature of Jesus' claim (cf. 8:27; labeling this an "aoristic imperfect," as Wallace [1996: 542] does, lacks explanatory power).

36. The plural "sins" in 8:24 (cf. 8:21) may refer to the multitude of sins that result from the primary sin of unbelief (Carson 1991: 342).

37. So Carson 1991: 344; Beasley-Murray 1999: 130–31; Schnackenburg 1990: 2.200. See especially Isa. 41:4; 43:10, 13, 25; 46:4; 48:12; cf. Deut. 32:39.

38. For a study of Jesus' words in 8:24 in light of Jewish messianic expectations, see Freed 1982.

39. The same phrase occurs in Epictetus, *Diatribai* 3.1.22: "Well, who are you?" (Σὺ οὖν τίς εἶ) (ca. A.D. 50–120).

40. So Carson 1991: 344; R. Brown 1966: 347; cf. Motyer 1997: 159, referring to 8:12 and 5:19–30.

41. Beasley-Murray (1999: 131, following M. Zerwick) prefers "Just what I am telling you." See also Michaels (1989: 149): "Just what I have been claiming all along."

42. Ridderbos 1997: 303. The expression κἀγώ (*kagō*, and I) creates a close link between Jesus and the Father (Morris 1995: 401 n. 54). The use of εἰς (*eis*, to) in the phrase "to the world" is interesting. R. Brown (1966: 348) suggests that it has an "aspect of motion."

43. Ridderbos (1997: 303) proposes that 8:27 relates to Jesus' words in 8:24b (rather than 8:25–26), translating, "They *had* not understood." If so, the Jews failed to understand that Jesus was actually referring to himself in 8:24.

8:28–30 It is their very action of crucifying Jesus that will cause them to become aware of who Jesus truly is (Ridderbos 1997: 303). The phrase "then you will know" (note the prophetic nature of this pronouncement [Beasley-Murray 1999: 131]) raises the specter of judgment yet leaves open the possibility that some of those who rejected Jesus as Messiah may later come to faith in him (Ridderbos 1997: 304).[44] The expression "lifted up" (ὑψώσητε, hypsōsēte [here in the active voice; contrast 3:14b]) probably harks back to the suffering Servant of Isaiah, who "will be raised and lifted up and highly exalted" (Isa. 52:13).[45] There is great irony in the fact that the Jews, by having Jesus crucified, are actually "lifting" Jesus up (Bultmann 1971: 350, followed by Witherington 1995: 176). Ironically, too, "at the very moment when they think they are passing judgment on him, he becomes their judge" (Bultmann 1971: 350).

"I do nothing on my own accord, but speak just what the Father has taught me" (cf. 5:19–20, 23). Jesus, as the sent Son, again affirms his dependence on the Father, in keeping with the Jewish maxim that "a man's agent [šālîaḥ] is like the man himself" (e.g., m. Ber. 5.5). The Father is with Jesus; he has never abandoned his Son (Ridderbos 1997: 304). Jesus can say this (ellipsis [Morris 1995: 402]) because he always does what pleases the Father (8:46; cf. 4:34). Hence, Jesus' actions are proof of the Father's presence with him. This comes into starkest relief at the outset of the cross: even when Jesus is deserted by all of his followers, he knows himself to be united with the Father (16:32b) (Morgan-Wynne 1980: 2.222). This, then, was Jesus' answer to those who said that anyone crucified was God-forsaken (Schlatter 1948: 211). Even David, the "man after God's own heart,"[46] was guilty of adultery and murder. Only Jesus could legitimately claim to be fully pleasing to God.

The "many" referred to in this verse could have been the crowds that followed Jesus rather than his opponents (Morris 1995: 402). More likely, though, the "many" of 8:30 and the "Jews" in 8:31 are the same group of people.[47] A comparable statement is found in 2:23. Quite apparently, the

44. See Schnackenburg (1990: 2.202–3), who notes the following: (1) the verb γινώσκω (ginōskō, know) is always used positively in John; (2) the words are similar to 19:37, a quote of the salvation oracle Zech. 12:10; (3) 12:32 describes Jesus' mission in terms of drawing "all [kinds of] people to himself"; and (4) 8:30–31 speaks positively about the Jews' response.

45. John is the only NT writer to use this term in a dual sense with reference both to Jesus' crucifixion (his literal "lifting up") and to his exaltation (metaphorical use). For NT instances of the verb ὑψόω, with the meaning "exalted" or "honored," see Matt. 23:12 (= Luke 14:11 = 18:14); Luke 1:52; Acts 2:33; 5:31; James 4:10; 1 Pet. 5:6. On the phrase "I am the one I claim to be," see commentary at 8:24 and at 8:58.

46. See Acts 13:22; 1 Sam. 13:14; 16:7; 1 Kings 11:4; cf. Jer. 3:15.

47. So the majority of commentators, including Ridderbos 1997: 305–6; Carson 1991: 346–47; Morris 1995: 404; Beasley-Murray 1999: 132; D. M. Smith 1999: 185; Borchert 1996: 301 n. 182; Burge 2000: 259; Bultmann 1971: 252 n. 2; contra R. Brown 1966: 354–55, 358; Schnackenburg 1990: 2.204–5; Moloney 1998: 277; Westcott 1908: 2.13–14.

faith of these "believers" is shallow.[48] What is required for true, lasting discipleship is not merely immediate assent, but continued adherence to Jesus' word (8:31) (Bultmann 1971: 434).[49] By definition, true faith perseveres. Jesus was more concerned about deepening the faith of his disciples than about numerical growth among his followers (Carson 1991: 345, 347–48).

ii. The Paternity Dispute: The Jews' and Jesus' Relationship to Abraham (8:31–59)

As on previous occasions, Jesus discerns the inadequate, shallow nature of people's faith and issues an ominous warning to those who would later deny him (Ridderbos 1997: 308). The Ἰουδαῖοι (*Ioudaioi*, Jews) addressed are neither "Judaizing Christians" (so, rightly, Carson 1991: 347) nor merely people from Jerusalem or Judea (contra R. Brown 1966: 355), but those Jews of 8:30 who had believed and who later turn out to be hostile to Jesus.[50] The measure of any disciple is the ability to hold to the master's teaching (cf. 2 John 9). The perfect follower was one who had "fully absorbed his master's teaching" and "was drawing on it to spread it abroad" (*b. Yoma* 28a; see Köstenberger 1998a: 123). The reference to being "truly" Jesus' disciples (μαθηταί, *mathētai*) implies that there is in Johannine thought such a thing as false (or temporary) disciples, that is, people who follow a teaching only for a season (cf. the Synoptic parable of the sower and the soils [Mark 4:1–20 pars.]).[51]

8:31–32

"And you will know the truth, and the truth will set you free." Though references to "truth" are common in this Gospel,[52] "freedom" vocabulary is limited to 8:32–36 (see also 2 Cor. 3:17; Gal. 5:1, 13; cf. 4:4–7; James 1:25). Truth in this context is not solely intellectual but centered in Christ, who can save people from moral darkness and sin.[53] Knowledge, too,

---

48. A semantic distinction between πιστεύω + εἰς (*pisteuō* + *eis*, believe + in) and the verb alone followed by an object in the dative case cannot be maintained (Carson [1991: 346–47] and the vast majority of commentators; see also Croteau 2002). Concerning the perfect participle πεπιστευκότας (*pepisteukotas*, having believed), Swetnam (1980 citing E. Abbott 1906: 365–66) notes that the perfect participle in Greek can also serve as a pluperfect. If so, the meaning here would be "those who had [previously] believed in him [but did so no longer]."

49. This is the point made by Jesus' parable of the sower and the soils (Mark 4:1–20 pars.).

50. Ridderbos (1997: 306–7) notes the anachronistic and incongruous nature of the tendency of modern scholars to associate statements such as those made in this verse with events in the early church while disassociating them from the life and ministry of Jesus. See also Carson 1991: 347.

51. A similar construction is found in John 13:35 (love) and 15:8 (fruitfulness).

52. Cf. 1:14, 17; 3:21; 4:23–24; 5:33; 8:40, 44–46; 14:6, 17; 15:26; 16:7, 13; 17:17; 18:37–38.

53. Morris 1995: 405; cf. R. Brown 1966: 355; Borchert 1996: 303. Carson (1991: 348–49) suggests that truth in 8:32 is similar to the notion of "gospel," that is, "the truth that has been revealed in and by Jesus" (cf. Barrett 1978: 344; Schnackenburg 1990: 2.205).

is not abstract, but entails an experiential dimension (Ridderbos 1997: 308; cf. Beasley-Murray 1999: 133; Bultmann 1971: 435). The freedom meant here "is not that of a person to manage his life free of all the ties that might hinder him in the development of his own 'identity' or 'authority'" (Ridderbos 1997: 308); rather, it is a freedom that comes from without, by the "liberation from the realm of sin and death" procured by Christ (Schnackenburg 1990: 2.206). Remarkably, this "eschatological gift" (Bultmann 1971: 437, 439) can be experienced already in the here and now (Schnackenburg 1990: 2.206).[54]

8:33–36 "We are Abraham's descendants" (lit., "seed," a collective singular; see R. Brown 1966: 355). Their descent from Abraham was the Jews' pride and major source of confidence regarding their salvation.[55] The Jews considered Abraham to be the founder of the worship of God; he recognized the Creator and served him faithfully.[56] Apart from descent from Abraham, it was God's deliverance of the Israelites from slavery in Egypt that was seen to ensure the Jews' freedom (*Exod. Rab.* 15.11). Several OT passages extol the blessings of descent from Abraham (e.g., Ps. 105:6; Isa. 41:8). However, even then, physical descent from Abraham was considered to be insufficient by itself.[57]

Asserting their "spiritual superiority as children of Abraham" (Ridderbos 1997: 309 [cf. Carson 1991: 349]), the Jews claimed that they had never been slaves to anyone; they had never been in a continuing state of bondage.[58] Freedom was considered to be the birthright of every Jew. The law laid down that no Jew, however poor, should descend to the level of slave (Lev. 25:39–42). The Mishnah states, "Even the poorest in Israel are looked upon as freemen who have lost their possessions, for they are the sons of Abraham, Isaac, and Jacob" (*m. B. Qam.* 8.6 [cited in Schlatter 1948: 212]). According to the Jewish Talmud, "All Israel are royal children" (*b. Šabb.* 128a; cf. Matt. 8:11–12). Jewish revolts often sprang from the conviction that the Jews were to obey no earthly ruler, because God was their only King (see Josephus, *Ant.* 18.1.6 §23; *J.W.* 7.8.6 §323; cf. Acts 5:29).

Nevertheless, it was commonly recognized that the Jewish nation had been subjected to the political control of at least four empires: Babylon, Persia, Greece, and Rome. However, these nations were frequently

---

54. For a brief sketch of the conceptions of freedom in Judaism and Greek philosophy, see Köstenberger 2002c: 85–86.

55. See especially Matt. 3:9 par., including John the Baptist's exhortation. On the importance assigned to ancestry in Judaism, see Jeremias 1969: 271–302.

56. See Philo's portrayal of Abraham in *Abr.* 1 §70; *Migr. Abr.* 9 §43; 24 §§132–33; *Heir* 6 §§24–27.

57. See Gen. 21:9–10; 25:21–34; cf. Jer. 4:4; 9:25–26; Ezek. 36:26–27; see also Rom. 9:6–13; Gal. 4:21–23.

58. Note the emphatic position of οὐδενί (*oudeni*, to no one) and the perfect tense verb δεδουλεύκαμεν (*dedouleukamen*, we have been slaves) in 8:33 (Morris 1995: 406 n. 66).

considered to operate as God's instruments, administering his judgment on the Jews as punishment for their disobedience. Yet in the end, God would break the dominance of these foreign powers and come to rule through his people Israel. This end-time scenario was tied to a believing remnant, the restoration of the Davidic kingdom, the coming of the Messiah, and the defeat of all of God's enemies.

"Everyone who perpetrates sin is a slave to sin" (see additional note to 8:34). At issue here is not so much the commission of distinct acts of sin, but remaining in a state of sin (Morris 1995: 406; Schnackenburg 1990: 2.208; contra Barrett 1978: 345).[59] Yom Kippur, the Day of Atonement, which had just passed, should have served as a reminder that the Jews, too, were sinners.[60] Jewish ethics viewed human existence as conflict between the evil and good impulses (*yeṣer*; e.g., *m. Ber.* 9.5). The law served to restrain the evil impulse and to help the good impulse prevail (Ridderbos 1975: 130–35, esp. 131 n. 98). The idea that serious offenses subject humankind to the power of sin is attested in Second Temple literature (T. Jud. 19:4; T. Ash. 3:2) and rabbinic Judaism (*Gen. Rab.* 22.6).[61]

By affirming that a slave has no permanent place in the family, but a son belongs to it forever, "so if the Son sets you free, you will be free indeed," Jesus is implicitly using his intimate relationship with the Father to highlight his authority to set sinners free (Schnackenburg 1990: 2.209).[62] Freedom from sin is not an innate characteristic even of Jews but rather is a gift of God, available only through Jesus the Son par excellence (Ridderbos 1997: 310). This is spoken against the backdrop of the Jews' claim of being the "seed of Abraham" in 8:33 (Barrett 1978: 346; cf. Burge 2000: 261).

In both Palestine and the Hellenistic world, households included slaves as well as sons. For Jewish slaves, this dependent relationship lasted only six years; in the seventh year, they must be set free. In the Greco-Roman world, too, slaves occasionally were granted freedom, though this was not formally mandated. The notion of a "son" being set over God's house "forever" is found in an important messianic text: "I will be his father, and he will be my son. . . . I will set him over my

59. Carson (1991: 350) helpfully notes that while the act of sinning proves that one is enslaved by sin, it is also true that "sin actively enslaves." Carson also points out that since the primary issue for Jesus was enslavement to sin, "the pursuit of social justice alone will always prove vain and ephemeral unless the deeper enslavement is recognized and handled" (ibid.).
60. Ridderbos (1997: 310) notes the similarity of this passage with Rom. 6:11–18; 7:7–25. See also commentary at 13:27.
61. See the references cited in Köstenberger 2002c: 87; Kruse 2003: 210.
62. Barrett (1978: 346) suggests that ὄντως (*ontōs*, indeed) in 8:36 is roughly equivalent to ἀληθῶς (*alēthōs*, truly) in 8:31.

house and my kingdom forever; his throne will be established forever" (1 Chron. 17:13–14) (Morris 1995: 407).[63]

8:37–40 Though Jesus concedes the Jews' literal physical descent from Abraham (cf. Luke 13:16; 19:9; but see Matt. 8:11–12; Kruse 2003: 209), he notes that their claim is spiritually contradicted by the plot against him. Hence, his message "has no (permanent) place" or cannot "gain a (firm) foothold" in them (Ridderbos 1997: 311 n. 180).[64] John 8:38 is dominated by contrasts such as those between "I" and "you" and between the two "fathers" (Morris 1995: 408) (see additional note to 8:38). In the following discussion, the operative distinction may be that between the "seed" (σπέρμα, *sperma*) of Abraham and being "children" (τέκνα, *tekna*) of Abraham (Beasley-Murray 1999: 134; Borchert 1996: 304; cf. 1:12).[65] Though the Jews unquestionably are the former, their claim to being the latter is denied. For the identity of the father is validated by the conduct of the child (Ridderbos 1997: 310): "If you were children of Abraham, you would do the works of Abraham."

In Gen. 18:1–8, Abraham welcomed divine messengers with eager hospitality (Witherington 1995: 177; R. Brown 1966: 357). In the Book of Genesis, Abraham displayed obedience to God (see 12:1–9; 15:1–6; 22:1–19; though less noble instances are recorded as well). The rabbis frequently upheld Abraham as a moral example to be emulated by the Jews (*m. ʾAbot* 5.19; *b. Beṣah* 32b); a distinction is made between people who act like Abraham and those who act like Balaam (*m. ʾAbot* 5.19; cf. Jub. 23:10). Generally, Abraham was believed to have fulfilled the whole Torah, even before it was given. The phrase "works of Abraham" also occurs in the Talmud, albeit not as a stereotypical description of Abraham's conduct (cf. *b. Beṣah* 32b). Interestingly, Jesus does not immediately state his position concerning the Jews' true paternity but instead leads them to draw their own conclusion about his opinion on this point (Ridderbos 1997: 312).

The anarthrous ἄνθρωπον (*anthrōpon*, a man) in 8:40 is used generically and lacks specific theological significance (Ridderbos 1997: 312; R. Brown 1966: 357; Moloney 1998: 281). The Jews' attempt to kill Jesus ultimately points to their hostility toward God (Morris 1995: 409). Jesus' claim that he has spoken to the Jews the truth he has heard from God draws a stark contrast between his opponents' obduracy toward his claims and his role as the mediator of divine revelation.[66] "This Abra-

---

63. The special status of sons even with regard to taxation by earthly kings is affirmed by Jesus in Matt. 17:25–26. In Heb. 3:5–6, Moses and Christ are contrasted in terms of the temporary status of servant and the permanent position of son.

64. Carson (1991: 351 n. 1) suggests the translations "my word has no place in you" or "my word does not operate in you" (cf. Barrett 1978: 346).

65. Contra Ridderbos (1997: 312 n. 185), who thinks that the terms are used synonymously.

66. Ridderbos (1997: 312) cites Gen. 15:6; 17:5; Rom. 9:16ff. (intending Rom. 9:6ff.); Gal. 3:7, 29.

ham did not do" implies, in context, that Abraham was receptive to divine revelation and acted in obedience to it (e.g., Gen. 12:1–4; 22:1–14; Kruse 2003: 212). He thus becomes "a witness to Christ, a voice urging faith in Christ and an accuser of non-believers" (Schnackenburg 1990: 2.211).

"You are doing the works of your father" continues the innuendo without **8:41** yet making explicit the equation: Jesus' opponents' father = the devil. "Children born out of wedlock" translates the literal "have been born of sexual immorality" (πορνεία, *porneia*; TNIV: "illegitimate children"). The Jews take Jesus' apparent denial of their descent from Abraham as an attack on their loyalty to God. The prophets had compared Yahweh's covenant with Israel to a marriage relationship: idolatry amounted to spiritual adultery.[67]

The Jews' rebuttal may imply the illegitimacy of Jesus' birth.[68] In the ancient Near East, "to question a man's paternity is a definite slur on his legitimacy" (Morris 1995: 393 n. 28, quoting Merrill Tenney). The earliest attestation of the Jewish belief that Jesus was born out of *porneia* may be *m. Yebam.* 4.13: "I found a family register in Jerusalem and in it was written, 'Such-a-one is a bastard through [a transgression of the law of] thy neighbour's wife (Lev. 18:20).'"[69]

In further defense against Jesus' charge, the Jews claim the greatest possible spiritual paternity, a close relationship with God: "The only Father we have is God himself." In 8:39, the Jews had said that Abraham is their father (cf. 8:33, 37). Now they say that they have only one father, God. This reference to Jewish monotheism (Ridderbos 1997: 313) is entirely in keeping with OT teaching (though not necessarily Jewish practice).[70] In the framework of John's Gospel, however, the Jews' claim to be born from God is ironic (cf. 8:41); the informed reader understands that those who lack the Spirit have not been born from God (3:1–8; Keener 2003: 759).

In response to his opponents' questioning of his paternity and their **8:42–44** assertion that they have God as their Father, Jesus maintains that he does not merely have God as his Father: he came from God—implying preexistence. In pagan religions, ἥκω (*hēkō*, I have come) was commonly used for the saving appearance of deity (Schneider, *TDNT* 2:926–28). In Jesus' case, it refers to his divine origin (cf., e.g., 16:28). This is part

---

67. See, e.g., Ezek. 16:15, 32–34; Hos. 1:2; 4:15; for the phrase "children of πορνεία," see Hos. 1:2; 2:6 LXX (2:4 Eng.).

68. So Carson 1991: 352; R. Brown 1966: 357; Barrett 1978; 348; contra Ridderbos 1997: 313; Borchert 1996: 305; Schnackenburg 1990: 2.212.

69. In 8:48, Jesus is called a Samaritan, but this may merely involve the charge of apostasy rather than questioning his Jewishness (for Samaritans being "illegitimate Jews," see 2 Kings 17:24).

70. Cf. Exod. 4:22; Deut. 32:6; Isa. 63:16; 64:8; Jer. 31:9; Mal. 2:10.

of John's portrayal of Jesus as coming from God and returning to him (metaphorically depicted in terms of descent/ascent; see Köstenberger 1998b: 121–30).

Rhetorically, Jesus then asks why the Jews do not recognize the true nature of his message.[71] Answering his own question, he asserts that the reason why they cannot do so is that they cannot hear his word (cf. 8:47).[72] Given the truthfulness of Jesus' words, the Jews' rejection of his message is therefore natural (cf. 8:45; see Morris 1995: 412). For they have the devil as their father and thus want to do his bidding—kill Jesus the Messiah.[73] The evangelist later makes clear that the plot to kill Jesus (cf. 8:37, 40) was ultimately inspired by Satan himself (13:2, 27). The phrase "murderer from the beginning" primarily refers to the fall narrative (Gen. 3) rather than the first murder (Gen. 4).[74]

Still, a reference to Cain, the murderer of Abel, may be secondarily in view (cf. 1 John 3:15, the only other reference featuring the term "murderer"; see R. Brown 1966: 358). If so, Jesus' comment may imply that the devil is the father of "the Jews" because they would kill Jesus, their fellow Jew, just as Cain had killed his brother Abel (Díaz 1963: 75–80; Dahl 1963). Other Jewish texts refer to those outside the community as "children of destruction" (Jub. 15:26), "sons of Beliar" (Jub. 15:33), or "sons of darkness" (1QS 1:10; 1QM passim).[75]

"Not holding to the truth" (cf. John 8:31–32) may refer to the fall of Satan (Isa. 14:12?), which preceded the fall narrative in Gen. 3.[76] This

71. Morris (1995: 410) and Barrett (1978: 348) claim to detect a contrast between Jesus' λαλία (*lalia*, speech) and his λόγος (*logos*, word), but it is hard to see why these two terms should not be understood as rough synonyms, in keeping with Johannine style.

72. On predestination in John's Gospel, see Schnackenburg 1990: 2.214–15. Carson (1991: 353) suggests that ἀκούω (*akouō*, hear) has the connotation of "obey." R. Brown (1966: 357) thinks that the verb means literally that the Jews "have become so obdurate that they cannot even hear him; they are deaf." Ridderbos (1997: 314) notes that Jesus' opponents' spiritual incomprehension results from their failure to combine hearing with faith.

73. Note the absence of the personal pronoun with τοῦ πατρός (*tou patros*, of the father), which harks back to 8:38. Cf. Ridderbos 1997: 315. Τοῦ διαβόλου (*tou diabolou*, of the devil) stands in apposition to τοῦ πατρός rather than implying that the devil has a father (Schnackenburg 1990: 2.213). For a study of 8:31–59 taking 8:44 as its point of departure, see Motyer (1997: esp. 160–210), who argues that the present interchange does not serve an anti-Jewish purpose, but rather is designed to persuade Jews that Jesus is the Christ.

74. So Morris 1995: 411; Ridderbos 1997: 315; Carson 1991: 353; Barrett 1978: 349; Beasley-Murray 1999: 135; Schnackenburg 1990: 2.213; Moloney 1998: 280; Borchert 1996: 305–6. It was commonly recognized in Second Temple literature that death was the result of Satan's initiative (Wis. 2:23–24; Sir. 25:24; cf. Rom. 5:12).

75. Antiochus Epiphanes IV, who erected the "abomination of desolation" in the temple in 167 B.C. and who serves as a type of the antichrist in biblical literature (see Dan. 9:27; 11:31; 12:11; cf. Matt. 24:15 par.) is called "murderer and blasphemer" in 2 Macc. 9:28 (see commentary at 10:36).

76. The phrase means, more literally, "not standing in the truth," which may imply that "the truth was not his starting point or standpoint" (Ridderbos 1997: 315; Barrett 1978:

narrative, in turn, makes clear that Satan flatly contradicted the truthfulness of God's word (Gen. 3:3–4; cf. 2:17). Parallels to the notion of not holding to the truth are found in the DSS (1QS 8:5–6; 1QH 12:14), which contrast the "spirit of truth" with the "spirit of deceit" (1QS 3:18–19; cf. John 14:17; 15:26; 16:13; 1 John 4:6). John does not use the expression "spirit of deceit," though the present passage does depict Satan as being diametrically opposed to truth.

Whenever the devil speaks a lie, he speaks ἐκ τῶν ἰδίων (*ek tōn idiōn*), which means either "he speaks from his own family" (Greek masculine) or "he speaks from his own things" (Greek neuter, in the sense of "doing what comes naturally," i.e., speaking his "native language" [so the TNIV]), with the latter being preferred (Barrett 1978: 349; Schnackenburg 1990: 2.214). In fact, the devil "is a liar and the father of lies" (lit., "father of it"; cf. Gen. 2:17; 3:4).[77] In all of this, Jesus and the devil are presented as complete opposites, with Jesus as the life-giver and truthful witness, and the devil as the quintessential murderer and liar (Witherington 1995: 178).[78]

The connection between Jesus' speaking the truth and the Jews' rejection of his message is by way of a causal ὅτι (*hoti*, because). The Jews fail to believe, not *in spite of* the truthfulness of Jesus' message, but *because of* it. In light of their true spiritual paternity, their response, according to Jesus, is entirely natural (Morris 1995: 412; cf. Ridderbos 1997: 316). Hence, unbelief is shown to be rooted ultimately in people's subjection to satanic lies and deception rather than merely lack of comprehension or human choice.

8:45–48

In the face of Jewish obduracy, Jesus affirms his absolute moral perfection and freedom from sin: "Who among you can convict me of sin?" (stated positively in 8:29). By issuing this challenge—and thus placing the burden of proof on his challengers (Ridderbos 1997: 317)—Jesus holds up his conduct as being consistent with his spiritual union with God the Father. The Jews may have accused him of individual "sins," such as breaking the Sabbath, but even they must admit that his general conduct is unassailable (Schnackenburg 1990: 2.216). In Isa. 53:9, it is said regarding the suffering Servant that there was no "deceit in his mouth."[79] Christ's sinlessness is affirmed by the unanimous testimony of the early church.[80]

---

349). The phrase "truth is not in him" asserts that Satan "has nothing in common with truth" (Barrett [1978: 349], who notes the absence of the article).

77. Notably, ψεῦδος (*pseudos*, lie) "does not refer here to a distinct act that can be immediately rectified but to a transindividual power of deception with paternity of its own" (Ridderbos 1997: 315).

78. In the DSS, the opponent of the "Teacher of Righteousness" is called the "Man of Lies" (1QpHab 2:1–2; 5:11; CD 20:15), with the Teacher saying of the people who want to divert him from his path, "They are sowers of deceit and seers of fraud, they have plotted evil against me . . . and are not firmly based in your truth" (1QH 12:9–10, 14).

79. Alluding to this passage, the Testament of Judah speaks of the "Star from Jacob," in whom "will be found no sin" (24:1 [Christian interpolation?]).

80. See 2 Cor. 5:21; Heb. 4:15; 1 Pet. 2:22 (citing Isa. 53:9); 1 John 3:5.

With sharp logic, Jesus exposes the Jews' inconsistency. If they have God as their Father, as they claim (harking back to 8:41; see R. Brown 1966: 365–66), why do they not listen to the message from God that Jesus came to bring?[81] For anyone who is from God listens to his words. As in 8:43, Jesus provides the answer to his own question (Morris 1995: 413). The reason why his opponents do not listen to him is that they are not from God. This undercuts Jewish presumption of their election by God and their own righteousness on account of keeping the law. Like Nicodemus, they must be born from above (3:3, 5, 7) with a birth that is not predicated upon human factors but is of God (1:13). Though in one sense they were God's children, in another, all-important sense, they first must "become" God's children by faith in Jesus (1:12).

Yet rather than ponder Jesus' assertions, his Jewish opponents sharpen the tone of their rhetoric: "You are a Samaritan and have a demon."[82] This is the only place in the four Gospels where Jesus is accused of being a "Samaritan."[83] Earlier in this Gospel, Jesus is shown to fraternize with Samaritans (esp. 4:40), but it is unclear whether Jesus' present audience is aware of this encounter (though certainly John's readers are).[84] In light of the fact that the entire present controversy revolves around paternity, and that Jesus has just insulted the Jews' own sense of paternity by Abraham their ancestor, this may best be seen as a riposte slandering Jesus' paternity in return: if he says that the Jews are of their "father the devil" (8:44), he will be charged with having been birthed by a Samaritan! Indeed, "for a *Jew* to question the paternity of other Jews was so despicable that only demon-possession could explain it" (Carson 1991: 355).

Ironically, though the Samaritan woman (4:9) and Pilate, the Roman procurator (18:35), acknowledge Jesus to be Jewish, his own people distance themselves from him. The reason for this may be, at least in part, that Jesus, like the Samaritans, called into question the legitimacy of the Jews' worship; hence his opponents' countercharge that it is he who is a "Samaritan," that is, a Jewish apostate.[85] Moreover, calling Jesus a Samaritan may intimate that Jesus' miracles are due to demonic influence

81. Ridderbos (1997: 317 n. 200) notes that 8:46 is missing from certain MSS because of the homoioteleuton in 8:45 and 8:46.

82. Morris (1995: 414) conjectures that the phrase "Do we not rightly say?" might refer to a charge brought against Jesus throughout his ministry, though he acknowledges the lack of direct evidence.

83. Cf. the charge of demon possession in 7:20; 8:52; 10:20.

84. Keener (2003: 764) seems to think that the present charge represents an extrapolation from reports of the welcome Jesus received in Samaria (4:40). He notes that the informed reader, who knows that Jesus denied the legitimacy of worship on Mount Gerizim and affirmed that salvation was from the Jews (4:21–22), recognizes the charge as slanderous (and perhaps motivated by envy).

85. This implies that Jesus neglects the traditional ways of Judaism and so is perceived as acting more like a Samaritan than like a true Jew (Morris 1995: 414; cf. Ridderbos

or magic.[86] In a talmudic passage, a person who learned Scripture and the Mishnah but did not study with a rabbi is described by one teacher as belonging to "the people of the land," by another as a Samaritan, and by a third as a magician.[87] Probably, the present insult is grounded in a whole cluster of ideas (Schnackenburg 1990: 2.218).

Given the lack of demons in this Gospel, it is natural for John's Jesus not to defend himself more fully against the charge of demon possession (cf. Mark 3:22 pars.; see Barrett 1978: 350). The personal pronouns ἐγώ (egō, I) and ὑμεῖς (hymeis, you) serve to accentuate the contrast between Jesus and his Jewish opponents (Morris 1995: 414 n. 100). Jesus offers his obedience to the Father as evidence of his freedom from demonic influence (Morris 1995: 414–15; cf. Carson 1991: 355). His calm, nonretaliatory response, "I honor my Father, and you dishonor me,"[88] evokes reminiscences of Isaiah's suffering Servant (cf. 1 Pet. 2:23, alluding to Isa. 53:7). According to Jewish law, rejection of someone's messenger was tantamount to rejection of the sender as well (see commentary at 5:25; 8:28). In many non-Western societies, honor and shame are of utmost importance; the dishonoring of a person is regarded as practically inexcusable (Malina 1981: 25–50). Jesus' charge, then, is that his opponents fail to give him due honor as the Father's Son (Barrett 1978: 350).

8:49–51

Nevertheless, despite his lofty claims, Jesus avers that none of his previous words should be construed as an attempt to elevate himself (Morris 1995: 415). He does not seek honor for himself, though "there is one who seeks it, and he is the judge."[89] This ominous statement serves as a reminder (and warning) that the Father will "vindicate the truth of his testimony and condemn his accusers for rejecting it" (Beasley-Murray 1999: 136; cf. Ps. 7:9–11; 35:22–28). That they "will never, ever see [i.e., experience] death" is a promise made to all who keep Jesus' word.[90] The earlier synonymous reference is to "abide by [Jesus'] teach-

1997: 318). Morris (1995: 414) suggests that the Jews might be addressing Jesus' failure to recognize their relationship with Abraham. Barrett (1978: 350) notes that since Dositheus and Simon Magus (both Samaritans who claimed to be sons of God) were described as demon-possessed, Jesus' opponents might be making a similar connection with him (cf. Moloney 1998: 286; R. Brown 1966: 358).

86. See Acts 8:9–11; Justin, *1 Apol.* 26.1–5; *b. Sanh.* 43a.

87. *b. Soṭah* 22a; the rabbis are Eleazar (A.D. 80–120), Jannai (ca. A.D. 240), and Aḥa b. Jacob (ca. A.D. 300).

88. The word ἀτιμάζω (atimazō, dishonor) occurs elsewhere in the NT in Mark 12:4; Luke 20:11; Acts 5:41; Rom. 1:24; 2:23; James 2:6.

89. A possible parallel is Isa. 16:5: "In love a throne will be established; in faithfulness a man will sit on it—from the house of David—one who in judging seeks justice and speeds the cause of righteousness."

90. Cf. 5:24; see also 6:40, 47; 11:25–26. Carson (1991: 355 [cf. Lindars 1972: 332]) suggests that this statement is in further development of 8:50. The word ἐμόν (emon, my) stresses that it is Jesus' word that must be kept; θάνατον (thanaton, death) is emphatic as well (Morris 1995: 416 n. 104), as is the negative οὐ μὴ . . . εἰς τὸν αἰῶνα (ou mē . . . eis

ing" (8:31). The phrase "will [never, ever] see death," a common Jewish idiom,[91] serves as "a graphic expression of the hard and painful reality of dying" (Behm, *TDNT* 1:677; Chilton 1980; Ridderbos 1997: 319 n. 205). Yet exceptions such as Enoch or Elijah showed that the power of death was not absolute.

8:52–53 Jesus' response to the charge of demon possession in 8:48, rather than defusing the charge, further exacerbates it. What was phrased as a question in 8:48 is now put as an emphatic statement: "Now we know that you have a demon!" How can Jesus promise eternal life to those who keep his word, when the greatest men in Israel's history, such as Abraham and the prophets, died?[92] Jesus' statement in Matt. 22:32 pars. (contra the Sadducees, who denied the resurrection) that God is "the God of Abraham, the God of Isaac, and the God of Jacob," and that he is "not the God of the dead but of the living," implies that Abraham is destined for eternal life with God (cf. Heb. 11:10, 13–16). Yet here the issue is not whether Abraham will be raised to eternal life but whether he (and the prophets) died in the first place.

The OT Scriptures, Jewish tradition, and Greco-Roman beliefs agree that death is the common lot of humanity. "What man can live and not see death, or save himself from the power of the grave?" writes the psalmist (Ps. 89:48). "Where are your forefathers now? And the prophets, do they live forever?" asks the prophet (Zech. 1:5). Even people whom the Jews believed to have been exceptionally close to God were not exempt from death.[93]

The Jews' quotation of Jesus' statement closely resembles the original at 8:51.[94] Thick Johannine irony laces the following question, "You are not greater than our father Abraham, are you?" (expecting a negative answer).[95] The Samaritan woman asked, "You are not greater than our

ton aiōna, never . . . ever) (Wallace 1996: 468–69). Note that when Jesus' opponents quote his statement in 8:52 (per the evangelist's rendering), they use the less marked pronoun μου (*mou*, my) instead of the possessive adjective ἐμόν and do not place θάνατον in an emphatic position.

91. See Ps. 88:49 LXX; Luke 2:26; Heb. 11:5; the close equivalent "will not taste death" is found in John 8:52.

92. Ironically, so did Jesus; yet in his case, the reason was substitutionary atonement, and his death was followed by resurrection.

93. Such as Abraham: see the midrash *Tanḥuma* 6.11. For Greco-Roman parallels, see Köstenberger 2002c: 90.

94. The majority of commentators believe that there is no significance in the slight alteration of Jesus' words in 8:52 (Morris 1995: 416 n. 104; Barrett 1978: 350–51; R. Brown 1966: 359; Borchert 1996: 307). Note, however, that "taste death" replaces "see death" (see Laney 1992: 168; cf. 5:24). The expression "taste death" is not found in the OT, but "to see death" is (see commentary at 8:51). The expression "taste death" occurs in the NT also in Mark 9:1 (cf. Barrett 1978: 351) and Heb. 2:9. See further Acts 2:27, 31 (citing Ps. 16:10); 1 Cor. 15:54–55 (citing Isa. 25:8; Hos. 13:14); 1 John 3:14. On other minor differences, see footnote for commentary at John 8:51.

95. Morris 1995: 416; Carson 1991: 356; Barrett 1978: 351. The pronoun ἡμῶν (*hēmōn*, our) in the phrase "our father Abraham" is likely exclusive, with Jesus not included as

father Jacob, are you?" (4:12), and Jesus elsewhere announced that one greater than Jonah and Solomon now was here (Matt. 12:41–42 par.). Operating along a salvation-historical continuum, John seeks to demonstrate that Jesus is far superior to any of his predecessors in God's plan of salvation, including not only Abraham and Jacob, but also Moses and John the Baptist. Moreover, what sets Jesus apart from his predecessors is not merely a difference of degree but a qualitative difference (cf. 8:58); for he is God incarnate.

The concluding question, τίνα σεαυτὸν ποιεῖς; (tina seauton poieis?) conveys impatience, exasperation, and the charge of arrogance on the part of the Jews ("Who do you think you are?" [TNIV]) and challenges Jesus' exalted and seemingly outlandish claims ("Who do you make yourself out to be?" [Carson 1991: 356; cf. Morris 1995: 417; Beasley-Murray 1999: 137]).

Jesus' response confirms the underlying thrust of the Jews' question at the end of the previous verse, that is, that Jesus' mission is self-appointed and his claims are self-exalting. Yet Jesus avers that self-glorification is irrelevant; what drives him is not a craving for recognition or self-aggrandizement but obedience (8:55). In fact, it is Jesus' Father—the very one whom the Jews call their God (cf. 8:41)—who brings honor and glory to him. This will be true at the cluster of events surrounding Jesus' crucifixion and resurrection (7:39; 12:16, 23; 13:31–32); it is true already during Jesus' earthly ministry (11:4; 12:28) (Schnackenburg 1990: 2.220). **8:54–57**

Staying on the offensive, Jesus asserts that his opponents' rejection of him proves that they really "do not know him," that is, the Father (cf. 8:27).[96] For if they did know the Father, they would acknowledge Jesus as the God-sent Messiah. A similar charge was leveled against the Jews by some of the OT prophets (e.g., Hos. 4:1; 6:6); several later prophetic passages predict a time when people would indeed know God (e.g., Isa. 11:9; Jer. 31:31–34; Hab. 2:14) (Carson 1991: 356). But even the prophets could not claim to be free from sin or to know God the way Jesus claimed. What his opponents are really asking him, Jesus notes, is to be unfaithful to his charge. If he were to deny God, he would be "a liar like" them (see commentary at 8:44; cf. 1 John 1:10).

"Abraham your father looked forward to the time when he would see my day, and he saw it and was glad" (cf. 8:39; see also 8:33, 37).[97] "To say

---

ancestor of Abraham (Wallace 1996: 398). Note also the relative pronoun ὅστις (hostis, who), which is both indefinite (R. Brown 1966: 359) and qualitative (Morris 1995: 416 n. 105) in import. Abraham serves as a type of others like him, and all of those were "of such a quality as to die" (Morris 1995: 416 n. 105).

96. The conjunction καί (kai, but) at the beginning of 8:55 is adversative ("yet" [Ridderbos 1997: 320 n. 209; Barrett 1978: 351]). Γινώσκω (ginōskō) and οἶδα (oida) for "know" are synonymous (Barrett 1978: 351; Borchert 1996: 307).

97. The term ἀγαλλιάω (agalliaō, be glad) occurs in this Gospel elsewhere only in 5:35. The sense is that of being "overjoyed" (Morris 1995: 417). The conjunction ἵνα (hina, that)

that Abraham saw the Messiah was neither new nor offensive to Jewish teachers; it was its application to Jesus that was unbelievable" (Beasley-Murray 1999: 138, paraphrasing Schlatter). Appealing to Gen. 15:17–21, Rabbi Akiba (d. ca. A.D. 135) taught that God revealed to Abraham the mysteries of the coming age (*Gen. Rab.* 44.22).[98] Abraham's "rejoicing" was taken by Jewish tradition to refer to his laughter at the prospect (or actual birth) of his son Isaac. This interpretation was based partly on Gen. 17:17 (seen as joy, not scorn, as in Philo, *Chang. Nam.* 29–31 §§154–69)[99] and partly on Gen. 21:6 (cf. Jub. 15:17; 16:19–29; see also Targum Onqelos on Gen. 17:17).[100]

The "day of the Lord" here has become *Jesus'* "day." Though this expression usually refers to the final judgment, here it probably denotes the incarnation (Morris 1995: 419).[101] "Abraham's joyful anticipation of the promise made to him [which involved a multitude of descendants] and of its (provisional) fulfillment in the birth of Isaac is placed here in the perspective of the eschatological salvation that has dawned with the coming (the 'day') of Jesus" (Ridderbos 1997: 321 [cf. Carson 1991: 357; R. Brown 1966: 360]). Since Jesus fulfills what is written of and announced in the OT, for the Jews to be true children of Abraham would have meant for them to share in his attitude of joyful expectation.[102]

The Jews' incredulous riposte, "You are not yet fifty years old, and you have seen Abraham?" involves misunderstanding in that Jesus had spoken of Abraham seeing *Jesus'* "day," not vice versa (Ridderbos 1997: 322; Moloney 1998: 286; Schlatter 1948: 221). According to Luke 3:23, Jesus was "about thirty years old" when he began his ministry (probably thirty-two). If the present dialogue occurs in the fall of A.D. 32, Jesus would be about thirty-five (perhaps almost thirty-six) years old (see introductions to 1:19–28 and 1:35–51). The age of fifty was commonly considered to mark the end of a man's working life and his attainment of full maturity (cf. Num. 4:3, 39; 8:24–25; *m. ʾAbot* 5.21; see Beasley-

---

is variously classified as referring to the content of Abraham's joy (Morris 1995: 417); as introducing "the ground of the rejoicing" (Barrett 1978: 351); as causal or explanatory (Beasley-Murray 1999: 126 n. l); or as conveying purpose (R. Brown 1966: 359).

98. Cf. 2 Esdr. (4 Ezra) 3:13–14; 2 Bar. 4:4; Apoc. Abr. 31:1–3; see Moloney 1998: 284.
99. So Moloney 1998: 286; R. Brown 1966: 360.
100. It has been suggested (e.g., Michaels 1989: 153; cf. Brodie 1993: 335) that the reference here may be to Abraham's rejoicing when he announced to Isaac on the way to the sacrifice, "God himself will provide the lamb for the burnt offering, my son" (Gen. 22:8). See also T. Levi 18:2, 6 (cf. 18:14; Matt. 8:11).
101. So Schnackenburg 1990: 2.222, citing 1 Enoch 61:5; 2 Esdr. (4 Ezra) 13:52. Similarly, Bultmann (1971: 326 n. 2). Brodie (1993: 335) opts for a broader scope, suggesting that "Jesus' day refers to the way in which, during his entire life, and especially in his death, he was revealed as the Anointed." Similarly, Whitacre (1999: 230), who says that the expression encompasses Jesus' "whole advent, ministry, death, resurrection and ascension."
102. Ridderbos 1997: 321–22; cf. Carson 1991: 357; Barrett 1978: 352; R. Brown 1966: 367; Burge 2000: 263.

Murray 1999: 139).[103] Jesus, the Jews may be saying, has not even reached full maturity, and he makes claims such as having seen Abraham.[104] His opponents' application of this measure to him may provide the context for Jesus' response in 8:58. Yet, according to Jesus, the sphere of his existence is beyond the scope of time.

The statement "Before Abraham came into being, I am" (cf. Ps. 90:2; see commentary at 8:24, 28) contrasts an allusion to Abraham's birth with a reference to Jesus' eternal existence, focused on his incarnation (Ridderbos 1997: 322–23). Jesus' language here echoes God's self-identification to Moses in Exod. 3:14.[105] Thus, Jesus does not merely claim preexistence— otherwise he could have said, "before Abraham was born, I *was*"—but deity (Motyer 1997: 159; note the reaction in 8:59).[106] The present instance of ἐγὼ εἰμί (*egō eimi*, I am) startlingly culminates earlier occurrences of this expression in this chapter (e.g., 8:24, 28) (Freed 1983b).

8:58–59

At this, they took up stones in order to cast them at him (cf. 10:31–33; 11:8).[107] This is in keeping with John's emphasis on Jesus' claim to deity. Stoning was the prescribed punishment for blasphemy (Lev. 24:16; cf. Deut. 13:6–11; *m. Sanh.* 7.4; see Carson 1991: 358). However, such punishment was to be the result of righteous judgment, not mob violence (Deut. 17:2–7; see Daube 1956: 306). Already in OT times, people considered stoning righteous men such as Moses (Exod. 17:4), Joshua and Caleb (Num. 14:10), and David (1 Sam. 30:6). Stephen, the church's first martyr, was stoned on account of alleged blasphemy (Acts 7:57–60). Paul, too, was stoned, although he escaped with his life (Acts 14:19; 2 Cor. 11:25), as were other saints (Heb. 11:37). The availability of stones in the temple area points to the fact that the temple area (though not the temple building proper [see commentary at 2:20]) was still being renovated.[108]

---

103. Kruse (2003:217) cites a stipulation in the Qumran writings (CD 14:7–10) that certain officeholders must be between thirty and fifty years of age. Schlatter (1948: 220) says that the present passage coheres with Matt. 17:24, for the obligation to pay the temple tax ended at age fifty: "hence Jesus was not yet a πρεσβύτερος." Also, the Book of Jubilees uses "fifty years" to measure the eras since the creation (M. Edwards 1994; followed by Moloney 1998: 286).

104. Keener (2003: 769) suggests that the Jews were probably "annoyed by his [Jesus'] claims to authority despite his relative youth."

105. Cf. Isa. 43:10, 13; so Ball 1996: 195–96; Schnackenburg 1990: 2.224; Burge 2000: 263.

106. Wallace (1996: 515, 530–31) contends that the present reference does not constitute an instance of the historical present of εἰμί (*eimi*, I am). Lindars (1972: 336) notes how the "striking change of tense and the use of the simple verb *einai* put all the emphasis on the timeless condition of eternal existence," drawing attention also to the escalating force of the "I am" sayings of the present chapter (8:12, 24, 28, 58).

107. John is the only evangelist who refers to the Jews' attempt to stone Jesus on account of blasphemy.

108. Josephus, *Ant.* 17.9.3 §216; *J.W.* 2.1.3 §§11–12; see Morris 1995: 420–21; R. Brown 1966: 360; cf. Laney 1992: 169.

But Jesus hid himself[109] and left the temple area, for his God-appointed destiny involved crucifixion, not stoning (Schlatter 1948: 221, citing also 10:31; cf. 10:39–40). With this, the narrative returns to the important Johannine theme of "the elusive Christ" (see esp. Stibbe 1991; cf. R. Brown 1966: 367).[110] Jesus consistently eludes his pursuers until the appointed "time" (cf. 7:30, 44; 8:20; see also Luke 4:30). "Hid himself" (cf. 12:36), coupled with leaving the temple area, may imply the departure of God's glory from among his people.[111] Jesus' action is reminiscent of his going up to the festival "not publicly, but in secret" in 7:10.

Additional Notes

8:16. Πατήρ is omitted in ℵ* and D, which would focus more on Jesus' mission and less on his relationship with the Father (Morris 1995: 392 n. 21). However, this reading is almost certainly secondary.

8:34. Τῆς ἁμαρτίας is almost certainly original (𝔓[66,75] ℵ B C; omitted in D). The meaning of the verse is only marginally affected in any case (Morris 1995: 406 n. 69; Ridderbos 1997: 309 n. 177), though the longer reading does heighten the character of slavery (Schnackenburg 1990: 2.208). The omission of the words may have been an attempt at stylistic improvement (Beasley-Murray 1999: 126 n. d; cf. Bultmann 1971: 438 n. 1). Conversely, R. Brown (1966: 355) suggests that a scribe may have added the words under the influence of Rom. 6:17.

8:38. The pronoun ὑμῶν probably is not original (so Morris 1995: 408; Beasley-Murray 1999: 126 n. e; contra Carson 1991: 351 n. 2). The word is not found in 𝔓[66], 𝔓[75], and B but is included in ℵ, C, and D. Nor is the pronoun μου original (absent from 𝔓[66,75] B C). Ridderbos (1997: 311) comments that the absence of pronouns suggests that "the emphasis does not yet lie on the different paternity of each but on the fact that both act in accord with their father and that the identities of their fathers therefore emerges [sic] in their action and speech." There is also a certain amount of textual instability as to the use of ἠκούσατε versus ἑωράκατε in 8:38b, with the former found in 𝔓[75], B, and C (plus ℵ[2]), and the latter in 𝔓[66], ℵ*, and D.

8:39. The reading ἐστε . . . ἐποιεῖτε is found in 𝔓[75] and ℵ* and supported by the majority of commentators (e.g., Morris 1995: 409 n. 77; Beasley-Murray 1999: 126 n. g; cautiously, Barrett

---

109. The passive verb ἐκρύβη (*ekrybē*) in 8:59 and 12:36 is customarily translated in English Bibles as reflexive/middle ("hid himself"; KJV; NKJV; NIV; TNIV; ISV; ESV; NLT; NET; NRSV; NASB) or even actively ("hid"; NAB; CEV). The sole exception is the HCSB, which renders the expression as a genuine passive. See also Morris (1995: 421), who contends that the NT usage is to take the form as a real passive and consequently argues that the passive form may imply the agency of God the Father in concealing Jesus. This is possible; *ekrybē* does function as a genuine passive in Luke 19:42 and Heb. 11:23, the only other two NT instances (besides here and in John 12:36) of the aorist passive indicative form of *kryptō*. But cf. BDAG 571, which treats both references as instances of the passive used in an active sense ("to hide"). Similarly, BDF §471 (4).

110. Cf. the Markan "messianic secret" motif.

111. Cf. 1:14; Ezek. 10–11; see Carson 1991: 358, citing W. Davies 1974: 290–96; Barrett 1978: 353. Keener (2003: 774) concurs that Jesus' withdrawing from the temple may "evoke a state of *Ichabod*, God's glory withdrawing from a polluted and rebellious sanctuary" (citing Ezek. 5:11; 8:4; 9:3; 10:4, 18). Ridderbos (1997: 324 n. 225) suggests that the meanings of the verbs ἐκρύβη and ἐξῆλθεν (*exēlthen*, he left) "mutually determine each other."

1978: 347). Properly, the form would be either a present (ἐστε . . . ποιεῖτε [so 𝔓⁶⁶ B*]) or a past condition (ἦτε . . . ἐποιεῖτε ἄν [so ℵ² C]). The presumed original reading therefore represents a mixed form (which makes it the "harder" reading), with the variants representing scribal attempts to correct the grammar of the phrase. The present tense ἐστε and the absence of ἄν may be intended to lend greater vividness to the statement ("If you *really* were . . ." [so Barrett 1978: 347]). The adversative δέ in 8:40 also supports reading the imperfect in 8:39. R. Brown (1966: 356–57) believes that the "mixed condition" indicates that Jesus affirms the Jews' kinship with Abraham yet charges that their conduct conflicts with their claim of Abrahamic descent.

8:44. The imperfect ἕστηκεν (𝔓⁶⁶ ℵ B* C) is to be preferred over the perfect ἕστηκεν (𝔓⁷⁵ B²) on both textual grounds (Ridderbos 1997: 315 n. 192; Bultmann 1971: 320 n. 4) and contextual grounds (Barrett [1978: 349] relates the phrase to ἀπ' ἀρχῆς in the previous clause), though Schnackenburg (1990: 2.214) notes that in light of 1 John 3:8, the difference may be rather inconsequential.

8:54. The difference in variants between ἡμῶν (𝔓⁷⁵ A B²) and ὑμῶν (𝔓⁶⁶* ℵ B* D) is, in the end, immaterial (Morris 1995: 417 n. 106). The external evidence is inconclusive; ἡμῶν appears favored by internal evidence (resulting direct speech; see Barrett 1978: 351; Beasley-Murray 1999: 126 n. k; Moloney 1998: 286).

8:57. The variant ἑώρακέν σε (𝔓⁷⁵ ℵ*) represents a rather transparent attempt at harmonizing the two statements.[112]

8:59. The various additions to the end of this verse are secondary; the ending ἱεροῦ enjoys excellent early and diversified support (𝔓⁶⁶, ⁷⁵ ℵ* B D) and surely is original (Beasley-Murray 1999: 126 n. n).

112. See Beasley-Murray 1999: 126 n. m; Schnackenburg 1990: 2.223; R. Brown 1966: 360; Bultmann 1971: 327 n. 3; contra Burge 2000: 263.

4. The Healing of the Blind Man and the Good Shepherd Discourse (9:1–10:42)

The present section brings a preliminary conclusion to the festival cycle, which extends from chapters 5 to 12 in John's Gospel. The *inclusio* pertaining to John the Baptist (10:40–42) brings some closure to chapters 5–10, setting the stage for the climactic seventh sign—the raising of Lazarus (ch. 11)—and its aftermath in the following chapter (ch. 12). The healing of the man born blind (ch. 9) is the sixth Johannine sign and the third healing recorded in John's Gospel. Hence, there is a certain symmetry between the Cana cycle (John 2–4) and the festival cycle (John 5–10) because both feature three signs of Jesus. The transitional section (John 11–12) contains the final, climactic seventh sign.

John 9–10 continues the Fourth Evangelist's agenda of demonstrating Jesus to be the messianic Son of God (cf. 20:30–31). There is no break between the end of chapter 9 and the beginning of chapter 10, making these two chapters a closely knit unit. Both literarily and historically, the healing in chapter 9 forms the backdrop for Jesus' good shepherd discourse in chapter 10. The Jewish leaders are shown to be blind guides and illegitimate usurpers, while Jesus is presented as the true, self-sacrificing shepherd of the sheep. Hence, the theme of escalating conflict between Jesus and the Jewish leadership, coming to the fore in chapters 5–12 and reaching peaks in chapters 5 and 8 (see esp. 5:18; 8:59), is continued in chapters 9–10 (see esp. 10:31–40, where the Jews again attempt to stone Jesus because of blasphemy, but Jesus again eludes their grasp and temporarily withdraws).

a. Jesus Heals a Blind Man (9:1–41)

The healing of the man born blind constitutes the sixth and penulti-mate sign chosen by John to demonstrate Jesus' messiahship.[1] Like the second (the clearing of the temple in ch. 2) and the fourth signs (the healing of the lame man in ch. 5), it takes place in Jerusalem, thus evincing an oscillating geographical pattern between Galilee and Judea. The parallels between the healings in chapters 5 and 9 are par-ticularly pronounced (Malina and Rohrbaugh 1998: 109; Culpepper 1983: 139 [cited in Witherington 1995: 194–95]). The sites for both healings are pools (5:2; 9:7), and both healings take place on a Sab-bath (5:9; 9:14). In both cases the healing is rendered difficult by the attending circumstances (lameness for thirty-eight years; blindness from birth), and in both instances Jesus' chosen method of healing is unconventional (5:8–9; 9:6–7). Yet the healed men's responses could not be more different (Carson 1991: 366; R. Brown 1966: 377; contra Beck 1997: 86–90).

Healings of blind men by Jesus are also featured in the other ca-nonical Gospels.[2] This is the sixth sign and the third healing selected by the Fourth Evangelist, following the healings of the royal official's son and of the lame man recorded in 4:46–5:15. Restoring sight to the blind is considered to be a messianic activity in the OT (Isa. 29:18; 35:5; 42:7).[3] In the context of his Gospel, John casts the healing in terms of light/darkness imagery. Just as Jesus is the light of the world by fulfilling Feast of Tabernacles symbolism (see 8:12), so also he shows himself to be the light of the world by giving sight to the blind man (Keener 2003: 779). The world, and the Jews with it, lies in darkness; whoever wants to walk in the light must come to Jesus.[4]

1. For a survey of source-critical scholarship on John 9, see Borchert (1996: 310–12). Carson (1991: 360–61) provides a brief summary and critique of Martyn's "two-level" reading of the chapter in light of the history of the putative "Johannine community." See also Bauckham (2001: esp. 103–6), who contends that Martyn's hermeneutic violates the genre of the Fourth Gospel.

2. Cf. Matt. 9:27–31 pars.; 12:22–23; Matt. 20:29–34 pars.; Mark 8:22–26.

3. Both Matthew and Luke set Jesus' healing of the blind in the context of the ministry of Isaiah's Servant of the Lord (Luke 4:18–19; Matt. 11:5 = Luke 7:21–22; Matt. 15:30–31; 21:14; cf. Isa. 35:4–6; 61:1–2; see also Isa. 29:18; 42:7). John, too, patterns Jesus' ministry to a significant extent after Isaiah's portrait of the Servant of the Lord (see esp. 12:38–41).

4. For an analysis of John 9 in light of the Johannine lawsuit motif, see Lincoln 2000: 96–105.

This contrast between light and darkness is illustrated by the two main characters (Lee 1994: 162).[5] The blind man progresses from calling Jesus a prophet (9:17) to defending him against the Pharisees' charges (9:25), inviting them to become Jesus' disciples (9:27), correcting their doctrine (9:34), confessing Jesus as Lord, and worshiping him (9:38), whereas the Pharisees, in a display of Johannine irony, are oblivious to their spiritual blindness (Talbert 1992: 158). Thus, while the Pharisees' guilt remains, the man walks home not only with his physical sight restored but also spiritually changed—a believer and worshiper of Jesus.[6] Jesus, the one supposedly under investigation, has the last word in a scathing pronouncement that exposes the Pharisees' spiritual blindness. More than a mere miracle, this sign represents a highly symbolic display of Jesus' ability to cure spiritual blindness. As the present story makes clear, the only sin against which there is no remedy is spiritual pride that claims to see while being, in fact, blind.

It is unclear exactly how much time has elapsed since Jesus' clash with the Jewish authorities at the end of the Feast of Tabernacles (chs. 7–8). But since the Feast was observed in September or October (in A.D. 32, Tabernacles fell on September 10–17); since both chapters 9 and 10 take place in Jerusalem (note the mention of the pool of Siloam in 9:7 and of Solomon's colonnade in 10:23); since there is no clear demarcation between chapters 9 and 10; and since 10:22 refers to the Feast of Dedication, which took place in Jerusalem in mid-December, it can be inferred that the healing of the man born blind must have taken place between October and mid-December (A.D. 32).[7]

In the ensuing investigation, John, with thinly veiled irony, keeps track of what people know or do not know (Duke 1985: 119; for a similar dynamic, see 3:1–15).[8]

---

5. For structural proposals, see especially Ridderbos (1997: 332), who divides the chapter into four major scenes (9:1–5, 6–12, 13–34, 35–41); Duke (1985: 125–26 [followed by Lincoln 2000: 97]), who contends that irony is intensified by the evangelist's juxtaposition of parallel scenes (9:1–7, 8–12, 13–17, 18–23, 24–34, 35–38, 39–41), which are arranged chiastically with 9:22 at the center; Lee (1994: 164–65), who sees a threefold structure (9:1–7, 8–34, 35–41); and Keener (2003: 775), who divides chapters 9 and 10 as follows: 9:1–34 (blindness and sin); 9:35–10:18 (true shepherd, sheep, and thieves); 10:19–21 (divided response); and 10:22–42 (conflict at Hanukkah). Lincoln (2000: 99) also follows Duke (1985: 126) in contending that in John 9 "the theme is clearly trial and judgment," with the elements of a trial emerging from 9:13 onward.

6. The paradoxical reversal between the blind seeing and the seeing being blind is in keeping with the dynamic unleashed by Jesus' ministry elsewhere (viz., Synoptic parables; cf. Matt. 9:12–13 pars.).

7. Due to the lack of a clear break between chapters 8 and 9 and the fact that the pool of Siloam was near the temple, Keener (2003: 776–77) contends that "[i]n the story world it therefore remains the final day of the Feast of Tabernacles." It is less clear when he thinks the events of chapter 9 took place historically.

8. The man's parents know that he is their son and that he was blind; but how he was healed and who opened the man's eyes, they do not know (9:20–21). The Pharisees know

Exegesis and Exposition

[1]And as he passed by, he saw a man who had been blind from birth. [2]And his disciples asked him, saying, "Rabbi, who sinned, he or his parents, so that he was born blind?" [3]Jesus answered, "Neither he sinned nor his parents, but this happened in order that the works of God may be manifested in him. [4]We must accomplish the works of the one who sent ⌜me⌝ as long as it is day. Night is coming, when no one can work. [5]While I am in the world, I am the world's light." [6]Having said these things, he spit on the ground, made some mud with his saliva, and put the mud on the man's eyes [7]and said to him, "Go, wash in the pool of Siloam" (which translated means "sent"). So he [the man] went and washed and returned seeing. [8]Then his neighbors and those who had formerly seen him—that he was a beggar—were saying, "Isn't this the one who used to sit there and beg?" [9]Others were saying, "It's him." Yet others were saying, "No, it's not him, but he looks like him." But he was saying, "It's me!" [10]So they were saying to him, "How, then, were your eyes opened?" [11]He answered, "The man called Jesus made mud and put it on my eyes and told me, 'Go to Siloam and wash.' So I went and, after having washed, was able to see." [12]And they said to him, "Where is he?" He said, "I don't know."

[13]They led him—the one who had formerly been blind—to the Pharisees. [14]Now it was a Sabbath on the day on which Jesus had made mud and opened his [the man's] eyes. [15]Again therefore the Pharisees also asked him how he had received his sight. And he told them, "He put mud on my eyes, and I washed myself, and now I see." [16]So some of the Pharisees were saying, "This man is not from God, because he does not keep the Sabbath." But others were saying, "How can a sinful man perform such signs?" And there arose a division among them. [17]Then they said to the blind man again, "What are you saying concerning him?—because it is your eyes he opened." And he said, "He is a prophet."

---

that Jesus is a sinner, or else he would not have broken the Sabbath (9:24). They also know that God spoke to Moses but do not know Jesus' background (9:29; cf. 9:30). The formerly blind man, finally, says that he does not know whether Jesus is a sinner or not (9:25; but see 9:31), but one thing he knows: he once was blind but now sees. He finds it curious that the Pharisees plead ignorance regarding Jesus' background, for "we know" that God does not listen to sinners but only to the godly man who does his will (9:30–31). Keener (2003: 784–85) calls this "battle of knowledge" an "epistemological conflict" (which is a bit too philosophical sounding).

¹⁸So the Jewish leaders still did not believe concerning him—that he had been blind and had received his sight—until they summoned the parents of the one who had received his sight ¹⁹and asked them, saying, "Is this your son, regarding whom you say that he was born blind? How, then, does he now see?" ²⁰Then his parents answered and said, "We know that he is our son and that he was born blind. ²¹But how he now sees, we don't know, or who opened his eyes, we don't know; ask him—he is old enough, he will speak for himself." ²²(His parents said these things because they were afraid of the Jewish authorities. For the Jews had already decided that anyone who confessed him as Christ would be put out of the synagogue. ²³For this reason his parents said, "He is old enough; ask him.")

²⁴Then they called the man—the one who had been blind—a second time and said to him, "Give glory to God! We know that this man is a sinner." ²⁵Then he answered, "Whether or not he is a sinner, I don't know. One thing I do know: I was blind but now I see!" ²⁶Then they said to him, "What did he do to you? How did he open your eyes?" ²⁷He answered them, "I've told you already, and you didn't listen. Why do you want to hear it again? You don't want to become his disciples, too, do you?" ²⁸So they hurled insults at him and said, "*You* are this man's disciple, but *we* are disciples of Moses. ²⁹We know that God spoke to Moses. But this man—we don't even know where he's from!" ³⁰The man answered and said to them, "Now this is amazing: you don't know where he's from, yet he opened my eyes. ³¹We know that God doesn't listen to sinners, but if anyone is God-fearing and does his will—to him God listens. ³²It is unheard of that anyone ever opened the eyes of one born blind. ³³If this man were not from God, he could do nothing." ³⁴They answered and said to him, "You—in sins you were born entirely, and *you* are teaching *us*?" And they threw him out.

³⁵Jesus heard that they had thrown him out, and when he found him, he said, "Do you believe in the Son ⌐of Man⌐?" ³⁶He answered and said, "And who is he, sir? [Tell me,] so that I may believe in him." ³⁷Jesus said to him, "You have seen him—in fact, he is the one speaking with you." ³⁸⌐And he said, "I believe, Lord"; and he worshiped him. ³⁹And Jesus said⌐, "For judgment I came into this world: that those who do not see may see, and those who do see may become blind."

⁴⁰Some of the Pharisees who were with him heard him say these things and said to him, "We are not also blind, are we?" ⁴¹Jesus said to them, "If you were blind, you would not have sin; but now that you say, 'We see,' your sin remains."

i. The Healing (9:1–12)

9:1–3a   "And as he passed by" (καὶ παράγων, *kai paragōn*) is the only instance of this descriptive phrase in John.⁹ The scene may have taken place in the area south of the temple at one of the two southern gates.¹⁰

9. The expression occasionally appears in the Synoptics (cf. Matt. 9:9; Mark 1:16; 2:14). Similar phrases occur in two accounts featuring the healing of blind men in Matthew (9:27; 20:30).
10. As to the time of the event, see the introduction to John 9 above.

4. The Healing of the Blind Man and the Good Shepherd Discourse
a. Jesus Heals a Blind Man
John 9:1–41

The man was blind from birth.[11] Lacking light, he also lacks life in the Johannine sense (Brodie 1993: 345). What is more, in the following narrative the healing is presented "not as an act of restoration, but as a creative act by him who is the Light of the World" (Lindars 1972: 341; so, earlier, Schlatter 1948: 222). The man's blindness from birth raises the ante for the ensuing miracle and makes it all the more striking (cf. 9:32; see commentary at 2:10). In ancient Palestine, blind people were cast wholly on the mercy of others. They frequently would position themselves near sanctuaries, hoping that passersby would be in a charitable mood.

"Rabbi, who sinned, he or his parents, so that he was born blind?" (cf. 9:34).[12] Jewish rabbis generally believed in a direct cause-and-effect relationship between suffering and sin (cf. the Book of Job, e.g. 4:7; b. Šabb. 55a). Jesus, however, while acknowledging the possibility that suffering may be the direct result of sin (cf. John 5:14), denied that such was invariably the case (cf. Luke 13:2–3a; see Ridderbos 1997: 333). Paul likewise acknowledged that a specific illness or experience of suffering may be the consequence of sin (Rom. 1:18–32; 1 Cor. 11:30), but he also made clear that this did not follow automatically (2 Cor. 12:7; Gal. 4:13; see Carson 1991: 361).

The disciples' statement can be placed squarely within the context of contemporary rabbinic views. Underlying the disciples' statement is the concern not to charge God with perpetrating evil on innocent people (cf. Exod. 20:5; Num. 14:18; Deut. 5:9).[13]

Jesus answers that this happened (ellipsis [Ridderbos 1997: 333; Morris 1995: 425 n. 11]) in order that the work of God may be manifested in the man's life (cf. 11:4; see Duke 1985: 118–19).[14] "Work of God" is literally "works of God."[15] The thought here is that even evil ultimately contributes to the greater glory of God. This is true supremely of human sinfulness

9:3b–5

---

11. This is the only place in the Gospels where the sufferer is said to have been afflicted from birth. The Book of Acts features two accounts of men crippled from birth, healed by Peter and Paul respectively: 3:2; 14:8.

12. On "rabbi," see commentary at 1:38. Apart from 9:2–3, the verb ἁμαρτάνω (hamartanō, sin) occurs elsewhere in this Gospel only in 5:14. The ἵνα (hina, so that) is consecutive, expressing result (Ridderbos 1997: 332 n. 246; Wallace 1996: 473).

13. Regarding the possibility that the man's blindness from birth may be the result of prenatal sin, compare Jewish speculation surrounding the struggle of Jacob and Esau in their mother Rebecca's womb (Gen. 25:22; cf. Gen. Rab. 63.6). There are also several parallels regarding the possibility that the man's blindness was the result of his parents' sin prior to his birth (Cant. Rab. 1.6 §3; Ruth Rab. 6.4; Tg. Ps.-J. of Deut. 21:20). However, several passages in the OT and Second Temple literature strongly challenge the notion that children suffer for their parents' sin (e.g., Jer. 31:29–30; Ezek. 18; cf. Tob. 3:3).

14. Poirier (1996), Burge (2000: 273), and Kruse (2003: 220–21) take the purpose clause in 9:3b with 9:4, which is less likely.

15. Noted by Calvin 1959: 239. See John 6:28; Ps. 64:9; 66:5; 78:7; Jer. 51:10; Tob. 12:6, 7, 11; 2 Macc. 3:36; 1QS 4:4.

resulting in Christ's crucifixion (e.g., 12:28, 37–41; 17:1, 5; cf. Rom. 8:28). Another instance of this dynamic is Pharaoh at the exodus.[16]

Jesus' pronouncement "We must accomplish the works of the one who sent me as long as it is day" has several rabbinic parallels (cf. *m. ʾAbot* 2.15; *b. Šabb.* 151b). "We" (emphatic [Ridderbos 1997: 334; Carson 1991: 362]) may include the disciples (Morris 1995: 426; Moloney 1998: 292); "the one who sent me" upholds Jesus' unique status as the Sent One of God (Carson 1991: 362).[17] The term δεῖ (*dei*, must), as elsewhere in John (e.g., 3:14; 4:4; 10:16; 12:34), connotes divine necessity (Köstenberger 1998b: 112–13; Ridderbos 1997: 333): God's work must be accomplished no matter how fierce the opposition (and in the present case, whether or not the day is a Sabbath; see Ridderbos 1997: 334; Bultmann 1971: 332).

The statement "Night is coming, when no one can work" (cf. 11:9–10; 12:35–36) has the ring of common sense, if not a proverbial saying.[18] It conveys the notion that Jesus' time to work is short (Ridderbos 1997: 334).[19] Apart from rare exceptions (such as shepherds, night watchmen, or special messengers), no one works in the dark (not even he who is the light of the world!).[20] Here, "night" also connotes the world's spiritual darkness apart from Jesus (cf. 9:5).[21]

Jesus' announcement that his earthly role would be limited in time (cf. 7:33–36; 12:35–36; 13:33) was contrary to the popular notion that the Messiah and the messianic age would last forever (cf. 12:34). The statement "I am the light of the world" links the present incident with the Feast of Tabernacles (cf. 8:12).

9:6–7 Once again, the miracle occurs entirely at Jesus' initiative; as earlier (5:6), there is no indication of requests or even prior conversations (Ridderbos 1997: 335; cf. Carson 1991: 363; Morris 1995: 427; Barrett

---

16. See Rom. 9:17; cf. Exod. 9:16; 14:4; Ps. 76:10.

17. On the phrase "he who sent me," see commentary at 1:33; 5:23; 8:18.

18. Similarly, Rom. 13:12: "The night is nearly over; the day is almost here. So let us put aside the deeds of darkness and put on the armor of light." Another proverb, which takes the night symbolism in a different direction, is found in Menander: "The night refreshes, the day brings forth work" (*Sententiae e codicibus Byzantinis* 532 = *Sent. Mono.* 1.385).

19. Michaels (1989: 160) comments, "Like a laborer determined to finish his job before nightfall, Jesus summons his disciples to join him in taking full advantage of the remaining daylight hours." D. M. Smith (1999: 192) notes that the time is short both for Jesus, who must complete his work on earth before his hour of departure arrives, and for his hearers, whose opportunity to respond positively to Jesus is close to gone (12:35–36). In this regard, compare the repeated references to Jesus' appointed "time" in John's Gospel (Beasley-Murray 1999: 155).

20. Bultmann (1971: 332 n. 1) finds this problematic and attributes the alleged difficulty to disparate sources; but see the responses by Ridderbos (1997: 334) and Carson (1991: 363).

21. Carson (1991: 363) sees the focus of the "darkness" in the period between Jesus' departure (i.e., the arrest prior to the crucifixion) and Pentecost.

4. The Healing of the Blind Man and the Good Shepherd Discourse
    a. Jesus Heals a Blind Man
John 9:1–41

1978: 358). The phrase "having said these things" ties 9:6 tightly to 9:5, making the sign an illustration of the saying in 9:5 (Carson 1991: 363; cf. Barrett 1978: 357–58). Jesus' use of saliva (9:6, cf. 9:11, 14–15) is reminiscent of the healing of the deaf and mute man in the Decapolis (Mark 7:33) and of the blind man in Bethsaida (Mark 8:23). According to some Jewish rabbis, the saliva of a firstborn had healing properties (*b. B. Bat.* 126b). In the surrounding pagan culture, however, saliva frequently was associated with magical practices,[22] so that many rabbis seem to have condemned the use of saliva.[23]

Like people in other cultures, Palestinian Jews apparently believed that human excreta (including saliva) were forms of dirt rendering a person ceremonially unclean. Under certain conditions, however, it was believed that that very "dirt" could become an instrument of blessing in the hands of authorized individuals. Thus, blood and saliva generally pollute, but in certain contexts blood cleanses and saliva cures. In the OT, saliva may convey ceremonial uncleanness (Lev. 15:8). If the reversal of this taboo also applies, then by using saliva to cure a man, Jesus claims to possess unusual spiritual authority (cf. Matt. 8:1–4).[24]

Jesus then tells the man to go and to wash in the pool of Siloam;[25] the man immediately obliges and returns seeing.[26] In the OT, Elisha does not heal Naaman immediately but sends him to wash in the Jordan (2 Kings 5:10–13). John 9 carries the only references to the pool of Siloam in the NT (cf. Luke 13:4). Isaiah speaks of "the gently flowing waters of Shiloah" (Isa. 8:6; cf. Neh. 3:15). The existence of a "basin of the latrines of Siloam" is attested by a reference in the Copper Scroll of Qumran (3Q15 10:16).[27] A part of the major water system built by King

22. Most frequently cited is the healing of the blind soldier Valerius Aper, apparently by Asclepius, in which an eye-salve was used (Deissmann 1927: 135; Rengstorf, *TDNT* 6:119). According to Boring, Berger, and Colpe (1995: 284), the inscription probably comes from the Asclepius temple on the island in the Tiber in Rome and dates to A.D. 138.

23. E.g., Rabbi Aqiba (ca. A.D. 130) in *t. Sanh.* 12.10.

24. Cf. D. Smith 1985, building on the work of Douglas 1984.

25. The double imperative constitutes a Semitism (Barrett 1978: 358). Ridderbos (1997: 336) lists three reasons why the blind man was sent to Siloam: (1) to wash the mud out of his eyes; (2) to evoke the blind man's faith; and (3) to carry out ritual purification (cf. Luke 7:14). Carson (1991: 365) adds (4) to correlate the Pharisees' unbelief with a prophecy of judgment in Isa. 8:6 (though he rejects any prefiguration of baptism, contra Lindars [1972: 344], who sees the man's bath as a "quasi-baptismal washing"; see also Ridderbos 1997: 337). Grigsby (1985) argues that the washing in the pool of Siloam constitutes a thematic anticipation of the Johannine cross.

26. Morris (1995: 428) notes the nonchalant fashion in which the miracle is described. Barrett (1978: 359) comments, "The man's obedience was complete and so was his cure." A connection with the previous chapters is established by the fact that the water for the water-pouring rites of the Feast of Tabernacles was drawn from the pool of Siloam (cf. *m. Sukkah* 4.9–10).

27. Josephus frequently refers to the pool of Siloam. See *J.W.* 2.16.2 §340; 5.4.1 §140; 5.6.1 §252; 5.9.4 §410; 5.12.2 §505; 6.7.2 §363; 6.8.5 §401.

Hezekiah, this rock-cut pool was located southwest of the city of David (excavated in 1880; see Michaels 1983: 150). Its water was "sent" (hence its name [cf. John 9:7]) via Hezekiah's tunnel from the Gihon spring in the Kidron valley (cf. 2 Chron. 32:30; see Ridderbos 1997: 336).[28]

As at other places, John translates Semitic words: "which translated means 'sent'" (see commentary at 1:38). The evangelist here establishes an allegorical connection between the water of the spring and Jesus as the Sent One of the Father (Carson 1991: 365; Morris 1995: 428).[29] Not only does the sign show Jesus to be the "light of the world," but also it reveals him as the sent Son (Ridderbos 1997: 336). The underlying OT reference may be Gen. 49:10, which was interpreted messianically by both Jewish and Christian interpreters: "The scepter will not depart from Judah until Shiloh comes."[30] Rabbinic sources mention the pool as a place of purification.

9:8–12   The phrase οὐχ οὗτός ἐστιν (*ouch houtos estin*, is not this) assumes an affirmative answer (Ridderbos 1997: 338 n. 263; cf. Morris 1995: 428–29).[31] The neighbors had become so accustomed to the man's begging that "they were flabbergasted to think the blind beggar could now see" (Carson 1991: 366). Begging (cf. Mark 10:46) as a way of life was a common feature in first-century Palestine (Jeremias 1969: 116–19). It was about the only way a blind person could make a living in that day. Beggars were "the truly poor," whose "hand-to-mouth existence was considered hardly worth living" (on the poor, see *m. Peʾah* 8; see also Davids, *DJG* 704). In Judaism, the giving of alms was considered to be of greater significance than all the commandments (*b. B. Bat.* 9a, b), constituting, together with the law and obedience, one of three pillars of the world (*m. ʾAbot* 1.2). Charitable deeds were viewed as a way to gain merit with God (*b. Šabb.* 151b; cf. Sir. 3:3–4, 30; 35:1–4) and as protection against the devil (*Exod. Rab.* 31.1).

"His neighbors . . . Others . . . Yet others . . . But he . . ." is another instance of the evangelist's skillful narrative art featuring lively interchange (cf. 7:12, 25–27, 31, 40–43).[32] The sequence of the three responses—

28. There is some debate as to whether it is to be identified with the "lower" or "old" pool (Isa. 22:9, 11; see Carson 1991: 365), the "upper" pool (cf. 2 Kings 18:17; Isa. 7:3; 36:2), or some other pool (Mackowski 1980: 56–58, 72, 74).

29. Kruse (2003: 222) suggests that the evangelist may have added the gloss "sent" to indicate that the miracle occurred because Jesus *sent* the man, not because the water had healing properties.

30. Barrett 1978: 358–59; Schnackenburg 1990: 2.243 (cited in Lee [1994: 167 n. 1], who also refers to Isa. 8:6 LXX). See *Gen. Rab.* 98.8; 99.8.

31. For other Johannine instances of questions with οὐ expecting an answer in the affirmative, see 4:35; 6:42, 70; 7:19, 25, 42; 8:48; 10:34; 11:37, 40; 14:10; 18:26; 19:10.

32. The imperfect verb tenses in 9:8–10 indicate ongoing discussion (Morris 1995: 429 n. 24). Morris (1995: 429) regards the NIV rendering of ἔλεγον (*elegon*, they were saying) as "they demanded" in 9:10 as too strong (note the change to "they asked" in the TNIV). The

(1) "It's him, isn't it?"; (2) "Yes, it's him"; (3) "No, it's not, but he looks like him"—plus the man's own testimony, "It's me!" establishes for the reader that the man in question is indeed the same man who formerly had been blind (Ridderbos 1997: 338). The man's limited response concerning "the man called Jesus" may indicate that he knew little about Jesus (Morris 1995: 429).[33] His repeated and humble confession of ignorance (9:12, 25, 36) stands in contrast with the Pharisees' brash statements (9:16, 24, 29) (R. Brown 1966: 377).

ii. The Pharisees' First Interrogation of the Formerly Blind Man (9:13–17)

The "they" who brought the man to the Pharisees presumably are the man's neighbors (9:8)—whose intentions were not necessarily hostile (Carson 1991: 366–67; Beasley-Murray 1999: 156; Morris 1995: 430)—though the subject is left indefinite to shift focus on the Pharisees' dealings with the formerly blind man.[34] As on other occasions, no mention is made of other Jewish sects, such as the Sadducees.[35]

    9:13–17

As in the case of the lame man in John 5, the day on which the blind man was healed was a Sabbath (cf. 5:9–18; 7:21–24; Matt. 12:1–14 pars.), and the fact is not mentioned until the point becomes relevant (Ridderbos 1997: 339).[36] It is clear that for the evangelist, christological concerns raised by the healing predominate (Carson 1991: 367; cf. Schnackenburg 1990: 2.247). According to the Pharisees, Jesus may have "broken" the Sabbath in the following ways (Carson 1991: 367): (1) since he was not dealing with a life-or-death situation, Jesus should have waited until the next day to heal the man; (2) Jesus had kneaded the clay with his saliva to make mud, and kneading (dough, and by analogy, clay) was included among the thirty-nine classes of work forbidden on the Sabbath (*m. Šabb.* 7.2; cf. 8.1; 24.3);[37] (3) later Jewish tradition stipulated that

---

passive "were opened" in 9:10 is an instance of agency being suppressed for rhetorical effect (Wallace 1996: 437).

33. See commentary at 9:6–7 and at 9:14–15.

34. Τόν ποτε τυφλόν (*ton pote typhlon*, the formerly blind man) is placed in apposition to αὐτόν (*auton*, him) earlier in the sentence, which is construed as emphatic by some commentators, including Ridderbos (1997: 339) and Morris (1995: 430 n. 29).

35. The reason for this may be that the Pharisees constituted the most popular and influential religious group in the Judaism of Jesus' day. John's focus on the Pharisees among Jesus' opponents may also reflect the fact (assuming a post–A.D. 70 date for the writing of the Gospel) that the Sadducees ceased to exist as a party after the destruction of Jerusalem in A.D. 70, so that they would have been of less interest to John's readers, especially in the Diaspora.

36. Morris (1995: 430) thinks it plain that the examination of the man before the Pharisees occurs "on a day subsequent to that of the cure." Borchert (1996: 317) perceives that the reference to the Sabbath "gives the effect of sounding a piercing alarm in the story."

37. See Ridderbos 1997: 335; Morris 1995: 427; Barrett 1978: 359; R. Brown 1966: 373; Borchert 1996: 318.

it was not permitted to anoint eyes on the Sabbath, although opinion seems to have been divided (*b. ʿAbod. Zar.* 28b).[38]

Interestingly, though the story revolves around Jesus and his actions, his name is not mentioned: "Jesus is the great absent and unmentioned one" (Ridderbos 1997: 339).[39] The imperfect ἠρώτων (*ērōtōn*, they were asking [noted in Morris 1995: 431]) may support the notion that the Pharisees launched a full inquiry, albeit condensed by the evangelist into the "how" of the miracle (Carson 1991: 367). Although the man is the one being interrogated, Jesus is the actual target of the Pharisees' investigation, though in the end it will be made clear that the tables have turned (9:39–41; see Barrett 1978: 360).

So some of the Pharisees were saying, "This man is not from God, because he does not keep the Sabbath."[40] But others were saying, "How can a sinful man perform such signs?"[41] The division apparent in this verse roughly follows the differing ways of reasoning followed by the schools of Shammai and Hillel (Carson 1991: 367, citing Schlatter).[42] The former based its argument on foundational theological principles ("Anyone who breaks the law is a sinner"), while the latter argued from the established facts of the case ("Jesus has performed a good work") (Schlatter 1948: 227).[43] Already in OT times, the Israelites were warned against the appearance of a prophet or dreamer who would perform "a miraculous sign or wonder" to lead people astray (Deut. 13:1–5).

The Pharisees said to the blind man again, "What are you saying concerning him?"[44] The fact that the Pharisees even care to ask the man what he

---

38. Schnackenburg (1990: 2.247) notes the active voice of ἀνέῳξεν (*aneōxen*, he opened), saying that it "brings Jesus into prominence as healer and sabbath-breaker."

39. Stibbe (1993: 107) notes that here, as in 5:1–15, Jesus is at the center of controversy even when he is offstage: "The narrator is employing the device of 'focus' in such a way as to leave Jesus in the centre of the reader's thinking even when he is not physically present in the narrative world of the Gospel." See further discussion below.

40. The separation of οὗτος (*houtos*, this) from ὁ ἄνθρωπος (*ho anthrōpos*, the man) suggests that the comment is meant contemptuously (Morris 1995: 431). Barrett (1978: 360) construes the intent underlying the statement as follows: " 'He is not from God—this man'; and certainly he is no more than [a] man." Both Morris (1995: 431) and Schnackenburg (1990: 2.248) believe that the word order is chosen by the evangelist to highlight the Pharisees' ignorance of the incarnation and ill-conceived notion of distance between Jesus and God.

41. The term ἁμαρτωλός (*hamartōlos*, sinner) occurs in John's Gospel only in the present chapter (9:16, 24, 25, 31; noted in Morris 1995: 431 n. 31).

42. Other examples of Jewish division over Jesus in John's Gospel include 6:66–69; 7:12–13, 30–31, 43; 10:19.

43. Incidentally, the second group apparently disregards the fact that Pharaoh's magicians were able to perform miracles as well (Exod. 7:11, 22; 8:7; but cf. 8:18–19). As Kruse (2003: 224) points out, their reasoning was defective—false prophets sometimes do perform miracles—but their conclusion was correct.

44. Contrast this with their contempt for the "people of the land" displayed in 7:49 (Schnackenburg 1990: 2.248). For a discussion of the reading σεαυτοῦ instead of αὐτοῦ in Codex Sinaiticus and 𝔓[75], see Bammel 1994: 455–56; Swanson 1995: 4.130.

4. The Healing of the Blind Man and the Good Shepherd Discourse
a. Jesus Heals a Blind Man
John 9:1–41

thinks of Jesus is an indication of their increasing perplexity and division among themselves (cf. 7:45–52; 11:46–48). The force of the conjunction ὅτι (*hoti*, that) may be "because" (so NASB, NKJV, RSV, ISV), yet with a twist, since the Pharisees obviously do not believe that the healing actually took place (9:18).[45] However, if the emphasis is indeed on the emphatic pronoun σου (*sou*, your), there is no problem, and the TNIV rendering would capture the essence of the statement very well: "It was *your* eyes he opened."

The blind man arrives at a verdict similar to that of the Samaritan woman: "He is a prophet" (4:19; cf. 4:44; 6:14; 7:40), though the precise nuances may differ (Ridderbos 1997: 340 n. 268; Carson 1991: 368).[46] "Prophet" may well have been the highest position that the man knew to ascribe to Jesus (Morris 1995: 432). Clearly, the man's verdict runs counter to the Pharisees' categorial denial, "This man is not from God" (9:16) (Ridderbos 1997: 340). Note the progression in the man's estimate of Jesus (Keener [2003: 775] calls the blind man a "paradigm of growing discipleship"): from "the man called Jesus" (9:11) to "a prophet" (9:17), to one who might be followed by disciples (9:27), to "from God" (9:33), to "Lord" to be worshiped (9:38) (Carson 1996: 368).

iii. The Pharisees' Interrogation of the Man's Parents (9:18–23)

In an effort to go through the facts of the case again in order to uncover some inconsistency that would resolve the current crisis, the Jews send for the man's parents (Carson 1991: 368; Morris 1995: 432–33; Schnackenburg 1990: 2.249).[47] (The man may have stayed under his parents' roof and spent his days begging in the temple courts.) The parents would be able to confirm whether he was actually born blind. Yet when the parents arrive, the Pharisees begin not by seeking to obtain more information, but by challenging the absurdity of their claim (Ridderbos 1997: 340). The parents' answer is predictably evasive: "Ask him—he is old enough, he will speak for himself."[48]

9:18–23

45. Ridderbos (1997: 339 n. 267) favors the sense "since *you say* he opened your eyes"; Barrett (1978: 360, citing LSJ) advocates ὅτι meaning "with regard to the fact that."

46. The only notable miracle-working prophets were Elijah and Elisha (cf. 2 Kings 5:10–14; see commentary at 9:7). Another possible antecedent figure is Moses (Deut. 18:15, 18; 34:10–12; see commentary at 1:21).

47. Bultmann (1971: 335) states that the authorities "now hit on the idea of questioning the fact of the miracle, as being the easiest way of putting an end to the whole business." Keener (2003: 786) notes how, incredibly, the Pharisees repeatedly ignore the testimony of the miracle itself, focusing instead on Jesus' alleged Sabbath violation. On "the Jews," see commentary at 5:10. Carson (1991: 368) attributes the shift from "Pharisees" to "the Jews" to John's penchant for stylistic variation. Schnackenburg (1990: 2.249) thinks that the change serves to indicate the "official character" of the inquiry. Duke (1985: 120, following Schnackenburg 1990: 2.248) suggests that the uneasiness of the Pharisees in 9:17–18 "is evident in the abrupt close of scene and their immediate change of tactic in what follows."

48. "He is old enough" probably means that the man is qualified to give legal testimony about himself—that is, he is at least thirteen (*m. Nid.* 5.6; Carson 1991: 369; Barrett 1978:

It will shortly become clear that despite their emphatic pleas of ignorance (note the double οὐκ οἴδαμεν [*ouk oidamen*, we don't know] in 9:21), the parents do in fact know more than they care to divulge (9:22–23) (Ridderbos 1997: 340; Carson 1991: 369); their emphatic statements indicate that they wish not to be dragged into the debate any more than they already have (Morris 1995: 433). In fact, as is duly noted by the evangelist, the parents spoke not from ignorance but out of fear, for the Jewish authorities had already decided to expel from the synagogue anyone who confessed Jesus as the Christ.[49] Since the synagogue was the center not only of Jewish religious life but also communal life, expulsion from it represented a severe form of social ostracism. This explains—though does not excuse—the parents' timidity and "readiness to submit tamely to the authority of their questioners" (Morris 1995: 433). Clearly, interrogating the man's parents did not greatly advance the Pharisees' investigation (Ridderbos 1997: 341).

The present reference to expulsion from the synagogue frequently is considered to be anachronistic.[50] The discussion revolves around the liturgical Eighteen Benedictions, which were recited by all pious Jews three times a day (Schürer 1973–79: 2.459–63). The twelfth of these benedictions is believed to have been rewritten by Samuel the Lesser, a rabbi at the school at Jamnia (ca. A.D. 85–90), in response to a request by Rabbi Gamaliel II, who headed the school (cf. *b. Ber.* 28b). It is believed that this revision, ironically called "the benediction of the heretics" (*birkat ha-minim*), was prepared for the Sanhedrin reconstituted after the fall of Jerusalem in A.D. 70. The purpose of this revision, it is thought, was to exclude Christian Jews from the synagogue by including in the liturgy a phrase that no Christian could utter.[51]

361; Kruse 2003: 225; Keener 2003: 788). Beyond this, his age is not known. The phrase may indicate that the man is sufficiently mature to reason and answer the Pharisees' questions for himself (Morris 1995: 433 n. 34).

49. Duke (1985: 120–21) detects irony in the fact that the parents' fear of the Jewish authorities sends the interrogators back to the man born blind, whom they had already questioned, yet it was precisely the Jews' dissatisfaction with that man's version that had caused them to change their tactic in the first place. This well illustrates not only the authorities' dilemma but also the cycle of futility in their investigation (cf. Bultmann 1971: 335). Confession of Jesus as Christ was the mark of the early Christians (e.g., Acts 9:22; 18:28; see Hurtado 1988b: 112–13). The phrase "fear of the Jews" occurs in this Gospel also at 7:13; 19:38; 20:19. The expression ἀποσυνάγωγος (*aposynagōgos*, expelled from the synagogue) occurs in the NT elsewhere only in John 12:42 and 16:2 (there with a future reference). Expulsion from the assembly of the exiles is reported already in Ezra 10:8 (Morris [1995: 434 n. 36], who also refers to Exod. 31:14).

50. See especially Martyn 1977; 1979; R. Brown 1979. But see the critique in Stibbe 1992: 59–61.

51. Cited by Köstenberger (2002c: 95), who also provides a basic critique of this reconstruction.

The agreement mentioned in 9:22, however, need not reflect an official decision and more likely points to an informal one.[52] In fact, it is not surprising that the same group that sought to arrest and kill Jesus would also seek to intimidate its followers by threatening synagogue expulsion. Also, the adverb νῦν (*nyn*, now) seems to suggest that opposition to Jesus had escalated to an advanced stage (cf. 7:13; see Ridderbos 1997: 343; Carson 1991: 371). The reference in 9:22 is therefore most likely to "an incidental measure adopted . . . with a view to a specific concrete situation."[53]

iv. The Pharisees' Second Interrogation of the Formerly Blind Man (9:24–34)

The phrase "give glory to God" constitutes a solemn exhortation to tell the truth and to make a confession, with the implication that the person so exhorted has done wrong.[54] In the context of the Gospel, this may constitute yet another instance of Johannine irony. For the blind man will indeed "give glory to God" (Beasley-Murray 1999: 158). Clearly, the veracity of the miracle is no longer the issue; discrediting Jesus is the only concern (Ridderbos 1997: 344). "This man is a sinner" (cf. 8:29, 46) would be the inference especially of the stricter rabbinic school of Shammai. Anyone who broke the Sabbath, and thus the law, was a sinner (cf. 9:16).

9:24–27

The man is willing to leave the question of Jesus' guilt to the theological experts: "Whether or not he is a sinner, I don't know."[55] But he nonetheless bears witness: "One thing I do know: I was blind but now I see!" Given the importance of witness in this Gospel, this may be an instance of the evangelist instructing his readers that a person of committed faith ought to bear personal witness (Carson 1991: 373). Thus, the Pharisees' theoretical and dogmatic assumptions ran into the indisputable and unalterable fact of the man's restored sight (Morris 1995: 436–37). From the two assertions—the man's sight and Jesus' guilt—the

---

52. Note the verb συνετέθειντο (*synetetheinto*, they decided among themselves; see Ridderbos 1997: 343 n. 281). Wallace (1996: 427) cites the form as an example of a reciprocal middle, with the pluperfect being extensive or consummative (p. 585). The same author classifies the ἵνα (*hina*, that) as complementary (p. 476).

53. Ridderbos 1997: 343; similarly, Morris 1995: 434 n. 36; contra Barrett 1978: 361; R. Brown 1966: 380; Schnackenburg 1990: 2.250; Bultmann 1971: 335.

54. Conway (1999: 131) suggests the idiomatic translation "Tell us the truth." See Josh. 7:19; 2 Chron. 30:8; Jer. 13:16; 1 Esdr. 9:8; *m. Sanh.* 6.2; cf. Ridderbos 1997: 344; Carson 1991: 372; Morris 1995: 436. Alternatively, the Jews exhort the man to give glory to God, who performed the miracle (but see Barrett 1978: 362).

55. Witherington (1995: 389) aptly notes that because the man is unsure of whether Jesus is a sinner, the evangelist hardly portrays him as a model believer. At the same time, however, he does bear witness to the change that Jesus brought about in his life, acts on the light he has been given, and shows continual progress in his understanding of who Jesus truly is.

only viable conclusion is that the law must have been superseded: "The Law condemns itself, and so do its exponents, when they try and condemn Jesus" (Barrett 1978: 362).

The Jews, now at a loss, ask the man to recount the details of the miracle, perhaps in hopes that he would contradict himself (Ridderbos 1997: 344–45; cf. Schnackenburg 1990: 2.251): "What did he do to you? How did he open your eyes?" In fact, Jewish jurisprudence considered diligent cross-examination to be vital in assessing the evidence (*m. Sanh.* 5.2). Yet once again, the man, whose understanding seems to grow as he is asked to repeat his story (Michaels 1989: 165), confounds the Jews' expectations: "I've told you already. . . ." In an instance of Johannine misunderstanding, he assumes that the reason why the authorities want him to repeat his story is that they are open to Jesus' claims; John's readers know better.

The man's question "You don't want to become his disciples, too, do you?" implies that he already considers himself to be Jesus' disciple (Morris 1995: 437; Michaels 1989: 169; Talbert 1992: 160; cf. 9:17). Though the man's response is steeped in Johannine irony and may reveal a certain naïveté as to the Jews' openness to consider Jesus' claims on their own merit (though note the interrogative particle μή [*mē*], which indicates expectation of a negative response [Ridderbos 1997: 345 n. 285; Morris 1995: 437]), it is not mocking (Moloney 1998: 294; contra Ridderbos 1997: 345).[56] Indeed, from here on, the man deploys "a quite marvellous gift for sardonic repartee" (Carson 1991: 373). The Pharisees, for their part, prefer being "disciples of Moses" (cf. 9:28).

9:28–29 Perhaps because they realize that the man has seen through their attempts to trip him up (Carson 1991: 373), the Pharisees "hurled insults" at him.[57] After giving their investigation an air of objectivity (9:13–27), the Pharisees' prejudice now erupts in full force (cf. 9:34). Employing sarcasm was a common way of dealing with people of perceived lower status, which conveyed the notion that they were unworthy of receiving a direct answer.[58] For their part, the Pharisees claimed to be "disciples of Moses" (cf. 1:17; 5:39–40, 45–47), considering Moses, through whom

---

56. Duke (1985: 81–82) describes the irony of the man's question as sarcastic and notes that it is one of four questions in this Gospel (cf. 7:26, 47–48, 52) that implicitly claim that the Jewish leaders have some form of belief in Christ (cf. 12:42; 19:38–39).

57. This is the only instance of λοιδορέω (*loidoreō*, insult) in the Gospel (elsewhere in the NT only in Acts 23:4; 1 Cor. 4:12; 1 Pet. 2:23). Note the emphatic juxtaposition of the personal pronouns σύ (*sy*, you) and ἡμεῖς (*hēmeis*, we), an "antithesis [that] is intended to expose the utter inferiority of the discipleship to which the man born blind refers" (Ridderbos 1997: 345), and the contemptuous force of ἐκείνου (*ekeinou*, that one's) (Carson 1991: 373; Morris 1995: 437 n. 42; Barrett 1978: 362).

58. For a similar dynamic, see John 8 (esp. 8:13, 19, 22, 25, 33, 39, 41b, 48, 52–53, 57, 59).

God gave the law to Israel, as the paradigmatic teacher (often called "our teacher" by the rabbinate).[59]

The Pharisees' claim "We know that God spoke to Moses" harks back to the establishment of Israel as a nation through the giving of the Mosaic covenant at Sinai, where "the Lord would speak to Moses face to face, as a man speaks with his friend" (Exod. 33:11; cf. Num. 12:2–8; see Ridderbos 1997: 345; Carson 1991: 373). According to the rabbis, this law consisted not merely of the written word (the Pentateuch) but also of oral tradition passed on from generation to generation (*m. ʾAbot* 1.1).[60]

"But this man—we don't even know where he's from!"[61] In other words, Moses is a proven quantity; Jesus is unproven, a Galilean upstart. The statement cuts to the very heart of the issue that came to divide Judaism and Christianity: the Jews insisted upon the revealed will of God as received through Moses, including both the Pentateuch and oral tradition, rather than choosing to attach themselves to the one who claimed to be the source of new revelation from God (Carson 1991: 374; cf. Beasley-Murray 1999: 158).[62] With regard to legal proceedings, it was important to check the background of a person charged with wrongdoing. This, by their own admission, the Pharisees had failed to do. The formerly blind man, on the other hand, knows what the Pharisees do not: Jesus is "from God."

Now the man born blind becomes the teacher, reasoning with the Jewish authorities on their own terms. His tenacity contrasts with the timidity of both his parents and even of Nicodemus (7:50–51; see Conway 1999: 132).[63] Unable to refute the man's logic, the authorities resort to personal

9:30–34

---

59. The perceptive reader will note that the Phraisees' claim to being disciples of Moses is refuted by the earlier statement in 5:45–47 (Keener 2003: 791). There is some debate as to how common this self-designation was among the Jews of Jesus' day (cf., e.g., Matt. 23:2). In *b. Yoma* 4a, it is applied to Pharisees as opposed to Sadducees. In *m. ʾAbot* 5.19, Jews are referred to as "the disciples of Abraham," while Christians are dismissed as "the disciples of Balaam the wicked" (that is, Jesus!). Schnackenburg (1990: 2.251) and Ridderbos (1997: 345 n. 287, referring to *TDNT* 4:443) consider this to be a characteristic rabbinic self-designation, while Carson (1991: 373–74, apparently following Barrett 1978: 362–63) says that this self-designation was not common.

60. Note also the close parallel to this verse in P.Eger. 2 (ca. A.D. 150).

61. Carson (1991: 373) points out that on a formal level, the present statement stands in contradiction with the Pharisees' earlier comment in 7:27 (cf. 6:42; 8:14b). He rightly notes that "both 7:27 and 9:29 are simultaneously false and ironically true" (almost identically, Barrett 1978: 363; similarly, Morris 1995: 437; Keener 2003: 792).

62. Carson (1991: 374) rightly notes that this raises a crucial hermeneutical question: how should previous revelation be understood in light of Jesus' teachings (cf. Matt. 5:17–18; John 1:17–18)?

63. As Rensberger (1988: 42 [cited in Conway 1999: 132]) notes, the man's attitude resembles that of Jesus before the high priest in 18:19–23, which is "why Jesus can be absent from the central episodes of the story; his role is taken over by the blind man himself."

attack (Conway 1999: 132). They cannot bear the truth he represents; hence, they expel him from the synagogue. This, too, anticipates the Jews' rejection of Jesus leading to his crucifixion.

"Now this is amazing" reads a bit awkwardly in the original Greek.[64] The personal pronoun ὑμεῖς (hymeis, you) in the statement "You don't know where he's from" mockingly contrasts with ἡμεῖς (hēmeis, we) in the previous verse and seems to note the irony: "You, the religious experts, cannot work out a simple thing like this?" (Morris 1995: 438). As it is, the Pharisees "are forced to listen to an uneducated man telling them that they, amazing as it may seem, are incapable of assessing God's activity" (Schnackenburg 1990: 2.251): "We know [turning the Pharisees' 'we know' in 9:29 against them (Ridderbos 1997: 345; Morris 1995: 438)] that God doesn't listen to sinners" is the major premise in the formerly blind man's argument. Scripture establishes a clear link between a person's righteousness and God's responsiveness to his or her prayer.[65] Accordingly, later rabbis shuddered at the thought of God listening to sinners (b. Sanh. 90a; b. Ber. 58a; see Barrett 1978: 363).

"But if anyone is God-fearing and does his will—to him God listens."[66] There is ample OT substantiation for the cured man's contention (Ps. 34:15; 145:19; Prov. 15:29).[67] "It is unheard of that anyone ever opened the eyes of one born blind"[68] is the minor premise of the formerly blind man: an extraordinary miracle has taken place (cf. Acts 3–4, esp. 4:14, 16).[69] Opening of the eyes of the blind is limited to unusual circumstances in the OT (e.g., 2 Kings 6:8–23). Instances of blind persons being healed in Jewish tradition are extremely rare (Tob. 11:10–14; cf. 2:10). But the healing of a man born blind is without parallel (Carson 1991:

64. Ridderbos (1997: 345 n. 289) notes that the γάρ (gar, for) "dangles somewhat," lacking an obvious referent.

65. See Job 27:9; Ps. 34:15; 66:18; 109:7; Prov. 15:8, 29; 21:27; 28:9; Isa. 1:15; John 14:13–14; 16:23–27; 1 Pet. 3:7; 1 John 3:21–22.

66. The term θεοσεβής (theosebēs, god-fearing [only here in the NT]) is occasionally used in Greek writings to mean "religious" or "pious" (Plutarch, Romulus 22.1; Dionysius of Halicarnassus, Antiquitates romanae 2.60.4; Epistula ad Pompeium Geminum 4.2). It is also found in Josephus, with reference to David (Ant. 7.7.1 §130; 7.7.3 §153) and others (Ant. 12.6.3 §284; 14.12.3 §308; 20.8.11 §195; Ag. Ap. 2.13 §140), and in Philo (Chang. Nam. 36 §197), who likewise uses the expression in a broad sense to refer to a "god-fearing" person.

67. There are also rabbinic parallels (b. Ber. 6b; Exod. Rab. 21.3; cf. Isa. 65:24).

68. A similar categorical statement is found in 4:29, 39. The phrase "nobody has ever heard" more literally reads "not heard from of old" (i.e., from the world's beginning), a common Jewish expression in both OT and rabbinic literature (e.g., Isa. 64:4). For Greek parallels, see MM 16, s.v. αἰών.

69. Carson (1991: 375) notes the dangers of a strict understanding of the man's logic, particularly the risks of associating powers with divine power (e.g., the Egyptian magicians). However, these are theological subtleties that do not concern the man. His conclusion thus is correct, even if his theological framework is somewhat precarious. Morris (1995: 438) says that the logic is admirable for a man who has been a beggar all his life.

374; Morris 1995: 422).[70] The man's conclusion, "If this man were not from God, he could do nothing" (cf. 3:2; see R. Brown 1966: 375),[71] is firmly in keeping with Judaism at large, which regarded miracles as answers to prayer.[72]

At this point the Pharisees are so enraged that they fail to recall the promises that sight will be restored at the dawn of the messianic age (Isa. 29:18; 35:5; 42:7; see Carson 1991: 375; Morris 1995: 422). The double pronoun σύ (sy, you) continues the pattern of verbal abuse, together with the emphatic position of ἐν ἁμαρτίαις (en hamartiais, in sins) (note also the modifier ὅλος [holos, entirely]) and the juxtaposition of "you" and "us": "*You—in sins* you were born entirely, and *you* are teaching *us*?"[73] This was excluded. Nevertheless, by alleging that the man was "steeped in sin at birth" (cf. 9:2–3), the Pharisees now tacitly acknowledge that the man had indeed been blind from birth (Carson 1991: 375; Morris 1995: 438), given the absolute connections that they found between sin and suffering (Ridderbos 1997: 346).[74] The common rabbinic view of human nature implicitly denied universal human sinfulness by maintaining that people could act on their good impulses (*yeṣer*) and resist evil ones. Yet, the reality of human sin is clearly taught in the OT (e.g., Ps. 51:5).[75] Thus, the Pharisees are unduly self-righteous in linking the man's sinfulness from birth with his physical defect of blindness while failing to include themselves under the rubric "sinful from birth."[76]

"And they threw him out." As in Acts 3–4, the Pharisees show that they are at their wit's end by resorting to (or threatening) violence. The phrase "they threw him out" refers to the man's expulsion from the synagogue.[77] The way in which this is carried out suggests an im-

---

70. Keener (2003: 792–93) acknowledges that Palestinian Jewish tradition provides no such reports, but he still holds out the possibility that the formerly blind man's statement is hyperbolic.

71. On the grammatical construction underlying the phrase "he could do nothing," see commentary at 14:30. Morris (1995: 438 n. 46) notes the emphatic double negative; Wallace (1996: 696) cites this as an example of a second-class condition (contrary to fact).

72. On Jewish opinions on Jesus' miracles, see van der Loos 1965: 156–65.

73. Duke (1985: 122–23) notes the irony inherent in 9:34 because the man born blind did in fact teach the Pharisees.

74. Jesus, likewise, is called a "sinner," because he is considered to have broken the Sabbath (9:24; cf. 9:16, 25, 28–33; see commentary at 8:29, 46).

75. The apostle Paul establishes the same truth in his letter to the Romans (cf. Rom. 1–3, esp. 3:23; cf. 6:23).

76. Keener (2003: 793–94) notes that the Pharisees' conclusion that the man must be a sinner (9:34) contradicts Jesus' affirmation that the man's blindness was not a result of personal sin (9:2–3). The fine irony will not escape the alert reader that the Pharisees themselves have not been born from God (3:3) but rather were born in sin as the devil's heirs (8:44) and destined to die in sin (8:21).

77. See Michaels 1989: 170. Contra R. Brown (1966: 375), who believes that the man was only cast from their presence rather than being formally expelled. Burge (2000: 275) and Laney (1992: 180) also seem to hold this view.

pulsive, impromptu decision rather than the culmination of a formal investigation issuing in a solemn, formal act of excommunication (see commentary at 9:22). In fact, the present verse seems to confirm that no official procedure was required for such an action (Ridderbos 1997: 347). Incidentally, the Pharisees' prejudiced procedure of interrogating the blind man and his parents violated their own laws, which stipulated that witnesses were to be examined fairly and without prejudice (see commentary at 5:31; 9:26–27).

v. The Pharisees' Spiritual Blindness (9:35–41)

9:35–38 Upon hearing of the man's expulsion from the local synagogue, Jesus tracks him down. Rather than finding the man accidentally, Jesus probably sought him out, having heard of his expulsion from the synagogue. If so, this would be in keeping with the portrait of Jesus as the "good shepherd" in the ensuing discourse (Ridderbos 1997: 347). Jesus' question "Do you believe in the Son of Man?" (see additional note) appears to assume a positive answer and may be designed to reveal more about the one for whose sake the man had been expelled (Ridderbos 1997: 347).[78] The term "Son of Man" here appears to be primarily a term of self-identification (Müller 1991).[79] Importantly, the man's growth in faith and understanding was predicated upon his decisive break with the Jewish leadership (Carson 1991: 375).

The vocative κύριε (kyrie) evolves from a polite "sir" (9:36) to an acknowledgment of Jesus as "Lord" (9:38).[80] The conjunction ἵνα (hina, in order that) in 9:36 is based on an elliptical "tell me" and conveys purpose (Morris 1995: 440). The double καί (kai) in Jesus' response is probably ascensive: "Not only have you seen him—in fact, he is the one speaking with you."[81] The man's "having seen" Jesus (the perfect ἑώρακας [heōrakas, you have seen] indicates a settled condition) is all the more significant since that man until very recently had not "seen" anything (Morris 1995: 440). By believing, he truly "gives glory to God" (cf. 9:24) and emerges as the one who sees in more than one sense (Ridderbos

---

78. The emphatic pronoun σύ (sy, you) points to the personal nature of faith (Morris 1995: 439) and draws a distinction between the man's positive response and the Pharisees' unbelief (Schnackenburg 1990: 2.253).

79. Though Carson (1991: 376 [cf. Morris 1995: 439]) also notes the judging role of the Son of Man (5:27), which coheres well with 9:39–41. Ridderbos (1997: 348) points out how Jesus repeatedly shifts to this title to reveal "greater things" about himself (1:51; 3:13; 6:27, 62; 8:28).

80. Carson 1991: 376; Morris 1995: 440; R. Brown 1966: 375. D. M. Smith (1999: 199) suggests that the ambiguity may be intentional, while Barrett (1978: 364) doubts that John intentionally meant to distinguish between these two meanings in 9:36 and 9:38. Regarding the question "Who is he . . . ?" see 12:34 (cf. Acts 9:5).

81. Ridderbos 1997: 348; Bultmann 1971: 339 n. 1. On the phrase "he is the one speaking with you," see 4:26.

1997: 349). "He worshiped him" is the only precrucifixion reference to worship of Jesus in this Gospel (cf. 20:28).[82]

Although the conversation was private, it must have occurred in a public place, so that the Pharisees were able to overhear what was said (Carson 1991: 377). John 9:39–41 serves as a kind of interpretive epilogue, transforming the preceding narrative into an acted parable with a message about sight and blindness in the spiritual realm (Carson 1991: 377–78; Beasley-Murray 1999: 160). The present passage anticipates the climactic conclusion in 12:37–40.[83] Jesus' pronouncement "For judgment I came into this world" harks back to 3:19–21. The saying formally appears to contradict 3:17 (see also 12:47), but with the clarification of 3:18–21 and the recognition that the saving of some entails the condemnation of others, such objections vanish (Carson 1991: 377). The judgment referred to here is the division of humanity into believers and unbelievers brought about by Jesus' coming into this world (Ridderbos 1997: 350).[84]

9:39–41

Both giving sight to the blind[85] and the blinding of those who see[86] are common OT themes (Barrett 1978: 365–66). The Pharisees regard their own illumination as sufficient, so when the true light shines, they refuse to look closely (Barrett 1978: 366). Elsewhere, Jesus calls the Pharisees "blind guides" (Matt. 23:16; cf. 15:14; 23:26).[87] The interrogative particle μή (*mē*) indicates the Pharisees' incredulity that they could be included among the blind (Ridderbos 1997: 350–51); the emphatic expression καὶ ἡμεῖς (*kai hēmeis*, we also) further underscores their surprise (Morris 1995: 441 n. 60). As Jesus makes clear, it is not the Pharisees' sin, but their repudiation of grace, that renders them lost (Ridderbos 1997: 351). There is no cure for people who reject the only cure there is (Barrett

---

82. Borchert (1996: 325) relates the present reference to 20:28 and believes that this confession is a high point in the festival cycle. The man's response to Jesus' self-revelation is in keeping with the standard OT reaction to theophany (e.g., Gen. 17:3). However, it is possible that the man's actions, while being "beyond that due to other men," fall "short of that due to God Almighty" (Beasley-Murray 1999: 160; similarly, Carson 1991: 377). Nevertheless, the majority of commentators favor a fuller sense of worship (Barrett 1978: 365; R. Brown 1966: 376; Bultmann 1971: 339 n. 3; Morris 1995: 440; Schnackenburg 1990: 2.254).

83. The ἵνα (*hina*, that) here may convey purpose or combine purpose and result (Schnackenburg 1990: 2.255). Carson (1991: 377–78) observes, "That tragic conclusion is the *foreseen* result of Jesus' coming, and in that sense part of its purpose."

84. R. Brown (1966: 381–82) seeks to make a case for the baptismal significance of the healing of the blind man in this chapter (but see Schnackenburg 1990: 2.257–58; see also Ridderbos 1997: 337).

85. See Ps. 146:8; Isa. 29:18; 35:5; 42:7, 18.

86. See Isa. 6:10; 42:19; Jer. 5:21 (cf. Matt. 13:13–15 pars.; and esp. John 12:40). See Lieu 1988: 90.

87. The phrase "blind ones in heart" is found in P.Oxy. 1.20–21. For the blinding effect of wickedness, see Wis. 2:21. In rabbinic Judaism, this metaphorical usage is very rare (Schrage, *TDNT* 8:281, 284–86), while Philo, under the influence of Greek philosophy, uses it frequently (e.g., *Husb.* 17 §81; *Heir* 9 §48; *Spec. Laws* 4.36 §189).

1978: 366; cf. Bultmann 1971: 341–42) and no hope for those who are wise in their own eyes (Prov. 26:12; Kruse 2003: 231).[88]

Additional Notes

9:4. Most commentators (Ridderbos 1997: 333; Carson 1991: 362; Morris 1995: 426 n. 13; Barrett 1978: 357; Beasley-Murray 1999: 151 n. b; Laney 1992: 173; contra Bultmann 1971: 331–32 n. 7) concur with the reading ἡμᾶς δεῖ . . . πέμψαντός με, though the best-attested variant is ἡμᾶς δεῖ . . . πέμψαντος ἡμᾶς (𝔓⁶⁶, ⁷⁵ ℵ* B). See the rationale in Metzger 1994: 194.

9:35. The variant "Son of God" (A) clearly is secondary (Metzger 1994: 194: the reading "Son of Man" is "virtually certain"; so also Lee 1994: 168; Barrett 1978: 364; Schnackenburg 1990: 2.253, 498; R. Brown 1966: 375; and virtually all the commentators).

9:38–39a. There is some question as to whether the words ὁ δὲ ἔφη, Πιστεύω . . . ὁ Ἰησοῦς are original (so the majority of MSS) or not (omitted in 𝔓⁷⁵ ℵ*). Despite the objections by R. Brown (1966: 375, 381) and C. Porter (1966–67), the longer reading is most likely original (so Metzger 1994: 195; Carson 1991: 377; Schnackenburg 1990: 2.254, 499 n. 51; cf. Beasley-Murray 1999: 151 n. i; Lee 1994: 169 n. 1). Also contra Lindars (1972: 351), who claims that the words are most likely "a liturgical interpolation from the use of this chapter in connection with baptism."

---

88. The construction of the clause "If you were blind, you would not be guilty of sin" occurs later also in 15:24 (cf. Rom. 4:15; 5:13). Regarding the phrase "Now that you claim you can see, your guilt remains," compare 10:25–26 (and see Prov. 26:12). The term μένειν (*menein*, to remain), which usually has a positive connotation in this Gospel, is here used negatively (as in 3:36).

---

b. Jesus the Good Shepherd (10:1–42)

As the last winter (A.D. 32/33) prior to Jesus' crucifixion approaches, Jesus elaborates on his relationship with his close followers, portraying himself as the messianic shepherd and his followers as his "sheep."[1] Jesus is both the gate to eternal life and the shepherd who lays down his life for the sheep.[2] The Jewish leadership, on the other hand, proud claimants of Abrahamic heritage but spiritually blind, are, strikingly, not even considered to be part of Jesus' flock. The reader is prepared for Jesus' establishment of a new messianic community in which his followers (but not the official Jewish leadership) play a pivotal role.[3]

Chapter 10 follows chapter 9 without transition (see also 10:21); thus, Jesus' audiences are likely the same (Ridderbos 1997: 352–53; cf. Morris 1995: 444, 446; Lincoln 2000: 97; Keener 2003: 797). Jesus' healing of the blind man had led to the man's expulsion from the local synagogue, an act viewed by Jesus as an arrogant assertion of usurped authority that called for further comment. For the Pharisees were not only blind themselves (9:40–41); they were also "blind guides" (cf. Matt. 23:16, 24) who led astray those entrusted to their care (cf. Luke 17:1–2; Matt. 23:15). The dark backdrop of Jesus' "good shepherd discourse" is therefore the blatant irresponsibility of the Jewish religious leaders.[4]

The present discourse bears a certain resemblance to Synoptic-style parables but is best classified as a "symbolic discourse," in which a given metaphor (here, shepherding) provides the backdrop for extended reflection (Köstenberger 2002b: 72–75).[5] With Jesus' appear-

---

1. For a thorough investigation of the OT background of John 10, especially 10:16, see Köstenberger 2002b. On sheep and shepherd imagery, see also Keener 2003: 799–802.

2. The reference is plainly to Jesus' substitutionary atonement (ὑπέρ [hyper, for] in 10:11, 15; cf. 15:13). On the nature of Jesus' work according to the Fourth Gospel, see Köstenberger 1998b: 74–81.

3. For a list of ways in which John appropriates old-covenant language to designate Jesus' new messianic community, see Köstenberger 1998b: 162, in adaptation of Pryor 1992a.

4. Cf. Zech. 9:9; 11:17; 12:10 (quoted in John 19:37; cf. Matt. 24:30; Rev. 1:7); 13:7 (alluded to in John 16:32; cf. Matt. 26:56; Mark 14:50). France (1971: 104 [cf. Köstenberger 1998b: 133–38]) argues that Zechariah's four images jointly portray the successive phases of the messianic shepherd-king's coming and people's reaction to him.

5. Dewey (1980), while acknowledging that the term παροιμία (paroimia, illustration) occurs only in 10:6 (with reference to 10:1–5) and 16:25, 29 (referring to 16:21–24), extends

ance at the Feast of Dedication, the "festival cycle" (chs. 5–10) comes to a close, ending the way it began: the Jews are persecuting Jesus on account of what they perceive to be blasphemy (10:30–31; cf. 5:16–18). The reference to Jesus' return to the place where the Baptist had baptized in the early days (10:40–41) rounds out chapters 1–10.

    i. The shepherd and his flock (10:1–21)
    ii. The unbelief of the Jews (10:22–42)

Exegesis and Exposition

[1]"Truly, truly, I say to you, whoever does not enter the sheep pen through the gate, but goes up another way, is a thief and robber. [2]But the one who enters through the gate is the shepherd of the sheep. [3]To him the gatekeeper opens, and to his voice the sheep listen. And he calls his own sheep by name and leads them out. [4]When he has brought out all his own, he goes before them, and the sheep follow him, because they recognize his voice. [5]But a stranger they will never follow, but they will flee from him, because they do not recognize the voice of strangers." [6](Jesus gave this illustration to them, yet they did not understand what it was that he was telling them.)

[7]Then Jesus said again, "Truly, truly, I say to you that I am the door for the sheep. [8]All who have come before me were thieves and robbers, but the sheep have not listened to them. [9]I am the gate: whoever enters through me will be saved, and will go in and out and find pasture. [10]The thief comes only to steal and to kill and to destroy; I have come that they may have life, and have it abundantly. [11]I am the good shepherd. The good shepherd ⌜lays down⌝ his life for the sheep. [12]In fact, the hired hand, since he is not the shepherd and the sheep are not his own, sees the wolf come and abandons the sheep and flees—and the wolf snatches them and scatters them— [13]because he is a hired hand and has no concern for the sheep. [14]I am the good shepherd, and I know those who are mine, and those who are mine know me— [15]just as the Father knows me and I know the Father—and I lay down my life for the sheep. [16]And I have other sheep that are not from this sheep pen; I must bring them also, and they will hear my voice, and ⌜there will be⌝ 'one flock, one shepherd.' [17]This is why the Father loves me: because I lay down my life, in order to take it up again. [18]No one ⌜takes⌝ it away from me, but I lay it down of my own accord. I have the power to lay it down, and I have the power to take it up again. This command I received from my Father."

[19]Again there arose a division among the Jews on account of these words. [20]And many of them were saying, "He has a demon and is raving mad. Why

---

the term to encompass as many as thirty-four proverbial sayings in the Gospel. This seems overzealous. For a more restrained treatment, comparing the Synoptic parables to their Johannine counterparts, see Schweizer 1996.

listen to him?" ²¹Others were saying, "These are not the words of one who is demon-possessed. A demon cannot open the eyes of the blind, can he?"

²²ᵀThenᵀ came the Feast of Dedication in Jerusalem—it was winter— ²³and Jesus moved about in the temple area at Solomon's colonnade. ²⁴So the Jews surrounded him and were saying to him, "How long will you keep us in suspense? If you are the Christ, tell us plainly." ²⁵Jesus answered them, "I did tell you, and you don't believe. The works I perform in my Father's name—these bear testimony concerning me. ²⁶But you don't believe, because you are not among my sheep. ²⁷My sheep hear my voice, and I know them, and they follow me, ²⁸and I give them eternal life, and they will never, ever perish, and no one will wrest them out of my hand. ²⁹My Father, ᵀwhoᵀ has given them to me, is greater than all, and no one can wrest them out of my Father's hand. ³⁰I and the Father are one [entity]."

³¹Again the Jews took up stones to stone him. ³²Jesus answered them, "I have shown you many good works from the Father; for which of these works do you stone me?" ³³The Jews answered him, "It is not for any good work that we are stoning you, but for blasphemy, even because you, a mere man, make yourself out to be God." ³⁴Jesus answered them, "Is it not written in ᵀyourᵀ law, 'I have said, "You are gods"'? ³⁵If it called those 'gods' to whom the word of God came—and Scripture cannot be broken— ³⁶how can you say, 'You are blaspheming,' to the one whom the Father set apart and sent into the world, because I said, 'I am the Son of God'? ³⁷If I don't perform the works of my Father, don't believe me; ³⁸but if I do perform them, even if you don't believe me, believe the works, so that you may come to know and ᵀrecognizeᵀ that the Father is in me and I am in the Father." ³⁹Again they tried to arrest him, yet he eluded their grasp.

⁴⁰And again he left the region beyond the Jordan and went to the place where John had at first been baptizing, and there he stayed. ⁴¹And many came to him and were saying, "John did not perform a single sign, but all the things John said regarding this man were true." ⁴²And many believed in him there.

i. The Shepherd and His Flock (10:1–21)

The double ἀμήν (*amēn*, truly) construction never begins a discourse in this Gospel, which suggests that the present pericope represents a continuation of the events recounted in the previous chapter (Morris 1995: 446; R. Brown 1966: 385). The metaphor of the "flock," an everyday feature of Jewish life, pervades the OT. God himself is called Israel's "Shepherd,"⁶ and his people are the "sheep of his pasture."⁷ Part of this   **10:1–6**

6. E.g., Gen. 48:15; 49:24; Ps. 23:1; 28:9; 77:20; 78:52; 80:1; Isa. 40:11; Jer. 31:10; Ezek. 34:11–31.
7. E.g., Ps. 74:1; 78:52; 79:13; 95:7; 100:3; Ezek. 34:31. A roughly contemporaneous passage, 2 Bar. 77:11–16, portrays the law as true shepherd (as well as light and water). Thus, Jesus here claims to fulfill the function that Jews generally attributed to the Torah

imagery was also the notion of chief shepherds and undershepherds and of hired hands. David, who was a shepherd before he became king, became a prototype of God's shepherd. Jesus saw himself as embodying the characteristics and expectations attached to this salvation-historical biblical figure as the good shepherd par excellence.[8]

The proper way to enter the sheep pen is by the gate. The sheep pen may have been a courtyard (cf. 18:15) near or bordering a house, surrounded by a stone wall and topped by briars, where one or several families kept their sheep. The gate, which probably could be locked, would have been guarded by a doorkeeper (cf. 10:3), who was hired to stand watch (Dalman 1928–39: 6.284–85).[9] The terms "thief" and "robber" overlap in meaning and may reflect Semitic parallelism (cf. Obad. 5; Let. Jer. 57), whereby "thief" may focus on the covert nature of entrance, and "robber" on violence (cf. Luke 10:30, 36).[10] Shepherds had to be on guard against either threat in order to avoid loss of sheep.

The shepherd was the authorized caretaker of the flock.[11] His task required dedication, courage, and vigilance. In Jesus' day, shepherds were regarded as vulgar and members of the lower class. This contrasted with the OT designation of both God and his Messiah as shepherds. "To him the gatekeeper opens." The gatekeeper (θυρωρός, *thyrōros*) was an undershepherd who provided access to the flock. The existence of a watchman suggests that the pen in mind here was large enough to house several flocks and hence warranted the need of a gatekeeper.[12]

(Moloney 1998; 307 [cited in Blomberg 2002: 158]). For a detailed treatment of John's appropriation of Ezekiel's shepherd motif in Ezek. 33–37, see Deeley 1997.

8. Though the OT is doubtless John's primary point of reference, the kind of imagery employed by the evangelist would not have been unknown to his Hellenistic audience. Cf. Themistius, *Peri Philanthr.* 9d–10c (fourth century A.D.), cited in Boring, Berger, and Colpe 1995: 286.

9. Barrett (1978: 368) suggests that ἀναβαίνων ἀλλαχόθεν (*anabainōn allachothen*, going up another way) refers to individuals who attempt to reach the heavenly realm through a method other than the cross, but it is doubtful that the symbolism can be extended this far. See the appropriate cautions against pressing an allegorical reading of every detail in the present discourse registered by Ridderbos 1997: 355 (Morris 1995: 447 cites the doorkeeper as an example; see below).

10. Later, Judas is called a thief (12:6), and Barabbas a robber (18:40; cf. Mark 15:7). At his arrest, Jesus asks why he is treated like a robber (Matt. 26:55 pars.), and in the end he is crucified with robbers on either side (Matt. 27:38, 44 pars.). The majority of commentators take both terms as referring to the same people (Ridderbos 1997: 354; Carson 1991: 381; Schnackenburg 1990: 2.281; contra Barrett 1978: 369). See further Hengel 1989a: 24–46; Simonis 1967: 101–3.

11. The lack of an article before ποιμήν (*poimēn*, shepherd) in 10:2 does not negate the specificity of the term (Ridderbos 1997: 354; Morris 1995: 446 n. 13, 453–54; contra Schnackenburg 1990: 2.282). Westcott (1908: 2.50) says that the "absence of the article fixes attention on the character as distinct from the person."

12. The term θυρωρός is used later for the doorkeeper of the high priest's courtyard in 18:16, 17. Morris (1995: 447) aptly notes that no special symbolic significance should be assigned to the doorkeeper in the present discourse.

The verb ἀνοίγω (*anoigō*, open) is used repeatedly in the context for Jesus' opening of the congenitally blind man's eyes (9:10, 14, 17, 21, 26, 30, 32; 10:21; 11:37).

"The sheep recognize his voice." In the OT, God communicated with his people preeminently through the law (which spelled out God's moral expectations for his people) and the prophets (who called people back to obedience to the law). People listened to God's voice by living in conformity with his revealed will. At the present time (from the perspective of the earthly Jesus), those who desire to follow God should do so by listening to Jesus' words and by obeying his commandments (e.g., 15:10). In the future, God (and Jesus) will speak to his own through the Spirit (16:13–15).

The shepherd calls his own sheep by name, that is, individually rather than collectively, which contrasts with the general call issued to the entire flock (Carson 1991: 383). There is evidence that Palestinian shepherds used to give nicknames to some of their sheep (Wilson 1906: 165; Dalman 1928–39: 6.250–51; Keener 2003: 805). In OT times, God called some of his closest servants, and Israel as a whole, "by name" (e.g., Exod. 33:12, 17; Isa. 43:1). In Jesus' case, the "sheep" are called out of Judaism (Carson 1991: 383; Barrett 1978: 369). One may infer that they were his sheep even prior to being called by him (cf. 6:37, 39, 44, 64–65; 17:6, 24; 18:9; see Carson 1991: 383).

The shepherd leads out his sheep until he has brought out all his own.[13] Jesus frequently refers to sheep to illustrate people's helplessness and need for guidance. The leading out of sheep is a delicate task. It involves pushing the flock from the fold, where many of them are crowded, through the gate.[14] The shepherd goes on ahead of his sheep (cf. Num. 27:17; Ps. 80:1). Western shepherds usually drive their sheep, often using a sheep dog. Their Near Eastern counterparts, on the other hand, both now and in Jesus' day, lead their flocks by beckoning them on with their voice. Often there is a helper watching the tail end of the flock (Dalman 1928–39: 6.249).[15]

The sheep follow him because they recognize his voice (see commentary at 10:3). They will never follow a stranger, but will flee from him, because they do not recognize the voice of a stranger. In ancient

13. The wording is reminiscent of OT passages such as Num. 27:15–17 and Ezek. 34:13. Carson (1991: 383 [cf. Barrett 1978: 369]) understands Num. 27:15–18 as a typological allusion to Christ (contra Schnackenburg 1990: 2.293; Moloney 1998: 308). Ridderbos (1997: 354) also mentions Ps. 80:1.

14. Lindars 1972: 357: "probably simply holding the gate open while the sheep run out past him." On the fold and the door, see also Keener 2003: 809–11.

15. Israel's exodus from Egypt occasionally is portrayed in terms of a flock being led by its shepherd (God, by the hand of Moses and Aaron [Ps. 77:20; Isa. 63:11, 14; cf. Ps. 78:52]). Old Testament prophetic literature holds out similar visions of end-time deliverance for God's people (Mic. 2:12–13).

times as well as today, sheep, while helpless and in need of guidance, are able to discern between their shepherd's voice and the call of a stranger (represented, in the present instance, by the "thieves and robbers" of 10:1).[16] This intimacy of a shepherd and his flock provides a beautiful illustration of the trust, familiarity, and bond existing between Jesus and his followers.

The term παροιμία (*paroimia*, illustration; TNIV: "figure of speech") occurs in John elsewhere only in 16:25, 29, where "speaking figuratively" is contrasted with "speaking plainly" (see also 10:24).[17] The genre of the present passage may best be described as an "image field" (Moloney 1998: 303, 309, citing K. Berger) or "symbolic discourse" (Barrett 1978: 367, 370) that allows Jesus to develop his message.[18] Those who fail to understand are likely the Jewish leaders featured in the previous chapter (Barrett 1978: 370; Ridderbos 1997: 356).[19]

10:7–10 The conjunction οὖν (*oun*, then) may indicate that the ensuing words serve to clarify what Jesus' listeners did not understand (Morris 1995: 449).[20] "I am the gate for the sheep."[21] The present verse appears to begin to present an alternate scenario (continued through 10:18) to that portrayed in 10:1–5: Jesus as the gate through whom people may enter and be saved.[22] Jesus' words may hark back to messianic readings

16. So Barrett 1978: 370; contra Ridderbos 1997: 354. See commentary at 10:8 and 10:10.

17. The word is absent from the Synoptics, where the roughly equivalent expression παραβολή (*parabolē*, parable) is found (not used in John; see Carson 1984: 301–4). Both terms apparently render the broad Hebrew expression *māšāl* (Borchert 1996: 329). They occur side by side in a few instances (e.g., Sir. 39:3; 47:17) and do not differ significantly in meaning (Dewey 1980).

18. Stibbe (1993: 113) characterizes παροιμία as "a symbolic word-picture with a cryptic meaning . . . essentially elusive discourse." Morris (1995: 445) suggests that this is a rather unique form of allegory. Ridderbos (1997: 355 [cf. Beasley-Murray 1999: 168]) opts for a parable with allegorical elements (cf. 10:7–9). Bultmann (1971: 375) describes the genre as a mixture between parable and riddle. See Köstenberger 2002b: 72–75. See also the long discussion in Schnackenburg 1990: 2.284–88.

19. Cf. the TNIV renderings in 10:1: "you *Pharisees*"; and 10:6: "but *the Pharisees* did not understand" (italics added).

20. Schnackenburg (1990: 2.288) suggests that πάλιν (*palin*, again) starts a new discussion. Carson (1991: 384) perceives that 10:7–9 does not necessarily expand on 10:1–5 but that it represents a treatment of the three dominant motifs (gate, shepherd, sheep) in those verses (cf. Barrett 1978: 370–71).

21. Some (e.g., Morris 1995: 450 n. 27; Barrett 1978: 371) seek to make a distinction between the meaning of ἡ θύρα τῶν προβάτων (*hē thyra tōn probatōn*, the door for the sheep) in 10:7 and ἡ θύρα (*hē thyra*, the gate) in 10:9, contending that in 10:7 Jesus is presented as the gate *to* the sheep, while in 10:9 he is the gate *for* the sheep. However, such a distinction is unnecessary (Carson 1991: 384; cf. Schnackenburg 1990: 2.289; Moloney 1998: 309).

22. For an interesting reconstruction of the background, see Barclay 1975: 2.58 (cited in Köstenberger 2002c: 99); cf. Bishop 1959–60. For links between "the door" and "the shepherd" in wisdom traditions, see Scott 1992: 121–23.

of passages such as Ps. 118:20: "This is the gate of the Lᴏʀᴅ through which the righteous may enter" (note that this psalm is used in John 12:13).²³

"All who have come before me were thieves and robbers" (see commentary at 10:1 and at 10:10).²⁴ The OT prophet Ezekiel refers to the "shepherds of Israel who only take care of themselves" and "do not take care of the flock" (Ezek. 34:2-4 [see the entire chapter]). "All who have come before me" hints at impostors who promised their followers freedom but instead led them into armed conflict and doom (Meyer 1956). Jesus' statement also may have more overtly political overtones, evoking reminiscences of then-recent events in Jewish history.²⁵

The spectrum of "thieves and robbers" may also encompass pseudo-prophets such as the ones mentioned by Luke and Josephus (cf. Acts 5:36–37; 21:38; *Ant.* 20.5.1 §§97–98; 20.8.5 §§169–72; 20.8.10 §188; *J.W.* 7.11.1 §§437–40; see commentary at 7:12), the Zealots, and even the high-priestly circles that controlled Judaism in Jesus' day. Sadducees in particular were known to use temple religion for their own profit, and elsewhere both the Pharisees (Luke 16:14) and the scribes (Mark 12:40) are denounced for their greed. Perhaps the closest connection in the present context is with the Pharisees, whose attitude toward the man born blind exemplifies a blatant usurpation of religious authority and a perversion of godly leadership (cf. John 9).

"I am the gate: whoever enters through me will be saved."²⁶ As is attested in Greek literature since Homer, people in ancient times frequently thought of entering heaven by a gate. Jesus' claim to be "the gate" would have resonated with this kind of thinking (cf. 1:51). The notion of a "gate to heaven" appears also in Jewish sources, both in OT and apocalyptic literature.²⁷ In the latter, the visionary receives a glimpse of the eternal truth of heaven that is the source of final salvation (cf. Rev. 4:1). Besides providing access to angels, the doors of heaven are the means by which knowledge and salvation are made known.²⁸ The Synoptics refer to "entering" God's kingdom as through a door or gate.²⁹

23. On the provision of access to God through Jesus, see John 14:6; Rom. 5:2; Eph. 2:18; Heb. 10:20; Rev. 3:7 (cf. Isa. 22:22).
24. "Were" is the rendering chosen in the ɴɪᴠ (but note the ᴛɴɪᴠ), ɴʟᴛ, and ɴᴇᴛ. If correct, this would constitute an instance in the Fourth Gospel of a historical present of εἰμί (*eimi*, am), whose existence is denied by Wallace (1990: 204; 1996: 531). But see Morris (1995: 451 n. 31), who says that the emphasis is on Jesus' own day. Another possible instance of this grammatical feature is found in 19:40 (so ɴɪᴠ = ᴛɴɪᴠ; ᴄᴇᴠ; see commentary at 5:2).
25. One thinks, for example, of the Maccabean times, when the high priests Jason and Menelaus betrayed their office and thus contributed to the desecration of the temple.
26. Note the emphatic placement of δι' ἐμοῦ (*di' emou*, through me), which focuses on Jesus' role as the one through whom sheep may enter the fold (Morris 1995: 452).
27. See Gen. 28:17; Ps. 78:23; 1 Enoch 72–75 (e.g., 72:2); 3 Bar. 6:13.
28. E.g., Odes Sol. 17:6–11; 42:15–18 (after ᴀ.ᴅ. 100).
29. See, e.g., Matt. 7:7, 13–14; 18:8–9; 25:10; cf. Acts 14:22.

"Will go in and out": Jesus' language here (a Semitism) echoes covenant terminology, especially Deuteronomic blessings for obedience (cf. Deut. 28:6; cf. Ps. 121:8). It is also reminiscent of Moses' description of Joshua (LXX: Ἰησοῦς, *Iēsous*), who led Israel into the promised land (Num. 27:16–17). "Find pasture" (νομή, *nomē* [only here in John]) is a common OT expression (e.g., 1 Chron. 4:40). The psalmist basked in the assurance of God's provision (Ps. 23:2), and God's people are frequently called "the sheep of his pasture" (e.g., Ps. 74:1; 79:13; 100:3; cf. Lam. 1:6). The pasture imagery is also found in OT references to Israel's final restoration (Isa. 49:9–10) and deliverance from the nations (Ezek. 34:12–15).[30]

Threefold repetition of parallel expressions such as "steal and kill and destroy" (whether positive or negative) is a characteristic device denoting emphasis in biblical literature. Here, three negative verbs are stacked to underscore the devastating effect of these usurpers on God's people. Such triads are attributed to Jesus (Matt. 7:7; John 14:6) and are used by Paul (1 Thess. 1:3; 5:23). The word for "kill" (θύω, *thyō* [only here in John]) is not the common term and may connote the abuse of the sacrificial system by the priestly authorities (R. Brown 1966: 386; Barrett 1978: 373).

Jesus came for his "sheep" to have life, and to have it abundantly.[31] "Have life" means "to have eternal life," that is, "to be saved" (see 10:9). Importantly, however, this does not merely entail participation in the age to come (as was the general view among Jews); according to John, Jesus gives a full life already in the here and now (which does not imply the absence of persecution [cf. 15:18–25]). In the OT, it is especially the prophet Ezekiel who envisions pasture and abundant life for God's people (cf. 34:12–15, 25–31). As the good shepherd, Jesus gives his sheep not merely enough but more than plenty (cf. Ps. 23; Ezek. 34; see Ridderbos 1997: 359).

10:11–13 "I am the good shepherd." The "good" (καλός, *kalos*) shepherd stands in contrast with the "thieves and robbers" who "steal and kill and destroy" (10:1, 8, 10).[32] God is portrayed as the shepherd of his flock in numerous OT passages (Thomson 1955; see commentary at 10:1). The people of Israel, in turn, are described as "the sheep of his pasture."[33] God as

30. Further ancient references are found in BDAG 675, including 1 Clem. 59:4 (psalm quotation) and Barn. 16:5 (an eschatological reference, possibly adducing 1 Enoch). The term is also used in Let. Arist. 112 and Josephus, *Ant.* 2.2.4 §18. Note also the messianic reference in Ps. Sol. 17:40.

31. On "life," see commentary at 1:4. Περισσόν (*perisson*, abundantly) is an adverbial accusative (Wallace 1996: 201, 293).

32. Schnackenburg (1990: 2.294) proposes a translation "right" or "true." Similarly, Borchert (1996: 333) suggests that the meaning of καλός is similar to that of ἀληθινός (*alēthinos*, true) (cf. Moloney 1998: 310; Bultmann 1971: 364). Carson (1991: 386) contends that the "good shepherd" should be thought of as "noble or worthy" but not "sentimental or effeminate." Lindars (1972: 361) favors the rendering "an ideal shepherd."

33. See commentary at 10:1. On "pasture," see commentary at 10:9.

the true shepherd is also contrasted with unfaithful shepherds, who are subject to divine judgment.[34] David (or the Davidic Messiah) is spoken of frequently as a (good) shepherd.[35] Moses, likewise, is portrayed as the "shepherd of his flock."[36]

The good shepherd lays down his life for the sheep.[37] Young David, first shepherd, then king, literally risked his life for his sheep (1 Sam. 17:34–37; cf. Sir. 47:3). The phrase "to lay down one's life" is rare in Greek and may reflect the Hebrew idiom "to hand over one's life."[38] Several OT passages hint at the Messiah's self-sacrifice (see esp. Isa. 53:12). In a cluster of messianic references (see Mark 14:27; John 19:37; Rev. 1:7), Zechariah refers to a figure who is "pierced" and for whom people mourn, a shepherd who is put to death and whose death brings about a turning point (Zech. 12:10; 13:7–9).

The "hired hand," in contrast to the shepherd, will abandon the flock in times of danger, putting self-interest first. This renders the flock easy prey for those (like wolves) who would attack it. Both OT and later Jewish literature are replete with references to leaders who fail to perform their God-given responsibilities and as a result render their charge vulnerable to attack.[39] Shockingly, the shepherds themselves had turned into wolves (Ezek. 22:27). The "hired hands" of Israel (whose function is temporary) are contrasted with those who hold a permanent shepherding office: God and his Messiah, whose role is patterned after God's "good shepherd" par excellence, David (1 Sam. 17:34–36; see commentary at 10:11). The figure of the hired hand who abandons his sheep in times of adversity was well-worn in Jesus' day (e.g., 2 Esdr. [4 Ezra] 5:18).

According to OT legislation, the hired hand was not required to make restitution for an animal torn to pieces by a wild beast (Exod. 22:13).[40]

34. Jer. 23:1–4; cf. 3:15; Ezek. 34; Zech. 11:4–17.
35. 2 Sam. 5:2; Ps. 78:70–72; Ezek. 37:24; Mic. 5:4; cf. Ps. Sol. 17:40–41; *Midr. Rab.* 2.2 on Exod. 3:1.
36. Isa. 63:11; cf. Ps. 77:20; *Midr. Rab.* 2.2 on Exod. 3:1. Philo speaks of a "good" (ἀγαθός) shepherd (*Husb.* 10 §44; 12 §49) and applies shepherd terminology not only to kings and wise men but also to both God and his firstborn Son or Word (*Husb.* 12 §§50–53; *Post. Cain* 19 §§67–68). In non-Jewish circles, too, gods and great men were described as shepherds (Barrett 1978: 374).
37. The preposition ὑπέρ (*hyper*, for) here, as elsewhere in this Gospel, has the connotation of a sacrificial, substitutionary death (Carson 1991: 386; Barrett 1978: 375; Borchert 1996: 334; Burge 2000: 291).
38. Possible parallels include Judg. 12:3; 1 Sam. 19:5; 28:21; Job 13:14; Ps. 119:109. Neyrey (2001 [see esp. chart on p. 287]) seeks to make a case (in my view, unsuccessful) for a Hellenistic background of John 10:11–18, contending that the burden of this passage (and 11:46–53) is to show that Jesus died a "noble death."
39. E.g., Jer. 10:21; 12:10; 23:1–4; Ezek. 34; Zeph. 3:3; Zech. 10:2–3; 11:4–17; 1 Enoch 89:12–76; 90:22–31; T. Gad 1:2–4.
40. Later mishnaic law stipulated that if one wolf attacked the flock, the hireling must protect it. However, if two wolves threatened the sheep, no blame attached to the

In Jesus' illustration, the "hired hand" is contrasted with "thieves and robbers" (10:1, 8, 10). Whereas the latter are thoroughly wicked, the hired hand merely proves to be more committed to his own safety than to the sheep entrusted to his care. Under normal circumstances, he is willing to shepherd the flock for pay. In the face of danger, however, he puts self-interest first.

Later in the Gospel, Jesus predicts that his disciples will be scattered, applying the present shepherding theme specifically to his followers at the salvation-historical juncture just prior to the crucifixion (16:32; the only other instance besides 10:12 of σκορπίζω [skorpizō, scatter] in John). Elsewhere, Jesus sends his disciples out "as sheep among wolves" (Matt. 10:16; Luke 10:3; cf. Acts 20:29). Jesus' appropriation of the title "shepherd" (see commentary at 10:11) places him firmly within the framework of OT and traditional Jewish messianic expectations.

10:14–18 The present verse continues the contrast between the shepherd and the hireling. John 10:14–15 reiterates but expands the saying in 10:11 by noting that Jesus' sacrificial death will institute a reciprocal relationship between believers and himself (cf. 10:3b–5; see R. Brown 1966: 396).[41] This relationship, in turn, will be patterned after Jesus' relationship with the Father.[42] Jesus' relationship with his followers ("know") is portrayed as an intimate, trusting relationship in which Jesus, the good shepherd, cares deeply for those in his charge. This relationship is patterned after God's relationship with OT Israel.[43]

"And I have other sheep that are not from this sheep pen; I must bring them also" (cf. 11:52; 17:20).[44] In light of OT expectations of the incorporation of the Gentiles among God's people, the "other sheep that are not from this sheep pen" probably are Gentiles (see esp. Isa. 56:8).[45] The "sheep pen" (αὐλή, aulē [cf. 10:1]) presumably is "the whole of historic Israel" (Ridderbos 1997: 363). The present passage clearly indicates that Jesus envisioned a full-fledged Gentile mission subsequent to his

---

hired man for any damage caused to the sheep (m. B. Meṣiʿa 7.8–9; see Dalman 1928–39: 6.233–35; Morris 1995: 454).

41. Barrett (1978: 370) notes how this deepens the Synoptic teaching on the kingdom of God by focusing on the personal, christological dimension of the relationship.

42. Cf. 1:18; 5:19–20; 7:29; 8:19, 55; 14:7, 31; 17:23, 25; see Carson 1991: 387; Ridderbos 1997: 361–62. Καθώς (kathōs, just as) entails not only a comparative but also a causal dimension (Schnackenburg 1990: 2.297).

43. See Exod. 3:7; 33:12, 17; Jer. 31:34; Hos. 6:6; 13:5; Nah. 1:7. For additional references and discussion, see Ridderbos 1997: 361. The saying "I know those who are mine, and those who are mine know me" has a proverbial ring to it; Boring, Berger, and Colpe (1995: 288) cite a Greek parallel: "I know Simon and Simon knows me."

44. For a full treatment of this passage in light of its OT background, see Köstenberger 2002b. See also additional note.

45. So the vast majority of commentators, including Barrett, Beasley-Murray, Burge, Carson, Moloney, Morris, Ridderbos, Schnackenburg, and Witherington. For Jewish material indicating that the Messiah would gather the Gentiles, see Hofius 1967.

death on the cross.[46] Though this mission is to be carried out through his followers, the pronoun "I" makes clear that Jesus will still be involved from his exalted position with the Father.[47] Together with his "own" (10:14–15), the "others" describe the full extent of Jesus' mission, both present and future (Ridderbos 1997: 362–63).

"There will be 'one flock, one shepherd'" (an allusion to Ezek. 34:23; 37:24). The notion of one flock being led by one shepherd as a metaphor for God's providential care for his united people is firmly rooted in OT prophetic literature[48] and continued in later Jewish writings.[49] Yet whereas the OT envisions primarily the gathering of the dispersed sheep of Israel, the present passage refers to the bringing together of Jews and Gentiles into one messianic community (cf. Eph. 2:11–22; 4:3–6; see Lindars 1972: 363). Hinted at in certain later OT prophetic passages (e.g., Isa. 56:6–8; Ezek. 37:15–28; Mic. 2:12), the full revelation of this truth awaited the NT era.[50] The theme of unity will be further developed in John 17 (Carson 1991: 388).[51]

John 10:17–18 continues and further explicates the thought of 10:15 (Ridderbos 1997: 365; R. Brown 1966: 399). There is no need to suppose that Jesus gained the Father's approval by sacrificing his life. Rather, his sacrifice is in obedience to the Father's command (Ridderbos 1997: 365; cf. Carson 1991: 388; Barrett 1978: 377; Beasley-Murray 1999: 171). The repeated reference to Jesus' sacrifice in 10:11–18 makes this the focal point of the characterization of the "good shepherd." The conjunction ἵνα (hina, in order that) in 10:17b probably conveys purpose rather than

---

46. Note the present tense ἔχω (echō, I have), which points to Christ's current possession of these sheep despite their absence from the fold (Morris 1995: 455). There is no basis for the supposition by some (e.g., Bultmann 1971: 383) that 10:16 represents a later addition (see Schnackenburg 1990: 2.299; ambivalent is Ridderbos 1997: 362). As a study of the Johannine mission theme makes clear (not to mention the mission theme in the other Gospels), this passage, far from representing an isolated reference to Jesus' anticipation of a future (Gentile) mission, coheres with a repeated and consistent emphasis on the extension of the scope of God's salvation beyond the boundaries of national Israel to the other nations (e.g., Matt. 28:19; Acts 1:8). See Köstenberger 1998b; Köstenberger and O'Brien 2001: 73–127, 203–26.

47. Cf. Matt. 28:18-20; see Carson 1991: 388; cf. Barrett 1978: 376; Beasley-Murray 1999: 171. John 10:16 presupposes Jesus' resurrection, which is referred to explicitly and repeatedly in the following verses (10:17, 18; cf. Michaels 1989: 181).

48. Jer. 3:15; 23:4–6; Ezek. 34:23–24; 37:15–28; Mic. 2:12; 5:3–5.

49. See Ps. Sol. 17:40; 2 Bar. 77:13–17; CD 13:7–9.

50. Cf. Paul's teaching regarding the μυστήριον (mystērion, mystery) in Eph. 3:1–10; Col. 1:26–27 (Ridderbos 1997: 363). Ridderbos (1997: 364–65) also provides a helpful discussion and critique of Martyn's (1977: 170–74) reading of 10:16 as "one great cryptogram" in terms of the "Johannine community hypothesis." See also the comments in Carson 1991: 390.

51. Leaders who promoted unity were also prized in the Hellenistic world (e.g., Plutarch, *De Alexandri magni fortuna aut virtute* 6 [cited in Boring, Berger, and Colpe 1995: 288]).

mere result (Carson 1991: 388; Morris 1995: 456 n. 50; contra Bultmann 1971: 384; Ridderbos 1997: 365).

"No one takes it away from me" may be a reference to past attempts at taking Jesus' life (5:18; 7:25; 8:59; see additional note) or to his future death and resurrection, or both.[52] "I have the power to lay it down, and I have the power to take it up again" bears a striking resemblance to Pilate's words in 19:10.[53] The statement is in keeping with the evangelist's consistent effort to portray Jesus being in charge throughout the events surrounding the crucifixion. It also highlights Jesus' power over life and death. Though more frequently it is God the Father who is credited with raising Jesus from the dead, the NT also teaches that Jesus himself "rose" (active or middle voice [e.g., Matt. 27:63]; see Morris 1995: 456–57 n. 53; cf. Beasley-Murray 1999: 172).

The reference to "this command I received" invokes covenantal language, relating Jesus' relationship with his disciples to God's relationship with OT Israel (Köstenberger 1998b: 162 n. 83, citing Pryor 1992a). This is the first of several references to "command" in the following chapters, whether to commands of the Father to the Son (10:18; 12:49–50; 14:31; 15:10) or of the Son to his followers (13:34; 14:15, 21; 15:10, 12, 14, 17).

10:19–21 The division among the Jews "again" probably alludes to 9:16 (Ridderbos 1997: 366).[54] "The Jews" here may refer not just to the Jewish leaders but more broadly to the people at large.[55] The charge that Jesus is demon-possessed and raving mad harks back to similar charges earlier in this Gospel (see 7:20; 8:48, 52). In ancient times, insanity and demon possession were frequently linked. The psalmist says that it is *the Lord* who gives sight to the blind (Ps. 146:8; cf. Exod. 4:11).

"Why listen to him?" may convey the notion of "continuing to listen" (durative present; see Ridderbos 1997: 367 n. 354). The reference to Jesus' opening the eyes of the blind in 10:21 links the good shepherd discourse with the preceding chapter and marks off 10:1–21 from the following section. The internal logic of the statement seems to be that demons were commonly considered to cause illnesses, so it would defy conventional wisdom that someone demon-possessed could heal others (Schnackenburg 1990: 2.303).[56] The reference also establishes that

52. Once again, Stibbe (1993: 115) detects here a reference to the "elusive Christ."

53. Ridderbos (1997: 366) also notes that the verb τίθημι (*tithēmi*, lay down) has the connotation of removing an article of clothing, and he points to the strong conceptual link between the present passage and Jesus' actions in 13:4, 12. Both passages feature Jesus' authority and compassion alongside each other.

54. Other times when schism occurred among the Jews in John include 7:12, 25–27, 31, 40–43. See further 5:16; 6:41–42, 52, 60, 66; 7:20, 32, 47–49; 8:22, 48, 52, 59; 9:22, 34.

55. So Morris 1995: 457; cf. Carson 1991: 390; Beasley-Murray 1999: 172; Schnackenburg 1990: 2.303; Burge 2000: 293.

56. The interrogative particle μή (*mē*) indicates expectation of a negative answer (Morris 1995: 458 n. 58).

Jesus' opponents were well aware of his amazing works (Ridderbos 1997: 367).

ii. The Unbelief of the Jews (10:22–42)

Unlike Tabernacles and the other two major annual feasts that were celebrated in Jerusalem, Dedication, with its festive candles, was joyously commemorated in Jewish homes as well as in the temple. The feast occurred near the time of the winter equinox (second half of December). A popular family celebration, it provided a stark contrast with the pagan Saturnalia, which were celebrated during the same period. Since there is no mention that Jesus went up to Jerusalem for the Feast of Dedication, it is possible that he spent the time from Tabernacles to Dedication (about two months) in Jerusalem. Alternatively, Jesus and his followers may have returned to Galilee subsequent to the Feast of Tabernacles, only to embark on what turned out to be Jesus' final journey to Jerusalem (Mark 10:1; Matt. 19:1; Luke 9:51; see Blomberg 2002: 161).

10:22–24

If, as is most likely, the healing of the blind man and the good shepherd discourse took place in October/November of A.D. 32, then the present incident occurred only about one month later (December 18–25).[57] This is the first reference to the Feast of Dedication by this name (τὰ ἐγκαίνια, *ta enkainia* [a typical "festive plural"]) in Jewish literature (Hengel 1999: 317). This eight-day festival (also called *Ḥanukkah* or the Feast of Lights [τὰ φῶτα, *ta phōta*]) celebrated the rededication of the temple in December 164 B.C. after its desecration by the Seleucid ruler Antiochus Epiphanes (1 Macc. 1:59; cf. Dan. 11:31; Josephus, *Ant.* 12.7.6 §§320–21) and the successful Maccabean revolt, which resulted in a period of Jewish independence lasting until 63 B.C. (1 Macc. 4:52–60; cf. 2 Macc. 10:5–8).[58]

There are similarities between the accounts of the Feast of Dedication, called "the festival of booths in the month of Chislev" (2 Macc. 1:9 [ca. 124 B.C.]; cf. 2 Macc. 10:6), and the Feast of Tabernacles (Lev. 23:42–43). Its association with the biblical Feast of Tabernacles lent Dedication a certain amount of scriptural legitimacy. Both festivals celebrated God's protection of the people Israel during their wanderings in the wilderness. Beyond this, the Feast of Dedication also commemorated God's intervention in the restoration of the temple, the apostasy among the Jews that had led to the temple's desecration, and the Jews' regaining of their religious (and national) freedom (Josephus, *Ant.* 12.7.7 §325 [cited in Köstenberger 2002c: 103]; cf. 12.7.6 §316).[59]

---

57. Barrett (1978: 379) suggests that the reference to the feast is meant to indicate that only a short period of time has elapsed since the events described in the previous narrative. See also the additional note to 10:22 below.

58. For a more detailed historical sketch, see Köstenberger 2002c: 103.

59. For discussions of the Feast of Dedication, see Barrett 1978: 378–79; Beasley-Murray 1999: 172–73. Moloney (1998: 317–19) suggests that 10:22–39 is a summary of John

It was winter, and Jesus moved in the temple area at Solomon's colonnade. Probably owing to the cold winter weather (in A.D. 32, Dedication fell on December 18), Jesus taught not in an open court but in the temple area called Solomon's colonnade, which, being about two hundred yards long (Hengel 1999: 318), offered protection from the raw east wind and was located on the east side of the temple.[60] This colonnade, which was commonly (but erroneously) thought to date back to Solomon's time but in fact derived from the pre-Herodian Hasmonean period, formed part of a magnificent covered structure that surrounded the outermost court of the temple on all sides. It later became the gathering place for the early Jerusalem church (cf. Acts 3:11; 5:12). It is possible that John's comment "it was winter" also has symbolic overtones.[61]

The Jews' "encircling" (κυκλόω, kykloō) Jesus indicates their resolve to elicit a definitive answer from Jesus.[62] "How long will you keep us in suspense?" (TNIV; cf. 8:25) may also be rendered "How long are you going to annoy us?" (Carson 1991: 392; Barrett 1978: 380).[63] If the TNIV rendering is accepted, the Jews questioning Jesus are not necessarily antagonistic but are merely requesting that he clarify the question of his status once and for all. If so, this would be one place in John where "the Jews" are not placed in so harsh a light. Then again, it is also conceivable that here they are preparing the kinds of charges later brought before Pilate (18:29–35).

5–10. See also his treatment of the narrative's structure on p. 314. Keener (2003: 822) notes the irony of Jesus the Messiah being rejected at a festival commemorating national deliverance.

60. See Josephus, *J.W.* 5.5.1 §§184–85; *Ant.* 15.11.3 §§396–401; 20.9.7 §§220–21. So the vast majority of commentators, including Carson, Barrett, Morris, Beasley-Murray, R. Brown, Moloney, and Burge; contra Ridderbos 1997: 368.

61. Cf. 18:18: "it was cold." If so, he is referring to the Jews' "chilling response" to Jesus (Hengel 1999: 319). See also Borchert 1996: 337. Contra Ridderbos 1997: 368; Carson 1991: 391–92. Stibbe (1993: 116) comments that the "sense of impending doom in 10.1–21 is heightened by the atmospheric statement of the narrator in v. 22." Bultmann (1971: 361) suggests that the reference to the season serves to indicate that "the end is near," as the "seasons of the year reflect the progress of the revelation."

62. Some see here a possible allusion to Ps. 118:10–12 (though not Barrett [1978: 380]). Burge (2000: 295) notes the presence of the same verb in Luke 21:20 with reference to Rome encircling Jerusalem before its destruction.

63. More literally, the Greek may be rendered "take away our life" (Ridderbos 1997: 368 n. 358). This translation is favored also by Morris (1995: 461, with reference to the same verb, αἴρω [airō, take away], in 10:18), who believes that the Jews are suggesting that Jesus is attempting to destroy Judaism. But in 10:18, αἴρω means "take up," not "take away." Bultmann (1971: 361 n. 5) thinks that this is "scarcely credible" and adduces the parallel expression in Josephus, *Ant.* 3.2.3 §48: οἱ δ᾽ ἦσαν ἐπὶ τὸν κίνδυνον τὰς ψυχὰς ἡρμένοι (LCL translation: "hearts elated"). R. Brown (1966: 403) proposes that Jesus is creating a pun on the word ψυχή (psychē, life), using it both with reference to Jesus' giving his life for his sheep and, ironically, to refer to Jesus' "taking away the life" of those who refuse to acknowledge him. In light of the fact that John's Gospel is laden with irony, this is possible but hard to verify.

"If you are the Christ, tell us plainly."[64] The request reveals, somewhat pathetically, that the entire significance of the preceding good shepherd discourse had eluded Jesus' opponents—a spiritual dynamic similar to that found in the Synoptic parables (see 10:26; cf. Mark 4:11–12 pars.). Owing to the political connotations of the term "Messiah" in first-century Palestine, Jesus generally avoided using the expression with reference to himself (cf. John 6:14–15; 11:48).[65] One wonders why the Jews repeatedly had tried to kill Jesus if they had not understood him to convey a plain message regarding his own identity (5:18; 7:25; 8:59; and esp. 10:33; Carson 1991: 392).[66]

"I did tell you" seems problematic at first blush. There appears to be no **10:25–30** explicit public statement to that effect recorded by the evangelist, though Jesus plainly identified himself as the Messiah to the Samaritan woman (where the aforementioned political connotations may have been less of a hindrance) (4:25–26) and disclosed himself as the Son of Man to the formerly blind man (9:35–37). Probably, the reference is not to a specific statement made by Jesus but to the general thrust of his ministry and teaching, which should have constituted more than sufficient evidence for the Jews to believe (see the latter part of this verse; cf. 12:37).[67] Perhaps statements such as "before Abraham came to be, I am" (8:58) are also in view.

Jesus' "works" (ἔργα, *erga*) include, but are not limited to, the miraculous (Morris 1995: 462). Most recently, Jesus had healed the blind man (see esp. 9:3–4; see R. Brown 1966: 406). The reason for the Jews' continual unbelief (present tense οὐ πιστεύετε [*ou pisteuete*, you do not believe] in 10:25, 26) is that they are not Jesus' "sheep" (see 8:47; additional note to 10:26). For Jesus' "sheep" listen to his voice; he knows them, and they follow him (10:3, 4, 8, 14, 16). Jesus gives them (present tense) eternal life (cf. 10:10), and they will never, ever perish (emphatic negative).[68] Together with the repeated assertion that no one can snatch his sheep out of his (or the Father's) hands, this conveys the image of utter security on the part of Jesus' followers.[69]

---

64. Cf. 10:6, 25. Similarly, note Luke 22:67 (cf. Matt. 26:63): "If you are the Christ, tell us."

65. So Carson 1991: 392; Burge 2000: 295. Compare the "messianic secret" motif in Mark (e.g., Mark 1:34; 5:43; 7:36; 8:30; 9:9; see Ridderbos 1997: 368; Barrett 1978: 378–80).

66. Borchert (1996: 338) suggests that the evangelist is relating Jesus' revelation by way of παροιμία (*paroimia*, illustration [10:6]) with the Jews' demand for παρρησία (*parrēsia*, frankness)—a possible play on words. Bultmann (1971: 361 n. 6), too, sees a contrast between these two terms (with reference to 16:25, 29; Mark 8:32).

67. So, in effect, Ridderbos 1997: 368; Carson 1991: 392–93; Morris 1995: 462; Beasley-Murray 1999: 174. Borchert (1996: 338) suggests that the "interplay between *paroimia* and *parrēsia* allows Jesus to tell the Pharisees that he has already answered their question."

68. Jesus' references to his "sheep" are regularly followed by an assurance introduced by "and I" (κἀγώ, *kagō*) (see Schnackenburg 1990: 2.307).

69. As Morris (1995: 463) notes, this makes clear "that our continuance in eternal life depends not on our feeble hold on Christ, but on his firm grip on us." Later, Paul affirms that nothing can "separate us from the love of God in Christ Jesus our Lord" (Rom. 8:39).

The term ἁρπάζω (*harpazō*, wrest), denoting the use of force, harks back to the use of that word in 10:12 with regard to the wolf attacking the sheep (see also the reference to "robbers" in 10:1, 8). The present assertion contrasts with the figure of the hireling who abandons the flock in the face of danger (cf. 10:12–13).[70] Jesus' reference to the Father's sovereign power recalls statements in both the OT and Second Temple literature that no one can deliver out of God's hand (Isa. 43:13) and that the souls of the righteous are in his hand (Wis. 3:1).[71]

Jesus' claim "I and the Father are one [entity]" (cf. 5:17–18; 10:33–38) forms the climax of the present chapter, much as 8:58 does for John 8 (Carson 1991: 395). The statement echoes the fundamental confession of Judaism: "Hear, O Israel: The LORD our God, the LORD is one" (Deut. 6:4).[72] For Jesus to be one with the Father yet distinct from him amounts to a claim to deity (cf. John 1:1–2). To be sure, the emphasis here is on the unity of their works (Ridderbos 1997: 371; Carson 1991: 394), yet an ontological (not just functional) unity between Jesus and the Father seems presupposed.[73] Though not an affirmation of complete identity, clearly this statement has more in view than a mere oneness of will between Jesus and the Father (so, rightly, Carson 1991: 395).[74]

Consequently, Jesus' assertion of oneness with the Father challenged narrow Jewish notions of monotheism, even though there are already hints in the OT of a plurality within the Godhead, some of which Jesus was careful to expose (e.g., Matt. 22:41–46 pars.). Jesus' present pronouncement constitutes the first major climax in John's Gospel; the second, no less important climax has Jesus cry, "It is finished," on the cross (19:30) (Hengel 1999: 319). Jesus' unity with the Father later constitutes the basis on which Jesus prays that his followers likewise will be unified (17:22; note again the neuter ἕν, *hen*).

10:31–33   Again, the Jews took up stones to stone him (see 5:18; 8:59). In the Judaism of Jesus' day, stoning was to be carried out on the basis of a judicial sentence rather than as an impulsive act of mob violence. But

---

70. See also the references to the "hands" of the prophet and of God in Ezek. 37:15–19, and the discussion below.

71. Keener (2003: 225) detects here an allusion to Ps. 95:7 (94:7 LXX), where people are called the "sheep of his [God's] hand."

72. The term "one" (ἕν, *hen*) in 10:30 is neuter rather than masculine; the latter would have suggested that Jesus and the Father are one person (Carson 1991: 394). Morris (1995: 464) suggests the rendering "one thing."

73. So, rightly, Carson (1991: 394–95), whose entire discussion repays careful reading (see also Morris 1995: 465; Beasley-Murray 1999: 174; Moloney 1998: 320; Burge 2000: 296; Laney 1992: 195; Stibbe 1993: 118; Westcott 1908: 2.68). Michaels (1989: 187) seems to conceive of Jesus' unity with the Father in functional terms (whether primarily or exclusively so), as both of them doing "the *same* work." Barrett (1978: 382) notes that the unity between the Father and the Son is also a unity of love and obedience.

74. Schlatter (1948: 242) says that ἕν denotes not identity but "inseparability"; nothing separates Jesus from the Father.

4. The Healing of the Blind Man and the Good Shepherd Discourse
b. Jesus the Good Shepherd
John 10:1–42

because the Roman authorities retained sole jurisdiction over capital punishment (cf. 18:31) and because large crowds could quickly turn volatile, especially in an oppressed nation replete with nationalistic fervor and religious fanaticism, lynching always remained a possible outcome (cf. Acts 7:54–60).[75] In light of the relationship between the Feast of Dedication and the consecration of the temple and John's portrayal of Jesus as the temple's replacement (2:19–21), the Jews' attempt to stone Jesus for blasphemy is presented by the evangelist as an effort on the Jews' part to blaspheme the "holy sanctuary of God," Jesus—and that at the feast commemorating the rededication of the temple (Hengel 1999: 318)!

Once again, Jesus displays striking serenity in the face of threats on his life.[76] As in 10:25, Jesus refers to his works done from the Father. There, reference is made to the works being done in the Father's name (i.e., as the Father's representative); here, the expression is "from the Father" (i.e., with the Father as his source as well as in order to reveal the Father). Owing to Jesus' oneness with the Father, his works display the characteristics of his Father (just as those of his Jewish opponents show the marks of their "father" [8:41, 44]). "It is as if, over against people who proved to be deaf to his words, Jesus here makes a final appeal to the undeniable character of his many 'good' deeds" (Ridderbos 1997: 372). But the Jews reject the witness of Jesus' works because they renounce his claim of unity with the Father. This, of course, places them in the dilemma of having to account for persecuting Jesus though his works indisputably are both "many" (πολλά, polla) and "good" (καλά, kala) (with both adjectives placed in an emphatic position; see Morris 1995: 466 n. 88).[77] By referring to his many "good works," though with the Father as his acknowledged source, Jesus avers that he is not guilty of disrespect for the Torah, nor is he a blasphemer, for if he were such, he would not be able to perform such works (Schnackenburg 1990: 2.309).[78]

75. In certain cases, Jewish law actually seems to have encouraged such a procedure (m. Mak. 3.2).
76. Whitacre (1999: 271–72) calls this "a most amazing scene." While the Jews are standing there, stones in hand, ready to kill Jesus, he calmly reasons with them in order to show them the error of their ways and to help them come to faith. The one who is life itself continues to offer life even to those who are determined to kill him.
77. R. Brown (1966: 403) suggests that καλός (kalos, good) here may also be intended to hark back to the description of Jesus as the "good" shepherd (10:11, 14) in the preceding narrative. The renderings by Carson (1991: 396) as "noble" or "beautiful," and by Barrett (1978: 383) as "deeds of power and moral excellence, resulting in health and well-being," may overreach as expositions of the meaning conveyed by the term.
78. Ridderbos (1997: 371 n. 373) identifies λιθάζετε (lithazete, you stone) as a conative present (cf. Morris 1995: 466 n. 90); Wallace (1996: 535) calls it a "tendential present," describing an act about to be performed.

The Jews, however, wanted to stone Jesus for blasphemy because he, whom they considered to be a mere man, claimed to be God.[79] Carson (1991: 396 [cf. Barrett 1978: 384; Burge 2000: 297]) notes the irony of this charge: in reality, Jesus "made" himself a man (cf. 1:14). With this statement, Jesus' controversy with "the Jews" in John 5–10 has come full circle (5:18; see Ridderbos 1997: 372).[80] Later Jewish law limited blasphemy to pronouncing the name of God, YHWH (the Tetragrammaton ["Yahweh"]; *m. Sanh.* 7.5; cf. 6.4), which Jesus is never recorded as doing. However, it is highly unlikely that the Sadducees, who controlled legal proceedings in the Sanhedrin, the highest Jewish court, ever adopted so narrow a definition of blasphemy in Jesus' day (Carson 1991: 396; Barrett 1978: 382–83; Beasley-Murray 1999: 175). Rather, a broader interpretation of blasphemy prevailed, based on passages such as Num. 15:30–31 ("anyone who sins defiantly . . . blasphemes the Lord") and Deut. 21:22 ("guilty of a capital offense").

10:34–36 "Is it not written in your law, 'I have said, "You are gods"'? If it called those 'gods' to whom the word of God came. . . .'"[81] By using the expression "your law," Jesus seems to distance himself not from the law itself, but from his opponents' approach to it (see 10:35b).[82] The passage quoted is Ps. 82:6.[83] In the OT, the phrase "to whom the word of God came" is often

79. Cf. Mark 14:64 par.; see Bock 1998: es p. 234–37. See the brief discussion of Synoptic parallels in Schnackenburg 1990: 2.310. John 10:33 is the only occurrence of the term βλασφημία (*blasphēmia*, blasphemy) in this Gospel; the verb βλασφημέω (*blasphēmeō*, blaspheme) occurs only in 10:36. The expression καὶ ὅτι (*kai hoti*, even because) (adverbial καί) further clarifies the charge made by the Jews (Morris 1995: 467 n. 92). The participle ὤν (*ōn*, being) in 10:33 is concessive: "even though you are a mere man" (Wallace 1996: 634–35). Ποιεῖς (*poieis*, you make) is identified by Ridderbos (1997: 372 n. 375) as a durative present.

80. Moloney (1998: 316) notes that at the Feast of Dedication the Jews affirmed their desire to remain faithful to God, yet in the present instance they are acting in a manner similar to Antiochus IV, who tried to destroy the presence of God.

81. The antecedent of εἶπεν (*eipen*, said) in 10:35 could be God ("he") or the law ("it"). The former alternative is chosen by the vast majority of versions, including the NIV = TNIV, NASB, ISV, ESV, HCSB, and KJV; the latter is preferred by the NAB. The issue is almost universally ignored by commentators, who apparently are almost exclusively preoccupied with adjudicating the appropriation of Ps. 82:6 in the present context. One of the few exceptions is Bernard (1928: 2.368), who favors the law as antecedent: "if then the Law (*i.e.* the Scripture) called them gods" (so also, apparently, Borchert 1996: 343). Against the majority of translations, there seems to be good reason to favor the law as antecedent, especially since the present passage is immediately followed by the statement that "Scripture cannot be broken," which thus would provide for a continuity of subjects in 10:34–35: "Is it not written in your *law*. . . . If *it* called . . . and *Scripture* cannot be broken. . . ."

82. Ridderbos (1997: 372) suggests, not implausibly, that the expression "in your law" may indicate the value placed on the law by the Jews resulting in their attempt to stone Jesus ("in the law that to uphold . . . is so important to you"). As noted by Carson (1991: 397), νόμος (*nomos*, law) here probably refers to the entire OT.

83. The expression "law" also covered the Psalter (for a broader conception of the term "the law," see 12:34; 15:25; Rom. 3:10–19; 1 Cor. 14:21), just as "Torah" in rabbinic literature

used with reference to those who speak or act in God's name. The phrase "the word of the Lord that came" is found at the opening of the prophetic books of Hosea, Joel, Micah, and Zephaniah (see also Luke 3:2). In the original context, the expression may have referred to (1) Israel's corrupt judges who were called "gods" because the administration of justice was a divine prerogative delegated to a few select individuals (Deut. 1:17; cf. Ps. 82:1–4); (2) angelic powers who abused the authority that God had given to them over the nations (unlikely in light of the scarcity of references to angels in John); (3) Israel at the time of the giving of the law.[84] Arguing, in typical rabbinic fashion, from the lesser to the greater (see commentary at 5:47),[85] Jesus' point here is that if Israel can in some sense be called "god" in the Scriptures, how much more is this designation appropriate for him who truly is the Son of God.[86]

Jesus' statement that the Scripture cannot be broken is evidence for his belief in the inviolability of God's written word (in the present instance, the Hebrew Scriptures). Elsewhere, Jesus contended that "until heaven and earth disappear, not the smallest letter, not the least stroke of a pen, will by any means disappear from the law until everything is accomplished" (Matt. 5:18). In this belief, Jesus knew himself united with his Jewish contemporaries (cf. Matt. 5:20). Paul and Peter concurred (2 Tim. 3:16; 2 Pet. 1:20–21). In the present instance, Jesus affirms, over against his opponents' claim that they alone upheld the authority of God's word, that he, too, has a high view of Scripture.

By his statement, Jesus emphatically (ὑμεῖς, hymeis, you) pits his Jewish opponents against the words of God and the inviolability of Scripture (Ridderbos 1997: 374). Once again, Jesus asserts that he is "the one whom the Father set apart and sent into the world."[87] In the OT and Second Temple

---

sometimes covers the Hebrew Scriptures in their entirety. Regarding this "generic sense" of law, see Pancaro 1975, especially 175–92.

84. See b. ʿAbod. Zar. 5a. For a variation of the first view, see Jungkuntz 1964; Schnackenburg 1990: 2.311; Morris 1995: 467; Beasley-Murray 1999: 176–77. The second position is held by Emerton 1960; 1966. For a variation of the third view, see Hanson 1964–65; 1967. See further Oepke, TDNT 4:1022–32, 1054–55. Most major commentators seem to favor the third view as well (e.g., Ridderbos 1997: 373; Carson 1991: 398; Barrett 1978: 384; Schnackenburg 1990: 2.311).

85. The presence of an argument from the lesser to the greater is denied by Ridderbos (1997: 374) against the overwhelming majority of commentators (e.g., R. Brown 1966: 410; Morris 1995: 469; Schnackenburg 1990: 2.310; Moloney 1998: 316). Carson (1991: 399, perhaps following Barrett 1978: 385), calls this an ad hominem argument, which he defines (somewhat idiosyncratically, it seems) as an argument that "does not require Jesus to subscribe to the same literal exegesis as his opponents."

86. For the charge of blasphemy against Jesus, see Hurtado 1999, especially 36–37. Jesus' practice of posing a question that proves too difficult for his opponents to answer is also attested repeatedly in the Synoptics (e.g., Matt. 22:41–46; Mark 12:35–37; Luke 20:41–44; see Borchert 1996: 343).

87. Barrett (1978: 385) appropriately describes the syntax of ὃν ὁ πατὴρ ἡγίασεν (hon ho patēr hēgiasen, whom the Father set apart) as "an accusative of reference, governed

literature, the term "set apart" was used for those appointed to fulfill an important task or office, be it Moses the lawgiver (Sir. 45:4), Jeremiah the prophet (Jer. 1:5), or the Aaronic priests.[88] Just as Jesus replaces the Sabbath (chs. 5, 9), the manna (ch. 6), and the light and water at the Feast of Tabernacles (chs. 7–9)—commonly called the "replacement theme" in John's Gospel (see also, in regard to the temple, 1:14; 2:21)—Jesus' reference to his own setting apart recalls the event behind the celebration of the Feast of Dedication: the consecration of the altar that replaced "the abomination of desolation" erected by Antiochus Epiphanes IV.[89]

10:37–39 The unit 10:37–39 brings closure to the entire chapter, even the section that started with 9:1. In the more immediate context, the phrase "works of the Father" in 10:37 harks back to the similar phrase in 10:32 (see also 10:25 and the equivalent opening reference in the festival cycle in 5:19–23). Jesus' point is that the Jews' unbelief would be justified if he did not back up his claims with action. Since he does so, however, his opponents' refusal to believe becomes inexcusable.[90] As before, Jesus emphasizes the unity between himself and the Father as exemplified in his works (Ridderbos 1997: 376; explained by R. Brown [1966: 411] in terms of the Jewish *šālîaḥ* concept), which include, but are not limited to, his miracles (Carson 1991: 400).

Once again, Jesus also confronts the Jews' unbelief (10:38; cf. 10:25, 26). The Jews are challenged to believe, if not in Jesus, at least in his works:[91] obedience out of inferior motives is better than outright disobedience. In the final analysis, of course, the distinction is immaterial, for by Jesus' own rationale it is by his very union with the Father that he is able to perform the works he does.[92] This is why faith in miracles

---

by λέγετε, and explaining the ὅτι clause." The verb rendered "set apart as his very own" is often translated "sanctified" or "consecrated." It occurs in John's Gospel only here and in 17:17, 19.

88. See Exod. 28:41; 40:13; Lev. 8:30; 2 Chron. 5:11; 26:18.

89. In the LXX, variants of the term τὰ ἐγκαίνια (*ta enkainia*, Feast of Dedication [John 10:22]) refer to the dedication of the tabernacle altar (Num. 7:10–11), Solomon's temple (1 Kings 8:63), and the second temple (Ezra 6:16–17). A connection between the present statement and the Feast of Tabernacles is made in, among others, Carson 1991: 399; R. Brown 1966: 411; Witherington 1995: 191; Moloney 1998: 317. Commentators differ as to the sacerdotal connotation of the term ἀγιάζω (*hagiazō*, set apart). R. Brown (1966: 411) is favorably disposed, while Barrett (1978: 385) denies such an association.

90. Morris (1995: 469 n. 102) notes the use of the adverb οὐ (*ou*) versus the particle μή (*mē*) in εἰ οὐ ποιῶ (*ei ou poiō*), giving the sense "if I were to leave undone" or "if I were to omit to do."

91. Morris (1995: 470) understands the dative τοῖς ἐργοῖς (*tois ergois*, the works) as "giving credence to" rather than full faith.

92. Old Testament figures recognized for performing unusual works were Elisha (who was given the key to the womb and enabled a barren woman to conceive), Elijah (who was given the key to the rain in answer to prayer), and both prophets together with Ezekiel (who were given the key to the graves and who raised the dead)—all three works usually being reserved for God's direct intervention (*Midr. Ps.* 78 §5).

apart from faith in Jesus remains inadequate (cf. 4:48; see Ridderbos 1997: 377).[93] Nevertheless, Jesus' shift from his own person to his works is in keeping with the principle that a tree is judged by the quality of its fruit, and a prophet by his deeds (Matt. 7:15–20).

Interestingly, coming to understand is presented as the result, rather than condition, of believing.[94] The required insight is wrapped up in an understanding of Jesus' union with the Father: "that the Father is in me, and I in the Father" (cf. John 10:30; see also 14:10–11; 17:21).[95] "Again they tried to arrest him" indicates that this was not the Jews' first attempt to arrest Jesus (cf. 7:30). The implication may be that Jesus' opponents were going to attempt to arrest Jesus in order to begin proper judicial procedures against him (Morris 1995: 470). Yet, as on previous occasions, Jesus eludes their grasp (though not necessarily by miraculous means; see Morris 1995: 470).[96]

Jesus again (πάλιν, *palin*) left the region beyond the Jordan and went to the place where John had at first been baptizing (see commentary at 1:28).[97] This presents all that has happened since then in the light of the Baptist's witness (Ridderbos 1997: 378).[98] "Beyond the Jordan" probably

10:40–42

93. C. Brown (1984) contends that one cannot have Christ or Christianity without the miracle-working Jesus of the Gospels. Carson (1991: 400) perceptively notes that the Jews' inability to discern God's presence in Jesus and his acts ultimately demonstrates their ignorance of God and how he acts. R. Brown (1966: 411–12) relevantly relates the present passage to modern attempts to use evidences as an apologetic tool (though I do not endorse all of Brown's comments here). Indeed, this verse does seem to suggest that evidence is helpful (if not necessary) in a person's coming to faith, though at the same time it is shown to be but a (limited) aid to faith rather than compelling faith in and of itself.

94. The distinction between γνῶτε (*gnōte*) and γινώσκητε (*ginōskēte*) is that of "coming to know" and "understanding" (Carson 1991: 400; Barrett 1978: 386; Morris 1995: 470; Laney 1992: 198). See also additional note to 10:38.

95. Some have seen a parallel to Jesus' assertion of oneness with God in Antiochus Epiphanes' boast that he was "God Manifest" (the meaning of the Greek epithet "Epiphanes"). This claim made by Antiochus may also lie behind the Jews' charge that Jesus (like the Seleucid ruler [see 2 Macc. 9:28]) was a blasphemer (cf. 10:33, 36; see VanderKam 1990: 211–14; followed by Moloney 1998: 321). See, however, the appropriate caution by Lindars (1972: 376), who distinguishes between Jesus' words here and the notion of family relationships among pagan gods. Lindars also points out that the present statement "preserves the logical priority of God, because the title Father is retained" and "denotes a personal intimacy which forestalls any suggestion of ditheism."

96. Morris (1995: 470) also suggests that the evangelist might be contrasting the "hand" of Jesus' opponents (unable to capture Jesus) with the "hand" of the Father (fully capable of protecting [10:29]), but this seems a bit far-fetched, since 10:28 refers to the "hand" of Jesus as the one protecting, while in the present instance it is Jesus who is being protected.

97. Ἧν . . . βαπτίζων (*ēn . . . baptizōn*) is a periphrastic, stressing the extended duration of the Baptist's baptizing ministry (contra Morris [1995: 471 n. 110], who proposes the rendering "where John was at first, baptizing").

98. R. Brown (1966: 414–15) seems to suggest that these verses are included to show that Jesus would not die until his hour had come and that he would go back to Jerusalem

refers to the region of Batanea in the tetrarchy of Philip in the northeast, at a safe distance from the jurisdiction of the Jerusalem leaders (Carson 1991: 400; contra Schnackenburg [1990: 2.314] and R. Brown [1966: 413], who suggest Bethany). And there Jesus stayed.[99] Notably, Jesus does not return to Galilee, his ministry there having come to a close (as far as the Fourth Evangelist is concerned) with the events of John 6.

The "many" who came and believed (note the repeated πολλοί [polloi] in 10:41–42) are, presumably, from the crowds that customarily followed Jesus (Ridderbos 1997: 378).[100] The evangelist notes that John did not perform a single sign, in obvious contrast to Jesus. Nevertheless, this does not diminish the importance of his witness. Jewish sources do not praise putatively great men unless some miracle is attributed to them (Bammel 1965; Carson 1991: 400; Beasley-Murray 1999: 178). The Synoptics likewise never attribute miracles to the Baptist, though Herod reportedly thought that Jesus, who did perform miracles, was John the Baptist come back to life (Mark 6:14).

The words "All the things John said regarding this man were true" (see commentary at 1:6–8 and 1:15) constitute the final reference to the Baptist in this Gospel.[101] The concluding comment "many believed in him" may mirror the similar statement "many believed in his name" (2:23) at the outset of Jesus' ministry.[102] It does not necessarily imply lasting success on Jesus' part in eliciting faith from among the crowds (contra Ridderbos 1997: 379).[103] In fact, "viewed through the eyes of Jesus' adversaries, his return to where his ministry began might have

---

when the hour had come. Schnackenburg (1990: 2.314) lists as many as six reasons why the evangelist included this portion: (1) to show that Jerusalem was too dangerous for Jesus; (2) to point out that Jesus received a more favorable response when he did not face opposition from the Jews; (3) to link Jesus' ministry in Jerusalem with the beginning of the Gospel when his identity was at issue as well; (4) to recall the Baptist's witness, which is fulfilled in Jesus' signs; (5) to indicate Jesus' supremacy over John the Baptist; and (6) to create a bridge to the following section.

99. The verb μένω (menō, remain) harks back to earlier similar uses with reference to Jesus in 1:38–39 and 2:12. The reading ἔμεινεν (aorist) rather than ἔμενεν (imperfect) is likely original (R. Brown 1966: 413; Morris 1995: 471 n. 111).

100. Ridderbos (1997: 378 n. 402) plausibly suggests that a period might be placed after πρὸς αὐτόν (pros auton, to him) in 10:41.

101. R. Brown (1966: 415, referring to Glasson) notes that after 3:30 ("He must increase, but I must decrease"), the references to the Baptist grow progressively shorter. However, this interesting observation should not be pressed too far.

102. Laney (1992: 199) thinks that the final word ἐκεῖ (ekei, there) represents an emphatic contrast between people's response "in that place" and the unbelief Jesus encountered in Jerusalem (10:36–39).

103. Ridderbos (1997: 379) proposes that the words of 10:42 are seeking to indicate that despite his rejection by the Jews elsewhere, Jesus' ministry was not ineffective. Ridderbos sees no reason to question the faith of these individuals. However, in light of the consistent string of instances of fleeting faith in John's Gospel, there seems to be good reason to do just that. Also doubtful is the contention by Morris (1995: 472) that 10:42 describes a process akin to what occurred in John 4 (the impact of the woman's testimony).

made of it the very picture of a failed mission. But the Evangelist views things quite differently" (Ridderbos 1997: 379).

Additional Notes

10:11. Some MSS have δίδωσιν ($\mathfrak{P}^{45}$ ℵ* D) rather than τίθησιν ($\mathfrak{P}^{66, 75}$ A B), presumably in dependence on Mark 10:45 (Beasley-Murray 1999: 165 n. d). R. Brown (1966: 386–87), against the majority of commentators and versions, believes that the former reading could be original.

10:16. Both readings γενήσονται ($\mathfrak{P}^{45}$ B D) and γενήσεται ($\mathfrak{P}^{66}$ ℵ* A) are attested, with the former more likely being original (Barrett 1978: 376; Beasley-Murray 1999: 165 n. e; Schnackenburg 1990: 2.300).

10:18. The textual evidence is divided between the readings αἴρει ($\mathfrak{P}^{66}$ A D and the majority of MSS; preferred by Beasley-Murray 1999: 165 n. f) and ἦρεν ($\mathfrak{P}^{45}$ ℵ* B; favored by Morris 1995: 456; Barrett 1978: 377; R. Brown 1966: 387; Lindars 1972: 364), with the former perhaps more likely to be original.

10:22. Of the two variants, τότε ($\mathfrak{P}^{75}$ B) and δέ ($\mathfrak{P}^{66*}$ ℵ A), the former is more likely original (favored by Morris 1995: 460 n. 64), the latter reading having arisen in order to solve a perceived chronological problem (Burge 2000: 294 n. 15). The presence or absence of both words in various other MSS further attests to some scribal turbulence surrounding this reading. Beasley-Murray (1999: 165 n. g, with reference to J. N. Sanders) supports the omission of both.

10:26. The phrase καθὼς εἶπον ὑμῖν ($\mathfrak{P}^{66*}$ A D) at the end of this verse is probably a secondary addition (Beasley-Murray 1999: 165 n. i).

10:29. Textual evidence for the relative pronoun divides between the neuter ὅ (ℵ B) and the masculine ὅς ($\mathfrak{P}^{66}$ A). The former (chosen by the UBS committee) is the harder reading, but the latter may well be original, for, as Barrett (1978: 381) observes, the masculine is "far more suitable to the context." Barrett discusses the almost insurmountable interpretive problems associated with adopting the neuter but notes that it is hard to account for the emergence of the neuter variant on the assumption that the masculine is original (see Metzger [1994: 198], who believes that the masculine pronoun "would almost certainly not have been altered"). He concludes by saying that any alternatives to reading the masculine pronoun here may be "so *difficilis* as to be *impossibilis*" (Barrett 1978: 382). Commentators are divided, with Ridderbos, Carson, Barrett, Moloney, Burge, and Bultmann favoring the masculine pronoun, and Morris, Schnackenburg, R. Brown, and Beasley-Murray preferring the neuter.

10:34. Barrett (1978: 384, perhaps dependent on Bultmann 1971: 389 n. 1) notes that ὑμῶν is omitted in some important MSS ($\mathfrak{P}^{45}$ ℵ* D) and expresses some doubt as to the wording being original (but note "your law" in 8:17 and "their law" in 15:25 [noted by Beasley-Murray 1999: 165 n. l]). Barrett contends that its later insertion would be natural. To the contrary, it appears that the term's omission can most likely be explained as "a scribal attempt to soften the seeming harshness of Jesus' attitude toward the OT and his tendency to dissociate himself from the Jewish heritage" (R. Brown 1966: 403).

10:38. Commentators are virtually unanimous in accepting γινώσκητε ($\mathfrak{P}^{45, 66, 75}$ B) rather than πιστεύ[σ]ητε (ℵ A) as the original reading (e.g., Morris 1995: 470 n. 106; Beasley-Murray 1999: 165 n. m; R. Brown 1966: 404; Moloney 1998: 321; Bultmann 1971: 391 n. 2).

C. Final Passover: The Climactic Sign—the Raising of Lazarus—and Other Events (11:1–12:19)

The present section is structured around the spectacular raising of Lazarus, who had been dead for four days. In anticipation of Jesus' seventh climactic sign, suspense is built in this Gospel by Jesus' delayed response (11:6) and the fact (mentioned by the evangelist in 11:17) that by the time Jesus arrived, Lazarus had already been dead four days. The disciples' misunderstanding (narrated in 11:11–15); Thomas's reminder of the danger awaiting Jesus in Judea (11:16); Lazarus's sisters' mourning, their partly resigned and partly hopeful attitude, and their struggle for faith (11:20–33, 39–40); and the presence and comments of their Jewish comforters (11:19, 31, 36–37, 42) build toward Jesus' climactic command to Lazarus to come out of the tomb and the dead man's due compliance (11:43–44). This powerful act reveals Jesus to be the resurrection and the life and the messianic Son of God (11:25; 20:30–31).

Jesus' miraculous restoration of Lazarus's life also turns the spotlight on Jewish unbelief (11:37; 12:37–43). Rather than finally eliciting faith from Jesus' opponents, the miracle actually hardens their resolve to kill—in an ironic paradox—the resurrection and the life. An emergency meeting is called, and the Jewish high priest prophetically presages Jesus' substitutionary cross-death (11:45–54). The chief priests decide that even Lazarus must be killed, since he constitutes an ever-present reminder to others of Jesus' miraculous, life-giving powers (12:10–11). Jesus' anointing for burial by Lazarus's sister Mary (12:1–8)—against the betrayer's objections—and the triumphal entry (12:12–19) constitute ominous events that signal to the readers of John's Gospel that Jesus' confrontation with the Jewish leadership is headed for a final showdown, resulting in his death and resurrection.

1. The Raising of Lazarus (11:1–57)

The significance of the raising of Lazarus in John's narrative as a whole cannot be exaggerated.[1] Only John records this event, clearly the most spectacular of any raisings recorded in the Gospels.[2] The pericope constitutes the climactic, seventh sign selected by the evangelist in order to show that Jesus is "the resurrection and the life" (11:25).[3] Raisings of the dead are very rare in both the OT[4] and the

1. Stibbe (1994: 39) calls the function of the present pericope "crucial" and "pivotal." Various attempts have been made to isolate sources underlying the existing narrative, but as Dodd (1963: 230 [cited in M. Harris 1986: 311]) points out, "Nowhere perhaps, in this gospel, have attempts to analyse out a written source, or sources, proved less convincing, and if the evangelist is following a traditional story of fixed pattern, he has covered his tracks." This observation also holds true for the attempts by Burkett (1994: 209–32) to isolate two previous accounts of Lazarus's resurrection that allegedly have been combined into one in John 11.

2. Though see the reference to "all the miracles" that the people of Jerusalem had seen in Luke 19:37 (noted by Ridderbos 1997: 383; R. Brown 1966: 429). For a defense of the historicity of the raising of Lazarus, see M. Harris 1986: 310–15. See also Morris (1995: 474–76), who, arguing for the historicity of the raising of Lazarus, presents several lines of reasoning: (1) the impressive amount of detail given, including names and geographical references; (2) Peter's absence from the Johannine narrative in 7:1–13:6 (cf. Matt. 19:27–26:33; Mark 10:28–11:21; Luke 18:28–22:8), which may account, at least in part, for the omission of the raising of Lazarus in Mark and Matthew; and (3) all the Jerusalem miracles are excluded from the Synoptic tradition, and Jerusalem itself is excluded, with the exception of the final week. Keener (2003: 836) conjectures that Mark may have "suppressed" (an infelicitous word choice) the Lazarus story to protect Lazarus and his sisters, who still lived near Jerusalem at the time of publication. Keener (2003: 837) also observes that the account of Jesus' raising of Lazarus is critical for John's plot development (the Lazarus account is at the heart of John's message: Jesus dies most immediately because he has given life to a disciple [11:14–16; cf. 3:16–17]); it constitutes the longest single sign account in the Fourth Gospel; and, apart from the passion narrative, it represents the longest narrative without a substantial discourse section.

3. Stibbe (1994: 40) proposes a pattern in which all but the seventh sign are paired up with another sign: 2:1–11 with 4:46–54; 5:1–15 with chapter 9; and 6:1–15 with 6:16–21. I have argued elsewhere that a more plausible structure is: Cana cycle: 2:1–11 / 2:14–22 / 4:46–54; festival cycle: 5:1–15 / 6:1–15 / chapter 9. In this structure the outer signs correspond (2:1–11 with 4:46–54 as the two Cana signs; 5:1–15 and chapter 9 as healings at pools in Jerusalem with negative versus positive responses). Stibbe (1994: 41) also suggests, quite implausibly, that the genre of the narrative is that of comedy.

4. Old Testament instances of raisings of the dead include Elijah's raising of the widow's son (1 Kings 17:17–24); Elisha's raising of the son of the Shunammite woman (2 Kings 4:32–37); Elisha's "posthumous" raising of a dead man (2 Kings 13:21); and the witch of Endor's illicit summoning of Samuel from the dead at King Saul's request (1 Sam. 28) (see also Ezekiel's vision of the valley of dry bones [Ezek. 37:1–14]). Raisings of the dead

Gospels.[5] Lazarus is known only from the present account;[6] Mary and Martha are featured also in Luke 10:38–42.

With the Feast of Dedication (which took place in mid-December) past (the year is now A.D. 33), and the threat to Jesus' life in Jerusalem and environs becoming increasingly severe, Jesus' impending death is casting an ever longer shadow forward, and his raising of Lazarus, the seventh and final Johannine sign, serves as the antitype (anticipatory pattern) of Jesus' own resurrection in the narrative.[7]

The raising of Lazarus thus provides the focal point of Jesus' escalating conflict with the Jews (esp. in chs. 5–10). Historically, the event triggers the Jewish leadership's resolve to have Jesus arrested and tried for blasphemy (11:45–57).[8] Structurally, John 11 serves a crucial bridge function between the narration of Jesus' ministry to the Jews (chs. 1–10) and his passion (chs. 13–20, esp. 18–20) (Ridderbos 1997: 381).[9]

---

were generally viewed in light of the final resurrection and as an expression of God's power to bring it about.

5. In all four Gospels combined there are only three such events: the raising of Jairus's daughter (Mark 5:22–24, 38–42 pars.); the raising of the widow's son at Nain (Luke 7:11–15); and the raising of Lazarus (John 11:1–44) (M. Harris 1986).

6. The conjecture that the designation "the one you love" in 11:3 points to Lazarus as the "disciple Jesus loved," the author of John's Gospel, is entirely speculative. Also, there is almost certainly no connection between this figure and the character in the parable about the rich man and Lazarus recorded in Luke 16:19–31 (rightly noted by Ridderbos 1997: 386 n. 14; Carson 1991: 404; contra Dunkerley 1959).

7. Though note that Jesus' resurrection also plays a role in the symbolism of the second sign recorded in John, the clearing of the temple (see 2:20–22). Stibbe (1994: 39; 1993: 121) points out that the seven signs of Jesus in John's Gospel span the whole gamut from the festive mood of a wedding to the aftermath of a funeral.

8. There is no reason to drive a wedge between history and theology and to diminish the historicity of the raising of Lazarus along the lines suggested by R. Brown (1966: 428–30 [but see Ridderbos 1997: 382]). R. Brown proposes that chapters 10–11 comprises a "later addition to the plan of the Gospel" (p. 427), attributing the present pericope more to "Johannine pedagogical and theological purpose than . . . historical reminiscence" (p. 430). Also precarious is the type of source-critical reconstruction attempted by Schnackenburg (1990: 2.316–21). Ridderbos (1997: 382) helpfully points to the "agains" in 11:7–8 (presupposing a long prior stay in Judea and Jerusalem) and the disciples' remarks about earlier attempts on Jesus' life by the Jews in 11:8 as evidence that chapter 11 constitutes an integral structural component of the overall Gospel. Ridderbos (1997: 386) rightly notes that the reality of the miracle and its theological significance cannot be separated (referring to 1:14). For a rebuttal of existentialist interpretations of chapter 11, see Carson 1991: 404.

9. M. Harris (1986: 311) divides the text as follows: setting (11:1–6); complication (11:7–37); and resolution (11:38–44). However, this does not adequately recognize the geographical movement from the location outside Judea where Jesus hears of Lazarus's condition (11:1–16), to his arrival in Bethany (11:17–37), to his arrival at Lazarus's tomb (11:38–44) (see Stibbe 1994: 41). According to Stibbe (1994: 43–44), the evangelist has arranged his material "in five sections using the technique of inverted parallelism or chiasmus" (11:1–16, 17–22, 23–27, 28–32, 33–44), with the "I am" saying in the center (11:25–26). Stibbe (1994: 41–42) notes that of all the Johannine signs, only the Lazarus narrative has

The raising of Lazarus is more than a miracle: it is a "sign," a demonstration of Jesus' true identity as the Christ and Son of God.[10] Moreover, as the culminating piece in the Fourth Evangelist's theodicy, this seventh, climactic sign constitutes the final damning piece of evidence against Jesus' opponents. No sign more powerful than the raising of Lazarus could be given. Hence, the period of Jesus' signs, confined to the first twelve chapters of this Gospel, comes to a close.

a. Jesus learns of Lazarus's death (11:1–16)
b. Jesus comforts Lazarus's sisters (11:17–37)
c. The raising of Lazarus (11:38–44)
d. The plot to kill Jesus (11:45–57)

Exegesis and Exposition

[1]Now a certain man was sick, Lazarus from Bethany, from the village of Mary and her sister Martha. [2](Now Mary was the one who had anointed the Lord with perfume and had wiped his feet with her hair; it was her brother Lazarus who was sick.) [3]So the sisters sent to him [Jesus], saying, "Lord, look, the one you love is sick." [4]Now when Jesus heard this, he said, "This sickness will not end in death but is for the glory of God, in order that the Son of God may be glorified through it." [5]Now Jesus loved Martha and her sister and Lazarus. [6]So when he heard that he [Lazarus] was sick, he remained in the place where he stayed two more days, [7]then after this said to the disciples, "Let's go to Judea again." [8]The disciples said to him, "Rabbi, just now the Jews have been trying to stone you, and you are going back there again?" [9]Jesus answered, "Are there not twelve hours in the day? If anyone walks around during the day, he does not stumble, because he sees the light of this world. [10]But if anyone walks around at night, he stumbles, because the light is not in him." [11]He said these things, and after this he said to them, "Our friend Lazarus has fallen asleep; but I am going to wake him up." [12]Then the disciples said to him, "Lord, if he has fallen asleep, he will get well." [13](Now Jesus had spoken concerning his death, but they thought he was talking about natural sleep.) [14]For this reason Jesus then told them plainly, "Lazarus has died, [15]and I am glad that I was not there, for

the miracle at the end, "as the grand finale of the story" (p. 42). The initial stance of Jesus in every instance is "outside": outside Judea; outside Bethany; outside the tomb (p. 43). The two main protagonists, Jesus and Lazarus, are far apart at the beginning and reunited at the end. Jesus is portrayed in his elusiveness and his humanity, and as the one who performs in his here-and-now ministry a function (raising the dead) reserved in traditional Jewish thought for God himself, even using the divine name (11:25) (Stibbe 1994: 44–45). Other ingredients of the present narrative are delay and misunderstanding.

10. Ridderbos (1997: 383) comments, "In the Lazarus story the miraculous event and Jesus' self-revelation in that event are completely interwoven."

your sake—in order that you may believe. But let's go to him." 16Then Thomas (the one called Didymus) said to his fellow disciples, "Let us go as well, so that we may die with him."

17So when Jesus came, he found that he [Lazarus] had already been in the tomb for four days. 18(Now Bethany was near Jerusalem, about fifteen stadia [less than two miles] away.) 19And many of the Jews had come to Martha and Mary to console them concerning their brother. 20So when Martha heard that Jesus was coming, she went to meet him; but Mary remained sitting in the house. 21Then Martha said to Jesus, "Lord, if you had been here, my brother would not have died. 22But even now I know that God will give you whatever you ask." 23Jesus said to her, "Your brother will rise again." 24Martha said to him, "I know that he will rise again in the resurrection on the last day." 25Jesus said to her, "I am the resurrection and the life: whoever believes in me will live even though he dies, 26and whoever lives and believes in me will never, ever die. Do you believe this?" 27She said to him, "Yes, Lord, I have come to believe that you are the Christ, the Son of God—the one who is coming into the world."

28And having said this, she left and called Mary her sister privately, saying, "The teacher is here and is calling for you." 29When she [Mary] heard this, she rose quickly and went to him. 30(Now Jesus had not yet come into the village, but was still in the place where Martha had met him.) 31Therefore, when the Jews who were with her in the house, consoling her, saw Mary—that she rose quickly and went out—they followed her, thinking that she was going to the tomb to weep there. 32So Mary, when she came to the place where Jesus was, upon seeing him, fell at his feet and said to him, "Lord, if you had been here, my brother would not have died." 33Then, when Jesus saw her weeping, and the Jews who had come with her weeping as well, he bristled in spirit and was stirred inside 34and said, "Where have you laid him?" They said to him, "Lord, come and see." 35Jesus burst into tears. 36Then the Jews were saying, "Look how much he loved him." 37But some of them said, "Could not he who opened the eyes of the blind man also have prevented this man [Lazarus] from dying?"

38Then Jesus, again bristling within himself, came to the tomb. (It was a cave, and a stone had been placed upon it.) 39Jesus said, "Take away the stone." The sister of the deceased, Martha, said to him, "Lord, there is already an odor, for it has been four days." 40Jesus said to her, "Did I not tell you that if you believe, you will see the glory of God?" 41Then they took away the stone. And Jesus lifted up his eyes and said, "Father, I give thanks to you because you heard me. 42I knew that you always hear me, but I said this for the sake of the crowd surrounding me, so that they may believe that you sent me." 43And when he had said this, he cried out in a loud voice, "Lazarus, come out!" 44The dead man came out, his feet and hands bound with strips of linen, and his face wrapped in a cloth. Jesus said to them, "Unbind him and let him go."

45Then many of the Jews who had come to Mary and had seen ⌜what⌝ he [Jesus] had done believed in him. 46But some of them went to the Pharisees and told them what Jesus had done. [47]Then the chief priests and Pharisees convened the Sanhedrin and kept saying, "What are we going to do? This man is performing many signs. [48]If we let him go on like this, all people will believe in him, and the Romans will come and take away both our place and our nation." [49]But one of them, Caiaphas, as the high priest of that year, said to them, "You know nothing at all! [50]You don't realize that it is better for ⌜you⌝ that one man die for the people than that the whole nation perish!" [51](Yet this he did not say of his own accord, but as high priest of that year he prophesied that Jesus was about to die for the nation, [52]and not for the nation only but in order that the children of God scattered everywhere might be gathered into one.) [53]Therefore from that day on they were plotting to kill him.

[54]For this reason Jesus no longer moved about publicly among the Jews, but left from there for the region near the wilderness, to a town called Ephraim, and there he stayed with his disciples.

[55]Now the Jewish Passover was near, and many went up to Jerusalem from the country prior to Passover in order to purify themselves. [56]So they kept looking for Jesus and were saying to one another as they were standing in the temple area, "What do you think? That he won't come to the feast at all?" [57]But the chief priests and the Pharisees had given orders that if anyone knew where he [Jesus] was, he should report it, so that they might arrest him.

a. Jesus Learns of Lazarus's Death (11:1–16)

"Now a certain man was" recalls the similar introduction in 5:5 (cf. 1 Sam. 1:1; Job 1:1).[11] "Lazarus" is a shortened form of "Eleazar" (Hebrew: *Elʿazar* ["whom God helps," "whose help is God"]).[12] This was the name of the third son and successor of Aaron, whose descendants were the high priests of the house of Zadok. Lazarus is mentioned in the NT only in John 11–12 (the same name is also found in Luke 16:19–31). Ossuary inscriptions show that the name "Eleazar" was common in NT times.

Lazarus was from a village called Bethany. The present Bethany (not previously mentioned in this Gospel) should be distinguished from the Bethany featured in 1:28 and alluded to in 10:40–42.[13] The village referred to here was situated east of the Mount of Olives, less than two miles from Jerusalem on the road to Jericho. This Bethany near Jerusalem is mentioned elsewhere (together with Bethphage) as the place where

11:1–2

---

11. This does not keep Ridderbos (1997: 386) from calling the introduction "choppy and cumbersome," or Barrett (1978: 387) from describing it as "clumsy."

12. Barrett (1978: 389) thinks it unlikely (though not impossible) that the etymological significance of Lazarus's name was in the mind of the evangelist.

13. Noted by Carson 1991: 405. On the relationship between the two Bethanys referred to in John's Gospel, see Brownlee 1972: 167–74. Morris (1995: 477 n. 10) rightly rejects the distinction made between "Bethany" as their present home and "the village" as their place of origin on the basis of the prepositions ἀπό (*apo*) and ἐκ (*ek*) in 11:1.

Jesus stayed when visiting Jerusalem (Matt. 21:17; 26:6). It is probably to be identified with the village of Ananyah mentioned in Neh. 11:32.[14] Today, the town is called El-ʿAzariyeh in commemoration of Lazarus. The term κώμη (kōmē, village) is elsewhere in John applied only to Bethlehem (7:42).[15]

Mary and her sister Martha are also mentioned in Luke 10:38–42. Apparently, Martha was the older of the two, since she acts as the hostess in the Lukan passage (so, e.g., Burge 2000: 312; cf. John 12:2; note also that she is named first in 11:5). The names "Mary," "Martha," and "Lazarus" were discovered in ossuary inscriptions in a tomb near Bethany in 1873.[16] "Mary" was a common name, the Greek form of the Hebrew "Miriam." "Martha" was an Aramaic name meaning "lady," feminine of mar, "Lord." The fact that of the three names in this family, one was Hebrew ("Lazarus"), one Aramaic ("Martha"), and one Greek ("Mary"), is typical of the end of the Second Temple period and attests to the way in which cultures had interpenetrated.[17]

The evangelist's aside in 11:2, "Now Mary was the one who had anointed the Lord with perfume and had wiped his feet with her hair," anticipates 12:3 (Ridderbos 1997: 386–87).[18] Since John does not recount the anointing until the following chapter, the present reference suggests that the evangelist expects his readers already to be familiar with the story (cf. Matt. 26:13 par.).[19] On the evangelist's reference to Jesus as "the Lord," see commentary at 6:23.

14. The name "Bethany" arose from a combination of the Hebrew word for "house," beth, and the name ananyah, whereby one of the two an syllables dropped out—a phenomenon known among linguists as syllabic haplology (so Albright 1923). Borchert (1996: 349) avers that Bethany means "house of suffering" and that this symbolic meaning may have been significant for the evangelist. However, even if Borchert's reconstruction of the etymology is correct, there is little evidence for his contention.

15. The term πόλις (polis, town, city) is used for Bethsaida (1:44), Sychar (4:5, 8, 28, 30, 39), Ephraim (11:54), and Jerusalem (19:20).

16. See Clermont-Ganneau 1874; Kraeling 1946 [cited in Bruce 1983: 253 n. 1]; Avi-Yonah 1964: 146.

17. Burge (2000: 312), contrary to conventional assumptions, insists that one must not assume that the three lived together and suggests that it would be natural for each of them to have been married.

18. Ridderbos (1997: 386–87) also notes the somewhat unusual placement of the final phrase "whose brother Lazarus was sick" in 11:2.

19. R. Brown (1966: 423 [cf. Schnackenburg 1990: 2.322]) claims that this verse is "clearly a parenthesis added by an editor," though it is unclear why the author himself (rather than a later editor) could not have added this kind of parenthetical statement. Carson (1991: 405 [approvingly cited by Borchert 1996: 349]) contends, against Barrett (1978: 390), that it does not follow that the intended audience was Christian, though clearly Carson's case is difficult here. More likely is the reconstruction by Witherington (1995: 201), who says that this verse may serve as "a simple reminder of Mary's identity to the Christians who would be using this Gospel as a missionary tool to bring outsiders to Christ." Yet Carson (1991: 405) rightly points out that regardless of this issue, and even if the anointing was

"Lord, look, the one you love is sick" (cf. 11:5; see also the possible *inclusio* in 11:36). The sisters sent word to Jesus regarding their brother's illness not merely for the purpose of information but as an urgent request for help, for they doubtless knew of Jesus' healing power.[20] The subtlety of the sisters' request is reminiscent of Jesus' mother's earlier words to Jesus at the Cana wedding (2:3).[21] Both cases reflect the practice, common in many ancient as well as modern cultures, of rather indirect, polite communication.[22] The phrase "the one you love" is reminiscent of the "disciple Jesus loved" (first in 13:23), but the similarity may be coincidental.[23] Jesus' confident assessment "This sickness will not end in death" may be compared with his words concerning Jairus's daughter, "The girl is not dead but asleep" (Matt. 9:24 pars.).

The signature statement here, "It is for the glory of God, in order that the Son of God may be glorified through it" (Beasley-Murray 1999: 188; cf. Moloney 1998: 322), parallels Jesus' earlier verdict regarding the man's blindness from birth (John 9:3). As Carson (1991: 406, perhaps following Barrett 1978: 390) is careful to point out, it is not that the sickness occurred *in order* for God to be glorified, but rather that it constituted an *occasion* for God's glory to be revealed. Here as elsewhere in the Gospel, God's self-disclosure takes place preeminently in his Son (13:31; 14:13; 17:4; see Carson 1991: 406; cf. Ridderbos 1997: 387).

The reference to Jesus' love for Martha and her sister[24] and Lazarus in 11:5 (the separate mention of all three may emphasize Jesus' love for each of them [Morris 1995: 479]) harks back to the phrase "the one you love" in 11:3 (cf. 11:36).[25] Yet rather than serving as "merely a superfluous confirmation of vs. 3b" (Ridderbos 1997: 388), the reference, in the wake of 11:4, adds Jesus' love to his desire for God's glory as the motivation

---

unknown to the reader, the proleptic reference to Mary still serves as a fine literary device, urging the first-time reader onward in the narrative.

20. Burge (2000: 312) notes the interesting fact that the women knew how to locate Jesus.

21. The absence of a specific request is noted by Morris (1995: 478).

22. Another Johannine example is Nicodemus's opening gambit in 3:2.

23. In any case, the mere reference to Lazarus as "the one you love" in the present passage hardly warrants the conclusion by Eller (1987), Brownlee (1990: 191–94), and Stibbe (1992: 79–81) that the beloved disciple is Lazarus. See the discussion in Charlesworth 1995: xiii (who advances the hardly more plausible theory that the beloved disciple is the apostle Thomas).

24. Contrast 11:1, where Mary is mentioned before Martha (presumably because of her prominence on account of the anointing [11:2]). Ridderbos (1997: 388 n. 22 [cf. Carson 1991: 411]) suggests (citing John 11:19ff. and Luke 10:38b, 40–41) that usually Martha is mentioned first because she more often appears as the initiator of events. Carson (1991: 406 [cf. Morris 1995: 478]) proposes that Martha may be the oldest of the three.

25. The Greek word for "love" used here is ἀγαπάω (*agapaō*); in 11:3 and 11:36 it is φιλέω (*phileō*). However, there appears to be little distinction in meaning between these two words, and the use of two different words for "to love" is best taken as an instance of the evangelist's penchant for stylistic variation.

for the ensuing miracle (Ridderbos 1997: 388; cf. Carson 1991: 406–7). Beyond this, the statement may also be intended to soften the implications of the next verse (see Morris 1995: 479; Carson 1991: 407).[26]

11:6–8 When Jesus heard that Lazarus was sick, he remained in the place where he stayed two more days.[27] On the face of it, this is a classic non sequitur. One would have expected Jesus to rush to the scene instantaneously. Yet once again the evangelist confounds conventional thinking in his presentation (cf. 2:4, see Schlatter 1948: 248; Ridderbos 1997: 389, citing Giblin 1980: 209). What defies human reasoning is upheld when the glory of God is the driving motivation and the sovereignty of God is the guiding force.[28] If the place where Jesus was staying when the news of Lazarus's illness reached him was the region of Batanea, located approximately one hundred miles to the northeast of Jerusalem (cf. 1:28; 10:40–42), then the following reconstruction of the events related to the raising of Lazarus best fits the evidence (Carson 1991: 407; contra Morris 1995: 479–80).

Apparently, Lazarus was still alive when the initial news regarding his illness reached Jesus (11:4). Two days later, Jesus, presumably by means of supernatural insight, announces to his followers that Lazarus has died, taking this as the divine signal to depart for Bethany (Riesner 1987: 44–45). The fact that Batanea (where Jesus was staying) was about one hundred miles from Bethany (a day's journey being about twenty to thirty miles in that day) accounts for the fact that four days passed between Lazarus's death and Jesus' arrival on the scene (11:17).[29] As Ridderbos (1997: 388–89) notes, "The whole of vss. 5–7 shows how the

---

26. R. Brown (1966: 423) postulates that 11:5 was added by a later editor, intending to "assure the reader that Jesus' failure to go to Lazarus does not reflect indifference." Brown may be right in construing the underlying intention, but once again it is hard to see why it could not have been the author himself rather than a later editor who was guided by this motivation.

27. For a similar delay, see 7:4–10 (noted by Moule 1975: 118). Keener (2003: 839) observes that in 4:40 Jesus also remains two additional days. Westcott (1908: 2.82) comments, "Because the Lord loved the family He went at the exact moment when His visit would be most fruitful, and not just when He was invited."

28. This is why Carson (1991: 407 [cf. Morris 1995: 479 n. 16]) is right in rejecting the NIV's rendering of 11:6 as "Yet when he heard" (retained in the TNIV), proposing instead the translation "When therefore he heard." Ridderbos (1997: 388 n. 24) avers that the particle μέν (*men*) in 11:6b is "more or less concessive" ("he [it is true] stayed where he was"). Similarly, Barrett (1978: 390) suggests that τότε μέν (*tote men*, then) in 11:6b anticipates the ἔπειτα μετὰ τοῦτο (*epeita meta touto*, then after this) in 11:7, stressing Jesus' deliberate delay.

29. Contra Keener (2003: 839–40), who says Bethany was only a single day's journey away. According to Keener's reconstruction, if Jesus delayed two days after receiving the message and arrived to find that Lazarus had been dead four days, Lazarus may have been dead by the time the messengers reached Jesus, dying shortly after they left Bethany. If so, even if Jesus had left immediately upon receiving the message, Lazarus would still have been dead, albeit only two (rather than four) days.

human and the divine—his love for his own *and* his regard for the times appointed for him by the Father—are inseparably intertwined in Jesus' conduct and therefore in his glorification as the Son of God (vs. 4)."

In the context of the Johannine narrative, Judea has become increasingly hostile to Jesus and his claims (most recently 10:39). Returning to Judea thus was fraught with considerable risk to Jesus' own life, if not that of his followers (cf. 11:8, 16).[30] In regard to the statement "Just now the Jews have been trying to stone you," it is possible that Thomas was the one among Jesus' followers who felt most strongly about this (cf. 11:16). The present reference is to recent events at the Feast of Dedication in Jerusalem (10:31, 39).

If the raising of Lazarus took place in March of A.D. 33, and the Feast of Dedication had taken place at the end of December of the previous year (Köstenberger 2002c: 12), then "just now" would be slightly hyperbolic (about two months would have passed since then), though the events would have been recent enough to be vivid in the disciples' memory. As their present comment reveals, Jesus' followers "still consistently allow themselves to be guided by purely human considerations" (Ridderbos 1997: 390), not recognizing "that his death, however appalling an event, would also be his glorification and the consummation of his ministry" (Carson 1991: 408; cf. Barrett 1978: 391).

In the context of the disciples' query in 11:8, Jesus' question in 11:9, "Are there not twelve hours in the day?" (an analepsis of 9:4–5 and a prolepsis of 18:4–8 [Stibbe 1994: 51]), assures them that his mission cannot be short of the allotted time (Schnackenburg 1990: 2.325).[31] Both Romans and Jews divided the day into twelve-"hour" periods. Since the length of daylight extended, according to season, anywhere from around ten to fourteen hours a day, the twelve "hours" of daylight varied accordingly. Most people did their work as long as there was daylight; once darkness came, it was time to stop working.

11:9–11

Jesus' rhetorical question underscores the urgency of his mission. The primary thrust of Jesus' illustration in 11:9–10 is to assure his disciples that as long as they are with him, the light of the world, they are secure

---

30. Morris (1995: 480) thinks that the present reference to returning to Judea (instead of the more specific Bethany) indicates that it is this entrance that is significant, for it will lead to Jesus' crucifixion. On the address "rabbi," see commentary at 1:38. The term is used here for the last time in John's Gospel (but see 20:16). The expression also occurs in 9:2 (note the similarities between 9:2–5 and 11:8–10).

31. Stibbe (1994: 51) paraphrases as follows: "I can return to Judea because the hour for my death (the hour of darkness) is not quite upon us. I will therefore not be killed ('stumble') at Bethany because I am still ministering in a season of pre-ordained security (daylight)." The saying is not without Jewish parallels (e.g., *b. Sanh.* 38b). Pollard (1973: 438, following Henderson 1920–21) somewhat implausibly suggests that the present statement indicates that Jesus "waited for light," that is, divine guidance, and hence the delay. But see the critique in Moule 1975: 118–20.

from stumbling (Laney 1992: 205).[32] Until his hour arrives, Jesus and his followers will be protected from the threats of the Jews (Ridderbos 1997: 391; cf. Acts 21:10–14). Moreover, while threats are looming on the horizon, Jesus must continue to be about his mission (Carson 1991: 409; Bultmann 1971: 399). The larger implication of Jesus' statement in its original historical context is that "people should make the most of the presence of Christ" while he is still in their midst; a time will come when it is too late (Morris 1995: 481).[33]

"He has no light" (NIV) or "they have no light" (TNIV) is rendered more literally "there is no light in him." This indicates a shift from the realm of nature (daylight) to symbolic language ("light" inside a person; cf. Matt. 6:22–23 par.). In Semitic thought the eye was regarded as light in a person's body (Schnackenburg 1990: 2.325). From there it is only a small step to the notion that a person is connected with the divine world of light. The shift in the image from *walking in* the light to light *in a person* is also attested in the Qumran texts.[34]

Jesus' statement "Our friend Lazarus[35] has fallen asleep; but I am going[36] to wake him up" (see 11:4) is a rather benign way of addressing a grim situation.[37] Similar language is used in the account of the raising of Jairus's daughter (Matt. 9:24 pars.; cf. 27:52). The equivalent OT phrase (esp. in the Books of Kings and Chronicles) is that a person "slept with his (or her) fathers" (i.e., the person died), suggesting falling into an irrevocable sleep (cf. Job 14:11–12). Occasionally, death is considered to be a sleep from which people will one day be awakened (Dan. 12:2; cf. 2 Esdr. [4 Ezra] 7:31–32; see Balz, *TDNT* 8:552).[38] The term ἐξυπνίζω (*exypnizō*, wake up [only here in the NT]) does not

32. Lindars (1972: 390) conjectures that "stumble" may constitute an allusion to Isa. 8:14.

33. Readings of 11:9–10 with reference to the coming of darkness leading to Jesus' crucifixion and the like (e.g., Ridderbos 1997: 391) seem to go beyond the image field conjured up by Jesus' saying.

34. E.g., 1QH 17:26. A similar statement is found in Gos. Thom. 24. A possible OT parallel is Jer. 13:16.

35. Keener (2003: 835, 840) says that since Lazarus was the friend of Jesus and the disciples (11:11), it was appropriate to die for him (15:13–15). If there is a connection, 15:13–15 serves as a commentary on the raising of Lazarus.

36. Keener (2003: 838) notes the contrasting dynamic between 7:1–10 (where others told Jesus to go to Jerusalem but he refused because his time had not yet come) and 11:1–16 (where Jesus goes to Jerusalem because his time is now close at hand).

37. See Morris (1995: 482), who refers to the universal fear regarding death in the ancient world. There is no reason to follow Barrett (1978: 392 [cf. R. Brown 1966: 431]), who, on the basis that φίλος (*philos*, friend) is a technical term for a Christian in the NT, proposes that this is the "true meaning" of this "pregnant saying." Carson (1991: 409) notes the "not accidental" switch from the plural "*our* friend" to the singular "*I* am going," saying that this indicates that Jesus alone is the resurrection and the life. "I am going" is identified as a futuristic present by Wallace (1996: 536).

38. Further references are provided by Borchert (1996: 352) and Lindars (1972: 394).

occur in secular Greek in the sense "to raise from death" (but see Job 14:12–15 LXX).[39]

As so often in this Gospel, the disciples misunderstand, taking Jesus' reference to sleep literally.[40] It is even possible that Jesus' followers take him to mean that Lazarus had taken a turn for the better, which for them would have been all the more reason to avoid Judea (Ridderbos 1997: 392; cf. Morris 1995: 482). The misunderstanding is promptly cleared up by Jesus.[41] Lazarus's death becomes occasion for rejoicing because it will serve to strengthen the disciples' faith in Jesus once Lazarus has been raised.[42] The syntax of Jesus' statement in 11:14b–15 is difficult. Perhaps most likely, it is to be construed as follows: "Lazarus has died, and I am glad that I was not there for your sake—in order that you may believe."[43]

11:12–16

The name "Thomas" (both Hebrew *tō'm* and Aramaic *tō'mā'* mean "twin") is not attested in literature prior to John's Gospel. However, the Greek term δίδυμος (*didymos*, twin) is known also to have served as a proper name. It is therefore likely that "Thomas" was a genuine Greek name patterned after its Hebrew or Aramaic equivalents (Fitzmyer 1971: 369–70). John consistently explains Thomas's name by adding the explanatory phrase "called Didymus" (cf. 20:24; 21:2). In the other Gospels, Thomas is mentioned only in the apostolic lists (Matt. 10:3; Mark 3:18; Luke 6:15; also Acts 1:13). John, on the other hand, refers to Thomas several times in his narrative (cf. 14:5; 20:24–29; 21:2).[44]

39. Hanson (1973) suggests that Job 14 lies behind John's narrative. Other LXX references featuring the term are Judg. 16:14, 20; 1 Kings 3:15.

40. For a defense of the historicity of this incident, see Carson (1991: 409), who points out that the disciples did not have the advantage of knowing the end of the story; that the messenger had announced sickness but not death; and that the disciples' anxiety about returning to Judea might have led to a certain amount of denseness. Carson also, rightly in my opinion, sees no double meaning in σωθήσεται (*sōthēsetai*, he will get well) (1991: 410; contra Barrett 1978: 393; R. Brown 1966: 424; Moloney 1998: 337; Westcott 1908: 2.84).

41. Whereby Jesus' clarification in 11:14 is preceded by the evangelist's aside in 11:13. Εἰρήκει (*eirēkei*, he had spoken) is an extensive pluperfect (Wallace 1996: 585); ἐκεῖνοι δέ (*ekeinoi de*, but they) emphasizes the difference in subject: "*they* in distinction from him" (Morris 1995: 482 n. 27). Κοίμησις (*koimēsis*, sleep) is used as an expression for death in Sir. 46:19; 48:13. On the phrase παρρησίᾳ (*parrēsia*, frankness), see 7:4; 16:29. Regarding the supernatural knowledge conveyed, see, e.g., 4:17–18.

42. See the reference to God's glory in 11:4; see also 2:11; cf. Barrett 1978: 393; R. Brown 1966: 432. Note the aorist subjunctive πιστεύσητε (*pisteusēte*, you may believe), which here refers to the strengthening of the disciples' faith (rather than the creation of new faith). This observation is significant in relation to the question of how the purpose statement in 20:30–31 should be construed. Morris (1995: 483) struggles to accommodate this form within his somewhat outmoded verbal theory.

43. Alternatively, the sentence should read, "Lazarus has died—and I am glad for your sake, in order that you may believe—because I was not there" (cf. Carson 1991: 411, citing Delebecque 1986; cf. Barrett 1978: 393).

44. Though there is little to justify the conclusion by Charlesworth (1995) that Thomas is the "beloved disciple" (see the critique by Beck 1997: 127–31).

The reference to Thomas's "fellow disciples" (συμμαθηταί, *symmathētai* [only here in the NT; cf. Mart. Pol. 17:3]) may indicate that Thomas was not alone in his sentiments (Morris 1995: 483). The "him" in "Let us go as well, so that we may die with him" is widely assumed to be Jesus (cf. 11:8), but it is possible that the reference is in fact to Lazarus.[45] It is unclear whether Thomas's words are sincere or sarcastic.[46] If the former (unlikely), then this would be evidence for unusual commitment on the part of Jesus' disciples.[47] If the latter, then Thomas, not reassured by the words of 11:9–10, would, as in 14:5 and 20:24–25, represent the sober, realistic human mind (Ridderbos 1997: 393).[48] Shortly thereafter, Peter tells Jesus that he will lay down his life for him (13:37), a statement that is as sincere as it is ironic in light both of Peter's imminent denial of Jesus and of Jesus' impending death *for him*.[49]

b. Jesus Comforts Lazarus's Sisters (11:17–37)

11:17–22 In John 2, Jesus is seen attending a wedding with some of his followers; in John 11, he is shown to mourn the loss of a loved one with close friends (Stibbe 1994: 39; 1993: 121).[50] In this and other instances, Jesus' actions clearly reflect his first-century Palestinian framework. By coming to console Martha and Mary after their brother Lazarus's death, Jesus fulfills one of the most essential obligations in the Jewish culture

45. See Larsen 2001: 215–20; Zahn 1921: 482 (called "a bizarre idea" by Bultmann [1971: 400 n. 6]); acknowledged as grammatically possible but rejected by Michaels (1989: 199).

46. Note that John does not record any comment on Jesus' part. Moloney (1998: 322) notes that this is the first time in the Gospel that ἀποθνήσκω (*apothnēskō*, die) is associated with Jesus, but from now on it will appear in that regard with frequency (cf. 11:50, 51; 12:24, 33). Keener (2003: 835 n. 1) says that Thomas ironically interprets Jesus as saying that he will go to the realm of death.

47. So Carson (1991: 410), who speaks of "raw devotion and courage"; similarly, Morris 1995: 484; Michaels 1989: 196. Keener (2003: 842), too, says Thomas's is an act of courage (contrasting him with Jesus' brothers in 7:5), though he notes that Thomas later failed to believe the disciples' testimony regarding Jesus' resurrection (20:25). Perhaps the strongest endorsement of Thomas's sincerity comes from Whitacre (1999: 283), who says that Thomas displays "an incredible picture of faith," is "following out of loyalty," and constitutes "a model disciple."

48. For Witherington (1995: 202), Thomas's comment "sounds more like fatalistic resignation to what seemed inevitable" (I would agree). Bultmann (1971: 400) speaks of "blind devotion" (with reference to 14:5 and 20:24–25); the exact same term is picked up by Beasley-Murray (1999: 189), who also notes the veiled irony in Thomas's statement. Stibbe (1993: 125) says that Thomas's comment "reveals an element of misunderstanding," manifesting "naiveté at best, insincerity at worst."

49. Stibbe (1994: 46) calls Thomas's statement one of "false bravado" and links it with Peter's similar statement in 13:37. According to Stibbe, both epitomize "a certain kind of false disciple: the kind which promises much in word (in this case, martyrdom) but delivers little in deed (where are Thomas and Peter when Jesus is crucified?)."

50. Talbert (1992: 172) perceives that 11:17–44 consists of two loosely corresponding cycles: a "Martha cycle" (11:17–27) and a "Mary cycle" (11:28–44).

of his day. The presence of a well-known teacher who had traveled a long distance would be particularly comforting to Lazarus's sisters. Yet, ultimately, Jesus has much greater things in mind (cf. 11:4, 11, 15).[51]

The evangelist's statement "Lazarus had already been in the tomb for four days" is part of John's repeated emphasis that Lazarus was truly dead.[52] Later Jewish sources attest the rabbinic belief that death was irrevocable three days after a person had died.[53] Burial usually followed quickly after death, as in the cases of Ananias and Sapphira (Acts 5:6, 10).

The reference to Bethany's close proximity to Jerusalem may serve to highlight the risk that Jesus took by coming (Carson 1991: 411).[54] It also explains the large number of Jews who had come from there to comfort Lazarus's sisters (Ridderbos 1997: 393).[55] The original wording specifies that Bethany was fifteen stadia from Jerusalem.[56] One stadion being approximately two hundred yards, fifteen stadia are equivalent to about three thousand yards, or just over 1.7 miles. If the "many Jews" who came to console Martha and Mary were indeed from Jerusalem, this would indicate that the family enjoyed considerable social standing, for although comforting the bereaved generally was regarded as a religious duty, not every villager would have been consoled by "many Jews" from the nearby city.[57]

It was customary for burial in ancient Palestine to take place on the day of death. Thus, mourning for the passing of a loved one must follow burial. In Jesus' time, men and women walked separately in the funeral procession, and after the burial the women returned from the grave alone to begin the thirty-day mourning period. This included frequent expressions of loud wailing and other dramatic displays of grief (R. Brown

---

51. Michaels (1989: 201) writes, "Jesus' arrival in Bethany is described like the visit of a conquering king, or in the way the early Christians later expected him to come gloriously to earth a second time."

52. See 11:14, 39; cf. 11:21, 32; see J. Martin 1964: 336–37. But note the dissenting voice of Michaels (1989: 205): "It is doubtful that such discussions shed light on the present passage. If the intent was to underscore that Lazarus was truly dead, the detail seems both unnecessary (he was, after all, buried!) and confusing (was Jesus *not* really dead because he was raised within three days?). Rather, the intent is simply to prepare the reader for Jesus' confrontation with death as decay and uncleanness in v. 39."

53. See *Lev. Rab.* 18.1 on Lev. 15:1; cf. *Eccles. Rab.* 12.6 (universally cited by commentators: e.g., Ridderbos 1997: 393; Carson 1991: 411; Morris 1995: 485). Cf. *m. Yebam.* 16.3; *Semaḥot* 8, rule 1 (cited in Köstenberger 2002c: 109). See also Hanson 1973. Keener (2003: 841 n. 63, citing Michaels 1984: 190) cautions, however, that the belief that the soul left the body three days after death is not widely attested in the early period.

54. Note that in Luke 10:38, Bethany is simply referred to as "a certain village," with no reference made to its proximity to Jerusalem (noted by Morris 1995: 485).

55. Again, Martha is mentioned first (cf. 11:5; noted by Ridderbos 1997: 393 n. 39).

56. Morris (1995: 485 n. 43) notes the "curious" Greek word order and explains it in terms of a measurement beginning "from" Jerusalem.

57. So Ridderbos 1997: 393; Carson 1991: 411 (but see Wis. 19:3; *m. Ketub.* 4.4).

1966: 424). The Talmud prescribes seven days of deep mourning and thirty days of light mourning (*b. Mo'ed Qaṭ.* 27b). Interestingly, in this section "the Jews" are treated in a neutral or even positive light by the evangelist (cf. 11:31, 33).[58]

Martha, in keeping with what is known of her personality elsewhere, takes the initiative and goes to meet Jesus, apparently without being summoned (so Morris 1995: 486; cf. 11:28). According to Keener (2003: 843), Martha, who was sitting *shiva*, should have stayed in the house and let Jesus come to her. Keener points out that Martha paid Jesus great respect by going out to meet him (also noting the verbal parallel with 12:13). Mary, by contrast, stays at home (the Greek text says that she "remained sitting in the house"). It was customary for those mourning the loss of a loved one to be seated when receiving the condolences of their friends (Morris 1995: 487).[59] John's characterization of Mary and Martha agrees with Luke's Gospel where Mary sits at Jesus' feet while Martha is busy with her household duties (cf. Luke 10:38–42; see Lindars 1972: 393; contra Pollard 1973: 438). Martha's words reveal that she had enough faith to believe that Jesus could have kept Lazarus from dying, though her words may betray a hint of disappointment at Jesus' delay.[60] Even now, she believes that Jesus can still intervene on her brother's behalf (though not necessarily that he will raise him from the dead [see 11:39–40]).[61]

11:23–27 Jesus' assurance here, "Your brother will rise again," appears to meet with a "clear undertone of dissatisfaction" (Ridderbos 1997: 396), for Jesus has told Martha nothing that she did not already know, and of which the Jews had undoubtedly reminded her: "I know that he will rise again in the resurrection on the last day."[62] Interestingly, all four previous references to raising the dead place the event "on the last day"

58. So, rightly, Carson 1991: 411; Barrett 1978: 394; Conway 1999: 139; Stibbe 1994: 48 (though he notes the return to a negative portrayal in 11:36, 45). Contra Morris (1995: 486), who finds the use of "the Jews" here "unusual" and suggests that it may imply that "though the mourners could bring themselves to sympathize with Martha and Mary, they were hostile to Jesus."

59. See Job 2:8, 13; Ezek. 8:14; cf. *Ruth Rab.* 2.14. A sitting posture was also common for mourners in ancient Rome, being adopted by, for example, Cato when learning of the defeat at Pharsalus (Plutarch, *Cato Minor* 56.4).

60. So Ridderbos 1997: 395. Wallace (1996: 703) goes further: "Although *formally* a second class condition, it is intended here as a *rebuke*. It is as if she had said, 'Lord, you should have been here!'" (contra Carson 1991: 412).

61. So, rightly, Carson 1991: 412; Ridderbos 1997: 395, with reference to 2:5; similarly, Keener 2003: 106–7, citing Barrett 1978: 390. The term κύριος (*kyrios*) probably means "Lord," as in 11:3 (Carson 1991: 411). Regarding the statement "God will give you whatever you ask," see commentary at 9:31.

62. Moloney (1998: 328) suggests, not implausibly, that Martha here interrupts Jesus: "*She tells* Jesus what resurrection means. . . . Jesus must wrest the initiative from the energetic Martha."

(6:39, 40, 44, 54; cf. 5:29).[63] Martha's affirmation of end-time resurrection was in keeping with Jesus' own teaching (cf. 5:21, 25–29; 6:39–44, 54), which in turn cohered with Pharisaic beliefs (cf. Acts 23:8; Josephus, *Ant.* 18.1.3 §14; *J.W.* 2.8.14 §163; see Barrett 1978: 395) and those of the majority of first-century Jews (Bauckham 1998b).[64] The Sadducees (as well as the Samaritans), on the other hand, flatly denied such a view.[65] The old idea of Jewish corporate personality, whereby one continued to exist only in the lives of one's descendants, hardly provided satisfactory hope for many pious Jews in Jesus' day.[66]

By identifying himself to Martha as "the resurrection and the life" in the present (on "life," see at 1:4; as another of Jesus' "I am" sayings, see at 6:35), Jesus seeks to shift Martha's focus from an abstract belief in resurrection on the last day to personal trust in the one who provides it in the here and now.[67] This transforms the sign into an action with symbolic significance that demonstrates the life-giving power of Jesus (Carson 1991: 412; cf. Barrett 1978: 395–96). Each of the juxtaposed statements, "Whoever believes in me will live even though he dies, and whoever lives and believes in me will never, ever die," expresses the same truth in a paradoxical manner (Bultmann 1971: 403; Hebrew *māšāl*),[68] the first from the viewpoint "of the deceased believer who will live," the second from that "of the one who lives in faith and will not die."[69] Every

---

63. John is the only NT author to use the expression "the last day" (cf. 6:39, 40, 44, 54; 12:48; cf. 5:29). Other writers prefer the plural, "the last days," usually referring to the times preceding the end (cf. Acts 2:17; 2 Tim. 3:1; James 5:3)—language that harks back to OT terminology (e.g., Isa. 2:2; Mic. 4:1; see Beasley-Murray 1999: 190).

64. The resurrection of the dead was the subject of lively debate between the Pharisees and their opponents (e.g., *b. Sanh.* 90b, referring to Deut. 31:16; Isa. 26:19; and Song 7:9). Other mishnaic passages likewise denounce those who refuse to affirm the resurrection of the dead (*m. Sanh.* 10.1; cf. *m. Ber.* 9.5). Belief in the resurrection is also evident from the second of the Eighteen Benedictions: "Lord, you are almighty forever, who makes the dead alive. . . . Blessed are you, Lord, who makes the dead alive" (cf. *m. Ber.* 5.2; *m. Soṭah* 9.15; see Schürer 1973–79: 2.456).

65. See Matt. 22:23–33 pars.; Acts 23:8; Josephus, *J.W.* 2.8.14 §165; *Ant.* 18.1.4 §16. See Oepke, *TDNT* 1:370; Meyer, *TDNT* 7:46–47.

66. For a discussion of the Jewish doctrine of corporate personality, see H. Robinson 1964.

67. Westcott (1908: 2.90) observes, "Martha had spoken of a gift to be obtained from God and dispensed by Christ. Christ turns her thoughts to His own Person. He is that which men need." See also the challenging question, "Do you believe this?" that concludes Jesus' statement at the end of 11:26. Cf. Brodie 1993: 393.

68. Morris (1995: 489) and Carson (1991: 413) note the one article tying closely together "everyone who lives and believes." Οὐ μή . . . εἰς τὸν αἰῶνα (*ou mē . . . eis ton aiōna*) is an emphatic negative: "never, ever" (plus subjunctive; see Wallace 1996: 468). In the question "Do you believe this?" the verb πιστεύω (*pisteuō*, believe) is followed by the accusative, which is unique in this Gospel (Bultmann 1971: 404 n. 1; Schnackenburg 1990: 2.332).

69. Ridderbos (1997: 396) persuasively argues that 11:25b refers to "death in the natural sense and to living in the sense of eternal life," while "lives" in 11:26a "refers to natural

believer in Jesus, "in life as in death, participates in the resurrection and 'the life' that Jesus is and that he imparts" (Ridderbos 1997: 396).[70]

Hence "physical death is not the important thing": believers "may die in the sense that they pass through the door we call physical death, but they will not die in the fuller sense. Death for them is but the gateway to further life and fellowship with God" (Morris 1995: 488). Martha's almost creedlike confession[71] of Jesus as "the Christ, the Son of God—the one who is coming into the world" strikingly anticipates the purpose statement at the end of the Gospel (20:30–31).[72] "The one who is coming into the world" takes up the messianic expression derived from Ps. 118:26 (so Beasley-Murray 1999: 192), which is applied to Jesus by others in the Gospels (see esp. Matt. 11:3 par.; John 12:13 pars.).

11:28–32   It attests to John's considerable narrative skill that he changes the scene while breaking off a conversation at its climax (cf. 4:26–27; 8:58–59). After uttering her confession, Martha calls her sister and informs her that "the teacher" is here and wants to see her.[73] Martha's unobtrusive way of proceeding may simply reflect an attempt to maintain a degree

---

human existence, while 'never die' refers to the eternal life that natural death can neither prevent nor affect" (so also Bultmann 1971: 403, Schnackenburg 1990: 2.331; Stibbe 1994: 51). Contra Carson (1991: 413), R. Brown (1966: 425), and Borchert (1996: 356) (also Calvin and Schlatter), who maintain that "lives" in 11:26a refers to eternal life. Wuellner (1991: 182) calls the present statement an oxymoron.

70. On the expression "Lord" in 11:27, cf. 11:3, 21.

71. Note the emphatic ἐγώ (egō, I) (Morris 1995: 489) and the perfect (labeled "intensive" by Wallace [1996: 574]) πεπίστευκα (pepisteuka, I have come to believe), which indicates a settled conviction (contra Moloney [1998: 328], who believes that the perfect suggests arrogance on Martha's part).

72. For this reason Witherington (1995: 203), who calls Martha's confession "the least inadequate confession yet in this Gospel," and R. Brown (1966: 433), who labels her belief "inadequate," are overly negative. More positive are Morris (1995: 489), who says, "She may not understand fully the implications of what he has just said, but as far as she can she accepts it," and Carson (1991: 414), who labels her faith as "a rich mixture of personal trust (fiducia) and of confidence that certain things about Jesus are true (assensus)." Keener (2003: 844–45) suggests that John, by including Martha's confession, likely sought to balance gender the way Luke does (cf. Peter's confession in 6:68–69). See also Stibbe (1994: 47), who perceives movement from two "I know's" (11:22, 24) to a climactic "I believe" (11:27); from propositional to personal understanding; and from confessor to witness. Ridderbos (1997: 399–400) calls the confession "spontaneous and uninhibited" and sees it as reminiscent of the man blind from birth, who confessed despite his lack of understanding concerning the Son of Man (9:38). On "the Christ," see commentary at 1:41; on "Son of God," see commentary at 1:34 and 1:49.

73. Morris (1995: 490 n. 62) perceptively notes that λάθρᾳ (lathra, privately) could modify ἐφώνησεν (ephōnēsen, she called) or εἰποῦσα (eipousa, saying), meaning either that Martha called her sister secretly or that she secretly (or privately) talked to her. The former is perhaps more likely. Morris also is critical of the NIV's gloss "aside." Borchert (1996: 358) suggests that Martha's statement to Mary may have been "an indication of Martha's controlling temperament."

of privacy in the middle of the commotion of the scene (Carson 1991: 414–15), or may indicate that Jesus intended to keep this a private visit rather than dealing with the public.[74] "The teacher" (ὁ διδάσκαλος, *ho didaskalos* [note the definite article]) would have been a natural way of referring to Jesus for any disciple in the preresurrection period.[75] The fact that the expression is used here by a woman (talking to another woman) is significant (Morris 1995: 491). Whereas contemporary rabbis regularly refused to instruct women, Jesus took a radically different approach.

Characteristically, Mary immediately rose and went to Jesus.[76] Jesus had not yet entered the village, but was still at the place where Martha had met him (cf. 11:20).[77] Despite Mary's unobtrusiveness, her departure did not escape the Jews who had been with her in the house to comfort her (see commentary at 11:19). Their assumption was that Mary, in keeping with Jewish custom (see Gen. 50:10; 2 Sam. 3:32; Jer. 38:15 LXX), had gone to the tomb to give way to her grief and mourn (TNIV; more literally, "weep") at the tomb.[78] The Jews' following Mary meant that the ensuing events "would have many witnesses and so receive wide publicity" (Morris 1995: 492). "But even now he could not remain hidden and again came into confrontation with 'the Jews' " (Ridderbos 1997: 400).

Upon her arrival, Mary fell at Jesus' feet and said, in words virtually identical to those of her sister earlier, "Lord, if you had been here, my brother would not have died."[79] Commentators differ over the nature of Mary's faith (or the lack thereof) and how Mary's response compares to that of her sister.[80] Bultmann (1971: 405) thinks that the

74. Ridderbos (1997: 400) comments, "The time of his public self-disclosure before 'the Jews' was past."

75. Though compare this designation with the immediately preceding confession of Jesus as the Christ and Son of God (noted by Barrett 1978: 397). The term is given as the Greek equivalent of *rabbi* in 1:38 and 20:16 and is used for Jesus in 3:2; 13:13, 14.

76. Note the progressive aspect reflected in the imperfect ἤρχετο (*ērcheto*, she went, was going) (see the discussion in Morris [1995: 491 n. 65], who does, however, believe that the present-tense form of the verb found in some MSS may be original here; cf. Maccini 1996: 149–50).

77. Schnackenburg (1990: 2.334) conjectures that Jesus did not return with Martha to the house in order to secure private conversations with the two sisters.

78. Compare Mary Magdalene's behavior at Jesus' tomb in 20:11, 15 (see also Wis. 19:3).

79. Cf. 11:21 (though note the absence of a further statement akin to 11:22 in the present instance). The sole difference between the two statements is the emphatic μου (*mou*, my), which may indicate that Lazarus had been especially dear to Mary.

80. An egregious example comes from Schnackenburg (1990: 2.333), who says that Mary "gives the impression of being nothing but a complaining woman," a comment for which he is sharply rebuked by Borchert (1996: 359), who calls this "a Western male's misunderstanding." Pollard (1973: 438–41) strongly contends that Martha's and Mary's responses are diametrically opposed (cautioning against reading the present pericope in light of Luke

lack of parallel to 11:22 indicates that Martha's faith is a step ahead of her sister's. Ridderbos (1997: 401) rejects this, pointing to the lack of privacy in the present instance, which may have cut the conversation short.[81] Carson (1991: 415) concurs, also noting that Mary's prostration may indicate that she showed less emotional restraint than her sister (cf. Keener [2003: 845], who says Mary was more forward and perhaps emotionally closer to Jesus; and Morris [1995: 492], who sees Martha as being "matter-of-fact"). Moloney (1998: 330), finally, views Mary's statement as an expression of simple trust in Jesus' presence, indicating acceptance of Jesus' revelation as the resurrection and the life.[82]

11:33–37 These verses present a scene of universal mourning.[83] According to Jewish funeral custom, even a poor family was expected to hire at least two flute players and a wailing woman (*m. Ketub.* 4.4), and Mary and Martha's family appears to have been anything but poor (cf. 12:1–3). This "professional mourning" doubtless provided the backdrop for the tears of Mary and her friends.[84] The present heartbreaking scene would have been preceded by a formal funeral procession and burial, in which wailing women and flute players as well as shouts of grief from the men in the procession punctuated laments sung in the house of death, on the way to the tomb, and during the burial itself (cf. Matt. 9:23 pars.; see Stählin, *TDNT* 3:151–52).

10:38–42): Martha exemplifies "confident trust," but Mary demonstrates "hysterical weeping," eliciting Jesus' reaction of "bitter disappointment" (p. 440). Similarly, Stibbe (1994: 47), who maintains that these two women "exhibit different types of grief," with Martha evincing "growth in resurrection faith," and Mary's grief being a "desperate, passionate and forlorn affair." For Pollard (1973: 441), "the lack of faith on the part of Mary and the Jews who were with her" is the actual reason why Jesus decides to raise Lazarus.

81. Morris (1995: 492) suggests that by moving quickly, Mary may have achieved some brief moments of privacy away from her comforters, who would have been confused over where she was going. If so, her "prostration and greeting" were private. At any rate, she was quickly rejoined by the party of mourners. We may add that it is quite likely that the evangelist does not record everything said at the present occasion.

82. Though, conversely, Martha understands Jesus as a thaumaturge. Thus, according to Moloney (1998: 330), "Mary is the character in the story reflecting true faith (vv. 29, 32) while Martha has fallen short of such faith (vv. 21–22, 24, 27)." Ironically, this conclusion is precisely the opposite of that drawn by Pollard 1973: 440–41 (see n. 80 above). Both instances seem to represent the kind of dichotomizations that Ridderbos (1997: 401) rejects.

83. Here Mary is shown weeping. Interestingly, there is no reference to her sister Martha doing likewise anywhere in this pericope. This may indicate that Martha was more task-oriented, and Mary more intuitive and emotional.

84. The evangelist uses a variety of terms for mourning to sketch people's behavior at Lazarus's tomb. The Jews "comfort" the deceased man's sisters (παραμυθέομαι, *paramytheomai* [11:19, 31]) in the midst of universal "weeping and wailing" (κλαίω, *klaiō* [11:31, 33; cf. 20:11, 13, 15]), and Jesus himself "weeps" (δακρύω, *dakryō* [11:35]).

When Jesus saw Mary and her Jewish friends weeping, he was visibly agitated.[85] "Deeply moved" (TNIV) hardly does justice to the underlying Greek word ἐμβριμάομαι (*embrimaomai*), which has the connotation of snorting (in animals).[86] Thus, Jesus is shown here not so much to express empathy or grief as to bristle at his imminent encounter with and assault on death (see further below).[87] "Stirred" (ἐτάραξεν, *etaraxen* [note the active voice here versus the passive in 12:27; 13:21]) has connotations of inner agitation and turmoil (cf. Esth. 4:4), as in the case of the waters of Bethesda (John 5:7) or the waves and breakers of a waterfall (Ps. 42:5–7).[88] Being thus in anguish is an experience frequently described by David in his psalms.[89]

A survey of the major commentators on this verse reveals a bewildering array of interpretations. Some say that Jesus was deeply moved but deny that he was angry (Morris 1995: 494).[90] But most insist that Jesus' emotions went beyond sorrow to actual indignation.[91] The object

85. The juxtaposition of the terms ἐνεβριμήσατο τῷ πνεύματι (*enebrimēsato tō pneumati*, bristled in spirit) and ἐτάραξεν ἑαυτόν (*etaraxen heauton*, was stirred inside) may well express the Johannine penchant for stylistic variation. If not, "it must be intended to underline the contention that Jesus was always master of himself and his circumstances" (Barrett 1978: 399).

86. The term, in verb or noun form, occurs rarely in the LXX (Dan. 11:30; Lam. 2:6; cf. Sir. 13:3), though the evidence is probably late and hardly conclusive (see Lindars 1992b: 94–95). For primary Greek references, see Lindars (1992b: 92–96), who cites Aeschylus, *Seven against Thebes* 1.461 (sixth to fifth century B.C.) as the only extracanonical reference preceding the present one. The term occurs three times in the Synoptics (Mark 1:43: Jesus "rebukes" a demon; Mark 14:5: some "reproach" a woman for wasting ointment; Matt. 9:30: Jesus "sternly warns" healed men to tell no one). Both τῷ πνεύματι (*tō pneumati*, in spirit) in John 11:33 and ἐν ἑαυτῷ (*en heautō*, in himself) in 11:38 represent Semitisms "for expressing the internal impact of the emotions" (R. Brown 1966: 425).

87. Note also that ἐνεβριμήσατο (*enebrimēsato*) in 11:33 is a middle deponent form, which may favor an active translation (such as "he bristled") over a passive one (such as "he was deeply moved").

88. Other occurrences in John are 12:27; 13:21; 14:1, 27. Burge (2000: 318 n. 18) may take things a bit too far when he says that the word's "active use here may refer to the Spirit (as living water) within him."

89. See Ps. 6:2–3, 7; 30:7; 31:9–13; 38:10; 55:2, 4; 109:22; 143:4. In the NT, Herod is "troubled" when he hears the news about Jesus' birth (Matt. 2:3); the disciples are alarmed at the sight of Jesus walking on the water (Matt. 14:26 par.); Zechariah is startled by the appearance of the angel at the altar (Luke 1:12), as are Jesus' disciples when they see the risen Jesus, thinking that he is a ghost (Luke 24:38). Later in John's Gospel, Jesus repeatedly expresses deep inner anguish in the face of his own impending death (12:27) and Judas's imminent betrayal (13:21).

90. Though Morris (1995: 494) does refer to Jesus' "deep concern *and indignation* at the attitude of the mourners." Morris cites the Synoptic occurrences of the term ἐμβριμάομαι related to Jesus (Matt. 9:30; Mark 1:43) and notes the lack of an expressed object of Jesus' anger. He favors the NRSV rendering "greatly disturbed in spirit."

91. Barrett (1978: 399) asserts that Jesus was angry "beyond question." Schnackenburg (1990: 2.335) calls attempts to render ἐμβριμάομαι as an emotional experience such as grief, pain, or sympathy "illegitimate." Beasley-Murray (1987 = 1999: 192–93, followed by

of Jesus' anger is variously identified as death itself (Michaels 1989: 203; Whitacre 1999: 289), or the realm of Satan represented by death (R. Brown 1966: 435), or the mourners' unbelief (Keener 2003: 846), or combinations of all three (Brodie 1993: 395).[92] However, the dichotomy may be false (note particularly the lack of an expressed object), for perhaps the primary reference is neither to grief nor to anger, and the term ἐμβριμάομαι simply indicates Jesus' excited anticipation of what he is going to do as he bristles and braces himself for his impending assault on death.[93]

Lindars 1992b: 89–90, noting that he changed his view from Lindars 1972: 398) marshals considerable evidence to support the reading "became angry in spirit." See also Carson (1991: 415), who contends that ἐμβριμάομαι means more than "deeply moved in spirit" and says that the term refers to "anger, outrage, or emotional indignation." Brodie (1993: 395), starting with Schnackenburg's view that Jesus was angry at the unbelief of Mary and the Jews, maintains that his anger is directed also at sin and death, and thus ultimately against the realm of Satan.

92. Among those who favor a reference to death itself is Ridderbos (1997: 402), who writes, "The emotion is the revulsion of everything that is in him against the power of death." See also Warfield (1950: 117 [cited in Morris 1995: 493 n. 72]); Michaels 1989: 203; Whitacre 1999: 289. The mourners' unbelief is favored by Bultmann (1971: 406); Schnackenburg (1990: 2.336); Witherington (1995: 203); Morris (1995: 494); Borchert (1996: 360); Beasley-Murray (1999: 192–93), several of whom adduce Paul's statement in 1 Thess. 4:13 that believers ought not to mourn as do those who have no hope (see also Pollard [1973: 441], who says that the raising of Lazarus was occasioned by lack of faith on the part of Mary and the Jews with her). Carson (1991: 416) maintains that we need not choose: Jesus' anger is directed toward both "the sin, sickness and death in this fallen world that wrecks so much havoc and generates so much sorrow" and the unbelief demonstrated by those wailing without hope (similarly, Brodie [1993: 395], who also includes Satan). Moloney (1998: 330), rather implausibly, sees Jesus' anger as occasioned by Mary's turning away from him toward the mourning crowd. An even more daring conjecture is that of Lindars (1992b: esp. 101–4), who rather ingeniously argues that the Fourth Evangelist used a source including a story comparable to Mark 9:14–29 (where the verb ἐπιτιμάω [epitimaō, rebuke] in Mark 9:25 refers to demon exorcism) and that he either "misunderstood the source and reproduced what he thought that it meant, or deliberately altered the meaning, and the syntax of the phrase, for the sake of his composition," to mean "moved in spirit." Finally, Story (1991) proposes that Jesus' struggle was entirely within himself, and renders the text, "He rebuked (his) spirit and troubled himself" (11:38 is translated "bearing the rebuke within himself"). According to Story, at the sight of people's grief, Jesus was overcome by "momentary self-regret," thinking, "Why did I not come sooner . . . ? I have only myself to blame. . . . Why did I cause the anxiety and sadness to this family and allow the one I love to die?" However, there is no contextual confirmation for this reading.

93. This is the meaning of the word in its only undisputed preceding reference in Aeschylus, *Seven against Thebes* 1.461, where mares are shown "snorting [ἐμβριμώμενας] in the bridles," "with their breath whistling in their nostrils (1.463–64), as they brace themselves for the rush upon the enemy" (the latter quote is a paraphrase by Lindars 1992b: 92). It is less clear that people's unbelief is the object of Jesus' indignation; if so, why would he join them in their grief by bursting into tears himself in 11:35 (Lindars 1992b: 92)? Schlatter (1948: 254) comments perceptively, "All that John is saying is that Jesus took on a threatening posture and that he was agitated as he went to Lazarus's tomb. John never provided an interpretation of the processes that moved the inner life of

Jesus' asking others for information ("Where have you laid him?") again accentuates his humanity. The speakers of the sentence "Lord, come and see" (a common Semitic phrase [see 1:39, 46]) are unidentified, but presumably they are the sisters (Morris 1995: 495). At this, the evangelist tells his readers, "without comment but all the more emphatically as a fact that needed to be mentioned by itself" (Ridderbos 1997: 401), that Jesus burst into tears (δακρύω, dakryō [only here in the NT; see commentary at 11:33]).[94] This is yet another, and perhaps the climactic, instance in this Gospel where Jesus' humanity comes to the fore.[95] In contrast to the loud wailing (κλαίω, klaiō [11:33]) around him, Jesus' grief is more subdued (Carson 1991: 416).[96] As in 11:33, the object of Jesus' grief is not so much the death of his friend (whom he is about to raise) as it is the presence of death itself.[97] Beyond this, Jesus, by weeping at the tomb of his friend, identifies with humanity by experiencing and participating "in the grief of all whose loved ones have gone to the grave" (Ridderbos 1997: 402).

Thus, the bystanders are at least partially correct when they interpret Jesus' tears as an expression of his love for Lazarus (cf. 11:5; see R. Brown 1966: 426),[98] though they err when they imagine "his grief to

---

Jesus." Conway (1999: 147–48) cautions similarly that "we should be wary of delving too deeply into the psyche of Jesus."

94. The term δακρύω occurs occasionally in the LXX (Job 3:24; Ezek. 27:35; Mic. 2:6; 2 Macc. 4:37; Sir. 12:16; 31:13). Owing to the force of the verb tense in the Greek original (an "ingressive aorist"), "Jesus burst into tears" is a better translation than the customary "wept" (Morris 1995: 495 n. 77; cf. Barrett 1978: 400; Pollard 1973: 441; Stibbe 1994: 45). This is suggested by comparison with instances of δακρύω in the same grammatical form in Greco-Roman and Hellenistic Jewish literature, where the term is regularly rendered this way (see Diodorus Siculus, Bibliotheca historica 17.66.4; 27.6.1; Plutarch, Camillus 5.5; Pyrrhus 34.4; Pompeius 80.5; Josephus, Ant. 11.5.6 §162; J.W. 5.10.5 §445; 6.5.3 §304).

95. Contra the unilateral docetic emphasis on Jesus' deity (see Ridderbos 1997: 402–3). See the brief discussion and references to Jesus' thirst, tiredness, and so on in Köstenberger 1998b: 50. See also Stibbe (1993: 124–25), who notes that Jesus "is not some mystical, neo-Platonic God who stands far beyond the harsh realities endured by those trapped within a frail mortality," but rather is "the deity who sheds tears, who feels anger, and who dares to look through the dark threshold of a place which he himself will have to enter."

96. Nevertheless, Kruse's (2003: 254) suggestion is doubtful that the use of a different word for Jesus' weeping may show that his crying was "of a different order" than Mary's.

97. So, essentially, Carson (1991: 416) and Morris (1995: 495), though both (in my view, illegitimately) speak of "unbelief" or "the misconceptions of those around him" as the primary target (similarly, Kruse [2003: 254] believes Jesus wept out of "deep disappointment" with the "faithless weeping and wailing" of Mary and "the Jews"). Schnackenburg (1990: 2.337) insightfully adduces the reference to Jesus' "tears" during his "life on earth" in Heb. 5:7, which there, as well as in the present reference, are related to the presence of and the need for salvation from death. The comment by Borchert (1996: 360) that Jesus' weeping is "directly related to the failure of his followers to recognize his mission as the agent of God" is sheer conjecture, as is Moloney's contention (1998: 331) that "he weeps because of the danger that his unconditional gift of himself in love . . . will never be understood or accepted."

98. Wallace (1996: 548) identifies ἐφίλει (ephilei, he loved) as a customary imperfect.

be as despairing as their own" (Carson 1991: 416–17).[99] The reasoning of those who asked, "Could not he who opened the eyes of the blind man also have prevented this man from dying?" is sound in principle, but "even to ask the question in this way betrays massive unbelief" (Carson 1991: 417).[100] On a literary level, the reference to the healing of the blind man establishes a link with the previous narrative unit—a repeated characteristic of Johannine style.[101] "The Jews were saying . . . But some of them said . . ." again shows the evangelist's skillful presentation of the back-and-forth cogitations of the bystanders (cf. 7:12, 25–27, 40–41; 9:16; 10:19–21).

c. The Raising of Lazarus (11:38–44)

11:38–40 "Then Jesus, again bristling within himself" harks back to 11:33.[102] As there, Jesus' inner state here seems to be that of excited anticipation.[103] As Ridderbos (1997: 403) comments, "He strides to the tomb, not in sovereign apathy of the great Outsider, but as the One sent into the world by the Father, as the Advocate who has entered human flesh and blood." The tomb was a cave with a stone laid across the entrance.[104] Though the shaft of the cave could have been vertical or horizontal, from the way Lazarus came out, as well as from archaeological evidence and mishnaic regulations, it appears that the cave was horizontal. The burial place was outside the village so that the living would not contract ritual

---

99. More negative are Morris (1995: 496), who says, "As always the Jews fail to enter the mind of Christ," and Beasley-Murray (1999: 194), who exclaims, "They did not perceive that the tears were more over them than over Lazarus!" Very possibly, Morris (1995: 496) is correct when he contends that the Jews misunderstood Jesus' tears to represent frustration.

100. As Barrett (1978: 401) writes, "They think of Jesus not as the Son of God who is light and life . . . but as a thaumaturge whose capacities, authenticated by the cure of the blind man, might conceivably have been expected to rise to this extremity." Carson (1991: 417 [cf. Morris 1995: 496]) says that we need not suppose that their attitude was "sneering," but Schnackenburg (1990: 2.337) points to the introductory δέ (*de*, but) and the negative connotation of οὐκ ἐδύνατο (*ouk edynato*, could he not have?).

101. Termed "narrative echo effect" by Stibbe 1994: 39, following R. C. Tannehill. R. Brown (1966: 436) further notes that this verse "calls forth the memory of the blind man, so that Jesus as the light and Jesus as the life will be juxtaposed."

102. Calvin (1961: 13) comments that Jesus comes "like a wrestler preparing for the contest": "no wonder that He groans again, for the violent tyranny of death which He had to overcome stands before His eyes." Wallace (1996: 631) takes ἐμβριμώμενος (*embrimō-menos*, bristling) to be a causal participle; my preference is attendant circumstance.

103. Again, Ridderbos (1997: 401), rightly in my opinion, dismisses attempts to link Jesus' anger to the unbelief of the Jews. Carson (1991: 417) perhaps construes the relationship between 11:38 and 11:37 too tightly when he states, "This unbelief is the reason the next verse [v. 38] reports that Jesus' quiet outrage flares up again." Similarly, Barrett (1978: 401) speaks of "inchoate faith" that draws Jesus' wrath.

104. See Avi-Yonah 1964: 147 (cited in Köstenberger 2002c: 112). For more information and examples of tombs from this period, see Mackowski 1980: 20–21, 157–59.

impurity from contact with the corpse. There is ample Jewish evidence for the use of natural caves for burial that were further prepared by artificial means (*m. B. Bat.* 6.8).[105] Jesus' own body would later be put in a similar tomb (Mark 15:46 pars.).

Jesus' command is terse, reflecting a quiet, persistent resolve: "Take away the stone."[106] There has been enough wailing; now it is time for action.[107] Martha, called "the sister of the deceased,"[108] retorts, presumably because she is the older sister and next of kin (Ridderbos 1997: 404), "Lord, there is already an odor, for it has been four days" (cf. 11:17).[109] Indeed, the Jews used spices at burials (though not embalming as did the Egyptians), but this did not prevent decomposition.[110] Martha's words express "her abhorrence at the mere thought that Jesus should expose the body of her brother—in the state in which it must be by this time—to the light of day" (Ridderbos 1997: 404). Similar to Jesus' previous signs, the comment serves to highlight the utter difficulty of the ensuing miracle. Clearly, it would have been hard for Martha, or anyone, to foresee what was about to happen (Ridderbos 1997: 404).

Jesus gently challenges Martha's faith: "Did I not tell you that if you believe, you will see the glory of God?"[111] By these words, which hark back to Jesus' words to his disciples at the outset of the miracle (11:4), Jesus seeks to remind Martha of their previous interchange in 11:23–26 (Carson 1991: 417–18; cf. Barrett 1978: 402). As in the case of the blind man (9:3–4), or at the wedding at Cana (2:11), and ultimately throughout Jesus' entire earthly ministry (1:14), Lazarus's death is viewed by Jesus as an occasion for the glory of God to be revealed.[112] This seventh, climactic sign demonstrates Jesus' power over death, thus foreshadowing his own resurrection. Though all present, believers and unbelievers alike, would

---

105. Regarding the stone being laid across the entrance, see *m. ʾOhal.* 2.4.

106. Ridderbos (1997: 403) calls Jesus' command "measured, almost gruff."

107. Ridderbos (1997: 403–4) construes the sense as follows: "Enough now of tears and wailing! Enough honor has been bestowed on death! Against the power of death God's glory will now enter the arena!"

108. The perfect participle τετελευτηκότος (*teteleutēkotos*, deceased) highlights the permanence of death (Morris 1995: 496–97).

109. Modern English translations almost universally take Lazarus to be the implied subject of τεταρταῖος γάρ ἐστιν ("he has been there four days" [see NIV = TNIV; NASB; KJV; ESV; ISV; NLT]; this also seems to be tacitly assumed by virtually all commentators, who devote themselves to discussing weightier matters), though the HCSB may well be right in rendering the phrase "It's been four days."

110. For the use of spices in the burial process, see J. N. Sanders 1968: 274.

111. On the phrase "you will see the glory of God," see 11:4; see also Jesus' previous interchange with Martha at 11:25–26.

112. R. Brown (1966: 436) thinks that the mention of "glory" here forms an *inclusio* within the chapter, an *inclusio* with the wine miracle at Cana, tying together the first and last signs, and serving to transition into "the Book of Glory." Schnackenburg (1990: 2.338) comments, "The two sayings, in v. 4 and v. 40, are like corner-posts supporting the interpretation of the raising as the greatest sign of the presence of God's saving power in Jesus."

see Lazarus come out of the tomb, only Jesus' followers would discern in this event the glory of God, that is, its messianic significance pointing to Jesus as God's Son and Sent One (Morris 1995: 497).

11:41–44   "They took away the stone" in its terseness mirrors Jesus' original command in 11:39. Jesus' prayer once again aligns him and his mission inextricably with the Father (Ridderbos 1997: 405).[113] Jesus' focus is not on the ensuing miracle but on the revelation of God's glory (and thus his own messianic calling) in and through it. In his humanity, Jesus, especially in light of his agitated state (11:33, 38), may draw strength from the assurance that the Father hears him and does so always (Ridderbos 1997: 405).[114] Of course, "Jesus is in constant communion with his Father, who always 'hears' even the unspoken thoughts of his heart, and therefore has already 'heard' his petition for Lazarus" (Barrett 1978: 402). By praying in public, Jesus does not engage in posturing but rather "seeks to draw his hearers into the intimacy of Jesus' own relationship with the Father" (Carson 1991: 418). Moreover, Jesus desires that the "sign" he is about to perform elicit a believing response.[115]

The Synoptists mention that Jesus looked up to heaven before the miraculous feeding of the multitudes (Matt. 14:19 pars.). The gesture of looking up, often accompanied by raised hands (Burge 2000: 319), is rarely attested for the later period.[116] Thanksgiving is also part of Jesus' prayer in the Synoptics (Matt. 11:25; Luke 10:21; see Hunter 1985: 59).

113. Westcott (1908: 2.101) draws a connection between Jesus' prayer here and his opening statement in 11:4. On the term "Father," see commentary at 1:14. "Father" is the customary address for God used by Jesus in prayer, occasionally adorned by a divine attribute, as in "holy Father" (17:11) or "righteous Father" (17:25). See 12:27–28; 17:1, 5, 21, 24; Luke 11:2; 22:42; 23:34, 46. At times, the address is "Our Father in heaven" (Matt. 6:9) or "Father, Lord of heaven and earth" (Matt. 11:25). The address "Father" is also found in the Qumran Scrolls (4Q372).

114. Hunter (1985: 59–60) suggests that the past tense ἤκουσας (ēkousas, you heard) be taken as a reference to "a previous (private) personal prayer offered by Jesus on behalf of his friend." An OT antecedent to Jesus' prayer here is that of Elijah: "Answer me, O Lord, answer me, so these people will know that you, O Lord, are God" (1 Kings 18:37; cf. Ps. 118:21; 121:1; 123:1). Cf. John 6:5; 17:1; Mark 7:34; Luke 18:13; Acts 7:55. See also Matt. 11:25; John 6:11. Hunter (1985: 62–70, citing J. M. Robinson 1964: 194–225) notes the similarity in form with Jewish prayers of thanksgiving (hodayot). Hanson (1973: 254) and Wilcox (1977: 130) contend that 11:41 is actually a quotation of Ps. 118:21a (see the discussion in Hunter 1985: 68); Wilcox (1977: 131) further argues that Ps. 118:22 also resonates in the present passage via the "stone" motif.

115. Lindars (1972: 401) maintains that it is Jesus' desire "that they may have the perception to see in the miracle the glory of God. . . . If it is urgent that Jesus should do this sign before his Passion, it is equally vital that its true meaning should be recognized." The phrase "that they may believe that you sent me" in 11:42 is later echoed repeatedly at the conclusion of Jesus' final prayer in 17:21, 23, 25, and in the purpose statement in 20:30–31, which mentions Jesus' "signs" and "believing" in his name.

116. Cf. 1 Esdr. 4:58; Josephus, Ant. 11.5.6 §162. Hunter (1985: 58, citing Dodd 1963: 183; Fortna 1970: 83) notes that "first-century Jewish custom dictated that 'prayers were generally said with downcast eyes'" (cf. Ps. 131:1a; b. Yebam. 105b).

The Jews generally believed that extraordinary things could be accomplished through the power of almighty God as a result of the prayer of his righteous servants (though magical practices made their way into Judaism as well).[117] Greco-Roman culture, on the other hand, attributed superhuman powers to "divine men." Jesus' contemporaries frequently viewed him as a thaumaturge who was able to perform extraordinary feats by virtue of his supernatural power. Jesus' prayer counters this perception. It shows that he has no authority apart from the Father and that he is neither a magician nor a "divine man" by Greco-Roman standards (Bultmann 1971: 408).

Jesus cried out in a loud voice, "Lazarus, come out!"[118] The Fourth Evangelist's use of the term κραυγάζω (kraugazō, cry out) is proleptic of Jesus' passion, where his opponents utter four shouts of death (18:40; 19:6, 12, 15). This underscores the utter irony that Jesus' act of giving life to Lazarus leads to his own life being taken away (Stibbe 1994: 50). The term δεῦρο (deuro) has a similar force to the English imperative "Here!" The command is "wonderfully succinct: 'Here! Outside!'" (Morris 1995: 498 n. 89; cf. Barrett 1978: 403). Jesus' shout is one "of raw authority" (Burge 2000: 320), and the power of his voice expresses "the power of God by which the dead are brought to life" (Ridderbos 1997: 406). The voice was loud, not so the dead could hear, but to a crowd accustomed to magic in which incantations and spells were muttered, Jesus stood entirely apart by performing the act by the creative, life-giving power of his sheer word (Morris 1995: 498; cf. 4:50; 5:8–9).[119]

The word the "dead man" (τεθνηκώς, tethnēkōs) is used in this Gospel elsewhere only in 19:33, establishing an interesting parallel between the accounts of the raising of Lazarus and Jesus' passion. Lazarus's feet and hands (the word order in the Greek; reversed in several standard translations to "hands and feet," though there may be a reason why the feet are mentioned first by the evangelist) were wrapped with strips of linen.[120]

117. See van der Loos 1965: 133–38; on the raising of Lazarus, 576–89.
118. Whitacre (1999: 293) notes perceptively that "Jesus could have healed Lazarus when he was still sick with a word of command, even across the miles [cf. 4:46–54]. But now he utters a mightier word across a much greater distance—that between the living and the dead."
119. Brodie (1993: 397) draws a connection with 5:24–29 and speaks of Jesus' exercise of "Creator-like power." See especially 5:28–29, where Jesus speaks of a coming time "when all who are in their graves will hear his [the Son of Man's] voice and come out." Keener (2003: 839) distinguishes between Jesus' "secret" sign in 2:1–11 and his public sign in chapter 11, the difference being that now his time is close at hand.
120. "The corpse was customarily laid on a sheet of linen, wide enough to envelop the body completely and more than twice the length of the corpse. The body was so placed on the sheet that the feet were at one end, and then the sheet was drawn over the head and back down to the feet. The feet were bound at the ankles, and the arms were tied to the body with linen strips. . . . Jesus' body was apparently prepared for burial in the same way (cf. 19:40; 20:5, 7)" (Carson 1991: 418–19; cf. Beasley-Murray 1999: 195). For mishnaic references to burial clothes and wrappings for corpses, see Kruse 2003: 256.

The custom of wrapping the feet and hands of a dead person in linen cloths is not attested elsewhere in Jewish texts. Frequently, deceased loved ones were dressed in flowing and valuable garments, a practice later abolished by Rabbi Gamaliel II.[121] Yet contrary to pagan custom, the Jews did not bind up their dead to prevent them from returning to life. In any case, one ought not suppose that Lazarus's graveclothes restricted his movement to the extent that his coming out of the tomb necessitated a "miracle within a miracle."[122]

The word for "strips of linen" (κειρίαι, *keiriai*) is used several times in fragments of medical papyri, suggesting narrow strips tied around the body. "Fine linen" is frequently mentioned as an Egyptian export and associated with the wealthy in the OT.[123] In rabbinic times, it was thought that at the final resurrection the dead would rise in their clothes (*b. Ketub.* 111b). Rabbi Eliezer (ca. A.D. 90) was reputed to have taught that all the dead would arise at the resurrection of the dead dressed in their garments, with reference to the prophet Samuel, who came up clothed in his robe (1 Sam. 28:14; cf. *Pirqe R. El.* 33). Lazarus's face was bound up with a cloth called *soudarion* (a loanword from the Latin *sudarium*, "sweat cloth"), which in life was often worn around the neck (cf. *b. Moʿed Qaṭ.* 27a).

Again, as in the case of the linen strips, there is a clear verbal link between the preparation of Lazarus and Jesus for burial (cf. 20:7; see Reiser 1973).[124] In fact, Stibbe (1994: 52–53) plausibly argues that Lazarus's emergence from the tomb is intended as a "prolepsis of the empty tomb" for the person rereading the Gospel.[125] Nevertheless, important differences remain between the raising of Lazarus and Jesus' resurrection: Lazarus rose to mortality, Jesus to immortality; Lazarus to his perishable body, Jesus to that which is imperishable. In fact, "The resurrection of Lazarus, occurring before that of Jesus, could only be a pale anticipation of what was yet to come" (Carson 1991: 419). Similar to previous directives, Jesus' command to unbind Lazarus and let him go is to the point; again, Jesus' quiet assertion of

121. About A.D. 90; see *b. Ketub.* 8b; *b. Moʿed Qaṭ.* 27b.

122. As is suggested by some modern commentators (e.g., Schnackenburg 1990: 2.340), with reference to Basil (ca. A.D. 330–379). But see the critique by Carson 1991: 418.

123. See Prov. 7:16; 31:22; Isa. 19:9; Ezek. 27:7.

124. Keener (2003: 850), however, observes that Lazarus's coming out of the tomb with his graveclothes contrasts with Jesus' leaving them behind at his resurrection (cf. 20:5, 7).

125. Stibbe (1994: 53) brilliantly elaborates that John expects the reader to follow the beginning and middle of a pericope from the point of view of its end, so that narrative form and christological claim coincide. Jesus Christ is portrayed as the eschaton personified, "the one who brings the end of history into the middle of time." Stibbe also notes the classic character of the story in which Jesus appears as one who is both sympathetic and yet able to transcend the situation. See also Reiser (1973: 52–54), who notes the parallels between 11:43–44, on the one hand, and 5:25, 28b, as well as 10:3, 10, 17–18 respectively.

authority and resolve emerges. There is nothing triumphalistic about his demeanor.[126] As at other occasions (e.g., Jairus's daughter in Mark 5:43), the aftermath of a miraculous healing consists of facilitating the person's "return to normal life" (Schnackenburg 1990: 2.340).[127]

The story ends rather abruptly because the evangelist's focus on Jesus and his signs excludes the "human interest" aspect of the story (Ridderbos 1997: 407). As Carson (1991: 420) notes, "Everything is sacrificed to the sign itself, to what it anticipates, and even to the way it precipitates it by arousing the animus of the authorities." Yet as Stibbe (1994: 53–54) points out, the greatest "gap" (citing Sternberg 1985: 186–229) is the omission of any response from Lazarus: "The silence of Lazarus is more deafening than the cry of Jesus. . . . The reader is left asking, 'How did Lazarus feel?' . . . Have you ever thought how he must have felt, as he stood blinking in the sunlight, looking anew on a world from which he had taken his last leave? . . . Nothing could ever be the same as it was before" (citing West 1981: 300–301).[128]

d. The Plot to Kill Jesus (11:45–57)

The phrasing, "Many of the Jews. . . . But some of them . . ." is typically Johannine (cf. 11:36–37).[129] The reference to "many" who had come to Mary and who now believed confirms that the characterization of "the Jews" in the previous section is essentially neutral rather than negative. That Mary, and not Martha, is mentioned here may indicate that it was primarily she who had an extensive circle of friends (Carson 1991: 419). The Jews' faith is based on having seen (θεάομαι, *theaomai* [cf. esp.

11:45–48

---

126. Ridderbos (1997: 406) perhaps goes too far when he says that Jesus' words are "the sovereign word of the conqueror." Also, his comment that Lazarus is brought out of "the half-darkness of the tomb into the full light of the day" is interesting, but is not a point actually made by the evangelist. Jesus is presented here as the resurrection and the life, not as the light.

127. Michaels (1989: 207) notes that all three raisings of the dead in the Gospels end "with a similarly warm human interest touch in which Jesus meets an additional, comparatively minor, need (cf. Mark 5:43; Luke 7:15)." Michaels also suggests that unbinding Lazarus may evoke the biblical imagery of "loosing" to convey the notion of victory over death and the powers of evil (citing Matt. 16:19; Luke 13:16; Acts 2:24; cf. John 8:32–36).

128. Along different lines, Keener (2003: 838) observes that Lazarus is wholly passive and silent in the entire narrative (which is hardly surprising, since he is dead for the vast majority of it) so that his sisters and their faith are the focal point of the story (apart from Jesus, one might add).

129. Barrett (1978: 404) thinks that "apparently" this section was substituted for the Synoptic accounts of Jesus' trial before the high priest, deeming it of "dubious historical value." He says that the present unit serves to raise the "dramatic tension of the gospel to a climax which is resolved only in the passion narrative." However, in light of the striking nature of the raising of Lazarus, it is entirely plausible historically that Jesus' opponents would have convened a meeting to respond to the perceived and increasing threat that Jesus represented to their own status and position.

1:14]) what Jesus did.[130] Notably, their positive stance does not prevent some of them from going and reporting to the Pharisees what Jesus did (an oblique reference to the raising of Lazarus).[131] The following events show that no amount of evidence will convince those who have already determined to reject Jesus' claims (Morris 1995: 502). Though recognizing that a miracle has taken place, these people respond, not in faith, but with hardened opposition. Thus, the raising of Lazarus, as the final climactic sign, also becomes the climactic occasion for judgment (cf. 12:36b–40).

The term συνέδριον (synedrion) in the sense of "council meeting" is rare in the NT, yet frequent in secular Greek (e.g., Diodorus Siculus, Bibliotheca historica 13.111.1), the LXX (e.g., Prov. 31:23; 2 Macc. 14:5), and Hellenistic Jewish literature (see Lohse, TDNT 7:861–62). Most large Jewish centers had a sanhedrin or local court, but the supreme or great Sanhedrin was located in Jerusalem. The Sanhedrin was the Jewish judicial, legislative, and executive body that, under Roman general jurisdiction, managed the nation's internal affairs. In Jesus' day, the council's members were controlled by the chief priests, who were drawn from the extended family of the high priest who presided over the Sanhedrin. The vast majority of these priests were Sadducees, with Pharisees (most of whom were scribes) constituting an influential minority.[132]

The calling of an official Sanhedrin meeting was legally the responsibility of the high priest. The wording of the TNIV suggests an official meeting of the Sanhedrin,[133] though a more informal gathering is equally plausible

130. Their signs-based response is reminiscent of 2:23. Morris (1995: 499) construes the relationship between "many of the Jews" and "who had come to Mary" in narrow terms as appositional, so that it would have been the Jews who had come to Mary who believed. However, R. Brown (1966: 438 [contra Bernard 1928: 2.401–2]) cogently contends that there is no need to overemphasize the agreement of the participle so as to conclude that all the Jews who had come to comfort Mary believed in Jesus.

131. On the Pharisees, see commentary at 1:19, 24. On the chief priests and Pharisees, see commentary at 7:32. Ridderbos (1997: 407 n. 84) plausibly argues that the evangelist's reference to the Pharisees as the key leaders of the people is a function not only of their influence in Jesus' day but also of their significance in the post-temple period in which the evangelist wrote. Thus, "Their name was particularly useful to him as a general term for the Jewish authorities." Carson (1991: 420), too, sees no hint of anachronism, pointing out also the Pharisees' more direct access to the people. This stands in marked contrast to the provocative statement by Barrett (1978: 405) that if the evangelist conceived of the Pharisees as an official body, "he was ignorant of Judaism as it was before A.D. 70." R. Brown (1966: 439) notes, "The reference to the Pharisees is more a question of simplification than of error."

132. For further information on the Sanhedrin, see Schürer 1973–79: 2.199–226; Lohse, TDNT 7:861–71. Hengel (1999: 330) questions whether the Sanhedrin had seventy members in Jesus' day, as is frequently alleged; he favors instead the view that the composition of the council depended on the particular ruling high priest, especially in the period between A.D. 6 and 41.

133. See Bammel 1970; J. A. T. Robinson 1985: 223–24. Inclusion of this account may explain John's omission of the later Jewish trial of Jesus before Caiaphas, implied in 18:24, 28 and narrated in Matt. 27:1–2 and Mark 15:1 (cf. Luke 23:1).

(in which case the word rendered "Sanhedrin" in the TNIV may simply mean "gathering" or "assembly"). The latter alternative would explain why Caiaphas is called "one of them" (11:49), even though in a formal Sanhedrin meeting he would have presided over the proceedings of the council. The casual way in which Caiaphas is introduced and the bluntness of his language also may indicate that this was not an official gathering of the Sanhedrin with the high priest presiding (contrast Matt. 26:57–66 pars.).[134] From this point on, the Pharisees are referred to infrequently in John's Gospel; control of the proceedings against Jesus has now been seized by the chief priests. This coheres with the other Gospels, all of which portray the Pharisees as Jesus' principal opponents throughout his ministry but rarely mention them in association with Jesus' passion.

The Pharisees' question can be rendered as deliberative, "What are we going to do?" (Ridderbos 1997: 408; R. Brown 1966: 439; Schnackenburg 1990: 2.347), or as rhetorical, "What are we accomplishing?" (Carson 1991: 420; Morris 1995: 502). The contrast between the Pharisees accomplishing nothing and Jesus performing many signs is apparent (Morris 1995: 502). The reference to Jesus "performing many signs" is probably to the healings in John 5 and 9, but especially to the raising of Lazarus (cf. 12:18; see also 2:23; 3:2; 7:31; 9:16). It seems that the signs performed in Judea and Jerusalem are particularly in view (cf. Luke 19:37; see Ridderbos 1997: 408). The proliferation of signs is an important part of the evangelist's message (cf. John 12:37; 20:30). In the present instance, the Jewish leaders "fear that popular messianic expectations will be fired to fever pitch, and, with or without Jesus' sanction, set off an uprising that would bring down the full weight of Rome upon their heads" (Carson 1991: 420; cf. Ridderbos 1997: 408).

"If we let him go on like this, . . . the Romans will come and take away both our place [TNIV: 'temple'] and our nation" (cf. 12:19). In Jewish literature, "the place" (Hebrew: māqôm) may refer metaphorically to the Lord (e.g., Gen. Rab. 68.9; b. ʿAbod. Zar. 40b), the promised land (2 Macc. 1:29), Jerusalem (m. Bik. 2.2), or the temple. Of these, the temple is the most concrete and climactic referent, since it is located in Jerusalem, the capital city of the promised land, and the place where God himself dwells.[135] Importantly, the temple assumes a central role

134. Note also the absence of the definite article before συνέδριον in the Greek (which may imply "a gathering" rather than "the Sanhedrin"), though not too much should be made of this (Morris 1995: 501 n. 99). For a complete list of high priests from 200 B.C. to A.D. 70, see Jeremias 1969: 377–78. For a list of high priests from 37 B.C. to A.D. 68, see Smallwood 1962: 31–32. For a list of the most important high priests from 200 B.C. to the time of Jesus, see Köstenberger 2002c: 114. R. Brown (1966: 439) suggests that there may be an intentional contrast between the gathering of the Sanhedrin here and the gathering of the children of God in 11:52.

135. The temple is favored by, among others, Ridderbos (1997: 408) and Carson (1991: 420).

in God's judgment of Israel (Jer. 7:14; cf. 1 Kings 9:7). The next major instance of God's judgment on his people Israel involving the temple is the desecration of the temple by the Seleucid ruler Antiochus Epiphanes IV (see commentary at 10:22).[136]

It appears, therefore, that the Jews' repeated, traumatic (albeit temporary) loss of land and temple elicited the fear (at least on part of its leaders) that God would once again visit the nation in judgment and allow them to be exiled and the temple to be destroyed if Israel was disobedient. This preoccupation, here expressed in relation to Jesus, surfaces once again in another, later Sanhedrin meeting when false witnesses testify that Stephen "never stops speaking against this holy place," predicting that Jesus would "destroy this place" (Acts 6:13–14). Still later, Paul is likewise charged with teaching "all men everywhere against our people and our law and this place" as well as with defiling "this holy place" by bringing Greeks into the inner temple area (Acts 21:28).

"Take away our nation" (ἔθνος, ethnos [outside of 11:48–52, only in 18:35]) refers to the feared removal of the Jews' semiautonomous status by the Romans.[137] The Roman overlords were concerned to preserve public order. The Pharisees had strained to be free from domination, be it by Hasmoneans, Pompey, or Herodians, ever since their party had come into existence, in order to devote themselves fully to the practice of the law. Jewish sources indicate that the authorites had been nervous for some time prior to the Jewish war of A.D. 66–74. This also comports with the Pharisees' initial opposition to the armed revolt against Rome that led to the destruction of the temple in A.D. 70 (cf. Josephus, J.W. 2.17.3–5 §§411–24).[138]

Again, the irony would be all too apparent to John's readers (especially after A.D. 70): what the Jewish leadership strenuously sought to avoid, namely, for history to repeat itself and for God's judgment to fall on Israel's nation as typified by the temple, is precisely what ensued in the wake of Jesus' crucifixion (cf. 2:13–22). "And so he died—but the nation perished anyway, not because of Jesus' activity but because of the constant mad search for political solutions where there was little spiritual renewal. Justice is sacrificed to expediency" (Carson 1991: 422). The irony would be most poignant if the destruction of the temple in A.D. 70 constituted one of the major occasions for the composition of the Fourth Gospel (Köstenberger forthcoming).

136. In an important apocryphal passage, the fortunes of "the place" (i.e., the temple) and the Jewish "nation" are said to be closely linked (2 Macc. 5:19).

137. Westcott (1908: 2.105) notes that the two finite verbs, ἐλεύσονται (eleusontai, they will come) and ἀροῦσιν (arousin, they will take away), rather than participle and finite verb, "give distinction to each element in the picture."

138. Josephus reports several portents of the end taking place in Jerusalem (J.W. 6.5.3–4 §§288–315). Earlier fears are indicated in Ant. 14.9.3–5 §§163–84.

Caiaphas was high priest that year (cf. 11:51; 18:13);[139] "that year" need **11:49–50** not imply that the high priestly office rotated annually but may simply indicate that Caiaphas happened to be high priest in "that fateful year" when Jesus was tried and crucified (Morris 1995: 503; cf. Schnackenburg 1990: 2.349).[140] In fact, Caiaphas held on to his office for a remarkably long time (eighteen years [A.D. 18–36]), longer than any other high priest in the first century. At the same time, John's remark may intend to convey the notion that the high priest's term generally lasted for a year but that considerable uncertainty attached to the high priestly office in that day (Beasley-Murray 1999: 197). In fact, if a single one of his actions displeased the Roman governor, the high priest was subject to removal. Valerius Gratus, Pilate's predecessor, repeatedly deposed high priests after a short length of office. Thus, the three high priests prior to Caiaphas (A.D. 15–18), as well as his immediate successor (A.D. 36), each held his office for only about one year; the same was the case with the three high priests under Agrippa (A.D. 41–44) and the majority of high priests from A.D. 44 to 66 (Hengel 1999: 332).

Caiaphas spoke up, "You know nothing at all!" His opening words display a rudeness that allegedly was characteristic of Sadducees. Josephus (who, though, apparently having been a Pharisee for some time as a young man, was hardly unbiased in this regard) states, "The Sadducees . . . are, even among themselves, rather boorish in their behavior, and in their intercourse with their peers are as rude as to aliens" (*J.W.* 2.8.14 §166).[141] "You don't realize that it is better for you [see additional note] that one man die for the people than that the whole nation perish!" Dying "for the people" invokes the memory of the Maccabean martyrs (2 Macc. 7:37–38). A similar principle is invoked in the OT when the prophet Jonah (though far from being innocent) is thrown overboard so that the rest of the passengers might be saved. The crew asks God not to hold them accountable for "killing an innocent man" and offers sacrifices to the Lord, who provides a great fish to swallow Jonah, who stays inside the fish three days and three nights (Jon. 1:14–17).

The question of whether or not Israelites should turn other Israelites over to the government was also discussed in rabbinic Judaism (Daube 1966a: esp. 18–47; cf. Beasley-Murray 1999: 197). Some argued that if there is good reason to turn over one person in particular, this was permissible. Others disagreed. One such passage takes its point of departure from 2 Sam. 20, where Sheba is slain while the city of Abel is spared, arguing that a person should be handed over rather than all

139. On the phrase "one of them," see commentary at 11:47.
140. Lindars 1972: 406: "in that memorable year." On Joseph Caiaphas, see the sidebar in Köstenberger 2002c: 116.
141. On the grammatical construction of the phrase "you know nothing at all," see commenary at 14:30. The parallel in 12:19 expresses similar exasperation.

people be killed only if this individual is specifically identified by name (*Gen. Rab.* 94.9; cf. *t. Ter.* 7.20).[142] Caiaphas's ruling thus is firmly rooted within Jewish thought. Ironically in Jesus' case, however, this coincided perfectly with God's plan that Jesus should serve as "God's lamb" (1:29, 36), a substitutionary sacrifice for the sins of humankind (cf. 3:14–16; 6:51; 10:14–18; 12:24, 32).[143] However, this did not render the Jewish nation free from guilt for rejecting its Messiah (Ridderbos 1997: 409).

11:51–53 However, Caiaphas did not say this of his own accord, but rather, as high priest of that year, he prophesied. "Israel's highest official, with all the authority associated with his office, spoke of Jesus' death as the only way in which the people could be saved. Israel had to hear this from the lips of its own high priest" (Ridderbos 1997: 410). It is not uncommon for John to point to a deeper meaning of a given saying in his Gospel (e.g., 2:19). The evangelist discerned in the high priest's pronouncement a deeper meaning, unknown to Caiaphas himself, that enunciated an important divine truth related to the nature of Jesus' cross-death.[144] Whereas Caiaphas thinks on a "purely political level, John invites his readers to think in terms of the Lamb of God who takes away the sin of the world" (Carson 1991: 422).

In the OT, prophecy occasionally was associated with the high priest (Num. 27:21). Zadok the priest is called a "seer" (2 Sam. 15:27 MT), and at one time the high priest sought to determine God's will by way of the Urim and Thummim (lots?). Josephus recounts how Saul ordered the high priest to don his high priestly garments and to prophesy whether or not an attack on the Philistines would be successful. The high priest predicted victory, which did in fact ensue in the battle that followed (*Ant.* 6.6.3 §§115–16; cf. 1 Sam. 14:15–23). As another instance in which the high priest functioned as a prophet, Josephus cites the high priest Jaddua's prediction that Alexander the Great would spare Jerusalem (*Ant.* 11.8.4 §327; see further Dodd 1968b). Josephus also points to the prophetic gift of the Hasmonean ruler John Hyrcanus (135–104 B.C.), who was said to unite in himself the offices of king, priest, and prophet.[145] Apparently, in the relative vacuum of prophetic voices in the Second Temple period, the priestly class claimed the gift of prophecy for itself.

---

142. The same case is taken up in the Jerusalem Talmud (*y. Ter.* 8.10). Another incident involved Ulla the son of Ḳosher, who was wanted by the government (*Gen. Rab.* 94.9; see also *Gen. Rab.* 91.10 on Gen. 48:10 [cited in Köstenberger 2002c: 117]). Cf. Daube 1966a: 18–47. M. Barker (1970) links Caiaphas's words with current messianic expectations.

143. Note the sacrificial language (ὑπέρ, *hyper*, for) in 11:51–52 (Carson 1991: 422; Wallace 1996: 387). On the irony in Caiaphas's statement, see especially Duke 1985: 87 (cited in Morris 1995: 503 n. 107).

144. Barrett (1978: 407) observes, "Caiaphas was made an unconscious vehicle of truth."

145. See Josephus, *J.W.* 1.2.8 §68; *Ant.* 13.10.3 §§282–83; 13.10.7 §299; cf. *t. Soṭah* 13.5, with 13.6 referring to Simeon the Righteous (after 200 B.C.).

Philo claims that "the true priest is necessarily a prophet" (*Spec. Laws* 4.36 §192). The view that utterances could on occasion have a deeper prophetic meaning is found elsewhere in Judaism, though not with particular reference to the high priest, and prophecy was often considered to be unwitting (cf. Philo, *Mos.* 1.49 §274; 1.50 §277; 1.51 §283; 1.52 §286; *Midr. Ps.* 90 §4).

Even "the scattered children of God" (cf. 1:12) would be gathered in the wake of Jesus' death.[146] This reference marks an (unexpected) *inclusio* with the reference to the "gathering" of the Sanhedrin in 11:47 (Beutler 1994: 400). Ironically, the "gathering" of the Sanhedrin, which decides on the death of the one who revealed himself as the "life," will prove to trigger (subsequent to Jesus' resurrection) the "gathering" of the scattered children of God (Nicklas 2000a: 594). Israel's end-time hopes were tied to the expectation that the "scattered children of God" (i.e., Jews in the Diaspora) would be regathered in the promised land by the Messiah (or messiahs [cf. 1QS 9:11]) to share in God's kingdom.[147] Yet at the same time, OT prophetic literature frequently depicts the Gentiles as streaming toward the mountain of the Lord,[148] and the Jerusalem temple is characterized as "a house of prayer for all nations" (Isa. 56:7 [cited in Mark 11:17]). In the present context ("for the Jewish nation, and not for the nation only but . . ."), it is clear that "the scattered children of God" refers to the Gentiles. Thus, Jesus is shown here to anticipate the Gentile mission (cf. esp. 10:16; see also 12:20–21, 32).[149]

From that day on they were plotting to kill him.[150] This decision seems to be underlying the Sanhedrin meeting two days before the Passover, whose only subject is how to dispense with Jesus (Matt. 26:4 pars.). With Caiaphas's words, an important threshold has been crossed (Ridderbos 1997: 411; Morris 1995: 505). From now on, "Jesus is not to be arrested in order to be tried; he is to be tried because he has already been found guilty (as Mk. 14:1–2 presupposes)" (Carson 1991: 423).

146. Cf. Matt. 23:37 = Luke 13:34 (noted by Beutler 1994: 403). Morris (1995: 504 n. 117) suggests that the perfect participle διεσκορπισμένα (*dieskorpismena*, scattered) may "indicate the permanence of the scattering, apart from Christ's work." The notion of the gathering of scattered "children of God" in the context of John's Gospel seems to presuppose the notion of divine election and predestination. R. Brown (1966: 443) sees eucharistic overtones in the term "gathered together," adducing 6:13 where fragments are gathered subsequent to the miraculous feeding. This reading seems far-fetched.

147. See Ps. 106:47; 107:3; Isa. 11:12; 43:5–7; 49:5; Jer. 23:3; 31:8–14; Ezek. 34:11–16; 36:24–38; 37:21–28; Mic. 2:12; cf. James 1:1.

148. Isa. 2:2–3; 56:6–8; 60:6; Zech. 14:16; cf. 1 Pet. 1:1.

149. See also Odes Sol. 10:5–6 (cf. Beutler 1994: 399–404). On the phrase "make them one," see commentary at 10:16; 17:21 (cf. Appold 1976: 236–45).

150. The verb βουλεύω (*bouleuō*, plan) occurs elsewhere in this Gospel only in 12:10.

11:54–57 Because of their plan to kill him, Jesus no longer moved about publicly among the Jews but left from there for the region near the wilderness, to a town called Ephraim. This again underscores that the final events in Jesus' earthly life would transpire not at the initiative of human courts or death plots but according to the predetermined plan of God, with which Jesus actively cooperated (Carson 1991: 423). The town of Ephraim probably is to be identified with OT Ophrah (Josh. 18:23) or Ephron (2 Chron. 13:19), site of the modern village of Et-Taiyibeh, four miles northeast of Bethel (cf. Josephus, *J.W.* 4.9.9 §551) and less than twenty miles north of Jerusalem.[151] It is unclear why Jesus withdrew to this particular location; perhaps someone provided him with lodging there (as in the case of Lazarus's family in Bethany; see Katz 1997: esp. 132, 134).[152]

The reference to the Jewish Passover signals to the alert reader that the time is near at which "the gospel story reaches its denouement and which has been referred to repeatedly" (Ridderbos 1997: 411). Now, "Jesus' hours are numbered" (Schnackenburg 1990: 2.364). Passover is one of the three pilgrim festivals for which men were required to travel to Jerusalem. This is the third and final Passover mentioned by John (cf. 2:13, 23; 6:4). If the first Passover took place in A.D. 30 (see commentary at 2:20), then the year of Jesus' passion is A.D. 33 (Hoehner 1977: esp. 44, 63, 143). Regarding the "many" who traveled from the country up to Jerusalem, recent scholarship estimates that the population of Jerusalem swelled from about one hundred thousand inhabitants to some one million during each of the three festivals.[153]

It is the height of irony that the people were concerned to purify themselves prior to Passover at a time when their leaders had "indelibly stained themselves as they ruthlessly plotted the death of the blameless Son of God" (Borchert 1996: 368). Such purification was necessary because ceremonial uncleanness prevented a person from celebrat-

---

151. See Riesner, *DJG* 49; Carson 1991: 423–24. But see Albright (1922–23), who argues that the Ephraim mentioned in John is not Et-Taiyibeh, but Ain Samieh, slightly to the northeast and lower in a valley. Cf. Schwank 1977.

152. Schwank (1977) helpfully points out that in the final analysis, the reason for the mention of Ephraim in 11:54 is most likely the Fourth Evangelist's conviction that Jesus did in fact withdraw to this location at this juncture of his ministry, whether or not this served the purpose of geographical symbolism or other theological purposes (cf. Olsson 1974: 28 [cited in Schwank 1977: 380]). He rejects the view of Bultmann (1971: 412 n. 3) that the reference is merely "schematic" (i.e., literary but not historical in nature) and also the contention by Kundsin (1925: 49–50) that the evangelist chose the name because the location was significant for Christians at the end of the first century (unsupported by evidence, as is admitted by Kundsin [p. 49]; see the discussions in Katz 1997: 131 n. 7; Schnackenburg 1990: 2.351).

153. See Reinhardt 1995: 262–63. Josephus (*J.W.* 6.9.3 §§422–25) provides the unlikely figure of over 2.7 million on the basis of a census taken by Cestius in the A.D. 60s.

ing the Passover.[154] This need arose particularly for those who lived in contact with Gentiles, since the latter frequently buried their dead near their houses, which would make their Jewish neighbors subject to the purification commanded by the law (Num. 19:11–12).[155] An OT law still operative in Jesus' day stipulated the need for ceremonial cleansing before the Passover for anyone who had become defiled, such as by touching a corpse (Num. 9:6–14). The appropriate purification rites might last as long as one week (Num. 19:12), so that many traveled to Jerusalem early, especially in light of the large numbers involved (Josephus, *J. W.* 1.11.6 §229; *m. Pesaḥ.* 9.1). Jesus, for his part, felt no need for ceremonial cleansing (see 12:1; contrast Paul in Acts 21:24–27).

The questions "What do you think? That he won't come to the feast at all?" reflect the "tense uncertainty" among the people and the prevailing opinion that Jesus would not "risk" coming to the festival (Ridderbos 1997: 412; cf. 7:11).[156] The general tone of the conversations taking place in the outer courts of the temple as reported by John is favorable. People here are wondering whether someone reputed to be as pious as Jesus would miss one of the major pilgrim festivals, knowing that he was in the immediate vicinity. But the chief priests and Pharisees had given orders that anyone who knew where Jesus was should report it so that they might arrest him (see commentary at 7:30).

In the wake of the questions of 11:56, the reference to the previously issued orders by the Pharisees and chief priests (note the pluperfect δεδώκεισαν [*dedōkeisan*, they had given]) serves to show that Jesus was already a marked man, highlighting the risk that Jesus would have to take if he were to appear publicly at the Passover (cf. the reference to his withdrawal in 11:54). Both OT and mishnaic legislation make provision for the kind of search ordered here by the chief priests and Pharisees. The Mosaic law obliged any Jew who heard a curse spoken aloud to report this to the authorities (Lev. 5:1). The Mishnah stipulates a procedure for covertly capturing a person who leads people into idolatry (*m. Sanh.* 7.10). In the present instance, the issue was not so much that Jesus' whereabouts were unknown; rather, the authorities simply were looking for an opportune time to arrest Jesus that would create the least stir possible (R. Brown 1966: 446).

---

154. See Num. 9:6; 2 Chron. 30:17–18; John 18:28; cf. *m. Pesaḥ.* 9.1.

155. The technical term ἁγνίζω (*hagnizō*, purify) (cf. Acts 21:24, 26; 24:18), used only here in John (but see 1 John 3:3), further indicates the evangelist's familiarity with Jewish customs (see also 18:28).

156. Barrett (1978: 410) opts for the rendering "He will not come, will he?" The imperfect verb forms ἐζήτουν (*ezētoun*, they were looking) and ἔλεγον (*elegon*, they were saying) indicate the ongoing search for Jesus and his being the subject of discussion. The former term need not be understood negatively but reflects "curious looking about for Jesus" (Ridderbos 1997: 411–12).

Additional Notes

11:45. Morris (1995: 499–500 n. 95), in a minority opinion, contends that the original reading is ὅ ($\mathfrak{P}^{66}$* [vid] B C* D) rather than ἅ ($\mathfrak{P}^{6, 45}$ ℵ A*), arguing that the latter reading represents an assimilation to the identical phrase in the following verse. If so, what induced faith in many was the singular act of raising Lazarus; when some went to the Pharisees, however, they spoke about a number of things Jesus had done.

11:50. The MS evidence is divided between ὑμῖν ($\mathfrak{P}^{45, 66}$ B D) and ἡμῖν (A) (ℵ has no pronoun). In light of both external and internal evidence, the former reading probably is original (contra Barrett [1978: 406] and Lindars [1972: 406], who favor omitting the pronoun; see the discussion in Nicklas 2000a: 590–91 n. 7).

2. The Anointing at Bethany (12:1–11)

In the context of John's narrative, the anointing scene casts a long shadow forward over Jesus' imminent arrest, trial, condemnation, crucifixion, and burial (12:7–8).[1] All four Gospels emphasize that Jesus foresaw his own violent, substitutionary death, underscoring that the condemning verdict did not take Jesus by surprise (see Mark 8:31–38; 9:30–32; 10:32–45 pars.). However, it is the Fourth Evangelist who stresses most explicitly that Jesus' death did not come as an accident but was fully willed and anticipated by him (e.g., 10:17–18; 18:4; cf. 13:1–3; 19:11).[2]

One incident in this pattern where Jesus interprets events (especially toward the end of his life) in light of the anticipated end is his anointing for burial. The account is closely linked with Jesus' raising of Lazarus, whose presence serves as a constant reminder that an amazing miracle has taken place and thus fuels the Jews' hostility toward Jesus still further.[3] Yet the focus in the anointing narrative is not on Lazarus but on his sister Mary, whom the evangelist introduced in the preceding chapter (11:2; cf. Mark 14:9; Matt. 26:13).

Three striking facts render Mary's anointing of Jesus particularly remarkable: the value of the perfume; Mary's pouring of oil on Jesus' feet (rather than his head); and her use of her hair to wipe his feet (it was considered improper for a woman to unbind her hair in public). Remarkably, a single verse is devoted to Mary's act of anointing Jesus,

---

1. Sabbe (1992: 2051–82) believes that John is literarily dependent on the Synoptics (esp. Mark, but also Luke) in the present instance. However, I am not convinced that the available evidence is sufficient to demonstrate redactional activity on John's part. Coakley (1988: 254) concludes that "the story of John 12:1–8 can without difficulty be understood on the hypothesis of the priority [i.e., independence] of John," and that the "details do not require to be explained as secondary developments of traditions preserved in more primitive form elsewhere [i.e., the Synoptics]" (though I do not share his skepticism regarding "the correctness of every detail in the account").

2. The evangelists' insistence that Jesus was not a tragic victim but was in full control of the events surrounding his passion is a crucial part of the gospel message, for it places the emphasis squarely on God's sovereignty and on his unfailing plan of the ages culminating in Jesus' sacrifice on the cross, relativizing the evil perpetrated upon God's suffering Servant by sinful people ultimately induced by Satan (cf. 13:2, 27). It is not as if in a dark hour evil took control and Jesus had to succumb to it; rather, he chose to die freely for our sake (cf. Matt. 26:52–54).

3. Lazarus is mentioned in the context of the setting of the anointing (12:1–2), at the conclusion of the anointing (12:9–11), and at the conclusion after the triumphal entry (12:17–19).

but five verses are given to Judas's taking offense and Jesus' rebuttal.[4] This indicates that the event sets the stage for Judas's imminent betrayal of Jesus.

A comparison with the parallel accounts by Mark and Matthew—Luke also records an anointing by a "sinful woman" (not Mary) but at an earlier occasion (at a Pharisee's house [7:36–50])—underscores the degree to which John chooses to focus on Judas.[5] Neither Mark (who obliquely refers to "some" [14:4]) nor Matthew (who speaks of "the disciples" [26:8]) reveals the identity of the persons objecting to the anointing. It is also John who alone adds the incriminating piece of information about Judas being a thief.

The account of the anointing is, at its core, a tale of contrasts: Mary's lavish devotion to Jesus is set against the backdrop of the looming prospect of Judas's betrayal of his master. In another contrast, the man whom Jesus had raised from the dead, Lazarus, takes part in the dinner, while Jesus himself is anointed for burial. This is the time for devotion or antagonism toward Jesus to be displayed. The narrative enters a crucial phase.

Jesus' Final Week (John 12–19)
March 27–April 3, A.D. 33

Friday, March 27, 33	Jesus arrives at Bethany	11:55–12:1
Saturday, March 28, 33	Dinner with Lazarus and his sisters	12:2–11
Sunday, March 29, 33	"Triumphal entry" into Jerusalem	12:12–50
Monday–Wednesday, March 30–April 1, 33	Cursing of fig tree, temple cleansing, temple controversy, Olivet discourse	Synoptics
Thursday, April 2, 33	Third Passover in John; betrayal, arrest	13:1–18:11
Friday, April 3, 33	Jewish and Roman trials, crucifixion, burial	18:12–19:42

Exegesis and Exposition

[1]Now Jesus, six days prior to the Passover, came to Bethany, where ⌜Lazarus⌝ was, whom Jesus had raised from the dead. [2]So they prepared a dinner for

---

4. For a detailed analysis of the present pericope (focused on verbal aspect), see Köstenberger 2001b: 49–63. The transitional nature of most of chapter 12 is noted by Keener 2003: 859.

5. See Köstenberger 2001b: 49–63. Ridderbos (1997: 413 [cf. Burge 2000: 336]) rightly contends that Mary is not the woman described in Luke 7 (though he perceives some degree of dependence on Mark 14:3–9 = Matt. 26:6–13). This view is rather common, though not universally so. Contra Holst (1976: 435–46), who on form-critical grounds believes that there is only one underlying historical event and that "variations arose in the course of oral transmission" (citing Dodd 1963: 172; other proponents include D. F. Strauss, Dibelius, and Bultmann).

him there, and Martha was serving, and Lazarus was one of those reclining with him. [3]Then Mary, taking a litra [about a pint or half a liter] of pure nard, an expensive perfume, anointed Jesus' feet and wiped his feet with her hair. And the house was filled with the fragrance of the perfume. [4]But Judas Iscariot, one of his disciples—the one who was about to betray him—said, [5]"Why wasn't this perfume sold for three hundred denarii [a year's wages] and the proceeds given to the poor?" [6](He said this not because he cared for the poor, but because he was a thief, and being in charge of the money box, he used to help himself to what was put into it.) [7]Then Jesus said, "Leave her alone, so that she may keep it for the day of my burial. [8]For you will always have the poor with you, but you will not always have me⌐." ⌐

[9]Then ⌐a⌐ large crowd of Jews learned that he was there, and they came not only on account of Jesus, but also to see Lazarus, whom he had raised from the dead. [10]But the high priests had decided to kill Lazarus as well, [11]because on account of him many Jews were coming and believing in Jesus.

The time reference "six days before the Passover" (cf. 11:55) significantly places Jesus' ensuing passion within the context of that important festival (Barrett 1978: 410), which may intend to remind the reader that Jesus is the paradigmatic sacrificial lamb (Carson 1991: 427). If, as is likely, John thinks of Passover as beginning Thursday evening (as do the Synoptics), then "six days before the Passover" refers to the preceding Saturday, which began on Friday evening. The evangelist identifies Bethany as the village where Lazarus lived, whom Jesus had raised from the dead.[6] This makes explicit the connection between the preceding chapter and the present account (Moloney 1998: 349), putting what is about to follow not only in the context of the death of Jesus but also of Lazarus (Brodie 1993: 407). Jesus frequently spent the night at Bethany during the closing days of his ministry (Matt. 21:17 par.; 26:6 par.).[7]

They prepared a dinner in Jesus' honor.[8] If Jesus arrived on Friday evening, then the festivity recounted here probably took place on Sat-

12:1–3

---

6. See 11:1 and commentary on John 11.

7. Curiously, Schnackenburg (1990: 2.366) questions the historical veracity of Jesus' trip to Bethany, arguing that it is unlikely that Jesus would have gone to a more dangerous location. However, there is solid, multiply attested evidence in favor of authenticity, and the Gospels make clear that Jesus was not exclusively, or even primarily, guided by concerns for his own safety, especially toward the end of his public ministry. Morris (1995: 510–11) notes that οὖν (oun, therefore) in 12:1 establishes a logical connection between the anointing and the preceding reference to the hostility of the Jewish leaders: despite their antagonism, Jesus was still willing to go to the place where he would eventually die.

8. The fronted ἐποίησαν (epoiēsan, they prepared) (which may be equivalent to a passive [so R. Brown 1966: 448]) is taken by some as indication of a very public occasion. If so, then the dinner may not have been prepared by Martha and her family and may not even have taken place at their house (Carson 1991: 428; Morris 1995: 511; contra Barrett 1978: 411; Moloney 1998: 356).

urday.[9] "Dinner" (δεῖπνον, *deipnon*) refers to the main meal of the day. It usually was held toward evening but could commence as early as the middle of the afternoon, so that there is no perfect correspondence to our contemporary terms "lunch" and "dinner." Nevertheless, Jesus' words in Luke 14:12, "when you give a luncheon [ἄριστον, *ariston*] or dinner [δεῖπνον, *deipnon*]," show that the midday and the evening meals were distinct. Moreover, "dinner" may refer to a regular meal or to a festive banquet (cf. Matt. 23:6 pars.; Mark 6:21). Elsewhere in John's Gospel, the term is used of the Last Supper (13:2, 4; 21:20). In first-century Palestine, banquets usually started in the later hours of the afternoon and quite often went on until midnight. Banquets celebrating the Sabbath could begin as early as midday.

Martha was serving, and Lazarus was one of those reclining with him.[10] Martha's serving at the table (a familiar posture [cf. Luke 10:38–42]) may indicate that by this time Sabbath had come to an end. Possibly, the meal was connected with the *Habdalah* service, which marked the end of a Sabbath (*m. Ber.* 8.5). It is probable that Lazarus, Mary, and Martha provided the meal, though a large dinner in this small village, celebrated in honor of a noted guest, might well have drawn in several other families to help with the work. Lazarus's presence at such a meal connects the dinner with the events recounted in the previous chapter. "Reclining" at the table may indicate a banquet rather than a regular meal (cf. 13:2–5, 23; see Keener 1993: 294).

Then Mary—here featured without introduction, presupposing John 11—took about a pint of pure nard, an expensive perfume. A λίτρα (*litra* [a measurement of weight equivalent to the Latin *libra*]) amounted to about eleven ounces, or a little less than three-quarters of a pound (half a liter; the only other NT reference is John 19:39). Then, as today, this represents a very large amount of perfume.[11] The elixir was pure nard, an expensive perfume (see Song 1:12; 4:13–16 LXX). Nard, also known as spikenard, is a fragrant oil derived from the root and spike (hair stem) of the nard plant, which grows in the mountains of northern India (Harrison 1966: 48–49). This "Indian spike," used by the Romans for anointing the head,

---

9. The vast majority of commentators holds that the dinner probably was eaten on Saturday at some point during the day, presumably in the evening. See Carson 1991: 427; Barrett 1978: 410; Morris 1995: 510 n. 10; see also Beasley-Murray 1999: 208; R. Brown 1966: 447; Burge 2000: 337. Schnackenburg (1990: 2.366) says that the meal could have been on Sunday or possibly Saturday evening.

10. Martha's serving suggests to some (e.g., Moloney 1998: 356) that the dinner was given at her (and Lazarus's) house. Others object that if the dinner had been at Lazarus's house, it likely would not have been stated that he was reclining with Jesus; his presence at the house would have been assumed (Morris 1995: 511; R. Brown 1966: 448; cf. Ridderbos 1997: 414). As on previous occasions, Martha is mentioned before her sister Mary (Schnackenburg 1990: 2.366).

11. Keener (1993: 294) mentions that normally a flask would contain no more than an ounce.

was "a rich rose red and very sweetly scented" (W. Walker 1958: 196). The Semitic expression is found in several papyri, including one from the early first century (P.Oxy. 8.1088, line 49). The rare term πιστικῆς (*pistikēs*, pure) may mean "genuine" (derived from πίστις, *pistis*, true, genuine) in contrast to diluted, since nard apparently was adulterated on occasion.[12] "Perfume" (μύρον, *myron*) is used here probably in the generic sense of "fragrant substance" (cf. Mark 14:3). The Synoptic parallels indicate that the perfume was kept in an "alabaster jar" (Matt. 26:7; Mark 14:3).[13]

She anointed Jesus' feet (cf. 11:2; Luke 7:38 refers to a different occasion of anointing). "Poured" (TNIV) translates the Greek word ἀλείφω (*aleiphō*), which more literally means "anoint." Anointing the head was common enough (Ps. 23:5; Luke 7:46), but anointing the feet was quite unusual (usually, simply water was provided), even more so during a meal, which definitely was improper in Jewish eyes.[14] In the present instance, it is hard not to see royal overtones in Mary's anointing of Jesus, especially in light of the fact that the event is immediately followed by Jesus' triumphal entry into Jerusalem, where he is hailed as the king of Israel who comes in the name of the Lord.[15] Attending to the feet was servant's work (see commentary at 1:27; 13:5), so Mary's action shows humility as well as devotion.[16]

Mary wiped Jesus' feet with her hair (cf. 11:2).[17] The use of hair rather than a towel for wiping Jesus' feet indicates unusual devotion. The act

12. The meaning "genuine" or "pure" is supported by most commentators (e.g., Carson 1991: 428; Barrett 1978: 412; Beasley-Murray 1999: 204 n. b; Schnackenburg 1990: 2.367; Ridderbos 1997: 414). Michaels (1989: 217), on the other hand, thinks that "it may have been the trade name under which the product was marketed" (i.e., "pistic nard").

13. See the illustration in Millard 1997: 179. For "expensive," see commentary at 12:5.

14. Though see the texts cited by Coakley (1988: 247–48), which illustrate that although Mary's act may have been unusual, it was "not unthinkable" (p. 248). Homer (*Odyssey* 19.503–7) speaks of Odysseus's feet being washed and subsequently anointed. The Greek poet Aristophanes cites an instance in which a daughter is washing, anointing (ἀλείφη), and kissing her father's feet (*Vespae* 608). Athenaeus (*Deipnosophists* 12.553) reports an Athenian custom among the wealthy of anointing "even the feet with perfumes." See also Pliny, *Natural History* 13.22 (putting scent on the soles of people's feet in Nero's day); Petronius, *Satyricon* 70; Curtius, *History of Alexander* 8.9.27 (bathing feet in perfumes as a custom of the kings of India); and, in a Jewish context, *t. Šabb.* 3.16; *Sipre* on Deut. 33:24. As Coakley (1988: 248) duly notes, of course, none of these passages suggests "that anointing of the feet was an everyday occurrence in Jesus' day in Palestine."

15. So Beasley-Murray 1999: 208–9; contra R. Brown 1966: 454. Witherington (1995: 207) notes the irony of Jesus being anointed at the same place where he raised someone from the dead. Carson (1991: 428) points out that in the following chapter, Jesus' disciples are told to "wash one another's feet," a command that may be anticipated by Mary anointing Jesus' feet in the present pericope.

16. This is further underscored by the repeated reference to Jesus' feet in 12:3 (Ridderbos 1997: 414–15; Morris 1995: 512).

17. According to Stibbe (1993: 132), 11:2 serves as an analepsis with 11:32 (where Mary falls at Jesus' feet) and as a prolepsis with chapter 13 (the footwashing) and 19:38–42 (Jesus' burial).

is all the more striking since Jewish women (esp. married ones) never unbound their hair in public, which would have been considered a sign of loose morals (cf. Num. 5:18; *b. Soṭah* 8a; see J. Lightfoot 1859: 3.376; Morris 1995: 512).[18] The fact that Mary (who probably was single, as no husband is mentioned) here acts in such a way toward Jesus, a well-known (yet unattached) rabbi, was sure to raise some eyebrows (see commentary at 4:7). Also unusual is the wiping off of the oil. Normally, anointing oil was not wiped off (Ridderbos 1997: 415 n. 111).

The house was filled with the fragrance of the perfume. In the Synoptic version of the account, Jesus issues the pronouncement, "Wherever this gospel is preached throughout the world, what she has done will also be told, in memory of her" (Matt. 26:13; Mark 14:9). Indeed, the Hebrew Scriptures teach that a good name is better even than fine perfume (Eccles. 7:1).[19] One Jewish work relates this verse to Abraham: before his call, he was like a flask of perfume sealed with a tight lid lying in a corner; but when God called him, and he obeyed, the reputation of his good works spread, just as when a jar of perfume is opened and the scent fills the air (*Cant. Rab.* 3.4 on Song 1:3).

12:4–8   This is the only place where Judas is named as the one who objected to the anointing (Matt. 26:8: "the disciples"; Mark 14:4: "some of those present"; see Calvin 1961: 25). The juxtaposition of Mary and Judas is meant to accentuate the contrast between their respective attitudes (Ridderbos 1997: 415–16; Westcott 1908: 2.112).[20] The question "Has the woman or the disciple rightly understood the significance of Jesus?" is posed and answered in the ensuing narrative (Moloney 1998: 349). Moreover, "the association of Judas with the death of Jesus also hints that Mary's action may be directed toward that event" (Moloney 1998: 357). The juxtaposition of the references to Judas as one of Jesus' disciples and as the one who would betray him (cf. 6:71) highlights the seriousness of Judas's actions (Morris 1995: 513).[21]

Judas's objection centered on the great value of the perfume: "a year's wages," that is, "three hundred denarii" (in Greek, a genitive of

---

18. See further Coakley (1988: 250 n. 51), who cites additional primary and secondary literature. Apparently, for a married woman to let down her hair in public constituted grounds for divorce (*t. Soṭah* 5.9; *y. Giṭ.* 9.50d; cf. *b. Yoma* 47a; *m. Ketub.* 7.6; *Num. Rab.* 9.16; more general, *b. Ned.* 30b; but see *m. Ketub.* 2.1). Yet note the conclusion by Coakley: "But none of these passages touches the question of what an unmarried woman might decently do in a neighbor's house among friends" (ibid.).

19. See also *Midr. Qoh.* 7.1 (cf. Morris 1995: 513).

20. Moloney (1998: 349) sees a contrast between Martha's objection in 11:39 and her acting in "a position of recognition" in 12:2b, on the one hand, and Mary's performance of "a humble act of love" in the present instance, but there is no explicit textual evidence to suggest that this contrast was intended by the Fourth Evangelist.

21. See especially Morris 1995: 513 n. 19. Contra Schnackenburg (1990: 2.367–68), who questions the originality of the phrase "the one who was about to betray him."

price [Wallace 1996: 122]). One denarius was the daily remuneration of a common laborer (cf. Matt. 20:2; see commentary at 6:7). Three hundred denarii is therefore roughly equivalent to a year's wages, since no money was earned on Sabbaths and other holy days. The perfume was outrageously expensive because it was imported all the way from northern India. Its great value may indicate that Mary and her family were very wealthy. Alternatively, this may have been a family heirloom that had been passed down to Mary. Though having the appearance of piety, Judas's objection turns out to be purely self-serving. And even if Judas's objection had been sincere, it is still true, as Carson (1991: 429) aptly observes, that "social activism, even that which meets real needs, sometimes masks a spirit that knows nothing of worship and adoration."

But as the evangelist notes, in a customary aside (Barrett 1978: 413), Judas had no true concern for the poor[22] and was in fact a thief (cf. 10:1, 8, 10).[23] The expression "money bag" (γλωσσόκομον, glōssokomon [the word recurs at 13:29, again in relation to Judas]) originally denoted any kind of box used to hold the reeds of musical instruments. Later, the term was employed for a coffer into which money is cast (2 Chron. 24:8, 10). In the present instance, therefore, the object in question is perhaps not a "bag" (TNIV), but a box made of wood or some other rigid material (cf. Plutarch, Galba 16.1; Josephus, Ant. 6.1.2 §11). The money kept in this container probably helped meet the needs of Jesus and his disciples as well as provide alms for the poor. The funds would have been replenished by followers of Jesus, such as the women mentioned in Luke 8:2–3 who supported his ministry. The term βαστάζω (bastazō, take away) can have the sense of "steal" (Carson 1991: 429; cf. Barrett 1978: 413; Beasley-Murray 1999: 205 n. d; Morris 1995: 514 n. 24).

Jesus' response is as startling (given the festive nature of the occasion) as it is firm. Clearly, Jesus' looming death weighs heavily on his mind (Morris 1995: 514). Most likely the statement involves some kind of ellipsis: "Leave her. [She did not sell it],[24] so that she may keep it

---

22. Morris (1995: 513 n. 21 [cf. R. Brown 1966: 448]) draws attention to the similarity between the wording of the phrase οὐχ ὅτι περὶ τῶν πτωχῶν ἔμελεν αὐτῷ in 12:6 and οὐ μέλει αὐτῷ περὶ τῶν προβάτων, the description of the hireling, in 10:13, noting that both are impersonal in tone.

23. This is the only NT passage in which Judas is called a thief, indeed, where he is charged with anything other than his ultimate betrayal of Jesus (though see Schnackenburg [1990: 2.368], who notes that the Synoptists, too, hint at Judas's greed: Matt. 26:14–15; 27:3–10; Mark 14:10–11; Luke 22:3–5). Carson (1991: 428–29 [cf. Burge 2000: 339]) suggests that the consistent description of Judas as the one who betrayed Jesus resulted from the "shocking force of their hindsight." It is as if the disciples' minds had been permanently seared by their memory of him as the one who betrayed their master.

24. That is, sell the perfume, as Judas had proposed (see 12:5; note the agreement in grammatical gender between αὐτό [auto, it] in 12:5 and μύρον [myron, perfume] in 12:7).

for the day of my burial."[25] According to Jesus, Mary had kept the perfume—unwittingly, no doubt, but in the providence of God—for just this purpose: the anointing of Jesus' body in anticipation of his burial (cf. 19:39–40).[26] Though it was not uncommon for people in first-century Palestine to spend considerable amounts on funeral-related expenses, it is unusual that Mary here lavishly pours out perfume on Jesus while he is still alive. The word "burial" (ἐνταφιασμός, *entaphiasmos* [elsewhere in the NT only in the parallel Mark 14:8]) refers not so much to the event itself as to the laying out of the corpse in preparation for burial (cf. 19:40; see Morris 1995: 514 n. 25; Moloney 1998: 357).

Jesus' concluding verdict, "For you will always have the poor among you, but you will not always have me,"[27] indirectly concedes that under normal circumstances Judas may have had a point, but these are not normal circumstances. Hence, Mary's extravagant act is vindicated as timely if not prophetic. The statement probably involves an allusion to Deut. 15:11: "There will always be poor people in the land." Jewish sources indicate that care of the dead was to take precedence over almsgiving. Thus *b. Sukkah* 49b praises the practice of kindness above charity because, among other reasons, it can be done to both the living and the dead (by attending their funeral; cf. *t. Peʾah* 4.19). In the present instance, Jesus' statement indicates that his "time" has almost come (cf. 12:23; see Ridderbos 1997: 419–20).[28]

12:9–11 A large crowd of Jews[29] (presumably the same as that referred to in 11:55–57 [Ridderbos 1997: 421]) learned of Jesus' whereabouts and

25. Most commentators view the statement in an elliptical fashion, though there is less consensus on precisely what ought to be supplied. Carson (1991: 429) suggests that the statement is to be construed as follows: "Leave her alone. [She has done this—i.e., held on to the jar] in order to keep it for the day of my burial." Ridderbos (1997: 417–19), too, holds that the ἵνα (*hina*, that) of 12:7 is independent (a "brachylogy" [cf. Schnackenburg 1990: 2.369]) and proposes that the phrase is best understood as a rhetorical question. Less likely is the construal of Witherington (1995: 208, appealing to Synoptic parallels), who thinks that Jesus is urging that Mary be left to keep the "burial ritual." Also doubtful is Maccini's (1996: 173–74) rendering: "Let her alone, so that she might keep what oil she has left for the day of my burial" (so, earlier, Schlatter 1948: 264).

26. Beasley-Murray (1999: 209) notes that there is no way of knowing whether or not Mary was aware of the significance of her act, while Laney (1992: 221) thinks that "Mary must have sensed the darkness of the hour." Calvin (1961: 27) observes that "a thing is said to be kept when it is held in store to be brought out appropriately and opportunely."

27. Note that in the Greek text, "me" is placed in the emphatic position (Morris 1995: 515 n. 30). See also the additional note on 12:8.

28. Ridderbos (1997: 420) speaks somewhat pompously of the "caesura in the manifestation of Jesus' glory" and notes the heightening of the distinction between the risen Christ and the historical Jesus implied in the present narrative. According to Ridderbos, the imminence of Jesus' burial highlights the separation between faith and unbelief that is illustrated radically in the contrast between Mary and Judas.

29. Literally, "from the Jews." The construction is somewhat unusual, featuring Greek ἐκ (*ek*), a partitive genitive (contra Brodie 1993: 408).

came to see not just him but also Lazarus.[30] Evidently, this crowd came to Bethany from Jerusalem. Crowds are mentioned at three junctures in the narrative: (1) those who heard about the miraculous raising of Lazarus and came to Bethany before Jesus left for Jerusalem (12:9); (2) those who likewise heard about the miracle and came out to meet Jesus at the triumphal entry (12:12, 18); and (3) those who saw Jesus raise Lazarus and spread the word (12:17).[31] The expression "raised from the dead" (i.e., from the realm of the dead) is used in keeping with the Jewish view that did not distinguish between the return of a dead person to the earthly world and the end-time resurrection of the dead.

At this the chief priests made plans to kill Lazarus as well (the term βουλεύω [bouleuō, counsel, plot] harks back to the identical term in 11:53; see Morris 1995: 517).[32] The presence of the resurrected Lazarus constituted a major embarrassment for the Sadducees (many of whom were among the chief priests), who held that there was no resurrection (see commentary at 11:23–24). Earlier, the high priest was talking about the death of "one man" (11:50); now, the chief priests plot to kill a second man as well.[33] The faith of the "many Jews" in Jesus in 12:11 again seems to be of the fleeting variety (so, rightly, Schnackenburg 1990: 2.370; contra Morris 1995: 518), despite the imperfect verb tenses of both ὑπῆγον (hypēgon, they went) and ἐπίστευον (episteuon, they believed).[34]

Additional Notes

12:1. The epithet ὁ τεθνηκώς (𝔓⁶⁶ A D, but not ℵ B) after "Lazarus" is almost certainly a scribal addition (so, rightly, Barrett 1978: 411).

12:8. Codex D omits 12:8, and 𝔓⁷⁵ omits μεθ᾽ ἑαυτῶν ἐμὲ δὲ οὐ πάντοτε ἔχετε (apparently owing to homoioteleuton), but the originality of 12:8 (included in 𝔓⁶⁶ ℵ A B and the overwhelming majority of MSS and versions) is not seriously in doubt (so Carson 1991: 430; Beasley-Murray 1999: 205 n. f; Schnackenburg 1990: 2.369; contra R. Brown [1966: 449] and Barrett [1978: 415], who suggests that it perhaps should be omitted).

30. Ἔγνω (egnō, learned) is best understood as an ingressive aorist (Morris 1995: 517). Most commentators (rightly, in my opinion) hold that the term "Jews" is not used in a negative sense here (so, e.g., Carson 1991: 431; Barrett 1978: 415; R. Brown 1966: 456; contra Morris 1995: 517). See also the additional note on 12:9.
31. See the discussion in R. Brown 1966: 456.
32. The verb ἐβουλεύσαντο (ebouleusanto, they counseled) is a reciprocal middle, suggesting interaction between the chief priests. BDAG 181 notes that βουλεύω occurs in our literature only in the middle voice. On the chief priests, see commentary at 7:32 and 11:47.
33. Contra Lindars (1972: 419), who claims that "the idea that Lazarus should also be put to death is an unhappy consequence of his own [i.e., the evangelist's] work, deriving not from the tradition, but from the logic of the situation which he has produced." I see no reason to question the historicity of this piece of information.
34. Contra Barrett (1978: 415 [cf. Morris 1995: 517]), who contends that the Jews mentioned here abandoned Judaism and aligned themselves with Christ.

12:9. There is some question as to the presence of the definite article ὁ before ὄχλος πολύς in 12:9. The article is found in ℵ* and B* but not in 𝔓⁶⁶* 𝔓⁷⁵ A D. Reading the article constitutes the harder variant, since the word order is reversed or the article is missing before the adjective, which may account for numerous apparent scribal attempts at correction. However, the reading without the article seems to be more Johannine (cf. 6:2, 5). On the whole, the anarthrous reading seems to be slightly preferable (contra Morris 1995: 517).

3. The Triumphal Entry into Jerusalem (12:12–19)

Entering Jerusalem, Jesus displays the determination and resolve portrayed also by Luke (9:51).[1] On a human level, the public acclaim for Jesus, which turns into a mob calling, "Crucify him! Crucify him!" in a matter of days, highlights the treacherous nature of popularity. Theologically, the triumphal entry is shown to fulfill OT prophecy.[2] Because palm branches commonly were used to convey the celebration of victory, the image of Jesus here is that of a victor who has defeated his enemies.[3]

This highly public scene stands in marked contrast to the intimacy of the preceding anointing of Jesus. In light of the reference to "Greeks" in 12:20, the evangelist likely perceived Jesus' entrance into Jerusalem "as the end point of his earthly self-manifestation as the Messiah of Israel" (Ridderbos 1997: 422). There is considerable narrative tension between Jesus being at the height of his popularity and the looming betrayal and arrest of Jesus, already plotted by the Pharisees (11:57; cf. 12:19).

The evangelist's presentation of Jesus as the signs-working, God-sent Messiah has already been completed. Now, one further messianic portrait is supplied: that of the Davidic king of Israel who triumphs in humility. But this brief flickering up of popularity is not to be trusted, for Jesus knows that he must die, and that his death is imminent (12:32–33).[4]

---

1. See the survey in Losie, *DJG* 854–59. Laney (1992: 222, 224) prefers the term "royal entry" because Jesus entered the city as Messiah and king.

2. Both OT passages featured in John convey the notion of Jesus' Davidic kingship. All four evangelists refer to Ps. 118:25–26, "Hosanna! Blessed is he who comes in the name of the Lord," to which John and Mark add references to "the king of Israel" (John 12:13d) or "the kingdom of our father David" (Mark 11:10).

3. John and Matthew also refer to Zech. 9:9 (see introduction to John 10). Riding on a donkey, a lowly animal, conveyed the notion of humility, so characteristic of Jesus throughout his ministry (cf. Matt. 11:29; 2 Cor. 8:9; Phil. 2:5–11). (But note the dissenting voice of Laney [1992: 225], who says that "a donkey was not considered a lowly creature in the ancient Near East," but that it was "the mount of princes [Judg. 5:10; 10:4; 12:14] and kings [2 Sam. 16:1–2]"; according to Laney, "Jesus came riding into Jerusalem on a mount appropriate to His royal position.") The donkey was also considered to be an animal of peace, in contrast to the war horse (cf. Zech. 9:10). The Synoptics provide additional information not given in John: Jesus' command to two of his disciples to go and get the colt in anticipation of his arrival in Jerusalem (Mark 11:2–3 pars.); John only mentions that "Jesus found a young donkey and sat upon it," without going into details here (12:14).

4. The popular observance of Jesus' triumphal entry on "Palm Sunday" does not adequately recognize that the crowd's waving of palm branches, rather than being based

Exegesis and Exposition

[12]On the next day the large crowd that had come to the festival, upon hearing that Jesus was coming to Jerusalem, [13]took palm branches and went to meet him, crying, "Hosanna! Blessed is he who comes in the name of the Lord, even the king of Israel!" [14]And Jesus, having found a young donkey, sat on it, just as it is written, [15]"Do not be afraid, daughter Zion: look, your king is coming, seated on the colt of a donkey." ([16]At first his disciples did not understand these things, but when Jesus had been glorified, then they remembered that these things had been written about him and that they had done these things to him.) [17]Now the crowd that was with him had been a witness ⌜when⌝ he had called Lazarus from the tomb and had raised him from the dead. [18](Therefore the crowd came to meet him, because they had heard that he had done this sign.) [19]Then the Pharisees said to one another, "See, it's useless. Look, the whole world has gone after him!"

12:12–13 In this scene, Jesus' entry into the Jewish capital "acquires the character of an acclamation by which Israel solemnly welcomes its Messiah into Jerusalem, the city and temple of the great king" (Ridderbos 1997: 423; cf. Matt. 5:35). "The next day" is probably Sunday of passion week (see commentary at 12:1, 2), called "Palm Sunday" in Christian tradition.[5] There was a large crowd at hand (see commentary at 12:9 and at 11:55). With Jerusalem's population at that time being about one hundred thousand, and the number of pilgrims amounting to several times the population of Jerusalem, the "large crowd" gathered at the Jewish capital at the occasion of the Passover may have totaled up to one million people.[6] Many of these pilgrims probably were Galileans who were well acquainted with Jesus' ministry (Morris 1995: 518). "The festival" refers to Passover (see commentary at 12:1 and at 2:13).

---

on a true understanding of Jesus, was in fact based on a misconception of Jesus' identity (editor's note following Farmer 1952: 66). Hence, it would be more proper to mourn people's inadequate notion of the Messiah at the present occasion than to perpetuate such misunderstanding by focusing on the externals of the event (waving of palm branches, celebration, etc.). Ironically, this kind of observance of Palm Sunday risks placing contemporary believers on par with the original Jerusalem crowd. But such an observance would miss the evangelists' universal portrayal of the triumphal entry as mistaken (though unwittingly fulfilling OT prophecy) rather than reflecting a true knowledge of Jesus' messianic calling and mission.

5. Contra Laney (1992: 224, citing Hoehner 1977: 91), who thinks that the "next day" refers to the day after the great crowds of Jews came to Bethany (12:9), "probably Monday, rather than Sunday." Ridderbos (1997: 422), among others, proposes that the triumphal entry occurred the day after the anointing at Bethany. Schnackenburg (1990: 2.373) contends that a definitive conclusion is not possible.

6. Kruse (2003: 265) cites Josephus (J.W. 6.9.3 §§422–25), who puts the figure at 2.7 million, which Kruse rightly finds "hard to believe." Cf. commentary at 11:54–57.

Upon hearing that Jesus was coming to Jerusalem, people took up palm branches.[7] Date palm trees grew in the vicinity of Jerusalem, especially Jericho, the "City of Palms" (Deut. 34:3; 2 Chron. 28:15; see Avi-Yonah 1964: 148). The palm tree in general served as a symbol of righteousness (Ps. 92:12). In the OT, palm branches are associated not with Passover but with the Feast of Tabernacles (Lev. 23:40). However, by the time of Jesus, palm branches had already become a national (if not nationalistic) Jewish symbol (Josephus, *Ant.* 3.10.4 §245; 13.13.5 §372; cf. Jub. 16:31; see Coakley 1995: 472). They were a prominent feature at the rededication of the temple by the Maccabeans in 164 B.C. (2 Macc. 10:7; see Burge 2000: 341), and they were used to celebrate Simon's victory over the Syrians in 141 B.C. (1 Macc. 13:51; see Farmer 1952: 65). Later, palms appear on the coins minted by the insurrectionists during the Jewish wars against Rome (A.D. 66–70 and 132–135), and even on Roman coins themselves. Apocalyptic end-time visions likewise feature date palms (T. Naph. 5:4; Rev. 7:9). In the present event, people's waving of palm branches may signal nationalistic hopes that in Jesus a messianic liberator had arrived (cf. John 6:14–15; see Farmer 1952).[8]

They went to meet him, crying, "Hosanna!" (see Ps. 118:25). The phrase "went to meet him" (rare in biblical literature: in the NT elsewhere only in Matt. 8:34; 25:1; in the LXX only in Judg. 11:34) was regularly used in Greek culture, where such a joyful reception was customary when Hellenistic sovereigns entered a city (Ridderbos 1997: 422; Morris 1995: 518 n. 39; Schnackenburg 1990: 2.374; R. Brown 1966: 460). An instance of this is recorded by Josephus, when Antioch came out to meet Titus (*J.W.* 7.5.2 §§100–101).[9] The term "hosanna," originally a transliteration of the identical Hebrew expression,[10] had become a general expression of acclamation or praise.[11] Most familiar was the term's occurrence in the Hallel (Ps. 113–18), a psalm sung each morning by the temple choir during various Jewish festivals (see *m. Pesaḥ.* 5.7; 9.3; 10.7). At such occasions, every man and boy would wave a *lulab* (a bouquet of willow, myrtle, and palm branches; see *b. Sukkah* 37b; Josephus,

---

7. Mark 11:8 adds that many spread their cloaks on the road (cf. Coakley 1995: 472–73).

8. Cf. *Lev. Rab.* 30.2. The Greco-Roman world knew palm branches as symbols of victory (e.g., Suetonius, *Caligula* 32).

9. For further primary source quotes, see Coakley 1995: 471–72 (Thucydides, *History* 4.121; Polybius, *Histories* 5.26.7–12; 20.7.5; 1 Macc. 10:86; Josephus, *Ant.* 13.4.4 §101; Plutarch, *Cicero* 43).

10. Literally, "Give salvation now!" "O save!" (cf. 2 Sam. 14:4; 2 Kings 6:26).

11. Ridderbos (1997: 423 n. 137) says that "hosanna" literally means, "Please help!"; Carson (1991: 432) prefers the meaning "Give salvation now!" But probably Barrett (1978: 417–18) is correct that at the time of Christ, the phrase might have been no more than a "jubilant shout of praise" as part of a "spontaneous ovation" (cf. Morris 1995: 516; R. Brown 1966: 457). Beasley-Murray (1999: 210) adds that it may have been a greeting as well.

Ant. 3.10.4 §245) when the choir reached the "Hosanna!" in Ps. 118:25 (*m. Sukkah* 3.9).[12]

People shouted, "Blessed is he who comes in the name of the Lord!" (see Ps. 118:26).[13] The citations of Scripture in 12:13 and 12:15 are the only ones in John's Gospel not preceded by a quotation formula. John's presentation here coheres quite closely with that of the Synoptic writers (cf. esp. Matt. 21:4–9). In its original context, Ps. 118 conferred a blessing on the pilgrim headed for Jerusalem (R. Brown 1966: 457), with possible reference to the Davidic king (Carson 1991: 432). Later rabbinic commentary interpreted this psalm messianically (*Midr. Ps.* 118.22 on Ps. 118:24).[14] The messianic application of the phrase "he who comes" is also evident in the Baptist's question to Jesus, "Are you the one who was to come, or should we expect someone else?" (Matt. 11:3 = Luke 17:19–20). The term "to come" (in the sense of "the Coming One") and the expression "Messiah" or "Christ" are repeatedly found juxtaposed in John's Gospel.[15]

The phrase "even the king of Israel"[16] may have been added by the people to the Psalms passage (recorded only in John; if so, it may constitute a separate acclamation of "the king of Israel" [so Coakley 1995: 477]) or represent an interpretive gloss by the evangelist (Barrett 1978: 418), with "the king of Israel" epexegetically defining "the one who comes in the name of the Lord" (Ridderbos 1997: 423; Barrett 1978: 418; Morris 1995: 520). The expression is in keeping with the emphasis on Jesus' royalty in this Gospel (esp. in the passion narrative).

12:14–16 Jesus, "for his part,"[17] found a young donkey and sat upon it.[18] By riding on a donkey, Jesus expresses his willingness to become the king of

---

12. Morris (1995: 518–19 n. 40 [cf. Schnackenburg 1990: 2.374]) denies that the branches waved on this occasion were the *lulab*s used at the Feast of Tabernacles.

13. Morris (1995: 520) prefers the translation "Blessed *is* he that comes" over "Blessed *be* the one." If this is correct, then the phrase constitutes a statement rather than a prayer. Freed (1961) maintains that the OT quotations in John 12:13–15 demonstrate Johannine literary dependence on the Synoptics; but see the rebuttal by D. M. Smith 1963.

14. Note also the interesting connection between a donkey and the "ruler from Judah" in Gen. 49:11 (see commentary at 12:15).

15. Cf. 4:25; 7:27, 31, 41, 42; 11:27; cf. 6:14. See the survey in Köstenberger 1998b: 94–96.

16. For the title "king of Israel," see commentary at 1:49. See also 18:37; 19:19.

17. This is the translation proposed by Ridderbos (1997: 424), who suggests that δέ (*de*, and, but) is not adversative here but rather serves as a transitional device.

18. For a fuller description of how Jesus "found" the donkey, see Matt. 21:1–3 pars. (note the harmonization proposed in Carson 1991: 433; Morris 1995: 520–21). Coakley (1995: 477) calls the reference here "intentionally uninformative," either because the evangelist had no information about how the donkey was found or because he chose not to disclose it (Coakley prefers the latter). However, his suggestion seems implausible that "Jesus did not intend to ride the donkey at all but was made to do so by enthusiastic followers" (p. 479, citing Luke 19:37; John 6:15). This is the only occurrence of the diminutive form ὀνάριον (*onarion*, young donkey) in the NT.

Israel (Ridderbos 1997: 424), though in more humble terms than those of the prevailing nationalism of the day.[19] Particularly in John's presentation, the account of Jesus' entry into Jerusalem is "the story of Jesus' hidden glory" (Ridderbos 1997: 424). Two associations with the donkey were dominant in first-century Palestine: humility (see commentary at 13:1–20) and peace (see commentary at 14:27). In contrast to the war horse (cf. Zech. 9:10), the donkey was a lowly beast of burden: "Fodder and a stick and burdens for a donkey" (Sir. 33:25; cf. Prov. 26:3). Donkeys were also known as animals ridden on in pursuit of peace, be it by ordinary folk, priests, merchants, or persons of importance (Judg. 5:10; 2 Sam. 16:2).

Jesus' choice of a donkey invokes prophetic imagery of a king coming in peace (Zech. 9:9–10), which contrasts sharply with notions of a political warrior messiah (cf. 1 Kings 4:26; Isa. 31:1–3). In OT times, donkeys were used by the sons of judges (Judg. 10:4; 12:14); Bathsheba's grandfather Ahithophel, a wise and respected counselor (2 Sam. 17:23); and Mephibosheth, Saul's son, at the occasion of his visit to Jerusalem to meet David (2 Sam. 19:26). The early Christians often were mocked as those worshiping a donkey, a man in the form of a donkey, or a donkey's head, such as in the famous graffito showing a crucified slave with the head of a donkey and another slave worshiping, with the inscription "Alexamenos worships God" (early third cent. A.D.?; see Michel, *TDNT* 5:284 n. 7; Ferguson 1993: 560–61).

"Do not be afraid, daughter Zion; look, your king is coming, seated on the colt of a donkey" (see Zech. 9:9). Note that John omits the characterization of the king riding on a donkey as "righteous and having salvation, gentle" (cf. Matt. 21:5). The words "do not be afraid" are not found in the Hebrew or other versions of Zech. 9:9, replacing instead the expression "rejoice greatly." It may be taken from Isa. 40:9, where it is addressed to the one who brings good tidings to Zion (cf. Isa. 44:2; Zeph. 3:16).[20] "Daughter Zion" is a common way of referring to Jerusalem and its inhabitants, especially in their lowly state as the oppressed people of God. An early messianic prophecy speaks of a ruler from Judah who

19. See commentary at 1:49–51 and at 6:14–15 (where both terms, "the one who comes" and "king," are used). Both Ridderbos (1997: 423) and Barrett (1978: 418) contend that by mounting the donkey, Jesus sought to correct the mistaken nationalism of the crowd (see also R. Brown 1966: 462; Witherington 1995: 221); though note Coakley (1995: 461–82), who contends that there is no evidence that the crowd understood at the time, so that, "if Jesus tried to make the crowd understand his actions in this way, he failed" (p. 463). Ridderbos (1997: 423) also points to the salvific context of Zech. 9 and notes that Jesus' action was intended to convey the fact that the time of salvation described in Zechariah (and other relevant OT texts) had arrived.

20. The possible reference to Isa. 40:9 is noted by Carson (1991: 433); cf. Barrett 1978: 418; contra Morris 1995: 521 n. 48. R. Brown (1966: 458) points to Zeph. 3:16. This kind of conflation of quotations from the OT is not uncommon in the NT (e.g., Matt. 27:9–10; Mark 1:2–3).

will command the obedience of the nations and who rides on a donkey (Gen. 49:10–11).[21]

This is not the first time in this Gospel that the disciples initially fail to understand the significance of Jesus' act (cf. 2:22; see also 14:26; 20:9; see Carson 1991: 434).[22] If people's waving of palm branches is reflective of false (nationalistic) notions of the Messiah, then both the crowd and Jesus' disciples are shown to misunderstand Jesus' true identity in the present scene.[23]

12:17–19 The present section mirrors 12:9–11 (R. Brown 1966: 463–64; Moloney 1998: 350). Both units begin with the Lazarus event and the reaction of the crowd, and both end with the attitude of the Jewish leaders. Both also refer to the effects of Jesus' sign. In an extended aside, the evangelist points out that the crowd that was with Jesus had been a witness when he had called Lazarus from the tomb and had raised him from the dead.[24] He is quick to add, however, that the reason why the crowd came to meet Jesus was that they had heard—rather than seen, which suggests hearsay rather than eyewitness testimony—that he had performed this sign.[25] The reference to the crowd, which forms an *inclusio* with 12:9, is plainly to the crowd featured in John 11,[26] though the evangelist makes

21. Though the rabbis had difficulty reconciling this humble notion of the Messiah with that of the Danielic Son of Man "coming on the clouds of heaven" (*b. Sanh.* 98a). However, riding on a donkey does appear as one of the three signs of the Messiah in *Eccles. Rab.* 1.9, where the latter redeemer in Zech. 9:9 is featured as the counterpart to Moses in Exod. 4:20.

22. Ridderbos (1997: 424 n. 145) notes that the first two occurrences of ταῦτα (*tauta*, these things) refer to the events narrated in 12:12–15. As to the third ταῦτα in 12:16, Morris (1995: 521) suggests that as the object of ἐποίησαν (*epoiēsan*, they had done), it refers to the role that the disciples played in acquiring the donkey (but see R. Brown [1966: 458], who proposes a general, passive sense of ἐποίησαν in 12:16, while Ridderbos [1997: 424] prefers to take it with reference to the manner in which the crowd greeted Jesus as he entered Jerusalem).

23. Barrett (1978: 419) notes that it is unlikely that the crowds would have understood the implications of Jesus' actions, when even his disciples did not.

24. See the additional note. The TNIV construes "when" as modifying "that was with him" rather than "was a witness," which is grammatically possible but results in a rendering that is hard to fit into the surrounding context: "Now the crowd that was with him when he called Lazarus from the tomb and raised him from the dead continued to spread the following word." Who, then, are the "many people" in the following verse, 12:18? Those to whom the crowd had "continued to spread the word"? (More likely, the ὁ ὄχλος [*ho ochlos*, the crowd] in 12:17 and the ὁ ὄχλος in 12:18 are identical: precisely the same people who had witnessed the previous miracle now came to meet Jesus at the triumphal entry.) Moreover, the crowd "spreading the word" is hardly a Johannine notion.

25. Note the *inclusio* between 12:12–13 and 12:18, with "they heard/they met" (ἀκούσαντες/ὑπάντησιν) and "they met/they heard" (ὑπήντησεν/ἤκουσαν) framing the "triumphal entry" pericope. Together with the *inclusio* of 12:9–11 and 12:17–19, and with 12:16 harking back to the account of the temple clearing in 2:22, the threefold pattern of inclusion between the present and previous sections in the narrative displays the literary artistry of the Fourth Evangelist.

26. Cf. 11:19, 33, 42, 45 (see Ridderbos 1997: 425; Schnackenburg 1990: 2.377).

clear that their faith was signs-based and thus inadequate by itself (Ridderbos 1997: 425–26).[27]

The words "See, it's useless" (cf. 11:47–48) reflect the Pharisees' growing exasperation in their attempt to endure the Roman occupation and the tension Jesus is creating with his popularity (Carson 1991: 435).[28] "The whole world" in the statement "The whole world has gone after him!" constitutes a common Jewish hyperbolic phrase.[29] The Fourth Evangelist perhaps seeks to exploit the potential for double meaning inherent in this phrase and intends this statement to be read as yet another unwitting prophecy (cf. 11:49–52), in the present instance of the effects of the preaching of the gospel.[30]

Additional Note

12:17. "When" (ὅτε [ℵ A B]) is preferable to "that" (ὅτι [𝔓[66] D]), the latter being an apparent scribal attempt to smooth out the meaning of this passage. So, rightly, Ridderbos 1997: 425 n. 148 (also citing 12:18); Schnackenburg 1990: 2.377; Barrett 1978: 420; Beasley-Murray 1999: 205 n. i; R. Brown 1966: 458; Moloney 1998: 359.

27. For previous reactions to Jesus' signs, see 2:23; 4:45, 48; 6:2; 11:47. The Fourth Evangelist repeatedly stresses that faith must not be based solely on signs (2:24–25; 4:48; 6:14–15).

28. Barrett (1978: 420) and, very tentatively, Morris (1995: 523) suggest that θεωρεῖτε (theōreite, see) is probably an indicative (rather than an imperative). Whitacre (1999: 308) notes that both verbs θεωρεῖτε and ὠφελεῖτε (ōpheleite, you accomplish) in 12:19 are in the second-person plural, suggesting that this captures "the mutual condemnation they are throwing at one another: 'You guys see that you are doing no good.'"

29. So it is said that "the whole world would not have room for the books that would be written" if all Jesus did was recorded (a possible *inclusio* with 12:19); that the early Christians "have caused trouble all over the world" (Acts 17:6); that "all the world know[s] that the city of Ephesus is the guardian of the temple of the great Artemis" (Acts 19:35); that "all over the world this gospel is bearing fruit and growing" (Col. 1:6); that "all the world" followed the high priest (*b. Yoma* 71b); that Hezekiah taught the Torah to "the whole world" (*b. Sanh.* 101b); that "the people [lit., 'the world'] were flocking to David" (*b. B. Meṣiʿa* 85a; cf. 2 Sam. 15:13); and that "all the people [lit., 'world'] came and gathered around" a certain rabbi (*b. ʿAbod. Zar.* 19b).

30. The ironic nature of the final part of the Pharisees' statement is noted by, among others, Ridderbos (1997: 426), Carson (1991: 435), and Beasley-Murray (1999: 211). Carson (1991: 435) further suggests that there is actually "irony within irony," given the reference to unbelief in 12:37–40.

D. Conclusion (12:20–50)

With Jesus' royal entry, the Messiah had been revealed in Jerusalem. What was needed now was not more instruction but action (Schlatter 1948: 267). The raising of Lazarus (ch. 11), the anointing at Bethany (12:1–11), and Jesus' triumphal entry into Jerusalem (12:12–19) mark a transition from Jesus' public ministry to the Jews to his private ministry to his disciples and his passion. In this context, the coming of some Greeks to Jesus (12:20–36) closes the gap, serving notice that the Jewish nation had turned its back on Jesus, while the Gentile mission was imminent.[1] Although Jesus does not grant the Greeks an audience, he speaks of the universal ramifications of his cross-death. This is followed by a closing of the book on Act I of the Johannine drama—a final, ringing indictment of the Jewish people who had failed to receive their Messiah despite a series of startling signs (12:37–50).

1. R. Brown (1966: 469) notes that this narrative provides an excellent conclusion to this section, suggesting numerous correspondences between the present section and John 11.

1. The Dawning Age of the Gentiles: Jesus Predicts His Death (12:20–36)

Apparently, the "whole world" that has gone after Jesus (12:19) includes certain "Greeks" who approach Jesus' disciples requesting to see him. Yet, rather than addressing their request directly,[1] Jesus announces that his "time" has now come (12:23; cf. 2:4; 8:20); the "Son of Man" will be "lifted up," that is, exalted from the earth, by way of crucifixion (cf. 3:13–15; 8:28). Jesus' gentle yet evasive response means that the Gentiles may "see" him, but only subsequent to his cross-death. Once lifted up from the earth, he will draw all (kinds of) people to himself (12:32; cf. 20:29; 1 Pet. 1:8). Indeed, Jesus has "other sheep" not of "this sheep pen" that he must bring as well (John 10:16; cf. Eph. 2:11–22; 4:3–6). Yet he will do this once exalted through the disciples by the Spirit (as recorded in the Book of Acts). Now he must complete his mission to the Jews by dying, in keeping with Caiaphas's prophecy, "for the Jewish nation," and "also for the scattered children of God" (John 11:52). Others will proclaim the message of salvation and forgiveness; only Jesus can give his flesh "for the life of the world" (6:51) and "lay down his life for the sheep" (10:11).

Unlike the Synoptists, who accentuate more keenly the shame and pain suffered by Jesus, John presents the cross primarily as the place of Jesus' glorification (12:28; 13:31–32; 17:1, 5).[2] According to John, Jesus is not glorified *despite*, but *through* and *in*, the cross. For it is there that Jesus is revealed as the obedient, dependent Son, who faithfully accomplished his mission (17:4; 19:30). The entire farewell discourse is cast plainly from the perspective of the exalted Jesus, who refers to his own death, in a major understatement, simply as his "going to the Father" (13:1; 14:12; 16:28). Though this Gospel does not contain an account of Jesus' struggle in Gethsemane, 12:27–28a is its equivalent.[3] Not only is it time for the Son of Man to be glorified,

1. For this request-and-response pattern, compare Mark 10:35–40; Acts 1:6–8.
2. The author of Hebrews, speaking of "Jesus . . . , who for the joy set before him endured the cross, scorning its shame, and sat down at the right hand of the throne of God" (Heb. 12:2), holds these two perspectives in tension. Jesus first suffered, and then was exalted. Peter, in his first epistle, likewise speaks of "the sufferings of Christ and the glories that would follow" (1 Pet. 1:11).
3. This is similar to, for example, Peter's watershed confession at the end of John 6, which is the Johannine equivalent of the Synoptic account of Peter's confession at Caesarea Philippi.

but also it is time for the world and its ruler to be judged (12:31; see 14:30; 16:11; cf. 1 John 3:8). The cross is cast as the final confrontation between Jesus and Satan (Kovacs 1995), in fulfillment of Scripture and in accordance with God's will. Those who choose to align themselves with Jesus by believing in him and following him join in his victory and participate in proclaiming the good news of his triumph to others. The crowd's question once again reveals misunderstanding, while the Greeks, for the time being, have to content themselves with an indirect response.

Exegesis and Exposition

[20]Now there were some Greeks among those who were coming up to worship at the festival. [21]So they approached Philip (the one from Bethsaida in Galilee) and asked him, saying, "Sir, we would like to see Jesus." [22]Philip came and told Andrew; Andrew and Philip came and told Jesus. [23]Yet Jesus answered them, saying, "The time has come for the Son of Man to be glorified. [24]Truly, truly, I say to you, unless a grain of wheat falls into the ground and dies, it remains by itself. But if it dies, it bears much fruit. [25]Whoever loves his life will lose it, yet whoever hates his life in this world will keep it for eternal life. [26]If anyone serves me, let him follow me, and where I am, there my servant will be as well. If anyone serves me, the Father will honor him.

[27]"Now my soul is troubled, and what shall I say: 'Father, save me from this hour'? But for this reason I came to this hour! [28][No!] Father, glorify your name!" Then a voice came from heaven: "I have both glorified it, and I will glorify it again." [29]Now the crowd that was standing there and heard this was saying that it had thundered; others were saying, "An angel has spoken to him." [30]Jesus answered and said, "This voice has come not for my benefit, but for yours. [31]Now is the judgment of this world; now the ruler of this world will be cast out. [32]And I, when lifted up from the earth, will draw ⌜all kinds of people⌝ to myself." [33](Now he was saying this in order to indicate by what kind of death he was about to die.) [34]Then the crowd answered him, "We heard from the law that the Christ remains forever, so how can you say that the Son of Man must be lifted up? Who is this 'Son of Man'?" [35]So Jesus said to them, "The light will be among you just a little while longer. Move about while you have the light, so that darkness may not overtake you; in fact, whoever moves about in darkness does not know where he is going. [36]While you have the light, believe in the light, in order that you may become sons of light." Jesus said these things, and left and hid himself from them.

12:20–22   The present section is connected with the previous narrative by the phrase "among those who were coming up to worship at the festival" (Ridderbos

1997: 427).[4] The reference to "some Greeks" (Ἕλληνες, *Hellēnes*) may invoke the Isaianic notion of Gentiles flocking to God in the end times (Isa. 42:4; 49:6; see Beutler 1990: 346; Kossen 1970: 103–4).[5] As elsewhere in the NT, the term Ἕλληνες refers not necessarily to people literally hailing from Greece but to Gentiles from any part of the Greek-speaking world, including Greek cities in the Decapolis.[6] The term "Greek" presumably was used as an umbrella term for Gentiles, owing to the dominance of Greek culture and language in the Greco-Roman world at large.[7] Most likely, then, the "Greeks" mentioned here were God-fearers, Gentiles who had come up to Jerusalem to worship the God of Israel at the feast (cf. Acts 17:4).[8] Like the Roman Cornelius (Acts 10) or the centurion who had a synagogue built (Luke 7:2–5), such God-fearers were attracted to the Jewish way of life without formally converting to Judaism. They were admitted to the court of the Gentiles but forbidden entrance into the inner courts on pain of death (see commentary at 2:14).

They approached Philip, requesting to "see" Jesus (cf. 1:39).[9] Philip came and told Andrew; both came and told Jesus (cf. 1:43).[10] It is pos-

---

4. Ridderbos (1997: 427 n. 154) notes that ἀναβαίνω (*anabainō*, go up) and προσκυνέω (*proskyneō*, worship) are often used with reference to pilgrims going to participate in cultic ceremonies. Barrett (1978: 421) suggests that the former expression may have a frequentative sense, indicating that these people regularly went up to these festivals.

5. Beutler (1990: 335–45) contends that John 12:20 echoes Isa. 52:15 LXX and suggests that John 12:20–50 may constitute a "great inclusion" with 1:19–34. Contra E. Schwartz's famous dictum (quoted in Busse 1992: 2085) that the Greeks here seem "ghostlike," Busse (1992) argues that 12:20–36 is part of the evangelist's literary strategy and consciously anticipates the epilogue in John 21 (compare esp. 21:18 with 10:11, 15, and 21:19 with 12:33).

6. See commentary at 7:35, the only other occurrence of the term in John's Gospel. A look at the remaining NT references indicates that in virtually all instances the term is used in contrast with "Jews" (Ἰουδαῖοι, *Ioudaioi*; see Acts 14:1; 16:1; 18:4; 19:10, 17; 20:21; Rom. 1:16; 2:9, 10; 3:9; 10:12; 1 Cor. 1:22, 24; 10:32; 12:13; Gal. 3:28; Col. 3:11). That the "Greeks" mentioned here were not Diaspora Jews (as Calvin [1961: 35] thought) is accepted by virtually all major commentators (e.g., Westcott [1908: 2.120], who likens these to the Gentile magi at the beginning of Matthew's Gospel; Ridderbos 1997: 427; Carson 1991: 436; Barrett 1978: 421; Schnackenburg 1990: 2.381; Witherington 1995: 223; Moloney 1998: 351; Burge 2000: 342).

7. Note that the term Ἑλληνιστής (*Hellēnistēs*, Hellenist) is used in Acts 6:1 and 9:29 for "Grecian [i.e., Greek-speaking] Jews" (NIV).

8. So, for example, Burge 2000: 343. Levinskaya (1996) demonstrates the presence of God-fearers in Jewish assemblies during the first-century Roman Empire. Cf. Josephus, *J.W.* 6.9.3 §§420–27; Acts 8:27–28.

9. The address κύριε (*kyrie*) is best rendered "sir" (Carson 1991: 437; Barrett 1978: 422). The verb ἰδεῖν (*idein*) here means "to visit with, to meet" (R. Brown 1966: 466) or "to have an interview with" (Carson 1991: 437; Barrett 1978: 422). Stibbe (1993: 136) contends that "the use of the verb 'see' points to the depth of their [the 'Greeks'] seeking." Moloney (1998: 352, 359) lists numerous instances in this Gospel where that verb is used with reference to "the acceptance or the refusal of Jesus' role as the revealer."

10. Philip is mentioned along with Andrew in 1:44 and 6:7–8 (cf. Mark 3:18). This may indicate that the two shared a close relationship. It may also suggest that they held

sible that the "Greeks" singled out Philip—and Andrew—because of their Greek names: although both were Jews, they were the only two members of the Twelve with Greek names (with the possible exception of Thomas [see commentary at 11:16]). If these "Greeks" were from the Decapolis or from the territories north or east of the Sea of Galilee (such as Batanea, Gaulanitis, or Trachonitis), they may have known (or found out) who among Jesus' disciples it was who came from the nearest town—Philip, who hailed from Bethsaida (located in Gaulanitis; see Barrett 1978: 422). Galilee, in fact, was more Hellenized than much of the rest of Palestine and bordered on pagan areas (cf. Matt. 4:15). Moreover, Philip, because of his origin, probably spoke Greek.[11]

12:23–26 The presence of the "Greeks" was directly responsible for Jesus' words in the present section (cf. 12:32; see Ridderbos 1997: 429), though Jesus transcends their immediate request in light of the circumstances before him (Carson 1991: 437; cf. Barrett 1978: 422; R. Brown 1966: 467). Jesus' assertion that his time "has come" is startling indeed. Up to this point, all references to Jesus' "time" in John's Gospel were future ("not yet": 2:4; 7:30; 8:20; cf. 7:6, 8). Now, the hour of Jesus' passion is said to be imminent (cf. 12:27; 13:1; 16:32; 17:1). The reference to the glorification of the Son of Man (12:23; cf. 1:51; 3:14; 8:28; 12:32–34) may well hark back to Isa. 52:13, where it is said that the Servant of the Lord "will be raised and lifted up and highly exalted" (LXX: δοξασθήσεται, *doxasthēsetai*). In pre-Christian usage, the glory of the Son of Man and his function of uniting heaven and earth are conceived in primarily apocalyptic terms (Dan. 7:13; cf. 1 Enoch 45–57, esp. 46, 48 [first century A.D.?]).

Jesus now plainly states that the glorification of the Son of Man will take place in his death: "Unless a grain of wheat falls into the ground and dies, it remains by itself. But if it dies, it bears much fruit." The principle of life through death is here illustrated by an agricultural example. In the rabbinic literature, the kernel of wheat is repeatedly used as a symbol of the eschatological resurrection of the dead. By argument "from the lesser to the greater," "If the grain of wheat, which is buried naked, sprouts forth in many robes, how much more so the righteous, who are buried in their raiment" (*b. Sanh.* 90b).[12] The cyclical pattern of sowing and reaping also constitutes a recurrent motif in ancient fertility cults and mystery religions. It is possible that the evangelist chose to record this saying of Jesus at least in part because this imagery would have resonated with his Hellenistic (as well as Jewish) audience.

---

a (minor?) leadership role among the disciples, though not comparable to Peter. See also 1:40 (Andrew) and 14:8 (Philip).

11. Philip's provenance from a bilingual region is cited by many commentators, including Ridderbos (1997: 427), Carson (1991: 436), Schnackenburg (1990: 2.382), R. Brown (1966: 470), Witherington (1995: 223), and Moloney (1998: 352).

12. Similarly, *Pirqe R. El.* 33. See also 1 Cor. 15:37.

The following verses (12:25–26) may be described as an "intermezzo" elucidating the relevance of 12:24 for the disciples (Ridderbos 1997: 431; cf. Mark 8:31–38; Matt. 16:21, 24–28; Luke 9:22–27).[13] "Whoever loves his life will lose it, yet whoever hates his life in this world will keep it for eternal life."[14] The love/hate contrast reflects Semitic idiom, pointing to preference rather than actual hatred.[15] The present statement is couched in Hebrew parallelism, taking the form of a *māšāl* with two antithetical lines, the basic message being that "loss of life is the condition for the emergence of new life" (Ridderbos 1997: 432; cf. Carson 1991: 438). Such wisdom sayings use paradox or hyperbole to teach a given truth in terms as sharp as possible (cf. *b. Taʿan.* 22a).[16]

"If anyone serves me, let him follow me, and where I am, there my servant will be as well" (cf. Mark 8:34 pars.; see Beasley-Murray 1999: 212). The imperative "let him follow me" carries within itself the double implications of peril and reward (Ridderbos 1997: 433). Being predicated upon the prospect of Jesus' imminent death, the saying alludes to the disciples' need for self-sacrifice, even to the point of martyrdom, with the expectation of eternal rewards. This teaching coheres closely with teacher-disciple relationships in first-century Palestine (Ridderbos 1997: 433). "Being a disciple required personal attachment to the teacher, because the disciple learned not merely from his teacher's words but much more from his practical observance of the Law. Thus the phrase 'to come after someone' is tantamount to 'being someone's disciple'" (Köstenberger 1998a: 119, esp. n. 90). What is more, the truth enunciated here extends beyond a disciple's earthly life to his or her eternal destiny (7:34, 36; 14:3; 17:24).

Attached to the requirements for true discipleship is the precious promise "If anyone serves me, the Father will honor him."[17] Jesus' disciples are to look for honor, not from others, but from God the Father. And this honor will sovereignly be bestowed upon Jesus' followers for committed and faithful service to *him*, Jesus. This is yet another instance of the close identification of Jesus and the Father in this Gospel. Serving Jesus will result in being honored by the Father, the one who sent Jesus and deals with people in accordance with the way they deal with

13. See the discussion of the relationship between 12:24 and the Synoptics in R. Brown 1966: 473–74, and of the relationship between 12:25 and the Synoptics in Schnackenburg 1990: 2.384.

14. Barrett (1978: 424) notes that εἰς (*eis*) in 12:25 has connotations of "with a view to" as well as "for the purpose of."

15. So, rightly, Carson 1991: 439; cf. Barrett 1978: 424; Beasley-Murray 1999: 211; R. Brown 1966: 467; Burge 2000: 344 n. 19. See Gen. 29:31, 33; Deut. 21:15; Matt. 6:24 par.; compare Luke 14:26 with Matt. 10:37.

16. As Carson (1991: 439) perceptively remarks, true discipleship involves not only denial of self but also the recognition of the importance of Christ.

17. Kruse (2003: 270) sees a resemblance between Jesus' pronouncement and 1 Sam. 2:30.

his Son. It goes without saying that the honor bestowed by the Father may well involve suffering or even martyrdom (as in the case of Peter [21:19]). Hence, even the honor bestowed by the Father upon Jesus' followers is different from the honor given by those in the world. Yet, because it is honor bestowed by the Father, it is sure and firm and lasting rather than the fleeting and precarious honor awarded in the eyes of humankind.

12:27–29 The present section illustrates "God's strength made perfect in weakness," presenting the "combined humiliation and glory of the earthly life of Jesus, both of which were to be consummated together in the cross" (Barrett 1978: 424–25). Paradoxically, "Jesus' death already belongs to his glorification, but is also the cause of his agitation" (Ridderbos 1997: 434).[18] As frequently in the events leading up to his crucifixion, Jesus' heart is troubled (see 11:33; 13:21; cf. 14:1, 27), whereby the term τα-ράσσω (tarassō, trouble) suggests strong inner turmoil and agitation.[19] One should not think of Jesus' emotion here as "a sense of dread that suddenly comes over" him, but rather as "the realization—which in the progress of his suffering (cf. 13:21) has repeatedly seized him—of the darkness of the path on which he is led by God" (Ridderbos 1997: 434). The scene is illumined by the Synoptic account of Jesus' struggle in Gethsemane (Matt. 26:38 par.) and by the depiction of Jesus offering up prayers and petitions "with loud cries and tears" in Hebrews (5:7).[20]

The ultimate sentiment of "What shall I say: 'Father, save me from this hour'? But for this very reason I came to this hour!"[21] matches

18. What is more, as Calvin (1961: 39) notes, "From this we learn better the enormity of sin, for which the heavenly Father exacted so dreadful a punishment from His only begotten Son. So we must learn that death was no pastime or game to Christ, but that He was cast into severest torments for our sake."

19. On the possible influence of Ps. 42 here and elsewhere in John's Gospel (11:33, 35, 37; 14:1–9, 27; 19:28), see the interchange between Beutler (1979, modifying Freed 1965b: 117–30) and Freed (1983a). See also Carson (1991: 440), who says that τετάρακται signifies "revulsion, horror, anxiety, agitation." This emphasis on the precrucifixion turmoil suffered by Jesus stands over against those who, in an effort to focus on the "glory" aspect of Jesus' death, overlook the real agony and anxiety he endured. So, rightly, Ridderbos (1997: 434), who argues, contra Witkamp, that 12:27a can "hardly refer to anything other than the natural human reaction in confrontation with death"; and Carson (1991: 439–40), who contends, contra E. Käsemann and G. C. Nicholson, that "even in John [with its realized eschatology], Jesus cannot contemplate the cross as a docetic actor, steeped in dispassionate unconcern." R. Brown (1966: 475) notes that here "we see the true humanity of the Johannine Jesus."

20. Though there is no need to suppose, as D. M. Smith (1999: 239) does, that "John and Hebrews knew a tradition about Jesus' agony without knowing the story as we find it in the Synoptics."

21. Morris (1995: 528) points out that the choice of verb may be significant here: "It may be important that the verb is 'say' rather than 'choose' or the like; there is no question about whether he will do the Father's will or not." On the address "Father," see commentary at 11:41.

Jesus' attitude in the Synoptic accounts of Gethsemane (Matt. 26:39, 42 pars.).[22] The deliberative subjunctive εἴπω (eipō, shall I say) and the strong adversative ἀλλά (alla, but)[23] both point "to a hypothetical rather than an actual prayer" that Jesus considers praying but rejects, expressing the "natural human shrinking from death" (Morris 1995: 528–29).[24] The saying underscores the genuineness of Jesus' humanity and points to his substitutionary sacrifice (2 Cor. 5:21). Jesus' unequivocal response, "Father, glorify your name!"[25] is in keeping with both OT theology, in which the glory of God is the ultimate goal of his salvific actions,[26] and the Fourth Evangelist's depiction of Jesus' motivation underlying his entire ministry (7:18; 8:29, 49–50; see Carson 1991: 440).[27] In particular, God is glorified by the Son's obedience (10:17) and by his exercise of delegated authority (14:13; 17:1b–2; see Ridderbos 1997: 435). Yet, though the ultimate object of glorification is the Father's name, this name is inextricably tied to the salvation-historical purposes pursued by the Father, supremely in and through his Son (Ridderbos 1997: 436).[28]

John 12:28 is one of only three instances during Jesus' earthly ministry when a heavenly voice attests to his identity.[29] In the present instance,

22. Commentators almost universally consider the present pericope to be the Johannine equivalent to the Synoptic account of Gethsemane (e.g., Morris 1995: 529; Barrett 1978: 424; R. Brown 1966: 475–76; Schnackenburg 1990: 2.386), though Ridderbos (1997: 435–36, pointing to Ps. 6) and Carson (1991: 440) rightly reject the notion that the Fourth Evangelist has simply refashioned the Synoptic Gethsemane scene to suit his purposes.

23. Ridderbos (1997: 435 n. 185) cites BDF §448.4 as evidence that ἀλλά after a question posed to oneself could be rendered more strongly as "No!" (cf. NRSV; Bultmann 1971: 427), though Ridderbos himself does not adopt this rendering. Cf. Whitacre 1999: 312, following Carson.

24. Contra Carson (1991: 440 [cf. Beasley-Murray 1999: 212; Burge 2000: 345]), who understands this to be a genuine question ("What shall I say?") and takes the following statement as a positive prayer ("Father, save me from this hour!"). As Morris (1995: 528) rightly notes, this interpretation, in an effort to do justice to the genuineness of Jesus' struggle, is unlikely in that it has Jesus utter a prayer and then immediately repudiate it. Moreover, even if the question is seen as rhetorical, this does not deny the reality of Jesus' struggle but simply shows how he overcomes succumbing to merely human reasoning.

25. On believing in Jesus' name and his having come in his Father's name, see 1:12; 5:43; 17:11.

26. E.g., Ps. 79:9; Isa. 63:14; 66:5; Ezek. 38:23.

27. Carson (1991: 441) finds it tempting to subsume this passage, and indeed all of Christ's redemptive work along with the new covenant, under Ezek. 36, particularly 36:22, 32. On Jesus' desire to glorify the Father, see further 13:31–32; 14:13; 17:1, 4–5 (cf. 15:8; 21:19). R. Brown (1966: 476 [cf. Schnackenburg 1990: 2.387]) sees 12:28 as analogous to the Lord's Prayer ("Hallowed be your name"); Beasley-Murray (1999: 207) regards it as the equivalent of Mark 14:36a.

28. Bultmann (1971: 427 n. 6) seems to draw the line too narrowly when he identifies the Father's name with the person of the Father himself and contends that "the Father is glorified precisely when he is acknowledged or named as Father."

29. The other two occasions are Jesus' baptism and his transfiguration: Matt. 3:17 pars.; 17:5 pars.; cf. 2 Pet. 1:17. Old Testament references to the "voice from heaven" include 1 Sam. 3:4, 6, 8; 1 Kings 19:13; Dan. 4:31–32. For other examples of a "heavenly voice"

the Father strengthens Jesus' resolve and calms his troubled soul[30] by affirming that his prayer has already been answered: "I have glorified it [i.e., the Father's name] and will glorify it again." Presumably, the former reference is to the entirety of Jesus' earthly ministry (including his signs), while the latter pertains supremely to the crucifixion (and related events).[31] The rabbis called the heavenly voice *bath qol* (literally, "daughter of a voice"). Since it was commonly believed that the prophetic office had ceased and would not be renewed until the onset of the messianic age, the *bath qol* was the most that could be expected in the interim.[32] The all-important difference between the NT instances of the heavenly voice and the rabbinic notion of the *bath qol* is that whereas the rabbis thought of the divine voice as a mere echo, the heavenly voice attesting Jesus is the voice of God himself.

Some people thought that it had thundered.[33] Hence, though not all heard the voice, all did hear a sound (Morris 1995: 530). Thunder was perceived to speak of the power and awesomeness of God (1 Sam. 12:18; 2 Sam. 22:14; Job 37:5). It was part of the theophany at Mount Sinai (Exod. 19:16, 19). God's intervention on behalf of his people is portrayed as a fierce thunderstorm sweeping down on his enemies (Ps. 18:7–15). In such instances, the power of the Creator is tied to that of Israel's redeemer (Exod. 9:28; 1 Sam. 7:10; Ps. 29:3; cf. Sir. 46:16–17). The manifestations of God's power also highlight the contrast between his omnipotence and the idols' powerlessness (Jer. 10:13 = 51:16). In NT times, light and sound accompanied the manifestation of the risen Christ to Saul (Acts 9:3–7; 22:6–9). In the Book of Revelation, peals of thunder emanate from God's throne (Rev. 4:5; 8:5; 11:19; 16:18; cf. 2 Esdr. [4 Ezra] 6:17).[34]

---

in Jewish literature, see 1 Enoch 65:4; 2 Esdr. (4 Ezra) 6:13, 17; 2 Bar. 13:1; 22:1; T. Levi 18:6. See also Acts 9:4–6; 11:7, 9–10; Rev. 10:4, 8; 11:12; 14:2, 13; 18:4; 19:5; 21:3. Evans (1981) notes the affinity of John 12:28 with Isa. 52–53.

30. For a similarly reassuring voice (prompting Paul to continue with his mission), see Acts 18:9–10.

31. Ridderbos (1997: 437) understands "I have glorified it" to refer to "the whole of Jesus' earthly activity." Carson (1991: 441) includes Jesus' earthly ministry, the incarnation, and the signs. Morris (1995: 530) seems to think that "I will glorify it" refers solely to the cross. Schnackenburg (1990: 2.388, citing Ps. 138:2; Ezek. 36:23; 38:23) takes the same phrase to point to the Son's exaltation and vindication: "He will justify the Son, raise him above the power of evil, and give him glory and saving power."

32. "Since the death of the last prophets, Haggai, Zechariah and Malachi, the Holy Spirit [of prophetic inspiration] departed from Israel; yet they were still able to avail themselves of the *bath qol*" (*b. Sanh.* 11a; cf. *t. Soṭah* 13.3; see Barrett 1970: 39–40; Dalman 1902: 204–5).

33. On the crowd, see commentary at 12:9, 12, 17.

34. The Sibylline Oracles speak of a "heavenly crash of thunder, the voice of God" (5:344–45). The notion of heaven answering human speech in thunder is also found in the ancient Greek world (Homer, *Odyssey* 20.97–104 [cited in Boring, Berger, and Colpe 1995: 292]).

Others said, "An angel has spoken to him." In OT times, angels (or the angel of the Lord) spoke to Hagar (Gen. 21:17), Abraham (Gen. 22:11), Moses (Acts 7:38), Elijah (2 Kings 1:15), and Daniel (Dan. 10:4–11). In the NT, angels are said to minister to Jesus (Matt. 4:11; Luke 22:43; cf. Matt. 26:53), and at one point it was surmised that Paul, too, might have heard an angelic voice (Acts 23:9). Angelic voices are commonplace in the Book of Revelation (e.g., 4:1; 5:2; 6:1). Regarding Jesus' statement "This voice has come not for my benefit, but for yours," see John 11:42. Similarly, compare the voice at the transfiguration (Matt. 17:5 pars.).

Calvin (1961: 41–42) aptly comments on the contemporary relevance of the present account by lamenting,

> It was a monstrous thing that the multitude was obtuse to so plain a miracle. Some were deaf, and caught what God had pronounced distinctly only as a confused sound. Others were less dull, but yet detracted greatly from the majesty of the divine voice by pretending that its author was an angel. But the same thing is common today [in Calvin's day as well as ours]. God speaks plainly enough in the Gospel, in which there is also displayed a power and energy of the Spirit which should shake heaven and earth. But many are as cold towards the teaching as if it came only from a mortal man, and others think God's Word to be a barbarous stammering, as if it were nothing but thunder.

When the crowds differ over whether the heavenly voice was the **12:30–33** sound of thunder or that of an angel, Jesus responds by pointing out that the voice came not for his sake but for theirs. The dynamic is similar to 11:41–42, where the purpose is for people to believe that the Father sent Jesus. In the present instance, whether or not the crowd was expected to have heard the contents of the divine utterance, they were to construe the sound as a divine attestation to Jesus' messianic mission.[35] In his response, Jesus sketches the significance of the hour: "now" (that "the light" is about to be snuffed out) is the time for judgment of this world (see 3:18–19; 9:39); "now" also the "ruler" or "prince of this world"[36] will be driven out (cf. 16:11; 1 John 5:19).[37]

---

35. Schnackenburg (1990: 2.390) here sees Jesus commenting on people's incomprehension and urging them to believe. Ridderbos (1997: 437), on the other hand, argues that Jesus refers to the sound of the voice, not the words, maintaining that Jesus "is not holding the crowd answerable for what it could not understand." Neither Barrett (1978: 426) nor R. Brown (1966: 477) seems able to reconcile the apparent tension in the voice being *for* the crowd yet unintelligible *to* the crowd. Carson (1991: 442) offers four points, most importantly that even if the crowd had not understood the voice, the voice itself should be a signal of divine activity.

36. "Prince" is more literally "ruler" (ἄρχων, *archōn*). See 14:30 and especially 16:11, the only other instance of "the prince of this world" in the NT; see also Luke 10:18. Similar terminology is also found in the Pauline writings (2 Cor. 4:4; 6:15; Eph. 2:2; 6:12).

37. There are several Jewish (though no rabbinic) parallels to the phrase "prince of the world" with reference to Satan (Segal 1981). The title "prince of this world" occurs

Yet, once "lifted up,"[38] Jesus will draw "all people" (not "all things" [see additional note]) to himself (the dynamic envisioned harks back to 6:37, 44, which speak of those who come to Jesus never ever being driven out and the Father drawing them [Beasley-Murray 1986: 76]).[39] Hence, the world's judgment precedes "all people's" salvation (Carson 1991: 443). Then, from heaven, the place to which he returns by way of the cross, the exalted Lord will draw people to himself, now that the power of sin, sickness, death, and the devil will have all been overcome (Ridderbos 1997: 440). At the present time, however, misunderstanding regarding Jesus' true identity still persists (12:34).

The double νῦν (*nyn*, now) in Jesus' response in 12:31 is most striking, harking back to Jesus' statement in 12:23 (in response to the Greeks' coming) that the hour has come for the Son of Man to be glorified.[40] Another link between 12:23 and 12:31 is the "Gentile connection." What is merely intimated in Jesus' evasive response to the Greeks in the earlier passage is now spelled out in greater detail (Carson 1991: 444; Barrett 1978: 427): it is only subsequent to his cross-death (the third link: compare 12:24 with 12:33) that Jesus will draw "all people," including

in relation to Beliar in Mart. Isa. (1:3; 10:29; cf. 2:4). In Jubilees, "Mastema" is called "chief of the spirits" or simply "prince" (e.g., 10:8; 11:5, 11). More generally, the Qumran texts contain the notion that the "dominion of Belial" extends to his entire "lot" (see 1QS 1:18; 2:5, 19; 1QM 1:5; 4:2; 13:2, 4, 11–12; 14:9; 15:3; CD 12:2). However, unlike extensive speculation in Second Temple literature regarding the demonic supernatural, John is much more restrained, limiting his treatment of Satan exclusively to his role in the plot against Jesus leading to the latter's crucifixion.

38. The term "lifted up" (see 3:14; 8:28) is likely chosen by John because of its potential double reference to physical lifting up as well as figurative lifting up, that is, exaltation (see esp. Isa. 52:13: see also R. Brown 1966: 146, 478; cf. Acts 2:33; 5:31; Luke 9:51; Phil. 2:9; Heb. 1:3; 1 Tim. 3:16).

39. The term "draw" brings out the truth that people do not come to Christ on their own initiative; only as God works in people and draws them can they come to him (Morris 1995: 531). The phrase "all people" does not imply universalism (the ultimate salvation of all [see commentary at 1:9]). Rather, the approach of Gentiles prompts Jesus' statement that after his glorification he will draw "all kinds of people," even Gentiles, to himself. For this interpretation and a brief discussion of the textual issues, see Köstenberger 1999a: 194. See also Ridderbos (1997: 439–40), who provides the glosses "the entire human world" and "'all' without distinction of people or race"; and Morris (1995: 531–32), who struggles but then interprets πάντας (*pantas*) to refer to "all kinds of men." In addition, Carson (1991: 443) sees a parallel with Rev. 12:11a and takes issue with the adversative NIV rendering, "But I, when I am lifted up" (changed in the TNIV to "And I, when I am lifted up").

40. Ridderbos (1997: 439) rightly notes that this is more than a mere proleptic reference to a future event, which effectively reduces 12:31b to a "prophetic vision" (contra Bultmann [1971: 431], who argues that the "nows" of 12:31 necessitate the purgation of traditional Christian eschatology). As Carson (1991: 444–45) aptly notes, "The end times have begun already. It is not that there is nothing reserved for the consummation; rather, it is that the decisive step is about to be taken in the death/exaltation of Jesus." See also R. Brown 1966: 477.

Gentiles, to himself (cf. 10:16; 11:51–52).[41] Yet, the anticipation of the inclusion of the Gentiles in the orbit of salvation also indicates that the Jewish rejection of the Messiah has all but reached its full measure. The crowd's final messianic misunderstanding—the law's portrayal of the Messiah as eternal[42]—is met with merely a faint exhortation on Jesus' part for them to "believe in the light" while they have it in order to become "sons of light."

In the present pericope, the Fourth Evangelist, just prior to Jesus' passion, crystallizes the spiritual dynamic of Jesus' crucifixion, resurrection, and exaltation. He reaches back all the way to the "great antithesis" between God and Satan, which is epitomized in Jesus' coming to "destroy the devil's works" (cf. 1 John 3:8). This power struggle has now entered its decisive stage (Kovacs 1995). What is at stake "is nothing less than the transfer of power over the present God-hating world into the hands of the Son of Man" (Ridderbos 1997: 438). The "coming of the ruler of this world" is the time of the devil's final assault on Jesus as God's Sent One (13:2, 27; 14:30; cf. Luke 22:31, 53), the world's final hour in its hostility and unbelief. Yet Satan fails, because with the crucifixion he has lost all grounds of appeal against sinful humanity; redemption has been achieved through Jesus' vicarious sacrifice (Ridderbos 1997: 439). Paradoxically, at the cross the world and its ruler are judged, while Jesus is glorified and salvation is procured for all.[43]

The people place their own expectation based on their scriptural understanding in stark contrast to Jesus: "The Christ remains forever."[44] Palestinian Judaism in Jesus' day generally thought of the Messiah as triumphant and frequently envisioned his reign to be without end in the future. Such hopes were rooted in the Son of David, of whom it was said that God would "establish the throne of his kingdom forever" (2 Sam. 7:13; cf. John 12:13, 15). This prospect was nurtured in both Psalms (e.g., 61:6–7; 89:3–4, 35–37) and prophetic literature (Isa. 9:7; Ezek. 37:25; cf. Dan. 2:44; 7:13–14). It was affirmed also in Second

12:34–36

41. The evangelist editorializes that "this was to show the kind of death Jesus was going to die" (with σημαίνων [sēmainōn, indicating] serving as a participle indicating purpose [Wallace 1996: 635]). "Kind of death" in the first instance refers to crucifixion (as opposed to, e.g., stoning) but also hints at the fact that Jesus' death is also "the pathway to his glorification, indeed an integral part of it" (Carson 1991: 444). The same phrase is used regarding Peter's eventual martyr's death in 21:19 (Köstenberger 1998b: 154–61, 168). It occurs frequently in connection with Greek oracles (e.g., Plutarch, *De Pythiae oraculis* 404.D.10), but also in regard to the meaning of names or prophecy (Josephus, *Ant.* 1.19.8 §308; 7.9.5 §214).

42. Whereby "the law" may refer to the Hebrew Scriptures in their entirety rather than merely to the five books of Moses (cf. 10:34; 15:25).

43. On Jesus' exaltation and glorification, see the excursus in Schnackenburg 1990: 2.398–410.

44. Note the emphatic personal pronouns ἡμεῖς (hēmeis, we) and σύ (sy, you) (Morris 1995: 532).

Temple literature (Ps. Sol. 17:4; Sib. Or. 3:49–50; 1 Enoch 62:14) and at the outset of Luke's Gospel (1:33).[45] Perhaps the closest parallel to the present passage is Ps. 89:37, where David's seed is said to "remain forever" (LXX: εἰς τὸν αἰῶνα μενεῖ, *eis ton aiōna menei*).[46] Notably, this psalm is interpreted messianically in both the NT (Acts 13:22; Rev. 1:5) and rabbinic sources (*Gen. Rab.* 97, linking Gen. 49:10, 2 Sam. 7:16, and Ps. 89:29), but probably reference is made not so much to any one passage as it is to the general thrust of OT messianic teaching (Barrett 1978: 427). Elsewhere in John, people express the expectation of a Davidic Messiah born at Bethlehem (7:42) and of a hidden Messiah to be revealed at the proper time (7:27; cf. 1:26). As to the juxtaposition of the terms "Christ" and "Son of Man," it is unclear whether Palestinian Jews in Jesus' day, whose concept of the Messiah was bound up largely with the expectation of the Davidic king, also linked the Coming One with the apocalyptic figure of the Son of Man (cf. Dan. 7:13–14; see de Jonge, *TDNT* 9:509–17).[47]

In response to people's messianic speculation, Jesus urges that this is the time for action, not idle conjecture, for they will have the light with them for just "a little while" longer. The closest verbal parallel to "a little while" is 7:33 (χρόνον μικρόν, *chronon mikron*).[48] In 16:16–19, Jesus predicts that "in a little while" his disciples will not see him, and then "after a little while" they will see him again, referring to the three-day interval between his crucifixion and resurrection. In response to the crowd's messianic misunderstanding, Jesus utters this final, almost laconic, exhortation: "Move about while you have the light, so that darkness may not overtake you; in fact, whoever moves about in darkness does not know where he is going. While you have the light, believe in the light, in order that you may become sons of light."

45. Carson (1991: 445) cites most of these passages and adds Ps. 72:17; 1 Enoch 49:1; and he contrasts 2 Esdr. (4 Ezra) 7:28–29.

46. So, rightly, Schnackenburg 1990: 2.395. For a summary and bibliographic references, see Köstenberger 1998b: 95 n. 180.

47. Regarding the people's question "Who is this 'Son of Man'?" see commentary at 1:51 and at 9:35–36. Ridderbos (1997: 441) takes the question to pertain to the nature of the Son of Man ("What kind of Son of man are you speaking of?") rather than his identity. Morris (1995: 532) thinks that the crowd asks what the function of the Son of Man is and whether or not he is one and the same as the Messiah. Carson (1991: 445) notes that though four months earlier the Jewish authorities were unclear about whether or not Jesus used the "Son of Man" title messianically, the less knowledgeable crowd, already ripe with messianic expectations, made the "Son of Man = Messiah" connection. To the contrary, if taken at face value, the crowd's question reveals not understanding, but misunderstanding, even ignorance, or at least confusion (so, rightly, Morris 1995: 533: "To the end they remain confused and perplexed, totally unable to appreciate the magnitude of the gift offered to them and the significance of the Person who offers it").

48. Other statements referring to the limited time that Jesus will be present among the Jews or with his disciples include 9:4–5 (cf. 11:9–10); 12:8; 13:33; 14:19.

Although Jesus does not answer the crowd's question directly, the discerning reader of the Gospel understands that he already has: his eternality is a function of his impending glorification (Carson 1991: 446). R. Brown (1966: 479) rightly notes that people's need was not so much to come to terms with the exact nature of the Son of Man but rather to face up to the judgment associated with him. Thus Jesus, in a way, really *does* address the crowd's deeper need at that hour: in light of the brevity of time, they must believe while this is still possible; messianic speculation will soon give way to the harsh realities of crucifixion and judgment. To be sure, the Messiah remains forever, "but it is only the incarnation of the Word and the descent of the Son of man in and from which the Messiah's 'remaining forever' can be known and understood" (Ridderbos 1997: 442).

The reference to "the light" harks back particularly to 9:4 and 11:10 and provides an inclusion with the references to Jesus as the light in the prologue. The term "move about" or "walk" (περιπατέω, *peripateō*) frequently occurs in John's Gospel in a figurative sense in conjunction with light and darkness.[49] Similar terminology can be found in the Qumran literature (1QS 3:20–21; cf. 4:11). The notion of "walking in the light/darkness" in John resembles the thought in the DSS that there are two ways in which people may walk: light and darkness. Probably both John and the DSS hark back independently to OT terminology, especially Isaiah (e.g., 50:10 [see Morris 1995: 533]; 9:2, quoted in Matt. 4:16). The important difference between John and the DSS is that the former calls people to "believe in the light," while the latter assume that the members of the community are already "sons of light."[50]

After Jesus said these things, he left and hid himself from them (see commentary at 8:59; see also 7:4, 10; 18:20). The present passage constitutes a dramatic illustration of the passing of the light (R. Brown 1966: 479) and an acted parable of the judicial warning that Jesus had just pronounced (Carson 1991: 447). What had begun with Jesus' prophetic visitation of the temple, when the temple area was cleared in a predictive display of divine judgment, now closes with an ominous reference to Jesus' self-concealment. Thus, the incarnate Word, who had come into the world to give a full account of the Father (1:18), concludes his revelatory work. The reference to Jesus' withdrawal thereby serves as a climax to the series of preceding warnings and as a transition to the

49. See 8:12; 11:9–10; cf. 1 John 1:6–7; 2:11; see also John 1:4–5, 7–9; 3:19–21; 9:4.
50. See Morris 1995: 534. "Son of . . ." reflects Hebrew idiom; the expression "sons of light," however, is not attested in rabbinic literature. A "son of light" displays the moral qualities of "light" and has become a follower of the "light" (cf. Luke 16:8; 1 Thess. 5:5; Eph. 5:8). The phrase is also common in the DSS, where it designates members of the Qumran community (e.g., 1QS 1:9; 2:16; 3:13, 20–21, 24–25; 4:11; 1QM 1:1, 3, 9, 11, 13). "Born of light" occurs in 1 Enoch 108:11. See also T. Naph. 2:10.

evangelist's theological reflections on unbelief that conclude the first major section of the Gospel (Carson 1991: 447).

Additional Note

12:32. The reading πάντας, "all people" ($\mathfrak{P}^{75\text{vid}}$ A B), is to be preferred over the reading πάντα, "all things" ($\mathfrak{P}^{66}$ ℵ* vg), primarily owing to internal contextual evidence. Not only is cosmic reconciliation not a major theme in John (contrast Paul), but also in the present instance Jesus clearly addresses the inclusion of Gentiles in the orbit of salvation, which makes the reading "draw all people"—including Gentiles—all but assured (so, rightly, Beasley-Murray [1999: 205 n. o] and the majority of commentators).

2. The Signs of the Messiah Rejected by the Old Covenant Community (12:37–50)

The final section of the first major unit of John's Gospel provides the denouement of Jesus' public ministry to the Jews, consisting of the Fourth Evangelist's putting of the Jewish rejection of the Messiah in a scriptural context (12:37–43) and a summary of Jesus' message (12:44–50) (Ridderbos 1997: 449; Schnackenburg 1990: 2.411).[1] The latter section almost has the feel of "an epilogue rather than a speech within the main structure of the play" (Barrett 1978: 429). As such, it matches the opening prologue and provides closure to the first half of the Gospel. Particularly pronounced in both cases is the note of failure, not on Jesus' part, but on that of the Jews (1:11; 12:37–43). This sets the stage for Jesus' work with the representatives of his new messianic community, the Twelve, in the ensuing section.

Exegesis and Exposition

[37]Yet even though he had performed such great signs before them, they were not believing in him, [38]so that the statement by the prophet Isaiah might be fulfilled which he uttered: "Lord, who has believed our report? And to whom has the arm of the Lord been revealed?" [39]For this reason they could not believe, because, again, Isaiah said, "He has blinded their eyes and hardened their hearts, so that they may not see with their eyes nor understand with their hearts and turn, and I heal them." [41]Isaiah said these things because he saw his [Jesus?] glory, and he spoke concerning him. [42]Even so, many even of the rulers believed in him, but on account of the Pharisees they were not confessing [him], so that

---

1. For a discussion of 12:37–50 in the context of the Johannine lawsuit motif (cf. Isa. 40–55), see Lincoln 2000: 105–10. Keener (2003: 882) notes that many find in 12:37–43 a theological summary of people's responses to Jesus' public ministry and in 12:44–50 an anthology of representative sayings. Whitacre (1999: 326) suggests that 12:37–43 emphasizes Jesus' deeds, and 12:44–50 his words (also adducing Moses' final words in Deut. 32:45–47 as a parallel). Both Ridderbos (1997: 443) and Schnackenburg (1990: 2.411) stress the relevance of this section for the evangelist's own day and the historical distance from which this section was presumably written. This surely is true but should not be exaggerated. Schnackenburg (1990: 2.421) also provides a defense of Johannine authorship against Boismard, who claims that 12:44–50 is non-Johannine. Bultmann (1971: ix), in a hardly defensible move, relocates both 12:34–36 and 12:44–50 to John 8, with only 12:37–43 remaining in the traditional position.

they might not be put out of the synagogue. ⁴³For they loved honor from people more than honor from God.

⁴⁴But Jesus cried out and said, "Whoever believes in me does not believe in me but in the one who sent me, ⁴⁵and whoever sees me sees the one who sent me. ⁴⁶I have come into the world as light, so that everyone who believes in me might not remain in darkness. ⁴⁷And if anyone hears my words and does not keep them, I do not condemn him; for I did not come to judge the world, but to save the world. ⁴⁸Whoever rejects me and does not receive my words, he has one who judges him: the message I have spoken—it will judge him on the last day, ⁴⁹because I did not speak of my own accord, but the Father who sent me himself has given me the command what I should say and what I should speak. ⁵⁰And I know that his command is eternal life. So what I am saying—just as the Father told me, this is what I say."

12:37–41   "Yet even though he had performed such great signs before them, they were not believing in him."[2] The Jews' failure to believe in Jesus' day is reminiscent of the unbelief of the wilderness generation, which had witnessed God's mighty acts of power (displayed through Moses) at the exodus (Deut. 29:2–4; see Carson 1991: 447; Ridderbos 1997: 444; R. Brown 1966: 485). No greater sign than the raising of Lazarus—the seventh, climactic sign in John—could be given.[3] And though faith apart from signs is preferable (20:29), faith based on signs is still better than no faith at all (2:11; 10:38; 14:11). The Jews' continued opposition to Jesus confirms them in their obduracy. However, as John makes clear in the verses to follow, rather than thwart God's purposes, the Jews' rejection of their Messiah actually fulfilled Scripture.

"So that the statement by the prophet Isaiah might be fulfilled." This first instance of the formula "this was to fulfill" (ἵνα . . . πληρωθῇ, hina . . . plērōthē) leads off a whole series of OT quotations that stress the fulfillment of prophecy in the events of Jesus' life, especially those surrounding his crucifixion.[4] The first passage cited is Isa. 53:1 LXX (cf. Rom. 10:16). In the original context, reference is made to the Servant of the Lord, who was rejected by the people but exalted by God (cf. Isa.

---

2. Οὐκ ἐπίστευον (ouk episteuon, they were not believing), using the imperfect tense, highlights the progressive nature of the Jews' unbelief (Ridderbos 1997: 443). Croteau (2002: 65–66) plausibly contends that the antecedents of the reference to people's unbelief in 12:37 include all previous instances of unbelief in the narrative, including 2:23; 4:45–48; 6:14; 7:31; 8:30–31; 11:47; 12:11 (viewed negatively by Croteau).

3. Thus, while τοσαῦτα (tosauta, so many, so great) may refer to both quantity and quality (Morris 1995: 536 n. 103), the latter is more likely in the present instance, since John selected only a few of Jesus' most striking signs and recorded them in vivid detail (so, rightly, Schnackenburg 1990: 2.413).

4. See 13:18; 15:25; 17:12; 19:24, 36. Cf. Evans 1982a; 1987: esp. 225–26. The formula is also found frequently in the Gospel of Matthew (1:22; 2:15, 17, 23; 4:14; 8:17; 12:17; 13:35; 21:4; 27:9).

52:13–15). In John, the verse is applied to Jesus the Messiah, who is that promised Servant, and to the rejection of his message and signs ("arm of the Lord") by the Jews.[5] Hence, Jewish rejection of God's words is nothing new in salvation history—just as Isaiah's message had been rejected, so was Jesus' (Ridderbos 1997: 444).

"For this reason they could not believe" (cf. 10:26). The present statement is unambiguously predestinarian yet compatibilist, including elements of human responsibility as well (Carson 1991: 447; Barrett 1978: 431).[6] In the scriptural quote, faith and the divine activity (the "arm of the Lord") are connected: "even unbelief has some place in the purpose of God" (Morris 1995: 536). John here accounts for the fact (surprising for some) that the Jews, God's chosen old covenant people, failed to accept their Messiah. His answer, far from implying that they are not responsible for their refusal to believe (19:11–12, 15), points to the ultimate purpose as God's judicial hardening of the Jewish people (similar to Pharaoh [cf. Rom. 9:17]). The quotation is from Isa. 6:10 (here closer to the Hebrew than to the LXX), a text frequently cited in the NT (cf. Matt. 13:13–15 pars.; Acts 28:26–27).[7]

In the wake of the two Isaianic quotes in 12:38 and 12:40, the evangelist concludes that "Isaiah saw Jesus' glory" (cf. 8:56). In light of the preceding quotation of Isa. 6:10, some say that the background for the present statement is the call narrative in Isaiah 6.[8] Yet though αὐτοῦ (autou, his) probably refers to Jesus,[9] John does not actually say that Isaiah saw *Jesus*, but that he saw Jesus' glory. Hence, it is not necessary to conclude that the evangelist believed that Isaiah saw "the pre-existent Christ" (Schnackenburg 1990: 2.416; cf. Talbert 1992: 180; D. M. Smith

5. The phrase "arm of the Lord" frequently serves as a figurative expression for God's power in the OT. See Deut. 5:15; Isa. 40:10; 51:9; 52:10; 63:5; cf. Luke 1:51.

6. The balancing emphasis is provided by Ridderbos (1997: 444–45), who notes, "Unbelief is not thereby blamed on God in a predestinarian sense, but is rather described as a punishment from God." Carson (1991: 448–49), too, engages in theodicy when he writes, "God's judicial hardening is not presented as the capricious manipulation of an arbitrary potentate . . . but as a holy condemnation of a guilty people who are condemned to do and be what they themselves have chosen."

7. For a helpful comparison and brief discussion of the MT, LXX, and Johannine forms of Isa. 6:10, see R. Brown 1966: 486. The Hebrew original moves from heart to ears to eyes and then back from sight to hearing to understanding. John does not refer to hearing but instead focuses on sight, probably owing to his mention of Jesus' signs in 12:37 (Carson 1991: 449; cf. Barrett 1978: 431). Keener (2003: 833) detects verbal ties between the quote of Isa. 6:9–10 (John 12:40) and John 9:39–41 (blindness) and 4:47; 5:13 (healing). The Jews considered the heart to be the seat of mental as well as physical life (cf. Mark 8:17–21).

8. This is confirmed by the Targumim: Tg. Ps.-J. on Isa. 6:1 changes "I saw the Lord" to "I saw the glory of the Lord," and the same Targum changes "the King, the Lord of hosts" in Isa. 6:5 to "the glory of the shekinah of the eternal King, the Lord of hosts" (first century B.C.–third century A.D.; see Carson 1991: 449).

9. This is the view of the majority of major commentators: e.g., Carson 1991: 449; Morris 1995: 538; Ridderbos 1997: 445; R. Brown 1966: 484.

1999: 244) or that he saw Jesus "in some pre-incarnate fashion" (Carson 1991: 449).[10] Rather, Isaiah foresaw that God was pleased with a suffering Servant who would be "raised and lifted up and highly exalted" (52:13), yet who was "pierced for our transgressions" and "bore the sins of many" (53:5, 12) (see esp. Evans 1987). Hence, Isaiah knew that God's glory would be revealed through a suffering Messiah—something deemed impossible by the crowds (John 12:34). Like Abraham, Isaiah saw Jesus' "day" (cf. John 8:56, 58).

12:42–43   Just as the sweeping indictment of 1:10–11 makes way to the positive examples of 1:12–13, the indictment of 12:37–41 is followed by the exceptions of 12:42 (Carson 1991: 450). Against the dark backdrop of 12:37–41, the evangelist notes that many even among the leaders (i.e., the Sanhedrin) believed in Jesus. This presumably included Nicodemus (3:1; 7:50–51; 19:39) and Joseph of Arimathea (19:38; cf. Mark 15:43; Luke 23:50). Even at this advanced stage of the plot against Jesus, opposition toward him was by no means monolithic. Yet the evangelist immediately qualifies what kind of faith these "believers" possessed. Fearing synagogue expulsion by the Pharisees, they did not confess Jesus openly (cf. 9:22);[11] for they loved honor from people more than honor from God (see 5:41–42, 44; 7:18; cf. Rom. 2:29).[12] The expulsion many feared would indeed have been exceedingly traumatic for any Sanhedrin member, amounting to virtual social and religious ostracism.[13] The description "crypto-believers" within the council fits the later characterization of Joseph of Arimathea in John's Gospel as "a disciple of Jesus, but secretly, because of fear of the Jews" (19:38). The

---

10. However, the notion of a preexistent Christ who was present and active in the history of Israel is found elsewhere in the NT (1 Cor. 10:4; see also Philo, *Dreams* 1.39 §§229–30, which, commenting on Gen. 31:13 and God's appearing to OT Israel, says, "Here it gives the title of 'God' to His chief Word"), and later interpreters, using texts such as Sir. 48:24–25, speculated that the prophet looked into the future and saw the life and glory of Jesus (see Ascension of Isaiah [second century A.D.]). Elsewhere the evangelist affirms the impossibility of a direct vision of God (cf. 1:18; 5:37; 6:46).

11. In conjunction with the chief priests, the Pharisees are consistently shown in the Gospel to function as the most influential body in Jewish national life (7:32, 45; 11:47, 57; 18:3). Note the imperfect tense in οὐχ ὡμολόγουν (*ouch hōmologoun*, they were not confessing), conveying these "believers' . . . continuing failure to confess" (Morris 1995: 538 n. 122; though Morris's overall analysis is hampered by use of an outmoded Greek verbal theory).

12. Michaels (1989: 234) detects in the present statement "a sense of tragedy, as if [the narrator was] aware that there were people like that in the synagogues of his own city." The term rendered "praise" in the NIV (though note the change to "glory" in the TNIV) is elsewhere in John translated "glory," which may tie in the present reference with John's use of the same word in 12:41. Examples of imperfect faith in this Gospel include 2:23; 4:48; 8:30–31.

13. Barrett (1978: 433) aptly notes that these individuals allowed "the decision of faith to be affected by a desire for personal security," yet that "the desire for the praise of men is a form of idolatry."

present verse serves as a reminder that living in the midst of mounting tension between Jesus and the Jews could endanger the disciples' very lives (cf. 15:18–16:4, esp. 16:2).

The final indictment of the Jews' unbelief in 12:37–43 is followed by a sort of epilogue (matching the prologue; see also the close resemblance to 3:16–21), which brings closure to the first major section of this Gospel and consists of a final appeal made by Jesus. Morris (1995: 539 n. 125, faulting the NIV rendering "then," which seems to connect the pericope immediately with what precedes) plausibly suggests that the present words may have been spoken at an earlier time and inserted here as an appropriate conclusion. This is suggested particularly by the reference to Jesus "being hidden" in 12:36 (see also R. Brown 1966: 490). In a somewhat stylized fashion, the evangelist here provides "a deft summary of many strands in his [Jesus'] teaching" (Carson 1991: 451) in form of a final appeal.[14] Nevertheless, this does not mean that the address is unhistorical (Burge [2000: 349] plausibly suggests the temple precincts as a possible setting), as is suggested especially by the strong verb κραυγάζω (*kraugazō*, cry out), a term that frequently denotes loud shouting or crying out with intensity.[15]

The principal notion that Jesus rejects is that he came on his own initiative and authority and for his own glory. Once again invoking a common Jewish maxim (yet transcending it [Carson 1991: 451–52]), Jesus asks people to believe in him, not in his own right, but as the emissary of the Father (12:44; see commentary at 5:23; Ridderbos 1997: 448). In fact, the entire closing section presupposes Jewish teaching on representation, according to which the emissary represents the one who sends him (see 14:9; cf. *m. Ber.* 5.5).[16] Once again, too, Jesus claims to have come as light into the world, to deliver anyone who believes in him from darkness (see 1:4, 5, 9; 3:19; 8:12; 9:5, 39).[17] The purpose of his coming is not condemnation (cf. 3:16–17; see Carson 1991: 452; Ridderbos 1997: 448) but transformation and deliverance from the wrath of God and the sentence of eternal death, which rest on humanity as a whole (Schnackenburg 1990: 2.422). Hence, one ought not to hold Jesus directly responsible for one's judgment; it is

---

14. Stibbe (1993: 140) views 12:44–50 as "a dramatic soliloquy, a form of discourse in which the hero voices his thoughts on an empty stage." According to Stibbe, this "anticipates much of the farewell discourses, where the reader *overhears* the Revealer speaking or praying in apparent isolation."

15. For other occurrences in this Gospel, see 1:15 (the Baptist) and 7:28, 37 (Jesus).

16. For a detailed account of the Jewish legal theory of envoys, see Rengstorf, *TDNT* 1:414–20.

17. Ridderbos (1997: 448 n. 128) and Morris (1995: 540) note that both "I" and "light" are emphatic.

the word that Jesus spoke that will condemn the unbeliever on the last day (cf. 5:45; 7:51).[18]

Jesus did not speak of his own accord (see Deut. 18:18–19; John 5:19–47; 7:17; 10:18) but rather took his cue from "the Father who sent" him (see commentary at 4:32–34). This is why Jesus' words are so definitive in pronouncing judgment on unbelief: in reality, they are words of the Father (Ridderbos 1997: 449; Carson 1991: 452).[19] For his part, Jesus knows that the Father's command represents eternal life (cf. 5:39; 6:68).[20] This is in keeping with the Book of Deuteronomy, in which God's commandments provide the framework within which Israel is to fulfill its calling as a people set apart for God (e.g., Deut. 8:3; 32:46–47). In later years, Jews commonly saw the law of Moses as the source of life (Deut. 32:45–47; cf. John 5:39), which, rightly understood, was unobjectionable (cf. Mark 10:17–19; Luke 10:25–28). The problem, however, was that no one could keep the law perfectly.

In closing, Jesus reiterates that he has spoken precisely as instructed by the Father.[21] By subordinating his person to his message, Jesus cuts off "any notion that in asking people to believe his words he is seeking to gratify his own ego, claiming something beyond the authority that the Father has given him" (Ridderbos 1997: 449). As Barrett (1978: 435) aptly sums up, "Jesus is not a figure of independent greatness; he is the Word of God, or he is nothing at all. In the first part of the gospel, which here closes, Jesus lives in complete obedience to the Father; in the second part he will die in the same obedience." By implication, the same unquestioning obedience must characterize Jesus' followers who are commissioned at the end of the Gospel by the paradigmatic Sent One become sender (20:21).

---

18. This emphasis is in keeping with instances in Second Temple literature, where the law seems to take a more active part in the process of judging (2 Bar. 48:47; 2 Esdr. [4 Ezra] 13:30–35; Wis. 9:3; cf. Philo, *Mos.* 2.10 §53). John 12:48–50 contains echoes of the Book of Deuteronomy (cf. Deut. 18:19; 31:19, 26; see O'Connell 1960; cf. R. Brown 1966: 491–92). There, it is God who takes vengeance on those who refuse to hear; in the Targumim, it is God's *memra*, or word: "And the man who does not listen to his words which he [the future prophet] will speak in the name *of my memra*, I *in my memra will be avenged of him*" (Tg. Neof. on Deut. 18:19); "*my memra* will take revenge on him" (Tg. Ps.-J. on Deut. 18:19). For "the last day," see 6:39–40, 44; 11:24 (the phrase, with "day" in the singular, does not occur elsewhere in the NT).

19. The emphatic αὐτός (*autos*, he) is noted by Morris (1995: 541), who also points to the perfects δέδωκεν (*dedōken*, he has given [12:49]) and εἴρηκεν (*eirēken*, he has told [12:50]) as underscoring the permanence of Jesus' message.

20. The TNIV's "leads to" eternal life perhaps is less than ideal (cf. Morris 1995: 541).

21. "Just what the Father has told me to say" reflects common Johannine parlance (see 8:28, 40; 14:31; 15:15).

III. The Book of Glory: Jesus' Preparation of the New Messianic Community and His Passion (13:1–20:31)

Chapters 13 through 20 constitute the second major unit in John's Gospel. They narrate the final days of Jesus' earthly ministry, including his cross-death and resurrection. In chapter 13, the new messianic community is cleansed (both literally and figuratively), first through the foot-washing (13:1–17) and then through the departure of Judas the betrayer (13:18–30). The farewell discourse proper (delivered to the Twelve minus Judas) comprises 13:31–16:33 and contains Jesus' final instructions to his followers. Chapter 17 features Jesus' final prayer, in which the sent Son reports to the Father who sent him that his mission has been accomplished (anticipating his cross-death in 19:30). Chapter 20 narrates Jesus' encounter with Mary Magdalene (20:1–18) and Jesus' appearances to the Eleven (first without Thomas [20:19–25] and then with him present [20:26–29]) and provides a preliminary conclusion (20:30–31).

The opening words of chapter 13 signal a distinctive shift in perspective over against the first half of John's Gospel. In light of the Messiah's final rejection by the old covenant community (12:37–42), Jesus' "own" are now his closest followers, the Twelve (13:1; cf. 1:11). These are given a final demonstration of Jesus' love and enjoined to love one another and to be unified so that the world may recognize them as Jesus' disciples and come to believe that the Father sent the Son (13:34–35; 15:12; 17:21, 23, 25). Jesus' performance of signs, demonstrating to the Jewish nation that he is the God-sent Messiah, no longer dominates the scene. Rather, the focus is on preparing his new messianic community for their Spirit-guided mission to the unbelieving world (which, significantly, includes the Jews). Hence, the disciples are drawn into the unity, love, and mission of Father, Son, and Spirit, culminating in the "Johannine Great Commission" (20:21–22).

A. The Cleansing and Instruction of the New Messianic Community, Including Jesus' Final Prayer (13:1–17:26)

In the face of obduracy on the part of the Jews, Jesus now turns his attention to the Twelve. After one final memorable demonstration of his love, and after exposing the betrayer, Jesus prepares his followers for the difficult times ahead.[1] The present section resembles the genre of farewell discourse.[2] Patterned after Moses' farewell discourse in Deuteronomy (31–33) and other similar OT farewells,[3] an entire genre of such works emerged during the Second Temple period.[4] Most of these testaments were written between the second century B.C. and the third century A.D. and include the following features:

1. Predictions of death and departure
2. Predictions of future challenges for the followers/sons of the dying man after his death
3. Arrangements regarding succession or continuation of family line
4. Exhortations to moral behavior
5. A final commission
6. An affirmation and renewal of God's covenant promises
7. A closing doxology

1. It is possible that John 13 represents a chiasm centering on Jesus' pronouncement in 13:18–20. See Moloney 1986: 372 (following Simoens 1981: 101). However, this proposal gives insufficient consideration to 13:31 as start of the farewell discourse proper. For a critique of chiastic proposals related to the Johannine farewell discourse, see Kellum 2005: 63–72. Kellum concludes that "on a structural level the farewell discourse resists a chiastic solution," both owing to "the lack of stated awareness of macro-chiasm in antiquity" and because "the text of the farewell discourse itself resists a chiastic arrangement" (ibid., 72). See also the recent paper by C. Smith (2002) pointing out foundational weaknesses of contemporary chiastic studies. John 13–17 in its entirety explicates 1:7.
2. The following material is adapted from Moloney 1998: 377–78 (for further bibliography, see pp. 389–91). See also Bammel 1993; Kurz 1985; 1990; Lacomara 1974; Paschal, *DJG* 229–33, esp. 232.
3. For example, Gen. 49; Josh. 23–24; 1 Sam. 12; 1 Kings 2:1–12; 1 Chron. 28–29.
4. For example, Testaments of the Twelve Patriarchs; Assumption of Moses; cf. Jub. 22:10–30; 1 Macc. 2:49–70; Josephus, *Ant.* 12.6.3 §§279–84. For Greco-Roman farewell passages, see Malina and Rohrbaugh 1998: 221–22.

However, John's presentation of Jesus' farewell discourse may not be consciously patterned after the Second Temple testament genre but may merely build on the precedent of patriarchal deathbed blessings and Moses' final words in Deuteronomy. There is the familiar instruction in virtue—"love one another" (13:34; 15:17); there is talk about Jesus' impending death or "departure" (13:33, 36; 14:5–6, 12, 28); and there are words of comfort to those about to be left behind (13:36; 14:1–3, 18, 27–28) (Attridge 2002a: 17). Also, in keeping with the genre's concern for proper succession, Jesus announces the coming of "another helping presence" (14:16; cf. 14:26; 15:26; 16:7), which would ensure continuation between his ministry and that of his disciples (see esp. 15:26–27; 16:8–11).

Yet important differences apply as well.[5] Jesus' farewell is but temporary—his followers will see him again "in a little while"—so that Jesus' final words focus on the future, while Jewish farewell discourses regularly consist of extended rehearsals of the past. Likewise, extensive detailed predictions regarding the future, common in Second Temple testaments, are almost entirely absent from Jesus' instructions to his followers. Also, the vine allegory in John 15 (with monologue replacing dialogue) is without precedent in Jewish farewell discourses. In short, the Johannine farewell discourse does not merely feature Jesus' prediction of his absence, but at the same time promises his abiding presence, so that, in a "bending" of the testament genre, a focus on the past is transposed to a (more hopeful) portrayal of the inaugurated permanent relationship between the Father, Jesus, and his followers.

The material contained in John 13–17 is unique to this Gospel. The underlying perspective of the farewell discourse is different from the first half of John's Gospel, which narrates Jesus' ministry to the Jews, with his followers playing only a minor role as disciples of Rabbi Jesus. The farewell discourse, on the other hand, presents Jesus' mission to the world, based on his cross-death and carried out through his followers in the power of the Spirit. The underlying assumption is that Jesus has been exalted; thus, he will answer prayer offered in his name, send his Spirit and direct the mission of his followers, and take his disciples into the loving and unified Father-Son relationship. The disciples have risen from lowly helpers to partners in ministry.[6]

5. For some of the following comments I am indebted to Attridge (2002a: esp. 9–10, 17–18), who points to differences between the Johannine farewell discourses and other ancient instances of this genre and says that John "bends" the genre here and elsewhere in his Gospel (i.e., the discourses in chs. 3, 4, 5, 6, 8, and 10).

6. Consider the more endearing terms used for Jesus' followers in the second half of John's Gospel (Köstenberger 1998b: 149–53): "his own" (οἱ ἴδιοι [13:1; cf. 1:11]); "little children" (τεκνία [13:33]); "friends" (φίλοι [15:15]); "those you gave me" (οἱ ἄνθρωποι οὓς ἐδωκάς μοι [17:6]); "those who are mine" (τὰ ἐμά [17:10]); "my brothers" (οἱ ἀδελφοί μου [20:17]); and "little children" (παιδία [21:5]).

The parallels between the present discourse and "covenant language" in Moses' parting Deuteronomic instructions[7] suggest that Jesus here is cast as the new Moses, who institutes a new covenant with his disciples.[8] Just as Moses was prevented by death from leading God's people into the promised land, so Jesus will be separated—albeit only temporarily—from his followers. Yet, in contrast to Moses, Jesus, as the new Joshua, entered heaven itself as our forerunner (cf. Heb. 4:8, 14; 6:20; 12:2). Or, to use Johannine terminology, Jesus will go to prepare a place for his disciples (14:2–3) and be glorified in the Father's presence with the glory he had with him before the world began (17:5).

These three larger observations—the unique character of the farewell discourse recorded in John, the shift in perspective from the earthly to the exalted Jesus, and the patterning of the farewell discourse after Moses' Deuteronomic farewell discourse—serve to set the study of John 13–17 into proper perspective. The entire section is controlled by one purpose: Jesus' preparation of his followers for the immediate future—that is, the trauma and loss resulting from his crucifixion and burial—and the time after his ascension.[9]

---

7. Note, for example, the preponderance of the five major verb themes of Exod. 33–34 and Deuteronomy—"love," "obey," "live," "know," and "see"—in John 14:15–24. See Lacomara 1974; Pryor 1992a: esp. 160, 166, 216 n. 8, referring also to Malatesta 1978: 42–77.

8. Note, for example, the "new commandment" in 13:34–35.

9. For the purposes of this present commentary, the farewell discourse will be treated as a literary unity. Writing in 1982, Segovia (1982: 82) could claim, "Nowadays hardly any exegete would vigorously maintain that John 13:31–18:1 is a literary unity as it stands." The past two decades have seen the emergence of many, often mutually contradictory, redaction-critical proposals, most notably the theory of the "relecture" of John 13–14 in John 15–16 (see esp. Dettwiler 1995). The primary grounds for such theories is the *magnus reus* ("great offender") of 14:31, which to many suggests a "literary seam" (*aporia*). However, Kellum (2005: esp. 205–33) recently has demonstrated the weaknesses of a disunity theory applied to the Johannine farewell discourse on stylistic, structural, and thematic grounds. Moreover, 14:31 is shown more likely to constitute an instance of the Johannine device of implied movement, which may in a given instance convey a shift in topic (cf. 11:16, 44; 20:11). This observation is significant not only on a micro level but also on a macro level. Within the context of the entire discourse, this device is employed to foster both discourse continuity and progression, moving in an increasingly exclusionary direction. In 13:30, Judas's departure leaves Jesus and the Eleven, triggering Jesus' initial cycle of instruction. In 14:31, it is Jesus and his followers whose departure is implied, followed by a metaphorical deepening of Jesus' words from 13:31–14:30. Finally, in 17:1 Jesus lifts his eyes to heaven, praying by himself. On the other end of the discourse, Jesus and the disciples are shown to cross the Kidron Valley in 18:1, with the subsequent arrest of Jesus and the ensuing events of his passion. Hence, there is no need to resort to redaction-critical relecture or chiastic or other theories, and 14:31 is not a "literary seam" but part of a carefully designed pattern of escalating narrative movement.

1. The Cleansing of the Community: The Footwashing and Judas's Departure (13:1–30)

Within the context of chapters 13–17, 13:1–30 constitutes a sort of preamble, with 13:31–16:33 representing the actual farewell discourse, and chapter 17 serving as the closing prayer that provides the transition to the subsequent passion narrative.[1] The material contained in 13:1–30 revolves around the motif of cleansing.[2] The disciples' need for continual cleansing is illustrated by the footwashing; the new messianic community is cleansed by the exposure and departure of the betrayer, Judas.[3] Continuity is provided by Peter, who is prominent throughout the chapter, including the footwashing, the exposure of the betrayer, and his plea of allegiance that elicits Jesus' prediction of Peter's denials.[4] Only after the community has been cleansed can Jesus proceed to prepare his inner circle for the coming events, most notably the sending of the Spirit subsequent to his exaltation.

---

1. This narrow delineation of the farewell discourse is affirmed by, among others, G. Johnston (1970), Segovia (1991, followed tentatively by Keener [2003: 891]), and Dettwiler (1995 [though note that Dettwiler starts the discourse at 13:1 to accommodate his relecture theory]). See also Kellum 2005. Many who do include chapter 17 do so by way of separate reference to Jesus' final prayer (e.g., Carson 1980).

2. For a defense of the literary and theological integrity of 13:1–30, see Carson 1991: 460. For a comprehensive discussion of various attempts at reconstructing putative sources, see Schnackenburg 1990: 3.7–15. Note that structurally, the cleansing motif in chapter 13 may correspond to the cleansing motif in chapter 2, both at the Cana wedding and at the clearing of the temple. While in chapter 2 Jesus' attempt to cleanse corrupt Jewish custom and worship must be pronounced a failure in human terms (though both events serve as Johannine "signs" with messianic significance), chapter 13 witnesses his successful cleansing of the new messianic community.

3. Westcott (1908: 2.159) comments, "The departure of Judas marked the crisis of the Lord's victory. By this the company was finally 'cleansed' (v. 10)."

4. See Wiarda 2000: 106–9, 136–39, 172–74.

a. The Footwashing (13:1–17)

The opening verse sets the scene not merely for the footwashing but for the entire farewell discourse. The time marker "just before the Passover" continues the buildup to Jesus' last Passover.[1] The first five verses set the scene, followed by the footwashing and Jesus' words of instruction.[2] The practice of footwashing, which has a long OT tradition,[3] usually was performed by slaves. In the present instance, however, Jesus stoops to perform this role, not in order to institute a permanent rite, but to teach his followers on the importance of humble, loving service (cf. Gal. 5:13; 6:2; Phil. 2:6–8).[4]

   i. The setting (13:1–5)
  ii. Jesus washes his disciples' feet (13:6–11)
 iii. The object lesson (13:12–17)

1. Cf. "six days before the Passover" in 12:1; "the next day" in 12:12. Carson (1991: 455–58) rightly concludes that Jesus and his disciples ate a true paschal meal on Thursday, 15 Nisan (contra Barrett 1978: 50–51; R. Brown 1970: 556; Schnackenburg 1990: 3.36). On the chronology of the passion narrative in John and the Synoptics (siding with Carson, despite Morris 1995: 688–90), see the sidebar in Köstenberger 1999a: 146, with further bibliographical references (see also Köstenberger 2002c: 130, 164, 173; Blomberg 1987: 175–80; Carson 1984: 530–32). Some seek to adjudicate apparent differences between the presentations in John and the Synoptics by the theory that differences in chronology are due to the use of different calendars. John, it is suggested, like the Judeans and the Sadducees, uses a lunar sunset-to-sunset calendar, while the Synoptics, like the Galileans, the Pharisees, and Jesus and his followers, employ a solar sunrise-to-sunrise reckoning (Hoehner 1977: 85–90; see chart on p. 89; Morris 1995: 684–95); or, John's calendric usage shifts: his light-darkness theme (rooted in the Genesis account) is conveyed by way of a solar calendar, while elsewhere a lunar system is found (building on exodus redemptive motifs) (Busada 2003). However, these theories seem to lack a clear textual base in the Gospels themselves and are unnecessarily complicated if the solution argued here is adopted.
   2. Lindars (1972: 448) notes, "The piling up of participial clauses is unusual in John, and gives a most solemn effect."
   3. See the concise summary of "footwashing in antiquity" in Hultgren 1982: 541–42. Hultgren understands the Johannine footwashing as a "symbol of eschatological hospitality." On the practice of footwashing, see also Keener 2003: 903–4 (who apparently, and implausibly, takes literally the reference to footwashing in 1 Tim. 5:10 [p. 904]).
   4. So Morris (1995: 544), citing Calvin (1961: 60), who denounces annual footwashing rites as "theatrical," "empty and bare," "ceremonial comedy," and "shameful mockery of Christ." See also Carson 1991: 458.

Exegesis and Exposition

[1]Now before the Passover festival Jesus, because he knew that the time had come for him to leave this world and go to the Father, and having loved his own who were in the world, showed them one final proof of his love. [2]And when ⌜it was time for⌝ dinner, and the devil had already thrust it into the heart of ⌜Judas⌝, son of Simon Iscariot, to betray him, [3]and because he knew that the Father had given all things into his hands and that he had come from God and was going back to God, [4]he rose from dinner, took off his outer clothing, and wrapped a towel around his waist. [5]Then he poured water into a basin and began to wash the disciples' feet and to dry them with the cloth wrapped around him.

[6]So he came to Simon Peter, who said to him, "Lord, are *you* washing *my* feet?" [7]Jesus answered and said to him, "What I'm doing you don't understand now, but after these things you will understand." [8]Peter said to him, "You must never, ever wash my feet!" Jesus answered him, "Unless I wash you, you have no part with me." [9]Simon Peter said to him, "Lord, then not only my feet, but also my hands and head!" [10]Jesus said to him, "One who has had a bath ⌜needs only to wash his feet⌝, but his whole body is clean. And you [disciples] are clean, but not all of you." [11](For he knew the one who would betray him; this is why he said, "Not all of you are clean.") [12]So when he had washed their feet, he put on his outer clothing and reclined again. He said to them, "Do you realize what I've done for you? [13]You call me 'Teacher' and 'Lord,' and you speak well, for this is what I am. [14]So if I, the Lord and Teacher, washed your feet, you also ought to wash one another's feet. [15]I have given you an example, so that just as I've done for you, you might also do for one another. [16]Truly, truly, I say to you, a servant is not above his master, nor is a messenger greater than the one who sent him. [17]Since you know these things, you are blessed if you do them."

i. The Setting (13:1–5)

Translations such as the TNIV conceal the fact that in the original, the introduction to the footwashing consists of a mere two sentences, 13:1 and 13:2–5. This sets the scene apart from the preceding narrative and lends added solemnity to the present occasion. The evangelist informs his readers that it was just before the Passover (cf. 2:13; 11:55; 12:1). According to the Synoptics (Mark 14:12; Luke 22:15), Jesus and his disciples celebrated the Passover during the early hours of 15 Nisan (Thursday evening, with days beginning at sundown), with preparations having been made earlier that day, 14 Nisan, the day on which the paschal lambs were slaughtered at the temple (usually between 3:00 and 5:00 P.M. in modern measure). Some believe that John places the supper on 14 Nisan, Wednesday evening, with Jesus' crucifixion occurring on Thursday afternoon, when the lambs are slaughtered at the temple in preparation for Passover. A closer look at the relevant passages, however, shows that none of these actually conflicts with the

13:1

Synoptic accounts.[5] The opening words thus place the footwashing immediately prior to the Passover meal that is about to begin.[6]

The time had come (see commentary at 12:23). The two major chronological markers running throughout the first part of John's Gospel, references to Jewish festivals (2:13, 23; 4:45; 5:1; 6:4; 7:2; 10:22; 11:55; 12:1) and to Jesus' "time" (2:4; 7:30; 8:20; 12:23, 27; 16:32; 17:1), now merge in a Jewish festival that also marks the "time" of Jesus. The term κόσμος (*kosmos*, world [on which, see commentary at 1:10]) occurs forty times in John 13–17, with "the world" replacing "the Jews" as the major reference point for Jesus and his followers. "His own" are now the Twelve, the representatives of the new messianic community, no longer the old covenant community, which had rejected Jesus as Messiah (cf. 1:11; see also 10:3–4, 12; cf. 15:19). The present reference is the first among several more endearing terms used for the disciples in the second half of John's Gospel (Köstenberger 1998b: 153, 162, 165–66).

The phrase εἰς τέλος (*eis telos*, one final proof [of his love]), in typical Johannine fashion combining a dual temporal and intensive meaning,[7] conveys the complete demonstration of Jesus' love, which is symbolized by Jesus' lowering himself to the status of a slave in the footwashing and realized in his vicarious cross-death.[8] Ridderbos (1997: 452 n. 4) calls it "love to the last breath" and "love in its highest intensity" that was exemplified by "the concrete expression of this love in the footwashing and in his self-giving 'to the end.'" In typical Johannine fashion, this elevates love to the highest principle underlying Jesus' mission and particularly the cross (cf. 3:16). It also is consistent with the picture of Jesus as the good shepherd who cares for his sheep by giving his life for them (10:15, 17–18; cf. Rev. 1:5; see Schlatter 1948: 178). The whole world is the object of God's love, but here Jesus' love is demonstrated specifically toward his "own," who are being readied for their mission to the world.

13:2–3 The "evening meal" (δεῖπνον, *deipnon*) was being served.[9] The ensuing references to Satan's prevenient act in Judas and Jesus' full knowledge of what was about to take place alert the reader that Jesus, in complete

---

5. See introduction to 13:1–17 and commentary at 18:28 and 19:14.

6. For the connection of Passover with Jesus' death, see also 11:55; 12:1; 18:28, 39; 19:14.

7. This is favored by Morris (1995: 545 n. 9) and Ridderbos (1997: 452); cf. Barrett 1978: 438; R. Brown 1970: 550. Carson (1991: 461), at least explicitly, remains undecided, though his translation reflects an intensive force.

8. Of the five other NT occurrences of the phrase εἰς τέλος, four are temporal (Matt. 10:22; 24:13; Mark 13:13; Luke 18:5) and one is intensive (1 Thess. 2:16). The present reference may contain an allusion to Moses' completing the writing of the law (and his song) in Deut. 31:24, 30.

9. See commentary at 12:2; cf. 1 Cor. 11:20. See also the time marker in 13:30 ("it was night") and the first additional note to 13:2.

awareness of what was about to take place, nonetheless went ahead to wash his disciples' feet, including those of Judas (Carson 1991: 461–62). It is hard to conceive of a more powerful demonstration of Jesus' command to love one's enemies (cf. Matt. 5:44 = Luke 6:27). The prospect of Judas's appalling action contrasts with Jesus' act of humble and loving service (Beasley-Murray 1999: 233).

The Greek underlying the phrase "the devil had already thrust [βεβλη-κότος, *beblēkotos*][10] it into the heart of Judas" (cf. 13:27, and see commentary at 12:31) allows for two interpretations: either Satan prompting Judas, or Satan deciding for himself, to betray Jesus (the former is more likely).[11] In any case, John shows that Judas's betrayal of Jesus was ultimately satanically inspired. The heart is "the seat of the will, and a heart moved by the devil wants what the devil wants" (Schlatter 1948: 279). As Ridderbos (1997: 458 n. 32) notes, "Here is the demonic starting point in the process that pervades the entire story from start to finish as a chain of faithlessness" that extended "from Judas to the Sanhedrin, from the Sanhedrin to Pilate, and from Pilate to the executioners."

In a Gospel that features no demons (and hence no exorcisms), all supernatural evil is centered in Satan and his grand scheme of bringing Jesus to the cross, though ultimately this worked into the hands of God's sovereign, eternal purposes (cf. 12:37–41; Acts 2:23; 3:18). In fact, the Father—no idle spectator at the events that are about to unfold (Morris 1995: 546)—was pleased to put all things into Jesus' hands.[12] Jesus' coming from God is a theme that pervades the entire Gospel (e.g., 3:2; 7:28; 8:14; 16:28, 30). What is about to follow took place precisely *because* Jesus knew (εἰδώς, *eidōs*; causal participle [Wallace 1996: 632]) his true status and position (cf. 10:17–18; see Schlatter 1948: 280).

Jesus got up from the meal,[13] took off his outer clothing, and wrapped a towel around his waist.[14] As Carson (1991: 462–63) notes, "His act of humility is as unnecessary as it is stunning, and is simultaneously a display of love (v. 1), a symbol of saving cleansing (vv. 6–9), and a model of Christian conduct (vv. 12–17)."[15] Jesus here adopts the stance of a

13:4–5

---

10. Brodie (1993: 448) notes that the term βάλλω (*ballō*, throw, put) is used twice at the beginning of chapter 13 (13:2, 5) and not otherwise in chapters 13–17 except for twice at the beginning of chapter 15 (both in 15:6).

11. Literally, the phrase reads, "the devil already having thrust it into the heart that Judas . . . should betray him." See the second additional note to 13:2.

12. Cf. Matt. 28:18; Eph. 1:22; Col. 2:15; see also Ps. 110:1, cited in Matt. 22:44 pars.

13. Ridderbos (1997: 459 n. 33, with reference to Friedrichsen 1939: 94) suggests the translation "after the meal," but this seems to be an unlikely rendering of the preposition ἐκ (*ek*).

14. Morris (1995: 547) notes the "vivid" historical presents used in this verse (see also 13:5a). The deponent form ἐγείρεται in 13:4 has an active meaning (as in 7:52; cf. BDAG 271).

15. Though Jesus' act may be characterized as a "display," a "symbol," and a "model," it is not therefore a "sign" in the Johannine sense, nor is it called that by the evangelist. Contra Whitacre 1999: 328–29.

menial, even non-Jewish (*Mek. Exod.* 21.2), slave, a position looked down upon by both Jews and Gentiles. Other rabbis also stressed the virtue of humility, yet with certain limitations (e.g., *y. Sanh.* 11.3 [cited in Keener 1993: 297]). Jesus, for his part, knew no such boundaries.[16]

The word rendered "took off" may echo the phrase "lay down" one's life in the good shepherd discourse (10:11, 15, 17, 18), especially since "take up" in 13:12 parallels 10:17, 18 (Ridderbos 1997: 458; cf. R. Brown 1970: 551). If so, then John links the footwashing with Jesus' sacrificial death.[17] "Outer clothing" translates the plural ἱμάτια (*himatia*, clothes), as in 13:12. The words "wrapped a towel around his waist" indicate that Jesus girds himself like a servant (Luke 12:37; 17:8). The term λέντιον (*lention*, towel), which occurs in the NT only here and is not attested in earlier Greek literature,[18] is a loanword from the Latin *linteum* (similar to *soudarion*; see John 11:44).[19] It refers to a long towel fastened to the shoulder, which allowed Jesus to gird himself and still to use the end to dry the disciples' feet (cf. 1 Pet. 5:5).

Jesus then poured water into a basin and began to wash his disciples' feet.[20] The OT recounts several instances of footwashing as part of ancient hospitality.[21] Several passages in Second Temple literature mention the washing of a guest's feet immediately prior to a meal.[22] The disciples probably reclined on mats around a low table, each leaning on his left arm, with his feet pointing outward. In first-century Palestine, where people walked long distances in sandals and roads were dusty, hospitality demanded that the host arrange for water to be available for the washing of feet (which was done upon arrival, not during the meal). Rather than washing the feet in the basin itself, water was poured over the feet from one vessel and caught in another (cf. 2 Kings 3:11).[23]

16. On Jesus' emphasis on service, see Matt. 20:25–28 pars.; cf. Phil. 2:5–11.

17. So, rightly, Talbert (1992: 191), who detects "prophetic symbolism" here (citing Isa. 8:1–4; Jer. 13:1–11; Ezek. 12:1–7).

18. The possible exception is *Vitae Aesopi* 61.13; 67.4 (Vita G); 61.9 (Vita W).

19. First-century B.C. and A.D. references include Plautus, *Mostellaria* 267; Catullus, *Carmina* 12.3; Petronius, *Satyricon* 28.4; Martial, *Epigrams* 12.70.1; Juvenal, *Satirae* 14.22. The term originally referred to a piece of linen cloth and was applied to various specific things made of linen, such as handkerchiefs, towels, and curtains.

20. Wallace (1996: 558) identifies ἤρξατο (*ērxato*, he began) as an ingressive aorist, but the verb already means "begin," which carries an ingressive notion, so that it is unclear what this identification contributes. Schlatter (1948: 281) notes that this is the only Johannine occurrence of the verb ἄρχομαι (except for the *pericope adulterae*, where the word appears at 8:9).

21. See Gen. 18:4; 19:2; 24:32; 43:24; Judg. 19:21; 1 Sam. 25:41.

22. See T. Abr. 3:7–9; Jos. As. 7:1. See Thomas (1991a: 35–40), who also cites instances of footwashing as part of hospitality in the Greco-Roman world (pp. 46–50).

23. The term νιπτήρ (*niptēr*, washbasin [only here in the NT]) occurs elsewhere in a Cyprian inscription from Roman times (see BDAG 674). The longer expression ποδανιπτήρ ("footbath") is found in Herodotus, *Historiae* 2.172 (fifth century B.C.); cf. ποδονιπτῆρα in 𝔓66 of John 13:5.

The performance of acts of service for his teacher was considered to be a common duty of a disciple.[24] In fact, it was maintained that "the service of the Torah is greater than the study thereof" (*b. Ber.* 7b). The washing of feet, however, was considered too demeaning for disciples (or even a Jewish slave) and thus assigned to non-Jewish slaves.[25] Thus, Jesus' adoption of the stance of (a non-Jewish) slave would have been shocking to his disciples and called for an explanation. For although there are occasional exceptions featuring people other than non-Jewish slaves washing the feet of others,[26] the washing of the feet of an inferior by a superior is not attested elsewhere in Jewish or Greco-Roman sources.

Thus, "Jesus the *teacher* renders a service to his *pupils* rather than vice versa, and the specific task performed exceeds that from which even *pupils* in contemporary Judaism were exempt" (Köstenberger 1998a: 117). Jesus' teaching style here follows the rabbinic pattern of "mystifying gesture–question–interpretation" (Köstenberger 1998a: 115–17), which was a didactic tool designed to elicit questions and to facilitate learning.[27] "The disciples" probably refers to the Twelve (cf. Matt. 26:20 par.).[28] "Dry" (ἐκμάσσειν, *ekmassein*) may echo 12:3.

ii. Jesus Washes His Disciples' Feet (13:6–11)

In the ensuing account of the footwashing, Peter serves as the foil for the lesson that Jesus seeks to impart to his followers.[29] Simon Peter's protest is not uncharacteristic (see Matt. 16:22 par.; cf. John 13:37).[30] The juxtaposed pronouns σύ and μου (*sy*, you; *mou*, my [noted by Morris 1995: 548]) convey Peter's inner revulsion at the thought that Jesus, his teacher and Lord, would stoop to wash *his* feet.[31] As Bultmann (1971: 468) aptly notes, Peter's stance reflects "the basic way men think, the

13:6–8

24. For further references and discussion, see Köstenberger 1998a: 122–23.

25. *b. Ketub.* 96a; *Mek. Exod.* 21.2 (cited in Köstenberger 2002c: 131).

26. For example, 1 Sam. 25:41; Jos. As. 20:1–5. See also the anecdote involving the mother of Rabbi Ishmael (d. ca. A.D. 135) recounted in Str-B 1:707.

27. Witherington (1995: 232–34) seems to overplay the Greco-Roman background when he compares Jesus to a resident guest teacher who leads the symposium (a teaching/dialogue following the meal).

28. Note also the parallel between John 13:18 and 6:70, which likewise may suggest that the Twelve were in view. On the word νίπτω (*niptō*, wash) in relation to λούω (*louō*, bathe), see commentary at 13:10. On "drying them with the towel that was wrapped around him," see commentary at 13:4.

29. Brodie (1993: 449) finds in the triple exchange between Jesus and Peter echoes of earlier conversations, particularly of the opening triple exchange between Jesus and the Samaritan woman in 4:7–15.

30. Ridderbos (1997: 459 n. 34 [cf. Schnackenburg 1990: 3.19]) notes the use of Peter's double name, "as elsewhere when his most striking and characteristic interventions are described" (e.g., 6:68; 13:9, 24, 36; 18:10, 15, 25; 21:3). On the designation "Lord," see 13:9, 36, 37, and commentary at 13:13.

31. The verb νίπτεις (*nipteis*, are you washing) has a futuristic force (Wallace 1996: 535).

refusal to see the act of salvation in what is lowly, or God in the form of a slave."[32] Jesus mildly replies (note again the two pronouns ἐγώ, *egō*, I; σύ, *sy*, you [Morris 1995: 548]) that while Peter does not understand the significance of what is about to transpire, he would do so later. In the immediate future, this may refer to the explanation given subsequent to the footwashing (13:12–17), though ultimately it may well relate to the time following Jesus' resurrection (cf. 2:22; 12:16; see Ridderbos 1997: 459; Carson 1991: 463), perhaps alluding to Peter's forthcoming denials of Jesus and his restoration to ministry.[33]

Jesus goes on to counter Peter's reluctance by noting that unless Peter allowed Jesus to proceed, he would have no part with Jesus (cf. 14:1–3; 17:24). The verb νίπτω (*niptō*, wash) carries a Johannine double meaning, referring both to the washing of feet and to the cleansing from sin (cf. 1 John 1:9). Only Jesus can do the latter, and without such spiritual cleansing no one can be in Christ (Morris 1995: 548). The notion of "having a part" (μέρος, *meros*) in something or someone occurs elsewhere in the NT with regard to inheritance (Luke 15:12). In OT times, each of the twelve tribes of Israel (except Levi) was to have its "share" (μερίς, *meris*) in the promised land (Num. 18:20; Deut. 12:12; 14:27). Later, μέρος is used with reference to people's being assigned a place in God's eternal kingdom, either in fellowship with God (Rev. 20:6; 21:8; 22:19) or separated from him (Matt. 24:51; Luke 12:46). In Acts 8:21, Peter rebukes Simon Magus using similar language (μερίς).

13:9–11   In a sudden turnabout, Peter reverses himself, saying, "If this is the case, wash not only my feet, but also my hands and head!" This is another instance of Peter's well-known overeagerness and penchant for hyperbole, with "feet, hands, and head" denoting his entire body.[34] Little did Peter know that "the basis of the cleansing foreshadowed by the washing of his feet lay ahead in the hideous ignominy of the barbarous cross" (Carson 1991: 464). However, what Peter failed to understand, and what emerged as an additional lesson, is that "the initial and fundamental cleansing that Christ provides is a once-for-all act. Individuals who have been cleansed by Christ's atoning work will doubtless need to have subsequent sins washed away, but the fundamental cleansing can never be repeated" (Carson 1991:

32. Schlatter (1948: 283, adducing 8:15) notes similarly that Peter here judges "according to the flesh" (κατὰ τὴν σάρκα).

33. So Schlatter 1948: 282. Morris (1995: 548 n. 22) notes the plural form ταῦτα (*tauta*, these things) and suggests that the expression "probably points to all the events associated with the Passion," though he does say that in part, the "later" may refer to the explanation that Jesus soon will give. The latter is ruled out categorically by Schnackenburg (1990: 3.19) and, less categorically but still firmly, by Carson (1991: 463). However, a radical disjunction between Jesus' explanation here and the events of the passion seems to be unnecessary.

34. Contra Carson (1991: 464), who discards a metonymic reading as "heavy-handed" and is content to interpret the statement as reflecting "unrestrained exuberance."

465; cf. Talbert 1992: 192–93; Calvin 1961: 59). Nevertheless, the present scene highlights the human failure to love and the human inability to serve apart from Christ's enablement (Schlatter 1948: 282–83).

"One who has had a bath needs only to wash his feet, but his whole body is clean."[35] Two terms for washing are contrasted here: λούω (*louō*, bathe) and νίπτω (*niptō*, wash).[36] To bathe, or "have a bath," may refer to Jewish ceremonial cleansing in preparation for Passover (cf. 11:55). Alternatively, Jesus may be alluding to the custom (at least in some quarters) "for guests at a meal to take a bath before leaving home, and on arrival at their host's house to have their feet, but only their feet, washed" (Barrett 1978: 441).[37] In any case, Jesus' disclaimer would caution his followers (and John's readers) against interpreting his actions as a mandate for ritual washings (καθαρισμός, *katharismos*) common in Judaism (cf. 2:6; 3:25). "They sit at table with Jesus as his disciples, clean not because they have purified themselves and made themselves worthy of this privilege but because of the word he has spoken to them" (Ridderbos 1997: 460–61). The footwashing thus serves as "a symbol for Jesus' act of total purification in his surrender for his own on the cross" (Ridderbos 1997: 464).[38]

iii. The Object Lesson (13:12–17)

In the present section, Jesus, upon returning to his seat, drives home the lesson that he intended to teach his disciples by washing their feet. Rather than focusing on the external act itself, Jesus points to the "principle that underlay that action" (Morris 1995: 550).[39] The verb γινώσκετε (*ginōskete*)

13:12–14

---

35. See 13:11 and 15:3, the only other two instances of καθαρός (*katharos*, clean) in John's Gospel. The aorist infinitive νίψασθαι (*nipsasthai*, to wash oneself) is identified by Wallace (1996: 427) as a "permissive middle."

36. Relevant instances of λούω in Scripture (LXX and NT) include Lev. 14:9; 15:11; 16:4; 17:16; Num. 19:7; Deut. 23:12; Acts 9:37; Heb. 10:22. Note especially Lev. 15:11, where νίπτω and λούω are found side by side. The word νίπτω occurs elsewhere in the NT for washing one's face (Matt. 6:17), hands (Matt. 15:2; Mark 7:3), eyes (John 9:7, 11, 15), and feet (John 13:5, 6, 8, 10, 12, 14; 1 Tim. 5:10). On the distinction in meaning between λούω and νίπτω, see Thomas 1991a: 51 n. 25; Oepke, *TDNT* 4:305; Hauck, *TDNT* 4:947.

37. Thus, according to Plutarch (first century A.D.), both Cato the Younger and Pompey had a bath before supper (λούω, δεῖπνον) (cf. *Cato Minor* 67.1; *Pompeius* 55.6; see also Lucian, *Gallus* 7.9; *Timon* 54; *De morte Peregrini* 6). Keener (2003: 909) suggests that the reference "may allude physically to the ritual purification preceding the eating of Passover."

38. A reference to Christian baptism is unlikely. Contra Moloney 1998: 375; Brodie 1993: 452; and R. Brown (1970: 562), who says that 13:6–10 represents a secondary allusion to baptism. Moreover, as Carson (1991: 466) notes, the washing of Judas's feet proves that "no rite, even if performed by Jesus himself, ensures spiritual cleansing." On "he knew," see 6:70–71; 13:3, 26–27.

39. Cf. the general application drawn by Carson (1991: 468): "[T]he heart of Jesus' command is a humility and helpfulness toward brothers and sisters in Christ." Talbert (1992: 194) rejects this general application and argues for a more specific one: "[F]or the disciples to wash one another's feet . . . means for them to forgive one another those daily trespasses that characterize one human being's infringement upon another."

could be either an indicative and hence introducing a question ("Do you realize what I've done for you?") or an imperative constituting a command ("Realize what I've done for you"). The former seems more likely (so the majority of commentators, contra Morris 1995: 551 n. 33).

"You call me 'Teacher' and 'Lord.'" John's Gospel regularly portrays Jesus being addressed in those terms by his disciples or others (Köstenberger 1998a: 97–128).[40] The designation "rabbi" was in keeping with Jewish teacher-disciple relationships; "Lord," on the other hand, was an expression commonly applied to God in the LXX.[41] Jesus acknowledges being both. In an argument "from the greater to the lesser," he drives home the lesson that if he, being Lord and teacher (the words are now reversed),[42] was willing to wash his disciples' feet, his followers should do the same for one another.[43]

13:15–17   "I have given you an example." The Greek word ὑπόδειγμα (*hypodeigma*) can denote both an "example," be it good[44] or bad,[45] and a "pattern" (Heb. 8:5; 9:23; cf. τύπος [*typos*, pattern] Acts 7:44). In several Second Temple texts, ὑπόδειγμα is associated with exemplary death[46] or other virtues such as repentance (Sir. 44:16). Greco-Roman writers likewise use the term to denote examples of various virtues.[47] Thus, the major difference between Jesus and the Greco-Roman world on this point was not the concept of leaving an example but the nature of this example: wheras Greeks and Romans prized virtues such as courage or military prowess, Jesus exemplified humility, self-sacrifice, and love.

The "aphoristic parenthesis" found in "nor is a messenger greater than the one who sent him" is paralleled by similar statements in the

40. "Teacher" is διδάσκαλος (*didaskalos*); the Aramaic equivalent is ῥαββί (*rabbi*): see 1:38, 49; 3:2; 4:31; 6:25; 9:2; 11:8; 20:16. "Lord" renders κύριος (*kyrios*): see 6:68; 9:38; 11:3, 12, 21, 27, 32, 34, 39; 13:6, 9, 25, 36, 37; 14:5, 8, 22; 20:28; 21:15, 16, 17, 20, 21. Schlatter (1948: 284, citing Matt. 23:8) detects in the pronoun ὑμεῖς (*hymeis*, you) an implied contrast: "You do it [call me 'Teacher' and 'Lord'], others don't."

41. Though it could also simply mean "sir"; see 4:11, 15, 49; 5:7.

42. This is noted by Morris (1995: 551), who says that the reversal "may be significant." R. Brown (1970: 553) theorizes that "the order in which the two titles are mentioned may reflect the development of the disciples' understanding, for 'Teacher' is more common in the earlier chapters of the Gospel and 'Lord' in the later chapters." Morris (1995: 551 n. 34, citing BDF §147 [cf. Barrett 1978: 443; Beasley-Murray 1999: 229 n. g]) says that the nominative ὁ διδάσκαλος καὶ κύριος "is equivalent to a vocative," though the phrase clearly functions as an apposition to ἐγώ in the present context.

43. As can be seen from 1 Tim. 5:10, the phrase "washing the feet of the saints," in extension of its literal application here, had already become an accepted figurative expression for Christian service by the time of the writing of John's Gospel.

44. For example, the prophets' patience: James 5:10; cf. Philo, *Heir* 51 §256.

45. For example, the disobedience of wilderness Israel (Heb. 4:11); godless Sodom and Gomorrah (2 Pet. 2:6); see also Philo, *Conf. Tong.* 15 §64.

46. 2 Macc. 6:28, 31; 4 Macc. 17:22–23; Sir. 44:16; cf. Josephus, *J.W.* 6.2.1 §§103, 106.

47. For example, Diodorus Siculus, *Bibliotheca historica* 30.8; Plutarch, *Marcellus* 20.1 (cited in Köstenberger 2002c: 132).

Synoptics.[48] This is the only instance of ἀπόστολος (*apostolos*, messenger) in this Gospel, and even here there are no overtones of the technical use of "apostle" with reference to the Twelve.[49] The solemn ἀμὴν ἀμήν (*amēn amēn*, truly, truly) signals a warning. Jesus' followers, still largely unaware of the dangers entailed by their allegiance to Jesus, "must not take too lightly the prospect that awaits them as disciples and emissaries of Jesus in the world" (Ridderbos 1997: 464). Messengers and servants should not think themselves exempt from tasks performed by their superiors (Carson 1991: 468; Morris 1995: 552).

Yet merely knowing these things will not suffice; a blessing is pronounced on those who put Jesus' words into practice (cf. 7:17; 12:26; see Ridderbos 1997: 464; Morris 1995: 552).[50] The importance of acting on one's knowledge is stressed repeatedly in the NT (e.g., Matt. 7:24–27 par.; James 1:22–25). Similar statements are attested in Greco-Roman sources.[51]

Additional Notes

13:2. Regarding the timing of the dinner itself, whether past or present, the MS evidence is divided between the present participle γινομένου (ℵ* B) and the aorist participle γενομένου (𝔓66 A D). Most commentators (as well as the majority of the UBS committee) favor the former (e.g., Morris 1995: 546 n. 10; Barrett 1978: 439; Schnackenburg 1990: 3.399 n. 35), though Carson (1991: 469) opts for the latter as the more difficult reading, construing the aorist as ingressive.

13:2. The MS evidence divides between a nominative and a genitive reading of Ἰούδας, whereby the former variant as the harder reading more likely accounts for the emergence of the latter reading. The nominative reading also has better external attestation (𝔓66 ℵ B). If so, then the heart in question would still be that of Judas, not that of the devil, though the expression would be rather awkward, hence the apparent attempt by later scribes to improve the grammar. See the competent discussion and sound conclusion by Carson 1991: 461–62.

13:10. The textual evidence in regard to the needs of one who has been bathed is complicated (Beasley-Murray [1999: 229 n. f] calls it a "*cause célèbre* of NT textual criticism"; see also Thomas 1987) but seems to favor the longer reading including εἰ μὴ τοὺς πόδας.[52] The shorter reading, whereby the bathed person has no need of further washing, is poorly attested, found in ℵ, but then only in vg, it, and some church fathers.

---

48. Cf. Matt. 10:24; Luke 6:40 (cf. 22:27). Jesus refers back to this saying in John 15:20. "Aphoristic parenthesis" is the term used by Carson (1991: 469); cf. Barrett 1978: 444; Beasley-Murray 1999: 236.

49. Similar occurrences of ἀπόστολος in the NT include 2 Cor. 8:23; Phil. 2:25. For references to the disciples being sent elsewhere in this Gospel, see 4:38; 17:18; 20:21 (Köstenberger 1998b: 180–97).

50. The only other instance of macarism (blessing) in John's Gospel is 20:29.

51. Hesiod, *Opera et dies* 826–27; Seneca, *Epistulae morales* 75.7 (cited in Köstenberger 2002c: 132).

52. So Morris 1995: 549 n. 27; apparently, Carson 1991: 464–66; and the UBS committee (Metzger 1994: 204), adducing the "preponderant weight of external attestation"; contra Barrett 1978: 442; Beasley-Murray 1999: 229 n. f; Lindars 1972: 451; D. M. Smith 1999: 254; Dunn 1970: 250–51.

b. The Betrayal (13:18–30)

In 13:18 the narrative rather abruptly shifts from the disciples' election to the imminent betrayal of Jesus by Judas. This continues the Johannine pattern of signaling this event ahead of time in order to forestall the notion that the betrayal came as a surprise to Jesus or that it went counter to the electing and providential purposes of God. The present section narrates the cleansing of the new messianic community from the unclean element in its midst (i.e., Judas the betrayer), after which the stage is set for Jesus' instruction of his followers in the farewell discourse proper (13:31–16:33). As at his arrest later on, Jesus is shown to be in full control of the circumstances of the betrayal (Keener 2003: 919).

Exegesis and Exposition

[18]"I am not talking about all of you; I know the ones I have chosen. But in order that the Scripture might be fulfilled, 'The one who is eating my bread has lifted up his heel against me.' [19]From now on, I'm telling you before it happens, in order that you may believe when it does happen that I am [the one I claim to be]. [20]Truly, truly, I say to you, whoever receives whom I send receives me, and whoever receives me receives the one who sent me."

[21]After he had said these things, Jesus was stirred up inside and testified and said, "Truly, truly, I say to you, one of you is going to betray me." [22]The disciples were looking at one another, without a clue as to whom Jesus had in mind. [23]One of his disciples was reclining at Jesus' side, the one whom Jesus loved. [24]So Simon Peter motioned to this disciple to find out to whom Jesus might be referring. [25]So while that disciple was reclining this way at Jesus' side, he said to him, "Lord, who is it?" [26]Jesus answered, "It is the one whose piece of bread I will dip and give to him." So when he had dipped the piece of bread, he gave it to Judas, son of Simon Iscariot. [27]And after Judas took the piece of bread, then Satan entered into him. Then Jesus said to him, "What you are about to do—do it quickly." [28]But none of those reclining understood why he said this to him. [29]For some were thinking that since Judas was in charge of the money box, Jesus said to him, "Buy what is needed for the festival, or give something to the poor." [30]So after taking the piece of bread, he [Judas] left at once. And it was night.

"But in order that the Scripture might be fulfilled, 'The one who is eat-   **13:18–20**
ing my bread has lifted up his heel against me.'" The text cited is Ps.
41:9.[1] The quotation brings out the "treacherous and faithless nature"
of Judas's deed: he was about to betray the one whose bread he had
eaten as a sign of intimate fellowship (Ridderbos 1997: 467). By Jesus'
day, David had become a "type" or model of David's "greater Son," the
coming Messiah, on the basis of passages such as 2 Sam. 7:12–16 or Ps.
2. Several aspects of David's life are given a messianic application in
the NT, especially his suffering, weakness, and betrayal (Carson 1991:
470).[2] Rabbinic interpretation took Ps. 41:9 to refer to Ahithophel's
conspiracy with Absalom against David.[3] In ancient Semitic cultures,
eating bread at the table of a superior amounted to a pledge of loyalty
(2 Sam. 9:7–13; 1 Kings 18:19; 2 Kings 25:29), and "to betray one with
whom bread had been eaten . . . was a gross breach of the traditions of
hospitality" (Bernard 1928: 2.467).

The expression "lifted up his heel against me" is open to several interpretations. Carson (1991: 471, citing Bruce) sees it as "has given me
a great fall" or "has taken cruel advantage of me" or "has walked out on
me." Morris (1995: 553) and others think that the imagery may be that
of a horse preparing to kick. R. Brown (1970: 554) notes, "To show the
bottom of one's foot to someone in the Near East is a mark of contempt.
. . . Some [though not Brown himself] would see here a reminiscence of
Gen iii 15: 'You shall bruise . . . his heel.'" Barrett (1978: 445) suggests
"the action of one who 'shakes off the dust of his feet against' another"
(cf. Luke 9:5; 10:11; see Bishop 1958–59: 331–33; Morris 1995: 553). From
Jacob (in whose case the heel connotes trickery) to Achilles (whose heel,
suggesting weakness, is perhaps the most famous of all), it appears that
the heel is patient of a wide variety of symbolic applications. At the heart
of the present issue seems to be Jesus' betrayal by a close friend (cf. Matt.
26:50 and Psalms references cited in commentary at 13:21).[4]

---

1. John's quotation is closer to the MT than to the LXX. Menken (1990) contends that
the rendering of Ps. 41:9 in the present passage represents the evangelist's own translation from the Hebrew. Moloney (1998: 384), on the strength of the evangelist's choice of
the verb τρώγω (trōgō [used also in 6:54–58]) in the place of the LXX's ἐσθίω (esthiō) for
"eat," postulates "eucharistic overtones" to the meal. On fulfillment quotations, see commentary at 12:38. Similar texts in the Psalms include 31:9–13; 38:10–12; 55:13–14 (see
commentary at 13:21). Ridderbos (1997: 467 [cf. R. Brown 1970: 554]) rightly argues for
a general sense of "this is to fulfill the scripture" rather than taking the statement to imply
that Jesus chose Judas in order to fulfill Scripture. This latter view seems to be held by
Carson (1991: 470), who writes, "The reason Jesus chose one who would betray him was
to fulfill the Scripture."

2. Note especially the use of Ps. 22 in the Gospel passion narratives and the Davidic
psalms noted in commentary at 11:33.

3. See *b. Sanh.* 106b; cf. 2 Sam. 15:12.

4. Schlatter (1948: 285) comments, "The kick with the foot symbolizes the entire dis-
solution of fellowship, just as 'eating his bread' portrays its reality and completeness."

"From now on, I'm telling you before it happens, in order that you may believe when it does happen that I am [the one I claim to be]" (cf. 8:58). Jesus' prescience is frequently reiterated in this section (14:29; 16:1, 4, 32, 33), which recalls similar expressions referring to God in the OT (Ezek. 24:24; Isa. 43:10 [cf. 41:26; 46:10; 48:3, 5–6]; see Ridderbos 1997: 467). The evangelist here stresses that Jesus was not "the deceived and helpless victim of unsuspected treachery, but the One sent by God to effect the divine purpose going forward calmly and unafraid" (Morris 1995: 553). "I am [the one I claim to be]," as in 8:24 and 8:28, very likely has overtones of deity (Morris 1995: 553; Moloney 1998: 381; Köstenberger 1999a: 261).[5]

A solemn statement introduced by ἀμὴν ἀμήν (amēn amēn, truly, truly), "Whoever accepts anyone I send accepts me; and whoever accepts me accepts the one who sent me," reiterates similar earlier statements in this Gospel (see 5:23; 12:44–50; esp. 13:16). This teaching (which mirrors Jewish teaching on representation [see commentary at 5:23]) is also found in the Synoptics (Matt. 10:40; Mark 9:37; Luke 10:16; cf. Matt. 25:40). In context, this statement, which is rather surprising at this juncture,[6] may serve the dual purpose of alluding to Judas's betrayal and of anticipating the disciples' future commission, which will entail identification with Jesus, their sender (20:21), and lead them to experience similar rejection as did their master (Carson 1991: 471–72). Perhaps in order to encourage his followers not to waver in the face of Judas's imminent defection, Jesus reminds them of their close association with him in their mission (Ridderbos 1997: 467).

13:21–22   "After he had said these things"—a transitional statement preparing the reader for what is about to follow—Jesus, "stirred up inside" (ταράσσω, tarassō [see commentary at 11:33; 12:27]), seizes the initiative by informing his disciples explicitly that one of them will betray him. The word ταράσσω provides the reader with another glimpse of Jesus' humanity and range of emotions. Notably, all three instances of Jesus being stirred up inside in this Gospel relate to the horror of human death (an effect of the work of Satan). In 11:33, Jesus is agitated in the face of Lazarus's death; in 12:27, he is stirred in light of the prospect of his own death. In 5:7, the term is used more concretely for water being stirred. In 14:1, 27, Jesus tells his followers not to be troubled by the specter of

5. Commenting on 13:19, Carson (1991: 471) notes that ἐγώ εἰμι (egō eimi, I am) is "an everyday expression that can be devoid of theological overtones" but also "can call to mind the ineffable name of God," without adjudicating the issue. At 13:20, however, he refers to "I am he" as a "stunning Christological claim."

6. Ridderbos (1997: 467) notes that at the outset, 13:20 does not seem to fit the apologetic thrust of 13:18–19. Barrett (1978: 445) observes the rapidly oscillating movement of thought between the intimate union sustained by Jesus with his disciples and the prediction of Judas's betrayal.

his death.[7] In the present passage, Jesus' emotions are shown to be in a state of turmoil, his whole inner self convulsing at the thought of one of his closest followers betraying him to his enemies.[8]

Jesus then solemnly "testified" (ἐμαρτύρησεν, *emartyrēsen*), again prefacing his remarks with the authoritative introductory formula ἀμὴν ἀμήν. The verb μαρτυρέω (*martyreō*, testify, witness) usually is associated in John's Gospel with the witness of others to Jesus, but in several passages Jesus himself is said to bear witness (e.g., 3:32; 7:7; 8:14; 13:21; 18:37). Thus far, Jesus, though cognizant of the identity of the betrayer (6:64; 13:11), had spoken of the impending betrayal in fairly oblique terms (6:70; 13:10, 18; though John's readers have known the identity of the betrayer all along [6:71; 12:4]). His followers may have believed that the betrayer was someone outside the circle of the Twelve or that the betrayal would be inadvertent. Perhaps their assumption was that Jesus would be able to avert any such threat by dint of his miracle-working abilities (Carson 1991: 472). Now he is broaching the issue more directly: "One of you is going to betray me."

The disciples, for their part, respond with bewilderment and confusion to Jesus' announcement that one from their own midst would betray him.[9] It surely would have been a highly unsettling feeling to know that a traitor was right in their midst. Not only was this revelation sure to engender self-doubt, but also it would have aroused suspicion of the genuine discipleship of others among the circle of the Twelve. The fact that neither here nor elsewhere do any of his fellow disciples express suspicion of Judas indicates that he had "covered his duplicity very well" (Morris 1995: 555).

Peter, always ingenious, motions to the disciple reclining next to him ("the one whom Jesus loved"), urging him to ask Jesus which one he meant. In the ensuing sequence of events, Judas—no surprise to the reader—emerges as the betrayer. Amazingly, the matter is still dealt with in such a private and inconspicuous manner that the disciples do not pick up the cue, interpreting Jesus' parting words to Judas as perhaps an instruction to buy what is needed for the festival or to give

13:23

---

7. This same word is chosen to depict the emotional turmoil suffered by Herod at reports of the birth of another king (Matt. 2:3) and by the disciples at the occasion of Jesus' walking on the water (Mark 6:50 = Matt. 14:26; see also Luke 1:12; Gal. 1:7; 5:10; 1 Pet. 3:14).

8. Jesus' experience closely parallels that of David, who expressed extreme anguish over the betrayal of a close friend (Ps. 55:2–14; see also Ps. 31:9–10; 38:10; and other references to Davidic psalms noted in commentary at 11:33).

9. This is the only instance of the verb ἀπορέω (*aporeō*, be at a loss) in this Gospel. The verb's other NT occurrences convey the notion of perplexity (Mark 6:20; Luke 24:4 [cf. 21:25]; Acts 25:20; 2 Cor. 4:8; Gal. 4:20). See also 1 Macc. 3:31; Josephus, *Ant.* 2.12.2 §271; *Life* 32 §161; the "Unknown Gospel" 1.63 (mid–second century A.D.) (see Bell and Skeat 1935: 13).

something to the poor. As John tells it, the scene could hardly be more ominous, for as soon as Judas takes the bread, Satan enters into him; and when Judas leaves the room, John remarks, in a phrase as terse as it is pregnant with meaning, "And it was night."

The expression "the disciple Jesus loved" probably refers to the historical figure of John the son of Zebedee as an oblique form of self-reference on part of the evangelist.[10] Since doubtless his recipients knew him well, the author can dispense with his proper name (Jackson 1999: 31). The character is here introduced for the first time. He reappears at the foot of the cross (19:26–27), at the empty tomb (20:2–9), by the Sea of Tiberias (21:1, 20–23), and in the final two verses that identify him as the author of this Gospel (21:24–25). The "other disciple" of 18:15–16 and 20:2–9 should in all likelihood also be identified as the "disciple Jesus loved," since 20:2 combines both expressions ("the other disciple, the one Jesus loved").

That disciple was reclining next to Jesus.[11] Literally, the expression means reclining "in his lap" or "at his side" (κόλπος, kolpos [cf. Luke 6:38; 16:22, 23; see also commentary at 13:25]). The reference constitutes an unmistakable echo of 1:18, where Jesus is said to be "at the Father's side" (Carson 1991: 473; R. Brown 1970: 577; Beck 1997: 113).[12] In both contexts, revelation is in view (Stibbe 1993: 149–50). Jesus' closeness to the Father enabled him to make God known in a unique, authoritative manner. Likewise, John's (physical) proximity to Jesus enables him to find out from Jesus the identity of the betrayer. Hence, the present passage legitimizes and authorizes the author of the present Gospel and the testimony contained therein.[13]

10. So, among others, Schlatter 1948: 286. On the "disciple Jesus loved," see Köstenberger 1998b: 154–61 (including further bibliographic references). For the identification of the "disciple Jesus loved" with John the son of Zebedee, see chapter 1 in Köstenberger 1999a; for the identification of the "disciple Jesus loved" with the Fourth Evangelist, see Jackson 1999. See also the discussion of authorial modesty in Vanhoozer 1993: 374, citing Augustine and Westcott. Contra Culpepper (1983: 121–23), who views the "beloved disciple" not only as an "ideal disciple" but also as the physical personification of the Paraclete. Beck (1997: 108–36) essentially aligns himself with Culpepper in characterizing this disciple as "the paradigm" or "embodiment of discipleship" (pp. 135–36).

11. Wallace (1996: 648) notes that ἦν ἀνακείμενος (ēn anakeimenos, he was reclining) is an imperfect periphrastic participle, which accentuates the ongoing, continual nature of the disciple's posture close to Jesus.

12. Barrett (1978: 446) maintains that "the specially favoured disciple is represented as standing in the same relation to Christ as Christ to the Father" (cf. Beasley-Murray 1999: 238). Morris (1995: 555 n. 53) argues that Barrett goes too far and that there is only "a tender regard" between Jesus and the "disciple he loved." Indeed, Barrett's statement seems somewhat hyperbolic, though Morris's reaction leads him to a wording that appears unduly minimalistic. The verbal allusion does suggest that an analogy is intended with regard to intimacy of relationship, without implying that the beloved disciple's relationship with Jesus is identical to Jesus' relationship with the Father in every respect.

13. Though the suggestion by Witherington (1995: 238–39) that the beloved disciple's "position at the head of the table next to Jesus may in fact suggest that it was his house in

As to the setting for a formal meal, usually several couches were placed in a U shape around a table. Those eating reclined with their heads toward the table and pointed their legs away from it. Leaning on the left elbow, the right hand was free to handle the food. The host sat in the middle of the main couch, flanked by the guest of honor to his left and the second guest of honor to his right.[14] The latter would have had his head close to the host's chest (Morris 1995: 555–56; cf. Jeremias 1966a: 48–49).[15] Clearly, this would have been the place where the "disciple Jesus loved" reclined. Though only second in importance, this nonetheless was the place of a trusted friend.

Peter apparently sat further away and so signaled (νεύω, neuō) to the "disciple Jesus loved," who reclined next to Jesus (cf. 20:8; see Schlatter 1948: 286). The word νεύω (elsewhere in the NT only in Acts 24:10) means "nodded [as a signal]."[16] Some have adduced here the practice at the Essene and Qumran meals whereby one could speak only in due order (Josephus, J.W. 2.8.5 §132; 1QS 6:10). If the analogy holds, then the "disciple Jesus loved" would have reclined in a more prominent position than did Peter and thus have had the right to speak before him (K. Kuhn 1957: 69). However, Peter, sitting at a distance, may simply have signaled to the "disciple Jesus loved," who reclined closer to Jesus, without reference to such a formal procedure.

13:24–26

In any case, one is struck by the noncompetitive relationship between Peter and John, though the latter is presented as being close to the source of revelation both literally and figuratively, which made him a primary candidate for writing an authoritative, spiritually penetrating Gospel (Ridderbos 1997: 470). The verb rendered "ask" in 13:24, πυνθάνομαι (pynthanomai), is found also in 4:52 with the meaning "inquire" (see commentary there). The easiest way for the "disciple Jesus loved" to address Jesus was to lean back until his head literally rested on Jesus' chest (στῆθος, stēthos [here and at 21:20]).[17]

---

which this banquet was held" is mere conjecture. Reclining at meals was first introduced into Judaism from the Hellenistic world (NewDocs 1 §1.9; 2 §26.75) and initially viewed as a sign of decadence (Amos 6:4–7). By NT times, however, reclining had become standard practice at banquets and feasts, including Passover celebrations. This leisurely way of observance, which symbolized freedom in contrast to Israel's bondage in Egypt (see b. Pesaḥ. 108a), stood in marked, self-conscious contrast with the haste that marked the first Passover on the night of the exodus (Exod. 12:11).

14. Contra Witherington (1995: 239), who, without substantiation, claims that "the side to the right of the host was the more favored side at such meals, while the left-hand side was less favored and sometimes even had negative associations."

15. "The senior takes his place first, the second next above him, and then the third one below him" (b. Ber. 46b).

16. Parallels cited in BDAG 670 include Lucian, Cataplus 15 (second century A.D.) and BGU 1978.9 (A.D. 39).

17. Elsewhere in the NT only in Luke 18:13; 23:48; Rev. 15:6; compare κόλπος in John 1:18; 13:23. On "Lord," see 13:6, 9, 36, 37 and commentary at 13:12–14.

In response to his beloved disciple's request, Jesus identifies the betrayer as "the one whose piece of bread I will dip and give to him," possibly recalling the quotation in 13:18 (Schnackenburg 1990: 3.30). Not only does this provide a clue to the identity of the betrayer, but also it places the "disciple Jesus loved" in the critical role of witness (Ridderbos 1997: 470). Jesus' reply must have been given discreetly, for in 13:27–30 the other disciples are still guessing as to the reason for Judas's departure (Carson 1991: 474). Intriguingly, there is no recorded response on the part of the "disciple Jesus loved," who may simply have watched as the events unfolded.[18]

The host at a festive meal (here Jesus) might well dip a tasty bit into a common bowl and pass it on to someone as a sign of honor or friendship (similarly, Ruth 2:14, though there Ruth dips her own bread). The term ψωμίον (*psōmion*, piece of bread), used only in this scene in the NT, refers to a morsel, usually bread, though sometimes meat. Perhaps, as Carson (1991: 474) suggests, the scene took place "at an early point of the paschal meal when bitter herbs were dipped into a bowl of fruit puree, the *harōset* sauce of dates, raisins and sour wine" (see *m. Pesaḥ.* 10.3; cf. Laney 1992: 247). The fact that Jesus could pass the sop to Judas Iscariot so easily suggests that he was close by, possibly on Jesus' left, the place of honor (Carson 1991: 474; cf. R. Brown 1970: 574; Morris 1995: 556).

Dipping the piece of bread, Jesus gives it to Judas Iscariot (the use of Judas's full name underscores the solemnity of the occasion).[19] Ridderbos (1997: 470–71) aptly sums up the significance of the event: "Everything that until now has awaited fulfillment becomes real: the bread prophecy of Psalm 41 (cf. vs. 18), the Satan-inspired plan to 'betray' Jesus (vs. 2), Satan himself moving into action. All these things have awaited the signal that Jesus—into whose hands the Father has put all things—had to give. He now gives that signal expressly to Judas." On a human level, Jesus' action constitutes an indication of friendship (Carson [1991: 474] calls it "a final gesture of supreme love") as well as a final appeal (rejected by the betrayer).

13:27–30 The evangelist ominously notes that at this point Satan entered into Judas (see 13:2; 1 Chron. 21:1; cf. 2 Sam. 24:1).[20] The term εἰσέρχομαι (*eiserchomai*, enter) is used by the Synoptics with regard to demon

---

18. Carson (1991: 474) suggests that "the momentous nature of Jesus' confidence left him temporarily paralysed." Barrett (1978: 447) says that the disciple's "inactivity is incomprehensible." Morris (1995: 558) thinks that the disciple "did not grasp the significance of the sop," an option sharply rejected by Barrett (1978: 447), who objects that "to say that he failed to grasp the meaning of the sign is to make him an imbecile."

19. On Judas Iscariot, son of Simon, see commentary at 6:71.

20. Two interesting parallels are found in T. Sim. 2:7 and T. Ash. 1:8. The DSS reveal the belief, also found in John (e.g., 8:44), that the relation between the devil and evil humans is

possession (e.g., Mark 5:12; Luke 8:30; 11:26). However, in the present passage it is not demons but Satan himself who is said to enter a person, which is without parallel in later Judaism (Foerster, *TDNT* 7:162–63). A crucial parallel is Luke 22:3, where Satan is said to have entered Judas prior to his betrayal (see also Matt. 16:23 par.). Judas's act of betrayal would have the most serious consequences for him personally. Jesus himself said, "It would be better for him if he had not been born" (Matt. 26:24 par.). Matthew reports how Judas later was overcome by remorse and in utter desperation hanged himself (27:3–5; cf. Acts 1:18–19).

"What you are about to do—do it quickly" (cf. John 13:11).[21] This command resembles the one issued by Jesus to Judas in Gethsemane according to Matt. 26:50: "Friend, do what you came for." Jesus gently prods Judas to go ahead and follow through with what he has already decided to do in his heart. This shows that Jesus is in charge rather than being a mere victim of events beyond his control (cf. John 10:11, 15, 16–18; and esp. 18:4–11).[22]

Some thought that Jesus was telling Judas to buy what was needed for the festival.[23] This being the night of the Passover, 15 Nisan, the disciples thought that Judas was dispatched to buy what was needed for the festival—not Passover, but the Feast of Unleavened Bread (the *hagigah*; see Carson 1991: 475; Morris 1995: 558). This festival started that very night and went on for seven days. Since the next day (Friday, still 15 Nisan) was a high feast day, and the following day was a Sabbath, Jesus might have considered it expedient to make necessary purchases (such as more unleavened bread) that night. Though there seems to have been some debate on the subject (*m. Pesaḥ.* 4.5), the making of

---

like that of father to child (see commentary at 12:36; cf. Wis. 2:24). In Judaism in general, however, a person's will was considered decisive in determining which of two impulses, that toward good or that toward evil, prevailed (see commentary at 8:34). The present verse is the only place in John's Gospel where the name "Satan" is found. Elsewhere the expression is διάβολος (*diabolos*, devil [6:70; 8:44; 13:2]). Schlatter (1948: 287) notes that Satan entering Judas is the converse of a disciple's "remaining in Jesus."

21. The present verb ποιεῖς (*poieis*, you are doing) is conative (Wallace 1996: 535), denoting an action not yet begun but about to be attempted. Carson (1991: 475) and Morris (1995: 557 n. 63; cf. Barrett 1978: 448) suggest that τάχιον (*tachion*, quickly) should be construed as a genuine comparative and rendered "more quickly" (than Judas had planned). This would be in keeping with the way the comparative form of this word is used in its only other Johannine reference (20:4), though in its other two NT instances the form is simply elative, to be rendered "soon" or "quickly" (Heb. 13:19, 23). Hence, caution seems to be called for in drawing conclusions from the comparative form of the term in the present passage.

22. Conversely, it appears that Satan was unaware of the ultimate outcome of Jesus' crucifixion, that is, his own demise (cf. 1 John 3:8; Heb. 2:14–15), or else he presumably would not have prompted Judas to betray Jesus (Kruse 2003: 289).

23. For in "charge of the money," see commentary at 12:6.

such purchases probably was both possible and lawful (though not necessarily convenient).[24]

Owing to the discreetness of the exchange between Jesus and "the disciple he loved," the other disciples (with the presumed exceptions of "the disciple Jesus loved" and Peter [R. Brown 1970: 575]) were still unaware of the significance of Judas's abrupt departure. This puts the beloved disciple in a position of privileged insight at this juncture of the narrative (Ridderbos 1997: 471). As to the reason for Judas's sudden errand, some thought that he may have been dispatched to give something to the poor (see 12:4–8 pars. and commentary at 9:8). Almsgiving was an important part of Jewish piety. As the famous rabbi Hillel used to say, "The more charity, the more peace" (*m. ʾAbot* 2.7). For pilgrims to Jerusalem, it was customary to give alms to the poor (Josephus, *Ant.* 4.8.19 §227).

On Passover night, the temple gates were left open from midnight on, allowing beggars to congregate (*Ant.* 18.2.2 §§29–30; see Jeremias 1969: 54). In fact, almsgiving was regarded as particularly meritorious when done in Jerusalem.[25] A talmudic maxim reflects a much older principle: "Even a poor man who himself lives from alms, should give alms" (*b. Giṭ.* 7b; cf. Luke 21:1–4 par.). Jesus himself was poor,[26] but this did not keep him from showing concern for others who were poor as well. "Sell your possessions and give to the poor" was his advice both to the disciples and to the rich young ruler (Luke 12:33; Matt. 19:21 pars.). The early church remembered this saying of Jesus, "It is more blessed to give than to receive" (Acts 20:35).

Possessed by Satan though he was, Judas obeys Jesus and leaves immediately (Carson 1991: 476).[27] The evangelist ominously adds, "And it was night" (cf. Matt. 26:20 = Mark 14:17: "when evening came"; 1 Cor. 11:23: "on the night he was betrayed").[28] The main meal usually was eaten in the late afternoon, but the Passover celebration took place at night.[29] The present reference in all likelihood also conveys the notion of spiritual darkness entered by the betrayer (cf. Luke 22:53: "this is your hour—when darkness reigns"). It was the night of whose coming Jesus had repeatedly warned, and now the separation between light and darkness was finally made (Ridderbos 1997: 473; cf. Laney 1992: 248).

---

24. But see Exod. 12:22, which indicates that at the original Passover, people were required to stay inside. A similar piece of legislation is found in *m. Šabb.* 23.1 (cited in Köstenberger 2002c: 135).

25. On acts of charity, see Jeremias 1969: 126–34; on begging, 116–19.

26. See Matt. 8:20 par.; 17:24–27; Luke 8:3; cf. 2 Cor. 8:9.

27. The term εὐθύς (*euthys*, immediately), extremely common in Mark, is rare in John. It occurs here for the first time and then only at 13:32 and 19:34, which highlights its deliberate use by the Fourth Evangelist.

28. Schlatter (1948: 287) infers from this reference that it was not dark when the meal started.

29. Exod. 12:8; cf. *m. Zebaḥ.* 5.8. See Jeremias (1969: 44–46), who also cites Jub. 49:1, 12; *t. Pesaḥ.* 1.34; and other references.

2. Jesus' Final Instructions: The Farewell Discourse (13:31–16:33)

While chapters 13 through 17 form a larger unit, 13:1–30 may be considered a preamble (the cleansing of the messianic community) and chapter 17 a postlude (Jesus' final prayer)[1] to the actual farewell discourse in 13:31–16:33.[2] After explaining that his followers cannot follow immediately (13:31–38), Jesus asserts that he is the way to the Father (14:1–14) and announces the imminent coming of the Spirit (14:15–31; 16:4b–15). The disciples must remain in close relationship with Jesus, just as branches derive their life from the vine (ch. 15). Once Jesus has left, the world's hatred will center on the disciples; but they must bear witness (15:18–16:4a). Though Jesus' followers will mourn his crucifixion, their sorrow will turn into joy when they see the resurrected Christ (16:16–33).

The farewell discourse proper is constrained fairly narrowly by the historical position of Jesus and the Eleven immediately prior to the crucifixion and by Jesus' need to prepare his followers for the brief interim (the "little while") between the crucifixion and the resurrection three days later. For this reason, certain elements of 13:31–16:33 can be understood only in reference to the historical vantage point of Jesus' original disciples (e.g., 15:27: "You also must testify, for *you have been with me from the beginning*," NIV, italics added). Readers today, looking back on both Jesus' crucifixion *and* resurrection, need not wait "for a little while" in grief before they can rejoice at seeing Jesus again (14:19; 16:16–22), nor need there be any delay in asking the Father in Jesus' name (16:23). Also, at that time Jesus' hearers had no concept of the coming Paraclete (e.g., 14:16–18, 26; 16:7–15) or of what it meant to live in organic relationship with their exalted Lord (ch. 15). The Gospel writer, and readers ancient and modern, living in the era subsequent to the giving of the Spirit at Pentecost, share a historical vantage point that enables them to understand life in the Spirit in a way not possible when the disciples first heard Jesus utter these words.

---

1. See the introductory ταῦτα ἐλάλησεν (*tauta elalēsen*, he said these things) in 17:1.

2. The outline of the structure of the first unit (13:31–14:31) below follows Carson (1991: 498) and Blomberg (2002: 199), who take 14:15–31 as a single unit. Others divide this section between 14:24 and 14:25 (e.g., Moloney 1998: 391–92; R. Brown 1970: 623). Schnackenburg (1990: 3.58), following Becker, sees a break between 14:17 and 14:18.

a. Jesus' Departure and Sending of the Spirit (13:31–14:31)

Now that the betrayer has left, the stage is set for Jesus to instruct the Eleven regarding life after his own departure (cf. 13:1). Jesus' reaction here is characterized by almost palpable relief. With Judas gone, the new messianic community has been cleansed (cf. 13:10–11). The time has come for Jesus' parting instructions to his disciples. To their minds, nothing could be worse than the loss of their beloved teacher. But according to Jesus, this actually will work out to their benefit. For he will send another "helping presence," who will take up Jesus'—and the disciples'—case. From his exalted position with the Father, Jesus will grant his followers' requests and enable them to accomplish even greater works than he performed during his earthly ministry.

  i. Jesus' departure and the disciples' inability to follow immediately (13:31–38)
 ii. Jesus' departure and sending of the Spirit (14:1–31)
    (1) Jesus is the way (14:1–14)
    (2) The promised "other helping presence" (14:15–31)

Exegesis and Exposition

[13:31]Then when he had gone, Jesus said, "Now is the Son of Man glorified, and God is glorified in him. [32]⌜If God is glorified in him⌝, God will also glorify him in himself, and he will glorify him at once. [33]Children, I will be with you for just a short while longer. You will look for me, and just as I told the Jews, so I tell you now: Where I am going you cannot come. [34]A new command I give you, to love one another, just as I loved you, that you also love one another. [35]By this all will know that you are my disciples, if you have love among one another."

[36]Simon Peter said to him, "Lord, where are you going?" Jesus answered, "Where I am going, you cannot follow me now—but you will follow me later."

[37]Peter said to him, "Lord, why can't I follow you now? I will lay down my life for you." [38]Jesus answered, "Will you really lay down your life for me? Truly, truly, I say to you, before the rooster crows, you will deny me three times.

[14:1]"Don't let your hearts be troubled. Believe in God; believe also in me. [2]In my Father's house are many dwellings; if it were not so, would I have told you ⌜that⌝ I am going to prepare a place for you? [3]And if I go and prepare a place for you, I will come again and take you with me, so that where I am, you will be as well. ⁴ʳAnd where I am going—you know the wayˀ."

⁵Thomas said to him, "Lord, we don't know where you are going; how can we know the way?" ⁶Jesus said to him, "*I* am the way and the truth and the life: no one comes to the Father except through me. ⁷If ˀyou have come to know meˀ, ˀyou will knowˀ my Father as well. And, certainly, you know him and have seen him."

⁸Philip said to him, "Lord, show us the Father, and it will be sufficient for us." ⁹Jesus said to him, "How long have I been with you and you still don't know me, Philip? Whoever has seen me has seen the Father. How can you say, 'Show us the Father'? ¹⁰Don't you believe that I am in the Father and the Father is in me? The words I speak to you I do not speak of my own accord, but the Father who resides in me—he performs his works. ¹¹Believe me that I am in the Father and the Father is in me; but if not, believe on account of the works themselves. ¹²Truly, truly, I say to you, whoever believes in me will also perform the works I am doing—and he will perform even greater works than these, because I am going to the Father. ¹³And whatever you ask in my name, this I will do, so that the Father may be glorified in the Son. ¹⁴If you ask me anything in my name, I will do it. ¹⁵If you love me, you will obey my commands. ¹⁶And I will ask the Father, and he will give you another helping presence, that he might be with you forever, ¹⁷the Spirit of truth, whom the world cannot receive, because it neither sees him nor knows him. You know him, because he resides with you and will be in you. ¹⁸I will not leave you as orphans; I will come to you. ¹⁹In just a little while, the world will no longer see me, but you will see me; because I live, you also will live. ²⁰On that day you will know that I am in my Father, and you are in me, and I am in you. ²¹Whoever has my commands and keeps them—he is the one who loves me. And the one who loves me will be loved by my Father, and I too will love him and disclose myself to him."

²²Judas—not Iscariot—said to him, "Lord, why is it that you are about to disclose yourself to us yet not to the world?" ²³Jesus answered and said to him, "If anyone loves me, he will keep my word, and my Father will love him, and we will come to him and make our dwelling with him. ²⁴Whoever does not love me does not keep my words. And the word you hear is not mine but the Father's who sent me. ²⁵I have told you these things while still with you. ²⁶The helping presence, the Holy Spirit, whom the Father will send in my name—he will teach you all things and remind you of all the things I told you. ²⁷Peace I leave with you—my peace I give you. I don't give to you as the world gives. Don't let your hearts be troubled and don't be unsettled. ²⁸You heard that I said to you, 'I am going away and I am coming back to you.' If you loved me, you would rejoice that I am going to the Father, because the Father is greater than I. ²⁹And now I have told you before it happens, so that you may believe when it does happen. ³⁰I will not say much more while I am with you, for the ruler of the world is coming; yet he has no hold on me, ³¹but in order that the world may

know that I love the Father and do just as the Father commanded me—come, let's go away from here."

i. Jesus' Departure and the Disciples' Inability to Follow Immediately (13:31–38)

13:31–32 Now that the new messianic community has been cleansed and the traitor has been removed, Jesus' final instruction of his followers can begin. Jesus begins by speaking of his imminent "glorification," that is, his cross-death, and notes that his time with his disciples prior to this event is short. This raises the specter of misunderstanding, since Jesus' followers still fail to grasp the import of Jesus' oblique references to his "glorification." Peter becomes the foil for this misunderstanding to be exposed.

The first two verses provide the reader with Jesus' commentary on the significance of Judas's departure. The traitor's exit marks the beginning of the farewell discourse, for now "the actual machinery of arrest, trial and execution" has been set into motion (Carson 1991: 482). The arrival of the Greeks triggered the first statement that Jesus' time had come; Judas's departure triggers the second (Moloney 1998: 385). The statement "Now has the Son of Man been glorified, and God in him" echoes the heavenly voice in 12:28. Hence, for the evangelist's eyes of faith, Jesus' darkest hour is transformed into the hour of his glorification (Schnackenburg 1990: 3.49).

The "Son of Man" was first mentioned at 1:51. Outside the NT, this figure is associated with glory (esp. Dan. 7:13–14; 1 Enoch 37–71); in the Synoptics, he is frequently associated with suffering. John brings these two elements together in striking fashion (Carson 1991: 482).[1] The "glorification of the Son" (cf. 12:23, 28; 17:5) is a Johannine euphemism for the events related to Jesus' crucifixion.[2] Once again, there are echoes of Isaiah (e.g., 49:3). "Immediately" constitutes a material parallel to the "three days" of John 2:19 (Schlatter 1948: 288).

13:33–35 The next topic that Jesus chooses to address is the temporary separation from his disciples owing to his impending departure (Ridderbos 1997: 474). Fulfilling the "paschal role of head of the family" (Carson 1991: 483), Jesus here affectionately addresses his followers as his "dear children."[3] Jesus' unconditional love is revealed in that "they remain his disciples, his 'little children,' lost yet loved in their misunderstanding,

---

1. This is the last time that the term "the Son of Man" is used in this Gospel. Whereas the title occurs twelve times in the first part of John's Gospel (chs. 1–12), this is the only reference to the Son of Man in the second part.

2. The reference point of εὐθύς (*euthys*, immediately) presumably is the resurrection.

3. The diminutive τεκνία (*teknia*, little children) is used only here in John's Gospel but seven times in John's first epistle (1 John 2:1, 12, 28; 3:7, 18; 4:4; 5:21). See Brodie 1993: 456; Westcott 1908: 2.160–61.

failure, and ignorance" (Moloney 1998: 385). The epithet is fitting also in that farewell discourses often feature a dying father instructing his children (e.g., T. Reub. 1:3; see R. Brown 1970: 611).

The content of Jesus' teaching is the same as that delivered to "the Jews" who rejected him (see 7:33; 8:21; 12:35), though here it is not a warning to believe before it is too late, but rather an announcement of another mode of existence, which will mean that his disciples' faith in him will face different demands (see 14:19; 16:16; see Ridderbos 1997: 474–75).[4] The startling effect that Jesus' announcement had on his followers is indicated by Peter's query in 13:36 (R. Brown 1970: 612). There is a marked difference between the implications of Jesus' departure for his disciples and for the Jews. The Jews will not be able to find him (7:34), but Jesus will prepare a place for his followers (14:2–3). The Jews will die in their sin (8:21); the disciples will have life in his name (14:19) (Carson 1991: 483).

Jesus' "new command" to his followers to love each other as he has loved them constitutes the third major topic.[5] This will be the mark of his disciples (cf. Matt. 5:43–48; Rom. 8:37; Rev. 1:5).[6] The command to love one's neighbor as oneself was not new.[7] Love within the community was also highly regarded at Qumran (e.g., 1QS 1:10; cf. Josephus, J.W. 2.8.2 §119), and neighbor love was emphasized by the first-century rabbi Hillel.[8] What was new was Jesus' command for his disciples to love one another *as he has loved them*—laying down their lives.[9] This rule of self-sacrificial, self-giving, selfless love, a unique quality of love inspired by

---

4. On "only a little longer," see 7:33; 12:35; 14:19; 16:16–19. The phrase is also used in the OT by the prophets to point to the shortness of time before God's salvation would come (Isa. 10:25; Jer. 51:33).

5. "New command" is in the emphatic position (Morris 1995: 562). The command probably harks back to the footwashing earlier in the chapter (Carson 1991: 484; Burge 2000: 376).

6. Words for "love" occur twelve times in John 1–12 and forty-five times in John 13–17 (Köstenberger 1999a: 149). The theme of commandment recurs frequently in Jesus' final discourse and in the Johannine Epistles.

7. Lev. 19:18; cf. Matt. 5:43. For a general survey, see Morris, *DJG* 492–95.

8. For example, *m.* ʾAbot 1.12. There are also several parallels in Testaments of the Twelve Patriarchs (T. Gad 4:1–2; 6:1; T. Zeb. 5:1; 8:5; T. Jos. 17:1–2; T. Iss. 7:6–7; T. Sim. 4:7; T. Reub. 6:9).

9. Cf. 13:1; 15:13; see also 1 John 3:23; 4:7–8, 11–12, 19–21. That the early Christians indeed did love one another is attested in the famous statement, quoting observers of Christians, recorded by the church father Tertullian: "See how they love one another" (*Apol.* 39). Regarding the Jews, on the other hand, the Roman historian Tacitus wrote, "The Jews are extremely loyal toward one another, and always ready to show compassion, but toward every other people they feel only hate and enmity" (*Historiae* 5.5; cf. Josephus, J.W. 2.8.14 §166). Keener (2003: 926) contends that "[l]ike the Qumran community, John's outlook is sectarian and dualistic," but he then proceeds to affirm that this does not negate love for those outside the community. It is unclear to me how, in light of the obvious missionary concern for the world evidenced in this Gospel, Keener can still maintain (even in a qualified sense) that "John's outlook is sectarian."

Jesus' own love for the disciples, will serve as the foundational ethic for the new messianic community.[10]

13:36–38 With reference to Jesus' words in 13:33, Peter now asks where Jesus intends to go.[11] Jesus provides an indirect response, not specifying his destination but merely telling Peter that for now (νῦν, *nyn*) he must stay behind (though he will follow him later; see 14:2–3; 21:18–19).[12] Peter, never one to take no for an answer, wants to follow Jesus immediately (ἄρτι, *arti*) and, in transparent Johannine irony (Morris 1995: 563), responds that he is willing to die for Jesus (it will have to be the other way around).[13] To which Jesus replies, in effect, "Really?"[14] When later given the opportunity to confess Jesus, Peter will deny his Lord three times.

All four Gospels record statements to this effect by Peter (Matt. 26:33–35 pars.). Peter's strong loyalty to Jesus is also shown in his later attempt to thwart Jesus' arrest (Matt. 26:51–54).[15] As to the crowing of the rooster, apparently roosters in Palestine frequently crowed in the late night hours, so that the Romans assigned the label "cockcrow" to the watch between midnight and 3:00 A.M. (cf. Mark 13:35; see commentary at 18:27; Carson 1991: 487). Jesus' prediction that Peter will disown him three times comes true in 18:27 (cf. Matt. 26:69–75 pars.). Fortunately, however, this is not the end of the story; John 21 narrates Peter's restoration by his risen Lord.[16]

ii. Jesus' Departure and Sending of the Spirit (14:1–31)
(1) Jesus Is the Way (14:1–14)

14:1–3 Now that the new messianic community has been cleansed, both literally (the footwashing) and figuratively (the exposure and departure of

---

10. Schlatter (1948: 289) notes that Jesus was first one who gave (*Gebende*) and only then one who commanded (*Gebietende*). Schlatter relates the "new commandment" to the "new grace of the new covenant" (p. 288, contra Calvin).

11. As Lindars (1972: 465) points out, the appearance of Peter at the beginning and at the end of John 13 is another Johannine instance of *inclusio*.

12. In the Greek, "you" here is singular (directed specifically to Peter), while in 13:33 it is plural (addressed to the disciples in general) (Morris 1995: 563).

13. Cf. 10:11. Carson (1991: 486) aptly notes that Peter's response "displays not only gross ignorance of human weakness, but a certain haughty independence that is the seed of the denial itself." Peter has no response to Jesus' prediction of his denials (Schnackenburg 1990: 3.57) and is not heard from again until 18:10 (Morris 1995: 564).

14. Ridderbos (1997: 478) says that Jesus hurls Peter's words back at him "almost contemptuously," though this is not required by the text. Jesus may just as well have responded mildly, albeit with some grief owing to Peter's inability to live up to his good intentions. The theme of the disciples' failure to understand their inability to follow Jesus now is continued throughout the discourse.

15. Note also the verbal similarity between Peter's words and those of the good shepherd (10:11, 15, 17, 18). Thomas voices similar sentiments in 11:16.

16. Schlatter (1948: 290) considers the present reference to be proleptic of the distinction made between Peter and John with regard to the outcome of their ministry.

Judas), and that Peter's denials have been foretold, Jesus can proceed to instruct his followers. Particularly, he must anticipate the aftereffects of his own departure in terms of loss of presence with his disciples. In this first piece of instruction, Jesus promises his followers that he will return (the "second coming" [14:3]) and elaborates on one of the purposes for his going to the Father: he will prepare a place for his disciples in heaven (Morris 1995: 567).[17]

Jesus' encouragement for his followers[18] is for them not to let their hearts be troubled.[19] In keeping with Semitic anthropology, "heart" denotes the seat of a person's will and emotions (Schnackenburg 1990: 3.58).[20] In the OT, God's chosen servants and his people Israel frequently were told not to be afraid, as when entering the promised land (Deut. 1:21, 29; 20:1, 3; Josh. 1:9) or facing threats from their enemies (2 Kings 25:24; Isa. 10:24). The psalmist repeatedly affirms his unwavering trust in God (e.g., Ps. 27:1; 56:3–4). Isaac, Jeremiah, and the apostle Paul alike were encouraged not to be afraid (Gen. 26:24; Jer. 1:8; Acts 27:24), as were Jesus' disciples (Matt. 8:26 par.; 10:31 par.).[21] Jesus continues to encourage his disciples by telling them to trust in God and to trust also in him.[22] The Greek term πιστεύω (pisteuō, believe) denotes personal relational trust, in keeping with OT usage (e.g., Isa. 28:16). In the OT, too, God's people were called upon to trust in God and in his servants (Moses: Exod. 14:31; the prophets: 2 Chron. 20:20; see Schlatter 1948: 291).

"In my Father's house are many dwellings." Earlier in the Gospel, Jesus had noted that "a son remains in the house [οἰκία, oikia] forever" (8:35; see Ridderbos 1997: 490). The only other NT occurrence of the term μονή (monē, single dwelling [from μόνος, monos, alone]) is found

17. As Talbert (1992: 203) notes, Jesus' soteriological priority is expressed here in terms of the chronological priority of Jesus' going: "[Jesus] is going before the disciples do; and until he goes they are unable to follow. . . . 14:1–6, focuses on where Jesus is going, for what purpose, and how one gets there."

18. Note the shift to the plural at 14:1, in contrast to Jesus' personal address to Peter in 13:36–38 (noted by Schnackenburg 1990: 3.57).

19. The Greek present imperative implies that the disciples were anxious already; the phrase therefore may be rendered as "stop being troubled" (Morris 1995: 565; Beasley-Murray 1999: 249; Köstenberger 1999a: 152).

20. On ταράσσω (tarassō, trouble) see commentary at 11:33; 12:27; 13:21. The term καρδία (kardia, heart) occurs, with the single exception of the Isaiah quotation in 12:40, in John only in the farewell discourse (cf. 13:2; 14:27; 16:6, 22).

21. In Second Temple farewell discourses, too, encouragement not to be afraid or dejected was common (1 Enoch 92:2; T. Zeb. 10:1–2; Jub. 22:23).

22. Most commentators take both occurrences of πιστεύετε (pisteute, believe, trust) in 14:1 as imperatives (e.g., Carson 1991: 488; Morris 1995: 566; Beasley-Murray 1999: 249; Burge 2000: 391; Westcott 1908: 2.167; Köstenberger 1999a: 163). Alternatively, the first form may be an indicative: "You trust in God; trust also in me" (NIV footnote) or interrogative: "Bultmann 1971: 600). Schnackenburg (1990: 3.59) notes that 14:1b forms a chiasm ("[You] Trust in God, also in me trust").

in 14:23, where it is said that Jesus and the Father will come and "make their dwelling" with the believer. However, whereas in 14:23 it is clear that spiritual indwelling of believers is in view, 14:2 refers to a reality external to Jesus' followers.[23] "Many" (πολλαί, *pollai* [cf. 2:12; 3:23; 10:32; 11:47; 20:30; 21:25]) dwellings stresses the large number of such dwelling places and thus the abundant space for all those who are prepared to follow Jesus.

In Jesus' day, many dwelling units[24] were combined to form an extended household.[25] It was customary for sons to add to their father's house once married, so that the entire estate grew into a large compound (called *insula*) centered around a communal courtyard. The image used by Jesus may also have conjured up notions of luxurious Greco-Roman villas, replete with numerous terraces and buildings, situated among shady gardens with an abundance of trees and flowing water. Jesus' listeners may have been familiar with this kind of setting from the Herodian palaces in Jerusalem, Tiberias, and Jericho (see Josephus, *J.W.* 5.4.4 §§176–83). Jesus thus conveys to his followers a vision of future heavenly living that surpasses even that enjoyed by the most exalted ruler or wealthy person of that day.[26]

As part of the farewell discourse, the present passage speaks of Jesus' provision for his followers after his departure (cf. 13:33–37; see Köstenberger 1998b: 124–26). Just as his first disciples asked him where he was staying (μένω, *menō*) and he invited them to "come and see" (1:38–39), he now assures his followers that he will not relinquish his responsibility as their teacher. In fact, his provision of permanent, eternal

---

23. This is inadequately recognized by Gundry 1967: 68–72 (see the critique in Carson 1991: 488–89).

24. The rendering "mansions" (rather than "rooms"), which crept into English translations through William Tyndale (1526) via the Vulgate, mistakenly suggests luxurious accommodations in modern parlance (the Latin word *mansio* referred to a stopover place, which was still the meaning of "mansion" in Tyndale's day). See R. Brown 1970: 619; Carson 1991: 489.

25. The expression "my Father's house" refers to the temple in 2:16 (cf. Luke 2:49), but there is no indication in the present context that the temple is in view (see McCaffrey 1988: 63). Note that even in 2:21 the temple is reinterpreted in terms of Jesus' body. On "father's house" as designating a (patriarchal) family in the LXX and extrabiblical literature, see McCaffrey 1988: 50–51.

26. Apocalyptic Second Temple literature provides descriptions of heavenly dwelling places for the saints (e.g., 1 Enoch 39:4–5; 41:2; 71:16; 2 Enoch 61:2–3). Note Luke 16:9, where Jesus speaks of his disciples' being "welcomed into eternal dwellings." Philo regards heaven as a paternal house or city to which the soul returns after death (*Dreams* 1.39 §256; cf. *Conf. Tong.* 17 §78; *Heir* 55 §274; *Mos.* 2.51 §288). The rabbis believed that there were seven classes or departments, graded according to merit, in the heavenly garden of Eden (*Midr. Ps.* 11 §6); the church fathers held similar views. John, however, is decidedly nonapocalyptic (the exception may be 1:51), and his treatment is much more restrained than Philo's existential allegorizing. The rabbinic notion of a compartmentalized heaven is likewise foreign to John.

dwellings for them will transpose this theme onto a higher, eternal plane.[27] Elsewhere, Jesus promises eternal rewards in exchange for "houses" left behind (Matt. 19:29 pars.). Here, rather than elaborating on the characteristics of the Father's house, Jesus is content to stress that there is plenty of room and that believers' future is bound up with a homecoming comparable to a son's return to his father's house (cf. Luke 15:11–32). In keeping with Jewish patriarchal culture, Jesus, the Son of the Father, establishes his followers "as members of the Father's household" and "makes his home accessible to them as a final place of residence" (Schrenk, *TDNT* 5:997).

"If it were not so, would I have told you that I am going to prepare a place for you? And if I go and prepare a place for you. . . ."[28] Ever the servant (cf. 13:1–20), Jesus will continue to serve his followers even after his departure. Once ascended, Jesus has further work to do: he will prepare (ἑτοιμάζω, *hetoimazō* [only here in John's Gospel]) a place for the disciples; for ultimately, they are not of this world (17:15–16). Jesus' provision seems to be patterned after Deuteronomy, where God is said to have gone ahead and to have prepared a place for his people in the promised land (e.g., 1:29–33; see P. Walker 1996: 186–90, esp. 188).[29] There may also be irony in the fact that the Jews fear that their "place" will be taken away from them by the Romans (11:48 [a fear that materialized in A.D. 70]), while Jesus' disciples can look forward to a "place" prepared for them by their master.

"I will come again and take you with me, so that where I am, you will be as well" (cf. 17:24). The reference is to the second coming.[30] Similar terminology is found in Song 8:2a, where the bride says that she will bring her lover to her mother's house. Here Jesus, the messianic bridegroom (3:29), is said first to go to prepare a place for his own in his Father's house and then to come to take them home to be with him.

---

27. On "remain," see at 1:39 and 15:1–4. On "follow," see at 1:37.

28. See additional note on 14:2. Similar language is used in Mark 10:40; 1 Cor. 2:9; Heb. 11:16; 1 Pet. 1:4. Jesus' words in the present passage are designed to further reassure his disciples (cf. Michaels 1989: 267). As Schnackenburg (1990: 3.59) notes, the point of reference probably is John 13:33.

29. Elsewhere in the NT, in the Book of Hebrews, Jesus is depicted as our "forerunner," who has finished the course and entered heaven (6:20; 12:2). In the same book, mention is made of a "heavenly country" or "city" prepared for the saints (11:16).

30. See John 21:22–23; 1 Thess. 4:16–17. So, rightly, Morris 1995: 568. Contra Schnackenburg (1990: 3.62), who says that a reference to the parousia would be in contradiction to the Fourth Evangelist's present eschatology, and Keener (1993: 299), who claims that Jesus' coming after the resurrection to give the Spirit is in view. This certainly is the case in 16:16 (cf. 14:17–24), but it is more than doubtful whether Jesus' comments in 14:2–3 indicate that he will prepare a place for the disciples in the interim between his crucifixion and his resurrection and then come back and take them with him at that time. After all, Jesus taught that the gospel must first be preached to all nations, and this will be done through Jesus' followers.

14:4–7   The present verse marks a progression from Jesus leaving his disciples to the identification of the way (Morris 1995: 569).[31] Jesus' statement "And where I am going—you know the way" (see additional note on 14:4) provokes a series of queries from among his disciples (as in 13:36–38), first by Thomas (who is known for his bluntness [14:5; cf. 11:16; 20:24–29]), then Philip (14:8; cf. 1:43–48; 6:5–7; 12:21–22), then Judas (not Iscariot, surfacing only here [14:22]). At the end of the discourse, the disciples raise one more question (16:17–18), which Jesus resolves to their satisfaction (16:29–30).[32] Once again, John's account reflects firsthand experience, including the recollection of who asked what question at a particular time. Thomas, no doubt representative of his fellow disciples (Ridderbos [1997: 493], who points to the plural "*we* do not know"), and serving as a convenient foil for Jesus' instruction (Schnackenburg 1990: 3.64), is the first to speak up. His remark, in turn, triggers the sixth "I am" saying featured in John's Gospel: "I am the way and the truth and the life: no one comes to the Father except through me."[33]

It is hard to exhaust the multifaceted nature of Jesus' statement here.[34] Thomas, interpreting the comment in the "most crassly natural way" (Carson 1991: 490), is looking for a literal road map, complete with specific directions that would enable him to know how to get to where Jesus is going. This is understandable; if Thomas and his fellow disciples have not come to terms with Jesus' departure itself, how can their thinking about the circumstances surrounding it be coherent (Carson 1991: 491)? But Jesus says that he himself *is* the way (Ridderbos 1997: 493; Carson 1991: 491). Tellingly, the early Christians were initially called the followers of "the Way" (cf. Acts 9:2; 19:9, 23; 22:4; 24:14, 22). Jesus' claim of himself being the way (with the corollary that no one can come to the Father but through him) is as timely today as it was when our Lord first uttered this statement. For in an age of religious pluralism, Christianity's exclusive claims are considered inappropriately narrow,

---

31. Schlatter (1948: 293–94) sees an affinity between the images of Jesus as "the door" (10:7, 9) and as "the way"; the former speaks of entrance into the community, while the latter refers to access to God and entering into eternal life.

32. The asking of clarifying questions was an important aspect of the teacher-disciple relationship in first-century Judaism. For specific rabbinic references and discussion, see Köstenberger 1998a: 120–22.

33. Ridderbos (1997: 493), failing to note 15:1, incorrectly refers to the present passage as the last "I am" saying in this Gospel. Compare also Heb. 10:20 where Jesus is said to have opened up a "new and living way" through his blood. The only other occurrence of ὁδός (*hodos*, way) in this Gospel is 1:23 (citing Isa. 40:3).

34. The importance of 14:6 in the context of the entire Gospel (not to mention Christian theology at large) can hardly be exaggerated. Ridderbos (1997: 493) calls it "the core statement of this entire Gospel." Schnackenburg (1990: 3.65 [cited approvingly by Beasley-Murray 1999: 252]) says that this text "forms a classical summary of the Johannine doctrine of salvation." Burge (2000: 392) calls it the premier expression of the Gospel's theology.

even intolerant, and pluralism itself has, ironically, become the criterion by which all truth claims are judged.[35]

Yet in a day when keeping the law and scrupulous observance of religious customs were considered paramount (cf. 5:10; 6:28; 9:16), Jesus claimed that allegiance to himself was the way. Jesus is the way; he is also the truth and the life.[36] It is sometimes argued that way, truth, and life should be read together as "the true way of life." Yet elsewhere in John three terms linked with the conjunction "and" remain distinct. In 2:14, for instance, "sheep and doves" does not further explicate "cattle," and in 16:8, "righteousness and judgment" does not further explicate "sin." It is true, though, that of the three terms used in 14:6, "the way" is the head term (Carson 1991: 491; cf. 14:4–5); since he is the way, Jesus is also truth and life.[37]

What is more, he is "*the* truth" and "*the* life," that is, truth and life par excellence. In the OT and Second Temple literature, "the way(s) of truth" is a life lived in conformity with the law (e.g., Ps. 119:30; Tob. 1:3; Wis. 5:6).[38] Both "truth" and "life" are applied to Jesus already in the prologue—where it is said that the Word-made-flesh was "full of grace and truth," that "grace and truth came through Jesus Christ" (1:14, 17), and that in that Word "was life" (1:4; cf. 5:26)—and constitute important Johannine concepts throughout.[39] To know the truth and to have life beyond the grave are the great aspirations of humankind. As John tells

---

35. For a comprehensive treatment and critique of religious pluralism within the larger framework of postmodernism, see especially Carson 1996. See also Carson's comments in his commentary (1991: 491–92) and his important rebuttal of Bruce (1983: 298–99 [picked up Beasley-Murray 1999: 253]), who alleges that "Jesus' claim, understood in the light of the prologue to the Gospel, is inclusive, not exclusive." On the exclusivism of 14:6, see also Keener 2003: 941–43.

36. Or perhaps better: truth and life—abstract nouns have the article in Greek but not necessarily in English. Schnackenburg (1990: 3.65) sums up the thrust of this passage well: "By revealing the truth that leads to life and mediating that true life to the one who accepts and realizes that truth in faith, Jesus takes everyone who believes in him to the goal of his existence, that is, 'to the Father'; in this manner, he becomes the 'way.'"

37. Keener (2003: 943) contends that "truth" and "life" in the present passage "merely clarify the 'way'" (following R. Brown 1970: 621).

38. The terms "way," "truth," and "life" frequently are combined in OT wisdom literature (e.g., Ps. 16:11; 86:11; Prov. 15:24). In the DSS, the ways of truth are contrasted with the ways of darkness and deceit. The Qumran covenanters considered themselves to be "the way" in absolute terms (perhaps on the basis of Isa. 40:3; cf. 1QS 8:12–16; 9:19–20), so that those who elected to join their ranks were said to have chosen "the way" (1QS 9:17–18). At Qumran, "the way" was understood to consist in strict legal observance as interpreted by the "Teacher of Righteousness."

39. The expression "truth," while virtually absent from the Synoptics (the only significant reference is Matt. 22:16 pars.), is found frequently in John's Gospel with reference to Jesus (1:14, 17; 5:33; 18:37; cf. 8:40, 45, 46; see also 1:9; 6:32; 15:1), the liberating effect of his word (8:31–32; cf. 17:17, 19), and the ministry of the Holy Spirit (16:13; cf. 14:17; 15:26). "Life" frequently is said to be the result of a person's coming to, and believing in, Jesus (e.g., 3:15, 16; 20:31) (Köstenberger 1998b: 75–76). The giving of life is said to be Jesus'

us, only in Jesus can these deepest of all human longings be fulfilled. For he in his very essence is truth and life; Jesus is the one and only way of salvation.

"No one comes to the Father except through me." In keeping with Jesus' claim, the early Christians maintained, "Salvation is found in no one else, for there is no other name under heaven given to men by which we must be saved" (Acts 4:12). In the OT, people expressed their faith in God by keeping the law; now that Jesus has come, he is the way. In the obstreperous Jewish and Greco-Roman world of the first century, as well as in today's pluralistic climate, Jesus' message is plain: he does not merely claim to be "a" way or "a" truth or "a" life, but "the way, the truth, and the life," the only way to salvation. As Morris (1995: 570) aptly notes, the words of this claim necessitated a faith perspective, "spoken as they were on the eve of the crucifixion. 'I am the Way,' said one who would shortly hang impotent on a cross. 'I am the Truth,' when the lies of evil people were about to enjoy a spectacular triumph. 'I am the Life,' when within a matter of hours his corpse would be placed in a tomb."

In 14:7–11, the focus changes to the "significance of Jesus as the only access to the Father and the guarantee for the ongoing life of the disciples in the world" (Ridderbos 1997: 493). The disciples will not be forced to find their own way by resorting to their own resources; rather, the knowledge of the Father mediated to them by the revelation provided in and through Jesus will serve as their continual source of spiritual life. "If you have come to know me, you will know my Father as well. And, certainly, you know him and have seen him."[40] The verb "know," in the sense of "acknowledge," was part of Near Eastern covenantal language.[41] In the OT, people frequently are exhorted to know God (e.g., Ps. 46:10; 100:3), with knowledge of God generally being anticipated as a future blessing (or being urged) rather than claimed as a present possession.[42] With Jesus' coming, however, the situation has changed dramatically: "we speak of what we know" (3:11); "we worship what we do know" (4:22); "you do not know him, but I know him" (7:28 = 8:55); "I know where I came from" (8:14); "I know my sheep and my sheep know (and follow) me" (10:14, 27); "this is eternal life: that they may know you, the only true God, and Jesus Christ, whom you have sent" (17:3).

14:8–11   Another benefit of Jesus' departure for his disciples will be the ensuing greater intimacy of relationship between them and Jesus. The subject of

---

purpose for coming (10:10) and is linked with two "I am" statements, "I am the bread of life" (6:35, 48) and "I am the resurrection and the life" (11:25).

40. See the additional note on 14:7. The rendering "certainly" takes ἀπάρτι (*aparti*) as one word (so, tentatively, Carson 1991: 493, with reference to A. Debrunner and Beasley-Murray; contra Moloney 1998: 399). This is also a possibility in 13:19 (note further the variant in 1:51; cf. Matt. 26:29, 64; Rev. 14:13; see BDAG 97).

41. See Hos. 13:4; Jer. 24:7; 31:34. Cf. Huffmon 1966 (cited by R. Brown 1970: 631).

42. But see Ps. 9:10; 36:10; Dan. 11:32.

the present interchange is one of the central themes of John's Gospel: the unity of God the Father and Jesus the Son (14:8–11).[43] What is at stake here is nothing less than Jesus' ability to provide firsthand revelation of God (cf. 1:18).[44] References to Jesus' unity with the Father pervade the entire Gospel and surface regularly in Jesus' confrontations with the Jewish leaders (e.g., 5:18; 10:30). John's presentation clearly implies *ontological* unity (unity of being); but the emphasis lies on *functional* unity, that is, the way in which God is revealed in Jesus' words and works (called "signs" by John; cf. 10:38).[45]

At this advanced stage of Jesus' ministry, it becomes clear that even the Eleven have yet to grasp this important truth. Philip's specific request is "Lord, show us the Father" (cf. 14:5, 22); this, he modestly allows, will be sufficient for him.[46] This marks another instance of Johannine misunderstanding (Morris 1995: 571; Moloney [1998: 396] says that Philip is "exasperatingly ignorant"), for, as Carson (1991: 494) notes, to the extent that the disciples have not yet grasped that in Jesus, God has made himself known, they do not know Jesus himself sufficiently well. Apparently, Philip here asks for some form of theophany (Morris 1995: 571). In the OT, Moses asked and was given a limited vision of God's glory (Exod. 33:18; cf. 24:10). Isaiah was granted a vision of "the Lord seated on a throne, high and exalted" (Isa. 6:1) and later predicted that in the day of the Messiah the glory of the Lord would be revealed (Isa. 40:5). In Jesus' day, many Jews longed for a firsthand experience of God. In keeping with OT teaching, John denies the possibility of a direct vision of God (unmediated by Jesus) in 1:18; 5:37; 6:46. Hence, Philip's request is utter foolishness (Bultmann 1971: 608).

Jesus responds to Philip's query with a gentle rebuke (Morris 1995: 571), perhaps with a tinge of sadness (Carson 1991: 494). "How long[47] have I been with you [plural, the Eleven] and you still don't know me, Philip?"[48] In a statement that is "staggering in its simplicity and its

---

43. On "in" terminology in John's Gospel, see the excursus in Köstenberger 1999a: 154–55.

44. In fact, the revelation mediated by Jesus exceeds that provided through Moses in the law (1:17; cf. 5:39–40, 45–47; 7:22–23).

45. Calvin (1961: 78) writes "I do not refer these words to Christ's divine essence, but to the mode of the revelation."

46. Again, "this will suffice" probably represents Johannine irony. Philip claims to be modest in his request—a direct vision of God—while in fact asking for something greater than the amazing revelation already provided in Jesus. On Philip, see commentary at 1:44; 12:21–22. The verb ἀρκέω (*arkeō*, suffice) occurs elsewhere in this Gospel only in 6:7, there, as in the present passage, on the lips of Philip (Moloney 1998: 399).

47. "How long" refers to the considerable duration of the disciples' association with Jesus (specifically, about three years) and is, like "with you," emphatic.

48. In principle, "Philip" could conclude this sentence or commence the following one, the preferable option being the former (contra Morris 1995: 572 n. 25). The perfect ἔγνωκάς (*egnōkas*, you know) has present meaning (Schnackenburg 1990: 3.69).

profundity" (Morris 1995: 572), Jesus claims, "Whoever has seen me has seen the Father."[49] Jesus' answer adduces the Jewish principle of representation (the *šālîaḥ*, messenger; see *m. Ber.* 5.5; Barrett 1978: 459), yet John's Christology surely transcends such teaching (Carson 1991: 494).[50] The reproach continues, "How can you [σύ, *sy*] say, 'Show us the Father?' Don't you believe that I am in the Father and the Father is in me?" (cf. 12:45; 13:20). This union with the Father is given expression both in Jesus' words (his teaching) and in his works (especially the "signs"): "The words I speak to you [plural] I do not speak of my own accord, but the Father who resides in me—he performs his works." The Fourth Evangelist consistently portrays Jesus' words as words of the Father,[51] and his works as works of the Father.[52]

Reiterating his just-voiced claim, Jesus asserts once more, "I am in the Father and the Father is in me." This mutual indwelling of Father and Son describes their unity yet does not obliterate their uniqueness (Carson 1991: 494). Although the relationship between the Father and the Son is not altogether reciprocal, "each can (in slightly different senses) be said to be in the other. The Father abiding in the Son does his works; the Son rests from, and to eternity in the Father's being" (Barrett 1978: 460). In Deut. 18:18, God says regarding the prophet like Moses, "I will put my words in his mouth, and he will tell them everything I command him." In Deut. 34:10–12, Moses is said to have been sent by the Lord to perform signs and works. If Jesus' followers are unprepared to take him at his mere word, they ought to include consideration of the witness added by his works. Faith on account of these works—"signs" from the evangelist's perspective, mere "works" from Jesus'—is better than no faith at all (Morris 1995: 573; cf. 5:36; 10:37–38).

14:12–14   The chapter started with Jesus' reference to his imminent departure in order to "prepare a place" for his followers. Queries by Thomas and Philip indicated that the disciples did not understand the way in which the Father was present in Jesus' works and words. In 14:12–14 the discussion moves beyond the question of Jesus' departure and destination and his unity with the Father to the disciples' future mission subsequent to Jesus' exaltation.[53]

---

49. Beasley-Murray (1999: 253) calls 14:10–11 "the needed counterpart of v 6b." Burge (2000: 393) contends that the present passage "at last explains statements hinted [at] in the public ministry" (10:30, 37–38).

50. Beasley-Murray (1999: 253–54) comments, "The reality is greater than human language can express." Contra Bultmann (1971: 609), who says that Jesus' unity with the Father must be understood exclusively in terms of revelation, and who, in turn, concludes that the "works" are all about Jesus' "words" because Jesus' miracles are superfluous.

51. See 3:34; 5:23–24; 8:18, 28, 38, 47; 12:49.

52. See 5:20, 36; 9:3–4; 10:25, 32, 37–38.

53. The present passage presupposes believers' identification with Jesus (see John 15).

Jesus' claim is nothing less than startling: "Whoever believes in me . . . will perform even greater works than these" (cf. 5:20; see Köstenberger 1995a: 36–45). Many early interpreters took the "greater things" to refer to the missionary successes of the early church. In relation to the Book of Acts, this certainly is true. Jesus' followers were in a position to influence a greater number of people and to spread out over a much larger geographical area. In the context of John's Gospel, however, "greater things" has primarily a qualitative dimension, marking Jesus' "signs" as preliminary and his disciples' ministry as "greater" in the sense that their ministry is based on Jesus' completed cross-work (12:24; 15:13; 19:30) and that it belongs to a more advanced stage in God's economy of salvation (cf. Matt. 11:11).[54] Jesus' followers are benefiting from others' labors, reaping what they have not sown, and will bear fruit that remains (John 4:31–38; 15:8, 16).

Thus, in keeping with motifs current in both Jewish life in general and farewell discourses in particular, the disciples are designated as Jesus' successors, taking their place in a long string of precedessors that ranges from the OT prophets to John the Baptist and climaxes in Jesus.[55] In this sense, Jesus' followers—not just his original disciples, but "whoever believes in me"—will do greater things than even Jesus did, aided by answered prayer in Jesus' name (14:13) and in close spiritual union with their exalted Lord (ch. 15).[56] In a real sense, these "greater works" will be performed by the exalted Jesus in and through his followers,[57] whereby "because I am going to the Father" is a somewhat oblique way of referring to Jesus' cross and resurrection (cf. 13:1; 16:28).[58] Jesus pledges that his leaving does not constitute a permanent withdrawal; rather, subsequent to his exaltation, he will be able to help his followers on earth (Ridderbos 1997: 498).

The reference to believers' future "greater works" in 14:12 marks a transition from the necessity of faith in Jesus (14:10–11) to the promise of God's help (14:13–14). In answer to the disciples' prayer, he will do "whatever you ask in my name."[59] Praying in Jesus' name does not

54. Carson (1991: 495–96) rightly contends that in the Johannine context "greater works" cannot mean (1) more works, (2) more spectacular works, or (3) more supernatural works. He correctly locates the clues to a proper understanding of 14:12 in the parallel in 5:20 and in the final clause "because I am going to the Father," and points to the disciples' greater understanding after the resurrection in the "new eschatological age that will then have dawned."

55. See 4:38; 17:18; 20:21. In another sense, it is the Spirit who is Jesus' "successor" (cf. 14:16); in 15:26–27, it is both the disciples and the Spirit.

56. For a fuller exposition of this passage, see Köstenberger 1998b: 171–75; 1995a.

57. Westcott (1908: 2.174) observes, "These 'greater works' are also works of Christ, being done by those who 'believe on Him.'"

58. Another Johannine euphemism for the events surrounding Jesus' crucifixion is "the glorification of the Son" (see commentary at 12:32; 13:32).

59. Note the sevenfold repetition of the phrase "in my name" in the farewell discourse (14:13, 14, 26; 15:16; 16:23, 24, 26). In the Johannine writings, cf. 15:7; 1 John 3:21–22;

involve magical incantations but rather expresses alignment of one's desires and purposes with God (1 John 5:14–15).[60]

(2) The Promised "Other Helping Presence" (14:15–31)

14:15–17 In 14:1–14, the focus is on the disciples' need to have faith in Jesus; in 14:15–24, the emphasis is on love (R. Brown 1970: 642). The entire section of 14:15–24 envisions the giving of the Spirit subsequent to Jesus' exaltation, at which time Jesus and the Father will make their dwelling in believers through the Spirit.[61] Jesus' identification with the Spirit, the "other παράκλητος," is so strong that he can say that *he himself* will return to his followers in the person of the Spirit (14:18). Though "yet a little while" in 14:19 and "on that day" in 14:20 at first blush may appear to refer to Jesus' resurrection appearances, Jesus' promise in 14:18 not to leave his disciples as orphans is hardly satisfied by his resurrection appearances, which were temporary in nature, and more likely refers to the permanent replacement of his presence with the Spirit.[62] This is suggested also by Jesus' response to Judas's question in 14:23 with reference to his and the Father's making their dwelling in believers as further explicating 14:18.[63]

Jesus' departure brings out his followers' love for him.[64] Jesus asks them to show their love by their obedience: "If you love me, you will obey what I command" (cf. 14:21, 23; 15:14; see also 15:10; 1 John 5:3).[65] In John, "obey my commandments" is used interchangeably with "keep my word" (8:51; 14:23, 24; 15:20; cf. 17:6; 1 John 2:5). Jesus' words echo the demands of the Deuteronomic covenant.[66] Yet, as Carson (1991: 498) aptly notes, "What the one who loves Jesus will observe is not simply an array of discrete ethical injunctions, but the entire revelation from the Father, revelation holistically conceived" (cf. 1 John 5:2).

The second entailment of the disciples' love for Jesus is that Jesus will petition the Father to provide "another helping presence" like Jesus. This prospect ought to encourage Jesus' disciples, who are struggling to come to terms with the implications of his upcoming departure. In fact, as Jesus is about to elaborate, the giving of the Spirit constitutes

---

5:14–15. Elsewhere, see Jer. 33:3; Matt. 7:7–8 = Luke 11:9–10; Matt. 18:19; 21:22. On "name," see commentary at 1:12 and at 5:43.

60. Jews frequently recalled the patriarchs in their prayers, hoping that God would be moved to hear them on account of these holy men. Regarding "so that the Son may bring glory to the Father," see commentary at 5:41; 7:18; 8:50, 54.

61. Keener (2003: 951) proposes a minor chiastic structure in 14:16–26, with 14:21–24 at the center (though he acknowledges the asymmetry in unit length).

62. See further commentary and interaction with alternative views below.

63. Note also Jesus' disparagement of belief based on "seeing" in 20:29.

64. The word "love" occurs eight times in 14:15–24 (Morris 1995: 575).

65. As Carson (1991: 498, citing Barrett 1978: 461) notes, the conditional clause of 14:15 controls the grammar of the next two verses and the thought of the next six. The condition is third class, with no assumption made as to its veracity.

66. See Deut. 5:10; 6:5–6; 7:9; 10:12–13; 11:13, 22.

another major advantage of his "going to the Father." For as John has made clear earlier in his Gospel, this giving of the Spirit was possible only subsequent to Jesus' glorification (7:39). With this glorification now imminent (cf. 12:23; 13:1), Jesus spends much of his time in the room of the supper preparing his followers for life in the age of the Spirit.

In the first half of this Gospel, John's treatment of the Spirit has largely resembled that of the Synoptics. Like them, he included the Baptist's reference to Jesus as the one who will baptize with the Holy Spirit (1:32–33; cf. Mark 1:8 pars.) and emphasized that the Spirit in all his fullness rested on Jesus during his earthly ministry (1:32; 3:34; cf. Luke 4:18). Moreover, John stressed the Spirit's role in regeneration (3:5, 6, 8; cf. 1:12–13), worship (4:23–24), and the giving of life (6:63). But as in John's presentation of Jesus' followers, his adoption of a postexaltation vantage point leads to a vastly enhanced portrayal in the farewell discourse, where the Spirit is featured primarily as the παράκλητος (paraklētos, helper, advocate [14:16, 26; 15:26; 16:7])[67] and as "the Spirit of truth" (14:17; 15:26; 16:13), two closely related terms (see 15:26).[68]

67. The term παράκλητος does not occur in the LXX (but see Aquila and Theodotion on Job 16:2: παράκλητοι), and elsewhere in the NT it appears only in 1 John 2:1, there with reference to Jesus "our advocate" with God the Father. For a survey of all known examples from the fourth century B.C. to the third century A.D., see Grayston (1981), who concludes that παράκλητος was a more general term that was sometimes (but not always) used in legal contexts, meaning "supporter" or "sponsor." The closest contemporaneous usage is found in Philo, who uses the expression to convey the notion of rendering general help, be it by giving advice or support (with the latter meaning being the more common). In later rabbinic usage, the term in its transliterated form is used alongside the transliterated term for a Greek expression meaning "advocate" (συνήγορος, synēgoros). Patristic references include Did. 5:2; 2 Clem. 6:9; and Clement of Alexandria, The Rich Man's Salvation 25.7 (for a study of the Johannine Paraclete in the church fathers, see Casurella 1983). Betz (1963) unconvincingly argues for a Qumran background (the archangel Michael; cf. Shafaat [1980–81], who likewise adduces DSS parallels; and Leaney [1972], who says that the Paraclete is God himself); Windisch (1968) advances the hardly more plausible hypothesis that the Paraclete is "a kind of angel . . . in human form," be it a prophet or teacher; G. Johnston (1970) unsuccessfully proposes that the παράκλητος is an active divine power that has become embodied in certain leaders of the apostolic church, such as the Fourth Evangelist (see the critiques by R. Brown [1967: 126; 1971: 268–70], for whom the Paraclete is the "alter ego of Jesus" [cited in Smalley 1996: 297]; cf. Burge 1987); Bultmann (1971: 566–72) views the concept as a Johannine appropriation of his gnostic source's figure of "helper"; Riesenfeld (1972) postulates a sapiential provenance, which is equally unlikely; Boring (1978) claims that the Paraclete is an angel demythologized as the "spirit of prophecy." For a discussion of the Paraclete as part of the Fourth Gospel's lawsuit motif (esp. in 15:26–16:15), see Lincoln 2000: 110–23, esp. 113–14. Billington (1995) appropriately stresses the Paraclete's role in mission. If the disciples are to witness to Jesus, they must understand the significance of his coming; witness to Jesus and the Paraclete's ministry thus are inseparable (15:26–27; 16:8–11; 20:21–23).

68. For a treatment of the Spirit-Paraclete in the context of the references to the Spirit in the entire Gospel narrative, see M. Davies 1992: 139–53. For a comparison of the treatments of the Spirit in John and the Synoptics, see Köstenberger 1999a: 156. On the Johannine Paraclete and Spirit of truth, see also the extended treatment in Keener 2003: 951–82.

First,[69] Jesus calls the Spirit "another παράκλητος."[70] This indicates that the Spirit's presence with the disciples will replace Jesus' encouraging and strengthening presence with them while on earth (cf. 14:17).[71] When the Spirit comes to dwell in believers, it is as if Jesus himself takes up residence in them.[72] Thus, Jesus is able to refer to the coming of the Spirit by saying, "I will come to you" (14:18).[73] This relieves a primary concern for Jesus' first followers in the original setting of the farewell discourse: Jesus' departure will not leave them as orphans

69. Ridderbos (1997: 500) perceptively notes that here, "spirit" designations such as "Spirit of truth," "Holy Spirit," and simply "Spirit" serve as further description of the παράκλητος rather than vice versa, as might be expected.

70. The translation of the term has proved particularly difficult since there does not seem to be an exact equivalent in the English language (see discussion in Carson 1991: 499). None of the expressions chosen in English translations seems fully adequate: "Counselor" (NIV) smacks of contemporary notions of counseling (marriage counselor, camp counselor), focusing primarily on emotional or psychological aspects (though the legal term "Counselor" or "Counsel" is more appropriate); "Helper" (NASB, ESV, ISV) is more neutral but conveys inferior status overtones not present in the text and lacks the legal connotation possibly present (cf. the discussion in Lindars 1972: 479); the fact that some translations give several alternative renderings in footnotes also suggests that any one English rendering may be inadequate (e.g., NLT: "the Counselor; or Comforter, or Encourager, or Advocate"). "Companion" (suggested by Brodie [1993: 466]) also falls short, as does Calvin's (1961: 82) "Patron." Some make reference to the root meaning of the word, "one called alongside to help," but it is unclear whether first-century usage consciously drew on this background. There is evidence that the expression was used in a legal setting, but it is less clear that the meaning should be restricted to "Advocate" (so, consistently, the TNIV) or the like (standard Greek reference works cite the following meanings: LSJ—one called to one's aid, legal assistant, advocate, summoned, intercessor; Behm, *TDNT* 5:800–814—legal advisor, helper, advocate in court [for a helpful survey, see Schnackenburg 1990: 3.144–50]). Perhaps "helping presence" captures the import of the term better than any other (Köstenberger 1999a: 157) for the following reasons: (1) this is what Jesus was while with the disciples; (2) this encompasses the various functions laid out for the Spirit in John 14–16; (3) this transcends (but may include) the legal context of the term (see esp. 16:7–11). See the discussion by Ridderbos (1997: 503), who issues a plea to let the Johannine context (rather than alleged extrabiblical parallels) determine the meaning of παράκλητος and concludes that "the dominant idea is of someone who offers assistance in a situation in which help is needed."

71. Talbert (1992: 207) calls the Paraclete "an abiding presence," "a teaching presence," and "a presence that both guides into all truth and declares the things to come."

72. "The Spirit is the divine presence when Jesus' physical presence is taken away from his followers" (Morris 1989: 159). Startlingly, Borchert (2002: 121), on the basis of the second-person plural pronoun, seems to deny that 14:17 should be understood with reference to the personal experience of believers. By his logic, believers are to show their love for Jesus by obeying him corporately but not individually—a transparent absurdity.

73. Though, as Moloney (1998: 407) points out, there are differences between Jesus and the Spirit as well: the latter neither becomes flesh nor dies for our sins. Alternatively, the statement refers to Jesus' postresurrection appearances to his followers (so Ridderbos 1997: 505; Carson 1991: 501; Morris 1995: 578–59; Beasley-Murray 1999: 258; Borchert 2002: 126). Barrett (1978: 464) says that the passage refers neither to Jesus coming in the person of the Holy Spirit nor to the parousia but rather is using language appropriate to both the resurrection and the parousia to refer to both.

(14:18); just as God was present with them through Jesus, so he will continue to be present with them through his Spirit.[74] The Spirit's role thus ensures the continuity between Jesus' pre- and postglorification ministry. What is more, the coming of the Spirit will actually constitute an advance in God's operations with and through the disciples (16:7; cf. 14:12).

The present is the first of five Paraclete sayings in the farewell discourse, in each case with reference to the Holy Spirit (cf. 14:26; 15:26; 16:7–11, 12–15).[75] In secular Greek, παράκλητος refers primarily to a "legal assistant" or "advocate" (though the word never became a technical term such as its Latin equivalent, *advocatus*). In John's Gospel, legal overtones are most pronounced in 16:7–11. In later rabbinic writings, the role of advocate (*sanêgôr*) is associated with the Holy Spirit (*Lev. Rab.* 6.1 on Lev. 5:1).[76] Also, both the noun παράκλησις (*paraklēsis*) and the verb παρακαλέω (*parakaleō*) are used in the OT with regard to the "consoling" expected to occur during the messianic era (e.g., Isa. 40:1; cf. *b. Mak.* 5b). "Encouragement" was also considered to be a spiritual gift in the early church (see Rom. 12:8).

As Jesus' emissary, the Spirit will have a variety of functions in believers' lives: he will bring to remembrance all that Jesus taught his disciples (14:26); he will testify regarding Jesus together with his followers (15:26); he will convict the world of sin, (un)righteousness, and judgment (16:8–11); and he will guide Jesus' disciples in all truth and disclose what is to come (16:13). Historically, this included the formation of the NT canon as apostolic testimony to Jesus. Though initially focused on the Eleven (cf. 15:26), the Spirit, in a secondary sense, fulfills similar roles in believers today. He illumines the spiritual meaning of Jesus' words and works both to believers and, through believers, to the unbelieving world. In all of these functions the ministry of the Spirit remains closely linked with the person of Jesus. Just as Jesus is portrayed everywhere in John's Gospel as the Sent One who is fully dependent on and obedient to the Father, so the Spirit is said to be "sent" by both the Father and Jesus (14:26; 15:26) and to focus his teaching on the illumination of the spiritual significance of God's work in Jesus (14:26; 15:26; 16:9).

The Spirit is also called "the Spirit of truth" (cf. 15:26; 16:13). In the context of the present chapter, Jesus has just been characterized as "the

---

74. As R. Brown (1970: 642) points out, the promise of the divine presence with Jesus' followers in 14:15–24 includes the Spirit (14:15–17), Jesus (14:18–21), and the Father (14:22–24), hence involving all three persons of the Godhead in the indwelling of believers.

75. In 1 John (2:1), the term refers to the exalted Jesus.

76. Rabbi Eliezer ben Jacob made this well-known statement: "He that performs one precept gets for himself one advocate [*peraqlît*]; but he that commits one transgression gets for himself one accuser [*qaṭêgôr*]" (*m. ʾAbot* 4.11).

truth" (14:6), in keeping with statements already made in the prologue (1:14, 17). The concept of truth in John's Gospel encompasses several aspects: (1) truthfulness as opposed to falsehood: "to speak the truth" means to make a true rather than false statement, that is, to represent the facts as they actually are (cf. 8:40, 45, 46; 16:7; "to witness to the truth" [5:33; 18:37]); (2) truth in its finality as compared to previous, preliminary expressions: this is its eschatological dimension (esp. 1:17: "the law was given through Moses; grace and truth came through Jesus Christ"); (3) truth as an identifiable body of knowledge with actual propositional content (e.g., 8:32: "you will know the truth"; 16:13: "he will guide you into all truth"); (4) truth as a sphere of operation, be it for worship (4:23–24) or sanctification (17:17, 19 [Swain 1998]); and (5) truth as relational fidelity (1:17; 14:6). The Spirit is involved in all five aspects: he accurately represents the truth regarding Jesus; he is the eschatological gift of God; he imparts true knowledge of God; he is operative in both worship and sanctification; and he points people to the person of Jesus.

The expression "spirit of truth" was current in Judaism (e.g., T. Jud. 20). Similarly, the Qumran literature affirms that God placed within humankind "two spirits so that he would walk with them until the moment of his visitation; they are the spirits of truth and of deceit" (1QS 3:18; cf. 4:23–26). Yet these parallels are merely those of language, not thought. For although these expressions are part of an ethical dualism in Second Temple literature (including Qumran), John's Gospel does not feature a "spirit of error" corresponding to the Spirit of truth (but see 1 John 4:6, where "the Spirit [or spirit] of truth and the spirit of falsehood" occur together). Rather, the Spirit of truth is the "other helping presence," who takes the place of Jesus while on earth with his disciples. This "other helping presence," the "Spirit of truth," the world cannot accept (see commentary at 1:10; cf. 10:26; 12:39; see also 1 Cor. 2:14), because it neither sees nor knows him. Yet, Jesus' followers do accept him, because "he resides with you and will be in you" (see 1 John 3:24; 4:13).[77]

14:18–21   Jesus' assurance here, "I will not leave you as orphans," is constrained by the farewell setting and evokes Moses' parting words to Israel: "The

---

77. D. M. Smith (1999: 274–75) notes that "you" here is plural, which leads him to infer that the statement does not necessarily refer to personal indwelling. In principle, this is true, but the statement could just as well be plural because Jesus is speaking to a group of followers (rather than a single person), not because reference is made to communal as opposed to individual indwelling. Despite the plural "you," the latter scenario seems more likely (note, e.g., the singular pronoun construction κἀκεῖνος [kakeinos, and that one] in 14:12, and compare the Pauline teaching on the Spirit's indwelling of individual believers). On some of the systematic-theological issues raised by the present verse, see Hamilton (2003), who takes the passage as a point of departure for arguing that OT believers were regenerated but not indwelt by the Spirit.

LORD . . . will never leave you nor forsake you" (Deut. 31:6; cf. Josh. 1:5; Heb. 13:5).[78] In OT times, orphans needed someone to plead their case. Here, the term ὀρφανός (*orphanos*, orphan) is used in a metaphorical sense in connection with Jesus' departure and the resulting loss that will be experienced by his disciples. In secular Greek, the term "orphans" occurs also with reference to children bereft of only one parent or to disciples left without their master (see *NewDocs* 4 §71; Carson 1991: 501).[79] In the only two other NT instances of the term, it is used in its literal sense in conjunction with widows (Mark 12:40 [some MSS]; James 1:27).

"Before long" is more literally, "yet a little while" (cf. 13:33; 16:16–19; see also Isa. 26:20; Heb. 10:37). Jesus' death will be but a brief interruption in the disciples' communion with him (Schnackenburg 1990: 3.77). Although the world will no longer see Jesus (cf. Judas's question in 14:22), his followers will (with the eyes of faith) (Schnackenburg 1990: 3.78–79); because Jesus lives, they will live as well (see 5:21, 26; 6:57). The phrase "on that day" frequently has end-time connotations and is commonly found in OT prophetic literature (e.g., Isa. 2:11; 3:7, 18; 4:1–2) and the NT (Matt. 24:36 par.). The majority of commentators takes "on that day" to refer to Jesus' resurrection (e.g., Morris 1995: 579; Borchert 2002: 126), though perhaps the more plausible view takes the statement as referring to Jesus' coming to his followers in the Spirit (see commentary at 14:18) at Pentecost.[80] This is the more likely point in time in the Johannine context at which Jesus' followers will understand his union with the Father and their union with Jesus.

---

78. For Jesus' earlier statements concerning leaving the disciples, see 13:33, 36; 14:2–4.

79. Plato wrote regarding the followers of Socrates that in the face of their teacher's imminent death, "they felt that he was like a father to us and that when bereft of him we should pass the rest of our lives as orphans" (*Phaedrus* 65). A similar phrase is also found in Lucian, *De mort. Peregrini* 6. See Barrett 1978: 463.

80. See Morris (1995: 579), who says that "if this is accepted it must be in the sense of 20:22, where the Spirit was in some sense given on the day of resurrection"; and Bruce (1983: 303), who points out that the resurrection appearances were but brief and temporary. See also Barrett (1978: 464), who maintains that the primary reference is to the resurrection but the expression also extends to the presence of Christ in his disciples (cf. Beasley-Murray 1999: 258). In the patristic period, the Eastern church fathers understood the phrase "in a little while" to refer to the resurrection, while the Latin church thought that Jesus meant the parousia. Bultmann (1971: 619) contends that John's source referred to the latter, with the evangelist demythologizing his source by reinterpreting it as the former. Hence, the second coming is swallowed up in Easter. However, this reconstruction is predicated upon Bultmann's source theory regarding John's Gospel as well as upon his existential approach to interpretation, including the categories of "myth" and "demythologization." Yet note how even after his resurrection, Jesus refers to a future time at which he will return (21:22, 23). Moloney (1998: 403) implausibly contends that "that day" is Jesus' hour and departure.

"Whoever has my commands and keeps them—he is the one who loves me" (see commentary at 14:15). In OT times, God had revealed himself to his people Israel preeminently through the law given at Mount Sinai; now, it is through Jesus (1:17; cf. Matt. 5:17; Rom. 10:4; Gal. 4:4–5). The Greek verb underlying "show" (ἐμφανίζω, *emphanizō*) and its cognates can, in the LXX, refer to theophanies, that is, manifestations of God (see Exod. 33:13 and the reading of Codex B at Exod. 33:18).[81]

14:22–24 Then Judas speaks up: "Lord, why is it that you will disclose yourself to us and not to the world?"[82] This Judas (not Iscariot) probably is the "Judas of James" mentioned in Luke 6:16 and Acts 1:13, not Jude the half-brother of Jesus (Matt. 13:55; Mark 6:3). Similarly, Jesus' brothers earlier had said, "Since you are doing these things, show yourself to the world" (John 7:4; see Schlatter 1948: 301). Judas's query shows no evidence of his understanding the idea of resurrection (Carson 1991: 504).[83] A certain mystery attached to the fact that Jesus did not press revelation onto people hostile to his claims. To them, he remained hidden (12:36b–40). Jesus' resurrection appearances are recorded in the final chapters of Matthew, Luke, and John (though not Mark; see also Paul's list in 1 Cor. 15:5–8).[84] As on previous occasions, Jesus does not answer Judas's question directly. Rather, he states positively that those who love him will obey his teaching (see commentary at 14:15) and, by implication, that these are the kinds of people to whom Jesus will be pleased to reveal himself.[85]

The reference to μονή (*monē*, dwelling) in 14:23 provides an *inclusio* with 14:2 (though there the reference is plural and the referents are different): "We will come to him and make our dwelling with him." Arguably, 14:23 provides the climax of the section that began in 14:18 (Schnackenburg 1990: 3.81). Hence, it stands to reason that since here the reference clearly is neither to the resurrection appearances nor to the second coming, but to believers' experience of God's presence subsequent to the giving of the Spirit (Morris 1995: 581), the same is true

81. The term occurs in Matt. 27:53 to describe the appearance of dead bodies raised to life after Jesus' resurrection. The related adjective ἐμφανής (*emphanēs*, manifest, visible) is used with regard to Jesus' resurrection appearance in Acts 10:40. By contrast, the noun ἐπιφάνεια (*epiphaneia*, appearance) approaches status as a technical term for Jesus' second coming (2 Thess. 2:8; 1 Tim. 6:14; 2 Tim. 1:10; 4:1, 8; Titus 2:13).

82. On "Lord," see 14:5, 8. On "disclose yourself," see commentary at 14:21.

83. Morris (1995: 580–81) perceives that Judas's question betrays a political hope.

84. As Carson (1991: 503) rightly notes, the reference is not limited to the resurrection appearances but also extends to Jesus' self-disclosure in later times (citing Matt. 28:20).

85. The synonymous use of the terms "word" and "commandment" harks back to the OT, where the Ten Commandments are called "words" (Hebrew *dābār*) of God (Exod. 20:1; cf. Deut. 5:5, 22). The expressions "commandments" and "word(s)" are used interchangeably in Ps. 119 (e.g., 119:10, 25, 28). Regarding Jesus' assertion "my Father will love him," see commentary at 14:21.

for 14:18–21.[86] This is the only place in the NT where the Father and the Son are both said to indwell believers.[87] In OT times, God dwelt among his people, first in the tabernacle (Exod. 25:8; 29:45; Lev. 26:11–12), then in the temple (Acts 7:46–47). In the NT era, believers themselves are the temple of the living God (1 Cor. 6:19; 2 Cor. 6:16; cf. 1 Pet. 2:5). This, in turn, anticipates the final state, when "the dwelling of God is with men, and he will live with them" (Rev. 21:3; cf. Ezek. 37:27).[88]

"And the word you hear is not mine but the Father's who sent me" reiterates Jesus' frequent assertions in dealing with his Jewish opponents (7:16; 8:26, 28; 12:49–50; cf. 5:19–20).

"I have told you these things" indicates the closing of this particular **14:25–27** portion of the farewell discourse (Schnackenburg 1990: 3.82; Beasley-Murray 1999: 261). "While still with you" likewise indicates that Jesus' instruction of his followers is about to come to a close. The former expression will recur a total of six times in the second part of the farewell discourse (15:11; 16:1, 4, 6, 25, 33). This kind of reiterated phrase is also found in prophetic writings such as Ezekiel (e.g., 5:13, 15, 17; 17:21, 24). The consistent use of the perfect tense λελάληκα (lelalēka, I have spoken) points to the completed impartation of Jesus' teaching to the disciples.

On the παράκλητος, see commentary at 14:16. This is the only reference to the Spirit as "Holy Spirit" in the farewell discourse (cf. 1:33; 20:22).[89] The "sending" terminology applied to the Spirit integrates him

---

86. Again, Bultmann (1971: 617–18) argues that the present reference collapses Easter and the parousia into one. This conclusion, however, is unwarranted. Rather, according to Jesus' statements in John, believers need not wait for the parousia to experience the indwelling presence of Christ. Just as the incarnate Lord's presence was with them during the time of his earthly ministry (1:14), his emissary, the Spirit (14:16), and the Father and the Son with him (14:23), will be present with the believer already in the here and now. As R. Brown (1970: 648) notes, the implicit message is "that in indwelling are fulfilled some of the expectations of the last period."

87. Elsewhere, it is Christ (Gal. 2:20; Eph. 3:17) or the Spirit (Rom. 8:9, 11; 1 Cor. 3:16).

88. Two interesting parallels to the phrase "make our home" (μονὴν ποιησόμεθα) in 14:23 are found in Josephus, where Jonathan is said to have "taken up residence" in Jerusalem (μονὴν ἐποιεῖτο [Ant. 13.2.1 §41]), and Elijah is shown to "make his dwelling" in a cave (ποιούμενος τὴν μονήν [Ant. 8.13.7 §350]). Philo frequently speaks of God or the Word as dwelling in people.

89. The term occurs infrequently in the OT (Ps. 51:11; Isa. 63:9–10). There are several references to the "Holy Spirit" in Second Temple literature (e.g., Wis. 9:17; Ps. Sol. 17:37; Odes Sol. 14:8). In the Gospels, the expression is used five times in Matthew (1:18, 20; 3:11; 12:32; 28:19), four times in Mark (1:8; 3:29; 12:36; 13:11), thirteen times in Luke (1:15, 35, 41, 67; 2:25, 26; 3:16, 22; 4:1; 10:21; 11:13; 12:10, 12), and three times in John (in the other two instances without the article: 1:33; 20:22). References to the "Holy Spirit" are frequent in the Book of Acts and the writings of Paul. I am puzzled by Moloney's (1998: 413) statement that "this is the only place in the NT where the expression 'the Holy Spirit' is found." There are about ninety references to the Holy Spirit in the NT.

into a network of sending relationships established in this Gospel. Jesus is the paradigmatic Sent One from the Father (9:4, 7); later, he becomes the sender of the disciples (17:18; 20:21). Here, it is the Spirit "whom the Father will send in my [Jesus'] name." In 15:26, it is "the helping presence . . . whom I [Jesus] will send to you from the Father, the Spirit of truth who goes out from the Father."[90] Hence, the Father is never sent; he is sender of both the Son and the Spirit. The Spirit is never sender; he is sent by both the Father and the Son. Only Jesus is both sent one and sender; sent by the Father, he sends both the Spirit and the disciples.

The Spirit's future ministry is described here in terms of teaching Jesus' followers all things (cf. 1 John 2:20, 27; see Schlatter 1948: 302) and of reminding them of the things that Jesus taught them.[91] The Spirit will not provide qualitatively new or independent revelation (neither did Jesus [see esp. 7:16]) but will bring to light the true meaning and significance of the revelation imparted by Jesus (Carson 1991: 505; Barrett 1978: 467). Hence, the Spirit's mission is the continuation of Jesus' mission (R. Brown 1970: 653), which continues the emphasis on the unity among the different persons of the Godhead in this Gospel. Teaching in the sense of authentic exposition of Scripture was a vital part of Judaism. In Qumran, the primary teaching office was occupied by the "Teacher of Righteousness," who interpreted the Hebrew Scriptures prophetically with reference to the Dead Sea community.[92]

Jesus' promise that the Spirit will remind his followers of everything he had told them has important implications for the life of the church and for the writing of the NT.[93] "Remembering" was

---

90. See also Gal. 4:6; 1 Pet. 1:12.

91. The vast majority of commentators (including R. Brown, Barrett, Borchert, Morris, Carson, and Ridderbos) believe that teaching and reminding are in synonymous parallelism. On the Spirit's teaching ministry, see the parallel in 16:13. Both verses together (14:26 and 16:13) echo Ps. 25:5 (cf. 25:9). See also Neh. 9:20 (cf. 1 John 2:20, 27). Regarding Jesus' teaching, see John 6:59; 7:14, 28, 35; 8:20; 18:20. It is often argued that the use of the Greek masculine pronoun ἐκεῖνος (ekeinos, he) for the Spirit in passages such as John 14:26; 15:26; and 16:13–14 affirms the personality of the Holy Spirit (Barrett 1978: 482; Borchert 2002: 159; Morris 1995: 583 n. 73 [citing Westcott]; 606 n. 64; 621 n. 27; and others cited in Wallace 1996: 331 n. 42). However, the most likely reason for John's use of the masculine pronoun in these passages is that the antecedent is the masculine noun ὁ παράκλητος (ho paraklētos, the helping presence). If so, John's use of a masculine pronoun to refer to the Spirit is best explained as a function of grammar rather than theology, and arguments for the personality of the Holy Spirit must be made on other grounds (so rightly Wallace 1996: 331–32, who points out that it is difficult to find any text where the neuter noun πνεῦμα [pneuma, spirit/Spirit] is grammatically referred to by the masculine).

92. However, one important difference between the Holy Spirit and the Teacher of Righteousness is that the former will guide people into truth definitively, while the latter will be followed by another "teaching righteousness" at the end of time (CD 6:11).

93. The theme of remembering is featured elsewhere in John's Gospel also in 2:17, 22; 12:17; 15:20 (cf. 13:16); 16:4. Other instances of "remembering" in the Gospels involve

also an important part of the Jewish testament tradition (Bammel 1993: 108).[94]

Following closely on Jesus' promise of the Spirit is his assurance of peace for his followers: "Peace I leave with you."[95] The statement reflects the customary Jewish greeting and word of farewell, whereby "leave" (ἀφίημι, *aphiēmi*) probably has the sense of "bequeath" (cf. Ps. 17:14; Eccles. 2:18). Here (as in 16:33), the context of greeting is farewell; after the resurrection, it is welcome (20:19, 21, 26). By invoking "that day" anticipated by the prophets (14:20), Jesus places this period squarely within the context of OT expectation. On the merits of his substitutionary death, the departing Lord bequeaths to his followers the permanent end-time blessing of a right relationship with God (cf. Rom. 1:7; 5:1; 14:17). Jesus' parting benediction is more than a "cheap wish" (see Ridderbos 1997: 511; Carson 1991: 506; Schnackenburg 1990: 3.84); Jesus' word is efficacious.

"My peace I give you. I don't give to you as the world gives."[96] The *pax Romana* ("Roman peace"), secured by the first Roman emperor, Augustus (30 B.C.–A.D. 14), had been obtained and was maintained by military might. The famous *Ara Pacis* ("altar of peace"), erected by Augustus to celebrate his inauguration of the age of peace, still stands in Rome as a testimony to the world's empty messianic pretensions (Beasley-Murray 1999: 262). The peace given by Jesus, on the other hand, was not af-

---

Jesus' prediction of Peter's denials and of future Spirit baptism, both remembered by Peter (Matt. 26:75 [cf. 26:34] pars.; Acts 11:16 [cf. 1:5]), and the prediction of Jesus' crucifixion and resurrection (Luke 24:6–8, 44; cf. 9:22; see also 2 Tim. 2:8). The disciples' failure to remember the miraculous feeding of the multitude is lamented in Mark 8:17–18 (cf. 6:43; 8:8), while on a different occasion they are challenged to "remember Lot's wife" (Luke 17:32). Other NT references include Acts 20:31, 35; 1 Cor. 11:2; 2 Thess. 2:5; 2 Tim. 2:11–14; 2 Pet. 1:12–15; 3:1–2; cf. Jude 5, 17.

94. There are several parallels in Second Temple literature between the consoling, teaching presence of the Paraclete and the period after the death of a revered leader in the testaments (e.g., 2 Bar. 77:11).

95. Hence, 14:27 continues 14:25–26. See Kellum (2005: 164), who cites Witherington 1995: 253 and Brodie 1993: 469. In the Greek world, peace (εἰρήνη, *eirēnē*) was essentially a concept stated negatively, denoting the absence of war. Though this is also part of the term's range of meaning in Hebrew thought (e.g., Josh. 9:15; 1 Sam. 7:14; 1 Kings 2:5), the expression *shālôm* usually had much richer connotations, conveying the notion of positive blessing, especially that of a right relationship with God (Morris 1965a: 237–44; Lindars 1972: 484). This is evident in the well-known blessing given by Moses and Aaron (Num. 6:24–26; cf. Ps. 29:11; Hag. 2:9). The OT prophetic writings in particular look forward to a period of peace inaugurated by the coming of the Messiah. The "prince of peace" (Isa. 9:6) would "command peace to the nations" (Zech. 9:10; cf. 9:9), and there would be good tidings of peace and salvation (Isa. 52:7; cf. 54:13; 57:19; Acts 10:36). Through the royal Messiah, God would make an everlasting "covenant of peace" with his people (Ezek. 37:26).

96. Along with his peace, the departing Jesus also bestows on his followers his love (15:9–10) and joy (15:11). This triad is found also in the Pauline teaching on the fruit of the Spirit (Gal. 5:22).

flicted with the burden of having been achieved by violence (cf. 18:11).[97] Moreover, in contrast to worldly conceptions of peace as the absence of war, Jesus' peace is not an exemption from turmoil, danger, and duress (all of which he is facing as he speaks). As Jesus is about to remind his followers, the world hates them (15:18), and in this world they will face affliction (16:33). Rather than extracting them from danger (cf. 17:15), Jesus, through the Spirit he would send, offers his followers poise and resolve in the midst of discomfiting circumstances. As Jesus was about to demonstrate, his peace is not the absence of conditions that intimidate but rather is the composure to be faithful in the face of adversity.

"Don't let your hearts be troubled" in 14:27 forms an *inclusio* (or at least constitutes an instance of back-referencing) with the identical phrase in 14:1 (Moloney 1998: 410–11), which provides a certain amount of closure to Jesus' instructions in the farewell discourse thus far (13:31–14:31). However, this does not relegate John 15–16 to secondary status, as is sometimes argued. Thus, Blomberg (2002: 218) plausibly suggests that 16:33 forms an *inclusio* with both 14:1 and 14:27 (which Blomberg [p. 203] calls "a small inclusio around this chapter"). Moreover, in any case, *inclusio*s do not necessarily appear at the end of a structural unit, so it is precarious to use the presence of such an *inclusio* at 14:27 as evidence for source-critical reconstructions (G. Guthrie 1994: 55; cf. Bultmann 1971: 599). Jesus' exhortation "Don't be afraid" evokes Moses' parting counsel in his farewell discourse, which likewise was "Don't be afraid" (Deut. 31:6, 8). The present negative statement complements the positive one regarding Jesus' peace, which excludes cowardice, fear, or anxiety and will be a natural result of the presence of the Holy Spirit (cf. Phil. 4:7; see Morris 1995: 584).

14:28–31 "You heard that I said to you, 'I am going away and I am coming back to you'" (see 13:33; 14:2–4, 12, 18–19, 21, 23). Jesus' statement "If you loved me [contrary-to-fact condition],[98] you would rejoice that I am going to the Father, because the Father is greater than I" (cf. Matt. 24:36 par.) seeks to expose the fact that the disciples are primarily focused on their own sense of loss in light of Jesus' imminent departure.[99] Yet, as Jesus reminds them, and as Paul would have agreed (Phil. 1:23), being with God is better by far, both for Jesus and for his followers, who subsequent to his exaltation will be able to draw on the assistance of both the exalted Jesus and the indwelling Spirit.

---

97. Philo, the Hellenistic Jew, calls peace "the highest of blessings . . . a gift no human being can bestow" (*Mos.* 1.55 §304; cf. *Dreams* 2.38 §250; see Foerster, *TDNT* 2:400–417).

98. So Carson 1991: 506; Morris 1995: 584; contra Ridderbos (1997: 511), who construes this clause not as conditional but causal (p. 494 n. 37).

99. For a similar dynamic, see commentary at 13:36–38.

Jesus' statement that the Father is greater than he is not meant to indicate ontological inferiority on his part. Elsewhere, Jesus affirms that he and the Father are one (10:30). Rather, Jesus stresses his subordination to the Father, which, as the NT makes clear, is not merely a part of his incarnate ministry but is rooted in his eternal sonship (cf. esp. 1 Cor. 15:28; see Beasley-Murray 1999: 262; contra Morris 1995: 584; see also Barrett 1982a: 19–36). The statement "I have told you before it happens, so that you may believe when it does happen" mirrors similar previous affirmations (see commentary at 13:19) and once again highlights Jesus' foreknowledge. The remark clarifies that Jesus' comment in 14:28b is designed not to shame his followers but rather to build their faith (Carson 1991: 508).

"I will not say much more" does not necessarily signal the ending of the discourse but rather the imminent nature of the arrest and final events in Jesus' earthly life (Carson 1991: 508). The prince of this world (lit., "the world's ruler") has no hold on Jesus (see commentary at 12:31 and at 16:11).[100] The double negative in the Greek (οὐκ . . . οὐδέν, *ouk . . . ouden*) is emphatic: "he does not have anything on me at all."[101] The present phrase constitutes an idiomatic rendering of a Hebrew expression frequently found in legal contexts with the sense "he has no claim on me" (BDAG 735; Carson 1991: 508–9; Beasley-Murray 1999: 263). The expression therefore means not "he has no power over me"[102] but "he has no legal claim or hold on me." The reason for this is Christ's sinlessness (cf. 8:46; see Morris 1995: 585).

In closing and by way of recapitulation, Jesus affirms his love for and obedience to the Father. This is to serve as a testimony to the world (cf. 14:17; see commentary at 1:10, at 15:18–25, and at 16:8–11, 33). Jesus' claim "I love the Father" is the only place in the NT where Jesus is said to love the Father. The term "Father" occurs twenty-three times in this chapter alone, the most references in any chapter of John's Gospel. "I do just as the Father commanded me" harks back to Jesus' earlier emphasis on his followers' need for obedience (14:15, 21, 23). In this regard, too, Jesus had set the example (cf. 4:34; 8:55; see also Phil. 2:8; Heb. 5:8).

The present portion of the discourse is concluded by Jesus' comment "Come now; let's go away from here." This may indicate that Jesus and his followers now leave the room of the supper and embark on a nocturnal walk that would lead them to Gethsemane, perhaps passing vineyards on the way, which would provide a fitting backdrop for Jesus' teaching

100. For the devil's role in the death of Jesus, see 6:70; 13:2, 27.
101. The vast majority of the instances of this construction in the Gospels are found in John (5:30; 6:63; 9:33; 11:49; 12:19; 14:30; 15:5; 16:23, 24; cf. 8:15; 18:9, 31; 19:41; elsewhere in the Gospels: Mark 14:60, 61; 15:4; Luke 4:2; 10:19).
102. So Schnackenburg 1990: 3.87; cf. 19:11: κατά (*kata*) not ἐν (*en*), though this is of course true as well. Schlatter (1948: 303) cites Matt. 5:23 and especially Rev. 2:4, but in both passages the preposition used is likewise κατά not ἐν.

on the vine and the branches (see John 15). Some have suggested that Jesus' "vine" metaphor was occasioned by the golden vine overhanging the main entrance to the temple.[103] Alternatively, Jesus may have told his disciples that it was time to go and then added some further instruction before finally getting underway (cf. 18:1).[104]

Additional Notes

13:32. The phrase εἰ ὁ θεὸς ἐδοξάσθε ἐν αὐτῷ is found in A but not 𝔓[66] ℵ* B C D. For this reason the shorter reading is to be preferred (Barrett 1978: 450; though see Metzger 1994: 205–6).

14:2. The word ὅτι (that, because) is found in ℵ A B C* D etc. but not in 𝔓[66*] and the Textus Receptus. The external evidence argues for inclusion. On internal grounds, too, Metzger (1994: 206) is probably right in saying that the conjunction may have been omitted by copyists who tried to simplify what they considered to be a superfluous ὅτι *recitativum*. Another reason for the omission of the conjunction may be the perceived difficulty of having Jesus say "If it were not so, would I have told you that I am going to prepare a place for you?" when he has not said this previously in this Gospel and does so only in the verse that follows (14:3; rightly noted by Barrett 1978: 457; Carson 1991: 490; but see Bultmann 1971: 601 n. 4, who refers to 12:26, 32). For these reasons, ὅτι is most likely original.[105]

A separate but related question is whether, assuming the originality of ὅτι, the verse is to be construed as a statement (NASB, rendering ὅτι as "for"; Carson [1991: 490] calls it "barely possible") or as a question (TNIV; ESV; ISV; favored by Bultmann 1971: 601 n. 4; very tentatively, Carson 1991: 490; and, with a slight variation, Ridderbos 1997: 489 n. 25; note that many other versions [e.g., NIV, NLT, NKJV] reject the ὅτι, rendering this question moot). Both renderings are possible, but the latter seems to make more sense contextually and is therefore adopted in the present commentary.[106]

103. Cf. Josephus, *J.W.* 5.5.4 §210; *Ant.* 15.11.3 §395; *m. Mid.* 3.8; Tacitus, *Historiae* 5.5.

104. The transition from 14:31 to 15:1 is frequently labeled an *aporia*, which is commonly taken to indicate a literary seam indicating the presence of different underlying sources (one of the first to see such a difficulty was C. H. Weisse 1856: 116; cf. Wellhausen 1907 and the influential series of essays by E. Schwartz 1907; 1908; see the historical survey in Kellum 2005: 10–78). However, this conclusion seems premature and unwarranted in light of preferable alternate explanations. Thielman (1991: 180), for instance, suggests that the present passage may be an instance of a "purposeful attempt at obscurity" common in ancient writers (he cites the transition from 5:47 to 6:1 as another possible example). Recently, Kellum (2005: 230) has suggested that statements indicating movement in the Fourth Gospel regularly serve as ways to move along the narrative. Stibbe (1993: 159), too, is able to make "very good sense" of the narrative as it stands without resorting to source-critical theories. For him, 14:31 is part of the Johannine theme of "the elusive Christ." After saying in 14:30 that the devil "has no hold" on him, Jesus, knowing that the "prince of this world" is now coming, is evading his captors for one final time. Schlatter (1948: 304), finally, makes the improbable suggestion that the unevenness may be due to a break in dictation.

105. See also the extended text-critical note in the NET (2d beta ed.), which arrives at the same conclusion for similar reasons.

106. Barrett (1978: 457) agrees that treating the sentence as a statement "does not seem to make good sense" but construes "and if it had not been so I would have told you" as a

14:4. The shorter reading ὅπου ἐγὼ ὑπάγω οἴδατε τὴν ὁδόν is found in ℵ B C; the longer reading ὅπου ἐγὼ ὑπάγω οἴδατε καὶ τὴν ὁδὸν οἴδατε is represented by 𝔓⁶⁶* A D. Presumably, the "syntactical harshness" of the shorter (original) reading invited efforts at amelioration (Metzger 1994: 207; so, rightly, Morris 1995: 569 n. 14).

14:7. The rendering of this verse depends on an adjudication of textual variants: the perfect ἐγνώκατε (𝔓⁶⁶ ℵ D*) and the pluperfect ἐγνώκειτε (A, B, and many later MSS). The latter, pluperfect reading, adopted by the NIV, is essentially negative: "If you really knew me—but you don't" (contrary-to-fact condition). The former, perfect reading, assumes that the disciples have in fact come to know Jesus, though now they must understand that this knowledge provides them access to the Father (so the TNIV). With the majority of the UBS committee (Metzger 1994: 207) and major commentators (Carson 1991: 493; Ridderbos 1997: 494; Moloney 1998: 398–99; Schnackenburg 1990: 3.67; Barrett 1978: 458–59; Bultmann 1971: 607 n. 3; Burge 2000: 393 n. 8; and the TNIV; contra R. Brown 1970: 621; Morris 1995: 570 n. 20; and the NIV [though see footnote ad loc.]), the perfect reading is to be preferred, not least because of its stronger external attestation. The pluperfect variant may have arisen under influence from the following verses (14:8–9) and because of Jesus' words in 8:19. The textual issue is similar with the corresponding verbs γνώσεσθε and the variant ἐγνώκειτε.

---

parenthesis in a sentence that otherwise reads, "There will be many abiding-places, for I am going to prepare a place for you" (see also Morris 1995: 568). But it is hard to see how this makes any better sense than the option Barrett rejects.

b. Jesus the True Vine (15:1–17)

Chapter 14 concludes with the statement "Come now; let's go away from here." Chapter 15 opens with Jesus' symbolic discourse on the vine.[1] It is possible that Jesus and the Eleven have left the room of the supper and are passing through scenery that illustrates Jesus' teaching (Westcott 1908: 2.187, 197). The next geographical piece of information is found in 18:1, where the group is said to cross the Kidron Valley, east of Jerusalem, and enter an olive grove on the other side. A vineyard setting would indeed be a highly suggestive environment for Jesus' teaching, especially since "God's vineyard" is a frequent OT designation for Israel.[2]

In the famous "Song of the Vineyard" in Isa. 5, the prophet makes the point that God carefully cultivated his vineyard (Israel) and in due time expected to collect fruit from it, but Israel had yielded only bad fruit; hence, God would replace Israel with a more fruitful nation.[3] Yet it is not the church that serves as Israel's replacement (Beasley-Murray 1999: 272); rather, the true vine is Jesus, who is the new Israel (R. Brown 1970: 670) as well as the new temple and the fulfillment of Jewish festival symbolism (Carson 1991: 513).[4] It is he who embodies God's true intentions for Israel; Jesus is the paradigmatic vine, the channel through whom God's blessings flow.

Theologically, John's point is that Jesus displaces Israel as the focus of God's plan of salvation, with the implication that faith in Jesus becomes the decisive characteristic for membership among God's people (Whitacre 1999: 372). Whereas OT Israel was ethnically con-

---

1. Carson (1991: 513) terms it "extended metaphor" or "illustrative comparison." He is not convinced that the parallels adduced by Bauckham (1987: 84–101) establish that the present passage constitutes a commentary on one of Jesus' parables (Carson 1991: 512). R. Brown (1970: 668) labels this a *māšāl* (so also Borchert 2002: 138; cf. 1996: 329); Schnackenburg (1990: 3.96) calls it "figurative discourse."

2. Although vine imagery is widespread in ancient literature, an OT background for the present passage is favored by the vast majority of commentators, primarily owing to the frequent OT references or allusions and the replacement motif in this Gospel (e.g., Carson 1991: 513; R. Brown 1970: 669–71; Morris 1995: 593; Ridderbos 1997: 515; contra Bultmann 1971: 530; Witherington 1995: 255–57).

3. This point is taken up by Jesus' parable of the wicked tenants (Mark 12:1–12 pars.).

4. Though it seems far-fetched to see in the present passage a secondary reference to the Eucharist, as do Brodie (1993: 482) and D. M. Smith (1999: 281) (citing Matt. 26:29; Mark 14:25).

strained, the new messianic community, made up of believing Jews and Gentiles, is united by faith in Jesus the Messiah. Jews still have a place in God's family; yet they must come to God on his terms rather than their own (Köstenberger 1998b: 166–67). A paradigm shift has taken place: faith in Jesus has replaced keeping the law as the primary point of reference.[5]

Exegesis and Exposition

[1]"I am the true vine, and my Father is the vinedresser. [2]Every branch in me that does not bear fruit he removes, and every branch that does bear fruit he prunes, so that it may bear even more fruit. [3]You are already cleansed on account of the message I have spoken to you. [4]Remain in me, as I also remain in you. Just as a branch cannot bear fruit by itself unless ⌜it remains⌝ in the vine, neither can you unless ⌜you remain⌝ in me. [5]I am the vine, you are the branches. Whoever remains in me and I in him—he bears much fruit, because without me you can do nothing. [6]Unless someone remains in me, he will be thrown away like a branch, and it will wither, and they will gather them and throw them into the fire, and they will be burned. [7]If you remain in me and my words remain in you, ask whatever you wish, and it will be done for you. [8]By this is my Father glorified, that you bear much fruit and ⌜prove yourselves to be⌝ my disciples. [9]Just as the Father has loved me, so have I loved you. Remain in my love. [10]If you keep my commands, you will remain in my love, just as I have kept my Father's commands and remain in his love.

[11]"I have told you these things so that my joy may be in you and that your joy may be complete. [12]My commandment is this: that you love one another just as I have loved you. [13]Greater love has no one than this, that he lay down his life for his friends. [14]You are my friends if you do what I command you. [15]No longer do I call you servants, because a servant does not know what his master is doing. But I have called you friends, because I have made known to you everything that I heard from my Father. [16]You did not choose me, but I chose you and appointed you to go and bear fruit—fruit that will last—so that whatever you ask the Father in my name he may do for you. [17]These things I command you: ⌜that⌝ you love one another."

Vine imagery was common in the ancient world, as in the case of the cult of Dionysos, the Greek god of wine. The OT frequently uses the vineyard or vine as a symbol for Israel, God's covenant people, especially in two "vineyard songs" found in Isaiah.[6] However, while the vine's purpose

15:1–4

---

5. For a discussion of the theological implications of the present passage, see Köstenberger 1999a: 159–60.

6. Ridderbos (1997: 515) calls it the "redemptive-historical description of the people of God." See Isa. 5:1–7; 27:2–6; cf. Ps. 80:8–16; Jer. 2:21; 6:9; 12:10–13; Ezek. 15:1–8; 17:5–10;

of existence is the bearing of fruit for its owner, references to Israel as God's vine regularly stress Israel's failure to produce good fruit, issuing in divine judgment (Carson 1991: 513).[7] In contrast to Israel's failure, Jesus claims to be the "true vine," bringing forth the fruit that Israel failed to produce. Thus Jesus, the Messiah and Son of God, fulfills Israel's destiny as the true vine of God (Ps. 80:14–17).[8]

The illustration of a vine and its branches, even more intimate than the shepherd imagery in John 10, focuses on the organic, vital connection between the branches and the vine. In a major paradigm shift, Jesus' presence among his disciples is about to be replaced with the Spirit's taking up residence in believers (cf. 14:16–18). This spiritual relationship must be nurtured if Jesus' followers are to remain connected to their exalted Lord.

"I am the true vine" (cf. Jer. 2:21 LXX) is the last of John's seven "I am" sayings and the only one adding a further assertion, namely, that the Father is the gardener. "True" (ἀληθινή, alēthinē) vine contrasts Jesus with OT Israel in its lack of fruitfulness and spiritual degeneracy (Morris 1995: 593; Ridderbos 1997: 515; Beasley-Murray 1999: 272; Moloney 1998: 419). In the ancient Near East, vines generally lie on the ground or wrap themselves around a tree. To this day, they are a common sight in the Holy Land, especially in Judea. Joseph is called a "fruitful vine" in Gen. 49:22. Building on the OT depiction of Israel as a vine, the vine in later years served as a symbol for wisdom (Sir. 24:17), the dominion of the Messiah (2 Bar. 39:7), and the Judaism of Jesus' day.[9] The Jerusalem temple was adorned with a golden vine with large clusters of grapes (see commentary at 14:31).[10]

"My Father is the vinedresser" (cf. 1 Cor. 3:6–9) indicates that he is "in supreme control of the whole process" (Barrett 1978: 473).[11] Though

19:10–14; Hos. 10:1–2; 14:7; see also Sir. 24:17–23; 2 Esdr. (4 Ezra) 5:23. An extensive allegorical depiction of Israel as a vine is also found in *Lev. Rab.* 36.2 (with reference to Ps. 80:9).

7. Since the OT develops the vine metaphor in predominantly negative terms, the notion of the vine as the source of life for the branches is largely absent (but see Sir. 24:17–21). Schnackenburg (1990: 3.98) notes that the vine is fruit-producing, not life-producing.

8. Sidebottom (1956–57: 234) points to similarities in vocabulary between John 15 and the *māšāl* of the vine in Ezek. 17. Other parallels are adduced by Vawter (1964). A general survey is found in Whitacre, *DJG* 867–68.

9. See Barrett 1978: 472. The term ἄμπελος (*ampelos*, vine) occurs elsewhere in the NT only in Matt. 26:29 pars.; James 3:12; Rev. 14:18–19. References to vines and vineyards occur frequently in Synoptic parables (Matt. 20:1–16; 21:28–32; 21:33–44 pars.; Luke 13:6–9).

10. Coins of the first Jewish revolt (A.D. 66–70) feature a vine and branches as a symbol of Jerusalem, and the rabbinic school at Jamnia headed by Rabbi Yoḥanan ben Zakkai after the destruction of the temple was known as a "vineyard" (*m. Ketub.* 4.6). Philo, characteristically, interprets Isa. 5:7 in terms of "that most holy vineyard," the virtuous soul (*Dreams* 2.26 §§172–73).

11. Some interpreters (e.g., Barrett 1978: 473; Carson 1991: 514; Witherington 1995: 258) view the depiction of the Son as the vine and the Father as the vinedresser in terms

the Father is not referred to frequently in the present passage, he does reappear in 15:8–10 (Borchert 2002: 138). The γεωργός (*geōrgos*, vine-dresser [translated "farmer" in 2 Tim. 2:6 and James 5:7]) may merely be the one who tills the soil, which in Palestine is frequently all that is done for the vineyard. Yet the term can also refer more specifically to a vinedresser, as in the Synoptic parable of the tenants (Mark 12:1–9 pars.; see Ridderbos 1997: 515 n. 113). Isaiah's first vineyard song, which constitutes the background of this parable, depicts God as spading, clearing, planting, and taking care of the vineyard, only to be rewarded with sour grapes (Isa. 5:1–7; cf. Ps. 80:8–9).[12]

The theme of mutual indwelling, already mentioned in 14:20, is now represented in terms of vine imagery (Carson 1991: 514). The statement in 15:2 prepares for an understanding of the critical expression μένω (*menō*, remain) in 15:4–16 (Bultmann 1971: 532). The vinedresser does two things to ensure maximum fruit production ("he removes . . . he prunes"; cf. Heb. 6:7–8).[13] In the winter, he cuts off the dry and withered branches. This may involve pruning the vines to the extent that only the stalks remain (Engel 1948–49). Later, when the vine has sprouted leaves, he removes the smaller shoots so that the main fruitbearing branches receive adequate nourishment (R. Brown 1970: 675; Schnackenburg 1990: 3.97).[14]

The pruning activity of the divine vinedresser resembles that of every earthly γεωργός.[15] Since the term underlying "cut" (αἴρω, *airō*) can mean either "cut off" (negative purpose) or "prop up" (restorative), some have argued that the present reference should be understood in the latter sense. But this is almost certainly erroneous.[16] More likely, the antitheti-

---

of the Son's subordination to the Father. Indeed, this seems to be the implication in the present allegory, though it is not at the front of the message. Borchert (2002: 140) affirms the functional, though not essential, subordination of the Son to the Father.

12. The Roman writer Lucian portrays God as γεωργός who acts without human collaboration (*Phalaris* 2.8 [second century A.D.]).

13. Westcott (1908: 2.198) notes, "Everything is removed from the branch which tends to divert the vital power from the production of fruit." The term καθαίρω (*kathairō*, prune) is rare in the LXX and occurs only here in the NT. It is found frequently with reference to agricultural processes (though not necessarily pruning) in secular Greek (e.g., Xenophon, *Oeconomicus* 18.6; 20.11). On cutting, see Matt. 3:10 par.; 7:19; Rom. 11:22, 24 (ἐκκόπτω, *ekkoptō*, cut off). On pruning, see Isa. 18:5; Jer. 5:10 (cf. Heb. 12:4–11). Commentators are virtually unanimous in detecting a play on words in the parallel use of αἴρω (*airō*, remove) and καθαίρω in 15:2 (e.g., Carson 1991: 515).

14. Philo refers to "superfluous shoots . . . which are a great injury to the genuine shoots, and which the husbandmen cleanse and prune" (*Dreams* 2.9 §64; cf. *Husb.* 2 §10). For Palestinian horticultural practice, see Dalman 1928–39: 4.312–13.

15. Note Horace, *Epodi* 2.13: "cutting off useless branches with the pruning knife."

16. See especially Carson (1991: 518), who notes that of the twenty-four occurrences of αἴρω in this Gospel, the term means "lift up" eight times and "remove" sixteen times, and states that no good evidence exists that the branches of vines were regularly lifted off the ground.

cal parallelism of the first part of each statement ("every branch in me that bears no fruit"/"every branch in me that does bear fruit") is matched by corresponding divine action, be it judgment (negative [see 15:6]) or discipline (positive [Laney 1989: esp. 58–60]). In the case of Jesus' followers, Judas was an example of the former, Peter of the latter.[17]

The term κλῆμα (klēma, branch [found in the NT only here and in 15:4–6]) occurs in the LXX regularly for the shoot of a vine (e.g., Num. 13:23; Ezek. 17:6) as distinct from the branch (κλάδος, klados) of other trees. The expression is used particularly of vine tendrils, though it occasionally refers to heavier branches as well. In 15:5, Jesus makes clear that the branches in the present symbolic discourse represent his followers. In the case of Jesus' followers, "in me" (15:2) would include Judas (cf. 13:10–11; see R. Brown 1970: 675–76; Morris 1995: 594 n. 10). In the church age, the designation may extend to nominal (but not true) believers.[18] Otherwise, Jesus' own credentials as true, fruit-producing vine would appear to be compromised (Carson 1991: 515).

The repeated references to "does not bear fruit . . . does bear fruit . . . bear even more fruit" draw attention to the fact that the bearing of fruit is God's primary creative (Gen. 1:11–12, 22, 28) and redemptive purpose (cf. John 15:8, 16). The OT prophets envisioned a time when Israel would "bud and blossom and fill all the world with fruit" (Isa. 27:6; cf. Hos. 14:4–8). Indeed, the bearing of fruit is the essential purpose of a vineyard (Morris 1995: 594). The term καρπός (karpos, fruit) occurs eight times in 15:1–16 and only twice in the rest of the Gospel (4:36; 12:24). The Father's intervention in 15:2 to ensure "more" fruit is continued by the "much" fruit borne by the one who remains in Jesus in 15:5 and is brought together in 15:8, where the bearing of "much" fruit brings glory to the Father and provides evidence of discipleship to Jesus.

In a reassuring statement, the disciples are pronounced "already clean" (or "cleansed") because of the word Jesus has spoken to them (cf. 15:7; 13:10–11; see R. Brown 1970: 676–77; see also 1 John 2:24; contrast John 8:31; 1 John 2:19). As Ridderbos (1997: 517) notes, the disciples are "so deeply bound" to Jesus "by his word that in virtue of that fellowship they are able and ready to do his word and to bear fruit." In relation to the purifying force here attributed to Jesus' word

17. Ridderbos (1997: 517 n. 119) rejects Judas and Peter as specific referents, yet it seems hard to deny that these two individuals (plus the rest of the Eleven alongside Peter) serve as excellent examples of the type of procedure described in the present verse.

18. Contra Barrett (1978: 473 [cf. R. Brown 1970: 675]), who believes that the reference is to apostate Christians, perhaps with unfruitful Jews in the background as well. But see Carson (1991: 515), who rightly notes that in John, true disciples by definition persevere (6:37–40; 10:28), while on the other hand, the NT as a whole acknowledges the existence of those who sustain some type of connection with Jesus but who nonetheless end up failing to exemplify the perseverance that would mark them as truly transformed, spiritually reborn individuals (e.g., 8:31–59; 1 John 2:19; 2 John 9; Matt. 13:18–23; 24:12).

(which may refer to the totality of Jesus' teaching [e.g., 14:23]; see Carson 1991: 515; R. Brown 1970: 660; Morris 1995: 595), see other references to Jesus' word in this Gospel (5:24; 6:63; 8:31, 51; 14:23; 17:17).[19] The logic of the present passage connects the bearing of "fruit" (most likely leading others to Christ) with believers' need for continual spiritual cleansing and sustained spiritual union with Christ (Schlatter 1948: 305).

In light of the farewell setting, Jesus proceeds to urge his followers to remain (μένω, menō) faithful to him after his departure (Ridderbos 1997: 517). Initially, "remaining with Jesus" had simply meant for Jesus' first followers to spend the night with Jesus (1:38–39). Yet already in 6:56, the term occurs with a spiritual connotation. In 8:31, "remaining in Jesus" involves continual holding to his teaching. The majority of theologically significant instances of μένω are found in John 14 and 15, with ten references in 15:4–10 alone.[20] The disciples must remain in Jesus, in particular in his love, by obeying his commandments (15:9–10).[21] The vine metaphor illustrates the close-knit relationship that Jesus desires with his disciples (cf. John 10).

Following the reference to Jesus' word in 15:3 (see also 15:7), his insistence in 15:4 that the Eleven must remain in him in order for him to remain in them entails first and foremost their holding fast to Jesus' teaching (cf. 6:56; 8:31).[22] The "in" language harks back to OT covenant theology, including prophetic texts regarding a future new covenant.[23] "Remain" is formally imperative (Morris 1995: 595; Wallace [1996: 720] calls it a "constative imperative"), which, especially in light of the elaboration in 15:4b, entails a conditional force (so the NIV; Carson 1991: 516), describing the dynamic involved in mutual spiritual indwelling.[24]

19. The adjective καθαρός (katharos, clean; cf. the verb καθαίρω [kathairō] rendered "prune" in 15:2) is occasionally used in Greek literature in connection with the growth of vines (Xenophon, Oeconomicus 20.20: καθαίραι αἱ ἄμπελοι). Westcott (1908: 2.199) suggests that the word may contain an allusion to Lev. 19:23.

20. This is what, in application of Robert E. Longacre's methodology, may mark 15:1–17 as the peak of the entire farewell discourse (Kellum 2005: 193–96). In the present chapter, "remain" seems to serve as a metaphorical substitute for "believe." On the "strange absence" of the word πιστεύω (pisteuō, believe) in John 15, see Morris 1995: 297 (cited in Croteau 2002: 111).

21. Though it cannot be explored in detail here, the implications for a biblical theology of sanctification are significant. Instead of focusing on self-effort in avoiding negative behavior (such as resisting sin), the believer ought to concentrate positively on nurturing his or her spiritual communion with Christ.

22. Schnackenburg (1990: 3.99) notes the elliptical nature of 15:4. The term μένω is found previously in the farewell discourse in 14:10, 17, 25. See also additional note on 15:4.

23. See Exod. 25:8; 29:45; Lev. 26:11–12; Ezek. 37:27–28; 43:9. See Malatesta 1978: esp. ch. 8; Pryor 1988: 49–50; and the excursus on "in" terminology in John's Gospel in Köstenberger 1999a: 154–55.

24. See Barrett 1978: 474; R. Brown 1970: 678. Contra commentators who view the statement in 15:4a as merely entailing a comparison (e.g., Bultmann 1971: 536).

Building on 15:4a (Carson 1991: 516), Jesus proceeds to explain in 15:4b that just as the branch cannot bear fruit by itself apart from the vine, so also the disciples must "remain" in Jesus. The vine imagery is, admittedly, strained when branches are given responsibility of remaining (Carson 1991: 516).[25] By implication, external, apparent growth that is not fueled by pulsating life within is not indicative of true, spiritual life (this is the context in which "nothing" is to be understood; see Ridderbos 1997: 517). The entire passage is reflective of new covenant theology (Carson 1991: 516, alluding to Ezek. 36 and citing Malatesta 1978; Pryor 1988: 49–50).

15:5–10 Jesus' statement in 15:5 reiterates the "I am" statement in 15:1 (though developing it in a different direction: in 15:1 toward the Father, in 15:5 toward the disciples) and then restates the essence of 15:4; 15:6 is the counterpart of both 15:5 and 15:7 (Barrett 1978: 474). "Without me you can do nothing" applies Jesus' assertion regarding himself to the disciples: "By myself I can do nothing" (5:30; see 5:19–20; cf. 2 Cor. 3:5). The "fruit" borne by Jesus' followers is an all-encompassing reference to the manifold evidences of growth and its results in the lives of believers (Bultmann 1971: 532–33; Beasley-Murray 1999: 273; see the warning against reductionism by Carson [1991: 517]). This would seem to include love (Moloney 1998: 420–21; R. Brown 1970: 676), Christian character (Morris 1995: 595), and outreach (Schnackenburg 1990: 3.100).[26]

John 15:6 and 15:7 further develop the contrast of 15:2.[27] The one who does not "remain" in Jesus is like a branch that is thrown away and withers; such branches are picked up, thrown into the fire, and burned.[28] The present imagery may hark back to the parallel in Ezek. 15, where a vine failing to produce fruit is said to be good for nothing but the fire (so Carson 1991: 517; cf. Ezek. 19:12). Fire (πύρ, *pyr*, only here in John's Gospel) is a common Jewish and biblical symbol for divine

---

25. Whitacre (1999: 376) contends that "remaining" is more than simply "believing"—though that is crucial—but that it also entails "being in union with him, sharing his thoughts, emotions, intentions and power."

26. Carson (1991: 517) lists as among the "fruit" obedience to Jesus' commands (15:10); experience of Jesus' joy (15:11; and peace [14:27]); love for one another (15:12); and witness to the world (15:16, 27).

27. See further Matt. 3:10 par.; 13:30; cf. Gos. Thom. 40. Similar imagery is used in Heb. 6:8. The word ξηραίνω (*xērainō*, wither) is used only here in this Gospel.

28. As mentioned, Judas seems to be the prime example (cf. 13:10–11; 15:2; see Stibbe 1996: 161–62). Both verbs ἐβλήθη (*eblēthē*) and ἐξηράνθη (*exēranthē*) are in the Greek aorist (lit., "has been thrown" and "has been withered"), indicating the completeness of the divine judgment (see the discussion in Carson 1991: 519). Of the four verbs in 15:6, the first two are passive and the second two active in the Greek, which is a bit awkward in English. Hence, several translations (such as the NIV, NLT, RSV, NRSV, and TNIV) render συνάγουσιν (*synagousin*, they gather), for example, as a passive (but see KJV, ASV, NASB, NKJV; Ridderbos 1997: 518). In either case, the agents are left unspecified.

judgment.[29] Some who appear to be members in good standing in the Christian community may eventually turn out never truly to have been part of it in the first place, Judas being the paradigmatic example (see esp. 1 John 2:19).

John 15:7 further develops 15:4 by adding the promise of answered prayer for continued adherence to Jesus and his teaching.[30] Jesus' "words" refers to the entire body of teaching composed of his individual pronouncements (Carson 1991: 517). Hence, mutual indwelling involves more than just obedience (though certainly no less); it also entails a growing absorption of Jesus' teaching in one's understanding and life practice that issues in the bearing of much fruit in one's own character, one's relationships with other believers, and outreach to those outside the faith. Because of this growing conformity to Jesus' teaching, obedient believers will be effective in their prayers, since these will be uttered in accordance with God's will (Carson 1991: 518).

What is paramount for Jesus is his "Father's glory" (cf. Isa. 61:3). Frequently in John's Gospel, God glorifies himself, and is glorified, in or through the Son (12:28; 13:31; 14:13; 17:4). Here, God is said to be glorified by the disciples (cf. 21:19) in their abundant bearing of fruit (cf. 15:16).[31] Hence, both Jesus' and his followers' missions culminate in the bringing of glory to God (Köstenberger and O'Brien 2001: 207–8; Moloney 1998: 421; R. Brown 1970: 662). The present statement establishes a close connection between fruitbearing and true Christian discipleship (see additional note on 15:8). The term γίνομαι (ginomai, become), which is capable of a wide range of meanings, here appears to convey the notion of "showing oneself to be" Jesus' disciple (note the dative ἐμοί [emoi, my]; lit., "to me").[32]

In 15:9, the subject introduced is love.[33] Hence, the bearing of spiritual fruit, referred to in 15:8, cannot be separated from the necessity of love (Schnackenburg 1990: 3.103). Jesus' statement "Just as the Father has loved me, so have I loved you" (cf. 5:20; 17:24)[34] makes

---

29. Lang, *TDNT* 6:934–47, especially 936–37, 942; Carson 1991: 517; R. Brown 1970: 679; Ridderbos 1997: 518. See, for example, Isa. 30:27; Matt. 3:12 par.; 5:22; 18:8; 25:41; Luke 12:49; Heb. 12:29; 2 Pet. 3:10; Jude 7, 23; Rev. 20:14.

30. On "my words remain in you," see 8:31; 14:21, 23. On "ask whatever you wish, and it will be given you," see commentary at 14:13.

31. Conversely, fruitlessness fails to give God the glory that he so amply deserves (Carson 1991: 518). The use of ἐδοξάσθη (edoxasthē, lit., he was glorified) resembles the similar instances of passive aorist forms (with the agents remaining unspecified) in 15:6 (Borchert 2002: 145). The conjunction ἵνα (hina) functions appositionally, meaning "namely" or "that" (Wallace 1996: 475–76).

32. Note the parallel in 13:35 with reference to mutual love. See the (not entirely convincing) efforts of coming to terms with this in Morris (1995: 597), who concludes that discipleship is a process, so that the true disciple is always "becoming more fully a disciple."

33. See, at the outset of the farewell discourse, 13:1. See also 13:34–35 (cf. 15:12).

34. The chiastic arrangement is noted by Schnackenburg 1990: 3.103.

the Father's love for Jesus the pattern for Jesus' love for his followers (Carson 1991: 520; Barrett 1978: 475). The same link is found in Jesus' final prayer, where reference is made to the Father's love having been extended to Jesus from the foundation of the world (17:24, 26). In 10:17, the Father's love for the Son is mentioned in relation to the Son's willingness to lay down his life (cf. 15:13). The Father's love for the Son is also the basis for his entrusting the Son with his mission (3:35; 5:20).

Having the Father's love for Jesus as the source, and assured of Jesus' love for them, his followers have a task that is comparatively simple: all they have to do is "remain" in Jesus' love.[35] Yet, importantly, this involves obedience to Jesus' commands (cf. 14:15, 21, 23; 15:14), which include that the disciples love one another (15:12, 17). Rather than obey Jesus out of a sense of obligation or fear, his followers ought to render obedience out of love (Carson 1991: 520; Ridderbos 1997: 519). In fact, not even Jesus is exempt from responding to the Father's love for him in obedience.[36] By his obedience, Jesus becomes a model for his disciples to emulate. The present reference to Jesus' obedience to the Father is in keeping with the evangelist's overall portrayal of Jesus as the Son sent by the Father.[37]

15:11–17 To forestall the notion that obedience is all gloom and doom (Carson 1991: 521), Jesus avers, to the contrary, that the goal of his instruction (telic ἵνα, *hina*, so that [Morris 1995: 598 n. 27]) is all about joy.[38] Jesus' desire is that his joy may be in his followers and that their joy may be complete (cf. 3:29; 4:34; see Ps. 19:8).[39] In keeping with John's focus on believers' present experience of salvation blessings, he grounds their

---

35. Similarly, Jude 21 (R. Brown 1970: 663). The noun ἀγάπη (*agapē*, love) occurred earlier in John's Gospel in 5:42 and, more significantly, in 13:35. It is found four times in 15:9–13 and once in 17:26. The corresponding verb ἀγαπάω (*agapaō*, love) is much more frequent; twenty-six of its thirty-seven occurrences in John are in the farewell discourse. The sober use of "love" terminology distinguishes John's Gospel from other writings such as the Odes of Solomon (e.g., 8:1, 11, 20–21).

36. The perfect τετήρακα (*tetēraka*, I have kept) sounds the notion of completeness (R. Brown 1970: 663; Morris 1995: 597 n. 26).

37. Cf. 4:34; 5:19–20; 6:38; 8:29, 55; 10:17–18; 12:27–28; 14:31.

38. Though "swept up into his dance" (Whitacre 1999: 378) might be a bit too exuberant. "I have told you these things" marks a recurring structural marker in the farewell discourse (see commentary at 14:25).

39. The theme of joy is also found elsewhere in John, in the illustration of the woman giving birth in 16:20–24 and in 17:13 (cf. 1 John 1:4; 2 John 12; see Barrett 1978: 476; R. Brown 1970: 681). The noun χάρα (*chara*, joy) occurs nine times in this Gospel (all but one of the references are in the farewell discourse), more than in any other NT writing (the verb χαίρω [*chairō*, rejoice] occurs nine times in John's Gospel as well). Similar to Jesus, Paul later expressed the hope that his joy might also be the joy of his followers (2 Cor. 2:3; cf. Phil. 2:2). As in the case of love, John's treatment of joy is remarkably restrained in comparison with other writings such as the Odes of Solomon (e.g., 15:1; 23:1; 31:3, 6; 40:4).

joy in OT prophetic notions of end-time rejoicing.[40] John the Baptist epitomizes this salvation-historical fulfillment of joy (3:29; even in his mother's womb [Luke 1:41, 44]), as does Jesus' mother, Mary (Luke 1:46–48). The early Christians likewise experienced this complete joy (Acts 13:52; Rom. 15:13; 2 Tim. 1:4). In rabbinic thought, joy was imperfect in the present age, marred by the certain prospect of death and the worries of this life (*Gen. Rab.* 42.3; attributed to Rabbi Samuel b. Naḥman [ca. A.D. 260]). Only the age to come, the messianic era, would see perfect joy.[41] Jesus' reference to "perfect joy" thus amounts to his claiming to be the Messiah.[42]

The previous verses leave Jesus' (and John's) audience wondering precisely what is Jesus' commandment(s).[43] The present passage gives the answer: "My commandment is this: that you love one another just as I have loved you."[44] References to Jesus' love commandment frame the unit between 15:12 and 15:17 (Moloney 1998: 424). What is more, 15:13–16 consists of specific illustrations of Jesus' love for the disciples: (1) giving his life for his "friends" (15:13, with 15:14–15 elaborating on the meaning of "friends"); and (2) their election by him (15:16; Kellum 2005: 172–74). This is not the first time that Jesus has issued this love command (called a "new" commandment in 13:34–35; see Moloney 1998: 424),[45] nor is it the last (cf. 1 John 3:11, 23; 4:7, 11). On the assumption that they are moved by love for God and Jesus, Jesus' followers are exhorted to act out this love in their relationships with one another (Carson 1991: 521).[46] Thus, John 15:9–12 features a chain of love (R. Brown 1970: 682; Moloney 1998: 424) that unites the Father with the Son, and believers with both Son and Father (Barrett 1978: 476).

In fact, Jesus' entire ministry, particularly in its redemptive aspect, is ultimately grounded in God's love (cf. 3:16), as is made clear by this

40. For example, Isa. 25:9; 35:10; 51:3; 61:10; 66:10; Zeph. 3:14–17; Zech. 9:9. Cf. Conzelmann, *TDNT* 9:362–63.

41. See Delling, *TDNT* 6:297–98; Conzelmann, *TDNT* 9:365.

42. Several commentators note that joy in the present passage is akin to peace (e.g., R. Brown 1970: 681; Burge 2000: 418, with reference to 14:27–28). R. Brown (1970: 681) also notes that joy is presented here as a salvific gift and points to 3:29; 4:36; 8:56; 11:15; 14:28.

43. Note that the reference in 15:10 is to "commandments" in the plural, while 15:12 employs the singular.

44. The conjunction ἵνα (*hina*, that) functions appositionally (Wallace 1996: 476). The distinction made by Moloney (1998: 424 [cf. R. Brown 1970: 663]) between the disciples being commanded to love "continuously" (present subjunctive) on the basis of Jesus' crucifixion, a single act of love (aorist), founders because of reliance on outmoded notions of Greek verbal theory.

45. Similar statements are found in the writings of Paul (Eph. 5:1–2; cf. Rom. 13:8) and Peter (1 Pet. 1:22).

46. Moloney (1998: 426) notes that the genre of farewell typically included a renewing of a covenant.

statement: "Greater love has no one than this, that he lay down his life for his friends."[47] This shows the intensity and quality of Jesus' love for his own (R. Brown 1970: 682; Moloney 1998: 425; Westcott 1908: 2.205; cf. 13:1).[48] Friendship was very important in the Greco-Roman world. It was commonly recognized that the supreme duty of friendship may involve self-sacrifice for one's friend even to the point of death.[49] The present statement thus would resonate particularly with John's Greco-Roman audience. Both the OT and rabbinic literature recognize the sanctity of risking one's life for another, though this was not commanded but left up to the individual, and one's own life was often considered to take precedence over the life of another.[50]

In light of Jesus' statement that the greatest love is to lay down one's life for one's friends, the question naturally arises, Who are Jesus' friends? (Carson 1991: 522).[51] Jesus' answer: "You are my friends if you do what I command you."[52] Not that obedience makes the disciples Jesus' friends; it simply characterizes them as such (Carson 1991: 522; cf. Ridderbos 1997: 520). In the OT, only Abraham (2 Chron. 20:7; Isa. 41:8) and, by metaphorical implication, Moses (Exod. 33:11) are called "friends of God."[53] Here, Jesus extends the same privilege of friendship to all believers, predicated on their obedience to his commands.

47. That is, for those he loves (Carson 1991: 521; R. Brown 1970: 664; Barrett 1978: 477; Witherington 1995: 259; Borchert 2002: 149). See 10:11, 15, 17–18; 1 John 3:16; cf. Rom. 5:6–8. The conjunction ἵνα (hina, that) in the present verse is epexegetical (R. Brown 1970: 664).

48. Some may object that love for one's enemies would be greater; but the present passage is concerned only with the greatest possible way to show love for one's friends (Bultmann 1971: 542 n. 4; Morris 1995: 599; Carson 1991: 522).

49. See the material cited in Köstenberger 2002c: 146.

50. Friendship was also the subject of extended reflection in Second Temple wisdom literature (esp. Sir. 6:5–17). For a study of the concept of friendship in Greco-Roman, Jewish, and early Christian literature with special focus on John's Gospel, see Ford 1997.

51. In the only two previous instances of φίλος (philos, friend) in John's Gospel, John the Baptist is the "friend of the bridegroom" (3:29) and Jesus calls Lazarus "our friend" (11:11). On friendship in the ancient world, see also Keener 2003: 1004–15.

52. Morris (1995: 599 n. 33) notes the emphatic personal pronouns ὑμεῖς (hymeis, you) and ἐγώ (egō, I), which set off Jesus' relationship with his disciples from the world. The converse does not follow: Jesus does not have to obey his followers in order to be called their friend (Carson 1991: 522; Kruse 2003: 321, who notes that Matt. 11:19 = Luke 7:34 is no real exception). Borchert (2002: 149) registers his concern that the hymn "What a Friend We Have in Jesus" may be unduly fraternizing.

53. Though R. Brown (1970: 664) notes that in Isa. 41:8, the verb used for "love" is ἀγαπάω (agapaō). Barrett (1978: 477) refers to Philo's (Sobr. 11 §55) rendering of Gen. 18:17 with the description of Abraham as "my friend" (τοῦ φίλου μου; the LXX reads τοῦ παιδός μου, my child/son). Other Jewish writings apply this designation to Abraham (Jub. 19:9; CD 3:2; Apoc. Abr. 9:6; 10:5; cf. James 2:23) and Moses (Philo, Heir 5 §21; Sacr. 38 §130; Cher. 14 §49; Mos. 1.28 §156), and also to other OT figures, including Isaac, Jacob, and Levi (Jub. 30:20; CD 3:3–4), or even the Israelites (e.g., Jub. 30:21), holy souls (Wis. 7:27), or students of Torah (m. ʾAbot 6.1).

No longer does Jesus call the disciples servants; now he calls them friends.[54] "Friends" is a status more elevated even than "disciples."[55] Whereas servants or slaves are simply told what to do, friends are given more information, which enables them to attain a fuller understanding in their obedience (Carson 1991: 523). This, in part, may be the reason why obedience to Jesus can be joyful rather than burdensome (see 15:11). Not that the disciples understand everything at this point (quite the contrary [cf. 16:29–32]), but they are prepared to follow Jesus in principle and thus become recipients of his revelation, which in due course (i.e., subsequent to Jesus' exaltation and the giving of the Spirit) will lead to greater understanding (Borchert 2002: 150).[56]

Yet the disciples' status as Jesus' "friends" is not an idle privilege; it carries with it a solemn responsibility and is granted in the context of being sent on a mission: "You did not choose me, but I chose you."[57] Election is rarely mentioned in the case of the OT "friends of God." Only once is it said of Abraham (Neh. 9:7) and Moses (Ps. 106:23) that they were "chosen" by God. The OT concept of election is primarily related to the king and people of Israel, God's "chosen people" (see commentary at 6:70; Quell, *TDNT* 4:155–68). In terms of teacher-pupil relationships, Jesus here broke with contemporary custom, for it was common in first-century Palestine for disciples to attach themselves to a particular rabbi, not vice versa.[58]

The term "appoint" (τίθημι, *tithēmi*) probably reflects Semitic usage (Barrett 1978: 478). The same or a similar expression is used in the OT for God's appointment of Abraham as father of many nations (Gen. 17:5; cf. Rom. 4:17), the ordination of Levites (Num. 8:10), and Moses'

54. The disciples' role as servants is intimated in 13:16 and implied in 13:13. On friends, see commentary at 15:13 and 15:14. The contrast between servants and sons is also found in Gal. 4:1–7 and Heb. 3:5–6. There are some interesting parallels between the present verse and John 8:31–36 (noted by Bultmann 1971: 543; Schnackenburg 1990: 3.110). The distinction between φίλοι (*philoi*, friends) and δοῦλοι (*douloi*, servants) is also found in Gnosticism and the mystery religions. See also Clement of Alexandria, *Stromata* 7.2.

55. The designation of the disciples as Jesus' "friends" is in keeping with the more intimate characterization of his followers in the second part of the Gospel (Köstenberger 1998b: 153).

56. "Everything that I heard from my Father I have made known to you" ties in with the present statement with previous passages in the Gospel (see esp. 5:19–20; 8:26, 40; 12:49–50). Philo cites the proverb "What belongs to friends is common" (*Mos.* 1.28 §156).

57. See Borchert 2002: 150; Carson 1991: 523; and Calvin (1961: 101), who notes that this "is as good as saying that they did not obtain by their own skill or industry whatever they have." The pronoun ἐγώ (*egō*, I) is emphatic (Barrett 1978: 478); the conjunction ἀλλά (*alla*, but) is strongly adversative and stresses the contrast between Jesus choosing his disciples and the contemporary practice of disciples choosing to attach themselves to a particular rabbi.

58. This is summed up by the well-known dictum of Rabbi Joshua b. Perahyah (ca. 100 B.C.): "Provide yourself with a teacher and get yourself a fellow disciple" (*m. ʾAbot* 1.6; see Morris 1995: 600 n. 36).

commissioning of Joshua (Num. 27:18). In the NT, the term refers to being "set apart" for a particular ministry, such as Paul's apostolic work (e.g., Acts 13:47, citing Isa. 49:6; 1 Tim. 1:12; 2:7; 2 Tim. 1:11), the role of pastor (Acts 20:28), or a great number of other callings in the church (1 Cor. 12:28); in Heb. 1:2, the expression even refers to Jesus' being made heir.

Jesus' calling and appointment for his followers is for them to "go and bear fruit—fruit that will last" (cf. 15:8). This most naturally refers to the making of new converts (Carson 1991: 523).[59] Once again, the disciples' mission is set in the context of needed, and answered, prayer. "That whatever you ask the Father in my name he may do for you" echoes similar statements elsewhere (14:13–14; 16:23–24, 26).[60] The "love commandment" in 15:17 reiterates 15:12 by way of *inclusio* (Ridderbos 1997: 522; Schnackenburg 1990: 3.113; Borchert 2002: 151 n. 241)—yet note that the phrase "as I have loved you" is absent here (Ridderbos 1997: 522)[61]—and brings closure to 15:9–17 before moving on to a new topic.

Additional Notes

15:4. The present subjunctive forms μένῃ and μένητε are found in ℵ B, the aorist subjunctives μείνῃ and μείνητε in 𝔓⁶⁶ᵛⁱᵈ D, and the evidence from A is mixed (μείνῃ, μένητε). The present subjunctives are probably original, the aorist subjunctives presumably arising by assimilation to verse 7 (Barrett 1978: 474), but in any case the difference in meaning is minimal.

15:8. The interpretation of this passage advocated in the present commentary stands, regardless of which variant (the aorist subjunctive γένησθε [𝔓⁶⁶ᵛⁱᵈ B D; Carson 1991: 519; Beasley-Murray 1999: 268 n. d] or the future indicative γενήσεσθε [ℵ A; Barrett 1978: 475; Moloney 1998: 423; Morris 1995: 597 n. 22]) is judged to be original (so, rightly, Barrett 1978: 475).

15:17. Barrett (1978: 478) appears to favor the omission of ἵνα because of its absence in 𝔓⁶⁶* D, which would give the sentence a harsher and stronger flavor.

59. See the discussions in Ridderbos 1997: 522 (greater emphasis on fruitbearing, but missionary activity is part of it); Barrett 1978: 478 (reference to apostles' mission to the world); and Schnackenburg 1990: 3.112 (leans against reference to missionary activity).

60. There is some debate as to whether the two ἵνα-clauses in 15:16 are coordinate (Ridderbos 1997: 521 n. 132; Barrett 1978: 478) or subordinate (Schnackenburg 1990: 3.112). The former seems more likely.

61. Also, "my commandment" (called a "new" commandment in 13:34) is replaced by "I command" (ἐντέλλομαι, *entellomai* [elsewhere in John only in 14:31; 15:14]).

c. The Spirit and the Disciples' Witness to the World (15:18–16:33)

Just as Jesus' "new commandment" for his disciples to love one another dominated the end of the previous section (15:9–17, elaborating on 13:34–35), the world's hatred of the disciples provides the dark backdrop to Jesus' words in the present unit.[1] Instruction on the world's hatred of the disciples is necessary, for during Jesus' earthly ministry it was he, not his followers, who bore the major brunt of the world's (including "the Jews'") persecution. But once Jesus has been removed, the world's hatred inevitably will turn toward them. James of Zebedee, John's brother, would be martyred by Herod Agrippa I in A.D. 42, and Peter almost followed suit (Acts 12). Their close identification with Jesus will mean that people's response toward them will mirror their response toward Jesus (John 15:20). People's response to Jesus, in turn, mirrors people's response to God (15:23). Thus, it is impossible for a person to claim to be someone who loves while at the same time hating Jesus or his followers.

Moreover, Jesus stresses that people persisted in their unbelief despite overwhelming evidence. Yet despite people's certain opposition (cf., e.g., 2 Tim. 3:12), the disciples must testify to what they have seen and heard (John 15:27; cf. 1 John 1:1–3; Acts 4:20; 1 Cor. 9:16; 1 Pet. 2:13–3:22). Jesus' words in the present passage are addressed primarily to the Eleven, the future leaders of the Christian movement. What in the case of the blind man in John 9 was still a local phenomenon (cf. 9:22), and what kept some in Jesus' day from openly confessing their faith (12:42), would soon be the norm: "they will put you out of the synagogue" (16:2). In fact, people would try to kill Christians on account of their faith. The history of the early church furnishes abundant proof of the accuracy of Jesus' predictions. This is clear from both biblical (Acts, Revelation) and extrabiblical sources (e.g., Tacitus, *Annales* 15.44).

    i. The world's hatred (15:18–16:4a)
   ii. The work of the Spirit (16:4b–15)
  iii. Grief will turn to joy (16:16–24)
   iv. Jesus' victory over the world (16:25–33)

---

1. Michaels (1989: 275) observes, "If the disciples are known by their love, the world is defined by its hatred."

Exegesis and Exposition

15:18"If the world hates you, know that it hated me before you. 19If you were of the world, the world would love you as its own. But because you are not of the world—but I have chosen you out of the world—for this reason the world hates you.

20"Do you remember ⌜the word⌝ I spoke to you, 'A servant is not greater than his master'? If they persecuted me, they will also persecute you. If they kept my word, they will also keep yours. 21But they will do all these things ⌜to you⌝ on account of my name, because they do not know the one who sent me. 22If I had not come and spoken to them, they would have no sin. But now they have no excuse for their sin. 23Whoever hates me also hates my Father. 24If I had not done the works among them that no one else has done, they would have no sin. But now they have both seen and have hated both me and my Father. 25But this happened in order that the word might be fulfilled that is written in their law—'They hated me without a cause.'

26"When the helping presence comes, whom I will send you from the Father—the Spirit of truth who proceeds from the Father—he will bear witness concerning me. 27And you too must bear witness, because you have been with me from the beginning.

16:1"I have told you these things so that you may not stumble. 2They will put you out of the synagogue; in fact, a time is coming when anyone who kills you will think he is rendering a service to God. 3Yet they will do these things because they know neither the Father nor me. 4But I have told you these things so that when their time comes you will remember that I told you about them.

"I did not tell you these things from the beginning, because I was with you. 5But now I am going to the one who sent me, and not one of you asks me, 'Where are you going?' 6But because I have told you these things, grief has filled your hearts. 7But I tell you the truth, it is better for you that I go away. For unless I go away, the helping presence will not come to you. But if I go, I will send him to you. 8And when he comes, he will convict the world about its sin and its lack of righteousness and its judgment. 9Concerning sin: that they don't believe in me; 10concerning righteousness: that I am going to the Father and they no longer see me; 11concerning judgment: that the ruler of this world stands condemned.

12"I still have many things to tell you, but you cannot bear them now. 13When he comes, the Spirit of truth, he will guide you ⌜in all truth⌝. For he will not speak of his own accord, but he will speak only what he hears, and he will proclaim to you what is to come. 14He will glorify me, because he will take from what is mine and will proclaim it to you. 15All things the Father has are mine; this is why I said that he will take from what is mine and will proclaim it to you. 16A little while and you will no longer see me, and again a little while and you will see me."

17Then the disciples said to one another, "What is this he is telling us: 'A little while and you will not see me, and again a little while and you will see me' and 'Because I am going to the Father'?" [18]So they were saying, "What is this he is saying: 'A little while'? We don't know what he is talking about."

[19]Jesus knew that they wanted to ask him, so he said to them, "Are you trying to find out from one another what I meant when I said, 'A little while and you will no longer see me, and again a little while and you will see me'? [20]Truly, truly, I say to you that you will weep and mourn, but the world will rejoice. You will grieve, but your grief will turn to joy. [21]When a woman gives birth, she has grief because her time has come. But when she has given birth to the child, she no longer remembers the affliction on account of the joy that a human being has been born into the world. [22]So you too now have grief. But I will see you again, and your hearts will rejoice, and no one will take your joy away from you. [23]And on that day you will not ask me anything. Truly, truly, I say to you, whatever you ask the Father in my name he will give to you. [24]So far you have not asked for anything in my name; ask, and you will receive, so that your joy may be complete.

[25]"I have told you these things by way of illustrations. The time will come when I will no longer talk to you by way of illustrations, but will talk to you about the Father in plain language. [26]On that day you will ask in my name, yet I am not saying to you that I will ask the Father for you; [27]for the Father himself loves you, because you have loved me and have believed that I came from God. [28]I came from the Father and have come into the world; I am leaving the world again and am going back to the Father."

[29]His disciples said, "See, now you are talking in plain terms and do not speak by way of illustration. [30]Now we know that you know everything and that you do not need anyone to ask you questions. By this we believe that you have come from God."

[31]Jesus answered them, "Do you now believe? [32]Look, a time is coming—and in fact has come—when each one of you will be scattered to his own home, and you will leave me all alone. Yet I am not alone, because the Father is with me. [33]I have told you these things so that in me you may have peace. In the world you will suffer affliction; but take heart, I have triumphed over the world."

i. The World's Hatred (15:18–16:4a)

The previous verse ended with a reference to Jesus' command for his disciples to love one another. Now, in a rather sharp turn, his attention focuses on the world's hatred toward those associated with him: "If the world hates you, know that it hated me before you."[2] Hence, Jesus' followers should not be surprised when, after their Lord's departure,   **15:18–19**

---

2. Keener (2003: 1019) finds another micro-chiasm in 15:18–25, with 15:20ab (a servant is not greater than his master) at the center. The six conditional clauses in 15:18–24 represent warnings pertaining to the future (or present) of the Christian community in relation to the world. Such parting exhortations are a common feature of farewell dis-

the world's hatred turns against them. As they grow more Christlike, it will become evident that though they are in the world, they are not of it (17:11, 14), and this, in turn, will convict the world (3:19–21; 7:7) (Carson 1991: 525). The Qumran community stressed love within the brotherhood but "everlasting hatred for the men of the pit" (1QS 9:21–22). Jesus, by contrast, preached love for one's enemies, though this did not necessarily alter the world's negative stance toward him or his followers.[3]

"If you were of the world, the world would love you as its own" (cf. 1 John 4:5). Unlike the previous condition in 15:18, this one is assumed not to be true (Borchert 2002: 154; Barrett 1978: 480). But the disciples do not belong to the world (see 8:21–23; 17:14, 16); rather, Jesus has chosen them out of the world (see 6:70–71; 15:16; 17:13–19). This election, not their intrinsic merit, is what constitutes the basis for their inclusion in the new messianic community. This should keep the disciples humble as they go into the world as Jesus' emissaries (Carson 1991: 525).

"For this reason the world hates you": they resent the disciples' status as Jesus' followers, and his spiritual presence in them stirs the world's antagonism toward God and his purposes in Christ. This does not call believers to physically separate themselves from the world; to the contrary, they are sent into the world to bear spiritual fruit (15:16; 17:18; 20:21). As they are being set apart spiritually as Christ's witnesses, the Spirit will use them to convict the world (15:26–27; 17:17; see Borchert 2002: 155). In this realistic yet loving stance toward the world, Jesus' followers stand apart from sectarians and gnostics alike (Borchert 2002: 153; Ridderbos 1997: 523).

---

courses (Moloney 1998: 433). The present condition is second class: "If the world hates you—and it does" (Wallace 1996: 696; Borchert 2002: 154). On the "world," see commentary at 1:9; the same phrase occurs in 1 John 3:13 (see also John 17:14). On the contrast between "above" and "below," see 3:31; 8:23 (cf. 18:36–37). The form γινώσκετε (ginōskete, you know) can be read as an imperative (NIV; NRSV; NLT; ISV; ESV; HCSB; TNIV; Barrett 1978: 480) or an indicative (NASB; KJV), though admittedly the difference is marginal (R. Brown 1970: 686). The pronoun με is emphatic (Morris 1995: 602 n. 42). The perfect verb form μεμίσηκεν (memisēken, it hated) stresses the settled, completed state of the world's hatred toward Jesus (Barrett 1978: 480; R. Brown 1970: 686; Morris 1995: 602 n. 44).

3. The world's hatred was experienced by Christians long before John wrote. The Roman historians Tacitus (Annales 15.44) and Suetonius (Nero 16) both called Christianity "a mischievous superstition." See also the charges leveled against the early Christians listed in Köstenberger 2002c: 147, citing Barclay 1975: 2.183–85. Still useful are Frend 1967 and Workman 1923. Keener (2003: 1017) claims that the worldview presupposed in 15:18–25 is "one common to sectarian groups, in which apocalyptic ideologies (in the modern sense of that expression) often prevail" (though he later acknowledges degrees of "sectarian" outlook [quotation marks his]). In his following paragraph, Keener does concede, however, that John's emphasis here "probably [but perhaps not?] stems from authentic Jesus tradition." Did Jesus, then, propagate a sectarian worldview? And, if so, in what sense?

Jesus' statement "A servant[4] is not greater than his master" reapplies the   **15:20–21**
truth previously enunciated at 13:16. Although Jesus' disciples have been
elevated to the status of "friends" (15:15), they are not therefore now
greater than he is (Ridderbos 1997: 524).[5] Jesus' message is couched in
the form of two first-class conditions (true to fact [Wallace 1996: 708]):
"If they persecuted me [and many of them did], they will also persecute
you. If they kept my word [and some of them did], they will also keep
yours."[6] The implication of this is that ultimately the disciples have no
control over how their message will be received (Ridderbos 1997: 524).
People's response to their proclamation will depend on their stance toward Jesus. As long as Jesus was on earth, he remained the prime target
of persecution; once his physical presence was removed, the world's
hatred would inevitably turn toward his disciples.[7]

The second first-class conditional sentence "If they kept my word,
they will also keep yours" has several formal OT parallels linking the
reception of a prophet's message with people's stance toward God himself (e.g., 1 Sam. 8:7; Ezek. 3:7). As Jesus sums up, "They will treat you
this way on account of my name, for they do not know the one who
sent me."[8] The three-step logic is as follows: when people oppose the
disciples, it is because they oppose Jesus; if people oppose Jesus, it is
because they do not know the Father (see 15:23); therefore, if people
oppose the disciples, it is ultimately because they do not know God. The
claim of Christians that Jesus—and he alone—is Lord (κύριος, *kyrios*)
pitted them against Roman imperial religion, which attributed that title
to the emperor. Domitian, who reigned probably when John's Gospel

---

4. Ridderbos (1997: 524) and Barrett (1978: 480) note the formal contradiction between
Jesus' statement that he no longer calls his followers "servants" in 15:15 and his application of the saying quoted in 15:20 to the disciples. Both conclude that there is no actual
contradiction here.

5. See Ridderbos 1997: 523; Carson 1991: 525. Compare Matt. 10:24 par. (Beasley-Murray 1999: 275). See also the additional note on 15:20.

6. So, rightly, Carson 1991: 525–26, with reference to 17:20, the NIV, and many major
commentators (e.g., Barrett 1978: 480; Bultmann 1971: 549; Lindars 1970: 494; Schnackenburg 1990: 3.115; Bruce 1980: 313; contra Borchert 2002: 156; Dodd 1963: 409; R. Brown
1970: 687; and the NLT). See the discussions in Beasley-Murray 1999: 275; Carson 1991:
525–26.

7. The Synoptics likewise record Jesus' warning that his followers would be persecuted
(Matt. 10:16–25 pars.). In this, too, the principle was true that a student is not above the
teacher (e.g., Luke 6:40). To persecute the church was to persecute Jesus himself (Acts
9:4). At the end of his life, Paul wrote to Timothy, "In fact, everyone who wants to live a
godly life in Christ Jesus will be persecuted" (2 Tim. 3:12).

8. See 7:28; 8:19, 27, 55; 16:3. Ταῦτα πάντα (*tauta panta*, all these things) presumably
includes both hatred (15:18–19) and the resulting persecution (15:20; cf. 16:1–3; see Bultmann 1971: 550 n. 1; Beasley-Murray 1999: 276; Ridderbos 1997: 524). The expression
"because of my name" reflects OT terminology pertaining to God and his great name (cf.
1 Sam. 12:22; 2 Chron. 6:32; Jer. 14:21; cf. Acts 5:41; 1 Pet. 4:14; 1 John 2:12; Rev. 2:3; see
R. Brown 1970: 687), though in the present context it is essentially synonymous with "me"
(Carson 1991: 526; Moloney 1998: 433).

was written (A.D. 81–96), insisted on the designation *dominus et deus*, Lord and God (cf. 20:28).[9]

15:22–25 Next follows a contrary-to-fact condition: "If I had not come and spoken to them, they would have no sin."[10] Positively stated, now that Jesus has come, the world is guilty. This does not mean that the world would have been in perfection if Jesus had not come; it is merely to stress the world's culpability in rejecting the divine revelation brought by Jesus (Carson 1991: 526). Moreover, there is a finality to both God's ultimate expression of his love in Jesus (3:16) and the world's final rejection of this love (Ridderbos 1997: 524).[11] The sin referred to in the statement "But now they have no excuse for their sin" may be specifically that of crucifying Jesus (8:40, 44), though this act is a direct result of people's unbelief (R. Brown 1970: 688) and rejection of divine revelation (Barrett 1978: 481), which are rooted in general human depravity (3:19–21; 5:40–44; 9:41).[12]

"Whoever hates me also hates my Father" continues the theme of the close identification between Jesus, the Father, and his followers sounded in 15:20 (see also 5:23; 1 John 2:23). The immediate point of reference surely is to the unbelieving Jews who were ultimately responsible for putting Jesus on the cross (Schnackenburg 1990: 3.116), though the reference is not limited to them. "Hate" (see 15:18–19) is a strong term that conveys the notion of rejection. It suggests that ultimately there is no middle ground: either people embrace Jesus and his message (and that of his followers) or they reject him and the good news of salvation (see 3:16–21).

John 15:24 adds to 15:22 a second contrary-to-fact conditional clause: "If I had not done the works among them that no one else has done [but Jesus did], they would have no sin [but now people do]." This is immediately followed by the conclusion: "But now they have both seen and have hated both me and my Father."[13] The double "both . . . and" construction has the cumulative effect of heightening people's culpability by contrasting the performance of Jesus' works and people's rejection of Jesus (Ridderbos 1997: 525).[14] Because Jesus' words and works are

9. See also 8:19, 27, 39–47, 54–55; 10:30; 12:44; 14:6–7, 9; 16:3; 17:3; cf. 1 John 2:23.

10. Several times in the NT, ignorance is attributed to those responsible for Jesus' suffering (Luke 23:34; John 15:24; Acts 3:17). Elsewhere, too, Jesus teaches that exposure to divine revelation brings about greater responsibility (Luke 12:48). For "to have [i.e., be guilty of] sin," see John 9:41; 19:11; cf. 1 John 1:8.

11. The finality of the sin of the world's unbelief in Jesus is stressed also by Barrett (1978: 481, citing 16:9) and Bultmann (1971: 550).

12. A possible parallel is Matt. 11:20–24, where those who have heard Jesus but rejected him will be judged more severely than Tyre and Sidon (see also Luke 11:31–32) (Carson 1991: 526).

13. The implied object of "seen" is Jesus' works (Schnackenburg 1990: 3.116; Barrett 1978: 481; R. Brown 1970: 688).

14. The perfect forms ἑωράκασιν (*heōrakasin*, they have seen) and μεμισήκασιν (*memisēkasin*, they have hated) highlight the enduring nature of the Jews' hatred toward Jesus.

those of the Father (5:36; 14:10), rejection and hatred of the former are rooted in rejection and hatred of the latter. Jesus' opponents have been urged to acknowledge the revelation of God in Jesus' works even if unable to accept his word (5:36; 7:21–24; 9:24–34; 10:31–39).[15] This is vital, especially since Jesus' works and words are "plainly visible" (cf. 18:20; see Barrett 1978: 481).

"But in order that the word might be fulfilled that is written in their law" is elliptical,[16] with the presumably required addition being "But *this happened* in order that . . ." (Ridderbos 1997: 525 and n. 141, citing BDF §448.7). "Their law" (see 12:34; cf. 8:17; 10:34) ironically highlights the discrepancy between the law and the actions of the Jews (Carson 1991: 527; Morris 1995: 605), who are convicted by "their own law" (Barrett 1978: 482), whereby "law" means broadly "Scripture" (Ridderbos 1997: 525). The introductory formula is the longest in this Gospel if not the entire NT (R. Brown 1970: 689, cf. Freed 1965b: 94; Schnackenburg 1990: 3.117).[17] The citation "They hated me without a cause" is from Ps. 35:19 or 69:4, reflecting Davidic typology (Carson 1991: 527). The latter is more likely, since Ps. 69 was widely regarded as messianic.[18]

Striking a forensic note (Morris 1995: 607; cf. Witherington 1995: 262), **15:26–27** Jesus proceeds to explain that his own as well as his disciples' vindication will come in the form of the παράκλητος (*paraklētos*, helping presence; Ridderbos 1997: 526). This is now the third Paraclete saying in John 14–16; παράκλητος and "Spirit of truth" are also juxtaposed in 14:16–17. The present instance of this term resumes the most recent reference to the παράκλητος in 14:26.[19] In the present context, truth is required for the Spirit's role as a witness.[20] The legal courtroom dimension brought

15. Compare with this the respect demanded by God for the prophet like Moses (Deut. 18:18–19).

16. So Ridderbos 1997: 525; R. Brown 1970: 688; Morris 1995: 605; Barrett 1978: 482; Carson 1991: 527 n. 2.

17. On fulfillment quotations, see commentary at 12:38.

18. So Ridderbos 1997: 525–26; Barrett 1978: 482; Carson 1991: 527; Beasley-Murray 1999: 276; contra Moloney (1998: 434), who contends that "most" favor Ps. 35. Cf. the citation of Ps. 69:9 in John 2:17. See also Ps. 119:161. Extrabiblical parallels include Ps. Sol. 7:1; *b. Yoma* 9b (cited in Köstenberger 2002c: 147; cf. Barrett 1978: 482; R. Brown 1970: 689).

19. Regarding the phrase "whom I will send to you," see 14:16, 26 (where the Son is said to be the sender of the Paraclete) and 16:7. "Whom I will send from the Father" and "who proceeds from the Father" are parallel (Schnackenburg 1990: 3.118; Beasley-Murray 1999: 276). Carson (1991: 528–29) rightly notes that what is in view is not ontological procession, but the mission of the Spirit is parallel to the mission of the Son (cf. Barrett 1978: 482). On "the Spirit of truth," see commentary at 14:17 (see also 16:13; 1 John 4:6).

20. See commentary at 16:8–11. At Qumran, the title "spirit of truth" is given to the leader of the forces of good against the forces of evil (e.g., 1QS 3:18). In 1QS 4:21, the expressions "spirit of holiness" (i.e., holy spirit) and "spirit of truth" occur in parallelism.

into play by the dual designation of the Spirit may foreshadow the upcoming trial scenes of Jesus.[21]

Note the coordination of witnesses in 15:26–27: "he will bear witness concerning me" (see 1 John 5:6); "you too must bear witness."[22] In OT prophetic literature (esp. Isaiah), God's end-time people are called God's "witnesses" to the nations (e.g., Isa. 43:10–12; 44:8). In the NT, believers are promised the Spirit's help in times of persecution (Matt. 10:20; Mark 13:11; Luke 12:12). Particularly in the Lukan writings, the Spirit is also presented as vitally engaged in missionary outreach (Acts 1:8; cf. Luke 24:48–49; Acts 5:32; cf. 6:10).[23] "From the beginning" refers to the beginning of Jesus' public ministry, at which time the disciples joined Jesus.[24]

16:1–4a   One of the major purposes of Jesus' parting instruction of his disciples was to prevent them from being taken by surprise (Barrett 1978: 484) or falling into apostasy (Carson 1991: 530).[25] "These things" refers to 15:18–27 (Carson 1991: 530).[26] "So that you may not stumble" features the semitechnical term for apostasy, σκανδαλίζω (*skandalizō*).[27] Encouraging words from the departing figure are a regular feature of Jewish farewell discourses. Those who will expel Jesus' disciples from the synagogue are referred to in 15:21–25.[28] The expression "a time is coming" is

21. Lindars (1972: 496) adduces Matt. 10:20 as evidence that the present passage probably refers to "legal testimony in a court of law."

22. Μαρτυρεῖτε (*martyreite*) is best taken as an imperative, "you must bear witness" (Carson 1991: 529; NIV; NLT; NRSV; TNIV), rather than as an indicative (ASV; RSV) or a future (NASB; NKJV), though there is little distinction in meaning (so, rightly, R. Brown 1970: 689). The imperative here is addressed to the Eleven, who in turn serve as representatives of later generations of believers (Köstenberger 1998b: 151 n. 33, as a mild corrective to Carson 1991: 505). On the implications (or lack thereof) of the use of the masculine form ἐκεῖνος (*ekeinos*, he) for the personality of the Spirit, see commentary at 14:26 (see also 16:13–14).

23. On the disciples' witness elsewhere in John's writings, see 1 John 1:2; 4:14. On the Spirit's role in the disciples' mission, see Simon 2002.

24. So Carson 1991: 529; Ridderbos 1997: 527; R. Brown 1970: 690; Moloney 1998: 434. See 16:4; 6:64; 8:25. See also Luke 1:2; Acts 1:21–22; 10:37. The present tense ἐστέ (*este*, you are) is perfective in meaning, "you have been" (R. Brown 1970: 690; contra Bultmann 1971: 554).

25. Cf. Pliny the Younger, *Epistulae* 10.96 (cited in Köstenberger 2002c: 148; cf. Stählin, *TDNT* 7:339–58).

26. Cf. the link between the "they" in 16:2 and those mentioned in 15:21–25 (Ridderbos 1997: 528).

27. According to Matt. 26:31, the first words that Jesus spoke after going from the supper to the Mount of Olives were, "This night you will all fall away [σκανδαλισθήσεσθε] because of me." For Johannine parallels, see John 6:61; 1 John 2:10; Rev. 2:14; cf. Did. 16:5.

28. On being "put out of the synagogue," see commentary at 9:22, 34 and at 12:42–43. There is no need to tie the present reference to the *birkat ha-minim* (Moloney 1998: 434). See also the references to "those who say they are Jews and are not, but are a synagogue of Satan" in the Book of Revelation (2:9; 3:9). Some rabbis taught that prayer was not effective unless offered in the synagogue.

reminiscent of prophetic or apocalyptic expressions such as "the days are coming."[29] In John, the "time" is bound up with the death, burial, and resurrection of Jesus.[30]

The statement "Anyone who kills you will think he is rendering a service to God"[31] (cf. Isa. 66:5) probably refers to Jewish rather than Roman persecution (R. Brown 1970: 691; Bultmann 1971: 556; contra Moloney 1998: 435).[32] The irony is apparent: when in fact the one martyred renders worship to God, it is his killers who attach pious motives to their acts of persecution (Carson 1991: 531; Barrett 1978: 485). In his pre-Christian days, Paul certainly reflected such misguided zeal for his ancestral traditions (see Acts 8:1–3; 26:9–12; Gal. 1:13–14). Later, he suffered similar persecution at the hands of others (2 Cor. 11:24). Some rabbinic authorities held that slaying heretics was an act of divine worship (*Num. Rab.* 21.3; cf. Num. 25:13; see Carson 1991: 531). However, these kinds of judgments rarely became public policy. For the most part, Jewish persecution of Christians was spontaneous, with seasoned voices counseling moderation.[33]

The reason for the persecution is made explicit in 16:3: "They will do these things because they know neither the Father nor me," a statement that repeats the thought of 15:21 (Ridderbos 1997: 529). As Carson (1991: 532) notes, to know the Son is to have eternal life; not to know him is "to spawn hostility toward those who do." The way Jesus states this makes clear that future persecution is a certainty, not merely a possibility (Morris 1995: 615). "I have told you these things so that when their time comes you will remember" harks back to 16:1 (Carson 1991: 532; cf. 13:19; 14:29). Rather than destroy their faith (cf. 16:1), persecutions thus have the potential of deepening the disciples' trust if they remember Jesus' prediction (Carson 1991: 532; Barrett 1978: 485; Beasley-Murray 1999: 278; Morris 1995: 616). "When their time comes" harks back to 16:2 (cf. Luke 22:53; see Carson 1991: 532).

---

29. For example, Isa. 39:6; Jer. 7:32; 9:25; 16:14; 31:31, 38; Zech. 14:1; 2 Esdr. (4 Ezra) 5:1; 13:29; cf. Mark 2:20; Luke 19:43; 23:29.

30. See Carson 1991: 530; Barrett 1978: 484. Though note the lack of the article in the present instance (Morris 1995: 615 n. 4). The same phrase, ὥρα ἔρχεται (*hōra erchetai*, a time, hour is coming), occurs in John also in 4:21, 23; 5:25, 28; 16:25, 32.

31. Wallace's (1996: 604) paraphrase.

32. See the use of λατρεία (*latreia*, service, worship) with reference to Jewish worship in Rom. 9:4; Heb. 9:1, 6. On Roman persecution, see Sordi 1994. The conjunction ἵνα (*hina*, that) is explanatory (Barrett 1978: 484).

33. For example, Acts 5:33–40; cf. *m. Sanh.* 9.6. According to Josephus, the Jewish authorities (i.e., the high priest Ananus II) were responsible for the stoning death of James the brother of Jesus in A.D. 62 (*Ant.* 20.9.1 §200). The Jews displayed similar zeal at the martyrdom of Polycarp, John's disciple (Mart. Pol. 13:1).

ii. The Work of the Spirit (16:4b–15)

16:4b–7 There was no need to talk about "these things" (i.e., the persecution mentioned in 15:18–25; see commentary at 16:4a) while Jesus was still with his followers.[34] He was the prime target of hostility and protected his disciples. But now Jesus is returning to the "one who sent" him (see 7:33; cf. 8:14, 21–22)—Johannine shorthand for God the Father. Gently chiding his followers for their self-absorption, Jesus notes that no one is asking him where he is going (though see 13:36; 14:5).[35] He is grieved that the Eleven do not show greater interest in the salvation-historical implications of his departure (cf. 16:17; see Ridderbos 1997: 530).[36]

"I have told you these things" in 16:6 continues 16:1 and 16:4 (see commentary at 14:25). The cause of the disciples' grief, lamentably, is largely preoccupation with their own fate (cf. 2 Kings 6:15).[37] This caused them to miss the positive implications of Jesus' departure both for themselves and for the continuation of his mission. "I tell you the truth" (see commentary at 1:51) introduces, with added gravity (Morris 1995: 618), the fourth Paraclete saying in John 14–16 (on which, see esp. Carson 1979: 547–66). The ramifications of Jesus' departure can be understood only from a salvation-historical vantage point (cf. 13:1, 3; see Ridderbos 1997: 530).

Contrary to what the announcement of Jesus' departure may signal for his followers, his work on earth has not come to an end; it will be continued by the Spirit. Rather than hold up God's purposes, the crucifixion actually will expedite it.[38] For, by eschatological necessity, the Spirit cannot come unless Jesus has first been exalted (see Acts 2). Since the work of atonement must first be accomplished for Jesus to be "glorified," and since the παράκλητος represents the presence of Jesus, Jesus by definition must depart before the Spirit can be given.

---

34. The phrase "at first" (ἐξ ἀρχῆς, *ex archēs* [lit. "from the beginning"]) also occurs at 6:64. A similar expression, ἀπ' ἀρχῆς (*ap' archēs*, from the beginning), is found in 8:44; 15:27 (cf. 1 John 1:1; 2:7, 13, 14, 24; 3:8, 11; 2 John 5–6).

35. On the surface, 13:36 and 14:5 seem to contradict Jesus' statement here, but in both previous passages the illocutionary force of the questions is a protest of Jesus' announced departure rather than a sincere inquiry as to his destination or the implications of his leaving (Carson 1991: 532–33; contra Schnackenburg 1990: 3.126; R. Brown 1970: 710, followed by Beasley-Murray 1999: 279; note also the curious attempt at resolving the difficulty by Borchert 2002: 164). Burge (2000: 436) notes the present tense ἐρωτᾷ (*erōta*, asks).

36. Though the point made by Stibbe (1993: 172) is likely apropos: "The silence of the disciples at this point reveals their caution. When Peter asked the question before, it led to a severe warning . . . (13.38). When Thomas asked this question in 14.5, it led to a thinly veiled rebuke. . . . The silence of the disciples in Jn 16.5 is therefore entirely explicable. [They] have become very cautious about asking questions."

37. The word λυπή (*lypē*, grief) occurs elsewhere in this Gospel only in 16:20–22.

38. The phrase "it is for your good" (συμφέρει, *sympherei*) also occurs in 11:50 and 18:14, and elsewhere in the Gospels only in Matthew (5:29, 30; 18:6; 19:10).

Only through the internal presence of the Spirit will the disciples truly understand Jesus (R. Brown 1970: 711).

Jesus' departure is both advantageous and necessary for the giving of the Spirit: "Unless I go away, the helping presence [παράκλητος] will not come to you." John paints successive events on a salvation-historical canvas: first Jesus' glorious "departure" via the cross, including his resurrection and exaltation (12:23, 32–33; 13:1, 31–32), then the sending of the Spirit (14:16, 26; 15:26; cf. 7:39). OT prophetic literature is full of anticipation regarding the inauguration of the age of the kingdom of God by the pouring out of the Spirit.[39] Jesus' breathing the Spirit on his followers in 20:22 is only a symbolic foreshadowing of this event.[40]

John 16:8 introduces in summary fashion what is spelled out in greater detail in 16:9–11.[41] John 16:8–11 deals with the Spirit's judgment of the world, and 16:12–15 with his revelatory ministry to believers (Whitacre 1999: 388). Ultimately, in John it is not Jesus who is on trial but the world. The anticipation of the Spirit's work of convicting the world of its guilt in effect represents a retrial of the trial of Jesus (R. Brown 1970: 711), who, despite the thrice-repeated "not guilty" verdict of Pilate, was put on the cross. When the evidence is properly weighed, it turns out that it is the world that is guilty of the sin of unbelief, convicted on the basis of Christ's righteousness (or of its lack of unrighteousness), and judged together with the supernatural "ruler of this world."[42]

16:8–11

When he comes, the παράκλητος will convict the world, that is, prove it guilty by producing definitive evidence regarding the world's guilt (Ridderbos 1997: 531; see 12:48a; cf. 8:44–47).[43] The world masquerades as righteous and suppresses any evidence to the contrary, and such behavior requires the Spirit to expose its guilt. This is the only place in Scripture where the Spirit is said to perform a work in "the world" (Morris 1995: 618–19). An early illustration of this convicting work is found in Acts 2:36–37, where the crowds who had heard Peter's Pentecost sermon were "cut to the heart" (cf. 1 Cor. 14:24–25).

---

39. For example, Isa. 11:1–10; 32:14–18; 42:1–4; 44:1–5; Jer. 31:31–34; Ezek. 11:17–20; 36:24–27; 37:1–14; Joel 2:28–32; cf. John 3:5; 7:37–39.

40. See commentary at 20:22.

41. The preceding statement in 15:26–27, linking the Spirit's witness with that of the disciples, shows that the Spirit's convicting work in the world also involves Jesus' followers (Schnackenburg 1990: 3.129).

42. According to Schlatter (1948: 311–12), the nature of sin, righteousness, and judgment were central Pharisaic concerns, and the Spirit's work is aimed at exposing false human views and expectations on these issues. Clearly, Christ and the Spirit work in tandem in this regard, and because of these false human conceptions the disciples require another "helping presence" that protects them and pleads their case.

43. Regarding the world, see commentary at 1:10. Jewish and Greek background material is cited in Köstenberger 2002c: 149.

With regard to sin, people's failure is that they do not believe in Jesus (see 15:21).[44] As Ridderbos (1997: 533, citing 9:41) notes, "the world's deepest misery and lostness [do] not consist in its moral imperfection but in its estrangement from God and its refusal to allow itself to be called out of that condition by the one whom God has sent for that purpose." In John's Gospel, faith is presented as the universal requirement for inclusion in the new messianic community (e.g., 1:12; 3:16), and unbelief as the quintessential sin for which there is no remedy and which will incur sure judgment.

The Spirit will also convict the world "in regard to righteousness."[45] This may refer either, by way of Johannine irony, to people's lack of righteousness (Carson 1979; 1991: 535–38; Westcott 1908: 2.220; contra Lindars 1970: 275–85; 1992: 501) or to Jesus' actual righteousness as the basis for the Spirit's judgment (Lincoln 2000: 117–19; Burge 1987: 208–10).[46] Regarding lack of righteousness, Isaiah averred that all the "righteous acts" of people in his day were "like filthy rags" (64:6).[47] Hence, the world's (and the Jews') self-perceived "righteousness" is in fact the very opposite: unrighteousness (cf., e.g., John 2:13–23; 5:16). Alternatively, and perhaps more likely, the Spirit of truth in his legal function of παράκλητος is said here to prosecute the world on the basis of the righteousness of Jesus, who is declared just and vindicated in court (see 1 Tim. 3:16; cf. Deut. 25:1; see Schnackenburg 1990: 3.132). If so, righteousness is explicated here as Jesus' going to the Father, which represents both Jesus' vindication (Ridderbos 1997: 533) and the reversal of the world's verdict against him (Billington 1995: 106).

The world's judgment is demonstrated by the fact that the "ruler of this world" (referring back to 12:31 and 14:30) now stands "condemned" (perfect tense in Greek; cf. 1 John 3:8; Heb. 2:14). But if the celestial ringleader of all evil is condemned, this also includes those who do his bidding, whether demons or human instruments (Carson 1991: 538).[48] Hence, John can write in his first epistle that believers *already have* "overcome the evil one" (1 John 2:13–14; see Schnackenburg 1990: 3.132). Significantly, this note of ultimate triumph concludes the pres-

44. Unbelief as sin is discussed at 8:21–24 (see also 1:11; 3:19; 15:22). Note also the reference to people's failure to believe Moses and the Scriptures in 5:46–47 (Schlatter 1948: 312).

45. The term δικαιοσύνη (*dikaiosynē*, righteousness) occurs in this Gospel only in the present context (16:8, 10).

46. Keener (2003: 1034) contends that Carson's interpretation of 16:8–11 is predicated "on his improbable view that v. 10 refers to the world's (pseudo-)righteousness." Keener prefers the traditional view that the righteousness is Christ's, or his people's (?).

47. Regarding the Isaianic "lawsuit motif" as background for 16:8–11, see Lincoln 2000: 122–23.

48. Lindars (1972: 503) rightly notes that the Spirit's convicting work in the world is critical, for people will see their need for salvation only "when the divine judgment becomes an inescapable reality to them."

ent farewell discourse: "Take heart, I have triumphed over the world" (16:33; cf. 1 John 5:4).

This is the fifth and final section on the Paraclete. Jesus has much more to say to his followers, but they cannot bear it now (presumably because they do not yet have the Spirit [Laney 1992: 290]).[49] Yet when the "Spirit of truth" comes (see 14:17; 15:26), he will guide (ὁδηγέω, hodēgeō) them in all truth.[50] "Guidance in all truth" (better than "into" all truth [see additional note on 16:13]) entails providing entrance to the revelatory sphere of God's character and ways.[51] In one very important sense, Jesus is the eschatological Word who has explained the Father (1:18). In another sense, however, by salvation-historical necessity it is the Spirit who guides his followers in "all" truth.[52] Such divine guidance was already the psalmist's longing (Ps. 25:4–5; 43:3; 86:11; 143:10). The prophet recounts how God led his people Israel in the wilderness by his Holy Spirit (Isa. 63:14) and predicts God's renewed guidance in the future (Isa. 43:19).[53]

16:12–15

Yet as he guides Jesus' followers in all truth, the Spirit will speak only what he hears—his dependence on Jesus enacting the pattern set by Jesus in his relation to the Father[54]—and also tell Jesus' followers what is yet to come.[55] The object of revelation is "what is yet to come" subsequent to the giving of the Spirit, which cannot be the passion, but must be events following Pentecost. The emphasis may lie not so much on predictive prophecy (Schlatter 1948: 314) but on helping the believing community understand their present situation in light of Jesus' by-then-

---

49. The "now" is the same as in 13:7 (see also 13:37). The term βαστάζω (bastazō, bear) is used figuratively also at Acts 15:10; it occurs in its literal sense in John 12:6.

50. This is the only instance of the verb ὁδηγέω in this Gospel. In Rev. 7:17, the term is used for the lamb leading the saints to "springs of living water." The noun form ὁδός (hodos) occurs in John's Gospel with reference to Jesus being "the way" (as well as "the truth") in 14:6.

51. An illustration of this is found in Acts 8:31, where the Ethiopian is unable to understand the true import of Isa. 53 until guided by Philip (and ultimately by the Spirit [cf. Acts 8:29]).

52. As Talbert (1992: 220) notes, this would include believing (1 John 2:21) as well as doing the truth (2 John 4; 3 John 4). The Johannine churches (better than Talbert's "community") may have used this saying as a "criterion to discern among the spirits, separating true from false (1 John 4:1–2)."

53. Second Temple literature applies guidance terminology to the figure of divine wisdom (Wis. 9:11; 10:10, 17). The illuminating function of God's Spirit (or Wisdom) is also prominent in Philo (Mos. 2.48 §265; Giants 12 §§54–55). See also 1QS 4:2.

54. See 3:34–35; 5:19–20; 7:16–18; 8:26–29, 42–43; 12:47–50; 14:10.

55. The verb ἀναγγέλλω (anangellō, proclaim), which is used thrice in 16:13–15, occurs over forty times in the Book of Isaiah (cf. R. Brown 1970: 708, citing Young 1955: 224–26), where declaring things to come is the exclusive domain of Yahweh (48:14). A close parallel to the present passage is Isa. 44:7 where Yahweh challenges anyone to declare the things to come (cf. 42:9; 46:10). Another striking parallel is found in 41:21–29 (esp. vv. 22–23; see also 45:19).

---

past revelation of God. This entails both "a more profound penetration into the content of revelation" and "the application of that revelation to the behaviour of the community within the world" (Schnackenburg 1990: 3.135).

In 16:14–15, the Father is identified as the ultimate source of both the Son's and the Spirit's revelatory ministry to believers. There is continuity between the Son and the Spirit: just as the Son brought glory to the Father (7:18; 17:4), so the Spirit will bring glory to Jesus. There is also continuity between the Father and the Son and hence between Father/Spirit and Son/Spirit, with the persons of the Godhead collaborating in the task of divine self-disclosure. Jesus' possession is the full revelation of God (1:18; 5:19–20). The Spirit's taking "what is Jesus'" draws on this reservoir.[56] Not that the Spirit materially advances the revelation brought by Jesus; Jesus, not the Spirit, is "the Word," God's definitive self-disclosure. The Spirit provides, rather, the filling out of revelation nodally present in Jesus (Carson 1991: 539).[57] "For as soon as the Spirit is severed from Christ's Word the door is open to all sorts of craziness and impostures" (Calvin 1961: 121).

iii. Grief Will Turn to Joy (16:16–24)

16:16–18 Jesus' statement at the end of his instructions about the Spirit provides the point of departure for the closing section of the farewell discourse. Somewhat cryptically, he speaks of "a little while" after which his followers will no longer see him and another "little while" after which they will see him again.[58] With the benefit of hindsight, John's first readers should have had no difficulty understanding that Jesus spoke here of the brief period between his crucifixion and his resurrection in the first instance and of the resurrection appearances in the second.[59] The

---

56. This free sharing of "possessions" was the mark of close relationship (see 15:15).

57. Burge (2000: 450) ventures into precarious territory when he suggests that the Spirit may "also lead into new territory, new doctrines, and new activities unknown in Jesus' historical ministry" (see, more fully, Burge 1987: 211–17). Clearly, the Spirit's ministry may lead believers to see the significance and relevance of Jesus' teaching in a way that would be impossible without his illuminating work, but it is less clear that the present passage should be construed along the lines of the mediation of substantively new revelation or even "new doctrines." For a critique of this view, see especially Carson (1991: 542), who rightly cautions against diminishing the salvation-historical uniqueness of the vantage point assumed in the present passage.

58. "In a little while" (μικρόν, *mikron*) harks back to previous instances of this expression (see, within the farewell discourse, 13:33; see also 7:33; 12:35; 14:19). Similar terms are used by the OT prophets for announcing both God's judgment (Hos. 1:4; Isa. 10:25; Jer. 51:33; Hag. 2:6) and his salvation (Isa. 29:17). The expression occurs seven times in John 16:16–19. "Then after a little while" is reminiscent of Isa. 26:20 (see also the reference to Isa. 26:17 at John 16:21).

59. So, rightly, Carson (1991: 543), who speaks of "Jesus' departure in death and his return after his resurrection" (cf. Morris 1995: 623; Burge 2000: 440), and makes the point

disciples' question in 16:17 brings an end to the longest monologue in John's Gospel (14:23–16:16). The disciples have not been heard from since Judas's query in 14:22. The resurfacing of the disciples' questions punctuating the discourse provides a sense of symmetry to the discourse, tying 13:31–14:31 together with 16:16–33 (Ridderbos 1997: 537).

The repetition of Jesus' words by the disciples underscores the extent of their incomprehension and perplexity, not just about the double use of "a little while" in 16:16 (repeated in 16:17a; cf. 16:18), but also concerning Jesus' reference to his departure to the Father in 16:5, 10 (reiterated in 16:17b). In confirmation of Jesus' earlier statement in 16:12, this shows that the disciples still had no category in which to place the notion of a dying and rising Messiah who would, upon his exaltation, send "another helping presence" in form of the Spirit (Carson 1991: 543). If Jesus planned to set up a messianic kingdom, the disciples may have reasoned, why first go away, and if not, why the need to come back (Morris 1995: 624, citing F. Godet)?

The authorial aside stating that Jesus perceived that his followers wanted **16:19–24** to ask him about this is in keeping with the evangelist's regular attribution to Jesus of the ability to know people's thoughts by way of supernatural discernment.[60] Reading between the lines, one can sense in Jesus' response his amazement at the disciples' lack of comprehension.[61] Even after the disciples' enthusiastic reply following his clarification (16:29–30), Jesus remains skeptical (16:31–33). The opening phrase in 16:20 once again signals a solemn pronouncement. In what follows, Jesus focuses on the rapid succession of grief at the occasion of his "departure" (i.e., crucifixion) and then joy when they see him again resurrected after a short interim (the prediction is fulfilled in 20:20). His primary point: their joy cannot come without being preceded by grief (Ridderbos 1997: 539).

First, Jesus' followers will weep and mourn, while the world (Jews and Romans alike) will rejoice.[62] Yet their temporary grief will, in short order, give way to joy.[63] OT Israel knew that it is God who is able to

---

that these verses cannot apply to the parousia, because according to Jesus' accompanying illustration in 16:20–24, there would have to be grief in the interim, while 15:11 promises joy. Contra Borchert (2002: 173 n. 295), who refers to Carson's view as "narrow."

60. See, for example, 1:47–48; 2:24–25; 4:17–18; 6:61, 64. See Barrett 1978: 492.

61. Note also what is now the third instance of Jesus' statement in 16:16 and the emphatic position of περὶ τούτου (peri toutou, about this) in 16:19.

62. Κλαίω (klaiō, weep) is also found in 11:31, 33; 20:11, 13, 15, regularly in conjunction with death (see also Luke 7:32); θρηνέω (thrēneō, mourn) does not occur elsewhere in John's Gospel. Both terms jointly refer to the loud wailing customary for mourning in the Near East. Similar terminology is found in the OT (Jer. 22:10).

63. "Grieve/grief" (λυπέω, lypeō; λύπη, lypē) refers to the profound inner sadness that the disciples will experience upon Jesus' death. The verb λυπέω denotes "hurt" in the other instance where it is used in John's Gospel (21:17).

"turn their mourning into gladness" and to give them "comfort and joy instead of sorrow" (Jer. 31:13; cf. Isa. 61:2–3; 2 Esdr. [4 Ezra] 2:27). The Jewish festival of Purim celebrates "the time when the Jews got relief from their enemies, and . . . when their sorrow was turned into joy and their mourning into a day of celebration" (Esth. 9:22). In the present instance, Jesus illustrates this psychological dynamic by the experience of childbirth. Although the labor preceding birth is intense, at the moment of birth, all anguish is forgotten out of joy that a new baby has been born.[64]

In the prophetic portions of the OT, the image of a woman in labor is quite common[65] and frequently applies to the coming of end-time salvation through the Messiah. The Day of the Lord is regularly portrayed as "a time of distress" (Dan. 12:1; Zeph. 1:14–15). Second Temple Judaism coined the phrase "the birth pains of the Messiah" to refer to the period of tribulation that precedes the final consummation.[66] This terminology is also used in Jesus' teaching on the end times, in which he speaks of "the beginning of birth pains" and times of "great distress" (Matt. 24:8, 21, 29 pars.; cf. Rom. 2:9). The early church likewise saw present challenges in this larger perspective (Acts 14:22: "many hardships"; 1 Cor. 7:26: "present crisis"; 2 Cor. 4:17: "light and momentary troubles"; Rev. 7:14: "great tribulation").

The expression "a child [more literally, 'human being,' ἄνθρωπος, *anthrōpos*] is born into the world" entails a certain amount of redundancy, since in rabbinic language "one born into the world" refers to a human being. "Now" (νῦν, *nyn*) replaces the "little while" of 16:16. The shift from "you will see me again" in 16:16 to "I will see you again" in 16:22 clarifies what is more foundational to their relationship (cf. 15:16; see also Gal. 4:19; see Carson 1991: 545). The phrase "you [more literally, 'your heart'] will rejoice" duplicates the words of Isa. 66:14, where the Lord speaks words of comfort regarding Jerusalem (cf. Isa. 60:5; more generally, Ps. 33:21).

---

64. While acknowledging that "the equation of the mother in labour with the disciples in bereavement seems to be the first order of reference and application," Stibbe (1993: 175) argues that the symbol is multivalent. According to Stibbe, the second order of reference is the impending agony of Jesus on the cross (citing 19:34; cf. 7:38). If so, then Jesus' death is described here as a childbirth experience. Calvin (1961: 125) takes the symbolism in a different direction, saying that believers are like women in labor both in that they have already entered God's kingdom and in that they are still "held captive in the penitentiary of the flesh" and long for their eternal destiny.

65. See Isa. 13:8; 21:3; 26:17–18; 42:14; 66:7–13; Jer. 4:31; 6:24; 13:21; 22:23; 30:6; 49:22–24; 50:43; Mic. 4:9–10; cf. 2 Esdr. (4 Ezra) 16:38–39. The anarthrous expression "a woman" is generic (Carson 1991: 544 n. 1). For a brief discussion and refutation of a Mariological interpretation of the woman (mostly by Roman Catholic interpreters), see Ridderbos 1997: 539 n. 188 (referring also to Schnackenburg 1990: 3.158–59).

66. For example, 1QH 11:8–12; cf. Rev. 12:2–5. See Brownlee 1956–57: esp. 29.

"In that day" or similar phrases in the NT frequently refer to the end of the age (e.g., Matt. 24:10, 19, 22 pars.; 26:29 par.; 2 Tim. 1:12, 18; 4:8). In the present context, however, what Jesus describes in 16:23–24 clearly precedes the parousia. Rather, the reference is to Jesus' resurrection and resurrection appearances, when "the great joy of seeing him again will put an end to the torment of uncertainty" (Ridderbos 1997: 539).[67] Not only will seeing Jesus again on the other side of the cross put an end to the disciples' confusion as to Jesus' departure and the two "little whiles," but also Jesus having died and been raised will open for them the way to prayer to the Father in Jesus' name (cf. 14:13; 15:16; see Burge 2000: 442).

This pattern of asking and receiving (cf. Matt. 7:7)[68] with resultant complete joy, which will be the mark of the new age inaugurated by Jesus' death and resurrection on behalf of believers, has already been sounded in John 15 (e.g., 15:7, 11, 16). Carson (1991: 546) aptly notes, "If that joy is part of the matrix of consistent obedience (15:11), that obedience, that remaining in Jesus (15:4) and his love (15:9) and his word (8:31), is the matrix out of which fruitbearing springs, the fruitbearing that is the direct consequence of prayer (15:7, 8)." Believing prayer grounded in obedience to Jesus' word thus will be the path to fruitful discipleship.

iv. Jesus' Victory over the World (16:25–33)

The opening phrase of the present section signals that the farewell discourse is coming to an end (R. Brown 1970: 734). "These things" in 16:25 most immediately refers to what Jesus is seeking to illustrate in 16:21 (cf. 16:16; see Moloney 1998: 453), though beyond this it probably encompasses at least the entire discourse.[69] The actual occurrence of the events depicted somewhat obliquely (i.e., the crucifixion and resurrection) will render the use of veiled language unnecessary (see the reference in 16:12 to "many things" that the disciples cannot yet

16:25–28

---

67. Bultmann (1971: 583) declares, "That . . . is *the eschatological situation*: to have no more questions!" Bultmann, of course, believes that the Fourth Evangelist has so conflated Easter and the parousia that for him they are one and the same. This, however, fails to understand the nature of Johannine-inaugurated (though not radically realized) eschatology, in which the end is shown to be anticipated in the here and now without the future being entirely swallowed up by the present.

68. Morris (1995: 628) notes the present tense of the imperative αἰτεῖτε (*aiteite*, ask) in 16:24, conveying the continual nature of the asking. Note also the presence of two different words for "ask," ἐρωτάω (*erōtaō*) in 16:23 and αἰτέω (*aiteō*) three times in 16:23–24, whereby the former refers to the barrage of questions that the disciples had for Jesus prior to the crucifixion (cf. 16:5, 30), and the latter to prayer requests subsequent to his exaltation (see Carson 1991: 545, apparently dependent on Barrett 1978: 494; contra Borchert 2002: 176).

69. So Carson 1991: 546; Barrett 1978: 495; R. Brown 1970: 735; Beasley-Murray 1999: 286; contra Schnackenburg 1990: 3.161.

grasp). A later horizon of understanding (plus the Spirit's revelatory ministry) will put Jesus' followers in a position to understand the true significance of Jesus' words (Ridderbos 1997: 541).[70] This is promptly misunderstood by the disciples in 16:29–30, when they erroneously conclude that this new salvation-historical epoch has already come (Borchert 2002: 177).

The distinction between "figurative" or enigmatic speech on the one hand and "plain" or clear speech on the other involves the use of the term παροιμία (*paroimia* [translating Hebrew *māšāl* in the LXX]). In biblical and extrabiblical literature, this covers a wide range of parabolic and allegorical discourse (e.g., Sir. 39:3; 47:17; see commentary at 10:6). In the present context, the phrase ἐν παροιμίας (*en paroimias*) does not necessarily mean "metaphorically" or "in a parable" but rather connotes the obscurity of Jesus' manner of expression from the disciples' precrucifixion vantage point.[71] The expression "plainly" occurs earlier in the Gospel with reference to the public nature of Jesus' ministry (7:4, 26; 11:54). More importantly, it has been used to denote plain language as opposed to enigmatic speech (10:24; 11:14). Similar to the Synoptics (esp. Mark), the disciples' lack of understanding pervades the entire Gospel (e.g., 2:22; 12:16; 13:7).

The expression "a time is coming" (see commentary at 4:21, 23) occurs in this chapter also in 16:2 and 16:32 (cf. 16:21). "Whatever you ask in my name" harks back to 16:23. Asking in Jesus' name does not mean that the disciples lack direct access to the Father as if they were restricted to asking Jesus for things that he then would present to the Father (Carson 1991: 547; Borchert 2002: 178); rather, now they are able to approach God in prayer directly on the basis of Jesus' finished cross-work on their behalf (Morris 1995: 629). In fact, "in interceding Jesus will not be a *tertium quid* between the Father and His children. Rather, Jesus' necessary role in bringing men to the Father and the Father to men (xiv 6–11) will set up so intimate a relationship of love *in and through Jesus* that Jesus cannot be considered as intervening" (R. Brown 1970: 735).

There is no necessary contradiction between this statement, "I am not saying to you that I will ask the Father for you," and the NT's affirmation of Christ's intercessory work elsewhere.[72] The affirmation that "the Father himself loves you" builds on 15:9–16 (Barrett 1978: 496). The Father's love is extended to believers on the basis of their confirmed love and

---

70. Calvin (1961: 129) comments, "He now says that His Word has hitherto been allegorical in comparison with that clear light of understanding which He would soon give them by the grace of His Spirit."

71. The statement involves no necessary contradiction with Mark 4:33–34 (Carson 1991: 546–47).

72. Rom. 8:34; Heb. 7:25; 1 John 2:1; cf. John 14:16; 17:9, 15, 20. See Carson 1991: 547; Ridderbos 1997: 543; Morris 1995: 629; Barrett 1978: 496.

settled faith in Jesus.[73] Their relationship, even friendship (15:15), with Jesus is extended to a direct relationship with God.[74] The characterization of Jesus as having come from the Father and going back to the Father (cf. 8:14; 13:3)[75] develops in chiastic fashion (Father/world/world/Father [Ridderbos 1997: 543]) the prophet's portrayal of the sent and returning word of God in Isa. 55:11–12 (R. Brown 1970: 735–36, citing Schwank; see commentary at 1:1).[76]

In another glaring and climactic instance of Johannine misunderstanding (Brodie 1993: 503), the disciples respond to Jesus' words in 16:25–28 with a claim to clarity that is as enthusiastic as it is impetuous: "Now you are talking in plain terms and do not speak by way of illustration. Now we know that you know everything and that you do not need anyone to ask you questions. By this we believe that you have come from God." Yet despite their confident confession, the disciples are no closer to understanding than before. Apparently, they think that the promise of 16:23a has already been fulfilled, failing to realize that "in that day" points to the time subsequent to Jesus' resurrection.[77]

16:29–33

In Jewish thought, the ability to anticipate questions and not needing to be asked is a mark of divinity (see e.g., Josephus, *Ant.* 6.11.8 §230). Thus, Jesus affirms, "Your Father knows what you need before you ask him" (Matt. 6:8). In the present instance, the disciples acknowledge that there is no further need to ask Jesus questions to test his religious knowledge; he has often been shown to know others' thoughts and intentions (e.g., 2:23–25; see Carson 1991: 548).

Jesus' question, with thinly veiled skepticism, amounts to a mild rebuke: "Do you now believe?" As in 13:38, Jesus' response apes the wording of the disciples' comment, revealing both irony and exasperation (with ἄρτι, *arti*, corresponding to νῦν, *nyn*, in 16:29–30 [Ridderbos

---

73. Note the two perfect-tense verbs πεφιλήκατε (*pephilēkate*, you have loved) and πεπιστεύκατε (*pepisteukate*, you have believed) in 16:27 (see Schnackenburg 1990: 3.163).

74. God's love for believers is affirmed also in 14:21, 23; 17:23; cf. 1 John 4:19.

75. On Jesus' "having come from the Father," see 8:42; 17:8. On "going back to the Father," see 7:33; 13:1; 14:12, 28. On modes of movement in Jesus' mission, see Köstenberger 1998b: 82–92, esp. 89.

76. Carson (1991: 548) notes how 16:28 sums up Jesus' entire mission, from his sending from the Father (3:16–17) through the incarnation (1:10–11, 14) to his departure from the world (14:19) and his return to the Father (the dominant theme of chs. 14–17). Similarly, Borchert 2002: 179. Barrett (1978: 496) even calls the verse "a complete summary . . . of the Christian faith," Beasley-Murray (1999: 287) "at once a summary of Johannine Christology and the heart of this Gospel" (combined by Burge 2000: 443), and Stibbe (1996: 174) "the parade example of this theme of the eternal origin and destiny of Jesus the Messiah."

77. For a comparable miscue, see Acts 1:6, where the disciples think that Jesus will restore the kingdom to Israel right then and there, even though he had just instructed them regarding the kingdom of God for forty days (Acts 1:3).

1997: 544 n. 205]).[78] The disciples' persistent lack of understanding will be transparent when they fail to stand by Jesus at his arrest (Morris 1995: 631). Whatever faith they have is inadequate to withstand persecution. Nevertheless, the disciples are to be commended for expressing their trust in Jesus (cf. 6:68–69; noted by Bultmann [1971: 590]).

Assuming a prophetic stance, Jesus now speaks of "a time that is coming" (see 16:2, 25) at which his followers "will be scattered," probably an allusion to Zech. 13:7 (quoted in Matt. 26:31 par.; cf. Matt. 26:56b; see also 1 Kings 22:17; Ridderbos 1997: 545). The image of shepherdless sheep and the scattering of God's flock is also the subject of other OT passages.[79] Yet in the present passage, it is not that the disciples will be left without a shepherd but rather that Jesus will be deserted by his "sheep" (though not by the Father). As in 1 Kings 22:17, the scattering is linked with everyone "going to his own home."[80] This likely refers to the disciples' temporary dwellings in Jerusalem rather than to their homes in Galilee.

However, though the disciples will desert Jesus, the Father will not (cf. 8:16, 29).[81] Even in the case of the disciples, Jesus looks beyond their defection to their restoration and promises them peace (cf. 14:27).[82] The "in me" language is an extension of Jesus' allegory of the vine and the branches in John 15. Jesus' assertion that in this world the disciples will have trouble harks back to his words in 15:18–16:4a regarding the world's hatred toward him and believers.[83] The farewell discourse proper ends

78. Jesus' statement is ironic whether it is a question (KJV, RSV, NRSV, NLT, HCSB, TNIV) or an exasperated comment (NIV).

79. For examle, Isa. 53:6; Jer. 23:1; 50:17; Ezek. 34:6, 12, 21. Note also the earlier references to the wolf scattering the flock in the present Gospel (though the circumstances are different [10:12]) and to Jesus' misson of gathering the "scattered children of God" (11:52).

80. So Schnackenburg 1990: 3.165. The phrase also occurs in the LXX (Esth. 5:10; 6:12), Second Temple literature (3 Macc. 6:27), and later in John (19:27).

81. Some find the present reference to the Father's presence with Jesus to contradict Jesus' cry of dereliction on the cross (Mark 15:34 = Matt. 27:46). However, the present passage simply contrasts the disciples' fickleness with the Father's faithfulness (Beasley-Murray 1999: 288), which does not rule out "Jesus' sense of total abandonment, for some brief period of time" (Carson 1991: 549). See also Borchert's (2002: 181–83) effort to adjudicate this issue in an excursus titled "Nonabandonment in John and the Cry of Dereliction."

82. Ταῦτα λελάληκα (tauta lelalēka, I have said these things) introduces the concluding statement of the whole discourse, whose purpose is to help the disciples overcome their discouragement by directing their view past the cross to the permanent victory won by Jesus. See Schnackenburg 1990: 3.166.

83. The only other reference to θλῖψις (thlipsis, affliction, trouble) in John is found in the illustration of the woman giving birth in 16:21. In the NT, θλῖψις can be a general expression of trouble (Acts 7:9–10) or refer to eschatological woes (Matt. 24:9, 21, 29) or persecution (Acts 11:19; Eph. 3:13), or both (Rev. 7:14). On "take heart," see commentary at 14:1, 27.

on a triumphant note, with Jesus anticipating his victory in the face of apparent defeat: "Take heart, I have triumphed over the world."[84]

Additional Notes

15:20. Concerning the minor variants related to τοῦ λόγου οὗ ἐγὼ εἶπον ὑμῖν, see the discussion in R. Brown 1970: 686–87 (without endorsing his suspicion that "a shorter text has been expanded by scribes").

15:21. The reading εἰς ὑμᾶς is strongly attested, though some favor the dative ὑμῖν or the omission of the phrase (see discussion in R. Brown 1970: 687).

16:13. The reading ἐν τῇ ἀληθείᾳ πάσῃ is found in ℵ[1] and D; εἰς τὴν ἀλήθειαν πᾶσαν is represented by A and B. The former, as the harder reading, is more likely original (Barrett 1978: 489; Metzger 1994: 210).

---

84. This is the only instance of the term νικάω (*nikaō*, triumph) in John's Gospel. The expression occurs several times in John's first epistle (2:13, 14; 4:4; 5:4, 5) and over a dozen times in the Book of Revelation (esp. in the letters to the seven churches in chs. 2 and 3; see Schlatter 1948: 317). The related noun νίκη (*nikē*, victory) occurs in 1 John 5:4. Other NT references to the victory won by Jesus (extended to believers) include John 12:31; Rom. 8:37 (ὑπερνικάω, *hypernikaō*); 1 Cor. 15:57 (νῖκος, *nikos*). The verb occurs rarely in the OT, with Ps. 50:6 LXX showing God as conqueror (cited in Rom. 3:4). It is also found in apocryphal and pseudepigraphical literature (see Wis. 4:2; 16:10; 18:22; 1 Esdr. 3:12). Bruns (1967) contends that John's portrayal of Jesus as victor echoes the pagan myth of Herakles, the conqueror of death and evil.

3. Jesus' Parting Prayer (17:1–26)

Like the material in chapters 13–16, Jesus' prayer[1] in chapter 17 is unique to John's Gospel.[2] It is by far the longest prayer of Jesus recorded in any Gospel[3] and comes at a strategic time in Jesus' ministry, sandwiched, as it were, between his final instructions to his closest followers and his passion.[4] Jesus' parting prayer affords us a rare glimpse into his consciousness and perspective on his imminent suffering. Once the prayer is ended, the final events of Jesus' earthly life ensue in rapid succession: the arrest (18:1–11); the Jewish and Roman trials (18:12–19:16); the crucifixion (19:17–37); the burial (19:38–42); the empty tomb and Jesus' resurrection appearances (chs. 20–21). But for one last time, Jesus pauses to take inventory, as it were, of his earthly ministry, giving his final account to the Father and, by praying, expressing his complete dependence on the Father even in this crucial hour.[5]

1. The prayer is often called Jesus' "high-priestly prayer" (a designation reaching back at least as far as the sixteenth century), though this label hardly fits with Johannine thought, which does not picture Jesus as a high priest (Ridderbos 1997: 546; Carson 1991: 552–53; though see commentary at 17:19 below). Westcott's and E. C. Hoskyns's title "prayer of consecration," though not without merit (see below), fails to encompass the contents of the entire prayer (Carson 1991: 553; Barrett 1978: 500). Hence, commentators now frequently opt for more generic titles of the present prayer, such as "The Farewell Prayer" (Ridderbos) or "The Prayer of Jesus" (Carson). Witherington (1995: 266) calls it "The Sage's Prayer," based on his view that the Fourth Evangelist portrays Jesus as a sage.

2. W. O. Walker (1982) seeks to show that the present prayer is a literary adaptation of the "Lord's Prayer" in the Synoptics. According to Walker, the Fourth Evangelist has reworked and expanded the basic themes of this prayer in keeping with Johannine theology, whereby 17:1–8 constitutes a midrash on the first three ("you") petitions, while 17:9–19 develops the three "we" petitions, and 17:20–26 recapitulates the major themes. However, the evidence set forth by Walker at best warrants only the conclusion that both prayers likely were prayed by the same individual, and not that there is in fact only one prayer, of which the Synoptics provide the original, and John a theological adaptation.

3. Other prayers of Jesus in John are found in 11:41–42 and 12:27–28, but both are very short.

4. Beasley-Murray (1999: 294) and others believe that the prayer of John 17 constitutes an expansion of the much shorter prayer in 12:27–28, but this is rightly rejected by Carson (1991: 552).

5. Hence, it was common especially in older commentators to refer to the present prayer as Jesus' "prayer of consecration" (e.g., Cullmann, E. C. Hoskyns, Bernard, W. F. Howard [cited in Agourides 1968: 138]; see also Westcott [1908: 2.238], who titles John 17 "The Prayer of Consecration" but later says that the chapter contains "what may be most properly called 'the Lord's Prayer'"). This designation has merit (esp. in light of 17:19 [so, rightly, Michaels 1989: 297]), as long as it is not used to imply a strong link between the

Various elements of prayers are found in both Jewish and Hellenistic farewell discourses (e.g., Gen. 49; Deut. 32; Jub. 22:7–23). It is not uncommon for farewell discourses to conclude with a prayer (Jub. 22:28–30; Sir. 51:1–12, 29; cf. Jub. 1:19–21; 2 Esdr. [4 Ezra] 8:19b–36); some testaments conclude with a short prayer of praise (T. Job 43:4–17; T. Isaac 8:6–7; T. Jacob 8:6–9). Occasionally, prayers are used to link sections of an apocalypse (e.g., 2 Esdr. [4 Ezra] 8:20–36; 2 Bar. 21; 34; 48:1–24). John 17 displays several thematic links with the Targumim to Exod. 19–20 (Marzotto 1977). Though the content of these prayers is markedly different from John 17, the form is present (see also Targumim to Deut. 32). More importantly still, Jesus' final prayer culminates John's portrayal of Jesus as the one sent from the Father who, after completing his mission, is about to return to the one who sent him (cf. Isa. 55:10–11; see Ridderbos 1997: 547).

Structurally, the prayer brings closure to the farewell discourse, forming the outer envelope corresponding to the preamble of 13:1–30 on the other end.[6] The prayer itself falls into three petitionary cycles: Jesus praying for himself (17:1–5), the disciples (17:6–19), and later believers (17:20–26).[7] It takes its point of departure from Jesus' declaration of victory in 16:33, and starting from this conviction, Jesus anticipates the cross in a mood not of despondence but of hope and

---

prayer and the liturgical practices of the church toward the end of the first century A.D. More modestly and soberly, Calvin (1961: 134) calls the prayer "the seal of the preceding teaching" of Jesus.

6. Hence, Bultmann (1971: 486, cf. 460–61) places chapter 17 between 13:30 and 13:31, with 13:1 serving as the introduction to the prayer. As R. Brown (1970: 745) rightly notes, however, although chapters 13 and 17 are indeed closely related, they are so by way of inclusion rather than direct sequence. Brown himself, incidentally, believes that chapter 17 was not part of the original Gospel but was added at the same time as chapters 15 and 16. He conjectures that the prayer may have been written by the same circle as the prologue. For a discussion of the literary structure of John 17, see also Malatesta 1971. Black (1988) breaks up the prayer into ninety-five "nuclear structures . . . embedded into 52 cola" (p. 145), also noting the frequent occurrence of ellipsis, anacolouthon, and parallelism (see also his chart of rhetorical features on pp. 149–53, listing instances of repetition, omission, and shifts in expectancy).

7. See Morris 1995: 634; with further delineation of subunits, Hunter 1979: 326–28. Lindars (1972: 515) further divides 17:20–26 into 17:20–23 and 17:24–26. Schnackenburg (1990: 3.168–69, with reference to a 1973 German article) provides a more complicated proposal, dividing at 17:1–2, 4–5, 6–11a, 11b–16, 17–19, 22–23, 24–26 (he considers 17:3 and 17:20–21 to be secondary glosses). Others favor division at 17:1–8, 9–19, 20–26 (e.g., R. Brown 1970: 748–51). Malatesta (1971: 191–92) divides at 17:1–5, 6–8, 9–19, 20–24, 25–26 and proposes a strophic arrangement. More eccentric is the suggestion by Appold (1976: 204) that there is an oscillating pattern of petition and review, featuring six petition and six review units. A survey of structural proposals for John 17 up to the late 1970s is found in Hunter 1979: 312–28. More recently, Borchert (2002: 185–89) has favored seven petitions, based on the address "Father." Yet, as Ridderbos (1997: 547) remarks, "The structure is not severe enough and the transitions are too fluid for us to speak of a detailed and sharply delineated thought scheme."

joy (Morris 1995: 634). On the other end of the prayer, the serenity of Jesus praying gives way to the harsh reality of a rapid succession of hostile encounters, from Judas's betrayal and Jesus' arrest to the Jewish and Roman trials and the events surrounding and issuing in the crucifixion.

    a. Jesus prays for himself (17:1–5)
    b. Jesus prays for his followers (17:6–19)
    c. Jesus prays for later believers (17:20–26)

Exegesis and Exposition

[1]Jesus said these things, and after lifting up his eyes toward heaven, he said, "Father, the time has come. Glorify your Son, in order that the Son may glorify you, [2]just as you gave him authority over all flesh, that he may give eternal life to everyone you have given to him. [3]And this is eternal life: that they may know you, the only true God, and the one you have sent—Jesus Christ. [4]I have glorified you on earth by completing the work you gave me to do. [5]And now, Father, *you* glorify *me* in your presence with the glory I had with you before the world came into being.

[6]"I have revealed your name to those you gave me from the world. They were yours, and you gave them to me, and they have kept your word. [7]Now they know that everything you have given me is from you; [8]because I have given them the words you gave me, and they accepted them and truly came to understand that I came from you and believed that you sent me. [9]I ask concerning them—I do not ask concerning the world but concerning those whom you have given me—because they are yours [10](indeed, all that is mine is yours, and all that is yours is mine), and I am glorified in them. [11]And I will no longer be in the world, yet they are still in the world, and I am coming to you. Holy Father, keep them by your name—⌜the name you gave me⌝—so that they may be one just as we are. [12]While I was with them, I kept them by your name which you gave me and guarded them, and not one of them perished except for the son of destruction, in order for Scripture to be fulfilled. [13]But now I am going to you, yet I say these things while still in the world, so that they may have my joy made complete within them. [14]I have given them your word. Yet the world has hated them, because they are not from the world, just as I am not from the world. [15]I do not ask that you take them out of the world, but that you keep them from the evil one. [16]They are not from the world, just as I am not from the world. [17]Make them holy in your truth—your word is truth. [18]Just as you sent me into the world, I have sent them into the world. [19]And I pursue holiness on their behalf, so that they too may be made holy in truth.

[20]"I do not ask solely concerning them, but also concerning those who will believe in me on account of their message, [21]so that all of them might be one,

just as you, Father, are in me and I in you, that they too might be in us, so that the world may believe that you have sent me. ²²And I—the glory you gave me I have given to them, so that they may be one just as we are one, ²³I in them and you in me, so that they may be made perfectly one, so that the world may know that you sent me and have loved them just as you have loved me. ²⁴Father, I want that those you have given me be with me where I am, so that they may see my glory, the glory that you have given me because you loved me before the beginning of the world. ²⁵Righteous Father, the world does not know you, but I know you, and they know that you have sent me. ²⁶And I have made your name known to them and will continue to make it known, so that the love you have for me may be in them and that I myself may be in them."

a. Jesus Prays for Himself (17:1–5)

"Jesus said these things" is a typical Johannine transitional statement **17:1** (see commentary at 14:25; cf. 18:1), whereby ταῦτα (*tauta*, these things) refers to the entire preceding farewell discourse (cf. 16:33).[8] It is impossible to be certain about the exact circumstances or location of Jesus' prayer.[9] Immediately before the prayer, Jesus is shown instructing his disciples; immediately after the prayer, Jesus is found leaving with his followers to cross the Kidron Valley. It is therefore reasonable to assume that Jesus uttered the prayer recorded in John 17 within the hearing of at least some of his disciples.[10]

---

8. Stibbe (1993: 178) memorably contends that "the Jesus of John's story [and of the present prayer] obeys very different laws of gravity [than mere mortals]. In our Newtonian perspective, 'what goes up must come down.' In the Johannine law of gravity, the opposite seems to be true: 'what comes down [Jesus] must go up!'" He adds (echoes of Käsemann?), "John's Jesus utters his prayer not as a human being on earth but as a divine being somewhere beyond both time and space." This is hardly an accurate reading of the prayer, however. In failing to understand the prayer's relation to John's depiction of Jesus as the sent Son whose mission is about to be completed (see commentary below), Stibbe erects a false dichotomy ("not as a human being . . . but as a divine being") and then disavows the former and unilaterally accentuates the latter, which hardly does justice to the sense of dependence expressed by Jesus on his sender, the Father.

9. Moloney (1998: 469, 473) seems to believe that the prayer was spoken while Jesus was still at the Passover meal, with his disciples still present at the table. D. M. Smith (1999: 308), too, insists on this presumption.

10. Contra those who, like Barrett, consider the entire prayer to be a creation of the Fourth Evangelist, "the greatest theologian in all the history of the church" (cited in Hunter 1979: 285). Lindars (1971: 77), too, thinks that the concern for unity pervading the prayer is "nothing else than the deepest expression of John's own personal experience" (cited in Hunter 1979: 302 n. 320). But see Hunter (1979), who argues that the prayer, including the "concept of the preexistent Son," is firmly rooted in "Jesus' own consciousness" (p. 301); and Agourides (1968: 138–39), who likewise contends that "no one can deny that what we really have is the formulation of the words, deeds, self-consciousness and evaluation of the work of Jesus by Himself" (p. 139; note also: "the Evangelist's recollections of an essential historic truth about Jesus' concern for the circle of His disciples before the Passion" [p. 141]).

Yet the focus of John's account of Jesus' prayer is on Jesus alone. As at 11:41, Jesus lifts his eyes toward heaven, a customary posture in prayer (cf. Mark 7:34; Luke 18:13; Ps. 123:1), and addresses God as "Father" (the term is repeated in conjunction with various attributes at 17:5, 11, 21, 24, 25), interceding first for himself, then for his disciples, and finally for those who would come to faith through his disciples' testimony. Jesus' address for God, "Father," is even more intimate than the address used in the "Lord's Prayer," "Our Father in heaven" (Matt. 6:9).

At the very outset of his prayer, Jesus acknowledges that in God's sovereignty, his time has come. The phrase "the time has come" is used as a dramatic device throughout the Gospel ("not yet come": 2:4; 7:30; 8:20; "has come": 12:23; 13:1; cf. 13:31–32), building toward the climax of the "glorification of the Son"—John's shorthand for the cluster of events comprising Jesus' crucifixion, burial, resurrection, ascension, and exaltation with God the Father. For Jesus, the arrival of his hour is not reason for resigned fatalism but incentive to increased prayer (Carson 1991: 553).

As Jesus commits his imminent death into God's hands (cf. 12:23–24, 32–33), his supreme concern is that his death glorify God (cf. 12:28; 21:19).[11] He does not ask God to "save him from this hour" (12:27) but to sustain him through this trying experience so that glory may accrue to God.[12] The prayer in John 17 culminates the Fourth Evangelist's portrayal of Jesus as the obedient, dependent Son of the Father (serving as the model for the disciples' mission [17:18; 20:21]; see Köstenberger 1998b: 96–121, esp. 107–11). The OT affirms that God will not give his glory to another (e.g., Isa. 42:8; 48:11); Jesus' sharing his Father's glory therefore implies that he is God.

17:2   "You gave him authority over all flesh, that he may give eternal life to everyone you have given to him." Jesus, the Son of Man who is about to be glorified and thus will fulfill his earthly mission, here anticipates his exalted, authoritative position subsequent to his crucifixion and resurrection. This authority enables him to bestow eternal life on all those whom God has given to him (cf. 6:39–40).[13] God's granting of authority to Jesus (cf. 1:12; 5:27) marks the inbreaking of a new era (cf. Isa. 9:6–7; Dan. 7:13–14).[14] All authority in heaven and on earth has been given to Jesus (Matt. 28:18), including the authority to judge (John 5:27).

11. On glory, see commentary at 1:14. See also 11:4; 12:23; 13:32; and also 17:4, 5, 10, 22, 24.

12. Ridderbos (1997: 548) says that the glory sought by Jesus here is none other than the one he already possessed on earth (e.g., 1:14; 2:11; cf. 9:3; 11:4, 40; 12:28). Carson (1991: 554) suggests that the petition is for the Father to reverse the self-emptying entailed in Jesus' incarnation and to restore Jesus to his preexistent glory (cf. 17:24).

13. "All people" reads literally, "all flesh," a Semitism (Lindars 1972: 518–19); compare 8:15, where "by human standards" translates "according to the flesh."

14. See also Matt. 11:27; 28:18; cf. Wis. 10:2. Carson (1991: 555) maintains that this authority was granted to Jesus by the Father in eternity past on the basis of the Son's

The phrase "eternal life," though also found in the Synoptics,[15] is a trademark of this Gospel, functioning as the Johannine equivalent to the Synoptic motif of the "kingdom of God."[16] The expression pervades John 3–12[17] and culminates in the present chapter (17:2, 3). The conviction that believing in Jesus is the only prerequisite for receiving eternal life runs through the entire Gospel (e.g., 3:36; 6:47, 68); the essence of such life is to know the only true God and Jesus Christ, whom he has sent (17:3). The possession of eternal life is not relegated to some time subsequent to death; rather, people can have eternal life already in the here and now (5:24).

In this emphasis on the present possession of eternal life (his "inaugurated eschatology"), John differs from the perspective conveyed by the Synoptics, which, in keeping with the Jewish attitude prevalent at the time of Christ, view eternal life primarily as a possession to be attained in "the age to come." But in John, the distinction between "the present age" and "the age to come" is collapsed; with Jesus, eternity has entered into human existence already in the present (Ladd 1993: 290–95). This realization is rooted in the knowledge that God is life itself, and that Jesus is the Son of God (cf. 1:4; 5:26; 20:31).

Remarkably, Jesus' authority to bestow eternal life extends only to those whom the Father has given to him (see 17:6, 9, 24).[18] This indicates again the subordination of the Son to the Father (see 14:28), a voluntary submission that pertains not just during Jesus' earthly ministry, but eternally (so 1 Cor. 15:28; cf. 11:3). As in creation, so also in redemption, Jesus is the Father's agent who gives eternal life to all those whom the Father has given to him. John juxtaposes, without embarrassment, God's sovereign election of certain ones to eternal life, his universal love for the world, and his condemnation of those who reject his mercy (Carson 1991: 555).

---

prospective obedience to the divine redemptive plan. Barrett (1978: 502) claims that the reference is to "a special empowering for the earthly ministry of the incarnate Son."

15. See Mark 10:17 pars.; 10:30 pars.; Matt. 25:46; Luke 10:25.

16. On life, see commentary at 1:4; on eternal life, see commentary at 3:15. The later expression last occurred at the conclusion of the first half of this Gospel (12:50). Its occurrences in the present and the following verse constitute the final references in John. Lindars (1972: 519) notes that, since "eternal life" is John's regular substitute for "the kingdom of God," the present prayer corresponds quite closely to the opening of the "Lord's Prayer" recorded in the Synoptics (though he stops short of saying that John actually used it as his model).

17. See 3:15, 16, 36; 4:14, 36; 5:24, 39; 6:27, 40, 47, 54, 68; 10:28; 12:25, 50.

18. According to 6:37–40, everyone who "looks to the Son and believes in him shall have eternal life" (cf. 1 John 2:23–25). In 10:27–28, Jesus is said to give life to "his sheep" who "listen to his voice." Morris (1995: 636 n. 6) notes the frequency of the term δίδωμι (didōmi, give) in the present prayer and elaborates on its significance. The neuter πᾶν ὅ (pan ho, all that) focuses less on the persons as such and more on the God-given nature of Jesus' authority (Morris 1995: 636 n. 9); R. Brown (1970: 741) suggests that it may "give a certain unity to the group."

17:3 Elaborating on 17:2, the present verse defines eternal life as knowing "the only true God, and the one you have sent—Jesus Christ."[19] Many religions relate life after death to the knowledge of God or of gods.[20] Yet in biblical parlance, "to know" God does not refer merely to cognitive knowledge (the Greek conception); it means living in fellowship with God.[21] Of course, God can also be known to a limited extent through creation (Rom. 1:18–25), but ultimately, as acknowledged also in Hellenistic Jewish literature (Wis. 15:3), knowledge of God is contingent upon salvation (Barrett 1978: 503).[22]

That God is the "only true God" is affirmed supremely in the Shema: "Hear, O Israel: The Lord our God, the Lord is one" (Deut. 6:4).[23] The verse is reminiscent of 1 Cor. 8:6: "There is but one God, the Father . . . and there is but one Lord, Jesus Christ." Similar expressions are found in confessions of faith and liturgical formulas.[24] Jesus, in turn, is

19. The explanatory phrase "now this is" is in keeping with Johannine style (cf., e.g., 3:19: "this is the verdict"). The conjunction ἵνα (*hina*, that) here, in typical Johannine idiom, is appositional (Wallace 1996: 475). Morris (1995: 638) notes that ἀληθινός (*alēthinos*, true) here precedes the noun (elsewhere in John also in 4:23), and he proposes that this indicates emphasis. The verse is regularly seen by critical scholars as a Johannine insertion (e.g., R. Brown 1970: 741; Schnackenburg 1990: 3.172; Barrett 1978: 503; but see Carson 1991: 556; Ridderbos 1997: 549).

20. These ties are most pronounced in the OT (e.g., Jer. 31:34). Hosea records the divine lament "My people are destroyed from lack of knowledge" (Hos. 4:6), while both Isaiah and Habakkuk envision a future day when "the earth will be full of the knowledge of the Lord as the waters cover the sea" (Isa. 11:9; Hab. 2:14). God's people are to acknowledge him in all their ways (Prov. 3:6) and to live lives of wisdom (the message of the OT Book of Proverbs, see Prov. 1:1–7). The principle of wise living is affirmed also in later rabbinic teaching (see *b. Ber.* 63a, citing Prov. 3:6; *Cant. Rab.* 1.4 §1, citing Hos. 4:6; *b. Mak.* 24a, citing Hab. 2:4).

21. Carson (1991: 556) writes, "Knowledge of God and of Jesus Christ entails fellowship, trust, personal relationship, faith." Similarly, Barrett (1978: 504) comments, "Saving knowledge is rooted in knowledge of a historical person; it is therefore objective and at the same time a personal relation." This is in keeping with the Hebrew use of the term "to know," which encompasses even the most intimate human relationship, sexual intercourse. Thus, Gen. 4:1 LXX says that Adam "knew" (ἔγνω, *egnō*) his wife, Eve, and she became pregnant and gave birth to her son.

22. In his first epistle, John disputes the communion with God falsely claimed by gnostic teachers. In the DSS, "life" and "eternal knowledge" are set in close parallelism (1QS 2:3; cf. 1QS 4:22; 11:3–4). The expression "eternal life" is found in those writings as well (CD 3:20). In Hellenistic and oriental cults, it was the vision of God received by the initiate that was considered to be the source of life and salvation. Philo spoke of "holding that the knowledge of him is the consummation of happiness. It is also agelong life" (*Spec. Laws* 1.63 §345; cf. *Unchang.* 30 §143).

23. See John 5:44 ("the only God"); cf. 1 Thess. 1:9 ("the living and true God"); 1 John 5:20 ("the true God and eternal life").

24. For example, 1 Tim. 1:17: "the only God"; 6:15–16: "God, the blessed and only Ruler, . . . who alone is immortal"; Rev. 6:10: "Sovereign Lord, holy and true." See also Philo (*Alleg. Interp.* 2.17 §68: "the only true God"; *Spec. Laws* 1.60 §332: "the one true God . . . the Being who truly exists, even God"; *Gaius* 45 §366: "the true God") and other Jewish writings (e.g., 3 Macc. 6:18: "most glorious, almighty, and true God").

the exclusive agent, the sole authorized representative of this one true God.[25] He is the God-sent Messiah, God's Anointed One, the Christ. Just as there is only one true God, there is only one way to the Father: Jesus Christ (Carson 1991: 556; Morris 1995: 638).[26]

Jesus now looks back on the entirety of his incarnate ministry and com-   **17:4**
mits his immediate future into the hands of his Father: "I have glori-
fied you on earth by completing the work you gave me to do." In the
framework of John's Gospel, Jesus' report to the Father in 17:4 that he
has completed his assigned work mirrors the statement at the beginning
of Jesus' ministry at 4:34 by way of *inclusio*.[27] The work that God gave
Jesus to do is focused on the cross (e.g., 12:23–24). When Jesus utters
his final prayer, the cross still lies ahead, but by faith, he anticipates
the successful completion of his mission (cf. 19:30; see Carson 1991:
557; Barrett 1978: 504).

"And now, Father, *you* glorify *me* in your presence with the glory I had   **17:5**
with you before the world came into being."[28] This verse alludes to
Jesus' existence prior to the incarnation—a reality already expressed in
John's prologue ("the Word" [1:1, 14]) and reaffirmed throughout the
Gospel ("the Son of Man" [3:13; 6:62]; the "I am" preceding Abraham
[8:58]; the one who came from the Father and is about to return to him
[16:28]).[29] Of all the Gospels, John's most clearly affirms the preexistence
of Jesus Christ.

In the present passage, Jesus looks beyond his imminent suffering to
the glory awaiting him once again in the Father's presence, the glory he
had known and enjoyed from eternity past (see 17:24). For John, however, the Son's "glorification" is not limited to his exaltation subsequent

25. Regarding the phrase "whom you have sent," note that sending terminology recurs
in this prayer in 17:8, 18 (twice), 21, 23, 25. Interestingly, even though elsewhere in John's
Gospel πέμπω (*pempō*, send) is used with similar frequency, all seven instances of "send"
in this chapter feature the verb ἀποστέλλω (*apostellō*).

26. The expression "Jesus Christ" is used in this Gospel only here and in 1:17 (see also
1 John 4:2), and it perhaps reveals hindsight: "Christ" has now become Jesus' last name
(but see Ridderbos 1997: 549). It may strike the modern reader as curious that Jesus would
call himself "Jesus Christ"; however, self-reference in the third person was common in
antiquity (cf. 21:24; see Jackson 1999: esp. 24–31).

27. These are the only two places in John where Jesus' work (ἔργον, *ergon*) is referred
to in the singular (see also 5:36; 14:31).

28. The phrase καὶ νῦν (*kai nyn*, and now) is also found in the OT in Yahweh's instructions to Moses (Exod. 19:5) and in the conclusion of David's prayer (2 Sam. 7:25–26) with
reference to a result that should follow on the basis of the truth of certain facts (Beasley-
Murray 1999: 292 n. c).

29. Westcott (1908: 2.245–46) distinguishes between the "glory of the Eternal Word"
(spoken of here) and the "glory of Christ, the Incarnate Word" (spoken of in 17:22), though
he notes that the two correspond to one another. Preexistence is ascribed also to Wisdom
in Second Temple literature (e.g., Wis. 7:25; 9:10–11) on the basis of its portrayal in the
OT Book of Proverbs (esp. 8:23, 30). But see commentary at 1:1.

to his passion but crucially encompasses the crucifixion. What is more, the crucifixion itself becomes the place where the Father glorifies ("lifts up") the Son. For Jesus' cross-death constitutes the final culmination of the obedient, faithful completion of his mission.[30]

b. Jesus Prays for His Followers (17:6–19)

17:6   John 17:6–8 recounts Jesus' obedience to his task as the basis for the following intercession (Ridderbos 1997: 550).[31] Everything is traced back to the Father: he has assigned the work; he has given the people; he is the one to whom Jesus is about to return; and he is the recipient of Jesus' petition (Ridderbos 1997: 552). Jesus' ministry to his disciples is described in terms of the revelation of God's name.[32] This echoes the affirmation in the prologue that Jesus "gave a full account of" the Father (1:18). The fact that John can subsume Jesus' entire ministry under the category of revelation has caused some to postulate that John knows Jesus exclusively as the revealer, in keeping with the gnostic "revealer myth." However, this is unlikely, since the revealer myth did not arise until the second century A.D., thus postdating John's Gospel, and since John demonstrably does not teach, as Gnosticism did, that knowledge constitutes salvation.[33]

Because of general Jewish obduracy (see 12:37–41), Jesus' disciples become the primary recipients of his revelation.[34] In a salvation-historical and eschatological sense, it is they who have been given to Jesus by the Father from out of the world (cf. 6:37, 39, 44; see Ridderbos 1997: 551; Whitacre 1999: 408–9).[35] What Jesus reveals to them is God's "name," which enshrines who God is in his character, his essential na-

---

30. Contra Michaels (1989: 294), who claims, "The Son will give glory to the Father *after* his death on the cross, and this glorification is defined as the giving of eternal life."

31. Note that 17:6 is echoed in the final verse of the prayer, 17:26, while 17:8 is echoed in 17:14.

32. Ἐφανέρωσα (*ephanerōsa*, I have revealed) globally refers to Jesus' entire ministry, including his imminent cross-death (Carson 1991: 558). See also the close parallel in 17:26, ἐγνώρισα (*egnōrisa*, I have made known) which, together with the present verse, brackets Jesus' intercession for others. The term φανερόω (*phaneroō*, reveal) occurs elsewhere in John in 1:31; 2:11; 3:21; 7:4; 9:3; 21:1, 14, and elsewhere in the Gospels only in Mark 4:22. The closest parallel in John is 2:11 (cf. 1:14; see also ἐξηγήσατο [*exēgēsato*, he has given full account] in 1:18).

33. For a refutation of the false dichotomy between revelation and redemption in John's Christology, see especially Köstenberger 1998b: 74–81.

34. On "your name," see also 17:26 (see commentary at 14:13). On "those whom you gave me," see 17:2. Regarding "out of the world," see 1:9–10; 15:19. Regarding the phrase "they were yours, and you gave them to me," Calvin (1961: 139) comments that this speaks of "the eternity of election," "not by faith, nor by any merit, but by pure grace." It might be added that God's election is presented here as the grounds for the perseverance of those so chosen ("they have kept your word").

35. Moreover, as Ridderbos (1997: 551) notes, "Jesus did not manifest God's name to those who had no knowledge of it but rather to those who were among the people to

ture;[36] because his name is glorious, God wants it to be made known.[37] The notion that Jesus reveals the Father in his whole person, both works and words, is foundational to John's Gospel.[38] In the OT, God's name is put on the central sanctuary (Deut. 12:5, 11), and knowledge of his name implies life commitment (Ps. 9:10). In John, too, Jesus' revelation of God's name must be met with obedience, and Jesus is shown to replace both tabernacle and temple, having become the "place" where God has put his name.[39]

Jesus' disciples are those who have obeyed Jesus' word (see commentary at 14:23).[40] Earlier in John's Gospel (8:51; 14:23) Jesus' (would-be) followers are enjoined to keep Jesus' word; here they are said to have obeyed that of the Father. This reinforces the theme of the Son's dependence, which pervades the Gospel (e.g., 5:19–20; 7:16).[41] Doubtless anticipating the postresurrection ministry of the Holy Spirit, Jesus reports to the Father that not only have the disciples obeyed the Father's word (17:6), but also they know that everything the Father has given Jesus comes from him (17:7), have accepted the words the Father has given Jesus, and have believed that the Father has sent Jesus (17:8). Hence, Jesus' mission has successfully imparted the conviction that Jesus is the Sent One from the Father and has engendered acceptance of and obedience to God's word.

Jesus' statement "Everything you have given me is from you" once again expresses his dependence on the Father (see commentary at 5:19–30). **17:7–8** "I have given them the words you gave me" sums up the result of Jesus' three-year teaching ministry among his disciples (see commentary at 15:15; see also 6:63; 7:16; 12:48–49; 17:14). The portrayal of Jesus in

whom God had from of old revealed 'his name' and to whom he had obligated himself to reveal his name in the future" (citing Isa. 52:6; Ezek. 39:7).

36. Cf. Exod. 3:13–15. See R. Brown 1970: 755; Carson 1991: 558; Morris 1995: 640; Schnackenburg 1990: 3.175.

37. For example, Ps. 22:22; Isa. 52:6; Ezek. 39:7. God's name is also the subject of John 17:11–12.

38. For example, 1:18; 8:19, 27; 10:38; 12:45; 14:9–11.

39. See also Isa. 62:2; 65:15–16. Speculation about the divine name was common in the Judaism of Jesus' day. In particular, people wondered about the angel of the Lord referred to in Exod. 23:20–21. In later Jewish literature, the name of God became enshrined in the sacred Tetragrammaton (YHWH), which served as a substitute for pronouncing the divine name. In fact, Schlatter (1948: 319–20) believes that John here alludes to the Jews' reluctance to pronounce God's name. In gnostic literature, "name" refers to the knowledge (γνῶσις, gnōsis) mediated by the redeemer. This name is revealed only to certain individuals who thereby acquire a share in God's life, light, and joy.

40. As Carson (1991: 559) rightly points out, the point of comparison here is not between the disciples' faith before and after the resurrection but between the disciples' faith and the world's unbelief prior to the resurrection. Barrett (1978: 505) thinks that hindsight has shaded the presentation of the disciples' faith in the present passage.

41. Elsewhere even Jesus himself is said to keep God's word (8:55).

the present passage is reminiscent of the description of the prophet like Moses in Deut. 18:18.

Though there was much that remained a mystery to the disciples prior to the crucifixion (see commentary at 16:25–33; Carson 1991: 559), they knew and believed with certainty that Jesus had been sent from the Father.[42] Hence, they are "worthy of Jesus' intercession and the Father's care" (Schnackenburg 1990: 3.178). The phrase "that you sent me" recurs in 17:21, 23, 25, being repeated like a solemn refrain (cf. 14:24; 17:18; 20:21).

17:9–12 After praying for himself in 17:1–5, and introducing his intercession for the disciples with a rehearsal of his own ministry to them in 17:6–8, Jesus now commences his actual prayer on his followers' behalf. In light of his imminent departure, Jesus' key concern is their protection while they are still in the world (17:11). While Jesus was with them, he protected them. No one has been lost except Judas; and he was lost only so that Scripture would be fulfilled (17:12). Jesus' prayer is not for God to take his followers out of the world but to protect them as long as they are in the world, particularly from the evil one (17:14–15). This protection will be realized as they are unified (17:11; cf. 17:21–23) and made holy in the truth, which is God's word (17:17).

Jesus is not praying for the world (see commentary at 14:30 and at 15:18–21; cf. 16:3).[43] To do so would be tantamount to praying that the world continue in its worldliness, which would be blasphemous (Carson 1991: 561). The only prayer for the world could be for it to desist from its hostility to God and Jesus his Son and for it to cease being "the world" in the Johannine sense of the term (Morris 1995: 642; Barrett 1978: 506). Yet the distinction between the disciples and the world is not absolute, since Jesus anticipates that some from out of the world will come and believe the disciples' message (17:20; see Witherington 1995: 270). The world, then, is included in Jesus' prayer to the extent that he desires for it to be won over by believers (Bultmann 1971: 500).[44]

There is close communion and free sharing between the Father and the Son (and also the Spirit [16:14–15]): "All that is mine is yours, and all that is yours is mine." This includes the disciples.[45] In 17:10b, Jesus'

42. Believing and knowing are similarly linked in Peter's seminal confession in 6:69. "Knew with certainty" (TNIV) reads more literally, "knew truly" (ἀληθῶς, *alēthōs*; cf. 1:47; 4:42; 6:14; 7:26, 40; 8:31). The same phrase occurs in 7:26 (there rendered "really concluded" in the TNIV) in an ironic reference to the Jewish authorities. Carson (1991: 560) points out that the references to the disciples' knowing and believing balance the strong predestinarian teaching of 17:2, 6.

43. An OT antecedent figure is Jeremiah, who was told by God not to pray for the Israelites, who were destined for judgment (Jer. 14:11; cf. Exod. 32:10). On the "world," see commentary at 1:9.

44. On the phrase "they are yours," see commentary at 6:37, 44, and below.

45. See also the references to Jesus' "own" (ἴδιοι, *idioi*) in 10:3–4; 13:1 (contrast 1:11; 15:19).

prayer focuses on the glory that has come to him through his followers. This is in keeping with his earlier statement that the disciples' bearing of spiritual fruit will be to the Father's glory (15:8, 16), which is Jesus' paramount desire (see commentary at 17:1). Now that Jesus is about to return to the Father (see 17:13; cf. 13:3; 14:12), he is concerned that his work for and in his followers be continued and completed (Ridderbos 1997: 552). Though Jesus will leave the world, his disciples will remain, which motivates his current intercession (Ridderbos 1997: 553).

"Holy Father" is a form of address found only here in this Gospel; in 17:1, 5, 24, the address is simply "Father" (cf. Luke 11:2; John 11:41; 12:27–28); in 17:25, it is "righteous Father" (note also Matt. 11:25: "Father, Lord of heaven and earth"). The conception goes back to Lev. 11:44 (cf. Ps. 71:22; 111:9; Isa. 6:3).[46] Similar addresses are found in Jewish literature: "O holy Lord of all holiness" (2 Macc. 14:36); "O Holy One among the holy" (3 Macc. 2:2); "You are holy and your Name is awesome" (*Shemoneh 'Esreh* 3). Holiness is ascribed to God also in the Book of Revelation (e.g., 4:8; 6:10; see Schlatter 1948: 321). In Jesus' case, however, addressing God as "holy" does not create a distance between him and God.

"Keep them by [the power of] your name" seems to refer primarily to protection from evil, though this also would include any resulting disunity (see Morris 1995: 643). The phrase "by the power of your name" probably is a Semitic expansion on "by [the instrumentality of] your name."[47] Yet because God's name is powerful, it can be viewed as synonymous with power (see, e.g., Ps. 54:1, where "your name" and "your might" occur in parallelism). The psalmist knows that deliverance from enemies and help in times of trouble are from the Lord (e.g., Ps. 44:5; 54:1; 124:8). More specifically, Jesus prays for God's protection of his own by "the name you gave me" (see additional note). References to Jesus' unique relationship with God the Father pervade the entire Gospel (see, e.g., 1:18; 10:30; 14:9).

"So that they may be one just as we are." Jesus proceeds to pray that as a result of God's protection, the disciples may be one, just as he and the Father are one.[48] Such unity is beyond human ability and is the result and gift of divine grace (Schlatter 1948: 321). In fact, "The unity prayed for is a unity already given: Jesus does not pray that they may 'become'

46. Carson (1991: 561) rightly notes that not only does the present address combine the notions of transcendence (holy) and familial intimacy (Father), but also it provides the foundation on the basis of which the Son and believers are consecrated for service (see 17:17–19; see Barrett 1978: 507).

47. R. Brown (1970: 759 [approvingly cited by Borchert 2002: 197]) says that ἐν (*en*, in, by) is both instrumental and local. Contra Carson (1991: 562) and Morris (1995: 644), who prefer a locative force ("in your name").

48. As Westcott (1908: 2.251) rightly affirms, the plural pronoun "we" signals the "sameness of essence" that "unites the Father and Christ. . . . Their nature is one."

one, but that they may 'continually be' one" (Morris 1995: 644; cf. Eph. 4:3). Moreover, their unity will be grounded in nothing less than the unity of God the Father and Son. This is important, not just as an end in itself, but as an indispensable prerequisite for effective and God-pleasing mission (Borchert 2002: 197). The importance of the disciples' unity for their mission to the world is developed further in 17:20–26.

"While I was with them, I kept them . . . and guarded them; . . . not one of them perished except for the son of destruction."[49] "The one doomed to destruction" (more literally, "son of destruction")[50] could refer either to Judas's character[51] or to his destiny.[52] The TNIV's "doomed to destruction" suggests the latter, though of course both are true. "Destruction" (ἀπωλεία, apōleia) commonly refers in the NT to final condemnation. "Son of perdition" also occurs in 2 Thess. 2:3, there with reference to "the man of lawlessness," the antichrist. This suggests that "son of destruction" labels Judas Iscariot as part of a typology of evil personages seeking to thwart God's sovereign purposes across the sweep of salvation history (cf. 1 John 2:18, 22; 4:3; see Carson 1991: 563; Borchert 2002: 199).[53]

In keeping with Johannine theodicy (cf. 12:38–40), even Judas's betrayal is said to have occurred "in order for Scripture to be fulfilled." This does not alter the fact that Judas made his decision as a responsible agent and that he will be held accountable and judged for his evil act (see Mark 14:21 = Matt. 26:24) (so, rightly, Calvin 1961: 143). Yet God,

---

49. See 6:37, 39, 70; 10:28–29; 18:8–9. The juxtaposition of the verbs "protect" and "keep safe" reflects Semitic parallelism (cf. Prov. 18:10). The verb ἐφύλαξα (ephylaxa, I guarded) may conjure up the image of a shepherd guarding his flock (Ridderbos 1997: 553). On "the name you gave me," see 17:11. R. Brown (1970: 764) views the events of 18:5–8 as a demonstration of how God's name protects the disciples: when Jesus identifies himself as ἐγώ εἰμι (egō eimi, I am [he]), his arresters fall down, and the disciples are allowed to leave. Similarly, Stibbe (1993: 176–77), who notes how both of Jesus' statements in his final prayer, that he protected his own (17:12) and that he completed his mission (17:4), anticipate realities still future from the vantage point of the Johannine narrative (cf. 18:1–11 and 19:30, respectively).

50. The phrase "son of" is a Semitism. See Matt. 23:15; Eph. 5:6 = Col. 3:6 (textual variant). Similar expressions (in the plural) are found in the DSS (1QS 9:16 = 10:19; CD 6:15 = 13:14). The phrase is attested also in classical Greek. Danker (1960–61) cites a passage in Menander's *Dyscolos* (published as part of Papyrus Bodmer IV) that contains the word "madman" (lit., "son of madness," ὀδυνῆς υἱός, odynēs huios).

51. So Morris 1995: 644–45: "characterized by 'lostness,' not . . . predestined to be 'lost.'" For example, in Isa. 57:4, "children of unrighteousness" in the MT becomes "children of perdition" in the LXX; the same phrase is found in Jub. 10:3.

52. In Isa. 34:5, "the people I have totally destroyed" in the MT becomes "the people of perdition" in the LXX.

53. Barrett (1978: 508) seems to go further, apparently suggesting that the Fourth Evangelist identified Judas and the antichrist. Note also Moloney's (1998: 467) startling assertion that what happened through "the son of perdition is beyond the control of Jesus." How does that cohere with the immediately ensuing assertion that Judas's betrayal occurred in fulfillment of Scripture?

---

for his part, sovereignly overrode Judas's evil designs to bring about his own good purposes (cf. Gen. 50:20; see Morris 1995: 645). The antecedent passage is probably Ps. 41:9 (applied to Judas in John 13:18). Other Scriptures fulfilled through Judas are Ps. 69:25 and 109:8 (cited in Acts 1:20; see also the reference to Isa. 57:4 above).

Once again, Jesus anticipates his return to the Father (cf., e.g., 14:28). **17:13–16** The reference to "these things" that Jesus spoke while in the world is probably to the entire farewell discourse (Carson 1991: 564). As on previous occasions, Jesus holds up as his desire for his followers that they experience "the full measure of my joy," which is predicated upon remaining in the Father's love and continued obedience to Jesus (see commentary at 15:11 and at 16:20–24). This joy, moreover, is to be known in the midst of the world's hostility. Once again, Jesus distinguishes sharply between the world aligned against Jesus in order to kill him (including the "son of perdition" and the "prince of this world") and those "not of the world" (cf. 15:18–19; 17:9; see Moloney 1998: 468).[54]

Jesus' petition is "not that you take them out of the world, but that you keep them from the evil one."[55] This is the first of two requests that Jesus makes for his disciples; the other is for their consecration in truth (17:17; cf. Titus 2:14). Moses (Num. 11:15), Elijah (1 Kings 19:4), and Jonah (Jon. 4:3, 8) all asked to be taken out of this world, but none of them were.[56] The phrase ἐκ τοῦ πονηροῦ (*ek tou ponērou*) could refer to evil in an abstract sense or to the "evil one" (i.e., the devil). Almost certainly the latter is in view.[57] Believers, then, are neither to withdraw from the world nor to become indistinguishable from it, but rather, as ones consecrated by the truth and separated from evil, they are to witness to God's Son, aided by the Spirit (Carson 1991: 565).[58]

Jesus' second petition is for their consecration for service: "Make them **17:17–19** holy in your truth."[59] The realm in which the disciples' consecration is to

---

54. On the necessity of spiritual rebirth, see 1:12–13; 3:3–8.

55. Parallel wordings are attested in rabbinic literature for both "take out of this world" (*y. Ber.* 2.7) and "protect from the evil one" (*y. Peʾah* 1.1; *Deut. Rab.* 4.4 [cited in Köstenberger 2002c: 210 nn. 519–20]; cf. Ps. 140:1; Matt. 6:13).

56. Though Elijah was taken up to heaven at a later time. The phrase τηρεῖν ἐκ (*tērein ek*, to keep from) is found elsewhere in the NT only in Rev. 3:10.

57. See the earlier references to the "ruler of this world" in John (12:31; 14:30; 16:11; see also Ridderbos 1997: 555). Cf. Matt. 6:13; 1 John 2:13–14; 3:12; 5:18–19.

58. Carson (1991: 565) says that believers have "neither the luxury of compromise . . . nor the safety of disengagement." Regarding the statement "they are not of the world, even as I am not of it," see 17:14.

59. Jesus' prayer is in keeping with common Jewish prayers, which regularly acknowledged that God sanctifies people through his commandments. On "truth" in John, see commentary at 1:14. Words relating to holiness occur infrequently in John's Gospel. The verb ἁγιάζω (*hagiazō*, make holy) is found in 10:36 and 17:17, 19; the adjective ἅγιος (*hagios*, holy) occurs as part of the expression "Holy Spirit" in 1:33; 14:26; 20:22, and

be realized is the truth of God's word and of his name (see 17:11).[60] This involves the work of both Son and Spirit; association with them—the one who in his person is the truth (14:6), and the one who is the "Spirit of truth" (14:17; 15:26; 16:13) who will lead believers into all truth (16:13)—will so sanctify believers that they will be equipped for service of God.[61] Critically, such service is ultimately grounded in divine revelation and predicated on an accurate understanding of and response to such revelation (Morris 1995: 647).

The prayer for the disciples' consecration highlights the balance and tension in which they must hold their mission in the world. As Ridderbos (1997: 555) points out, "Within that realm the disciples are not only safe in the world but also capable of continuing the work for which Jesus has destined them, their mission in the world." Hence, personal holiness is not to be an end in itself but a means to an end: reaching the lost world for Christ. Believers' consecration serves the purpose of preparing them for their God-given mission in the world (Ridderbos 1997: 555; cf. Carson 1991: 565–66). They are not to be inwardly focused, cultivating merely intracommunitarian love and unity, but rather to reach out together to a lost and needy world.

"Just as you sent me into the world, I have sent them into the world."[62] Just as Jesus was "set apart" and sent into the world (10:36; see Morris 1995: 647–48 n. 56), so also the disciples are set apart in order to be sent into the world. The world, not some other place, will be their place of service (Ridderbos 1997: 555). Jesus' prayer anticipates the disciples' commissioning in 20:21 (cf. 4:38; 13:20; 15:26–27; see Ridderbos 1997: 556). Jesus' relationship to the Father as his sender is now presented as the pattern for the disciples' relationship to Jesus as their sender (Köstenberger 1998b). A partial OT parallel is the instruction to Moses,

---

otherwise in 6:69; 17:11. See also the address "Holy Father" in 17:11, which to the Jewish mind would suggest that holiness was also expected of Jesus' followers according to the principle enunciated in the Book of Leviticus (11:44; 19:2; 20:26).

60. Barrett (1978: 510) rightly contends that "truth" here "means the saving truth revealed in the teaching and activity of Jesus." Earlier references to the word in this chapter are 17:6 and 17:14 (see also 17:20, and 14:23–24; 15:3, 20, earlier in the farewell discourse). The present phrase is similar to Ps. 119:142: "Your law is true" (cf. 119:151, 160). David likewise acknowledged, "Your words are trustworthy" (2 Sam. 7:28; cf. Ps. 19:7). D. M. Smith (1999: 315) perceptively observes that the reference to God's word here seems sudden, since according to the prologue it is Jesus who is the Word. As Smith duly notes, however, the difficulty is alleviated by the fact that "after Jesus is named (1:17), he is never again called the Word in the Gospel."

61. R. Brown (1970: 766) notes the lack of explicit reference to the Spirit in the present passage and suggests that "truth" in 17:17 ought to be identified not only with God's word but also with the Spirit, who makes God's word intelligible.

62. The coordination of two clauses by way of "as" is found in this Gospel also with regard to life (6:57), knowledge (10:14–15), love (15:9; 17:23), and unity (17:22).

who had himself been consecrated by God (Sir. 45:4) in order to consecrate others so that they too may serve God as priests (Exod. 28:41).

"And I pursue holiness on their behalf" (cf. John 10:36). Jesus' sanctification "on behalf of" (ὑπέρ, *hyper*) others involves self-sacrifice (Ridderbos 1997: 556; cf. Carson 1991: 567) and is evocative of atonement passages elsewhere in the NT (e.g., Mark 14:24; John 6:51; 1 Cor. 11:24).[63] Jesus' willingness to give his life on behalf of others in obedience to the Father is frequently reiterated in John's Gospel[64] and not uncommonly involves the prepositions "for" or "in place of."[65] Significantly, the purpose of Jesus' self-sacrifice is that the disciples too may be truly sanctified, that is, set apart for their redemptive mission in the world.[66]

c. Jesus Prays for Later Believers (17:20–26)

Jesus does not stop at praying for himself and his disciples; his vision   **17:20–21**
transcends the present, reaching beyond his immediate followers to those who will believe through their message (17:20; cf. 17:18; 15:27; Rom. 10:14).[67] Jesus' concern for his followers' unity is his greatest burden as his earthly mission draws to a close, and it pervades this entire section.[68] Their unity, in turn, is to be rooted in Jesus' own unity with the Father (Ridderbos 1997: 560). Together with love (13:34–35; 15:12–13; 17:26), unity constitutes a vital prerequisite for their mission (see 17:23) (Köstenberger 1998b: 189–90).[69] Importantly, this unity is not merely a unity of love; it is predicated upon the acceptance and transmission of the revelation imparted to the disciples by the Father through the Son (cf. 17:6, 8, 20; see Carson 1991: 568).

63. It is also reminiscent of the OT notion of "setting apart" sacrificial animals (e.g., Deut. 15:19; see Michaels 1989: 297).

64. See 10:17–18; 12:23–28; 18:11; 19:11, 17, 30.

65. See 6:51; 10:11, 15; 11:50–52; 15:13; 18:14. Along similar lines, the author of Hebrews writes, "We have been made holy through the sacrifice of the body of Jesus Christ once for all" (10:10; cf. 2:10–11; 9:12–14).

66. "Truly" translates the phrase ἐν ἀληθείᾳ (*en alētheia*), which refers adverbially to the unique nature of the disciples' consecration (Ridderbos 1997: 556). Borchert (2002: 204) remarks, "In consecrating himself, Jesus modeled for his disciples what is meant to be both alien from the world and yet committed to a mission in and to the world, even to the point of death." See also the short excursus in which Ridderbos (1997: 557) responds to the charge that the farewell discourse and prayer are world-avoiding.

67. See the parallel in Deut. 29:14–15. The present participle πιστευόντων (*pisteuontōn*, believing) clearly is future-referring (Ridderbos 1997: 558 n. 248, citing BDF §339.2b). "Message" translates the term λόγος, *logos* (see commentary at 17:17).

68. R. Brown (1970: 769) notes a "grammatical parallelism" between six lines of 17:20–21 and six lines of 17:22–23. Morris (1995: 649) points to structural similarities between 17:21 and 17:23 and says the effect is to "add solemnity and emphasis." See also the helpful thoughts in Black 1988: 155–59 on the kind of unity envisioned by Jesus.

69. As Carson (1991: 568) notes, believers are dependent on Jesus "for life and fruitfulness."

"Just as you, Father, are in me and I in you, that they too might be in us." Jesus' vision of a unified community, transcending mere institutional unity,[70] encompasses present as well as future believers (Ridderbos 1997: 559).[71] Just as the Father is active in and through the Son (10:38; 14:10–11, 20), so also the Son is to be active in and through believers (see 15:4; 1 John 1:3; 2:5–6; see Barrett 1978: 512). The desired result is this: "that the world may believe that you have sent me." Similar to the display of authentic love among believers, the display of their genuine unity ought to provide a compelling witness to the truth of the gospel (Carson 1991: 568). The same concern was expressed in Jesus' prayer at Lazarus's tomb (11:42; cf. 13:34–35; 17:23, 25). The coordination between unity and love is paralleled by exhortations to fraternal love and harmony in Jewish testamentary literature.[72]

17:22–23 Jesus has completed his revelatory task; it now remains for his followers to pass on the message to others (Carson 1991: 569; cf. 2 Tim. 2:2). The glory that the Father has given to Jesus and that he has passed on to his disciples is not Jesus' preexistent glory, which he is yet to reclaim (see 17:5), but the glory that Jesus was awarded in order to carry out his earthly mission (e.g., 1:14; 2:11; 11:4, 40; see Ridderbos 1997: 563).[73] As they continue his mission, Jesus wants his followers to share in the glory that has been a hallmark of his own ministry, including at the cross (Ridderbos 1997: 563). This implies that the disciples' path, too, entails lowly service and suffering on behalf of others (Morris 1995: 650).[74]

Believers' unity is neither self-generated nor an end in itself (Borchert 2002: 208; similarly, Moloney 1998: 475). Believers' "complete" (τετελει-ωμένοι, *teteleiōmenoi*)[75] unity results from being taken into the unity of

70. Carson (1991: 568) maintains that such unity is achieved not by finding "the lowest common theological denominator, but by common adherence to the apostolic gospel, by love that is joyfully self-sacrificing, by undaunted commitment to the shared goals of the mission." Similarly, Morris (1995: 644) and Beasley-Murray (1999: 306–7). Schlatter (1948: 325) points out that unity is all the more important as the circle of believers in Jesus grows. He also notes the contrast between such unity and the existence of various sects in contemporary Judaism.

71. The notion of being "in Christ" is found elsewhere in the NT especially in Paul's writings (e.g., Rom. 8:10; 2 Cor. 13:5; Gal. 2:20; 4:19), though it is not unknown to other NT authors, such as Peter (cf. 1 Pet. 5:14). Barrett (1978: 512) believes that the final phrase of 17:21 implies universalism, though this is arguably not the case. The statement speaks to Jesus' desire rather than to his actual expectation.

72. This parting concern is attributed to Noah (Jub. 7:26), Rebecca (Jub. 35:20), Isaac (Jub. 36:4), Zebulon (T. Zeb. 8:5–9:4), Joseph (T. Jos. 17:2–3), and Dan. (T. Dan 5:3).

73. Contra Calvin (1961: 149), who interprets this reference in terms of the restoration of God's image in sinful humankind through Christ. On "glory," see 17:1, 4, 5.

74. Regarding "that they may be one as we are one," cf. 17:11, 21.

75. The same verb, τελειόω (*teleioō*, complete) is used in 4:34; 5:36; 17:4; 19:28. Other Johannine parallels include the "one flock and one shepherd" (10:16) and the "gathering of the scattered children into one" (11:52). The Qumran covenanters, too, saw themselves

God,[76] and, once unified, believers will be able to bear witness to the true identity of Jesus as the Sent One of God.[77] Unless they are unified, how can they expect to give authentic, credible testimony to the Father, who is united with the Son and the Spirit in revealing himself and his salvation in Christ?[78] Secure in the Father's love, the same love with which he loved his Son, believers will be able to express and proclaim the Father's love to a dark and hostile world.[79]

Jesus has one more request: he wants his followers to see the preexistent **17:24–26** glory that the Father has given him.[80] This echoes his earlier words to the disciples that he is going to prepare a place for them (14:1–4). As he concludes his prayer, Jesus reiterates his conviction that his disciples have truly come to know the Father in him. With this assurance, Jesus is prepared to die, for he has ensured that subsequent to his departure there remains a circle of his followers able to proclaim the true knowledge of God to others. As John 13–17 makes clear, training the Twelve has been the centerpiece of his three-year mission.[81] Now, his death and resurrection will give them the message that they must proclaim to the world.

"Father" and "righteous Father" indicate the close filial tie between Jesus and God the Father as well as Jesus' appeal to the Father as righteous (cf. Ps. 119:137; Rev. 16:5) and thus inclined to grant the Son's requests. Hence, "Jesus does not pray here as a claimant, but as *the Son*, as one who knew he could rightly assume ownership over the many rooms in the Father's house (cf. 14:2, 3)" (Ridderbos 1997: 564). The closeness of Jesus' relationship with the Father is further underscored by the striking phrase "I desire" (θέλω, *thelō*; cf. 5:21; see Ridderbos 1997: 564). Since Jesus' will is elsewhere in this Gospel presented as congruent

---

as a *yaḥad* (union) and displayed a keen consciousness of their election (for a discussion of Qumran parallels to the notion of unity in John 17, see R. Brown 1970: 777).

76. See 10:38; 14:10–11, 20, 23; 15:4–5; 1 John 1:3; 2:23–24; 5:20. On the relationships of mutual indwelling, see Whitacre 1999: 418–19. Brodie (1993: 516) contends that this "ideal" of "a community based on God and mutual care" is "the high point and synthesis of the discourse and of the chapter—indeed of the whole gospel. As the incarnation is the finale of the prologue, so is the idea of unity the finale of chap. 17."

77. The phrase "to let the world know that you sent me" (cf. 17:21) is reminiscent of OT passages such as Zech. 2:9.

78. Lindars (1972: 530) asserts, "A disunited Christian community denies by its behaviour the message which it proclaims." For an interesting example of the use of John 17 in church history, see Payton 1992: 26–38 on Martin Bucer's 1531 sermon on John 17 in the context of the Reformation controversy regarding the Eucharist. Bucer reminded his listeners that Jesus himself is the one praying, and God alone is all-knowing.

79. See Carson 1991: 569; Ridderbos 1997: 564. On "you . . . have loved them," see 14:23; 16:27.

80. Westcott (1908: 2.260) writes, "The words distinctly imply the personal pre-existence of Christ. The thought of an eternal love active in the depths of divine Being presents, perhaps, as much as we can faintly apprehend of the doctrine of the essential Trinity."

81. See Coleman 1963; 1977.

with that of the Father (e.g., 4:34; 5:21, 30; 6:38), one may reasonably expect that the Father will do what the Son asks of him.

Specifically, Jesus' request is that his followers be granted to see his preexistent glory with the Father, which in turn is grounded in the Father's love for the Son. Then Jesus' earlier pronouncement will become reality that "where I am, my servant also will be" (12:26), and his promise will have been fulfilled that "I will come back and take you to be with me that you also may be where I am" (14:3).[82] "Before the creation of the world" (TNIV) reads more literally, "before the foundation of the world," an echo of 17:5.[83] The term καταβολή (katabolē, foundation) occurs only once in the LXX (2 Macc. 2:29), for the foundation of a house. The phrase "from the beginning of the world" is frequently used in Judaism.[84]

The foundation for Jesus' following appeal is his recognition of God as the "righteous Father" (see commentary at 17:11). The OT commonly teaches that God is righteous and just.[85] With Jesus' betrayal and innocent suffering imminent, he affirms the righteousness of God his Father. In the NT, this righteousness is shown to have both positive and negative effects: God will save believers but will judge unbelievers. Jesus proceeds to speak of three states of knowledge: "The world does not know you [see 1:10; 8:55; 16:3], but I know you [see 7:29; 8:55; 10:15], and they know that you have sent me."[86] Jesus has made God's name known,[87] and he will continue to do so (once exalted, through his Spirit?),[88] so that God's love for Jesus may be in them as he is in them.[89]

---

82. See also Luke 22:30; John 13:36; Rom. 8:17; 2 Tim. 2:11. On "to see my glory," see 2 Cor. 3:18; 1 John 3:1–3. On "you loved me," see 17:26.

83. Cf. Matt. 13:35; 25:34; Luke 11:50; Eph. 1:4; Heb. 4:3; 9:26; 1 Pet. 1:20; Rev. 13:8; 17:8.

84. For example, *Gen. Rab.* 1.10; 2.5; *Lev. Rab.* 25.3; *Num. Rab.* 12.6; *Deut. Rab.* 10.2; *As. Mos.* 1:13–14. For further Jewish references, see Hauck, *TDNT* 3:620–21. A suggestive parallel is found in Odes Sol. 41:15, where the Messiah is said to have been "known before the foundations of the world, that he might give life to persons forever by the truth of his name." Compare 17:6 with 17:26. Note also the strong affinity between 17:24–26 and 1 John 3:2.

85. For example, Ps. 116:5; 119:137; Jer. 12:1; cf. Rom. 3:26; 1 John 1:9; Rev. 16:5.

86. Beasley-Murray (1999: 293 n. k [contra Barrett 1978: 515]), following J. N. Sanders, suggests "that the καὶ ... δὲ construction has been combined with the καὶ ... καὶ construction used to introduce a contrast, so giving the sequence καὶ ... δὲ ... καὶ ..., which should be rendered, '*although* ... *yet* ... *and* ...'" (all accents contextual).

87. Schlatter (1948: 326) observes, "Jesus' divine sonship consists not in possession of a secret name but in his ability to make God's name known."

88. So Carson 1991: 570; cf. R. Brown 1970: 781; Schnackenburg 1990: 3.197; Borchert 2002: 211. Contra Morris (1995: 653), who thinks that it is through the cross. Ridderbos (1997: 566) suggests that this is not so much an anticipation of the passion as it is a reference "to Jesus' continuing work in heaven."

89. The term γνωρίζω (gnōrizō, make known) occurs elsewhere in John's Gospel only in 15:15 (see commentary on "revealed" at 17:6). On "the love you have for me," see 17:24.

The phrase "I myself may be in them" is replete with covenantal overtones.[90] Subsequent to the giving of the law at Sinai, the glory of God that was displayed on the mountain (Exod. 24:16) came to dwell in the midst of Israel in the tabernacle (Exod. 40:34). As God's people moved toward the promised land, God frequently assured them that he was in their midst (Exod. 29:45–46; Deut. 7:21; 23:14). In John's prologue, Jesus is said to have come to dwell (lit., to "pitch his tent" [1:14]) among his people, and now Jesus' earthly presence is about to be transmuted into his spiritual presence in his followers, in keeping with OT notions of a new covenant (see commentary at 17:6). The closing words of Jesus' prayer conclude his final instruction of his disciples prior to the events of his passion.

Additional Note

17:11. The reading ᾧ [δ]έδωκάς μοι is strongly favored by the external evidence and is adopted by the majority of commentators (e.g., Ridderbos 1997: 553 n. 237; Barrett 1978: 508; Beasley-Murray 1999: 293 n. f).

More literally, the phrase reads, "the love [with] which you loved me"; the construction is similar to one found in Eph. 2:4. As Carson (1991: 570) notes, the present reference goes beyond 17:23 in that it "promises that they will be so transformed, as God is continually made known to them, that God's own love for his Son will become their love. The love with which they learn to love is nothing less than the love amongst the persons of the Godhead" (cf. Calvin 1961: 152). The preposition ἐν (*en*) could mean either "in" or "among" or both (Carson 1991: 570; Barrett 1978: 515; Morris 1995: 653). Most likely, the initial reference is to Jesus' spiritual presence "in" a given disciple individually, though secondarily this would yield a group of Spirit-indwelled believers collectively, so that Jesus could also be said to be "among" his followers spiritually.

90. See commentary at 14:20 and at 17:23; see also Matt. 28:20.

B. The Passion Narrative (18:1–19:42)

The major theme of John's passion narrative is the otherworldly kingship of Jesus.[1] The evangelist shows that the case against Jesus is groundless: three times Pilate states that he finds no basis for a charge against Jesus (18:38; 19:4, 6).[2] Pilate is cast as a cowardly and superstitious political opportunist who is easily manipulated and intimidated by the Jewish leaders, while the Jews charge Jesus with blasphemy, contending that they have no king but Caesar (19:15). Ironically, Barabbas, a convicted insurrectionist, whose name means "son of the father," is released rather than Jesus, the "Son of the Father," whom Pilate finds innocent of any criminal charges. But all of this fulfills scriptural predictions regarding the Messiah (19:24, 28–29, 36–37).

Overall, the Johannine passion narrative coheres closely with that of the Synoptics, yet occasionally with different emphases. As in the previous narrative (e.g., 10:15, 17–18; 13:1–5), John stresses Jesus' sovereign control over what happens to him (18:3–4). Although John omits Jesus' formal Jewish trial by the Sanhedrin, he does feature the informal hearing before Annas (not found in the Synoptics) and provides the most detailed account of Jesus' Roman trial before Pilate. Events unfold with Judas' betrayal of Jesus and Jesus' arrest (18:1–11), followed by Jesus' informal hearing before Annas, the former Jewish high priest (18:12–14, 19–24), into which John skillfully intersperses Peter's denials (18:15–18, 25–27). Jesus' appearance before Pilate includes an initial interrogation (18:28–38a), culminating in Pilate's verdict that he finds no basis for a charge against Jesus, and a final summons (18:38b–19:16), during which Jesus is sentenced to die. The passion then ensues, with Jesus' crucifixion, death, and burial (19:16b–42).

---

1. Stibbe (1992: 111–12) contends that John's characterization of Jesus in his passion narrative consists of three aspects: Jesus as judge, king, and elusive God. Stibbe also suggests that 18:1–27 serves as an "implicit commentary on the truth enunciated in 1:5" (i.e., the victory of the light over the darkness [p. 100]). On the relationship between the Johannine and the Synoptic passion narratives, see Ridderbos 1996: 569–72; Carson 1991: 571–76; Westcott 1908: 2.262–64. Burge (2000: 485–86) addresses the historical trustworthiness of the Johannine passion narrative. Moloney (1998: 482) divides 18:1–19:42 into five scenes on the basis of the introduction of new people and places. He also notes that this section begins and ends with κῆπος (kēpos, garden). R. Brown (1970: 813–17), too, has an extensive discussion of the structure and historicity of John's passion narrative. See also the examination of theological and literary features of this section in Schnackenburg 1990: 3.218–19.

2. For Jesus' trial before Pilate in the context of the "lawsuit motif" in the Fourth Gospel (with echoes of Isa. 40–55), see Lincoln 2000: 123–38 (with further bibliography on p. 123 n. 93).

1. The Betrayal and Arrest of Jesus (18:1–11)

Again, the passion narrative reflects eyewitness testimony (esp. 19:35; cf. 13:23; 20:2; 21:24; see Ridderbos 1997: 581).[1] Only this Gospel mentions the name of the servant whose ear was cut off and identifies Simon Peter as the one who drew the sword (18:10); features the informal hearing before Annas, Caiaphas's father-in-law (18:12–14, 19–24); and provides the information that Nicodemus accompanied Joseph of Arimathea at the occasion of Jesus' burial (19:39).

In keeping with the introduction to the second half of the Gospel (cf. 13:1, 3), Jesus' arrest is portrayed from the vantage point of God's sovereign plan (conversely, references to Jesus' agony in the garden are conspicuously absent [Ridderbos 1997: 573; Morris 1995: 655]). Jesus, "knowing all the things that were about to happen to him," is shown to take the initiative throughout the entire arrest proceedings (18:3–4).[2]

The preservation of Jesus' disciples, in turn, fulfills Jesus' previous words (18:8–9; cf. 6:39; 10:28–29; 17:12). Peter seeks to resist Jesus' arrest by taking things into his own hands (18:10–11; cf. Matt. 16:22–23). But Jesus rebukes him; Jesus' methods are not those of the Zealots. He is determined to "drink the cup the Father has given" him (18:11), certain that God is in perfect control.

Exegesis and Exposition

¹After he had said these things, Jesus left with his disciples to the other side of the Kidron ravine, where there was a garden into which he and his disciples entered. ²Now Judas—the one who would betray him—also knew the place, because Jesus had often gathered there with his disciples. ³So Judas came there, having taken a cohort [of soldiers] and some officials from the chief priests and the Pharisees with torches, lanterns, and weapons. ⁴Then Jesus, because he knew all the things that were about to happen to him, came out and said to them, "Whom are you looking for?" ⁵They answered him, "Jesus of Nazareth."

---

1. Contra Moloney (1998: 483), who, puzzlingly, urges that 18:1–11 should not be described as "the arrest of Jesus." He actually suggests that "Jesus is not betrayed, led out, or questioned" (p. 485).

2. In the Synoptics, it is Judas, rather than Jesus himself, who identifies Jesus to those who would arrest him (Ridderbos 1997: 574).

He said to them, "I am he." Now Judas—the one who would betray him—also was standing there with them. ⁶So when he [Jesus] said to them, "I am he," they drew back and fell to the ground. ⁷Then he asked them again, "Whom are you looking for?" And they said, "Jesus of Nazareth." ⁸Jesus answered, "I told you that I am he. So, then, if you are looking for me, let these men go." ⁹([He said this] so that the word may be fulfilled which he had spoken, "Of those you have given me, not one perished.") ¹⁰Then Simon Peter, who had a sword, drew it and struck the high priest's servant and cut off his right ear. (The servant's name was Malchus.) ¹¹Then Jesus said to Peter, "Put the sword back into the sheath. Shall I not drink the cup the Father has given me?"

18:1–2   "After he had said these things" probably refers to Jesus' words in John 14–17.[3] The last recorded movement was in 14:31, where Jesus initiated the group's departure from the room of the supper. After further discourse material and the final prayer (chs. 15–17), 18:1 shows Jesus and his disciples[4] leaving the location of Jesus' prayer[5] and crossing the Kidron Valley,[6] a location frequently mentioned in the LXX and Jewish intertestamental literature (though in the Gospels only in John).[7] Literally, the phrase is "the brook [χείμαρρος, *cheimarros*] of Kidron," whereby "brook" refers to an intermittent stream that is dry most of the year but swells up during rainfalls, particularly in the winter (Josephus, *Ant.* 8.1.5 §17). The Kidron Valley, called Wadi en-Nar, continues variously south or southeast until it reaches the Dead Sea (cf. Ezek. 47:1–12; Zech. 14:8; John 7:37–38).

To the east of the Kidron rises the Mount of Olives. The olive grove (κῆπος, *kēpos*, lit., "garden") on its slopes is called Gethsemane (meaning "oil press") in the Synoptics.[8] This garden may have been made available to Jesus and his followers by a wealthy person who supported Jesus' ministry.[9] The terminology ("entered," later "came out") suggests

3. So Carson 1991: 576; Barrett 1978: 517; Beasley-Murray 1999: 321.

4. "With" here is σύν (*syn*) rather than μετά (*meta*), another instance of Johannine stylistic variation (Morris 1995: 655 n. 2). Moloney (1998: 484) notes the emphasis placed on the disciples in this Gospel in contrast with the Synoptics, contending that the "passion of Jesus in the Fourth Gospel may not only be about what happens to Jesus, but may also determine the future of the disciples."

5. Morris (1995: 655) suggests that ἐξῆλθεν (*exēlthen*, they left) means they "went out of the house" (cf. Barrett 1978: 517). Carson (1991: 576) proposes that it means they left the city (cf. Bultmann 1971: 638).

6. However, there is no need to postulate the later insertion of John 15–17 into the narrative (contra, e.g., Ridderbos 1997: 573). Ridderbos (1997: 573) notes that the Fourth Evangelist begins the passion narrative completely independent of the Synoptic accounts.

7. See 2 Sam. 15:23; 1 Kings 2:37; 15:13; 2 Kings 23:4, 6, 12; 2 Chron. 29:16; 30:14; Jer. 31:40; 1 Macc. 15:39, 41; cf. Neh. 2:15.

8. See Matt. 26:36; Mark 14:32. See Green, *DJG* 265–68, esp. 267–68.

9. The phrase "there was" rather than "there is" may indicate that the garden had been destroyed by the time of writing of John's Gospel (Morris 1995: 655–56 n. 3).

a walled garden.[10] According to Jewish custom (with reference to Deut. 16:7), Passover night was to be spent in Jerusalem, but in light of the large number of pilgrims, city limits were extended as far as Bethphage on the Mount of Olives (though Bethany lay beyond the legal boundary; Jeremias 1966b: 55). As to Judas, John's readers have been repeatedly alerted to the identity of Jesus' betrayer (6:64, 71; 12:4; 13:2, 11, 21–30). As one of the Twelve, Ju1as knew the place where Jesus had often met with his disciples (note Luke 22:39: "as usual").

Judas is now shown to have officially switched sides. Rather than stand-   **18:3**
ing with Jesus and his followers, he appears with those who would arrest Jesus (Ridderbos 1997: 574; cf. Morris 1995: 658). Since Judas's remorse and suicide are not mentioned (cf. Matt. 27:3–5), this is the final refer- ence to Judas in this Gospel (Ridderbos 1997: 574). The forceful arrest initiated by Judas's leading[11] a sizable number of soldiers and officials to Jesus stands in ironic contrast to Jesus' peaceful nature (Borchert 2002: 219). Moreover, the approaching cohort would have been visible (and audible) from some distance, so that it very well may have been possible for Jesus and his followers to flee if they had chosen to do so; but they did not (Talbert 1992: 233).

The Greek (σπεῖρα, *speira*) indicates that the detachment of soldiers consisted of a cohort of Roman soldiers.[12] A full cohort was led by a "chiliarch" (lit., "leader of a thousand," rendered "tribune" or "com- mander") and consisted of one thousand men, though in practice it often numbered only six hundred.[13] The Romans could use surprisingly large numbers of soldiers even in dealing with a single person (like the 470 soldiers protecting Paul in Acts 23:23), especially when they feared a riot.[14] Roman troops were stationed in Caesarea, but during festivals they gathered northwest of the temple by the fortress of Antonia. This

10. The present passage has been subjected to several highly creative but rather improb- able readings (see esp. Whitacre 1999: 425; Brodie 1993: 529; Stibbe 1993: 182–84).

11. The participle λαβών (*labōn*) here has the sense of "leading" rather than "taking" (Carson 1991: 577; Barrett 1978: 518).

12. So Blomberg 2002: 228–30; Burge 2000: 491; Morris 1995: 656 (though both the LXX and Josephus use the term also with reference to non-Roman military [2 Macc. 8:23; 12:20, 22; Josephus, *Ant.* 17.9.3 §215; *J.W.* 2.1.3 §11]). Cf. the cautious assessment by Ridderbos (1997: 575). Contra Keener (1993: 306), who maintains that both the "de- tachment of soldiers" and the "officials from the chief priests and Pharisees" refer to the temple police.

13. The term χιλίαρχος (*chiliarchos*) was used to translate the Roman *tribunus militum*, a commander of a cohort of six hundred or even as few as two hundred soldiers (e.g., Polybius, *Histories* 11.23; the LXX features twenty-nine instances of χιλίαρχος for civil or military officials). Stibbe (1992: 170) thinks that the σπεῖρα probably consisted of two hundred soldiers. See the discussion by Morris (1995: 656 n. 5), who suggests that the use of σπεῖρα with the definite article here may indicate that a specific cohort is meant.

14. As presumably is the case here (so Morris 1995: 656 n. 5; cf. Carson 1991: 577; Witherington 1995: 285; Borchert 2002: 218).

enabled the Romans to keep a close watch on the large crowds during Jewish festivals and to quell any mob violence at the very outset.

Judas also brought with him "some officials from the chief priests and the Pharisees."[15] The officials (ὑπηρέται, hypēretai) from the chief priests and the Pharisees represented the temple police, the primary arresting officers. This unit was commanded by the captain of the temple guard (cf. Acts 4:1), who was charged with watching the temple at night (m. Mid. 1.1–2).[16]

The chief priests (made up predominantly of Sadducees) and the Pharisees are regularly linked in this Gospel (7:32, 45; 11:47, 57; cf. Josephus, Life 5 §21). The Pharisees are not mentioned again in John's narrative. The rubric of chief (or high) priests included the incumbent high priest, former high priests who were still living (such as Annas), and members of aristocratic families from whom high priests were chosen (Schürer 1973–79: 2.203–6).

Torches (λαμπάς, lampas) consisted of resinous strips of wood fastened together.[17] Lanterns (φανός, phanos) were "roughly cylindrical terracotta vessels with an opening on one side large enough for a household lamp to be inserted, its wick facing outward; a ceramic ring—or strap—handle on the top permitted easy carrying. Occasionally lanterns may have had built-in lamps" (R. Smith 1966: 7). Roman soldiers carried both kinds of lighting devices;[18] the temple guard went on their rounds with "lighted torches" (m. Mid. 1.2). Although this was the time close to the full paschal moon, lanterns might still be needed to track down a suspect who (it probably was suspected) was hiding from the authorities in the dark corners of this olive grove.[19]

18:4–6 From the beginning, John has emphasized Jesus' supernatural knowledge, so that Jesus' knowing beforehand "all the things that were going to happen to him" comes as no surprise to the reader.[20] In the

---

15. Ridderbos (1997: 574) suggests that the two groups are mentioned jointly here to underscore Jesus' authority. Carson (1991: 577) concludes that the two groups are described to imply that the whole world is against Jesus (cf. Beasley-Murray 1999: 322). See the further references in 18:12, 18, 22; 19:6 (cf. 18:36).

16. Their arms and methods are recalled in a "street-ballad" (see Köstenberger 2002c: 157, following Klausner 1925: 337); various versions circulated, depending on the high priests targeted (cf. b. Pesaḥ. 57a; t. Menaḥ. 13.21).

17. See the discussions in R. Smith 1966; Jeremias 1968: 83–87.

18. Cf. Dionysius of Halicarnassus, Antiquitates romanae 11.40.2: "carrying torches [φανούς] and lamps [λαμπάδας]."

19. "They were carrying" (not in the Greek text, supplied by the TNIV) should in any case not be taken to imply that all carried torches; it would have been sufficient for some to do so. Regarding the carrying of weapons (ὅπλον, hoplon; only here used literally in the NT; cf. Josephus, Life 19 §99 [cited in BDAG 716]), it may be noted that sometimes the temple guards were unarmed (see Josephus, J.W. 4.4.6 §293), but in the present instance both they and the Roman soldiers took no chances.

20. See, for example, 1:47–48; 2:24–25; 4:17–18; 6:61, 64; 11:11. In other places, similar expressions refer to a calamity befalling someone (e.g., Matt. 18:31).

disciples' case, it will be the Spirit who will tell them "what is yet to come" (16:13). The adjective "Nazarene" occurs outside the present context in John only in 19:19 (the inscription on the cross); the term, denoting origin (Schnackenburg 1990: 3.224), may carry a derogatory connotation here (cf. 1:46; see Moloney 1998: 485; contra R. Brown 1970: 810). "I am he" reads more literally, "I am."[21] In light of the response (see below), the phrase probably has connotations of deity (see commentary at 8:24).[22] Judas "standing" with the arresting forces may later in the narrative be echoed by Peter "standing" outside the gate (18:16) and then by the fire warming himself (18:18, 25). If so, both Judas and Peter are shown standing with the world against Jesus (Stibbe 1993: 182).[23]

"They drew back[24] and fell to the ground."[25] Repeated previous efforts at arresting or harming Jesus had failed (7:30, 44–49; 8:20, 59; 10:39; 12:36); now, at long last, the captors catch up with the "elusive Christ," not only finding him, but also binding him (Stibbe 1993: 184).[26] Falling

21. As Whitacre (1999: 426) notes, in the present passage we find juxtaposed references to Jesus' humble humanity and his exalted deity: he acknowledges that he is Jesus "the Nazarene," and in doing so he evokes the paradigmatic OT self-designation of God, "I am" (see further commentary below).

22. So Ridderbos 1997: 576; with reference to the threefold repetition of this phrase in this section, Morris 1995: 658 and Ball 1996: 201; cf. Beasley-Murray 1999: 322; Moloney 1998: 485; R. Brown 1970: 818; Borchert 2002: 219; Burge 2000: 492.

23. Stibbe (1993: 182–84) takes this one step further when he says that in 18:1–11, Jesus "plays the part" of the good shepherd, and Judas that of the thief; and that in 18:15–27, the beloved disciple "plays the part" of the shepherd who walks in and out of the fold; the girl at the gate "plays the part" of the gatekeeper; and Peter is equated with the role of the hired hand who runs away in the hour of danger. Stibbe may be right in the case of Jesus acting as the good shepherd, Judas as the thief, and Peter as the hired hand. But if the beloved disciple is said to play the part of the shepherd just because he is shown to walk in and out of the high priest's courtyard, one may perhaps also argue that Pilate is portrayed as a shepherd, since he too is shown repeatedly going in and out of his palace when oscillating back and forth between the crowds and Jesus. Stibbe's reading here is too allegorical and lacks restraint; construing John 18 as, in essence, an allegorical outplaying of John 10 seems to take careful literary analysis a step too far.

24. Brodie (1993: 526) draws attention to the fact that the only other previous reference to "drawing back" in the Johannine narrative was in 6:66, where many of Jesus' followers left in unbelief. At that time Judas remained one of the Twelve; now he is the leader of the arresting forces.

25. Contra Lindars (1972: 541: "scarcely . . . an historically reliable detail . . . John's way of expressing . . . theological fact"), apparently echoed by D. M. Smith (1999: 330: "scarcely conceivable historically . . . John's way of conveying theological points"), I see no reason to question the historicity of the account.

26. This, then, becomes the climax of the "elusive Christ" motif in John's Gospel. However, Stibbe (1993: 184) unduly dichotomizes when he says that the soldiers drew back in amazement "not so much because Jesus is divine as because they have at last apprehended the elusive Christ." It is unclear to me how this reading can be firmly established from the text.

to the ground is regularly a reaction to divine revelation.[27] This striking response also conveys the powerlessness of Jesus' enemies when
confronted with the power of God (Schnackenburg 1990: 3.224). The
phrase is reminiscent of certain passages in Psalms.[28] Jewish literature
recounts the similar story of the attempted arrest of Simeon (*Gen. Rab.*
91.6). The reaction also highlights Jesus' messianic authority, in keeping
with passages such as Isa. 11:4 (cf. 2 Esdr. [4 Ezra] 13:3–4; see Calvin
1961: 154).

18:7–9 In 18:7–8, the interchange of 18:4–5 is repeated. Once again, Jesus is
shown to take the initiative, which serves to secure the safety of his followers, in keeping with Jesus' previous assertions. By having the soldiers
repeat his name, Jesus draws all attention to himself and away from the
disciples (Morris 1995: 659).[29] The statement "Of those you have given
me, not one perished" summarizes 17:12, which in turn harks back to
6:39 and 10:28 (Ridderbos 1997: 577).[30] Jesus is portrayed as the good
shepherd who voluntarily chooses death to save the life of his sheep (cf.
10:11, 15, 17–18, 28).[31] John frequently parallels Jesus' sayings with OT
references that are fulfilled in Jesus' life (cf. 12:38; 13:18; 15:25; 19:24,
36–37).[32]

18:10–11 All four canonical Gospels mention the incident of the attack on the
servant, but only John provides the names of the major characters involved, Simon Peter and Malchus.[33] The name Malchus is not uncommon in the first century A.D. It occurs several times in Josephus, almost
entirely of Nabatean Arabs,[34] as well as in the Palmyrene and Nabatean

---

27. See Ezek. 1:28; 44:4; Dan. 2:46; 8:18; 10:9; Acts 9:4; 22:7; 26:14; Rev. 1:17; 19:10;
22:8. Contra Carson (1991: 578–79), who argues that the evangelist is not attempting to
describe a theophanic manifestation, concluding that the soldiers simply responded "better
than they knew" (cf. Witherington [1995: 286], who calls this an example of "Johannine
double-entendre"; but see Bultmann 1971: 639; Burge 2000: 492; Conway 1999: 173). See
also the legend cited in Köstenberger 2002c: 158.

28. See Ps. 27:2; 35:4; cf. 56:9; see also Elijah's experience in 2 Kings 1:9–14.

29. As Barrett (1978: 521) notes, by failing to mention the disciples' flight (cf. Mark
14:50), John presents them in more sympathetic terms than do the Synoptists.

30. Moloney (1998: 485), rather idiosyncratically, claims that the "son of perdition" in
17:12 is not Judas but Satan and that Jesus does not exclude anyone, even Judas, from
his request to the soldiers (p. 483). R. Brown (1970: 811–12) suggests that Judas was
not given to Jesus by the Father. Borchert (2002: 220) rightly notes that the exception is
already stated in 17:12.

31. For an extensive literary examination of the links between the good shepherd
discourse and 18:1–27, see Stibbe 1992: 101–4.

32. For the disciples having been "given" to Jesus, see the verbal parallel in 2 Esdr.
(4 Ezra) 2:26 (cf. John 3:35; 17:2, 6).

33. On Peter's characterization in 18:10–11, see Wiarda 2000: 110–11, 139, 174–75.

34. See *Ant.* 1.15 §240; 13.5.1 §131; 14.14.6 §390; 15.6.2–3 §167–75; *J.W.* 1.14.1 §276;
1.15.1 §286; 1.18.4 §360; 1.22.3 §440; 3.4.2 §68 (see Schlatter 1948: 329).

inscriptions.[35] The name probably derives from the common Semitic root *m-l-k* (*melek* means "king").

According to Luke 22:38, the group had two swords. The term μάχαιρα (*machaira*) may refer to a long knife or a short sword, with ῥομφαία (*rhomphaia*) being a large sword (see Laney 1992: 319, referring to Luke 22:38). The fact that Peter's action was unforeseen suggests the short sword, which could be concealed under one's garments. It may have been illegal to carry such a weapon at Passover.[36]

Peter struck Malchus's "right ear" (cf. Luke 22:50; John 21:6). Both Mark (14:47) and John use the term ὠτάριον (*ōtarion*), a double diminutive, equivalent to our "earlobe." It is possible that Peter deliberately chose the right ear (which was considered to be the more valuable [BDAG 217]) as a mark of defiance. Generally, an injury to a slave would not have aroused much interest, but Jesus shows concern even for this (by human standards) insignificant (Arab?) slave.[37]

The reference to Jesus' "cup" climaxes the arrest narrative (Ridderbos 1997: 578).[38] "Cup" serves here as a metaphor for death. In the OT, the expression refers primarily to God's "cup of wrath," which evildoers will have to drink.[39] Similar terminology is found in later Jewish writings and in the NT.[40] This imagery may have been transferred to the righteous, guiltless one taking upon himself God's judgment by way of substitutionary suffering.[41]

35. Hence the suggestion that Malchus was an Arab; cf. 1 Macc. 11:39: "Imalkue the Arab"; Josephus, *Ant.* 13.5.1 §131: "Malchus the Arab," referring to an earlier namesake. Cf. R. Brown 1970: 812; BDAG 614.
36. "A man may not go out with a sword" (*m. Šabb.* 6.4; so the sages with reference to Isa. 2:4, but not Rabbi Eliezer [A.D. 90–130]: "They are his adornments").
37. "Put your sword away" (cf. Jer. 47:6) reads more literally, "put the sword into the sheath" (θήκη, *thēkē*; related to the Greek word for "put," τίθημι, *tithēmi*). The term does not occur elsewhere in the NT.
38. The word ποτήριον (*potērion*, cup) is not used elsewhere in John (Synoptic parallels are Matt. 20:22–23 par.; 26:39 pars.). This is the only place where the Father is said to be the originator of the cup.
39. For example, Ps. 75:8; Isa. 51:17, 22; Jer. 25:15–17; Ezek. 23:31–34; Hab. 2:16.
40. See 1QpHab 11:10–15; Rev. 14:10; 16:19; 18:6.
41. See Delling 1957: esp. 110–15; Goppelt, *TDNT* 6:149–53.

2. Jesus Questioned by the High Priest, Denied by Peter (18:12–27)

The Gospels narrate two trials of Jesus, one Jewish and one Roman.[1] The former started with an informal hearing before Annas (18:12–14, 19–24), while Sanhedrin members probably were summoned for the purpose of staging a more formal trial. A meeting of the highest Jewish body (Matt. 26:57–68; Mark 14:53–65) then led to formal charges and the sending of a delegation to Pilate (Matt. 27:1–2; Luke 22:66–71). The Roman trial consisted of an initial interrogation by Pilate (Matt. 27:11–14; John 18:28–38a), followed by an appearance before Herod (Luke 23:6–12) and a final summons before Pilate (Matt. 27:15–31; John 18:38b–19:16).[2]

Though Jewish law contained numerous stipulations regarding legal proceedings against those charged with serious offenses, many such stipulations could be breached if the matter was judged to be urgent (including the possibility of mob violence).[3] Another factor in Jesus' case was that executions could proceed on feast days but not on a Sabbath. Thus, if Jesus' arrest took place on Thursday evening, little time remained if he was to be tried and put to death by the onset of Sabbath at sundown of the following day. Moreover, Roman officials such as Pilate worked only from dawn until late morning, so that the Jews' case against Jesus had to be prepared overnight.[4]

The present section oscillates between Jesus' informal hearing before Annas (18:12–14, 19–24) and Peter's denials of Jesus (18:15–18, 25–27).[5] By providing an account of Jesus' appearance before Annas,

---

1. See Bammel 1970; Corley, *DJG* 841–54.

2. Jeremiah almost suffered a similar fate when the high officials of the Jewish nation conspired against him (Jer. 26:11). The Qumran "Teacher of Righteousness" likewise claims to have suffered persecution by the hands of the "Wicked Priest" (1QpHab 11:4–7).

3. The earliest references to Jesus' death in Jewish literature frankly acknowledge involvement in the crucifixion (see esp. *b. Sanh.* 43a). Josephus's "Testimonium Flavianum" states that Jesus was "accused by men of the highest standing amongst us" (*Ant.* 18.3.3 §64).

4. On Roman and Jewish administrative policies in first-century A.D. Palestine, see Egger 1997.

5. For the various ways in which Peter's characterization is contrasted with that of Jesus, see the discussion in Stibbe 1992: 97–98. Stibbe notes that Jesus is presented twice answering under interrogation with the construction ἐγώ εἰμι (*egō eimi*, I am) while Peter twice answers with οὐκ εἰμί (*ouk eimi*, I am not). Also, Peter attacks a servant of the high priest, while Jesus is assaulted by a servant of the high priest. Finally, Peter is on trial

John again fills an important gap, since the Synoptics do not record this event but rather focus exclusively on the formal Jewish trial before Caiaphas. By way of background: Annas was deposed by the Romans in A.D. 15; his son-in-law Caiaphas held the high priesthood from A.D. 18–36 ("the high priest that year" in 18:13 means "the high priest at that time").

    a. Jesus taken to Annas (18:12–14)
    b. Peter's first denial (18:15–18)
    c. Jesus before the high priest (18:19–24)
    d. Peter's second and third denials (18:25–27)

Exegesis and Exposition

[12]Then the soldiers and the commander and the Jewish officials took Jesus into custody and bound him [13]and led him first to Annas; for he was the father-in-law of Caiaphas, who was high priest that year. [14](Now Caiaphas was the one who had counseled the Jewish leaders that it would be better for one man to die on behalf of the people.)

[15]So Simon Peter and another disciple were following Jesus. Now that disciple was known to the high priest and went with Jesus into the high priest's courtyard. [16]But Peter stood by the door outside. Then the other disciple, who was known to the high priest, came and talked to the girl at the door and brought Peter in. [17]The servant girl at the door said to Peter, "You aren't one of this man's disciples too, are you?" He said, "I'm not." [18]Now the servants and officials who stood there had made a fire, because it was cold, and were warming themselves.

[19]Meanwhile the high priest asked Jesus about his disciples and about his teaching. [20]Jesus answered him, "I have spoken openly to the world, I always taught in a synagogue or at the temple, where all the Jews come together, and I spoke nothing in secret. [21]Why do you ask me? Ask those who heard what I said to them. Look, they know what I said." [22]When he had said these things, one of the nearby officials gave Jesus a blow, saying, "Is this the way you answer the high priest?" [23]Jesus answered him, "If I misspoke, testify concerning the wrong; but if I spoke correctly, why do you strike me?" [24]Then Annas sent him bound to Caiaphas the high priest.

[25]Meanwhile Simon Peter was standing and warming himself. Then they said to him, "You aren't one of his disciples too, are you?" He denied it and said, "I'm not." [26]One of the high priest's servants, a relative of the one whose ear Peter had cut off, said, "I saw you in the garden with him, didn't I?" [27]So again Peter denied it, and at once a rooster began to crow.

---

outside, while Jesus is on trial inside. Duke's (1985: 96–99) discussion of the characterization of Peter focuses on its ironic aspects.

a. Jesus Taken to Annas (18:12–14)

18:12–14   Jesus' preliminary hearing before Annas is recorded only in John.[6] Apparently, in deference to Annas's continuing power and stature, Jesus was first brought to him. The absence of witnesses suggests that this hearing was informal. In the ensuing narrative John alternates between Jesus' hearing before Annas (18:12–14, 19–24) and Peter's denials (18:15–18, 25–27). He uses a similar oscillating pattern in his narration of Jesus' trial before Pilate (see introduction to 18:28–40).

The detachment of soldiers, its commander (by implication), and the Jewish officials, were first introduced in 18:3. To be "bound" (δέω, *deō*) is a customary expression in conjunction with arrest or imprisonment (e.g., Acts 9:2, 14, 21; earlier in Plato, *Leges* 9.864E).[7] Yet while powerless in human terms, Jesus' spirit is unbroken (cf. 18:23; see Schnackenburg 1990: 3.233). "First" anticipates the later arraignment before Caiaphas (Ridderbos 1997: 578; Morris 1995: 664; Barrett 1978: 524).

Annas held the office of high priest from A.D. 6 until A.D. 15.[8] He was appointed by Quirinius, the Roman prefect and governor of Syria, and removed from office by Pilate's predecessor, Valerius Gratus (A.D. 15–26) (cf. Josephus, *Ant.* 18.2.2 §34). Annas continued to wield considerable influence, not only because his removal from office was deemed arbitrary by many Jews, but also because as many as five of his sons, as well as Joseph Caiaphas his son-in-law, held the office at one point or another (*Ant.* 20.9.1 §§197–98 [A.D. 6–41]).[9]

Thus, even though Caiaphas held the official position of high priest that year (in the sense of "at that time" [Morris 1995: 664]), many still considered Annas, the patriarch of this preeminent high-priestly family, to be the real high priest (Morris 1995: 663; Carson 1991: 581), especially since under Mosaic legislation the appointment was for life (Num. 35:25).[10] Caiaphas, the high priest that year, was the one who

---

6. Though Annas is also mentioned by Luke (Luke 3:2; Acts 4:6). On the historical plausibility of such a trial, see Ridderbos 1997: 579–80. See also the excursus on the political and judicial situation in Israel during the time of Jesus in Borchert 2002: 224–26 and the chart showing the relationship of the four Gospels to one another concerning Jesus before the Jewish authorities in R. Brown 1970: 830–31. John 18:12a–b can be construed either with 18:1–11 (Beasley-Murray 1999: 324; Moloney 1998: 486; Barrett 1978: 523) or with 18:12c–14 (so Ridderbos 1997: 578; Morris 1995: 664; R. Brown 1970: 819).

7. The same word is used in 11:44 for Lazarus and in 19:40 for Jesus. Jesus is still bound when sent to Caiaphas by Annas in 18:24 and when handed over to Pilate by the Sanhedrin (Matt. 27:2 par.). The same term is used for John the Baptist (Mark 6:17), Barabbas (Mark 15:7), Peter (Acts 12:6), and Paul (Acts 21:11, 13; 24:27; Col. 4:3).

8. He is called "Ananus the son of Seth[i]" by Josephus (*Ant.* 18.2.1 §26). Ridderbos (1997: 578) lists the dates as A.D. 5 to 16.

9. On John's portrayal of Annas and Caiaphas his son-in-law, see Hengel 1999: 322–34.

10. See *m. Hor.* 3.4; cf. *m. Meg.* 1.9; *m. Mak.* 2.6; *t. Yoma* 1.4. See also Luke 3:2, where the appearance of John the Baptist is placed "during the high priesthood of Annas and

had counseled the Jewish leaders that it would be better (more accurate than "good" as in the TNIV) for one man to die on behalf of the people (see commentary at 11:49–52).

Under Roman occupation, the high priests were the dominant political leaders of the Jewish nation (Smallwood 1962). The mention of Caiaphas in 18:14 may serve the purpose of reminding John's readers of Caiaphas's and the Sanhedrin's opinion about Jesus, thus rendering a full account of the hearing held later that night unnecessary (Ridderbos 1997: 578–80; Morris 1995: 671); presumably, John judged that the information regarding this hearing had "been adequately circulated elsewhere" (i.e., in the Synoptic Gospels) (Carson 1991: 581).

b. Peter's First Denial (18:15–18)

At this point in his narrative the evangelist skillfully interposes Peter's[11] initial denial of Jesus; his second and third denials follow in 18:25–27.[12] **18:15–18** The "other disciple" known to the high priest is probably none other than "the disciple Jesus loved" (i.e., the apostle John).[13] John was a fisherman, but this does not mean that he came from an inferior social background.[14] John's father, Zebedee, is presented in Mark 1:20 as a man having hired servants, and either John and his brother James or their mother (or both) had prestigious ambitions (Matt. 20:20–28 par.). Moreover, it is not impossible that John himself came from a priestly

---

Caiaphas." Josephus indicates that it was customary for former high priests to continue to be called by that term (*J.W.* 4.3.7 §151; 4.3.9 §160; see Ridderbos 1997: 579; Moloney 1998: 490; Pancaro 1975: 66–67). The family is mentioned several times in later Jewish writings; it was noted not only for its great size, wealth, and power (*b. Pesaḥ.* 57a; *t. Menaḥ.* 13.18), but also for its greed (see the street-ballad referred to in commentary at 18:3). Its wealth is reported later to have been destroyed by the Zealots.

11. John never uses the short form "Peter" at the beginning of a narrative. In the present passage, he starts with "Simon Peter" (18:15), followed by "Peter" (18:16, 17, 18). When the courtyard scene is resumed, it is again "Simon Peter" (18:25), then "Peter" (18:26, 27).

12. Peter's three denials are recorded in all four Gospels. See the comparison chart in R. Brown 1970: 838–39.

13. This is suggested by the juxtaposition of both expressions in 20:2 and the close association between Peter and this disciple in the Gospels and Acts (see commentary at 13:23; Köstenberger 1999a: 22–24). This is held by the majority of commentators (e.g., Ridderbos 1997: 580; Westcott 1881: 255; Borchert 2002: 229; Carson 1991: 582 ["tentatively"]; Witherington 1995: 288; Beasley-Murray 1999: 324). Contra Calvin 1961: 159 (but see Morris 1995: 666 n. 37); Bultmann 1971: 645 n. 4 (followed by Conway 1999: 179); Schnackenburg (1990: 3.235). Alternative suggestions include Judas (Abbott), Nicodemus (Tindall) (both mentioned in R. Brown 1970: 822), James the son of Zebedee (Zahn [cited in Bultmann 1971: 645 n. 4]), and Lazarus (Stibbe 1992: 79, 98–99).

14. Talbert (1992: 235–36) points to a reference in the Gospel of the Hebrews to the effect that John used to supply fish to the court of the high priest while still working for his father, Zebedee. This is also noted by D. M. Smith (1999: 335), who adds that "fishermen were entrepreneurs, not common laborers at the bottom of the social spectrum" (citing Wuellner 1967: 45–61).

family (Morris 1995: 666 n. 37).[15] "Known" (γνωστός, *gnōstos* [used in 18:15, 16]) may suggest more than mere acquaintance.[16]

Where was the high priest's courtyard? The official high priest was Caiaphas, though Annas may have been referred to under this designation as well (see commentary at 18:13). Presumably, he lived in the Hasmonean palace on the west hill of the city, which overlooked the Tyropoeon Valley and faced the temple. It is possible that Caiaphas and Annas lived in the same palace, occupying different wings bound together by a common courtyard. The sequence of references to "the high priest" in this chapter (esp. 18:13–14, 19, 24) shows that Annas is in view and that the courtyard (αὐλή, *aulē*) is the atrium connected with his house (Carson 1991: 582; contra Barrett 1978: 526).

The mention of a "girl at the door" confirms that the scene took place outside the temple area, for there only men held such assignments (Carson 1991: 582; see further below).[17] Caiaphas's quarters may have shared the same courtyard, so that even the second stage of the investigation would have been relatively private (though with at least some Sanhedrin members present). The formal action taken by the Sanhedrin (at about dawn) is not recorded in John's Gospel (cf. Matt. 27:1–2 pars.). The "other disciple" known to the high priest spoke to "the servant girl on duty" (TNIV; more literally, "the servant girl at the door") and brought Peter in.[18] Apparently, this doorkeeper was a domestic female slave, probably of mature age, since her role was one of responsibility, requiring judgment and life experience.[19]

The girl's question to Peter, though apparently worded as if expecting a negative answer (Ridderbos 1997: 582; Morris 1995: 667; R. Brown 1970: 824), may more likely be viewed as a cautious assertion (Carson 1991: 583; Barrett 1978: 526, citing J. H. Moulton). "You too" may allude to the "other disciple" (Carson 1991: 583; Barrett 1978: 526; Schlatter

---

15. Yet Borchert (2002: 230 n. 40, citing Culpepper 1994: 61–63) remains skeptical.

16. So Morris 1995: 665–66 n. 35, citing Dodd; Carson 1991: 581; Barrett 1978: 526; but see Bultmann 1971: 645 n. 3. The term is used for a "close friend" in the LXX (e.g., 2 Kings 10:11; Ps. 54:14 [55:13 Eng.]; cf. Luke 2:44; see also *NewDocs* 4.44; Homer, *Iliad* 15.350).

17. Schlatter (1948: 333) maintains that it almost certainly was not the norm for the high priest's courtyard to be guarded by a woman. This presumably was done only when all the men were otherwise engaged. Schlatter further conjectures that a man probably would not have allowed Peter and John to enter, but the girl did. John, in turn, attributed this to divine providence enabling Jesus' prediction in 13:38 to be fulfilled. What is more, John himself had a part in this without realizing it at the time.

18. This construes the "other disciple" as the subject of εἰσήγαγεν (*eisēgagen*, he/she brought in) (Schlatter 1948: 333); alternatively, it is the slave girl who led Peter in. On women gatekeepers, see 2 Sam. 4:6 LXX; Acts 12:13 (R. Brown 1970: 824). MM 295 cites inscriptions dating from 14 B.C. and A.D. 34. The word παιδίσκη (*paidiskē*, servant girl) in John 18:17 is rendered "bondwoman" (in distinction from "free woman") in Gal. 4:22–31.

19. See Ramsay 1915–16 and the supplement by J. Mann (pp. 424–25) pertaining to talmudic literature.

1948: 333; contra R. Brown [1970: 824], who says that the reference is to the disciples with Jesus when he was arrested). Peter's reply is characterized by maximum terseness: "I'm not" (Ridderbos 1997: 582).[20] Perhaps Peter simply wanted to get access to the courtyard without having to engage in conversation with this woman (Carson 1991: 583).

It was cold (cf. 10:22). Nights in Jerusalem, which is half a mile above sea level, can be quite cold in the spring. The servants and officials (referring to "the domestic servants of the high priest" and the "officers of the Sanhedrin" respectively [Ridderbos 1997: 582 n. 42; Morris 1995: 667 n. 42]) had returned to their barracks, entrusting the role of guarding Jesus to the temple guards. Only John mentions that the fire was a charcoal fire (ἀνθρακιά, anthrakia; cf. 21:9; see Carson 1991: 583).[21] The presence of a fire confirms that these preliminary proceedings against Jesus took place at night, when the cold would move people to make a fire to stay warm. Even at night, fires were not normally lit, other than in exceptional circumstances,[22] and night proceedings generally were regarded as illegal (Carson 1991: 583). Moreover, the fact that a fire was kept burning in the chamber of immersion so that the priests on night duty could warm themselves there, and that lamps were burning even along the passage that leads below the temple building (m. Tamid 1.1), suggests that the courtyard referred to in the present passage is private.

The description of Peter here suggests that he was trying to be as inconspicuous as possible (Ridderbos 1997: 582). Like Judas earlier (18:5), Peter here "stands" with Jesus' enemies (Michaels 1989: 309; Stibbe 1993: 182).[23]

c. Jesus before the High Priest (18:19–24)

The conjunction οὖν (oun, meanwhile) indicates that John now resumes his account of Jesus' hearing before Annas (from 18:12–14; see Ridderbos 1997: 582). Again, Annas is referred to as "the high priest"

18:19–21

---

20. Calvin (1961: 159) puts it memorably: "He had boasted that he would prove an invincible fighter and triumphant unto death. Now, at the voice of one maid, and that without any threatening, he is confounded and throws down his weapons." Conway (1999: 174) cites O'Day (1995: 808): "The words of Peter's denial . . . are the antithesis of Jesus' words of self-identification and revelation from 18:1–12, 'I am.'"

21. Morris (1995: 667 n. 44) sees this as a mark of the Fourth Evangelist's "fondness for exact detail." Borchert (2002: 231) notes the literary link established between the present verse and the reference to a "charcoal fire" in 21:9 (the only two occurrences of this term in the NT).

22. Sherwin-White (1963: 45) asks, "Why light a fire—an act of some extravagance—if everyone was sleeping through the night?" He cites the younger Pliny's astonishment at his uncle's habit of studying at night and an instance where a protracted session of the Senate was concluded by lamplight.

23. Symbolic interpretations of this verse (such as those by Witherington 1995: 288; Moloney 1998: 490; and Whitacre 1999: 432) fail to convince.

(Carson 1991: 583; contra Barrett 1978: 525). The appropriateness of such a designation even after such an official was removed from office is confirmed by the Mishnah (*m. Hor.* 3.1–2, 4) and by Josephus (*J.W.* 2.12.6 §243; cf. 4.3.7–9 §§151–60). There may even be an element of defiance in the Jewish practice of continuing to call previous high priests by that name, challenging the Roman right to depose officials whose tenure was meant to be for life according to Mosaic legislation (cf. Num. 35:25). Apparently, the seasoned, aged Annas still wielded considerable high-priestly power while his relatives held the title.

The fact that Jesus is questioned—a procedure considered improper in formal Jewish trials, where a case had to rest on the weight of witness testimony (e.g., *m. Sanh.* 6.2)—suggests that the present hearing was more informal.[24] The question addressed to Jesus regarding his disciples and his teaching (διδαχή, *didachē* [cf. Rev. 2:14–15]) suggests that the authorities' primary concern was theological, despite the political rationale given to Pilate (cf. 19:7, 12).[25] The Jewish leadership seems to have viewed Jesus as a false prophet (see, later, *b. Sanh.* 43a) who secretly enticed people to fall away from the God of Israel—an offense punishable by death (Deut. 13:1–11).[26] Apparently, Annas hopes that Jesus might incriminate himself on those counts.

Jesus does not directly address the question from the high priest, who already knew the answer in any case (Ridderbos 1997: 582–83), but merely points to the public nature of his instruction.[27] Jesus' (non)answer takes the attention off his disciples and places it squarely upon himself (note the emphatic "I" statements in 18:20–21).[28] The point of Jesus' reference to the public nature of his instruction seems to be that the Jewish authorities would have been more than able to gather eyewitness testimony from those who had heard Jesus teach.[29] "Temple" refers to

---

24. Among those viewing the present hearing in more unofficial terms are Carson (1991: 584), Ridderbos (1997: 582), and R. Brown (1970: 826). Most other major commentators consider this to be an official trial (e.g., Morris, Barrett). On the Sadducees' reputation for judging in general, Josephus writes that "the school of the Sadducees . . . are indeed more heartless than any of the other Jews . . . when they sit in judgment" (*Ant.* 20.9.1 §199).

25. Carson (1991: 583) thinks that the authorities' main concerns were "the size of his following and the potential for any possible conspiracy."

26. The charge that Jesus leads the people astray surfaces earlier in John's Gospel at 7:12, 47.

27. As R. Brown (1970: 826) points out, the only previous reference to Jesus teaching in a synagogue in this Gospel is found in 6:59 (though there are other instances recorded in the Synoptics). The perfects λελάληκα (*lelalēka*, I have spoken) in 18:20 and ἀκηκοότας (*akēkootas*, [those who] heard) in 18:21 present Jesus' teaching from the perspective of having been completed, so that it is now possible to look at it as a finished product in terms of both delivery and reception (though not everything that commentators deduce from the perfects here seems warranted [see, e.g., Moloney 1998: 488]).

28. Some see in the present statement an echo of the motif of Wisdom speaking to the people in public (Prov. 8:2–3; 9:3; Wis. 6:14, 16; cf. Bar. 3:37).

29. See further comments below on "I spoke nothing in secret."

the temple precincts, usually translated "temple courts" in the TNIV (cf. 2:14; 7:14, 28; 8:20; 10:23; see Wallace 1996: 561 n. 15).

"I spoke nothing in secret."[30] Jesus' words here echo those of Yahweh in the Book of Isaiah (e.g., 45:19; 48:16; see R. Brown 1970: 826; Schlatter 1948: 334). The point is not that Jesus never spoke privately with his disciples but that his message was the same in private and in public (Morris 1995: 669; Carson 1991: 584; Borchert 2002: 232); he was not guilty of plotting a sinister conspiracy.[31] Jesus' statement may also seek to establish an ironic contrast between the charge that he pursued his teaching ministry in a secretive fashion (which is manifestly untrue) and the covert way in which the authorities went about Jesus' arrest (enlisting Judas, coming at night, etc.) (see Westcott 1908: 2.276).

"Why ask me? Ask those who heard me. Look, they know what I said." Jesus' challenge is understandable, especially if the questioning of prisoners was considered improper in his day (see commentary at 18:19). This is further confirmed by the recognized legal principle that a person's own testimony regarding himself was deemed invalid (see 5:31). Though an accused person could raise an objection (which must be heard [see 7:50–51]), a case was to be established by way of testimony, whereby witnesses *for* the defendant were to be questioned first (*m. Sanh.* 4.1; cf. Matt. 26:59–63 par.). If the testimony of witnesses agreed on essential points, the fate of the accused was sealed. The violation of this formal procedure here strongly suggests that Jesus' hearing before Annas was unofficial (R. Brown 1970: 826).

"Ask those who heard me." Jesus is not being uncooperative and evasive, but rather he urges a proper trial in which evidence is established by interrogation of witnesses; the present informal hearing did not meet such qualifications (Morris 1995: 669). This assertive display of self-confidence before authority was in all likelihood startling. As Josephus shows, those charged would normally maintain an attitude of humility before their judges, assuming "the manner of one who is fearful and seeks mercy" (*Ant.* 14.9.4 §172; see Schlatter 1948: 335). The official (ὑπηρέτης, *hypēretēs*) who strikes Jesus in response is one of the temple guards mentioned earlier as having taken part in his arrest (see 18:3, 12).

The official dealt Jesus a blow in the face—another illegal action. This **18:22–24** insult (R. Brown 1970: 826; Moloney 1998: 491) is not the only ill-treatment that Jesus had to endure during his Jewish trial before the Sanhedrin. According to Matthew, "They spit in his face and struck him with their fists. Others slapped him" (26:67). The term used here (ῥάπισμα,

---

30. Note the earlier acknowledgment by the people of Jerusalem that Jesus was "speaking publicly" (7:26).

31. Socrates answered his judges similarly (Plato, *Apologia* 33B). The Qumran community, on the other hand, preferred secret teaching, as did the mystery religions.

rhapisma) denotes a sharp blow with the flat of one's hand (cf. Isa. 50:6 LXX). Striking a prisoner was against Jewish law (Morris 1995: 670; Keener 1993: 307). Compare the similar incident involving Paul in Acts 23:1–5, where the high priest Ananias ordered those standing near Paul to strike him on the mouth.

"Is this the way you answer the high priest?" A proper attitude toward authority was legislated by Exod. 22:28: "Do not blaspheme God or curse the ruler of your people" (quoted by Paul in Acts 23:5; see Ridderbos 1997: 583; R. Brown 1970: 826).[32] "If I said something wrong" (TNIV) reads more literally, "spoke in an evil manner," that is, "if I said something that dishonored the high priest." Jesus implicitly refers to the law of Exod. 22:28 and denies having violated it.[33] The LXX uses the expression "speak evil" for cursing the deaf and blind (Lev. 19:14), one's parents (Lev. 20:9), the king and God (Isa. 8:21), and the sanctuary (1 Macc. 7:42) (Moloney 1998: 488).[34]

Annas's only response is to send Jesus, still bound, to Caiaphas the high priest (Ridderbos 1997: 583).[35] Before Jesus can be brought to Pilate, charges must be confirmed by the *official* high priest, Caiaphas, in his function as president of the Sanhedrin (Alexander 1988: esp. 46–49; Schürer 1973–79: 2.199–226).[36] Precisely where the Sanhedrin met at that time is subject to debate; a chamber on the south side of the temple or the marketplace are both cited (Blinzler 1959: 112–14).[37] In any case, "sent" need not imply movement to another building but may merely refer to changing courtrooms in the temple.

32. See also Josephus, *Ag. Ap.* 2.24 §194: "Anyone who disobeys him [the high priest] will pay the penalty as for impiety towards God himself."

33. Apparently, Jesus did not consider his response to be in violation of his "turning the other cheek" principle (see the discussions in Ridderbos 1997: 583; Morris 1995: 670 n. 55; Carson 1991: 585). Schlatter (1948: 335) resolves the apparent difficulty by noting that Jesus merely pointed out the abuse without fighting for his rights. In fact, "Turning the other cheek without bearing witness to the truth is not the fruit of moral resolution but the terrorized cowardice of the wimp" (Carson 1991: 585). Contrast also Jesus' response with Paul's in Acts 23:2–5, where the apostle lost his temper and called the high priest "you whitewashed wall" (see Carson 1991: 584–85).

34. Regarding the phrase "testify as to what is wrong," cf. 8:46; 15:25.

35. "Bound" in 18:24 corresponds to "bound" in 18:12 (though it is unclear whether Jesus had been bound throughout the entire proceedings or whether he was rebound after those; see Morris 1995: 670–71).

36. The lack of detail devoted to the trial before Caiaphas in this Gospel may be due to John's presupposing knowledge of the Synoptics among his readers as well as to the conviction "that these exchanges with the Jews settled nothing" (Witherington 1995: 289).

37. A mishnaic source specifies the chamber of hewn stone on the south side of the temple court (*m. Mid.* 5.4), while the Babylonian Talmud indicates that the Sanhedrin ceased meeting in this location "forty years" (not necessarily a literal time marker [e.g., *b. Yoma* 39a]) prior to the destruction of the temple, moving to the marketplace (*b. Šabb.* 15a; *b. Sanh.* 41b; *b. 'Abod. Zar.* 8b).

d. Peter's Second and Third Denials (18:25–27)

Again, John shifts back to Peter (δέ, *de*, in the meantime; see R. Brown 1970: 827), who has already denied his Lord once (18:15–18; see Ridderbos 1997: 584). The "they" who spoke to Peter in 18:25 may have been the same (Mark) or a different girl (Matthew) or a group (cf. Luke; see Morris 1995: 672). The connotation of the question in 18:25 closely conforms to that in 18:17.[38] The repetition of "warming himself" in 18:18 and 18:25, rather than being redundant or incongruous, reflects a literary device frequently used in Greek literature to resume the thread of a previous narrative, especially in cases where two plot lines are developed side by side.[39]

The third question heightens Peter's discomfort further in light of who asked it: the man was a relative of Malchus, whose ear Peter had cut off.[40] Being one of Jesus' disciples was not a legal offense, though it could have been surmised that open confession of Jesus might lead to trouble, especially if he was found guilty and executed (cf. 20:19). Of more immediate concern for Peter might have been the earlier incident in which he had drawn a weapon (perhaps carried illegally) and assaulted one of the high priest's servants. Peter's denial of association with Jesus[41] may therefore stem from a basic instinct of self-preservation and a self-serving desire not to incriminate himself in this matter that may have led to legal troubles of his own.[42]

At once a rooster began to crow (see commentary at 13:38).[43] Mark (14:72) notes that it was then that Peter remembered Jesus' prediction and

38. Ridderbos (1997: 584 n. 46) and Morris (1995: 672) claim that the wording indicates the expectation of a negative answer, though once again the force may be more that of a cautious assertion (see commentary at 18:17).

39. In the present instance, the two plot lines of Jesus' trials and the denials of Peter (Evans 1982b [cited in Carson 1991: 586]).

40. As in the case of the naming of Malchus and Peter earlier (see commentary at 18:10), John is the only evangelist to specify the identity of Peter's third accuser. Note also the rhetorical shift between the two earlier questions (μή, *mē*; expecting a negative answer) and the present, third question (which starts with οὐκ, *ouk*; expecting a positive answer), which accentuates the fact that the third question amounts to an accusation that could be rendered, "I saw you in the garden with him, didn't I?"

41. Though note that in the third instance Peter's exact words are not cited (Morris 1995: 673). Barrett (1978: 529) considers John's "abrupt ending" even more effective than Mark's presentation.

42. The contrast with Jesus is stark: "Jesus confronts his critics denying nothing, Peter wilts before his inquisitors denying everything" (Witherington 1995: 289). As Stibbe (1993: 181) notes, the poignancy of the contrast between Jesus and Peter is "carefully explored in the use of echo effects," with Jesus' twice-repeated self-identification "I am" (18:5, 8) corresponding to Peter's twice-repeated denial "I am not" (18:17, 25). The repeated term "deny" brings to mind Matt. 10:33 and Luke 12:9 (Carson 1991: 586).

43. The Greek wording is identical to Matt. 26:74. The translation "began to crow" reflects the understanding that the aorist verb ἐφώνησεν (*ephōnēsen*) is ingressive (cf., e.g., the TNIV). If so, D. M. Smith's (1999: 337) point is moot that "it is only in Mark that

broke down and wept; John immediately moves on to Jesus' encounter with Pilate.[44] Exactly when cocks crowed in first-century Jerusalem is subject to debate; estimates range from between 12:30 and 2:30 A.M. to between 3:00 and 5:00 A.M.[45] Some have argued that the present reference is not to the actual crowing of a rooster but to the trumpet signal given at the close of the third watch, named "cockcrow" (midnight to 3:00 A.M.) (Bernard 1928: 2.604). If so, then Jesus' interrogation by Annas and Peter's denials would have concluded at around 3:00 A.M.

the cock crows twice (14:72; cf. 14:30)," but that "like Matthew and Luke, John reports only one cock-crowing" (cf. Laney 1992: 326). Mishnaic legislation prohibited the raising of fowl in Jerusalem (*m. B. Qam.* 7.7), but it is unlikely that this prohibition was strictly obeyed in Jesus' day (Jeremias 1969: 47–48).

44. The Fourth Evangelist's omission of Peter's tears probably assumes what everyone knew at that point: Peter subsequently repented, and he had been restored to service by Jesus, as is recorded in the epilogue in John 21.

45. The former is suggested by Kosmala 1963; 1967–68; the latter by Lattey 1953–54; R. Brown 1970: 828 (both citing Lagrange). See also commentary at 13:36–38.

3. Jesus before Pilate (18:28–19:16a)

John's account of Jesus' Roman trial is by far the most detailed in the Gospels.[1] The entire Roman portion of Jesus' trial is narrated by John in seven units with an oscillating pattern of outdoor and indoor scenes: outside (18:29–32); inside (18:33–38a); outside (18:38b–40); inside (19:1–3); outside (19:4–7); inside (19:8–11); and outside (19:12–15).[2] This "carefully planned structure" is intended "to exhibit the paradoxical outcome of the whole process—how they [Pilate and the Jewish leaders] found each other in a single unprincipled alliance against Jesus" (Ridderbos 1997: 587; cf. Acts 4:27).[3]

By now it is early morning. Mark seems to indicate that the chief priests held a second Sanhedrin meeting to lend their actions the appearance of legality (Mark 15:1). After this the Jews lead Jesus from Caiaphas to the palace of the Roman governor. Throughout the following proceedings, Pilate displays the customary reluctance of Roman officials to get involved in internal Jewish religious affairs.[4] Although Pilate keeps referring to Jesus somewhat mockingly as "king of the Jews," the Jews claim to have no king but Caesar. If Pilate were to let Jesus go, he would prove himself to be no friend of Caesar. He sees no choice but to acquiesce to their demands.

    a. Jesus interrogated by Pilate (18:28–40)
    b. Jesus sentenced to be crucified (19:1–16a)

---

1. R. Brown (1970: 861) comments, "With all its drama and its theology, John's account of the trial is the most consistent and intelligible we have." Further positive evaluations of John's historicity are offered by Ridderbos (1997: 587–88) and by Carson (1991: 587), who suggests as possible Johannine sources Jesus after the resurrection, court attendants who later became believers, or possibly some public court records. Barrett (1978: 530) believes that most of the material is based on the Markan passion narrative.

2. See R. Brown 1970: 858–59, followed by Lincoln 2000: 124; Schnackenburg 1990: 3.220, 242; Moloney 1998: 493.

3. For a narrative exegesis of 18:15–19:22, see Larsen 2001: 122–39. Larsen views Pilate as an archetypal tragic figure, in application of the work of Northrop Frye with further reference to Culpepper (1983) and Stibbe (1992; 1994). Keener (2003: 1097) proposes another chiasm for 18:29–19:16, with 19:1–3 (scourging and crown of thorns) at the center. On John's Passover chronology, see Keener 2003: 1100–1103. Keener (2003: 1103) does not favor Blomberg's and Carson's harmonization and concludes that the Synoptics and John "at least imply (perhaps for theological reasons) the Passover on different days." I have similar problems here with Keener's reconstruction as with his view on the temple cleansing.

4. Cf. Acts 19:35–41; 23:23–26:32. In his discussion of the characterization of Pilate in the Fourth Gospel, Culpepper (1983: 143) summarizes the role of Pontius Pilate by suggesting that he "represents the futility of attempted compromise." Stibbe (1992: 109) disagrees, concluding that the reader should not necessarily view Pilate in a negative light.

Exegesis and Exposition

^{18:28}Then they led Jesus from Caiaphas to the Praetorium. By now it was early morning, and in order not to defile themselves they did not enter the Praetorium, so that they would be able to eat the Passover.

²⁹So Pilate came out to them and said, "What charge are you bringing against this man?" ³⁰They answered and said to him, "If he were not a criminal, we would not have handed him over to you." ³¹Then Pilate said to them, "*You* take him and judge him according to your own law." The Jews said to him, "It is not lawful for us to execute anyone." ³²([This happened] so that the word of Jesus might be fulfilled which he had spoken indicating by what kind of death he was going to die.)

³³Then Pilate entered the Praetorium again, and called Jesus and said to him, "Are you the king of the Jews?" ³⁴Jesus answered, "Are you saying this on your own accord or did others talk to you about me?" ³⁵Pilate answered, "Am I a Jew? Your own nation and the chief priests handed you over to me. What have you done?" ³⁶Jesus answered, "My kingdom is not of this world. If my kingdom were of this world, my servants would fight, so that I would not be handed over to the Jews. But now my kingdom is not from here." ³⁷Then Pilate said to him, "Then you are a king, aren't you?" Jesus answered, "You say that I'm a king. I was born for this purpose, and for this purpose I came into the world: to bear witness to the truth. Everyone who is of the truth listens to my voice." ³⁸Pilate said to him, "What is truth?"

And having said this, he went out to the Jews again and said to them, "I find no basis for a charge against him. ³⁹You have a custom that I release for you one prisoner at the Passover. Would you therefore like me to release to you 'the king of the Jews'?" ⁴⁰Then they cried out again, saying, "Not this one, but Barabbas!" Now Barabbas was a revolutionary.

^{19:1}So, then, Pilate took Jesus and had him flogged. ²And the soldiers twisted together a crown of thorns and placed it on his head and wrapped him in a dark red robe. ³And they kept coming to him and were saying, "Hail, king of the Jews!" And they buffeted him with blows.

⁴And Pilate came out again and said to them, "Look, I bring him out to you, so that you may know that I find no basis for a charge against him." ⁵Then Jesus came outside, wearing the thorny crown and the dark red robe. And he [Pilate] said to them, "See, the man!" ⁶So when the chief priests and the officials saw him, they cried out, saying, "Crucify! Crucify!" Pilate said to them, "*You* take him and crucify him. I find no basis for a charge against him." ⁷The Jews answered him, "We have a law, and according to that law he ought to die, because he made himself out to be the Son of God."

⁸Now when Pilate heard this statement, he grew even more afraid, ⁹and entered the Praetorium again and said to Jesus, "Where do you come from?" But Jesus gave him no answer. ¹⁰Then Pilate said to him, "Will you not talk

to me? You realize, don't you, that I have authority to release you and I have authority to crucify you?" ¹¹Jesus answered, "You wouldn't have any authority over me unless it had been given to you from above; for this reason the one who handed me over to you has a greater sin." ¹²From this moment on Pilate sought to release him; but the Jews cried out, saying, "If you release him, you are no friend of Caesar. Everyone who makes himself out to be a king opposes Caesar."

¹³So when Pilate heard these words, he led Jesus out and sat down on the judgment seat at a place called Lithostratos (Gabbatha in Aramaic). ¹⁴Now it was the day of preparation of Passover week, about the sixth hour [noon]. And he said to the Jews, "See, your king!" ¹⁵Then they cried out, "Take him away, take him away! Crucify him!" Pilate said to them, "Shall I crucify your king?" The chief priests answered, "We have no king but Caesar." ¹⁶ªSo, then, he gave him over to them, so that he might be crucified.

a. Jesus Interrogated by Pilate (18:28–40)

Jesus was led to the Praetorium, the headquarters of the Roman governor. Though based in Caesarea in a palace built by Herod the Great (cf. Acts 23:33–35), Pilate, like his predecessors, made it a practice to go up to Jerusalem for high feast days in order to be at hand for any disturbance that might arise. It is unclear whether Pilate's Jerusalem headquarters is to be identified with the Herodian palace on the Western Wall (suggested by the TNIV's "palace") or the Fortress of Antonia (named after Mark Antony [Josephus, *J.W.* 1.21.1 §401) northwest of the temple grounds.[5]

18:28

Herod the Great had had both palaces built, the former in 35 B.C. (on the site of an older castle erected by John Hyrcanus [Josephus, *Ant.* 18.4.3 §91]), the latter in 23 B.C., whereby especially Philo identifies the (former) Herodian palace as the usual Jerusalem headquarters of Roman governors.[6] Yet the discovery of massive stone slabs in the Fortress of Antonia in 1870 has convinced some that it is this building that is in view (see further commentary at 19:13; see also Vincent 1954). On balance, the Herodian palace is more likely, especially in light of the aforementioned evidence from Philo and Josephus.[7]

"Early morning" (πρωΐ, *prōi*) is ambiguous. The last two watches of the night (from midnight to 6:00 A.M.) were called "cockcrow" (ἀλεκτο-ροφωνία, *alektorophōnia*) and "early morning" (πρωΐ, *prōi*) by the Ro-

5. Acts 21:35, 40; see the extensive description in *J.W.* 5.5.8 §§238–46; both locations are mentioned in *Ant.* 15.8.5 §292. Cf. the discussion in R. Brown 1970: 845.
6. *Gaius* 39 §306; see also the incident involving Pilate recounted in *Gaius* 38 §§299–305.
7. See also Kopp 1963: 368–39. R. Brown (1970: 845) also notes that the term αὐλή (*aulē*, palace), used in Mark 15:16 to describe the Praetorium, occurs frequently in Josephus with reference to the Herodian palace but never with regard to the Fortress of Antonia.

mans. If this is the way the term is used here, then Jesus was brought to Pilate before 6:00 A.M. This coheres with the practice, followed by many Roman officials, of starting the day very early and finishing their workday by late morning.[8] Because Jews rarely tried capital cases at night (see commentary at 18:18), "early morning" more likely means some time after sunrise, when the Sanhedrin had met in formal session and pronounced its verdict on Jesus (Matt. 27:1–2 pars.).[9]

The references to the Jews not entering the palace in order to avoid ceremonial uncleanness so that they could eat the Passover serves the purpose of explaining Pilate's comings and goings. There is deep irony in the fact that the Jews are scrupulously avoiding ceremonial uncleanness while not being concerned about burdening themselves with the moral guilt of condemning an innocent man to death.[10] Also ironic is that they use a Gentile to achieve their ends yet will not enter a Gentile's house (R. Brown 1970: 866). Jews who entered Gentile homes were considered to contract uncleanness,[11] which prevented them from celebrating Passover.

The present reference may not merely be to Passover itself but to the Feast of Unleavened Bread, which lasted seven days (note Luke 22:1: "the Feast of Unleavened Bread, called the Passover"; see further commentary at 19:14, 31), and in particular to the feast-offering (*hagigah*), which was brought on the morning of the first day of the festival (cf. Num. 28:18–19). "Eat the Passover" probably simply means "celebrate the feast" (cf. 2 Chron. 30:21).[12]

18:29 Pontius Pilate, governor of Judea, was appointed to his post by the emperor Tiberius in A.D. 26 and held this position for about ten years until A.D. 36/37.[13] Pilate owed his appointment to Sejanus, the commander of the praetorian guard in Rome (cf. Philo, *Gaius* 24 §159). If the chronology presented in the introduction above is correct, then Pilate by now

8. See the evidence cited in Sherwin-White 1963: 45, with primary references. See also Seneca, *De ira* 2.7.3.

9. See Carson 1991: 588; Beasley-Murray 1999: 317 n. h; Morris 1995: 674–75. R. Brown (1970: 844) sees the hearing before Annas as concluding at 3:00 A.M., Jesus before Caiaphas from 3:00 to 6:00 A.M., and before Pilate from 6:00 A.M. until noon.

10. Ridderbos 1997: 589; Carson 1991: 589; Duke 1985: 127–28. Duke (1985: 128 [cf. R. Brown 1970: 866]) notes the further irony that the Jews are concerned about not being able to eat the Passover, yet they ultimately kill the true Passover.

11. See *m. ʾOhal.* 18.7; cf. uncleanness contracted from contact with corpses in Num. 9:7–14; 31:19.

12. That is, "the many meals and celebrations that week in the Passover season" (Burge 2000: 499; cf. Carson 1991: 590; see also Torrey 1931: 239–40). Contra Keener (1993: 307–308), who says that different calendars or John's "making a symbolic point" account for the apparent discrepancy between John and the Synoptics (different calendars are also the "solution" presented by Laney [1992: 330, following Hoehner]).

13. See Hoehner, *DJG* 615–17. "Pontius" appears only in Luke 3:1; Acts 4:27; 1 Tim. 6:13.

would have been governor for about seven years (the year of Jesus' trial being A.D. 33).[14] Apparently, Pilate could act from a position of strength until the death of his mentor Sejanus (October 18, A.D. 31), after which he had to tread much more lightly (P. Maier 1968).[15] Since the Gospels portray Pilate's conduct at Jesus' trial as accommodating the Jews and reflecting personal vulnerability, it is likely that Jesus' trial took place after A.D. 31 (i.e., in A.D. 33).[16]

Rather than providing specific charges, the Jews answer somewhat   **18:30–32** evasively (Morris 1995: 676), "If he were not a criminal [cf. Matt. 27:23], we would not have handed him over to you." The Jews' response tacitly acknowledges their inability to "bring a water-tight charge against Jesus" (Schnackenburg 1990: 3.245) and reveals their distaste for Roman interference in their own affairs. By calling Jesus a "criminal," they "seek both to impress on Pilate the danger Jesus presents to the public order and at the same time to avoid a concrete charge" (Ridderbos 1997: 590–91).[17]

Pilate, for his part, was well aware of the weakness of the Jews' case against Jesus: "*You* take him and judge him according to your own law."[18] Like Gallio after him (Acts 18:14–15), Pilate was not interested in being a judge of internal Jewish disputes. The Jews reply, "It is not lawful for us to execute anyone."[19] Despite instances where the Jewish authorities

14. The Synoptists use the generic title "governor" (ἡγεμών, *hēgemōn*) with regard to Pilate (e.g., Matt. 27:2, 11; Luke 20:20). Tacitus, the Roman historian, calls him *procurator* (*Annales* 15.44); Josephus uses the equivalent expression ἐπίτροπος, *epitropos* (*J.W.* 2.9.2 §169). The famous Latin "Pilate inscription," found in Caesarea in 1961, identifies him as "prefect" (*praefectus*) of Judea: [PON]TIUS PILATUS [PRAEF]ECTUS IUDA[EA]E (Vardaman 1962).

15. For example, Josephus, *J.W.* 2.9.2–3 §§169–74; *Ant.* 18.3.1–2 §§55–62; Luke 13:1 (?).

16. Jesus' trial and crucifixion under Pilate are also attested by non-Christian sources such as the Roman historian Tacitus (*Annales* 15.44). Pilate's tenure came to an end in A.D. 36/37, when he was deposed and sent to Rome by Vitellius, legate of Syria, on account of his brutal action in a Samaritan uprising (Josephus, *Ant.* 18.4.2 §§88–89; see Smallwood 1954). He arrived in Rome after Tiberius's death (March 16, A.D. 37).

17. Carson (1991: 590) comments insightfully, "The fact that Pilate had sufficiently agreed with their legal briefs to sanction sending a detachment of troops had doubtless encouraged them to think that he would ratify the proceedings of the Sanhedrin and get on to other business. To find him opening up what was in fact a new trial made them sullen."

18. As will be seen, this statement involves irony on multiple levels, because not only did the Jews lack the right to impose capital punishment under Roman law, but also, more importantly, they were forbidden under God's law to execute anyone not formally convicted of a capital offense (see Michaels 1989: 314). Moreover, in yet further irony, the Jewish authorities' response to Pilate's teasing remark amounts to a public acknowledgment of the illegality and illegitimacy of their dealings with Jesus (so, rightly, Stibbe 1993: 190).

19. Literally, "kill" (ἀποκτείνω, *apokteinō*), in possible reference to the sixth commandment of the Decalogue (Michaels 1989: 314). Schlatter (1948: 338) notes the emphatic position of ἡμῖν (*hēmin*, for us), contrasting the Jews and Pilate.

are involved in executions[20] (all of which involved lynch law or breaches of authority) the Sanhedrin did not have the power of capital punishment.[21] This was consistent with general Roman practice in provincial administration, and capital punishment was the most jealously guarded of all governmental powers (Sherwin-White 1963: 24–47, esp. 36).

Moreover, an equestrian procurator such as Pilate in an insignificant province such as Judea had no assistants of high rank who could help him carry out his administrative and judicial duties. Thus, he had to rely on local officials in minor matters while retaining the right to intervene in major cases, including "crimes for which the penalty was hard labor in mines, exile, or death."[22] Also, in handling criminal trials, the prefect or procurator was not bound by Roman law that applied only to Roman citizens and cities.[23] For this reason, it is difficult to determine with certainty Pilate's motives in offering to give the case back to the Jewish authorities.

Crucifixion was looked upon by the Jews with horror.[24] Execution on a cross was considered to be the same as hanging (Acts 5:30; 10:39), for which Mosaic law enunciated the principle "Anyone who is hung on a tree is under God's curse" (Deut. 21:23; cf. Gal. 3:13). If Jesus had been put to death by the Sanhedrin, stoning would have been the likely mode of execution, since it is the penalty specified in the OT for blasphemy,[25] the most common charge against Jesus in John.[26] Other forms of capital punishment sanctioned by mishnaic teaching are burning, beheading, and strangling (m. Sanh. 7.1).

The statement "[This happened] so that the word of Jesus might be fulfilled which he had spoken indicating by what kind of death he was going to die" once again underscores the notions of Jesus' supernatural foresight (cf. 18:4) and of divine sovereignty and theodicy.[27] There

---

20. One thinks of the stonings of Stephen (Acts 7) and of James the half-brother of Jesus in A.D. 62 (Josephus, Ant. 20.9.1 §200), as well as the burning of a priest's daughter accused of committing adultery (m. Sanh. 7.2).

21. Barrett 1978: 533–35; Morris 1995: 695–97; Hengel 1999: 330; Winter 1974. See especially the references in Josephus (J.W. 2.8.1 §117; Ant. 20.9.1 §§197–203 [cited in Köstenberger 2002c: 164]). Cf. the acknowledgment in talmudic literature that the Jews had lost this power "forty years" before the destruction of Jerusalem (y. Sanh. 1.1; 7.2; on "forty years," see commentary at 18:24 above; loss of this power may have occurred as early as A.D. 6; see also Legasse 1997: 54–56).

22. Sherwin-White 1965: 99 (summarized by R. Brown [1970: 848]).

23. Such provincial trials were known as extra ordinem ("trials outside the system").

24. As when Alexander Jannaeus had eight hundred of his captives crucified in the center of Jerusalem (Josephus, J.W. 1.4.6 §97). Note 4QpNahum 1:6–8: "It is horrible for the one hanged alive from the tree."

25. Lev. 24:16; cf. John 10:33; Acts 7:57–58; m. Sanh. 7.4; 9.3.

26. Kruse (2003: 359) suggests that the Jewish leaders may have wanted crucifixion to show that Jesus was under God's curse.

27. Duke (1985: 129) also notes irony: the Jewish leaders have Jesus "shamefully crucified to prevent the world from going after him, when in fact he long ago had chosen just such a way to gather the world unto himself."

are also verbal links with the Johannine "lifted-up" sayings (12:32–33) and the destiny predicted of Peter at his commissioning (21:19). John's point is that even the fact that the Romans had ultimate jurisdiction over capital punishment coheres with Jesus' prediction that he was going to be "lifted up," a Johannine euphemism for crucifixion (Carson 1991: 592).

After this interchange, Pilate went back inside the palace to interrogate Jesus.[28] In contrast to Jewish practice (see commentary at 18:19, 21), Roman law made provisions for detailed questioning of persons charged with crimes, whether they were Roman citizens (*accusatio*) or not (*cognitio*) (Sherwin-White 1963: 13–23). These hearings were public and gave the accused person sufficient opportunity for self-defense against the charges, as seems to be presupposed in Jesus' case by the Synoptics.[29]

18:33–35

The question "Are you the king of the Jews?"[30] is recorded in all four Gospels (Bammel 1984: 417–19). One wonders if Pilate, upon seeing this prisoner bound before him, has a first impression of incredulity: Is *this* the man accused of claiming to be king of the Jews? (Ridderbos 1997: 593; Morris 1995: 679). If so, then the personal pronoun σύ (*sy*, you) may be emphatically scornful: "You, a prisoner, deserted even by your friends, are a king, are you?" (Barrett 1978: 536).[31]

"King of the Jews" may have been used by the Hasmoneans, who ruled Judea prior to the Roman subjugation of Palestine.[32] The title is also applied to Herod the Great (Josephus, *Ant.* 16.10.2 §311). Pilate's question seeks to determine whether or not Jesus constituted a political threat to Roman imperial power (Bammel 1984: 417–19). His gubernatorial tenure was punctuated by outbursts of ethnic nationalism that rendered him ever more alert to potential sources of trouble, especially since Judea was "infested with brigands" (*Ant.* 20.9.5 §215) and "anyone might make himself king as the head of a band of rebels" (*Ant.* 17.10.8 §285 (Jensen 1941: esp. 261–62).

Jesus' response in 18:34–37 is more extensive than that recorded in the Synoptics (Ridderbos 1997: 593).[33] His initial counterquestion draws attention away from himself to the Jews who had lodged their charges against him and possibly shows awareness of Pilate's disgust at having

---

28. Πάλιν (*palin*) here hardly means "again," since there is no previous reference to Pilate entering the palace. Here the term means "back," as in 6:15; 10:40 (Morris 1995: 679 n. 78).

29. On "the palace," see commentary at 18:28.

30. See 1:49; 12:13; 18:33–37, 39; 19:3, 12, 14–15, 19–22.

31. Beyond this, Michaels (1989: 317) may have a point when he writes, "All that happens . . . is the product of Pilate's sick and anti-Semitic sense of humor. He seems obsessed throughout with the grim joke that Jesus is the Jews' king."

32. See, for example, Josephus, *Ant.* 14.3.1 §36 (cited in Köstenberger 2002c: 166).

33. Schlatter (1948: 339) notes the connection between 18:34 and 4:42.

to interfere in internal Jewish matters.[34] Jesus is fully aware that the epithet "king of the Jews" is capable of more than one definition, especially given the different cultural, political, and religious backgrounds of Jews and Romans. Hence, he cannot simply answer Pilate's question; he must first define the sense in which he is and is not a king.[35]

Pilate's riposte "Am I a Jew?" reveals the depth of his exasperation (Witherington 1995: 291). He realizes that he is getting drawn more and more deeply into a Jewish internecine dispute without being able to extricate himself. Moreover, though Pilate harbors contempt and resentment toward the Jews, ironically, he will be forced in the course of the investigation to adopt their position (Carson 1991: 593).

18:36–37 "My kingdom is not of this world. . . . But now my kingdom is not from here."[36] Earlier, Jesus had rebuffed people's efforts to make him king (6:15).[37] Apart from 3:3 and 3:5, this is the only instance of "kingdom" terminology in this Gospel, which stands in stark contrast with the Synoptics, where the phrase "kingdom of God" is exceedingly common. In both cases in the present Gospel, the use of the term seems to be constrained by the specific encounters of Jesus with Nicodemus and with Pilate and their notions, respectively, of a Jewish kingdom or the Roman Empire. In John, Jesus consistently disavows all political aspirations.

If Jesus were seeking political rule, his servants[38] would fight to prevent his arrest by the Jews.[39] Jesus here makes no mention of Peter's

34. Jesus' response also seizes the initiative rather than merely passively responding to Pilate's question. Duke (1985: 129) suggests that Jesus is not simply seeking information but instead is asking an ironic question in import similar to the blind man's question in 9:27. In this manner, Jesus is now placing Pilate on trial and calls him to make his own decision. Likewise, Michaels (1989: 315) notes that Jesus' reply in 18:34 "addresses Pilate at a very personal level, as if to ask him, 'Do you really want to know the answer for your own sake, or are you simply carrying out your duty as magistrate?'" Pilate quickly removes all doubt: it is strictly the latter.

35. Witherington (1995: 291) claims that another reason for Jesus' reserve is that "Jesus as a loyal Jew was expected to say nothing against his fellow Jews in a Gentile court."

36. As Brodie (1993: 535) points out, Jesus' reference to the nature of his "kingdom" in the present passage coheres with the thrust of John 13–17: his washing of feet to set the example of humble service, the kind of union depicted by the vine, and the disciples' sanctification by the truth of God's word.

37. The answer given by the grandchildren of Jude, Jesus' half-brother, at a trial before Domitian echoes Jesus' words (Eusebius, *Hist. eccl.* 3.20.6 [cited in Köstenberger 2002c: 166]). Jesus' description of the nature of his kingdom is reminiscent of certain passages in Daniel (e.g., 2:44; 7:14, 27).

38. The term ὑπηρέτης (*hypēretēs*), which previously has been used for the temple police, refers in the LXX to the minister or officer of a king (Prov. 14:35; Isa. 32:5; Dan. 3:46) or even to kings themselves (Wis. 6:4).

39. But since Jesus' kingdom is otherworldly, the use of force is uncalled for in the present instance. Lindars (1972: 559) remarks, "For the Kingdom understood in this way military action is not appropriate—a fact which the Church has not always remembered."

earlier efforts (recorded in 18:10–11) to do just that. Yet although Jesus disavows any political aspirations, he does not deny being a king. If he did, he would fail to testify to the truth. The phrase "I was born" constitutes the sole reference to Jesus' birth in this Gospel (Carson 1991: 594–95; Barrett 1978: 537). "Bear witness to the truth" harks back to similar language used earlier regarding John the Baptist (5:33).

When Jesus says, "Everyone on the side of truth listens to me," he makes Pilate palpably uncomfortable (see commentary at 18:38). For in truth, it is not Jesus who is on trial but rather Pilate, who is confronted with the "light of the world" and must decide whether he prefers darkness or light (R. Brown 1970: 868). Yet although Jesus' disavowal of an earthly kingship could have been reassuring for Pilate in that Jesus obviously was no threat to Roman hegemony, the procurator finds himself challenged to accept or reject the truth that Jesus has come to reveal (R. Brown 1970: 869; cf. Michaels 1989: 316).

"What is truth?" With this flippant remark, Pilate dismisses Jesus' claim **18:38–40** that he came to testify to the truth and that everyone on the side of truth listens to him.[40] Rather than being philosophical in nature, Pilate's comment may reflect disillusionment (if not bitterness) from a political, pragmatic point of view. In his seven years as governor of Judea, he had frequently clashed with the Jewish population. And recently, his position with the Roman emperor had become increasingly tenuous (see commentary at 18:29).

After this, Pilate went out again to the Jews, returning to the outer colonnade (cf. 18:28–29). His statement "I find no basis for a charge against him" (cf. Luke 23:4, 14) indicates that he did not perceive Jesus as a rival aspirant to political office. At the same time, Pilate's thrice-repeated exoneration of Jesus (cf. John 19:4, 6) stands in blatant contrast with the actual death sentence pronounced in deference to the Jewish authorities.

"It is your custom for me to release to you one prisoner at the time of the Passover" (more literally, "at Passover").[41] There is little

---

Yet one must be careful not to construe Jesus' statement here as a wholesale endorsement of pacifism. Though the institutional church ought to be cautious about endorsing military action, Christians are at times in their capacity as citizens called on to take up arms; in that sense, "the church" may well engage in military action and not be in any conflict with Jesus' refusal (in a very different if not unique situation). One thinks here of the forceful abolition of slavery in the United States and of Dietrich Bonhoeffer's participation in a plot to assassinate Adolf Hitler.

40. Witherington (1995: 292) writes, "Apparently Pilate concludes that Jesus is a deluded quack whom he can banter with but not take seriously." Carson (1991: 595) describes Pilate's response as "curt and cynical" and thinks that his reply is terse "either because he is convinced there is no answer, or, more likely, because he does not want to hear it." Ridderbos (1997: 596) sees Pilate "shrugging his shoulders, in effect."

41. The expression refers to the entire festival in Deut. 16:1–2; Ezek. 45:21; Luke 2:41; 22:1; John 2:13, 23; 6:4; 11:55; Acts 12:4; Josephus, *Ant.* 17.9.3 §213; cf. *y. Pesaḥ.* 9.5 (cited in Köstenberger 2002c: 212 n. 577).

extrabiblical evidence for the custom of releasing one prisoner at Passover.[42] The release probably served as a gesture of goodwill designed to lessen political antagonism and to assure people that "no one coming to Jerusalem would be caught in the midst of political strife."[43] Roman law provided for two kinds of amnesty: pardoning a condemned criminal (*indulgentia*) and acquitting someone prior to the verdict (*abolitio*); in Jesus' case, the latter would have been in view (Keener 1993: 309).

The term "king of the Jews" in Pilate's mouth is used in a mocking, derogatory sense (cf. 19:14, 15, 19–20), "expressing what he regards as the absurd nature of the charge made by the Jews" (Ridderbos 1997: 597–98). The strong word "shout" (κραυγάζω, *kraugazō*) is consistently used by John to describe the escalating dynamic of the mob's demands for Jesus' crucifixion.[44] They then demanded, "No, not him! Give us Barabbas!"[45] Generally, Zealot-style political extremism was condemned. Yet here the Jews, at the instigation of the high priests, ask for the release of Barabbas, a terrorist, while calling for the death of Jesus of Nazareth, who renounces all political aspirations (6:15; 18:36–37; see Burge 2000: 502). Apart from the irony of making such a person out to be a political threat, this demonstrates both the influence that the Sanhedrin had over the Jewish people at large and the Jewish authorities' determination to have Jesus executed in order to preserve their own privileged position (11:49–52; see also Acts 17:7).

Nothing is known of Barabbas apart from the Gospel evidence.[46] He is called a ληστής (*lēstēs*, lit., "one who seizes plunder"), which probably means not merely "robber" but "insurrectionist" (cf. Mark 15:7).[47] Luke (23:19) indicates that Barabbas "had been thrown into prison for an insurrection in the city, and for murder." In Matt. 27:16, Barabbas is

42. The practice may go back to Hasmonean times and may have been continued by the Romans after taking over Palestine. See Josephus, *Ant.* 20.9.3 §209; Livy, *Roman History* 5.13; *b. Pesaḥ.* 91a. See Blinzler 1959: 218–21.
43. See Chavel 1941 (the quotation is from p. 277). One mishnaic passage (*m. Pesaḥ.* 8.6 [cited in Köstenberger 2002c: 167]) suggests that such releases were common enough to warrant legislation.
44. Cf. 19:6: "Crucify! Crucify!"; 19:12: "kept shouting"; 19:15: "Crucify him!"
45. For a chart comparing the Synoptic and Johannine accounts of the Barabbas scene, see R. Brown 1970: 870–71.
46. "Barabbas" is not a personal name but a patronymic (like Simon *Barjonah*, "son of Jonah") that occurs also in the Talmud (see Twomey 1956). Very possibly John saw in this designation a play on words (Stibbe 1993: 190): "Barabbas" literally means "son of the father," and John has presented Jesus as the Son of the Father throughout the Gospel.
47. Josephus frequently uses the term for those engaged in revolutionary guerilla warfare who, harboring mixed motives of plunder and nationalism, roamed the Jewish countryside in those volatile days. The term applies particularly to the Zealots, who had made armed resistance against Rome the consuming passion of their lives and who were committed to attaining national liberty by all means, including risk of their own lives (Rengstorf, *TDNT* 4:257–62).

characterized as "notorious" (ἐπίσημος, *episēmos*).[48] The irony is plain: the crowd prefers someone who had a track record of political subversiveness over someone who had no such record but who, to the contrary, had refused to define his mission primarily in political terms and who hardly represented a threat to the Roman Empire (Duke 1985: 131).

b. Jesus Sentenced to Be Crucified (19:1–16a)

After the Jewish phase of the trial and Jesus' interrogation by Pilate, the sentencing stage begins. The day is April 3, A.D. 33,[49] and Jesus' execution is imminent. Despite the governor's own personal conclusion that Jesus is innocent, he yields to Jewish demands for Jesus' crucifixion. The preferred Roman capital punishment for non-Roman citizens, crucifixion, is one of the most cruel and tortuous forms of death ever invented and inflicted in human history.

19:1–3

Pilate had Jesus flogged.[50] From least to most severe, there were three forms of flogging administered by the Romans: (1) the *fustigatio*, a beating given for smaller offenses such as hooliganism, often accompanied by a severe warning; (2) the *flagellatio*, a more brutal flogging to which criminals were subjected whose offenses were more serious; and (3) the *verberatio*, the most terrible form of this punishment, regularly associated with other reprisals such as crucifixion.[51]

In the present instance, the flogging probably in view is the least severe form, the *fustigatio*, which was intended in part to appease the Jews and in part to teach Jesus a lesson.[52] After the sentence of crucifixion, Jesus was scourged again, this time in the most severe form, the *verberatio*. This explains why Jesus was too weak to carry his own cross very far (see commentary at 19:17). Also, the nearness of the special Sabbath meant that the agony of crucifixion

48. The word is used by Josephus to describe Zealot leadership (e.g., John of Gischala, son of Levi [*J.W.* 2.21.1 §585]).

49. See Humphreys and Waddington 1992, with particular reference to the lunar eclipse occurring on that day (cf. Mark 15:33).

50. On Pilate, see commentary at 18:29. Ἐμαστίγωσεν (*emastigōsen*) is a causative active form: "Pilate *caused* Jesus to be scourged, but did not perform the act himself" (Wallace 1996: 412). The juxtaposed expressions ἐμαστίγωσεν (scourged [19:1]) and ῥαπίσματα (*rhapismata*, blows [19:3]) echo the Servant Song in Isa. 50:6 LXX, where the same two words (the former in noun form) are featured (Ridderbos 1997: 599 n. 102; cf. R. Brown 1970: 874).

51. For ancient references on flogging and torture, see Malina and Rohrbaugh 1998: 263.

52. Sherwin-White 1963: 27–28; Carson 1991: 596–97. Contra Schnackenburg (1990: 3.254), who believes that John misplaced the scourging and who, seeing only one scourging, believes that this scourging was the *verberatio*. R. Brown (1970: 858–59) thinks that John has moved the scourging from its original position (cf. Mark and Matthew) in order to fashion a chiastic arrangement.

must be kept short in order not to interfere with religious festivities (19:31–33).[53]

Apparently, the "crown of thorns" consisted of some branches twisted together from the long spikes of the date palm, shaped into a mock "crown," the radiant *corona*, which adorns rulers' heads on many coins of Jesus' time (Bonner 1953).[54] The thorns may have come from the common thorn bush (Isa. 34:13; Nah. 1:10) or from date palms that have thorns near the base.[55] These thorns, which could be up to twelve inches long, would sink into the victim's skull, resulting in considerable pain. It is reasonable to surmise that onlookers would observe profuse bleeding and distortion of facial features.

The purple robe, probably a military cloak, was used as a mock royal garment (Carson 1984: 573). The Matthean parallel (27:28) refers to a "scarlet robe," a red chlamys or outer cloak worn by emperor, minor officials, and soldiers alike. John uses the term ἱμάτιον (*himation*), which denotes a person's "outer clothing" or "robe." Like Mark (15:17), John gives the robe's color as purple, the imperial color (1 Macc. 8:14); yet in the Book of Revelation, "purple and scarlet" are mentioned side by side (Rev. 17:4; 18:16). Because purple dye (taken from shellfish) was expensive, a genuine purple cloak was not as easily obtained as a red one. On the whole, ancient nomenclature of color appears to have been somewhat fluid.

"Hail, king of the Jews!"[56] The soldiers' greeting mimics the "Ave Caesar" extended to the Roman emperor. Their mocking of Jesus as king seems to copy scenes frequently featured on stage and in Roman circuses (Winter 1974: 148–49). The game of "mock king," scratchings of which are preserved on the stone pavement of the fortress of Antonia (see commentary at 19:13), was played by soldiers during the Roman Saturnalia.[57] On the word for "slap in the face" or "blow" (ῥάπισμα, *rhapisma*), see commentary at 18:22. The imperfect ἐδίδοσαν (*edidosan*, they were giving) indicates repeated blows to the face (Schlatter 1948:

53. Similar floggings are recorded in Acts 22:24 (cf. 16:22) and by Josephus, *J.W.* 2.14.9 §306.

54. The crown is also reminiscent of depictions of oriental kings who were worshiped as gods (Hart 1952: esp. 71–74).

55. The former is favored by Ha-Reubéni 1933; the latter by Hart 1952. Goodenough and Welles (1953) and Avi-Yonah (1964: 151) suggest acanthus.

56. Wallace (1996: 58, citing BDF §147) says that articular nominatives with simple substantives were used in Attic Greek only to address inferiors: "Thus, although they call him 'King,' the *form* in which they make this proclamation denies the address."

57. Philo tells of people mocking a certain madman named Carabas in the gymnasium of Alexandria in A.D. 38. Dressed in a rug for a royal robe, with a sheet of byblus as a diadem on his head and a papyrus scepter in his hand, Carabas received homage and was saluted as king and hailed as lord, apparently in imitation of familiar pantomimes (*Flacc.* 6 §§36–42 [ca. A.D. 50]). See also the reference to a similar Persian custom in Dio Chrysostom, *De regno* 4.67–68 (cited in Köstenberger 2002c: 169).

343). Matthew and Mark record the soldiers hitting Jesus on the head with a staff used as a mock scepter (Matt. 27:30 par.).

The scourging and the mockery of Jesus are part of Pilate's plan to convince the Jews of the absurdity of their accusation against Jesus (Ridderbos 1997: 600). The statement "I find no basis for a charge against him" reiterates 18:38. Usually, this "not guilty" verdict reached by the Roman governor would stand (especially if repeated three times [see 19:6]). But the Jewish leadership is not to be deterred.

19:4–7

"Here is the man!"[58] "Man" may hark back to OT messianic passages such as Zech. 6:12 (Meeks 1967: 70–71). In classical literature the expression occasionally means "the poor fellow," "the poor creature."[59] To be sure, in his mock regal garments, Jesus must have been a heartrending sight (Ridderbos 1997: 600; Carson 1991: 598). In John's context, Pilate's statement may also accentuate Jesus' humanity: Jesus is *the* man," the God-sent Son of Man.[60]

But similar to Pilate's attempt to release Jesus as part of a Passover custom, so also this attempt to sidestep his judicial authority failed (Ridderbos 1997: 601). The chief priests (see commentary at 7:32) called all the louder for Jesus' crucifixion.[61] For the third and final time, Pilate asserts, "I find no basis for a charge against him" (19:6; cf. 18:38; 19:4). In first saying, "You take him and crucify him," Pilate uses sarcasm: he knows full well that the Jews do not have the authority to impose the death penalty, and if they did, they would stone rather than crucify Jesus (see commentary at 18:31).[62]

"We have a law, and according to that law he must die, because he claimed to be the Son of God."[63] A Roman prefect was responsible both for keeping peace and for maintaining local law. Jesus has frequently been accused of blasphemy (5:18; 8:59; 10:31, 33); yet in both the OT and other Jewish literature, the claim of being God's son need not be blasphemous and may refer to the anointed king of Israel (2 Sam. 7:14;

58. Wallace (1996: 221) says that the article preceding ἄνθρωπος (*anthrōpos*, man) is deictic (pointing).
59. For example, Demosthenes, *In Midiam* 91; *De falsa legatione* 198.
60. As Carson (1991: 598) notes, "All the witnesses were too blind to see it at the time, but this Man was displaying his glory, the glory of the one and only Son, in the very disgrace, pain, weakness and brutalization that Pilate advanced as suitable evidence that he was a judicial irrelevance." So also D. M. Smith (1999: 346): "In typical Johannine fashion, and with a touch of irony, Pilate is saying more than he could possibly know theologically."
61. R. Brown (1970: 890) draws attention to the verbal connection between the Jews' calling for Jesus' crucifixion in the present passage and the crowd hailing Jesus as the king of Israel in 12:13.
62. Carson (1991: 599) reads this as a sarcastic taunt: "You bring him to me for trial but you will not accept my judgment."
63. "We have a law" may refer to Lev. 24:16: "Anyone who blasphemes the name of the Lord must be put to death" (Carson 1991: 599; Barrett 1978: 541; Ridderbos 1997: 602).

Ps. 2:7; 89:26–27) or to the Messiah (4QFlor; see commentary at 1:49; Michel, *NIDNTT* 3:637).[64]

19:8–11 "Now when Pilate heard this statement, he grew even more afraid."[65] Though Roman officials may have been cynical, they also were often deeply superstitious. In pagan ears, the designation "son of god" conjured up notions of "divine men," persons believed to enjoy certain divine powers.[66] Ancient pagans concluded commonly enough that "the gods have come down to us in human form" (Acts 14:11). If Jesus was a "son of god," Pilate may have reasoned, he might incur the wrath of the gods for having Jesus flogged (cf. Matt. 27:19).

Alternatively, the root of Pilate's apprehension may have been political. He may have feared that the Jewish leaders would report to Rome that he failed to respect local religious customs, which was an accepted principle of provincial administration.[67] This depiction of Pilate hardly fits with Josephus's portrayal of the early years of the Roman governor's tenure, where he ruthlessly broke up riots and stubbornly resisted Jewish demands. Yet it fits perfectly with Pilate's tenuous position subsequent to the execution of his mentor Aelius Sejanus in A.D. 31.[68]

Pilate seeks to assuage the fear welling up inside by asking Jesus, "Where do you come from?"[69] The question is profound, but once again Pilate is in no position to comprehend the truth regarding Jesus (cf. 18:38). In a parallel recorded by Josephus, the Roman procurator Albinus summons the prophet Jesus, son of Ananias, who had proclaimed the destruction of Jerusalem and the temple, inquiring who he is and where he comes from (*J.W.* 6.5.3 §305). During the course of Jesus'

---

64. Even Israel could be called God's son (Exod. 4:22; Hos. 11:1; cf. John 10:33–38). In Greco-Roman circles, "son of god" (υἱὸς θεοῦ; *divi filius*) frequently occurs in inscriptions as a title for the emperor, especially Augustus (Deissmann 1901: 167), which is why the present charge has possible political implications. However, Pilate seems to find it hard to see Jesus as a threat to Roman imperial power (Whitacre 1999: 449).

65. Similarly most translations (including the TNIV, NASB, NLT, NKJV); alternatively, the meaning is "very afraid," since there is no previous reference to Pilate being afraid (see Carson 1991: 600; Morris 1995: 704; Barrett 1978: 542; Conway 1999: 159).

66. Two instances of such fear on the part of a judge of one accused whom he came to recognize as a higher being are relayed by Philostratus (*Vita Apollonii* 1.21; 4.44 [cited in Köstenberger 2002c: 212 n. 596]). See Bultmann 1971: 661 n. 4.

67. See the later incident recounted in Philo, *Gaius* 38 §§299–305, and the parallel in Josephus, *J.W.* 2.9.2–3 §§169–74. So Carson 1991: 600; cf. Morris 1995: 704. Yet see P. Maier 1969.

68. See Hoehner, *DJG* 121. Contra Keener (1993: 311) and R. Brown (1970: 891), who conjectures, "Perhaps the tremors that presaged the fall of Sejanus were already felt by sensitive political observers, and Pilate feared that soon he would have no protector at court" (thus placing Jesus' trial and crucifixion prior to Sejanus's demise in October, A.D. 31). Another pertinent issue is the designation "friend of Caesar," on which, see commentary at 19:12. Regarding "the palace," see commentary at 18:28.

69. Kruse (2003: 362) notes that in the ancient world, one's identity and honor were closely tied to one's place of origin (Acts 21:39).

ministry, his origins frequently had been at issue in his dealings with his opponents (e.g., 7:27–28; 8:14; 9:29–30). On a literal level, Jesus' Galilean provenance places him under Herod Antipas's jurisdiction (cf. Luke 23:6–7). In the Johannine context, however, there are clearly spiritual overtones as well (18:36–37).

Jesus gave Pilate no answer. He and Pilate occupy entirely different worlds, and no answer, short or long, would have been sufficient to adequately address Pilate's question (Carson 1991: 600). Jesus' silence also brings to mind the suffering Servant of Isaiah (53:7; cf. 1 Pet. 2:22–23). If Nicodemus and the Jewish authorities could not understand where Jesus had come from, how could this Roman governor be expected to grasp his true origin? The Greco-Roman pantheon was replete with gods having sexual union with women resulting in human offspring; a mind saturated with such myths would have grave difficulty comprehending Jesus' relationship with his Father. Jesus' silence obviously had an irritating effect on Pilate (cf. 19:10).

In issuing what Pilate must have known was a somewhat hollow threat in light of the Jews' leverage over him (Whitacre 1999: 450–51), he reminded Jesus, "I have power" (see commentary at 18:31; 19:6).[70] Jesus' response is "typical of biblical compatibilism, even the worst evil cannot escape the outer boundaries of God's sovereignty—yet God's sovereignty never mitigates the responsibility and guilt of moral agents who operate under divine sovereignty, while their voluntary decisions and their evil rebellion never render God utterly contingent" (Carson 1991: 600).

Pilate finds himself in charge ultimately only because of God's sovereign action (Carson 1991: 601; Kruse 2003: 363, citing Dan. 2:20–21; 4:25). The Roman procurator is responsible for failing to act to preserve truth and justice, but "he did not initiate the trial or engineer the betrayal" (Carson 1991: 602). In good Jewish manner, Jesus here uses "from above" as a circumlocution for God.[71] As to the identity of "the one who handed me over to you," Judas is a possible candidate (6:71; 13:21; 18:2), but the more likely person is Caiaphas (18:30, 35; cf. 11:49–53; Mark 14:61–64), since Judas drifts from view subsequent to Jesus' arrest in 18:12.[72]

---

70. According to Josephus, Coponius, the first Roman governor of Judea (A.D. 6–9), "was sent out as procurator, entrusted by Augustus with full powers, including the infliction of capital punishment" (*J.W.* 2.8.1 §117).

71. On the use of the phrase earlier in John, see notes in commentary at 3:3, 7, 31.

72. So, rightly, Carson 1991: 601; cf. Morris 1995: 705; Beasley-Murray 1999: 340; Burge 2000: 505; Borchert 2002: 254. Contra Barrett (1978: 543), who thinks that the singular participle constructed from the verb παραδίδωμι (*paradidōmi*, I hand over) suggests Judas. See also the discussions by Schnackenburg (1990: 3.261–63) and Ridderbos (1997: 603), both of whom ultimately point to the Jews as the most likely referent. Stibbe (1992: 170)

19:12   From then on, Pilate tried to set Jesus free. Apparently, Pilate remained unconvinced of Jesus' guilt (cf. 18:38; 19:4, 6). "Neither the charge of sedition nor the additional charge of blasphemy held up in Pilate's eyes" (Carson 1991: 602).[73] Perhaps also owing to his superstitious nature (19:8) and because he was impressed by Jesus' courage in the face of death (considered virtuous in the Greco-Roman world), he was reluctant to have Jesus crucified. Yet as in other instances, Pilate, despite his boast to Jesus that he had power to release and power to crucify (19:10; see R. Brown 1970: 894), would eventually yield to Jewish demands (see Philo, *Gaius* 38 §§301–2).

Pilate had reason to fear the threat of the Jewish leaders—they had conveyed their displeasure with Pilate to the emperor on earlier occasions—for Tiberius was known to act decisively when suspicions were cast on the conduct or loyalty of his subordinates.[74] By the time of Vespasian (A.D. 69–71), "friend of Caesar" had become virtually an official title; even in Jesus' day, the term may have had semitechnical force.[75] It is possible that Pilate had acquired "friend of Caesar" status through his mentor Sejanus.[76] But since Sejanus recently had fallen from grace (executed October 18, A.D. 31), Pilate would have ample reason to be concerned that his favored status with the emperor likewise would be removed.[77]

19:13   After several futile attempts to elude the Jews' grasp, Pilate finally sits down[78] on his judgment seat to render "his judicial decision on the one

concludes that "the one" in 19:11 probably refers to Caiaphas as a representative of the Jewish nation, as the evangelist has a propensity to implicate the Jews in Jesus' death.

73. Carson (1991: 603) helpfully puts Jesus' kingship in historical perspective: "Jesus *claims to be a king*, but a king of such a nature (18:36–37) that he is far less of an immediate threat to Caesar than are the people who are levelling the charge—as is made clear by the Jewish revolt, which lay ahead of the crucifixion but was almost certainly behind John the Evangelist when he wrote. And when the Jews eventually revolted, they were ruthlessly crushed and their temple was razed, while even as John writes the kingship of the crucified Master is running from strength to strength."

74. See Suetonius, *Tiberius* 58; Tacitus, *Annales* 3.38.

75. See Bammel (1952), who consequently insists on a post–A.D. 31 crucifixion date for Jesus. On "Caesar" as a title for the Roman emperor in Jesus' day, see Köstenberger 2002c: 172.

76. Note especially Tacitus's statement "The closer a man's intimacy with Sejanus, the stronger his claim to the emperor's friendship" (*Annales* 6.8). See also commentary at 19:8; on Sejanus's anti-Semitism, see Philo, *Gaius* 24 §§159–61.

77. In Hellenistic times, "Friends of the King" constituted a special group honored by the ruler for their loyalty and entrusted by him with responsible tasks (1 Macc. 2:18; 3:38; 10:65; 11:27; 3 Macc. 6:23; Josephus, *Ant.* 12.7.3 §298). In the early empire, "Friends of Augustus" was a well-known group. Later, the inscription **PHILOKAISAR**, "friend of Caesar," frequently occurs on coins of Herod Agrippa I (A.D. 37–44) (cf. Philo, *Flacc.* 6 §40).

78. The verb ἐκάθισεν (*ekathisen*, he sat) is intransitive, with Pilate, not Jesus, being the one sitting down (so, rightly, Ridderbos 1997: 605; Carson 1991: 608; Morris 1995: 707 n. 31). Barrett (1978: 544) thinks that this is an instance of Johannine double meaning, though, as R. Brown (1970: 881) rightly objects, "the phenomenon [of double meaning]

who alone is the promised Messiah, the one to whom the Father himself entrusted all (eschatological) judgment (5:22)" (Carson 1991: 603). The βῆμα (bēma, judge's seat), or *sella curilis*, normally stood in the forecourt of the governor's residence. It was elevated, so the judge could look out over the spectators. Matthew depicts the entire trial with Pilate seated on the judge's seat and Jesus standing before him.[79]

The Greek term λιθόστρωτον (*lithostrōton*) may refer to different kinds of stone pavement, ranging from simple ones consisting of identical pieces to elaborate ones of fine mosaic. In light of the pavement's location in front of the governor's residence, where traffic would have been heavy, a simple pavement of large stones is most likely.[80] The meaning of "Gabath" (cf. Gibeah, birthplace of Saul [1 Sam. 11:4]) is given as "hill" by the Jewish historian Josephus (*J.W.* 5.2.1 §51).[81]

Some argue that παρασκευή (*paraskeuē*, Day of Preparation) refers to **19:14** the day preceding Passover, that is, the day on which preparations for Passover are made (in the present case, Thursday morning). If so, then John indicates that Jesus is sent to be executed at the time at which Passover lambs are slaughtered in the temple. The Synoptists, however, clearly portray Jesus and his disciples as celebrating the Passover on the night prior to the crucifixion. Moreover, Matthew, Mark, Luke, and Josephus all use παρασκευή to refer to the day preceding the Sabbath.[82] The term therefore should be taken to refer to the day of preparation for the Sabbath (i.e., Friday).[83]

If this is accurate, then τοῦ πάσχα (*tou pascha*) means not "of the Passover," but "of Passover week."[84] Indeed, "Passover" may refer to the (day of) the actual Passover meal or, as in the present case, the entire

---

has not been based on syntactical ambiguity, nor is it usual for the second meaning to be opposite of the first."

79. Similar accounts are given of trials before the governors Festus (Acts 25:6, 17) and Florus (Josephus, *J.W.* 2.14.8 §301).

80. A paved court measuring about 2,300 square yards has been excavated on the lower level of the fortress of Antonia, one of the two possible sites of the governor's residence (the other is Herod's Palace in the northwest part of the upper city; see commentary at 18:28; Avi-Yonah 1964: 152). The blocks making up this pavement are more than a yard square and a foot thick. This kind of structure may well have been famous as "the stone pavement." However, it is unclear whether the excavated pavement was part of the fortress of Antonia in Jesus' time or not (Kopp [1963: 372–73] suggests a date ca. A.D. 135).

81. Similar kinds of descriptions of geographical locations in John are found in 5:2; 19:17.

82. Matt. 27:62; Mark 15:42; Luke 23:54; Josephus, *Ant.* 16.6.2 §§163–64.

83. Cf. Did. 8:1; Mart. Pol. 7:1. See Torrey 1931 (including his critique of Str-B 2:834–85 on pp. 235–36); Higgins 1954–55: 206–9; Story 1989: 318; Blomberg 1987: 177–78; Morris 1995: 708; Ridderbos 1997: 606.

84. So, correctly, the NIV; see also Carson 1991: 604; contra Barrett 1978: 545; R. Brown 1970: 882–83, 895. Also contra those who, like Morris (1995: 684–95, esp. 604–95), contend that Jesus and the temple authorities followed different calendars, with the Synoptics using Jesus' calendar (according to which the meal was the Passover) and John using

Passover week, including Passover day as well as the associated Feast of Unleavened Bread.[85] "Day of Preparation of Passover week" is therefore best taken to refer to the day of preparation for the Sabbath (i.e., Friday) of Passover week (so, rightly, Carson 1991: 603–4; see also commentary at 19:31). Thus, all four Gospels concur that Jesus' last supper was a Passover meal eaten on Thursday evening (by Jewish reckoning, the onset of Friday).

For the time reference to "about the sixth hour," see commentary at 1:39. Reckoning time from dawn to dark, "sixth hour" would be about noon. Mark 15:25 indicates that Jesus' crucifixion took place at the "third hour," that is, about 9:00 A.M. But since people related the estimated time to the closest three-hour mark, any time between 9:00 A.M. and noon may have led one person to say that an event occurred at the third (9:00 A.M.) or the sixth hour (12:00 noon) (Blomberg 1987: 180; Morris 1995: 708). Mark's concern likely was to provide the setting for the three hours of darkness (15:25, 33), while John seeks to stress the length of the proceedings, starting in the "early morning" (18:28) before Pilate.[86]

"Here is your king." Once again, Pilate caustically presents the Jews with "their king," mocking their implicit contention that "even the emperor in Rome has to be on his guard" in light of Jesus' claims (Ridderbos 1997: 606). By his sarcastic "acclamation," Pilate "simultaneously throws up with bitter irony the spurious charge of sedition in their face, and mocks their vassal status by saying that this bloodied and helpless prisoner is the only king they are likely to have" (Carson 1991: 605). Yet, like Caiaphas earlier (11:49–52), Pilate spoke better than he knew. Jesus was indeed the "king of the Jews," the king of Israel (1:49), as John had come to believe, and the present travesty of justice is part of God's paradoxical plan of reversal by which the world's judgment is confounded by God's judgment of sin in Christ.

19:15 At this the members of the Sanhedrin strike the exceedingly "cynical pose . . . of loyal subjects of the emperor" (Ridderbos 1997: 606): "We have no king but Caesar!"[87] The OT frequently reiterates that Yahweh alone is the true king of Israel (e.g., Judg. 8:23; 1 Sam. 8:7). None of the

---

that of the temple authorities (according to whom the sacrificial animals were slain the following day; hence, Jesus was sacrificed as our Passover).

85. Cf. Josephus, *Ant.* 14.2.1 §21; 17.9.3 §213; *J.W.* 2.1.3 §10; Luke 22:1; see commentary at 18:28.

86. So, rightly, Carson 1991: 605. Unlikely proposals are those of Barrett (1978: 545), who suggests that confusion of the Greek numerals for 3 and 6 may have led to the apparent discrepancies; and Witherington (1995: 294), who believes "that a Roman form of reckoning is being used, in which case the sixth hour is near dawn, at six in the morning."

87. See commentary at 19:12. For a more inclusive statement indicting the entire nation, see Matt. 27:25: "All the people answered, 'Let his blood be on us and on our children!'" (Schnackenburg 1990: 3.266).

foreign overlords qualified, whether Persian, Greek, or Roman (cf. Isa. 26:13). The very Feast of Passover, which the Jews are in the process of celebrating, is built on God's unique and supreme role in the life of the nation. The eleventh of the ancient Eighteen Benedictions prays, "Reign over us, you alone."[88]

Yet here, by professing to acknowledge Caesar alone as their king, the Jewish leaders betray their entire national heritage, as well as deny their own messianic expectations based on the promises of Scripture (Beasley-Murray 1999: 343). This, then, is the Fourth Evangelist's point, especially for his first Jewish readers: the Jewish rejection of the Messiah involved religious compromise and a failure to worship God. Yet the Jews, too, spoke better than they knew. For in truth, the Jews joined the world in its rejection of the God-sent Messiah, thus failing to give homage to God and showing that they had, in fact, no king but Caesar (Morris 1995: 710).[89]

At that point Pilate handed Jesus over to "them" to be crucified, whereby **19:16a** "them" presumably refers in the immediate instance to the soldiers, but secondarily also indicates that Pilate handed Jesus over in order to satisfy the Jews.[90] The usual form of death sentence was *Ibis in crucem*, "On the cross you shall go" (Petronius, *Satyricon* 137).[91] Upon pronouncement of the sentence, the criminal was first scourged, then executed (Josephus, *J.W.* 2.14.9 §308).

---

88. Several commentators (e.g., Kruse 2003: 365; Keener 2003: 1132, referring to Meeks 1967: 77 citing *b. Pesaḥ.* 118a) add that the Jews concluded the Greater Hallel in the Passover haggadah with the prayer "From everlasting to everlasting, you are God; beside you we have no king, redeemer, or savior; no liberator, deliverer, provider. . . . We have no King but you."

89. As Westcott (1908: 2.306) points out, the Jews' words here amount not merely to a rejection of Jesus as the Jewish Messiah but to a denial of their messianic hope per se: "The kingdom of God, in the confession of its rulers, has become the kingdom of the world. In the place of the Christ they have found the emperor. They first rejected Jesus as the Christ, and then, driven by the irony of circumstances, they rejected the Christ altogether."

90. So, rightly, Carson 1991: 606. See also Schnackenburg (1990: 3.267), who suggests that the evangelist "intentionally allowed the uncertainty to remain." The present statement is echoed by Tertullian, who says that the Jews extorted from Pilate a sentence giving Jesus up *"to them* to be crucified" (*Apol.* 21.18, italics added).

91. Latin literature usually uses the indirect expression *Duci iussit*, "He ordered him to be led off" (e.g., Pliny, *Epistulae* 10.96; see Sherwin-White 1963: 27).

4. Jesus' Crucifixion and Burial (19:16b–42)

John's account of Jesus' crucifixion is somber and restrained.[1] Jesus carried his own cross. He went to the Place of the Skull and was crucified with two others, one on his left, the other on his right. After Jesus had entrusted care of his mother to the "disciple he loved" and expressed his thirst in fulfillment of Scripture, he pronounced his mission complete, bowed his head, and gave up his spirit. Later, Joseph of Arimathea and Nicodemus, both Sanhedrin members, ensured that Jesus receive a proper burial.

    a. The crucifixion (19:16b–27)
    b. The death of Jesus (19:28–37)
    c. The burial of Jesus (19:38–42)

Exegesis and Exposition

[16b]Then they took Jesus, [17]and carrying the cross by himself, he went out to what is called the Place of the Skull (Golgotha in Aramaic), [18]where they crucified him, and two others with him—one on either side, and Jesus in the middle.

[19]Now Pilate also had a sign written and placed it on the cross. And it was written, "Jesus of Nazareth, the king of the Jews." [20]So many Jews read this sign, because the place where Jesus was crucified was near the city; and it was written in Aramaic, Latin, and Greek. [21]Then the Jewish chief priests were saying to Pilate, "Don't write, 'The king of the Jews,' but, 'This man said, I am the king of the Jews.'" [22]Pilate answered, "What I have written, I have written."

[23]When the soldiers crucified Jesus, they took his garments and divided them into four pieces, one for each soldier, and then there was also the undergarment. Now the undergarment was in one piece, woven seamlessly from top to bottom. [24]So they said to one another, "Let's not divide it, but let's cast lots to see whose it shall be." ([This happened] so that the Scripture might be fulfilled

---

1. For discussions of this passage's relationship to the Synoptics, see Barrett 1978: 546–48 (on the assumption of John's use of Mark and the superiority of Markan material); Beasley-Murray 1999: 343–44; Bultmann 1971: 667; R. Brown 1970: 913–16. R. Brown (1970: 910–12) divides 19:16b–42 into five chiastically arranged episodes plus introduction and conclusion; Moloney (1998: 502, following Donald Senior) sees the five scenes but not the chiasm (see also Moloney's literary analysis of John 18–19 on pp. 511–12).

which says, "They divided my clothes among themselves and cast lots for my undergarment.") So this is what the soldiers did.

[25]Now there were standing by the cross of Jesus his mother, and his mother's sister, and Mary the wife of Clopas, and Mary Magdalene. [26]So when Jesus saw his mother and the disciple he loved standing beside her, he said to his mother, "Mother, see, your son." [27]Then he said to the disciple, "Look, your mother!" And from that time on, the disciple took her into his home.

[28]After this, because Jesus knew that everything had already been accomplished, in order that Scripture might be fulfilled, he said, "I am thirsty." [29]A jar of wine vinegar was there; so they soaked a sponge in it and put the sponge on a stalk of hyssop and lifted it to his mouth. [30]So when Jesus had taken the vinegar, he said, "It is accomplished." And bowing his head, he gave up his spirit.

[31]Now the Jews, since it was the day of preparation of Passover week, in order that the bodies on the cross might not be defiled on the Sabbath—for the next day was a special Sabbath—asked Pilate to have their legs broken and to have them taken down. [32]So the soldiers came and broke the legs of the first man who had been crucified with him and then those of the other one. [33]But when they came to Jesus, they saw that he was already dead and did not break his legs, [34]but one of the soldiers pierced his side with a spear, and at once blood and water came out. [35]And the one who has seen it has borne witness, and his testimony is true, and he knows that he speaks truthfully, so that you too may believe. [36]For these things happened so that the Scripture may be fulfilled, "They did not break his bones." [37]And again, another Scripture says, "They will look at the one they have pierced."

[38]Now after these things Joseph of Arimathea, a disciple of Jesus, but secretly because of fear of the Jews, asked for Pilate's permission to take Jesus' body. And Pilate permitted it. So he came and took his body. [39]And Nicodemus (the one who had come to him [Jesus] at first by night) came as well, carrying a mixture of myrrh and aloes, about a litra [sixty-five pounds] each. [40]So they took Jesus' body and wrapped it in strips of linen with the spices, as was the burial custom among the Jews. [41]Now at the place where he was crucified was a garden, and in the garden was a fresh tomb, in which no one had ever been laid. [42]So it was there, on account of the Jewish day of preparation, because the tomb was nearby, that they laid Jesus.

a. The Crucifixion (19:16b–27)

They (i.e., the Roman soldiers)[2] took charge of Jesus. It was at this point **19:16b–17** that Jesus received his second flogging, the brutal *verberatio*. In this form of punishment, the victim was stripped naked, tied to a post, and beaten

2. So, rightly, Ridderbos 1997: 608; Carson 1991: 608; Morris 1995: 711; Beasley-Murray 1999: 344; Borchert 2002: 260; Burge 2000: 524. Contra Moloney (1998: 506, following R. Brown), who contends that "the Jews" are the subject of the verb.

by several soldiers with a whip "whose leather thongs were fitted with pieces of bone or lead or other metal." The scourgings were so severe that persons subjected to this torture sometimes died; others were left with their bones and entrails exposed (Carson 1991: 597).[3]

According to John, Jesus carried the cross "by himself" (ἑαυτῷ, *heautō*).[4] According to the Synoptics, he was aided by Simon of Cyrene. Despite the appearance of conflict between the Synoptics and John, such is hardly required; John's account may indicate nothing more than that Jesus carried the cross himself when setting out to the site of crucifixion.[5] The lack of reference to Simon of Cyrene may be due to the evangelist's desire to portray Jesus as continuing to be in charge of events, as has been his practice throughout the passion narrative.[6]

The condemned man would carry his cross to the site of crucifixion, where the upright beam (*stipes* [about nine feet high]) had already been staked into in the ground. There, he would be made to lie with his back on the ground, his arms stretched out and his hands, wrists, or forearms tied or nailed to the crossbar.[7] After this, the crossbar was stood up and affixed to the upright beam. To this beam the victim's feet were tied or nailed, often not very high off the ground, whereby the legs were bent and twisted so that a single nail was driven through both heels. An optional piece of wood (*sedecula*) served further to increase the victim's agony by prolonging the time of suffering.[8]

3. Josephus reports that a certain Jesus, son of Ananias, was brought before Albinus and "flayed to the bone with scourges" (*J.W.* 6.5.3 §304). Eusebius writes that certain martyrs at the time of Polycarp were "lacerated by scourges even to the innermost veins and arteries, so that the hidden inward parts of the body, both their bowels and their members, were exposed to view" (*Hist. eccl.* 4.15.4).

4. This most likely is to describe the custom that called for those who were to be crucified to carry their own cross (see the primary references cited in Köstenberger 2002c: 174–75; cf. Ridderbos 1997: 608 n. 128; Beasley-Murray 1999: 345). "By himself" is probably more accurate than the TNIV's "carrying his own cross." Note also the emphatic position of ἑαυτῷ (Barrett 1978: 548).

5. Traditional reconstruction has Jesus bear the cross, that is, the horizontal crossbar called a *patibulum*, until he collapses on the way, at which time Simon of Cyrene is pressed into service (Matt. 27:32 pars.).

6. So, with a variety of nuances, Witherington 1995: 308; R. Brown 1970: 917; Schnackenburg 1990: 3.270; and Moloney 1998: 502, 506. Carson (1991: 609), who says that the omission is due to John's desire to further highlight Jesus' willing obedience to the Father, dismisses as unduly speculative the view that the omission is part of a polemic against the theory that Simon of Cyrene was himself crucified (contra Beasley-Murray 1999: 345). Barrett (1978: 548) proposes that the omission is due to the evangelist's effort to highlight the "all-sufficiency of Jesus . . . in effecting the redemption of the world." Beasley-Murray (1999: 345 [cf. Borchert 2002: 261; R. Brown 1970: 917–18; contra Schnackenburg 1990: 3.270]) suggests that the omission serves to create an allusion to Isaac carrying the wood for his sacrifice.

7. The upper palm of the hand is considered most likely by Zugibe 1989: 41–43.

8. Later Jewish literature draws parallels between the crucifixion and Isaac's carrying the wood "like one carries his stake [= cross] on his shoulder" (*Gen. Rab.* 56.3 on Gen. 22:6; see R. Brown 1970: 917–18).

"He went out." Jewish custom prescribed that stonings take place outside the camp or city.[9] By extension, the same principle applied to crucifixions (cf. Heb. 13:12). The wording of the phrase "the Place of the Skull (Golgotha in Aramaic)" recalls the earlier description of "the place called Lithostratos (Gabbatha in Aramaic)" in 19:13. Greek "Golgotha" transliterates the Aramaic expression for "skull." The Latin equivalent (found in the Vulgate of all four Gospels) is "Calvary." The location may have derived its name from its skull-like appearance. A site just outside Gennath Gate, not far from the Church of the Holy Sepulchre, is the most likely option.[10]

They crucified him.[11] In ancient times, crucifixion was synonymous **19:18** with horror and shame, a death inflicted on slaves (Cicero, *In Verrem* 2.5.65.168), bandits (Josephus, *J.W.* 2.13.2 §253), prisoners of war (*J.W.* 5.11.1 §451), and revolutionaries (*Ant.* 17.10.10 §295).[12] Josephus terms it "the most pitiable of deaths" (*J.W.* 7.6.4 §203; cf. 1.4.6 §97), Cicero calls it "that cruel and disgusting penalty" (*In Verrem* 2.5.64.165). Those crucified were made a public spectacle, often being affixed to crosses in bizarre positions, and their bodies left to be devoured by vultures.[13] No Roman citizen could be subjected to this terrible punishment without the penalty being sanctioned by the emperor himself.

For hours (if not days), the victim would hang in the heat of the sun, stripped naked and struggling to breathe. In order to avoid asphyxiation, he had to push himself up with his legs and pull with his arms, triggering muscle spasms that caused almost unimaginable pain. The end would come through heart failure, brain damage caused by reduced oxygen supply, suffocation, or shock.[14] Atrocious physical agony, length of torment, and public shame combined to make crucifixion a most horrible form of death.[15] The crucifixion of Jesus is corroborated by extrabiblical writers (Tacitus, *Annales* 44.3; Josephus, *Ant.* 18.3.3 §§63–64).

---

9. See Lev. 24:14, 23; Num. 15:35–36; Deut. 17:5; 21:19–21; 22:24; Acts 7:58; cf. Luke 4:29.

10. See Riesner, *DJG* 43; Taylor 1998. "Gordon's Calvary" is ruled out by Parrot 1957: 59–65.

11. For an extensive discussion of Roman crucifixion, see Witherington 1995: 303–6. See also Borchert 2002: 263–64.

12. See Hengel 1977; Green, *DJG* 147–48; Malina and Rohrbaugh 1998: 263–64; D. Chapman 2000.

13. Seneca, *Ad Marciam de consolatione* 20.3 (A.D. 37–41); Pliny, *Natural History* 36.107–18; Josephus, *J.W.* 5.11.1 §451; Philo, *Dreams* 2.31 §213.

14. Shock as the cause of death is strongly argued by Zugibe (1989: 41): "Shock is unquestionably the cause of Jesus' death on the cross," referring also to the opinion of a surgeon who contends, "There is overwhelming evidence that Christ died from heart failure due to extreme shock caused by exhaustion, pain and loss of blood."

15. The remains of a crucified man, aged 24–28 years, dating roughly to Jesus' day were found in north Jerusalem in 1968. The man's name is incribed on his bone ossuary as Yehoḥanan ben Hagkol. See Charlesworth 1972–73.

Two others were crucified with Jesus, with him between the two. In the context of the Johannine narrative, this strikes one as a rather cursory remark (Witherington 1995: 308), anticipating the later reference in 19:32 (R. Brown 1970: 918). Possibly, the evangelist finds Jesus' crucifixion between two criminals reminiscent of Ps. 22:16: "A band of evil men has encircled me."[16] There is little direct evidence for the common assertion that Jesus' placement in the middle indicates greater importance.[17] Matthew and Mark identify these two others as bandits (λησταί, lēstai [Matt. 27:38 par.; cf. Luke 22:52; John 18:40]), possibly insurrectionists like Barabbas (Mark 15:7).[18]

19:19 "Pilate had a notice prepared" (TNIV) reads more literally "Pilate wrote a notice."[19] As the TNIV rendering reflects, Pilate probably did not write this notice himself but rather used the services of a literate slave.[20] The "notice" (Latin, titulus) was prepared—presumably written on a board whitened with gypsum (sanis, leukoma)—and fastened to the cross. Its purpose was most likely the public exposition of the person's specific crime, presumably to serve as a deterrent to others.[21]

The text of the sign (on whose trilingual nature, see below) was, "Jesus of Nazareth, the king of the Jews." This notice serves to indicate at least three things: (1) Jesus' conviction on the charge of treason; (2) Pilate's resentful exacting of a small measure of revenge upon the Jews; and (3) symbolism regarding Jesus being the Savior of the world (Carson 1991: 611).[22] The reference to Nazareth may constitute a further insult directed toward the Jews (Witherington 1995: 308).

16. The passage may also echo Isa. 53:12: "numbered with the transgressors" (Beasley-Murray 1999: 346; Bultmann 1971: 669 n. 1; R. Brown 1970: 900; more cautious is Carson [1991: 611–12]).

17. So, for example, Ridderbos 1997: 608; Beasley-Murray 1999: 346; Schnackenburg 1990: 3.270; Moloney 1998: 502; Schlatter 1948: 348; Westcott 1908: 2.308.

18. Although later Jewish legislation forbids condemning two persons on the same day (m. Sanh. 6.4), it is unlikely that this law was in effect in Jesus' day, and even if it was, that it would have been honored by the Romans. Earlier, the Jewish high priest Alexander Jannaeus (88 B.C.) had crucified eight hundred persons at the same time (Josephus, J.W. 1.4.6 §97).

19. Morris (1995: 713) suggests that the καί (kai, also) of 19:19 may indicate that the notice was another means used by Pilate to disgrace the Jews.

20. Cf. the causative use of "flogged" in 19:1. So the majority of commentators, including R. Brown 1970: 901; Carson 1991: 610; Morris 1995: 713; Barrett 1978: 549 (but see Borchert 2002: 265). See also commentary at 19:40.

21. See Suetonius, Domitian 10.1 (cited in Köstenberger 2002c: 176). Though instances are known in which a condemned man carried the notice around his neck or had it carried in front of him—such as "Attalus the Christian" during Marcus Aurelius's reign in the amphitheater in Lyons (Eusebius, Hist. eccl. 6.44)—there is little or no evidence for the custom of affixing it to a cross.

22. Bultmann (1971: 669) suggests that the title serves as a universal judgment of Judaism and the world, which have rejected their Savior; Barrett (1978: 549) notes that the title is symbolic of the world's universal condemnation of Jesus.

Many Jews (an instance of a neutral instance of this term in John's   19:20–22
Gospel) read this sign. The literacy level among first-century Palestinian Jews was high: "A pious Jew [in Jesus' day] . . . could read and
write" (Riesner 1981: 199). The comment that the place where Jesus was
crucified was near the city (see commentary at 19:17) associates Jerusalem with the death of Jesus (Morris 1995: 714). The sign was written
in Aramaic, Latin, and Greek.[23] If the order given reflects the order in
which the inscriptions were written, then Aramaic, the language most
widely understood by the Jewish population of Palestine, took pride of
place.[24] Aramaic (see commentary at 5:2) was the language commonly
in use in Judea (cf. Acts 21:40); Latin was the official language of the
Roman occupying force; and Greek was the "international language"
of the empire, understood by most Diaspora Jews as well as Gentiles.[25]
By writing the sign in those three languages, the Romans (including
Pilate in the present instance [Ridderbos 1997: 609]) ensured widest
possible circulation of its contents as a deterrent to every segment of
the population.[26]

Upon seeing the sign, the chief priests of the Jews[27] register their
protest to Pilate, urging that the sign be changed to reflect the notion
that Jesus ("this man" may carry a derogatory connotation [R. Brown
1970: 902]) only claimed to be the king of the Jews.[28] Yet, with newly
resurgent resolve (Borchert 2002: 266), now that he has given in to the
Jews on the big issue (having Jesus crucified), Pilate is resolute on a
minor matter: "What I have written, I have written."[29] "No longer faced
with the possibility of mob unrest or a complaint to Tiberius, Pilate

23. For a reconstruction of the sign, see Köstenberger 2002c: 177; Avi-Yonah 1964:
153.

24. R. Brown (1970: 901) notes that some MSS alter the order by placing Greek before
Latin, in which case the Latin would occupy the "place of dignity at the end."

25. Inscriptions warning Gentiles against entering the inner temple were written mainly
in Greek (see commentary at 2:14).

26. Polyglot notices were quite common in the Hellenistic era. Examples include those
cited by Josephus (*Ant.* 14.10.2 §191; *J.W.* 6.2.4 §125) and the *Res Gestae Divi Augusti*,
which existed in both Latin and Greek. Schlatter (1948: 349) also refers to *m. Giṭ.* 9.8 (bills
of divorce written in both Greek and Hebrew). See also Esth. 8:9. Blinzler (1959: 254–55)
refers to still extant Roman tombstones.

27. According to Morris (1995: 714 n. 51), the reference to the "chief priests of the
Jews" may be designed to create a contrast with the "king of the Jews."

28. "Do not write" in 19:21 somewhat unexpectedly involves a present-tense verb (γράφε,
graphe). Wallace (1996: 487–88) classifies the form as an imperative of entreaty. Barrett
(1978: 549, following N. Turner 1963) proposes the translation "Alter what you have written" (i.e., "Do not go on writing [what you have written]"; cf. R. Brown 1970: 902).

29. The double perfect of γέγραφα (*gegrapha*, I have written) conveys a sense of finality,
portraying Pilate's action as a fait accompli (Ridderbos 1997: 609 n. 134; Morris 1995: 714
n. 54). Bultmann (1971: 670 n. 2 [cf. R. Brown 1970: 902]) suggests that the first perfect
is aoristic; Wallace (1996: 577) lists 19:22 as an example of an extensive perfect focusing
on the completion of an action in the past. Similar word combinations are found also in

returns to his characteristic lack of cooperation" (Keener 1993: 313). The request of the Jewish authorities clashed with the Roman respect for written documents, a legal decision that could not be reversed. For John, Pilate's firmness may again relate to his speaking better than he knew: for Jesus is the King of kings and Lord of lords, and there is no other.[30] Hence, Pilate is portrayed as in some sense favorable toward declaring Jesus "king of the Jews," despite his verdict of crucifixion, which is shown to be merely a means of appeasing the Jews for political expediency (see R. Brown 1970: 919).

19:23–24 They took his clothes—presumably, Jesus' belt, sandals, head-covering, and outer garment (Carson 1991: 612).[31] Romans normally stripped crucified persons naked. It is possible, however, that in deference to the Jewish aversion to public nudity Jesus was left with his underclothing.[32] This may be suggested by the use of the word ἱμάτια (*himatia*), which generally referred to the outer garment in distinction from the undergarment (called χιτών, *chitōn*) (Barrett 1978: 550).[33]

They divided his clothing into four pieces, one for each soldier.[34] "Four pieces" indicates that the execution squad consisted of four soldiers, half the size of the basic unit of the Roman army—that is, eight soldiers sharing a tent (the *contubernium*)—which sometimes was assigned to particular tasks (in Acts 12:4, Peter is "guarded by four squads of four soldiers each"; see Keener 1993: 313). According to the Synoptics, a centurion was present as well. It is possible that additional soldiers were involved in preparing the other two men for crucifixion.

Jesus' undergarment was of one piece, woven seamlessly from top to bottom.[35] Using a seamless piece of cloth precluded the possibility that

---

the LXX (Gen. 43:14; Esth. 4:16; 1 Macc. 13:38) and in rabbinic literature (*b. Menaḥ.* 3a; *b. Ketub.* 96a; *b. Yebam.* 106b) (cited in Köstenberger 2002c: 177; further instances are cited in Schlatter 1948: 349). Perhaps significantly, similar phrases are found also in a Roman context (note Cicero, *Epistulae ad Quintum fratrem* 1.2.2; 1.2.13: *scripsi, scripsi*). Keener's (2003: 1138) observation that every other instance of "written" in this Gospel refers to Scripture (2:17; 6:31, 45; 8:17; 10:34; 12:14, 16; 15:25), which cannot be broken (10:35), seems of doubtful relevance here.

30. Carson (1991: 611) notes that Caiaphas and Pilate unwittingly serve a prophetic function in the Johannine narrative (cf. Beasley-Murray 1999: 346; Bultmann 1971: 669).

31. If a later collection of Roman law also reflects earlier practice, then the soldiers were to take Jesus' clothes into custody but not necessarily keep them for themselves. See Justinian, *Digesta* 48.20 (cited in Köstenberger 2002c: 177; contra Barrett 1978: 550).

32. A dispute about whether or not a man about to be stoned should be completely stripped is recorded in *m. Sanh.* 6.3.

33. People of that day wore a loin cloth, undergarments, an outer garment, a belt, a head covering, and sandals (Daniel-Rops 1962: 211–18).

34. It is unclear whether the soldiers overstepped legal bounds when dividing up Jesus' robe among themselves.

35. The general conclusion of commentators is that the reference to the "seamless robe" may not necessarily have theological significance (e.g., Ridderbos 1997: 610 n. 136;

two materials had been joined together, something that was forbidden (Lev. 19:19; cf. Deut. 22:11). Such a garment could be woven without exceptional skill and was not necessarily a luxury item.[36] In the OT, it was Joseph who was stripped of his robe (Gen. 37:3, 23), which in later Jewish thought was interpreted in salvific terms (*Gen. Rab.* 84.8).

"This happened in order that the Scripture may be fulfilled." OT references become more frequent in the Johannine narrative with Jesus' passion approaching, presumably because John's Jewish audience would have been particularly skeptical about a crucified Messiah (Carson 1991: 612; Witherington 1995: 308). The OT reference in view clearly is Ps. 22:18, a Davidic messianic passage regarding the righteous sufferer, which the Fourth Evangelist sees fulfilled in Jesus.[37]

The Greek construction μὲν . . . δέ (*men . . . de*) links the soldiers in 19:24b with those associated with Jesus who stood near the cross.[38] **19:25–27** Several people stood by the cross of Jesus. Although there is little direct evidence to confirm the notion, it appears that crucified persons may have been surrounded by family, friends, and relatives.[39] In an apparently conflicting statement, the Synoptic writers mention that at one

---

cf. Morris 1995: 715, esp. n. 56; Bultmann 1971: 671). Both Witherington (1995: 309) and R. Brown (1970: 920–22) note several possibilities yet caution against dogmatic conclusions (see also Carson 1991: 614). Barrett (1978: 550) sees an allusion to Jesus' death resulting in "the scattered children of God."

36. See Repond 1922; Dalman 1928–39: 5.126–29. Josephus notes that the high priestly robe (χιτών, *chitōn*) was "not composed of two pieces, . . . [but] one long woven cloth" (*Ant.* 3.7.4 §161; cf. Exod. 28:31; Rev. 1:13), while Philo uses a robe as symbolic of the Logos, which binds all things together in unity (*Flight* 20 §§110–12). However, it is far from certain whether the present passage alludes to the high-priestly garment (or the unity of the church, for that matter) (so, rightly, Carson 1991: 614; contra Moloney 1998: 503, 507). Carson (1991: 614–15) and Beasley-Murray (1999: 347–48), following Schnackenburg (1990: 3.274), see in the preservation of the seamless tunic an allusion to the Father's preservation of the Son; Carson also sees a connection with the footwashing.

37. See the extensive discussion by Carson (1991: 614), who contends that "the Evangelist sees in the *entire* distribution of Jesus' clothes a fulfillment of *both* lines of Psalm 22:18, but mentions the peculiarity of the decision about the tunic because he was an eyewitness, and possibly because he saw something symbolic in the seamless garment." Regarding the use of Ps. 22 in ancient Jewish writings, see Str-B 2:574–80. Regarding the "fulfillment quotations" in the latter half of John's Gospel, which reach their crescendo in the passion narrative, see commentary at 12:38. "So this is what the soldiers did" seeks to bring closure to the section narrating the soldiers' actions (19:16b–24).

38. There is no agreement, however, on the exact way in which soldiers and bystanders are related by the evangelist. Ridderbos (1997: 610 [cf. R. Brown 1970: 903]) thinks that there is no implied contrast between these two groups. Other commentators believe that the construction does imply such a contrast (e.g., Carson 1991: 615; Barrett 1978: 551; Beasley-Murray 1999: 348; Schnackenburg 1990: 3.273, 276). If a contrast is intended, it is hardly a sharp one; more likely, the two groups are distinguished as the narrative moves from one to the other.

39. According to one talmudic passage, a rabbi stood under the gallows of a hanged disciple and wept (*b. B. Meṣiʿa* 83b; see Stauffer 1960: 111–12, 179 n. 1).

---

point the women stood far off.[40] However, during the several hours of vigil, it is possible, even likely, that there would be a certain amount of coming and going on the part of Jesus' acquaintances.[41]

As to the group composed of Jesus' mother, his mother's sister, Mary the wife of Clopas, and Mary Magdalene, the Greek wording allows for the reference to indicate the presence of two, three, or four women.[42] The wording adopted by the TNIV plausibly interprets there to be four women:[43] (1) Mary, Jesus' mother (here, as elsewhere, not named in this Gospel [see commentary at 2:1–5]); (2) his mother's sister (perhaps Salome, the mother of the sons of Zebedee, mentioned in Matthew and Mark);[44] (3) Mary the wife of Clopas (cf. Luke 24:18?); and (4) Mary Magdalene (cf. John 20:1–18).[45]

The focal point prior to Jesus' death in the Fourth Gospel is the moving scene involving "the disciple Jesus loved"[46] and Jesus' mother.[47] Jesus'

---

40. Beasley-Murray (1999: 348–39) actually suggests that the women who stood afar could have been different women.

41. The historicity of 19:25 is buttressed by several factors (Carson 1991: 615; cf. Beasley-Murray 1999: 349; Witherington 1995: 309; contra Barrett 1978: 551–52): (1) the Roman soldiers most likely would not have cared to remove women from the vicinity of the cross; (2) Jesus' disciples would not have been seen as a threat by the Roman administration; (3) the fact that the sign affixed to the cross was intended to be read, and in fact was read (19:20), by many implies that people could get close enough to the cross to read it; (4) the Gospels record as many as seven statements by Jesus on the cross, suggesting that people were close enough to hear him speak.

42. See the extensive discussions in Carson 1991: 616; R. Brown 1970: 905–6. Symbolic interpretations (such as Brodie 1993: 549; Stibbe 1993: 194) fail to convince.

43. So also the vast majority of commentators: e.g., Ridderbos 1997: 611; Carson 1991: 615; Barrett 1978: 551; Morris 1995: 716–17; Beasley-Murray 1999: 348; Bultmann 1971: 672; Borchert 2002: 268; R. Brown 1970: 904; Schnackenburg 1990: 3.276. Ridderbos (1997: 611 n. 142) notes that in light of Mark 15:40 and Matt. 27:56, there could have been other women there as well. See also Luke 23:49.

44. See Ridderbos 1997: 611; Carson 1991: 616; Beasley-Murray 1999: 348; Burge 2000: 528; contra Barrett 1978: 551–52; Bultmann 1971: 672 n. 5; Schnackenburg 1990: 3.277. Carson (1991: 616 [cf. Morris 1995: 717]) notes that, like Jesus' mother's sister, Jesus' mother is also unnamed here and elsewhere in the Gospel (as is the "disciple Jesus loved" in 19:26–27).

45. Westcott (1908: 2.313) notes how Mary Magdalene is "introduced abruptly, as well known, without any explanation." According to Luke 8:2–3, this Mary is a woman from Magdala, a village on the western shore of the Sea of Galilee, from whom Jesus had exorcized seven demons.

46. Many view the "disciple Jesus loved" as an ideal disciple, often in conjunction with the "ideal faith" of Jesus' mother (e.g., Moloney 1998: 503–4; but see the dissenting voice of Carson 1991: 618; cf. Ridderbos 1997: 614–15). Witherington (1995: 310) suggests that these two unnamed individuals are models for potential disciples to follow. Ridderbos (1997: 613) has an extensive discussion of Mary and the "disciple Jesus loved" as representatives of the new community that is established with the death of Jesus.

47. Commentators have detected various types of symbolism in this scene. Bultmann (1971: 673), true to F. C. Baur, sees Mary as representative of Jewish Christianity, and the beloved disciple of Gentile Christianity, the latter being charged to honor the former as its

mother, who almost certainly was widowed and probably in her early fifties with little or no personal income, was dependent on Jesus, her oldest son. In keeping with the biblical injunction to honor one's parents (Exod. 20:12; Deut. 5:16), Jesus makes here provision for his mother.[48] It may be surprising that Jesus entrusts his mother to the "disciple Jesus loved" rather than to one of his brothers, but this may be explained by his brothers' unbelief (7:5) (so, e.g., Laney 1992: 348).[49]

Jesus' mother is addressed as "woman." As in 2:4, the only other place where Jesus' mother is featured in John's Gospel (apart from brief mentions in 2:12 and 6:42), the term translated "dear woman" in the NIV is γύναι (gynai; TNIV: "mother"), which more literally means simply "woman." Ἀπ' ἐκείνης τῆς ὥρας (ap' ekeinēs tēs hōras) intends "from," not "because of," that hour (contra Moloney 1998: 503). The phrase εἰς τὰ ἴδια (eis ta idia) means "home,"[50] as in the beloved disciple taking Mary into his home (Morris 1995: 718), and nothing more (contra Ridderbos 1997: 613–14; Barrett 1978: 552).

b. The Death of Jesus (19:28–37)

The phrase μετὰ τοῦτο (meta touto, after this) sets off from the present one the preceding small pericope regarding the beloved disciple and Jesus' mother. "Because Jesus knew that everything had already been accom-   **19:28–30**

"mother," from whom it originated (cf. Brodie 1993: 549). Witherington (1995: 309) views these two characters as symbolic of a new Adam and Eve, who are obedient whereas the former were not. Carson (1991: 618, following M. Gourgues) suggests that Mary, on account of her faith in Christ, is now able metaphorically to become a mother to a new son supplied for her by Jesus (cf. Matt. 19:29; see also Witherington 1995: 310). Beasley-Murray (1999: 350, following Schnackenburg 1990: 3.278) sees Mary as representing that part of Israel that is willing to believe in Jesus as the Messiah. Refreshingly, and refusing to resort to symbolism or allegory, Morris (1995: 718) says the beloved disciple simply "provided her [Mary] with a roof" and took her under his care. Others focus on lessons (to be) learned by Mary, such as needing to "step back in submission to the law of life that the Father has set for her son" (Ridderbos 1997: 612) or to receive the gift of salvation that she desired to receive at the wedding in Cana (Schnackenburg 1990: 3.278; Beasley-Murray 1999: 350; Borchert 2002: 269).

48. In antiquity, a dying person ordinarily would entrust his mother to another with a direct charge such as this: "I leave to you my mother to be taken care of" (Lagrange 1925: 494 [cited in R. Brown 1970: 907]; cf. Lucian, *Toxaris* 22). In the LXX, the adoption formula is generally "you are" rather than "here is" as in the present passage ("'Mother, here is your son' . . . 'Here is your mother'"; cf. Ps. 2:7; Tob. 7:12). The form of expression used in John has a Semitic ring. Speaking of "the official formula of the old Jewish family law," one commentator refers to a crucified man's "right to make testamentary dispositions, even from the cross" (Stauffer 1960: 13; cf. Borchert 2002: 269; Schnackenburg 1990: 3.278).

49. Some Roman Catholic interpreters contend, implausibly, that this statement proves that Mary did not, in fact, have other children after Jesus, for if he had had siblings, he would not have entrusted his mother to "the disciple he loved." For a discussion on 19:26–27 in the ancient cultural context, see Keener 2003: 1144–45.

50. Though not necessarily in allusion to 1:11, where the identical phrase is found (see Carson 1991: 617 n. 2; Moloney 1998: 503–4).

plished" marks the point immediately prior to Jesus' death at which everything that brought Jesus to the cross in keeping with God's sovereign plan
had taken place.[51] "In order that the Scripture might be fulfilled" continues
19:24.[52] The reference to Jesus saying, "I am thirsty," for the purpose of
Scripture being fulfilled[53] is in keeping with the evangelist's emphasis on
Jesus actively bringing about the respective events of his passion.

The present reference most likely represents an allusion to Ps. 69:21:
"They . . . gave me vinegar for my thirst."[54] Beyond this, the allusion may
involve the entire psalm in its portrayal of the righteous sufferer (Ridderbos 1997: 616; Carson 1991: 620). The substance called "vinegar" in
the current passage was a cheap, sour wine that was used by soldiers to
quench their thirst (Mark 15:36; cf. Ps. 69:21). It differs from the "wine
mixed with myrrh" that Jesus was offered, and that he refused, on the
way to the cross (Mark 15:23). Whereas the latter was a sedative, "wine
vinegar" prolonged life and therefore pain.

They put the sponge on a stalk of the hyssop plant (Carson 1991:
621; Beasley-Murray 1999: 318 n. q).[55] Hyssop is "a small bushy plant
that can grow out of cracks in walls, a plant that 1 Kings iv 33 classifies as the humblest of shrubs" (R. Brown 1970: 909).[56] It was used for
the sprinkling of blood on the doorpost at the original Passover (Exod.
12:22).[57] In the present instance, the branches at the end of the stalk
would have formed a little nest into which the soggy sponge would have
been placed (Nestle 1913). Since crucified people were not raised very
high off the ground, the soldiers would have had to lift the stalk barely
above their own heads.[58]

---

51. As Carson (1991: 619) points out, this is not obviated by the presence of fulfillment
quotations subsequent to the present reference. The adverb ἤδη (ēdē, already) further
stresses the notion of fulfillment.

52. The verb used here for "fulfill" is τελειόω (teleioō) rather than πληρόω (plēroō),
perhaps to connect it with the cognate form τελέω in the previous clause and in 19:30
(Carson 1991: 620; Barrett 1978: 553).

53. The vast majority of commentators connect the reference to Scripture being fulfilled
with Jesus' statement (e.g., Carson 1991: 619; Barrett 1978: 553; Schnackenburg 1990:
3.283; though Morris [1995: 719] seems to suggest that it might be deliberately ambiguous). Contra R. Brown (1970: 908), who seems to prefer linking Jesus' statement with his
words to Mary and the beloved disciple.

54. So Ridderbos 1997: 616; Carson 1991: 619; Barrett 1978: 553; Schnackenburg 1990:
3.283; Schlatter 1948: 351. Psalm 69:21 is also cited in the Qumran hymn 1QH 12:11. Another relevant passage is Ps. 22:15 (Schlatter 1948: 351; Kruse 2003: 369). The suggestion
that Jesus here refers back to his statement in 18:11 is improbable (so, rightly, Ridderbos
1997: 617; contra Schnackenburg 1990: 3.283; R. Brown 1970: 930).

55. This detail is provided only by John.

56. There is some uncertainty as to the exact species of hyssop referred to here; see the
discussion in Wilkinson 1964: 77; Shewell-Cooper 1962: 75–76; Beetham 1993.

57. Hence, Stibbe (1993: 196) says that it is very probable that Passover symbolism
is intended here.

58. The action of lifting the stalk to Jesus' lips seems unusual for a member of the
Roman execution squad, especially in light of their earlier treatment of Jesus. For this

"It is accomplished" (cf. 4:34; 17:4).[59] In this, the second and major climax of John's Gospel (see commentary at 10:30), Jesus triumphantly announces the completion of his mission entrusted to him by the Father at what may be considered the lowest point of his life, his death by crucifixion. Jesus dies on Friday afternoon, with the Sabbath approaching, just as God completed his work of creation at the end of the sixth day in order to rest on the seventh (Hengel 1999: 319). Bowing his head was not a sign of weakness on Jesus' part but rather a deliberate act prior to giving up his spirit.[60]

The entire following section of 19:31–42 answers the question "What happened to Jesus' body?" (Ridderbos 1997: 618). In the first unit (19:31–37) the body is removed from the cross by the soldiers; in the second unit (19:38–42) the body is given proper burial by Joseph of Arimathea and Nicodemus (Bultmann 1971: 666). The "day of preparation of Passover week" was Friday, Nisan 15 (see commentary at 19:14).[61] The Sabbath following it was special because it was the Sabbath of Passover week. An important sheaf offering was made on this day as well (Lev. 23:11; see Str-B 2:582; Carson 1991: 622; Ridderbos 1997: 618). **19:31–34**

Because the Jews did not want the bodies left on the crosses during the Sabbath, they asked Pilate to have the legs broken and the bodies taken down. The Jews' attitude was based on Deut. 21:22–23 (cf. Josh. 8:29), according to which bodies of hanged criminals must not defile the land by remaining on a tree overnight. The Romans would leave crucified persons on their crosses until death ensued (which could take days) and their bodies were devoured by vultures.[62] There is also evidence that at times, especially during feast days, bodies were taken down and given to relatives (Philo, *Flacc.* 10 §83).[63]

In order to hasten death, the victims' legs (and sometimes other bones) would be smashed with an iron mallet, a practice called *crurifragium*

---

reason some have conjectured that there may be a link with the centurion acknowledging Jesus as "Son of God" in Mark 15:39.

59. Beasley-Murray (1999: 353) suggests that this might be the "loud cry" referred to in Mark 15:37. Westcott (1908: 2.317) provides a helpful chronological synthesis of Jesus' "seven words" from the cross.

60. Borchert 2002: 272–73; Schnackenburg 1990: 3.284; contra Bultmann 1971: 675. The same word, παραδίδωμι (*paradidōmi*, give up) is used in Isa. 53:12 to describe the death of the suffering Servant (Morris 1995: 721 n. 81).

61. So the vast majority of commentators (e.g., Ridderbos 1997: 618; Carson 1991: 622; Barrett 1978: 555; Morris 1995: 730; Bultmann 1971: 676). Contra Borchert (2002: 273 [cf. R. Brown 1970: 933]), who seems to suggest that Jesus died on Nisan 14 and thus was being portrayed as the Passover lamb.

62. Though Roman law does seem to have allowed burial of crucified people, as is suggested by a passage attributed to the first-century A.D. rhetorician Quintilian (*Declamationes* 6.9 [cited in Köstenberger 2002c: 179]).

63. Josephus indicates that application of this passage was later extended to cover the crucified (*J.W.* 4.5.2 §317; cf. Gal. 3:13).

("breaking of the shinbone"). This prevented the person from prolonging life by pushing himself up with his legs in order to breathe. Arm strength soon failed, and asphyxiation ensued. In the case of the body of a man crucified in the first century and found in 1968 north of Jerusalem (see commentary at 19:18), one leg had been fractured, the other broken to pieces (Haas 1970; Zias and Sekeles 1985; Shanks 1985). The Jews' request is their last action recorded in this Gospel.

When the soldiers came to Jesus, they saw that he was already dead. The series of floggings would have substantially weakened Jesus.[64] What is more, Jesus probably had not slept since the previous day. The spear may have pierced Jesus' heart,[65] resulting, either directly or via chest and lung, in the flow of blood and water.[66] The flow of blood and water underscores that Jesus died as a fully human being.[67] Perhaps "blood and water" also points to Jesus' two natures, human and divine.[68] The parallel 1 John 5:6–8 refers to spirit, water, and blood; Jesus gave up his spirit when he died (19:30), leaving behind blood and water.[69]

John also may be alluding to Exod. 17, especially v. 6: "Strike the rock, and water will come out of it for the people to drink" (cf. Num. 20:11; see Carson 1991: 624).[70] An allusion to the Passover may also be

64. See commentary at 19:1, 17 on Jesus' two floggings.

65. Roman soldiers used primarily two kinds of weapons: a short sword for close combat and a lance or javelin for attacks from a distance. The lance (*pilum*) was about three and a half feet long and was made up of an iron point or spearhead (λόγχη, *lonchē*) joined to a shaft of light wood (Avi-Yonah 1964: 154). Later, the term λόγχη (the word used in the present passage) came to be used for a spear or lance itself.

66. See the summary in Carson 1991: 623–24, and the fuller treatment in Beasley-Murray 1999: 355–58. For further discussion, see Barbet 1953; W. Edwards, Gabel, and Hosmer 1986; Sava 1960.

67. See *Lev. Rab.* 15.2 on Lev. 13:2. Commentators disagree as to whether or not the present reference is intended to counter incipient Docetism, which denied Jesus' full humanity at his death. Some consider this unlikely (Ridderbos [1997: 620], who thinks that the present passage is simply designed to further support the reliability and eyewitness nature of the account; R. Brown 1970: 949–52), while a majority favors such a polemic purpose (e.g., Carson [1991: 623], who sees this verse as the "counterpoint" to 1:14; Barrett 1978: 556; Morris 1995: 724; Beasley-Murray 1999: 356; Borchert 2002: 276–77; Burge 2000: 532).

68. Homeric mythology held that the gods were bloodless and had a kind of blood-water flowing through their veins (*Iliad* 5.339–42; cf. Plutarch, *Moralia* 180E). Stibbe (1992: 118, with reference to Barrett) sees in the flow of blood and water "the paradoxical association of life-giving properties with a dead man's body." Less likely is Whitacre's (1999: 466) "sacramental" interpretation of blood and water symbolizing the Eucharist and baptism.

69. Burge (1987: 93–95), referring to 7:37–39, views 19:34 as "a proleptic symbol of the release of the Spirit," which is realized in 20:22. He views this as an instance of Johannine paradox: what was meant to ensure the victim's death resulted in the unleashing of the life-giving water/Spirit within. However, Burge's understanding of 19:34 is predicated upon a christological reading of 7:37–39 (see commentary and critique there).

70. Later Jewish thought held that Moses struck the rock twice and that it yielded first blood, then water (*Exod. Rab.* 3.13 on Exod. 4:9).

in view (*m. Pesaḥ.* 5.5–8; cf. *m. ʾOhal.* 3.5), consisting of (1) the hyssop (19:29); (2) the unbroken bones (19:33, 36); and (3) the mingled blood (19:34) (Barrett 1978: 557; Burge 2000: 532; Ford 1969). If so, then John may witness to all three events that portray Jesus as the Passover lamb. Moreover, Jewish sacrificial law required that the victim's blood not be congealed, but rather flow freely at the moment of death so that it could be sprinkled (*m. Pesaḥ.* 5.3, 5).[71]

"The one who has seen it has borne witness."[72] The author (identified in the   **19:35–37** concluding verses of the Gospel as the beloved disciple [Ridderbos 1997: 620; Carson 1991: 625; Morris 1995: 725]) here plainly claims to be an eyewitness of Jesus' crucifixion. The eyewitness character of the entire Gospel is affirmed in the concluding statement of 21:24–25 (see also 20:30–31). The pronoun ἐκεῖνος (*ekeinos*, he) in the phrase "*He* knows that he speaks truthfully" presumably refers to that same eyewitness, identical to the Fourth Evangelist.[73] The use of ὑμεῖς (*hymeis*, you) as an address to John's readers is startling and unprecedented in this Gospel. As in 20:31, the purpose of the evangelist's testimony is to engender faith in Jesus as the Messiah.

This call to faith, in turn, is issued on the basis of Scripture being fulfilled in Jesus (γάρ, *gar*, for; see Ridderbos 1997: 622): "They did not break his bones." Remarkably, not only did Jesus escape the breaking of his legs (unlike those crucified with him), but also his body was pierced by a spear without sustaining bone damage.[74] Two sets of Scripture converge: (1) Ps. 34:20, depicting God's care for the righteous man: "[The Lord] protects all his bones, not one of them will be broken"; and (2) Exod. 12:46 and Num. 9:12, specifying that no bone of the Passover lamb may be broken (applied to Jesus in 1 Cor. 5:7; 1 Pet. 1:19).[75]

"And again, another Scripture says, 'They will look at the one they have pierced.'" The passage in view is plainly Zech. 12:10 (cf. Rev. 1:7). Though the Hebrew of this passage appears to refer to the piercing of Yahweh himself (figuratively, with sorrow), later messianic interpretation developed this notion into the belief that the Messiah would be

---

71. Jewish law also insisted that the priest "slit the [lamb's] heart and let out its blood" (*m. Tamid* 4.2).

72. The double perfect ὁ ἑωρακὼς μεμαρτύρηκεν (*ho heōrakōs memartyrēken*, the one who has seen has testified) conveys the settled, established nature of this witness.

73. Contra Bultmann (1971: 678), who seems to suggest that the pronoun refers to Jesus. See the extensive discussion of this verse in Carson 1991: 625–26.

74. Apparently, "in Jewish thought disfiguration was an obstacle to resurrection," which may further explain why John takes pains to stress that no bone was broken (Daube 1956: 325–29).

75. So R. Brown 1970: 952–53; Moloney 1998: 509. Beasley-Murray (1999: 355) suggests that the source of the Fourth Gospel was alluding to Passover typology, while the evangelist is alluding to the righteous sufferer of Ps. 34. Somewhat ironically, Barrett (1978: 558) proposes the exact converse: the source is alluding to the Psalms typology, while the evangelist is alluding to Passover typology. Ridderbos (1997: 622–23) opts for the Psalms typology but denies the Passover allusion.

pierced and people would look to Yahweh (*b. Sukkah* 52a; but see 5/6 HevPsalms: "They have pierced my hands and feet"). John, for his part, saw the fulfillment of Zech. 12:10 at the crucifixion as confirmation that the Messiah was Jesus (cf. 20:31).

Significantly, the fulfillment entails a reversal: it is as the one pierced that Jesus becomes the source of salvation for those who look at him in faith. In fact, all humanity will have to look at the pierced Messiah at the last judgment—to receive either final deliverance or final punishment (Ridderbos 1997: 623–24). A related OT figure that may have been in John's mind is that of the suffering Servant of Isa. 53:5, 10, who was "pierced for our transgressions" and "crushed" and "caused to suffer."

c. The Burial of Jesus (19:38–42)

19:38 As a member of the Sanhedrin (Mark 15:43 par. Luke 23:50), Joseph of Arimathea was wealthy (Matt. 27:57; cf. Isa. 53:9) yet "waiting for the kingdom of God" (Mark 15:43 = Luke 23:50). Although Joseph is mentioned in all four Gospels in relation to Jesus' burial, apart from John only Matthew (27:57) refers to him as a disciple of Jesus; John adds that he was a disciple secretly for fear of the Jews. This reluctance to identify with Jesus openly is hardly commendable (cf. 12:42–43), but Joseph's present action shows considerable courage and respect (if not devotion); for it was common for disciples to arrange for their teacher's burial.[76] Joseph's intervention fulfilled another Scripture: "He was assigned a grave with the wicked, and with the rich in his death" (Isa. 53:9) (Witherington 1995: 313).[77] Of the several suggestions for the location of Arimathea, none is in Galilee, which would make Joseph one of Jesus' Judean followers.[78]

Joseph asked Pilate's permission to take Jesus' body. The Romans usually handed over executed criminals to the closest relative. In the case of crucifixion, however, the rotting bodies were left to the vultures, both as a stern public warning and as the epitome of shame. The Jews, on the other hand, buried even such people, yet rather than allowing their corpses to desecrate previously buried ones (the result if placed in a family tomb), a separate burial site was provided just outside the city.[79] Doubtless the Jewish authorities' request that the bodies be taken down (19:31) presupposed this arrangement. Joseph of Arimathea, however,

---

76. R. Brown (1970: 939) conjectures that Pilate's releasing the body to Joseph suggests that he was not an overt disciple of Jesus, because the Roman governor would not have done this for an ardent follower of Jesus. Contra Ridderbos (1997: 625, reacting against Martyn), who claims that Joseph of Arimathea and Nicodemus are symbolic of the "true Israel."

77. For a survey of funerary customs in antiquity and a discussion of the likely location of Jesus' burial site, see Green, *DJG* 88–92.

78. One possibility is the Judean village Ramathaim-Zophim (1 Sam. 1:1).

79. See Josephus, *Ant.* 5.1.14 §44: Achar "given the ignominious burial proper to the condemned." Cf. *m. Sanh.* 6.5.

used his position as a member of the Sanhedrin to gain access to Pilate and to secure a more dignified burial for Jesus. As mentioned, Joseph's act took some courage, since Jesus had been accused of subversive activities against both the Jews and the Romans.

Like Joseph of Arimathea, Nicodemus was a member of the Sanhedrin, **19:39–40** a "ruler" (see commentary at 3:1; 7:50–52).[80] The men brought along a mixture of myrrh and aloes—literally, one hundred λίτραι (*litrai* [see commentary at 12:3]), or about sixty-five pounds (rather than seventy-five pounds, as in the TNIV), a considerable amount (noted by Keener 2003: 1163).[81] Myrrh, a fragrant resin used by Egyptians in embalming (Herodotus, *Historiae* 2.86 [the Romans often cremated their dead]), was turned by the Jews into a powder and mixed with aloes, itself a powder of aromatic sandalwood, with which it is regularly associated in the OT (cf. Ps. 45:8; Prov. 7:17; Song 4:14).

In the Jewish context, the mixture was intended to overcome the smell of putrefaction. From the narrative, it appears that Joseph took care of legal matters, while Nicodemus brought the spices. Very possibly, servants were used to carry the aromatic mixture, take Jesus' body down from the cross and transport it to the burial place, and prepare it for burial. During the times of Israel's monarchy, King Asa died and was laid on "a bier covered with spices and various blended perfumes" (2 Chron. 16:14). Later, "five hundred servants carrying spices" participated in the funeral procession of Herod the Great (Josephus, *Ant.* 17.8.3 §199).

The two of them wrapped Jesus' body, along with the spices, in strips of linen. This was in accordance with Jewish burial customs.[82] "They wrapped" need not necessarily imply that Joseph and Nicodemus performed this task themselves (see commentary at 19:19). More likely, they used slaves in order not to contract ritual impurity (Num. 19:11), which would have prevented them from celebrating the Passover (cf. 18:28). Apparently, spices were spread along the linen wrappings (ὀθόνια, *othonia* [see commentary at 11:44; Hepper 1989]) as well as underneath and perhaps around Jesus' body. Then the strips were wound around the corpse. Additional spices may have been spread near the entrance of the tomb. In Jesus' day, burial clothes still tended to be luxurious; in around A.D. 90, Rabbi Gamaliel II simplified procedures by having the dead buried in simple linen robes (*sadin*). Remarkably, the washing of

---

80. Nicodemus's description by the evangelist as "the man who had earlier visited Jesus at night" harks back to 3:2 (see there the discussion, and ultimately the negative evaluation, of Nicodemus's putative "progression" in faith throughout the narrative). Contra Carson (1991: 629 [cf. Witherington 1995: 312]), who believes that Nicodemus is, in the present context, presented as "stepping out of the darkness and emerging into the light."

81. Though not necessarily an exaggeration (as Lindars [1972: 592] charges).

82. This is but one place in his Gospel where John provides information regarding Jewish customs (cf. 2:6; 4:9; 11:55; 18:28).

Jesus' body, the most important service rendered to a dead person, is not mentioned by any of the evangelists.[83]

19:41–42 Providentially, "everything in the immediate surroundings proves to be available to him [Jesus] as though it has long been reserved and made ready for him" (cf. Mark 11:2).[84] At the place where Jesus was crucified (see 19:17, 20) there was a garden.[85] The term for "garden" (κῆπος, *kēpos*) points to a more elaborate structure, such as an orchard or a plantation.[86] Later Jewish legislation discouraged the planting of fruit trees near burial sites. In OT times, King Manasseh of Judah was buried in the family tomb in his "palace garden" (2 Kings 21:18), as was his son and successor, Amon (2 Kings 21:26). According to Neh. 3:16 LXX (cf. Acts 2:29), the popular tomb of David was situated in a garden as well.

"In the garden was a fresh tomb, in which no one had ever been laid" (cf. Matt. 27:60).[87] Burying a crucified person in a fresh tomb was doubtless less offensive to the Jewish authorities than using a grave that had previously been used (Lindars 1972: 593).[88] The tomb's proximity to Golgotha and its location in a garden concur with speculation that the site of the crucifixion is just outside the second north wall of the city (see commentary at 19:17). In fact, one of the four openings in the north wall was the Garden Gate ("Gennath" [cf. Josephus, *J.W.* 5.4.2 §146]). This (prestigious) area also housed the tombs of the Hasmonean high priests John Hyrcanus and Alexander Jannaeus (*J.W.* 5.6.2 §259; 5.7.2 §304]).[89]

Because the tomb was nearby, they laid Jesus there. Sabbath was rapidly approaching, when all work must cease, including that of carrying spices or transporting a corpse (though in emergency situations

83. It is possible that this service was not rendered in Jesus' case because of the lack of time.

84. Ridderbos 1997: 628; cf. Beasley-Murray 1999: 360; Bultmann 1971: 680.

85. John alone provides this information (as well as that regarding the presence of a tomb nearby).

86. So Carson 1991: 631; Barrett 1978: 560. Cf. 18:1: "olive grove." Note also the later mention of a gardener in 20:15.

87. Carson (1991: 631 [cf. R. Brown 1970: 959]) suggests that by mentioning that no one had previously been placed in the tomb, the evangelist intends to help the reader realize that only one person was in the tomb and that only that same person could have been resurrected three days later. This may find support in the emphatic way in which this is stated in the original Greek: οὐδέπω οὐδείς (*oudepō oudeis*, no one ever before) (Morris 1995: 730 n. 115). Matthew 27:60 indicates that this was Joseph of Arimathea's "own new tomb, which he had cut in the rock."

88. The location of the tomb is probably on the site of the Church of the Holy Sepulchre (built by Constantine) rather than the popular "garden tomb" (Taylor 1998: 180, referring also to Barkay 1986). The vestiges of a nearby garden were still visible in Cyril of Jerusalem's day (*Catechesis* 14.5 [ca. A.D. 350]).

89. On tombs in first-century Palestine, see commentary at 11:38. On the Jewish Day of Preparation, see commentary at 19:14.

it probably was permissible to wash and anoint a dead person's body even after sundown; see the cases adjudicated in *m. Šabb.* 23.4–5). Although it may have been permissible for a dead body to remain without burial overnight if time was needed to obtain "a coffin and burial clothes" (*m. Sanh.* 6.5), the nearby tomb was a welcome instance of divine providence (Calvin 1961: 190). The shortness of time for Jesus' burial in 19:38–42 prepares for the events of John 20, which starts with Mary Magdalene setting out for the tomb early on Sunday morning.

C. Jesus' Resurrection and Appearances and the Commissioning of His Disciples (20:1–29)

John 20 provides the conclusion of the passion narrative[1] and the penultimate conclusion of the entire Gospel.[2] Again, though there are similarities with the Synoptic accounts, the Fourth Evangelist forges his own path.[3] John 20 consists of three scenes plus a conclusion. At the heart of the chapter is the commissioning of Jesus' followers, encircled by narratives focusing on Mary Magdalene and Thomas respectively.[4] The chapter also continues the parallel feature of Peter and the beloved disciple in the second half of the Gospel, which will be brought to a final resolution in John 21.[5]

There are several connections that tie the present chapter to the preceding one and the following one.[6] The empty tomb narrative follows the account of Jesus' burial. Considerable narrative suspense and expectation has also been created by Jesus' farewell discourse, in which he promised to return shortly, at least for a "little while,"

1. On the structure of John 20, see the discussion in Schnackenburg 1990: 3.301–2. See also Beasley-Murray 1999: 367–70; Moloney 1998: 517; Borchert 2002: 289; R. Brown 1970: 995–96. Schnackenburg (1990: 3.321) considers 20:11–18 to be a "prelude" to 20:19–29. Borchert (2002: 289–90, 296) perceives in 20:1–18 an "envelope effect or sandwich pattern" whereby the narratives involving Mary have been framed around 20:3–10, with the statement about the beloved disciple in 20:8 serving as the focal point of this chapter. Moloney (1998: 515–16) finds an *inclusio* between 1:35–51 and chapter 20.
2. See the introduction to John 21 below.
3. Note the lack of consensus on the relationship between the Johannine empty tomb narrative and those found in the Synoptics: see, for example, the studies by Neirynck (1984), who detects a "determinative" Synoptic influence on the Fourth Evangelist; Lindars (1956), who says that John's sources are traditions that lie behind the Synoptics rather than the Synoptics themselves; and Curtis (1971), who makes the implausible suggestion that Luke used John rather than vice versa.
4. Lee (1995: 38) speaks of a "narrative partnership" between those characters within the literary plan of the chapter.
5. See the introduction to John 21 below. On the parallel development of Peter and the beloved disciple in the Fourth Gospel, see Quast 1989 (though see the critical interaction in Köstenberger 1998b: 154–61).
6. Apart from the connections mentioned below, Stibbe (1993: 204) detects aspects of "the elusive Christ" again in John 20 (he says that this is the "primary characteristic" of the portrayal of Jesus in this chapter). As Stibbe notes, "Jesus' resurrection body is not immediately recognizable as the same as his pre-resurrection body," which makes him "a Messiah who is not easy to grasp in any conventional sense."

to his followers. The present chapter narrates the fulfillment of this promise. The time references in 20:1, 19, 26 structure the chapter and provide the point of reference for 21:14.[7] The chapter concludes with a purpose statement that summarizes virtually all the major themes of the Gospel.

---

7. On the literary connections between John 20 and 21, see Talbert 1992: 248; Schneiders 1989 (cited in Lee 1995: 40 n. 7).

1. The Empty Tomb (20:1–10)

Saturday is passed over in silence.[1] The preceding chapter closed with Jesus' hasty burial on Friday afternoon, just prior to the onset of the Jewish Sabbath. It is now Sunday morning, "the first day of the week," and once again permissible for observant Jews to resume regular activities. Mary Magdalene and several other women, as devoted followers of Jesus, waste no time attending to some unfinished business; carrying spices, they head for the tomb to anoint Jesus' body (Mark 16:1). It is unclear how they expect to be able to roll away the heavy stone sealing Jesus' tomb. Perhaps they are still so immersed in their grief that they have given little forethought to what would await them at the tomb. Or perhaps they simply hope that somehow they would receive help upon their arrival there. Great is Mary's shock when she gets to the tomb and finds that the stone had already been removed from the entrance.

Exegesis and Exposition

[1]Now on the first day of the week Mary Magdalene came to the tomb early in the morning, while it was still dark, and saw that the stone had been removed from the tomb. [2]So she ran and came to Simon Peter and the other disciple, the one Jesus loved, and said to them, "They've taken the Lord out of the tomb, and we don't know where they've put him!" [3]So Peter and the other disciple set out for the tomb. [4]Now both were running, but the other disciple ran ahead of Peter and came to the tomb first, [5]and bending down, he saw the linen strips lying there, but he did not enter. [6]Then Simon Peter also came, following him, and entered the tomb, and saw the linen strips lying there, [7]and the face cloth that had been on his [Jesus'] head, not lying there with the linen strips, but separately rolled up by itself. [8]Then the other disciple, who had come to the tomb first, also came, saw, and believed. [9](For they did not yet understand Scripture—that he must rise from the dead.) [10]Then the disciples returned home.

---

1. For a discussion of this pericope's relationship to the Synoptics, see Ridderbos 1997: 629–30 (see also Morris 1995: 732; R. Brown 1970: 996). Ridderbos (1997: 630–31) also defends the historicity of the event over against Bultmann (1971: 685), who denies historicity and takes an allegorical approach. On historical questions surrounding the Johannine account of Jesus' resurrection and appearances, see also Keener 2003: 1167–78.

Like the Synoptists, John introduces his account of Jesus' resurrection **20:1**
with a reference to "the first day of the week" rather than "the third
day after the crucifixion."² The reference to the "early" hour may imply
Roman reckoning, since for the Jews the day had begun on the previous
evening after sunset. Mark indicates that the time was "just after sunrise"
(16:2; Matt. 28:1: "at dawn"; Luke 24:1: "very early in the morning");
John indicates that "it was still dark."³ Perhaps Mary was the first among
a group of women to reach the tomb, or John refers to Mary's leaving
home while Mark speaks of her arrival at the grave site.

The portrayal of Mary Magdalene stresses her determination (Lee
1995: 40–42). Earlier, she is found near the cross as part of a group of
women (19:25). Her surname suggests that she was from Magdala, on
the northwest shore of the Sea of Galilee, approximately seven miles
southwest of Capernaum. She is featured prominently in the first resurrection account of all four Gospels. After her initial visit to the tomb,
she seems to have returned with some other women, possibly following Peter and the "disciple Jesus loved." At some point after her arrival,
she apparently was separated from the others and at that time saw the
risen Lord (20:10–18).⁴

Mary came to the tomb.⁵ A seven-day mourning period was customary—though people often would visit tombs within three days after
the burial—so that Mary might have remained at home had she not
sought to complete work left undone because of the Sabbath (cf. 19:42;
see Morris 1995: 733; contra Borchert 2002: 290).⁶ Doubtless to Mary's
surprise, the stone had already been removed. The cave tomb, which
probably was horizontal rather than vertical (see commentary at 11:38),

2. Cf. Matt. 28:1; Mark 16:2; Luke 24:1; cf. 1 Cor. 15:4; see Carson 1991: 635. The expression "on the first day of the week" reads more literally, "on one of the Sabbath [week]"
and may allude to the week of creation (cf. *Gen. Rab.* 11.9 on Gen. 2:3). Morris (1991: 733
n. 7 [cf. Beasley-Murray 1999: 366 n. a]) notes that σαββάτων (*sabbatōn*) can mean either
"Sabbath" or "week" (contra R. Brown [1970: 980], who claims that the meaning "week"
emerged only later). The use of the cardinal numeral ("one") for the ordinal ("first") may
represent a Semitism (Barrett 1978: 562; cf. Morris 1995: 733 n. 6; Beasley-Murray 1999:
366; Moloney 1998: 521; Lindars 1972: 599).

3. Often, though not always, in John, darkness connotes evil or unbelief (see 1:5; 8:12;
9:4; 11:10; 12:35, 46; 13:30). It is not clear that it does so here (contra Maccini 1996: 208;
Carson 1991: 635–36; Borchert 2002: 291; R. Brown 1970: 981; Schnackenburg 1990:
3.308; Moloney 1998: 518).

4. Carson (1991: 635–36 [cf. Beasley-Murray 1999: 371]) suggests that Mary was alone
during her first trip to the tomb (contra Morris 1995: 734; Moloney 1998: 522; Witherington 1995: 323; Burge 2000: 553). Mary's witness was not used as significantly in the
preaching of the early church as that of Peter, doubtless because evidence provided by a
woman was held in lesser esteem (e.g., *m. Roš Haš.* 1.8). This is underscored by the fact
that Jesus' encounter with Mary is not included in the resurrection appearances to the
disciples cited in 21:14.

5. Regarding mourning at a grave site, see commentary at 11:31.

6. See the rabbinic material cited in Köstenberger 2002c: 186.

was entered on ground level through a small doorway. This opening was usually no higher than a yard, so that people had to bend down to crawl in (20:5).[7]

20:2   Mary went first to Peter, then to the beloved disciple.[8] Even after his denial of Jesus, Peter is still the leading figure among his disciples.[9] "The other disciple" (mentioned already in 18:15–16) is explicitly identified here as "the disciple Jesus loved" (cf. 13:23–24; 19:25–27).[10] This means that the person reclining close to Jesus at the last supper in the upper room; the person providing Peter with access to the high-priestly courtyard; the person to whom care for Jesus' mother is entrusted at the foot of the cross; the person featured along with Peter in chapters 20 and 21; and the Fourth Evangelist (21:24; cf. 21:20) are all one and the same individual.

"They've taken the Lord out of the tomb."[11] Mary has no thought of resurrection.[12] The charge of the Jewish leaders that Jesus' disciples stole Jesus' body (Matt. 27:62–66; 28:11–15) suggests that grave robbery was not uncommon.[13] The plural "we" in Mary's statement "We don't know where they've put him!" may indicate that she came in the company of other women (Maccini 1996: 208–10).[14] This is further suggested by the fact that she went to the tomb while it was still dark (20:1), which she would hardly have done on her own, especially during religious festivals, when Jerusalem was crowded with visitors of uncertain character.[15]

7. On the presumed layout of the tomb, see Köstenberger 2002c: 186.

8. The repetition of the preposition πρός (*pros*, to) may indicate that Peter and the beloved disciple were at different locations (see Whitacre 1999: 472; Brodie 1993: 561). The reference to "Simon Peter" is the first mention of this disciple since his denial of Jesus (18:27). As is his custom, John uses Peter's full name when reintroducing him into his narrative (see commentary at 18:15).

9. Cf. 21:2–3, 7–8, 11, 15–23. On Peter as prime resurrection witness, see Kessler 1998.

10. The verbs ἐφίλει (*ephilei*) and ἠγάπα (*ēgapa*) are used synonymously for "loved" in this expression (cf. 13:23; 19:26; 21:20; see Ridderbos 1997: 632 n. 7; Carson 1991: 636; Barrett 1978: 562).

11. Three times in this chapter Mary expresses her conviction that Jesus' body had been taken by grave robbers (cf. 20:13, 15; see Lee 1995: 40).

12. Carson (1991: 636) rightly notes that Mary's use of κύριος (*kyrios*, lord, master) here does not constitute a christological confession and that she simply spoke "better than she knew" (cf. Moloney 1998: 521; contra R. Brown 1970: 984).

13. An inscription discovered in the neighborhood of Nazareth indicates that the emperor Claudius (A.D. 41–54) subsequently ordered capital punishment for those convicted of this crime (Barrett 1978: 562–63).

14. Cf. Matt. 28:1; Mark 16:1; Luke 24:10. See R. Brown 1970: 984. Contra Bultmann (1971: 684 n. 1), who suggests that the term is an Oriental idiom. Also contra Moloney (1998: 518–19), who claims that the term suggests that Mary is being associated with the two disciples.

15. Morris 1995: 734; cf. Bernard 1928: 2:262. Contra Carson (1991: 635, following Bultmann), who maintains that the plural "we" is "merely a mode of speech, without plural referent."

Both were running, but the other disciple ran ahead of Peter and came to   20:3–10
the tomb first.[16] The other disciple's greater speed has been taken by some
as an indication that he was the younger of the two (see commentary at
20:8), but any number of variables might account for contrasting foot
speed.[17] He bent over and saw the linen strips lying there. Apparently,
by now there was enough daylight to see inside the burial chamber
through the small, low opening in the cave tomb.[18] For the "disciple
Jesus loved," the linen strips (τὰ ὀθόνια, *ta othonia* [see commentary
at 19:40]) were sufficient evidence that the body had not simply been
moved. Moreover, grave robbers certainly would not have left behind
expensive linen wrappings or spices (Borchert 2002: 281, 293; R. Brown
1970: 1007–8). "There" probably refers to the place where the body had
been, on the *arcosolium*.[19]

The beloved disciples' eyes then fell on the face cloth that had been
around Jesus' head. In contrast to Lazarus, who came out of the tomb
still wearing his graveclothes (11:44), Jesus' resurrection body apparently
passed through the linen wrappings very much in the same way as he
later was able to appear to his disciples in a locked room (20:19, 26; see
Talbert 1992: 250). The cloth (σουδάριον, *soudarion*), presumably used
to keep Jesus' jaw in place (cf. *b. Moʿed Qaṭ.* 27a; see Morris 1995: 735
n. 18; R. Brown 1970: 986; Burge 2000: 554), was folded up in a place
(εἰς ἕνα τόπον, *eis hena topon*; see Carson 1991: 637) by itself (χωρίς,
chōris; see Ridderbos 1997: 633 n. 14, following BDF; Schnackenburg
1990: 3.311, 468 n. 26), separate from the linen. John draws attention
to the care that had been taken in the way the tomb was left.

The expression "folded up" (NIV; somewhat paraphrastically and ag-
nostically, TNIV: "still lying") may actually mean "rolled up" (ἐντυλίσσω,
entylissō; so NASB; NRSV; cf. Matt. 27:59 and Luke 23:53, of Joseph wrap-

---

16. The approach of several disciples here coheres with the plural ἀπῆλθον (*apēlthon*,
they went) in Luke 24:24 (Carson 1991: 636). Wallace (1996: 401) notes the singular
ἐξῆλθεν (*exēlthen*, he went out) in 20:3 and seems to conclude that here the evangelist is
emphasizing Peter. If so, this would counter the notion (advanced by some) that Johannine
supremacy is affirmed in the present pericope (see the following note).

17. This is disputed by Brodie (1993: 561), who says that the beloved disciple is "in
better running order," which he takes to be symbolic of superior discipleship (though on
p. 564 he sees both disciples as symbolic of the unity achieved through faith in the ascending Christ). Beasley-Murray (1999: 371–72) contends that the beloved disciple's speed was
due to the extent of his love for Jesus; Moloney (1998: 522) suggests that he had stronger
faith that a miracle had occurred. Yet others have seen in this statement an affirmation of
John's superiority over Peter (e.g., Schnackenburg 1990: 3.310, 312; Moloney 1998: 520;
R. Brown 1970: 1004–7). More likely, however, both the beloved disciple and Peter are
presented here as a duo of eyewitnesses to the resurrection (so, rightly, Ridderbos 1997:
632; Carson 1991: 636–37; Bultmann 1971: 684).

18. The word παρακύπτω (*parakyptō*, stoop to see) is in the LXX regularly used to
describe peering through a door or window (Judg. 5:28; Prov. 7:6; Song 2:9; Sir. 14:23;
21:23). See Morris 1995: 735 n. 17, following BAGD 619 (= BDAG 767).

19. See the reference to Köstenberger 2002c: 186 at 20:1.

ping Jesus' body in a linen cloth),[20] which either points to neatness or indicates that the cloth was still in the exact same position as when Jesus' body had been wrapped in it, or both.[21] This rules out grave robbers, who would have acted in haste (and probably taken these items with them; see Westcott 1908: 2.340). Also, it renders the Jewish story of the disciples stealing Jesus' body highly implausible, because they likewise would hardly have left face cloth and linen wrappings behind.[22]

Finally, the other disciple saw and believed.[23] The fact that two men saw the items mentioned in 20:5–7 renders the evidence admissible under the Jewish legal system (Deut. 17:6; 19:15). The evangelist does not specify precisely what "the other disciple" believed (presumably, that Jesus had risen from the dead);[24] nor is there any indication given as to Peter's response.[25] Other instances where the "other disciple/whom Jesus loved" compares favorably with Peter are 13:22–26 (where he inquires for Peter about the identity of the betrayer) and 21:7 (where he is the first to recognize Jesus standing on the shore of the Sea of Galilee).

Yet the beloved disciple's "believing" has no apparent immediate narrative impact (Lee 1995: 39). The reason for this is that he and Peter

20. Contra Moloney (1998: 520), who suggests that the participle ἐντετυλιγμένον (*entetyligmenon*, rolled up) is a divine passive.

21. Carson (1991: 637) denies that the burial cloths still retained the shape of Jesus' body (cf. Morris 1995: 735; Beasley-Murray 1999: 372; R. Brown 1970: 1007–8). But Whitacre (1999: 473) says, "With the body gone, the clothes were presumably collapsed, though perhaps retaining much of their shape due to the spices."

22. So, rightly, Carson 1991: 637; Barrett 1978: 563; Morris 1995: 735; Schnackenburg 1990: 3.311; Moloney 1998: 523. Carson also suggests that the fact that the graveclothes were still in the tomb is intended to create a contrast with Lazarus, who left the tomb with his graveclothes on (11:44) (cf. Barrett 1978: 563; Schnackenburg 1990: 3.311; Beasley-Murray 1999: 372; Moloney 1998: 519–20).

23. In this he compares favorably with Thomas later in this chapter (Moloney 1998: 538; see commentary at 20:24–29). Ridderbos (1997: 633 n. 15 [cf. Schnackenburg 1990: 3.312; Beck 1997: 117–18]) suggests that ἐπίστευσεν (*episteusen*, he believed) is an ingressive aorist. He also contrasts Mary's reaction (concern that the body had been stolen) with that of the beloved disciple (faith).

24. So, rightly, Carson 1991: 638; Schnackenburg 1990: 3.312; Borchert 2002: 295; R. Brown 1970: 987; Bultmann 1971: 684; Burge 2000: 554; Laney 1992: 360. Witherington (1995: 325) suggests, less plausibly, that the beloved disciple believed that Jesus had been taken by God similar to Elijah. Morris (1995: 736) notes that the two verbs do not have explicit objects, supplying the graveclothes as the object of the beloved disciple's "seeing" and Jesus' resurrection as that of the disciple's "believing" (albeit without understanding its full theological significance). Hardly plausible is the suggestion by Minear (1983: 91 n. 14, with reference to 1976 [followed by Conway 1999: 189–90]) that what the disciples believed was the statement of Mary Magdalene in 20:2.

25. Carson (1991: 638–39 [contra Bultmann 1971: 684]) suggests, on the basis of Luke 24:12, that Peter did not believe at this time (cf. D. M. Smith 1999: 374). Byrne (1985: 92) calls him "the odd-man-out" within the context of John 20. Morris (1995: 737, following Michaels 1989: 336) says that Peter could have believed, and the evangelist may have chosen to present the beloved disciple's reaction as his own while describing Peter from an external point of view.

still did not understand *from Scripture* that Jesus must rise from the dead.[26] The point is that the "disciple Jesus loved" believed on the basis of seeing (the empty tomb left in a certain condition) rather than believing (from Scripture) (Ridderbos 1997: 634; contra Bultmann 1971: 685). However, as is made clear later in the narrative, faith apart from seeing is superior (20:29). Thus, the "disciple Jesus loved" shares with Thomas his position as follower of Jesus during his earthly ministry, which must be transformed through the Spirit-Paraclete subsequent to Jesus' glorification.[27] This also proves that the disciples did not fabricate a story in order to fit their understanding of Scripture; rather, they were confronted with certain facts without initially relating them (or being able to relate them) to Scripture.

The singular γραφή (*graphē*, Scripture) may indicate that a specific OT text is in view—suggestions include Ps. 16:10, Isa. 53:10–12, and Hos. 6:2—though it cannot be ruled out that the reference is to Scripture in its entirety.[28] "Must rise" points to divine necessity (see commentary at 4:4). In the following transitional verse, "home" reads more literally "to them" (πρὸς αὐτούς, *pros autous*), that is, the things belonging to them—their homes (cf. Josephus, *Ant.* 8.4.6 §124; Morris 1995: 738 n. 27; contra Barrett 1978: 564). Elsewhere, John uses the equivalent expression εἰς τὰ ἴδια (*eis ta idia* [1:11; 16:32; 19:27; cf. Num. 24:25]). In all probability, the "disciple Jesus loved" brought the good news of Jesus' resurrection to Jesus' mother, whom he had taken "into his home" (19:27).

---

26. Note the plural "they" (Beasley-Murray 1999: 373). As Lee (1995: 40) points out, the present pericope thus acts as a prolepsis to John 21. Specifically, the beloved disciple recognizes the risen Jesus in 21:7.

27. This is inadequately recognized by those who see in the "disciple Jesus loved" a model disciple par excellence. See Ridderbos 1997: 633; Whitacre 1999: 474; contra Schnackenburg 1990: 3.312; R. Brown 1970: 1005; Borchert 2002: 295.

28. Cf. Luke 24:25–27, 32, 44–47; see commentary at 2:19–22; Ridderbos 1997: 634; Barrett 1978: 564.

2. Jesus Appears to Mary Magdalene (20:11–18)

Although not numbered among Jesus' resurrection appearances to his "disciples" in John (see 21:14), Jesus' encounter with Mary is nonetheless momentous in that it is the first recorded instance of anyone seeing the risen Lord. After serving as a witness to the empty tomb for Peter and the beloved disciple, Mary now comes face to face with Jesus himself. This is followed in the context of the Johannine narrative by three resurrection appearances of Jesus to his disciples.

The focal point of the present section is Jesus' self-revelation to Mary and the touching recognition scene in 20:16. Up until that point, Mary, throughout the entire chapter, had consistently reasoned and acted on a physical plane: mourning Jesus' passing, suspecting foul play in the disappearance of Jesus' body, and so on (see 20:1–2, 11–15). This marks her joyful response to Jesus' appearance as a truly remarkable reversal (Moloney 1998: 525–26).

Exegesis and Exposition

[11]Now Mary stood ⌜outside⌝ the tomb crying. So as she was crying, she bent down [to look] into the tomb [12]and saw two angels in white, seated where Jesus' body lay, one at the head and one at the feet. [13]And they said to her, "Woman, why are you crying?" She said to them, "They have taken my Lord away, and I don't know where they've put him." [14]When she said these things, she turned around and saw Jesus standing there (yet she did not realize that it was Jesus). [15]Jesus said to her, "Woman, why are you crying? Who are you looking for?" Thinking that he was the gardener, she said to him, "Sir, if you've carried him away, tell me where you've put him, and I will take him." [16]Jesus said to her, "Mary." Turning around, she said to him in Aramaic, "Rabbouni!" (which means Teacher). [17]Jesus said to her, "Don't hold on to me, for I have not yet ascended to the Father; but go to my brothers and tell them, 'I am ascending to my Father and your Father, to my God and your God.'" [18]Mary Magdalene went and announced to the disciples, "I have seen the Lord!" and told them that he had said these things to her.

20:11–13 The disciples went back to their homes, but (δέ, *de*, indicating contrast [Carson 1991: 639; Morris 1995: 739]) Mary stood outside the tomb crying (see additional note).[1] Mary weeps, not because Jesus has died, but because his body has vanished; abuse of the dead was considered an abhorrent offense.[2] Yet in what follows, the Johannine narrative turns the attention away from the possibility of grave robbers to the reality of the invasion of God's power, with angels adduced as witnesses to the activity of the Father (Carson 1991: 640; Schnackenburg 1990: 3.315–16; Witherington 1995: 330; Burge 2000: 555).

She bent over to look into the tomb,[3] and she saw two angels in white.[4] Notably, the theme of fear, which is usually associated with such manifestations, is absent here (cf. Matt. 28:2–10 pars.). Angels or celestial visitors are often depicted as clad in white.[5] The appearance of angels in pairs is likewise not uncommon in descriptions of heavenly visitations.[6] All the angels do is ask Mary a question, posed from the vantage point of the resurrection: "Woman, why are you crying?" This question constitutes a call for Mary to set aside her anguish and recognize the reality of Jesus' return to life (Ridderbos 1997: 636; Carson 1991: 640).[7]

Mary saw Jesus standing there, but she did not realize that it was Jesus. As **20:14–18** is commonly the case in resurrection narratives, Jesus is not recognized immediately (see 21:4; Luke 24:16; cf. Matt. 28:17; see Breck 1992: 32). Though Jesus' resurrection body can be seen and touched (John 20:27; Luke 24:39) and still bears the marks of crucifixion (John 20:20, 25, 27), and though Jesus continues to share meals with his followers (John 21:9, 13; Luke 24:41–43), his resurrected body apparently rose through the linen wrappings (John 20:6–8), is able to walk through closed doors (John 20:19, 26), and is often not recognized immediately.[8]

Mary's failure to recognize Jesus continues the pattern of misunderstanding that characterizes the Fourth Evangelist's portrayal of Mary throughout this chapter up to this point. Neither the removal of the stone

---

1. The term κλαίω (*klaiō*, cry) denotes the loud wailing typical of people in the ancient Near East (Morris 1995: 739 n. 30; Borchert 2002: 297–98; see commentary at 11:31).

2. An OT example is the Philistines' exposure of the bodies of Saul and his sons and the bodies' recovery and proper burial by the brave men of Jabesh-Gilead (1 Sam. 31:9–13).

3. Cf. Peter at 20:5. Note that this is the first time Mary actually looks inside the tomb (Lee 1995: 41). When she first arrived at the tomb, it was still dark (20:1), and upon noticing that the stone had been removed, she immediately ran to tell Peter and the beloved disciple.

4. In that day and culture, angelic appearances were no less real than what in modern parlance is called "evidence." Matthew speaks of one angel (28:2), Mark of a young man in white (16:5), and Luke of two men who were angels (24:4, 23).

5. Dan. 10:5–6; Ezek. 9:2; Rev. 15:6; cf. 1 Enoch 87:2.

6. For example, Acts 1:10; 2 Macc. 3:26. The reference to one angel at the head and the other at the feet probably pertains to an angel sitting at either end of the burial shelf (see commentary at 20:1).

7. Mary's response notably replaces her earlier "the Lord" and "we" (20:2) with the more personal "my Lord" and "I" (20:13) (Okure 1992: 180).

8. The primary NT passage dealing with this issue is 1 Cor. 15:35–58.

(20:1) nor the angels inside the tomb (20:12) nor even the risen Jesus himself fail to remove it. Yet, characteristically, Mary does not abandon her search (Lee 1995: 41). The address "woman," not particularly endearing but not harsh either, is elsewhere in this Gospel also directed at Jesus' mother (see commentary at 2:4; 19:26). Of the two questions asked by Jesus of Mary, the first, "Why are you crying?" (reiterating the angels' question [20:13]) may be a mild rebuke (Carson 1991: 641), though it is also possible that this is a nonjudgmental, caring way of empathizing with Mary's grief. The second question directs Mary's attention away from herself to Jesus (Schnackenburg 1990: 3.317): "Who are you looking for?" Jesus, of course, knew the answer, but he, characteristically, nonetheless elicited the answer in anticipation of his imminent self-revelation to Mary. Not only was he aware of who it was that Mary was looking for; he, in his very person, was that individual.

Apart from grave robbers or other mourners, neither of which would have been likely visitors at this early morning hour, gardeners attending to the grounds where the tomb was located (cf. 19:41) would have been the only people around.[9] Mary's guess indicates that at first blush the resurrected Jesus was indistinguishable from an ordinary person. The word βαστάζω (bastazō, carry away) is found elsewhere in the context of disposing of a corpse (Josephus, Ant. 3.8.7 §210; 7.11.7 §287). The irony of Mary's question is palpable: "The one whose body she is seeking is asked for a solution to the mystery of the empty tomb" (Moloney 1998: 525).[10] The repetition of Mary's complaint, first to the angels (20:13) and now to Jesus, heightens the tension in the narrative, accentuating both Mary's distress and the comfort about to be provided by Jesus (Schnackenburg 1990: 3.314, 317).

Jesus says, "Mary." Turning around, she saw.[11] The present scene validates Jesus' words in 10:3, "My sheep know my voice" (Schnackenburg 1990: 3.317; Okure 1992: 181). John here records the Aramaic, "Rabbouni!" (which means Teacher; see commentary at 1:38).[12] The evangelist's use of the original language creates a heightened sense of intimacy (Moloney 1998: 528). The present reference is the only instance of the term "rabbi" in the second half of John's Gospel. Since John 13–21 is told from the vantage point of the exalted Jesus, Mary's

9. The term κηπουρός (kēpouros, gardener; keeper of a κῆπος, kēpos, garden) occurs only here in the NT.

10. Moloney (1998: 525) notes that at previous instances Mary referred to those whom she believed to have taken Jesus' body in the third person ("they" [20:2, 13]); now she addresses Jesus directly in the second person ("you").

11. Similar recognition scenes are found in stories of Greco-Roman gods walking among people (Dibelius 1918 [cited in R. Brown 1970: 1008–9]).

12. The only other NT instance is Mark 10:51. John here translates the word for his Hellenistic audience (see commentary at 1:38, 41). For targumic background material, see Morris 1995: 741 nn. 39–40.

address of Jesus as "rabbi" indicates that she has not yet come to terms with the reality of Jesus' resurrection. Nevertheless, the address seems to have a "strong personal and affective component" (Ridderbos 1997: 637; cf. Maccini 1996: 212–13) in light of Mary's use of κύριος (*kyrios*, lord, master) in 20:13 and the fact that Jesus had saved her from a dire condition (Witherington 1995: 331).

Jesus' reply to her, "Don't hold on to me, for I have not yet ascended to the Father," highlights the change that has occurred in Jesus' relationship with his disciples (Ridderbos 1997: 637).[13] In fact, what all of Jesus' resurrection appearances in John 20–21 reveal is that the disciples now find themselves in a transition period in which they cannot revert to their familiar pattern of relating to their Master during his earthly ministry, yet at the same time they cannot fully grasp the nature of the new spiritual relationship with their Lord that soon will be mediated to them by the Holy Spirit. This transitory condition explains the awkwardness that surrounds the interim between the resurrection of Jesus and the sending of the Spirit.

In the present instance, Mary, upon Jesus' self-identification to her, presumably had proceeded (or at least attempted) to embrace Jesus.[14] Her reaction is entirely natural; yet, once again, it reveals misunderstanding.[15] Apparently, Mary is determined not to lose a second time what it cost her such effort to find again; yet she must not cling to the unascended Jesus, for "his permanent abiding with her is to be not in the flesh as she supposes . . . but in the Spirit" (Lee 1995: 42; see 20:22).

---

13. Lee (1995: 42) notes the interesting narrative tension introduced by the fact that Jesus asks Mary not to cling to him (20:17) but invites Thomas to touch him later on in the narrative (20:27). She also points out that in the end, it is inconsequential whether or not Thomas actually does touch Jesus (p. 43; see discussion below). For an alternate way of construing the syntax of 20:17 by taking γάρ (*gar*, for) to be anticipatory, see McGehee (1986), who translates, "Don't cling to me. Since I have not yet ascended to the Father, go to my brothers and tell them I am ascending to my Father and your Father and my God and your God." D'Angelo (1990) adduces Apoc. Mos. 31 as a parallel, taking the present passage to relate to a concern for purity "because the appearance takes place in some sort of intermediary stage."

14. Commentators are not agreed as to whether Mary had already touched Jesus or was about to do so. Some say that Mary had already touched him (e.g., Morris 1995: 742; Schnackenburg 1990: 3.318; Witherington 1995: 331; R. Brown 1970: 992; Burge 2000: 555), while others seem to allow for the possibility that she was about to but had not yet done so (e.g., Beasley-Murray 1999: 366 n. g, 376; Bultmann 1971: 687). Regarding Mary's devotion, see Ruth 1:16. Stibbe (1993: 205) says that the present passage is "most stylized" and detects intertextual echoes with Song 3:1–3.

15. That Mary's reaction is natural may be illustrated by one incident in the life of Alexander the Great (see Arrian, *Anabasis* 6.13.3 [cited in BDAG 126]). That it reveals misunderstanding is well argued by Lindars (1972: 607), who writes, "The desire to hold Jesus must be restrained, because it is an attempt to recapture the conditions of the incarnate life in place of the universal and abiding relationship which is the object of his mission."

"Do not hold on to me"[16] probably has the sense of "Stop clinging to me" (NASB), while "I have not yet ascended to the Father" indicates that Jesus is not yet in an "ascended" state (ἀναβαίνω, *anabainō* [cf. 6:62]); his process of glorification has not yet been completed (Ridderbos 1997: 638).[17] By salvation-historical necessity, Jesus must move on; the Spirit will take his place (14:16–17).[18]

This is not the time for sentimentalities; rather, Jesus calls for action: "but go . . . and tell them." In light of the limitations placed on women's witness in first-century Judaism (*m. Roš Haš.* 1.8), Jesus' entrusting Mary with this important message surely is significant (Maccini 1996: 207–33). "My brothers" most likely means the disciples, particularly the Eleven (cf. 20:18).[19] This culminates the more endearing terms used by John in the second half of his Gospel.[20] The message to be conveyed by Mary to Jesus' disciples is that Jesus is "in the process of ascending" to God the Father (Carson 1991: 644). Jesus' distinction between "my Father and your Father" and "my God and your God" highlights the different sense in which God is God and Father of both Jesus and of believers (cf. 1:12, 14, 18, 34; see Carson 1991: 645).[21]

Additional Note

20:11. All major commentators except R. Brown (1970: 988) argue in favor of ἔξω being in the original (e.g., Carson 1991: 640 n. 1; Schnackenburg 1990: 3.315; Beasley-Murray 1999: 366 n. e; Moloney 1998: 527).

16. The Latin for this phrase, *noli me tangere*, famously inspired a medieval painting (Okure 1992: 177).

17. D. M. Smith (1999: 378) observes, "Jesus' permanent postresurrection state will not obtain until he has ascended to the Father, which he will now do"; Schlatter (1948: 358) comments, "Jesus' entry into fellowship with the Father in heaven is the prerequisite for his fellowship with the disciples." On Jesus' return to the Father, see also 3:13; 7:33; 13:1, 3; 14:4, 12, 28; 16:5, 17, 28; 17:11.

18. R. Brown (1970: 1012, 1015–16) relates Jesus' words to Mary with his promised giving of the Spirit. In 14:18–19, Jesus promised that he would return to his disciples. On the basis of these words, Mary may have thought that Jesus had returned and would continue their former relationship on a permanent basis. Jesus corrects her misunderstanding in the present passage by showing that this permanent relationship would be established by the giving of the Spirit (see Burge 2000: 556–57, with further reference to the "not yet" in 7:39).

19. Though see the discussion and bibliographic references in Lee 1995: 45 n. 22.

20. Cf. 13:1, 33; 15:15; 17:6, 10; 21:4–5. See Köstenberger 1998b: 153.

21. Wallace (1996: 274, 277) briefly discusses the implications of this construction for the Granville Sharp rule. On Mary Magdalene, see commentary at 20:1. On the disciples, see commentary at 20:19. Regarding the statement "I have seen the Lord," see 20:25. On "the Lord," see commentary at 20:2; see also 20:13; 21:7. On "seeing" Jesus, see 20:20 and commentary at 20:29.

3. Jesus Appears to His Disciples (20:19–23)

The present pericope is related to Jesus' encounter with Mary Magdalene in 20:11–18 through the reference to "the evening of that first day" in 20:19 and through the mention of Mary's and the disciples' "seeing the Lord" in 20:18 and 20:20b (Schnackenburg 1990: 3.321–22). The pericope also serves as a bridge that links the preceding narrative with the events described in 20:24–29 (Moloney 1998: 530). The present is the first of three resurrection appearances of Jesus to his disciples recorded in this Gospel; the second one follows one week later (20:24–29); the third one occurs some time later at the shores of the Sea of Galilee (21:1–23; cf. 21:14).

Exegesis and Exposition

[19]Now when it was evening on that first day of the week, and the doors were locked where the disciples were on account of fear of the Jews, Jesus came and stood in their midst and said to them, "Peace be with you." [20]And having said this, he showed them his hands and side. So the disciples rejoiced, because they had seen the Lord. [21]Then Jesus said to them again, "Peace be with you. As the Father has sent me, so I am sending you." [22]And having said this, he breathed on them and said to them, "Receive the Holy Spirit. [23]If you forgive any their sins, ⌜they have been forgiven⌝ them; if you retain them, they are retained."

The reference to the "evening of that first day of the week" provides continuity with 20:1–9 and 20:10–18.[1] Since the Twelve are mentioned very infrequently in John, at least under that designation (see 6:67, 70, 71; 20:24), it is not always clear whether "disciples" in this Gospel refers to them or to a larger circle of Jesus' followers (Köstenberger 1998b: 142–69). In light of the characterization of Thomas as "one of the Twelve" in 20:24, it is possible that this resurrection appearance is to the Twelve minus Judas and Thomas, though it is not unlikely that others joined them as well.[2] The location of their gathering probably is a house in

20:19–20

---

1. Note also the connective οὖν, *oun* (R. Brown 1970: 1019). The suggestion by Borchert (2002: 303) that the darkness of the evening corresponds to the darkness of the disciples' understanding is of doubtful relevance.
2. Cf. Luke 24:33. Barrett (1978: 568) contends that it is impossible to know the extent of the gathering but that even if only "the ten" were present, they are still representative of

Jerusalem, presumably the same place where the disciples were when Mary Magdalene came to them with the news that she had seen the Lord (20:18; cf. Luke 24:33). The disciples probably are still there to mourn. Also, the Feast of Unleavened Bread is still in progress.

The doors were "locked" (not merely shut: note the perfect κεκλει-σμένων, *kekleismenōn*; see Morris 1995: 745) for fear of the Jews.[3] This underscores the miraculous nature of Jesus' entry (Ridderbos 1995: 641; Carson 1991: 646).[4] Concerning the plural "doors" (cf. 20:26), the reference may be to a door at the house entrance and one into the room (Morris 1995: 745 n. 50). "Proper residences were equipped with bolts and locks. Bolted doors would prevent anyone from entering (a heavy bolt could be slid through rings attached to the door and its frame)" (Keener 1993: 317). Jesus came and stood in their midst.[5] This reunion marks the fulfillment of Jesus' promise to the disciples (15:11; 16:20–24; 17:13; see Ridderbos 1995: 642; Beasley-Murray 1999: 379; contra Moloney 1998: 534).

"Peace be with you."[6] This common Jewish greeting (e.g., 1 Sam. 25:6; see Morris 1995: 745), representing Hebrew *šālōm ʿalêkem* and repeated in 20:21 and 20:26, is still used today. In Jesus' case, "peace" was uniquely his gift to his followers by virtue of his vicarious sacrificial death on the cross.[7] The expression may also function as a formula of revelation (cf. Judg. 6:23; Dan. 10:19; see Borchert 2002: 304–5). Jesus' greeting was given to dispel any fears of his followers owing to their desertion prior to the crucifixion (16:32; see Morris 1995: 745). This pertains particularly to Peter, who doubtless was in their midst as well (see further ch. 21; cf. Mark 16:7).

Jesus' scars on his hands and his side (cf. 19:34) are marks not only of his suffering but also of his victory (Ridderbos 1995: 641).[8] In fact, his mere presence among his followers is evidence of his triumph (cf.

---

the entire church. Morris (1995: 745) and R. Brown (1970: 1022, 1034) favor a larger group beyond the apostles including also other disciples (contra Carson 1991: 646, 656).

3. The phrase "fear of the Jews" is first used in 7:13 (see also 9:22; 12:42) and regularly points to people's dread that the Jewish religious authorities would use their authority to inflict recriminations on anyone who dissented from the "party line."

4. Lindars (1972: 610) says, "This does not mean that his body is ethereal, able to pass through locked doors," but "rather that he can make himself present at any time and place 'where two or three are gathered in my name.'" Similarly, Calvin 1961: 202.

5. The preposition εἰς (*eis*, into) may convey motion toward the disciples (Morris 1995: 745 n. 52).

6. On "peace," see commentary at 14:27.

7. See commentary at 14:27; 16:33. So Beasley-Murray 1999: 379; Carson 1991: 647; Witherington 1995: 339–40; Moloney 1998: 530.

8. Only John mentions that Jesus showed his followers his side (Morris 1995: 745 n. 53). Note also the opening καί (*kai*, and) in 20:20, which is unusual for John, who normally prefers asyndeton. Morris (ibid.) suggests that the use of the double καί may seek to stress "the completeness of the process."

20:5–7; Moloney 1998: 530–31, 534). According to Luke 24:37, the disciples "were startled and frightened, thinking they saw a ghost" (as at previous occasions: e.g., Matt. 14:26; cf. John 6:19–20). Whereas John focuses on Jesus' hands and side (which would have shown the wound inflicted by the Roman soldier's spear [19:34]), Luke 24:39–40 refers to his hands and feet (which would have borne the nail marks from the crucifixion; see commentary at 19:18). Both the Hebrew (*yad*) and the Greek (χείρ, *cheir*) words for "hand" include the wrist and forearm, so that the nails could have been driven either through Jesus' hands or his wrists.[9] Nails were driven through the feet, with one foot placed on top of the other.

"So the disciples rejoiced, because they had seen the Lord" (see commentary at 20:19).[10] The scars of Jesus proved to them that the person before them really was their resurrected Lord.[11] The response of joy is also attributed in this Gospel to John the Baptist (3:29) and Abraham (8:56). In 14:28, the disciples are encouraged, but are not yet able, to rejoice (cf. also 4:36; 11:15; 16:20, 22). Jesus is called "the Lord" also in 20:2, 18 (see also 20:13). Significantly, for the evangelist, calling Jesus "Lord" in a true christological sense frequently presupposes either hindsight (6:23; 11:2) or at least Jesus' resurrection having occurred (20:28; 21:7, 12), though there are occasional instances where disciples address Jesus as "Lord" during his earthly ministry (e.g., 9:38 [cf. 9:36]; 11:12, 21, 27, 32, 34, 39).

Once again, Jesus utters the familiar greeting "Peace be with you" (see commentary at 20:19). Peace is what Jesus bequeaths to them, and peace is what they will need to fulfill their commission (Schnackenburg 1990: 3.323). The focus of the present unit is Jesus' commissioning statement "As the Father has sent me, so I am sending you" (cf. Matt. 28:18–20; Luke 24:46–49),[12] which climaxes the characterization of Jesus as the sent Son (Köstenberger 1998b: esp. 96–121, 180–98).[13] The disciples are drawn into the unity and mission of Father and Son (cf. 17:21–26; see Ridderbos   **20:21–23**

9. See Carson 1991: 656; R. Brown 1970: 1022; Beasley-Murray 1999: 366 n. i.

10. The aorist ἐχάρησαν (*echarēsan*, they rejoiced) may point to a sudden influx of joy at the sight of their resurrected Lord (Morris 1995: 746 n. 54).

11. Morris (1995: 746) sees the conjunction οὖν (*oun*, then, so) conveying the notion that the disciples' rejoicing was the result of their recognition of Jesus on the basis of his showing them his hands and side.

12. The statement harks back to 17:18, albeit without reference to the sphere of the disciples' commission (i.e., the world), indicating that the emphasis in the present passage is on the disciples' authorization rather on the realm of their activity (Ridderbos 1997: 643). Compare also the general statement in 13:20, which suggests that the present passage extends beyond the original disciples to later generations of believers (Morris 1995: 746 n. 55).

13. The vast majority of the instances of "sending" in John's Gospel relate to Jesus' having been sent by the Father. "Sending" terminology also occurs with regard to God's sending of the Baptist, the Father's and the Son's sending of the Spirit, and Jesus' sending of his

1997: 642). Succession is important both in the OT and in Second Temple literature. In the present Gospel, Jesus succeeds the Baptist and is followed by both the Spirit and the Twelve (minus Judas), who serve as representatives of the new messianic community. OT narratives involving succession feature Joshua (following Moses) and Elisha (succeeding Elijah).[14]

Jesus breathed on them and said, "Receive the Holy Spirit."[15] The present reference represents a symbolic promise of the soon-to-be-given gift of the Spirit, not the actual giving of it fifty days later at Pentecost (cf. Acts 2; see Carson 1991: 649–55; cf. Witherington 1995: 340–41).[16] Otherwise, it is hard to see how John would not be found to stand in actual conflict with Luke's Pentecost narrative in Acts 2, not to mention his own disclaimers earlier in the narrative that the Spirit would be given only subsequent to Jesus' glorification, which entailed his return to the Father.[17] The disciples' behavior subsequent to the present incident

---

disciples. The present passage features two "sending" verbs, πέμπω (pempō) and ἀποστέλλω (apostellō), with no apparent difference in meaning (as is the virtual consensus among major commentators, including Ridderbos, Morris, Carson, Barrett, Schnackenburg, and R. Brown; see also Köstenberger 1999c: 125–43). Morris (1995: 746 n. 56) notes that this is already suggested by the use of καθώς (kathōs, just as) linking the two verbs.

14. See Deut. 31:1–8; 2 Kings 2:1–14. The concept of a person empowered for and sent on a mission by God is attested also in Hellenistic literature.

15. The absence in the Greek of the article in the expression "Holy Spirit" may indicate a focus on "the quality of the gift of the Holy Spirit rather than on the individuality of the Spirit" (Morris 1995: 747 n. 59).

16. The critique by Hatina (1993), who says that the reference is to the indwelling Paraclete, fails to convince. Contrary to the view of many commentators, the present pericope does not constitute the Johannine equivalent to Pentecost (e.g., R. Brown 1970: 1038; Barrett [1978: 570], who says that the present passage cannot be harmonized with Acts 2; Bultmann 1971: 691), nor is Calvin's (1961: 205) proposal satisfactory that at 20:22 the disciples "were only sprinkled with His grace and not [as at Pentecost] saturated with full power." Beasley-Murray (1999: 382 [followed by Borchert 2002: 307–8]) believes that John telescoped the giving of the Spirit without concern for chronology (citing the reference to the ascension in 20:17 as a parallel). M. Turner (1977) thinks that the reference is not to the Spirit at all but to Jesus' message as Spirit and life. The treatment by Moloney (1998: 532, 535) is rather idiosyncratic. Schnackenburg (1990: 3.325), too, surprisingly contends that the Johannine instance involves all believers, while the events in Acts 2 pertain to the apostles. If anything, one might have expected the opposite kind of reasoning, with John's account anticipating the general outpouring narrated in Acts 2. Against the view of Burge (2000: 558 [cf. Burge 1987: 148–49]), who notes the connection between the present passage and Jesus' promise to send the Spirit in John 14 and 16, the present event does not mark the actual fulfillment of these promises other than by way of anticipatory sign. Keener's (2003: 1196–1200, see also 1204–6) discussion, including an attempted refutation of M. Turner (1998), remains inconclusive and, on the whole, fails to convince.

17. See 7:39; 14:12, 16–18, 25–26; 16:12–15; cf. 20:17. Luke's account of Pentecost hardly reads as though Acts 2 represents merely "one of several additional empowerings of the Spirit," as Hatina (1993: 201) alleges. Talbert (1992: 252) concludes from 20:22 that Jesus must have ascended by then because otherwise, according to 7:39, he could not yet have given the Spirit. But this presupposes that the Spirit was in fact imparted at 20:22. If not, there is no need to suppose that Jesus had already ascended by then.

would also be rather puzzling had they already received the Spirit.[18] The present gesture is made to the group in its entirety rather than to its separate individuals, just as the authority to forgive or retain sins is given to the church as a whole (Morris 1995: 747, 749). As the TNIV properly translates, the Greek verb ἐνεφύσησεν (*enephysēsen*) means "breathed *on*" rather than "breathed *into*." The theological antecedent plainly is Gen. 2:7, where the exact same verb form is used.[19] There, God breathes his Spirit into Adam at creation, which constitutes him as a "living being." Here, at the occasion of the commissioning of his disciples, Jesus constitutes them as the new messianic community in anticipation of the outpouring of the Spirit subsequent to his ascension.[20]

"If you forgive any their sins, they are forgiven them; if you do not forgive them, they are not forgiven" (cf. Job 42:9 LXX; Rev. 1:5).[21] The second part of this saying reads literally, "if you retain [the sins of any], they are retained." In Matthew, this power is attributed to Peter in a universal, salvation-historical sense (16:19; cf. Acts 1–12) and to the disciples in an intrachurch context (18:18).[22] Both evangelists perhaps echo the reference to the one who is given "the key to the house of David" in Isa. 22:22 (cf. Rev. 3:7; see Emerton 1962). If so, what is at stake is the authority to grant or deny access to God's kingdom. However, whereas in Matthew the focus is on Peter's and the new messianic community's didactic and intracommunitarian authority, John focuses on the pronouncement of the forgiveness (in case of repentance) or the retention of sins (in the case of a person's refusal to believe) (Ridderbos 1997: 644; Witherington 1995: 343).

In a Jewish context, the expression "binding and loosing" described the activity of a judge who declared persons innocent or guilty and thus "bound" or "loosed" them from the charges made against them.[23] The

18. In 20:26, the doors are still locked (as prior to 20:22 in 20:19), presumably still "for fear of the Jewish leaders"; in 21:3, Peter decides to go fishing and is joined by six others, but they catch nothing. Hatina's (1993: 200) argument that the latter may have been "an atypical circumstance" fails to convince, as does his claim that Peter's threefold confession of love suggests reception of the Spirit (cf. Peter's earlier offer in 13:37 to lay down his life for Jesus).

19. See also 1 Kings 17:21; Ezek. 37:9; Wis. 15:11; cf. Philo, *Creat.* 46 §135.

20. This "new creation" theme is noted by several commentators, including Morris 1995: 747 n. 58 (who also cites Ezek. 37:9); Barrett 1978: 570; R. Brown 1970: 1035, 1037; Witherington 1995: 342; Keener 2003: 1204. Whitacre (1999: 482) speaks of the event in John 20:22 as the church's "conception," and of Pentecost as its "birth."

21. The two perfect verbs ἀφέωνται (*apheōntai*, they are forgiven) and κεκράτηνται (*kekratēntai*, they are retained) denote the settled state of the pronounced forgiveness or retention of sins (see esp. Carson 1991: 655; Wallace [1996: 581] calls these "proleptic perfects"). See additional note.

22. The Greek words used for "binding and loosing" in Matthew are δέω (*deō*) and λύω (*lyo*); John has ἀφίημι (*aphiēmi*) for "forgive" and κρατέω (*krateō*) for "retain."

23. See Schlatter 1959: 511; Beasley-Murray 1999: 383; Borchert 2002: 310. The rabbis used the terms "binding" and "loosing" to declare what was forbidden or permitted by

same terminology was applied to the imposition or rescindment of a ban or to a person's expulsion from or restitution to the synagogue. If this meaning resonates here, then Jesus is declaring that his new messianic community, versus the Jewish leadership represented by the Sanhedrin and the Pharisees, is authorized to affirm or deny acceptance into the believing (new) covenant community (cf. 9:22, 34, 35; 12:42; 16:2). On a secondary level, if Jewish nonmessianic synagogues in John's day had begun to expel Christians (*minim*?) on a larger, more formal and organized scale, then the reference served as a reminder that Christians, not nonmessianic Jewish synagogues, now held the key to membership in the messianic community.

Additional Note

20:23. Very probably, the perfect ἀφέωνται, rather than the present ἀφίενται or the future ἀφεθήσεται, is the original reading (so, e.g., Morris 1995: 749 n. 68; Beasley-Murray 1999: 366 n. j; the UBS committee; contra Barrett 1978: 571).

the law. See Str-B 1:738–41; Büchsel, *TDNT* 2:60–61; J. Lightfoot 1859: 2.237–41; Dalman 1902: 213–17.

4. Jesus Appears to Thomas (20:24–29)

This is now the second resurrection appearance proper, included here no doubt in part because the lesson taught to Thomas applies also to later believers and because the encounter culminates in the climactic christological confession in this Gospel, which mirrors the lofty christological designations of the prologue.

Exegesis and Exposition

²⁴Now Thomas, one of the Twelve, the one called Didymus, had not been with them when Jesus had come. ²⁵So the other disciples were telling him, "We've seen the Lord!" But he said to them, "Unless I see the nail marks on his hands and put my finger on the nail marks and put my hand into his side, I will certainly not believe." ²⁶And eight days later his disciples were inside again, and Thomas with them. Even though the doors were locked, Jesus came and stood in their midst and said, "Peace be with you." ²⁷Then he said to Thomas, "Put your finger here and see my hands, and take your hand and put it into my side, and stop being faithless and believe." ²⁸Thomas answered and said to him, "My Lord and my God!" ²⁹Jesus said to him, "Because you have seen me, you have believed; blessed are those who have not seen and yet have believed."

Thomas, one of the Twelve (an expression used of Judas Iscariot in 6:71), called Didymus (see commentary at 11:16), had not been with the group when Jesus came earlier.[1] So the other disciples kept telling (imperfect ἔλεγον, *elegon*; see Morris 1995: 751 n. 74) or attempted to tell (conative sense; see Beasley-Murray 1999: 367 n. k; R. Brown 1970: 1025; Moloney 1998: 539) him, "We've seen the Lord!" (cf. 20:18, 20). Ever the skeptic,[2] he insists that he will "certainly not" (οὐ μή, *ou mē*) believe unless he sees the nail marks in Jesus' hands and puts (βάλλω, 20:24–25

---

1. The present unit is introduced by δέ (*de*, and, but), perhaps creating a contrast between Thomas and the disciples in the previous narrative (Moloney 1998: 538). The existence of the Twelve is in this Gospel presupposed rather than explicitly narrated (see commentary at 6:67; see also the brief excursus in Borchert 2002: 311). The reference to Thomas's designation "the twin" hardly constitutes an allusion to his double-mindedness (so, rightly, Borchert 2002: 312; cf. R. Brown 1970: 1024; Bultmann 1971: 694 n. 2). Lee (1995: 43, citing Robert Alter) notes that "absence is a favourite literary device of this narrator."
2. Contra Lee (1995: 43), who says that Thomas is no more doubtful than the other disciples.

ballō—a rather strong term; see Moloney 1998: 539; R. Brown 1970: 1025) his finger on the nail marks and his hand into Jesus' side.[3]

Earlier in the narrative, Jesus had disparaged people's need for "signs and wonders" (4:48). In the present instance, Thomas asks not merely for a sign but for hard evidence. Perhaps he thinks that the disciples actually saw a ghost, not the resurrected Jesus in the flesh (cf. 6:19–21 pars.), and his statement expresses lack of confidence in his fellow disciples' judgment as much as skepticism regarding the possibility of Jesus having risen from the dead.

From the evangelist's perspective, Thomas's objection becomes a welcome foil for forestalling the incipient gnostic notion that Jesus only appeared to be human (the heresy later termed "Docetism," from δοκέω, *dokeō*, seem). Just as in the case of the incarnation (1:14), John takes pains to affirm that Jesus "came in the flesh" (a major concern in John's epistles; cf. 1 John 4:2–3; 2 John 7), which entails also that his resurrection body was not merely that of a phantom or spirit apparition but a "fleshy" (albeit glorified) body.

20:26–27 "A week later" (TNIV) reads more literally, "after eight days." By inclusive reckoning, this refers to Sunday, one week after Easter (Carson 1991: 657).[4] His disciples were inside again (see commentary at 20:19). Now that the Feast of Unleavened Bread was over, the disciples soon would be returning home to Galilee (barring instructions to the contrary). Thomas, in the present instance, compares unfavorably with the beloved disciple, who in 20:8 saw the condition of the empty tomb (but not Jesus himself) and believed (Moloney 1998: 538; though see the disclaimer in 20:9).

As on the previous occasion, the doors were locked (not merely closed; see commentary at 20:19), which seems to imply that the disciples' fears of the Jewish leaders had not subsided (cf. 20:19). This, in turn, seems to support the notion that the event described in 20:22 constitutes a symbolic gesture rather than the permanent impartation of the Spirit to the disciples (so, rightly, Carson 1991: 657; contra Barrett 1978: 572). Moreover, once again, the doors being locked provides occasion for Jesus'

---

3. Thomas's comments at 11:16 perhaps display similar skepticism (if not sarcasm). Ridderbos (1997: 646–47) believes that Thomas's response does not represent "a serious condition for belief" but rather shows how ridiculous he thought his fellow disciples' statement was. Morris (1995: 752) suggests that Thomas's response shows how traumatized he was by the circumstances of Jesus' death and the degree of his injuries. Both of these views are possible but hard to verify and not necessarily accurate. See further discussion below.

4. Schlatter (1948: 361, citing Rev. 1:10) thinks that the celebration of Sunday as the Lord's Day is in view. Carson (1991: 657) suggests that the continued reference to the Lord's Day in the resurrection narrative may represent a polemical attempt to demonstrate the basis of Christian worship to John's Jewish readers.

miraculous manifestation to his disciples (Schnackenburg 1990: 3.331). The greeting "Peace be with you," too, is the same (see 20:19, 21).

Jesus' encounter with Thomas bears a certain resemblance to his earlier meeting with Nathanael (1:47–51; see Schnackenburg 1990: 3.331–32; Borchert 2002: 313). Jesus' words "Put your finger here and see my hands, and take your hand and put it into my side" closely mirror Thomas's earlier statement (see 20:25). As he had done previously, by showing awareness of the disciple's objection, Jesus displays supernatural knowledge (see commentary at 2:24). "Stop doubting and believe" (TNIV) reads, more literally, "Stop being faithless [ἄπιστος, apistos] and believe [πιστός, pistos]."[5] On a narrative level, Jesus' words in 20:27 constitute a bridge to the blessing pronounced in 20:29 (Schnackenburg 1990: 3.332).

Apparently, Thomas no longer has need to touch Jesus' wounds in order **20:28–29** to verify that his resurrection really has taken place: in his case, seeing was believing.[6] Rather, in a peak (at least) akin to the recognition scene in 20:16, Thomas acknowledges Jesus as his Lord and God.[7] Although "Lord" may have simply expressed respect, the reluctant disciple now realized that Jesus was in fact somehow God incarnate (Ridderbos 1997: 647–48; Morris 1995: 753).[8] This climactic confession forms an *inclusio* with the ascription of deity to Jesus as the Word-made-flesh in 1:1, 14, 18.[9] In the Johannine narrative, the evangelist desires that the reader respond in the same way Thomas did (Carson 1991: 659; Beasley-Murray 1999: 386).[10]

In the OT, "Lord" and "God" are frequently juxtaposed with reference to Yahweh (e.g., Ps. 35:23–24).[11] In the Greco-Roman world, the

5. So, essentially, Schnackenburg (1990: 3.332): "Do not be faithless, but believing." Carson (1991: 657) translates both terms substantively: "Do not be an unbeliever, but a believer." Neither word occurs elsewhere in John. In the NT epistles, "unbelieving" refers to people who are not Christians, but these categories are not as firmly in place at this earlier stage of salvation history.

6. So, rightly, Ridderbos (1997: 647) and most major commentators (e.g., Morris 1995: 753; Witherington 1995: 344; Carson 1991: 657; Moloney 1998: 537; Barrett 1978: 572; Schnackenburg 1990: 3.332; contra Borchert 2002: 314; R. Brown 1970: 1027).

7. Stibbe (1996: 203) comments, "Like Mary Magdalene, Thomas has made the journey to 'owned' faith . . . his own faith in Jesus as Yahweh, 'Lord and God.'" Note the double personal pronoun μου (*mou*, my), which accentuates the personal nature of Thomas's confession (Carson 1991: 659; Beasley-Murray 1999: 386; Schnackenburg 1990: 3.332; Wallace 1995: 82).

8. As Carson (1991: 659) astutely observes, however, the present narrative shows that "Jesus' deity does not exhaust deity" (cf. 5:16–30; 20:17).

9. See M. Harris 1992: 284–86; Ridderbos 1997: 648. On 20:28, see M. Harris 1992: 105–29. For a defense of the historicity of the present pericope, see Carson 1991: 657–58; M. Harris 1992: 111–19.

10. Thomas's function in John thus is similar to that of the Roman centurion in Mark 15:39. Keener (2003: 1211) perceptively comments, "Thomas's very skepticism makes him the ideal proponent of a high Christology" in John's Gospel.

11. Though this does not necessarily mean that Thomas (or the evangelist) consciously sought to allude to this or other similar OT passages in the present instance (so Ridderbos

expression seems to have made its way into Roman emperor worship via Mediterranean cults.[12] The Roman emperor Domitian (A.D. 81–96) in particular, during whose tenure the Fourth Gospel most likely was written, wished to be addressed as *dominus et deus noster*, "our Lord and God" (Suetonius, *Domitian* 13.2).[13] Hence, the present reference may on a secondary level be designed to counter Roman emperor worship (Schnackenburg 1990: 3.333; Witherington 1995: 349; contra Borchert 2002: 315–16).

Jesus' response to Thomas in fact constitutes a mild rebuke (cf. 20:9).[14] The point of Jesus' remark is not so much to pronounce Thomas's faith inferior (Ridderbos 1997: 648; Carson 1991: 660)—after all, the confession has a climactic function in the Johannine narrative—but rather to show the limitation of a faith in Jesus based on seeing him risen and to signal the transition from such faith to believing in the apostles' testimony.[15] Even Thomas should have believed his fellow disciples rather than demanding further proof (Ridderbos 1997: 649; Morris 1995: 754; contra Barrett 1978: 573).[16] Hence, Jesus' blessing really pertains to John's readers.[17]

This concludes the "literary partnership" shared by Mary Magdalene and Thomas in John 20. The readers have traced their journey from misunderstanding and doubt to a recognition of the risen Lord and positive witness and confession. "Mary is not a weak, helpless woman moving blindly from one misapprehension to another, nor is Thomas a pessimistic character prone to existential doubt. Just as Magdalene is the witness to the resurrection and announces its meaning, so Thomas brings that faith to a climax and acts as a bridge for future believers" (Lee 1995: 49). Such a believing response to Jesus, in turn, is the pathway to eternal life, which transcends living merely in terms of physical presence and earthly relationships.

1997: 647; contra Borchert 2002: 315). See also 2 Sam. 7:28; 1 Kings 18:39; Ps. 29:3; 86:15; 88:1; Jer. 31:18; Zech. 13:9.

12. An inscription dated 24 B.C. dedicates a building "to the god and lord Socnopaeus" (Deissmann 1927: 361–62).

13. Keener 2003: 1211–12. A Greek parallel is "O Lord God" in Epictetus, *Arriani epistula ad Lucium Gellium* 2.16.13. Only decades later, Pliny attests that Christians worshiped Christ as God (*Epistulae* 10.96 [before A.D. 115]). Other confessions in John include 1:49; 4:42; 6:69; 9:38; 11:27; 16:30; 20:16.

14. So, rightly, the majority of commentators (e.g., Ridderbos 197: 648; Morris 1995: 754; Carson 1991: 659; Beasley-Murray 1999: 386; Burge 2000: 563; Barrett 1978: 573; Schnackenburg 1990: 3.334; contra Borchert 2002: 316; R. Brown 1970: 1027).

15. For an in-depth study of the Thomas narrative, see Bonney 2002, who argues that 20:24–29 "serves to reveal Jesus' identity rather than to criticize the manner in which Thomas comes to faith" (p. 172).

16. Note also John's (and Jesus') negative evaluation of people's dependence on miracles (e.g., 4:48; 6:26). The saying in 20:29, which encompasses future believers as well (cf. 17:20), probably is echoed in 1 Pet. 1:8; similarly, Paul in 2 Cor. 5:7: "We live by faith, not by sight."

17. The only other macarism (pronouncement of blessing) in John is 13:17.

D. Conclusion: The Signs of the Messiah Witnessed by the New Messianic Community (20:30–31)

John 20:30–31 contains perhaps the clearest purpose statement found in any of the Gospels. The present concluding passage makes reference to virtually all the major themes covered in the preceding narrative: certain selected signs of Jesus; the necessity of believing that the Christ, the Son of God, is Jesus; and the promise of present (not merely future) possession of eternal life.[1]

Exegesis and Exposition

[30]So, then, Jesus also performed many other signs before his disciples that are not written in this book. [31]Yet these are written so that ⌜you may believe⌝ that it is Jesus who is the Christ, the Son of God, and that by believing you may have life in his name.

Coming as it does on the heels of Jesus' implicit rebuke to Thomas (οὖν, **20:30–31** *oun*, so then),[2] the present penultimate concluding statement shows that faith based on Jesus' "signs" ought not to be disparaged (Ridderbos 1997: 650): "but these [signs] are written so that you may believe."[3]

---

1. Keener (2003: 1213) says that 20:30–31 is the conclusion of the book, followed by the epilogue of chapter 21. Keener (2003: 1221, with reference to Whitacre 1999: 489) also cites other places in the Johannine writings where summary conclusions are followed by additional material (e.g., John 12:36–37; 1 John 5:13; Rev. 22:5).

2. Carson (1991: 660–61) construes the connection between 20:29 and 20:30 as follows. Individuals who have not seen the risen Christ, yet believe, are blessed; therefore, the present Gospel has been written in order that its readers may believe on the basis of its testimony to Jesus' signs. The construction μὲν . . . δέ contrasts the totality of Jesus' signs with those recorded in John's narrative.

3. Parallels to this type of concluding statement can be documented from both secular and intertestamental Jewish literature (Bultmann 1971: 697–98 n. 2). After describing God's creative work and the marvels of nature, one intertestamental book concludes a section with these words: "We could say more but could never say enough; let the final word be: 'He is the all'" (Sir. 43:27). Even closer in wording is 1 Macc. 9:22: "Now the rest of the acts of Judas . . . and the brave deeds that he did . . . have not been recorded, but they were very many." Schlatter (1948: 362) also refers to Luke 3:17; Josephus, *Ant.* 3.15.3 §318; 7.7.5 §161; he also notes the exact verbal parallel of γεγραμμένα ἐν τῷ βιβλίῳ τούτῳ found in Rev. 22:19.

As mentioned, Jesus' signs in John's Gospel are confined to the period of Jesus' public ministry to the Jews in John 1–12 (see commentary at 2:1; cf. Köstenberger 1995b).[4] The present reference harks back to the first half of the Gospel culminating in a similar summary statement in 12:37.

The signs selected for inclusion in the present Gospel are presented as evidence that it is Jesus who is the Christ, the Son of God (see 1:41, 49; 11:27).[5] Believing on account of these signs (cf., e.g., 1:12) leads to having life in Jesus' name (see commentary at 1:4). Reading this programmatic purpose statement ought to send the reader back to the preceding narrative in order to revisit the description of Jesus' signs and to ponder once more what it means to have faith in Jesus and hence to have life in his name. This is true regardless of whether those readers are unbelievers or believers.[6] Moreover, the emphasis here probably lies on identifying the Messiah as Jesus rather than Jesus as Messiah (see Carson 1991: 662; contra Wallace 1995: 46–47).

Additional Note

20:31. It is hard to determine which of the two major extant variants, the present subjunctive πιστεύητε ($\mathfrak{P}^{66vid}$ ℵ* B [so Ridderbos 1997: 652; Barrett 1978: 575; R. Brown 1970: 1056; Moloney 1998: 544; Fee 1992: 2193–2205]) or the aorist subjunctive πιστεύσητε (A C D [so Morris 1995: 755 n. 88; Carson 1991: 662]), is original (cf. the stance adopted by the UBS committee, per Metzger 1994: 219–20). On balance, the aorist subjunctive (which is the virtually undisputed reading in 19:35) may be more likely, though as mentioned in the preceding commentary, this is not essential for construing the thrust of the purpose statement in the present passage.

4. Contra Carson (1991: 661), who contends that the preeminent sign is Jesus' death, resurrection, and exaltation; and Beasley-Murray (1999: 387), who maintains that the resurrection appearances should also be viewed as signs.

5. Contra those who would see ταῦτα (*tauta*, these) in 20:31 referring not to the antecedent πολλὰ ἄλλα σημεῖα (*polla alla sēmeia*, many other signs) in 20:30 but, on the contrary, to "these things" other than those signs. The term "Christ" is mentioned with possible or definite reference to Jesus in 1:41; 4:25, 29; 7:26, 27, 31, 41, 42; 9:22; 10:24; 11:27; 12:34; 20:31. "Son of God" occurs in 1:34, 49; 3:18; 5:25; 10:36; 11:4, 27; 19:7; 20:31. Though closely related, the two terms are not synonymous (Ridderbos 1997: 653; contra Beasley-Murray 1999: 388). "Christ" primarily relates to Jewish messianic expectations; "Son of God" also has messianic connotations but beyond this accentuates more keenly relationship with God, especially in the context of the Johannine characterization of Jesus as the Son of the Father.

6. So, rightly, Bultmann 1971: 698–99. The question does not hinge on adjudicating which of the textual variants, πιστεύητε or πιστεύσητε, is original (see additional note), for verb tenses are less distinctive in nonindicative moods (cf. 19:35, where most MSS have the aorist reading). It is sometimes alleged that the present subjunctive would imply a purpose of strengthening the faith of believing readers, while the aorist would imply an evangelistic purpose (Metzger 1994: 219–20). However, as Carson (1991: 662) points out, the present tense of πιστεύω (*pisteuō*, believe) is used in this Gospel with reference to both coming to faith and continuing in faith. Carson also notes that the aorist subjunctive is more common after ἵνα (*hina*, that) than the present subjunctive.

IV. Epilogue: The Complementary Roles of Peter and the Disciple Jesus Loved (21:1–25)

Throughout the Johannine narrative, Jesus is repeatedly identified as Christ and Son of God. If the Gospel were to conclude with 20:30–31, this purpose statement would, at least on those grounds, provide sufficient closure.[1] In fact, it has been conjectured that John originally planned to finish his Gospel at this point and only later appended an additional chapter.[2] Alternatively, it has been suggested that someone other than John, perhaps some of his disciples, added chapter 21 after the apostle's death (e.g., Roberts 1987). This is possible. However, the presence of an epilogue[3] seems required by the opening prologue in order to preserve balance and

---

1. Barrett (1978: 577) states, "Ch. 20 is a unit which *needs* no supplement"; even more strongly, R. Brown (1970: 1078) asserts, "The clear termination . . . seems to *preclude* any further narrative" (both cited in Schenk 1992: 530). Gaventa (1996: 240–52, citing B. Smith 1968: 34) notes that closure "allows the reader to be satisfied by the failure of continuation." On one level, it is impossible to expect closure for Jesus' incarnation and public ministry (cf. 21:25); on another level, however, a reasonable form of closure is for Jesus to return to the Father, from whom he came, and to leave behind a well-trained group of followers who will continue his ministry. Moreover, the treatment of Peter and the beloved disciple in the final chapter creates a sense of open-endedness with regard to the situation faced by the church at the time of writing, similar to the teaching on the Paraclete in chapters 14 and 16.

2. So the majority of commentators, including Morris 1995: 753; Schnackenburg 1990: 3.335; R. Brown 1970: 1047–48; Burge 2000: 563; contra Borchert 2002: 317 (but see n. 94). See Reim 1976: 330 (cited in Minear 1983: 85).

3. On ancient epilogues, see Schenk 1992: esp. 528–30. Schenk argues that it is intrinsic to the nature of epilogues that they appear (at least at first glance) to be superfluous. According to Schenk, the function of John 21 is one of legitimation of the work by way of a conventional legal συγγραφή. Breck (1992) distinguishes between appendix, epilogue, and conclusion, contending that John 21 is a conclusion rather than an epilogue (e.g., R. Brown 1970: 1081; Osborne 1981: 294) or an appendix (e.g., Bacon 1931: 71; Lindars 1972: 618). He points to the Johannine pattern of double endings (cf. 1 John 5:13, followed by vv. 14–21), contends that 20:30–31 and 21:25 form an "inclusion-conclusion" parallelism enveloping a macrochiasm, and claims that 20:30–31 is a more fitting conclusion to chapter 20 than to the Gospel as a whole (following Minear 1983: esp. 87; cf. Vorster 1992: 2219; but see Spencer 1999: 52). He also points to 21:14 as indicating that 21:24–25 rather than 20:30–31 serves as the conclusion of the Gospel. I concur that John 21 forms an integral part of the Gospel. However, I would add that labeling that chapter as an "epilogue" does not necessarily imply

symmetry of structure. The prologue, in turn, is tied in so closely with the remainder of the Gospel that its composition cannot be easily relegated to a later follower of John.[4] Hence, both prologue and epilogue frame the Gospel in such a way that they form an integral part of the theological and literary fabric of the entire narrative.[5] Particularly notable is the way in which the relationship between Peter and the beloved disciple is resolved in terms of noncompetition.[6] Another crucial element of resolution is the identification of the beloved disciple as the Fourth Evangelist.[7] What is

---

attributing it to later disciples; John, as the original author, could just as well have written it himself. Moreover, Breck's proposal seems to diminish unduly the vital function and structural significance of 20:30–31 as embracing the entire Gospel rather than merely concluding chapter 20 (cf. esp. 12:37).

4. Gaventa (1996: 246–47), drawing on Torgovnick's (1981) insights on closure, suggests that chapters 20 and 21 pursue different "strategies of closure." According to Gaventa, chapter 20 structurally corresponds primarily to the prologue (cf., e.g., 20:17 with 1:10; 20:24–31 with 1:7, 13; and 20:28, 31 with 1:18), while chapter 21 recalls a number of scenes throughout the Gospel (cf., e.g., 21:24 with 1:6–8; 21:18–19 with 10:11; 21:15–23 with 13:36) (on the connections between the call narratives of chapters 1 and 21, see Franzmann and Klinger 1992). What is more, chapters 20 and 21 also differ in focus, with chapter 20 centering primarily on Jesus, and chapter 21 foregrounding (two select representatives of) the disciples. There is some truth in this, but oversimplifications should be avoided. John's narrative strategy is doubtless more complex than is often thought.

5. So Ridderbos (1997: 656), who states, "There is much that argues for ascribing the majority of ch. 21 to the Evangelist, as the completion of his narrative, albeit as a striking . . . addition to a provisionally concluded whole." Among the tie-ins between chapters 21 and 1–20, Ridderbos cites 21:1, 14 (referring back to the preceding resurrection account, in which Peter and the beloved disciple are linked) and the connection between Peter's reinstatement in 21:15–23 and 13:38/18:16ff. According to Ridderbos (1997: 658), the chapter "was added to describe the passage from Jesus' work on earth to its continuation through his disciples." Keener (2003: 1219–22), too, makes a strong case for the literary unity of John 21 as a chapter and as an integral part of the entire Gospel. He notes that, apart from special vocabulary needed for the matters at hand (such as fishing terminology), chapter 21 does not differ significantly from the rest of the Gospel. Keener (2003: 1219, citing Bruce 1983: 398) lists the following commonalities: the variation of synonymous terms in 21:15–17; the double ἀμήν (21:18); the construction "This he said, indicating" (21:19; cf. 12:33); and the reference to the Sea of Tiberias (21:1; cf. 6:1). Contra, for example, Dodd (1953: 290), who claims that chapter 21 "falls outside the design of the book as a whole" (cited in Minear 1983: 87 n. 11).

6. So Culpepper 1983: 96. See also Schlatter (1948: 366), who contends that the sustained characterization of Peter and John in 1:35–42; 13:23–29; 18:15–17; 20:2–10; and chapter 21 cannot be assigned to different hands; Ridderbos (1997: 656), who says that the final chapter is designed to bring into sharper profile the roles of Peter and the beloved disciple; and Carson (1991: 667), who notes that their relationship is removed from the realm of competition and their complementarity strongly and explicitly affirmed. Minear (1983: 91) writes, "Only in chapter 21 do we discover an adequate end to the story of the two disciples who, from chapter 13 on, have played the most conspicuous supporting roles in the gospel: Simon Peter and the beloved disciple."

7. This is astutely observed by Minear (1983: 95), though I disagree that the "we" of 21:24 and the "I" of 21:25 are two different persons or groups (see further below).

more, not only do language and style in chapter 21 not differ significantly from chapters 1–20,[8] but also there are actually positive terminological links between this final chapter and the rest of the Gospel.[9] Also, there is no textual evidence that the Gospel ever circulated in any form other than the present, canonical one (Ellis 1992: 18; Mahoney 1974: 12 [cited in Minear 1983: 86]). Finally, ending the Gospel immediately after Jesus' encounter with Thomas would have seemed rather abrupt.[10] For these reasons it must be maintained that the epilogue constitutes an integral part of John's Gospel.[11] It is part of John's overall literary

8. See Ridderbos (1997: 656 n. 3), who cites Schlatter: "The attribution of the new narrative to another author is impossible, however, since the identical linguistic conventions have been fully maintained." Even Bultmann (1971: 700) declares, "*Language and style* admittedly afford no sure proof." Similarly, Neirynck (1990: 336) concludes that "the evidence of style and vocabulary . . . is ambiguous and not decisive." Barrett (1978: 576) provides a list of words used in chapter 21 but not in chapters 1–20. See also Breck (1992: 36), who notes that words unique to chapter 21 in John's Gospel are either "technical expressions linked to the fishing trade" (ἁλιεύω, πιάζω, αἰγιαλός, προσφάγιον, δίκτυον, σύρω, ἀποβαίνω) or particular expressions required by their respective contexts (πρωΐα, ἐπενδύτης, γυμνός, βόσκω, ἀρνίον, ποιμαίνω, προβάτιον [variant of πρόβατα, the more likely reading in 21:16–17]).
9. See Schlatter 1948: 363–77. Note, for example, the references to a charcoal fire in 21:9 and 18:18 and to "drawing" in 21:8 and 12:32, as well as the links between 21:20; 13:23; 1:18 (see Ellis 1992: 18–19). See also the common elements between the good shepherd discourse in chapter 10 and Peter's commissioning in 21:15–19 (Cassian 1956–57: 132–36 [cited in Minear 1983: 95 n. 24]). Minear (1983: 96–97) further notes the appellation of Thomas as "the twin" in 20:24 and 11:16; the references to Nathanael in 21:2 and 1:45–51 and to Cana in chapters 2, 4, and 21; and several other terminological and thematic connections. Gaventa (1996: 245) notes the similarity between μετὰ ταῦτα (*meta tauta*, after these things) in 21:1 and 19:38. To this may be added the term "Sea of Tiberias" (21:1; cf. 6:1); Simon Peter "son of John" (21:15; cf. 1:42); Jesus' taking (λαμβάνω, *lambanō*) and distributing (δίδωμι, *didōmi*) bread (21:13; cf. 6:11 [close verbal parallels with 6:11, where Jesus' giving thanks is explicitly mentioned, may imply thanksgiving in 21:13]); the double ἀμήν (*amēn*, truly) (21:18; cf., e.g., 1:51); the connection between Peter's and Jesus' death established by the evangelist's parenthetical comment (21:19; cf. 12:33); Jesus' call for his disciples to "follow" him (21:19, 22; cf. 1:43); and other verbal links, grammatical features, and thematic connections (Osborne 1981: 294). Spencer (1999) finds the following "narrative echoes" of earlier portions in John's narrative: (1) the feeding of the five thousand (ch. 6); (2) Peter's threefold denial (18:15–18, 25–27); (3) the footwashing and the final meal (13:3–5, 36–38); and (4) the good shepherd discourse (10:1–18). Note, however, that Spencer considers chapter 21 to be a "later redactional addition" (p. 68).
10. Carson's (1991: 666) comments are particularly insightful: "But as in a 'whodunit' where all the pieces have finally come together . . . , there remains certain authorial discretion: the book may end abruptly . . . or it may wind down through a postscript that tells what happens to the characters, especially if what happens to them sheds a certain light backward onto the principal plot of the work." Contra Barrett (1978: 577), who expresses doubt that an author would spoil the effect of the commissioning in 20:21–23 by representing the disciples thereafter as returning to their former employment and as at first being unable to recognize their Lord; and R. Brown (1970: 1078) who attributes chapter 21 to a later redactor.
11. Carson (1991: 667) mentions one additional possible purpose of chapter 21: "The death of Peter and its relation in God's providence to the Evangelist's long life provide an

plan and provides the culmination of various strands carefully woven earlier in the Gospel. In fact, both the prologue and the epilogue can be shown to be integrally connected to the body of the Gospel by way of anticipation and resolution.

Prologue/Anticipation		Body/Explication		Epilogue/Resolution	
1:1 (and 1:18)	Word was God	20:28	My Lord and God		
		5:18; 8:59; 10:31–39; 19:7	Charges of blasphemy		
1:4a	In him was life	5:26	Jesus has life in himself		
		11:25	Jesus is resurrection and life		
		14:6	Jesus is way, truth, and life		
1:4b–5, 9–10	People's light	3:19–21; 8:12 = 9:5; 12:35–36, 46	Believe in the light		
1:6–8, 15	Testimony of John the Baptist	1:19–37; 3:22–30; 5:31–36; 10:40–42	Ministry of John the Baptist		
1:10–11	Jesus' rejection by the world (including Israel)	12:37–43; 15:18–27; 18:1–19:42	World and Israel reject Jesus	21:19	Peter glorifies God by dying same death as Jesus
1:12–13	Children of God	3:3, 5–8	Born of God		
		8:31–58	Children of the devil		
		11:51–52	Scattered children of God		
1:14 (and 1:16–17, 18)	We have seen his glory	2:11; 9:3; 11:4, 40; cf. 3:2	Jesus' signs display God's glory to disciples		
	One-of-a-kind Son	3:16, 18	One-of-a-kind Son		
	Full of grace and truth	14:6; 18:36–37	Jesus is the truth		
		1:51; 3:3, 5, 11, etc.	Jesus speaks the truth		
1:17	Law through Moses; true, ultimate grace through Jesus Christ	2:6; 5:10, 45–47; 7:19; 9:14–16; 13:1–17:26	Jesus transcends limitations of Jewish law; delivers farewell discourse		
1:18	Jesus at the Father's side has given full account of him	1:19–21:19 (esp. 13:23)	Entire Gospel is evangelist's full account of Jesus' explication of the Father	21:20–25	Disciple Jesus loved = Fourth Evangelist

opportunity to articulate at a practical level some implications of the sustained tension throughout the Gospel between the dominant inaugurated eschatology (congruent with the Evangelist's long life and therefore with the 'delayed' parousia) and the futurist eschatology of apocalyptic expectation." See also Gaventa (1996), who conceives of 20:30–31 and chapter 21 as "dual" or "parallel" endings featuring an "archive of excess" (McCracken's term). Whereas McCracken (1994: 151) applies this solely to the concluding hyperbole in 21:25, Gaventa extends the notion of "excess" to the entire chapter, encompassing also the 153 fish, the breakfast prepared even before the fish are hauled ashore, the strength of the nets, Jesus' threefold question to Peter, and, of course, the boundless number of Jesus' deeds. Though chapters 20 and 21 may indeed constitute an instance of "double closure," however, it may still be meaningful to speak of chapter 21 as an epilogue mirroring the prologue within the context of John's overall literary structure.

A. Jesus Appears to Seven Disciples (21:1–14)

John 20 has already chronicled two of Jesus' resurrection appearances to his disciples. John 21 adds the third and final appearance featured in this Gospel.

Exegesis and Exposition

¹After these things Jesus revealed himself again to the disciples at the Sea of Tiberias. And this is the way in which he revealed himself. ²Simon Peter, Thomas (called Didymus), Nathanael (the one from Cana in Galilee), the sons of Zebedee, and two other disciples were together. ³Simon Peter said to them, "I'm going fishing." They said to him, "We'll also come with you." They went and got into the boat, but that night they caught nothing. ⁴Now when it was already early morning, Jesus stood at the shore. (Yet the disciples did not realize that it was Jesus.) ⁵So Jesus said to them, "You don't have anything to eat, guys, do you?" They answered him, "No." ⁶Then he said to them, "Cast the net on the right side of the boat, and you will find some." So they cast it, and they were unable to haul it in owing to the large number of fish. ⁷Then that disciple whom Jesus loved said to Peter, "It's the Lord!" So when Simon Peter heard that it was the Lord, he wrapped his outer garment around him—for he had taken it off—and plunged himself into the lake. ⁸And the other disciples went in the boat, towing the net full of fish, for the distance from the shore was no more than about a hundred yards. ⁹So when they stepped onto the shore, they saw a charcoal fire there with fish on it and bread. ¹⁰Jesus said to them, "Bring some of the fish you've just caught." ¹¹Then Simon Peter climbed aboard and dragged the net ashore, full of large fish, 153; yet even though there were so many, the net was not torn. ¹²Jesus said to them, "Come, have breakfast." Yet none of the disciples dared ask him, "Who are you?" because they knew that it was the Lord. ¹³Jesus came and took the bread and gave it to them, and likewise the fish. ¹⁴This was now the third time that Jesus had revealed himself to the disciples since he had been raised from the dead.

21:1–3 "After these things" (see commentary at 2:12) signals that with the week-long Feast of Unleavened Bread now past, the disciples have left Jerusalem and returned to Galilee (cf. Luke 2:43; see Moule 1957–58).

"Again" explicitly identifies the following account as a resurrection narrative (cf. 21:14; see Ridderbos 1997: 658). "Sea of Tiberias" is an alternate designation for the Sea of Galilee (see commentary at 6:1).[1] The word φανερόω (phaneroō, reveal) designates the subsequent appearance of the risen Lord Jesus as a "revelatory act."[2] Indeed, Jesus' progressive self-disclosure is the constitutive element of John 21, which moves "from lack of knowledge to knowledge limited to the Beloved Disciple to knowledge shared by all" (Gaventa 1996: 243).

Of the seven, Simon Peter[3] is named first, as would be expected (6:68; 13:6, 9; 20:2–7). The readers are by now familiar with Thomas ("the twin"; see 11:16; 20:24). Nathanael, who has not been heard from since 1:45–51, is here said to come from Cana, the site of the first two of Jesus' signs (2:1–11; 4:46–54).[4] The sons of Zebedee are mentioned only here in this Gospel. Their names are given in the Synoptics as James and John (e.g., Matt. 4:21 par.). Luke mentions that they were "Simon's partners" in fishing prior to being called by Jesus (Luke 5:10). Regarding the "two other disciples," it is not uncommon for John to leave disciples unnamed (cf. 1:35–39; 18:15–16; 20:2, 4, 8).[5]

A group of (seven) disciples "were together."[6] The disciples probably had returned to Galilee in obedience to Jesus' command (Matt. 26:32; 28:7, 10 par.). Perhaps while waiting for further instructions, Peter, the commissioning in 20:21–23 notwithstanding, temporarily returns to his old occupation. Characteristically, he takes the initiative and is joined

1. Perhaps the gloss is added with a view toward the Gospel's Greek-speaking readership, though there is no reason why this should be relegated to the redactional (rather than authorial) level (contra R. Brown 1970: 1067; Schnackenburg 1990: 3.351; Witherington 1995: 405).

2. As always, undertaken at Jesus' initiative (Carson 1991: 668; cf. Morris 1995: 760). The term also occurs in 21:14, marking off 21:1–14 as the first of two scenes in this chapter (Gaventa 1996: 242).

3. The customary designation for Peter in this Gospel (see 1:40; 6:8, 68; 13:6, 9, 24, 36; 18:10, 15, 25; 20:2, 6; 21:2, 3, 7, 11).

4. Breck (1992: 27–49, following Ellis 1984; 1992) lays out 1:19–51 and 20:19–21:25 in inverted parallelism involving Nathanael.

5. The important implication for the authorship of John's Gospel is that since the "disciple Jesus loved" is identified as the author in 21:24 (cf. 21:20), and since he is one of the seven (21:7), the author must be one of the seven mentioned in 21:2. This makes it eminently plausible that the author (the "beloved disciple") is John, one of the two sons of Zebedee (Köstenberger 1999a: 22–24).

6. Ridderbos (1997: 658–59) detects in this a reference to "the unity they [the disciples] recovered after Jesus' resurrection." Similarly, Talbert (1992: 259) sees in this "unity" an answer to Jesus' prayer in 17:11 and a result of the Spirit's enabling. This seems to rest too much interpretive weight on the rather inconspicuous expression "were together," however. Little else in the context suggests that these disciples are Spirit-filled (note that they caught no fish). The presence of symbolism in the number seven is doubtful as well (so, rightly, Ridderbos 1997: 650; Carson 1991: 669; contra Schnackenburg 1990: 3.352; Beasley-Murray 1999: 399; Borchert 2002: 324); it is hard to see what would connote "completeness" in the present instance (contra Brodie 1993: 582).

by six associates.[7] They get into "the" boat,[8] yet, as on previous occasions, "that night they caught nothing."[9] Nighttime was the preferred
time for fishing in ancient times, including first-century Galilee (e.g.,
Luke 5:5). That way, fish caught before daybreak could be sold fresh
in the morning.[10]

Early in the morning,[11] Peter and his friends (who are by now doubtless   **21:4–6**
weary and hungry) are addressed by a stranger from the shore.[12] The
disciples' not realizing that it was Jesus, in keeping with other instances
where disciples are kept from recognizing their risen Lord (Luke 24:16,
37; see commentary at 20:14), serves to underscore Jesus' transcendent
glory.[13] Alternatively, the early morning hour (cf. 20:1) or the distance

7. This, incidentally, is yet another argument against reading 20:22 as indicating an
actual impartation of the Spirit at that point. Had they already received the Spirit, it would
be almost inexplicable why Peter went back to fishing so soon after that event. So, rightly,
Carson (1991: 669–70 [cf. Morris 1995: 760]): "It is impossible to imagine any of this taking place in Acts, *after Pentecost* . . . this is not the portrait of believers who have received
the promised Paraclete." Barrett (1978: 579) considers it "unthinkable" that Peter and his
fellow disciples "should contemplate a return to their former occupation after the events
of chapter 20." Contra Keener (2003: 1227), who argues against negative interpretations
of the disciples' return to fishing in 21:3, saying that the disciples simply made use of free
time (citing Bruce 1983: 399). Keener also cites Beasley-Murray's (1999: 399) contention
that, even though Jesus had risen from the dead, the disciples must still eat.
8. The definite article with πλοῖον (*ploion*, boat) may imply that "this is the boat habitually used for fishing" (R. Brown 1970: 1069).
9. Cf. Luke 5:1–11. Stibbe's (1993: 210) characterization of the event that Peter initiates
is insightful: "Having failed Jesus so obviously in 18.15–27, he now seeks to suppress and
even obliterate the shame in his life by reverting to 'life before Christ,' to fishing. He seeks
to deny the three denials. This attempt to fill his 'hole in the soul' with work fails dismally.
The narrator laconically remarks that 'they caught nothing.'"
10. Carson (1991: 670) here (as elsewhere) detects symbolism in the "night" reference,
citing 3:2, 19–21; 13:30; 20:1. However, though 3:19–21 and 13:30 qualify, it is less clear
that 3:2, 20:1, and the present instance do. Stibbe (1993: 210) draws attention to the
fact that "the time between night and the early hours of the morning was precisely the
time when Peter denied Jesus in 18.15–27." Brodie's (1993: 583) casting of the symbolism as setting "their boat in an atmosphere of alien darkness" seems overdone, as does
Whitacre's (1999: 490) contention that the early morning hour symbolizes "the dawning
of spiritual light."
11. "Early morning" is reminiscent of the similar phrase at the beginning of the previous chapter (see commentary at 20:1). Borchert's (2002: 326) symbolic interpretation
("a new morning having arrived not only physically but also as a Johannine theological
symbolization of the arrival of a new era") fails to convince.
12. The reference to Jesus "standing" (ἵστημι, *histēmi*) at the shore is part of a pattern
of describing Jesus' presence in the resurrection narratives (cf. 20:14, 19, 26; see Ridderbos
1997: 659). Morris (1995: 761) notes, "It is not said that he came there or the like, and the
choice of language may be a hint at the kind of thing we see in earlier passages, where
Jesus suddenly appears behind closed doors."
13. So, rightly, Beasley-Murray 1999: 400: "The Jesus whom they were meeting in his
Easter glory was living in a different mode of existence from that of his former earthly
conditions."

from the shore may have made it difficult for the disciples to see Jesus clearly.[14]

"Friends" (TNIV) reads more literally "children" (παιδία, *paidia*), perhaps used in a colloquial sense equivalent to the English "lads" (R. Brown 1970: 1070), the Irish "boys," or the American "guys" (Carson 1991: 670).[15] Jesus' question once again reveals supernatural insight.[16] The rare term προσφάγιον (*prosphagion*, fish), not found elsewhere in biblical literature, is the first of three different expressions for "fish" in the present narrative. The reference is most likely to a "bite to eat," which in first-century Galilee often would have been a piece of fish. Remarkably, the disciples never catch a fish in any of the Gospels without Jesus' help.

With regard to Jesus' command for the disciples to throw out their net, three different kinds of nets were used: one that was cast by hand; one that was spread out from a boat and trawled through the water with cables on poles; and one that was stretched out in deep water. In the present instance, the trawl net is most likely (Dalman 1928–39: 6.346–51, esp. 349; Keener 1993: 318). Peter was told to cast his net on the right side of the boat.[17] The right side was the auspicious one.[18] More importantly, Jesus knows which side is the right one, and the disciples follow his instructions.

In light of the disciples' questions as to whether and how their relationship with Jesus will continue beyond the cross, the present account places them one more time in the Johannine narrative in the familiar setting of following the earthly Jesus, who elsewhere had promised to

14. Barrett (1978: 579) and R. Brown (1970: 1070) have difficulty accommodating this statement within a unified authorial framework. The former finds it hard to fathom the disciples' failing to recognize Jesus, on the assumption that they had seen him twice since the resurrection. The latter uses the opportunity to reaffirm his belief that the present pericope represents Jesus' first resurrection appearance rather than a later incident.

15. Cf. 1 John 2:14, 18; in John 13:33, the word for "children" is τεκνία (*teknia*). However, understanding this as a familiar reference must be tempered with placing it in the larger context of first-century teacher-disciple relationships (so, rightly, Ridderbos 1997: 660; Moloney 1998: 552, with further reference to 1 John). On this topic, see Köstenberger 1998a: 119–26.

16. Ridderbos (1997: 660) suggests, alternatively, that Jesus may know the answer "because the disciples were still fishing at the break of day." However, this hardly seems to be an adequate explanation in the light of John's characterization of Jesus both before and especially subsequent to the resurrection (note, e.g., Jesus' prediction of Peter's martyrdom in 21:18–19).

17. Morris (1995: 762 n. 17, citing H. V. Morton) conjectures that an individual on the shore may be able to see better than the one fishing and thus may plausibly direct the latter on where to cast the net. Similarly, Laney (1992: 375) suggests that "perhaps the disciples thought the stranger on the shore could see a school of fish near the surface of the water."

18. See Matt. 25:33; cf., e.g., Xenophon, *Cyropaedia* 7.1.3. See Str-B 1:980; BDAG 217. Brodie (1993: 584) draws rather precarious conclusions from the fact that the only other instance of the term "right" in this Gospel is Peter's cutting off of Malchus's right ear in 18:10.

make them "fishers of people." In the interim between the anticipatory sign of giving the Spirit and Pentecost, Jesus reassures his followers that there is no vacuum and that he will keep his promise and enable them to fulfill their commission. Hence, what Jesus promised his followers at the very outset over three years ago is now on the verge of fulfillment.[19]

Again, Peter and the beloved disciple appear together.[20] In characteristic fashion, the beloved disciple displays spiritual discernment, while Peter exhibits decisive action (Carson 1991: 671; cf. Ridderbos 1997: 660). In yet another recognition scene (cf. 20:16; see also 20:28), the "disciple Jesus loved" exclaims, "It's the Lord!" "Lord" has previously served as a christological confession in the resurrection narrative in 20:18, 25, 28.

21:7–10

Simon Peter "wrapped his outer garment around him—for he had taken it off—and plunged himself into the lake."[21] People would tuck up and tie up their clothes so that they had freedom of movement.[22] The "outer garment" in the present case was probably a fisherman's coat (ἐπενδύτης, *ependytēs*) that Peter wore in the morning chill (R. Brown 1970: 1072). The Greek underlying "for he had taken it off" means literally "for he was naked," but this may merely mean that Peter wore only his undergarment (so, rightly, the TNIV), probably the short tunic of the Greek workman (Avi-Yonah 1964: 155).[23] He tucked in his outer garment in order to be able to swim (rather than wade—the shoreline drops off rather rapidly at most parts of the lake) ashore more easily and to be properly dressed for greeting Jesus.[24]

19. In that sense, but only in that sense, R. Brown is right in seeing parallels between the present incident and Luke 5. Regarding the interpretation taken here, compare especially Ridderbos 1997: 660, though he sees more overt symbolism in the present pericope than I do.

20. Cf. 13:23–25; 18:15–18; 20:2–10; 21:20–24; see Köstenberger 1998b: 154–61. On "the disciple Jesus loved," see commentary at 13:23; 19:26; 21:2 (see also 18:15; 20:3, 8; and commentary at 21:20). For Peter's characterization in John 21, see Wiarda 2000: 111–14, 139–40, 175–78.

21. The verb "wrap [clothes] around [oneself]" (διαζώννυμι, *diazōnnymi*) occurs in the NT only in John (Luke employs the LXX form περιζώννυμι, *perizōnnymi*). Burge (2000: 583–84) adduces some interesting evidence regarding fishing practices on the Sea of Galilee (see also Burge 1998), though there appears to be some incongruity in his suggesting at one point that Peter dove into the water "checking the cast nets (21:7)" and his comments elsewhere that Peter jumped in in order to swim to Jesus.

22. See Ridderbos 1997: 661 n. 17; Soards 1983. In 13:4–5, the same term is used for Jesus' wrapping a towel around himself in preparation for washing his disciples' feet.

23. Note the translation by R. Brown (1970: 1066): "Simon Peter tucked in his outer garment (for he was otherwise naked)." Similarly, Morris (1995: 763) contends "that here the word means that parts of the body normally covered were exposed, so that Peter was not naked but rather 'stripped for work.'"

24. So, rightly, Barrett 1978: 580–81; Morris 1995: 762 n. 19 (though Soards [1983: 283] may have a point when he says "that the impetuous Peter met in this story would not have modesty uppermost in his mind"). Cf. *t. Ber.* 2.20.

The other disciples went in the boat, towing the net full of fish.[25] The distance was about a hundred yards, more literally "about two hundred cubits," one cubit being about half a yard. Ever the servant (cf. 13:1–17; see also 21:13; see Carson 1991: 671), Jesus had made a fire of burning coals (see commentary at 18:18).[26] There was already fish on the fire (the singular ὀψάριον, *opsarion*, fish [cf. 6:9, 11] may suggest that just one large fish was being cooked).[27] Moreover, Jesus encourages the disciples to bring some of the fish they just caught, which indicates that Jesus both enables his followers and then uses what they procure.[28]

21:11–14 Simon Peter climbed aboard and dragged the net ashore. Earlier, the entire group was unable to haul in the net because of the large number of fish (21:6). Now, with Peter—a man no doubt very strong physically to begin with—further energized through the appearance of his risen Lord, the net is dragged ashore. Even so, the phrase "Peter . . . dragged the net ashore" need not be taken to imply that he did so all by himself (Morris 1995: 764; Barrett 1978: 581; contra Witherington 1995: 354).

25. Wallace (1996: 155) classifies τῷ πλοιαρίῳ (*tō ploiariō*, in the boat) as a dative of sphere and τῶν ἰχθύων (*tōn ichthyōn*, of the fish) as a genitive of content (1996: 93). The word for "towing" or "dragging" (σύρω, *syrō*; used elsewhere in the NT only figuratively) occurs in connection with a trawl net in Plutarch, *De sollertia animalium* 977.F. Carson (1991: 671) sees in the narrator's staying with the disciples in the boat rather than following Peter in his encounter with Jesus "a small indication of eyewitness integrity." If the narrator is none other than John, the son of Zebedee, of course, he himself would have been in that boat, which may further explain why the story is told the way it is.

26. Borchert (2002: 329) insightfully compares the references to a charcoal fire in 18:18 and the present passage, commenting, "Although the earlier fire marked the symbol of an uninviting situation of cold, hostile questioning, this second fire with its fish and bread must be seen as an inviting setting . . . providing a new commissioning for Peter." Similarly, Stibbe (1993: 211–12) says, "Jesus is recreating the setting in which Peter denied him."

27. The heading "The Banquet" for 21:9–14 in Keener (2003: 1230) seems overdone; one would hardly call a few fried fish at a lakeshore a banquet. Barrett (1978: 581), seeking to resolve the apparent difficulty of Jesus already cooking fish before the disciples had brought the fish ashore, suggests a literary solution in which two stories, one featuring the disciples catching and bringing the fish and another describing Jesus providing the meal, were being combined. More likely, the presence of fish prior to the disciples bringing theirs is yet another hint at Jesus' supernatural powers of provision.

28. Ridderbos (1997: 662) notes how Jesus involves his followers as those who will continue his work on earth (more restrained is Morris [1995: 764]). This, of course, has already been his practice during his earthly ministry (e.g., 6:5–13). Moreover, care must be taken not to overreach in finding symbolism in every detail of this or other Johannine narratives. For instance, it would be wrong to infer from the present instance a kind of synergism in which believers collaborate with Jesus in his provision as if what Jesus provides were insufficient to meet their needs.

The net was full of large fish, 153 of them.[29] Various attempts have been made to interpret the full net,[30] and specifically the number 153, symbolically (most recently, Brooke 1999), but more likely it simply represents the number of fish counted.[31] The inclusion of the specific number most likely reflects eyewitness recollection and points to the generous provision of Jesus.[32] Indeed, an abundant catch of fish was considered to be evidence of God's favor (T. Zeb. 6:6). The fact that even with so many fish the net was not torn seems to be attributed by the evangelist to divine intervention (Morris 1995: 766)—yet one more detail in the present account that adds to the aura of an encounter with the risen Jesus.[33]

Jesus' invitation to his disciples must surely have been welcome: "Come, have breakfast" (cf. 21:15). First-century Jews normally ate two meals a day (cf. Luke 14:12), with "breakfast" (ἄριστον, ariston) being the first of these, generally eaten before starting a day's work (though it could be an

29. Whatever symbolism there may be in the present reference (see below), the event does not, in my opinion, constitute a Johannine sign, since the signs are confined to the period of Jesus' public ministry to the Jews (John 1–12). See Köstenberger 1995b. Contra, among others, Keener (2003: 1234), who seems to imply that the catch of 153 fish is a Johannine sign.

30. For example, R. Brown (1970: 1097), who interprets the full net allegorically as the absence of schism in the Christian community; Bultmann (1971: 709), who speaks of the "indestructible unity of the Church"; Michaels (1989: 354–55), who contends that the full net indicates the successful completion of Jesus' mission; and Talbert (1992: 260), who says that the 153 fish symbolize the universal outreach of the church. For a virtually exhaustive list of interpretations of the number 153, no matter how implausible, see Keener (2003: 1231–33). He properly concludes that "the number could simply stem from an accurate memory of a careful count on the occasion, because fish had to be counted to be divided among fishermen." Keener (2003: 1233) also notes that 153 fish may be no more symbolic than Peter swimming 100 yards in 21:8.

31. Contra efforts to unlock the alleged numerical symbolism, as does Brodie (1993: 586–88), who notes that 153 is the triangular number of 17, which is the sum of both 10+7 and 12+5, all four of which are significant numbers in the Gospel. Calvin (1961: 217) called these kinds of efforts "childish trifling." On a different note, Ridderbos (1997: 663) categorically states that "carefully counting the fish after a catch was probably never done," but it is unclear on what basis he can make such a sweeping pronouncement.

32. So, for example, R. Brown (1970: 1076), who sees the origin of the number in authentic eyewitness, citing 21:24. Note also the presence of the sons of Zebedee, according to 21:2. Large numbers elsewhere in John are meant literally as well (e.g., 2:6; 12:3); Schlatter (1948: 368) notes that the large number of fish caught points to Jesus' generous, abundant provision, citing 2:6; 6:13. More questionable are Burge's (2000: 586) reference to 153 being "numerically important" for "Greek mathematicians" and Bultmann's (1971: 709) assertion that the number is allegorical "since it is not a round number." For proper cautions against allegorical interpretations, see Ridderbos 1997: 663.

33. The unbroken net frequently is interpreted symbolically as conveying the preservation of all that is caught (Ridderbos 197: 663, adducing 6:12; Witherington 1995: 355; Michaels 1989: 354–55), or the limitless number of Christian converts (Carson 1991: 673, following Bruce 1983: 401–2), or the unity of the church (Talbert 1992: 260). For surveys, see Carson 1991: 672–73; R. Brown 1970: 1074–76.

early lunch as well; cf. Luke 11:37–38). Yet despite the promise of fellowship as in days past, none of the disciples dared ask him, "Who are you?"[34] They knew that it was the Lord (cf. John 4:27; 16:18–19). The marvel of Jesus' resurrection, still unfamiliar to his followers, had further added to the aura of respect commanded by Jesus (Carson 1991: 674).[35]

"Jesus came[36] and took the bread and gave it to them, and likewise the fish."[37] Jesus here performs the act of the Jewish host pronouncing the blessing at a meal (cf. verbal parallels with the thanksgiving in 6:11, 23). As Schnackenburg (1990: 3.359) observes, however, the way the present meal is narrated makes clear that this is no ordinary meal: "There is no mention of a conversation, not even of the disciples' eating. . . . Jesus, the host, is absolutely central; his gestures speak for themselves." The mundaneness of the simple breakfast is dwarfed by the presence of the risen Lord and the implications of his resurrection for the life of his followers.

The reference to this being "the third time" Jesus appeared to his disciples after he was raised from the dead, plus the verb φανερόω (*phaneroō*, reveal), ties the present account in with the previous two appearances of Jesus to his disciples (20:19–23, 26–29)[38] and provides an *inclusio* with 21:1 (Carson 1991: 674–75; R. Brown 1970: 1083), marking off 21:1–14 as a unit.

---

34. Witherington (1995: 354) considers this to be "a fellowship meal, a family reunion of a sort" (similarly, Michaels 1989: 356, 358), contra those who would detect the presence of "eucharistic symbolism" (e.g., R. Brown 1970: 1098–1100; D. M. Smith 1999: 394; Stibbe 1993: 212; Whitacre 1999: 494). In fact, Beasley-Murray (1999: 404) points out that what is celebrated here is not Jesus' death but his resurrection, which enabled his followers to enjoy fellowship with their Lord subsequent to his death. He classifies the present meal as "an epiphany celebration of the risen Lord" (following Rissi 1979: 81–86). Schlatter (1948: 369) says that the disciples' present disposition fulfills 16:23.

35. So also Ridderbos (1997: 664), though, as elsewhere, Ridderbos may somewhat overstate his point when he speaks of "the miracle of the 'wholly-otherness' of his [Jesus'] presence and of their 'knowing' him." On "the Lord," see 21:7.

36. As previously, indicative of his appearance (see Ridderbos 1997: 664).

37. On the strength of the fact that only here and in John 6 is there mention of fish and bread, and that John 6 includes Jesus' "bread of life discourse," which displays eucharistic overtones, Shaw (1974) contends that the present pericope and Jesus' encounter with Mary Magdalene (seeing parallels between 20:17 and 3:13; 6:62) constitute "eucharistic narratives." He also perceives the presence of a "quasi-eucharistic meal" in the Lukan Emmaus narrative (24:13–35). According to Shaw, the point made in the two Johannine "eucharistic narratives" is that believers on this side of the ascension are able to encounter Christ by way of participation in the Eucharist. Despite its considerable sophistication, however, Shaw's effort represents an unsuccessful effort to impose eucharistic theology onto the narratives in question. Not only are the links between chapter 6 and chapters 20 and 21 not as pronounced as he alleges, but also there is in fact a rather stark contrast between the extensive elaboration on Jesus as the "bread of life" in chapter 6 and the absence of such "eucharistic" elaboration in chapters 20 and 21.

38. Not counting the episode with Mary Magdalene, who was not one of the Twelve (cf. 1 Cor. 15:5, 7–8).

B. Jesus and Peter (21:15–19)

After breakfast, Jesus takes Peter aside in order to commission him for service. In the context of John's Gospel, Peter's threefold affirmation of his love for Jesus mirrors, and offsets, his threefold denial of Jesus preceding the crucifixion (cf. 18:15–18, 25–27). Although Jesus had expressed forgiveness to Peter and apparently had appeared to him privately prior to the present encounter (cf. Luke 24:34; 1 Cor. 15:5), the public nature of his denial of Jesus demands that his reinstatement to service be equally public in full view of his fellow disciples. There is also a connection between the present scene and Peter's earlier pledges of loyalty in the presence of the other disciples (cf. 13:8, 37–38; 18:10–11; see Carson 1991: 675–76).

Exegesis and Exposition

[15]So when they had had breakfast, Jesus said to Simon Peter, "Simon, son of John, do you love me more than these?" He [Peter] said to him, "Yes, Lord, you know that I love you." He [Jesus] said to him, "Tend my lambs." [16]He said to him again a second time, "Simon, son of John, do you love me?" He [Peter] said to him, "Yes, Lord, you know that I love you." He [Jesus] said to him, "Shepherd my sheep." [17]He said to him a third time, "Simon, son of John, do you love me?" Peter was grieved that he said to him a third time, "Do you love me?" and he said to him, "Lord, you know all things; you know that I love you." He [Jesus] said to him, "Tend my sheep. [18]Truly, truly, I say to you, when you were younger, you girded yourself and went where you wanted; but when you are old, you will stretch out your hands, and someone else will gird you and bring you where you don't want to go." [19](Now he said this in order to indicate by what kind of death he [Peter] would glorify God.) And having said this, he said to him, "Follow me."

There is an element of déjà vu in the ensuing scene: a charcoal fire and **21:15–17** three questions regarding Peter's stance toward Jesus (Borchert 2002: 335).[1] The setting matches rather closely that of Peter's previous denials of Jesus, though this time the outcome will be markedly different. The address of Peter as "Simon, son of John" may constitute an *inclu-*

---

1. On the way in which 21:15–23 brings closure to the entire Gospel narrative, see the introduction to John 21 above. For interesting thoughts on the contribution of 21:15–25, see Barrett 1982b.

sio with 1:42.[2] Predictably, Roman Catholic interpreters tend to see in the present passage evidence for Petrine primacy.[3] But nothing in the present passage suggests "a *distinctive* authority for Peter. . . . These verses deal with Peter's reinstatement to service, not with his elevation to primacy" (Carson 1991: 679). Peter is neither charged to serve as "Jesus' earthly vicar" nor appointed as the "chief shepherd to whom all the other shepherds are subordinate" (Ridderbos 1997: 666). In fact, in his first epistle, Peter pointedly calls Jesus "the chief shepherd" (1 Pet. 5:4) and places himself as "fellow elder" alongside other shepherds of God's flock (1 Pet. 5:1–2).

It surely is significant that the one thing about which Jesus questions Peter prior to commissioning him for service is love, specifically, supreme love for Jesus himself.[4] Paradoxically, one who loves Jesus supremely will love those entrusted into his charge more, not less. In this call to love, Jesus does not treat Peter differently from other individuals whom he called to follow him in discipleship.[5] The fact that there are two different verbs for "love" used in the present passage has led some to believe that ἀγαπάω (*agapaō*) and φιλέω (*phileō*) are distinct in meaning, but this is doubtful for at least two reasons: (1) the fact that the word ἀγαπάω, said to convey the notion of divine love, is used with reference to human love—and evil humans at that—in texts such as 3:19 and 12:43, and that φιλέω, said to connote human love, is used for God the Father in 5:20 (where he is said to love the Son) and 16:27 (where he is said to love the disciples); (2) the presence of other close synonyms in the same section, such as the use of two words for "know" (γινώσκω, *ginōskō*; οἶδα, *oida*), and stylistic variants of "tend/shepherd" (βόσκω, *boskō*; ποιμαίνω, *poimainō*) "my sheep/lambs" (ἀρνία, *arnia*; πρόβατα, *probata*) in 21:15–17 (Köstenberger 1999a: 193–94; Carson 1991: 676–77, citing Barr 1987: esp. 15).[6]

2. There is some affinity between the present passage and Peter being given the "keys of the kingdom" in Matt. 16:19. Note also the primacy of Peter in the early stages of the Christian movement as seen in the Book of Acts.

3. Though see the disclaimers by R. Brown (1970: 1112–17), who says that Peter's authority is not absolute, and Schnackenburg (1990: 3.365), who cautions that later Roman Catholic exegesis should not be read into this passage.

4. This is somewhat overlooked by Morris (1995: 772), who notes that love is indispensable for Christian service and adduces as a parallel 1 Cor. 13:1–3.

5. Though it is fascinating to contemplate the contrast in John 21 between the beloved disciple, who knows himself to be loved by Jesus (21:7a, 20a), and Peter, who is called to love Jesus (21:15–17). See Schenk 1992: 516–17, referring to Stenger 1990: 240 and Ruckstuhl 1977: 340, 343, 356.

6. But see the dissenting opinion of McKay (1985: esp. 323), who concludes that "the pattern of variation of forms of ἀγαπάω and φιλέω in this passage are not pointless [in apparent reaction to N. Turner 1976], but constitute a contextual distinction which is not blatant, but gently significant" (p. 333). However, it is unclear what McKay means by "not blatant, but gently significant," especially since he never elaborates on this assertion with reference to the use of these two verbs in 21:15–17.

But we must discern the thrust of the question "Do you truly love me more than these?" Is Jesus' question whether Peter loves him more than he loves these men (Witherington 1995: 356, citing Osborne 1981: 308)? Is it whether Peter loves him more than these men do (Morris 1995: 768; Carson 1991: 675–76)? Or is Jesus asking whether Peter loves him more than he loves these fish—that is, his profession (Wiarda 1992: esp. 62–64; Keener 2003: 1236)? On one level, all three are true: Peter must love Jesus more than he loves other people (Matt. 10:37; Luke 14:26) or his natural profession (Mark 1:16–18; Luke 5:1–11), and he is called to love Jesus more than these other men do and to be willing to render extraordinary sacrifice on behalf of his master (John 6:67–69; 13:36–38; 21:18–19). Indeed, Peter earlier had claimed a devotion to Jesus exceeding that of the other disciples (Matt. 26:33; Mark 14:29; John 13:37; cf. 15:12–13). Hence, in context, the second alternative seems most likely here: Jesus challenges Peter to love him more than the other disciples do. Notably, the love required of Peter is primarily for Jesus rather than for the flock; it is to be "a love of total attachment and exclusive service" (cf. Deut. 6:5; 10:12–13; see R. Brown 1970: 1115). Those who want to be used significantly in God's service must be willing to make greater sacrifices for the Lord they serve.

"Tend my lambs. . . . Shepherd my sheep. . . . Tend my sheep." Shepherd imagery abounds in the OT, which is pervaded by a yearning for shepherds who are devoted to God, care for his sheep, and carry out his will (Ezek. 34; Jer. 3:15; cf. Isa. 44:28; see commentary on ch. 10).[7] The term βόσκω (boskō, tend) regularly occurs in the LXX for feeding sheep (e.g., Gen. 29:7; 37:12); the metaphorical sense is already found in Ezek. 34:2. The two verbs βόσκω and ποιμαίνω (poimainō, shepherd) jointly span the fullness of the task given to Peter (R. Brown 1970: 1105; cf. Schnackenburg 1990: 3.363).[8] Three decades later, Peter wrote similar words to the churches entrusted to his care (1 Pet. 5:1–3; cf. Paul in Acts 20:28–31). Jesus' threefold repetition of his question may reflect the Near Eastern custom of reiterating a matter three times before witnesses in order to convey a solemn obligation, especially with regard to contracts conferring rights or legal dispositions. By analogy, Jesus' threefold question lends solemnity to the occasion of his commissioning Peter to his special shepherding task (Gächter 1947: 328–44).[9]

When Jesus, the third time he asks the question, finally adopts Peter's word for "love," Peter is not relieved but rather saddened that Jesus has asked him the same question a third time (Ridderbos 1997: 667; Michaels

---

7. At Qumran, the metaphor is applied to the authoritative overseer, mebaqqer (CD 13:9).

8. Stibbe (1993: 213) notes that Peter had acted like a hired hand at his three denials of Jesus in John 18; now, Jesus evokes pastoral imagery to call him back to his vocation as a model shepherd.

9. Regarding "Lord, you know all things," see commentary at 2:25.

1989: 364; cf. Barrett 1978: 585).[10] Peter's response, "Lord, you know all things," rather than pointing to actions of his own that prove his loyalty, defers to Jesus' knowledge of him: "If Jesus does not know that Peter loves him, what can Peter say to assure him?" (R. Brown 1970: 1106). Perhaps at long last Peter has learned that he cannot follow Jesus in his own strength and has realized the hollowness of affirming his own loyalty in a way that relies more on his own power of will than on Jesus' enablement (cf. 13:36–38—significantly, in response to Jesus' "new" love commandment). Likewise, we should soundly distrust self-serving pledges of loyalty today that betray self-reliance rather than a humble awareness of one's own limitations in acting on one's best intentions.

21:18–19 Jesus now makes clear what prompted his questioning in 21:15–17 in the first place: "Jesus has sought not so much Peter's triple retraction of his denial, and even less to embarrass him again before the other disciples; it is rather what awaits Peter in the future that prompts Jesus to reinforce his ties with him as never before" (Ridderbos 1997: 667). The contrast "when you were younger . . . but when you are old" is found in a different context in Ps. 37:25.[11] In the ancient world, the expression "stretch out . . . hands" (ἐκτείνω τὰς χεῖρας, *ekteinō tas cheiras*) was widely taken to refer to crucifixion.[12] The "stretching" occurred when a condemned man was tied to the horizontal crossbar, the *patibulum* (see commentary at 19:17) and compelled to carry his cross to the place of execution.[13] Hence, Jesus almost certainly refers not merely to an unspecified martyr's death on the part of Peter in the future but more specifically to martyrdom by crucifixion—the same kind of death that he himself had suffered.[14]

Jesus said this "in order to indicate by what kind of death Peter would glorify God." This text sheds light on the more cryptic reference in 13:36, where Jesus had said to Peter, "Where I am going, you cannot follow now, but you will follow later." Note also the verbal link with 12:33 (cf.

10. Contra Laney (1992: 381), who says that Peter was hurt "when Jesus used his own word to ask about his love."

11. Bultmann (1971: 713) sees the origin of this saying in a proverb; but see the critique by Carson (1991: 679).

12. This is illustrated by the following passages: Epictetus, *Diatribai* 3.26.22; Seneca, *Ad Marciam de consolatione* 20.3; Dionysius of Halicarnassus, *Antiquitates romanae* 7.69; Tertullian, *De pudicitia* 22 (cited in Köstenberger 2002c: 194). See Bauer (1925: 232) and Haenchen (1984: 2.226–27), who also note passages in Artemidorus and Plautus; Beasley-Murray 1999: 408–9; Hengel 1977: esp. chapter 4.

13. Note also that patristic interpreters read Isa. 65:2 with reference to the crucifixion (Barn. 12; Justin Martyr, *1 Apol.* 35; Irenaeus, *Epid.* 79; see Barrett 1978: 585).

14. Note further the verbal link between the reference to Jesus' "lifting up" (i.e., crucifixion) in 12:32–33 and the reference to Peter's future destiny in 21:19. See Carson 1991: 679–80; Beasley-Murray 1999: 408–9; Barrett 1978: 585. Contra Ridderbos (1997: 667); Morris (1995: 773); and Schnackenburg (1990: 3.366–67), who believe that the reference is more generally to martyrdom.

18:32).[15] Peter follows Christ not only in the kind of death he suffers (i.e., crucifixion) but also in thus bringing glory to God (cf. 12:27–28; 13:31–32; 17:1). By the time John wrote his Gospel, Jesus' prediction had been fulfilled. According to Clement of Rome (ca. A.D. 96), Peter had suffered martyrdom under Nero (A.D. 54–68) (1 Clem. 5:4), probably during the final years of Nero's reign (ca. A.D. 64–66).[16] Later, Tertullian (ca. A.D. 212) asserted that Peter was crucified.[17]

Jesus' injunction to Peter here, "Follow me" (cf. 21:22), may, on a literal level, constitute an invitation to a private walk. On a more profound note, the command reiterates Jesus' initial call for the disciple to follow him (cf. 1:43; see Carson 1991: 680). There may also be an allusion to Jesus' words in 13:36–38 (Ridderbos 1997: 668; cf. Schnackenburg 1990: 3.367). In light of Jesus' words in 21:18–19, his call to Peter to follow him now takes on a new and deeper meaning. The rest of Peter's life must be lived in the shadow of the cross, just as Jesus' was. As such a man, who has renounced all earthly ties and who has declared his supreme loyalty to Jesus, Peter is commissioned to serve as shepherd of Jesus' flock as the Great Shepherd takes his leave (Ridderbos 1997: 668).

The Fourth Evangelist's characterization of the disciple Jesus loved and Peter in relation both to Jesus and to each other finds its resolution in the final chapter of John's Gospel.

Verbal Echoes Linking Jesus' Roles to Those of Disciple Jesus Loved and Peter

Prologue	Body: First Half	Body: Second Half	Epilogue
1:1–18	1:19–12:50	13:1–20:31	21:1–25
Jesus		**Disciple Jesus Loved**	
1:18 At Father's side (*kolpos*), full account		13:23, 25 At Jesus' side (*kolpos; stēthos*)	21:20–25 At Jesus' side (*stēthos*), full account
		Peter	
	12:33 Indicating what kind of death		21:19 Indicating what kind of death

Relationship between Disciple Jesus Loved and Peter in Second Half of John's Gospel

	Upper Room 13:23–24	High Priest's Courtyard 18:15–16	Empty Tomb 20:2–9	Sea of Galilee 21:15–23
Peter	Motions to disciple Jesus loved	Waits outside	Arrives second; no response recorded	Admonished by Jesus
Disciple Jesus Loved	Asks Jesus	Secures access for Peter	Outruns Peter; believes	Special assignment from Jesus

15. A different parallelism links Jesus and the "disciple Jesus loved" (cf. 1:18 with 13:23).

16. In 1 Pet. 5:13, Peter is placed in Rome not too much earlier.

17. *Scorpiace* 15 (cited in Köstenberger 2002c: 214 n. 666). Blomberg (2002: 278) also cites Acts Pet. 37–39 and Eusebius, *Hist. eccl.* 3.1.

C. Jesus and the Disciple Jesus Loved (21:20–25)

The Gospel concludes with a final interchange between Jesus, Peter, and "the beloved disciple," which gave rise to a rumor that is promptly dispelled.[1] The postscript claims eyewitness testimony for the entire Gospel (cf. 19:35), and by identifying the Fourth Evangelist with the "disciple Jesus loved" (21:24; cf. 21:20; 13:23), it implicitly points to Johannine authorship.[2]

Exegesis and Exposition

[20]Turning around, Peter saw the disciple whom Jesus loved following [them]—the one who had leaned against his chest at the dinner and said, "Lord, who is the one who will betray you?" [21]So when Peter saw this disciple he said to Jesus, "Lord, but what about him?" [22]Jesus said to him, "If I want him to stay until I come, is that any of your business? You follow me!" [23]So the word went out to the believers that this disciple would not die; but Jesus did not say that he would not die, but, "If I want him to stay until I come, is that any of your business?"

[24]This is the disciple who testifies concerning these things and who wrote these things down, and we know that his testimony is true.

[25]And there were also many other things that Jesus did, which, if they were written down one by one, I suppose the whole world could not contain the books that would be written.

21:20–23 Apparently, after breakfast Jesus and Peter go for a walk by the lake (see commentary at 21:19), with the beloved disciple (on whom, see commentary at 13:23, 25; 21:7) within earshot (Carson 1991: 675; Ridderbos 1997: 668 n. 38).[3] The evangelist's parenthetical comment here,

1. Interestingly, part of Matthew's last chapter is likewise devoted to dispelling a false rumor, in his case that Jesus' disciples had stolen Jesus' body (Matt. 28:11–15; cf. 27:62–66).
2. See Vanhoozer 1993 and also the brief summary of the relevance of Vanhoozer's contribution to the case for the apostolic authorship of the Fourth Gospel in the section on hermeneutical presuppositions in the introduction to the present commentary.
3. Barrett (1978: 586) detects in the reference to the beloved disciple as "following" Jesus (and Peter) in 21:20 yet another hint at this disciple's superiority over Peter: "The beloved

"the one who had leaned against his chest at the dinner and said, 'Lord, who is the one who will betray you?'" is one of several references to characters or events mentioned earlier in the narrative.[4] The reference points once again in conclusion to the disciple's closeness to Jesus during his earthly ministry (cf. 13:24–25), which is presented as lending special credibility to the present Gospel account (21:22, 24; see Carson 1991: 681).

When Peter, perhaps emboldened by his restoration to leadership (Morris 1995: 774), inquires about the beloved disciple's destiny, Jesus' answer is, in effect, that this is none of his business.[5] Peter (note the emphatic σύ, *sy*, you) must follow Jesus. Yet some among "the believers" (ἀδελφοί, *adelphoi*, lit., "brothers") apparently understood this to mean that the beloved disciple would not die prior to Jesus' return.[6] It is not impossible that these final verses were penned by John's disciples subsequent to his death in order to counter the charge that Jesus' prediction had been proven erroneous by John's death.[7] More likely perhaps is the suggestion that John himself, while still alive, sought to lay to rest the rumor that Christ had promised to return during his lifetime.[8] This would be even more plausible if ancient patristic testimony is correct

disciple was already doing what Peter had just been bidden to do" (yet see the skepticism voiced by R. Brown [1970: 1108]). Schlatter (1948: 372–73) notes how the beloved disciple here, as elsewhere in the Gospel (at his first recorded encounter with Jesus [1:37], at his entry into the high priest's courtyard, and at the cross), is the silent listener.

4. Cf. 4:46; 6:23; 7:50; 9:13, 18, 24; 10:40; 12:1–2, 9; 18:14, 26; 19:39. See the excursus "Asides" in Köstenberger 1999a: 250–52.

5. Most likely, Peter, just having been told that he would be martyred in the future, wants to know if, once again, the beloved disciple will fare better and be spared a similar fate. Contra Morris (1995: 774), who construes Peter's motivation much more positively: "Happy in his own position, Peter now gave thought to his friend." The words "if I want him to remain" emphasize Jesus' authority and power, which is not accountable to Peter (Ridderbos 1997: 668–69).

6. Augustine (*In Iohannis Evangelium* 124.1 [cited in Volfing 2001: 51 n. 79]) already acknowledges the difficulty of understanding the import of Jesus' words. While presupposing Peter's martyrdom and John's dying a natural death, he follows an allegorical line of interpretation, seeing the two apostles as representing, respectively, the *vita activa* ("active life") and the *vita contemplativa* ("contemplative life"), with the latter being superior to the former (Volfing 2001: 51–53). Literal interpretations are advocated by Bede and Rupert of Deutz (Volfing 2001: 53 n. 83). Some patristic and medieval authors also seek to alleviate the apparent difficulty that Jesus predicted that both sons of Zebedee would drink from his bitter cup (Matt. 20:23; see references in Volfing 2001: 55).

7. So Barrett 1978: 587; Schnackenburg 1990: 3.371; R. Brown 1970: 1117–19.

8. So Carson (1991: 682), who contends, "It seems simpler to think that the circulating rumour is making the rounds while the beloved disciple is still alive, but advancing in years, and he is determined to stifle it as well as he can for fear of the damage that would be done if he died before the Lord's return" (cf. Morris 1995: 775). Jackson (1999: 21–22) maintains that 21:23 "makes perfectly good sense as a corrective from a living Beloved Disciple anxious to dispel what he feels are overly enthusiastic eschatological inferences being drawn by some from Jesus' words."

that John's life span extended to the reign of Trajan (Irenaeus, *Haer.* 2.22.5; 3.3.4).[9]

Possibly some, including Peter, were tempted to mistake the beloved disciple's closeness to Jesus as favoritism. Indeed, if this disciple is none other than John the son of Zebedee, he (or at least his mother) was not entirely innocent in fostering this impression (see Mark 10:35–45, esp. v. 41; cf. Matt. 20:20–28). Yet Jesus does not see a need to justify his different treatment of the "disciple he loved" here.[10] Peter is called to pastoral ministry and martyrdom, John to a long life and strategic, written witness—both callings are vital and equally important (Carson 1991: 681). In a personal lesson on discipleship, Jesus tells Peter to be content with his own calling and to leave that of others to him. This, in turn, becomes a general lesson relevant also for the readers of the Gospel.[11]

As Ridderbos (1997: 669) comments incisively, the evangelist "suggests that, while Peter's destiny lay in the God-glorifying significance of his death, Jesus' purpose with the other disciple lay rather in his *continuing*, though not in the sense—as the Evangelist expressly states—that this disciple could not die before the coming of Jesus. Instead, by continuing, he would serve Jesus as his disciple throughout his life. . . . What applies to both disciples is the call to follow Jesus, each with his own destiny." For Peter, Christlikeness is found in martyrdom (cf. 21:19 with 12:33); for the beloved disciple, Christlikeness manifests itself in witness grounded in unparalleled intimacy with Jesus (cf. 21:20, 24 with 13:23; see Köstenberger 1998b: 154–61, esp. 161).

21:24–25   The concluding verses, 21:24–25 (esp. 21:24), should be read in the context of 21:20–23 rather than in isolation (Carson 1991: 683).[12] The

---

9. Volfing (2001: 48 n. 74) also cites Jerome (*Vir. ill. 9*), according to whom John "died sixty-eight years after the passion of the Lord" (assuming a crucifixion date of A.D. 33, this would be A.D. 101). Volfing (2001: 48–59) chronicles the emergence of legendary materials surrounding the mysterious reference to John "remaining" in 21:22.

10. Stibbe (1993: 214–15) contends that it "makes no sense at all for a rumour to spread concerning the immortality of a Galilaean fisherman," and on that basis he suggests that the beloved disciple is Lazarus, the one who had already been raised from the dead once, "the founder of the community and the authority behind the Gospel." This is intriguing indeed but highly conjectural and based on a very small amount of textual evidence.

11. Carson (1991: 682 [cf. Beasley-Murray 1999: 410]) suggests that the Fourth Evangelist may be encountering a situation similar to the one Paul faced in Corinth (see 1 Cor. 1–4, esp. 1:10–11). Thus, the evangelist is stressing that the mode of Christian service will vary from person to person and that the important thing is to follow Christ as his disciple. Hence, there will be one flock (John 10:16) in unity (ch. 17).

12. Keener (2003: 1240–42) seems open (if not favorable) toward the possibility that the author of the entire Gospel wrote the Gospel's final two verses, though he maintains that at least the plural in 21:24 would seem to represent others, discarding the possibility of an "editorial we" (see further below). Keener does not address the first-person singular verb in 21:25.

beloved disciple, the one who was close to Jesus at the last supper (21:20), is in fact the one who wrote the entire Gospel. His "staying" (rather than dying a martyr's death, as did Peter) enabled him to do so and thus served an important purpose, just as Peter's martyrdom did (Ridderbos 1997: 671). Hence, 21:24 is to be understood as part of the answer to Peter's question in 21:21: "Lord, but what about him?" (Carson 1991: 683; cf. Barrett 1978: 587)—though now it is no longer Jesus speaking but the evangelist.

Other intertextual links are evident between 21:24 and 19:35, which also establishes an explicit connection between the Fourth Evangelist and eyewitness testimony of Jesus' crucifixion, and between 21:25 and 20:30–31. The concluding verse reiterates the principle of selection operative in the composition of the Gospel, which has already been noted in the penultimate ending of 20:30–31. Yet "far from being a pale imitation of 20:30–31, they [21:24–25] make their own contribution to the credibility of the entire book" (Carson 1991: 667; contra Barrett 1978: 577; Lindars 1972: 642). Moreover, by moving from an indirect self-reference (see further below) to a statement regarding the inexhaustible wealth of material about Jesus, the evangelist directs attention to where it is due, similar to what occurs in 20:30–31.[13]

The statement in 21:24, "This is the disciple who testifies to these things and who wrote them down. We know that his testimony is true" (see 19:35; 1 John 1:1–4), in its formal, solemn tone, represents the signature and statement of autography also common in epistolary postscripts.[14] It comes on the heels of two retrospective references to "the disciple Jesus loved" in 21:7 and 21:20 and a third resumptive passage in 21:14. The function of the entire chapter is "to confirm the Beloved Disciple as author of the body of the document and to substantiate the credibility of his eyewitness authority for its content" (Jackson 1999: 9).[15]

The present verse identifies the Fourth Evangelist, the author of John's Gospel, with the literary character of "the disciple Jesus loved." This

13. As Carson (1991: 686) perceptively notes, "It is as if John had identified himself (v. 24), but is not content to focus on himself, not even on his veracity. He must close by saying his own work is only a minute part of all the honours due the Son."

14. See Gal. 6:11; Col. 4:18; 2 Thess. 3:17; Philem. 19. Morris (1995: 776) notes the present participle ὁ μαρτυρῶν (ho martyrōn, the one testifying) as "another indication that he [the beloved disciple] was still living" (see also Breck 1992: 33; contra Schnackenburg [1990: 3.372], who says that the evangelist "lives on in his testimony"). On the Johannine "witness" motif, see commentary at 1:7.

15. The most natural way to take the participle ὁ γράψας (ho grapsas, the one who wrote) is to see it as affirming that the evangelist himself wrote the Gospel. See the important critique of amanuensis theories formed on the basis of a suggested parallel with 19:19 (where Pilate caused things to be written down rather than writing them down himself) in Carson 1991: 685 (with reference to Bruce 1983: 3). As Carson points out, it is especially dubious to construe an amanuensis theory on the basis of later disciples writing down material on behalf of their deceased master.

figure, in turn, relates historically to John the apostle, the son of Zebedee.[16] The present verse is cast in the third person in order to affirm the credibility of the author's own witness.[17] In the second part of the verse, he shifts to the first-person plural,[18] and in the next verse to the first-person singular (οἶμαι, *oimai*, I suppose).[19] Here the author strikes a more informal, familiar tone to underscore his personal involvement and not to appear unduly detached from the events recorded earlier (Jackson 1999: 8).[20]

The identity of the "we" in 21:24 is subject to much debate, with most scholars identifying the expression as referring to the "community that formed around the beloved disciple, to which he left his Gospel and his legacy" (so, e.g., Ridderbos 1997: 671; cf. R. Brown 1970: 1125). Others see it more globally as the "apostolic church" (Barrett 1978: 588).[21] In this case it would be the community tracing its origin to the beloved disciple, or the larger church, that seeks to attest to the reliability of the evangelist's witness (Ridderbos 1997: 672). Nevertheless, taking "we" as a self-reference of the evangelist is preferable, with the first-person plural functioning editorially, as in other places in the present Gospel or elsewhere in the NT.[22]

16. See the introduction to the commentary.

17. "This is the disciple," "his testimony." See especially 19:35. Compare also Jesus' final prayer, where Jesus refers to himself as "Jesus Christ" (17:3), and Thucydides' practice of introducing himself in the third person (*History of the Peloponnesian War* 1.1.1; 5.26.1) and of referring to himself as "Thucydides" (ibid., 4.104.4: "Thucydides, the son of Oloros, who composed this history"; this is also true of Julius Caesar in *Gallic Wars*). See Jackson 1999: 27; see also there pp. 28–20 on Josephus.

18. An "associative collective," where the "you" subsumed under the "we" are the book's Christian readers, but where the "I" included in the "we" is the author (Jackson 1999: 23–24).

19. Contra Ridderbos (1997: 672), who takes the change in grammatical person as indication of "another hand." For a vigorous refutation of the view that 21:25 was added by a later editor, see J. Chapman (1930: 386–87), who contends that it is "quite inconceivable" that an interpolator composed this "very Johannine" verse. The main burden of Chapman's essay is to argue that "we know" in 21:24 constitutes a "plural of authorship."

20. On the implications of the use of the first-person singular verb οἶμαι for the Gospel's authorship, including a survey of interpretations of 21:24–25 and a discussion of pertinent first-century references featuring the term, see Köstenberger 2004.

21. Similarly, Morris (1995: 775), who vaguely refers to "people respected in the church who knew the facts of the case." Osborne (1981: 327, following Dodd) favors "the community as a whole as separate from the author of the epilogue." Moloney (1998: 562) focuses more on the way in which the "we" of 21:24 "involves [later] generations of Christian readers who know that this witness is true and who can give witness to their own belief."

22. Carson (1991: 684) adduces 1:14; 3:2, 11; 20:2; 1 John 1:2, 4, 5, 6, 7; 3 John 12; 2 Cor. 12:2–4; Schlatter (1948: 376), with reference to John 3:2 and 20:2, where the speaker is included in the plural, speaks of the possible presence of collaborators. Minear (1983: 95) believes that 1:14–18 and 21:24 are intended by the evangelist "to enclose his entire message to his audience." Wallace (1996: 399) lists the present passage as a (debatable) example of the exclusive "we," "in which the first-person plural restricts the group to the author and his associates" (p. 397).

In conclusion, the evangelist reinforces the selection principle already mentioned in 20:30–31 and further draws attention to the multitude of remarkable works performed by Jesus the Messiah. A particularly interesting feature of the final verse of John's Gospel (21:25) is the interjected word "I suppose" (οἶμαι, *oimai*; rare in the NT [cf. Luke 7:43; Acts 16:13; 1 Cor. 3:18; Phil. 1:17; James 1:7] but not uncommon in extrabiblical sources). As mentioned, it is widely held that the final two verses of the Gospel, perhaps together with the last chapter in its entirety, were added by the church or some later redactor. This appears to find support by the third-person reference to "this disciple who testifies concerning these things" and the first-person plural verb οἴδαμεν (*oidamen*, we know) in 21:24. This conclusion also nicely undergirds a variety of source-critical and redaction-critical theories surrounding the composition of the Fourth Gospel. The Johannine community, it is argued, here comes to the fore as the community responsible for the final version of the Gospel.[23]

These views would perhaps be more convincing if it were not for the presence of the first-person verb οἶμαι in 21:25. As Morris (1995: 775 n. 64) points out, if John 21:24–25 were added by a later group, one would expect the first-person plural to continue through verse 25. The stubborn fact is that it does not.[24] Indeed, a study of instances of οἶμαι in first-century Greek literature suggests that the expression is frequently used by historians to convey the notion of authorial modesty in stating a claim or opinion (e.g., Diodorus Siculus, *Bibliotheca historica* 8.12.15.10; Dionysius of Halicarnassus, *Antiquitates romanae* 4.74.2; 5.48.1; 6.35.2; *De Thucydide* 49.3; Plutarch, *Mulierum virtutes* [*Bravery of Women*] 243. D.7).[25] In its extrabiblical instances, the expression regularly forms an inextricable part of the author's argument and cannot easily be separated from the larger context by means of source or redaction criticism.

What is more, there seems to be no ancient precedent for a later editor or group of editors using the term in the context of authenticating the message of an original author or witness. While the convention of an "authorial we" is well-attested in ancient literature, the converse feature of a "communal I" is not found. This evidence appears to render untenable any redaction-critical proposals that the last one or two verses (21:24–25) be separated from the rest of the Gospel and assigned to a

---

23. Some view the statements in John 21:24–25 more narrowly as an authentication of the preceding Gospel by its recipients. Others draw more far-reaching implications from these final verses, holding that the Johannine community was responsible for writing the body of the Gospel. According to these interpreters, John's Gospel tells the story of Jesus in terms of the history of this Johannine community.

24. The rather bewildering array of interpretations attempting to come to terms with the shift from the first-person plural in 21:24 to the first-person singular in 21:25 is documented by a survey of the state of research in Köstenberger 2004.

25. For extensive documentation, see Köstenberger 2004.

different author, and it seems to bolster the case for the unity of chapter 21, if not also for apostolic authorship of the Fourth Gospel. Hence, we conclude that 21:24–25 was most likely written by the Fourth Evangelist rather than a later community, with "we know" in 21:24 reflecting an authorial "we" and "I suppose" in 21:25 constituting a self-reference by the evangelist.

"And there were also many other things that Jesus did, which, if they were written down one by one, I suppose the whole world could not contain the books that would be written." Hyperbolic statements such as these were a well-established literary convention at the time in both Greco-Roman and Jewish literature. The OT Book of Ecclesiastes ends with the acknowledgment that the wise Teacher had searched out many proverbs, but "of making many books there is no end" (12:9–12). Rabbi Yoḥanan ben Zakkai (ca. A.D. 80) reportedly said, "If all the heavens were sheets, all the trees quills and all the seas ink, they would not suffice for recording my wisdom which I acquired from my masters" (*Soperim* 16.8).[26] John's hyperbole, however, extols neither the books people write nor the wisdom people acquire, but rather the deeds Jesus performed. Taken together with the prologue's stress on Jesus' person, the epilogue's reference to his works renders John's christological portrait not exhaustively comprehensive but sufficiently complete.

---

26. Examples in Philo (*Post. Cain* 43 §144; *Drunk.* 9 §32; *Mos.* 1.38 §213) are cited in Köstenberger 2002c: 195 (see also Boring 1995: 308).

Works Cited

Abbott, E. A.
1906   *Johannine Grammar.* London: Black.

Abbott, L.
1879   *Illustrated Commentary on the Gospel according to St. John.* New York/Chicago: Barnes.

ABD   *The Anchor Bible Dictionary.* Edited by D. N. Freedman et al. 6 vols. New York: Doubleday, 1992.

Abegg, M. G., and C. A. Evans
1998   "Messianic Passages in the Dead Sea Scrolls." Pp. 191–203 in *Qumran-Messianism: Studies on the Messianic Expectations in the Dead Sea Scrolls.* Edited by J. H. Charlesworth et al. Tübingen: Mohr-Siebeck.

Abrahams, I.
1917   *Studies in Pharisaism and the Gospels.* 2 vols. Cambridge: Cambridge University Press.

Ådna, J.
2000   *Jesu Stellung zum Tempel: Die Tempelaktion und das Tempelwort als Ausdruck seiner messianischen Sendung.* Wissenschaftliche Untersuchungen zum Neuen Testament 2/119. Tübingen: Mohr-Siebeck.

Agourides, S.
1968   "The 'High Priestly Prayer' of Jesus." Pp. 137–45 in *Studia Evangelica,* vol. 4: *Papers Presented to the Third International Congress on New Testament Studies Held at Christ Church, Oxford, 1965.* Edited by F. L. Cross. Texte und Untersuchungen 102. Berlin: Akademie.

Albright, W. F.
1922–23   "Ophrah and Ephraim." *Annual of the American Schools of Oriental Research* 4:124–33.

1923   "New Identifications of Ancient Towns: Bethany in the Old Testament." *Bulletin of the American Schools of Oriental Research* 9:8–10.

1924   Untitled article. *Harvard Theological Review* 17:193–94.

1956   "Recent Discoveries in Palestine and the Gospel of St. John." Pp. 153–71 in *The Background of the New Testament and Its Eschatology: In Honour of C. H. Dodd.* Edited by W. D. Davies and D. Daube. Cambridge: Cambridge University Press.

Alexander, P. S.
1988   "Jewish Law in the Time of Jesus: Towards a Clarification of the Problem." Pp. 44–58 in *Law and Religion.* Edited by B. Lindars. Cambridge: Clarke.

1992   " 'The Parting of the Ways' from the Perspective of Rabbinic Judaism." Pp. 1–25 in *Jews and Christians: The Parting of the Ways A.D. 70 to 135.* Edited by J. D. G. Dunn. Tübingen: Mohr-Siebeck.

Anderson, P. N.
1996   *The Christology of the Fourth Gospel: Its Unity and Disunity in the Light of John 6.* Wissenschaftliche Untersuchungen zum Neuen Testament 2/78. Tübingen: Mohr-Siebeck.

Appold, M. L.
1976   *The Oneness Motif in the Fourth Gospel: Motif Analysis and Exegetical Probe into the Theology of John.* Wissenschaftliche Untersuchungen zum Neuen Testament 2/1. Tübingen: Mohr-Siebeck.

Argyle, A. W.
1971   "Note on John 4:35." *Expository Times* 82:247–48.

Ashton, J.
1986   "The Transformation of Wisdom: A Study of the Prologue of John's Gospel." *New Testament Studies* 32:161–86.

Asiedu-Peprah, M.
2001   *Johannine Sabbath Conflicts as Juridical Controversy: An Exegetical Study of John 5 and 9:1–10:21.* Wissenschaftliche Untersuchungen zum Neuen Testament 2/132. Tübingen: Mohr-Siebeck.

Attridge, H. W.
1980   "Thematic Development and Source Elaboration in John 7:1–36." *Catholic Biblical Quarterly* 42:160–70.
2002a   "Genre-Bending in the Fourth Gospel." *Journal of Biblical Literature* 121:3–21.
2002b   "Response to 'The De-historicizing of the Gospel of John' by Robert Kysar." Paper presented at the annual meeting of the Society of Biblical Literature, Toronto, November 23–26.

Augenstein, J.
1997   " 'Euer Gesetz'—Ein Pronomen und die johanneische Haltung zum Gesetz." *Zeitschrift für die neutestamentliche Wissenschaft* 88:311–13.

Aus, R.
1988   *Water into Wine and the Beheading of John the Baptist: Early Jewish-Christian Interpretation of Esther 1 in John 2:1–11 and Mark 6:17–29.* Brown Judaic Studies 150. Atlanta: Scholars Press.

Auwers, J.-M.
1990   "La nuit de Nicodème (*Jean* 3,2; 19,39) ou l'ombre du langage." *Revue biblique* 97:481–503.

Avi-Yonah, M.
1964   *The World of the Bible: The New Testament.* Yonkers, N.Y.: Educational Heritage.

Bacchiocchi, S.
1981   "John 5:17: Negation or Clarification of the Sabbath?" *Andrews University Seminary Studies* 19:3–19.

Bacon, B. W.
1929   "The Place of Jesus in the Religious Life of His Day." *Journal of Biblical Literature* 48:40–81.
1931   "The Motivation of John 21:15–25." *Journal of Biblical Literature* 50:71–80.

Badcock, F. J.
1935   "A Note on St. John ii.20." *Expository Times* 47:40–41.

BAGD   *A Greek-English Lexicon of the New Testament and Other Early Christian Literature.* By W. Bauer, W. F. Arndt, F. W. Gingrich, and F. W. Danker. 2d edition. Chicago: University of Chicago Press, 1979.

Baird, W.
1992   *History of New Testament Research,* vol. 1: *From Deism to Tübingen.* Minneapolis: Fortress.

Ball, D. M.
1996   *"I Am" in John's Gospel: Literary Function, Background and Theological Implications.* Journal for the Study of the New Testament: Supplement Series 124. Sheffield: Sheffield Academic Press.

Bammel, E.
1952   *"Philos tou Kaisaros." Theologische Literaturzeitung* 77:205–10.
1957   "Zu 1QS 9:10f." *Vetus Testamentum* 7:381–85.
1965   "John Did No Miracles: John 10:41." Pp. 197–202 in *Miracles.* Edited by C. F. D. Moule. London: Mowbrays.
1984   "The Trial before Pilate." Pp. 415–51 in *Jesus and the Politics of His Day.* Edited by E. Bammel and C. F. D. Moule. Cambridge: Cambridge University Press.
1993   "The Farewell Discourse of the Evangelist John and Its Jewish Heritage." *Tyndale Bulletin* 44:103–16.
1994   "Johannes 9.17." *New Testament Studies* 40:455–56.

Bammel, E. (ed.)
1970   *The Trial of Jesus.* Studies in Biblical Theology 2/13. London: SCM.

Barbet, P.
1953   *A Doctor at Calvary.* New York: Kennedy.

Barclay, W.
1975   *The Gospel of John.* Revised edition. 2 vols. Philadelphia: Westminster.

Barkay, G.
1986   "The Garden Tomb—Was Jesus Buried Here?" *Biblical Archaeology Review* 12/2:40–53, 56–57.

Barker, M.
1970   "John 11.50." Pp. 41–46 in *The Trial of Jesus: Cambridge Studies in Honour of C. F. D. Moule.* Edited by E. Bammel. Studies in Biblical Theology 2/13. London: SCM.

Barnett, P. W.
1980–81 "The Jewish Signs Prophets—A.D. 40–70: Their Intentions and Origin." *New Testament Studies* 27:679–97.

Barr, J.
1961 *The Semantics of Biblical Language.* London: SCM.
1987 "Words for Love in Biblical Greek." Pp. 3–18 in *The Glory of Christ in the New Testament: Studies in Christology in Memory of George Bradford Caird.* Edited by L. D. Hurst and N. T. Wright. Oxford: Clarendon.

Barrett, C. K.
1970 *The Holy Spirit and the Gospel Tradition.* Revised edition. London: SPCK.
1971 *The Prologue of St John's Gospel.* London: Athlone.
1975a *The Gospel of John and Judaism.* Translated by D. M. Smith. Philadelphia: Fortress.
1975b "The House of Prayer and the Den of Thieves." Pp. 13–20 in *Jesus und Paulus.* Edited by E. E. Ellis and E. Grässer. Göttingen: Vandenhoeck & Ruprecht.
1978 *The Gospel according to St. John.* 2d edition. Philadelphia: Westminster.
1982a " 'The Father Is Greater Than I' John 14.28: Subordinationist Christology in the New Testament." Pp. 19–36 in *Essays on John.* Philadelphia: Westminster.
1982b "John 21.15–25." Pp. 159–67 in *Essays on John.* Philadelphia: Westminster.

Barrosse, T.
1959 "The Seven Days of the New Creation in St. John's Gospel." *Catholic Biblical Quarterly* 21:507–16.

Bassler, J. M.
1989 "Mixed Signals: Nicodemus in the Fourth Gospel." *Journal of Biblical Literature* 108:635–46.

Bauckham, R.
1987 "The Parable of the Vine: Rediscovering a Lost Parable of Jesus." *New Testament Studies* 33:84–101.
1993 "Papias and Polycrates on the Origin of the Fourth Gospel." *Journal of Theological Studies* 44:24–69.
1996 "Nicodemus and the Gurion Family." *Journal of Theological Studies* 47:1–37.
1997 "Qumran and the Fourth Gospel: Is There a Connection?" Pp. 267–79 in *The Scrolls and the Scriptures: Qumran Fifty Years After.* Edited by S. E. Porter and C. A. Evans. Journal for the Study of the Pseudepigrapha: Supplement Series 26. Sheffield: Sheffield Academic Press.
1998a *God Crucified: Monotheism and Christology in the New Testament.* Grand Rapids: Eerdmans.
1998b "Life, Death, and the Afterlife in Second Temple Judaism." Pp. 80–95 in *Life in the Face of Death: The Resurrection Message of the New Testament.* Edited by R. N. Longenecker. Grand Rapids: Eerdmans.
2001 "The Audience of the Fourth Gospel." Pp. 101–11 in *Jesus in Johannine Tradition.* Edited by R. T. Fortna and T. Thatcher. Louisville: Westminster John Knox.

Bauckham, R. (ed.)
1998 *The Gospels for All Christians: Rethinking the Gospel Audiences.* Grand Rapids: Eerdmans.

Bauer, W.
1925 *Johannesevangelium.* 2d edition. Tübingen: Mohr.

BDAG *A Greek-English Lexicon of the New Testament and Other Early Christian Literature.* By W. Bauer, F. W. Danker, W. F. Arndt, and F. W. Gingrich. 3d edition. Chicago: University of Chicago Press, 2000.

BDF *A Greek Grammar of the New Testament and Other Early Christian Literature.* By F. Blass, A. Debrunner, and R. W. Funk. Chicago: University of Chicago Press, 1961.

Beasley-Murray, G. R.
1986 "John 12,31–34: The Eschatological Significance of the Lifting Up of the Son of Man." Pp. 70–81 in *Studien zum Text und zur Ethik des Neuen Testaments: Festschrift für H. Greeven.* Berlin: de Gruyter.
1992 "The Mission of the Logos-Son." Vol. 3 / pp. 1855–68 in *The Four Gospels 1992: Festschrift Frans Neirynck.* Edited by F. van Segbroeck et al. Bibliotheca ephemeridum theologicarum lovaniensium 100. Leuven: Leuven University Press.
1999 *John.* 2d edition. Word Biblical Commentary 36. Waco, Tex.: Word.

BEB *Baker Encyclopedia of the Bible.* Edited by W. A. Elwell. 2 vols. Grand Rapids: Baker, 1988.

Beck, D. R.

1993 "The Narrative Function of Anonymity in Fourth Gospel Characterization." *Semeia* 63:143–58.

1997 *The Discipleship Paradigm: Readers and Anonymous Characters in the Fourth Gospel.* Biblical Interpretation Series 27. Leiden: Brill.

2001 "Review of *Encountering John*, by A. Köstenberger." *Faith & Mission* 18/2:87–89.

Becker, U.

1963 *Jesus und die Ehebrecherin: Untersuchungen zur Text- und Überlieferungsgeschichte von Joh. 7:53–8:11.* Beihefte zur Zeitschrift für die neutestamentliche Wissenschaft 28. Berlin: Töpelmann.

Beetham, F. G., and P. A.

1993 "A Note on John 19:29." *Journal of Theological Studies* 44:163–69.

Behr, J.

2000 "The Word of God in the Second Century." *Pro Ecclesia* 9:85–107.

Bell, H. I., and T. C. Skeat (eds.)

1935 *Fragments of an Unknown Gospel.* London: British Museum.

Belle, G. van

1998 "The Faith of the Galileans: The Parenthesis in Jn 4,44." *Ephemerides theologicae lovanienses* 74:27–44.

Ben-David, A.

1969 *Jerusalem und Tyros: Ein Beitrag zur palästinensischen Münz- und Wirtschaftsgeschichte (126 a.C.–57 p.C.).* Kleine Schriften zur Wirtschaftsgeschichte 1. Basel: Kylos/Tübingen: Mohr.

Bernard, J. H.

1928 *A Critical and Exegetical Commentary on the Gospel of John.* 2 vols. International Critical Commentary. Edinburgh: Clark.

Bettenson, H. (ed.)

1967 *Documents of the Christian Church.* 2d edition. Oxford: Oxford University Press.

Betz, O.

1963 *Der Paraklet: Fürsprecher im häretischen Spätjudentum, im Johannes-Evangelium und in neu gefundenen gnostischen Schriften.* Arbeiten zur Geschichte des Spätjudentums und Urchristentums 2. Leiden: Brill.

Beutler, J.

1979 "Psalm 42/43 im Johannesevangelium." *New Testament Studies* 25:33–57.

1990 "Greeks Come to See Jesus (John 12,20f)." *Biblica* 71:333–47.

1994 "Two Ways of Gathering: The Plot to Kill Jesus in John 11.47–53." *New Testament Studies* 40:399–404.

BGU *Aegyptische Urkunden aus den Königlichen (Staatlichen) Museen zu Berlin: Griechische Urkunden.* 15 vols. Berlin, 1895–1983.

Bieringer, R., et al. (eds.)

2001a *Anti-Judaism and the Fourth Gospel.* Louisville: Westminster John Knox.

2001b *Anti-Judaism and the Fourth Gospel: Papers of the Leuven Colloquium, 2000.* Jewish and Christian Heritage Series 1. Assen: Royal Van Gorcum.

Billington, A.

1995 "The Paraclete and Mission in the Fourth Gospel." Pp. 90–115 in *Mission and Meaning: Essays Presented to Peter Cotterell.* Edited by A. Billington, T. Lane, and M. Turner. Carlisle: Paternoster.

Bishop, E. F. F.

1956 "The Authorised Teacher of the Israel of God." *Bible and Theology* 7:81–83.

1958–59 " 'He That Eateth Bread with Me Hath Lifted Up His Heel against Me.'—Jn xiii.18 (Ps xli.9)." *Expository Times* 70:331–33.

1959–60 "The Door of the Sheep—John x.7–9." *Expository Times* 71:307–9.

Black, D. A.

1984 "The Text of John 3:13." *Grace Theological Journal* 6:49–66.

1988 "On the Style and Significance of John 17." *Criswell Theological Review* 3:141–59.

Blinzler, J.

1959 *The Trial of Jesus.* Cork: Mercier.

Blomberg, C. L.

1987 *The Historical Reliability of the Gospels.* Downers Grove, Ill.: InterVarsity.

1993 "To What Extent Is John Historically Reliable?" Pp. 27–56 in *Perspectives on John: Method and Interpretation in the Fourth Gospel.* Edited by R. B. Sloan and M. C. Parsons. NABPR

Special Studies Series 11. Lewiston, N.Y.: Mellen.

1995 "The Globalization of Biblical Interpretation: A Test Case—John 3–4." *Bulletin of Biblical Research* 5:1–15.

2001 "The Historical Reliability of John: Rushing in Where Angels Fear to Tread?" Pp. 71–82 in *Jesus in Johannine Tradition*. Edited by R. T. Fortna and T. Thatcher. Louisville: Westminster John Knox.

2002 *The Historical Reliability of John's Gospel*. Leicester: Inter-Varsity.

Bock, D. L.

1998 *Blasphemy and Exaltation in Judaism and the Final Examination of Jesus*. Wissenschaftliche Untersuchungen zum Neuen Testament 2/106. Tübingen: Mohr-Siebeck.

Boers, H.

1988 *Neither on This Mountain nor in Jerusalem: A Study of John 4*. Society of Biblical Literature Monograph Series 35. Atlanta: Scholars Press.

Boismard, M.-E.

1956 *Du baptême à Cana (Jean 1,19–2,11)*. Paris: Cerf.

1957 *St. John's Prologue*. Translated by Carisbrooke Dominicans. London: Blackfriars.

1993 *Moses or Jesus: An Essay in Johannine Christology*. Translated by B. T. Viviano. Minneapolis: Fortress/ Leuven: Peeters.

Bokser, B. M.

1985 "Wonder-Working and the Rabbinic Tradition: The Case of Ḥanina ben Dosa." *Journal for the Study of Judaism* 16:42–92.

Bonner, C.

1953 "The Crown of Thorns." *Harvard Theological Review* 46:47–48.

Bonney, W.

2002 *Caused to Believe: The Doubting Thomas Story at the Climax of John's Christological Narrative*. Biblical Interpretation Series 62. Leiden: Brill.

Booser, K. D.

1998 "The Literary Structure of John 1:1–18: An Examination of Its Theological Implications concerning God's Saving Plan through Jesus Christ." *Evangelical Journal* 16:13–29.

Borchert, G. L.

1996 *John 1–11*. New American Commentary 25A. Nashville: Broadman & Holman.

2002 *John 12–21*. New American Commentary 25B. Nashville: Broadman & Holman.

Borgen, P.

1965 *Bread from Heaven*. Novum Testamentum Supplements 10. Leiden: Brill.

1970 "Observations on the Targumic Character of the Prologue of John." *New Testament Studies* 16:288–95.

1972 "'Logos Was the True Light': Contributions to the Interpretation of the Prologue of John." *Novum Testamentum* 14:115–30.

1977 "Some Jewish Exegetical Traditions as Background for Son of Man Sayings in John's Gospel (Jn 3,13–14 and Context)." Pp. 243–58 in *L'Évangile de Jean: sources, rédaction, théologie*. Edited by M. de Jonge. Bibliotheca ephemeridum theologicarum lovaniensium 44. Gembloux: Duculot.

Boring, M. E.

1978 "The Influence of Christian Prophecy on the Johannine Portrayal of the Paraclete and Jesus." *New Testament Studies* 25:113–23.

Boring, M. E., K. Berger, and C. Colpe (eds.)

1995 *Hellenistic Commentary to the New Testament*. Nashville: Abingdon.

Bowman, J.

1958 *Samaritan Studies*. Manchester: Manchester University Press.

Braun, F.-M.

1959 *Jean le théologien*, vol. 1: *Jean le théologien et son évangile dans l'église ancienne*. Paris: Gabalda.

Breck, J.

1992 "John 21: Appendix, Epilogue, or Conclusion?" *St. Vladimir's Theological Quarterly* 36:27–49.

Brodie, T. L.

1993 *The Gospel according to John: A Literary and Theological Commentary*. New York: Oxford University Press.

Broer, I.

2001 "Knowledge of Palestine in the Fourth Gospel?" Pp. 83–90 in *Jesus in Johannine Tradition*. Edited by R. T. Fortna and T. Thatcher. Louisville: Westminster John Knox.

Brooke, G. J.
1999 "4Q252 and the 153 Fish of John 21:11." Pp. 253–65 in *Antikes Judentum und frühes Christentum: Festschrift für Hartmut Stegemann zum 65. Geburtstag.* Edited by B. Kollmann, W. Reinbold, and A. Steudel. Beiheft zur Zeitschrift für die neutestamentliche Wissenschaft und die Kunde der älteren Kirche 97. Berlin and New York: de Gruyter.

Brown, C.
1984 *Miracles and the Critical Mind.* Grand Rapids: Eerdmans/Exeter: Paternoster.

Brown, R. E.
1966 *The Gospel according to John I–XII.* Anchor Bible Commentary 29A. Garden City, N.Y.: Doubleday.
1967 "The Paraclete in the Fourth Gospel." *New Testament Studies* 13:113–32.
1970 *The Gospel according to John XIII–XXI.* Anchor Bible Commentary 29B. Garden City, N.Y.: Doubleday.
1971 "The Spirit-Paraclete in the Gospel of John." *Catholic Biblical Quarterly* 33:268–70.
1979 *The Community of the Beloved Disciple: The Lives, Loves, and Hates of an Individual Church in New Testament Times.* New York: Paulist Press.
1997 *An Introduction to the New Testament.* Anchor Reference Library. New York: Doubleday.

Brown, R. E., et al. (eds.)
1978 *Mary in the New Testament.* Philadelphia: Fortress.

Brownlee, W. H.
1956–57 "Messianic Motifs of Qumran and the New Testament." *New Testament Studies* 3:12–30.
1972 "Whence the Gospel according to John?" Pp. 166–94 in *John and Qumran.* Edited by J. H. Charlesworth. London: Chapman. Reprinted in *John and the Dead Sea Scrolls.* Edited by J. H. Charlesworth. Christian Origins Library. New York: Crossroad, 1990.

Bruce, F. F.
1978 *The Time Is Fulfilled.* Exeter: Paternoster.
1983 *The Gospel of John.* Grand Rapids: Eerdmans.
1988 *The Canon of Scripture.* Downers Grove, Ill.: InterVarsity.

Bruns, J. E.
1967 "A Note on John 16:33 and 1 John 2:13–14." *Journal of Biblical Literature* 86:451–53.

Bryan, S. M.
2002 *Jesus and Israel's Traditions of Judgement and Restoration.* Society for New Testament Studies Monograph Series 117. Cambridge: Cambridge University Press.

Buchanan, G. W.
1991 "Symbolic Money-Changers in the Temple?" *New Testament Studies* 37:280–90.

Bultmann, R.
1923 "Der religionsgeschichtliche Hintergrund des Prologs zum Johannesevangelium." Vol. 2 / pp. 1–26 in *Eucharistērion: Studien zur Religion und Literatur des Alten und Neuen Testaments: Hermann Gunkel zum 60. Geburtstage.* Edited by H. Schmidt. Forschungen zur Religion und Literatur des Alten und Neuen Testaments 36. Göttingen: Vandenhoeck & Ruprecht.
1955 *Theology of the New Testament,* vol. 2. Translated by K. Grobel. New York: Charles Scribner's Sons.
1960 "Is Exegesis without Presuppositions Possible?" Pp. 342–51 in *Existence and Faith.* Translated by S. M. Ogden. New York: World.
1971 *The Gospel of John.* Translated by G. R. Beasley-Murray. Oxford: Blackwell.
1973 "Die Bedeutung der neuerschlossenen mandäischen und manichäischen Quellen für das Verständnis des Johannes-evangeliums." Pp. 402–64 in *Johannes und sein Evangelium.* Wege der Forschung 82. Edited by K. H. Rengstorf. Wissenschaftliche Buchgesellschaft: Darmstadt. Reprint of *Zeitschrift für die neutestamentliche Wissenschaft* 24 (1925): 100–146.

Burge, G. M.
1984 "A Specific Problem in the New Testament Text and Canon: The Woman Caught in Adultery (John 7:53–8:11)." *Journal of the Evangelical Theological Society* 27:141–48.

1987   *The Anointed Community: The Holy Spirit in the Johannine Tradition.* Grand Rapids: Eerdmans.

1998   "Fishers of Men: The Maritime Life of Galilee's North Shore, Jesus' Headquarters." *Christian History* 59:36–37.

2000   *The Gospel of John.* NIV Application Commentary. Grand Rapids: Zondervan.

Burkett, D.
1994   "Two Accounts of Lazarus' Resurrection in John 11." *Novum Testamentum* 36:209–32.

Burns, J. A.
1971   "The Concept of Time in the Fourth Gospel." Ph.D. diss., New Orleans Baptist Theological Seminary.

Burrows, E. W.
1974   "Did John the Baptist Call Jesus 'The Lamb of God'?" *Expository Times* 85:245–49.

Busada, C. J.
2003   "Calendar and Theology: An Investigation into a Possible Mutable Calendric System in the Fourth Gospel." Ph.D. diss., Southeastern Baptist Theological Seminary, Wake Forest, N.C.

Busse, U.
1992   "Die 'Hellenen' Joh 12,20ff. und der sogenannte 'Anhang' Joh 21." Vol. 3 / pp. 2083–100 in *The Four Gospels 1992: Festschrift Frans Neirynck.* Edited by F. van Segbroeck et al. Bibliotheca ephemeridum theologicarum lovaniensium 100. Leuven: Leuven University Press.

Byrne, B.
1985   "The Faith of the Beloved Disciple and the Community in John 20." *Journal of the Study of the New Testament* 23:83–97.

Calvin, J.
1959   *The Gospel according to St. John 1–10.* Translated by T. H. L. Parker. Edited by D. W. Torrance and T. F. Torrance. Edinburgh: Oliver & Boyd.

1961   *The Gospel according to St. John 11–21.* Translated by T. H. L. Parker. Edited by D. W. Torrance and T. F. Torrance. Edinburgh: Oliver & Boyd.

Campbell, R. J.
1982   "Evidence for the Historicity of the Fourth Gospel in John 2:13–22." Pp. 101–20 in *Studia Evangelica,* vol. 2: *Papers Presented to the Fifth International Congress on Biblical Studies Held at Oxford, 1973.* Edited by E. A. Livingstone. Texte und Untersuchungen 126. Berlin: Akademie.

Cantwell, L.
1983   "Immortal Longings in Sermone Humili: A Study of John 4.5–26." *Scottish Journal of Theology* 36:73–86.

Caragounis, C. C.
1998   "Jesus, His Brothers, and the Journey to the Feast (John 7:8–10)." *Svensk Exegetisk Årsbok* 63:177–87.

Carson, D. A.
1979   "The Function of the Paraclete in John 16:7–11." *Journal of Biblical Literature* 98:547–66.

1980   *The Farewell Discourse and Final Prayer of Jesus: An Exposition of John 14–17.* Grand Rapids: Baker.

1981   *Divine Sovereignty and Human Responsibility: Biblical Perspectives in Tension.* Atlanta: John Knox.

1984   "Matthew." Vol. 8 / pp. 1–599 in *The Expositor's Bible Commentary.* Edited by F. E. Gaebelein. Grand Rapids: Zondervan.

1991   *The Gospel according to John.* Pillar New Testament Commentary. Grand Rapids: Eerdmans.

1996   *The Gagging of God: Christianity Confronts Pluralism.* Grand Rapids: Zondervan.

Carson, D. A. (ed.)
1993   *Worship: Adoration and Action.* Carlisle: Paternoster/Grand Rapids: Baker.

Carson, D. A., D. J. Moo, and L. L. Morris
1992   *An Introduction to the New Testament.* Grand Rapids: Zondervan.

Casey, M.
1996   *Is John's Gospel True?* London/New York: Routledge.

Casey, P. M.
1997   "Culture and Historicity: The Cleansing of the Temple." *Catholic Biblical Quarterly* 59:306–32.

Cassian, B.
1956–57   "John XXI." *New Testament Studies* 3:132–36.

Casurella, A.
1983   *The Johannine Paraclete in the Church Fathers: A Study in the History of Exegesis.* Beiträge zur

Geschichte der biblischen Exegese 25. Tübingen: Mohr-Siebeck.

Chapman, D. W.
2000   "Perceptions of Crucifixion among Jews and Christians in the Ancient World." Ph.D. diss., University of Cambridge.

Chapman, J.
1930   "We Know That His Testimony Is True." *Journal of Theological Studies* 31:379–86.

Charles, J. D.
1989   " 'Will the Court Please Call in the Prime Witness?' John 1:29–34 and the 'Witness'-Motif." *Trinity Journal*, n.s., 10:71–83.

Charlesworth, J. H.
1972–73   "Jesus and Jehohanan: An Archaeological Note on Crucifixion." *Expository Times* 84:147–50.

1995   *The Beloved Disciple: Whose Witness Validates the Gospel of John?* Valley Forge, Pa.: Trinity.

Chavel, C. B.
1941   "The Releasing of a Prisoner on the Eve of Passover in Ancient Jerusalem." *Journal of Biblical Literature* 60:273–78.

Chilton, B.
1980   " 'Not to Taste Death': A Jewish, Christian, and Gnostic Usage." Vol. 2 / pp. 29–36 in *Studia Biblica 1978*. Edited by E. A. Livingstone. Journal for the Study of the New Testament: Supplement Series 3. Sheffield: JSOT Press.

Clermont-Ganneau, C. S.
1874   "Sarcophagi." *Palestine Exploration Quarterly* 6:7–10.

Coakley, J. F.
1988   "The Anointing at Bethany and the Priority of John." *Journal of Biblical Literature* 107:241–56.

1995   "Jesus' Messianic Entry into Jerusalem (John 12:12–19 par.)." *Journal of Theological Studies* 46:461–82.

Cohee, P.
1995   "John 1.3–4." *New Testament Studies* 41:470–77.

Cohon, S. S.
1955   "The Unity of God: A Study in Hellenistic and Rabbinic Theology." *Hebrew Union College Annual* 26:425–79.

Coleman, R. E.
1963   *The Master Plan of Evangelism*. Old Tappan, N.J.: Revell.

1977   *The Mind of the Master*. Old Tappan, N.J.: Revell.

Collins, C. J.
1995   "John 4:23–24, 'in Spirit and Truth': An Idiomatic Proposal." *Presbyterion* 21:118–21.

Coloe, M.
1997   "The Structure of the Johannine Prologue and Genesis 1." *Australian Biblical Review* 45:40–55.

2001   *God Dwells with Us: Temple Symbolism in the Fourth Gospel*. Collegeville, Minn.: Liturgical Press.

Colwell, E. C.
1933   "A Definite Rule for the Use of the Article in the Greek New Testament." *Journal of Biblical Literature* 52:12–21.

Conway, C. M.
1999   *Men and Women in the Fourth Gospel: Gender and Johannine Characterization*. Society of Biblical Literature Dissertation Series 167. Atlanta: Scholars Press.

Cortés, J. B.
1967   "Yet Another Look at Jn 7,37–38." *Catholic Biblical Quarterly* 29:75–86.

Cory, C.
1997   "Wisdom's Rescue: A New Reading of the Tabernacles Discourse (John 7:1–8:59)." *Journal of Biblical Literature* 116:95–116.

Cotterell, P.
1985   "The Nicodemus Conversation: A Fresh Appraisal." *Expository Times* 96:237–42.

Cox, S. L.
2001   "Is Jesus Still the Only Begotten Son?" Paper presented at the annual meeting of the Evangelical Theological Society, Colorado Springs, November 14–16.

Cribbs, F. L.
1970   "Reassessment of the Date of Origin and the Destination of the Gospel of John." *Journal of Biblical Literature* 89:38–55.

Croteau, D. A.
2002   "An Analysis of the Concept of Believing in the Narrative Contexts of John's Gospel." Th.M. thesis, Southeastern Baptist Theological Seminary.

2003 "An Analysis of the Arguments for the Dating of the Fourth Gospel." *Faith and Mission* 20/3:47–80.

Crown, A. D. (ed.)
1989 *The Samaritans*. Tübingen: Mohr-Siebeck.

Cullmann, O.
1956 "Samaria and the Origins of the Christian Mission." Pp. 185–92 in *The Early Church*. Edited by A. J. B. Higgins. London: SCM.
1976 *The Johannine Circle*. London: SCM.

Culpepper, R. A.
1980–81 "The Pivot of John's Prologue." *New Testament Studies* 27:1–31.
1983 *Anatomy of the Fourth Gospel: A Study in Literary Design*. Philadelphia: Fortress.
1993 "John 5:1–18: A Sample of Narrative-Critical Commentary." Pp. 193–207 in *The Gospel of John as Literature: An Anthology of Twentieth-Century Perspectives*. Edited by M. Stibbe. New Testament Tools and Studies 17. Leiden: Brill.
1994 *John, the Son of Zebedee: The Life of a Legend*. Columbia: University of South Carolina Press. Reprinted Minneapolis: Fortress, 2000.

Curtis, K. P. G.
1971 "Luke xxiv.12 and John xx.3–10." *Journal of Theological Studies* 22:512–15.

Dahl, N. A.
1963 "The Murderer and His Father (8:44)." *Norsk Teologisk Tidsskrift* 64:129–62.
1969 "The Atonement—an Adequate Reward for the Akeda? (Ro 8:32)." Pp. 15–29 in *Neotestamentica et Semitica: Studies in Honour of Matthew Black*. Edited by E. Ellis and M. Wilcox. Edinburgh: Clark.

Dahms, J. V.
1983 "The Johannine Use of Monogenēs Reconsidered." *New Testament Studies* 29:222–32.

Dalman, G.
1902 *The Words of Jesus*. Edinburgh: Clark.
1928–39 *Arbeit und Sitte in Palästina*. 6 vols. Gütersloh: Bertelsmann. Reprinted Hildesheim: Olms, 1964.
1935 *Sacred Sites and Ways*. London: SPCK.

Danby, H.
1933 *The Mishnah*. Oxford: Oxford University Press.

D'Angelo, M. R.
1990 "A Critical Note: John 20:17 and Apocalypse of Moses 31." *Journal of Theological Studies* 41:529–36.

Daniel-Rops, H.
1962 *Daily Life in Palestine at the Time of Christ*. London: Weidenfeld & Nicolson.

Danker, F. W.
1960–61 "The *Huios* Phrases in the New Testament." *New Testament Studies* 7:94.

Danna, E.
1999 "A Note on John 4:29." *Revue biblique* 106:219–23.

Daube, D.
1950 "Jesus and the Samaritan Woman: The Meaning of *Synchraomai* (Jn 4:7ff)." *Journal of Biblical Literature* 69:137–47.
1956 *The New Testament and Rabbinic Judaism*. London: Athlone.
1966a *Collaboration with Tyranny in Rabbinic Law*. London: Oxford University Press.
1966b *He That Cometh*. London: SCM.

Davies, M.
1992 *Rhetoric and Reference in the Fourth Gospel*. Journal for the Study of the New Testament: Supplement Series 69. Sheffield: JSOT Press.

Davies, W. D.
1974 *The Gospel and the Land*. Berkeley: University of California Press.

Deeley, M. K.
1997 "Ezekiel's Shepherd and John's Jesus: A Case Study in the Appropriation of Biblical Texts." Pp. 252–64 in *Early Christian Interpretation of the Scriptures of Israel*. Edited by C. A. Evans and J. A. Sanders. Journal for the Study of the New Testament: Supplement Series 148. Studies in Scripture in Early Judaism and Christianity 5. Sheffield: Sheffield Academic Press.

Deines, R.
1993 *Jüdische Steingefässe und pharisäische Frönmigkeit: Ein archäologisch-historischer Beitrag zum Verständnis von Joh 2,6 und der jüdischen Reinheitshalacha zur Zeit Jesu*. Wissenschaftliche Untersuchungen zum Neuen

Testament 2/52. Tübingen: Mohr-Siebeck.

Deissmann, A.
1901   *Bible Studies.* Edinburgh: Clark.
1927   *Light from the Ancient East.*
        Revised edition. London: Hodder &
        Stoughton.

Delebecque, E.
1986   "Lazare est mort (note sur Jean
        11:14–15)." *Biblica* 67:89–97.

Delling, G.
1957   "*Baptisma Baptisthēnai.*" *Novum
        Testamentum* 2:92–115.

Derrett, J. D. M.
1970   *Law in the New Testament.* London:
        Darton, Longman & Todd.
1988   "The Samaritan Woman's Purity
        (John 4.4–52)." *Evangelical Quarterly*
        60:291–98.
1993   "*Ti ergaze?* (Jn 6,30): An
        Unrecognized Allusion to Is 45,9."
        *Zeitschrift für die neutestamentliche
        Wissenschaft* 84:142–44.

Dettwiler, A.
1995   *Die Gegenwart des Erhöhten:
        Eine exegetische Studie zu den
        johanneischen Abschiedsreden (Joh
        13, 31–16, 33) unter besonderer
        Berücksichtigung ihres Relecture-
        Charakters.* Forschungen zur
        Religion und Literatur des Alten und
        Neuen Testaments 169. Göttingen:
        Vandenhoeck & Ruprecht.

Dewey, K. E.
1980   "*Paroimiai* in the Gospel of John."
        Semeia 17:81–99.

Díaz, J. R.
1963   "Palestinian Targum and New
        Testament." *Novum Testamentum*
        6:75–80.

Dibelius, M.
1918   "Die alttestamentlichen Motive in
        der Leidensgeschichte des Petrus-
        und des Johannes-Evangeliums."
        Pp. 125–50 in *Abhandlungen zur
        semitischen Religionskunde und
        Sprachwissenschaft.* Edited by
        W. Frankenberg and F. Küchler.
        Beiheft zur Zeitschrift für die
        alttestamentliche Wissenschaft 33.
        Giessen: Töpelmann.

Dixon, L.
1992   *The Other Side of the Good News:
        Confronting the Contemporary
        Challenges to Jesus' Teaching on Hell.*
        Wheaton, Ill.: Victor.

Dixon, P. S.
1975   "The Significance of the Anarthrous
        Predicate Nominative in John."
        Th.M. thesis, Dallas Theological
        Seminary.

DJG   *Dictionary of Jesus and the Gospels.*
        Edited by J. B. Green, S. McKnight,
        and I. H. Marshall. Downers Grove,
        Ill.: InterVarsity, 1992.

Dockery, D. S.
1988   "Reading John 4:1–45: Some Diverse
        Hermeneutical Perspectives."
        Criswell Theological Review 3:127–40.

Dodd, C. H.
1953   *The Interpretation of the Fourth
        Gospel.* Cambridge: Cambridge
        University Press.
1963   *Historical Tradition in the Fourth
        Gospel.* Cambridge: Cambridge
        University Press.
1968a   "A Hidden Parable in the Fourth
        Gospel." Pp. 30–40 in *More New
        Testament Studies.* Grand Rapids:
        Eerdmans.
1968b   "The Prophecy of Caiaphas: John
        11:47–53." Pp. 58–68 in *More New
        Testament Studies.* Manchester:
        Manchester University Press.

Douglas, M.
1984   *Purity and Danger: An Analysis of
        Concepts of Pollution and Taboo.*
        London: Ark.

Draper, J. A.
1997   "Temple, Tabernacle and
        Mystical Experience in John."
        Neotestamentica 31:263–88.

Droge, A. J., and J. D. Tabor
1991   *A Noble Death: Suicide and
        Martyrdom among Christians and
        Jews in Antiquity.* San Francisco:
        HarperSanFrancisco.

Duke, P. D.
1985   *Irony in the Fourth Gospel.* Atlanta:
        John Knox.

Dunkerley, R.
1959   "Lazarus." *New Testament Studies*
        5:321–27.

Dunn, J. D. G.
1970   "The Washing of the Disciples' Feet
        in John 13:1–20." *Zeitschrift für
        die neutestamentliche Wissenschaft*
        61:247–52.

EDNT   *Exegetical Dictionary of the New
        Testament.* Edited by H. Balz and
        G. Schneider. 3 vols. Grand Rapids:
        Eerdmans, 1990–93.

Works Cited

Edwards, M. J.
1994 " 'Not Yet Fifty Years Old': John 8:57." *New Testament Studies* 40:449–54.
1995 "Justin's Logos and the Word of God." *Journal of Early Christian Studies* 3:261–80.

Edwards, R. B.
1988 "Χάριν ἀντὶ χάριτος (John 1.16): Grace and the Law in the Johannine Prologue." *Journal for the Study of the New Testament* 32:3–15.

Edwards, W. D., W. J. Gabel, and F. E. Hosmer
1986 "On the Physical Death of Jesus Christ." *Journal of the American Medical Association* 255/11:1455–63.

Egger, P.
1997 *"Crucifixus sub Pontio Pilato."* Neutestamentliche Abhandlungen, Neue Folge 32. Münster: Aschendorff.

Ehrman, B. D.
1988 "Jesus and the Adulteress." *New Testament Studies* 34:24–44.

Eller, V.
1987 *The Beloved Disciple: His Name, His Story, His Thought.* Grand Rapids: Eerdmans.

Ellis, P. F.
1984 *The Genius of John: A Compositional-Critical Commentary on the Fourth Gospel.* Collegeville, Minn.: Liturgical Press.
1992 "The Authenticity of John 21." *St. Vladimir's Theological Quarterly* 36:17–25.

Emerton, J. A.
1960 "Interpretation of Psalm 82 in John 10." *Journal of Theological Studies* 11:329–32.
1962 "Binding and Loosing—Forgiving and Retaining." *Journal of Theological Studies* 13:325–31.
1966 "Melchizedek and the Gods: Fresh Evidence for the Jewish Background of John 10:34–36." *Journal of Theological Studies* 17:399–401.

Engel, F. G.
1948–49 "The Ways of Vines." *Expository Times* 60:111.

Ensor, P. W.
2000 "The Authenticity of John 4.35." *Evangelical Quarterly* 72:13–21.

Epp, E. J.
1975 "Wisdom, Torah, Word: The Johannine Prologue and the Purpose of the Fourth Gospel." Pp. 128–46 in *Current Issues in Biblical and Patristic Interpretation.* Edited by G. F. Hawthorne. Grand Rapids: Eerdmans.

Eppstein, V.
1964 "The Historicity of the Cleansing of the Temple." *Zeitschrift für die neutestamentliche Wissenschaft* 55:42–58.

Evans, C. A.
1981 "The Voice from Heaven: A Note on John 12:28." *Catholic Biblical Quarterly* 43:405–8.
1982a "On the Quotation Formulas in the Fourth Gospel." *Biblische Zeitschrift* 26:79–83.
1982b "Peter Warming Himself: The Problem of an Editorial 'Seam.'" *Journal of Biblical Literature* 101:245–49.
1987 "Obduracy and the Lord's Servant: Some Observations on the Use of the Old Testament in the Fourth Gospel." Pp. 221–36 in *Early Jewish and Christian Exegesis: Studies in Memory of William Hugh Brownlee.* Edited by C. A. Evans and W. F. Stinespring. Homage Series 10. Atlanta: Scholars Press.
1989 "Jesus' Action in the Temple: Cleansing or Portent of Destruction?" *Catholic Biblical Quarterly* 51:237–70.
1993 *Word and Glory: On the Exegetical and Theological Background of John's Prologue.* Journal for the Study of the New Testament: Supplement Series 89. Sheffield: Sheffield Academic Press.
1997 "From 'House of Prayer' to 'Cave of Robbers': Jesus' Prophetic Criticism of the Temple Establishment." Pp. 417–42 in *The Quest for Context and Meaning: Studies in Biblical Intertextuality in Honor of James A. Sanders.* Edited by C. A. Evans and S. Talmon. Biblical Interpretation Series 28. Leiden: Brill.

Farmer, W. R.
1952 "The Palm Branches in John 12:13." *Journal of Theological Studies* 3:62–66.

Fee, G. D.
1978 "Once More—John 7:37–39." *Expository Times* 89:116–18.

1982 "On the Inauthenticity of John 5:3b–4." *Evangelical Quarterly* 54:207–18.

1992 "On the Text and Meaning of Jn 20,30–31." Vol. 3 / pp. 2193–205 in *The Four Gospels 1992: Festschrift Frans Neirynck*. Edited by F. van Segbroeck et al. Bibliotheca ephemeridum theologicarum lovaniensium 100. Leuven: Leuven University Press.

Ferguson, E.
1993 *Backgrounds of Early Christianity*. 2d edition. Grand Rapids: Eerdmans.

Fernando, A.
1994 *Crucial Questions about Hell*. Wheaton, Ill.: Crossway.

Feuillet, A.
1968 *Le prologue du quatrième évangile: Étude de théologie johannique*. Paris: Desclée de Brouwer.

Finegan, J.
1992 *The Archeology of the New Testament*. Revised edition. Princeton, N.J.: Princeton University Press.

Fisher, M. C.
2003 "God the Father in the Fourth Gospel: A Biblical Patrology." Ph.D. diss., Southeastern Baptist Theological Seminary.

Fitzmyer, J. A.
1971 *Essays on the Semitic Background of the New Testament*. London: Chapman.

Ford, J. M.
1969 "Mingled Blood from the Side of Christ, John 19:34." *New Testament Studies* 15:337–38.

1997 *Redeemer—Friend and Mother: Salvation in Antiquity and in the Gospel of John*. Minneapolis: Fortress.

Forestell, J. T.
1974 *The Word of the Cross: Salvation as Revelation in the Fourth Gospel*. Analecta biblica 57. Rome: Biblical Institute Press.

Fortna, R. T.
1970 *The Gospel of Signs: A Reconstruction of the Narrative Source Underlying the Fourth Gospel*. Society of New Testament Studies Monograph Series 11. Cambridge: Cambridge University Press.

1989 *The Fourth Gospel and Its Predecessor: From Narrative Source to Present Gospel*. Studies of the New Testament and Its World. Edinburgh: Clark.

France, R. T.
1971 *Jesus and the Old Testament*. London: Tyndale.

Franzmann, M., and M. Klinger
1992 "The Call Stories of John 1 and John 21." *St. Vladimir's Theological Quarterly* 36:7–15.

Freed, E. D.
1961 "The Entry into Jerusalem in the Gospel of John." *Journal of Biblical Literature* 80:329–38.

1965a "John IV.51 Παῖς or Ὑιός?" *Journal of Theological Studies* 16:448–49.

1965b *Old Testament Quotations in the Gospel of John*. Novum Testamentum Supplements 11. Leiden: Brill.

1982 "*Egō eimi* in John viii.24 in the Light of Its Context and Jewish Messianic Belief." *Journal of Theological Studies* 33:163–67.

1983a "Psalm 42/43 in John's Gospel." *New Testament Studies* 29:62–73.

1983b "Who or What Was before Abraham in John 8:58?" *Journal for the Study of the New Testament* 17:52–59.

Frend, W. H. C.
1967 *Martyrdom and Persecution in the Early Church: A Study of a Conflict from the Maccabees to Donatus*. New York: New York University Press.

Freyne, S.
1980 "The Charismatic." Pp. 223–58 in *Ideal Figures in Ancient Judaism: Profiles and Paradigms*. Edited by J. J. Collins and G. W. E. Nickelsburg. Society of Biblical Literature Septuagint and Cognate Studies 12. Chico, Calif.: Scholars Press.

Friedrichsen, A.
1939 "Bemerkungen zur Fusswaschung Joh 13." *Zeitschrift für die neutestamentliche Wissenschaft* 38:94–96.

Gächter, P.
1947 "Das dreifache 'Weide meine Lämmer.'" *Zeitschrift für katholische Theologie* 69:328–44.

Gaffney, J.
1965 "Believing and Knowing in the Fourth Gospel." *Theological Studies* 26:215–41.

Gaventa, B. R.
1996 "The Archive of Excess: John 21 and the Problem of Narrative Closure."

Pp. 240–52 in *Exploring the Gospel of John: In Honor of D. Moody Smith.* Edited by R. A. Culpepper and C. C. Black. Louisville: Westminster John Knox.

Gese, H.
1981   "The Prologue to John's Gospel." Pp. 167–222 in *Essays on Biblical Theology.* Translated by K. Crim. Minneapolis: Augsburg.

Giblin, C. H.
1980   "Suggestion, Negative Response, and Positive Action in St John's Portrayal of Jesus (John 2.1–11; 4.46–54; 7.2–14; 11.1–44)." *New Testament Studies* 26:197–211.

1999   "What Was Everything He Told Her She Did?" *New Testament Studies* 45:148–52.

Glasson, T. F.
1963   *Moses in the Fourth Gospel.* Studies in Biblical Theology 40. London: SCM.

Goldin, J.
1980   "The First Pair (Yose Ben Yoezer and Yose ben Yohanan) or The Home of a Pharisee." *Association for Jewish Studies Review* 5:41–61.

Goodenough, E. R., and C. B. Welles
1953   "The Crown of Acanthus?" *Harvard Theological Review* 46:241–42.

Goodman, M.
1992   "Diaspora Reactions to the Destruction of the Temple." Pp. 27–38 in *Jews and Christians: The Parting of the Ways* A.D. *70 to 135.* Edited by J. D. G. Dunn. Tübingen: Mohr-Siebeck.

Goulder, M. D.
1991   "Nicodemus." *Scottish Journal of Theology* 44:153–68.

Gower, R.
1987   *The New Manners and Customs of Bible Times.* Chicago: Moody.

Grappe, C.
2000   "Jean 1,14(–18) dans son contexte et à la lumière de la littérature intertestamentaire." *Revue d'histoire et de philosophie religieuses* 80:153–69.

Grayston, K.
1981   "The Meaning of Paraklētos." *Journal for the Study of the New Testament* 13:67–82.

Grese, W. C.
1988   " 'Unless One Is Born Again': The Use of a Heavenly Journey in John

3." *Journal of Biblical Literature* 107:677–93.

Grigsby, B. H.
1985   "Washing in the Pool of Siloam—A Thematic Anticipation of the Johannine Cross." *Novum Testamentum* 27:227–35.

1986   " 'If Any Man Thirsts . . .': Observations on the Rabbinic Background of John 7,37–39." *Biblica* 67:101–8.

Grillmeier, A.
1975   *Christ in Christian Tradition,* vol. 1: *From the Apostolic Age to Chalcedon (451).* Translated by J. Bowden. 2d revised edition. Atlanta: John Knox.

Gundry, R. H.
1967   "In My Father's House Are Many *Monai* (John 14:2)." *Zeitschrift für die neutestamentliche Wissenschaft* 58:68–72.

Gundry, R. H., and R. W. Howell
1999   "The Sense and Syntax of John 3:14–17 with Special Reference to the Use of Οὕτως . . . Ὥστε in John 3:16." *Novum Testamentum* 41:24–39.

Guthrie, D.
1981   *New Testament Theology.* Downers Grove, Ill.: InterVarsity.

Guthrie, G. H.
1994   *The Structure of Hebrews: A Text-Linguistic Analysis.* Leiden: Brill. Novum Testamentum Supplements 73. Reprinted Grand Rapids: Baker, 1998.

Haas, N.
1970   "Anthropological Observations on the Skeletal Remains from Giv'at-ha-Mivtar." *Israel Exploration Journal* 20:38–59.

Haenchen, E.
1984   *A Commentary on the Gospel of John.* Translated by R. W. Funk. Edited by R. W. Funk and U. Busse. 2 vols. Hermeneia. London: SCM/ Minneapolis: Fortress.

Ham, C.
1998   "The Title 'Son of Man' in the Gospel of John." *Stone-Campbell Journal* 1:67–84.

Hambly, W. F.
1968   "Creation and Gospel: A Brief Comparison of Genesis 1:1–2:4 and John 1:1–2:12." Pp. 69–74 in *Studia Evangelica,* vol. 5: *Papers Presented to the Third International Congress on New Testament Studies Held at Christ*

Church, Oxford, 1965. Edited by F. L. Cross. Texte und Untersuchungen 103. Berlin: Akademie.

Hamilton, J.
2003   "He Is with You and He Will Be in You: The Spirit, the Believer, and the Glorification of Jesus." Ph.D. diss., Southern Baptist Theological Seminary.

Hanhart, K.
1970   "The Structure of John I 35–IV 54." Pp. 22–46 in *Studies in John: Presented to Professor Dr. J. N. Sevenster on the Occasion of His Seventieth Birthday.* Novum Testamentum Supplements 24. Leiden: Brill.

Hanson, A. T.
1964–65   "John's Interpretation of Psalm 82." *New Testament Studies* 11:158–62.
1967   "John's Interpretation of Psalm 82 Reconsidered." *New Testament Studies* 13:363–67.
1973   "The Old Testament Background to the Raising of Lazarus." Pp. 252–55 in *Studia Evangelica*, vol. 6: *Papers Presented to the Fourth International Congress on New Testament Studies Held at Oxford, 1969.* Edited by E. A. Livingstone. Texte und Untersuchungen 112. Berlin: Akademie.

Ha-Reubéni, E.
1933   "Recherches sur les Plantes de l'Évangile." *Revue biblique* 42:230–34.

Harnack, A. von
1892   "Über das Verhältnis des Prologs des Vierten Evangeliums." *Zeitschrift für Theologie und Kirche* 2:189–231.

Harner, P.
1973   "Qualitative Anarthrous Predicate Nouns: Mark 15:39 and John 1:1." *Journal of Biblical Literature* 92:75–87.

Harris, E.
1994   *Prologue and Gospel: The Theology of the Fourth Evangelist.* Journal for the Study of the New Testament: Supplement Series 107. Sheffield: Sheffield Academic Press.

Harris, M. J.
1986   " 'The Dead Are Restored to Life': Miracles of Revivification in the Gospels." Pp. 295–326 in *Gospel Perspectives,* vol. 6: *The Miracles of Jesus.* Edited by D. Wenham and C. Blomberg. Sheffield: JSOT Press.
1992   *Jesus as God.* Grand Rapids: Baker.

Harris, R.
1917   *The Origin of the Prologue of St. John's Gospel.* Cambridge: Cambridge University Press.

Harrison, R. H.
1966   *Healing Herbs of the Bible.* Leiden: Brill.

Harstine, S.
2002   *Moses as a Character in the Fourth Gospel: A Study of Ancient Reading Techniques.* Journal for the Study of the New Testament: Supplement Series 229. Sheffield: Sheffield Academic Press.

Hart, H. J.
1952   "Crown of Thorns in John 19:2–5." *Journal of Theological Studies* 3:66–75.

Hartley, D. E.
1996   "Criteria for Determining Qualitative Nouns with a Special View to Understanding the Colwell Construction." Th.M. thesis, Dallas Theological Seminary.
1999   "John 1:1, Colwell, and Mass/Count Nouns in Recent Discussion." Paper presented at the fifty-first annual meeting of the Evangelical Theological Society, Danvers, Mass., November 17–19.

Hatina, T. R.
1993   "John 20,22 in Its Eschatological Context: Promise or Fulfillment?" *Biblica* 74:196–219.

Hayward, C. T. R.
1978   "The Holy Name of the God of Moses and the Prologue of St John's Gospel." *New Testament Studies* 25:16–32.

Heil, J. P.
1991   "The Story of Jesus and the Adulteress (John 7,53–8,11) Reconsidered." *Biblica* 72:182–91.

Heine, R. E. (trans.)
1993   Origen, *Commentary on the Gospel according to John,* vol. 2. The Fathers of the Church 81. Washington, D.C.: Catholic University of America.

Henderson, A.
1920–21   "Notes on John xi." *Expository Times* 32:123–26.

Hengel, M.
1977   *Crucifixion.* Philadelphia: Fortress.

1989a   *The Johannine Question*. London: SCM/Philadelphia: Trinity.

1989b   *The Zealots: Investigations into the Jewish Freedom Movement in the Period from Herod I until 70 A.D.* Translated by D. Smith. Edinburgh: Clark.

1993   *Die johanneische Frage.* Wissenschaftliche Untersuchungen zum Neuen Testament 67. Tübingen: Mohr-Siebeck.

1995   "The Dionysiac Messiah." Pp. 293–331 in *Studies in Early Christology*. Edinburgh: Clark.

1999   "Das Johannesevangelium als Quelle für die Geschichte des antiken Judentums." Pp. 293–334 in *Judaica, Hellenistica et Christiana: Kleine Schriften II*. Wissenschaftliche Untersuchungen zum Neuen Testament 109. Tübingen: Mohr-Siebeck.

Hepper, F. N.

1989   "Flax and Linen in Biblical Times." *Buried History* 25:105–16.

Hiers, R. H.

1971   "Purification of the Temple: Preparation for the Kingdom of God." *Journal of Biblical Literature* 90:82–90.

Higgins, A. J. B.

1954–55   "Origins of the Eucharist." *New Testament Studies* 1:200–209.

Hill, C. E.

1997   "The Identity of John's Nathanael." *Journal for the Study of the New Testament* 67:45–61.

1998   "What Papias Said about John (and Luke): A 'New' Papian Fragment." *Journal of Theological Studies* 49:582–629.

Hirsch, E. D., Jr.

1967   *Validity in Interpretation*. New Haven: Yale University Press.

Hodges, Z.

1979a   "Problem Passages in the Gospel of John. Part 6: Those Who Have Done Good—John 5:28–29." *Bibliotheca sacra* 136:158–66.

1979b   "Problem Passages in the Gospel of John. Part 7: Rivers of Living Water—John 7:37–39." *Bibliotheca sacra* 136:239–48.

Hoehner, H. W.

1972   *Herod Antipas*. Society of New Testament Studies Monograph Series 17. Cambridge: Cambridge University Press.

1977   *Chronological Aspects of the Life of Christ*. Grand Rapids: Zondervan.

Hofius, O.

1967   "Die Sammlung der Heiden zur Herde Israels (Joh 10,16; 11,51f.)." *Zeitschrift für die neutestamentliche Wissenschaft* 58:289–91.

1983   "Das Gesetz des Mose und das Gesetz Christi." *Zeitschrift für Theologie und Kirche* 80:262–86.

1989   "'Der in des Vaters Schoß ist,' Joh 1,18." *Zeitschrift für die neutestamentliche Wissenschaft* 80:163–71.

1999   " 'Er gibt den Geist ohne Mass' Joh 3,34b." *Zeitschrift für die neutestamentliche Wissenschaft* 90:131–34.

Hollis, H.

1989   "The Root of the Johannine Pun—Ὑψωθῆναι." *New Testament Studies* 35:475–78.

Holst, R.

1976   "The One Anointing of Jesus: Another Application of the Form-Critical Method." *Journal of Biblical Literature* 95:435–46.

Hooker, M.

1969–70   "John the Baptist and the Johannine Prologue." *New Testament Studies* 16:354–58.

Horbury, W.

1998   *Jesus Messianism and the Cult of Christ*. London: SCM.

Horsley, R. A.

1984   "Popular Messianic Movements around the Time of Jesus." *Catholic Biblical Quarterly* 46:471–95.

Hoskins, P. M.

2002   "Jesus as the Replacement of the Temple in the Gospel of John." Ph.D. diss., Trinity Evangelical Divinity School.

Huffmon, H. B.

1966   "The Treaty Background of Hebrew Yādaᶜ." *Bulletin of the American Schools of Oriental Research* 181:31–37.

Hultgren, A. J.

1982   "The Johannine Footwashing (13.1–11) as Symbol of Eschatological Hospitality." *New Testament Studies* 28:539–46.

Humphreys, C. J., and W. G. Waddington
1992   "The Jewish Calendar, a Lunar Eclipse, and the Date of Christ's Crucifixion." *Tyndale Bulletin* 43:331–51.

Hunter, W. B.
1979   "The Prayers of Jesus in the Gospel of John." Ph.D. diss., University of Aberdeen.
1985   "Contextual and Genre Implications for the Historicity of John 11:41b–42." *Journal of the Evangelical Theological Society* 28:53–70.

Hurtado, L. W.
1998a   "First-Century Jewish Monotheism." *Journal for the Study of the New Testament* 71:3–26.
1998b   *One God, One Lord: Early Christian Devotion and Ancient Jewish Monotheism.* Edinburgh: Clark.
1999   "Pre-70 C.E. Jewish Opposition to Christ-Devotion." *Journal of Theological Studies* 50:35–58.

ISBE   *The International Standard Bible Encyclopedia.* Edited by G. W. Bromiley et al. 4 vols. Grand Rapids: Eerdmans, 1979–88.

Jackson, H. M.
1999   "Ancient Self-Referential Conventions and Their Implications for the Authorship and Integrity of the Gospel of John." *Journal of Theological Studies* 50:1–34.

Jensen, E. E.
1941   "The First Century Controversy over Jesus as a Revolutionary Figure." *Journal of Biblical Literature* 60:261–72.

Jeremias, J.
1966a   *The Eucharistic Words of Jesus.* London: SCM.
1966b   *The Rediscovery of Bethesda.* Louisville: Southern Baptist Seminary.
1968   "*Lampades* in Matthew 25:1–13." Pp. 83–87 in *Soli Deo Gloria: New Testament Studies in Honor of William Childs Robinson.* Edited by J. M. Richards. Richmond: John Knox.
1969   *Jerusalem in the Time of Jesus.* London: SCM.
1971   *New Testament Theology.* London: SCM.

Jervell, J.
1956   " 'Er kam in sein Eigentum': zum Joh 1,11." *Studia Theologica* 10:14–27.

Johnson, B.
2001   "The Temple in the Gospel of John." Pp. 110–33 in *Christ's Victorious Church: Essays on Biblical Ecclesiology and Eschatology in Honor of Tom Friskney.* Edited by J. A. Weatherly. Eugene, Ore.: Wipf & Stock.

Johnston, E. D.
1962   "The Johannine Version of the Feeding of the Five Thousand: An Independent Tradition?" *New Testament Studies* 8:151–54.

Johnston, G.
1970   *The Spirit-Paraclete in the Gospel of John.* Society for New Testament Studies Monograph Series 12. Cambridge: Cambridge University Press.

Jonge, M. de
1971   "Nicodemus and Jesus: Some Observations on Misunderstanding and Understanding in the Fourth Gospel." *Bulletin of the John Rylands Library* 53:337–59.

Julian, P.
2000   *Jesus and Nicodemus: A Literary and Narrative Exegesis of Jn. 2,23–3,36.* European University Studies 23/171. Frankfurt: Lang.

Jungkuntz, R.
1964   "Approach to the Exegesis of John 10:34–36." *Currents in Theology and Mission* 35:556–65.

Käsemann, E.
1968   *The Testament of Jesus.* Translated by G. Krodel. Philadelphia: Fortress.

Katz, P.
1997   "Wieso gerade nach Efrajim? (Erwägungen zu Jh 11,54)." *Zeitschrift für die neutestamentliche Wissenschaft* 88:130–34.

Keener, C. S.
1993   *Bible Background Commentary: New Testament.* Downers Grove, Ill.: InterVarsity.
1999   "Is Subordination within the Trinity Really Heresy? A Study of John 5:18 in Context." *Trinity Journal,* n.s., 20:39–51.
2003   *The Gospel of John.* 2 vols. Peabody, Mass.: Hendrickson.

Kellum, L. S.

2005   *The Unity of the Farewell Discourse: The Literary Integrity of John 13:31–16:33*. Journal for the Study of the New Testament: Supplement Series 256. London/New York: Clark.

Kenyon, F.

1939   *Our Bible and the Ancient Manuscripts*. London: Eyre & Spottiswoode.

Kerr, A. R.

2002   *The Temple of Jesus' Body: The Temple Theme in the Gospel of John*. Journal for the Study of the New Testament: Supplement Series 220. Sheffield: Sheffield Academic Press.

Kessler, W. T.

1998   *Peter as the First Witness of the Risen Lord*. Rome: Gregorian University Press.

Kilpatrick, G. D.

1963   "John IV.51 Παῖς or Ὑιός?" *Journal of Theological Studies* 14:393.

Kippenberg, H. G.

1971   *Garizim und Synagoge: Traditionsgeschichtliche Untersuchungen zur samaritanischen Religion der aramaischen Periode*. Religionsgeschichtliche Versuche und Vorarbeiten 30. Berlin: de Gruyter.

Klaiber, W.

1990   "Der irdische und der himmlische Zeuge." *New Testament Studies* 36:205–33.

Klausner, J.

1925   *Jesus of Nazareth*. London: Allen & Unwin.

Klein, W. W., C. L. Blomberg, and R. L. Hubbard Jr.

1993   *Introduction to Biblical Interpretation*. Dallas: Word.

Knapp, H. M.

1997   "The Messianic Water Which Gives Life to the World." *Horizons in Biblical Theology* 19:109–21.

Koester, C. R.

1990a   "Messianic Exegesis and the Call of Nathanael (John 1.45–51)." *Journal for the Study of the New Testament* 39:23–34.

1990b   " 'The Savior of the World' (John 4:42)." *Journal of Biblical Literature* 109:665–80.

2003   *Symbolism in the Fourth Gospel: Meaning, Mystery, Community*. 2d edition. Minneapolis: Fortress.

Koester, H.

1989   "Hearing, Seeing, and Believing in the Gospel of John." *Biblica* 70:327–48.

Kopp, C.

1963   *The Holy Places of the Gospels*. Edinburgh/London: Nelson.

Kosmala, H.

1963   "The Time of the Cock-Crow." *Annual of the Swedish Theological Institute* 2:118–20.

1967–68   "The Time of the Cock-Crow (II)." *Annual of the Swedish Theological Institute* 6:132–34.

Kossen, H. B.

1970   "Who Were the Greeks of John XII 20?" Pp. 97–110 in *Studies in John: Presented to Professor Dr. J. N. Sevenster on the Occasion of His Seventieth Birthday*. Novum Testamentum Supplements 24. Leiden: Brill.

Köstenberger, A. J.

1995a   "The 'Greater Works' of the Believer according to John 14:12." *Didaskalia* 6:36–45.

1995b   "The Seventh Johannine Sign: A Study in John's Christology." *Bulletin for Biblical Research* 5:87–103.

1996   "Review of Martin Hengel, *Die johanneische Frage*." *Journal of the Evangelical Theological Society* 39:154–55.

1997   "What Does It Mean to Be Filled with the Spirit?" *Journal of the Evangelical Theological Society* 40:229–40.

1998a   "Jesus as Rabbi in the Fourth Gospel." *Bulletin for Biblical Research* 8:97–128.

1998b   *The Missions of Jesus and the Disciples according to the Fourth Gospel*. Grand Rapids: Eerdmans.

1999a   *Encountering John: The Gospel in Historical, Literary, and Theological Perspective*. Encountering Biblical Studies. Grand Rapids: Baker.

1999b   "Review of David R. Beck, *The Discipleship Paradigm*." *Journal of the Evangelical Theological Society* 42:749–51.

1999c   "The Two Johannine Verbs for Sending: A Study of John's Use of Words with Reference to General Linguistic Theory." Pp. 125–43 in *Linguistics and the New Testament: Critical Junctures*. Edited by S. E.

Porter and D. A. Carson. Journal for the Study of the New Testament: Supplement Series 168. Studies in New Testament Greek 5. Sheffield: Sheffield Academic Press.

2000 "John." Pp. 280–85 in *New Dictionary of Biblical Theology*. Edited by D. Alexander and B. Rosner. Leicester: Inter-Varsity/Downers Grove, Ill.: InterVarsity.

2001a "Review of Andrew Lincoln, *Truth on Trial*." *Trinity Journal*, n.s., 22:269–72.

2001b *Studies on John and Gender: A Decade of Scholarship*. Studies in Biblical Literature 38. New York: Lang.

2002a "Diversity and Unity in the New Testament." Pp. 144–58 in *Biblical Theology: Retrospect and Prospect*. Edited by S. J. Hafemann. Downers Grove, Ill.: InterVarsity.

2002b "Jesus the Good Shepherd Who Will Also Bring Other Sheep (John 10:16): The Old Testament Background of a Familiar Metaphor." *Bulletin for Biblical Research* 12:67–96.

2002c "John." Vol. 2 / pp. 1–216 in *Zondervan Illustrated Bible Background Commentary: New Testament*. Edited by C. E. Arnold. Grand Rapids: Zondervan.

2002d "Review of Marianne Meye Thompson, *The God of the Gospel of John*." *Journal of the Evangelical Theological Society* 45:521–24.

2003 "Translating John's Gospel: Challenges and Opportunities." Pp. 347–64 in *The Challenge of Bible Translation: Communicating God's Word to the World*. Edited by G. G. Scorgie, M. L. Strauss, and S. M. Voth. Grand Rapids: Zondervan.

2004 " 'I Suppose' (Οἶμαι): The Conclusion of John's Gospel in Its Literary and Historical Context." Pp. 72–88 in *The New Testament in Its First Century Setting: Essays on Context and Background in Honour of B. W. Winter on His 65th Birthday*. Edited by P. J. Williams, A. D. Clarke, P. M. Head, and D. Instone-Brewer. Grand Rapids: Eerdmans.

forth-coming "The Destruction of the Second Temple and the Composition of the Fourth Gospel." In *Historical and Literary Studies in John:*

Challenges to Prevailing Paradigms. Edited by P. Head and J. Lierman. Wissenschaftliche Untersuchungen zum Neuen Testament. Tübingen: Mohr-Siebeck.

Köstenberger, A. J., and P. T. O'Brien

2001 *Salvation to the Ends of the Earth: A Biblical Theology of Mission*. New Studies in Biblical Theology 11. Leicester: Apollos/Downers Grove, Ill.: InterVarsity.

Kovacs, J. L.

1995 " 'Now Shall the Ruler of This World Be Driven Out': Jesus' Death as Cosmic Battle in John 12:20–36." *Journal of Biblical Literature* 114:227–47.

Kraeling, C. H.

1946 "Christian Burial Urns." *Biblical Archaeologist* 9:18.

Kreitzer, L. J.

1998 "The Temple Incident of John 2.13–25: A Preview of What Is to Come." Pp. 92–101 in *Understanding, Studying, and Reading: New Testament Essays in Honour of John Ashton*. Edited by C. Rowland and C. H. T. Fletcher-Louis. Journal for the Study of the New Testament: Supplement Series 153. Sheffield: Sheffield Academic Press.

Kruijf, T. C. de

1970 "The Glory of the Only Son (John I 14)." Pp. 111–23 in *Studies in John: Presented to Professor Dr. J. N. Sevenster on the Occasion of His Seventieth Birthday*. Novum Testamentum Supplements 24. Leiden: Brill.

Kruse, C. G.

2003 *The Gospel according to John*. Tyndale New Testament Commentary. Leicester: Inter-Varsity.

Küchler, M.

1999 "Zum 'Probatischen Becken' und zu 'Betesda mit den fünf Stoën.' " Pp. 381–90 in *Judaica, Hellenistica et Christiana: Kleine Schriften II*. By M. Hengel. Wissenschaftliche Untersuchungen zum Neuen Testament 109. Tübingen: Mohr-Siebeck.

Kuhn, H.-W., and R. Arav

1991 "The Bethsaida Excavations: Historical and Archaeological Approaches." Pp. 77–106 in *The Future of Early Christianity:*

Festschrift für H. Koester. Edited by
B. A. Pearson. Minneapolis: Fortress.

Kuhn, K. G.
1957   "The Lord's Supper and the
Communal Meal at Qumran." Pp.
65–93 in *The Scrolls and the New
Testament*. Edited by K. Stendahl.
New York: Harper.

Kundsin, K.
1925   *Topologische Überlieferungsstoffe im
Johannes-Evangelium*. Forschungen
zur Religion und Literatur des Alten
und Neuen Testaments, Neue Folge
22. Göttingen: Vandenhoeck &
Ruprecht.

Kurz, W. S.
1985   "Luke 22:14–38 and Greco-Roman
and Biblical Farewell Addresses."
Journal of Biblical Literature
104:251–68.
1990   *Farewell Addresses in the New
Testament*. Collegeville, Minn.:
Liturgical Press.
1997   "Intertextual Permutations of the
Genesis Word in the Johannine
Prologues." Pp. 179–90 in *Early
Christian Interpretation of the
Scriptures of Israel: Investigations
and Proposals*. Edited by C. A.
Evans and J. A. Sanders. Journal
for the Study of the New Testament:
Supplement Series 148. Sheffield:
Sheffield Academic Press.

Kuyper, L. J.
1964   "Grace and Truth: An Old Testament
Description of God and Its Use in the
Johannine Gospel." *Interpretation*
18:3–19.

Kysar, R.
2002a   "The De-historicizing of the Gospel
of John." Paper presented at the
annual meeting of the Society
of Biblical Literature, Toronto,
November 23–26.
2002b   "Expulsion from the Synagogue: A
Tale of a Theory." Paper presented
at the annual meeting of the Society
of Biblical Literature, Toronto,
November 23–26.

Lacomara, A.
1974   "Deuteronomy and the Farewell
Discourse (Jn 13:31–16:33)." *Catholic
Biblical Quarterly* 36:65–84.

Ladd, G. E.
1993   *A Theology of the New Testament*. 2d
edition. Grand Rapids: Eerdmans.

Lagrange, M.-J.
1925   *Évangile selon Saint Jean*. 2d edition.
Paris: Gabalda.

Lamarche, P.
1964   "Le Prologue de Jean." *Recherches de
science religieuse* 52:529–32.

Laney, J. C.
1989   "Abiding Is Believing: The Analogy
of the Vine in John 15:1–6."
Bibliotheca sacra 146:55–66.
1992   *John*. Moody Gospel Commentary.
Chicago: Moody.

La Potterie, I. de
1977   *La vérité dans Saint Jean*. 2 vols.
Rome: Biblical Institute Press.
1984   "Structure du Prologue de saint
Jean." *New Testament Studies*
30:354–81.

Larsen, B.
2001   "An Interaction of Theology and
Literature by Means of Archetypal
Criticism with Reference to the
Characters Jesus, Pilate, Thomas,
the Jews, and Peter in the Gospel."
Ph.D. diss., University of St.
Andrews.

Lattey, C.
1953–54   "A Note on Cockcrow." *Scripture*
6:53–55.

Laughlin, J. C. H.
1993   "Capernaum: From Jesus' Time and
After." *Biblical Archaeology Review*
19/5:54–61, 90.

Leaney, A. R. C.
1972   "The Johannine Paraclete and the
Qumran Scrolls." Pp. 38–61 in
John and Qumran. Edited by J. H.
Charlesworth. London: Chapman.

Lee, D. A.
1994   *The Symbolic Narratives of the
Fourth Gospel: The Interplay of Form
and Meaning*. Journal for the Study
of the New Testament: Supplement
Series 95. Sheffield: JSOT Press.
1995   "Partnership in Easter Faith: The
Role of Mary Magdalene and
Thomas in John 20." *Journal for the
Study of the New Testament* 58:37–49.

Legasse, S.
1997   *The Trial of Jesus*. London: SCM.

Leidig, E.
1979   *Jesu Gespräch mit der Samaritanerin
und weitere Gespräche im
Johannesevangelium*. Theologische
Dissertationen 15. Basel: Reinhardt
Kommissionsverlag.

1980 "Natanael, ein Sohn des Tholomäus." *Theologische Zeitschrift* 36:374–75.

Levinskaya, I.
1996 *The Book of Acts in Its Diaspora Setting*. The Book of Acts in Its First Century Setting 5. Grand Rapids: Eerdmans/Carlisle: Paternoster.

Lieu, J. M.
1988 "Blindness in the Johannine Tradition." *New Testament Studies* 34:83–95.
1999 "Temple and Synagogue in John." *New Testament Studies* 45:51–69.

Lightfoot, J.
1859 *A Commentary on the New Testament from the Talmud and Hebraica.* 4 vols. Oxford: Oxford University Press. Reprinted Peabody, Mass.: Hendrickson, 1989.

Lightfoot, R. H.
1956 *St. John's Gospel*. Oxford: Oxford University Press.

Lincoln, A. T.
2000 *Truth on Trial: The Lawsuit Motif in the Fourth Gospel*. Peabody, Mass.: Hendrickson.

Lindars, B.
1956 "The Composition of John xx." *New Testament Studies* 7:142–47.
1970 "Δικαιοσύνη in Jn 16.8 and 10." Pp. 275–85 in *Mélanges bibliques en hommage au R. P. Béda Rigaux*. Edited by A. Descamps and A. de Halleux. Gembloux: Duculot.
1971 *Behind the Fourth Gospel*. Studies in Creative Criticism 3. London: SPCK.
1972 *The Gospel of John*. New Century Bible. Grand Rapids: Eerdmans/London: Marshall, Morgan & Scott.
1981 "John and the Synoptic Gospels: A Test Case." *New Testament Studies* 29:287–94.
1992a "Capernaum Revisited: John 4,46–53 and the Synoptics." Vol. 3 / pp. 1985–2000 in *The Four Gospels 1992: Festschrift Frans Neirynck*. Edited by F. van Segbroeck et al. Bibliotheca ephemeridum theologicarum lovaniensium 100. Leuven: Leuven University Press.
1992b "Rebuking the Spirit: A New Analysis of the Lazarus Story of John 11." *New Testament Studies* 38:89–104.

Liver, J.
1963 "The Half-Shekel Offering in Biblical and Post-biblical Literature."

Harvard Theological Review 56:173–98.

Loader, W.
1991 "John 1:50–51 and the 'Greater Things' of Johannine Christology." Pp. 255–74 in *Anfänge der Christologie: Festschrift für Ferdinand Hahn zum 65. Geburtstag*. Edited by C. Breytenbach and H. Paulsen. Göttingen: Vandenhoeck & Ruprecht.

Loos, H. van der
1965 *The Miracles of Jesus*. Translated by T. S. Preston. Novum Testamentum Supplements 9. Leiden: Brill.

Louw, J. P.
1968 "Narrator of the Father: Ἐξηγεῖσθαι and Related Terms in Johannine Christology." *Neotestamentica* 2:32–40.
1986 "On Johannine Style." *Neotestamentica* 20:5–12.

Lowery, D. K.
2003 "Review of *A Greek-English Lexicon of the New Testament and Other Early Christian Literature*, 3d ed., by Walter Bauer [*BDAG*]." *Bibliotheca sacra* 160:119–21.

LSJ *A Greek-English Lexicon*. By H. G. Liddell, R. Scott, and H. S. Jones. 9th edition. Oxford: Clarendon, 1968.

Lund, N. W.
1931 "The Influence of Chiasmus upon the Structure of the Gospels." *Anglican Theological Review* 13:42–46.

Luthardt, C. E.
1875 *St. John the Author of the Fourth Gospel*. Translated and revised by C. R. Gregory. Edinburgh: Clark.

Luther, M.
1957 *Luther's Works*, vol. 22: *Sermons on the Gospel of St. John Chapters 1–4*. Edited by J. Pelikan. Saint Louis: Concordia.

MacAdam, H. I.
1999 "Σκότος Ἐγένετο: Luke 3:1; 23:44 and Four First Century Solar Eclipses at Antioch." *Irish Biblical Studies* 21:2–33.

Maccini, R. G.
1994 "A Reassessment of the Woman at the Well in John 4 in Light of the Samaritan Context." *Journal for the Study of the New Testament* 53:35–46.
1996 *Her Testimony Is True: Women as Witnesses according to John*. Journal

for the Study of the New Testament: Supplement Series 125. Sheffield: Sheffield Academic Press.

Macdonald, J.
1964   *The Theology of the Samaritans.* Philadelphia: Westminster.

Mackowski, R. M.
1979   " 'Scholar's Qanah.' A Re-examination of the Evidence in Favor of Khirbet-Qanah." *Biblische Zeitschrift* 23:278–84.
1980   *Jerusalem, City of Jesus.* Grand Rapids: Eerdmans.

MacLeod, D. J.
2003   "The Eternality and Deity of the Word: John 1:1–2." *Bibliotheca sacra* 160:48–64.

Mahoney, R.
1974   *Two Disciples at the Tomb.* Frankfurt: Lang.

Maier, G.
1994   *Biblical Hermeneutics.* Translated by R. W. Yarbrough. Wheaton: Crossway.

Maier, P. L.
1968   "Sejanus, Pilate, and the Date of the Crucifixion." *Church History* 37:3–13.
1969   "Episode of the Golden Roman Shields at Jerusalem." *Harvard Theological Review* 62:109–21.
1989   "The Date of the Nativity and the Chronology of Jesus' Life." Pp. 113–30 in *Chronos, Kairos, Christos: Nativity and Chronological Studies Presented to Jack Finegan.* Edited by J. Vardaman and E. M. Yamauchi. Winona Lake, Ind.: Eisenbrauns.

Malatesta, E.
1971   "The Literary Structure of John 17." *Biblica* 52:190–214.
1978   *Interiority and Covenant: A Study of EINAI EN and MENEIN EN in the First Letter of Saint John.* Analecta biblica 69. Rome: Biblical Institute Press.

Malina, B. J.
1981   *The New Testament World: Insights from Cultural Anthropology.* Atlanta: John Knox.

Malina, B. J., and R. L. Rohrbaugh
1998   *Social-Science Commentary on the Gospel of John.* Minneapolis: Fortress.

Marcus, J.
1998   "Rivers of Living Water from Jesus' Belly (John 7:38)." *Journal of Biblical Literature* 117:328–30.

Marshall, I. H.
1974   "The Problem of New Testament Exegesis." *Journal of the Evangelical Theological Society* 17:67–73.

Martin, J. P.
1964   "History and Eschatology in the Lazarus Narrative John 11.1–44." *Scottish Journal of Theology* 17:332–43.

Martin, T. W.
1998   "Assessing the Johannine Epithet 'the Mother of Jesus.'" *Catholic Biblical Quarterly* 60:63–73.

Martyn, J. L.
1977   "Glimpses into the History of the Johannine Community." Pp. 149–75 in *L'Évangile de Jean: sources, rédaction, théologie.* Bibliotheca ephemeridum theologicarum lovaniensium 44. Edited by M. de Jonge. Gembloux: Duculot.
1979   *History and Theology in the Fourth Gospel.* 2d edition. Nashville: Abingdon.

Marzotto, D.
1977   "Giovanni 17 e il Targum di Esodo 19–20." *Rivista biblica italiana* 25:375–88.

Mathews, K. A.
1988–89   "John, Jesus, and the Essenes: Trouble at the Temple." *Criswell Theological Review* 3:101–26.

McCabe, R. V.
1999   "The Meaning of 'Born of Water and the Spirit' in John 3:5." *Detroit Baptist Seminary Journal* 4:85–107.

McCaffrey, J.
1988   *The House with Many Rooms: The Temple Theme of Jn. 14,2–3.* Analecta biblica 114. Rome: Pontifical Biblical Institute.

McCracken, D.
1994   *The Scandal of the Gospels: Jesus, Story, and Offense.* New York: Oxford University Press.

McDonald, J. I. H.
1995   "The So-Called *Pericope de Adultera.*" *New Testament Studies* 41:415–27.

McGaughy, L. C.
1972   *Toward a Descriptive Analysis of EINAI as a Linking Verb in New Testament Greek.* Society of Biblical Literature Dissertation Series 6.

Missoula, Mont.: Society of Biblical Literature.

McGehee, M.
1986 "A Less Theological Reading of John 20:17." *Journal of Biblical Literature* 105:299–302.

McKay, K. L.
1985 "Style and Significance in the Language of John 21:15–17." *Novum Testamentum* 27:319–33.
1994 *A New Syntax of the Verb in New Testament Greek: An Aspectual Approach*. Studies in Biblical Greek 5. New York: Lang.

Mead, A. H.
1985 "The Βασιλικός in John 4.46–53." *Journal for the Study of the New Testament* 23:69–72.

Meeks, W. A.
1966 "Galilee and Judea in the Fourth Gospel." *Journal of Biblical Literature* 85:159–69.
1967 *The Prophet-King*. Novum Testamentum Supplements 14. Leiden: Brill.
1972 "The Man from Heaven in Johannine Sectarianism." *Journal of Biblical Literature* 91:44–72.

Mees, M.
1986 "Die Heilung des Kranken vom Bethesdateich aus Joh 5:1–18." *New Testament Studies* 32:596–608.

Meier, J. P.
1994 *A Marginal Jew: Rethinking the Historical Jesus*, vol. 2: *Mentor, Message, and Miracles*. Anchor Bible Reference Library. Garden City, N.Y.: Doubleday.
2001 *A Marginal Jew: Rethinking the Historical Jesus*, vol. 3: *Companions and Competitors*. Anchor Bible Reference Library. Garden City, N.Y.: Doubleday.

Melick, R. R.
1976 "A Study in the Concept of Belief: A Comparison of the Gospel of John and the Epistle to the Romans." Th.D. diss., Southwestern Baptist Theological Seminary.

Menken, M. J. J.
1985 "The Quotation from Isa 40:3 in John 1:23." *Biblica* 66:190–205.
1988 "The Provenance and Meaning of the Old Testament Quotation in John 6:31." *Novum Testamentum* 30:39–56.

1990 "The Translation of Psalm 41.10 in John 13.18." *Journal for the Study of the New Testament* 40:61–79.
1996 "The Origin of the Old Testament Quotation in John 7:38." *Novum Testamentum* 38:160–75.

Messner, B.
1998 "'In the Fifteenth Year' Reconsidered: A Study of Luke 3:1." *Stone-Campbell Journal* 1:201–11.

Metzger, B. M.
1994 *A Textual Commentary on the Greek New Testament*. 2d edition. Stuttgart: Deutsche Bibelgesellschaft.

Metzner, R.
1999 "Der Geheilte von Johannes 5—Repräsentant des Unglaubens." *Zeitschrift für die neutestamentliche Wissenschaft* 90:177–93.

Meyer, P. W.
1956 "A Note on John 10 1–18." *Journal of Biblical Literature* 75:232–35.
1996 "'The Father': The Presentation of God in the Fourth Gospel." Pp. 255–73 in *Exploring the Gospel of John: In Honor of D. Moody Smith*. Edited by R. A. Culpepper and C. C. Black. Louisville: Westminster John Knox.

Michaels, J. R.
1966–67 "Nathanael under the Fig Tree." *Expository Times* 78:182–83.
1983 *John: A Good News Commentary*. San Francisco/Cambridge: Harper & Row.
1989 *John*. New International Bible Commentary. Peabody, Mass.: Hendrickson.

Michel, M.
1981 "Nicodème ou le non-lieu de la verité." *Revue des science religieuses* 55:227–36.

Millard, A.
1997 *Discoveries from Bible Times*. Oxford: Lion.

Miller, E. L.
1989 *Salvation-History in the Prologue of John: The Significance of John 1:3–4*. Novum Testamentum Supplements 60. Leiden: Brill.
1993 "The Johannine Origins of the Johannine Logos." *Journal of Biblical Literature* 112:445–57.
1999 "'In the Beginning': A Christological Transparency." *New Testament Studies* 45:587–92.

Milne, B.
1993   *The Message of John: Here Is Your King.* Leicester: Inter-Varsity/ Downers Grove, Ill.: InterVarsity.

Minear, P. S.
1976   "We Don't Know Where . . . John 20:2." *Interpretation* 30:129–39.
1983   "The Original Functions of John 21." *Journal of Biblical Literature* 102:85–98.

MM   *The Vocabulary of the Greek Testament: Illustrated from the Papyri and Other Non-literary Sources.* By J. H. Moulton and G. Milligan, 1930. Reprinted Grand Rapids: Eerdmans, 1976.

Moloney, F. J.
1977   *The Word Became Flesh.* Theology Today Series 14. Dublin/Cork: Mercier.
1978   *The Johannine Son of Man.* 2d edition. Bibliothèque des sciences religieuses 14. Rome: LAS.
1986   "The Structure and Message of John 13:1–38." *Australian Biblical Review* 34:1–16.
1993   *Belief in the Word: Reading John 1–4.* Minneapolis: Fortress.
1998   *The Gospel of John.* Sacra Pagina 4. Collegeville, Minn.: Liturgical Press.
2002   "Narrative and Discourse at the Feast of Tabernacles: John 7:1–8:59." Pp. 155–72 in *Word, Theology, and Community in John.* Edited by J. Painter, R. A. Culpepper, and F. F. Segovia. St. Louis: Chalice.

Montgomery, J. A.
1939   "Hebrew *Hesed* and Greek *Charis.*" *Harvard Theological Review* 32:97–102.

Moody, D.
1953   "God's Only Son: The Translation of John 3:16 in the Revised Standard Version." *Journal of Biblical Literature* 72:213–19.

Morgan-Wynne, J. E.
1980   "The Cross and the Revelation of Jesus as ἐγώ εἰμι in the Fourth Gospel (John 8.28)." Pp. 219–26 in *Studia Biblica 1978: Sixth International Congress on Biblical Studies, Oxford, 3–7 April 1978,* vol. 2: *Papers on the Gospels.* Edited by E. A. Livingstone. Journal for the Study of the New Testament: Supplement Series 2. Sheffield: JSOT Press.

Morgenthaler, R.
1958   *Statistik des neutestamentlichen Wortschatzes.* Zürich: Gotthelf.

Morris, L.
1965a   *The Apostolic Preaching of the Cross.* 3d edition. London: Tyndale.
1965b   *The Cross in the New Testament.* Grand Rapids: Eerdmans.
1969   *Studies in the Fourth Gospel.* Grand Rapids: Eerdmans.
1974   *The Lord from Heaven.* Downers Grove, Ill.: InterVarsity.
1989   *Jesus Is the Christ.* Grand Rapids: Eerdmans.
1995   *The Gospel according to John.* Revised edition. New International Commentary on the New Testament. Grand Rapids: Eerdmans.

Motyer, S.
1997   *'Your Father the Devil'? A New Approach to John and 'the Jews.'* Carlisle: Paternoster.

Moule, C. F. D.
1954   "A Note on 'under the Fig Tree' in John I.48, 50." *Journal of Theological Studies* 5:210–11.
1957–58   "The Post-resurrection Appearances in the Light of Festival Pilgrimages." *New Testament Studies* 4:58–61.
1975   "The Meaning of 'Life' in the Gospels and Epistles of St John." *Theology* 78:114–25.

Mowvley, H.
1984   "John 1^{14-18} in the Light of Exodus 33^{7}–34^{35}." *Expository Times* 95:135–37.

Müller, M.
1991   " 'Have You Faith in the Son of Man?' (John 9.35)." *New Testament Studies* 37:291–94.

Munck, J.
1959   "Presbyters and Disciples of the Lord in Papias: Exegetic Comments on Eusebius, Ecclesiastical History, III, 39." *Harvard Theological Review* 52:223–43.

Murphy-O'Connor, J.
2000   "Jesus and the Money Changers (Mark 11:15–17; John 2:13–17)." *Revue biblique* 107:42–55.

NA^{27}   *Novum Testamentum Graece.* Edited by [E. and E. Nestle], B. Aland, K. Aland, J. Karavidopoulos, C. M. Martini, and B. M. Metzger. 27th revised edition. Stuttgart: Deutsche Bibelgesellschaft, 1993.

NEAEHL   *The New Encyclopedia of Archaeological Excavations in the Holy Land.* Edited by E. Stern. 4 vols. Jerusalem: Israel Exploration Society & Carta/New York: Simon & Schuster, 1993.

Neirynck, F.
1984   "John and the Synoptics: The Empty Tomb Stories." *New Testament Studies* 30:161–87.
1990   "John 21." *New Testament Studies* 36:321–36.

Nelson, D. P.
2001   "In Spirit and Truth: The Holy Spirit and the Interrelation of Doxology and Doctrine with Implications for Evangelical Congregational Worship." Ph.D. diss., Southeastern Baptist Theological Seminary.

Nestle, E.
1913   "Zum Ysop bei Johannes, Josephus und Philo." *Zeitschrift für die neutestamentliche Wissenschaft* 14:263–65.

Neuer, W.
1996   *Adolf Schlatter: A Biography of Germany's Premier Biblical Theologian.* Translated by R. W. Yarbrough. Grand Rapids: Baker.

Neusner, J.
1989   "Money-Changers in the Temple: The Mishnah's Explanation." *New Testament Studies* 35:287–90.

NewDocs   *New Documents Illustrating Early Christianity.* Edited by G. H. R. Horsley and S. Llewelyn. North Ride, N.S.W.: Ancient History Documentary Reseach Centre, Macquarie University, 1981–.

Neyrey, J. H.
1979   "Jacob Traditions and the Interpretation of John 4:10–26." *Catholic Biblical Quarterly* 41:419–37.
1982   "The Jacob Allusions in John 1.51." *Catholic Biblical Quarterly* 44:586–605.
1987   "Jesus the Judge: Forensic Process in John 8,21–59." *Biblica* 68:509–42.
1994   "What's Wrong with This Picture? John 4, Cultural Stereotypes of Women, and Public and Private Space." *Biblical Theology Bulletin* 24:77–91.
1996   "The Trials (Forensic) and Tribulations (Honor Challenges) of Jesus: John 7 in Social Science Perspective." *Biblical Theology Bulletin* 26:107–24.
2001   "The 'Noble Shepherd' in John 10: Cultural and Rhetorical Background." *Journal of Biblical Literature* 120:267–91.

Nicklas, T.
2000a   "Die Prophetie des Kaiaphas: Im Netz johanneischer Ironie." *New Testament Studies* 46:589–94.
2000b   " 'Unter dem Feigenbaum': Die Rolle des Lesers im Dialog zwischen Jesus und Natanael (Joh 1,45–50)." *New Testament Studies* 46:193–203.

NIDNTT   *The New International Dictionary of New Testament Theology.* Edited by L. Coenen, E. Beyreuther, and H. Bietenhard. English translation edited by C. Brown. 4 vols. Grand Rapids: Zondervan, 1975–86.

Nixon, J. A.
2003   "Who Wrote the Fourth Gospel? The Authorship and Occasion of the Fourth Gospel according to Patristic Evidence from the First Three Centuries." *Faith and Mission* 20/3:81–98.

Nortjé, S. J.
1986   "The Role of Women in the Fourth Gospel." *Neotestamentica* 20:21–28.

O'Connell, M. J.
1960   "The Concept of Commandment in the Old Testament." *Theological Studies* 21:352.

O'Day, G. R.
1986   *Revelation in the Fourth Gospel: Narrative Mode and Theological Claim.* Philadelphia: Fortress.
1992   "John 7:53–8:11: A Study in Misreading." *Journal of Biblical Literature* 111:631–40.
1995   "John." Vol. 9 / pp. 493–865 in *The New Interpreter's Bible.* Edited by L. E. Keck. Nashville: Abingdon.
2002   "Response to 'Expulsion from the Synagogue: A Tale of a Theory' by Robert Kysar." Paper presented at the annual meeting of the Society of Biblical Literature, Toronto, November 23–26.

Odeberg, H.
1968   *The Fourth Gospel.* Amsterdam: Grüner.

Okure, T.
1992   "The Significance Today of Jesus' Commission to Mary Magdalene."

International Review of Mission 81:177–88.

Olsson, B.

1974 *Structure and Meaning in the Fourth Gospel: A Text-Linguistic Analysis of John 2:1–11 and 4:1–42.* Coniectanea Biblica, New Testament 6. Lund: Gleerup.

O'Neill, J. C.

1991 "The Word Did Not 'Become' Flesh." *Zeitschrift für die neutestamentliche Wissenschaft* 82:125–27.

1995 *Who Did Jesus Think He Was?* Biblical Interpretation Series 11. Leiden: Brill.

Osborn, E. F.

1973 *Justin Martyr.* Beiträge zur historischen Theologie 47. Tübingen: Mohr-Siebeck.

Osborne, G. R.

1981 "John 21: Test Case for History and Redaction in the Resurrection Narratives." Pp. 293–328 in *Gospel Perspectives*, vol. 2: *Studies of History and Tradition in the Four Gospels.* Edited by R. T. France and D. Wenham. Sheffield: JSOT Press.

1991 *The Hermeneutical Spiral: A Comprehensive Introduction to Biblical Interpretation.* Downers Grove, Ill.: InterVarsity.

Osburn, C. D.

1989 "Some Exegetical Observations on John 3:5–8." *Restoration Quarterly* 31:129–38.

Pagels, E. H.

1999 "Exegesis of Genesis 1 in the Gospels of Thomas and John." *Journal of Biblical Literature* 118:477–96.

Painter, J.

1977 "Christ and the Church in John 1,45–51." Pp. 359–62 in *L'Évangile de Jean: sources, rédaction, théologie.* Edited by M. de Jonge. Bibliotheca ephemeridum theologicarum lovaniensium 44. Gembloux: Duculot.

Pamment, M.

1985 "Focus in the Fourth Gospel." *Expository Times* 97:71–75.

Pancaro, S.

1972 "The Metamorphosis of a Legal Principle in the Fourth Gospel: A Closer Look at Jn 7,51." *Biblica* 23:340–51.

1975 *The Law in the Fourth Gospel.* Novum Testamentum Supplements 42. Leiden: Brill.

Parrot, A.

1957 *Golgotha and the Church of the Holy Sepulchre.* London: SCM.

Payton, J. R.

1992 "On Unity and Truth: Martin Bucer's Sermon on John 17." *Calvin Theological Journal* 27:26–38.

Pazdan, M. M.

1987 "Nicodemus and the Samaritan Woman: Contrasting Models of Discipleship." *Biblical Theology Bulletin* 17:145–48.

Pendrick, G.

1995 "Μονογενής." *New Testament Studies* 41:587–600.

Petersen, W. L.

1997 "Οὐδὲ ἐγώ σε [κατα]κρίνω: John 8:11, the *Protevangelium Iacobi*, and the History of the *Pericope Adulterae*." Pp. 191–221 in *Sayings of Jesus: Canonical and Non-canonical: Essays in Honour of Tjitze Baarda.* Edited by W. L. Petersen, J. S. Vos, and H. J. de Jonge. Novum Testamentum Supplements 89. Leiden: Brill.

Peterson, R. A.

1995 *Hell on Trial: The Case for Eternal Punishment.* Phillipsburg, N.J.: Presbyterian & Reformed.

Pixner, B.

1985 "Searching for the New Testament Site of Bethsaida." *Biblical Archaeologist* 48:207–16.

Poirier, J. C.

1996 "'Day and Night' and the Punctuation of John 9.3." *New Testament Studies* 42:288–94.

Pollard, T. E.

1970 *Johannine Christology and the Early Church.* Society for New Testament Studies Monograph Series 13. Cambridge: Cambridge University Press.

1973 "The Raising of Lazarus (John xi)." Pp. 434–43 in *Studia Evangelica*, vol. 6: *Papers Presented to the Fourth International Congress on New Testament Studies Held at Oxford, 1969.* Edited by E. A. Livingstone. Texte und Untersuchungen 112. Berlin: Akademie.

1977 "The Father-Son and God-Believer Relationships according to St John: A Brief Study of John's

Use of Prepositions." Pp. 363–69 in *L'Évangile de Jean: sources, rédaction, théologie*. Edited by M. de Jonge. Bibliotheca ephemeridum theologicarum lovaniensium 44. Gembloux: Duculot.

Porter, C. L.

1966–67 "John 9:38, 39a: A Liturgical Addition to the Text." *New Testament Studies* 13:387–94.

Porter, S. E.

1989 *Verbal Aspect in the Greek of the New Testament, with Reference to Tense and Mood*. Studies in Biblical Greek 1. Bern: Lang.

1992 *Idioms of the Greek New Testament*. Sheffield: JSOT Press.

2002 "Jesus, the Jews, and John's Gospel: A Conflict of Religious Paradigms." Paper presented at the annual meeting of the Evangelical Theological Society, Toronto.

Potter, R. D.

1959 "Typography and Archaeology in the Fourth Gospel." Pp. 329–37 in *Studia Evangelica*, vol. 1: *Papers Presented to the International Congress on "The Four Gospels in 1957" Held at Christ Church, Oxford*. Edited by K. Aland et al. Texte und Untrsuchungen 73. Berlin: Akademie.

Prest, L. A.

1992 "The Samaritan Woman." *Bible Today* 30:367–71.

Pryor, J. W.

1987 "John 4:44 and the *Patris* of Jesus." *Catholic Biblical Quarterly* 49:254–63.

1988 "Covenant and Community in John's Gospel." *Reformed Theological Review* 47:44–51.

1990 "Jesus and Israel in the Fourth Gospel—John 1:11." *Novum Testamentum* 32:201–18.

1991a "The Johannine Son of Man and Descent-Ascent Motif." *Journal of the Evangelical Theological Society* 34:341–51.

1991b "John 3.3, 5: A Study in the Relation of John's Gospel to the Synoptic Tradition." *Journal for the Study of the New Testament* 41:71–95.

1992a *John, Evangelist of the Covenant People: The Narrative and Themes of the Fourth Gospel*. Downers Grove, Ill.: InterVarsity.

1992b "Justin Martyr and the Fourth Gospel." *The Second Century* 9:153–69.

1997 "John the Baptist and Jesus: Tradition and Text in John 3.25." *Journal for the Study of the New Testament* 66:15–26.

Quast, K.

1989 *Peter and the Beloved Disciple: Figures for a Community in Crisis*. Journal for the Study of the New Testament: Supplement Series 32. Sheffield: JSOT Press.

Ramsay, Lady W. M.

1915–16 "Her That Kept the Door." *Expository Times* 27:217–18, 314–16.

Reich, R.

1995 "6 Stone Water Jars." *Jerusalem Perspective* 48:30–33.

Reim, G.

1976 "Johannes 21: Ein Anhang?" Pp. 330–37 in *Studies in New Testament Language and Text: Essays in Honour of George D. Kilpatrick on the Occasion of His Sixty-fifth Birthday*. Edited by J. K. Elliott. Novum Testamentum Supplements 44. Leiden: Brill.

Reinhardt, W.

1995 "The Population Size of Jerusalem and the Numerical Growth of the Jerusalem Church." Pp. 237–65 in *The Book of Acts in Its Palestinian Setting*. Edited by R. Bauckham. The Book of Acts in Its First Century Setting 4. Grand Rapids: Eerdmans.

Reiser, W. E.

1973 "The Case of the Tidy Tomb: The Place of the Napkins of John 11:44 and 20:7." *Heythrop Journal* 14:47–57.

Rensberger, D.

1988 *Johannine Faith and Liberating Community*. Philadelphia: Westminster.

Repond, C.

1922 "Le Costume du Christ." *Biblica* 3:3–14.

Richardson, P.

1992 "Why Turn the Tables? Jesus' Protest in the Temple Precincts." Pp. 507–23 in *SBL Seminar Papers*. Edited by E. H. Lovering Jr. Atlanta: Scholars Press.

Ridderbos, H.

1975 *Paul: An Outline of His Theology*. Grand Rapids: Eerdmans.

1997   *The Gospel according to John.*
         Translated by J. Vriend. Grand
         Rapids: Eerdmans.

Riesenfeld, H.
1970   "The Pericope *de adultera* in the
         Early Christian Tradition." Pp.
         95–110 in *The Gospel Tradition.*
         Translated by E. M. Rowley and
         R. A. Kraft. Oxford: Blackwell.
1972   "A Probable Background to the
         Johannine Paraclete." Vol. 1 / pp.
         266–74 in *Ex Orbe Religionum:
         Studia Geo Widengren.* Edited by
         C. J. Bleeker et al. Studies in the
         History of Religions 21. Leiden:
         Brill.

Riesner, R.
1981   *Jesus als Lehrer: Eine Untersuchung
         zum Ursprung der Evangelien-
         überlieferung.* Wissenschaftliche
         Untersuchungen zum Neuen
         Testament 2/7. Tübingen: Mohr-
         Siebeck.
1987   "Bethany beyond the Jordan (John
         1:28): Topography, Theology, and
         History in the Fourth Gospel."
         Tyndale Bulletin 38:29–63.
2002   *Bethanien jenseits des Jordan:
         Topographie und Theologie im
         Johannes-Evangelium.* Studien
         zur biblischen Archäologie und
         Zeitgeschichte 12. Giessen: Brunnen.

Rissi, M.
1979   "Voll grosser Fische,
         hundertdreiundfünfzig: Joh 21,1–
         14." *Theologische Literaturzeitschrift*
         35:73–89.

Roberts, C.
1987   "John 20:30–31 and 21:24–25."
         Journal of Theological Studies
         38:409–10.

Robertson, A. T.
1934   *A Grammar of the Greek New
         Testament in the Light of Historical
         Research.* Nashville: Broadman.

Robinson, H. W.
1964   *Corporate Personality in Ancient
         Israel.* Philadelphia: Fortress.

Robinson, J. A. T.
1959   "The 'Others' of John 4,38: A Test
         of Exegetical Method." Pp. 510–15
         in *Studia Evangelica,* vol. 1: *Papers
         Presented to the International
         Congress on "The Four Gospels in
         1957" Held at Christ Church, Oxford.*
         Edited by Kurt Aland et al. Texte

         und Untersuchungen 73. Berlin:
         Akademie.
1962–63 "The Relation of the Prologue to the
         Gospel of St. John." *New Testament
         Studies* 9:120–29.
1976   *Redating the New Testament.* London:
         SCM.
1985   *The Priority of John.* Edited by J. F.
         Coakley. London: SCM.

Robinson, J. M.
1964   "Die Hodajot-Formel in Gebet und
         Hymnus des Frühchristentums."
         Pp. 194–225 in *Apophoreta:
         Festschrift für Ernst Haenchen
         zu seinem siebzigsten Geburtstag
         am 10. Dezember 1964.* Edited
         by W. Eltester. Beihefte zur
         Zeitschrift für die neutestamentliche
         Wissenschaft und die Kunde
         der älteren Kirche 30. Berlin:
         Töpelmann.

Robinson, M. A.
1998   "Preliminary Observations regarding
         the *Pericope Adulterae* Based upon
         Fresh Collations of Nearly All
         Continuous-Text Manuscripts and
         over One Hundred Lectionaries."
         Paper presented at the annual
         meeting of the Evangelical
         Theological Society, Orlando,
         Florida.

Rodgers, P. R.
1999   "The Text of John 1:34." Pp. 299–305
         in *Theological Exegesis: Essays in
         Honor of Brevard S. Childs.* Edited by
         C. Seitz and K. Greene-McCreight.
         Grand Rapids: Eerdmans.

Rowland, C.
1984   "John 1.51, Jewish Apocalyptic and
         Targumic Tradition." *New Testament
         Studies* 30:498–507.

Ruckstuhl, E.
1977   "Zur Aussage und Botschaft von
         Johannes 21." Pp. 339–62 in *Kirche
         des Anfangs: Festschrift für Heinz
         Schürmann zum 65. Geburtstag.*
         Edited by R. Schnackenburg, J.
         Ernst, and J. Wanke. Erfurter
         theologische Studien 38. Leipzig:
         St. Benno.

Ruckstuhl, E., and P. Dschulnigg
1991   *Stilkritik und Verfasserfrage
         im Johannesevangelium: Die
         johanneischen Sprachmerkmale
         auf dem Hintergrund des Neuen
         Testaments und des zeitgenössischen
         hellenistischen Schrifttums.*

Göttingen: Vandenhoeck & Ruprecht.

Saayman, C.
1995 "The Textual Strategy in John 3:12–14: Preliminary Observations." *Neotestamentica* 29:27–48.

Sabbe, M.
1992 "The Anointing of Jesus in John 12,1–8 and Its Synoptic Parallels." Vol. 3 / pp. 2051–82 in *The Four Gospels 1992: Festschrift Frans Neirynck*. Edited by F. van Segbroeck et al. Bibliotheca ephemeridum theologicarum lovaniensium 100. Leuven: Leuven University Press.

Safrai, S.
1976 "Home and Family." Vol. 2 / pp. 728–92 in *The Jewish People in the First Century: Historical Geography, Political History, Social, Cultural and Religious Life and Institutions*. Edited by S. Safrai and M. Stern. Compendia rerum iudaicarum ad Novum Testamentum 1/2. Assen: Van Gorcum/Philadelphia: Fortress.

Safrai, S., and M. Stern (eds.)
1976 *The Jewish People in the First Century: Historical Geography, Political History, Social, Cultural and Religious Life and Institutions*. Compendia rerum iudaicarum ad Novum Testamentum 1/2. Assen: Van Gorcum/Philadelphia: Fortress.

Sanders, E. P.
1985 *Jesus and Judaism*. London: SCM.

Sanders, J. A.
1990 " 'Nor Do I . . .': A Canonical Reading of the Challenge to Jesus in John 8." Pp. 337–47 in *The Conversation Continues: Studies in Paul and John in Honor of J. Louis Martyn*. Edited by R. T. Fortna and B. R. Gaventa. Nashville: Abingdon.

Sanders, J. N.
1943 *The Fourth Gospel in the Early Church: Its Origin and Influence on Christian Theology up to Irenaeus*. Cambridge: Cambridge University Press.

1968 *A Commentary on the Gospel according to St John*. Edited and completed by B. A. Mastin. London: Black.

Sandy, D. B.
1991 "John the Baptist's 'Lamb of God' Affirmation in Its Canonical and Apocalyptic Milieu." *Journal of*

the *Evangelical Theological Society* 34:447–59.

Sava, A. F.
1960 "Wound in the Side of Christ." *Catholic Biblical Quarterly* 19:343–46.

Schenk, W.
1992 "Interne Strukturierungen im Schluss-Segment Johannes 21: Συγγραφη + Σατυρικον Ἐπιλογος." *New Testament Studies* 38:507–30.

Schenke, L.
1989 "Joh 7–10: Eine dramatische Szene." *Zeitschrift für die neutestamentliche Wissenschaft* 80:172–92.

Schlatter, A.
1948 *Der Evangelist Johannes*. 2d edition. Stuttgart: Calwer.
1959 *Der Evangelist Matthäus*. 5th edition. Stuttgart: Calwer.
1962 *Das Evangelium nach Johannes: Ausgelegt für Bibelleser*. Erläuterungen zum Neuen Testament 3. Stuttgart: Calwer.
1997 *The History of the Christ*. Translated by A. J. Köstenberger. Grand Rapids: Baker. Original German edition published in 1923.

Schlosser, J.
1990 "La parole de Jésus sur la fin du temple." *New Testament Studies* 36:398–414.

Schnackenburg, R.
1990 *The Gospel according to St. John*. Translated by C. Hastings et al. 3 vols. New York: Crossroad.

Schneiders, S.
1989 "John 21.1–14." *Interpretation* 43:70–75.

Schnelle, U.
1996 "Die Tempelreinigung und die Christologie des Johannesevangeliums." *New Testament Studies* 42:359–73.

Schürer, E.
1973–79 *The History of the Jewish People in the Age of Jesus Christ*. Revised and edited by G. Vermes et al. 4 vols. Edinburgh: Clark.

Schwank, B.
1977 "Efraim in Joh 11,54." Pp. 377–83 in *L'Évangile de Jean: sources, rédaction, théologie*. Edited by M. de Jonge. Bibliotheca ephemeridum theologicarum lovaniensium 44. Gembloux: Duculot.

Schwartz, E.
1907   "Aporien im 4. Evangelium I."
        Pp. 342–72 in *Nachrichten von
        der Königlichen Gesellschaft der
        Wissenschaften zu Göttingen*. Berlin:
        Weidmannsche Buchhandlung.
1908   "Aporien im 4. Evangelium II,"
        "Aporien im 4. Evangelium III,"
        and "Aporien im 4. Evangelium
        IV." Pp. 115–48, 149–88, 497–560
        in *Nachrichten von der Königlichen
        Gesellschaft der Wissenschaften zu
        Göttingen*. Berlin: Weidmannsche
        Buchhandlung.

Schweizer, E.
1996   "What about the Johannine
        'Parables'?" Pp. 208–19 in *Exploring
        the Gospel of John: In Honor
        of D. Moody Smith*. Edited by
        R. A. Culpepper and C. C. Black.
        Louisville: Westminster John Knox.

Scott, M.
1992   *Sophia and the Johannine Jesus.*
        Journal for the Study of the New
        Testament: Supplement Series 71.
        Sheffield: Sheffield Academic Press.

Segal, A. F.
1981   "Ruler of This World: Attitudes
        about Mediator Figures and the
        Importance of Sociology for Self-
        Definition." Vol. 2 / pp. 245–68,
        403–13 in *Jewish and Christian Self-
        Definition*. Edited by E. P. Sanders.
        Philadelphia: Fortress.

Segovia, F. F.
1982   *Love Relationships in the Johannine
        Tradition: Agapē/Agapan in 1 John
        and the Fourth Gospel*. Society of
        Biblical Literature Dissertation
        Series 58. Chico, Calif.: Scholars
        Press.
1991   *The Farewell of the Word:
        The Johannine Call to Abide.*
        Minneapolis: Fortress.

Seim, T. K.
1987   "Roles of Women in the Gospel
        of John." Pp. 56–73 in *Aspects
        on the Johannine Literature:
        Papers presented at a Conference
        of Scandinavian New Testament
        Exegetes at Uppsala, June 16–19,
        1986*. Edited by L. Hartman and B.
        Olsson. Uppsala: Almqvist & Wiksell.

Shafaat, A.
1980–81 "Geber of the Qumran Scrolls and
        the Spirit-Paraclete of the Gospel
        of John." *New Testament Studies*
        27:263–69.

Shanks, H.
1985   "New Analysis of the Crucified
        Man." *Biblical Archaeology Review*
        11/6:20–21.

Shaw, A.
1974   "Breakfast by the Shore and the
        Mary Magdalene Encounter as
        Eucharistic Narratives." *Journal of
        Theological Studies* 25:12–26.

Sherwin-White, A. N.
1963   *Roman Society and Roman Law in
        the New Testament*. Oxford: Oxford
        University Press.
1965   "The Trial of Christ." Pp. 97–116 in
        *Historicity and Chronology in the
        New Testament*. D. E. Nineham et al.
        London: SPCK.

Shewell-Cooper, W. E.
1962   *Plants and Fruits of the Bible.*
        London: Darton, Longman & Todd.

Shidemantle, C. S.
2001   "Nehemiah 9 in John 7:37–39." Ph.D.
        diss., Trinity Evangelical Divinity
        School.

Sidebottom, E. M.
1956–57 "The Son of Man in the Fourth
        Gospel." *Expository Times* 68:231–35.

Silva, M.
1991   "Bilingualism and the Character
        of Biblical Greek." Pp. 205–26 in
        *The Language of the New Testament:
        Classic Essays*. Edited by S. E.
        Porter. Journal for the Study of the
        New Testament: Supplement Series
        60. Sheffield: JSOT Press.

Simoens, Y.
1981   *La gloire d'aimer: structures
        stylistiques et interpretatives dans
        de la Cegagne (Jn 13–17)*. Analecta
        biblica 90. Rome: Pontifical Bible
        Institute.

Simon, W. B.
2002   "The Role of the Spirit-Paraclete in
        the Disciples' Mission in the Fourth
        Gospel." Ph.D. diss., Southern
        Baptist Theological Seminary.

Simonis, A. J.
1967   *Die Hirtenrede im Johannes-
        Evangelium: Versuch einer Analyse
        von Johannes 10,1–18 nach
        Entstehung, Hintergrund, und Inhalt*.
        Analecta biblica 29. Rome: Pontifical
        Biblical Institute.

Skarsaune, O.
1987   *The Proof from Prophecy: A Study in Justin Martyr's Proof-Text Tradition: Text-Type, Provenance, Theological Profile.* Novum Testamentum Supplements 56. Leiden: Brill.

Sloyan, G. S.
1996   "The Gnostic Adoption of John's Gospel and Its Canonization by the Church Catholic." *Biblical Theology Bulletin* 26:125–32.

Smalley, S. S.
1996   " 'The Paraclete': Pneumatology in the Johannine Gospel and Apocalypse." Pp. 289–300 in *Exploring the Gospel of John: In Honor of D. Moody Smith.* Edited by R. A. Culpepper and C. C. Black. Louisville: Westminster John Knox.

Smallwood, E. M.
1954   "The Date of the Dismissal of Pontius Pilate from Judaea." *Journal of Jewish Studies* 5:12–21.
1962   "High Priests and Politics in Roman Palestine." *Journal of Theological Studies* 13:14–34.

Smith, B. H.
1968   *Poetic Closure: A Study of How Poems End.* Chicago: University of Chicago Press.

Smith, C. A.
2002   "The Leaning Tower: Foundational Weaknesses of Contemporary Chiastic Studies." Paper presented at the annual meeting of the Evangelical Theological Society, Toronto.

Smith, D.
1985   "Jesus and the Pharisees in Socio-Anthropological Perspective." *Trinity Journal,* n.s., 6:151–56.

Smith, D. M.
1963   "John 12:12ff. and the Question of John's Use of the Synoptics." *Journal of Biblical Literature* 82:58–64.
1990   "The Contribution of J. Louis Martyn to the Understanding of the Gospel of John." Pp. 275–94 in *The Conversation Continues: Studies in Paul and John in Honor of J. Louis Martyn.* Edited by R. T. Fortna and B. R. Gaventa. Nashville: Abingdon.
1992   *John among the Gospels: The Relationship in Twentieth-Century Research.* Minneapolis: Fortress.
1999   *John.* Abingdon New Testament Commentaries. Nashville: Abingdon.

Smith, R. H.
1966   "The Household Lamps of Palestine in New Testament Times." *Biblical Archaeologist* 29:2–27.

Smothers, E. R.
1958   "Two Readings in Papyrus Bodmer II (Jn 7:52, 8:25)." *Harvard Theological Review* 51:109–22.

Soards, M.
1983   "Critical Notes: Τὸν ἐπενδύτην διεζώσατο, ἦν γὰρ γυμνός." *Journal of Biblical Literature* 102:283–84.

Sordi, M.
1994   *The Christians and the Roman Empire.* London/New York: Routledge.

Spencer, P. E.
1999   "Narrative Echoes in John 21: Intertextual Interpretation and Intratextual Connection." *Journal for the Study of the New Testament* 75:49–68.

Staley, J. L.
1986   "The Structure of John's Prologue: Its Implications for the Gospel's Narrative Structure." *Catholic Biblical Quarterly* 48:241–63.
1988   *The Print's First Kiss: A Rhetorical Investigation of the Implied Reader in the Fourth Gospel.* Society of Biblical Literature Dissertation Series 82. Atlanta: Scholars Press.
1991   "Stumbling in the Dark, Reaching for the Light: Reading Character in John 5 and 9." *Semeia* 53:55–80.

Stauffer, E.
1960   *Jesus and His Story.* London: SCM.

Steele, M.
1988   "Where Does the Speech Quotation End in John 3:1–21?" *Notes on Translation* 2/2:51–58.

Stegemann, E.
1990   "Zur Tempelreinigung im Johannesevangelium." Pp. 503–16 in *Die Hebräische Bibel und ihre zweifache Nachgeschichte: Festschrift für Rolf Rendtorff zum 65. Geburtstag.* Edited by E. Blum, C. Macholz, and E. W. Stegemann. Neukirchen-Vluyn: Neukirchener Verlag.

Steinmetz, D.
1980   "The Superiority of Pre-critical Exegesis." *Theology Today* 37:27–38.

Stenger, W.
1990   *Strukturale Beobachtungen zum Neuen Testament.* Leiden: Brill.

Sternberg, M.
1985   *Poetics of Biblical Narrative.* Bloomington: Indiana State University.

Stibbe, M. W. G.
1991   "The Elusive Christ: A New Reading of the Fourth Gospel." *Journal for the Study of the New Testament* 44:19–38.
1992   *John as Storyteller: Narrative Criticism and the Fourth Gospel.* Society for New Testament Studies Monograph Series 73. Cambridge: Cambridge University Press.
1993   *John.* Readings: A New Biblical Commentary. Sheffield: JSOT Press.
1994   "A Tomb with a View: John 11.1–44 in Narrative-Critical Perspective." *New Testament Studies* 40:38–54.

Stimpfle, A.
1992   "Das 'sinnlose γάρ' in Joh 4:44: Beobachtungen zur Doppeldeutigkeit im Johannesevangelium." *Biblische Notizen* 65:86–96.

Story, C. I. K.
1989   "The Bearing of Old Testament Terminology on the Johannine Chronology of the Final Passover of Jesus." *Novum Testamentum* 31:316–24.
1991   "The Mental Attitude of Jesus at Bethany: John 11.33, 38." *New Testament Studies* 37:51–66.

Strachan, R. H.
1955   *The Fourth Gospel.* London: SCM.

Str-B   *Kommentar zum Neuen Testament aus Talmud und Midrasch.* By H. L. Strack and P. Billerbeck. 6 vols. Munich: Beck, 1922–61.

Strickert, F.
1998   *Bethsaida: Home of the Apostles.* Collegeville, Minn.: Liturgical Press.

Stuhlmacher, P.
1997   "Der Kanon und seine Auslegung." Pp. 263–90 in *Jesus Christus als die Mitte der Schrift: Studien zur Hermeneutik des Evangeliums.* Edited by C. Landmesser et al. Beihefte zur Zeitschrift für die neutestamentliche Wissenschaft 86. Berlin: de Gruyter.
2002   "My Experience with Biblical Theology." Pp. 174–91 in *Biblical Theology: Retrospect and Prospect.* Edited by S. J. Hafemann. Downers Grove, Ill.: InterVarsity.

Swain, S. R.
1998   "Truth in the Gospel of John." Th.M. thesis, Southeastern Baptist Theological Seminary.

Swanson, R. J. (ed.)
1995   *New Testament Greek Manuscripts: Variant Readings Arranged in Horizontal Lines against Codex Vaticanus.* Sheffield: Sheffield Academic Press/Pasadena: William Carey International University Press.

Swetnam, J.
1980   "The Meaning of Πεπιστευκότας in John 8,31." *Biblica* 61:106–9.

Sylva, D. D.
1988   "Nicodemus and His Spices (John 19:39)." *New Testament Studies* 34:148–51.

Talbert, C. H.
1970   "Artistry and Theology: An Analysis of the Architecture of Jn 1,19–5,47." *Catholic Biblical Quarterly* 32:341–66.
1992   *Reading John.* Reading the New Testament. New York: Crossroad.

Taylor, J. E.
1998   "Golgotha: A Reconsideration of the Evidence for the Sites of Jesus' Crucifixion and Burial." *New Testament Studies* 44:180–203.

TDNT   *Theological Dictionary of the New Testament.* Edited by G. Kittel and G. Friedrich. Translated and edited by G. W. Bromiley. 10 vols. Grand Rapids: Eerdmans, 1964–76.

Thatcher, T.
1999   "The Sabbath Trick: Unstable Irony in the Fourth Gospel." *Journal for the Study of the New Testament* 76:53–77.

Thielman, F.
1991   "The Style of the Fourth Gospel and Ancient Literary Critical Concepts of Religious Discourse." Pp. 169–83 in *Persuasive Artistry: Studies in New Testament Rhetoric in Honor of George A. Kennedy.* Edited by D. F. Watson. Journal for the Study of the New Testament: Supplement Series 50. Sheffield: JSOT Press.

Thomas, J. C.
1987   "A Note on the Text of John 13:10." *Novum Testamentum* 29:46–52.
1991a   *Footwashing in John 13 and the Johannine Community.* Journal for the Study of the New Testament: Supplement Series 61. Sheffield: JSOT Press.

1991b   "The Fourth Gospel and Rabbinic Judaism." *Zeitschrift für die neutestamentliche Wissenschaft* 82:159–82.

1995   " 'Stop Sinning Lest Something Worse Come upon You': The Man at the Pool in John 5." *Journal for the Study of the New Testament* 59:3–20.

Thompson, M. M.

2000   *The Promise of the Father: Jesus and God in the New Testament*. Louisville: Westminster John Knox.

2001   *The God of the Gospel of John*. Grand Rapids: Eerdmans.

2002   "A Response to 'The De-historicizing of the Gospel of John' by Robert Kysar." Paper presented at the annual meeting of the Society of Biblical Literature, Toronto, November 23–26.

Thomson, J. G. S. S.

1955   "The Shepherd-Ruler Concept in the Old Testament and Its Application in the New Testament." *Scottish Journal of Theology* 8:406–18.

Tobin, T. H.

1990   "The Prologue of John and Hellenistic Jewish Speculation." *Catholic Biblical Quarterly* 52:252–69.

Tolmie, D. F.

1998   "The Characterization of God in the Fourth Gospel." *Journal for the Study of the New Testament* 69:57–75.

Torgovnick, M.

1981   *Closure in the Novel*. Princeton: Princeton University Press.

Torrey, C. C.

1931   "The Date of the Crucifixion according to the Fourth Gospel." *Journal of Biblical Literature* 50:227–41.

1936   *Our Translated Gospels: Some of the Evidence*. New York: Harper.

Tovey, D.

1997   *Narrative Art and Act in the Fourth Gospel*. Journal for the Study of the New Testament: Supplement Series 151. Sheffield: Sheffield Academic Press.

Trudinger, L. P.

1982   "An Israelite in Whom There Is No Guile: An Interpretive Note on John 1:45–51." *Evangelical Quarterly* 54:117–20.

Trudinger, P.

1997   "The Cleansing of the Temple: St John's Independent, Subtle Reflections." *Expository Times* 108:329–30.

Turner, M. M. B.

1977   "The Concept of Receiving the Spirit in John's Gospel." *Vox Evangelica* 10:24–42.

1990   "Atonement and the Death of Jesus in John: Some Questions to Bultmann and Forestell." *Evangelical Quarterly* 62:99–122.

1998   *The Holy Spirit and Spiritual Gifts in the New Testament Church and Today*. Revised edition. Peabody, Mass.: Hendrickson.

Turner, N.

1963   *Syntax*. Vol. 3 of *A Grammar of New Testament Greek*, by James Hope Moulton. Edinburgh: Clark.

1976   *Style*. Vol. 4 of *A Grammar of New Testament Greek*, by James Hope Moulton. Edinburgh: Clark.

Twomey, J. J.

1956   "'Barabbas Was a Robber.'" *Scripture* 8:115–19.

UBS⁴   *The Greek New Testament*. Edited by B. Aland, K. Aland, J. Karavidopoulos, C. M. Martini, and B. M. Metzger. 4th revised edition. Stuttgart: Deutsche Bibelgesellschaft/ United Bible Societies, 1993.

Valentine, S. R.

1996   "The Johannine Prologue—a Microcosm of the Gospel." *Evangelical Quarterly* 68:291–304.

VanderKam, J. C.

1990   "John 10 and the Feast of the Dedication." Pp. 203–14 in *Of Scribes and Scrolls: Studies on the Hebrew Bible, Intertestamental Judaism, and Christian Origins Presented to John Strugnell*. Edited by J. J. Collins and T. H. Tobin. Lanham, Md.: University Press of America.

van der Watt, J. G.

1995   "The Composition of the Prologue of John's Gospel: The Historical Jesus Introducing Divine Grace." *Westminster Theological Journal* 57:311–32.

Vanhoozer, K. J.

1993   "The Hermeneutics of I-Witness Testimony: John 21.20–24 and the 'Death' of the 'Author.'" Pp. 366–87 in *Understanding Poets*

*and Prophets: Essays in Honour of
George Wishart Anderson*. Edited by
A. G. Auld. Journal for the Study
of the Old Testament: Supplement
Series 152. Sheffield: JSOT Press.
Also published as pp. 257–74 in
*First Theology: God, Scripture, and
Hermeneutics*. By K. J. Vanhoozer.
Downers Grove, Ill.: InterVarsity,
2002.

1995   "The Reader in New Testament
Interpretation." Pp. 301–28 in
*Hearing the New Testament:
Strategies for Interpretation*. Edited
by J. B. Green. Grand Rapids:
Eerdmans/Carlisle: Paternoster.

1998   *Is There Meaning in This Text? The
Bible, the Reader, and the Morality of
Literary Knowledge*. Grand Rapids:
Zondervan.

2002   *First Theology: God, Scripture, and
Hermeneutics*. Downers Grove, Ill.:
InterVarsity.

Vardaman, E. J.

1962   "A New Inscription Which Mentions
Pilate as 'Prefect.'" *Journal of Biblical
Literature* 81:70–71.

1963   "The Pool of Bethesda." *Bible and
Theology* 14:27–29.

Vawter, B.

1964   "Ezekiel and John." *Catholic Biblical
Quarterly* 26:450–58.

Vermes, G.

1972–73   "Ḥanina ben Dosa: A Controversial
Galilean Saint from the First
Century of the Christian Era."
Journal of Jewish Studies 23:28–50;
24:51–64.

Vincent, L. H.

1954   "L'Antonia, palais primitif d'Hérode."
Revue biblique 61:87–107.

Viviano, B. T.

1998   "The Structure of the Prologue
of John (1:1–18): A Note." *Revue
biblique* 105:176–84.

Volfing, A.

2001   *John the Evangelist in Medieval
German Writing: Imitating the
Inimitable*. Oxford: Oxford
University Press.

Vorster, W. S.

1992   "The Growth and Making of John
21." Vol. 3 / pp. 2207–21 in *The
Four Gospels 1992: Festschrift
Frans Neirynck*. Edited by F.
Van Segbroeck et al. Bibliotheca
ephemeridum theologicarum

lovaniensium 100. Leuven: Leuven
University Press.

Waheeb, M.

1999   "Site of Jesus' Baptism Found—
Again." *Biblical Archaeology Review*
25/3:14–15.

Walker, N.

1960   "The Reckoning of Hours in
the Fourth Gospel." *Novum
Testamentum* 4:69–73.

Walker, P. W. L.

1996   *Jesus and the Holy City: New
Testament Perspectives on Jerusalem*.
Grand Rapids: Eerdmans.

Walker, W.

1958   *All the Plants of the Bible*. London:
Lutterworth.

Walker, W. O., Jr.

1982   "The Lord's Prayer in Matthew and
in John." *New Testament Studies*
28:237–56.

1994   "John 1.43–51 and 'the Son of Man'
in the Fourth Gospel." *Journal for the
Study of the New Testament* 56:31–42.

Wallace, D. B.

1990   "John 5,2 and the Date of the Fourth
Gospel." *Biblica* 71:177–205.

1993   "Reconsidering 'The Story of Jesus
and the Adulteress Reconsidered.'"
New Testament Studies 39:290–96.

1996   *Greek Grammar beyond the Basics*.
Grand Rapids: Zondervan.

Waltke, B. K.

1958   "The Theological Significance
of Ἀντί and Ὑπέρ in the New
Testament." 2 vols. Th.D. diss.,
Dallas Theological Seminary.

Warfield, B. B.

1950   *The Person and Work of Christ*.
Edited by S. G. Craig. Philadelphia:
Presbyterian and Reformed
Publishing Company.

Weisse, C. H.

1856   *Die Evangelienfrage in ihrem
gegenwärtigen Stadium*. Leipzig:
Breitkopf & Härtel.

Wellhausen, J.

1907   *Erweiterungen und Änderungen im
vierten Evangelium*. Berlin: Reimer.

Wenham, D.

1997   "The Enigma of the Fourth Gospel:
Another Look." *Tyndale Bulletin*
48:149–78.

West, M.

1981   *The Clowns of God*. London: Hodder
& Stoughton.

Westcott, B. F.
1881   *The Gospel according to St John.*
        London: Murray.
1896   *A General Survey of the History of
        the Canon of the New Testament.*
        7th edition. London/New York:
        Macmillan.
1908   *The Gospel according to St. John:
        The Greek Text with Introduction and
        Notes.* 2 vols. London: Murray.

Whitacre, R. A.
1999   *John.* IVP New Testament
        Commentary 4. Downers Grove, Ill.:
        InterVarsity.

Wiarda, T.
1992   "John 21.1–23: Narrative Unity and
        Its Implications." *Journal for the
        Study of the New Testament* 46:53–
        71.
2000   *Peter in the Gospels: Pattern,
        Personality, Relationship.*
        Wissenschaftliche Untersuchungen
        zum Neuen Testament 2/127.
        Tübingen: Mohr-Siebeck.

Wieand, D. J.
1965–66 "John V.2 and the Pool of Bethesda."
        New Testament Studies 12:392–404.

Wilcox, M.
1977   "The 'Prayer' of Jesus in John
        xi.41b–42." *New Testament Studies*
        24:128–32.

Wilkinson, J.
1964   "Seven Words from the Cross."
        Scottish Journal of Theology 17:69–
        82.

Williams, R. H.
1997   "The Mother of Jesus at Cana: A
        Social-Science Interpretation of
        John 2:1–12." *Catholic Biblical
        Quarterly* 59:679–92.

Wilson, C. T.
1906   *Peasant Life in the Holy Land.*
        London: Murray.

Windisch, H.
1968   *The Spirit-Paraclete in the Fourth
        Gospel.* Translated by J. W. Cox.
        Philadelphia: Fortress.

Winter, P.
1953   "Μονογενὴς παρὰ Πατρός."
        *Zeitschrift für Religions- und
        Geistesgeschichte* 5:335–65.
1974   *On the Trial of Jesus.* 2d edition.
        Berlin/New York: de Gruyter.

Witherington, B.
1995   *John's Wisdom.* Louisville:
        Westminster John Knox.

Witkamp, L. T.
1985   "The Use of Traditions in John 5:1–
        18." *Journal for the Study of the New
        Testament* 25:19–47.

Workman, H. B.
1923   *Persecution in the Early Church:
        A Chapter in the History of
        Renunciation.* 4th edition. London:
        Epworth.

Wright, N. T.
1986   "*Harpagmos* and the Meaning of
        Philippians 2:5–11." *Journal of
        Theological Studies* 37:321–53.
1992   *The New Testament and the People of
        God.* Minneapolis: Fortress.

Wuellner, W.
1967   *The Meaning of "Fishers of
        Men."* New Testament Library.
        Philadelphia: Westminster.
1991   "Rhetorical Criticism and Its Theory
        in Culture-Critical Perspective: The
        Narrative Rhetoric of John 11." Pp.
        171–85 in *Text and Interpretation:
        New Approaches in the Criticism of
        the New Testament.* New Testament
        Tools and Studies 15. Edited by P. J.
        Hartin and J. H. Petzer. Leiden: Brill.

Yarbrough, R. W.
1983   "The Date of Papias: A
        Reassessment." *Journal of the
        Evangelical Theological Society*
        26:181–91.

Young, F. W.
1955   "A Study of the Relation of Isaiah to
        the Fourth Gospel." *Zeitschrift für
        die neutestamentliche Wissenschaft*
        46:215–33.

Zahn, T.
1921   *Das Evangelium des Johannes.* 6th
        edition. Kommentar zum Neuen
        Testament 4. Leipzig: Deichert.

Zias, J., and E. Sekeles
1985   "The Crucified Man from Giv'at-
        ha-Mivtar." *Israel Exploration
        Journal* 35:22–27.

Zimmermann, M., and R. Zimmermann
1999   "Der Freund des Bräutigams
        (Joh 3,29): Deflorations- oder
        Christuszeuge?" *Zeitschrift für die
        neutestamentliche Wissenschaft*
        90:123–30.

ZPEB   *Zondervan Pictorial Encyclopedia of
        the Bible.* Edited by M. C. Tenney. 5
        vols. Grand Rapids: Zondervan, 1975.

Zugibe, F. T.
1989   "Two Questions about Crucifixion."
        Bible and Review 5/2:35–43.

Index of Subjects

Jacob 47, 85, 153, 192, 270–
71, 281n13, 411
Jacob's well 141, 147, 150–51
James 461
Jehovah's Witnesses 28
Jeremiah 316
Jericho 369
Jerusalem 62n21, 154, 177,
241, 349, 367
Jesus
anger 340
anointing 357–58, 360–64
as apocalyptic warrior
66–67n35
ascension 219, 569–70
authority 233, 486–87
baptism 44, 66, 69
as bridegroom 99n35, 133,
138n12, 427
brothers 101, 229–30
burial 554–57
as chosen one 71
as consummate Israelite
69
crucifixion 260n45, 422,
475, 538, 540, 541–
49
death 9, 102, 306, 308, 363,
549–54
deity 28n27, 256, 271,
507n21
divine sonship 44
dwelling with his people
501
emotions 412–13
entrance into Jerusalem
367–74
eternal existence 273
exaltation 260n45, 382n31,
384n38, 433
flesh 215–16
friends of 458–59
as fulfillment of Old
Testament 14, 18, 35
glorification 99, 435, 486,
489, 565, 570
glorification on cross 375,
378, 380, 422, 490
as good shepherd 508
heavenly origin 210
humanity 99, 141, 151,
412, 507n21, 533
humility 403–4
intercession 492–93
isolation 231
kingship 502

knowledge of people
116–17
as light of the world 253–
54, 277, 282, 284
love 327, 402–3, 422–24,
456, 458
as Messiah 9, 85, 91, 99,
158, 230, 235–37, 259,
582
mission 13–15, 53, 307,
329–30, 382, 489–90
name 38, 478
as new Moses 398
as new temple 313, 491
obedience to Father 269,
381, 394, 445, 486
as only begotten 42–44
passion 345, 378
paternity 251, 265
power over death 343
prayer 344–35, 482–84
for followers 490–97
for future believers
497–501
for himself 485–90
preexistence 19, 25, 45, 68
prescience 412, 506
as Prophet 153, 155, 203,
482n1
as prosecutor 255n17
as rabbi 74, 120, 569
rejection of 23, 36, 37, 51
resurrection 322, 343, 346,
439, 475, 479, 560–65,
573, 594
resurrection appearances
9, 566–70, 571, 587
sacrifice 306–7, 359, 385
as savior of the world
164–65
sent by Father 483, 492
sinlessness 267, 445
"stirred up inside" 410,
412–13
as teacher 405
temptation 230
time 378, 402
trial 512–39
triumph over world 481
as true vine 448
trustworthiness of sayings
85
unity with Father 216,
312–13, 316–17, 414,
431–32, 445, 493–94,
497–98

walks on water 204–5
weeping 341
as Word 40
work 14, 161
works 192, 311, 313, 316
wounds 579
Jesus Christ (expression),
489n26
Jewish monotheism 28, 185,
194, 265, 312
Jewish Passover 104n9
Jewish weddings 92
Jews 15
persecution of Christians
469
rejection of God's words
390–91
rejection of Jesus 224–25,
266–67
rejection of Messiah 51,
90, 352, 385, 389, 395,
539n89
unbelief 309–17, 320, 393
Job 182
Johannine community 3, 4,
277n1, 605
Johannine Great Commis-
sion 395
Johannine irony 81, 149, 151,
157, 164, 168, 181,
208, 213, 234, 235,
238, 270, 278, 289,
290, 431n46, 472.
See also irony
Johannine misunderstanding
96n28, 257, 259, 290,
431, 479
John, Gospel of
authorship 1, 3, 6–8, 33
chronology in 11–13
hermeneutical
presuppositions 3–6
historical setting 5, 6–8
historicity of 2n5
literary features 9–13
original audience 8
place in canonicity 16–17
theological themes 13–
16
John Hyrcanus 523, 556
John son of Zebedee 7, 414,
602
John the apostle 1, 7, 32
John the Baptist 22, 32–34,
133–40, 145, 271, 435,
457

judgment of 471–72
rejection of Jesus 131, 230
spiritual darkness 282
on trial 250, 131
worldliness 492

worship 103, 148, 153–56,
    435, 438
wrath 140

zeal 107, 193, 200, 469

Zealots 107, 203, 208, 303,
    530–31
Zebedee 414, 513, 588
Zechariah 32, 61, 83
Zion 371

Index of Authors

Index of Greek Words

Index of Scripture and
Other Ancient Writings

Old Testament

Genesis

1   27
1:1   19, 25, 28
1:1–2:4   20n8
1:2   69, 219
1:3   25, 219
1:3–4   13
1:3–5   30
1:6   219
1:9   25, 219
1:11   25, 219
1:11–12   452
1:14   219
1:14–18   30
1:15   25
1:20   219
1:20–31   30
1:22   452
1:24   25, 219
1:26   219
1:28   452
1:30   25
1:31   29n29
2:2   161
2:2–3   185
2:3   561n2
2:7   15, 30, 189n70, 219, 575
2:17   267
3   49, 131, 266
3:3–4   267
3:4   267
3:15   100n39, 411
3:20   30
4   266

4:1 LXX   488n21
5:24   85, 127
7:1–4   192
9:4   217n83
9:5   258n34
12:1–3   192
12:1–4   265
12:1–9   264
12:7   153
15:1–6   264
15:6   34n42, 265n66
15:17–21   272
16:13   49
17:3   295n82
17:5   265n66, 459
17:9–14   234
17:17   272
18:1–2   192
18:1–8   264
18:4   404n21
18:17   458n53
18:25   188
19:2   404n21
21:6   272
21:9–10   262n57
21:11   218
21:17   383
21:20   121
22   129
22:1–14   265
22:1–19   264
22:2 LXX   43
22:2   43, 43n74
22:6   542n8
22:8   67

22:11   383
22:12 LXX   43
22:12   43, 43n74
22:13   67
22:16 LXX   43
22:16   43
24:7   138
24:10–61   142n5
24:11   148
24:17   148
24:32   404n21
25:21–34   262n57
25:22   281n13
26:19   150
26:24   121, 425
27:35–36 LXX   82
28:10   152n37
28:12   85
28:15   121
28:17   86, 154, 303n27
29:1–20   142n5
29:4   236n34
29:7   597
29:7–8   148
29:10   148
29:31   379n15
29:33   379n15
31:3   121
31:13   392n10
31:19   154n45
32:3   138
32:24–30   192
33:18–19   146
33:19   151
33:20   153

35:4   154n45
37:3   547
37:12   597
37:23   547
37:30 LXX   201n12
40:13   127n40
40:19   127n40
40:20–22   127n40
41:55   96
42:7   218
43:14 LXX   546n29
43:24   404n21
45:5   138
46:28   138
48:10   352n142
48:15   299n6
48:21–22   146
48:22   151
49   396n3, 483
49:3   45
49:10   83, 284, 386
49:10–11   372
49:11   97n31, 370n14
49:22   450
49:24   299n6
50:10 LXX   337
50:20   495

Exodus

2:15–21   142n5
2:16   148
3:1   305n35, 305n36
3:4–4:17   192
3:6   49

New Testament

Old Testament Apocrypha

Old Testament Pseudepigrapha

Apocalypse of Abraham

9:6 458n53
10:5 458n53
31:1–3 272n98

Apocalypse of Moses

31 569n13

Assumption of Moses

1:13–14 500n84
11:17 194n100
12:6 194n100

2 (Syriac) Baruch

4:4 272n98
13:1 382n29
21 483
22:1 382n29
29:3 77n73
29:3–30:1 200n6
29:5 93n16
29:8 200n6, 209
30:1 77n73
30:1–2 190n73
34 483
39:7 450
40:1 77n73
42:7–8 190n73
48:1–24 483
48:3–4 125
48:47 394n18
50:2 190n73
59:2 31
70:9 77n73
72:2 77n73
77:11 443n94
77:11–16 299n7
77:13–17 307n49

3 (Greek) Baruch

6:13 303n27

4 Baruch (Paraleipomena Jeremiou)

9:3 254n12

1 (Ethiopic) Enoch

10:19 93n16
22:13 190n73

37–71 188n63, 422
39:4–5 426n26
41:2 426n26
41:3 125
42:2 36n50
45–57 378
46 378
48 378
48:1 152
48:6 235n33
48:10 77n73
49:1 386n45
49:2 99n38
49:3 70
49:4 188n63
51 190n73
52:4 77n73
58:3 254n12
58:4–6 254n12
60:12 125
61:5 272n101
61:9 188n63
62:2–6 188n63
62:14 386
63:11 188n63
65:4 382n29
71:16 426n26
72–75 303n27
72:2 303n27
87:2 567n5
89:12–76 305n39
90:9–12 66n36
90:22–31 305n39
90:28–36 102n2
92:2 425n21
92:4 254n12
105:2 84n112
108:11 387n50

2 (Slavonic) Enoch

61:2–3 426n26

4 Ezra

see 2 Esdras on p. 691

Joseph and Aseneth

7:1 404n22
20:1–5 405n26

Jubilees

1:19–21 194n100, 483
1:23 70, 71
1:23–25 124
5:14 258
7:26 498n72
7:29 258

8:19 241n61
10:8 384n37
11:5 384n37
11:11 384n37
15:17 272
15:26 266
15:33 266
16:19–29 272
16:31 369
18:2 43
18:11 43
18:15 43
19:9 458n53
22:7–23 483
22:10–30 396n4
22:22 258
22:23 425n21
22:28–30 483
23:10 264
30:20 458n53
30:21 458n53
35:20 498n72
36:4 498n72
49:1 418n29
49:12 418n29

Letter of Aristeas

112 304n30
132–38 186n51
210 185n47

Martyrdom and Ascension of Isaiah

1:3 384n37
2:4 384n37
10:29 384n37

Odes of Solomon

8:1 456n35
8:11 456n35
8:20–21 456n35
10:5–6 353n149
14:8 441n89
15:1 456n39
17:6–11 303n28
23:1 456n39
31:3 456n39
31:6 456n39
40:4 456n39
41:15 500n84
42:15–18 303n28

Psalms of Solomon

3:12 254n12
7:1 467n18

8:28 239n46
9:2 239n46
14:8 117n7
17:4 386
17:21–27 188
17:25 117n7
17:30 102n2
17:30–32 99n38
17:32 77n73, 214n70
17:37 70, 441n89
17:40 304n30, 307n49
17:40–41 305n35
18:4 43

Pseudo-Philo

Biblical Antiquities
25.10 154n45

Sibylline Oracles

3:11–12 186n51
3:49 209
3:49–50 386
3:545–61 186n51
5:344–45 382n34
12:104 199n3

Testament of Abraham

3:7–9 404n22

Testament of Asher

1:8 416n20
3:2 263

Testament of Benjamin

3:8 66n36
9:2 61n16

Testament of Dan

5:3 498n72

Testament of Gad

1:2–4 305n39
4:1–2 423n8
6:1 423n8

Testament of Isaac

8:6–7 483

New Testament Apocrypha

Nag Hammadi

Rabbinic Writings

Qumran / Dead Sea Scrolls

Papyri

Josephus

Philo

Classical Writers

Justinian

Digesta
48.20 546n31

Juvenal

Satirae
14.22 404n19

Livy

Roman History
5.13 530n42

Lucian

Cataplus
15 415n16
De morte Peregrini
6 407n37, 439n79
Gallus
7.9 407n37
Phalaris
2.8 451n12
Timon
54 407n37
Toxaris
22 549n48

Martial

Epigrams
12.70 404n19

Menander

Sententiae
e codicibus
Byzantinis
532 282n18
Sent. Mono.
1.385 282n18

Petronius

Satyricon
28.4 404n19
70 361n14
137 539

Philostratus

Vita Apollonii
1.21 534n66
4.44 534n66

Pilate inscription

in toto 525n14

Plato

Apologia
33B 517n31
Leges
9.864E 512
Phaedrus
65 439n79
Republic
7.1–11 131n51

Plautus

Mostellaria
267 404n19

Pliny the Elder

Natural History
2.188 75n65
13.22 361n14
36.107–18 543n13

Pliny the Younger

Epistulae
10.96 468n25,
539n91, 580n13

Plutarch

Camillus
5.5 341n94
Cato Minor
56.4 334n59
67.1 407n37
Cicero
43 369n9
De Alexandri
magni fortuna aut
virtute
6 307n51
De Pythiae oraculis
404.D.10 385n41

De sollertia
animalium
977.F 592n25
Galba
16.1 363
Marcellus
20.1 408n47
Moralia
180E 552n68
Mulierum virtutes
243.D.7 605
Pompeius
55.6 407n37
80.5 341n94
Pyrrhus
34.4 341n94
Romulus
22.1 292n66

Polybius

Histories
5.26.7–12 369n9
11.23 505n13
20.7.5 369n9

Quintilian

Declamationes
6.9 551n62

Res Gestae Divi Augusti

in toto 545n26

Seneca

Ad Marciam de
consolatione
20.3 543n13,
598n12
De ira
2.7.3 524n8
Epistulae morales
75.7 409n51

Suetonius

Caligula
32 369n8

Domitian
10.1 544n21
13.2 580
Nero
16 464n3
Tiberius
58 536n74
73 55n2

Tacitus

Annales
3.38 536n74
4 §4 55n2
6.8 536n76
15.44 461, 464n3,
525n14, 525n16
44.3 543
Historiae
5.5 185n51, 423n9,
446n103

Themistius

Peri Philanthropias
9d–10c 300n8

Thucydides

History of the
Peloponnesian War
1.1.1 604n17
4.104.4 604n17
4.121 369n9
5.26.1 604n17

Vitae Aesopi

61.9 (Vita
W) 404n18
61.13 404n18
67.4 (Vita
G) 404n18

Xenophon

Cyropaedia
7.1.3 590n18
Oeconomicus
18.6 451n13
20.11 451n13
20.20 453n19

Church Fathers